# Carta's New Century Handbook and Atlas of the Bible

(overleaf) *The Valley of Aijalon.*

# Carta's New Century Handbook and Atlas of the Bible

**Anson F. Rainey**
Emeritus Professor of
Ancient Near Eastern Cultures and Semitic Linguistics
Tel Aviv University
Adjunct Professor of Historical Geography, Bar-Ilan University
and American Institute for Holy Land Studies

**R. Steven Notley**
Professor of Biblical Studies
Nyack College, New York City campus
Former Chairman of the Department of New Testament Studies
American Institute for Holy Land Studies

carta
Jerusalem

First published in 2007 by
**CARTA Jerusalem**

This volume is the concise version of
*The Sacred Bridge: Carta's Atlas of the Biblical World*
Carta, Jerusalem 2006

**Academic Editor and Art Adviser:** Shmuel Ahituv, Ph.D.,
Professor Emeritus of The Bible and Ancient Near Eastern Studies, Ben-Gurion University of the Negev, Be'er Sheva

**Text and Art Editor:** Barbara Laurel Ball
**Map Editor:** Lorraine Kessel
**Map Art:** Prof. Pinchas Yoeli, Vladimir Shestakovsky
**Maps and Graphics:**
Amnon Shmaya, Evgeny Vasenin, Adi Friedman,
Irena Shnitman, Tsahi Ben-Ami
**Systems Administrator:** Daniel Wanoun
**Production Manager:** Shlomo Abergel



ISBN: 965-220-703-9

**Cover Art:** Evgeny Vasenin
**Cover Photo:** NASA

## Picture Sources

*The New Encyclopedia of Archaeological Excavations in the Holy Land*, The Israel Exploration Society and Carta, Jerusalem, 1993
pp. 11 (bottom), 25, 26, 28, 32, 37, 41 (bottom), 42, 44, 46, 47, 51, 57 (left), 58, 59, 60, 66, 67, 77 (bottom), 83, 90, 92, 100, 103, 107, 110, 113, 118, 137 (bottom), 139, 143, 145, 159 (top), 167, 170, 174, 180 (top), 200, 205, 212, 221, 222, 230, 235, 265

A. Alon: p. 19
D. Bahat: p. 201
S. Ben-Yosef: p. 52 (and frontispiece)
H. Bünting, *Itinerarium Sacrae Scripturae*, c. 1580
R. Gherson: p. 38
G. Nalbandian: pp. 20, 21, 23, 71, 127 (bottom), 204, 216, 220, 226, 229, 231, 236 (top), 239, 255
NASA: pp. 14, 22
Palestine Exploration Fund: p. 11 (top)
L. Ritmeyer: pp. 235, 253 (bottom)
P. H. Wright: pp. 57, 77 (top), 217, 258 (top)
Y. Yadin: pp. 264, 267
A. Yardeni: pp. 137 (top), 144, 147, 208 (bottom)

All other illustrations or photographs are from the archives of Carta, Jerusalem and the authors.
Originals of the following may be found in:
British Museum, London: pp. 75, 106, 116, 124, 135
Egyptian Museum, Cairo: p. 131
Israel Museum, Jerusalem: p. 114
Oriental Institute of the University of Chicago: pp. 31, 39, 161
Reuben and Edith Hecht Museum, Haifa: p. 253
School of Oriental and African Studies, London: p. 153
Staatliche Museen, Berlin: p. 133

Great care has been taken to establish sources of illustrations. If inadvertently we failed to do so, due credit will be given in the next edition.

Carta, Jerusalem
18 Ha'uman Street, POB 2500
Jerusalem 91024, Israel
E-mail: carta@carta.co.il
Website: www.holyland-jerusalem.com

# Contents

**Anson F. Rainey**
Chapters 1–11

**R. Steven Notley**
Chapters 12–20

**FOREWORD** ........ **7**

**INTRODUCTION** ........ **9**
Dimensions and Disciplines of Historical Geography ........ 9
Archaeology ........ 10

**CHAPTER 1 The Ancient World View** ........ **12**
Other Ancient Views of the World ........ 13

**CHAPTER 2 The Land Bridge** ........ **14**
The Levant ........ 14
The Southern Levant ........ 15
The Land of Israel ........ 17
Climate ........ 23

**CHAPTER 3 The Bronze Age Fourth Millennium to Twelfth Century BCE** ........ **25**
Early Bronze Age (4th to 3rd Millennia BCE) ........ 25
Middle Bronze Age (c. 2200–1550 BCE) ........ 26
Late Bronze Age (c. 155s0–1200 BCE) ........ 28

**CHAPTER 4 Crisis and Transition Twelfth Century BCE** ........ **31**
The Southern Levant ........ 31
Israelite Ancestral Traditions ........ 33
The Epic of the Exodus and Wilderness Wanderings ........ 37
Conquest Traditions ........ 41

**CHAPTER 5 Survival and Renewal Eleventh Century BCE** ........ **49**
The Southern Levant ........ 49
The Judges ........ 52
Saul ........ 61
Tribal and Clan Mobility and Stability ........ 67

**CHAPTER 6 Territorial States Tenth Century BCE** ........ **70**
The Southern Levant ........ 70
Solomon's Reign ........ 74
The Kingdom Split ........ 79
The Solomonic Administrative Districts ........ 82
Tribal Border Descriptions ........ 86

**CHAPTER 7 Regional Conflicts Ninth Century BCE** ........ **93**
Mesopotamia ........ 93
The Southern Levant ........ 94
The Omride Dynasty ........ 96
Political Developments ........ 105
Prophetic Traditions ........ 107

**CHAPTER 8 Window of Opportunity Early Eighth Century BCE** ........ **108**
Aram-Damascus' Period of Supremacy ........ 108
Adad-nirāri's Last Campaign to the West ........ 109
The Resurgence of Israel and Judah ........ 110
The Prophet Amos—Political Critique ........ 114

**CHAPTER 9 Imperial Domination Mid-Eighth to Mid-Seventh Centuries BCE** ........ **116**
Assyria Under Tiglath-pileser III ........ 116
Conflicts in the Southern Levant ........ 117
Assyrian Intervention in the Southern Levant ........ 119
The Reign of Sargon II ........ 123
Sennacherib's Third Campaign ........ 127
The Aftermath ........ 132
Assyrian Activity Renewed in the West ........ 132

CHAPTER 10 Crisis and Turmoil Late Seventh to Early Sixth Centuries bce ..... 136
Trouble from the North ..... 136
Philistia ..... 137
The Kingdom of Judah ..... 137
The Fall of Assyria—The Rise of the Neo-Babylonian Kingdom ..... 140
Egyptian Intervention and Occupation of the Levant ..... 141
Nebuchadnezzar's Conquest of the Levant ..... 143
Life on the Edge: The Kingdom of Judah in the Vise of Levantine Geopolitics ..... 146
Further Conflicts in the Levant ..... 149
Developments in Egypt ..... 150
The Final Stages of the Neo-Babylonian Dynasty ..... 151
The Medes and the Persians ..... 155

CHAPTER 11 Persian Domination Late Sixth to Fourth Centuries bce ..... 157
Population and Political Organization ..... 157
Historical Outline ..... 160

CHAPTER 12 Alexander and the Early Hellenistic Period ..... 173
Judea Under the Diodochi (323–301 bce) ..... 176
Judea Under the Ptolemies (301–200 bce) ..... 177
Judea Under Seleucid Rule ..... 179

CHAPTER 13 The Hasmonean Struggle for Independence 167 to 142 bce ..... 183
The Early Battles ..... 183
Hasmonean Campaigns Outside of Judea ..... 186
Judas' Final Battles ..... 188
The Campaigns of Jonathan and Simon ..... 192
Jonathan's Final Campaigns ..... 196

CHAPTER 14 The Hasmonean Kingdom 142 to 76 bce ..... 200
John Hyrcanus (135–104 bce) ..... 203
Aristobulus I (104–103 bce) ..... 205
Alexander Jannaeus (103–76 bce) ..... 206

CHAPTER 15 Hasmonean Decline and the Rise of Herod 67 to 37 bce ..... 210
Qumran ..... 216

CHAPTER 16 Herod and His Sons 37 bce to 6 ce ..... 217
Herod's Early Years (37–25 bce) ..... 217
Herod's Building Projects ..... 219
The Declining Years of Herod ..... 223
Herod's Death and the Division of His Kingdom ..... 223

CHAPTER 17 Historical Geography of the Gospels ..... 224
The Birth of Jesus and the Flight into Egypt ..... 224
The Ministry of John and the Baptism of Jesus ..... 225
The Travels of Jesus ..... 227
The Last Days of Jesus ..... 233
From the Empty Tomb to the Road to Emmaus ..... 237

CHAPTER 18 The Early Days of the Church First Century ce ..... 239
Jerusalem, Judea and Samaria ..... 239
The Apostle Paul ..... 241
The Seven Churches of the Apocalypse (Rev 1:4–3:21) ..... 249

CHAPTER 19 The First Jewish Revolt Against Rome 66 to 74 ce ..... 250
The End of the Herodian Dynasty ..... 250
The Outbreak of Violence ..... 252
The Aftermath of the Revolt ..... 263

CHAPTER 20 The Bar Kochba Revolt 132 to 135 ce ..... 265

Abbreviations ..... 269

Index ..... 270

# FOREWORD

*Carta's New Century Handbook and Atlas of the Bible*, a concise version of *The Sacred Bridge: Carta's Atlas of the Biblical World*, is meant for use by all those who have a love for biblical history. College teachers may find it useful for undergraduates alongside the standard *Carta Bible Atlas*, which it complements by being more of a historical geography.

*Carta's New Century Handbook and Atlas of the Bible* also serves as a stepping stone to the elaborate scholars' edition, *The Sacred Bridge: Carta's Atlas of the Biblical World* itself, where a great deal of material not directly related to biblical history and lands has been discussed in detail and special attention has been paid to citing all available historical sources in their original languages, sometimes in their original script. With its emphasis on linguistics and supported by a detailed and easy to use bibliography. *The Sacred Bridge* has been highly praised and enthusiastically received by scholars worldwide.

The object of this concise version is to augment the personal Bible study of all who seek a straightforward understanding of biblical history. Nevertheless, the reader will still have the sense that sacred history came about in a real world, a realm illumined by a multitude of discoveries and studies during the past two hundred years. Furthermore, the geographical dimension of the Bible accounts is being thoroughly presented. Every Bible student may thus put himself in the ancient reality and feel the events as they were experienced by the ancient Israelites and their neighbors.

If wanted, foreign scripts, transcriptions and their rendering in English, along with the complete bibliographical apparatus, can be easily accessed by turning to *The Sacred Bridge*. The latter work is based on the research of many scholars and the present text without references is not intended to obscure that dependence. One of its innovative principles was the attempt to deal with the history of the whole Levant, i.e. North Syrian as well as Palestinian history. That guideline has been largely reserved for the more elaborate *Sacred Bridge*, but the reader should always keep in mind that events in the north, as in Egypt, often had a decisive effect on "biblical" history.

It is our sincere hope and that of the publishers, that this new historical atlas will enrich the Bible reading experience of a yet wider audience for whom the Sacred Canon enjoys special significance in their lives.

**Anson F. Rainey**
**R. Steven Notley**

# Solomon's Prayer

When a foreigner, who is not of your people Israel, comes from a distant land because of your name—for they shall hear of your great name, your mighty hand, and your outstretched arm—when a foreigner comes and prays toward this house, then hear in heaven your dwelling place, and do according to all that the foreigner calls to you so that all the peoples of the earth may know your name and fear you, as do your people Israel, and so that they may know that your name has been invoked on this house that I have built.

(1 Kings 8:41–43)

# INTRODUCTION

The twenty-first century has burst upon the stage of history in a worldwide epidemic of racial and ethnic violence. Whereas the twentieth-century pundits sought to eliminate the natural human instinct for self- and group identification (partly as a reaction to the gross misuse of that instinct that led to the Second World War), the end of the Cold War saw an outbreak of local conflicts between peoples of diverse cultures seemingly no longer able to share a small piece of the planet with their neighbors.

In times of such crisis, wise men everywhere have mainly turned to their ancient sacred writings for wisdom to overcome their plight. Globalization has led to the development of a vast constituency of people who find their guidance in the Judeo-Christian Scriptures: the Jewish Diaspora on every continent, and the spread of Christianity through the enterprise of evangelization.

Of all the writings held sacred by the world's religions, only the Bible presents a message linked to geography. This is not just the location of religious centers but the experience of a people in its land, a people that has insisted on its God-given right to self-identity throughout the ages and in defiance of all forces that sought to deny it. All Jews and Christians who profess to find the source of their faith in these Scriptures look to the experiences of that people depicted in the Bible as examples and role models for their search after the Divine will and for their moral conduct among men. The religious experiences of that ancient people took place in relation to a geographical setting, generally a small postage stamp on the face of the globe, a patch of terrain in the southern part of the eastern Mediterranean littoral.

The Bible is replete with geographical information, not as a guidebook for travelers or a textbook on geography, but often almost incidental to the message. Yet without the geography, that message is often obscured or vitiated for the uninformed reader. The present atlas seeks to introduce the reader to the geographical elements that can help to make real the social, historical and spiritual experience of the People of the Book.

This is not meant to be a textbook in geography, not even biblical geography. It is an attempt to view the geographical setting through the eyes of the ancient inhabitants. It concentrates on the terms and places that have enjoyed their attention; it seeks to define them in terms of their ancient understanding. On the other hand, recognizing that the geography of the Land of the Bible is not complete and that many other peoples have contributed to its history, our attention will be turned to every available documentary source, Egyptian, Akkadian, Moabite, Phoenician, Greek, Latin, Arabic, etc., that may provide geographical details and perspective. Many ancient towns escaped mention in the Bible but are known from Late Bronze sources and reappear again in the Hellenistic Age. They were there all along as their archaeological mounds often testify. The Canaanites, Amorites, Moabites, Edomites, Ammonites, Nabateans and others had a share in the historical vicissitudes of the land in question. Their experiences are treated as equally worthy of attention and every possible source must be exploited to fill in the picture. This inclusive approach, utilizing all possible sources in addition to the Bible, is consciously meant to be a continuation of the scholarly tradition established by the patriarchs of modern historical geography in the Holy Land: George Adam Smith, Albrecht Alt, and my own personal mentors, Benjamin Mazar and Yohanan Aharoni.

*Jerusalem as the Center of the World, the pivot of three continents, with America—Terra Nova—in the lower left-hand corner.*

Not only the religious Jew or Christian may gain insight and inspiration from this historical and geographical story. In the past, one might have pointed to the biblical tradition as one of the foundations of "Western" culture. Globalization is making that Western conceit obsolete. The ideologies and technologies of the Western world are becoming the possession of a world constituency. Even those populations with equally venerable and ancient cultural traditions may find understanding and insights from the human experience that derived from the ancient Near East in general and from the Levantine and East Mediterranean peoples in particular.

## Dimensions and Disciplines of Historical Geography

The **Spatial** dimension naturally plays an important role in historical geography. The focus will be on the geographical entities known to us from the "eastern Mediterranean" and the "ancient Near East."

The **Temporal** dimension requires the exposition of the country's and the peoples' experiences over time. This is the "Historical" aspect of this endeavor. As a working definition, history as intended here is "man's reflection on his past." The human animal had been given the blessing and the curse of reflection. We can think about and evaluate the events of our past, our present and our prospective future. The written sources we study may all have an agenda, e.g. Pharaonic propaganda, religious exhortation, but the allusions to geographical details are seldom a matter of invention. The ancient writers often

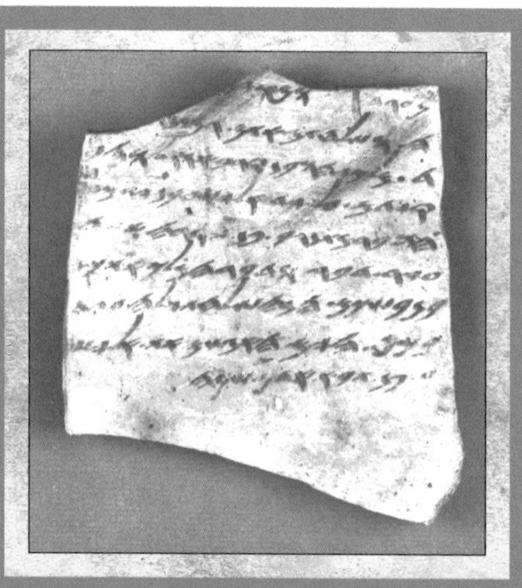

*Reinforcements to Ramoth-negeb "lest Edom come there." Arad Ostracon No. 24, the most detailed historical/geographical information from the pre-exilic period ever found in Cisjordan.*

framed their tendentious messages in a geographical framework. That framework often helps us to reveal a more objective situation than the original writer may have intended (consciously or unconsciously). The scholarly, scientific exposition of ancient sources using all the tools of paleography, epigraphy, grammar, syntax and discourse analysis, is an honorable and worthy enterprise. There is nothing to be gained by the pretext born of intellectual laziness known as Post-modernism.

The **CULTURAL** dimension requires that the Bible and its contemporary sources must be interpreted in the light of ancient Near Eastern culture. Each generation pictured biblical history in terms of its own culture, e.g. medieval and Renaissance art. The past two centuries and a half of archaeological research have provided us with graphic representations and actual objects from real life: buildings, artifacts, facial and hair styles, etc. Modern historical study must seek to interpret events in the matrix of that ancient culture.

The **SPIRITUAL** dimension derives from the fact that religion in antiquity was not a separate compartment of life; it was integral to everyday living. Furthermore, the expressions "Holy Land" and "Holy Places" reflect the religious motivation of many of the ancient writers and more specifically the motivation of myriads of students of biblical history. While the approach in this atlas is meant to be entirely secular in the scholarly sense, the sensibilities of the religious constituency are respected and no apologetic agenda is intended in that sphere. Every interested person of every persuasion should be able to partake of the fruits of our labors and derive whatever religious benefit he or she may be seeking. But on that score, the onus is on the reader; only the receptive can receive.

Historical geography is not a discipline of itself. It is rather the synthesis of data from several fields of research.

**Physical Geography.** Though this is not a textbook of physical geography, the study of the physical makeup of the geographical area of our interest must play a major role. The emphasis is on what may be learned about the ecology within which the historical events had taken place. Today all the modern techniques of scientific research, including space technology, are utilized to help us understand the nature of our planet and its living surface. All scientific methodologies must be welcomed in the study of historical geography. The most important elements that must be considered are:

1. *Geology and Orography:* geomorphology.
2. *Ecology:* soils and rocks and their potential, flora and fauna and their contribution.
3. *Hydrology:* water sources and the means of their utilization.
4. *Meteorology:* changing weather patterns as affecting the way of life in the various periods.
5. *Cartography:* recording of data and representing it on paper.

Complete certainty in defining the ancient geographical terms cannot be attained with the sources available. But one must make the effort in any serious historical research. The modern geographers must not be allowed to apply the biblical terms in any manner that suits their fancy without reference to the ancient sources. Furthermore, maps for biblical atlases should be based on the best in modern topographical recording, i.e., on the latest scientific maps.

An effort will be made throughout this atlas to apply the ancient names properly, restricted to the areas they designated in ancient times. The following is a description of the country using the ancient terms for the respective features and area.

**Historical Philology**. This is the study of ancient texts and will comprise the main activity of this present study. Historical geography begins with the Bible itself and a good example is the narrative of Genesis, chapter 14. The author has at his disposal a geographical tradition older than his own day. This is reflected in the ancient toponyms. Sometimes he makes a comment such as "Bela, that is, Zoar" (Gen 14:2), or "En-mishpat, that is, Kadesh" (Gen 14:7), which show us that the other double names in the chapter must be likewise understood. He reveres his older tradition, but he wants his reader to have geographical orientation relevant to his own day so he gives the more recent names of the older sites. Without geographical orientation, he is saying that one cannot get the full impact of the narrative.

**Toponymy**. The third major discipline is the study of place names. An important aspect of any ancient culture is its corpus of geographical names. These reflect many aspects of local psychology, society, and religion. The corpus of geographical names in any region comprises a rich source of linguistic, ethnic, historical, and folkloristic information. This is especially true of Palestine.

## ARCHAEOLOGY

Archaeology is the scholarly investigation of past human life, especially as it is revealed through relics, i.e. material objects, that have survived from ancient times.

The emphasis on everyday life as the legitimate study of archaeology can be seen in nineteenth-century works on biblical and Jewish antiquities based on the written documents. The biblical and talmudic references to buildings, utensils, rituals, foodstuffs and agriculture were collected systematically and studied philologically like any other cultural or historical subject.

Today archaeology of the Near East is a specialty in its own right. Within this field there is what many call "biblical archaeology." One cannot divide them very easily because some parts of the Bible

*The "way of the sea" is the route known later as the road from Paneas (Banias) to Tyre. "Beyond the Jordan" is Gilead (Perea in Herodian times), and the "Galilee of the Gentiles (foreigners/nations)" is the Jezreel Valley (= Harosheth-ha-goiim of Judges 4) where the Assyrians soon established an administrative center.*

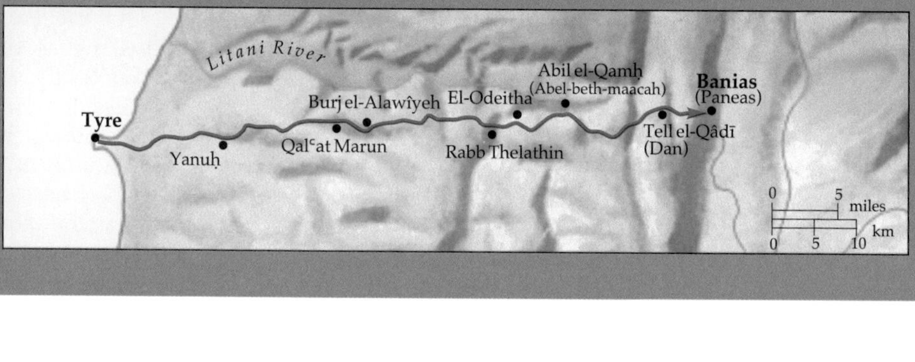

*Members of the Sinai Survey team, 1868–69: (left to right) guides Hassan and Salem, E. H. Palmer, H. S. Palmer, C. W. Wilson, F. W. Holland and C. Wyatt.*

deal with adjacent countries such as Egypt, Mesopotamia, Iran, and others. From a logical point of view, the archaeology of Palestine (Eretz-Israel) is a special area of study which greatly overlaps but is not necessarily the equivalent of biblical archaeology. The legitimacy of the latter term has recently been brought into question. It is best to admit that the Bible, the most extensive written document to survive from the ancient Near Eastern world, deals with the life of Israel and its neighbors: therefore, it is reasonable and desirable that the material side of Israelite and contemporary cultures be elucidated by archaeological research.

Interpretation of archaeological information, even when it includes many laboratory reports and the most careful and objective recording, is still a subjective affair. Though the objects found have an objective reality, their meaning as witnesses to life at the site can only be grasped by the exercise of human judgment. For example, two major activities in the past, public building works in times of prosperity and brutal destruction in times of war, usually leave their traces in the ruins of an ancient site. However, the dating of such features as structures and destruction levels depends on some precise link with known historical events. In even the best of cases that essential link between material finds and historical or even ethnic factors is tenuous in Palestinian archaeology. This is due to the paucity of written materials discovered in stratified contexts. Recently, there has been some criticism of the "biblical" archaeologist for being too bound up with his philological and historical studies to do objective work in the field. If anything, the "biblical" archaeologist has given too much credence to the "objectivity" of his material finds at the expense of sound historical analysis apart from mute archaeological evidence. One must work in the two disciplines separately and then exercise the utmost caution when trying to link them up. Most archaeologists' historical syntheses are highly tentative at best.

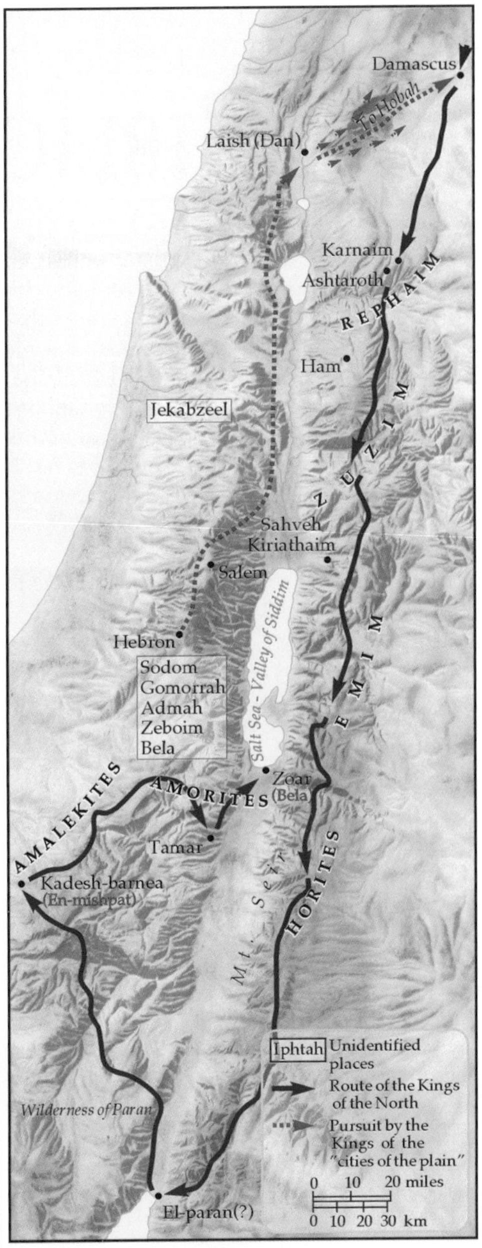


**THE KINGS OF THE NORTH (GENESIS 14)**

*A tel is an artificial mound consisting of the cultural remains of ancient towns or structures that accumulated on top of each other through the ages. Each layer came about as a result of deliberate obliteration in war or as a result of natural disasters such as earthquakes. These destructions were often followed by conflagrations, leaving layers of ashes separating the different strata, an aid to archaeologists in assigning the various layers to their respective periods.*

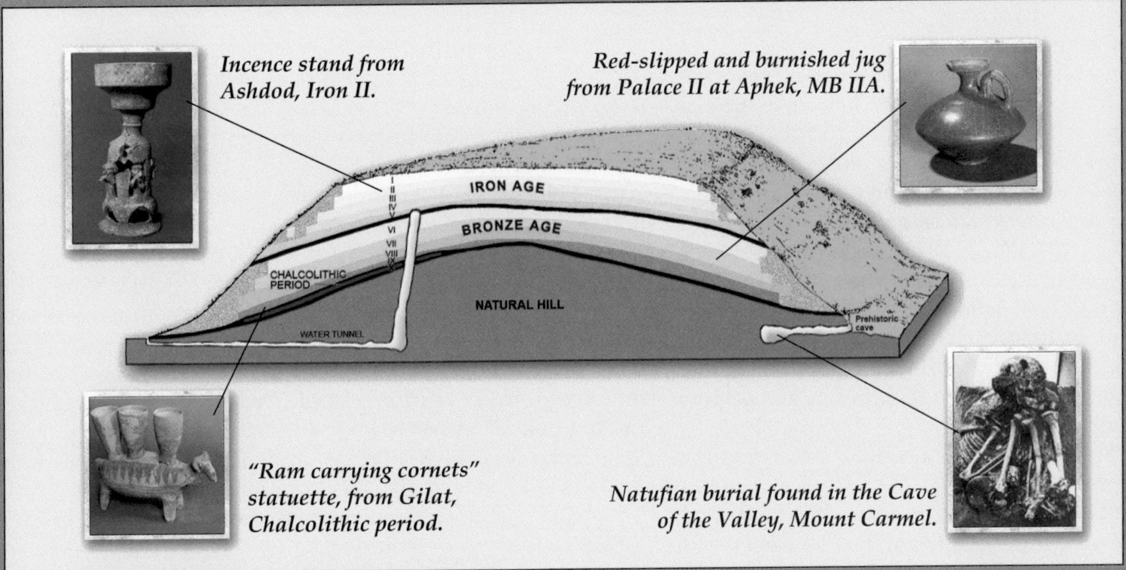


*Incence stand from Ashdod, Iron II.*

*Red-slipped and burnished jug from Palace II at Aphek, MB IIA.*

*"Ram carrying cornets" statuette, from Gilat, Chalcolithic period.*

*Natufian burial found in the Cave of the Valley, Mount Carmel.*

# CHAPTER ONE

# THE BIBLICAL VIEW OF THE WORLD

The epigraphic and artistic sources of the ancient peoples are replete with allusions to the various ethnic groups that peopled the Eastern Mediterranean and the Near East. In most traditions, such as that of the Egyptian artists, there were standard models of facial and sartorial types denoting the peoples that they encountered. This is also true of Mesopotamia and especially of ancient Persia (note the wall reliefs of Persepolis).

THE FAMILY OF NATIONS (GENESIS 10)

For the biblical view of world anthropology we have the "Table of Nations" in Genesis 10 and its parallel in 1 Chronicles 1:4–23. These two texts and their Septuagint counterparts can be used to clarify some of the obscure ethnicons but many of them still remain unknown to us. For a detailed exegesis of these passages one may consult critical and linguistic commentaries. The treatment here will touch only on those elements and ethnic groups about which something is known and which shed light on the outlook of the passage as a whole.

One may see that the "Table" presents three main branches of the population of the known world as viewed from the standpoint of the land of Canaan/Israel. These are subsumed under the headings of the three sons of Noah, the legendary ancestors of all who came after the Flood. The relations between certain groups are not always comparable to modern knowledge of the language families or generic ties as modern research has defined them. But the general picture is instructive for understanding the ancient mentality.

The descendants of Japheth (Gen 10:1–5; 1 Chr 1:5–7) are:

(1) *Gomer*, the Cimmerians of classical sources, a people from the Caucasus who threatened the civilized nations in the seventh century BCE and later, and Magog, probably a kindred group;

(2) *Madai*, the Indo-European nation situated in northwestern Iran; the Persians of southeast Iran are not mentioned.

(3) *Javan*, viz. Ionia.

(4) *Tubal* and *Meshech* and *Tiras*. Three nations in Anatolia; the first two are Tabal and Mushki, Phrygian kingdoms of Cappadocia known from Assyrian inscriptions. Tiras might be the "Tyrsenoi" of the Greek sources, viz. the Etruscans who migrated from Lydia in the eighth century BCE at the earliest.

(5) The sons of Gomer are *Ashkenaz* (the Scythians), *Riphath* (unknown) and *Togarmah*, the Til-garimmu of the Assyrian texts.

(6) The sons of Javan are *Elishah* (presumably=ancient Alashia on the south coast of Cyprus), *Tarshish* in Cilicia, *Kittim* (the kingdom of Kition?) and *Dodanim*, which must be corrected to Rodanim, in accordance with LXX Rhodes, and with 1 Chronicles 1:7, which also has Rodanim.

Surprisingly, the sons of Ham encompass groups which we would arrange in a different order:

(7) *Cush*, *Mizraim*, *Put* and *Canaan* (Gen 10: 6–10; 1 Chr 1:9–16). This group includes three elements in Africa. Cush is presumably the same as Egyptian Cush, which is in Nubia, i.e. modern Sudan. Mizraim is the Semitic term for Egypt; it derives from Semitic *miṣru* (as in Akkadian), "border, district." The dual form evidently reflects the awareness that Egypt was known by its two logical geographical parts: the Nile Valley (Upper Egypt) and the Delta (Lower Egypt). Put is on the Libyan coast.

What has surprised modern scholars is the inclusion of Canaan as a descendant of Ham. Linguistics discerned long ago that the Canaanite dialects are part of the family which modern scholarship has called the "Semitic" languages. The appropriateness of that latter title is itself questionable since the biblical ethnographic division in this chapter included Elam as a son of Shem as well as other elements whose languages are hardly "Semitic" in the modern linguistic sense.

The Cushites in this list are then linked with elements that all seem to be either in northeast Africa or on the southern "heel" of the Arabian Peninsula, viz. Seba, Havilah and Sabtah, Raamah and Sabteca. The sons of Raamah are said to be Sheba and Dedan, two elements in south and north Arabia respectively.

Furthermore, the link between Cush and Nimrud the mighty hunter is strange. Nimrud is associated with a group of cities in Mesopotamia: Babel, Erech, Accad and Calneh, in the land of Shinar (=Sumer in Mesopotamian terminology), and Ashur (Assyria), and its political capital, Nineveh, as well as Rehoboth-ir (possibly="the open space around the city") and Calah along with Resen (unknown) between Nineveh and Calah. The Chronicler mentions the connection between Nimrud and Cush but he ignores the list of Mesopotamian cities.

Mizraim is surprisingly associated with the Ludim (Lydians in southwest Turkey) and an obscure group called Casluhim from whom the author derives the Philistines, but also the Caphtorim, i.e. the people of Crete (from which Amos 9:7 derives the Philistines).

Canaan, as a supposed descendant of Mizraim, is called the ancestor of a number of well-known peoples: Sidon, his firstborn (Sidonians is the biblical generic name for the Phoenicians); Heth (the Neo-Hittite states that survived the collapse of the Hittite empire and continued to exist in North Syria); the Jebusite (the occupants of pre-Davidic Jerusalem) and the Amorite (originally the population of North Syria in the Middle Bronze Age); the Girgashite and Hivite (among the unknown ethnic groups mentioned elsewhere in the Bible); and the people of several well-known city-states: Arkite (of ᶜArqat) and the Sinite (of Siyannu), Arvadite (of Arvad) and the Zemarite (of Ṣumur, Ṣimirru, classical Simyra) and the Hamathite (the Neo-Hittite/Aramaic city-state of Hamath). In general, one may note that all the identifiable elements in this group were speakers of one of the so-called Northwest Semitic dialects (according to current terminology), viz. Canaanite and Aramaic. None of them are in Transjordan.

The descendants of Shem (Gen 10: 21–32; 1 Chr 1:23) are even more obscure and speculative. The main emphasis is on the descendants of Eber (*ᶜEḇer*) since Abram is called an *ᶜIḇrî* (Hebrew).

The list as a whole includes some overlaps and duplications. What is especially surprising is the absence of some of the most important ethnic groups of the earlier periods, such as the Hurrians and the Urartians. The similarity to the ethnic picture in Ezekiel 27 indicates that it reflects a viewpoint of a very late period. One might think of the Persian period but it does not seem to match what is known about the many nations of the Persian Empire and the neighboring areas (as described, e.g., by Herodotus). In general, one may note that the three sons of Noah and their descendants are roughly placed in three areas, north, south and east of the Levant. Perhaps this is its main object: to show how the eastern Mediterranean littoral is the land bridge between the main branches of the human race.

An ancient view of the peoples of the world as comprising a vast feudal society with each nation assigned to the care of a specific heavenly being is clearly reflected in the original text of Deuteronomy 32:8–9.

When the Most High gave the nations their inheritance,
When He separated the sons of man,
He set the boundaries of the peoples
According to the number of the sons *of God*.
*And* YHWH's portion was His people; Jacob was the allotment of His inheritance.

At the end of line 8, the Masoretic Text as we have it now reads, "according to the number of the sons of Israel." However, the Septuagint reads here, "according to the number of the messengers (angels) of God." The existence of a Hebrew version with the reading, "according to the number of the sons of God," has been found at Qumran.

Therefore, the passage, as properly restored, indicates that the people of the world were placed in their respective homelands by the Most High God, who established their boundaries in accordance with the number of His heavenly servants/messengers, assigning one nation to each of them. But among those feudal allotments, God, i.e. YHWH, kept one for Himself, viz. Jacob (Israel). The great preoccupation of the non-canonical Jewish literature of the Hellenistic and Roman periods with the "sons of God" in Genesis 6 (who begat the "giants" on the daughters of men) apparently caused a counter-reaction among the more conservative rabbinic scholars (Pharisees?), who deliberately altered the poem to get rid of the "angelic" beings of the original text.

During the pre-exilic period in Judah, the society of men was viewed as a company of nations (ethnic groups), each with its own specific territory assigned to the oversight of a particular "son of God" who received the people/land as a feudal fief. But Israel/Jacob was viewed as the special inheritance (feudal fief) of the Most High God, with whom YHWH was identified.

## Other Ancient Views of the World

*Babylonian World Map*
*1) Mountain; 2) city; 3) Urarṭu; 4) Ashur; 5) Der; 6) Euphrates; 7) swamp; 8) Susa; 9) channel; 10) Bīt Yakin; 11) city; 12) Ḫabbān; 13) Babylon; 14) ocean (salt sea); 15) [ocean]; 16) [o]cean; 17) oce[an]; 18) Great Wall; 19) region, six leagues in between; 20) [regi]on [...]; 21) [regi]on [...]; 22) region, eight leagues in between; 23–25) No inscription.*

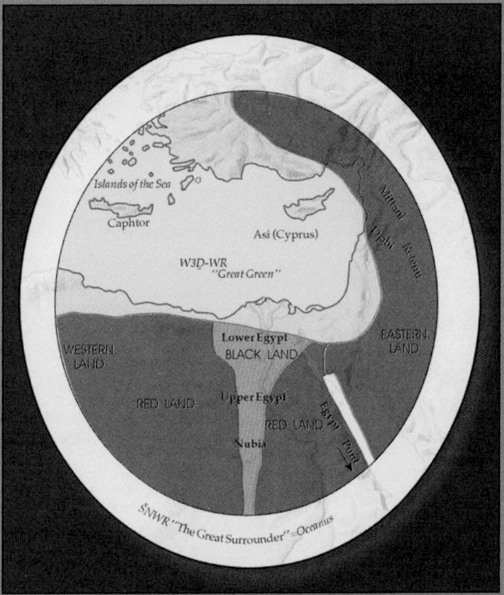


*The Egyptian world view is expressed in the Poetical Stele of Pharaoh Thutmose III in which the god Amon recounts the many nations and peoples that he has placed under the feet of the king. Like the Mesopotamians (and the Greeks), the Egyptians believed that a river encircled the known earth. The nations listed are those with whom Thutmose interacted during his many military campaigns and commercial ventures.*

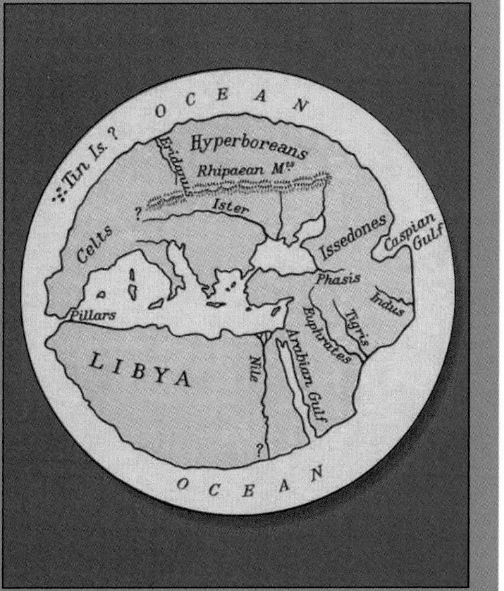


*The World According to Hecataeus (500 BCE)*
*Hecataeus, the early geographer, produced a map as Greeks envisioned it. No copies have survived but other Greek writers described it in detail. It had a striking resemblance to the Babylonian and Egyptian conceptions.*

# CHAPTER TWO
# THE LAND BRIDGE

The southern part of the eastern Mediterranean littoral is a clearly defined concept in the Bible and as such must be understood as part of the ancient Israelite concept of geography. Characterized by the coastal plain, from the border with Cilicia of classical times (the Plain of Adana in southwest Turkey) to approximately the line formed by the Suez Canal, that plain is bordered on the east by a series of mountain ranges, viz. the Jebel Noṣairah (Anṣarîyeh) in northern Syria, the mountains of Lebanon, their extension in Galilee and the mountains of Ephraim and Judah. The highlands south of Beer-sheba continue the chain to the border of the Sinai expanse. Beyond the western mountain ranges is the Great Rift, which may be seen in the Orontes Valley, the Lebanese Beqa$^{c}$, the Huleh and Jordan valleys, and the Arabah down to the Gulf of Elath (Gulf of Aqaba). East of the Great Rift one finds the Anti-Lebanon range, which swerves eastward (here called Jebel Bishrī) towards the middle Euphrates area, with the southern extension, called the Sirion, culminating in Mount Hermon. The plateaus of Golan and Gilead, Moab and Edom and Midian (the Hejaz) border the Rift on the east, south of Mount Hermon. Eastward of those ranges and plateaus there begin the deserts of Syria, Jordan and Arabia, which delimit the extreme eastern boundary of the littoral. A more detailed description of the respective areas of the littoral and their ancient names will be given below.

The eastern Mediterranean littoral is now commonly referred to in archaeological discussions as the Levant, which reflects a restriction and delimitation of its broader nineteenth-century usage. As a geographical unit, it was distinguished by a number of terms in the various languages.

The history of the eastern Mediterranean littoral is inexorably linked with the history of the adjacent regions, Mesopotamia and Egypt, the ancient seats of the beginnings of civilization and especially of many technological advances in the human struggle, including the art of writing. Together they comprise the "Fertile Crescent" of which the Levant is the western arm.

## THE LEVANT

This geographical entity is the subject of several biblical passages and also of some terms applied by writers in Mesopotamia and Egypt. As a unit it achieved its permanent status as a geographical factor in the ancient world during the Persian period and eventually became known as "Syria" or today, "Greater Syria" (Arabic *esh-Shâm*). Since the focus of this atlas is historical, some ancient terminology applied to the whole land bridge will be reviewed. A historical and physical description of the zone in question will reflect the fact that the northern Levant and southern Levant have had their own separate histories, overlapping and cross-influencing, to be sure, but nevertheless distinctive.

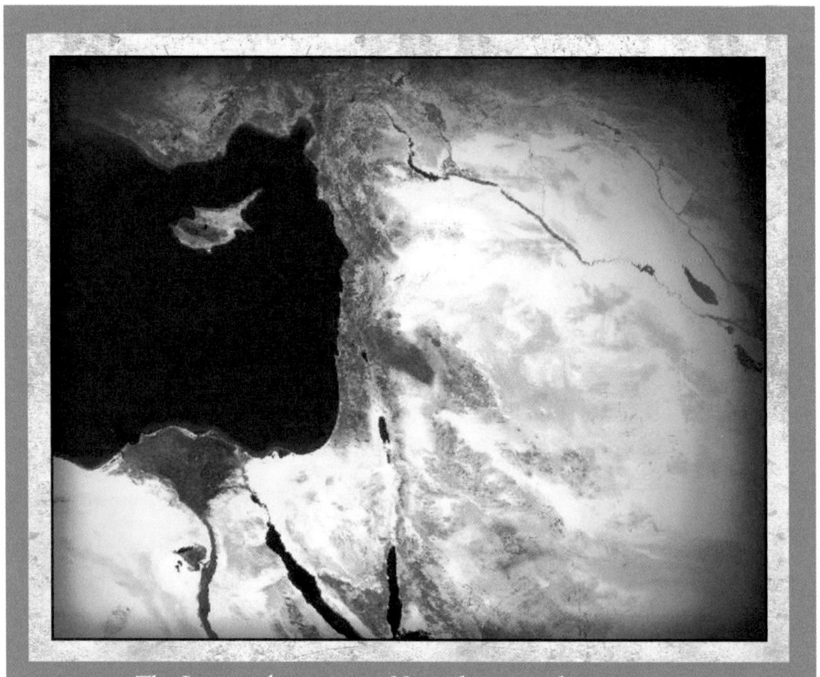

*The Levant from space. Note the great desert areas.*

**The Promised Land**. Although it is widely used in religious circles, the term "Promised Land" is not documented in the Bible. There is one passage, however, that furnished the basis for this term; it is the promise to Abram recorded in Genesis 15: 18–21.

On that day YHWH made a covenant with Abram, saying, "To your descendants I have given this land, from the **River of Egypt** as far as the great river, **the River Euphrates**...." (Gen 15:18–19)

The area encompassed here begins in the south at the "**River of Egypt**," the eastern, Pelusiac arm of the Nile River, which was well known as the border of Egypt through the ages down to classical times:

he encamped at Pelusion, for here is the entryway (to Egypt). (Herodotus 2.141)

The "River of Egypt" is in no way the equivalent of the "Brook of Egypt," Wâdī el-$^{c}$Arîsh, discussed below.

"The great river, the **River Euphrates**," is of course obvious. One biblical reference makes specific allusion to Tiphsah (1 Kgs 5:4), classical Thapsakos, at the bend in the Euphrates where convenient fords existed in antiquity. Tell Meskeneh, the site of ancient Emar, is also located here. The geographical entity envisioned in the Genesis promise is repeated in the opening chapter of the Book of Deuteronomy (*see* 1:7).

And likewise in the introduction to the Book of Joshua (*see* 1:1–4).

It must be stressed that the geographical unit depicted here contains Canaanites, to be sure, but it is *not* the equivalent of "the Land of Canaan." There is no legitimacy to the popular expression "Greater Canaan." This issue will be discussed more in detail below.

**Solomon's Sphere of Influence**. The biblical historian, writing after 561 BCE, sought to clarify for his readers the sphere of influence exercised by King Solomon of Israel. He used some geographical terms that were in vogue in his own time.

For he had dominion over everything Beyond the River, from Tiphsah even to Gaza, over all the kings of Beyond the River; and he had peace on all sides around about him. (1 Kgs 5:4)

The epithet, "Beyond the River," is documented first in the inscriptions of Esarhaddon, king of Assyria, in the seventh century BCE:

I called up the kings of the land of Ḫatti and "Beyond the River." (Prism B = Nin. A, V, 54–76)

Solomon's area of political dominance

is further defined by this same author in a passage which today precedes the verse cited above, but which probably had served as a geographical conclusion to the Solomonic chapters since it does come just at that place in the Chronicler's account (*see* 1 Kgs 5:1 [= Eng. 4:21] should probably be 10:26a || 2 Chr 9:26)

By "the River," the Euphrates is certainly meant, but at the other extreme the territory is said to extend to "the land of the Philistines" and to the "border of Egypt." It seems obvious that the intention here is that Philistia went as far as Wâdī el-ᶜArîsh, where the associated town was called Ienysus in Persian times, while the land from there to the Pelusiac branch of the Nile was the "border of Egypt." Herodotus clarifies the situation:

> Only through this (Arabian desert) is there entry into Egypt. For from Phoenicia to the boundaries of Kadytis belongs to the Syrians known as "Palestinian": from Kadytis, a town, I should say, not much smaller than Sardis, the seaports as far as Ienysus belong to the Arabian; from Ienysus as far as Lake Serbonis it is again Syrian, near which Mount Casius runs down to the sea; and after Lake Serbonis (where Tryphon is supposed to be buried), from there it is already Egypt. The whole area between Ienysus on the one side, and Mount Casius and the Lake on the other—and it is of considerable extent, not less than three days' journey—is desert and completely without water. (Herodotus 3.5)

Of course in Herodotus' day, Gaza (Kadytis) was in the hands of an Arabian king and not the Philistines. The description in Kings 5:1 relates to the situation prior to the Arabian (Kedarite) conquest of Gaza.

**The Province Beyond the River**. The Aramaic equivalent of Akkadian "Beyond the River" (Ezra 4:20) became the official name of the Persian satrapy that encompassed the eastern Mediterranean littoral in the Persian period. There was a familiar tradition about times when kings in Jerusalem had dominated this province.

> And mighty kings have ruled over Jerusalem, governing all of Beyond the River, and tribute, custom and toll were being paid to them. (Ezra 4:20; Deut 1:7)

## The Southern Levant

The ensuing section will treat the southern part of the eastern Mediterranean littoral, the "Southern Levant," which has enjoyed more geographical documentation than the northern, ancient part (modern Syria).

**The Province of Canaan**. Although the Egyptian records of the Late Bronze Age, when the pharaohs were overlords of Canaan, do use the term "Canaan" from time to time (alongside Khurru and Djahi and perhaps Retenu), there is no record of an official designated specifically as the governor or viceroy of Canaan. Neither is there any specific reference to a "Province of Canaan/Khurru/Djahi." However, one Alashian scribe, trained in the true Middle Babylonian tradition (as against the usual peripheral), does refer to the Egyptian-controlled area as "the province of Canaan."

On the other hand, there does not seem to be any record of a specific individual in the Egyptian governmental structure who was overall governor of the province.

The geographic extent of Canaan is also never described in Egyptian or Akkadian documents of the Late Bronze Age. Nevertheless, there are some indications to the effect that the northern border of Canaan as described in the Hebrew Bible reflects a geographic reality.

The passage in question is Numbers 34: 1–12, paralleled by Ezekiel 47:15–20. The southern border is identical with the southern border of the idealized Judean tribal inheritance in Joshua 15:2–4. For that reason, it is probably dealt with first in the Numbers passage. It does not conform to the geographical understanding of the Egyptian documents of the New Kingdom (Dynasties XVIII and XIX). Gaza would appear to be the first city along the coast that is reckoned as Canaan, e.g. in

*Fortress of "the town of the Canaan"; detail from relief of Seti I on north wall of temple at Karnak.*

the march across Sinai by Thutmose III and the itinerary followed by Seti I (and in Papyrus Anastasi I). However, for the sake of defining the biblical literary concept, the southern border will be discussed here (*see* Num 34:3b–5).

Many of the points along this route are not identified with any degree of certainty. The location of "the ascent of Akrabbim (scorpions)" is unknown, and there is no solid evidence for identifying it (as is done on modern maps) with Naqb eṣ-Ṣafa. Zin is also unknown, unless we assume that it is a general name for the steppe land that

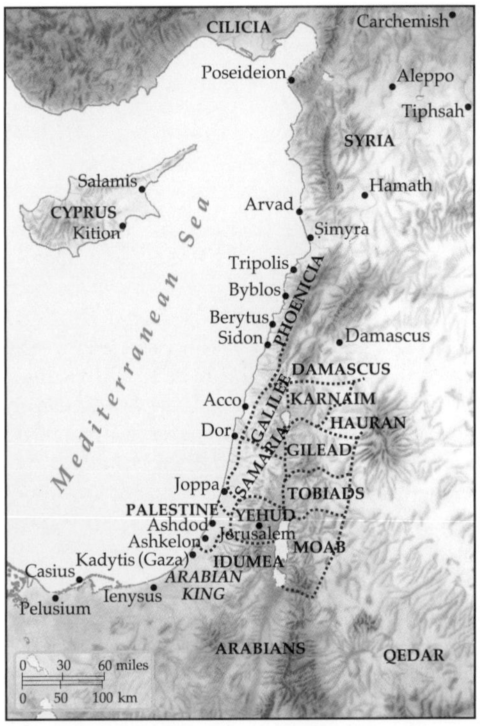


**The Satrapy Beyond the River: The Levant under Persian Administration**

extended as far as Kadesh-barnea. Here Ezekiel lists Tamar, which was the most important station in the northern Arabah, possibly the modern ᶜAin Ḥuṣb, southwest of the Dead Sea. The next reference point is "south of Kadesh-barnea." Since this is a place nearly halfway from the eastern to the western end of the border being described, it seems hardly contestable that Kadesh-barnea must be sought at or near the spring called ᶜAin Qedeis. However, the Iron Age Kadesh-barnea is more likely to be located a bit farther north at the fort beside ᶜAin el-Qudeirat, the richest and most centrally located of a group of springs on the southern edge of the steppe. It had been suggested that the whole region was called Kadesh-barnea, but that the name was preserved only at the southernmost well. The Book of Numbers, chapter 34, has only two points after Kadesh-barnea (Hazar-addar and Azmon) while Joshua 15 has four (Hezron, Addar, Karka, Azmon). From ᶜAin el-Qudeirat westward there are three additional wells which led to the following suggested identifications: ᶜAin Qedeis = Hazar-addar; ᶜAin Qeseimeh = Karka; ᶜAin Muweiliḥ = Azmon. Above ᶜAin Qedeis a small Iron Age fort was discovered which may be identified with Hazar-addar. From here the boundary continued on to the Mediterranean, following the "Brook of Egypt."

The most important point to note here is that the southern border of the entity known as the Land of Canaan is at the Brook of Egypt which is at Wâdī el-ᶜArîsh, while the southern border of the "Land of Promise" (= the satrapy "Beyond the

THE TRAVELS OF THE SPIES AND THE LIMITS OF THE LAND OF CANAAN (NUM 13)

River") was at the "River of Egypt," which was the Pelusiac branch of the Nile. The date that this southern border had some validity is another question.

On the west, the Mediterranean was of course the border of Canaan (Num 34:6).

The northern border is the most significant for our discussion. There are certain key points in this description on the basis of which the others may be conjectured with some degree of certainty (*see* Num 34:7).

From the seacoast the line is said to run to a prominent feature called Mount Hor, like the Mount Hor in the Negeb. This is obviously one of the northern summits of the Lebanese range in the vicinity of the coast. Various conjectures for identifying it, such as Jebel ᶜAkkar east of Tripolis or Jebel Makmel farther south, are unlikely since these ridges are far from the coast. The northern border of "the land that remains" (Josh 13:4) included Byblos and extended to Aphek to the Amorite territory (i.e. the Late Bronze Age kingdom of Amurru). Mount Hor is most likely one of the northwestern summits of the Lebanese range, north of Byblos, such as Râs Shaqqah, the hallowed *Theouprosopon* located between Byblos and Tripolis.

The key points for defining the northern border are Lebo-hamath and Zedad. As for Lebo-hamath, most translations have assumed that it is not the name of a city but only an adverbial expression: "the **entrance** of Hamath" (e.g. RSV), referring to Hamath on the Orontes. But Lebo is shown to be an important city on the border of the kingdom of Hamath and is to be identified with Lebweh, situated at one of the sources of the Orontes River, north of Baalbek.

The next point, Zedad, is easily identifiable since its name is preserved to this day in the village Ṣadâd east of the Anti-Lebanon range, near the Damascus–Homs highway, northeast of Lebweh. Zedad is situated on the fringe of the desert; therefore, it is most likely that the next two places, Ziphron and Hazar-enan, are to be equated with the two desert oases found east of Zedad, Ḥawwārîn and Qaryatein.

The eastern border has a series of reference points, none of which have been properly identified (*see* Num 34:10). Ain may be Khirbet ᶜAyyûn, not far from the Sea of Chinnereth.

Comparison with Ezekiel's version (*see* Ezek 47:18) reveals that the prophet defines the eastern border in terms of the provinces that had been established by the Assyrians after 732 BCE.

In Numbers, "the shoulder on the east side of the Sea of Chinnereth," and the continuation of the border southward along the course of the Jordan River, suggest that from Hazar-enan the border included a large portion of the Damascene, perhaps as far as Jebel Druze.

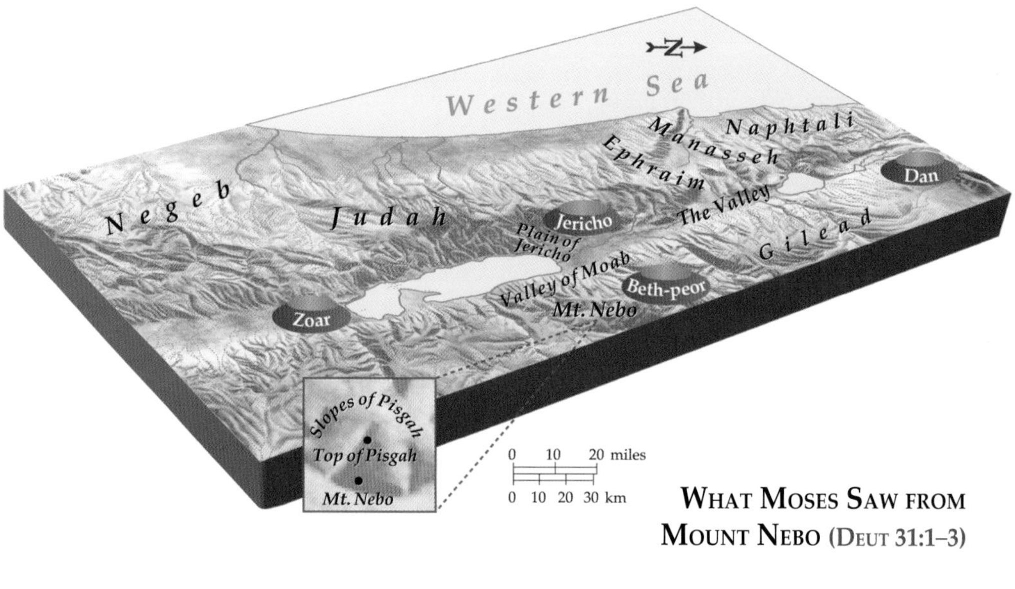


WHAT MOSES SAW FROM MOUNT NEBO (DEUT 31:1–3)

In any case, the Dead Sea is the "Eastern Sea" from which the southern border was delineated.

That the Jordan River below Chinnereth was considered the border of Canaan is illustrated by the affair described in Joshua 22. When the delegation was sent from Cisjordan to confer with the tribes of Transjordan, they were going from Canaan to Gilead (cf. Josh 22:9, 22:32).

One ethnographic tradition placed the Canaanites on the plains and the Jebusites, Amorites and Hittites in the hills (*see* Num 13:29; cf. Deut 1:7). This concept of Canaan's northern border finds confirmation from the Hellenistic-Roman period in the coins minted by Beirut. The numismatic evidence pertaining to the name of Beirut on its coins, "Laodicea which is in Canaan," along with a Greek monogram, is decisive. Other coins have *lbyrt*, "of Beirut," also with the same Greek monogram, which rightly surmised should represent "Laodicea which is in Phoenicia." Besides the equation of Phoenicia with Canaan, the most important fact is that the Laodicea of Beirut is identified as being in Canaan, thus distinguishing it from "Laodicea on the sea" (Strabo *Geog.* XVI, 2: 9), which is modern-day Latikia (Laḍiqîyeh), just 7 miles (11 km) south of Râs Shamra. This latter Laodicea is thus not in Canaan/ Phoenicia. So the Hellenistic geographical concept that the northern limits of Canaan = Phoenicia seems to correspond to the same conception going back to the Late Bronze Age sources.

## The Land of Israel

As mentioned above, the editor of the Book of Kings envisions the sphere of Solomon's political influence in terms of "Beyond the River," reaching as far north as the bend of the Euphrates. But he makes a clear distinction between that geographic entity and the territory where the sons of Israel (Judah and Israel) actually reside.

> So **Judah and Israel** lived in safety, every man under his vine and his fig tree, from **Dan** even to **Beer-sheba**, all the days of Solomon.
>
> (1 Kgs 5:5 [Eng. 4:25])

The same concept is embodied in the land as defined in the view of Moses from Mount Nebo (*see* Deut: 31:1–3). The same may be said for the summary in the Book of Joshua (*see* Josh 11:17). Moreover, the census ascribed to David was to cover essentially the same area (*see* 2 Sam 14:2).

All this does not imply that the respective borders ran close to the actual tels of these two cities, Dan and Beer-sheba. It simply means that they were the principal towns at the two extremities of the territory recognized as being occupied by the Israelite tribes. At least during periods of national strength, the real southern border of Judah must have passed just south of

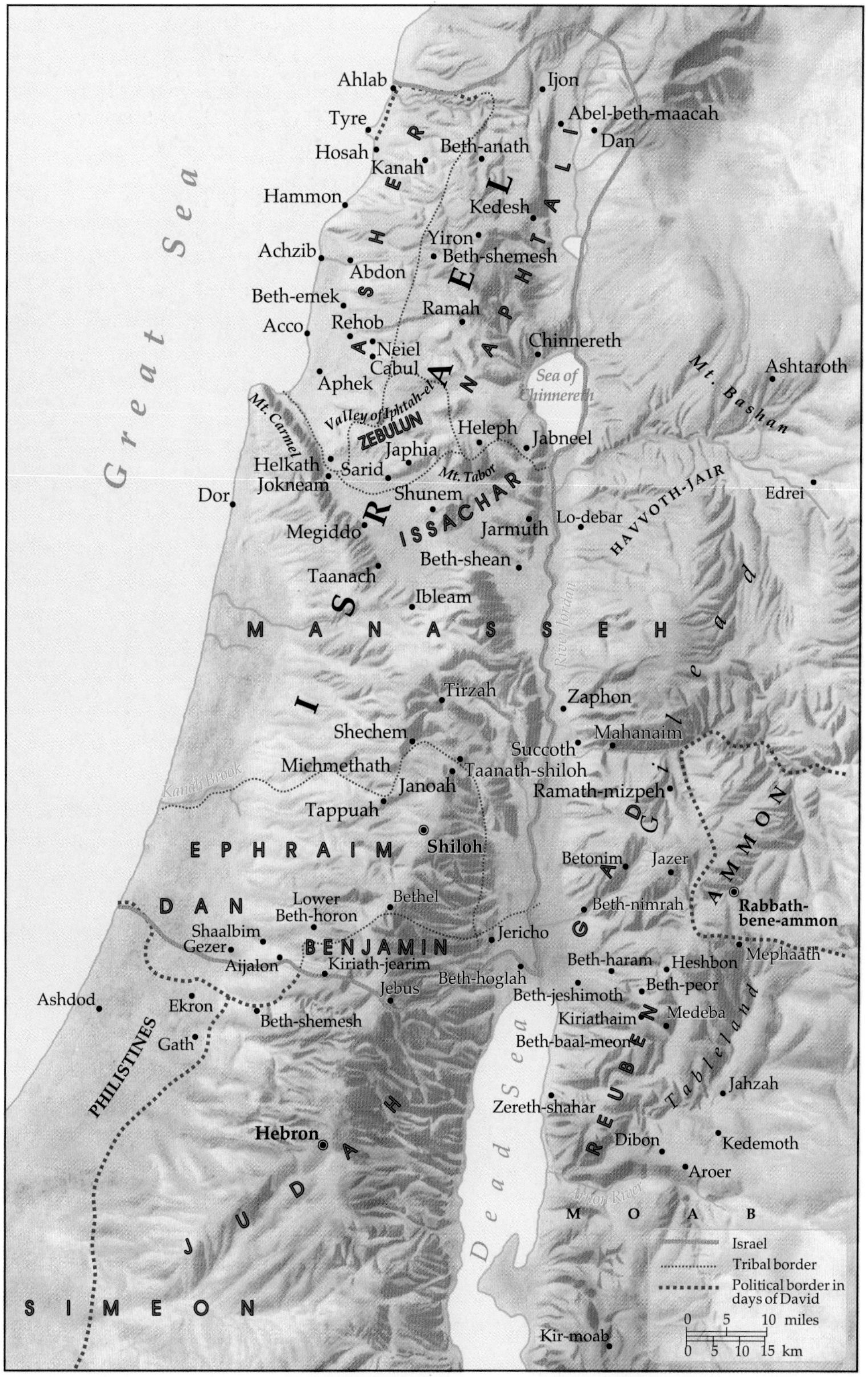


**The Borders of the Tribal Territories (Josh 13–19)**

Kadesh-barnea and the northern border of Israel must have approached Lebo-hamath (cf. e.g. 2 Kgs 14:25).

The incident described in Joshua 22 about the misunderstanding with the tribes in Transjordan underscores the view that those tribes were also a genuine part of Israel, "beyond the Jordan toward the sunrise, from the valley of the Arnon as far as Mount Hermon, and all the Arabah to the east" (Josh 12:1b). In the eighth century BCE the Cisjordanian governments of Judah and Israel had occasion to conduct their censuses in Transjordan (1 Chr 5:17).

There are a number of east-west or west-east cross-sectional descriptions of the land but they represent a Judahite viewpoint since they include the Shephelah, that intermediate range of foothills that borders the Judean hill country on the west (but is not present on the Sharon Plain to the north) (*see* e.g. Deut 1:7a; Josh 10:40; Judg 1:9).

To these may be compared the cross section of Judah in the days of King Uzziah (*see* 2 Chr 26:10). Finally, one such passage does include the northern Shephelah of

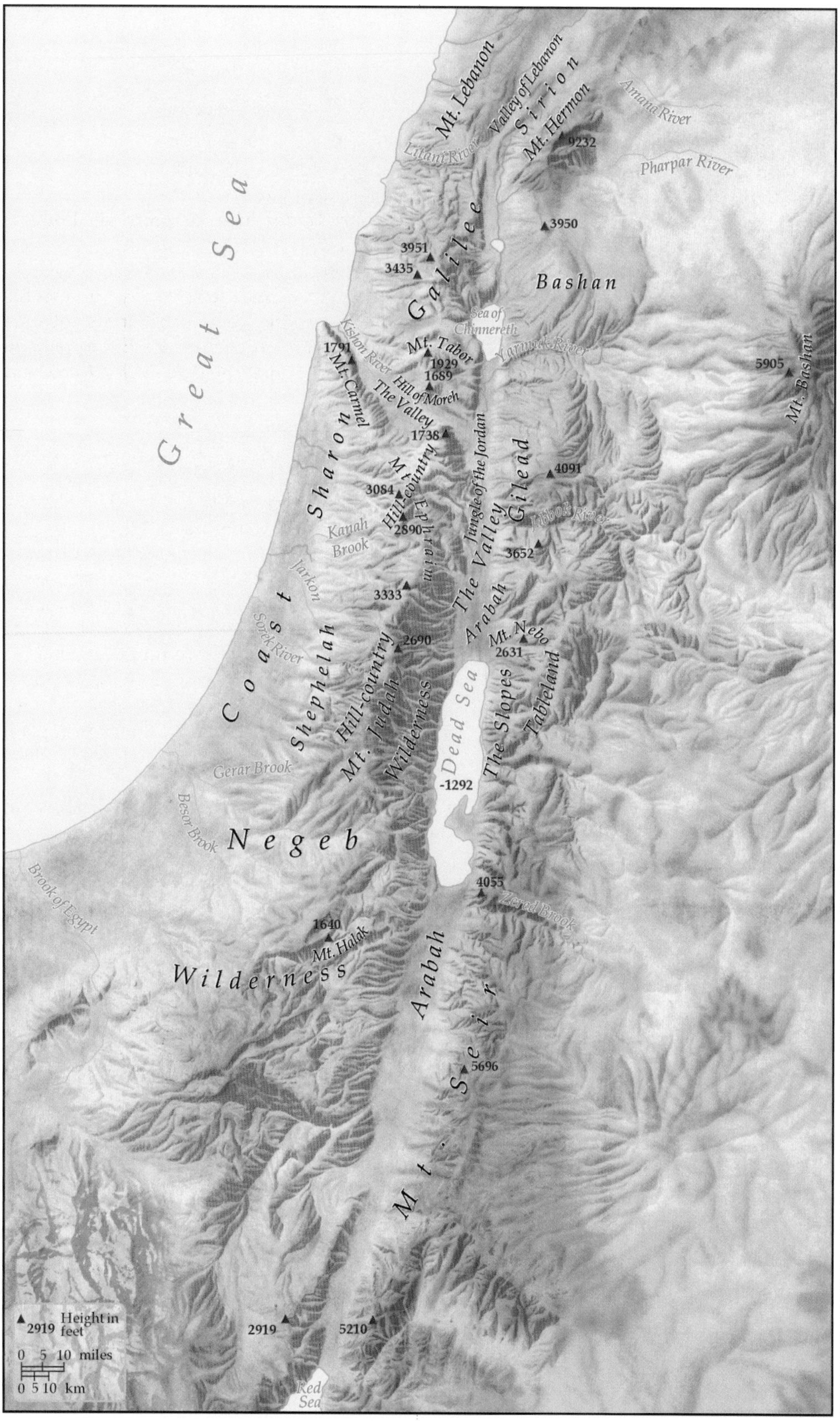


**The Geographical Regions of the Southern Levant**

Israel, viz. the foothills of western Galilee (*see* Josh 11:16–17).

**Topographical Description**. The overall character of the terrain is succinctly stated in Deuteronomy 8:7–8. Note that these agricultural products can be divided in accordance with their usual venue of production: some on the hills and the others on the plains.

**Description and Nomenclature**. The terrain will be briefly described from north to south and west to east. Stress is upon the biblical terminology as it was applied in Old Testament times, though later terms (especially Greco-Roman) and even some modern names are unavoidable. Though many topographical terms have survived in biblical Hebrew, there are many local and regional names that have been lost. A few of the latter may have survived in rabbinic sources, or in the Arabic toponymy of today.

## Coastal Plain

***Phoenicia***. The northern coast, that of modern Lebanon, is characterized by the closeness of the mountains to the shore. The major harbors of the east Mediterranean were here, viz. those of the Phoenician cities: Byblos, Beirut, Sidon and especially the two islands, Tyre and Arvad. Cultivable land is scarce on the plain but the mountains of the hinterland provided the timber and other products so famous in antiquity. The northern coastal zone is called Phoenicia in Greco-Roman times (Acts 21:2) but has no name in the Old Testament except Canaan (Isa 23:11) or simply Sidon (Judg 18:28). The population was mainly engaged in maritime activities (Ezek 27:8–9) so agricultural workers were absorbed in working the land (Judg 1:31–32). The promontory of Râs en-Naqûra (Rosh ha-Niqra), called Ladder of Tyre in Crusader times, sets off the plain to the south of it from the rest of Phoenicia. On the south it is bounded by the Carmel. The coast is bounded by cliffs of considerable height accompanied by an extensive abrasion platform that shows up as reefs running parallel to the shore about 1 mile (1.5 km) or more out in the water. No sand dunes encroach on the fertile plain that is about 4.4 miles (7 km) at its maximum length, being bounded on the east by the mountains of Upper Galilee. The soil is mainly alluvial deposited by the streams coming from these latter hills. The principal harbor was near Acco-Ptolemais since the sands block most of the southern shore. The coast north of Acco is also too rocky; thus the cove by Acco was the only convenient landing point. The Na$^{c}$mân (Belus) breaks to the surface in the center of the plain between Acco and Carmel and flows north till it finds an outlet to the sea south of Acco. No cliff formations appear on the south; instead, there is a wide beach and a dune area about 1 mile (1.6 km) wide. Extensive swamps that once existed on the eastern side are now left with rich alluvial soil. Important antiquity sites stand around the edge of this plain: ancient Acco in the north and others around the eastern perimeter. Two impressive tels stand in the center: one in the north, Tell Keisan (Tel Kison), is perhaps biblical Achshaph (Josh 11:1, 12:20, 19:25) or Mishal (Josh 19:26), and the other, Tell Kurdâneh, is most likely Aphek (Josh 19:30), at the headwaters of the Na$^{c}$mân/Belus.

Mount Carmel is the mass of Cenomanian limestone running northwest to southeast from its headland to Wâdī Milḥ (Naḥal Yoqne$^{c}$am). It forms a wedge-shaped barrier that divides the coastal plain; within its ridges were plentiful orchards and vineyards, making it a symbol of fertility (Isa

*Ancient ruins of Ashkelon.*

33:9; Amos 1:2; Nah 1:4). The Carmel formed its watershed along the northeastern ridge; the main streams flow westward through steep ravines, the caves of which gave shelter to prehistoric man.

The coastal zone from the Carmel headland south to the Crocodile River (Naḥal Tanninim) was evidently called Naphoth-(Dor) (Josh 11:2, 12:23, 17:11; 1 Kgs 4:11). It is bounded by ridges of sandstone along the shore which shelter a fertile plain at the foot of the Carmel. Though Dor was the principal harbor town, there were a few smaller sites such as Tell es-Samak (Tel Shiqmona).

***Sharon Plain***. From Naphoth-dor to Joppa the Sharon (Eus. *Onom.* 162:5–6) consists of alluvial soil from the Samarian Hills on the east, a band of red Mousterian sand in the middle, and then ridges of sandstone (*kurkar*) which blocked the passage of the several streams crossing the plain from east to west. This caused swamps and scrub forests to develop behind the sandstone ridges. The Nahr el-ᶜAuja (modern-day Yarkon) cuts across the southern third of the plain forming an additional barrier. Thus, the ancient towns grew up along the eastern side of the Sharon where the ground was higher, more fertile and rich in water sources. In modern times added fertilizers have made the red sand the citrus area par excellence but in Old Testament times the plain was mostly used for pasturage (1 Chr 27:29; Isa 65:10). From Aphek north to Gath-padalla ran a key segment of the great coastal trunk route connecting Egypt with Syria and Mesopotamia.

At Aphek the waters of the Nahr el-ᶜAuja (modern Yarkon) rise and flow in a tortuous course to the sea north of Joppa (Josh 19:46). The ancient north-south route led eastward around Aphek because of this barrier. Near the mouth of the Nahr el-ᶜAuja was a town (Tell Qasîleh, still unidentified) and a small harbor settlement (Tell Qudadi).

According to the Phoenician inscription of Eshmunazer (line 19) the hinterland of Joppa was also included in "the mighty grain lands in the territory of Sharon." Eusebius (*Onom.* 162:5–6) confirms this dictum. Therefore, the southern border of the Sharon must be placed at the Valley of Sorek (Judg 16:4; Wâdī Ṣarâr; Naḥal Soreq) which was also the southern border of the Danite inheritance. Another wadi (Wâdī Musrârah; modern Naḥal ᵓAyyalon) runs from the Valley of Aijalon diagonally across the plain towards Joppa; in geological antiquity it had debouched in the sea where the port of Joppa was formed, but prior to human habitation it was deflected northward by the intrusion of sand and had to flow behind a sandstone ridge until it joined Nahr el-ᶜAuja. It thus bounds the coastal segment from Joppa to Tell Qasîleh. It forms a boundary (with the adjacent sandstone ridge) to the "district of Joppa," and it was "seaward," i.e. "on the west" (Judg 19:46 LXX) of the Danite inheritance (which never included Joppa). Therefore, the ancient name of this wadi must have been Jarkon (rather than Nahr el-ᶜAuja, i.e. modern Yarkon). South of the modern Naḥal ᵓAyyalon lies a large field of Mousterian red sand (Arabic: *ḥamra*), useful in antiquity only for grazing (cf. 1 Chr 7:21).

***Philistia***. From the border of Joppa (Josh 19:46) southward was the coast wherein dwelt the Canaanites (Josh 13:29; Deut 1:7). Its shore is typified by long stretches of sand that have encroached on the sandstone ridges. While Joppa and Ashkelon stood right on the shore, along with Yavneh-yam, two other major towns, Ashdod and Gaza, were located inland behind the sand dunes. They had access to the sea by means of small harbor settlements on the coast, usually at the mouth of a wadi.

The plain of Philistia is much wider in the south, 15.5 miles (25 km), and narrows progressively towards the north to about 10.5 miles (17 km). Behind the dune belt the soil is wind-blown loess in the south and red *ḥamra* in the north. Just behind the sands there is a sort of topographic corridor, somewhat troughlike, which gradually rises toward the Shephelah foothills to the east.

Along the sand dunes, especially around Gaza, there were extensive vineyards. The inland soils are excellent for grain crops and also olive orchards (Judg 15:5). The area supported a dense human population from earliest times.

The great trunk route from Egypt across northern Sinai and northward to Damascus and the Phoenician coast followed the "trough" east of the line of dunes. After Jabneel it had to turn northeast towards Aphek.

The main cities in this area were those known later as the five Philistine principalities: Gaza, Ashkelon, and Ashdod along the coast, and Gath and Ekron farther inland (Josh 13:3 *et passim*). Other towns of lesser importance but with a history of their own were Jabneh/Jabneel/Jamnia (Josh 15:5, 15:11; 2 Chr 26:6; 1 Macc 4:15, 5:58; 2 Macc 12:8–9) and Mahoz (in the Amarna letters and in post-biblical sources), a seaport near the mouth of the Sorek.

Several wadis cut across the Philistine plain, bringing alluvial soil from the Judean hills. Most of them were forced to turn northward in order to find passage through the coastal dunes. This was an ancient geological process reflecting the retreat of the coastline westward.

The commercial route from Egypt to Mesopotamia was not the only source of caravan trade. The seaports of Philistia were the destination of the caravans coming from Arabia across the Negeb to the Mediterranean. This heavy commercial traffic led to the frequent alliances between the Philistine cities and the Edomites and Arabs (e.g. 2 Chr 21:16–17; cf. 2 Chr 17:10–13 and 26:7–8).

## Central Range

***Lebanon***. The mountains of Lebanon, a range about 100 miles (160 km) long, are the most prominent orographic feature of the Levant (Jer 18:14). It was the source of timber for both Egypt and Mesopotamia (1 Kgs 5:6–10; 2 Kgs 19:23; Isa 60:13; Zech 11:1). The southern extension of this range, beyond the Litani River, forms the western highlands of Palestine, which consist of several distinct units. The foothills behind the coastal plain of Tyre and of Acco were called "shephelah" (i.e. "lowlands," Josh 11:2).

***Galilee***. The northernmost is Galilee, in turn divided into two, Upper and Lower. This is documented only in Roman times (Josephus, *War* 3.3.1) but stands behind the order of towns in Joshua 19:35–38. The plateau in the north is lower to the northwest and slopes upward toward the south. It was known as an area of Canaanite cities (Judg 1:33; Josh 11:2); the ancient Meron (Maron) was near Jebel Marûn er-Râs. The southern part of Upper Galilee is a massif (Jebel Jarmaq, now wrongly Mount Meiron), largely uninhabited until the Israelite period. It looks down on the Valley of Beth-haccerem that separates it from Lower Galilee.

Lower Galilee consists not of a plateau or plain but a series of ridges running east-west, the most important being the ridge now wrongly called Mount Atzmon and the Nazareth hills. In between these ridges were some latitudinal valleys, especially that of Bêt Neṭôfa (Sahl el-Baṭṭôf), the plain of Asochis in Greco-Roman sources. The watershed between east and west is east of the center line of Galilee; to the east the ridges slope steeply down to the Huleh Valley and the Sea of Chinnereth; to the west they point long slender fingers down to the coastal plain. There is considerable basalt on the east while the west is limestone. Upper and Lower Galilee were divided between Asher (west) and Naphtali (east) in biblical times, though the exact line of their boundary is unknown (Josh 19:34). From the end of the tenth century BCE Tyre inherited all of Asher, and Galilee was restricted to the east.

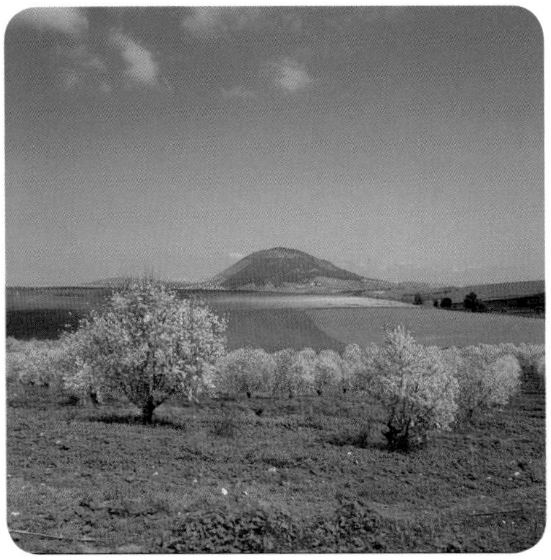

*Mount Tabor in the Jezreel Valley.*

***Jezreel.*** Later historians (e.g. Josephus) include the Jezreel Valley in Galilee. This triangular depression between the hills of Lower Galilee and Samaria was the main thoroughfare between the coast and the Jordan Valley. On its eastern edge stood Mount Tabor and the Hill of Moreh and to the east of these two hills is a basalt plateau comprising the inheritance of Issachar. The valley was named after its most ancient Israelite town, Jezreel; its form in Greek and Latin sources is Esdraelon. The Harod Valley led from Jezreel down to Beth-shean. The Jezreel Valley was famous for its grain production. Megiddo stood near the mouth of the main thoroughfare from Egypt as it enters the valley; a famous string of Canaanite towns lined the southwestern edge of the valley (Josh 17:16; Judg 1:27). It seems evident that the term "Valley of Jezreel" included not only the great plain but also the Valley of Harod and the Beth-shean Valley of today.

The low-lying plateau behind Megiddo and Jokneam (Bilâd er-Rûhah; Ramat Menashe) separates the Valley of Jezreel from the Sharon Plain and connects the Carmel Range with the mountains of Samaria. The southeastern point of the Jezreel, partly encircled by the arm of Mount Gilboa (1 Sam 28:4), is bounded by a low ridge leading up to the Valley of Dothan (Gen 37:17–28), which provided another easy passage to the Sharon.

***Samaria.*** The mountains of Samaria are called Mount Shechem in an Egyptian source from the Canaanite period (Papyrus Anastasi I). Opinions are divided as to whether it could all be called Mount Ephraim. Manasseh occupied the northern part (Josh 17:7–13). A central feature is the Shechem Valley between Mount Gerizim on the south and Mount Ebal on the north. Samaria had several valleys leading out to the west providing easy access to the mountain area. The Dothan Valley and the Shechem Valley in the north and west, respectively, are matched by the Wâdī el-Farᶜah, a dramatic gash in the mountains running down to the Jordan Valley at Adam(ah) (Josh 3:16; 1 Kgs 7:46). Southwest from the Shechem Valley, via the Valley of Michmethath (Josh 16:6, 17:7), ran the Valley of Kanah (Josh 16:8, 17:9), the principal boundary between Manasseh and Ephraim (though Ephraimite towns were north of it and Manassite towns were south of it). This happens to prove that streams and wadis do not form natural boundaries between social groups. Whoever established the Kanah as a boundary had administrative and not social issues in mind.

The mountains of Samaria are not separated from the Sharon by an intermediate zone; their foothills slope naturally down to the west in a gentle continuity. The eastern side is largely steppe land while the west is good for vineyards, orchards and grain, the latter especially in the valleys.

The term Mount Ephraim includes the northern portion of Benjamin's inheritance (1 Sam 1:1). The hill country of Ephraim and Benjamin is a continuity but one major subdivision is the district occupied by the people of Gibeon (Josh 9:3). It forms a sort of topographic saddle between Mt. Ephraim and Mt. Judah. The four Gibeonite cities were located in the southern half of Benjamin (Josh 18:25–28), including the ridge of Nebī Samwîl and the plain through which passes the road to Beth-horon. This latter joins the "highway" (Judg 21:19) that follows the watershed from Shechem past Lebonah to Ramah in Benjamin, going west of Jerusalem to Bethlehem, Halhul, Hebron, and finally to Beer-sheba.

***Jerusalem.*** In the vicinity of Jerusalem there are two ravines, the Wâdī Beit Ḥanînah and the Valley of Rephaim (Josh 15:8), which bisect the mountain chain from the watershed west. They are steep and dangerous and anyone approaching from the west was easily threatened by ambushes (1 Chr 14:9–16). So the route through Gibeon to Beth-horon was the favorite link between Jerusalem and the coast. Jerusalem is situated, therefore, at a point where three major approaches connect the shore with the central range. To the east was the Jericho road (Lk 10:30), facilitating passage to the Jordan Valley and beyond. The ridge west of Jerusalem (Josh 15:8) above the Valley of Hinnom was a link between Mount Ephraim to the north and Mount Judah to the south.

*The Valley of Shechem, between Mount Gerizim and Mount Ebal.*

***Mount Judah.*** The heart of Cisjordan is the high watershed zone known as Mount Judah or "the hill country of Judah" (Josh 15:48; cf. also Josh 10:40, 11:16, 12:8; Judg 1:9, *et passim*). Comprised of limestone and dolomite strata with layers of chalk and marl, the hill country forms a massive block incised from the west by some deep ravines and bordered on that side by a trough of Cenomanian chalk. To the east lies the Wilderness of Judah.

The highest point in the Judean Hills is at Halhul (c. 3,280 feet [1,000 m]). The central plateau is dominated by Hebron. It is situated in a depression, the meeting place of deep valleys running westward. Bethlehem and its general area was occupied by the families of Hur, of the tribe of Judah; south of them, e.g. around Tekoa, was a mixture of Calebites and Judahites, and in the center, Hebron was Caleb's main city. The southern district was the Negeb of Caleb, occupied by the related Kenizzites, the principal town being Debir (Josh 15:15–17; Judg 1:11–12). The soil here was less fertile and enjoyed less moisture than the central hills. Six districts represent the groupings of towns in the hill country (Josh 15:48–60), one of which is preserved only in the Septuagint (Josh 15:59a).

***Shephelah.*** The "Lowland" or Shephelah is a separate unit of later limestone on the western flank of the Judean Hills, from which it is separated by a trough valley of soft chalk running north to south. The rounded hills of the Shephelah are fairly uniform in height, about 656 feet (200 m) above sea level. The zone reaches to the area around Gezer in the north and the southern end of its hills trails off towards Beer-sheba. Several wadis bisect the Shephelah from east to west, the most prominent being the Valley of Aijalon, the Sorek, the Vale of Elah and the Valley of Zephathah (Wâdī Beit Jibrîn) plus two others (by Lachish and Adoraim) that are unnamed in the Bible.

The Shephelah was divided into three districts from north to south (Josh 15:33–42), following the pattern of the wadis. Towns such as Keilah and Nezib, located in the trough at the foot of the Judean Hills, were joined with the Shephelah districts. The northernmost district lay between the Sorek and Elah; the southern included Lachish and many as yet unidentified towns; the central one had Mareshah and the Levitical city of Libnah as its main towns.

***Negeb.*** To the south of the hill country was the zone called Negeb (Josh 15:21–32), often translated "south" or "extreme south" in English versions of the Bible. One went up from Kadesh-barnea to the Negeb (Num 13:17, 13:22); therefore, the biblical Negeb was mainly the valley east of Beer-sheba and the

*Wilderness (Steppe-land) of Judah. This zone had few towns (Josh 15:61) because it was the chalky waste in the rain shadow to the east of the Judean watershed. The infertile soil and the lack of water left the area unsuitable for cultivation except with special care for water collection; even then the territory remained a steppeland, a pastoral zone for the flocks of the hill-country settlements. Actually there are several "wildernesses," always attached to towns, e.g. the wilderness of Tekoa (2 Chr 20:20), Ziph (1 Sam 23:14–15, 26:2), and Maon (1 Sam 23: 24–25). The areas above the cliffs bordering on the Dead Sea were even more barren and could be accurately called "wasteland."*

rolling plain encircled by the Besor Brook to the west. This Negeb of Judah was in fact inhabited by various satellite tribes or ethnic groups, e.g. Simeon (Josh 19:1–9), the Kenites (Judg 1:16; 1 Sam 15:6), the Jerahmeelites (1 Sam 27:10), and the Cherethites (1 Sam 30:14; cf. Deut).

The local administrative center was at Beer-sheba during the United Monarchy (2 Sam 24:7). It is beside the junction of the Hebron wadi from the hill country and the Beer-sheba wadi from the east; after they join they form the Besor (1 Sam 30:10) which winds its way west and northwest to empty into the sea south of Gaza.

The Negeb should not be thought of as wilderness though it is a zone of very marginal rainfall. Its main significance was as a link in the caravan route from the Arabah to the Philistine seacoast. It was to the kingdom of Judah what the Jezreel Valley was to the northern kingdom of Israel; control of the Negeb was a sign of Judean strength and prosperity; loss of the Negeb with incursions from the Philistines and the Edomites or the Arabs, meant a time of weakness and lack of political power. In the Persian period (fifth to fourth centuries BCE) the Negeb was controlled by the Arab king of Kedar, known in the Book of Nehemiah as Geshem (Neh 2:19).

Just south of the Negeb was a steppeland called "the wilderness (= steppe) of Beer-sheba" (Gen 21:14; cf. Gen 16:7), through which passed a road called the "Way to Shur" (leading to Egypt). At a copious water source was Beer-lahai-roi (Gen 16:14), between Bered (unknown) and Kadesh (= Kadesh-barnea). Kadesh was in another zone, called the "wilderness of Zin" (Num 33:36), which bordered on the wilderness of Paran (the Sinai expanse; Num 13:26).

The highlands south of the Negeb were considered by the author of Chronicles to be Mount Seir (1 Chr 4:42; probably also 2 Chr 20:10). In antiquity they were never called Negeb. The modern term Negev encompasses all the area from Beer-sheba to Elath but this derives from a misconception of the biblical term Negeb.

## The Rift Valley

The geographical feature which determined the north-south orientation of the main physical features of the entire land is the so-called Great Rift running the length of the Levant and extending down into Africa.

***The Beqa*^c^**. In the north the "Rift" is known as the Beqa^c^ "Valley" and to the biblical writers it was the "Valley of Lebanon" (Josh 11:17, 12:7), the rich plain between the mountains of Lebanon and the Hermon-Sirion (Anti-Lebanon). At its watershed was Lebo-hamath (Num 34:8 *et passim*), northwards it is drained by the Orontes, southwards by the Litani. The southern half of the valley was known as the "Land of Amqi" in the Amarna letters; the valley at the foot of Mount Hermon was called Valley or Land of Mizpeh (Josh 11:8, 11:11).

***Mount Hermon***. This is the highest mountain in the Land of Israel (9,230 feet [2,814 m]). Its snows furnish most of the water for the Jordan River, of which there are four sources, two from the ^c^Ayyûn (Ijon) Valley and two from Hermon.

***Huleh Valley***. The principal sources for the Jordan are the waters by Tell el-Qâḍī (Tel Dan) and the spring at Banias (Paneas). They join in the Huleh Valley (Ulatha in Josephus) and formed the shallow Lake Huleh. This latter has generally been taken to be the waters of Merom but the site of Merom must be located in the plateau above, near Marûn er-Râs. The lake was surrounded by swamps (since drained in the 1950s) and served as a filter cleansing the waters of the Jordan before they flowed down to the Sea of Galilee.

From the north, one entered the Huleh via the pass beside Abel-beth-maacah or that coming down past Dan. The major town in the valley was Hazor, the largest urban center of the Canaanite period.

Between the formerly swampy basin in the northern part of the valley and the Sea of Galilee is a massive dyke of ancient basalt. The Jordan cuts its way through this lava deposit in a narrow gorge on the eastern side of the valley. The Huleh and the mountain ridges on the west were part of the land of Naphtali (1 Kgs 15:2; 2 Kgs 15:29; Isa 9:1).

***Sea of Galilee***. The Jordan River comes out of the gorge, crosses a small alluvial plain and enters the lake of Chinnereth, or the Sea of Galilee. This is a heart-shaped body of water, about 656 feet (200 m) below sea level. It is 11 miles (18 km) long by 7.5 miles (12 km) across and is shut in by the hills on nearly all sides. The slopes are mostly of basalt; at their base is a flat area nearly around the entire lake, leaving room for a road. The waters are generally fresh

*The Sea of Galilee and the Plain of Gennesaret. The ancient name was the "sea of Chinnereth" (Num 34:11; Josh 13:27) after the city on the northwestern shore (Josh 19:35; Deut 3:17) and the area around it (1 Kgs 15:20), the "land of Chinneroth." Greco-Roman times saw the use of the term Genessar, Ginnosar (1 Macc 11:67) for the fertile plain behind the town; the lake was Gennesaret (Lk 5:1) or the Sea of Galilee or the Sea of Tiberias (Josh 21: 1). More is known about the towns of the Greco-Roman period, e.g. Capernaum on the north, Tiberias on the west, and Hippus on the east. At the outlet to the Jordan stood Beth-yerah, or Sennabris.*

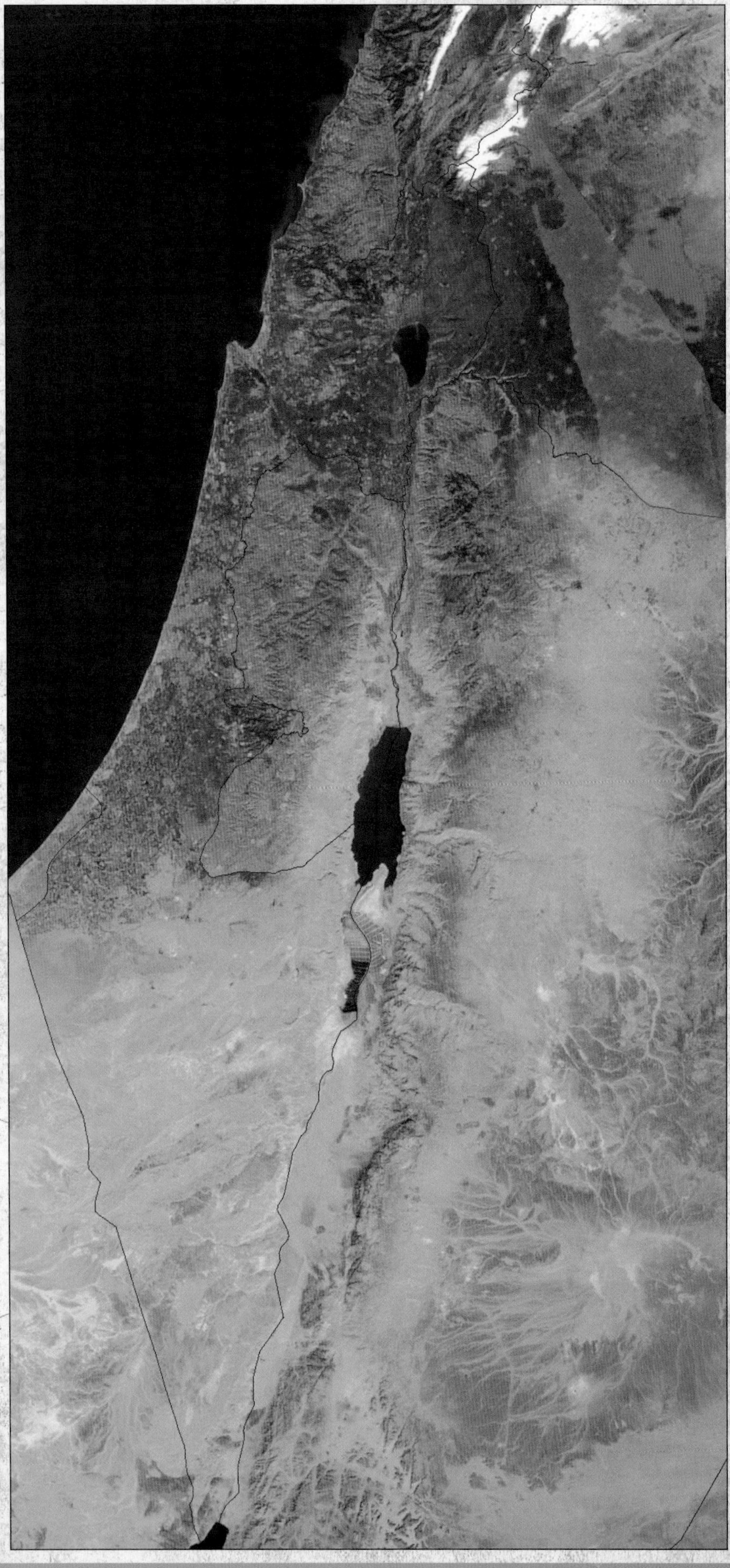

This satellite photo, taken in January 2003, shows the "Great Rift" from the Red Sea to the Lebanese Beqa<sup>c</sup> Valley.

though highly mineral springs once fed the northwestern shore. Hot springs break forth along the western side, leaving a small arm of land isolated to the east, but within the past century the course has cut to the south of that split and now flows out in a western direction.

***Jordan River***. The Jordan flows in a tortuous course through the deep Rift Valley down to the Dead Sea. In a straight line it covers about 65 miles (105 km) and descends from 656 feet (200 m) below sea level to nearly 1,310 feet (400 m) below. The first part of its course is through steep clay banks until it reaches the confluence of the Jabbok (Nahr ez-Zerqā) from the east and the Wâdī el-Far<sup>c</sup>ah on the west. At this point, denoted by the town of Adam (Josh 3:16), modern ed-Damieh, the riverbed cut through a more open plain.

The valley was part of the biblical Arabah (Deut 1:7; 2 Sam 2:29, 4:7 *et passim*); it served as the boundary of Canaan (Num 34:12; Ezek 47:18). Along the eastern edge of the valley were rich water sources that encouraged the rise of towns in the Canaanite period, e.g. Peḥel (Pella), Succoth, etc., while the western side was more arid except for the Beth-shean Valley and the Jericho region, which was a tropical paradise (*War* 4.8.3).

***Southern Arabah***. The name Arabah was preserved in Arabic only with relation to the valley south of the Dead Sea. It also appears as such in the Bible (Deut 1:1, 2:9). The valley floor rises gradually southward to about 656 feet (200 m) above sea level before sloping down again at the Gulf of Elath (Aqabah). It is a desert area with heavy alluvial sands in the middle and saline soils just south of the Dead Sea. The red cliffs of Mount Seir rise to the east and the yellow limestone of the Cisjordan desert highlands stand on the west. The two main oases are <sup>c</sup>Ain Ḥuṣb in the north and <sup>c</sup>Ain Ghaḍyân in the south. The latter is the Arabic reflex of Ezion(-geber), the fortified outpost beside Elath. The Arabah was a natural border between Israel and Edom but was also a line of communication with South Arabia, by land and also by sea. As such it was a contested zone between the neighboring states. The main lines of communication in the Arabah were east to west and there was much more traffic in that direction than there was from north to south.

***Reed Sea***. The Gulf of Elath, the eastern arm of the Red Sea, is called "Reed Sea" in the Bible (1 Kgs 9:26), often rendered "Red Sea" in the English translations, following Greek usage (Herodotus 2.8).

## TRANSJORDAN

In Transjordan the history of biblical times touches mainly on those districts bordering on the deep Rift Valley; they were bounded on the east by the wastelands of the Arabian Desert. The geopolitical importance of

*The Dead Sea. The biblical name for the great lake into which the Jordan flows was the Sea of Salt (Gen 14:3; Num 34:12; et passim) or the Sea of the Arabah (Deut 3:17; Josh 3:16; 2 Kgs 14:25). Josephus called it Asphaltitis (*Ant. *1.9.1). By the latter half of the second century CE it was called the Dead Sea by the Greco-Roman writers. It formerly received about 6,000,000 tons of water daily from the Jordan. On the east it is bordered by the steep cliffs of Moab with only the "Tongue" (Arabic Lisân), a boot-shaped peninsula, projecting across its width. South of the Lisân it is a shallow basin but on the northeastern side it is over 1,310 feet (400 m) deep. At times one could cross dry-shod from the Lisân to the western shore. The most famous site on the western shore was the oasis of En-gedi, where water is found in abundance. At the southwestern corner, alongside the shallow basin, is Jebel Usdum, Mount Sodom. The water of the Dead Sea is of such a high mineral content as to be poisonous to normal life forms. The arid valley south of the Dead Sea was called the Valley of Salt (2 Kgs 14:7).*

Transjordan was due to the "King's Highway" (Num 20:17, 21:22), the route from Damascus to Elath which also led to Midian and thence to South Arabia.

***Bashan***. The northern districts, often disputed with Aram-Damascus, were part of the land of Apum/Upe in the Canaanite period. The biblical name for the whole district was Bashan (Deut 3:13 *et passim*) which included various territories including the "whole region of Argob," with its sixty walled cities (Deut 3:4–5; 1 Kgs 4:13). In Greco-Roman times it was divided into Gaulanitis (named after the town Gaulana) along the western edge of the plateau and east to the Nahr Allân, and Batanea (from the Aramaic form of Bashan), the zone east of the same Allân Valley, and Auranitis (from biblical Hauran, Ezek 47:16, 47:18), mainly the mountain called Jebel Druze, the highest peak of which is Jebel Ḥaurân. The lava region northwest of the Hauran mountains was called Trachonitis (Gk. for "rough country"), the modern Leja.

The entire area was included in Canaan and contained the Aramean district of Geshur (just east of Chinnereth). Its southern border was the Yarmûk Valley. The latter, though not mentioned in the Bible, is an ancient name, known from rabbinic sources. It is the largest river in Transjordan, and flows through a steep gorge to join the Jordan below the Sea of Galilee. Its waters originate in streambeds far to the east, especially from the Hauran region. The Yarmûk Valley thus separated the Bashan/Golan from Gilead. The rail line developed in the beginning of the twentieth century echoed the ancient trade route by which the Jezreel Valley was linked with the King's Highway, as described in an ancient Egyptian treatise on roads in Canaan.

The Havvoth-jair (Num 32:41 *et passim*) and the half-tribe of Manasseh were the main occupants of the area in biblical tradition. The previous ones were called Rephaim (Gen 14:5).

***Gilead***. Central Transjordan is a mountainous area of Cenomanian limestone like the hills of Ephraim and Judah. It is known throughout biblical history as Gilead, or the land of Gilead (Josh 22:9 *et passim*). It is not reckoned as part of Canaan (Josh 22), but was occupied by the tribe of Gad (Josh 13:29–31) as well as Bashan. Thus, the division of the area into two halves by the Jabbok was recognized in the Israelite settlement.

The mountains reach over 2,950 feet (900 m), with the highest point at ᶜAjlûn. The western slopes and the hills take up most of the area; to the east is a narrow tableland bordering on the desert. The high ridges catch a larger amount of precipitation than elsewhere. There is a double watershed, one near the west from whence steep ravines flow to the Jordan Valley; the easterly flowing streams are largely collected by the course of the Jabbok that runs north along the eastern plateau before turning west to bisect the entire uplifted dome reaching the valley by Mahanaim and Succoth.

***Ammon***. Rabbath-ammon, the center of the land of the Ammonites, is located on the east at the head of another series of valleys separating Gilead from the tableland of Moab. Ammon is structurally a basin 20 by 10 miles (32 by 16 km), aligned northeast to southwest.

***Moab***. The tableland, the northern half of the territory claimed by the Moabites (disputed by Israel), consists of a lovely plain behind the ridges sloping down to the Dead Sea (from Mount Nebo = Pisgah; Deut 32:49, 34:1). The entire plateau east of the Dead Sea is divided into two halves by the Arnon Valley (Wâdī el-Môjib) which formed the border between Israel and Moab proper (Josh 13:96). Dibon, on the northern side of the Arnon, was, nevertheless, the capital of the Moabite state in the ninth century BCE. The term *mîshôr*, "tableland," applies only to this northern plain (Deut 3:10 *et passim*) while the area between the Arnon and the Zered (Wâdī Ḥasā) was considered as Moab's original home since the tableland had belonged to the Amorites (Judg 11:18). This latter area, to the south of the Arnon, also has other wadis cutting their way down to the Dead Sea, one being the "ascent of Luhith, the road to Horonaim" (Isa 15:5).

***Edom***. The final region of the land is southern Transjordan, viz. Mount Seir or Edom (Gen 36:21; Ezek 35:15). There is some evidence that Edom/Seir also applied to the high country south of the Negeb (e.g. 1 Chr 4:42–43), but in monarchial times the red sandstone mountains south of the Zered are usually meant. Some of the peaks reach as high as 5,696 feet (1,736 m). The territory of Edom proper, though 75 miles (120 km) long, is only about 12.5 miles (20 km) wide. There is room in the mountain range for a single line of towns. The embayment behind Feinân (biblical Punon) divides the area into two halves. The Old Testament capital was Sela (Arabic Silaᶜ) while the Nabatean and Roman capital moved to Rekem, known in Greek sources as Petra (and not to be identified with Sela, or with Kadesh-barnea). The people of Edom were in constant rivalry with Judah for control of the Arabah south of the Dead Sea, and Elath/Ezion-geber changed hands several times between them. To the south of Edom was the territory of Midian and to the east was Kedar, whose king gained control of the entire area across to Gaza and Egypt during the Persian period.

## CLIMATE

***Seasons***. Although rabbinic tradition knows four seasons: Fall, Winter, Spring and Summer, the Old Testament recognized only two; cf. Genesis 8:22, "seedtime and harvest" equal "cold and heat," and "winter" and "summer." Westerners in Europe and North America have failed to grasp this situation and its role in the life of ancient Israel. The year is divided into two halves, one beginning with Nisan, the first month, and another beginning with Tishri, the seventh month. These Babylonian month names were not in vogue in pre-exilic Israel. They were adopted only afterwards. The Old Testament sacred festivals fell in the seven-month period embracing the Passover (in Nisan) and the Tabernacles (in Tishri). During the winter, the main agricultural activities are devoted to grain crops expected in the spring and summer; in the summer the work was on vines and in orchards, for the summer fruits (Amos 8:1–2; Jer 40:10, 40:12; Mic 7:1; 2 Sam 16:1). Every month there was something to do; there was never an unfertile season in the Levant, either north or south. The "eyes of the Lord" were upon the land from the beginning to the end of the year (Deut 11:12). Theories of an annual "dying and rising" fertility deity, based on misuse of the

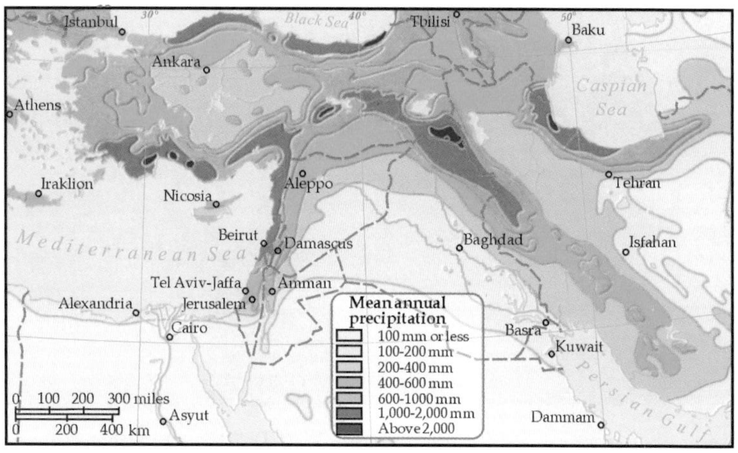


**Average Annual Rainfall**

Ugaritic myths and descriptions of fertility rites in the Hellenistic period, have no relation to reality in the Levant. The farmers were afraid of a series of bad years, to be sure, in which case they might assume that Baal/Hadad had been defeated by the god of Death. But they also nurtured the belief that someday he would be revived and bring back the fertility of the land by giving his voice in the heavens.

The weather pattern in winter consists of low-pressure systems that arrive from the west and northwest. Those from northern Italy pass along the Adriatic to Greece and the Aegean, reaching Syria. The others come from southern Italy to the central Mediterranean and across to Palestine. The rains of a given year usually come in three phases, the "early rain," "rain" and "latter rain" (Deut 11:13–17; Jer 5:24 *et passim*). The "early rain" is hoped for just after the Feast of Tabernacles; it is a light sprinkling to soften the hard earth and to facilitate plowing with the crude implements of antiquity. It may come in September but usually arrives sometime in October. The principal rain, about 75 percent, falls between December and February. The main sowing takes place from November through December and late sowing usually is done during a break in the rains in January. By March the grass is high enough to cut for fodder and in April the "latter rain" is needed as a final dose to swell the grain. But if the rain in April/May is too heavy, it can bring disaster (1 Sam 12:17).

The rains are deposited more intensively on the mountain ranges of Judah, Ephraim and Galilee. There is a difference of several degrees in temperature during the winter between Jerusalem and the seacoast, the latter being obviously the milder. Beyond the watershed in Ephraim and Judah there is a rain shadow since most of the precipitation has fallen on the hills; thus the dry chalk wastes of the Judean Wilderness have little chance of getting moisture. However, the same winds that brought the rains from the west descend again to the humid depression of the Jordan Valley and the Dead Sea where they pick up more moisture to be deposited in the ranges of Gilead and Moab. In a drought year for western Palestine, the dry winds and high temperatures cause higher evaporation in the Rift Valley so that Transjordan actually may have a slightly higher precipitation for a change (Ruth 1:1).

The snows of Mount Hermon provide the principal water source for the Jordan. Most of the winter rainwater is absorbed by the limestone mountains of Cisjordan and descend to a deep underground water table which was not utilized in antiquity. However, some of the water did break through to the surface in the form of springs and wells. These were generally located along the edge of the plains at the foot of the hill ranges.

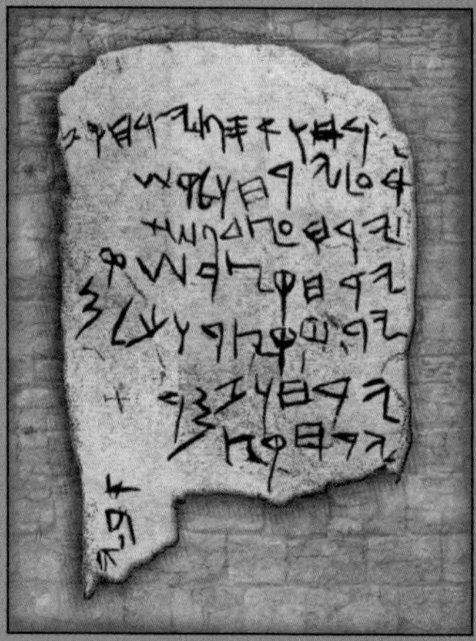

### The Gezer Calendar

*The true agricultural cycle is reflected in a school exercise from approximately the tenth century* BCE, *viz. the Gezer Calendar.*

**Translation:**

(1) His two months: Ingathering;
His two months: Sowing

(2) His two months: Late sowing

(3) His month: Chopping flax (or grass)

(4) His month: Barley harvest

(5) His month: Harvest and measuring

(6) His two months: Vine harvest

(7) His month: Summer fruit

Lower edge Abiya

*There is no doubt that the calendar deals with twelve months, four periods of two months each and four periods of only one month. The grammatical forms leave no doubt of this. Moreover, the series matches the real cycle of agricultural activities in the country.*

**Modern States (left) and the Ancient Near East (right)**

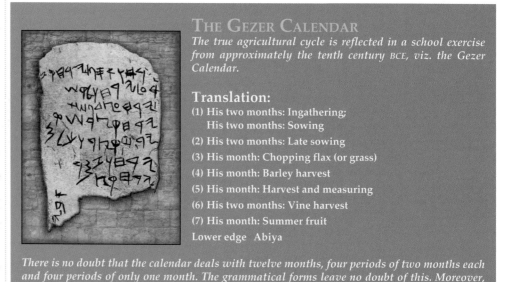

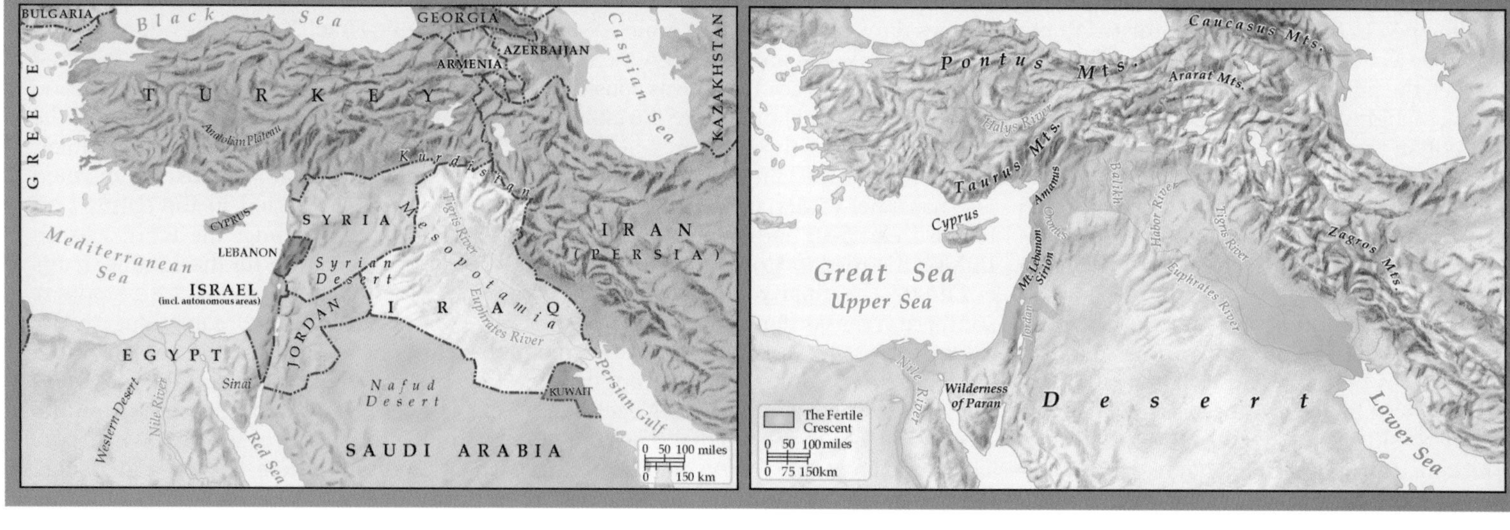

# CHAPTER THREE
# The Bronze Age
## FOURTH MILLENNIUM TO TWELFTH CENTURY BCE

### Early Bronze Age (4th to 3rd Millennia BCE)

Toward the end of the fourth millennium BCE, significant activities in Mesopotamia and Egypt led to the establishment of social and economic frameworks in the valleys of the Nile and the Tigris and Euphrates which became the basis for all subsequent cultural developments. Recent excavations in North Syria, at Tell Hamoukar, indicate that an impressive urban center had arisen there in the mid-fourth millennium BCE. So urban development was not exclusive to Sumer. However, among the cultural advances in Sumer during this period was the discovery of writing. It may well have been developed first in southern Mesopotamia but there may be attempts to challenge this on the basis of some new discoveries in Egypt. Be that as it may, the third millennium saw the production of inscribed records for daily needs and also for wider religious and political goals.

Between the two great riverine cultures, the Levant did not seem to benefit from the use of writing, at least not on nonperishable materials, until the mid-third millennium and then it was in North Syria but not in the southern Levant. Therefore, although the process of establishing organized settlements in Palestine, Lebanon and Jordan can now be observed at many of the major sites in the country's archaeological history during what we call the Early Bronze Age I, there are no written testimonies to illuminate the process or the actors in that social drama.

An archaeological description of the Early Bronze Age is possible and it is now much richer in detail than was possible fifty years ago. But where the objective is historical geography, the stages of the Early Bronze Age will have to be discussed in relation to the neighboring cultures and their epigraphic expressions. While North Syria is now illuminated by the tablets from Ebla, no light is shed on the southern Levant. The main links, those which contribute to some degree of chronological arrangement, are with Egypt. Those early links will be discussed first.

*Clay box in the shape of a broadroom with a flat roof, from Arad, Early Bronze II.*

**Early Bronze I**. Toward the end of the fourth millennium and the beginning of the third millennium BCE there was a marked change in the settlement pattern throughout the southern Levant. Marginal areas such as the southern steppe land (the Negeb) saw the disappearance of the Chalcolithic culture. Instead, settlements were being established at sites in the valleys of the more central areas and also in some places in the hills, and even along the coast. The pattern of settlements near good water sources, rich cultivable land and pasturage and on elevated, easily defensible locations is established at this time. A number of the newly founded settlements became fortified during Early Bronze IB (e.g. probably Tel $^{c}$Erani=Tell Sheikh el-$^{c}$Areinī) but most seem to have been unwalled villages (as at Arad).

Although the archaeological testimony from excavations and surveys is still somewhat haphazard and incomplete, there is a mounting data base of substantial evidence to the effect that while EB IA was mainly a village-level beginning, the EB IB saw the emergence of numerous fortified sites throughout the country. Not only that, but the relative sizes of some of the sites indicate a quantitative hierarchy of settlements with very few really large fortified towns, some medium-size towns and many smaller, unfortified sites. During this growth process, there were extensive contacts with Egypt. The Egyptians were interested in products such as wine and oil. EB IB settlements expanded into the hill country areas and contributed to the increased production of those commodities.

**Early Bronze II**. The Early Bronze II period was characterized by the construction of impressive fortifications at major urban centers. Public buildings such as palaces and temples also appear. Most of the EB I sites developed into large fortified towns though the urban pattern is but a diluted reflection of the great developments in Mesopotamia.

The discovery between 1974 and 1976 of an extensive cuneiform archive at Tell Mardikh (the ancient town of Ebla) has opened up a hitherto unknown world of Semitic society in the Early Bronze Age. Dynastic lists indicate that the kingdom must date back at least as far as 2700 BCE, making the history of the site parallel to that of the Mesopotamian Early Dynastic II (c. 2700–2500 BCE) and Early Dynastic III (c. 2500–2300 BCE). Palace G at Tell Mardikh, in which the archive and a few other texts were housed, was destroyed by a conflagration. On the floor of the administrative quarter were found fragments of diorite and alabaster bowls with short hieroglyphic inscriptions containing two of the names from the titles of Khafre (Chephren), the fourth pharaoh in Dynasty IV (and builder of the second Giza Pyramid, c. 2550 BCE). A lid was also found in this Ebla assemblage having the name of Pepi I, the prominent pharaoh of Dynasty VI. Thus, we have now a synchronism between the last king of Ebla and the VI$^{th}$ Dynasty of Egypt.

**Early Bronze III**. The Early Bronze II and III periods in the south remain mute. Fortified cities, palaces and temples testify

*EB II storage jar from Arad.*

to a sophisticated social and economic regime but the ethnic identification of the population(s) is still a mystery. The transition to Early Bronze III is marked archaeologically by the appearance of "Khirbet Kerak Ware," a special type of pottery, the style and manufacture of which originated in Armenia and the Caucasus.

Although the style is foreign, examination of many vessels has shown that they were made in the southern Levant at the site of their discovery. The conclusion is that this ware represents the arrival of people (at least craftsmen) who had brought their ceramic tradition with them from the north. How they arrived and in what circumstances is a mystery. It is likely that they had come by stages, passing through eastern Turkey, the $^{c}$Amuq Plain, and some areas of western Syria before arriving in Palestine. Such a movement of people does not seem to have left any echo in the Ebla archives about North Syria.

**Early Bronze IV (EB IIIC).** Israeli archaeologists prefer to denote the latest phase of the third-millennium urbanization as a separate period, EB IV, corresponding roughly with the VI$^{th}$ Dynasty of Egypt. This EB IV is not to be confused with the period denoted by most scholars outside of Israel as EB IV, which is called the Intermediate Bronze Age in Israel (which terminology will be adopted here).

Mesopotamia saw the rise of the Akkad Dynasty which spread its authority over most of Sumer and Akkad (the central Euphrates and Tigris valleys). In the west, the founder, Sargon I, conquered Mari and his successors converted it into a client state under governors. His grandson, Naram-Sin, extended the empire to Anatolia and to the Persian Gulf.

EB IV is evidently a time when the cities of Canaan were in economic and cultural decline and were being destroyed. At northern sites the evidence for this phase is extremely scanty; places like Megiddo, Beth-shean and Dan seem to have maintained their "urban" character right to the end of EB III, but the southern sites, especially Jarmuth, show the clearest evidence for this final phase.

Lack of historical documentation makes it impossible to know the causes for the destruction of the towns in the Early Bronze Age.

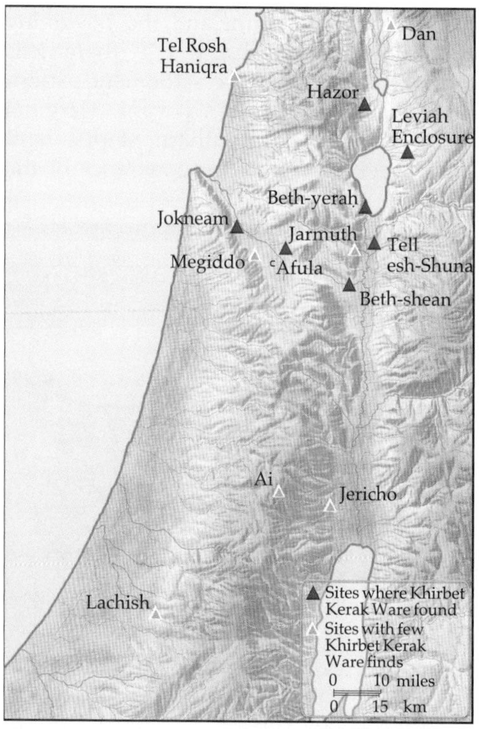


**SITES WITH KHIRBET KERAK WARE**

*Typical Khirbet Kerak Ware, EB III, found at Afula.*

**Intermediate Bronze Age (Late Third Millennium BCE).** During the last two centuries of the third millennium BCE, Egyptian society seems to have withdrawn unto itself; connections with the Levant apparently had ceased entirely. This was the Egyptian First Intermediate Period, Dynasties IX through mid-XI, when central authority in the land had broken down.

However, in the southern Levant, i.e. Canaan, the Early Bronze III and IV towns all underwent violent destructions. In their place came a new culture of people who were apparently originally pastoralists but who were driven by the ecological and social circumstances to develop a village culture. Following Israeli practice, this will be called the Intermediate Bronze Age (rather than EB IV). It truly is an intermediate period and it lasts for a considerable length of time (perhaps a century or more); it would correspond to the end of the Akkad Dynasty and the Neo-Sumerian period under the Ur III Dynasty.

One of the most common manifestations of this new culture is the vast number of cemeteries. The burials are of individuals and the skeletons are disarticulated. Many copper implements and weapons were found with the human remains. The pottery repertoire is distinctly different from the EB ceramics though one can see some reflections of the older traditions. The habitation sites are usually unimpressive.

## MIDDLE BRONZE AGE (C. 2200–1550 BCE)

The first half of the second millennium BCE is commonly known as the Middle Bronze Age in Levantine archaeology. The three main phases of this period will be denoted by the modern terminology in contrast to that used in the mid-twentieth century. The new terms with their equivalents in the older system are MB I (=MB IIA), MB II (=MB IIB) and MB III (=MB IIC).

**Middle Bronze I in the Southern Levant.** The culture of the Intermediate Bronze population seems to have disappeared. Whether the people were absorbed into the population of the new Middle Bronze I or simply retreated back to their desert steppes is an open question. The settlement patterns of the first stage of the Middle Bronze Age are a sharp departure from the site distribution of the previous Intermediate Bronze. The former Early Bronze II–III sites in the valleys and on the coastal plains were usually rebuilt during the MB I (=MB IIA). The earliest renewals were along the coast and on the inner coastal plain.

As for contacts with Egypt in the MB I, there seem to be many less Egyptian artifacts present in remains of that period in the southern and inner Levant (Canaan) than there are at coastal sites and especially in Lebanon and farther into Syria. Dynasty XII developed extensive trade connections with the Levant; they seemed to have preferred the sea route as did their counterparts in northern Lebanon and Syria. The people of the inland MB I sites in Canaan evidently used the land routes. It was the renewal of the Egyptian demand for timber and other North Syrian products that motivated their return to the Levantine coast, principally via Byblos. The concomitant establishment

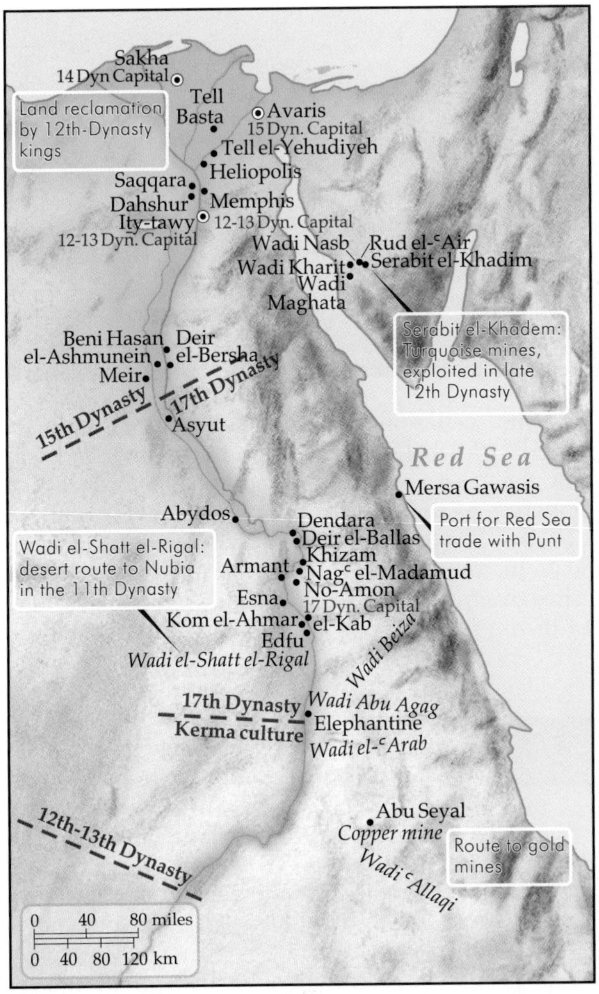


**Dynasties XII to XV (Mid-2nd Millennium BCE)**

*The Sinuhe story is perhaps a novel but more likely a real tomb inscription so well written that the scribal schools chose to use it as a text for many generations. It is the tale of an Egyptian nobleman who, for an unspecified reason, fled from Egypt at the death of Amenemhet I and found sanctuary with a ruler of (Re)tenu (i.e. Syria-Canaan). This literary masterpiece is in the format of a tomb inscription but is composed of various elements of narrative, poetry and drama. The eulogy of Senwoseret I within this text and the portrayal of that king as a generous monarch point to the early XIIth Dynasty as the time of composition.*

*The story culminates with Sinuhe's return to Egypt and his reception by Senwoseret I. He achieves the ultimate dream of every Egyptian: to be buried with all due honors in Egypt.*

*Wooden figure of Senwoseret I, from Lisht.*

of MB I sites along the coast was probably inspired by the need to service the ships plying this coastal sea lane from Egypt to Byblos and back. These same coastal anchorages (seldom real harbors like those in Lebanon) were also usually linked via wadis and streams flowing west across the coastal plain to larger inland towns, and including some smaller intermediate sites (also fortified in the main).

In the north of the country, it has been stressed that the coastal plain and the Huleh Valley have sites much larger than those south of the Carmel range, viz. Acco and Hazor. This could very well be because the northern sites have closer affinities with Syria and Mesopotamia where large cities were prevalent. Several archaeological features have been noted that point to a northern origin: the early use of brick-built arched gates in Mesopotamian style which were soon abandoned for wood and stone construction more suitable to southern conditions (Dan, Acco, Ashkelon); new burial practices, supplementing but not entirely superceding the former ones; osteological evidence pointing to changes too distinct to be explained by mere local developments in an indigenous population.

As for the burial practices, there are innumerable graves of males with accompanying weapons, mostly implements needed for personal combat. Thus, one may surmise that the MB I people, at least the leading stratum in the population, were a warrior class. This detail is especially relevant when assessing the background of the Execration Texts and the Tale of Sinuhe.

**Middle Bronze II in the Southern Levant.** The two later phases of the Middle Bronze Age, MB II (MB IIB) and MB III (MB IIC), are often treated together because the transition from one to the other is gradual.

The distribution of major and mid-sized centers and the increase in rural settlements as well, show that the MB II constituted the pinnacle of cultural and political development in the southern Levant during the second millennium BCE. The material culture, including ceramics, metal objects and other items, is of the highest quality. The various imports discovered in excavations and tombs testify to an active role played by the Levant in the MB II as a bridge for trade between the flourishing Amurrite states of North Syria and Mesopotamia and Egypt plus contacts with the Aegean, especially Crete. The southernmost anchor in this trade network was evidently Avaris

*Execration text on a clay figurine from Saqqara. These figurines or other pottery were inscribed with curses against Pharaoh's enemies at the time of the Middle Kingdom. The figurines were then smashed in the belief that this act would break their power. Among those cursed—Asian kings, hostile Egyptians and everything evil.*

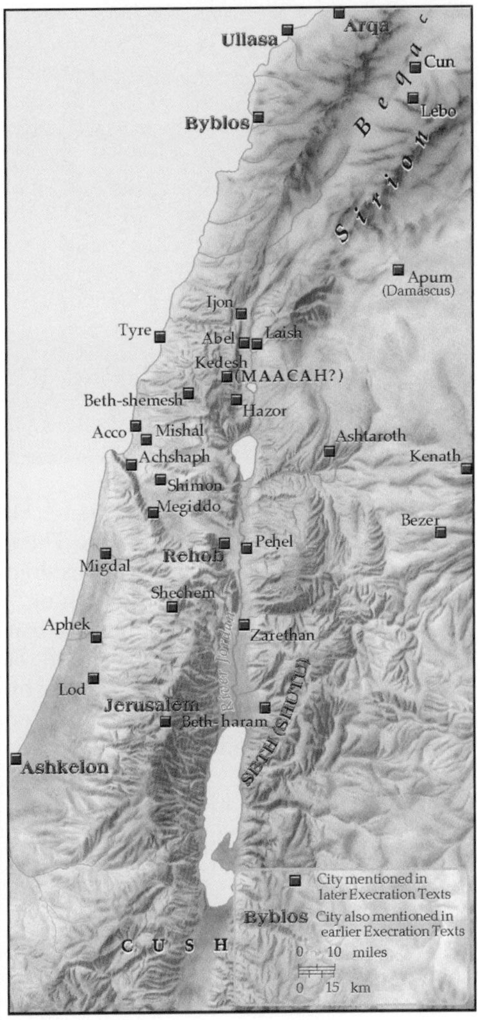


**Sites Mentioned in the Execration Texts**

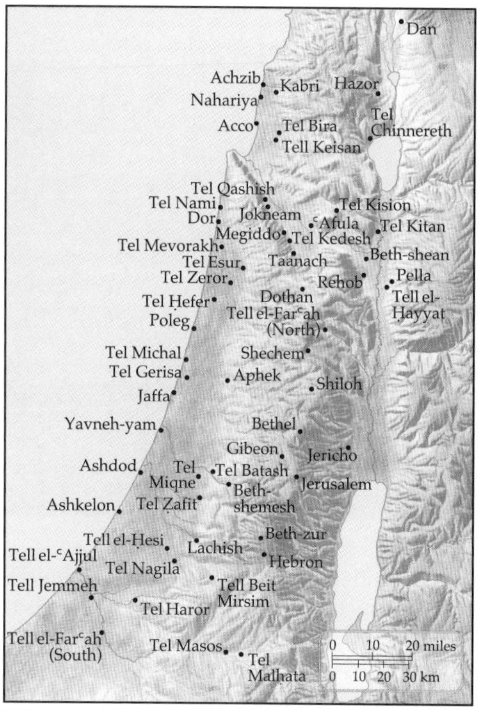


**MIDDLE BRONZE AGE SITES IN THE SOUTHERN LEVANT**

*City gate at Tel Dan, MB II.*

(Tell ed-Dabʿa) on the Pelusiac branch of the Nile in the eastern delta of Egypt. There a commercial colony, undoubtedly fostered by the Egyptians, was already flourishing.

Given the evidence for mighty urban centers, heavy agricultural utilization of resources and international commerce by sea and land, it is ironic that so few written records have survived to illuminate this period.

The largest city in Canaan during the second millennium BCE was Hazor. During MB II its connections with the great Amurrite kingdom of Mari are attested in cuneiform documents from the latter site.

**Middle Bronze III in the Southern Levant** (and the Second Intermediate Period in Egypt). Even though there does not seem to be a sharp transition in the material record between strata of MB II and MB III, all students of material culture have noted developments in the artifactual evidence, especially in pottery. One outstanding feature seems to be the proliferation of scarabs dating to the XVth Dynasty of Egypt. All of the major sites of MB II are still occupied and many of them are expanded.

*Akkadian cuneiform tablet listing animals, from Tell Ramada, MB II (front and side views).*

## LATE BRONZE AGE (c. 1550–1200 BCE)

The mid-second millennium BCE was a time of crisis. Political and social frameworks were collapsing and new formations were taking shape. There is an unfortunate dearth of written sources for the seventeenth and sixteenth centuries BCE. However, this presumed "dark age" is surely a matter of chance. The capital of the Mittanian kingdom, Washshukanni, has yet to be identified. It would surely have had cuneiform archives with documents from this period. The Hittite records of the "Old Kingdom" provide some details, such as the campaigns of Hattusili I and his successors.

The ensuing period, the second half of the second millennium BCE (down to c. 1150 BCE) has several historical phases which match to some extent the development of aspects of the material culture. The division of the Late Bronze Age adopted here is LB I, LB II and LB III.

**Late Bronze I.** The material evidence from Late Bronze Age Canaan reveals a drastic decline in comparison with the Middle Bronze Age. Throughout the country, most of the major MB sites suffered destruction. Not all of them were restored in the Late Bronze Age; of fifty-four excavated sites, only twenty-two show signs of being rebuilt during LB I. During LB II the number of sites inhabited was doubled but some of the large MB sites never recovered. The extensive hill-country settlement of small MB habitation sites just disappeared. Some of that population may have retreated to the Transjordanian steppe lands; others may have gravitated to the urban centers.

In contrast to most of the country, the seacoast did see the founding of relatively small harbor sites or anchorage points, e.g. Tell Abū Hawâm, Tel Megadim, and Tel Michal. At Hazor, the huge lower city was again occupied during the Late Bronze Age as well as the upper tel but that is unusual for this period. Though the overall surface area of Cisjordanian sites increases slightly from LB I to LB II, sites with more than five hectares (c. 12 acres) in area are the exception.

The long-held assumption that there was no appreciable occupation in Transjordan during the Late Bronze must now be abandoned in the light of research during the last several decades. Some major sites have been investigated in the eastern Jordan Valley (especially Tabaqât Faḥil=Hellenistic/Roman Pella, Tell es-Saʿīdîyeh, Tell Deir ʿAllah) and other sites along the main north-south highway on the Transjordanian plateau. There are also burial grounds and sedentary and pastoralist villages.

While the MB towns were usually surrounded by mighty earthen ramparts

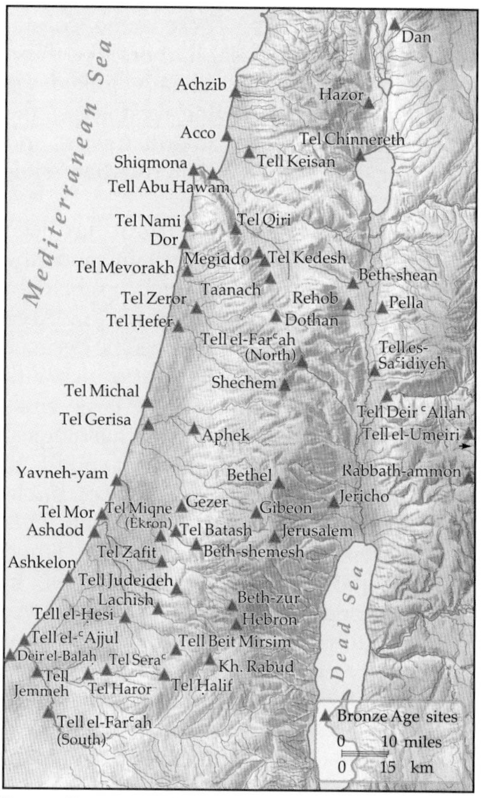


**LATE BRONZE AGE SITES IN THE SOUTHERN LEVANT**

held in place by various technological methods, the LB towns do not seem to have been surrounded by fortifications. This may be due to Egyptian restrictions placed on their subjects. The local towns were also less populated and probably did not command the resources necessary for major defensive projects. Hazor, as an exception, was evidently still protected by the MB earthworks. Some of the sites may have been ringed with houses, the back walls of which formed a continuous line around the crest of the city mound on top of the MB ramparts, but that was not the case everywhere.

The social structure of the local "city-states" is reflected in the architecture. There are more substantial buildings, i.e. "palaces," for the local rulers and their senior personnel. When written sources begin to appear (e.g. Thutmose III's topographical list and the Amarna tablets), it is clear that the country is divided between small city-states, each having a limited area of direct control. There are also temples, sometimes more than one at a site. A remarkable feature is the lack of storage facilities for the temples. This might lead to the assumption that the shrines were closely associated with the local governments and thus shared storage places with the political authority.

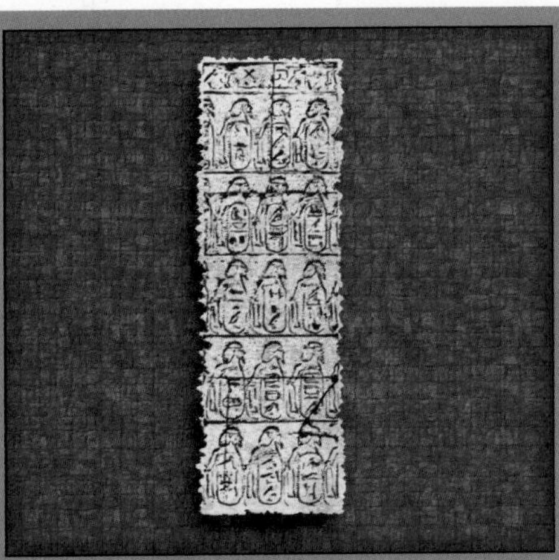

*City list of Thutmose III. Pharaohs of the XVIII[th] Dynasty boasted their victories with lists of conquered towns.*

The relative dearth of inscriptional evidence found at local sites means that the history of the country at this time is almost entirely dependent upon records found in Egypt. This is, of course, in sharp contrast with the situation in North Syria, where major cities, usually capitals of large territories, have produced an abundance of cuneiform and other documents.

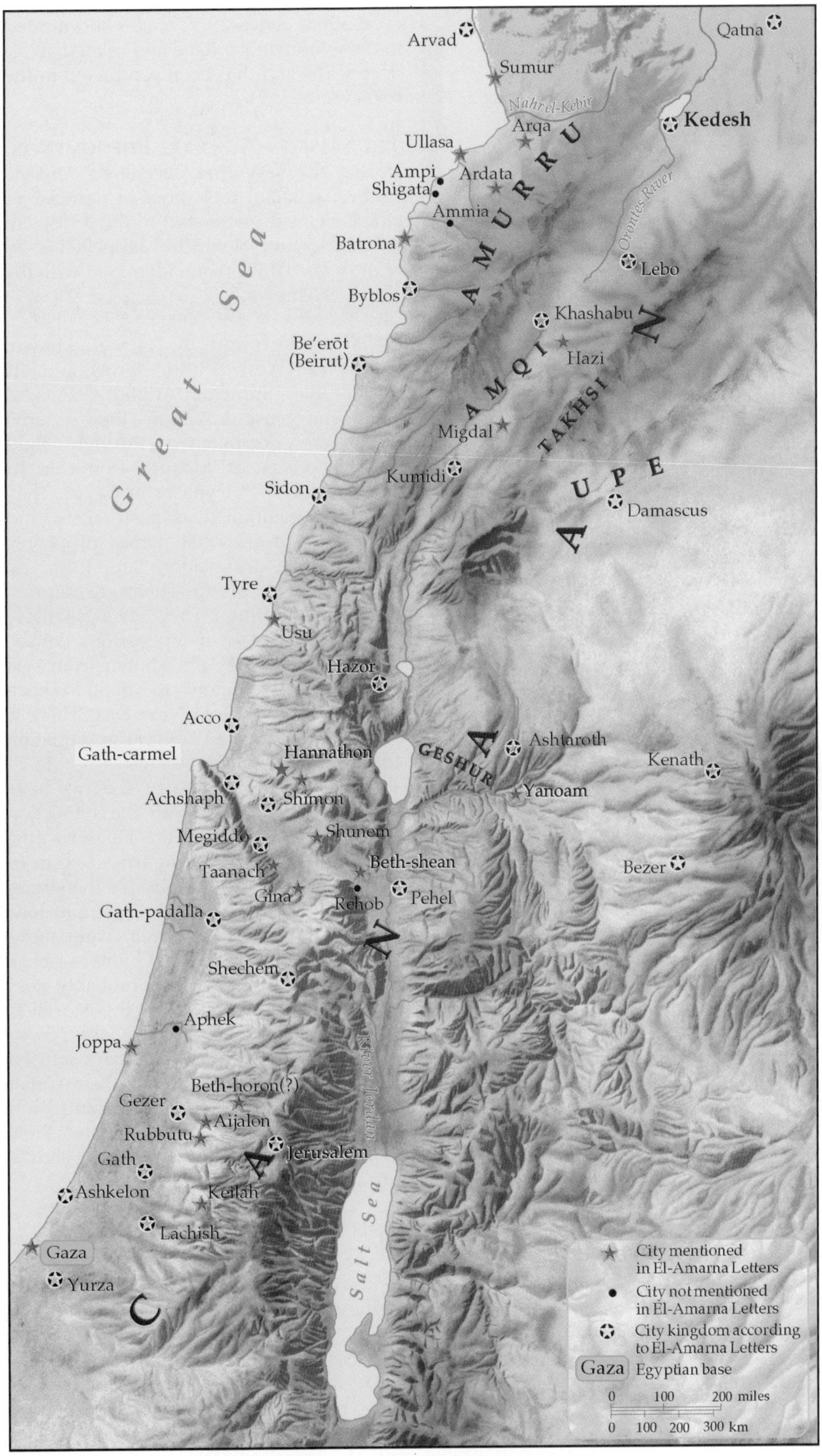


**THE KINGS OF CANAAN IN THE AMARNA AGE (MID-14[TH] CENTURY BCE)**

**Late Bronze Age II.** The fourteenth century BCE began as a golden age of peace and ended as a time of war and tension. It is illumined by a relative abundance of inscriptional material, especially in cuneiform, from Mesopotamia, from Anatolia (Hattusas=Boghazköy) and from Egypt. This historical period in North Syria is also enriched by important cuneiform archives (especially from Ugarit). Central Syria and Canaan are likewise known by means of cuneiform documents found mainly in Egypt (the Amarna texts).

The events documented for the Levantine littoral during the fourteenth century BCE are closely linked to the events in Egypt. The testimony to those events derives mainly from the collection of cuneiform letters

*Queen Nefertiti, first lady of Akhenaten, the founder of Ahhetaten (el-Amarna); partially restored.*

discovered in the ruins of the Amarna site. Over a century of studying those texts has produced a reasonable synthesis of several "case histories" concerning city-states and other elements in central Syria and in the province of Canaan (the southern Levant) as well as a limited number of international communications between the major political states of the region.

**Tell el-Amarna and the Amarna Tablets.** A central component in the cultural and political life of the ancient Near Eastern Late Bronze Age is the collection of cuneiform documents known as the Amarna Tablets.

**Discovery.** The semi-legendary accounts of their discovery 120 years ago are fairly well known to the scholarly world but less so today to the general public. The ancient ruins are about midway between No-amon (Thebes; modern Luxor) and Noph (Memphis; modern Mit Rahina and surrounding sites). The present name of the site was an artificial creation derived from a misunderstanding by scholars of the local toponyms: the villages et-Tîl and el-ᶜAmarîyah and a local tribe settled in the region, the Banî ᶜAmrân (plural ᶜAmarna). The first use of the term Tell el-Amarna was on the map of John Gardner Wilkinson in 1830. Today, the post office at the train station on the western side of the Nile opposite the site bears the official name "Tell el-Amarna."

This is the location of the ancient capital founded by Amenḥotep IV (Akhenaten). He named it Akhetaten, "the Horizon of the Sun Disc." The project was inaugurated in his fourth regnal year and he evidently moved his family and entourage there by his sixth year. The full city plan was never achieved but many prominent temples to the sun disc, Aten, and palatial buildings were constructed, as revealed by the excavator's spade during the late nineteenth and early twentieth centuries. Further excavations since 1977 have concentrated in the workman's village and related areas. Special research has been conducted in the royal tombs.

**The ᶜ*Apîru*—A Social Phenomenon.** During the very first decade of Amarna studies, scholars took note of a social or ethnic element mentioned in the Jerusalem letters the name of which was spelled *ḫa-bi-ru* or *ḫa-bi-ri*. It was soon identified with the *ᶜibrîm*, "Hebrews."

**Social Background.** As is well known, the *ᶜapîru* (West Semitic term) and its ideographic Sumerian reflex, SA.GAZ (sometimes just GAZ in the Amarna texts), are documented through eight hundred years of history, from Ur III down to the XX<sup>th</sup> Dynasty in Egypt. They are never mentioned as pastoralists, and the preserved personal names of people bearing this designation are from no single linguistic group. There are Semites, Hurrians and others. They never belong to tribes. They may worship various deities. Geographically they are known from east of the Tigris, to Anatolia, to Egypt, in short, over the entire ancient Near East. There is absolutely nothing to suggest an equation with the biblical Hebrews!

For more than a century, theories have been promulgated to explain the connection between the *ᶜapîru* and the Hebrews (the patriarchs and the invading tribes). None of them are sound, but because of the strong desire to find some extra-biblical allusions to the patriarchs and to Joshua's campaigns, the theories continue to have their appeal. Actually, the proto-Israelites probably stem from another group, the tribal pastoralists called *Sutû* in cuneiform and *Shâsu*/*Shôsu* in Egyptian; these latter are never confused with the *ᶜapîru*. The popular theory, that the *ᶜapîru* were revolting peasants, has no textual support, either in the Bible or in extra-biblical documents or in the archaeological record.

**Late Bronze Age III.** The last stage of the Late Bronze Age as defined by archaeologists and historians corresponds to the thirteenth century BCE. In terms of Egyptian history, this is parallel to Dynasty XIX. While the transition from Dynasty XIX to Dynasty XX was a time of serious crisis in Egypt, the latter dynasty considered itself the heirs of the great works of Ramesses II and thus the line of kings took the same throne name, viz. Ramesses III to XI. From the standpoint of material culture, a decided downgrading in the standard of living and in the character of the luxury items imported and produced in the Levant is observable. Evidence of closer Egyptian control over the southern Levant is seen in the presence of buildings at numerous towns in Canaan which have a clearly Egyptian plan and Egyptian artifacts and inscriptions. These are the so-called "governors' residences."

While it is convenient to maintain the traditional division here at the end of the thirteenth century BCE, the real cultural break is not so sharp, at least not on the coastal plains, and events of the reigns of Ramesses III and IV can be treated as a continuation of Late Bronze III. It was a time of great conflicts but also of intensive trade and cultural interchange. The eastern Mediterranean was being plied by merchant ships delivering luxury goods as well as staples between Egypt, the Levant and the Aegean regions. All the major players on the geopolitical scene: Ḫatti, Egypt, Babylonia and Assyria, were striving to share in the shipping and the caravan trade across the Middle East.

**The Shâsu Pastoralists.** In the New Kingdom texts concerning activities in the Levant, there are numerous references to a socio-ethnic group called Shâsu. These Shâsu pastoralists begin to appear during the XVIII<sup>th</sup> Dynasty and occur with increasing frequency in the Egyptian texts of Dynasty XIX. The earliest reference dates to the early fifteenth century BCE, from the inscription of Aḥmose-Pennekhbet.

The reaction of the pastoralists during times of stress, especially drought and famine, was to seek refuge in the settled area. The Tigris and Euphrates Valley, the Lebanese Beqaᶜ, the Jezreel Valley and the Egyptian Delta are all well known as refuge zones to which the pastoralists would turn in times of trouble.

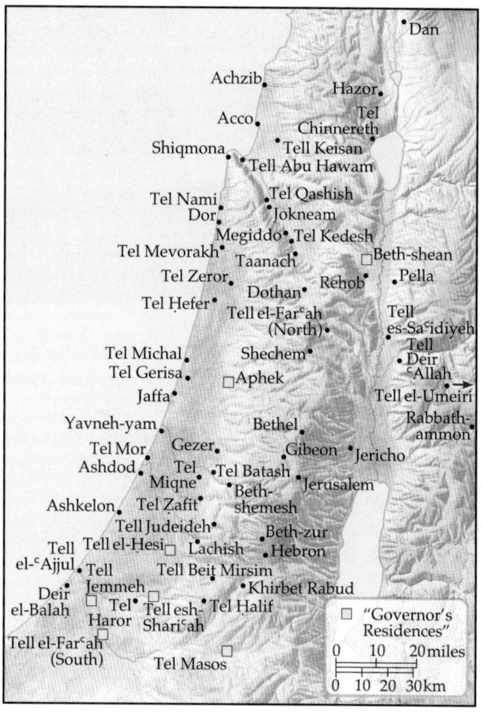


**Late Bronze Age III Sites in the Southern Levant**

# CHAPTER FOUR

# Crisis and Transition

## TWELFTH CENTURY BCE

Most of the Late Bronze centers of the eastern Mediterranean saw violent destruction sometime during the first quarter of the twelfth century BCE. The archaeological evidence is clear and widespread: the main palaces of the Mycenaean world, the capital of the Hittite Empire and other major Anatolian centers, Alalakh and Ugarit on the Syrian coast, several coastal towns, such as Ashkelon and Ashdod, and inland sites such as Hazor and Aphek, all in the southern Levant, i.e. southern Canaan. None can deny that these destruction levels represent outbreaks of unprecedented violence throughout the region. The explanations in the respective areas, and the identifications of suspected perpetrators are numerous and varied. In the wake of all this violence new frameworks of social and political organization emerged; the process continued through the twelfth century BCE into the tenth. That transition is one of the most difficult periods to assess because there are practically no written sources to document the course of events. Only at the two extremities of the Fertile Crescent is there inscriptional evidence: Mesopotamia and Egypt. To a large extent, one must rely on archaeological data, especially the results of excavations and surveys from the last quarter of the twentieth century.

## The Southern Levant

A burning question about this area is the radical change that came about during the age of crisis and transition. The major Canaanite towns on the Lebanese coast do not seem to have been damaged by the conflict initiated by the seafarers. Ramesses III apparently stopped the invaders at the border of Amurru and Djahi, north of Byblos. On the other hand, the Late Bronze towns and seaports along the southern coast suffered violent destruction. The ensuing renewal of occupation reveals a complex of traits in the material culture and point unequivocally to the arrival of a new ethnic entity. The most obvious feature is the new ceramic style. The vessels are locally made but reflect a distinct Aegean tradition. This is the Mycenaean IIIC1b. It was the pottery style that prevailed in Greece itself and related areas in the wake of the destruction of the Late Helladic palaces.

*Prisoners from among the Sea Peoples, relief of Ramesses III at Medinet Habū.*

To be more precise, it reflects what is called in Greece the Late Helladic IIIC, Middle Phase. It replaced the Mycenaean IIIB (Late Helladic IIIB) which was in vogue during the end of the Bronze Age in Greece and as imports in all the major urban centers of the eastern Mediterranean seaboard. The Mycenaean IIIB was generally imported from the Aegean area. The new Mycenaean IIIC1b which appears in southern Canaan is locally made. The newcomers had brought their potters with them. The same cities of the southern coastal plain—Gaza, Ashkelon, Ashdod, Gath and Ekron—had all been important towns in the Late Bronze Age. Now they were destroyed and the succeeding occupation was characterized by this new pottery. In the background of this material analysis is the fact that in biblical and later in non-biblical sources, those five cities (and various others) are known as cities of the Philistines. The Philistines seem obviously to be the *Pu-l-śa-tá* of the northern war described by Ramesses III. Apart from the *Onomasticon of Amenope*, they are not mentioned in earlier or later Egyptian texts of this period. The coastal city of Dor, near Mount Carmel, was occupied by another of Ramesses' enemies, the Sicels.

**The Cisjordanian Highlands and Transjordan.** The late thirteenth and early twelfth centuries BCE saw a new phenomenon in the hill-country areas of the southern Levant. This was the establishment of a plethora of small campsite-like settlements; they appeared in the uplands of Upper Galilee, Lower Galilee, the hill country of Manasseh and Ephraim, the hill country of Judah and the biblical Negeb. Collateral surveys were conducted in adjacent areas, such as the Shephelah of Judah and the Beth-shean Valley. Surveys on the eastern side of the Jordan Valley have also contributed to the overall picture.

As a typical case history, the analysis of the Ephraim survey furnishes a basic framework for the process as a whole. The earliest sites were apparently on the eastern side of the watershed, on the fringe of the steppe land (the ridges leading down to the Jordan Valley). The occupants may have begun by seasonal usage, utilizing some adjacent fields for dry farming and the adjacent steppe for grazing their herds. Eventually, as the population grew, settlements developed on the western side of the watershed and some of them eventually grew into the main occupied tels of the later Iron Age. In the westward migration from the watershed, where the ridges and slopes were wild and rocky, the settlers evidently began to develop terraces in order to create more cultivable land.

In some cases, new sites of this period also developed in the low-lying plains (e.g. on the Sharon Plain and the Jezreel Valley).

The archaeological facts are becoming clearer. The material culture of these new

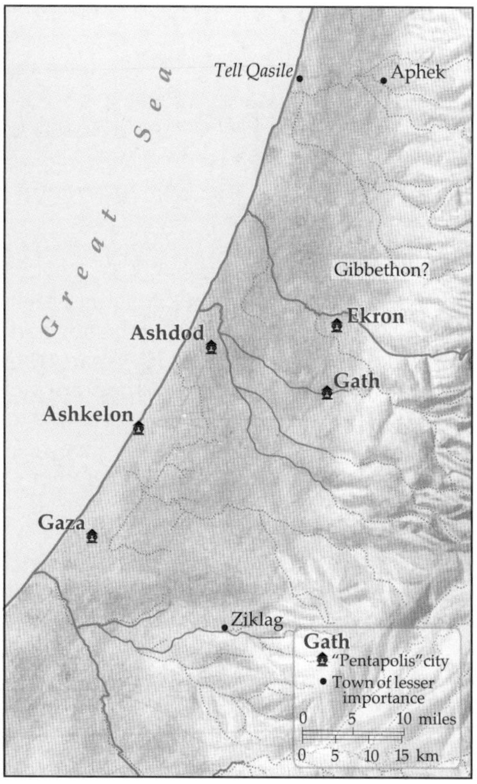


THE CITIES OF PHILISTIA

*The Iron Age I witnesses the appearance of the Philistines, a clearly foreign entity, in the southern coastal plain. The Philistines brought with them Aegean cultural traditions, including different pottery, architecture and settlement planning. The Philistines settled five major cities (Gaza, Ashkelon, Ashdod, Ekron and Gath) at first, yet with time they spread farther to the east, south and north with smaller settlements. The Philistine cities were strongly fortified (as seen at Ashdod and Ekron). Of the most distinct public buildings is the Philistine temple. While certain temples contain Canaanite local elements (as those found at Tell Qasile), there seem to be unique features, such as the hearth (which is well known from Cyprus and the Aegean), which was placed in the center of the main hall. Another foreign element concerning Philistine religion is the "Ashdoda," a sitting goddess found at Ashdod and Ekron (opposite, left). The most diverse feature of the Philistine material culture is the pottery. A number of stages can be discerned concerning this pottery, yet clearly its most characteristic feature is the painted decorations and forms (e.g. bell-shaped bowls). The Philistine arrival is marked with the appearance of locally produced Mycenaean IIIC1b pottery, which develops into the well-known Philistine Bichrome Ware (opposite, right). The pottery is handmade and typically decorated with swirls, birds and fish painted red, or black and red, on a light buff. The pottery seems to lose certain elements of its individuality as the period progresses, and at the same time integrates Egyptian and Canaanite influences. It is important to note that Philistine assemblages usually also contain local pottery as well.*

settlements shows some affinities with the Late Bronze Age culture known from the larger cities of the thirteenth century BCE, but other, distinctive features are even more striking (e.g. the ceramics). But from the standpoint of historical geography, the identification of these apparently new socioethnic elements is fraught with the same problems as that of the new socioethnic elements in mainland Greece (Dorians) and the Aramaic pastoralists in Syria and Mesopotamia. Apart from the Egyptian references (e.g. Shâsu and "Israel" in the Merneptah stele), only the biblical traditions are available. Those traditions now comprise a national epic, edited and arranged by much later writers. But like the Dorians/Heracleidae, the late traditions surely have a basic twelfth-century BCE reality. As literary compositions, they are discussed below.

The whole controversy surrounding these archaeological sites and their development is linked to the question of Israel's origins. The biblical tradition is unanimous that Israel's ancestors were pastoralists, the patriarchs (Gen 46:34, 47:3–4) and the later tribes (Num 20:19, 32:1). But the modern tendency is to deny the validity of that tradition. The historical (pseudo-) philological arguments based on the Late Bronze epigraphic material have been treated elsewhere. But explanations other than the arrival of pastoral immigrants in Cisjordan from Transjordan have been dominant in the field. So much so, that archaeologists have denied any ethnic distinctiveness to the new dwellers in the campsites. They are supposedly Canaanites who have changed their subsistence strategy from sedentary to pastoral. The same thinking underlies much of the discussion about other parts of the eastern Mediterranean world.

Analysis of the material finds from two excavations of such sites in the hill country of Ephraim (at et-Tell [biblical Ai] and at Khirbet Raddana), led to the conclusion that the inhabitants were "Hivites" who had migrated to the hills from the western coastal areas. Years later it was argued that the occupants of all the strata from these and other Iron Age I sites in the hill country had migrated from the north and west, certainly not from the south and east as formerly assumed. In other words, the material culture from the plethora of hill-country sites that sprang up at the end of the Late Bronze Age must point to a coastal or lowland origin for the settlers.

Everyone agrees that there is an amazing multiplication of small village sites in the hill-country areas during this period and it has even been admitted that there probably weren't enough people from the depleted Canaanite population to furnish occupants for the new Iron Age I sites.

It must be kept in mind that during the Late Bronze Age (and during the Middle Bronze Age before it), there were always pastoralists in the steppe lands living in symbiosis with the sedentary, agricultural populations.

Today Transjordan and the eastern side of the Jordan Valley cannot be ignored as the most probable source for the new immigrants who established the small villages on the heights of Mount Ephraim (the Samarian hills). That their pottery and other artifacts show some continuity with the Late Bronze material culture is no deterrent. The recent survey of known Late Bronze materials in Transjordan shows just how extensive is the spread of Late Bronze material culture there. Today the excavations at Tell el-ʿUmeiri add more weight to the argument that there was plenty of Late Bronze material culture in Transjordan during the Late Bronze Age and the transition to the twelfth century BCE. A pillared house excavated there produced an abundance of collared-rim

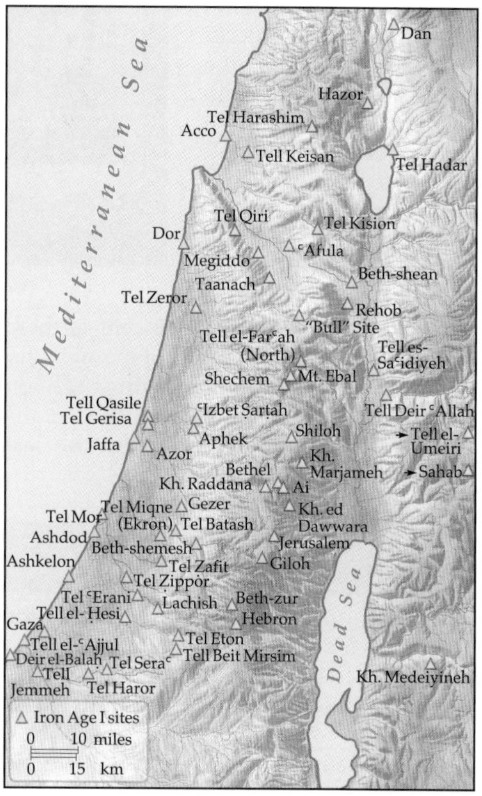


**THE MAJOR EARLY IRON AGE SITES**
*Recent surveys have recorded dozens of small sites, especially in the Hill Country (both Arabic and Hebrew names are used).*

store pithoi. But we can go a step further, as a result of ethnographic surveys of the Jordan Valley; it was possible to correlate the results of archaeological excavations and surveys in the Tell Deir Allah area from the Late Bronze and Iron Age I with nineteenth-century developments among the Bedouin. The case of the Mihdawi tribe is most instructive. Due to pressures from more dominant tribes, it had been forced to migrate to the Jordan Valley but then further pressures eventually forced it to migrate to the hills of Cisjordan!

Another factor which has never been taken into account is the linguistic affinities of ancient Hebrew with the eastern dialects of Moabite and southern old Aramaic. Hebrew, in fact, did not develop from coastal Canaanite. Its connections are with Transjordan and not with Phoenicia. The language and religion of the early Israelites evidently originated in Transjordan and were brought to Cisjordan by the pastoralists migrating in the twelfth century BCE.

## Israelite Ancestral Traditions

The people of ancient Israel, like other ethnic groups in the eastern Mediterranean, preserved traditions about the ancestral, and eponymous, personalities who had been the progenitors of the nation. The Israelites' concept of their own origins is embodied in various biblical passages, many of them of considerable literary merit in their present form. This final written formulation of the traditions derives from a time when certain intellectuals sharing a strong theological and ethnocentric viewpoint sought to explain some basic questions: "Who are we? And how did we get here?" The narratives are thus incorporated into what may be called "The National Epic." The men and women who comprised the parents of the nation as a whole and its respective tribal units are depicted as real people, subject to the foibles of human nature but also partaking of heroic dimensions. The origin of these narratives, their oral and literary history, are complex subjects which have been the object of scholarly attention for generations. An essential feature of the tradition is its geographical outlook and its geographical content. Study of these aspects of the ancestral narratives makes it possible to delineate the viewpoint of the Israelite authors about the place of their people in time and space.

**Mesopotamian Origin—Egyptian Captivity.** An awareness of the location of the Israelite people on the great land bridge between Asia and Africa is basic to their ancestral history. The "Deuteronomistic" oration by the heroic personality of the conquest narratives expresses this consciousness in the Book of Joshua 24:2–4.

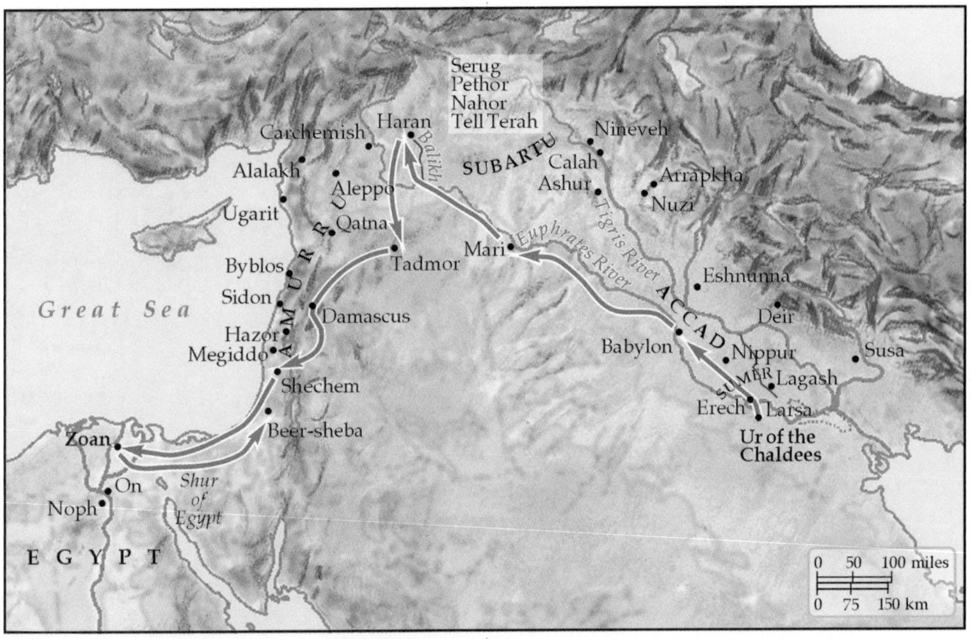


**The Tradition of Abraham's Migration**

The story begins in Mesopotamia, "beyond the River." This is a unique instance when that expression refers to the eastern side of the Euphrates unlike the later usage when it defines the Levant from a Mesopotamian stance. The ancestors are said to have worshipped other deities until YHWH Himself called them out to come to Canaan. The Book of Genesis gives a more detailed account (*see* Gen 11:27–32).

At the culmination of the post-diluvian ancestors, Terah is said to have lived a relatively "modest" two hundred and five years. He had his origin in southern Mesopotamia, characterized as "Ur of the Chaldees." The epithet serves to help the reader (late Israelite or Persian period) orient himself. The Chaldeans may have entered the land of the two rivers sometime prior to the tenth century BCE but the earliest documentation is in the ninth century BCE (878 BCE inscription of Ashurnaṣirpal II). At any rate, the Chaldeans were not present in lower Mesopotamia during the Bronze Age. The ancestors' second station was Haran, the great crossroads (the meaning of its name in Akkadian is road or caravan) city of northern Mesopotamia. The temptation to associate the son of Terah, Haran, with the geographical name Haran must be strenuously resisted. On the other hand, some of the principal names, e.g. Nahor, appear as geographical entities in the Mari letters of the Middle Bronze Age. The common feature of Ur and Haran was the worship of the moon god, Sin. This is prominent in the mid-sixth century BCE during the reign of Nabu-naid (Nabonidus), who gave substantial support to the temple of Sin at Haran.

The later narratives about acquisition of the principal tribal matriarchs, Rebekah (Gen 25:20), Leah and Rachel and the secondary wives, Bilhah and Zilpah (Gen 28:2), in the land of Paddan-aram, and the kinship with the Arameans in that area, i.e. Laban (whose name reflects the moon worship of the Haran area) and his kinship group, confirm the Israelite consciousness that they were related to the Arameans (*see* Deut 26:5).

The Aramean tribal matriarchs are later called "Hittites" (Ezek 16:3, 16:45) using the late terminology for the Neo-Hittite elements in what the Assyrians and Babylonians called "the land of Ḫatti." Those "Hittites" were thoroughly Aramean in Ezekiel's day.

In the light of cuneiform inscriptions, the Arameans are only documented for the late twelfth, early eleventh centuries BCE, viz. in the texts of Tiglath-pileser I. There is no justification for seeking a generic link between the Aramean tribes and the Amurrites of the Mari era. So even the biblical recollections (in some elaborate genealogical detail) link the origins of the Israelite tribes with the emerging pastoralist tribes in the upper and middle Euphrates Valley who appear on the stage of history at the beginning of the eleventh century BCE. The stress on Aramean affinity is coupled with an awareness that the tribes were not related to the indigenous Canaanite population of the southern Levant.

**The Land of Canaan.** The connection of Israel to the land of Canaan, i.e., the southern Levant, is attributed to migration, under divine guidance (*see* Gen 12:1–5).

***Central Hill Country and the Southern Steppe.*** The ensuing narratives take place within the geographical framework of Canaan (except for Jacob's sojourn in Paddan-aram and the Joseph novella). The principal sites mentioned in the patriarchal peregrinations are in the central hill country (later called Mount Ephraim

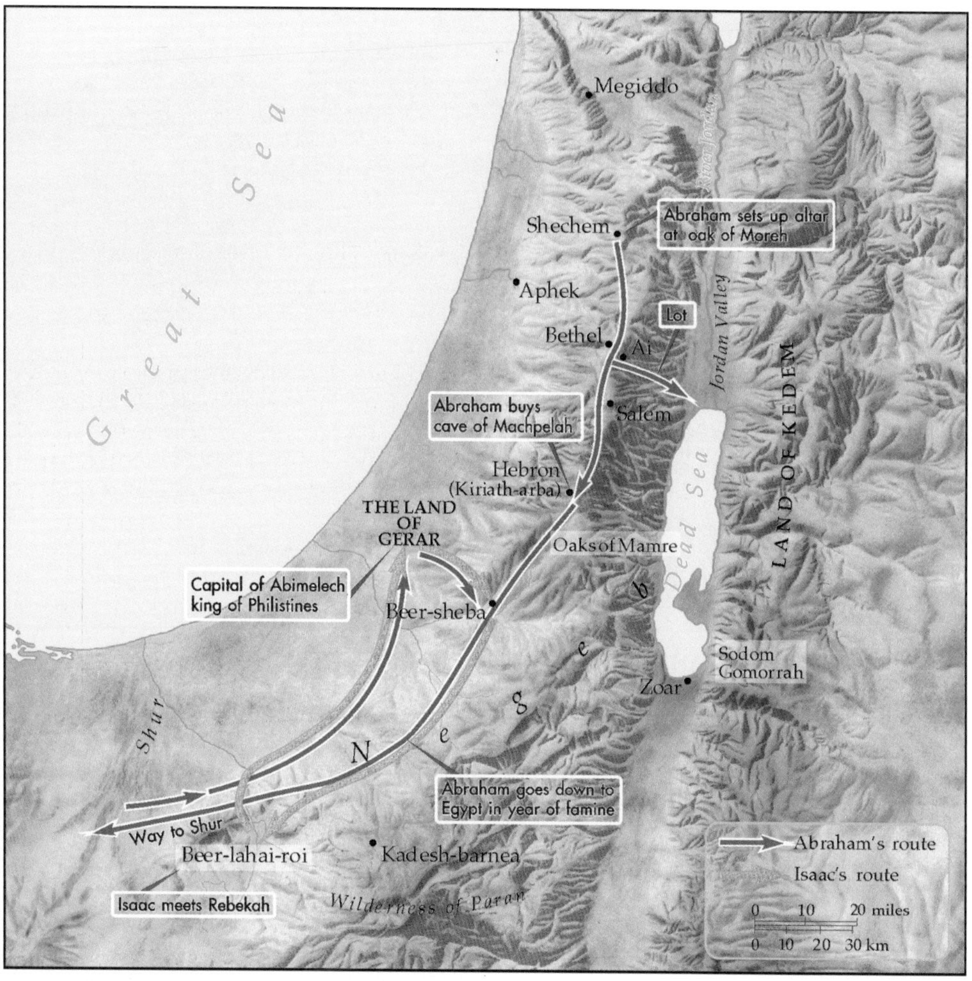


**Abraham and Isaac in the Land of Canaan**

and Mount Judah) along the watershed route. It has long been observed that the frequent discussion of altars, sacrifices, and sometimes theophanies must be based on local cultic traditions at shrines that functioned at the respective places. These same places are generally known as cultic sites during the monarchy.

> Abram passed through the land as far as the "place" of **Shechem**, to the **Oak of Moreh**. Now the Canaanite was then in the land. YHWH appeared to Abram and said, "To your descendants I will give this land." So he built an altar there to YHWH who had appeared to him. (Gen 12:6–7)

"Place" is evidently a designation for a holy site and the oak was most probably a sacred tree, a central icon in the ritual practiced there. Its name is obviously etiological, relating to the theophany vouchsafed to the patriarch.

Genesis 12:8 is the first reference to Bethel, a site later made famous as the southern border cult place of the northern kingdom of Israel. The ancestral narratives make several important references to this town, thus linking it firmly with the national foundational epic. Abram returned to the site of his first altar and theophany after a sojourn in Egypt (Gen 13:1–4). The geographical location of Bethel at the town of Beitîn is unimpeachable.

The steppe land, the Negeb, across the southern belt of the country with Beer-sheba as its focus, is also a major venue for the experiences of the national ancestors (*see* Gen 12:9). However, Abram's chief adventure there will occur later (regarding Gerar). In the meantime, the patriarch's descent to Egypt is paralleled by other migrations to the delta by the other figures. Altogether, they happen to match the phenomenon reflected in the XIXth Dynasty sources about the Shâsu seeking refuge from famine and drought. The folk motif of the "wife-sister" and the fear engendered by the beauty of the matriarch (Gen 12:10–20) will be dealt with more in detail with reference to its third occurrence in Genesis, about Isaac and Rebekah at Gerar (Gen 26).

Another venue included in the ancestral narratives is the "valley of the Jordan," obviously on the eastern side of the "rift," since it was not included in the land of Canaan (Gen 13:10–12). It provided the scene for the razzia narrative of Genesis 14 as well as the "great catastrophe" of chapter 19.

Finally, the southern hill country residence of Hebron becomes the place of burial for the matriarch Sarai/Sarah and other members of the founding family. Again, an altar is associated with the site (*see* Gen 13:18).

Here the tradition introduces an ethnicon suitable for the ancestral family, "Abram the Hebrew." This term is derived from Eber, the name of a figure in the genealogical matrix (Gen 10:21, 10:24–25, 11:16–17 *et passim*). Thus, the ethnic group that became Israel is an offshoot of the "sons of Eber," a line that descended from Shem, the son of Noah. Abram the Hebrew is juxtaposed to the three Amorite eponyms of the Hebron area, namely "Mamre the Amorite, brother of Eshcol and brother of Aner" (Gen 14:13). Not only is Abram not a Canaanite, he is also not an Amorite. That *ᶜib̲rî* has absolutely no connection with the ubiquitous Late Bronze term *ᶜapîru*, is discussed above.

The narrative in Genesis 14 about the four kings who came to attack the five kings of the "cities on the plain" is the oldest military tradition preserved in the Bible. It contains pre-Israelite geographical data exemplified by the double names of most of the towns, e.g. "Bela, that is Zoar." Besides a reverence for that ancient tradition, there is a concern that the reader be able to orient himself geographically; thus the venerable names are updated by contemporary Israelite names. None of the characters mentioned have been identified with known historical figures. Amraphel can by no means be equated with ᶜAmmurapi, the Amurrite king of Babylon; Chedorlaomer has an Elamite look to it but has no exact parallel among known Elamite names. Tidal does match the alphabetic spelling of the name of known Hittite kings, conventionally spelled Tudkhaliya. Two of the geographical names are well known: Shinar (southern Mesopotamia; originally Shanghar; the land otherwise known as Sumer, the home of the Sumerians) and Elam (the national homeland in the hill country to the east of the lower Tigris Valley, in western Iran). Ellasar is unknown, nor have Sodom, Gomorrah or the other towns appeared in ancient Near Eastern documents (certainly not from Ebla).

It is especially noteworthy that the course of the invasion followed the watershed route on the Transjordanian plateau. The conflicts, from north to south, are against indigenous peoples, most of whom do not appear on the map of Israelite national consciousness (*see* Gen 14:5–7).

The Rephaim are considered to be the early inhabitants of the Bashan area; they were believed to have been or to have included many giant warriors. Their city was Ashtaroth (modern Tell ᶜAshtarah). In the Iron Age, it seems to have been overshadowed by Karnaim (Sheikh Saᶜd). Thus, the editor of the narrative chose to update the locale for his readers. The Zuzim from Ham (modern Hâm) are otherwise unknown. The Emim are said to have been the indigenous inhabitants of the land of the Moabites, who displaced them. They are said to have been giants like the Anakim but reckoned with the Rephaim (Deut 2: 10–11). The Horites are the autochthonous dwellers of Mount Seir who were displaced by the descendants of Esau. They can hardly have any association with the Hurrians of northern Mesopotamia or Syria. The resemblance in names is strictly accidental.

Ashtaroth-karnaim, Shaveh-kiriathaim, En-mishpat (i.e. Kadesh[-barnea]), and Bela (i.e. Zoar) all are updates of geographical names. They testify to the archaic nature of the narrative which needed clarification by the editor/redactor so that his contemporaries could grasp the geographical matrix of the campaign. But the total lack of any link with known ancient Near Eastern sources leaves the story, like Melchizedek, hanging in limbo without genealogy. It is a Transjordanian tradition, linked to the ancestral history by means of the connection between Lot in the valley (the progenitor of Moab and Ammon) and Abram in the Hebron hills. The mysterious Melchizedek, king of Salem, is introduced to confirm an association with most ancient Jerusalem (Ps 110:4).

A further sojourn by Abraham in the southern steppe land (the Negeb) around Beer-sheba is recorded in Genesis 20. The opening verse requires some geographical comment (*see* Gen 20:1).

The verbal forms here indicate a progression: first the patriarch went toward the southern district known as the Negeb. Then he evidently shifted to a more distant venue in the Sinai between Kadesh and the wilderness of Shur, i.e. western Sinai bordering on the Egyptian Delta (Ex 15:22). After that, he moved to Gerar. Gerar is almost as mysterious as Salem and Melchizedek. Abraham's experience there is a repeat of the folk motif from his Egyptian sojourn (Gen 12:10–20). It is repeated again, with more important coloring, in the life of Isaac (Gen 26).

An ancestral association with the holy mount in Jerusalem (2 Chr 3:1) is encapsulated in the account of the sacrifice of Isaac (*see* Gen 22:2).

***Gerar.*** As mentioned above, there is a narrative about Abram/Abraham and Sarah sojourning in a place called Gerar. A doublet narrative features Isaac and Rebekah (Gen 26). Both instances involve the danger felt because of the unusual beauty of the matriarch and the threat that someone will slay the patriarch in order to capture the wife. However, the Isaac/Rebekah version contains other details of a sociological nature.

First of all, in both versions the residents of Gerar are Philistines, so there is no doubt that they represent Israelite storytelling no earlier than the eleventh century BCE. Attempts to find a pre-twelfth-century Aegean ethnic presence in the western Negeb (Middle or Late Bronze Age) are nothing more than exercises in futility. The strange factor is that the ruler has a Semitic name, Abimelech (which contaminates also the later Gath tradition, Ps 34:1). The identification of the site for the city of Gerar has moved from Tel Gamma (Tell Jemmeh) to Tel Haror (Tell Abū Hureirah). Gerar is never mentioned in any non-biblical source and its role as the principal city in the western Negeb during the "ancestral period" is fraught with difficulties. Of course, making the residents Philistines may be a simple anachronism on the part of later reciters or redactors. Still, even in the Late Bronze Age, Gaza is the mightiest urban center at the western end of the Negeb (cf. Gen 10:19) though several interesting tels stand along the courses of the wadis (Tell el-Far$^c$ah; Tell Jemmeh=Tel Gamma; Tell Abū Hureirah=Tel Haror; Tell esh-Sharî$^c$ah=Tel Sera$^c$). Its only later occurrence is in a ninth-century BCE narrative preserved in 2 Chronicles (14:13–14). There it is not treated as a city but more like an area. The Medeba Map shows a Saltus Gerariticus but no city. Nevertheless, there is no doubt that Isaac is depicted as living in a town.

Abimelech saw Isaac and Rebekah, probably on the roof of their house (*see* Gen 26:8). Of more significance is Isaac's participation in local agriculture (Gen 26:12).

Elsewhere, the Genesis narratives describe altars built or real estate acquired by the patriarchs, certainly as underpinnings for local traditions at various shrines and cult centers. Nothing is said about Isaac purchasing fields or houses. The implication seems to be that as a prosperous sojourner, he was permitted to invest in local agriculture. He may have financed the crops for local farmers for which he was granted an abundant profit. His success in this enterprise aroused the jealousy of the agriculturalists and led to his being expelled from Gerar.

Both narratives see the patriarch and his entourage moving away from Gerar until they arrive back at Beer-sheba where they establish themselves and then enter into a treaty agreement with Abimelech. The impression is that Abimelech was reconciled to the Hebrew presence on the periphery of his own territory. But he sought to establish a covenant relationship with that large pastoral element in hopes of avoiding future conflicts. In both stories, the name Beer-sheba is linked to the oath taking; the verb for swearing an oath (as required in treaty ratification) is a denominative from the numeral "seven." "To seven oneself" is the act of affirming your word by oath. The praxis behind this semantic development is unknown but in the Genesis accounts seven sacrifices or seven altars are emphasized. There is nothing in these traditions about seven wells.

The steppe land immediately to the south of Beer-sheba consisting of Eocene rock like the Shephelah, farther north, was known as the "steppe land of Beer-sheba" (Gen 21:14).

***Jacob and His Sons.*** Unlike the narrative about Abram, that describing Jacob's return from Paddan-aram is quite explicit. In fact, it probably provides the paradigm for the immigration movement during the transition period (*see* Gen 31:20–23).

The time frame may or may not be valid, but the direction and the destination are clear. This is also confirmed by the etiological narrative about a sacred stele and a circular platform of stones (*see* Gen 31:44–49).

Another etiological account explains the name of an important town in the valley of the Jabbok, i.e. Mahanaim (*see* Gen 32:1–2). Mahanaim (probably Tell edh-Dhahab el-Gharbī) is one of two impressive tels in the Jabbok Valley. There seems to be a hint at the morphologically dual suffix, *-aim*, in Jacob's dividing his entourage into two camps (Gen 32:7). Mahanaim is known as a Levitical city that plays a significant role in the administration of Transjordan during the later monarchial period (e.g. 1 Kgs 4:14; also Josh 21:38; 1 Chr 6:65).

The continuation of this pericope explains the name of the twin site, Penuel (*see* Gen 32:24–31). Penuel became the Transjordanian administrative center for the newly established northern kingdom of Israel (1 Kgs 12:25).

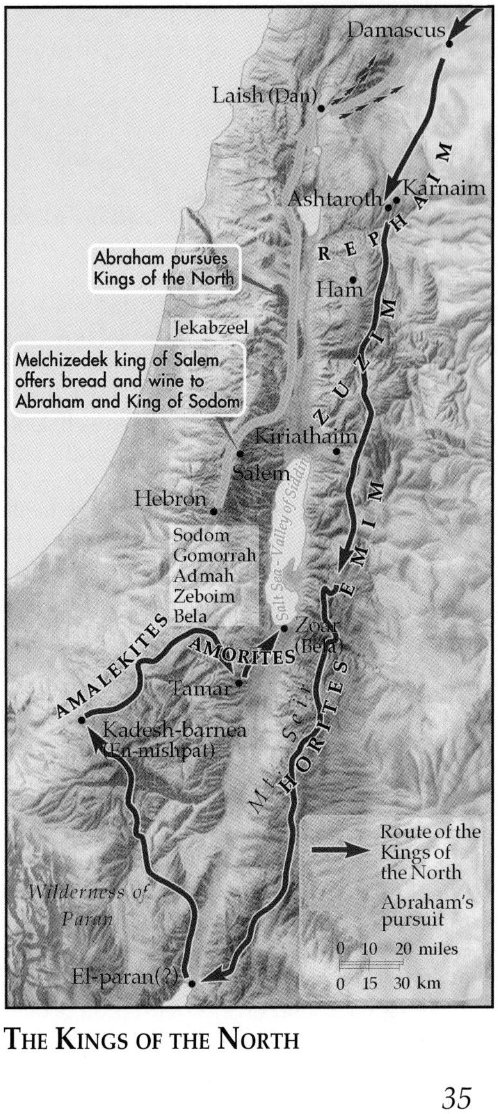


THE KINGS OF THE NORTH

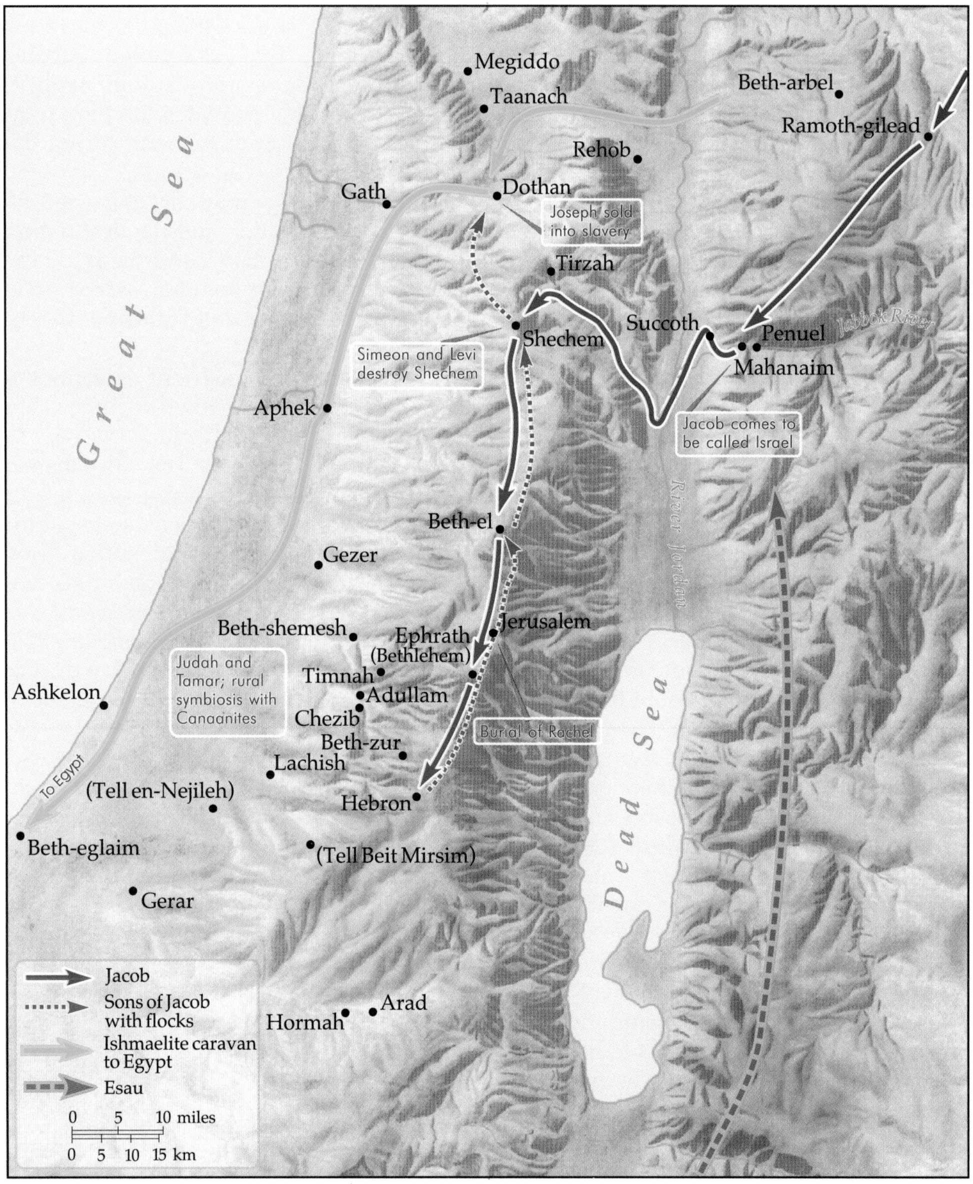


## Jacob and His Sons

The third site, where the Jabbok has debouched onto the plain of the Jordan Valley, is next explained. The most likely site for Succoth (*see* Gen 33:17) is Tell Deir ᶜAllah. Evidence for an ancient cult there includes a Late Bronze temple and a much later structure with plastered walls that bore a West Semitic inscription of a prophetic nature (about Baalam). The early Iron Age occupants were known for their belligerent attitude (Judg 8:5–6). Industrial activity during the United Monarchy is also described (1 Kgs 7:46; 2 Chr 4:17).

Crossing the Jordan westward brought Jacob and his entourage to the land of Canaan (*see* Gen 33:18–20). Purchase of a piece of land and establishment of an altar confirm an ancient cultic tradition. The conditions of settlement in the Shechemite territory illustrate the relationship of symbiosis that could prevail between a permanent settlement and tribal pastoralists (*see* Gen 34: 9–10).

The town center of Shechem could benefit from an infusion of new blood. Jacob's cattle was still at Succoth showing that his ties with Transjordan were not broken. Thus, his association with Shechem would also bring the benefits of the typical huckstering practiced by such pastoralists. This is a striking parallel with the nineteenth-century Bedouin activities from Transjordan to the Nablus hills. But the violence that erupted between Jacob's sons and the residents of Shechem also hints at a different scenario when relations became disrupted (Gen 34: 25–31, also 35:5).

The later phase of the ancestral narratives pertaining to Jacob and his sons is restricted almost entirely to the central hill country. Esau is now living on Mount Seir, which may be on the eastern or the western side of the Arabah valley. Jacob and his entourage migrated south following the watershed road. He came to Bethel, the site of his original theophany before the sojourn in Paddan-aram. There he enjoyed another theophany and built an altar accompanied by a stele (Gen 35:6–14).

The next leg of his journey brought him across the saddle connecting what are later called the hill country of Ephraim and the hill country of Judah. The intermediate zone became known as the inheritance of the tribe of Benjamin and Rachel's birth of that son took place here (Gen 35:16–18). Finally, he came to Mamre of Kiriath-arba (Gen 35:27), which is identified as the Hebron area. Though this remains their principal venue, the Joseph story demonstrates that they could migrate northward as far as the Valley of Dothan during the grazing season (*see* Gen 37:14–17). As an interesting curiosity, it should be noted that to this day, residents of the area north of Hebron transfer their flocks to the Dothan Valley for summer, post-harvesting, grazing!

In the Valley of Dothan, Joseph was sold to a caravan passing through the valley (on the southern route from the Jezreel Valley to the Sharon Plain as defined by Thutmose III). This fits in with the evidence for that link in the international trade route known from the Late Bronze Age (*see* Gen 37:25).

Further evidence for peaceful symbiosis with sheep-raising Canaanites is reflected in the story of Judah and Tamar, which takes place in the northern Shephelah near the junction of the Valley of Elah with the geographical "trough" separating the Shephelah from the hill country of Judah (Gen 38). Jacob established a partnership with a Canaanite named Hirah who was from Adullam (Gen 38:1; Khirbet esh-Sheikh Madhkûr=Ḥorbat ᶜAdullam). They pastured their flocks during shearing time in the vicinity of a certain Timnah (Gen 38:12). The other toponyms in the story prove that this Timnah must be Khirbet et-Tabbâneh (Hebrew Ḥorbat Tivna) east of the Valley of Elah in the foothills. It cannot be the Timnah in the Sorek Valley (Josh 15:10; Judg 14:1). Judah acquired a wife in that area who lived at Chezib (Gen 38:5), otherwise known as Achzib (Josh 15:44), between Keilah and Mareshah (which points to Khirbet Tell el-Beiḍā, unfortunately now called Ḥorbat Lavnin in Hebrew) and thus slightly south of the Valley of Elah. Tamar had disguised herself and pretended to be a harlot:

> And she sat in the **entrance of Enaim**, which is on the road to **Timnah**. (Gen 38:14)

Enaim is evidently "the Enam" (Josh 15:34) in the northern district of the Shephelah. It has to be south of Zanoah and near Jarmuth, therefore in or near the trough valley and presumably not far from Adullam, i.e. either just across the Valley of Elah or in the basin formed by the turn westward of the Elah stream as it departs from the trough valley.

The narrative serves to explain the location of some Judahite clans in the Shephelah (Gen 46:12; Num 26:21–22). It also illustrates the possibilities for symbiosis between mountain pastoralists and Canaanites in the lowlands. It is significant that there are no later conquest traditions about the northern Shephelah where the Judah/Tamar incident took place.

Another tradition, completely independent of the tendentious Deuteronomistic history, and therefore representing authentic tribal lore, is the story of Ephraim's sons. It shows the other side of the coin from the Judah/Tamar narrative, viz. the hostile relations that sometimes prevailed between hill country pastoralists and ethnic elements living on the plain below (*see* 1 Chr 7:20–24).

Here the native-born residents of Gath are not Philistines and the Gath is not Philistine Gath; it is Gath/Gittaim/Gath-rimmon (Josh 19:45; 2 Sam 4:3; Neh 11:33; 2 Chr 18:10), at or near modern Ramleh. They are synonymous with the Amorites (Judg 1:34–35; cf. 1 Sam 7:14) who prevented the Danites from coming down out of the hills and settling in the plain later known as the Plain of Ono (Neh 6:2; modern-day "Gush Dan" or the greater Tel Aviv area).

The eponymous ancestor is seen living in the hills above the plain and being there long enough to begat two generations of children. This is in sharp contrast to the Genesis account where Manasseh and Ephraim are said to have been born in Egypt and therefore must be presumed to have either died before the Exodus or at least in the wilderness. The chronicler included this story about the death of the sons to authenticate the clans who established settlements at Beth-horon but also as an expression of his bias against the Deuteronomistic conquest tradition.

*Faience vase with the name of the Egyptian queen Tawesret, from the LB sanctuary at Tell Deir ʿAllā, identified with Succoth.*

***Chronological Considerations.*** Finally, the ethnic horizon of the ancestral narratives must be considered. Nothing chronological can be deduced from the campaign described in Genesis 14; no confirmed contacts with the sources of the Bronze or Iron Age have been found. Reference has already been made above to the Philistines at Gerar. The society depicted at Gerar, considerably acclimatized to the Canaanite milieu, certainly suggests a time after the initial arrival of the Philistines after the mid-twelfth century BCE. The strong tradition of the associations with the Arameans in Upper Mesopotamia again points to the late twelfth or, more likely, the eleventh century BCE. Laban and his people are well along in the settlement process. Other groups, such as the Ishmaelites and Midianites (e.g. Gen 37:28), are also part of the Iron Age population. They might have originated as branches of the generic Shâsu of the Bronze Age, just like the Edomites, but their ability to conduct caravan trade between Transjordan and Egypt, and their use of camels, puts them in the Iron Age. In short, these Genesis pericopes open a window on life in the southern Levant during the transition out of the crisis that had so disrupted life at the end of the Late Bronze Age. Even the reference to "the land of Ramesses" (Gen 47:11) is compatible with a late XX^th^ Dynasty outlook or even later.

## THE EPIC OF THE EXODUS AND WILDERNESS WANDERINGS

There are two foundation stones in Israelite belief. These are embodied in the commandment to keep the Sabbath. The earlier version predicates Sabbath observance on the belief in YHWH as creator (*see* Ex 20:11). The Deuteronomistic version bases it on the belief in YHWH as deliverer (*see* Deut 5:13–15).

Those who formulated the national epic saw their ethnic identity as being rooted in an experience of deliverance from bondage in Egypt. The narratives recounting their collective memories and legendary elaborations of this event (Ex 1–15) find many echoes in poetry of the temple cult (e.g. *see* Ps. 78:12–13).

Such a powerful folk memory with so many ramifications can hardly be a strictly pure invention. Some major segment of the Iron Age settlers in the hills of Canaan during the crisis years must have brought with them this tradition. Their experience was grounded in reality and the Egyptian records of Shâsu tribes seeking refuge in the Delta provide a reasonable background for it. The actual component of ancient Israel that underwent such an experience in Egypt is impossible to identify now. Whether or how they became absorbed into the socioethnic group called "Israel" in the Merneptah stele cannot be determined. The "House

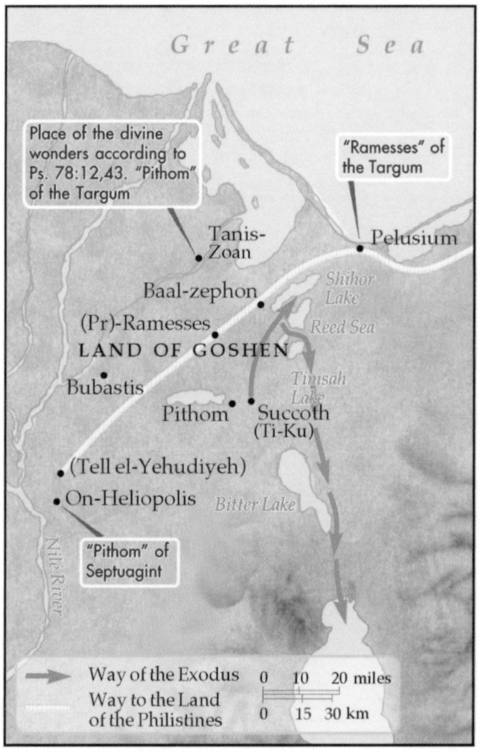


EGYPT OF THE EXODUS (AFTER BIETAK)

of Joseph tribes" (Ephraim and Manasseh; perhaps with Benjamin), descendants of the beloved favorite wife, Rachel, come to mind as likely candidates. Their position in the "hills of Ephraim" would have placed them in a position to influence the tradition that must have developed at Shiloh. This is in spite of the fact that the birth of the two eponymous ancestors in Egypt (Gen 46:20, 48:1–20) is belied by another tradition (1 Chr 7:20–24). Later, when the tribe of Judah and Jerusalem became predominant, their ancestor assumed a favorable role in the Joseph novella.

In spite of the literary character of the biblical tradition, it does embody considerable geographic information. Researches by the Austrian expedition to the eastern Delta have elucidated the geography and ecology of the eastern Delta and provided new insights into the geographical background of the biblical narratives. The ensuing discussion will deal with various identifications for places and terms in those relevant chapters.

It is emphasized that Jacob and his sons were allowed to settle in a choice portion of "the land of Ramesses" called "the land of Goshen" (*see* Gen 47:3–6, 47:11).

The mention of "the land of Ramesses" and the later building of the city of Ramesses would possibly suggest a time in the XIX^th^ Dynasty, especially during the reign of Ramesses II. But this is not mandatory; pharaohs of the XX^th^ Dynasty also had the name Ramesses and in any case the cult of Ramesses II thrived for generations afterward at Tanis (Zoan) and Bubastis. Furthermore, the story of the spies sent to scout out the land from the south

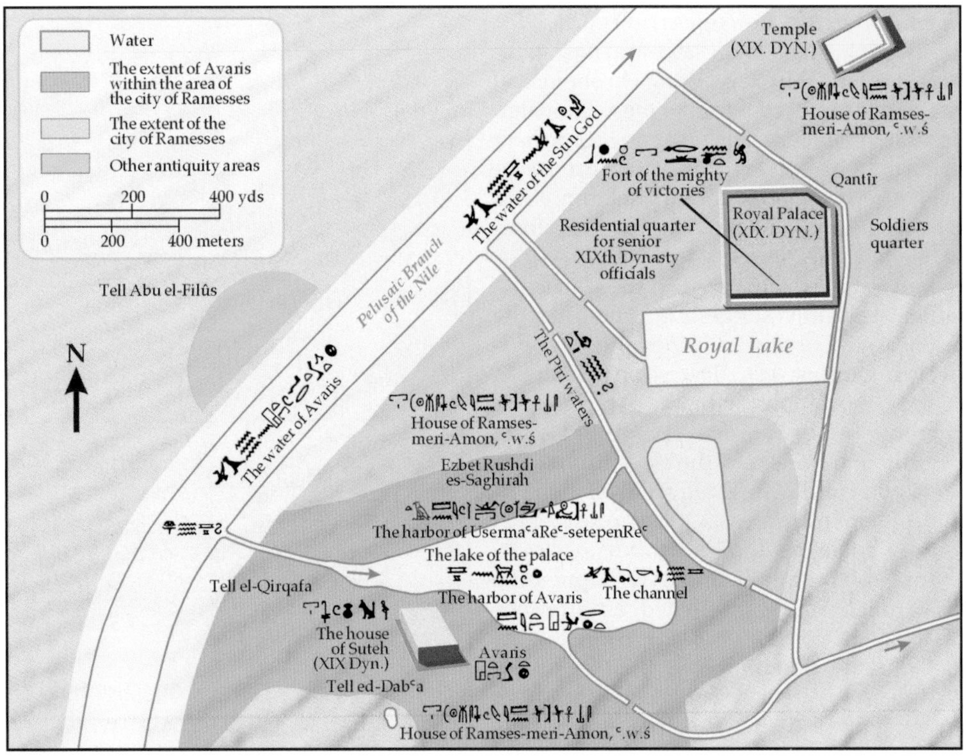


**The City of Ramesses** (after Bietak)

(Num 13) mentions their arrival at Hebron and adds the chronological note: "Hebron was built seven years before Zoan in Egypt" (Num 13:22), meaning that in the eyes of the narrator (or annotator) the presence of the sons of Israel in the Kadesh area was during the last days of the XX^th^ Dynasty.

The city of Ramesses (Egyptian: *Pr-Rᶜmss*, "the House of Ramesses") was built on the former site of the Hyksos capital, Avaris. It served as the northern capital for the pharaohs of Dynasties XIX and XX. By the end of the twelfth century BCE, the branch of the Nile beside Ramesses had silted up, forcing the pharaohs of Dynasty XXI to build a new capital at Zoan (Tanis). They plundered the ruins of Ramesses and brought many statues, stelae and other ornamented architectural pieces to their new city. The pharaohs of Dynasty XXII established a second delta capital at Bubastis and also brought in statues and other pieces from the ruins of Ramesses. During the fourth century BCE, the worship of a deified Ramesses was practiced at both Tanis (Zoan) and Bubastis, while the gateway city to Egypt had become Pelusium. This led late Jewish writers to identify Zoan as the venue for the Israelites' Egyptian experience (Ps 78:12, 78:43). The Targums also make a similar association with Pithom and they placed Ramesses at Pelusium; in this they were followed by Josephus. The translators of the Greek Septuagint speak of three cities: "Pithom and Ramesses and On, which is Heliopolis" (Ex 1:11). The Septuagint identifies Goshen with "Gesem Arabias," the name of the northeastern nome encompassing the Wâdī Tumeilât during the Ptolemaic period.

During their stay in Egypt, the Israelites are said to have been reduced to forced labor (*see* Ex 1:11). Egyptian inscriptions point to Pithom (Egyptian *Pr-Atum*) as Tell er-Raṭâbah, the site at the western end of an ancient overflow lake in the Wâdī Tumeilât.

The Pentateuch records the itinerary of the Israelites in the wilderness in two ways. First there is the narrative sequence punctuated by pericopes of ethical and moral instruction, narrative parables defining the religious lessons of

*Ramesses II and his queen, Nefertari, at the temple of Abu Simbel.*

the wilderness experience. Then, there is a more concise itinerary (Num 33). The first group of names in the sequence is dictated by the cycle of narrative events connected with the Exodus. But there is also a basic itinerary in which the continuation has all the earmarks of an official document or a compilation of official documents. They are hardly a guide for pilgrimage to Mount Sinai. Rather, it seems more plausible that they are itinerary routes compiled for use by caravans, military and commercial, or better, commercial caravans with the prerequisite military escort (*see* Num 33:1–3).

**Leaving Egypt**. The geography of the first stage, leaving Egypt (Ex 13:19–14:9), contains several geographical points that square with the recent study of the northeastern delta from an archaeological point of view. The land of Goshen was the plain between Ramesses and Pithom. The Shihor was evidently an elongated lake or pond lying alongside the course of the ancient eastern branch of the Nile between Baal-zephon (Daphne) and Pelusium. The "Reed Sea" was the large marshy area that once existed to the southeast of Baal-zephon. Between these two bodies of water passed the "Way of Horus," the route taken by New Kingdom pharaohs (incarnates of Horus) on their military campaigns to Canaan and Syria. The Bible calls it "the way of the land of the Philistines" (Ex 13:17).

The pharaonic campaigns to Canaan required logistic bases at intervals of about 15 miles (20–25 km) across the northern Sinai coastal route. Seti I included a depiction of the forts and water sources along this route in his reliefs on the north wall of the hypostyle hall at Karnak. This route was too heavily fortified to serve as an escape route for the people of Israel (Ex 13:17).

Instead, the Israelites are depicted as avoiding the "way of the land of the Philistines," and going instead by way of the steppe land (wilderness) (*see* Ex 13:18).

The Hebrew word for "reeds" is actually a loan from Egyptian, meaning papyrus reeds. Marshes of papyrus are known from Egyptian sources to have existed in the area of Ramesses. In the monarchial period the name Reed Sea was transferred to the Gulf of Elath (1 Kgs 9:26 *et passim*).

Up to this point, the city of Ramesses and/or the land of Ramesses was the starting point for the start of this new adventure; it was seen as a break with Ramesside Egypt (*see* Num 33:3–4).

Leaving the immediate territory of Ramesses, they journeyed to the key point on the eastern end of the Wâdī Tumeilât, namely Succoth (Num 33:5):

They began their trek from Succoth (Egyptian *Tj-ku*), a known pasturage area for the Shâsu bedouin during the XIX^th^ Dynasty (*see* Ex 13:20; Num 33:6). Biblical Succoth is the name associated with watering pools farther

*Campaigns of Seti I on the north wall of the hypostyle hall at Karnak.*

west of Pithom, toward the modern Timsah Lake, at Tell el-Mashkhûta. Then they are said to have gone to Etham, on the fringe of the steppe land (of Shur). The identification of Etham with a Ramesside fort known as *Ḫtm* is problematic from a phonetic point of view.

From there they turned back to a position in front (east) of Pi-hahiroth (possibly a site near Sillû/Sillô) "between Migdol and Baal-zephon" (Ex 14:2, 14:9; cf. Num 33: 7). The identification of Baal-zephon with Tell Defeneh (classical Daphne, biblical Tahpanes) is supported by the testimony of a Phoenician inscription found at Saqqâra.

The identification of Migdol, thought to have been at Tell el-Kheir, is still in question. Surveys of northwestern Sinai have found mainly Saitic remains there. Its approximate location, hardly very far from Tell el-Kheir, is dictated by its place in the reliefs of Seti I. It is interesting to note that no reference is made to the most important fortress of all, viz. Sillû/Sillô (Selle), the headquarters of the Egyptian forces guarding all the eastern border of the delta. Evidently it was avoided as the anchor point on the "Way of Horus" (="the way of the land of the Philistines").

The Israelite withdrawal in the face of the pursuing Egyptians was through the marshes east of Baal-zephon, the "sea of reeds" (Egyptian *P-Tjufy*). Thence, they entered the wilderness of Shur (*see* Ex 15:22) and evidently headed south (*see* Ex 15:23; Num 33:8).

**The Road to Sinai**. Firm identifications for the remaining stations on their march are difficult since practically none of the ancient names have survived on the Sinai Peninsula. In spite of many alternate suggestions, none of which have any objective supporting evidence, the present state of our knowledge does not preclude a route commensurate with the Byzantine traditions for the location of Mount Sinai at Jebel Mûsā (*see* Ex 15:27; Num 33:9). At this stage, Numbers 33 adds another point which is hard to explain:

> They journeyed from **Elim** and camped by the **Reed Sea**. Then they journeyed from the Reed Sea and camped in the **wilderness of Sin.** (Num 33:10–11)

The Exodus account is more logical:

> Then they set out from Elim, and all the congregation of the sons of Israel came to the **wilderness of Sin**, which is between Elim and Sinai, on the fifteenth day of the second month after their departure from the land of Egypt. (Ex 16:1)

On the other hand, the itinerary of Numbers 33 adds two more stations skipped over in Exodus (*see* Num 33:12–14; Ex 17:1). The places, Dophkah and Alush, cannot be identified but it would seem reasonable that the journey would have had to entail some intermediate stops:

The stages in the Exodus narrative, which are marked between the pericopes of edification, are also accompanied by date formulae (*see* Ex 19:1). Those chronological notations are absent from the Numbers itinerary (Num 33:15).

**Mount Sinai=Horeb=Mount Paran**. The wilderness itinerary (Num 33:1–49) seems to point to a location for Mount Sinai in the southern Sinai Peninsula. Mount Sinai is mentioned fifteen times in the books of Exodus, Leviticus, and Numbers as the

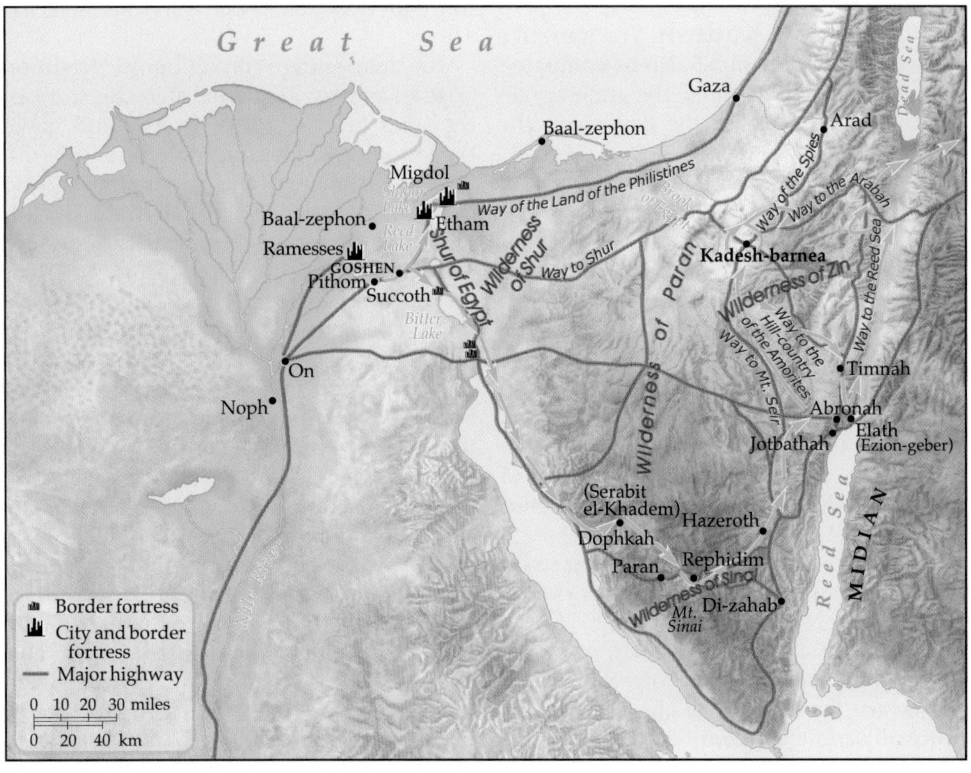


**The Exodus and Wandering in the Wilderness**

place where the people of Israel received the revelation of the Torah. Poetic passages (e.g. Judg 5:5; Ps 68:9 [Eng. 8; note also v. 18=Eng. 17]) depict it as the dwelling place of YHWH. Two call it Mount Paran (Deut 33:2; Hab 3: 3). The steppe land (wilderness) of Paran (e.g. Num 10:12, 12:16, 13:3) seems to be the generic name for the main Sinai expanses of which there are various subdivisions. Its name may be preserved in that of the oasis of Feirân known as Faran in Byzantine sources. In Numbers 10:33 Sinai is called "the mountain of YHWH." Seventeen times in the Hebrew Bible, especially throughout Deuteronomy and three passages in Exodus (3:1, 17:6, 33:6) and elsewhere (1 Kgs 8:9, 19:8; 2 Chr 5:10; Ps 106:9; Mal 3:22), the name Horeb is used, evidently for the same place. A few passages make reference to "the mountain of God" (e.g. Ex 4:27, 18:5, 24:13), and Exodus 3:1 equates it with Horeb. Attempts to see in Horeb and Sinai two separate mountains have been shown to be unproductive. A most significant allusion is the following Deuteronomistic passage:

It is eleven days' journey from **Horeb** by way of **Mount Seir** to **Kadesh-barnea**. (Deut 1:2)

The location of Kadesh-barnea will be discussed below. An eleven-day journey from Kadesh-barnea can only point to a place in southern Sinai and rules out most alternatives, especially the Hejaz. The text is also an additional testimony to the location of a Mount Seir on the western side of the Arabah which will also help to understand something in the subsequent narratives.

There have been at least a dozen proposals for alternate locations, in different districts of Sinai or in Saudi Arabia. All of them will be ignored in this study.

**From Sinai to Kadesh**. The narrative entries in Numbers must also be compared with the same section of the itinerary in Numbers 33:16–36. For the first stage, the narrative gives a date (*see* Num 10:11–12), while the itinerary mentions a time span of three days' journey (*see* Num 10:33):

Two experiences of punishment for rebellion are the background for etiological names, Taberah and Kibroth-hattaavah (*see* Num 11:3, 11:34), while the itinerary has only the second name (*see* Num 33:16):

Both are mentioned together in Deuteronomy (9:22). The next station, Hazeroth, has been identified with ᶜAin el-Khuḍra, c. 22 miles (35 km) northeast of Jebel Mûsā. Both traditions record it (*see* Num 11: 35, 33:17).

The itinerary then supplied a long series of further stations, none of which can be identified (*see* Num 33:18–32).

The next station, Jotbathah, may be located at Ṭâbeh. Archaeological research points to the island of Jezîrat Farᶜûn. Abronah cannot be identified (cf. Deut 2:8, 10: 6–7) and Ezion-geber is also controversial, though the name survives in the cognate ᶜAin Ghaḍyân (*see* Num 33:33–35).

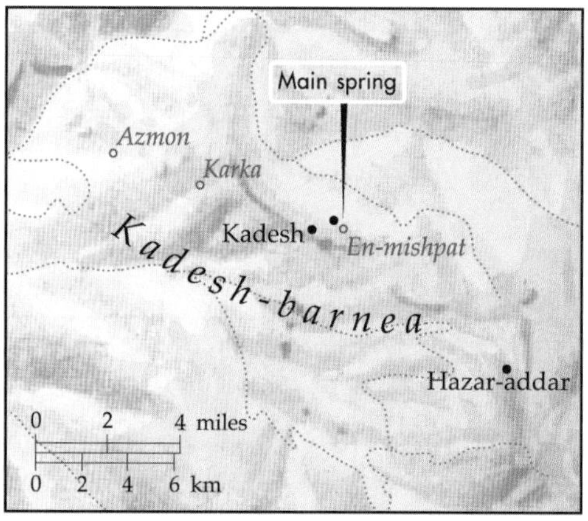


**KADESH-BARNEA (NUM 20:13; DEUT 1:19–46)**

Deuteronomy (1:1) introduces some other names into this segment of the route. The narrative entry apparently lumps all of these stations into a general statement (*see* Num 12:16).

There follows the focal narratives of the "wilderness experience," the chapters about experiences in the vicinity of Kadesh-barnea. The narratives of the Book of Numbers call it simply Kadesh (e.g. Num 20: 1, 33:36) until Numbers 32:8 where the full epithet, Kadesh-barnea, is used. Several passages in Deuteronomy (viz. 1:2, 1:19, 2:14, 9:23) use the full name and confirm that one place is intended.

Here were enacted the famous incidents of the twelve spies (Num 13), and the ill-fated attempt to invade the country from the south (treated below), the death of Miriam (Num 20:1) and the later version of the rebellion at the "waters of Meribah" which were paradigmatic in the didactic poetic tradition (Num 20:13; Deut 33:8; Ps 81:8, 95:8, 106: 32).

An interesting chronological tradition appears almost incidentally in the story of the spies (*see* Num 13:22). That would make the founding of Hebron contemporary with the establishment of the city of Zoan during the late XX$^{th}$ Dynasty, i.e. late in the twelfth or early eleventh century BCE. The town of Zoan is first documented in the 23$^{rd}$ year of Ramesses XI from Dynasty XX (c. 1083 BCE). It became the residence of Smendes, the officer assigned to the administration of Lower Egypt. When Ramesses died and Smendes succeeded him as founder of the XXI$^{st}$ Dynasty (c. 1176–931 BCE), Zoan became the official residence, replacing the old Ramesside capital, Pi-Ramesses, c. 19 miles (30 km) to the south. Pi-Ramesses declined and was abandoned due to a shifting of the Nile branch that deprived its harbor of water; its monumental buildings and installations were dismantled and much of the architectural pieces were transferred to Zoan. Statues and stelae which had once stood at Pi-Ramesses were incorporated into the new capital. Early excavators mistakenly identified Zoan with Pi-Ramesses and Avaris, an identification now recognized as false.

The first great builder to turn the small provincial town into a monumental city was Psusennes I, son of Smendes and second king of Dynasty XXI. He laid out the enclosure and built the temple of Amon, which was later enlarged by Siamon (984–965 BCE). The synchronization given in Numbers 13:22 accords well with all the other chronological indicators in the Pentateuchal narratives about the birth of the nation of Israel. The question is, "How did the biblical writer obtain such a piece of information?" As the story of Wenamon reveals, the early eleventh century BCE was a time of great commercial activity along the sea of Canaan and such active maritime enterprise would perforce require a well-developed agricultural hinterland.

The identification of Kadesh-barnea is based on the convergence of three lines of evidence. Textually, the decisive testimony is its place in the southern border description, ascribed to Canaan (Num 34:4) or Judah (Josh 15:3) or the idealized eschatological land (Ezek 47:19, 48:28). It is obvious that Kadesh-barnea must be located roughly halfway between the lower extremity of the Dead Sea on the east and the estuary of the "Brook of Egypt" (Wâdī el-ᶜArîsh). It is not surprising, therefore, that at just about the right position required by the texts (also assuming a more or less uniform distance between the points on that southern border) a spring was found called ᶜAin Qedeis. During the early nineteenth century, scholars looked for Kadesh-barnea somewhere in the Arabah because of Numbers 20:16, which places the site on the border of Edom. The misunderstanding of that passage will be discussed below. Later, the search shifted westward because of the other biblical references, viz. to its place on the southern border of Canaan/Judah. ᶜAin Qedeis, an oasis in northern Sinai which preserves an echo of the biblical name and which is located about where one would expect from the border descriptions, was discovered. In 1905 N. Schmidt recognized that a more appropriate archaeological site was located at neighboring Wâdī el-ᶜAin with its water source at ᶜAin el-Qudeirât. C. L. Woolley and T. E. Lawrence made an archaeological survey of the region soon after, and confirmed Schmidt's conclusion. Subsequent archaeological excavation has uncovered the Iron Age fortress at ᶜAin el-Qudeirât. It stands near the junction of a road leading from Suez to Beer-sheba/ Hebron, the "way of Shur" (Gen 16:7) and the road branching from the coastal highway, the "way of the land of the Philistines" (Ex 13:17) near el-ᶜArîsh, which leads to ᶜAqabah. This area is now the largest oasis in the northern Sinai and has a spring that produces about 40 cubic meters of water per hour. Finds from the excavations will

*Psusennes I, king of Dynasty XXI, was the first to turn the small town of Zoan into a monumental city.*

be discussed subsequently in their proper historical contexts. Obviously, one should not expect archaeological evidence for the presence of the Israelites in the area during their "wilderness wanderings."

The next stage in their journey involved an encounter with the "king of Edom" (Num 20:14). It will be noted below that after the Edomite refusal, the texts report a violent encounter with the "king of Arad" (Num 21: 1, 33:40).

The key to understanding the geography here is the recognition that Israel's encounter with Edom took place on the western side of the Arabah. This might be a seventh/sixth century BCE outlook since it is now well documented that Edom did move westward in that period. But it could also represent a time in the early Iron Age; the Edomites may have been another element in the Shâsu who had roamed the Sinai expanses during the time of the XIXth Dynasty. Once the western location of these Edomites is understood, the subsequent itinerary, going around them, makes sense. It also obviates the late Jewish (Targums) and Christian (Eus. *Onom.* 112:8–12) misconception that Kadesh-barnea was located at or near Petra.

The next site, Mount Hor, where Aaron is said to have died, is not identified (*see* Num 20:22–23, 33:37). The above-mentioned misapprehension about Kadesh being at Petra has given birth to the burial site of Aaron in the Petra area. A tradition going back at least to the Herodian period (*Ant.* 4:7) identifies Mount Hor with Jebel Nebī Harûn ("mountain of Aaron") near Nabatean Petra; however, this two-topped sandstone mountain, some 4,800 feet (1,460 m) high, is in the middle of the eastern Edomite territory. On its rugged summit is a tomb, traditionally that of Aaron, the upper portion of which is a Muslim mosque. It is more likely a reconstructed Christian church dating to the reign of Justinian (527–565 CE). The same approach to the geography of the Edomite encounter also precludes the proposed identification with Jebel Maḍrah in the Naḥal Zin (Wâdī Fuqrah). On the other hand a height named ʾImaret el-Khureiseh, which towers over an important road junction about 8 miles (12 km) north of Kadesh-barnea deserves consideration.

**From Kadesh to Moab**. After the hostile reception by the Edomites, the people of Israel are said to have sought to circumvent the Edomite territory. Both traditions, the narrative and itinerary, record a clash with the ruler of Arad (*see* Num 21:1, 33:40).

So the general picture is of the Negeb and Sinai expanses inhabited by various tribal groups (generically Shâsu) who seem to have each laid claim to a particular territory. The "king" of Edom in our narrative was the chieftain of such a group. The "king" of Arad was designated as a "Canaanite," i.e. of original Cisjordanian origin. Arad as a site probably did not exist except as the Early Bronze ruin. But the name Arad, "wild ass," looks like a totem name like Simeon (from *šemaᶜ*, "hyena"). So this particular "king" was probably also a tribal chieftain who did not want a new tribal group like the Israelites encroaching on his territory, the Negeb. The Cisjordanian Edomites were apparently in the modern "Negev highlands" east of the route from Kadesh-barnea to Beer-sheba (*see* Num 21:4).

How and why the name "Reed Sea" had become transferred from the Egyptian border to the Gulf of Elath/ᶜAqabah is not known. The itinerary gives two stations that followed Mount Hor not mentioned by name in the narrative chain. The first, Zalmonah (Num 33:41), should be compared with the Roman fort of Calamon in the Arabah. But the next place can surely be identified, viz. Punon (Num 33:42) with Feinân, in Wâdī Feinân.

Another moralizing pericope comes next in the narrative sequence (*see* Num 21:6–9). The story is an etiological explanation attached to a cult object worshipped in the Jerusalem temple in the eighth century BCE. When King Hezekiah purged the temple compound from many cult objects and installations no longer considered acceptable,

> he also broke in pieces the copper (bronze) **serpent** that Moses had made, for until those days the sons of Israel burned incense to it; and it was called **Nehushtan**. (2 Kgs 18:4)

*Cult stand with birds and serpents, from Beth-shean, c. 11th century BCE.*

The venue of the fiery serpent incident is not stated but comparison with the itinerary reveals that it must have been at Punon, which also happens to be an ancient center for copper mining from the Chalcolithic to Roman times, including the Iron Age. Among the sites in the Feinân area was Khirbet en-Naḥas, the name of which is from the same root as Hebrew *nāḥāš*, "snake."

The next station, Oboth (*see* Num 21:10, 33:43), must be sought north of Feinân but before entering the Zered (Wâdī el-Ḥasā). An unidentified site north of Feinân has been suggested.

The next station is called Iye-abarim, "ruins of the fords" or "ruins of the stream banks"; its shorter name was Iyim, "ruins" (*see* Num 21:11, 33:44–45). At least two sites in this area have been proposed: Muhai, located about 6.5 miles (11 km) southeast of Mazâr, but north of the Wadī el-Ḥasā, and Medeiyineh, on a hilltop rising out of the canyon of the Wâdī el-Ḥasā. The latter site might be more appropriate for the place of encampment "in the Valley of Zered" that followed Iye-abarim.

The itinerary list in Numbers 33 does not list the Zered. On the other hand, the narrative sequence does refer to it explicitly after the encampment at Iyim (Num 21:12).

It is also a key turning point in the Deuteronomy narrative (*see* Deut 2:13–14).

The activity on the Moabite tableland and the plains of Moab will be described below.

## CONQUEST TRADITIONS

The Book of Numbers, with parallels in the summary of Deuteronomy, and the Book of Joshua present a series of narrative traditions about Israelite conquests. The historicity of these narratives is a matter of controversy.

**Attempt from the South**. As discussed above, the rebellion in the Kadesh-barnea area was a paradigm of national rebellion in the cultic and religious traditions of the monarchial period (Num 20: 13; Deut 33:8; Ps 81:8, 95:8, 106:32). After rejecting the recommendation of Caleb and Joshua in favor of the negative urging of the other ten reconnaissance scouts, the people are said to have changed their minds on the following day and resolved to launch the campaign. Their leader, Moses, informed them that the divine guidance would be withheld since

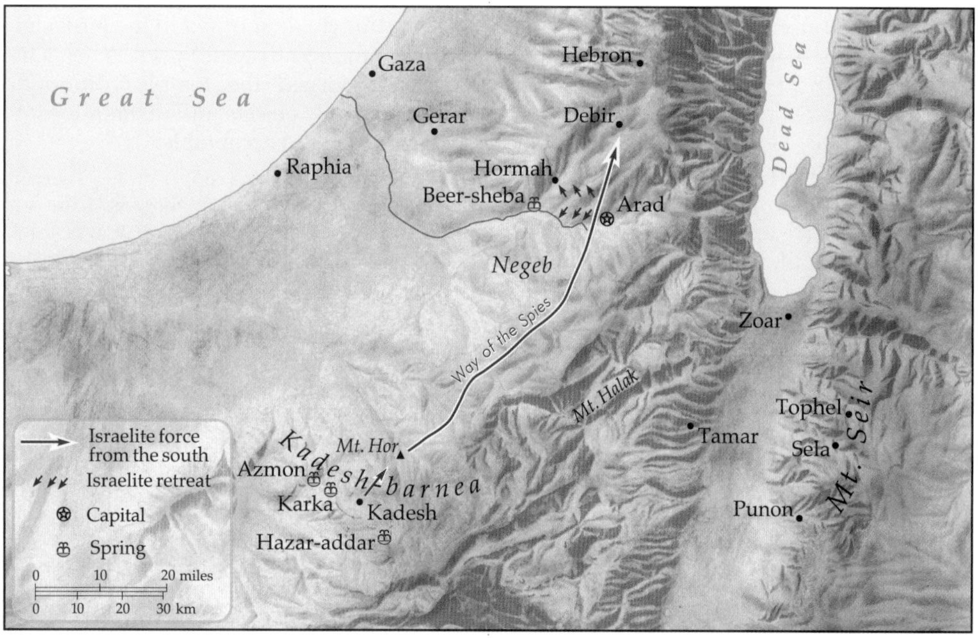


**Ill-fated Invasion from the South**

they had already offended YHWH.

Numbers 13:29 succinctly summarizes the Genesis traditions; the "sons of Heth" and the Amorites are encountered by Abraham at Hebron. The Jebusites are in the Jerusalem area during the conquest narratives, including David's campaign to take the city, and the Canaanites are viewed as the lowland inhabitants. However, this is changed in the present narrative of an attempted conquest. The Israelites' ill-fated razzia is narrated in two passages. The Amalekites, at that time the inhabitants of the Negeb, and the Canaanites, who are here called the hill dwellers, are the forces that repulsed the Israelite attack (*see* Num 14:40–45).

On the other hand, the parallel in Deuteronomy (*see* Deut 1:41–46) conforms to the picture in Numbers 13:29. Canaanites and Amalekites are ignored. The victorious enemies were the Amorites, in conformance with a widely held concept that hill dwellers are Amorites while Canaanites lived on the plains below.

The focus of these narratives is Hormah, a place name which may be interpreted to mean "set apart for the deity" (cf. Lev 27:28). In the subsequent narrative, there may be a double entendre, i.e. "set apart for destruction" (cf. Judg 1:17). The eventual conquest of Hormah was also linked to Israel's vow after the ill-fated encounter with the "king of Arad" (*see* Num 21:2–3).

The fulfillment of that vow is then linked with the conquest of Hormah, under the name Zephath, by the tribe of Simeon assisted by Judah (*see* Judg 1:17). The town of Hormah is listed as a real place (Josh 12:14, 15:30, 19:4) and thus invites efforts at identification. None of the passages cited above give any indication other than it must be in the Negeb and probably in a spot compatible with a retreat from the southern Judean hill country. Among sites proposed are Tell el-Milḥ (=Tel Malḥata), about 6.5 miles (11 km) northeast of Beer-sheba; Tell esh-Sharîʿah (=Tel Seraʿ), about 12 miles (20 km) northwest of Beer-sheba; Khirbet el-Meshâsh (=Tel Masos); and Khirbet Gharrah (=Tel ʿIra; as Zephath). It also should most likely be a site with pre-Israelite occupation and possibly fortified. One determining factor should be the order of sites in the Negeb list of Judean towns (Josh 15:21–32). It has been noted that the list seems to run more or less (but not entirely) from east to west. That Hormah comes after Beer-sheba (Josh 15:30) and just before Ziklag (Josh 15:31) should be indicative. Beer-sheba must have been the central town in the list while Ziklag should be in the west. So the suggestion that Hormah was located at Tell el-Khuweilifeh (Tel Ḥalif) is logical. The site does guard, in effect, the traffic from the Negeb to the southern hill country and thus could have been a point of retreat for people fleeing from a defeat in the hills. It was also the strong point in World War I at which the Turkish army held up the British advancing from Beer-sheba for some days, thus allowing the main Turkish force to retreat northward from Gaza.

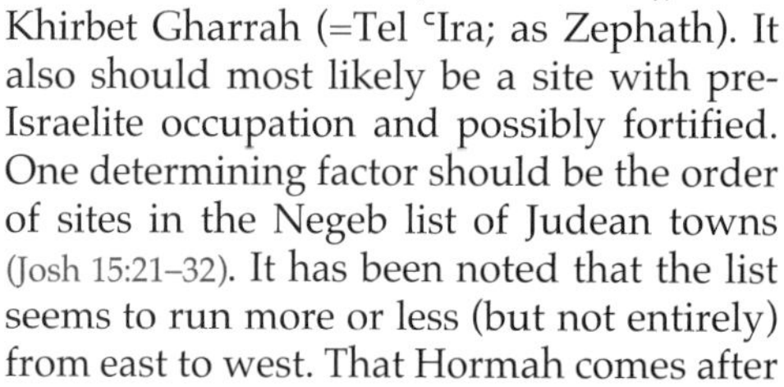

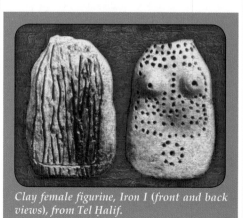

*Clay female figurine, Iron I (front and back views), from Tel Ḥalif.*

## Campaign from the East.

The Israelite conquest narratives began in Transjordan, beyond the borders of the land of Canaan. In this sparsely settled region, there were extensive lands for pasturage (Num 32:14). Related peoples, Edom and Moab, are depicted as being settled in the southern parts of Transjordan. The Amorite kingdom of Heshbon was located between Moab and Ammon; its ruler, Sihon, is said to have warred with Moab's first king and conquered the entire plateau of Moab to the Arnon River (Num 21:26). For the Moabite segment of the conquest tradition, there are contrasting sequences of places between the narrative pericopes and the itinerary list of places. There are also variants from Deuteronomy. This has led to the assumption that two separate "campaigns" or "waves" of immigration are reflected in the sources. The summary that was preserved in Numbers 33 denotes a line of stations and settlements on the main road from Kadesh-barnea to Edom and Moab as far as the plains of Moab, which is one of the major branches of the King's Highway.

Dibon (Dhibân) is the first important town on the road north of the Arnon (*see* Num 33:45). The author of the Book of Joshua assigned it to Reuben (Josh 13:17) while according to Numbers 32:34, it belonged to Gad. The latter assignment has more credence because of the testimony of the Mesha inscription. Here it receives the anachronistic designation Dibon-gad. The last two stations, Almon-diblathaim and the mountains of Abarim (Num 33:46–47), are in the vicinity of Mount Nebo on the road from Dibon to the plains of Moab by the Jordan, at Jericho (*see* Num 33:48–49).

The narrative pericope brings them around to the headwaters of the Arnon and from there across to Pisgah (=Nebo in the itinerary) (*see* Num 21:13–20). The citations from the "Book of the Wars of YHWH" reveal something of the original source from which these tales have been adapted to the narrative sequence in the Book of Numbers.

Numbers 21:20–21 indicates that the negotiations with Sihon, king of Heshbon, were initiated from the vicinity of Pisgah/Mount Nebo, i.e. west of Medeba, overlooking the Dead Sea. On the other hand, the Deuteronomy account places the approach to Sihon and his refusal from the steppe land of Kedemoth (*see* Deut 2:26).

Kedemoth has not been identified but several suggestions have been made. It would most likely be on the southeast periphery of the Moabite tableland. That it had its associated "steppe land" suggests that it faced the eastern expanses and its function as a "Levitical city" (Josh 21:37; 1 Chr 6:79) also implies that it was guarding a frontier. Possible sites are ʿAleiyân or es-Salîyeh. That the battle with Sihon and his forces is said to have taken place near Jahaz enforces the impression of authenticity for the Deuteronomy version (*see* Num 21:21–31).

Apparently, with the organization of the kingdom of Moab, the king of Heshbon took from its first king the tableland between Heshbon and the Arnon, a district over which the Moabites claimed right of possession throughout their history. Henceforth, the Arnon was the traditional border for the Israelite tribes in eastern Transjordan. On the other hand, the Moabites considered this an encroachment upon their land. The pressure of Moabite expansion was always directed northward, and in later periods they succeeded in restoring this region to themselves as far as Medeba on the border of Heshbon and sometimes as far as the southern end of the eastern Jordan Valley, which was known even in biblical tradition as "the plains of Moab."

Essentially, Deuteronomy preserves the same story, but based on a more logical geographical sequence (*see* Deut 2:32–34). Jahaz (Deut 2:32) is most likely to be located on the eastern side of the Moabite tableland. So the Deuteronomy version brings the Israelites into the Moabite tableland from the southeast, to the vicinity of Kedemoth east of the Arnon (Deut 2:26), whence they invaded the land of Sihon, the Amorite king of Heshbon. Extensive archaeological excavations have been conducted at Tell Ḥisbân. There are no Late Bronze remains and the Iron Age levels were badly disturbed. There can be hardly any doubt that this is the ancient biblical site of Heshbon and the Esbus of Eusebius (*Onom.* 46:1, 76:12, 84:4,13; 132:2, 136:8,13), which he identifies with biblical Essebon (*Onom.* 84: 1–6). The results of the excavations again suggest a twelfth- to eleventh-century BCE date for the tradition of its conquest.

The next pericope has to do with Jazer (*see* Num 21:32), a town reckoned as bordering on the territory of the Ammonites (Num 21:24 LXX). The strongest candidate for Jazer may be Khirbet Jazzîr where there is Iron Age and Hellenistic ceramic evidence. Khirbet Jazzîr is located 2.5 miles (4 km) south of es-Salt, at the head of the Wâdī Shuᶜeib which flows into the Jordan. Less than a kilometer from Jazzîr is ᶜAin Ḥazer.

The final pericope of the Transjordanian campaign traditions has to do with the northern Gilead and the Bashan, the kingdom of Og (*see* Num 21:33–35). Og was associated with Ashtaroth, an important city in the Amarna Age (*see* Josh 13:12).

The Israelite view of the geography of Transjordan is summarized as being comprised of three units from north to south. It is the conquest of those districts (Deut 3:10) that are covered by the pericopes in Numbers 21.

During the stay on the "plains of Moab" two other events are recorded as paradigms of moral and religious significance. One is the prophecies of Balaam (Num 23–24) and the other is the apostasy at Baal-peor (Num 25). The Israelites were encamped at Shittim "in the valley opposite Beth-peor" (Deut 3:29). The venues of the three oracles pronounced by Balaam follow a consistent progress from south to north. The first was at Bamoth-baal (Num 22:42), a site mentioned in the Mesha inscription. Perhaps it was on the ridge above Beth-baal-meon (Māᶜîn).

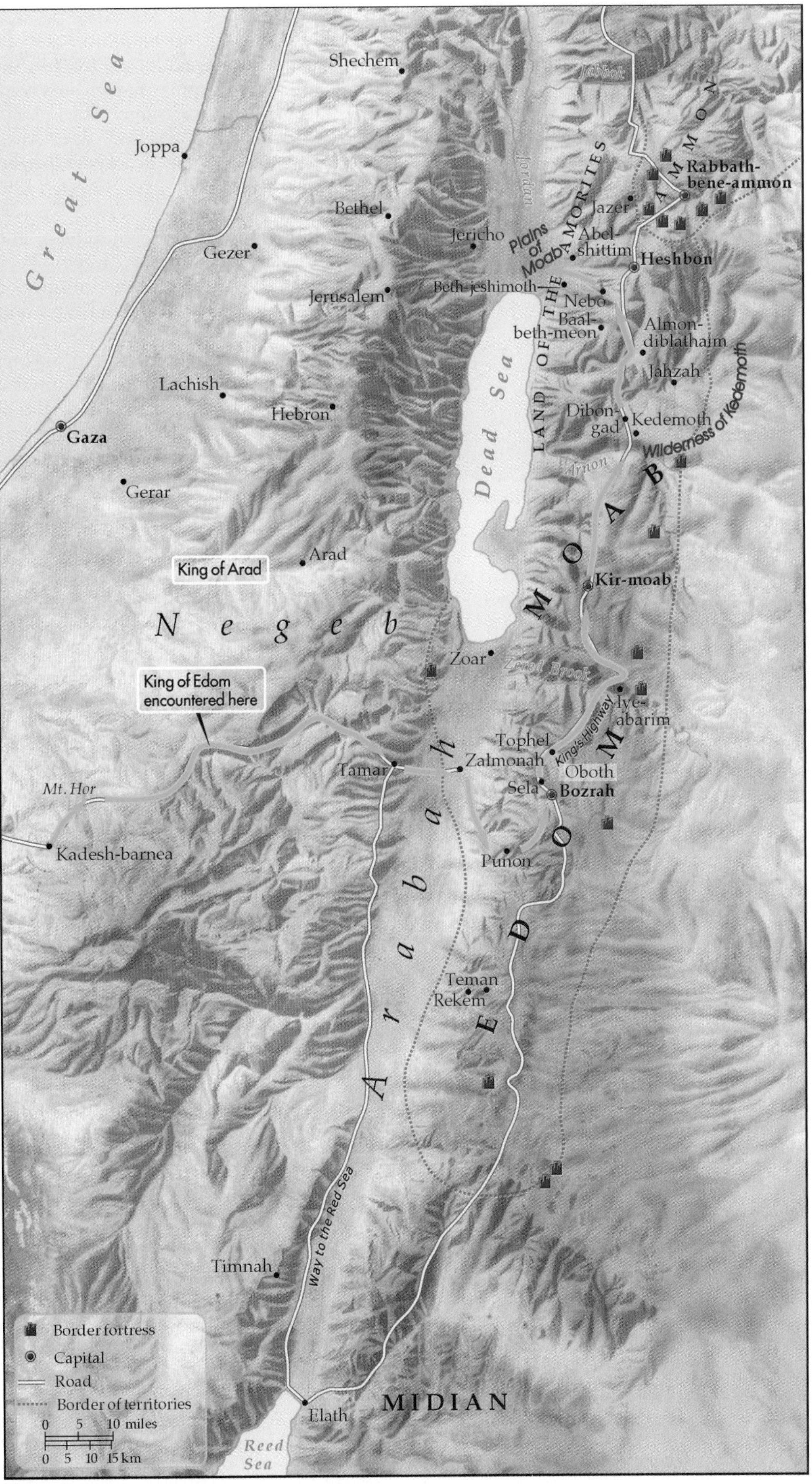

THE PENETRATION INTO THE TRANSJORDAN

*The Mesha Stele from Dibon.*

Khirbet el-Quweiqiyeh was noted, c. 3 miles (5 km) northwest of Medeba and 1.5 miles (2.5 km) south of Khirbet el-Mekhaiyet, often identified with the town of Nebo. That location fulfills the geographical requirements of the biblical account though archaeological data are unavailable. The second was the "field of Zophim, to the top of Pisgah" (Num 23:14) and the last was the "the top of Peor which overlooks the wasteland" (Num 23:28). Each place was the site of a sacred cult center where sacrifices were offered. At the final vantage point, the prophet would have had a clear view of the plains of Moab below.

The second account (Num 25) concerns relations with the cult center of Baal-peor, located at Beth-peor, placed by Eusebius (*Onom.* 48:3–5), along with Mount Phogor, 6 Roman miles east of Livias (Beth-haram=Tell Iktanû?), on the road to Esbus (Heshbon=Tell Ḥisbân). The Israelites were encamped at this time,

> . . . from **Beth-jeshimoth** as far as **Abel-shittim** in the plains of Moab. (Num 33:49)

The ancient name of Jeshimoth seems to be echoed in Khirbet es-Suweimeh, although archaeological survey suggests that nearby Tell ᶜAẓeimeh was the actual ancient site. Abel-shittim is the same as Shittim (Num 25:1); its location was east of the Jordan and north of the Dead Sea. Two sites have been proposed, originally, Tell el-Kefrein, on a hill overlooking the plains of Moab, 6 miles (10 km) north of the Dead Sea and east of the Jordan, and another, perhaps the more probable site, Tell el-Ḥammâm, about 2 miles (3 km) farther east in the Wâdī el-Kefrein. Here, remains of Iron Age fortresses with 1.2-meter-thick outer walls have been discovered. The foundations of massive towers at each end and an impressive glacis supporting the wall indicate that Tell el-Ḥammâm was a strategic fortification. The confusion over the identification of the site exists because the biblical name, Abel-shittim, and its Roman name, Abila, no longer exist in the area. While other familiar names survived, Abel-shittim was forgotten. The names "Shittim," meaning "acacias," and Abel-shittim, "stream of the acacias," suggest that the place was in the once-forested hills of Moab.

The pericopes of the wilderness and Transjordanian conquests have been interpreted as evidence for two migration traditions that have been molded into one. The role of Midian is a case in point. When Moses fled from Egypt, he found asylum in Midian and married into a renowned priestly family there. While in the service of his father-in-law, Jethro, he received his first theophany in Sinai. Later Jethro is credited with instructing him about worship and about organizing the exercise of judgeship in the desert (Ex 2:15 *et passim*, 18). The other strand of tradition reflects extremely hostile relations between Israel and Midian (Num 25, 31). This encounter is associated with the plains of Moab and nearby Baal-peor, i.e. the region to which a straight march through Edom had led. In the Balaam narrative the elders of Midian usually appear beside the elders of Moab (Num 22 *passim*).

The roles of the tribes of Gad and Reuben may also reflect the earlier and the later migration. It is not clear whether a settlement process in Transjordan, particularly in Gilead, took place at an earlier or a later stage. The territory of Jazer and the land of Gilead remained noteworthy as good cattle country (Num 32 *passim*), and this did not change in its essentials even in the monarchial period (1 Chr 5:9). Evidently Gad took possession of the Gilead expanses early on so that the names Gad and Gilead became interchangeable and almost synonymous in later texts. The settlements of Gad were dispersed as far as the Arnon and included Dibon and Aroer (Num 32:34). Dibon is called Dibon-gad (Num 33:45–46), and Mesha, the king of Moab, indicated on his stele that ". . . the men of Gad had dwelt in the land of Ataroth from of old" (line 10). In the north the inheritance of Gad reached as far as the Jabbok. The eastern Jordan Valley was nearly all reckoned as Gadite from Beth-haran and Beth-nimrah in the south through the Plain of Succoth and the city of Zaphon up to the shore of the Sea of Galilee (Josh 13:27). It would appear that the Gadites had infiltrated into this region while it was still occupied by Canaanites; later these Canaanite cities were added to the inheritance of Gad. In the story of Jephthah a tradition is preserved that the Israelite settlement had been rooted in Gilead for a considerable period (300 years; Judg 11:26), but no exact chronology can be built on such figures. It is also worthy of note that Gad is the brother of Asher, both of them being sons of Zilpah, the handmaiden of Leah. Asher certainly belonged to an early migration and this is evidently expressed in the genealogical scheme.

By contrast, Reuben apparently belongs to a later migration. In tradition he is the firstborn of the tribes of Israel but his position declined during the course of time. According to Numbers 32:37–38 the Reubenites settled in Heshbon and its environs and the conquest of this region is certainly connected with the later migration tradition. Thus the Reubenites encountered serious difficulties in the process of their settlement, especially since other tribes had preceded them. They remained partially nomadic on the fringe of the desert (1 Chr 5:8–10), while certain of its clans apparently crossed over to Cisjordan. There are clear witnesses to connections between Reuben and Judah and Benjamin. On the border between Judah and Benjamin, west of Jericho, there was "the stone of Bohan the son of Reuben" (Josh 15:6, 18:17). On the boundary between Judah and Benjamin lay the Valley of Achor (Josh 15:7), where Achan the son of Carmi from the tribe of Judah was stoned (Josh 7:26), but Carmi also was one of the chief clans of Reuben (Gen 46:9; Num 26:5–6; 1 Chr 5:3). The clan of Hezron is known both among the clans of Reuben (Num 26:6) and those of Judah (Num 26:21), and the clan of Bela is shared with Reuben (1 Chr 5:8–10) and Benjamin (Gen 46:21; 1 Chr 8:1).

It is also worthy of note that Reuben's assignation with Bilhah, his father's concubine (Gen 35:21), is said to have been perpetrated at Migdal-eder, a place in Judahite territory. As a result, the narrative

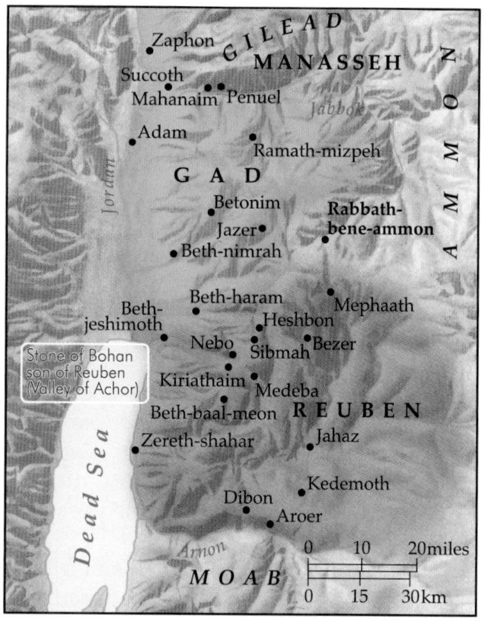


**The Cities of Gad and Reuben**

explains the decline of Reuben's seniority among the tribes.

The biblical tradition about the conquest of the land of Og, the king of Bashan who was defeated at Edrei, is related to the settlement there of the half-tribe of Manasseh. The concept of the half-tribe of Manasseh in this region is related to the later phase of the period of the Judges, after Machir migrated thither from the hill country of Ephraim where he had still been dwelling at the time of the battle of Deborah (Judg 5:14). Whatever the origin of the tradition about Og, the king of Bashan, it is shared with the neighboring people of Ammon (Deut 3:11). His sixty cities which were "fortified with high walls, gates and bars" (Deut 3:5; 1 Kgs 4:13) is a reminder that such cities were known in the region during the Late Bronze Age as attested by the Amarna letters and the inscriptions of pharaohs such as Thutmose III and Seti I. It cannot be demonstrated whether they were really fortified with high walls. The Cisjordanian Late Bronze cities certainly were not.

In any case, the title half-tribe of Manasseh also includes other tribes whose origin is obscure. Prominent among them was Jair who is counted as a son of Manasseh (Num 32:41; Deut 3:14; 1 Kgs 4:13), and whose settlements are called Havvoth-jair ("encampments of Jair"). The Havvoth-jair were in northern Gilead (1 Kgs 4:13; 1 Chr 2:23) and on the border of Bashan (Deut 3:14; Josh 13:30). A local judge is also known in this area named Jair the Gileadite, who dominated twenty-three cities (cf. 1 Chr 2:22) which were called Havvoth-jair (Judg 10:3–5).

Another tribal element that settled the eastern Bashan was Nobah, who "went and took Kenath and its villages, and called it Nobah, after his own name" (Num 32:42). Kenath is probably Qanawat in eastern Bashan, but we have no additional information about Nobah, and even his connections with Manasseh are not confirmed.

One might conclude from these traditions that in the early migration, some tribal entities established themselves in the southern regions of Transjordan from the Arnon in the south to the Jabbok in the north. Various other related tribes penetrated into northern Gilead and the Bashan at about the same time. Only under the impetus of Machir's later eastward migration was the region transformed into an Israelite entity and the various tribal groups incorporated in the "sons of Machir and of Manasseh."

## Central Cisjordan

**Central Cisjordan**. The penetration of Cisjordan is the subject of the Book of Joshua. The author intended to depict a unified conquest by a twelve-tribe league under the leadership of one commander, Joshua the son of Nun from the tribe of Ephraim. It has been seen that a rival tradition exists (1 Chr 7:20–28) whereby Ephraim, as eponymous ancestor, was in the land very early (rather than being born in Egypt). That same passage brings the genealogy down to Joshua son of Nun (1 Chr 7:28). Joshua's home and place of burial is Timnath-serah (Josh 19:50, 24:30) or Timnath-heres (Judg 2:9), identified with Khirbet Tibnah on the southern slopes of the Ephraimite territory. Joshua was most probably an Ephraimite military leader who distinguished himself in some conflict against Canaanite elements, perhaps concerned with the area of Beth-horon and the Benjaminite plateau. His notoriety in that action won him the honor of being appointed as the commander-in-chief in the conquest tradition devised in the Deuteronomistic history.

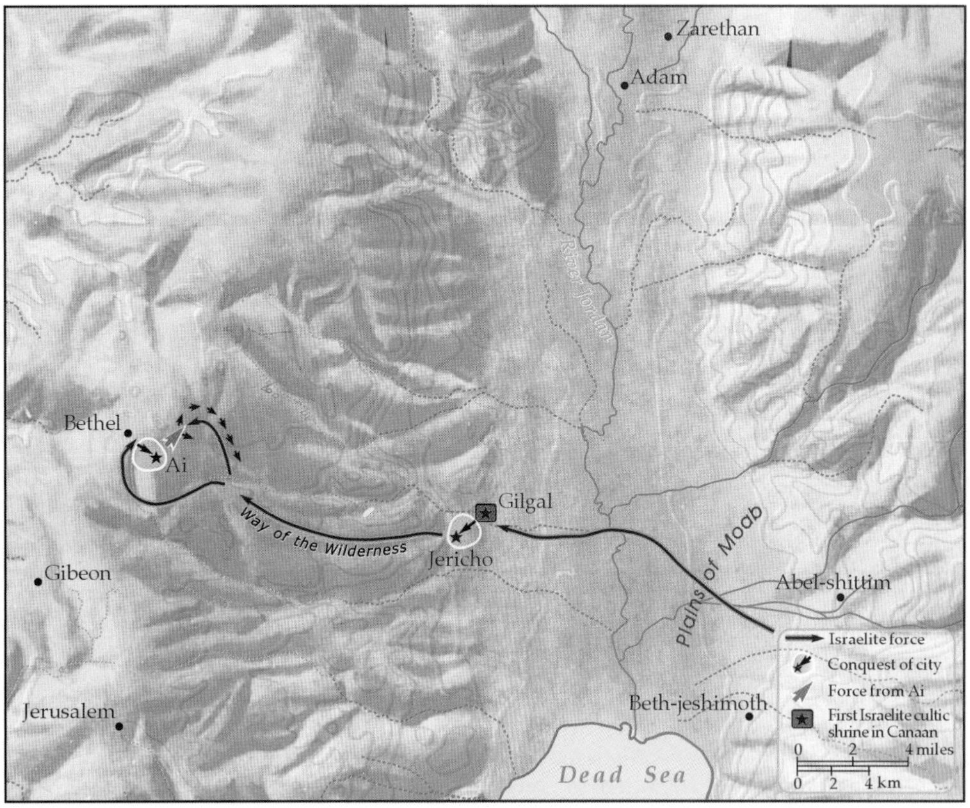


The Narrative of the Initial Penetration into the Land of Canaan

***The Initial Thrust***. The miracle stories of crossing the Jordan and the conquest of Jericho are well known and elicit the most heated debate and the strongest emotions. The waters of the Jordan are said to have piled up at Adam, near Zarethan (Josh 3:15b–16), traditionally located at Tell ed-Dâmiyeh. This is logical in itself as the clay banks in that area, north of the juncture with the Jabbok from the east and the Wâdī Far<sup>c</sup>ah from the west, could easily block the course of the river for a period of time. The new Cisjordanian base of operations was established at Gilgal, a site that acquired importance as a cultic center (*see* Josh 4:19).

After the conquest of Jericho, the next pericope concerns a penetration into the mountains to attack the city of Ai (Josh 7–8). The same geographical relation in Joshua 7:2 was expressed in the story of Abraham (see Gen 12:8). Since Bethel is unquestionably located at Beitîn, the most likely site for Ai is still et-Tell, the great Early Bronze Age city mound that was crowned by an early Iron Age village of substantial proportions. The ambush motif whereby the men of a site are lured out and then surprised from behind was evidently well known (cf. a similar account in Judg 20:29–46). It may have been a real tactic used in internecine conflicts (*see* Josh 8:10–15).

The Israelites are not said to have occupied the site of Ai, which strengthens the impression that the story is an etiological tale to explain the ruin. In the Joshua narrative, Israel returned to their base at Gilgal.

The next pericope deals with the Gibeonite ruse and the resultant battle with the ruler of Jerusalem and his allies. The narrative (Josh 9:3–10:15) recounts how Joshua and the Israelites were deceived into making a solemn oath of peace with the Hivite population at the center of the plateau north of Jerusalem. The Hivites had disguised themselves as travelers from afar and came seeking Israel's protection. As punishment for this successful ruse, the Gibeonites were reportedly forced to become "wood-cutters and water-carriers" for the Israelites, who, for their part, felt contractually obliged to rescue Gibeon from a retaliatory attack by their erstwhile overlord, the ruler of Jerusalem. In the ensuing battle, Joshua's warriors drove the Canaanites from Gibeon into the descent of Beth-horon while God "hurled huge hailstones from heaven" (cf. Isa 28:21) on them as the sun and moon stood still in their courses. This famous story is

*Aerial view of et-Tell (Ai) showing the main structures: temple, palace and city wall, EB.*

*Examination of the topography in and around et-Tell has demonstrated that the details of the Joshua narrative fit amazingly well with the physical configuration of the site and the surrounding terrain. The saddle connecting the tel with the adjacent ridge and the ravine all answer to the details of the story. There is every likelihood that this is a legend about the real conquest of an Iron Age settlement.*

probably based on an etiological tradition explaining the subservient relationship of the Hivites of Gibeon to the Israelites.

The Gibeonites-Hivites lived in four towns. The territory encompassed by these towns is possibly intended in some cases when speaking of Gibeon, though the expression "land of Gibeon" does not appear. There is a "valley in Gibeon" (Isa 28: 21). As for their four towns:

> Now their cities were **Gibeon** and **Chephirah** and **Beeroth** and **Kiriath-jearim**. (Josh 9:17)

The Gibeonites were said to be vassals of the king of Jerusalem. Their desertion to Israel was a cause for alarm in Jerusalem since their territory straddled the most important routes leading to the coastal plain. The controversies during the Amarna Age between Jerusalem and her coastal neighbors were concerned with the same problem. Now the ruler of Jerusalem called up his Amorite allies to help him punish his errant vassals (*see* Josh 10:4–5).

At this point, Joshua and the warriors of Israel came up from Gilgal and surprised the Amorite coalition (*see* Josh 10:10–11). Beth-horon, both Upper and Lower, have been correctly identified with twin sites, Beit ʿÛr el-Fôqā and Beit ʿÛr et-Taḥtā respectively, on the easiest route from the coastal plain to the hill country north of Jerusalem. Azekah is a town in the northernmost district of the Shephelah of Judah (Josh 15:35). It was first identified with Tell Zakarîyeh by Rabbi Yehoseph Schwartz in 1840.

Makkedah was usually sought in the vicinity of Azekah, i.e. in the northern Shephelah, because of this passage. But in the Shephelah list, Makkedah was assigned to the Lachish (Josh 15:41) district and an administrative text must take precedence over a war legend. However, it has been shown that the distance from Beth-horon to Azekah is about the same as the distance from Azekah to Khirbet el-Qôm when one takes into account the "trough valley" separating the Shephelah from the hill country. Eusebius says of Makkedah:

> It is now east of Eleutheropolis from the eighth milestone. (*Onom.* 126:24–25)

At about that point, there is a Roman-Byzantine ruin called Khirbet Beit Maqdûm about 0.6 mile (1 km) from Khirbet el-Qôm. The latter site is an impressive tel on the eastern side of the trough valley but definitely not in the hill country. It is a Shephelah site like all the tels in the trough. So the pursuit described in Joshua 10:11 as far as Azekah and as far as Makkedah can describe two legs on the journey: first to Azekah and then in the Valley of Elah and south along the trough to Makkedah at Khirbet el-Qôm, which is just where one would expect to find Iron Age Makkedah according to Eusebius! In recent years the identification of Khirbet el-Qôm with Makkedah has been virtually confirmed by a plethora of fourth-century BCE Aramaic ostraca that have reached the antiquities market from Khirbet el-Qôm. Some were discovered in the possession of villagers from Khirbet el-Qôm during a routine search at a military checkpoint. Many of the texts make reference to Makkedah in Aramaic.

Of course, the phrase, "as far as Makkedah," may very well be literary glue to link this pericope with the following, but to be credible it ought to make geographic sense. That disparate legends are being patched together may be obvious from Joshua 10:15 whereby Joshua and his troops are said to have returned to Gilgal in the Jordan Valley. But that verse is missing from the Septuagint and it may, in fact, be a later, post-third-century BCE addition to the Hebrew text. It does not seem likely that the translator into Greek had removed an awkward piece of editorial glue. After that, Joshua was summoned to the cave at Makkedah where the five kings were in hiding. But this leads into the next pericope

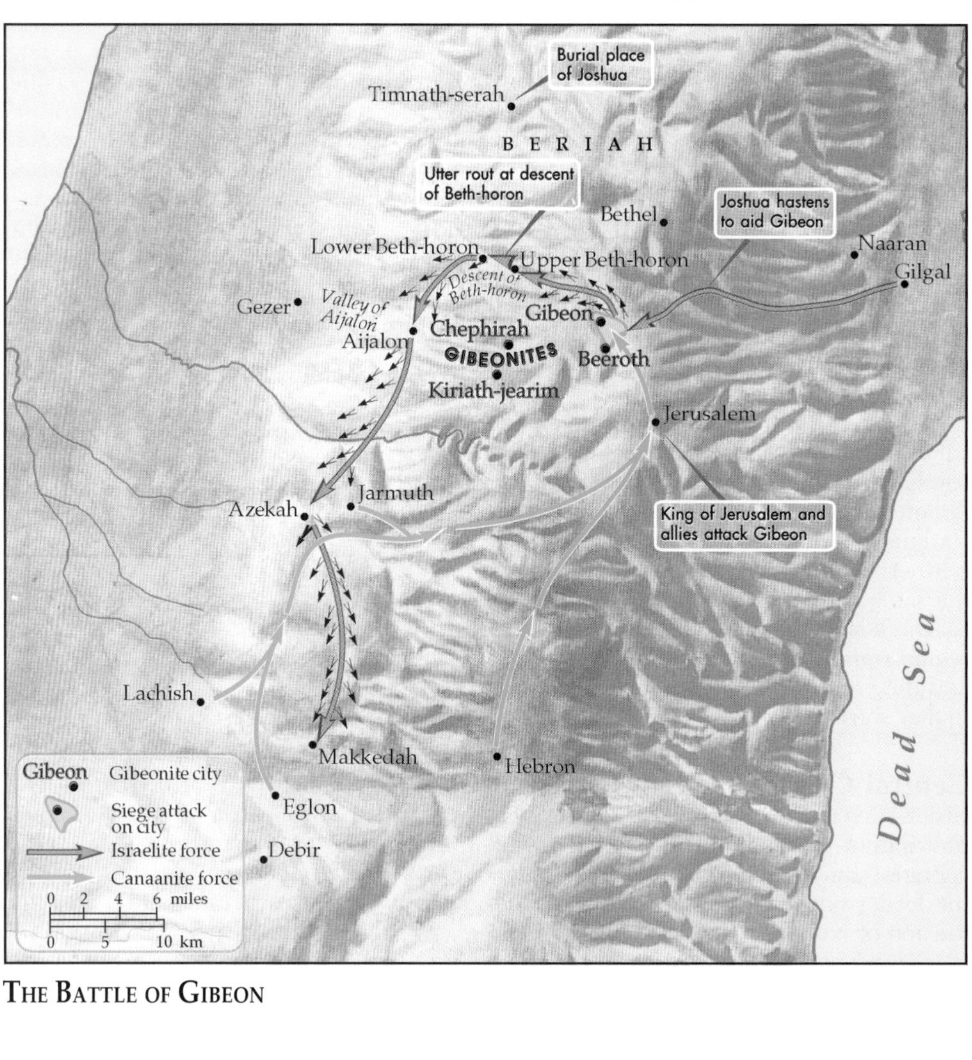


**THE BATTLE OF GIBEON**

about the conquest of towns in the central and southern Shephelah.

**The Southern Campaign**. It is interesting to note that there are no conquest stories about places in the northern district of the Shephelah in Joshua 15:33–36. Apparently, the relationship between the Israelites and the Canaanite/Amorite dwellers in that district is reflected accurately in the story of Judah and Tamar (Gen 38).

Later in Joshua 10:21, Joshua had a camp at Makkedah (=Khirbet el-Qôm) on the eastern edge of the trough valley, at the foot of the Hebron hills. It becomes the first in a cycle of conquests in the central and southern districts of the Shephelah (*see* Josh 10:28).

The next target in the sequence was Libnah (*see* Josh 10:29–30). Libnah's identification is still not confirmed, but there is ample evidence pointing to Tell Bornâṭ. Many suggestions have been made for the identification of Libnah. One of the most frequent was Tell eṣ-Ṣâfī, but the Arabic name of that mound means "bright, shining" and not "white." In the Sennacherib campaign, it hardly makes sense that the Assyrians would have taken Ekron (Tel Miqne=Khirbet el-Muqannaʿ) and then gone around to Tell eṣ-Ṣâfī to attack Lachish, only to return to Tell eṣ-Ṣâfī later. Furthermore, it is impossible to visualize an administrative district reaching from Mareshah to Tell eṣ-Ṣâfī. The apostasy of Libnah during the reign of Jehoram (2 Kgs 8:22) indicates that it was in close proximity to Philistia. Placing it to the east, with the entire Lachish district blocking the way, never made any sense. Furthermore, its status as a Levitical city (Josh 21:13) also suggests a role as border fortress facing the west. Therefore, one seems compelled to accept the arguments for placing Libnah at Tell Bornâṭ (Tel Burna).

Eusebius merely says:

Now it is a village called **Lobana** in the district of Eleutheropolis. (*Onom.* 120:23–25)

That he does not give a direction or mileage suggests that Libnah was just too close to Beth Govrin (Beit Jibrîn). Another hint is the fact that "Libnah and Ether" appear together in the town list of Judah (Josh 15:42). Ether can hardly be disassociated from Khirbet ʿAtar, 1 mile (1.5 km) west of Beth Govrin. It is a similar distance from Tell Bornâṭ.

The size and impressiveness of Tell Bornâṭ is obscured by the fact that it is located down in the depression of Wâdī ez-Zeitā (Naḥal Guvrin). Its location on the western border of the Shephelah facing Philistia suits the account of its rebellion against the king of Judah (2 Kgs 8:22; 2 Chr 21:10).

From Libnah, the sequence continues to Lachish (*see* Josh 10:31–32). Tell ed-Duweir was recognized as the most likely site for Lachish when it became clear that Tell el-Ḥesī (Tel Ḥasi) was not a viable candidate.

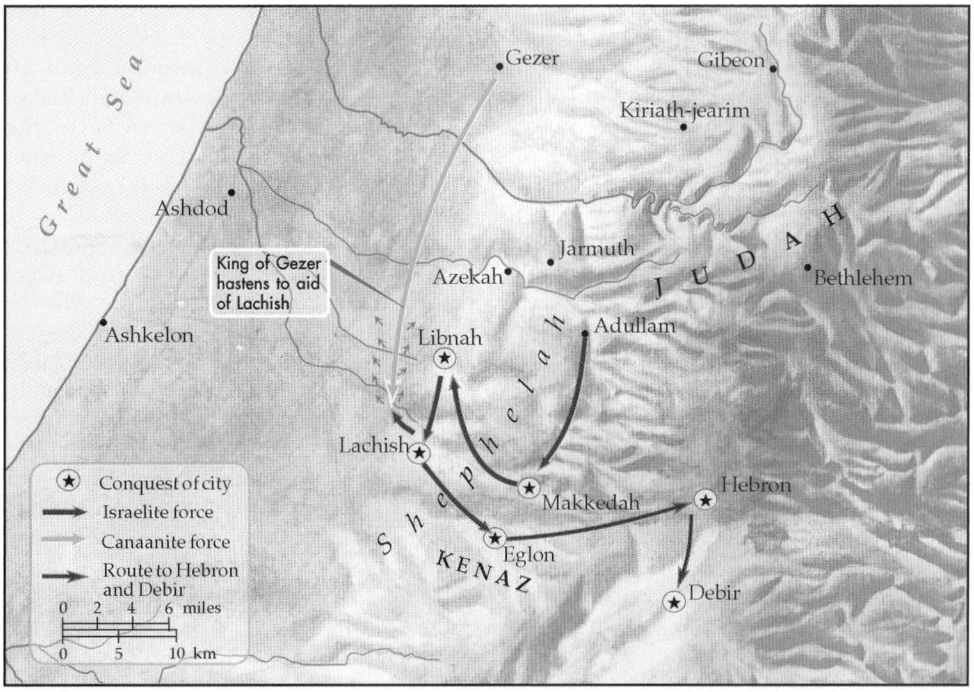


**Conquest of the Southern Shephelah and Central Hill Country (Late 12th Century bce)**

The identification of Tell ed-Duweir with Lachish was firmly established by the discovery of the "Lachish Letters." One of them, No. 4, mentioned Lachish in such a way as to preclude all doubt that it was sent to Lachish by someone located within eye contact of Tell ed-Duweir, which he calls Lachish.

At this point the progress of conquest is interrupted by the attempted intervention by the king of Gezer in support of Lachish (*see* Josh 10:33).

The sequence of conquests resumes with the progress towards Eglon (*see* Josh 10:34–35). Eglon ought to be somewhere between Lachish, now firmly identified, and Hebron. The site that answers best to the demands of the text is Tell ʿAitûn (now Tel ʿEton), which would be on a more natural route from Lachish to Hebron via Wâdī el-Jizâʾir (Naḥal Adorayim). There is no doubt today that Tell ʿAitûn has all the physical and archaeological characteristics for biblical Eglon.

Thus a geographically logical route, from Libnah (Tell Bornâṭ) to Lachish (Tell ed-Duweir) and on to Eglon (Tell ʿAitûn) is established, a fitting prelude to the author's next stage, the conquest of the central hill country.

**The Central Hill Country**. Here one finds the most striking literary evidence for the composite nature of Joshua 10 (pericopes patched together). Three versions of this section are extant in the Hebrew Bible. The original version ascribed the conquest of Hebron and Debir to the Kenizzites. The leading personality is Caleb. The account is accommodated to the conception of the author of Joshua by making this an assignment of territory during Joshua's allocation of the land (*see* Josh 15:13–19).

A second version associated Caleb with the tribe of Judah (*see* Judg 1:19–20).

And finally, the conquest of Hebron and Debir is attached to the southern campaign of all Israel under the leadership of Joshua (*see* Josh 10:36–39). The identification of Debir has been another long and wearisome process. It should have been the major pre-Israelite town south of Hebron, later converted into a priestly city. Analysis of the biblical sources leaves no room for doubt that Debir was located in the southern Judean hill country (Josh 15:49). Thus, it is not surprising that in the nineteenth century attention was focused on the Arab town of edh-Dhâherîyeh, the southernmost town in the Judean hills.

Survey and excavation at Khirbet Rabûd have demonstrated that it has Late Bronze

*View of Lachish (Tell ed-Duweir), looking northeast.*

*The Iron Age fortified city excavated at Tell ed-Duweir bears a striking resemblance to Lachish on Sennacherib's reliefs, and one of the ostraca found there mentions Lachish in such a way that the most logical inference is that the writer means the town at Tell ed-Duweir.*

occupation and that during Iron Age II it was surrounded by a massive stone wall encompassing an area larger than Lachish. It has also been demonstrated that Khirbet Rabûd and its vicinity are a perfect match for the conditions reflected in the written sources. This includes the location of two water sources, Bîr el-ᶜAlaqah el-Fōqânī (=colloquial el-ᶜAliyeh) and Bîr el-ᶜAlaqah et-Taḥtânī (colloquial et-Taḥtā), in an adjacent valley, which correspond to the upper and lower springs in the narrative about Achsah, daughter of Caleb. The location also makes sense out of that story. Khirbet Rabûd does not have a natural water source of any consequence right next to it. The valley with the two wells could be placed under its jurisdiction though that was not obligatory from its location.

**Upper Galilee**. There are many areas for which the author of the Book of Joshua seems not to have acquired conquest narratives. He concludes that portion of his book with a campaign in Upper Galilee. Once again, Joshua is the commander.

Only four Canaanite cities are mentioned in the narrative about the conflict at the so-called waters of Merom. The Madon and Shimron and also Merom, of the Hebrew version, are ghost words; the Greek Septuagint translation, based on a superior Hebrew text, proves that the originals were *Maron and *Shimᶜon (Simeon; it also survives correctly in 2 Chr 16:9, 34:6).

The proper understanding of the geography of this pericope requires the use of the Septuagint for the correct forms of the place names (*see* Josh 11:1–3; cf. LXX). The actual location of Maron (LXX) is probably Tell el-Khureibeh, just over 2 miles (3 km) south of Marûn er-Râs. Shimᶜon (Simeon) is of course at Khirbet Sammûniyeh (today Tel Shimron). Achshaph was one of the major sites on the Acco Plain. Its location remains uncertain, possibly Tell Keisân (Tel Kison), 6 miles (10 km) southeast of Acco, or Khirbet el-Harbaj (Tel Regev), situated at the southern end of the Plain of Acco. The idea in the description of the allies is to present a picture of the main centers of non-Israelite settlement in the northern part of the country, all of them presumably subordinate to the king of Hazor. There must have been a longer list of towns but it has been intentionally truncated and summarized in terms of the general areas.

The reference to a "Shephelah" in the north indicates a configuration of low-lying hills between the narrow coastal strip and the central mountain range. These are the north-south foothills of western Galilee extending up to the coastal plain of Tyre in southern Lebanon. Here a Shephelah-like geomorphology lies between mountains and the coastal plain. This region was well recognized throughout history as distinctive, and consequently finds expression in administrative arrangements, during Crusader times and especially during the nineteenth century. In Talmudic times, the "Shephelah of Galilee" was differentiated as a "Land of Gentiles," while the mountains to the east were included in the "Land of Israel."

The Canaanites had gathered at a well-known water source near Marûn er-Râs, a centrally located mountain in Upper Galilee. This places the venue of the battle on the relatively level ground north of the southern, uplifted block of Upper Galilee called Jebel Jarmaq. The modern name, Mount Meiron, hardly reflects any early nomenclature. It is a modern invention.

Merom (*see* Josh 11:5) has been identified with the village of Meiron on the eastern slopes of Jebel Jarmaq. But this is to ignore the correct text as reflected in the Septuagint. Excavations at Meiron have demonstrated that it is a much later village.

The line of the Canaanite retreat confirms that the battle took place in Upper Galilee and not at some other venue such as the Horns of Hattin (*see* Josh 11:8). Apparently, the Israelites cut off the escape routes to the south from Upper Galilee because the overthrown Canaanites escaped by the only available routes to the west, to Misrephoth, near Khirbet Musheirefeh, via Iqrit (Ḥorbat Yoqrat) and Abdon (Khirbet ᶜAbdā=Tel ᶜAvdon), north toward Sidon via Yattir and Kanah, and northeast to the Mizpeh valley via Taphnith and Beth-anath (Ṣafed el-Baṭṭîkh), as indicated in Joshua 11: 6–9. Joshua then is said to have destroyed Hazor.

The original clans involved were probably those of Naphtali and perhaps of Asher, whose initial settlements were in the high mountainous area of southern Upper Galilee as demonstrated by archaeological surveys. Joshua and the entire people of Israel are introduced in accordance with the conception being promulgated by the author of the Book of Joshua. It has been noted that the author of Chronicles does not agree with this conception.

### The List of Conquered Kings.

*After recounting his conquest narratives, the author of the Book of Joshua presents a list of the conquered kings. For Transjordan he reviews the traditions about Sihon and Og, thus showing his dependence on the narratives in Numbers. For Cisjordan he gives a list. Unfortunately, the Masoretic version of this list has become somewhat corrupt. However, by using the Septuagint version, which is known to be superior textually to the MT for Joshua and Samuel, a fairly comprehensible list can be reconstructed. It may be that there were originally conquest traditions for some of the places not mentioned explicitly in the previous chapters. A partially reconstructed text is as follows:*

#### Partially Corrected King List of Joshua 12:9–24

9 The king of Jericho, one;
The king of Ai, which is beside Bethel, one;
10 The king of Jerusalem, one;
The king of Hebron, one;
11 The king of Jarmuth, one;
The king of Lachish, one;
12 The king of Eglon, one;
The king of Gezer, one;
13 The king of Debir, one;
The king of Geder, one;
14 The king of Hormah, one;
The king of Arad, one;
15 The king of Libnah, one;
The king of Adullam, one;
16 The king of Makkedah, one;
The king of Bethel, one;
17 The king of Tappuah, one;
The king of Hepher, one;
18 The king of Aphek of the Sharon, one;
19 The king of Hazor, one;
20 The king of Shimᶜon, one;
The king of Maron, one;
The king of Achshaph, one;
21 The king of Kedesh, one;
The king of Taanach, one;
22 The king of Megiddo, one;
The king of Jokneam of the Carmel, one;
23 The king of Dor in the heights of Dor, one;
The king of Goiim in Galilee, one;
24 The king of Tirzah, one:
All the kings: thirty-one.

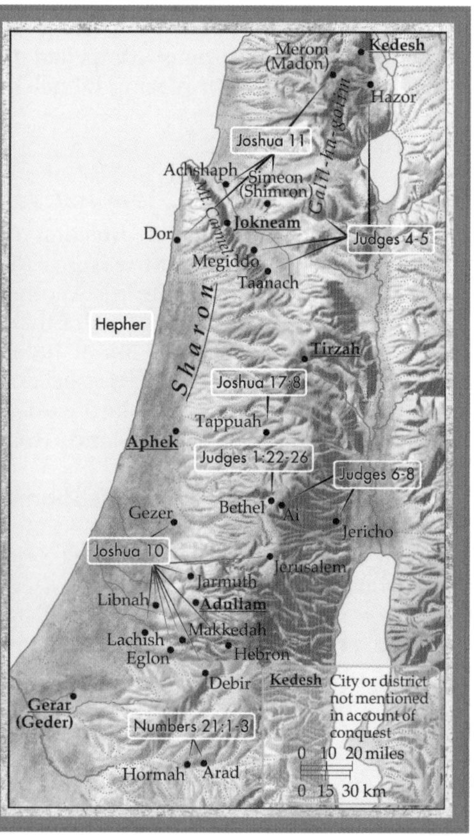

# CHAPTER FIVE
# SURVIVAL AND RENEWAL
## ELEVENTH CENTURY BCE

The eleventh century BCE in the ancient Near East is not rich in written sources. Nevertheless, there are some epigraphic windows opened here and there and, with some extrapolation from later periods, it is possible to learn something about life in the Levant.

## THE SOUTHERN LEVANT

By the twelfth century BCE the principal rival peoples in Palestine were becoming well established in their respective areas. The Canaanites continued to dwell in the northern valleys and plains, the Philistines (with other "sea peoples"?) in the southern coastal plain, and the tribes of Israel in the hill country. The biblical tradition confirms that Israelites were unable to dislodge the Canaanites and Amorites in the lowland areas, for they had "chariots of iron" (Josh 17:18). A list of the areas where the non-Israelites continued to dwell is given in Judges 1 and similar allusions appear here and there in the Book of Joshua (15:63, 17:11–13).

The Book of Judges is meant to be a link in the national epic, taking up the story after the conquest narratives in the Book of Joshua. Judges 1:27–35, discussed below, lists the unconquered areas according to tribe. No tradition exists about the conquest of Shechem, whose situation may have been like Gezer (Judg 1:19), a Canaanite population living in symbiosis with the Israelites. Jebus-Jerusalem, Gezer and the Amorite towns that resisted the Danites were in the center of the country. Very ancient traditions reveal that the Ephraimites came into early contact with the indigenous population of the area where the Danites had been prevented from settling (1 Chr 7:20–24; Judg 1:35). Some clans from Benjamin also migrated to the same area (1 Chr 8:12–13; 2 Sam 4:3–4).

Recent archaeological surveys in the hill-country areas confirm the arrival of pastoralists who began their settlement along the fringes of the steppe land, east of the watershed. Gradually they expanded and established settlements in the areas of mixed agriculture and eventually moved into the western hill zones where it became necessary to develop terraces and plant orchards and vineyards. Thus, originally pastoral groups became transformed into a thoroughly sedentary society with varied subsistence strategies. The tribal groups that settled in Upper Galilee went through a similar process; their material culture reflects a certain cultural affinity with the Phoenicians on the coast below.

All of these data confirm the new population revolution brought about in the twelfth and eleventh centuries BCE. In the Late Bronze Age the main concentrations of population were in the plains; the hill-country areas were relatively uninhabited, providing refuge for ʿapîru outlaws and for the Shâsu pastoralists. The latter became more and more numerous and adopted sedentary ways of life, perhaps because of a decline in the overall Canaanite agricultural productivity. Though a process of significant growth among the hill-country rural population can be deduced from the archaeological surveys, in the ensuing discussions of biblical narratives, all numbers of participating warriors will be ignored as elements of pure historiography or of oral heroic tradition. This will apply to accounts in both the books of Judges and Samuel.

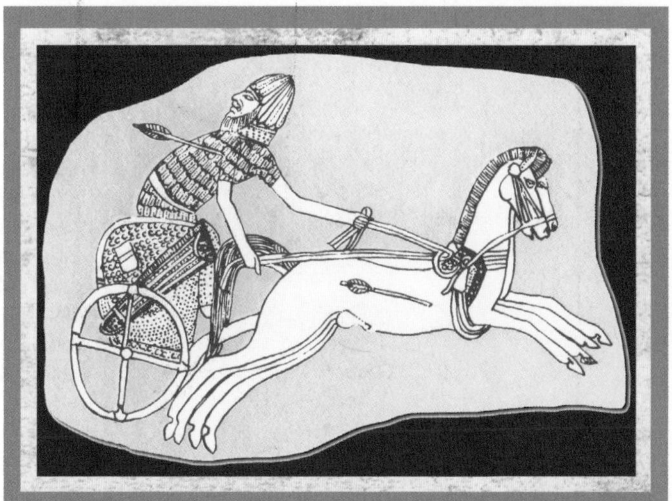

*Canaanite charioteer wounded by arrow (decoration on chariot of Thutmose IV).*

The dichotomy between Canaanites on the plains and Israelites in the hills characterizes the narratives throughout the books of Judges and Samuel. Before proceeding to a discussion of biblical sources for this period, it is necessary to say a few words about the Book of Judges. This is a political treatise with strong religious overtones. The final statement of the book is:

In those days there was no king in Israel; every man was doing what was right in his own eyes.
(Judg 21:25)

And it has always been obvious that in the time of the final author, there already was a king in Israel. This closing statement was preceded by two narratives illustrating the social and moral chaos of the period in question. They will be addressed subsequently.

Attention is usually focused more on the body of the work, viz. a series of hero stories, chosen from most of the Israelite tribes. The narratives have been arranged in a tendentious chronological framework explained by the Deuteronomist (*see* Judg 2:11–19).

A period of oppression by some neighboring element is met with the rise of a hero, a "judge/leader" who led the people to victory. The country was then said to enjoy rest for forty years until the next danger arose. There is a strong Deuteronomistic overtone to the whole arrangement, the times of suffering usually blamed on the people's apostasy to the worship of local Canaanite deities. The work of the champion would bring the people back to loyalty to YHWH. This cyclic framework is thoroughly artificial and can by no stretch of the imagination be used to establish absolute dates for the stories. Neither are there any literary contacts with outside sources or chronology.

A salient feature of the treatment of these hero stories is the attempt to give credit where credit is due. The heroes of the pre-monarchial era of settlement and consolidation are honored as true servants of the people and of YHWH, albeit with individual personal weaknesses. But in the final analysis, as encapsulated in the concluding verse, life is now much easier and orderly under a monarchy.

What usually goes unnoticed is that the first chapter also has a strong pro-monarchic flavor. The list of "tribal failures" (Judg 1:27–35) draws a contrast between the geo-sociological situation following the initial entrance into the land and that prevailing under the monarchy. How is this

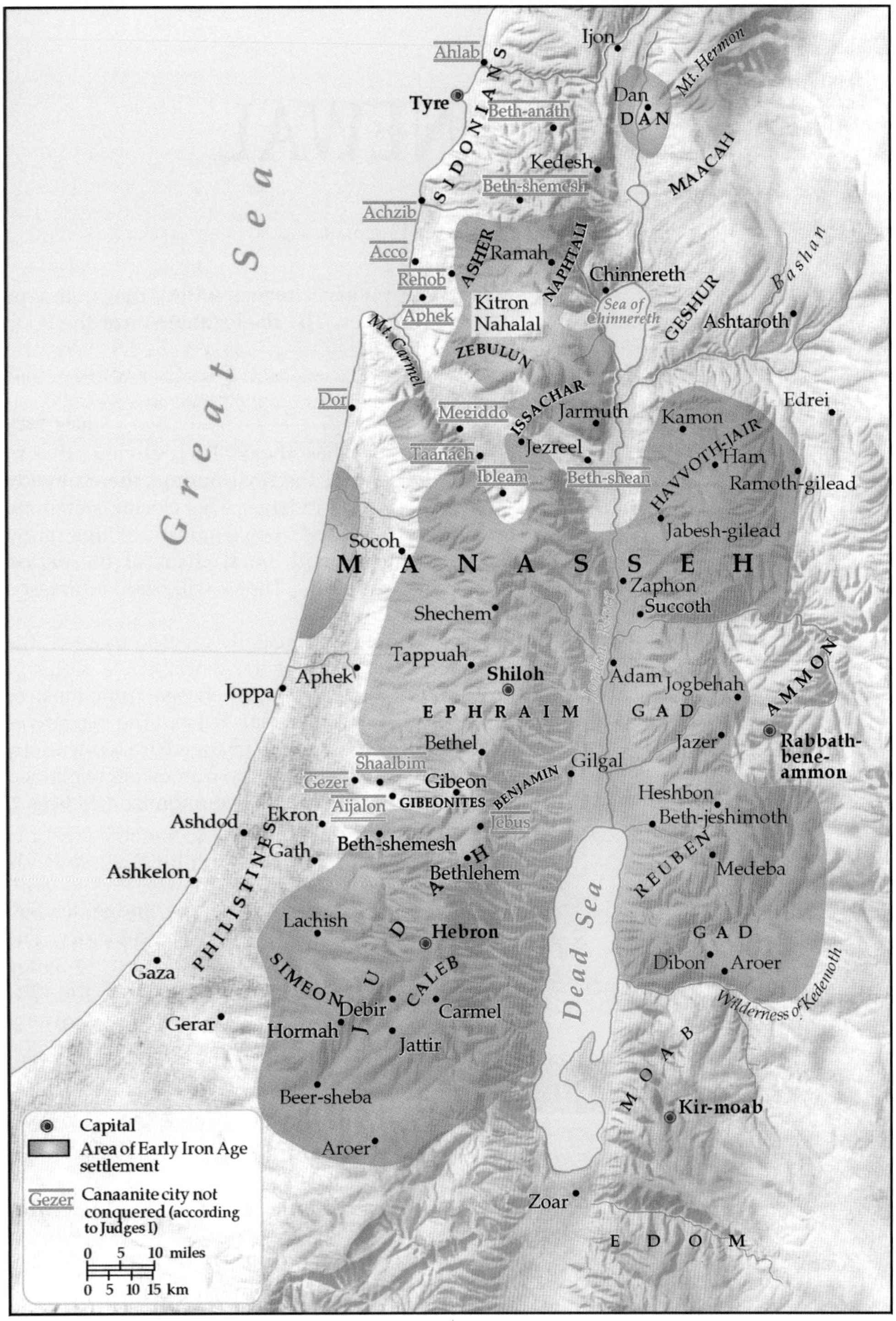


**The Limits of Israelite Presence (12th–11th Centuries BCE)**

expressed? By the allusions to the forced labor imposed on the conquered peoples, the author/editor was emphasizing the new sociological alignment under the consolidated, centralized monarchial regime. It should also be remarked that there is a striking correlation between the list of unconquered enclaves and the list of administrative districts under the monarchy (1 Kgs 4). Apart from its tendentious character, the geographical details of this chapter tell a remarkable story.

**The Southern Tribes**. Verses 1 to 8 recount a strange story about Judah as the supposed leader in the continued conquest. There is a mysterious account of conflict at a place called Bezek which hardly seems commensurate with the small town by that name in northeastern Samaria (Khirbet Ibzîq). The captured king, Adoni-bezek, is brought to Jerusalem, which is then conquered and burnt. The impression is that it is a veiled allusion to some phase in the conquest of the Jerusalem area, of which Adoni-bezek may have been considered the ruler.

Verses 9 to 15 are a doublet of the capture of Hebron and Debir. In this version the initiative is from Judah while the ultimate capture is still accomplished by the Kenizzites, Caleb and his nephew Othniel.

Another special ethnic group, the Kenites, is listed in verse 16.

> The sons of ‹Hobab the› (LXX) the Kenite, Moses' father-in-law, went up from the **city of palms** ***to*** (LXX) the sons of Judah, (to) the wilderness of Judah which is in the Negeb **‹at the descent›** (LXX) of **Arad**; and they went and lived with the Am‹alekites›. (Judg 1:16)

The Simeonite conquest of Zephath/Hormah is given next (Judg 1:17) followed by a summary of Judah's activity (Judg 1:18–19).

> And Judah **‹did not›** (LXX) take **Gaza** with its territory and **Ashkelon** with its territory and **Ekron** with its territory. Now YHWH was with Judah, and they took possession of the hill country; but **they could not dispossess the inhabitants of the valley because they had iron chariots**. Then they gave **Hebron** to Caleb, as Moses had promised; and he drove out from there the three sons of Anak. (Judg 1:18–20)

The positive Masoretic verse 18 contradicts the Septuagint. It was certainly a deliberate alteration of the Hebrew text, apparently in an attempt to portray Judah as successful in contrast to the other tribes. The emender overlooked the glaring contradiction with verse 19. The subsequent biblical narratives about confrontations between Judah and his Philistine neighbors confirms the Septuagintal version, viz. that Judah did not conquer the cities of Philistia.

So Judges 1:18–19 (LXX) confirms that Judah did not subdue the Philistines. There is evidence that the Philistines had expanded northward during the eleventh century BCE. The original appearance of this Aegean people in the southern Levant was marked by the appearance of the Mycenaean IIIC1b ceramics, mainly confined to sites in the south, i.e. up to Ekron. The later development of Philistine pottery, which demonstrates a symbiosis with local Canaanite traditions, the "classical" Philistine ware, appears also in the area of Joppa and its hinterland. It will also be seen from some later biblical narratives that the Philistines were controlling the territory up to Aphek, which they used as a military staging ground.

Benjamin, the tribe located just north of Judah, is discussed next, here with regard to the Jebusite enclave at Jerusalem. The evident contradiction between this passage and the previous account of a putative capture of Jerusalem by Judah (v. 8) is ignored (*see* Judg 1:21).

Then there follows an entry about the House of Joseph (Ephraim) and the city of Bethel (*see* Judg 1:22–26).

This is the record of a successful conquest. A major Canaanite town in the central hill country is taken by force. The contrast with the subsequent entries is striking. Hill-country sites such as Hebron in the south and Bethel in the center are conquered. Canaanite centers on the plains below are not dispossessed. The same will hold true for Gezer on the plain, which the Ephraimites did not occupy at first.

**The Northern Tribes**. The remainder

*Decorated Philistine jug from Tell eṣ-Ṣâfī, probable site of Philistine Gath.*

of the list deals mainly with tribes in the north and in Transjordan, particularly those tribes that had some propinquity to lowland areas.

The first entry in this section establishes the tone and the intention of the subsequent entries (*see* Judg 1:27–28). The towns in this list are all on the plains and in the lowlands. In fact they represent a geographical and population belt reaching from the seacoast to the Jordan Valley, i.e. the district of Dor and the plain of Megiddo and the Jezreel Valley (which included the Beth-shean Valley). This text has its parallel in Joshua 17:11–13 where the cities in question are said to be "in Asher and Issachar." When was Israel sufficiently strong to impose forced labor on the population dwelling on the plains? Certainly not during the "period of the judges" or under the leadership of Samuel. There was no central government or administrative mechanism to impose and operate such a program. Even Saul, an experimental king, did not have control over the Jezreel Valley. It was while attempting to penetrate into that area that he lost his life. To every ancient reader of this text it would have been obvious that the reference is to the monarchial regime founded by David and developed by his son, Solomon. So this passage in the first chapter corresponds to the final verse of the book in proclaiming that only under the monarchy was the country organized at last into a cohesive entity, geographically, administratively and socially. Also, the moral and social chaos that prevailed in the pre-monarchial era was brought under control by the royal institution.

The subsequent entries follow the same vein. In spite of the capture by the House of Joseph of Bethel in the hill country, the tribe of Ephraim did not dispossess the Canaanite enclave at Gezer.

And Ephraim did not dispossess the Canaanites who lived in **Gezer**; but the Canaanites lived among them in Gezer [LXX, and they became subject to forced labor]. (Judg 1:29)

The Septuagint shows that the Hebrew text has lost the ever-recurring phrase, "and they became subject to forced labor."

This passage raises some interesting questions about the population in the greater Gezer district. The story about Ephraim's sons slain by the autochthonous dwellers of a certain Gath in this area (1 Chr 7:21–23), undoubtedly the Gath-rimmon/Gittaim near modern Ramla, does not call them Canaanites. The same area is said to be inhabited by Amorites in the passage below about the tribe of Dan. That might be a biblical way of saying that they had more ancient roots in the land. Ephraim will appear again in the entry pertaining to the Danites.

Attention is turned next to the northern side of the Great Plain, the Jezreel Valley, where Zebulun did not gain a foothold (*see* Judg 1:30). Kitron is to be equated with the Kattath of Joshua 19:15 but has not been identified on the ground. Nahalal/Nahalol was correctly identified by Rabbi Yosi son of Haninah in the Jerusalem Talmud (*Megillah*, I, 77a) with Mahalûl, the site of which was preserved in the Arabic name Ma$^{c}$lûl (where the modern moshav Nahalal was later established). Its proximity to Tell Seimûnia and Beit Laḥm (which Rabbi Yosi called "the Tyrian Bethlehem") confirms that the intention here is to the northwestern quadrant of the Jezreel Valley. A likely ancient tel for Nahalal is nearby Tell el-Beiḍā. It is located 0.6 mile (1 km) south of Ma$^{c}$lûl in a rich area with a good water supply. At the southern foot of the tel is a spring; around Tell el-Beiḍā there are tributaries of the Kishon. Incidentally, the sequence of verb tenses here makes it clear that becoming subject to the forced labor was a later development.

The statement concerning the tribe of Asher is unique in that it records just the opposite process (*see* Judg 1:31–32). The secondary status of this tribe is reflected in its being assigned to the handmaiden Zilpah. The area of its biblical "inheritance" was to include the western foothills of Lower Galilee and the Plain of Acco from the Carmel headland north to the hinterland of Tyre. But they are said not to have dispossessed any of the Canaanite populations in this area. The answer lies in the nature of this coastal zone. The Canaanite population was, since time immemorial, engaged in maritime activities: fishing, sailing commercial ships, building and maintaining the ships and boats. Such an industrialized population still had to eat. In the Amarna letters from Byblos, the hapless ruler there was always worried about his yeomen farmers. Would they remain loyal or would they rebel or perhaps abandon Byblos for another venue where working conditions were better?

Therefore, it seems obvious that the Asherites managed to settle among the industrially oriented Canaanites because they were welcomed as agricultural workers. They also were thus able to share in the benefits of the coastal enterprises (Judg 5:17; along with the Danites up north).

The story of Naphtali is similar but the geographical matrix is somewhat different (*see* Judg 1:33). The two towns in question are not in the plains below but rather in the hill country of Upper Galilee. However, Upper Galilee has a dual configuration. Rising above the Valley of Beth-haccerem, which separates it from Lower Galilee, is the Jebel Jarmaq (called Mount Meiron in modern Israeli geography), a mountain massif that rises 3,960 feet (1,208 m) above sea level. Archaeological survey has shown that this very high and isolated area saw the appearance of a plethora of humble new sites at the beginning of the Iron Age. At the foot of its northern slopes there is a zone of ridges and good agricultural land at a lower altitude. There, in the *relatively* lower hills, were some Canaanite towns. Two of these were Beth-shemesh (Kh. Tell er-Ruweisī?) and Beth-anath (Safed el-Baṭṭîkh?), the names of which testify to the presence of cult centers dedicated to two Canaanite deities, the sun god and

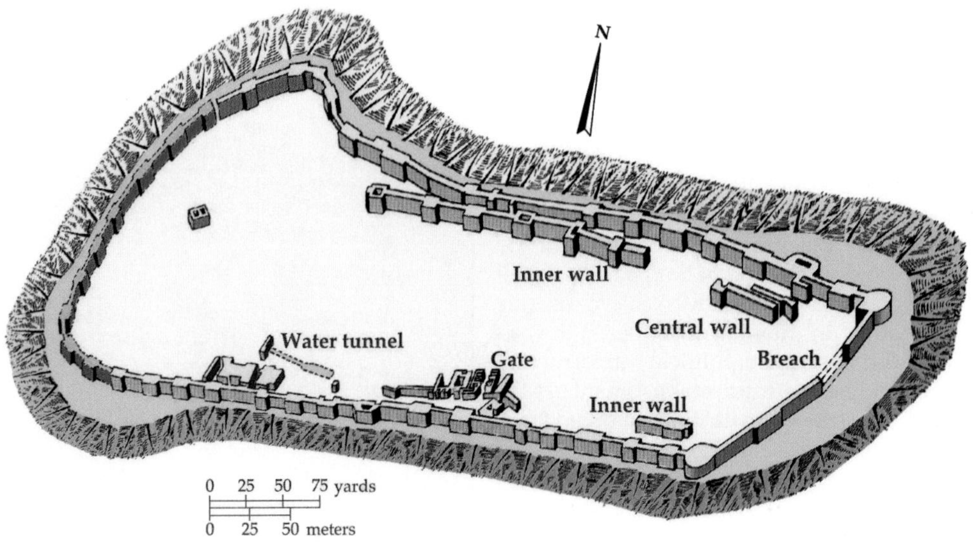


*Plan of Canaanite Gezer.*

*The Valley of Aijalon.*

the huntress goddess. It is this Canaanite enclave that maintained its integrity during the eleventh century BCE while the clans of Naphtali occupied the uplifted peaks of the Jebel Jarmaq. Archaeological excavations have shown that Canaanite Hazor had been destroyed violently and subsequently occupied by a new and less sophisticated culture in the early Iron Age.

The final entry has to do with the tribe of Dan (*see* Judg 1:34–35). There is considerable disagreement about the location of Har-heres. The reference here is most likely to the hilly slopes east of the Valley of Aijalon. The settlements of Aijalon and Shaalbim are on the eastern and western margins, respectively, of the Aijalon Valley. So the indigenous population here is called Amorite while elsewhere they are Canaanites. In the story of the slain Ephraimite sons (1 Chr 7:21) they are called "the men of Gath who were born in the land. . . ." At stake was the strategic hub of land between modern-day Ramla and Laṭrûn. The "House of Joseph" here must be the tribe of Ephraim, as indicated by the reference to the Ephraimites in relation to Gezer (Judg 1:29). Some clans from Benjamin also migrated to the same area (1 Chr 8:12–13; 2 Sam 4:3–4).

In these passages the institution of "forced labor" has been emphasized. It should be obvious that through the period of the Judges and till the end of Saul's reign, Israel did not have control over the Canaanite population in those unconquered towns. Israel did not have a political infrastructure that could facilitate the establishment of such an administrative institution as forced labor or corvée. The main surviving Canaanite enclaves were in the Valley of Jezreel, and along the Phoenician coast. The Asherites gained acceptance among the Phoenicians (Sidonians), apparently as client farmers for a society whose manpower was heavily committed to maritime activities (Judg 1:31–32). No tradition exists about the conquest of Shechem, whose situation may have been like Gezer (Judg 1:19), a Canaanite population living in symbiosis with the Israelites. Jebus-Jerusalem, Gezer and the Amorite towns that resisted the Danites were in the center of the country. Very early traditions reveal that the Ephraimites came into early contact with the indigenous population of the area where the Danites were driven out (1 Chr 7:20–24; Judg 1:35).

The dichotomy between Canaanites on the plains and Israelites in the hills characterizes the narratives throughout the books of Judges and Samuel. This reflects the archaeological settlement patterns of villages in the hills vis-à-vis the town sites on the plains.

## The Judges

The ensuing catalog of tribal heroes contains much geographic material. Some of the details are obscure but wherever they can be understood, they elucidate important aspects of the society and the mentality of this period. There are relatively few "miraculous" elements such as theophanies (Gideon's "call" and Samson's birth narrative are exceptions; they belong to a special genre). The collector/editor has arranged them in what he considered a chronological order. There are no contacts with non-biblical sources that might assist in establishing some dates for these accounts. The sequence of narratives starts in the south and then progresses to the

The Judges According to Their Tribes (12th to 11th Centuries BCE)

center and the north, reflecting the author/editor's Judean orientation.

**Othniel** son of Kenaz (*see* Judg 3:8–11). The first example brought is Caleb's nephew (1 Chr 4:13), Othniel son of Kenaz. He is credited with winning Caleb's daughter Achsah by capturing the town of Debir (Josh 15:15–19; Judg 1:11–15). Othniel is also a clan eponym (1 Chr 27:15).

As a Kenizzite, he represents one of the southern tribes that became joined to Judah. Therefore, it would make sense if the enemy against whom Othniel prevailed also came from the south. The full title, "king of Aram-naharaim" obviously points to North Syria/Mesopotamia, the area of Laban in the ancestral tradition. This would strengthen the connection with the Aramean tribes along the Euphrates. On the other hand, the name Cushan evokes associations with the Midianites (*see* Hab 3:7).

It would make more sense if this particular enemy had posed a threat to the tribal elements in the southern part of the country. His epithet, "rishathaim," literally "doubly evil," derives from the epic tradition and his title, "king of Aram-naharaim," remains enigmatic.

**Ehud** (Judg 3:12–30). Attention now moves north to the tribe of Benjamin where a hero named Ehud son of Gera delivered his people from Transjordanian aggression. The various geographical allusions in the passage (*see* Judg 3:12–15), e.g. Gilgal and the hill country of Ephraim strongly suggest that the City of Palms is, in fact, Jericho (e.g. *see* Deut 34:3; 2 Chr 28:15). A misunderstanding of Deuteronomy 34:3 evidently led to the talmudic application of the term "City of Palms," to Zoar (m. *Yebam.* 16:7).

What is being depicted here is evidently an act of extortion on the part of combined tribal elements from across the Jordan. They were forcing the residents of the central hill country (and perhaps from the central western Jordan Valley) to pay "protection" in the form of produce. Cisjordan enjoyed a higher average rainfall and was usually more productive than Transjordan so the rough tribes on the eastern side oppressed the villagers on the west.

The drama of the assassination story is built of the play on Ehud's tribe (Benjamin, "son of the right hand") and his ambidextrous ability to hide a weapon on his right thigh. Additional folk humor is injected by the allusion to Eglon's toilet. When Ehud had escaped from the Moabite enclave, he fled past the cult site at Gilgal to *hass$^{ec}$îrāṭāh* which is not an attested place name but is best understood as a topographical feature with the meaning "the woody hills." Ehud rallied support from his own tribal area (*see* Judg 3:27).

The "hill country of Ephraim" is a generic geographical term for the entire block of hills that included the territory of Benjamin, Ephraim and Manasseh. However, it seems likely that the participants in this action would have been from Ehud's own tribe. By blocking the fords across the Jordan, the Israelite warriors trapped many of their enemies and brought an end to their intervention in Cisjordan.

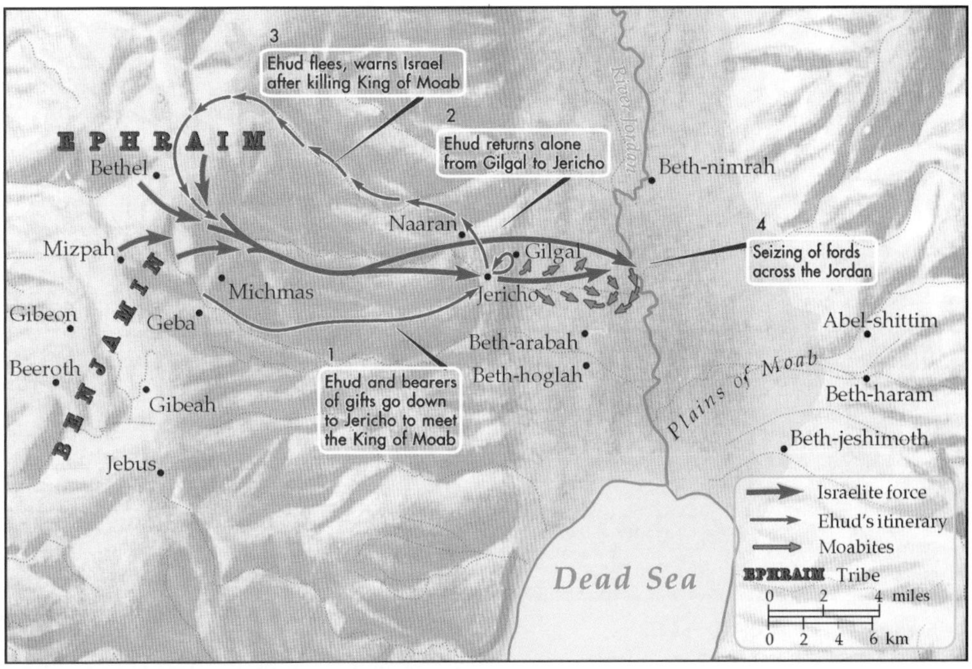

THE CONFLICT OF EHUD (12$^{th}$ TO 11$^{th}$ CENTURIES BCE)

**Shamgar** son of Anath (Judg 3:31). The reference to this personage seems intrusive in the sequence of hero stories. The venue of his activity is not given. The name of possibly Hurrian origin and the epithet "son of Anath" just might indicate membership in a warrior guild or clan bearing the name of the warrior/huntress goddess of North West Semitic tradition (*see* Judg 3:31, 5:6).

Because of the mention alongside Jael, it has also been suggested that Shamgar's activity represented conflict with the Sea Peoples' enclave in the north. However, the reference to Philistines and an oxgoad (anticipating that theme in the Samson story) plus the place in the series (after Othniel) indicate that a southern venue must be sought. The detailed legend was either unavailable to the editor of Judges or else it was so fraught with "heretical" features that he preferred to skip over it. The hero was just too well known to be ignored altogether. None of these conjectures can be substantiated and the role of Shamgar remains a mystery.

**Deborah and Barak** (Josh 12:19–23; Judg 4–5). The link to the next pericope lies in the location of the prophetess Deborah (*see* Judg 4:4–5). Her influence was said to be more widespread so that she could intervene in the emergency being faced by the tribes living in Galilee (*see* Judg 4:2–3).

Jabin, it will be remembered, is the ruler of Hazor in the conquest narrative pertaining to the upper Galilean "waters of Maron" (LXX Josh 11:5, 11:7). There it is stated that Hazor was burned with fire and its king slain (Josh 11:10–11). Various theories have been offered to explain the anomaly. Some would excise the reference to Jabin from the present text; another would simply reverse the order of the narratives, placing Joshua 11 later than Judges 4–5. In any case, both texts are from the northern repertoire of conflict narratives, the former about Upper and the latter about Lower Galilee. It is barely credible that the tradition of Hazor's seniority as "head of all those kingdoms" is a memory deriving from the Middle Bronze Age. At the same time, excavations have shown that Late Bronze Hazor did not survive into the twelfth century BCE. The origin of the central role of Hazor probably is a tradition learned during the early arrival of tribes, known later as Naphtali (from the Lebanese Beqa$^{c}$; from the Syrian Desert?) that settled in the mountain massif of Jebel Jarmaq, considerably earlier than the tribal penetrations in the central and southern hill-country areas.

This conflict is enshrined not only in a prose version (Judg 4) but also in a poem (Judg 5) formulated in a most archaic language. The prose text concentrates on the details of how the conflict played out, including numerous key geographical points that require explication. The poetic version deals with the deteriorating social situation that led to the confrontation and to the enthusiasm or indifference of the respective tribes. But it also gives some complimentary details about the geography and course of the conflict.

First, it is necessary to follow the course of the prose narrative in Judges chapter 4.

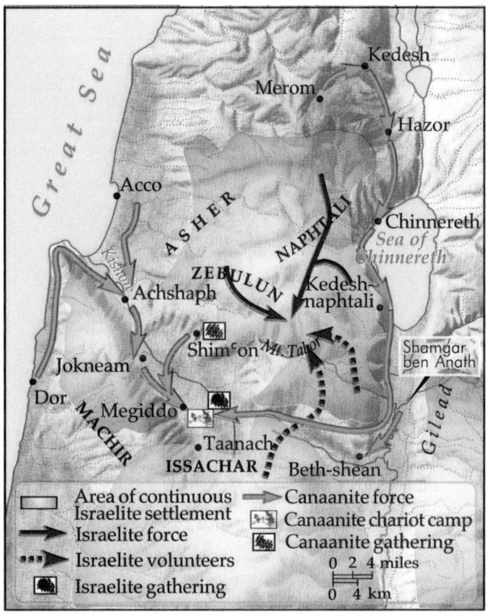


**The War of Deborah—The Deployment of Forces**

The oppressor was the ruler of Hazor and his army commander, Sisera. From Judges 4:2–8 cited above, it is learned that Sisera dwelt in **Harosheth-ha-goiim**. This is the expansive plain east of Megiddo, a well-known area for assembling troops down through the ages.

The initiative for the action against Sisera originated with the prophetess Deborah (*see* Judg 4:6–7). One of the geographical problems is the location of Kedesh-naphtali, the home of Barak (Judg 4:6). The assumption that combat was staged on the side of the valley near Taanach and Megiddo suggested an identification with Tell Abū Qudeis (Tel Qedesh), a small mound 2.5 miles (4 km) north of Taanach on the plain. However, it was clear from the prose narrative that the Kedesh in Judges 4:11 must be east of Mount Tabor, since it is associated with the Oak in Zaanannim, which itself must be on the border between Naphtali and Issachar between Mount Tabor and the Jordan Valley (Josh 19:33) near the lower Galilean Adami-nekeb (Kh. et-Tell ed-Dâmiyeh) and Jabneel (Tell en-Naʿam = Tel Yinʿam). A suitable archaeological and geographical location for Kedesh-naphtali is thus Khirbet Qedîsh (Ḫ. Qedesh) on the slope above the Sea of Chinnereth on the western side (*see* Judg 4:9b–11).

The battle itself is described in brief in Judges 4:12–16. When Deborah gave the command to charge, the Israelite warriors rushed down the mountain slope, gathering speed and adrenaline as they went. Something happened to the chariotry and foot troops of the Canaanites and they broke into a frantic retreat back toward their campground at Harosheth-ha-goiim. What made them break ranks and flee? The answer is supplied by a passage in the poem (*see* Judg 5:4–5).

As in the Exodus traditions, the Edom here is most likely on the western side of the Arabah which is supported by its parallelism with Mount Sinai. The approach of YHWH is expressed by the beginning of rain. Anyone who has seen the Kishon during a downpour will understand what happened to the chariots of Sisera. The plain turned into a massive flood of muddy water. The chariots sank in the quagmire and the crews dismounted and fled. The Israelite foot troops used their momentum to pursue the fleeing Canaanites, most likely along the geological dike from modern Tel Adashim toward the present-day Megiddo junction. Deborah had read the weather correctly.

Against this background, a key passage in the poem becomes brilliantly intelligible (*see* Judg 5:19–21a). In the Masoretic verse division, "At **Taanach** on the waters of **Megiddo**" is linked with the fighting by the kings of Canaan and the collection of spoil is associated with the geographical area. This is in line with the age-old tradition of military encampments at that spot. "**Taanach** on the waters of **Megiddo**" is the poetic synonym of the prose Harosheth-ha-goiim. The poem concludes with an ironic allusion to the intended division of spoil (Judg 5:30) that did not take place because of the resounding defeat.

The death of Sisera, who had sought refuge at the holy shrine maintained by Heber and Jael, is the classic story of a heroic woman who recognized that the death of a tyrant took precedence over the usual rules of sanctuary and hospitality (Judg 4:17–22).

The epitaph to this story, depicting the gradual defeat of Jabin, king of Hazor (Judg 4:23–24), shows, if nothing else, that this battle tradition was independent from that concerning the "Battle of the Waters of Merom" (Josh 11:1–15).

It remains to note some observations about the praises and rebukes in the poem concerning those tribes that did or did not take part in the battle. The prose narrative credits only Zebulun and Naphtali while the poem (Judg 5:14–15a) adds some from Ephraim, Benjamin, and Machir (prior to the consolidation of Manasseh). Others who did not take part were Reuben, Gilead (not yet subsumed under Gad), Dan and Asher. The first two, especially Reuben, were chided for not leaving their flocks to join the battle. Dan and Asher are derided for their connections with the Phoenician maritime society. Concerning Asher, this was clear from Judges 1:31–32 that they had found a niche in the coastal social regime. The allusion to Dan, however, has led to much speculation. The theory that the Danites were originally Danunians of the Sea Peoples who had settled at Joppa has been summarily dealt with in the preceding chapter. The passage here says: "And as for Dan, why does he abide in ships?" (Judg 5:17). The cryptic reference must be understood in terms of the Danite location at the former Laish. When they went to spy it out they had found:

> . . . the people who were in it living in security, after the manner of the Sidonians, quiet and secure; for there was no ruler disputing (with them) in the land, and they were far from the Sidonians and had no communication with **anyone**. (Judg 18:7)

The Septuagint had read "Aram" in this place: "and they had no affair with Syria," but not in the later passage when the Danites arrive *en masse* (*see* Judg 18:27b–28). The Danites had attacked an isolated people and took their city. Later they rebuilt the place. Now these people with their affinity to the Sidonians (Phoenicians) were independent but their agricultural abundance, extolled in the narrative (Judg 18:10), could have been sold to the Sidonians on the coast. As is now well known, there was a mountain route connecting Banias, at the foot of Mount Hermon, with Tyre (the true "Way of the Sea").

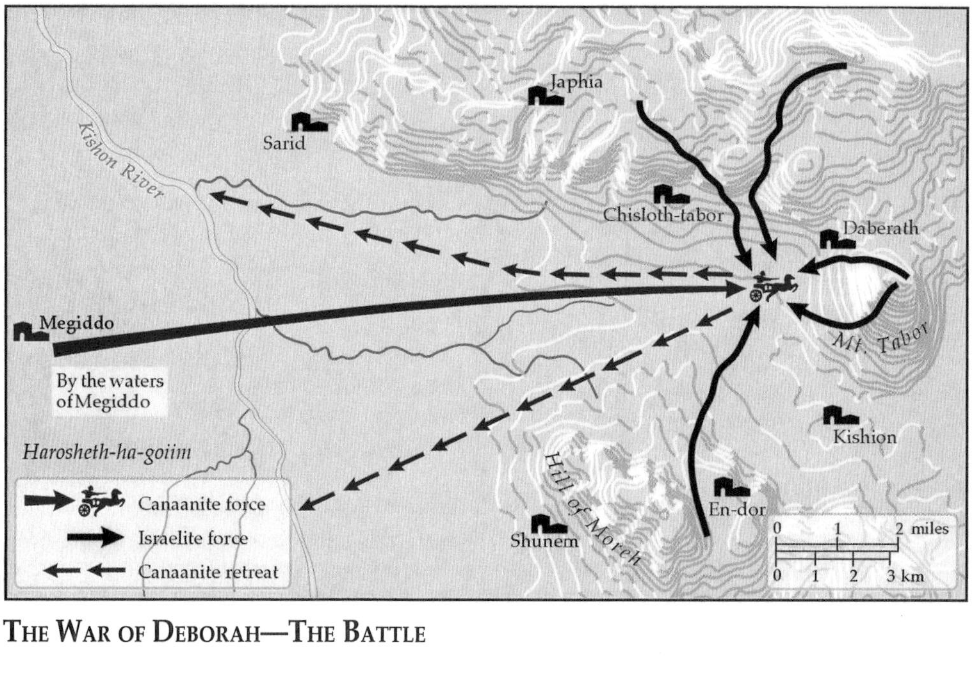


**The War of Deborah—The Battle**

When the Danites had established their new town, called Dan, they must have used the route to Sidon to sell their produce and by that means, their young men became enamored with the maritime society they found there and to which they became suppliers. They would have chosen not to jeopardize their lucrative commercial links with Phoenicia and thus did not come to the aid of Barak. The irony in their rebuke by the Song of Deborah takes on a realistic flavor in this light.

Meroz (Judg 5:23) is evidently a settlement, but its identity remains a mystery. It might have been a Canaanite or related enclave ostensibly allied with Israel.

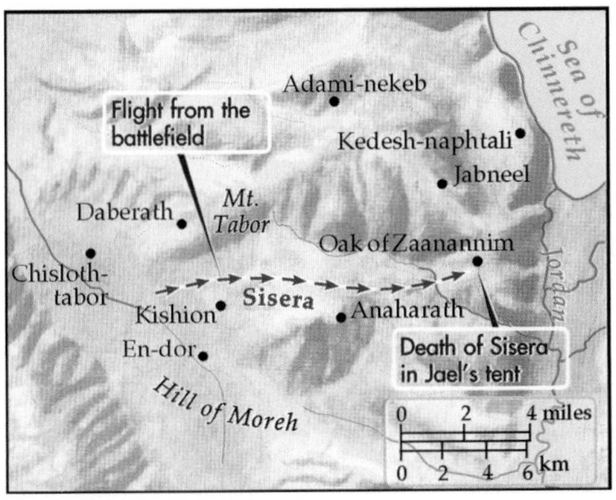


**The Death of Sisera**

**Gideon** (Judg 6–8; Ps 83:10–11). Three chapters are devoted to the career of a hero from the central hills of Ephraim, from the clan of Abiezer, a branch of the tribe of Manasseh. The core of the narrative has to do with a known phenomenon: the oppression of the agricultural villagers by the camel nomads of the desert. The raiders would come seasonally to plunder the crops collected in the harvest. The desert incursions may have been made possible by the weakening of the Canaanite forces in the area due to the disaster of Sisera's defeat. This same

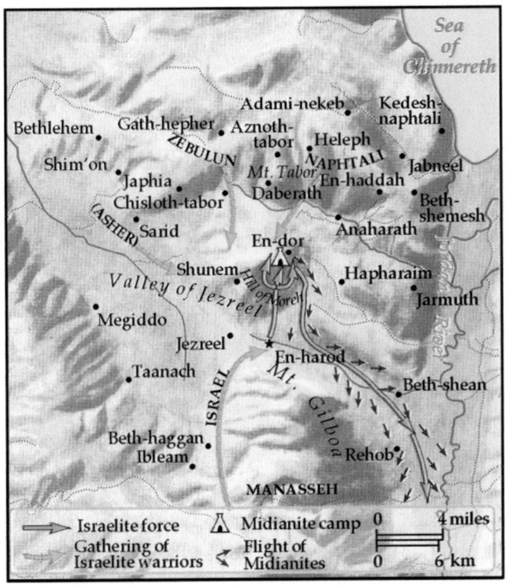


**The War of Gideon**
**(12th to 11th Centuries BCE)**

situation prevailed in the nineteenth century when Ottoman rule from Damascus was largely ineffective. There are many witnesses to the domination of the Lower Galilee and the Jordan Valley by aggressive Bedouin tribes (*see* Judg 6:1–5).

The reference to the Gaza area is linked to the Amalekites who must have invaded the Negeb from the south. The "sons of the east" indicates that there were other nomadic elements on the desert fringe as well as the Midianites.

The mantel of deliverance falls on a youth from the Abiezer clan, Gideon, whose other name was Jerubbaal (which was probably the original name in the war narrative, cf. Judg 7:1). The need for deliverance from the nomads is interwoven with another genre, viz. the conflict of Yahwism with Baalism so crucial to the Deuteronomistic point of view. The literary composition of the entire Gideon narrative is complex and cannot be dealt with here. Suffice it to say that Gideon's hometown, Ophrah, was the center of a cultic installation where pre-monarchial Baal elements were intertwined with Yahwism. This monarchial version must go to great lengths to make it a deliverance vouchsafed by YHWH as a reward for turning away from Baalism. The location of this Ophrah has to be somewhere in Mount Ephraim (as discussed with relation to Jotham, *infra*).

The highly embellished narrative about the assembling of the Israelite warriors takes place at "the spring of Harod," traditionally, the spring that flows today at ᶜAin Jalûd on the opposite side of the valley from the enemy encampments (*see* Judg 7:1).

A poetic allusion to the battle indicates that the Midianites were mainly to the north of the Hill of Moreh near En-dor (*see* Ps 83: 10–11 [Eng. 9–10]).

The reference to the slaughter of Gideon's brothers at Tabor (Judg 8:18–19) is commensurate with the location of the Midianite camp north of the Hill of Moreh. Thus, the nomads would not have seen the assembly of the village farmers at the spring. After the surprise night attack, the nomads

> ... fled as far as **Beth-shittah** toward **Zererah**, as far as the edge of **Abel-meholah**, by **Tabbath**.
> (Judg 7:22b)

Warriors from Naphtali, Asher and Manasseh joined in the pursuit (Judg 7: 23) and the Ephraimites were urged to seize the fords across the Jordan (Judg 7:24) and they managed to capture two of the Midianite leaders, Oreb and Zeeb (Judg 7: 25). Gideon pursued the main force of the enemy eastward beyond Nobah (location unknown) and Jogbehah (Jubeihât), 15 miles (24 km) southeast of Penuel. Karkor (Judg 8:10) should be in the Wâdī Sirḥân in the northern Ḥejâz, 150 miles (93 km) from Jubeihât and 50 miles (31 km) southeast of Azraq.

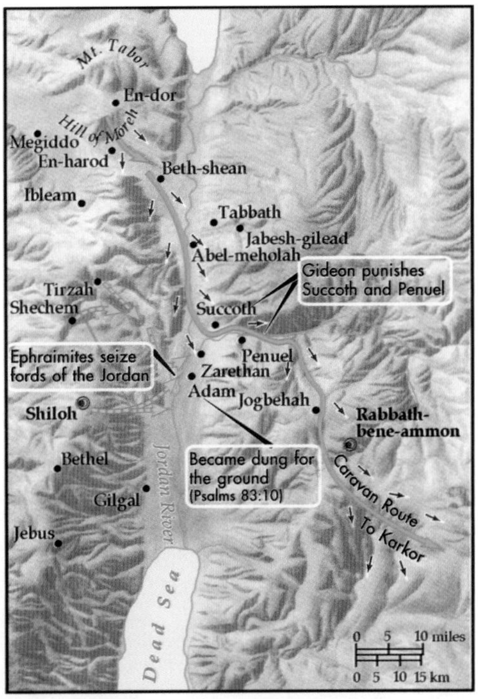


**The Pursuit of the Midianites**
**(12th to 11th Centuries BCE)**

The punishment of the elders of Succoth (Deir ᶜAllah) and Penuel (Tell edh-Dhahab esh-Sharqī) is illustrative of the age of violence and enmity that prevailed (Judg 8: 5–9, 8:13–16).

Gideon is said to have donated an ephod to the cult center at his hometown of Ophrah (Judg 8:27). Much of the Gideon narrative was probably from the oral legacy of that shrine.

**Abimelech** (Judg 8:30–9:57). There follows the story of Abimelech, the son of Gideon by a Shechemite woman. The narrative centers

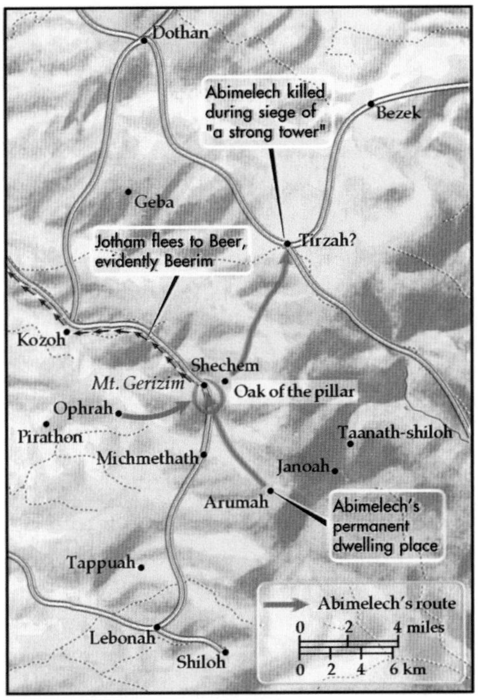


**The Kingdom of Abimelech**
**(12th to 11th Centuries BCE)**

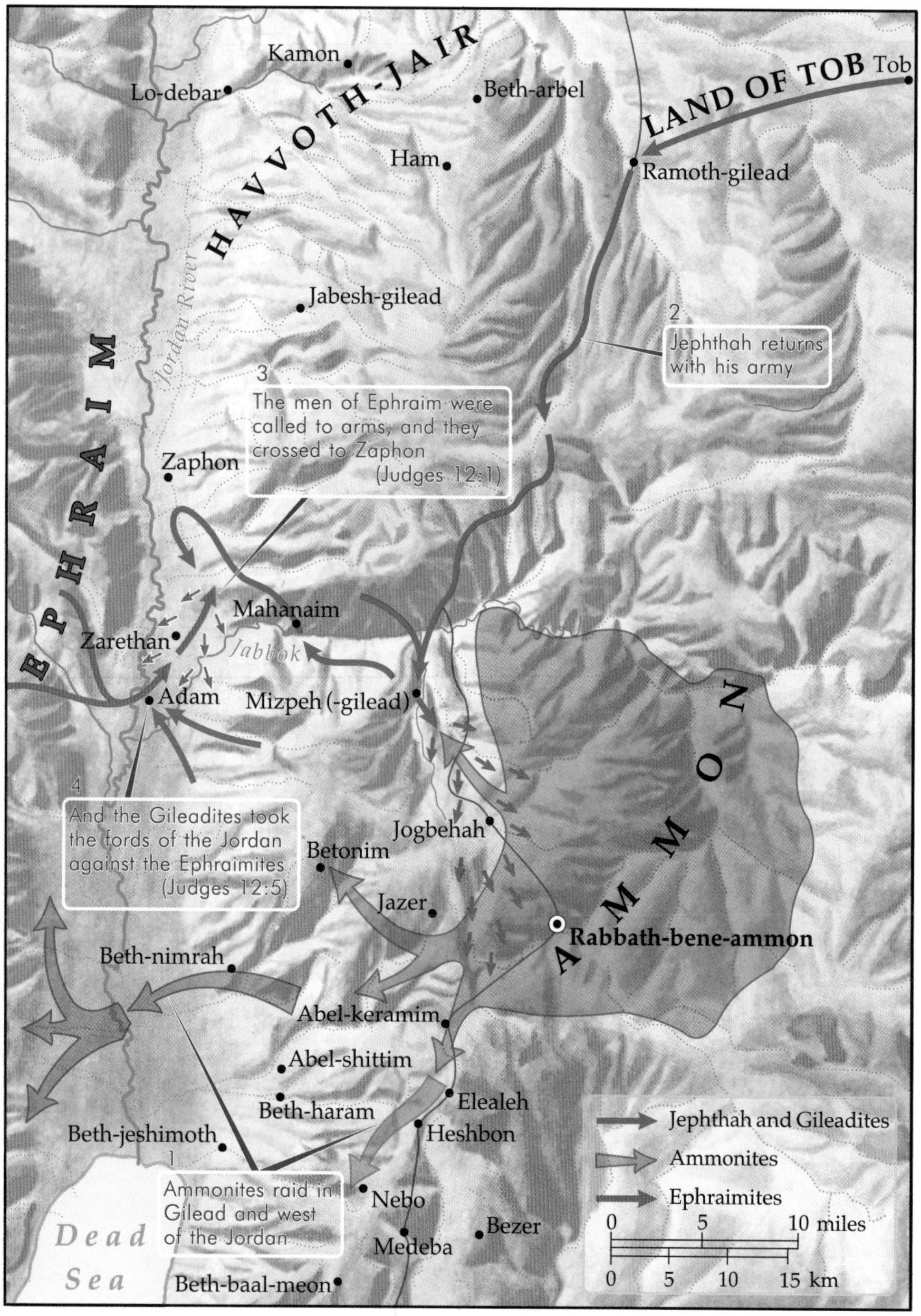


**THE WAR OF JEPHTHAH (END OF 12TH TO 11TH CENTURIES BCE)**

around Shechem and its surrounding hinterland. Abimelech persuaded the elders of Shechem to make him their king, in the manner of the Canaanite city rulers. He then proceeded to slaughter his siblings, the seventy sons of Gideon. Abimelech still maintained his home base at Arumah (Kh. el-ʿUrmah).

Abimelech exercised his position of power by the support of a band of ruffians. Abimelech himself had to fight another attempt by a rival gang leader (Judg 9:23–49). Ultimately Abimelech destroyed the city of Shechem and slew its leaders. He himself was killed during the siege of another town, Thebez. The identification of Thebez with Tubas is not attractive phonetically. Perhaps Thebez is an early corruption of Tirzah.

The story of Jotham (Judg 9:7–21), the surviving son of Gideon, adds to the impression that Ophrah must be in the Manassite area of the Samarian Hills somewhere southwest of Mount Gerizim. Khirbet ʿAwfar, about 3.7 miles (6 km) southwest of Shechem, has been suggested.

**More Hero Stories** (Judg 10:1–5). There follow allusions to two other heroes whose stories would have been of exceptional interest. But alas, the editor/author of Judges did not see fit to include them. Of course, they may not have been fully at his disposal (*see* Judg 10:1).

Tola was from Issachar, a tribe that might have lost its identity but for the reorganization during the early monarchy. But he is found living in Mount Ephraim in a place the name of which might be related to Shemer, a leading eponym of Manasseh (1 Kgs 16:24).

The famous Jair, eponym from the tribe of Manasseh (Num 32:41), whose clan occupied a large section of Gilead, gave his name to "thirty" settlements in Argob in Bashan (Deut 3:14). No exploits are described but he is listed as one of the heroes (*see* Judg 10:3–5). He is not credited here with any special military exploit. His burial place is not located with any certainty.

**Jephthah** (Judg 10:6–12:7). After Jair, attention is still focused on Transjordan with the legend of Jephthah, a hero whose life reflects a number of themes from this type of literature, not only in the Levant but in the eastern Mediterranean in general. He is of noble lineage through his father but a supposed outcast because his mother was a harlot. When he is ousted by his siblings, he gathers a band of outlaw warriors and establishes himself at Tob, identified with eṭ-Ṭaiybeh southeast of Edrei (Derʿā). The place was known from the city list of Thutmose III and in the Amarna letters. Sociologically, it can be said that Jephthah and his militia had become like the Late Bronze Age *ʿapîru* men.

The Jephthah story is prefaced by a long homily of dialogue with YHWH about the people's apostasy (Judg 10:6–16). Seven foreign gods have detracted Israel from their national deity, YHWH. As a result Israel was subjected successively to seven neighboring peoples until they cried out to YHWH for relief. The new oppressors are the Ammonites in Transjordan while the Philistines are mentioned as well, looking forward to the Samson cycle to follow (*see* Judg 10:7–9).

It is surely not accidental that the East Mediterranean features of the Jephthah and the Samson narratives come at a time when Philistine influence is recorded. This is the story of an outcast in spite of his worthy lineage (descendant of Gilead) who leads the people in victory but tragically sacrifices his own daughter as the result of a hasty, ill-advised vow. He also slaughtered members of the Ephraimite tribe as the result of an inter-tribal dispute (*see* Judg 10:17–18).

As for this Mizpah (Judg 10:17), the location is uncertain but surely to be sought south of the Jabbok, in the vicinity of Jebel Jelʿad and Khirbet Jelʿad. It is probably to be equated with Ramath-mizpeh (Josh 13:26). The leaders of Gilead needed someone to start the fighting against the Ammonites. That these Israelites are called "Gileadites" indicates a period prior to the tribal reorganization which assigned the area to Manasseh, north of the Jabbok, and Gad, south of the Jabbok.

The war narrative is interrupted by a lengthy dialogue between Jephthah and the

Ammonites which expresses the standard Israelite view about the sequence of historical events that led to Israelite claims in Transjordan (Judg 11:12–28).

When the battle was joined it ranged over an extensive area, evidently to the west of the Ammonite territory (*see* Judg 11:32–33). This Aroer (Judg 11:33) must be distinguished from the Aroer on the Arnon. It was mentioned in Joshua 13:25 in the presumed tribal territory of Gad.

So this Aroer was "before" Rabbah (modern Amman) and formed part of the boundary between the Israelite tribe of Gad's territory and Ammonite country. As for Abel-keramim, it is probably the Abila in Eusebius' *Onomasticon* (32:14–16), six milestones from Philadelphia (Rabbath-bene-ammon, modern Amman). Various identifications have been proposed: Nāᶜûr, Khirbet es-Sûq, Kôm Yājûz, and Saḥâb, deduced from early Islamic tradition about a battle in 634 CE that was fought between "Âbil, Zîzāᵓ, and Qasṭal." Saḥâb was a walled city in the Late Bronze Age, and extensively occupied during the Iron Age. Minnith is equated by Eusebius (*Onom.* 132:1–2) with a certain Maanith, four milestones from Esbus (Heshbon) as one goes to Philadelphia (Amman); Umm el-Basaṭîn is a likely candidate.

The dispute with the Ephraimites took place at Zaphon, a town in the Jordan Valley (*see* Josh 13:27a). There are two main candidates for identification with Zaphon, Tell Mezâr and Tell es-Saᶜīdîyeh. The Ephraimites seem to have come too late to be of any assistance in the conflict with the Ammonites but were jealous of not sharing in the spoil.

The Hebrew text says that Jephthah was buried "in the cities of Gilead" (Judg 12:7), but the Septuagint says, "in his city, Gilead," while there is also textual evidence for Zaphon.

*Clay figurine of a horseman from an Ammonite tomb, Rabbath-bene-ammon (modern Amman).*

**Three "Minor" Judges**. The stories about these heroes may have been just as interesting as those recounted at length. Either the author/editor did not have them or he suppressed them because they contained pre-monarchial material unacceptable to him for religious reasons. From a literary and geographical point of view, we are the losers (*see* Judg 12:8–10).

The first is the story of a clan leader, Ibzan, who is surely from the Galilean Bethlehem (Josh 19:15; Beit Laḥm) of the tribe of Zebulun. He may have been an example of too close relations with the neighboring Phoenicians; therefore, his other anecdotes are suppressed.

The second hero was Elon, also from Zebulun (Judg 12:11–12). Nothing is recorded about him except his burial place. The Hebrew text has "Aijalon," but the Septuagint has "Ailim" and the original was more likely "Elon," which was a major clan in the tribe of Zebulun (Num 26:26).

The third was Abdon from Pirathon (Farᶜatā) in the territory of Ephraim. Only his status as patriarch of a great clan is mentioned, followed by his place of burial, "at Pirathon in the land of Ephraim, in the hill country of the Amalekites" (Judg 12:15). Why a hill region in the land of Ephraim was called "Amalekite" is unknown.

**Samson** (Judg 13–16). The Samson cycle of heroic legends concludes the circle of narratives about charismatic leaders in the pre-monarchic period. It is replete with all the features of a divinely chosen deliverer, e.g. a miraculous birth announcement, a conception by a previously barren woman, Nazarite restrictions on his mother during the pregnancy and on the child after his birth, imbuement with the divine spirit in times of crisis. Above all, there are amazing, single-handed victories in combat, one with the "jawbone of an ass," reminiscent of the enigmatic exploits of Shamgar the son of Anath who used an oxgoad (Judg 3:31).

The protagonists are Samson and the Philistines, in a period after which the latter had thoroughly established themselves as the dominant force in the southern coastal area (*see* Judg 14:4b).

This supremacy entailed the extortion of agricultural produce from the Judean villages, no doubt especially in the Shephelah and the western hills. Although the hero and his family are Danites, they must represent a remnant of that tribe that had not migrated north (*see* Judg 13:2a).

Zorah (Kh. Ṣarᶜah = Tel Ẕorᶜa) is located on the ridge bounding the Sorek stream on the north, opposite Beth-shemesh, which is on the south side of the wadi.

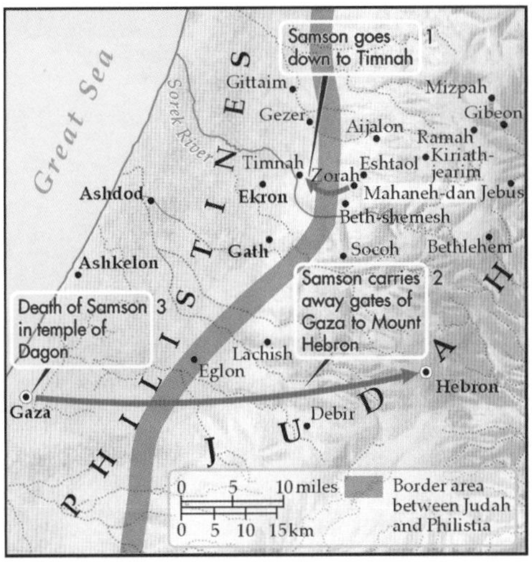


**Judah and Philistia in the Days of Samson (Early 11th Century BCE)**

The venue for the hero's inspired youth is said to be:

. . . in **Mahaneh-dan**, between **Zorah** and **Eshtaol**. (Judg 13:25b)

Mahaneh-dan appears also in Judges 18:5 where it denotes a camping ground of the Danites on their migration north; it was west of Kiriath-jearim. It seems to be a folk epithet for places associated with the tribe of Dan within the territory of Judah. Eshtaol is evidently to be located at Khirbet Deir Shubeib beside the village of Ishwaᶜ, which may preserve a distorted echo of the ancient name, on a hill east of the ridge of Zorah. Eshtaol is an archaic name built on the infinitive of a reflexive verb stem that was no longer in use in biblical Hebrew.

The first account of the conflict (Judg 14) takes place in a clear geographical matrix. It happened in the Sorek Valley (Wâdī eṣ-Ṣarâr), a relatively broad valley in the Shephelah some 13 miles (21 km) west of Jerusalem. Actually, it is only mentioned in Judges 16:4 regarding Samson's more famous paramour, Delilah. If it were not for Eusebius (*Onom.* 160:2–4), we would not know that the Sorek was near Zorah whence Samson came. It is the western extension of the system which starts in Wâdī Beit Ḥanînah and includes the Rephaim and Chesalon valleys that join the Sorek to drain a 10-mile (16-km) section of the watershed

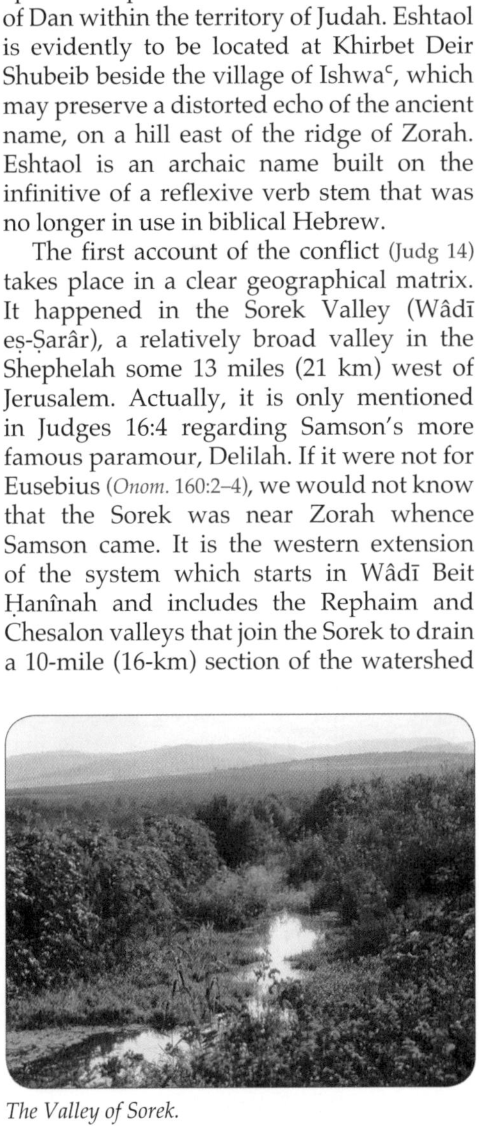

*The Valley of Sorek.*

*Aerial view, looking south, of Tel Batash, identified with biblical Timnah.*

from Ramah to Bethlehem. These wadis drop about 2,000 feet (610 m) through the Judean mountains, cutting deep V-shaped canyons into the hard limestone as they flow from east to west. As the Sorek reaches the softer limestone and chalk of the Shephelah, the valley broadens out and alluvial soil is deposited, making a rich fertile valley (*see* Judg 14:1).

Zorah was on top of the ridge; Timnah was below in the valley. Thus the statement is correct that Samson "went down." The location of Timnah is deduced from Joshua 15:10–11, the putative northern border of Judah.

Given the measurable distances between most points along this border and the fact that Timnah is found in the sequence—Chesalon (Keslā=Kesalon), Beth-shemesh (Tell er-Rumeileh=Tel Bet Shemesh) on the east and Ekron (Kh. el-Muqanna$^{c}$=Tel Miqne) on the west—the logical candidate is Tell el-Baṭâshī (Tel Baṭash), located about equidistant from Beth-shemesh and Ekron. Archaeologically, it has all the requisite remains.

His inspired act of vengeance took him as far as Ashkelon (Judg 14:19). But his withdrawal to the "cleft of the rock of Etam" (Judg 15:8) is something of a mystery. Is it near the Etam (Kh. el-Khôkh) east of the watershed south of Bethlehem (2 Chr 11:6; Josh 15:59a LXX) or the Etam that belonged to the Simeonites (1 Chr 4:32) which must have been either in the southern Shephelah or the very northern side of the Negeb?

The location of a placed called Lehi, where the Philistines formed a battle line with the view of capturing Samson (Judg 15:9), is not known though suggestions have been made, but none carry conviction. There must be some folkloristic connection with Samson's slaying of a host of Philistines with the jawbone of an ass (*see* Judg 15:15–16).

Another of his superman-like escapades has the only oblique allusion to the road from Gaza to Hebron (*see* Judg 16:3). Appropriately, Samson was buried "between Zorah and Eshtaol in the tomb of Manoah his father" (Judg 16:31).

**Concluding Stories** (Judg 17–21). The collection called the Book of Judges is concluded by two narratives about events which must have occurred chronologically at an early stage in the period. Both of them take place in the "hill country of Ephraim" which in this case refers to the territory of Benjamin (at least in the second story and most likely in the first also). Both narratives have to do with members of the tribe of Levi and both of the Levites have connections with Bethlehem. This early connection between Levites and David's home town may have something to do with the special status and function of the Levites during the newly established monarchy later on.

***The Danite Migration.*** The account begins with a family in the Ephraimite hill country which had enough silver to make expensive cult objects, viz. "a graven image and a molten image" (Judg 17:4). The unnamed matriarch seems to have been the head of the family; her eldest son was Micah (*see* Judg 17:7–8). The young Levite was hired because of his cultic skills, to officiate at the family shrine on the estate of Micah and his mother.

At this juncture, the scouts sent out by the Danites to find a more suitable venue get an oracle from the same Levite and as a result, they reconnoitered Laish (Judg 18:2–10), at the foot of Mount Hermon. The Danite fighting force came to the hill country on their way north. It may be significant that they were unable to travel by the coastal highway, doubtless because it was controlled by the Canaanite cities that would threaten any such tribal movement in their vicinity (*see* Judg 18:12; cf. Judg 5:6).

The Danite scouts, remembering the favorable oracle from the Levite, "recruit" him for the tribe and confiscate the cultic paraphernalia from Micah's shrine (Judg 18:15–20). This episode was meant to explain the origin of the northern cult center at Dan. One is inclined to accept the Septuagint version ascribing the priests' family connection to Moses. The change to Manasseh looks like another late Hellenistic (or Herodian) emendation to satisfy pharisaic sensibilities (*see* Judg 18:30–31).

***The Outrage at Gibeah of Benjamin.*** The final pericope has to do with Gibeah in Benjamin. Its name appears in various formulations, e.g. "the Gibeah" (Judg 19:13), "Gibeah which belongs to Benjamin" (Judg 19:14), "Gibeah of Benjamin" (1 Sam 13:2), "Gibeah of the Benjaminites" (2 Sam 23:29), "Gibeah of Saul" (1 Sam 11:4, 15:34; Isa 10:29), "Gibeath Elohim (of God)" (1 Sam 10:5; but LXX "the high place/hill of God").

In the official tribal inheritance of

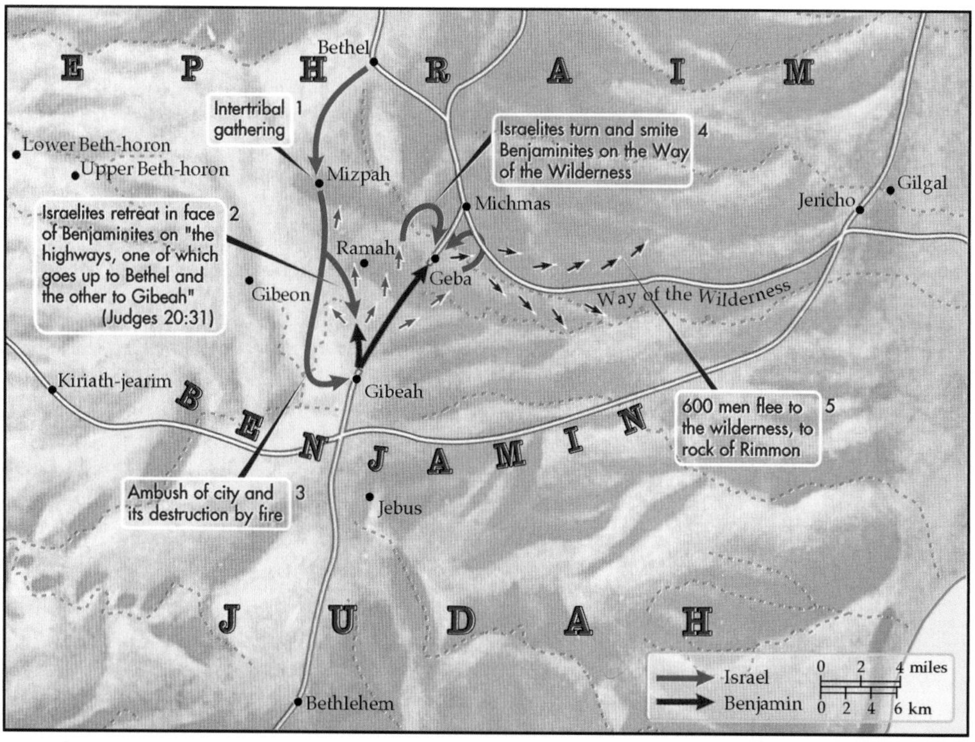


**The Story of the Concubine at Gibeah (12th to 11th Centuries BCE)**

Benjamin as recognized in biblical sources (e.g. Josh 18:11–28) three towns with similar names are known: Gibeon (el-Jîb), Geba (Jeba$^{c}$) and Gibeah. In the various biblical pericopes there may have been a certain degree of confusion between these three, especially when the Septuagint is taken into account. In any case, the identification with Tell el-Fûl, on the grounds that the present narrative requires a town on the watershed road north of Jerusalem, still stands as the best solution.

The Bethlehem connection supports the assumption that both of these final pericopes had their origins in that town (*see* Judg 19:1). Just what is intended by the "farthest limit" of Mount Ephraim is not clarified. Given the fact that Mount Ephraim included all the hill region from Benjamin to Manasseh (at least as far as Shechem, 1 Kgs 12:15), the Levite's venue may have been far to the north. At any rate, it was much too far to reach before sundown if one was opposite Jebus (Jerusalem) on the watershed road.

After finally managing to leave Bethlehem with his concubine, his servant and his two pack animals, they arrived late on the watershed road opposite Jebus (*see* Judg 19:10–13). Of course, Jebus-Jerusalem was located on the southern extension of a ridge that ran southeast from the watershed and was bounded on its eastern side by the Kidron Valley and on the west by another valley (the Tyropoeon which had been filled up by Herodian times). An adjacent valley (today Mamilla) curved around to the southern end of the Jebusite ridge (the Valley of the Sons of Hinnom; Josh 15:8). The Levite and his entourage were on the watershed road that led from Bethlehem, passing below Ramat Raḥel (probably Beth-haccerem) and running along the ridge on which the Montefiore windmill and the King David Hotel are situated today.

Their fateful decision to continue northward toward an Israelite settlement would logically bring them to a place that could be reached before sundown. El-Jîb and Jeba$^{c}$ were surely too far away and Ramah (er-Râm) was evidently an extreme limit. So Tell el-Fûl is the most likely place for the site of Gibeah.

The first major thrust of the story is the infamous behavior of the men of Gibeah, likened to that of the legendary Sodom and Gomorrah. The criminals had sought to rape the male visitors but finally contented themselves with the concubine (Judg 19:22–25). The ignoble Levite used her body parts to call together the forces of Israel.

The present version of the story credits a unified Israel (twelve body parts had been sent out) "from Dan to Beer-sheba" (Judg 20:1) that assembled at Mizpah. The location of Mizpah at Tell en-Naṣbeh is still the most likely (especially in view of 1 Kgs 15:22). First Mizpah and then Bethel (Judg 20:18, 20:26, 21:2–4) figure in the narrative as

*Photograph and drawing of a fragment of a cultic stand from Shiloh, Iron I.*

cultic centers where oaths can be taken and where oracles can be sought. The officiating priest was said to be Phinehas the son of Eleazar, Aaron's son (Judg 20:28); so the story is ostensibly dated to the first generation of the conquest.

The conduct of the battle and the tactic of the feigned retreat and ambush (Judg 20:18–44) must have been a common theme and may even have been a common practice in the local conflicts of that time. The "rock of Rimmon" (Judg 20:45–47; cf. also 1 Sam 14:2) must have been a prominent feature east (toward the wilderness/steppe) of Gibeah. It could hardly be the village of Rammûn, 5.5 miles (9 km) northeast of Jeba$^{c}$. It was once proposed that the "pomegranate (= *rimmon*) tree" might have stood near the el-Jaiʾā cave in the Wâdī eṣ-Ṣuweinît, 1.2 miles (2 km) east of Jeba$^{c}$. The cave itself, some 98 feet (30 m) high, pitted on the inside with hundreds of small caves and holes (thus resembling a split pomegranate), would be a more likely candidate for the Rock of Rimmon. At least it would have made an ideal refuge for besieged warriors.

The theme of preventing a tribe from being entirely wiped out is reflected in the brutal measures taken to provide wives for the surviving Benjaminite warriors. The city of Jabesh-gilead is ravaged for not taking part in the general muster and their virgins are spared and given to the Benjaminites (Judg 21:8–15). Thus was formed a tie between that Transjordanian town and Gibeah of Benjamin (and of Saul) which bears fruit later on. The second act, kidnapping women from Shiloh, provides one of the rare examples of specific geographical description (*see* Judg 21:19).

Shiloh (Kh. Seilûn) is some short distance east of the main road. Soon after passing the gentle valley that leads from the foot of the tel to the highway, one comes to the descent towards Lebonah (el-Lubbân or Lubbân esh-Sherqîyeh).

The chaos and low moral state of life among the newly settled tribes and clans is condensed in this narrative. The author, writing from the vantage point of the monarchy, has a vision of a twelve-tribe Israel with acknowledged cult centers and priesthood and a primitive "ethic" of oaths, covenants and a sense of "brotherhood" among the tribes, all this in spite of bloody warfare and depraved violation of the accepted rules of hospitality (*see* Judg 21:25).

Such a view of the pre-monarchial society, though colored by later preconceptions, preserves a number of features that can be trusted as reliable:

1. The tribal settlements are almost entirely in the hills; hostile elements dwell on the plains.
2. There is no central leadership despite the generalizations in the editorial summaries linking the respective stories; each hero actually operates in a limited sphere with a particular number of tribal elements (Barak and Gideon have the widest believable following).
3. The hostile actions are conducted by the able-bodied warriors from the respective villages; there is no standing army.
4. The Israelites are by now engaged not only in pastoralism but also in agriculture even though they are mostly confined to the hill country; this includes vineyards as well as fields of grain.
5. This age of heroes is one of violence and enmity. The "spirit of YHWH" can inspire a warrior to slaughter massive numbers of enemy troops. All of these elements, and the tendentious nature of the composition as a whole, can be understood more clearly to the degree that the geographical matrix can be accurately defined.

## SAMUEL

The Book of Samuel (now divided into 1 Sam and 2 Sam) is a kind of semi-novella explaining how the dynasty of David was established. Today, it is well recognized that the Hebrew text has undergone many corruptions; the Septuagint often represents a better original Hebrew text as does the material preserved by the Chronicler and sometimes by Josephus. Fragments of the book discovered in Qumran Cave 4 have tended to confirm this textual situation and sometimes hint that there were several versions of the text circulating in the Herodian period.

What is now called 1 Samuel recounts the leadership of Samuel, the last of the "judges," a prophet of Levitical lineage who exercised his office mainly within the territory of Benjamin (*see* 1 Sam 1:1–3). His father, Elkanah, was a descendant of Zuph in the Levitical line of Kohath (1 Chr 6:22–28).

Ramathaim is the town of Ramah in Benjamin. It is Ramathaim of (the clan of) the Zuphim. The "hill country of Ephraim"

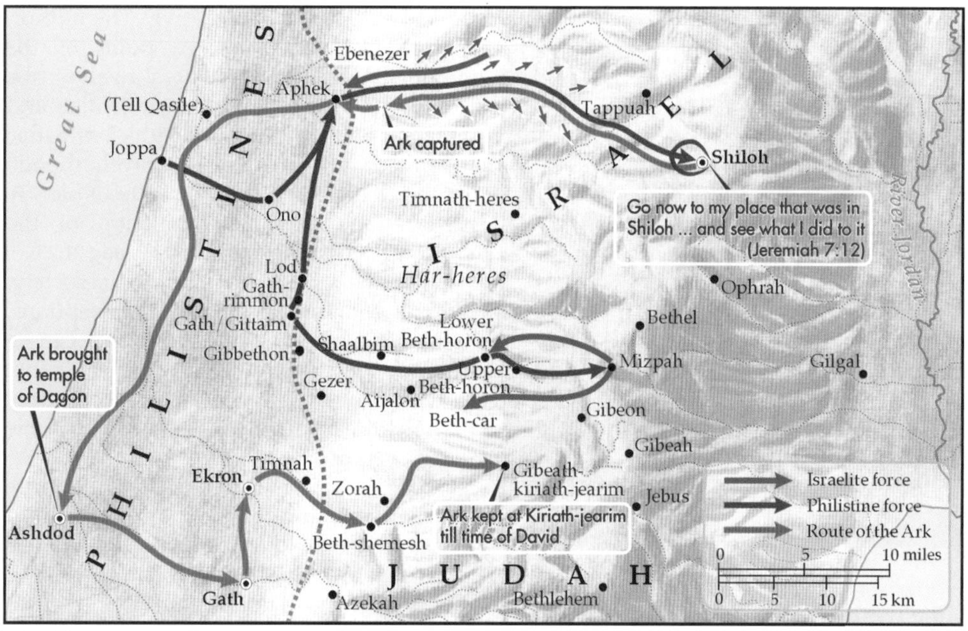


**The Battle of Ebenezer: The Peregrination of the Sacred Ark (Mid-11th Century BCE)**

is a geographical, not a tribal, term and includes the territory of Benjamin (and Manasseh) as well as that of Ephraim. Elkanah's ethnicon is homophonous with the ethnicon for a member of the Ephraimite tribe (cf. Judg 12:5; 1 Kgs 11:26) but here it makes more sense to interpret it as an Ephrathite. If that be accepted, then the Elkanah-Samuel tradition is Levitical, located in the tribal area of Benjamin, and associated with those Levites who lived in or around Bethlehem. They are, therefore, in line with the Levites who played a decisive role in the final two pericopes of the Book of Judges. So the spotlight is still on Levites operating within the topographical saddle between Mount Ephraim and Mount Judah. This provides another logical link between this book and the Book of Judges.

The focus of the Samuel birth narrative is the cult center at Shiloh. The high priesthood, the "tent of meeting" (tabernacle), and the ark of the covenant are all said to be there. Excavations at the site of Khirbet Seilûn have uncovered a storeroom full of the "collared-rim" storage jars so typical of Early Iron Age archaeological contexts in Transjordan and Cisjordan that might have been the storeroom of the cultic center itself. Otherwise, there were no traces of the cultic installations as such, probably due to later occupation levels.

A serious confrontation with the rival ethnic group, the Philistines, is said to have occurred near a place called Ebenezer, "The Stone of Deliverance" (*see* 1 Sam 4:1).

The Septuagint version makes the Philistines the initiators of the action:

> And it came about in those days that the uncircumcised ones were gathered against Israel and Israel went out for a confrontation with them to fight and they encamped beside Ebenezer while the uncircumcised ones encamped at Aphek.
>
> (1 Sam 4:1 LXX)

In view of their lack of success, the Israelites brought to their camp the ark of the covenant from Shiloh (1 Sam 4:3–9) which was captured during their defeat in the ensuing battle (1 Sam 4:10–11). News about the capture of the ark and the death of its attending priests was brought from the battlefield to Shiloh by a runner (*see* 1 Sam 4:12).

These details seem to place Ebenezer in a position opposite Aphek (Râs el-ᶜAin=Tel Afeq) at the headwaters of Nahr el-ᶜAujā (so-called Yarkon River), but also on a route that could be traversed in less than a day by a runner going to Shiloh.

The aftermath of this conflict is not described in this narrative, but later passages speak in retrospect of the destruction of Shiloh, presumably by the Philistines. Destruction of the archaeological loci from this period at the site tends to support that thesis. The destruction of the Tent of Meeting is mentioned in Psalm 78:60.

*The small antiquity site at ᶜIzbet Ṣarṭah has been suggested as the location of Ebenezer. Someone at this Early Iron Age site was learning to write the "Phoenician" alphabet as attested by this small sherd with the Proto-Canaanite alphabet and various practice combinations of letters.*

The same tradition is the basis for Jeremiah's exhortations not to depend on the presence of the Jerusalem temple as insurance against destruction (*see* Jer 7:12–14, 26:6–9).

It is not known when the priesthood transferred its focus to Nob (1 Sam 21:2 ff.), a site overlooking Jebus/Jerusalem from the east, but such a move might have been motivated by a desire to establish a safer venue, not as exposed as other cult sites (e.g. Mizpah, Bethel) that were closer to the watershed highway.

The peregrinations of the ark (1 Sam 5–6) when in Philistine captivity reflect a reasonable geographical sequence in spite of the folkloristic elements (*see* 1 Sam 5:1–10). Ashdod (Esdûd) and Ekron (Kh. el-Muqannaᶜ=Tel Miqne) are firmly identified. This passage suggests that Gath must be somewhere between them and strengthens the impression that Gath must be sought in northern Philistia.

The divinatory test by which the ark was returned to Israelite territory also contains some realistic geographical details (*see* 1 Sam 6:12–14).

Ekron and Beth-shemesh are at opposite ends of an east-west segment of the Sorek Valley, before it makes a swing to the northwest. The cows are said to have made a beeline for Beth-shemesh in spite of their unhappiness at being separated from their calves. The leaders of the Philistines followed it up to the boundary line of the Beth-shemesh fields. From the Samson story and from the border description in Joshua 15:10–11, we learn that between Beth-shemesh and Ekron was the town of Timnah, at this time in Philistine hands, and it must have been on the north side of the streambed (Tell el-Baṭâshī=Tel Baṭash). But the cows headed straight for Beth-shemesh; that is the significance of "on a single trail." Timnah and Beth-shemesh each had their own fields in the valley (cf. Judg 15:5) and the respective farmers knew quite well where the fields of one met the fields of another. Therefore, the Philistine chieftains wisely stopped at a clearly recognized boundary between the agricultural zones of the two towns.

In the end, the ark was passed on to Kiriath-jearim to await its transfer to Jerusalem by King David (*see* 1 Sam 7:1). Topographically, it is hardly a coincidence that Beth-shemesh and Kiriath-jearim are both reference points on the boundary described in Joshua 15:9–10.

As for the socioethnic situation whereby Judahites lived at one end of the valley (Beth-shemesh) and Philistines at another (Ekron), the evidence of pig domestication at Ekron and its absence at Beth-shemesh is a valuable confirmation and a reliable marker of ethnic distinction.

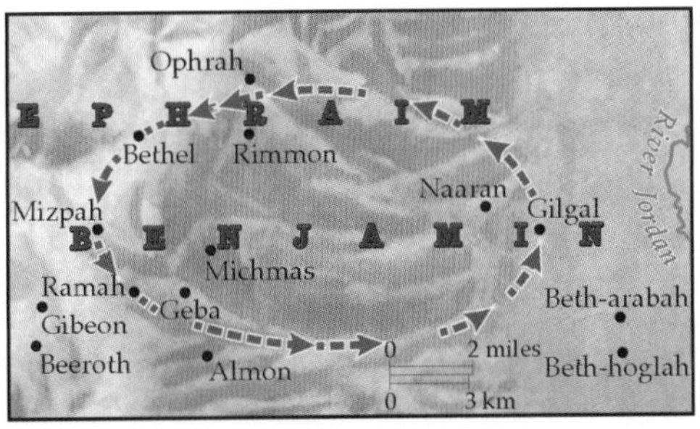


**Samuel's "Judicial Circuit" (c. 1040 BCE)**

Philistine strategy in trying to extort agricultural produce from the hill-country tribes was often concentrated on the topographical saddle between Bethlehem and Bethel. The northern segment of this physical bridge is the land of Benjamin. A final narrative about conflict with the Philistines under the leadership of Samuel is focused on preventing Philistine incursion into that very zone (*see* 1 Sam 7:5–11).

After the successful Israelite campaign to oust the Philistines from the Benjaminite territory, it is said:

> So the Philistines were subdued and they did not come anymore within the border of Israel. And the hand of YHWH was against the Philistines all the days of Samuel. The cities which the Philistines had taken from Israel were restored to Israel, from **Ekron** even to **Gath**; and Israel delivered their territory from the hand of the Philistines. So there was peace between Israel and the Amorites. (1 Sam 7:13–14)

The question at once arises as to which Gath is meant here. Its association with Ekron naturally would suggest Gath of the Philistines and this text was used as proof for a Gath in southern Philistia, far from Ekron in northern Philistia. The Hebrew syntagma, "from (one extremity) to (the other)," is more likely to indicate two towns close to one another rather than far away (cf. 1 Sam 27:8). On the other hand, the very same passage was employed to prove that there really was another Gath in the north, close to Ekron, which must be equated with Gittaim. The Gath in this context is most likely Gittaim/Gath-rimmon of the Danite territory. That the Amorites were at peace with Israel must mean that the settlements around "Har-heres, Aijalon and Shaalbim" (Judg 1:35) were now on good terms with the Israelites. Those Amorites were "the men of Gath who were born in the land" (1 Chr 7:21) who had been at such enmity with the Ephraimite clans at an earlier stage. In the meantime, the Philistine incursion to the territory north of the Sorek had made them the mutual enemies of the native Amorites and the people of Israel. Now the Philistines have been at least temporarily driven out of that area and the new reconciliation between the Amorites and the Israelites would have facilitated the occupation of Aijalon by the Beriah clan (1 Chr 8:13).

One fact is abundantly clear: all of the relevant texts, from the topographical list of Thutmose III (No. 63) to the Medeba map, point to a location for Gath/Gittaim/Gath-rimmon in the area just south or southwest of Lod. It could have been in the spot of present-day Ramla (Ramleh) or possibly Râs Abū Ḥumeid.

It was in the central hill-country area, the strategic "saddle" that Samuel, prophet/judge/Levite, had his "circuit" of ministry (*see* 1 Sam 7:15–17). All of the sites mentioned are in the central zone and all have cultic associations as places where oracles were sought and sacrifices were made. It is not surprising that another altar was set up at Ramah. Any judicial process required access to the expressed will of the deity, for validating testimonies of witnesses, for administering oaths, or even for deciding legal cases.

It could be that, due to various reasons, more stories survived from the Benjaminite territory than from other areas, probably due to the influence of Samuel. But apart from that, there is geographical logic in trying to control that saddle between Mount Judah and Mount Ephraim as the key to domination of both those ranges.

In his old age, Samuel is said to have appointed his two sons to judgeship and stationed them at Beer-sheba (1 Sam 8:1–2). That would have had to be well into Saul's reign, after the Negeb campaign of 1 Samuel 15, and might have been an effort to bring that southern area into the orbit of a broader Israelite control.

## SAUL

The king chosen by oracular lot had his home at Gibeah (1 Sam 10:26), known often as Gibeah of Benjamin (e.g. 1 Sam 13:2) but also as Gibeah of Saul (1 Sam 11:4). He thus continues the tradition of leadership from the northern side of the "saddle." There is no record of formal institutions of state. In one instance there is a hint at what a king would do for his loyal followers but the satirical text may be more of a later commentary than an expression of reality (*see* 1 Sam 22:7).

The implication would be that Saul had already started to provide gifts of productive land to those in his service. But this remains in the realm of theory, and probably was not seriously realized in fact.

At one point in the Saulide narrative there is an insertion summarizing Saul's "victories" (*see* 1 Sam 14:47–48). The preserved battle narratives, discussed *infra*, can account for several of these conflicts but not all. Unless Moab and Edom supported the Ammonite king, Nahash, nothing is said about campaigns against them. There is, however, a tradition of a desert war on the part of the tribe of Reuben during the reign of Saul (*see* 1 Chr 5:10).

On the other hand, it seems hardly credible that someone like Saul, who had not even a foothold in the Jezreel Valley, could have ever campaigned against the Arameans of Zobah. Of course, some narratives might have been skipped over or perhaps were not available to the author of the Book of Samuel, but this would be indeed surprising. Beth-rehob would have made a natural pair with Zobah (cf. 2 Sam 10:6). In any case, the possibility must be considered that a summary appropriate for David happened to get inserted into the narrative of Saul.

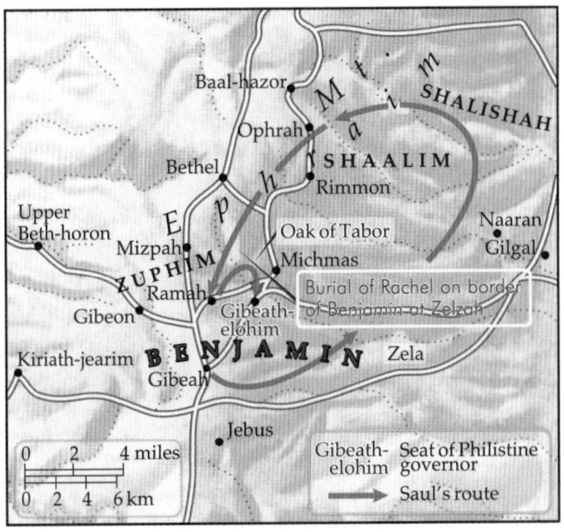


**Saul Searches for His Asses (c. 1035 BCE)**

When the actual conflict narratives of Saul are reviewed, he is seen mainly protecting the central core of Israelite settlement in Mount Ephraim, later in Mount Judah and the Negeb and Shephelah.

**Rescue of Jabesh-gilead.** Saul's first trial as a military leader was the rescue of the beleaguered residents of Jabesh-gilead (1 Sam 11:1–11). Nahash, king of the sons of Ammon, laid siege to their town and had demanded cruel and humiliating terms of surrender. Saul mustered his forces at Bezek (Kh. Ibzîq) in the northeastern hills

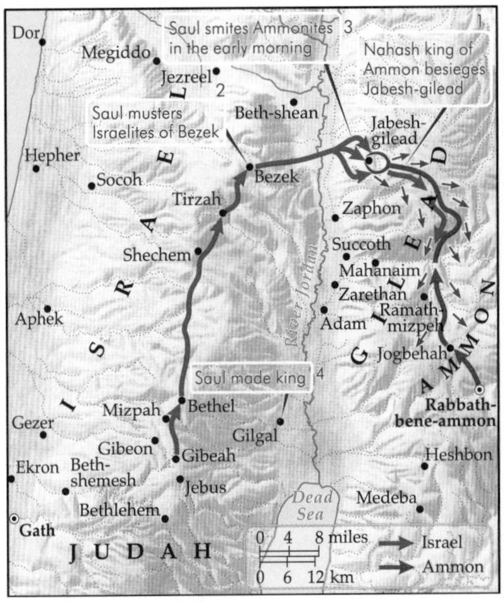


**The Rescue of Jabesh-gilead (c. 1035 BCE)**

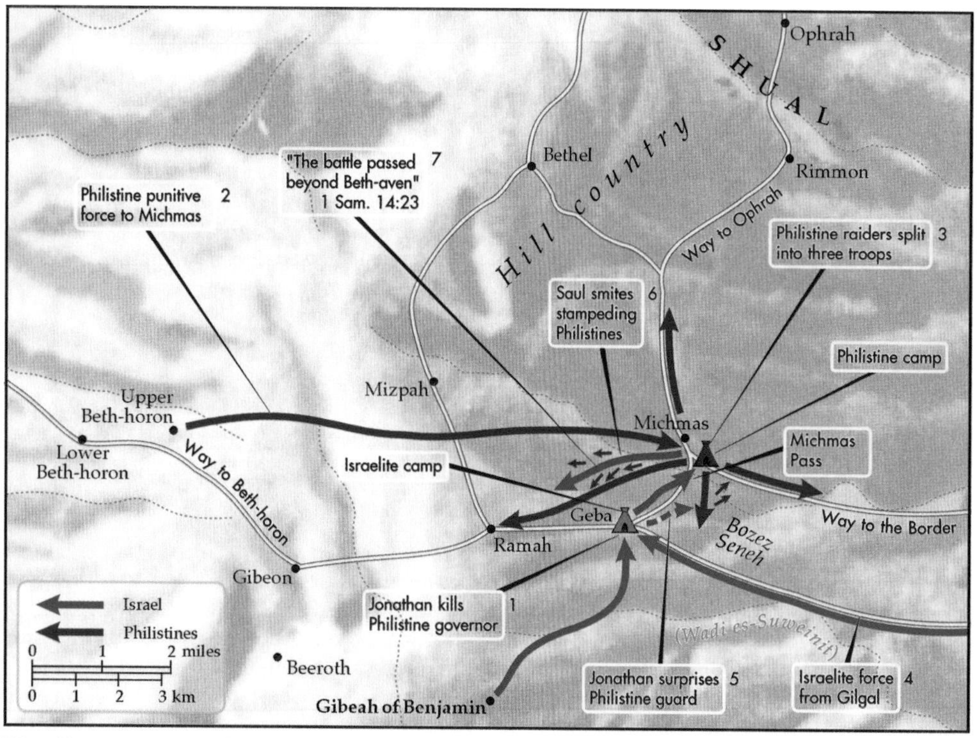


**The Rebellion of Saul Against the Philistines: The Battle of Michmas**

of Mount Ephraim. From there Saul and his forces made a surprise dash across the Jordan Valley to attack the Ammonite camp during the early morning watch. It will be remembered that there were ancient family ties between the people of Gibeah and Jabesh-gilead (Judg 21:14). Now there was a special relationship between Saul and the population of the town. They would not forget his act of deliverance.

**Central Hill Country**. The first, and crucial stage in Saul's war against his most formidable enemy, the Philistines, was his expulsion of their oppressive military presence in the central hill country. Saul was, in effect, the commander of a militia comprised of three units posted at key points in this sensitive area (*see* 1 Sam 13:2).

The first move was made by Jonathan, who slew the Philistine representative (commissioner, or "garrison") at nearby Geba (*see* 1 Sam 13:3). This is one good context for demonstrating that Gibeah and Geba were two separate places. Jonathan was posted at the former (Tell el-Fûl), while the Philistines had an officer (garrison commander?) at nearby Geba (Jeba$^{c}$).

The Philistine response was to send an expeditionary force to Michmas, where Saul had been staying (*see* 1 Sam 13:5). For fear of Philistine reprisals, the Israelites gathered at Gilgal to confer with Saul. Samuel was also to come there. Saul's impatience and his subsequent quarrel with Samuel over matters of authority are a theme of the book as a whole, painting Saul as a tragic figure unworthy of ultimate dynastic rule (1 Sam 13:6–16). The important point for the conflict narrative is that Saul's forces had assembled at a safe distance away to offer sacrifices and to seek an oracle, but that they had dwindled in size (many of his people fled to Transjordan). Saul could not return to Michmas, where the enemy had set up their camp; and he could not go to Gibeah because the angry Samuel had gone there (it was perhaps too dangerous for him to return to Ramah), so Saul and his meager force went to Geba, on the opposite side of a deep valley from Michmas.

The Philistine response was to send an expeditionary force to the area in order to restore order and to discourage any Hebrew efforts to rebel (*see* 1 Sam 13:16–18). One unit went north toward Ophrah (eṭ-Ṭaiyibeh) to block the junction of the main road leading up from the Jordan Valley. The second unit went west toward the main road coming up from the coastal plain, past Beth-horon. The third unit went out into the steppe, overlooking the Zeboim ("Hyenas") Valley to see if any Israelites might be seeking to ascend that way. Their march southeastward took them along the northern rim of the Wâdī eṣ-Ṣuweinît toward the steppe. About 5.5 miles (9 km) southeast of Mukhmas (Michmas), near the conjunction of Wâdī eṣ-Ṣuweinît with the Wâdī el-Qelt, there is the Wâdī Abū Ḍibâ$^{c}$ (Arabic: "Valley of the Father of Hyenas"), which apparently preserves the ancient Hebrew toponym.

Saul, in the meantime, had withdrawn to the vicinity of Gibeah, at Migron, which is here probably a synonym or related term for *gōren*, "threshing floor," and not the same as the Migron in Isaiah 10:28 which is a town near Michmas.

> Saul was staying in the **outskirts of Gibeah** under the pomegranate tree which is in **Migron**. And the people with him numbered about six hundred men.
> (1 Sam 14:2)

Left alone in charge of the troops at Geba, Jonathan conceived and carried his surprise attack on the advanced guardpost of the Philistines. This was achieved by crossing the deep ravine between the two cliffs, Bozez and Seneh (*see* 1 Sam 14:4–5). Jonathan's surprise move led to confusion and an ultimate rout of the Philistines, especially exacerbated by the uprising of the Hebrews who up to now had supported the Philistines (1 Sam 14:6–46).

> And they struck on that day among the Philistines from **Michmas** to **Aijalon**. (1 Sam 14:31a)

As a result of this action, the entire route from the central hill country to the Valley of Aijalon was cleared of the enemy. There was no follow-up, however; the fight was not taken further into the Philistine territory on the plain.

**The Negeb**. Saul's next recorded campaign was against Amalek in the Negeb. The objective was to bring security to the settlements there, many of them probably newly established by clans of Judah (*see* 1 Sam 15:4). If the assembly point at Telaim is a real place it may be identical with the Telem of Joshua 15:24.

> So Saul came to the **city of Amalek** and set an ambush in the valley. And Saul said to the **Kenite**, "Go, turn aside, go down from among the **Amalekites**, so that I do not destroy you with them; for you showed kindness to all the sons of Israel when they came up from Egypt." So the **Kenites** departed from among the **Amalekites**. And Saul defeated the **Amalekites**, from **Havilah** as you go to **Shur**, which is adjacent to **Egypt**. (1 Sam 15:5–7)

Amalek was reckoned among the "chiefs of Eliphaz in the land of Edom" (Gen 36:15–16). They were descendants of Eliphaz and linked with the land of Edom like Esau. This

*Carts of Sea People drawn by oxen, from relief of Ramesses III at Medinet Habu.*

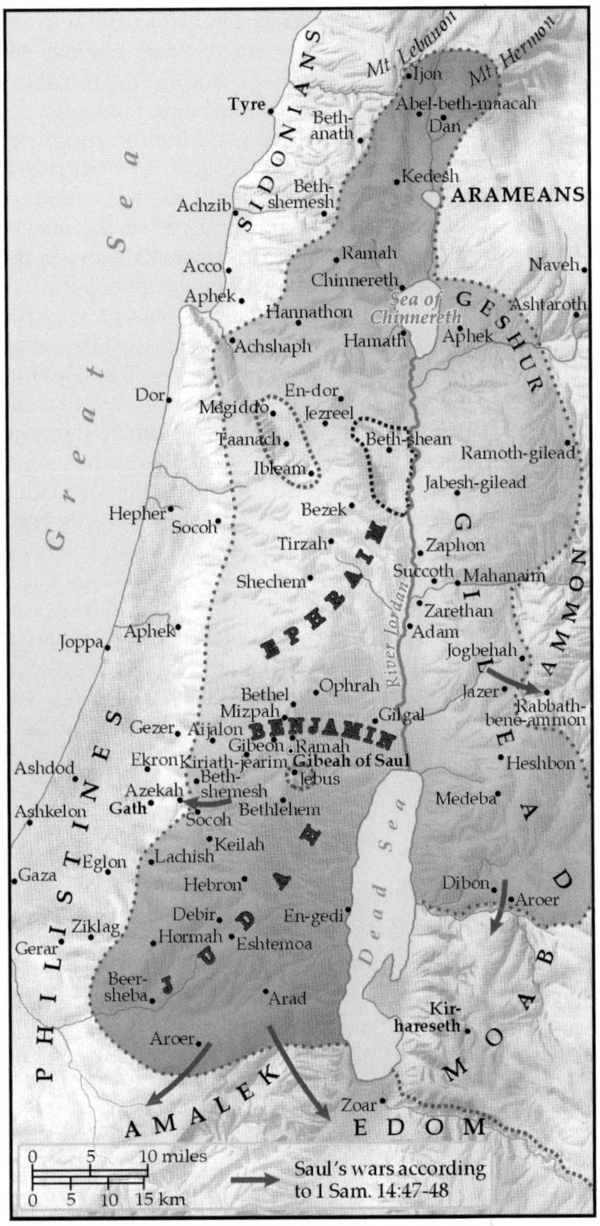


**HYPOTHETICAL TERRITORY OWING ALLEGIANCE TO SAUL (C. 1035 BCE)**

is another clear indication that Edom (and Seir) refers to an area west of the Arabah. The Amalekites were a nomadic people, descendants of Esau and a constant threat to the settled population in the Negeb. For the Kenites, cf. Judges 1:16 (discussion *supra*).

The "city of Amalek" is still a mystery. One interesting suggestion was to locate it at Tel Masos (=Kh. el-Meshâsh), an impressive Early Iron Age settlement in the middle of the Beer-sheba basin. However, it is more likely that Masos represents ancient Baalath-beer (Josh 19:8).

Failure to observe the complete *herem* by Saul is marked as another stage in the growing rift between him and the prophet Samuel, a basic theme throughout the Saul tradition.

**The Shephelah**. Saul's further effort to win the allegiance of Judah is reflected in the clash between his forces and the Philistines in the Valley of Elah (1 Sam 17). The "duel of champions" so typical of Homeric tradition (but also of the ancient Near East) is perhaps the most widely known tale from all of biblical military lore; in fact there is a rival tradition that Elhanan son of Jaare-oregim of Bethlehem was the actual champion on the Israelite side (2 Sam 21:19) though the parallel passage in Chronicles makes it the *brother* of Goliath that he slew (1 Chr 20: 5). The various divergencies in the two texts leave the question open. Concerning Elhanan (2 Sam 21:19; 1 Chr 20:5; 1 Sam 21:10, 22:10; cf. Ps 151 LXX) this might be a hero story that gravitated to the more famous personality of David.

Nevertheless, the geographical details of the narrative (especially in the Greek version) reflect a first-hand knowledge of the terrain. The two armies were facing one another across the valley, the Philistines on the south, Israel on the northern ridge (*see* 1 Sam 17:1–3).

The anchor point for identifying the venue of this battle and the geographical elements therein is the mention of Socoh. Clear remains of the Roman road from Eleutheropolis (Beit Jibrîl/Jibrîn=Beth Govrin) to Ailia (Jerusalem) are evident in the Shephelah and it went, beyond doubt, through the Wâdī es-Sunṭ ("Valley of the Acacia"). In the clearest east-west segment of that wadi, on the south side, there is a ruin called Khirbet esh-Shuweikeh (Roman-Byzantine and later) situated at the southern end of a low hill with a high, Iron Age tel (Kh. ᶜAbbâd). Shuweikeh is the Arabic correspondent to the Hebrew Socoh, "thicket," so the antiquity site is preserving a biblical name in Arabic form and that site happens to be beside a valley named after a tree. The Valley of Elah means "valley of the terebinth," so the tree has changed but the convergence of these details cannot be coincidental.

Given the location of Socoh and the Valley of Elah, it is then easy to see that Tell Zakarîyeh, to the west of Socoh, should be biblical Azekah.

From the hill on which Khirbet ᶜAbbâd and Khirbet esh-Shuweikeh are located the situation described in 1 Samuel 17:1–3 becomes abundantly clear. The opposing forces were lined up on the ridges on the north and south of the valley, respectively. This is a segment where the valley (which begins by flowing north along the trough valley between the Shephelah and the hill country) has taken a turn westward (today's "valley of the [satellite] dishes"); it continues in this direction for a matter of one or two miles (2–3 km) before again turning north for a short distance (having been deflected by the ridge on which Tell Zakarîyeh stands) until it veers once more to the west. The east-west segment that runs past Shuweikeh would have been the venue for the duel between the two opposing champions and for the subsequent battle which became a rout (*see* 1 Sam 17:52).

After the defeat of their heroic protagonist, the Philistines began their retreat by running west and as they turned northward (to go around Azekah=Tell Zakarîyeh) they were on the "way to Shaaraim." The Israelites were waiting there and inflicted many casualties on the Philistines. Shaaraim has not been identified but according to the list of towns in the northern Shephelah district (Josh 15:33–36), which has been shown to run clockwise, it comes after Azekah and is most likely somewhere between Azekah and Beth-shemesh. In other words, the "way to Shaaraim" would be linked to that south-north segment of the road leading from the Valley of Elah out to the west. At the junction where the Elah road diverges west while the Shaaraim road continues north, Saul's warriors must have ambushed many of the fleeing Philistines.

The pursuit then followed the course of the valley westward beyond Azekah toward the gates of Gath and Ekron. Ekron, of course, has recently been proven to be located at Kh. el-Muqannaᶜ (Tel Miqne); Tell eṣ-Ṣâfī is directly south of it and in fact on the south bank of the Elah Valley. This passage is one of the key texts supporting the location of Philistine Gath in northern Philistia and seems to point unequivocally to Tell eṣ-Ṣâfī as the site of Philistine Gath.

**David's Life as a Fugitive**. The personal conflict between King Saul and his protégé, David, is the topic of several

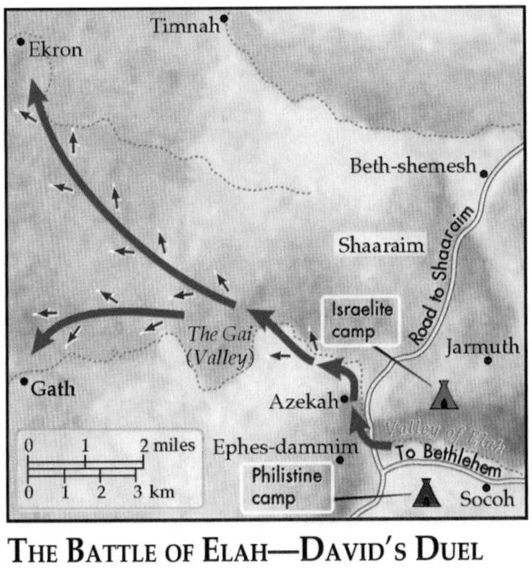


**THE BATTLE OF ELAH—DAVID'S DUEL WITH GOLIATH (C. 1020 BCE)**

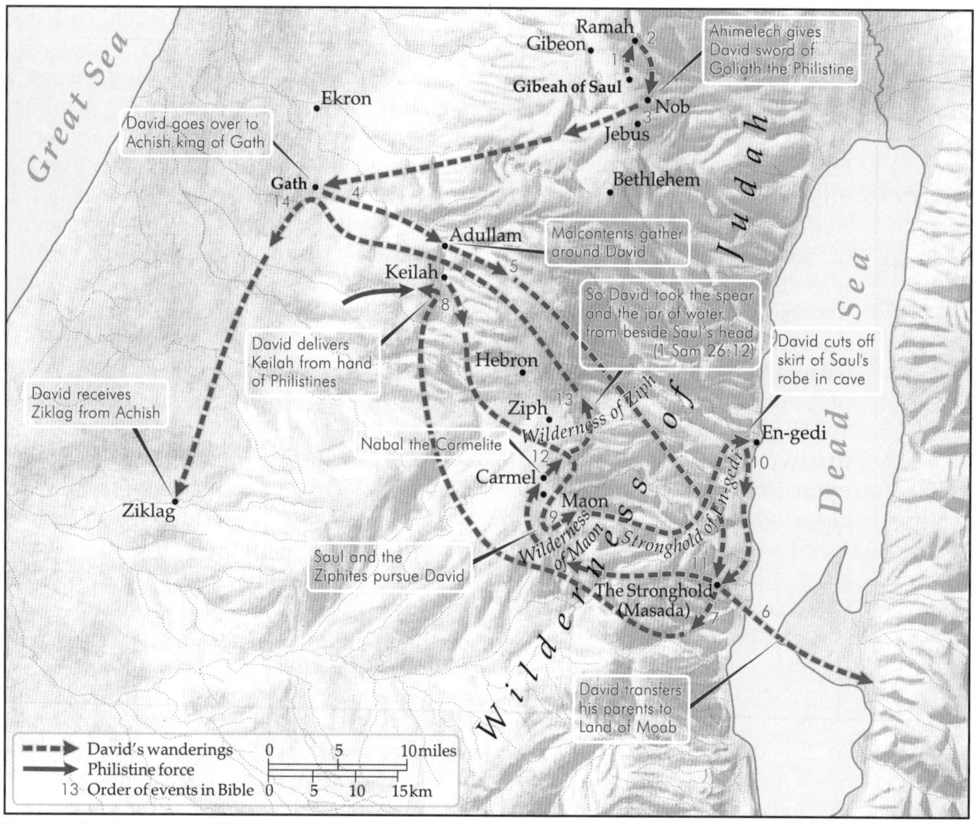


**David's Life as a Renegade (c. 1018 BCE)**

chapters in the Book of Samuel. The function of those narratives is as royal propaganda for the Davidic dynasty, justifying its attainment of power over a united Israel. Every effort is made to show that David was neither a usurper nor a traitor. The ensuing discussion deals with the geographical information that can be gleaned from the fugitive adventures of David. Most of it comes from rural and pastoral areas that might otherwise not play a role in royal narration.

When the final rift had become a reality, David is seen seeking refuge and counsel from Samuel at Ramah. The two of them went to an apparently safe place at "**Naioth** in Ramah" (1 Sam 19:18). It would appear that this is an encampment within the district of Ramah where a band of prophets lived and practiced their profession. Later, when David made a covenant with Jonathan, he awaited behind the "stone Ezel" (1 Sam 20:19) but the Septuagintal rendering, "by that Ergab," suggests that the Hebrew text is corrupt and that the original was *hāʾargab hallaāz* (or *hallaāzeh*), "this cairn."

After receiving Jonathan's message that Saul was determined to slay him, David and a few followers went to the sacred shrine at Nob (1 Sam 21:2 [Eng. 21:1]). This place had evidently become the chief shrine after the destruction of Shiloh since it was administered by Ahimelech, grandson of Eli. Its place and role in Isaiah 10:32, where the invader shakes his fist at Jerusalem, has led to the suggestion that Nob was on Râs el-Meshârif, a slope of Mount Scopus having clear eye contact with the Temple Mount. While alternate proposals have been made, this one makes the most sense. At Nob, David was given some holy bread for supplies and also the great sword of Goliath that had been placed there as a trophy. Saul executed all the priests of Nob except Abiathar, who escaped to David (1 Sam 22:6–19).

In desperation, David then sought asylum (1 Sam 21:10–15) with the king of Gath, called Achish in the Hebrew Bible. At this juncture, David was not well received by the Philistines (*see* 1 Sam 22:1–2).

Adullam was in the northern Shephelah district (Josh 15:35); its name did not survive intact in Arabic but there was a water source called *ʿîd el-mâ*, "Festival of the water," or *ʿîd el-Miʾah*, "Festival of the hundred." The echo of the biblical name was noted. But *ʿîd el-mâ* is located near the foot of an antiquity site called Tell esh-Sheikh Madhkur which satisfies the demand for a suitable Iron Age town. (A local Christian tradition placing David's hideout in a large cave in the Bethlehem area has nothing to support it.)

At this stage, David took his followers and his parents to Mizpeh of Moab (1 Sam 22:3–4). Its location is purely a matter of conjecture; both Kerak and Rujm el-Meshrefeh southwest of Medeba have been proposed. Soon David returned to the land of Judah and entered the forest of Hereth (1 Sam 22:5). There are no hints in the source and no valid toponymic echoes to help identify this forest. Subsequent events in the narrative focused on the town of Keilah, which is nearby. David and his men successfully intervened there against the Philistines, who were raiding the threshing floors of the people of Keilah. However, the people of Keilah showed their gratitude by reporting David's presence to Saul (1 Sam 23:1–13). Keilah is identified with modern Khirbet Qîlā, an important tel on the eastern side of the trough valley; like all sites in the trough it is reckoned as a Shephelah town (Josh 15:44). The discussion about whether to make the trek to Keilah in the Shephelah and the reservations expressed by David's men suggest that the forest of Hereth must have been some distance from Keilah and not close by.

After the perfidy of the people of Keilah, David and his band withdrew to the hilly country in "the steppe land of Ziph" (1 Sam 23:14), "in the wooded height" (1 Sam 23:15). This is further defined by the Ziphites as "in the strongholds of the wooded height on the hill of Hachilah, which is on the south of **Jeshimon** (=wasteland)" (1 Sam 23:19). This Ziph (Josh 15:55) is logically identified with Tell Zîf about 4.4 miles (7 km) to the south-southeast of Hebron. The toponymy is perfect and the location on the eastern border of the Hebron Hills facing the wilderness area suits the present narrative. Adjacent to the hill country of Judah is the large zone of Cenonian chalk in the rain shadow east of the watershed. The segments of that steppe land are habitually designated in accordance with the closest hill-country town. Thus, the steppe land (so-called wilderness) of Ziph is that area of the Judean "wilderness" adjacent to the town of Ziph. Those areas too rugged and rocky for

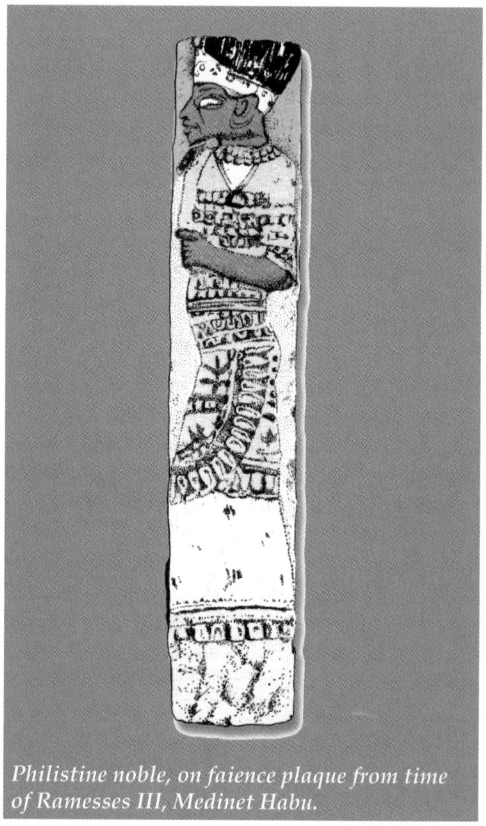

*Philistine noble, on faience plaque from time of Ramesses III, Medinet Habu.*

pasturing flocks were called "wasteland."

When it became known to David that the residents of Ziph sought to hand him over to Saul, he and his band moved south to the "steppe land of **Maon**, in the desert plain to the south of the wasteland" (1 Sam 23:24–28). Maon is located at Khirbet el-Maᶜîn, about 8 miles (13 km) south-southeast of Hebron. A standard theme in these pericopes is the opportunities afforded David to assassinate Saul in which he steadfastly declines to lay hand on the "anointed of YHWH."

When Saul was called away from the search after David because of trouble on the Philistine front, David again changed his venue, this time to "the strongholds of En-gedi" (1 Sam 23:29). He was therefore in "the steppe land of En-gedi" (1 Sam 24:1). En-gedi (ᶜAin Jidī) is the oasis created by a copious spring that flows into the Dead Sea about midway down the western shore. This is the venue for the story about David's chance to slay Saul in a cave.

From En-gedi, David returned to the steppe land of Maon (1 Sam 25:1 LXX instead of MT "steppe land of Paran"). This introduces a pericope about the clash with a local Calebite landowner, Nabal. The latter refuses to grant provisions to David's men and insults him. Before David can requite the insult, he is intercepted by Nabal's beautiful and gifted wife, Abigail, who brings the supplies and asks for forgiveness in the name of her churly spouse. When she returns home, her husband conveniently suffers an attack and expires. David then married Abigail, thus obtaining the lands and property of Nabal, particularly at Carmel. This Carmel (Josh 15:55) is Khirbet el-Kirmil, also about 8 miles (13 km) southeast of Hebron, not far from Maon. It is also mentioned in this context (1 Sam 25:43) that David had taken Ahinoam of Jezreel, and they both became his wives. This Jezreel (Josh 15:56) must also have been somewhere south or southwest of Hebron. Its name has not survived in the local toponymy.

The final episode in David's fugitive experience (1 Sam 26) takes place in the wilderness of Ziph, near "the hill of Hachilah (darkness) facing the wasteland" (1 Sam 26:1). After once again showing that he had no intention of assassinating Saul, David decided to make another try to obtain asylum with Achish of Gath. This time, his status as a fugitive was well known and the Philistines thought they could trust him (*see* 1 Sam 27:1–2).

Rather than staying at Gath, David proposed to his new master that he be assigned a place in Philistine territory (i.e. Ziklag) where he could serve as a vassal to Achish (*see* 1 Sam 27:5–6). One mound which fits this description admirably is Tell esh-Shārîᶜah (Tel Seraᶜ), in the Wâdī esh-Shārîᶜah (Naḥal Gerar), approximately 15.5 miles (25 km) southeast of Gaza. A site is required where David's subsequent activities and behavior while at Ziklag can make sense. Strata of the appropriate periods matching the biblical references to Ziklag have been uncovered in recent excavations, including evidence of a substantial Philistine presence in the later part of the Iron I period.

Thus, David is depicted as a vassal of the king of Gath. His placement at a site like Ziklag was probably meant to cover the Philistines' southeastern flank facing the various tribal settlements that later became part of Judah. Achish thought he was entrusting a sector vital to the Philistines to a newly acquired loyal vassal. While he was there, he was joined by more disaffected warriors from Saul's own tribe of Benjamin (1 Chr 12:1) and from Manasseh (1 Chr 12:21). As will be seen, the narrative also makes more sense if David is located far enough away from Achish for the latter to have to take David's word concerning his military activities without access to first-hand knowledge (*see* 1 Sam 27:8–12).

In fact, David was deceiving his master. Instead of attacking the settlements belonging to Judah and its affiliated tribes, David was actually using his militia as a desert patrol, attacking those very nomadic elements that threatened the newly settled inhabitants of the Negeb. By that means he was gaining their respect while leading Achish to think just the opposite. If Ziklag were close to Gath, such a tactic would have been most difficult, even impossible.

This passage must be compared with the statement of the rescued Egyptian slave of an Amalekite about a recent razzia:

> We made a raid on the **Negeb of the Cherethites**, and on **that which belongs to Judah**, and on the **Negeb of Caleb**, and we burned **Ziklag** with fire.
> (1 Sam 30:14)

The Negeb is described in terms of the various tribal and ethnic components in the population, e.g. "Negeb of...."

The groups that appear here in the Book of Samuel are: (1) Judah (in both passages) showing that some families of that tribe had settled in that area; (2) the Jerahmeelite, called the firstborn son of Hezron the son of Perez the son of Judah by Tamar; the brother of Ram and Chelubai=Caleb? (1 Chr 2:4–5, 2:9, 2:18, 2:25, 2:42). He had two wives and six sons, and numerous progeny through them, including thirteen descendants through the marriage of the daughter of his distant descendant Sheshan to the Egyptian slave Jarha (1 Chr 2:25–41). The fact that he has a "Negeb" separate from Judah suggests that the Jerahmeel group was also originally

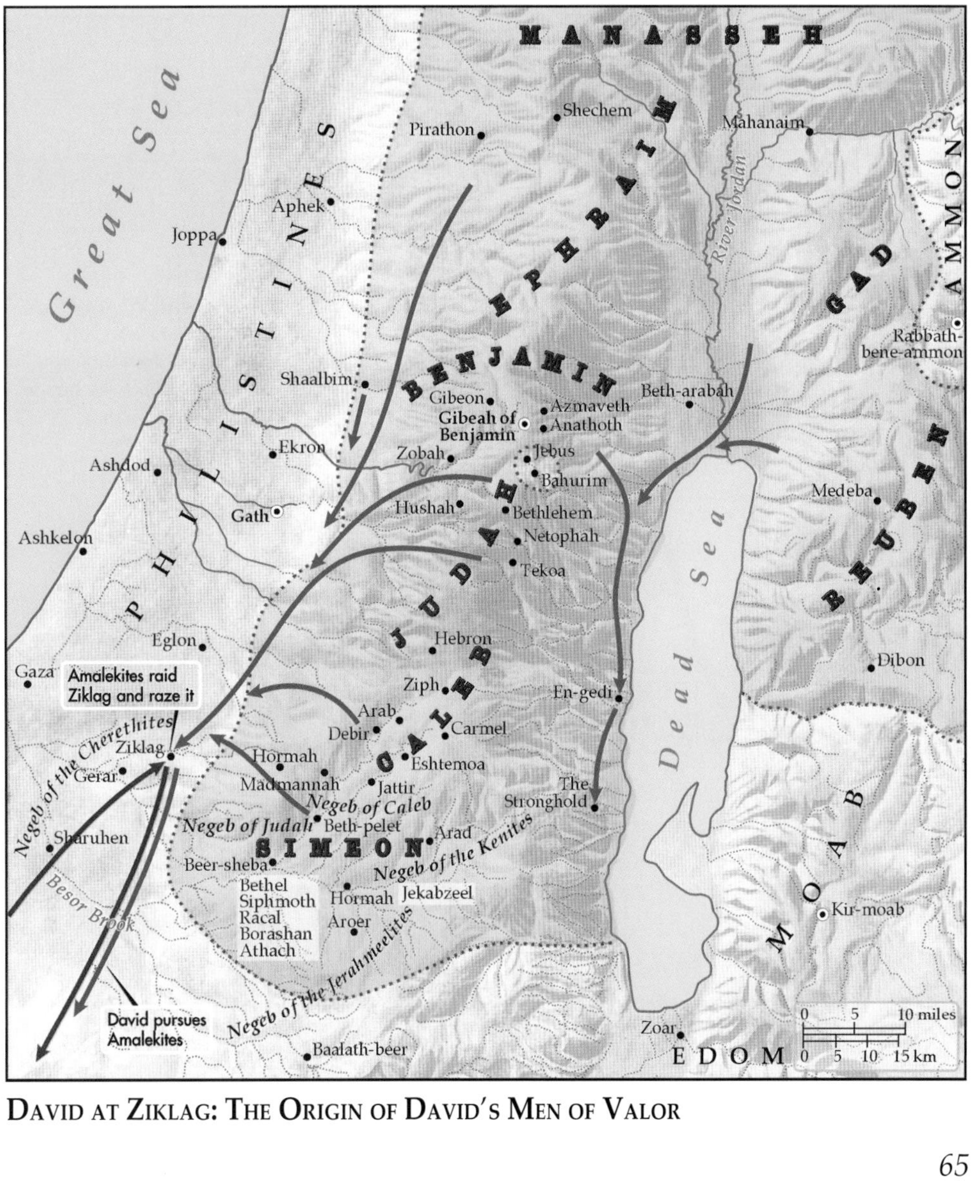


DAVID AT ZIKLAG: THE ORIGIN OF DAVID'S MEN OF VALOR

some outside element that later became incorporated into Judah by intermarriage or adoption. (3) The Kenites, who had settled in the eastern area in the vicinity of Arad (Judg 1:16). These were definitely not originally part of the Israelite tribes (cf. 1 Sam 15:6). The Cherethites are synonymous, or rather related, to the Philistines (Ezek 25:16; Zeph 2:5) and their very name is probably from the name of the island of Crete. Another name of Crete in ancient sources is Caphtor and biblical tradition cites Caphtor as the place of origin of the Philistines (Am 9:7). Their "Negeb" would logically be in the western Negeb, adjacent to Gaza, and it also would follow that Ziklag itself would have been located in the Negeb of the Cherethites. Thus David later recruited them for his personal bodyguard, but more of that later. The Calebites and the Othnielites are actually Kenizzite descendants or relatives of Kenaz (Num 32:12; Josh 14:6, 14:14). Kenaz is listed as the son of Eliphaz, the firstborn son of Esau and Adah (Gen 36:11; 1 Chr 1:36), who also appears as the chief of an Edomite clan (Gen 36:15, 36:42; 1 Chr 1:53). The Negeb of Caleb could, in fact, be the southern hill country where Debir (Kh. Rabûd) is located. Achsah, Caleb's daughter, is quoted as complaining about the location of Debir: "You have given me a Negeb land" (Josh 15:19; Judg 1:15).

So the Kenites were in the eastern Negeb near Arad. The Cherethites must have been in the west and the Jerahmeelites must have been in the Beer-sheba basin adjacent to the Kenites. The Judahites would have been in the center, with Beer-sheba as one of their principal settlements (later given to Simeon). The five Negebs extended from east to west with Caleb in the north. It is notable that the tribe of Simeon is not mentioned in these pre-monarchial contexts, especially not at Ziklag which was later to be assigned to them.

It remains to review the account of David's sharing the spoil from his rescue operation against the Amalekites. The list of the towns that received this largess is a contribution to the historical geography of the Negeb and the southern Judean hill country (1 Sam 30:26–31).

*Lid of an anthropoid coffin, grotesque style, from Beth-shean, c. late 12th century BCE.*

**Saul's Final Demise**. To understand the preliminary stages of Saul's final confrontation with the Philistines, one must recognize the objectives of the author of the Book of Samuel. He seeks to exonerate David from any responsibility for military action against his own people or against Saul. The literary arrangement chosen to emphasize this goal has caused untold confusion in historical geography. The solution is simple. Chapter 28 introduces the disposition of forces in the Jezreel area on the eve of the battle. Chapter 29 provides a "flashback" to the earlier mustering of the Philistine forces at Aphek (Râs el-ᶜAin) where they had previously assembled for the battle of Ebenezer (1 Sam 4:1, 5:1). This site marked the northern border of the territory under direct Philistine control at that time (*see* 1 Sam 29:1).

In the review of the troops, Achish and his brigade came last, accompanied by the vassal, David. The Philistine leaders objected to David's participation and he and his men were sent back to Ziklag. Therefore, David, exempted from the battle against his own people, Israel, could not be charged with an act of treason against his Philistine overlord. The ensuing account of the rescue of their families and property from the marauding Amalekites by David and his men is meant to stress David's attempts to win the favor of all the ethnic and clan groups living in the south of the country.

The "spring which is in Jezreel" may be the spring of Harod (Judg 7:1) though there was another spring in the valley below the ancient site of the town of Jezreel.

When the Philistines finally marched to the Jezreel Valley they took up a position near Shunem (Solem; 1 Sam 28:4), a town on the southern slopes of the Hill of Moreh (Jebel ed-Dahi, Nebī Dahi). Saul seems to have withdrawn from the valley and moved his troops to the slopes of Gilboa (Jebel Fuqûᶜah) on the south side of the valley. Chapter 28 goes on to recount the affair of the witch of En-dor (Kh. Ṣafṣâfeh near Indûr or possibly Tell el-ᶜAjjûl). The battle

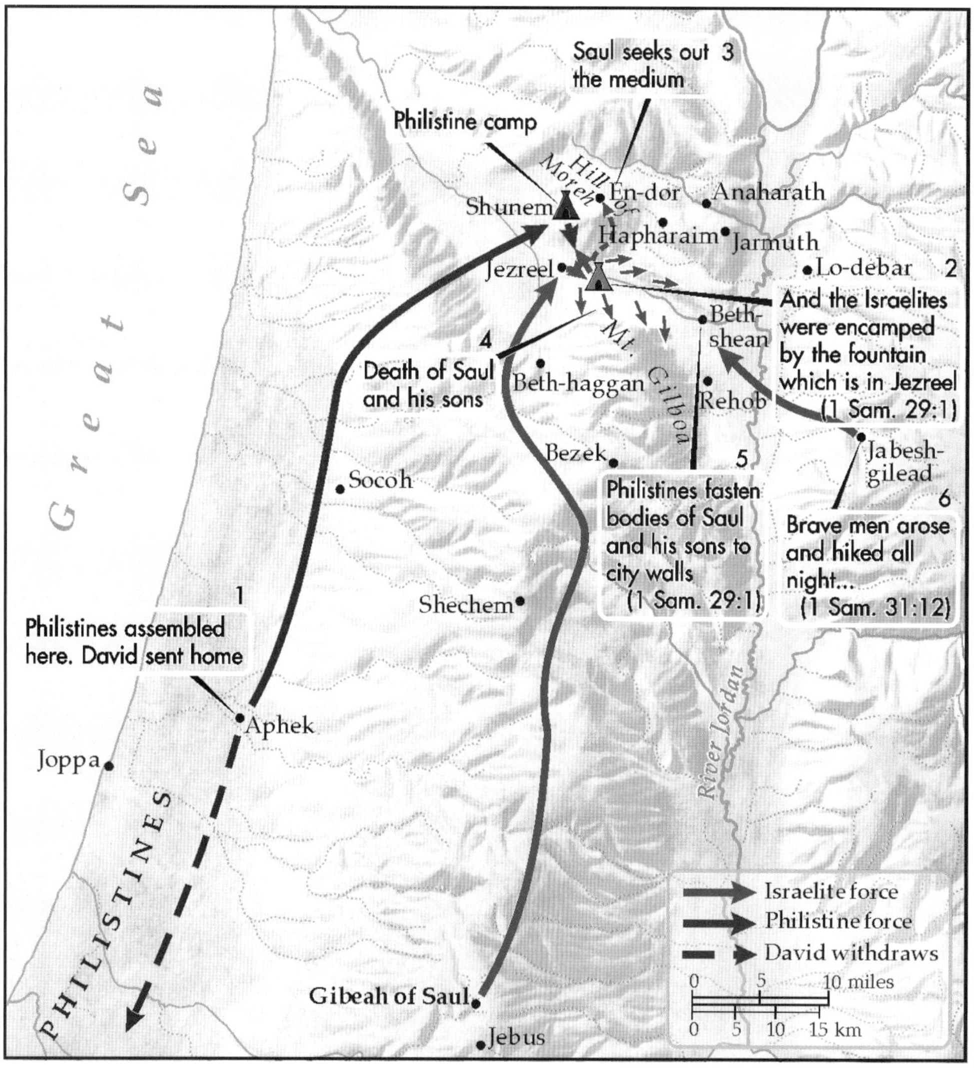


DEPLOYMENT FOR THE BATTLE OF GILBOA AND THE DEATH AND BURIAL OF SAUL

narrative continues in chapter 31, skipping over the David account.

The Philistines gained the victory and Saul and his sons were slain on the field of battle (*see* 1 Sam 31:8–13). The Philistine presence at Beth-shean, which permitted them to hang the bodies of the slain heroes on its walls, remains unexplained. In any case, the men of Jabesh-gilead acted in accordance with the ties they had with Saul, both family and political. The style of the burial, in the manner of that afforded to Homeric heroes, might be due to Aegean influence in the Jezreel and Jordan valleys.

## Tribal and Clan Mobility and Stability

The picture presented in the Book of Joshua is an idealized twelve-tribe nation. The author had an agenda, to create this ideal nation, descendants from twelve sons of the eponymous ancestor, with every tribe occupying its allotted inheritance. These tribal areas were said to have been assigned by Joshua and the priesthood by divinely inspired lot. In reality the settlement by the respective tribes in their "assigned" areas was a complex process not crowned by uniform success in every instance. Tribal societies have always demonstrated fluidity in structure and organization. Due to pressures of ecology, rivalry and spatial constraints, various clans or smaller tribes have sometimes gravitated to larger coalitions or have broken off from them and moved to some other framework. It was then often felt necessary to create legendary relationships between eponymous ancestors with resulting genealogies. Ultimately, such coalitions of clans that have emerged as tribes usually have a link with territory. Besides the power struggles over territory that may arise between tribal units, some new central authority may seek to stabilize the situation under its jurisdiction by allotting and confirming tribal ownership over specific territories, as did Salah ed-Din and later the Ottoman Empire. Just such an allotment of tribal areas is envisioned by the author of the Book of Joshua. The resulting literary product must be evaluated in the light of other biblical references that belie the reality of the idealized picture. Supplementary information can be gleaned from certain narratives, and scrutiny of the genealogical tables demonstrates that some reshuffling of the tribal territories had taken place. The records provide evidence for three processes:

1. Certain tribes picked up and migrated to other regions after their first attempts were unsuccessful in their original choice of territory.
2. Particular clans shifted from one tribe to another according to the exigencies of their local situation. There are even families of one clan that became affiliated with more than one tribe, so that the name of the clan or its eponym may be found in more than one tribal genealogy.
3. There are explicit records of intermarriage between members of different tribal groups (e.g. 1 Chr 2:21) and the resulting offspring.

In all these processes, the role of geography cannot be ignored.

**The Danite Migration.** The best-known narrative of a tribe's migration after failure to occupy its assigned territory is that of the Danites (Judg 17–18). It should not be assumed that this was the only such movement. The Danite story was preserved as an illustration of the chaos in the period of the Judges and also because it supported the alleged founding of a temple at Dan by Moses' grandson (Judg 18:30 in some MSS of the LXX, the Vulgate, and the Talmud, *Baba Bathra* 109). The MT assigns it to a son of Manasseh by adopting an orthographic modification; this is a transparent attempt to deny any Mosaic claim on the part of the northern priesthood. The priesthood there continued to function until "the day of the captivity of the land," i.e. the invasion by Tiglath-pileser III (733 BCE). The putative grandson of Moses was said to have come to Dan from Bethlehem of Judah by way of Mount Ephraim (Judg 17: 7–8). There is no reason to cast aspersions on the Danite tradition. Attempts to occupy the northern Shephelah region met with stiff opposition from the Amorites dwelling there (Judg 1:34–35). The Philistines were not yet present.

Certain Danite clans remained in the south, as illustrated by the Samson narratives (cf. *supra*). The Danite clan of Hushim (Gen 46:23; Shuham according to Num 26:42) also is found in Benjamin (1 Chr 8: 8). Samson was a Danite from Zorah (Judg 13: 2), but his narratives belong to the eleventh century BCE at the earliest, because the Philistines were already present and were enjoying the upper hand over the Judeans.

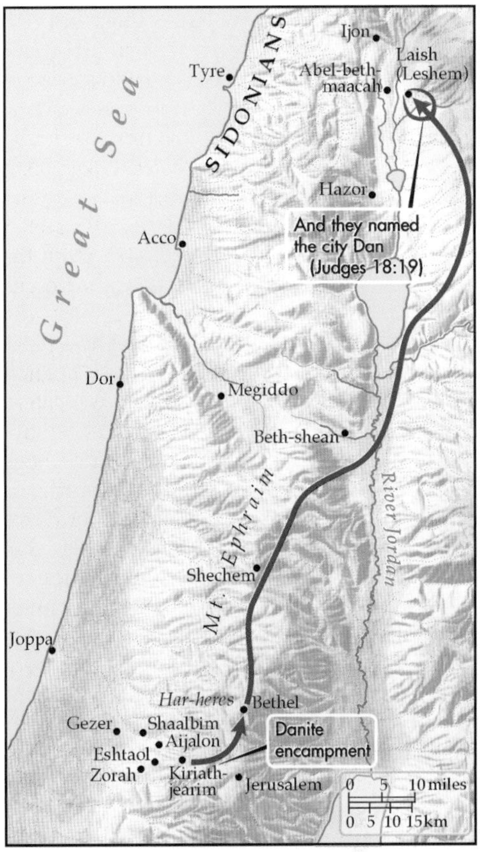


**The Migration of the Tribe of Dan (12th Century BCE)**

**The Machir Migration Eastward.** Various allusions indicate that similar movements took place among other tribes, though the respective traditions have been lost. This is mainly documented in the genealogical tables. For example, Machir, now listed as the father of Gilead, was still found among the tribes of Mount Ephraim in the Song of Deborah (Judg 5:14). After Machir migrated thither from Mount Ephraim, the western tribe was called Manasseh, who became its eponymous ancestor. The concept of "the half-tribe of Manasseh" in Transjordan is related to this

*Excavations at Tell el-Qâḍī (Tel Dan) have shown that the early Iron Age strata contained storage jars, as assembled here, of the northern type, with affinities to Galilee and Phoenicia, alongside the typical "collared-rim" jars used in the central hill country. That unusual archaeological evidence gives credence to the narrative of the Danite migration.*

**THE GENEALOGY OF MANASSEH**

Num 26:28–34, 27:1–4 (5–11), 36:10–12 (cf. 1–8); Josh 17:1–6; 1 Chr 7:14–19

Manasseh
|
Machir
|
Gilead
|
Abiezer Helek (A)sriel Shechem [Hepher] Shemida
|
Zelophehad
|
Mahlah Noah Hoglah Milcah [Tirzah]

Underlined: Clans appearing in Samaria Ostraca

later phase of the period of the Judges. Thus a complicated genealogy of Manasseh was created in which Machir became the father of Gilead which is then inserted into the main stem of the family tree (*see* Num 26:29–33).

The formative stages of this genealogy are still reflected in another pericope: Machir is called the firstborn of Manasseh, the father of Gilead, while the western clans, viz. Abiezer, Helek, Asriel, Shechem, Hepher and Shemida, are called "the rest of the tribe of Manasseh" (Josh 17:1–2); they are thus sons of Manasseh and brothers of Machir. But in the next verse a mixed family line is given: "Zelophehad the son of Hepher, son of Gilead, son of Machir, son of Manasseh" (Josh 17:3; *see* Josh 17:1–6).

The genealogical table in 1 Chronicles 7:14–17 purports to describe this development but the passage is obviously corrupt. In accordance with the other passages cited above, one may venture to correct it (the proposed additions are italicized):

The sons of Manasseh: ‹*Abiezer, Helek*›, **Asriel**, ‹*Shechem, Hepher,* and *Shemida, these are the male descendants of Manasseh the son of Joseph according to their families;*› ‹*and*› whom his Aramean concubine bore: she bore **Machir** the father of **Gilead**. Machir took a wife for **Huppim** and **Shuppim**, whose sister's name was Maacah. And the name of the second was **Zelophehad**, and Zelophehad had daughters. **Maacah** the wife of Machir bore a son, and she named him **Peresh**; and the name of his brother was **Sheresh**, and his sons [were] **Ulam** and **Rakem**. The son of **Ulam** [was] **Bedan**. These are the sons of **Gilead** the son of **Machir**, the son of **Manasseh**. (1 Chr 7:14–17)

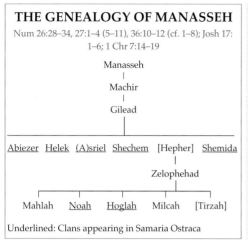

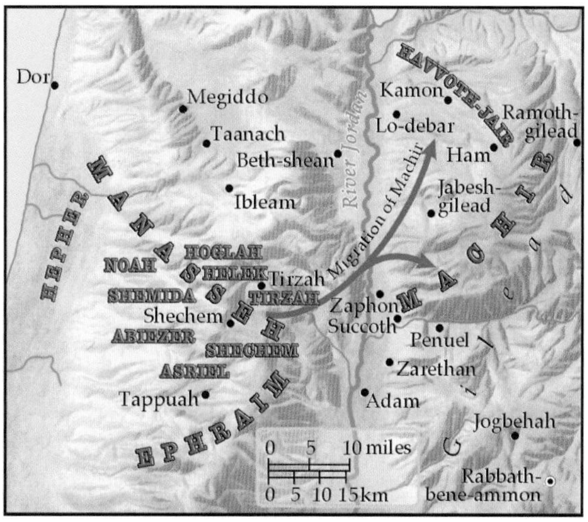


**MACHIR THE SON OF MANASSEH**
**(12TH CENTURY BCE)**

Actually, the western clans, for whom there is independent documenta-tion in the Samaria Ostraca, had surely been the original sons of Machir but when a major portion of that tribe migrated eastward, they were transferred directly to Manasseh and could be called the descendants of Manasseh's first wife while those in Transjordan were the progeny of his Aramean concubine, starting with Machir. Maacah was also the name of an Aramean group in the north around Mount Hermon and the Golan (Deut 3:14; Josh 13:11; 2 Sam 10:6–8). It is therefore admitted that the Gilead population was comprised of different elements with a strong Aramean component. Attempts to form a unified genealogy for Manasseh led to the combining and intertwining of the two strands on the respective sides of the Jordan.

**The Issachar Dispersal.** Some clans from the tribe of Issachar had connections with the Ephraimite hill country. Among the judges was "Tola the son of Puah, son of Dodo, a man of Issachar; and he lived at Shamir in the hill country of Ephraim" (Judg 10:1). Puah is also listed as one of the main clans of Issachar (1 Chr 7:1; also Gen 46:13; Num 26:23). Two other clan names from Issachar show affinities to place names in Mount Ephraim: Shimron-Shemer, owner of the hill of Samaria (1 Kgs 16:24; also the Shamir mentioned above); Jashub (Jashib in 1 Chr 7:1) with Yashub, a place name from the Samaria Ostraca. Issachar's early arrival is hinted in the allusion to its subservience to Canaanite corvée (*see* Gen 49:14–15).

This one tribe, to which Jezreel is associated (Josh 19:18), had early on been able to settle on or close to the Great Plain, but in order to do so, the tribe had to submit to corvée labor on behalf of the occupants of the Canaanite cities there.

**The Tribe of Asher.** The genealogical table of Asher clearly indicates clan connections with southern Mount Ephraim (Gen 46:17–18; 1 Chr 7:30–40). Three Asherite clans have associations with districts along the mutual border between Benjamin and Ephraim: Japhlet (1 Chr 7:33) with the Japhletite (Josh 16:3); Shual (1 Chr 7:36) and the land of Shual (1 Sam 13:17) and also the land of Shaalim (1 Sam 9:4); Shelesh (1 Chr 7:35) and Shilshah (1 Chr 7:37) and the land of Shalishah (1 Sam 9:4). Malchiel was the "father of Birzaith" (1 Chr 7:31), i.e. the clan had settled in Birzaith. The place can be identified with Khirbet Bîr Zeit north of Beitîn (Bethel). Two Asherite clans are also reckoned to the House of Joseph, Beriah in Ephraim and Benjamin (1 Chr 7:30, 8:13) and Shemer in Benjamin (1 Chr 8:12). There might be some connection between Serah (1 Chr 7:30) and Timnath-serah, the town of Joshua in Mount Ephraim (Josh 19:50, 24:30; called Timnath-heres in Judg 2:9). These names seem to indicate that certain Asherite clans and families had settled very early in Mount Ephraim, where they eventually were incorporated into Benjamin and southern Ephraim.

**Reuben.** In the conquest narratives, the Reubenites settled in Heshbon and its environs (Num 32:37–38). Nevertheless, they remained partially nomadic in the desert expanses (1 Chr 5:8–10), while some families of this tribe evidently crossed over to Cisjordan. There is some genealogical evidence for connections of Reuben with Judah and Benjamin. On the border between Judah and Benjamin, west of Jericho, one finds "the stone of Bohan the son of Reuben" (Josh 15:6, 18:17). The Valley of Achor lay on the boundary between Judah and Benjamin (Josh 15:7); there Achan the son of Carmi from the tribe of Judah was stoned (Josh 7:26), Carmi also being one of the leading clans of Reuben (Gen 46:9; Num 26:5–6; 1 Chr 5:3). The clan of Hezron is known among the clans of Reuben (Num 26:6) and Judah (Num 26:21), and the clan of Bela is shared by Reuben (1 Chr 5:8–10) and Benjamin (Gen 46:21; 1 Chr 8:1). The tradition is also interesting that at Migdal-eder, in the vicinity of Jerusalem (Mic 4:8), Reuben is said to have lost his seniority by having sex with Bilhah, his father's concubine (Gen 35:21).

**Judah.** In the genealogies of Judah the affiliated southern tribes have prominent connections with the area of the Arabah and Mount Seir, which refers at least partially to the area west of the Arabah. Of the four Calebite clans from Hebron (1 Chr 2:43), two are of southern origin: Korah, known as an Edomite chief (Gen 36:16), and Rekem, a Midianite prince (Num 31:8; Josh 13:21) as well as being the ancient name of Petra (*Ant.* 6.1.161). Shema also has affinities with that region. The Shimeathites were a Kenite clan (1 Chr 2:55), and among the Simeonites one finds a clan named Shimei (1 Chr 4:26–27) for which the Negeb settlement of Shema might have been named (Josh 15:26). Kenaz also appears as an Edomite chieftain (Gen 36:15). The powerful and widely connected Judean clan of Hezron established an association with Machir and Gilead (*see* 1 Chr 2:21) as well as with Reuben (Num 26:6, 26:21). Hezron is also the clan that absorbed (or adopted?) the two originally independent tribes of Caleb (1 Chr 2:18–24) and Jerahmeel (1 Chr 2:25–33). The family of David came from Hezron through his son Ram (1 Chr 2:10–15; Ruth 4:18–19).

These subsidiary tribes had ancient

connections with the ancient Horites of Mount Seir. For example, among the sons of Seir there was the clan of Shobal (Gen. 36:23, 36:29; 1 Chr 1:38), and a clan by this same name is found at Kiriath-jearim, being associated with "Hur the firstborn of Ephrathah" (1 Chr 2:50b–52). The Horite element is especially prominent among the sons of Jerahmeel (1 Chr 2:25–28): Jether (1 Chr 2:17) and Onam (1 Chr 2:26, 2:28) are included among the Horite sons of Seir (Gen 36:23; 1 Chr 1:40). The Onan of Judah (Gen 38:4–10, 46:12) might have some connection with the Jerahmeelite (and Horite) Onam.

The Kenite "house of Rechab" (1 Chr 2: 55) is associated with the clans of Caleb and Kenaz on the one hand and with the Edomite Ir-nahash ("Serpent City" [probably modified from "City of Copper"]) and Ge-harashim ("Valley of Craftsmen") on the other (1 Chr 4:12–14).

Zerah of Judah also appears among the Simeonites (Num 26:13; 1 Chr 4:24) and also the Edomites (Gen 36:13, 36:17; 1 Chr 1:37).

**Geneaologies and Geography**. The genealogical tables of the various tribes include geographical information of great importance which can be classified under three headings:

1. Names of settlements mentioned among the genealogical records of the tribes and clans in the initial chapters of 1 Chronicles, which derive from different periods. This includes the list of Simeon's towns (1 Chr 4:28–33) and Simeonite expansion toward Gedor (LXX: Gerar) and Mount Seir (1 Chr 4:39–43); the Reubenite settlements "in (from?) Aroer, as far as Nebo and Baal-meon" and his eastward expansion "as far as the entrance of the desert this side of the Euphrates" (1 Chr 5:8–10); the border towns of Ephraim and Manasseh (1 Chr 7:28–29); the history of the Beriah clan which was associated with Gath, Aijalon and Beth-horon (1 Chr 7:21–24, 8:13); the building of Ono and Lod by Benjaminite clans (1 Chr 8:12).
2. Geographical names (such as settlements and regions) integrated into the genealogical framework, discussed above in relation to tribal migrations. The structure of these genealogies expressed the patriarchal viewpoint, viz. that all members of a tribe are the descendants of one venerable eponym including towns and villages within the tribal inheritance. Some of these latter may have been founded by the tribesmen, e.g. Anathoth, Alemeth, Azmaveth and Mozah, which appear among the sons of Benjamin (1 Chr 7:8, 8:36), but others are ancient pre-Israelite settlements that came to be absorbed into the tribal framework, e.g. Shechem, Hepher and Tirzah among the clans of Manasseh (Josh 17:2–3).
3. In the genealogy of Judah (1 Chr 2–4), the sons of various clans are mentioned along with the names of their respective settlements in such a way that a clansman becomes the father of the place occupied, e.g. "Laadah the father of Mareshah" (1 Chr 4:21), "Ezer the father of Hushah" (1 Chr 4:4), etc.

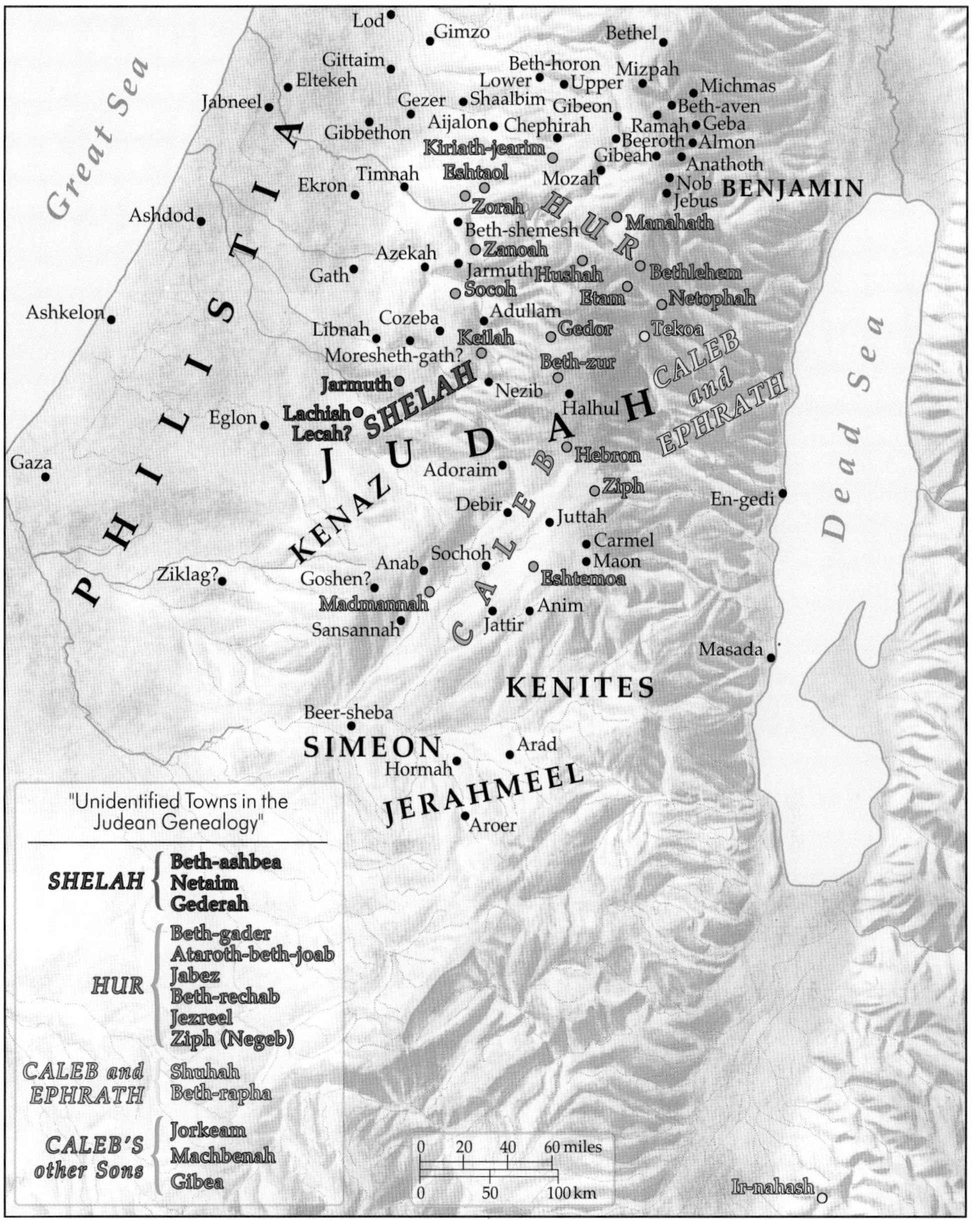


CLANS AND TOWNS/VILLAGES OF THE TRIBE OF "GREATER" JUDAH

By combining the various references in these two chapters one may obtain an approximate reconstruction of the geneaological list. The genealogy of Judah seems to consist of four main branches:

1. The sons of Shelah who settled in Lecah, Mareshah, Beth-ashbea, Cozeba (Cezib), Netaim and Gederah. Of these sites only Mareshah in the Shephelah is identified with certainty, but occupation of the Shephelah by Shelah is indicated by the Judah and Tamar tradition (Gen 38:5).
2. The sons of Hur (from the Hezron-Ephrath[ah] union), who dwelt in Kiriath-jearim, Bethlehem, Beth-gader, Manahath, Zorah, Eshtaol, Netophah, Ataroth, Jabez, Beth-rechab, Etam, Gedor, Hushah, Eshtemoa, Socoh, Zanoah and Keilah. These towns are in the vicinity of Bethlehem and the northeastern Shephelah around the Valley of Elah.
3. The sons of Caleb and Ephrathah, who occupied Tekoa, Shuhah, Beth-rapha and Ir-nahash. Of these the only known location is that of Tekoa, which would seem to indicate that the region between Bethlehem and Hebron is intended.
4. Caleb's other sons, who settled in Ziph, Hebron, Jorkeam, Beth-zur, Madmannah, Machbenah and Gibea, i.e. in the central Judean Hills from Beth-zur, Hebron and the area to the south of them.

Regardless of the accuracy, one important feature stands out. Throughout the two chapters of Judean genealogy, there are place names interwoven with the clans. There is a close relationship between the people and the territory. The study of the ancient society cannot be divorced from geography. A map, no matter how conjectural, still can reflect this relationship.

# CHAPTER SIX

# TERRITORIAL STATES

## TENTH CENTURY BCE

During the course of the tenth century BCE, it was clear that certain territorial states came into being in the Levant. In North Syria, the Neo-Hittite city-states had managed to survive the crisis at the end of the thirteenth century BCE. The emerging Assyrian sources at the end of the tenth and the beginning of the ninth century BCE reveal the presence of territorial states with Aramaic eponyms alongside the Neo-Hittite states. Unfortunately, those new Aramean states have not left behind a body of literary tradition that would reveal the process of settlement, assimilation and consolidation that led to their establishment. There can be no doubt that such oral and written traditions existed and would have provided a rich source of cultural and social information. The Neo-Hittite monumental art comprises a special field of study but it is hard to distinguish specific Aramean elements. In the southern Levant, a literary, historiographic tradition does exist while monumental art is absent. Even architectural remains from the tenth century BCE are hotly disputed in some circles.

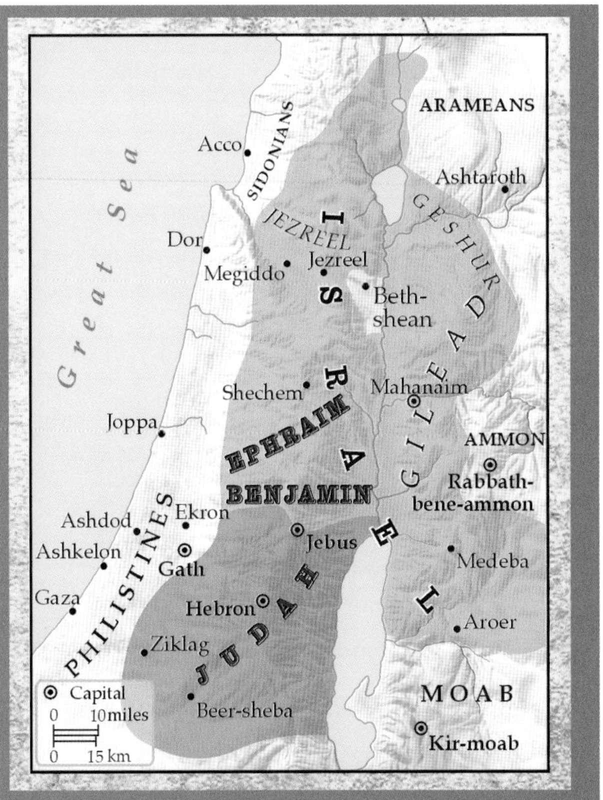

THE KINGDOM OF DAVID AND ESHBAAL

The Assyrians were engaged in a struggle for survival against the Arameans. They had managed to deflect the thrust of the Aramean tribes southward toward Babylonia. However, the Arameans had managed to settle along the eastern bank of the Tigris. More important, they had occupied areas in the northern Jezîrah and along the Euphrates and had succeeded in overrunning some Assyrian territories and driving out the Assyrian population, for example in the reign of Shalmaneser II in the mid-eleventh century BCE and in that of Ashur-rabi II in the late eleventh to early tenth centuries BCE. This situation would only be righted toward the end of the tenth century BCE.

The Arameans had penetrated northern Mesopotamia and founded large tribal states, Bīt-Zamāni (in the Diyarbakir region), Bīt-Bakhiāni (at Guzānu=Gozan, Tell Ḥalâf and Nāṣibīna=Niṣībīn), Bīt-Khalūpe (in the Khabūr/Euphrates triangle) and Bīt-Adini (Til-Barsip=Tell Aḥmar), which was probably the oldest. Henceforth, those areas remained Aramaized in population. West of the Euphrates lay Bīt-Agusi, encompassing Ḥalab (Aleppo) and especially its capital, Arpad (Tell Rifʿat). There was also the kingdom at Samʾal (Sinjirli), possibly called Bīt-Gabbāri.

The process of penetration, occupation and acculturation for the late eleventh and early tenth centuries BCE is undocumented by written sources. The process can only be surmised from the results. However, one thing is certain from the Assyrian records: the Arameans were viewed as original tribal elements, the descendants of those Akhlamû and Sutû who had harassed the caravan routes from Mesopotamia to Syria during the Bronze Age. As such they penetrated the lands between the two rivers, threatened the Assyrians and Babylonians and established territorial states usually named after an eponymous ancestor. Those latter individuals were obviously famous tribal chieftains. Around them there may have been a fascinating body of traditions but alas, none has survived.

## THE SOUTHERN LEVANT

There are no Philistine epigraphic sources from the tenth century BCE. Their role in local history is recorded in a negative way by the biblical sources through the interactions between the Philistines and the tribes of Israel. The tenth century BCE is the story of the consolidation of the Davidic dynasty among the Israelite tribes.

**David's Rise to Power**. The eponymous founder of the Judean dynasty, David, son of Jesse, is immortalized in an essay that comprises the later chapters of the biblical Book of Samuel.

After the death of Saul, David moved his power base from Ziklag to Hebron (*see* 2 Sam 2:1–4). So in effect, David united Judah and the other client tribes, viz. Caleb, Kenaz, the Kenites, the Jerahmeelites, and probably the Cherethites in the western Negeb around Ziklag. The choice of Hebron was a wise one. It was centrally located between David's own Judahite clan on the north, and the client clans on the south. Hebron had, or developed, strong Abrahamic traditions as well.

**Simeon**. Another tribe was also within David's sphere of influence and it cannot be determined if the expansion of that tribe's inheritance took place during David's tenure at Hebron or later, when he had established a new capital in Jerusalem. The record (in three parallel pericopes) of Simeon's towns is comprised of two lists, a long and a short one. They are best represented in 1 Chronicles 4:24–31a.

It is important to note carefully that verses 28–31a list towns *after* David began to reign while verse 32 lists towns *prior* to David's reign. The ill-advised division of the verses broke up the true heading for the short list and left the impression that Simeon had lived in the towns of the long list "until David's reign." The short list is recorded in 1 Chronicles 4:31b–33.

It must be remembered that while David and his troop were at Ziklag, there was no mention of Simeon. Furthermore, there was no "Negeb of Simeon." The only problem city is Hormah because in Judges 1:17 it seems to be described as an early Simeonite conquest albeit in conjunction with Judah.

What seems to have happened is that

*The water shaft of Gibeon, Late Iron Age.*

David found he could use the Simeonites to protect his southern frontier. Whether he took this step at Hebron or later is a moot point. It will be observed that David did not establish any Levitical cities in the Negeb. In the ancestral tradition Simeon and Levi are brothers, eponyms whose violent behavior (Gen 34) prevented them from having an inheritance of their own (Gen 49:5–7).

The tribal town list needs some textual adjustments, not all of them capable of final decisions. The Simeonite list in Joshua (Josh 19:1–8; included also in Josh 15:21–32) can correct a few obvious errors from the Chronicles list, also vice versa, not to mention the LXX versions. The following passage emphasizes only the differences with the better readings in bold and the inferior ones in italics:

> Then the second lot fell to Simeon, to the tribe of the sons of Simeon according to their families, and their inheritance was in the midst of the inheritance of the sons of Judah. So they had as their inheritance Beer-sheba and *Sheba* (correct to read Shema as in Josh 15:32) and Moladah, and Hazar-shual and *Balah* and Ezem, and **Eltolad** and *Bethul* and Hormah, and Ziklag and Beth-marcaboth and Hazar-susah, and **Beth-lebaoth** and *Sharuhen*; thirteen cities with their villages; Ain, Rimmon and Ether and Ashan; *four* cities with their villages; and all the villages which are around these towns as far as **Baalath-beer** (Kh. el-Meshâsh=Tel Masos), **Ramath-negeb** (Kh. Gharrah=Tel ᶜIra). This is the inheritance of the tribe of the sons of Simeon according to their families.
>
> (Josh 19:1–8)

**The Intertribal War**. For seven years it is said that war raged between the Davidic coalition in the south and the Saulide coalition in the north. This reflected age-old differences in the two regions and the two tribal "leagues" (*see* 2 Sam 2:8–9, 4:2, 4:7).

To what degree this description reflects a political reality from that time is impossible to assess. The tribes of Galilee are not included and that is true to the situation attending Saul's death when he died trying to gain a foothold in the north. The conflict is illustrated in the narrative by a battle that took place in the vicinity of Gibeon (*see* 2 Sam 2:12–32).

There is no way that the "pool of Gibeon" could be the water shaft excavated at el-Jîb. It must have been a water-collection facility outside the confines of the town, probably in the field close to the point where the spring water flows out from its source. In such a place the opposing forces could have arranged themselves for the ensuing contest. The opening gambit by twenty-four champions from each side is again reminiscent of a well-known Mediterranean theme.

The chain of events that developed from the battle at Gibeon led to the death of Joab's brother, Asahel, at the hand of Abner, and the subsequent assassination of Abner by Joab. This was considered the run-up to the assassination of Ish-bosheth/Eshbaal and the subsequent uniting of the two coalitions under David (*see* 2 Sam 4:1–3).

The two assassins were from a clan of Gibeonites reckoned as part of Benjamin, but their clan had fled to Gittaim, which must also have been known as Gath-rimmon. Their act of regicide may have been in revenge for Saul's acts of cruelty against their clan.

The tragic deaths of Abner and Eshbaal led to David's kingship over the northern tribal coalition. Just as David had chosen Hebron as a capital to unite Judah and the client tribes in the south, he now chose to conquer the Jebusite enclave at Jerusalem and make that city his dynastic possession ("the city of David"). By now the Philistines realized that the unification of all the tribes under David posed a threat to their hegemony in the hill country. Twice they came up against him via the Valley of Rephaim (cf. Josh 15:8). The first time, they had a garrison positioned at Bethlehem (2 Sam 23:14) to prevent David from getting help from the south. David smote them and called the place of his victory Baal-perazim (2 Sam 5:20).

The second time that the Philistines came, David ambushed them by blocking their retreat at the western end of the Valley of Rephaim: "and he smote the Philistines from **Geba** as far as **Gezer**" (2 Sam 5:25).

Having expelled the Philistines from the central hill country, David was free to bring the Ark of the Covenant from Kiriath-jearim to his new capital in Jerusalem (2 Sam 6; 1 Chr 13, 15). Then he took the initiative against the Philistines on the coastal plain (*see* 1 Chr 18:1).

Geographically, this text seems superior to the "bridle of the forearm(?)" of 2 Samuel 8:1. The reference here is probably not to "Gath of the Philistines" (Am 6:2; Tell eṣ-Ṣâfī = Tel Ẓafit), of the pentapolis, but rather the Gath/Gittaim/Gath-rimmon northwest of Gezer. This victory secured David's control over the corridor from Gezer, where David left the indigenous Canaanites unmolested, to the seaport at Joppa.

**David's Transjordanian and Syrian Conquests**. The course of David's Transjordanian conquests may be traced chronologically by correlating the information in 2 Samuel 8:2–11 (=1 Chr 18:2–11) with that of 2 Samuel 10:1–19, 11:1 and 11:26–31 (=1 Chr 19:1–19, 20:1–3). The development was apparently as follows:

1. ***Moab***. Moab was conquered and reduced to vassal status, thus giving David firm control over the tableland north of the Arnon (2 Sam 8:2 || 1 Chr 18:2).

2. ***Ammon***. At this point, the suggestion can be accepted to treat 2 Samuel 10:1–11:1, 12:26–31 || 1 Chronicles 19:1–20:3 as the next stage in the course of events. As was his wont, the author of the Book of Samuel gave precedence to certain crucial events in the career of David. Here he is concerned with the affair of David, Bath-sheba and Uriah the Hittite. Thus, he strove to set the political and geographic scene and the course of events that brought the Israelite army to the walls of Rabbath-bene-ammon where Uriah could be exposed and killed. To do so, he must begin with the initial conflict with the Ammonites.

The new Ammonite ruler, Hanun, showed his displeasure at the new Israelite military presence so close to his borders by insulting David's ambassadors (2 Sam 10:1–5 =

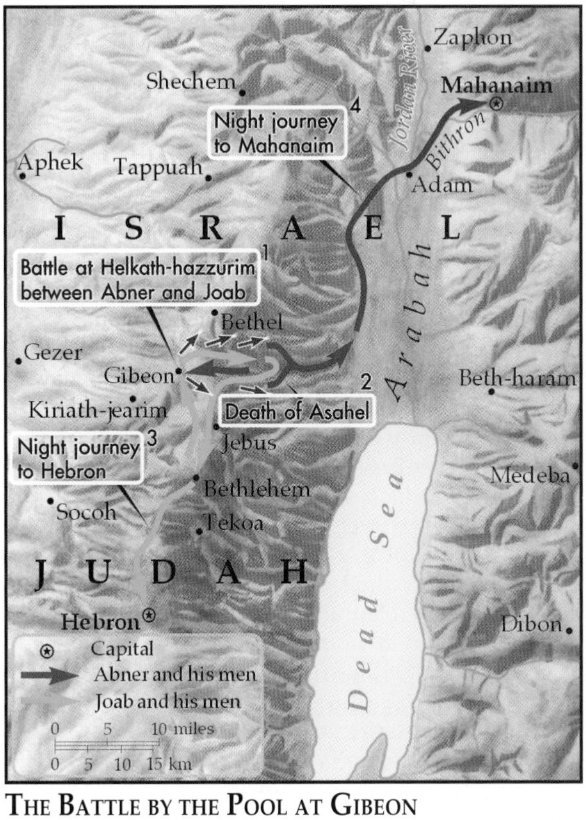


THE BATTLE BY THE POOL AT GIBEON

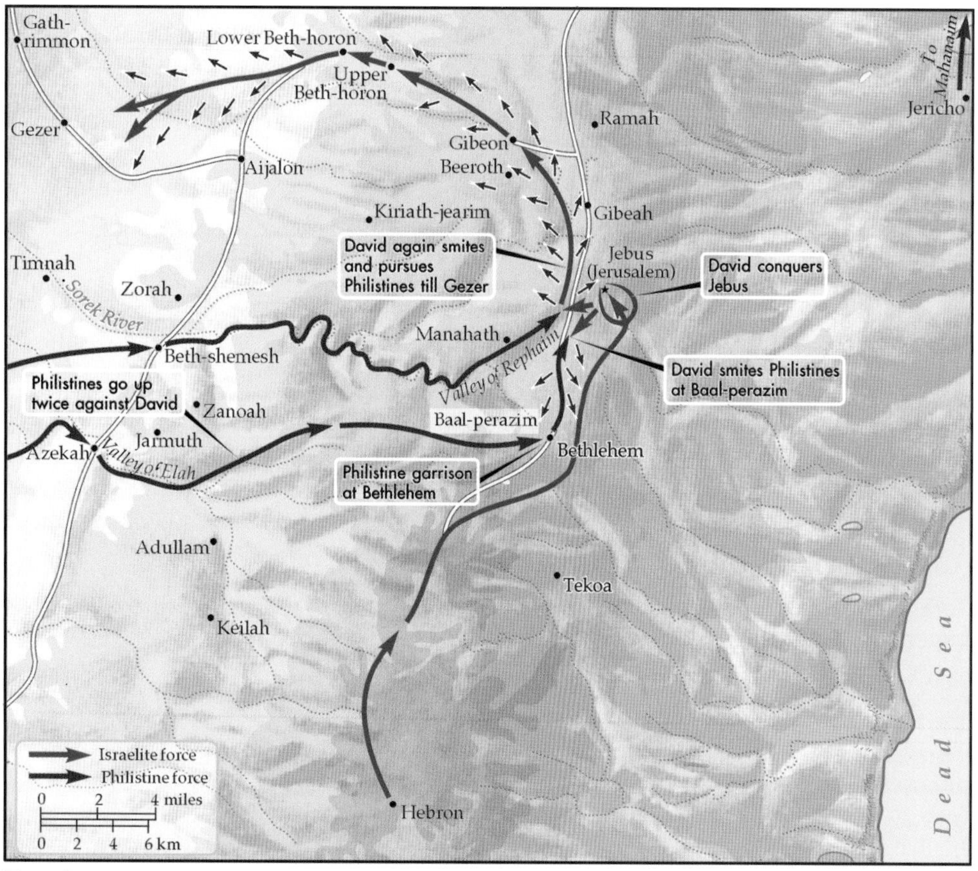


**The Assassination of Eshbaal, The Conquest of Jerusalem and The Subsequent Philistine Wars**

1 Chr 19:1–5). David's subjection of Moab led him and his counselors to suspect that the Israelite monarch had further designs on Transjordan. Then he sent for help from the Aramean kingdoms that had developed in northern Transjordan and in the Lebanese Beqa$^{c}$ Valley, namely Aram-beth-rehob and Aram-zobah, Maacah, and the men of Tob (*see* 2 Sam 10:6–14 || 1 Chr 19:6–8).

David sent forth his army under the command of Joab; seeing the opposing forces on two sides, Joab divided the command with his brother, Abishai. The Arameans were routed by Joab and then the Ammonites retreated to their fortified city.

3. ***Hadadezer, king of Aram-zobah.*** Stung by the defeat of the Aramean forces, Hadadezer sent for all his vassals and associates among the Aramean kingdoms and tribes as far as the Euphrates (*see* 2 Sam 10:15–16 || 1 Chr 19:16).

They assembled at Helam where David confronted them with the army of Israel (*see* 2 Sam 10:17–19 || 1 Chr 19:17–19). David's victory caused Hadadezer's vassals to defect and to offer allegiance to David (2 Sam 10:15–19; 1 Chr 19:16–19). As for this Helam, the town of Alema, modern $^{c}$Almā, northeast of Derâ$^{c}$a on the plain of Hauran on the southern border of Syria in northern Transjordan, is mentioned in 1 Maccabees 5:26, 35 in a context with Bezer (Buṣra Eski Shâm) and Bosor (=Buṣr el-Ḥarîrī, 45 mi./72 km east of the Chinnereth). This is a logical locale for the confrontation though Helam appears also in the Septuagint of Ezekiel 47:16 and 48:1, but not in the Hebrew; there the site is between Damascus and Hamath, not far from Hadadezer's main cities, Tebah and Berothai (2 Sam 8:8).

4. ***Rabbath-bene-ammon.*** The way was now clear to settle accounts with Rabbath-bene-ammon. After the next harvest, David sent the army under Joab to attack the city and following a protracted siege, Joab was able to send for David to receive the enemy's surrender (2 Sam 11:1, 12:26–11; 1 Chr 20:1–3). During this time, Uriah was sent to his death on the order of David and with the connivance of Joab.

5. ***Hadadezer defeated.*** Now that David was the undisputed master of Transjordan, he could give his attention to his Aramean rival in the north. While Hadadezer was trying to restore his authority over his former vassals along the Euphrates, David invaded his home territory and captured most of his military forces. This made David the nominal leader of the Aramean league over which he appointed governors at Damascus. The two parallel passages correct mistakes in one another and provide a comprehensive picture (*see* 2 Sam 8:3–8 || 1 Chr 18:3–8).

By this sequence of fortuitous events, David was drawn into confrontation with the Arameans to the east and north. The picture fits perfectly with the information from Assyrian sources about the widespread conflicts and violence due to the Aramean tribes and their movements. By the tenth century BCE, many of those Aramean elements had begun to form more stable political entities with which the Assyrians would subsequently have to deal. But the biblical picture of David's conflicts and interaction with the many Aramean groups is thoroughly compatible with what is known about the Arameans in that period. Leaders like David and Hadadezer were doubtless typical of the kind of leadership that had developed among the various Aramean tribes and coalitions of tribes that came to dominate the banks of the Euphrates and who also invaded lower Mesopotamia and settled in trans-Tigris and also formed the new territorial states in northern Syria.

6. ***Treaty with Hamath.*** As a result, Toi, king of Hamath on the Orontes, the archenemy of Hadadezer, sought an alliance with David (2 Sam 8:9–11; 1 Chr 18:9–11). So Toi sent **Joram** (1 Chr 18:10, **Hadoram**), his son, to seal the treaty. This was to be the beginning of a long-standing tradition of friendship between the two states. It also gave the Israelite king an entrée into the world of northern Syria. During a brief window of opportunity in the tenth century BCE, Israel came to represent a strong military power in the southern Levant with allies and alliances in central Syria.

7. ***Conquest of Edom.*** Finally, the way was now open to extend Israel's control over the southern expanses of Edom. The military victory was accomplished by Abishai (probably under Joab; cf. the superscription

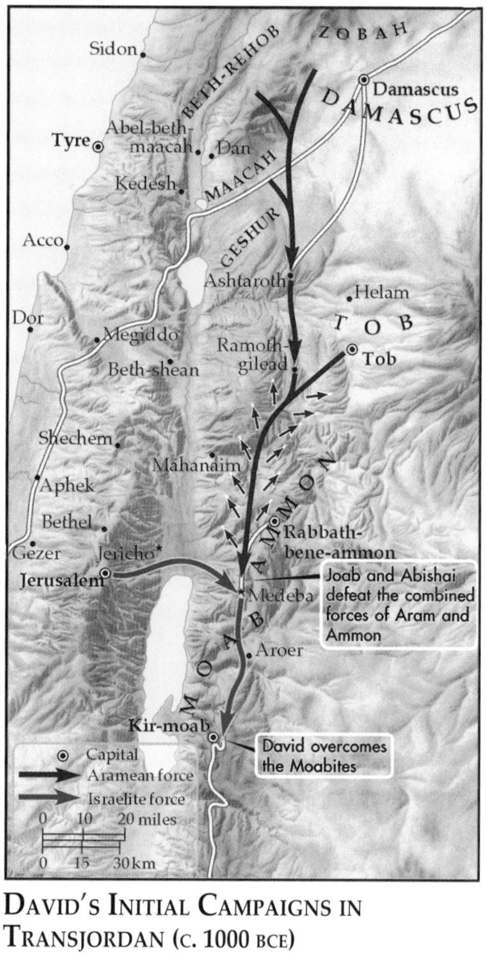


**David's Initial Campaigns in Transjordan (c. 1000 BCE)**

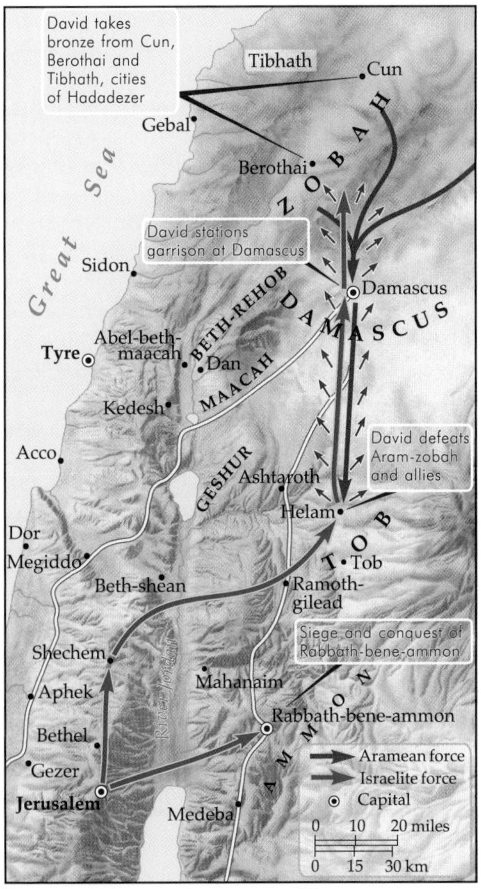


**Defeat of the Aramean Coalition and the Conquest of Rabbath-bene-ammon**

to Ps 60); commissioners were appointed to administer the Edomite domains (1 Chr 18: 12–13; cf. 2 Sam 8:13b–15). At this time, Hadad, a child from the Edomite royal house, was smuggled to Egypt where he received political asylum (1 Kgs 11:15–20).

**The Davidic Census.** The reign of David culminated in an administrative act, a census, which is condemned by the seers and prophets but is linked, nevertheless, with the purchase of the threshing floor of Araunah the Jebusite, the rocky outcrop which became the site of the altar for the Jerusalem temple (2 Sam 24:18–25). The description of the census (2 Sam 24:4-7) is not without textual corruptions but it still gives a fascinating geographical survey of the newly consolidated kingdom (*see* 2 Sam 24:4–7).

The territory covered represents all of the area directly under control of the monarchy in Jerusalem. Although the text of Joab's itinerary (2 Sam 24:5–7) is badly preserved in spots, the general course of the census can be discerned. He began at **Aroer** on the traditional border with Moab whenever Israel held the tableland. Then they progressed through the territory of **Gad**, in the western tableland itself according to Mesha's inscription. Note that Reuben is not mentioned at all. Then they continued on to Jazer/Jaazer, a strongpoint facing the kingdom of the Ammonites (Num 21:24; Kh. eṣ-Ṣâr?) and on through Gilead. The next stage of the journey is obscured by a textual corruption, but the best Greek version, albeit unclear, suggests that **Bashan** was the area visited. This makes sense since Joab went from there to Dan at the foot of Mount Hermon, and on to Jaan, an obvious metathesis for Ijon. This latter is Tell ed-Dibbîn in Marj ᶜAyyûn. The Septuagint interprets Tahtim-hodshi as "to the land of the Hittites, Kadesh," which might have made some sense if it came after Ijon in the southern Beqaᶜ Valley. But the usual geographical marker in that area would have been Lebo-hamath. Next the census team moved across Upper Galilee along the border with Sidon, past the "fortress of Tyre," probably the Usû known from Egyptian and Assyrian inscriptions (Hellenistic *Palaeotyrus*, "Old Tyre").

The next entry is the most tantalizing: "All the cities of the Hivites and the Canaanites." It is unfortunate that those towns are not listed by name. However, it seems obvious that the intention is all those towns that had initially been

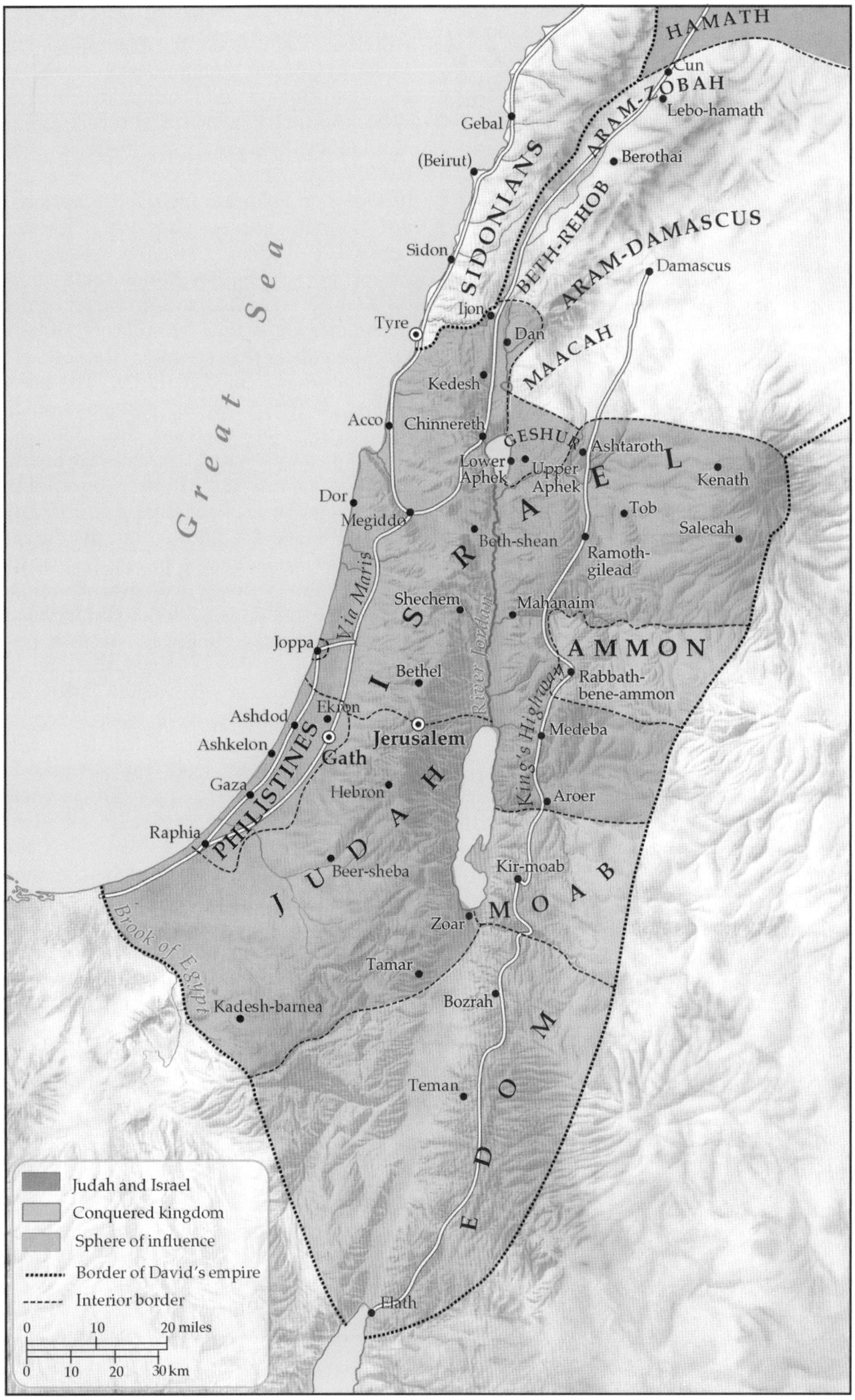


**The Kingdom of David**

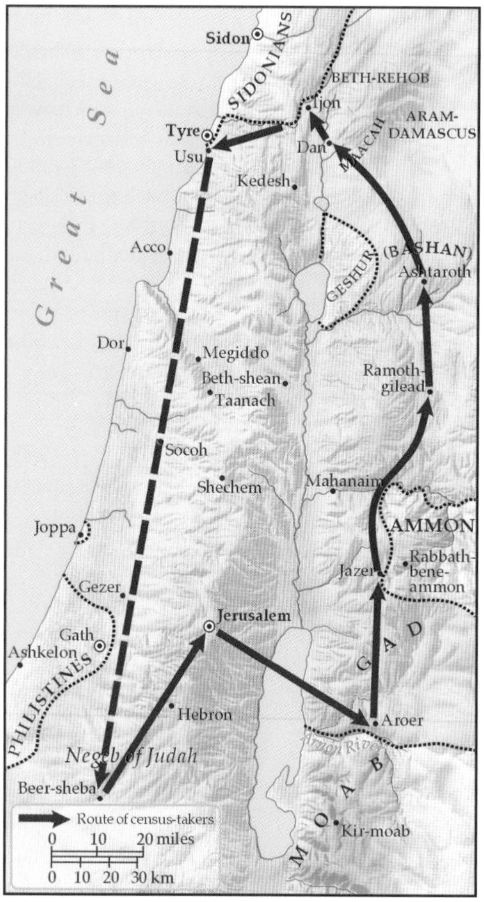


JOAB'S CENSUS (C. 980 BCE)

unconquered (Judg 1:27–35). Here is the tacit admission that those centers of the pre-Israelite population that had maintained their social and political integrity up to now had finally succumbed to the new, united Israel. Specific details about how David subdued those Hivite and Canaanite cities is not found in any ancient source. Was it by force? Was it by diplomacy? The *Landesausbau*, the expansion of the Israelites during the course of time until, under the monarchy, they occupied the entire land, is rightly seen as the key to understanding the conquest traditions. It is indeed sad that that process is shrouded in mystery. However, the end result can be seen in the dispersal of Levitical settlements and in the Solomonic commissioners' districts. The main concentrations of Canaanite towns were in the Plain of Acco, the Jezreel Valley, and in the Sharon Plain (including the district of Dor and the hinterland between Gezer and Joppa).

The final area to be visited was the Negeb of Judah, the southern frontier zone occupied mainly by subsidiary tribes such as the Kenites, the Jerahmeelites, and the Simeonites recently settled there by David. Joab went to the new regional capital, Beer-sheba, located at the center of the Judean Negeb (today's Be'er Sheva[c] and Besor valleys).

Therefore, the census passage provides a description of the territory now under the aegis of the founder of the new dynasty, the "House of David."

## SOLOMON'S REIGN

**Spheres of Influence.** Later tradition has imbued Solomon, the son of David, with an aura of glory that continued into post-biblical times, on to the Qurân and other fable traditions. The beginning of this trend is an editorial comment in the prophetic summary of his reign (*see* 1 Kgs 10: 23–24 ‖ 2 Chr 9:22–23).

In order to achieve a more realistic appraisal of the Solomonic tenure, the geographical data in the pericopes dealing with that reign must be evaluated. The framework of the kingdom is presented in two dimensions, a wider sphere of influence and a narrower zone of direct Israelite population. The LXX arrangements and the Book of Chronicles suggest that originally, the essay on Solomon included "captions" that defined the geographical "frame." Verses 4:20–5:1 (Eng. 4:20–21) of 1 Kings do not appear in the Septuagint; the equivalent to 1 Kings 5:1 (Eng. 4:21) in Chronicles comes much later in a final summary (2 Chr 9: 26). Therefore, the second "framework" combination is treated here first. The other passage, when placed in juxtaposition to its partner, would create the following scheme: Levant—Israel ‖ Israel—Levant. In any event, that is the proper geographical approach in order to define the political, military, economic and social picture as reflected in the sources (*see* 1 Kgs 5:4 [Eng. 4:24]).

The editor who added this comment evidently wanted his readers to understand that Solomon's political domination extended across the Levant as defined in the Mesopotamian expression "Beyond the River." He must have been living in a time when that geographical term was in vogue, any time from the seventh to the fourth century BCE. Since the narrative of Kings ends with the reign of Evil-merodach, it seems more likely that the mid-sixth century BCE would be the time that final editorial comments were added. Nevertheless, the reign of Josiah is also a possibility. The northern geographical point, Tiphsah (classical Thapsakos, modern Dibseh), was on the bend of the Euphrates, a very convenient fording point that often played such a role in later history (Xenophon, *Anabasis* 1.4.11). However, it never appears in the abundant Assyrian records in the ninth, eighth or seventh centuries BCE.

If the allusion to military action against Hamath of Zobah has a historical basis, it would suggest a brief rift in the relationship between the two states (*see* 2 Chr 8:3–4). The enigmatic Hamath-zobah seems to suggest that Hamath had incorporated the former kingdom of Zobah. Hamath may also have gained hegemony over the districts to the north of it, viz. Luġath and Hadrach. If Solomon had gained some form of dominance there, it would indeed bring his influence as far as the Euphrates.

On the other hand, there is no intimation that Solomon exercised direct rule over this broad area. He dominated the kings of the Levant. The picture is of an eastern Mediterranean littoral occupied by many small kingdoms from the north to the south. Gaza was evidently the senior city-state along the southern coast and surely had control of the route across Sinai to Egypt.

In contrast to that wider sphere of influence, there was the limited area of actual Israelite occupation (*see* 1 Kgs 5:5 [Eng. 4:25]).

The other passage, missing in the Septuagint and partially inserted later in the Solomonic narrative as 1 Chronicles 9: 26, gives the two contrasting geographical entities in the opposite order (*see* 1 Kgs 4:20).

The next verse, the second part of the description, has suffered corruption but can easily be corrected. The river can only be the Euphrates as comparison with passages such as Deuteronomy 1:7, 11:24 and Joshua 1:4 readily demonstrates. In the south, the "land of the Philistines" is the first limit but afterwards "and to the border of Egypt." The restored passage is as follows:

> Now Solomon ruled over all the kingdoms from the ‹‹Great›› **River** ‹‹the River Euphrates›› ‹to› the **land of the Philistines** and to the **border of Egypt**; [they] brought tribute and served Solomon all the days of his life. (1 Kgs 5:1 [Eng. 4:21])

So there was the nation of Israel proper, as defined by the two major religious and

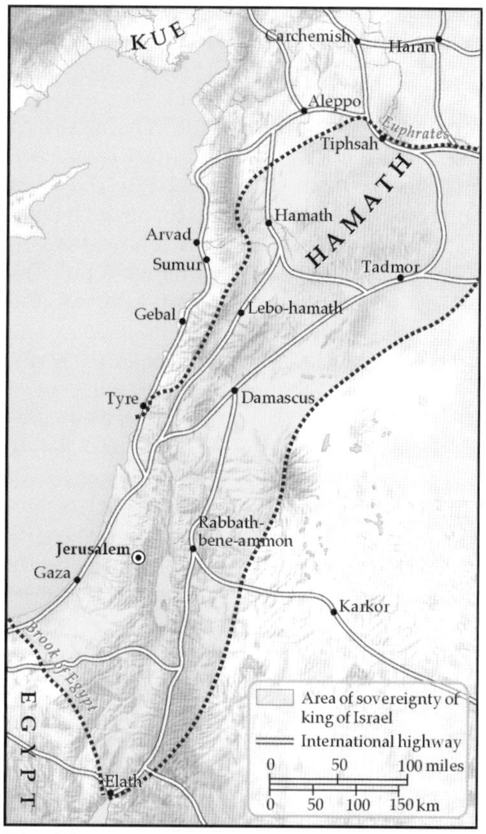


THE PRESUMED ISRAELITE HEGEMONY DURING THE REIGNS OF DAVID AND SOLOMON

*Bringing tribute to an overlord; relief on obelisk of Ashurnasirpal II, from Calah.*

administrative centers at the north and south extremities, Dan and Beer-sheba respectively. And there was the wider zone of influence from the Euphrates bend to the border of Egypt. The latter was undoubtedly identical to the "River of Egypt" of Genesis 15:18.

How plausible is this picture? Obviously, such hegemony over the Levant would have been short-lived. By 925 BCE Shishak would have brought an end to any such aspirations of power by his campaign against both Judah and Israel. The Assyrian resurgence at about the same time, under Ashur-dan II, did not yet reach into central Syria, so there is no reason to expect cuneiform references to such a "Solomonic power bloc." It will be seen below that Solomon was said to have had diplomatic relations with the Neo-Hittite states (possibly including the Aramean dynastic states that were coalescing at this time). It cannot be said that an Israelite period of influence during this window of opportunity is impossible. Obviously, it is not the glorious empire that ancients and moderns often ascribe to Solomon. But a time of seniority in the Levant is compatible with all that is known of the tenth century BCE.

**Strong Military Establishment**. Solomon is credited with maintaining a strong army with modern equipment—horses and chariots (*see* 2 Chr 1:14 || 1 Kgs 10:26 also || 1 Kgs 5:6 [Eng. 4:26] and 2 Chr 9:25; *see also* 1 Kgs 9:17–19).

It is still not clear what is meant by a "chariot city" or a "horseman city." The need for this military organization was to control the highways and to police the territories through which the caravan trade could move. At the outposts and storage depots along the routes and at major junctions, there were also stores of supplies to sell to the caravans and to support the troops stationed there.

**Diplomacy**. The relationship between Solomon and other neighboring states is described in a number of passages. The most striking is the reported alliance with the king of Egypt (*see* 1 Kgs 3:1, 9:16).

The name of this pharaoh is unknown though it has often been assumed to be Siamon (978–959 BCE). The enigmatic allusion to the conquest of Gezer is also without explanation. Was it at first an act of aggression? Was the marriage recognition that Israel was really a force to be reckoned with? Since there is no outside confirmation to this relationship, it has often been doubted. It must be said, however, that the daughter of Pharaoh appears in key passages about the planning of public construction and its realization. Given the nadir of Egyptian political and military clout during the XXI$^{st}$ Dynasty, it seems unlikely that a fictitious link with Egypt would have served to glorify the king of Israel. No answers to these questions are forthcoming.

Marriage alliances with neighboring states can be deduced from the list of Solomon's wives (*see* 1 Kgs 11:1). Moab, Ammon and Edom were reduced to tributary status by the conquests of David. The Sidonians could be from any of the Lebanese coastal states since that is the Hebrew generic term for Phoenicians. The diplomatic relationship with Tyre is discussed below.

As for the "Hittites," they would have been from some of the Neo-Hittite states in northern Syria, especially Hamath and its satellites. There is a hint (2 Chr 8:3) that Solomon had employed strong-arm tactics to gain bases in central Syria and at Tadmor on the route to Mesopotamia. Specific links with the emerging Aramean states in northern Syria are not mentioned in the sources.

The diplomatic relationship with Hiram/Hirom, king of Tyre, is more complicated. From the census passage it would appear that David had managed to include the coastal dependencies of Tyre in his own new political entity (2 Sam 24:7). This comes at a time when the Tyrians and the other cities were engaged in active maritime activity. Therefore, the two parties had much to gain from each other (2 Sam 5:11).

Josephus (*Apion* 1.106–111) reports that Tyre kept very detailed chronicles of its political and foreign affairs but he is dependent on two Hellenistic/Roman sources, especially Menander of Ephesus (*Apion* 1.116–121; *Ant.* 8:144–460). Menander gives the name of Hiram's father, Abibalos (Abi-Ba$^{c}$al) and says Hiram lived for fifty-three years and reigned for thirty-four years. Another of Josephus' sources was a historian, Dius (*Apion* 1:112–115; *Ant.* 8:147–149), whom he calls "an accurate historian of Phoenicia." Nevertheless, the "historical data" include folkloristic matters such as the contests of wisdom with Solomon.

Hiram is said to have supplied workmen and raw materials for the palace of David (2 Sam 5:11). That context, 2 Samuel 5:9–12, is an editorial moralizing summary and cannot be related to the chronological context. David surely did not do any building in Jerusalem until long after he had removed the Philistine threat and had defeated the Aramean coalition in the north. Hiram's assistance would have come near the end of David's reign when the latter could devote time to building and fortifying his capital.

Concerning Hiram's relationship with Solomon, there are two biblical accounts (1 Kgs 5:15–32 [Eng. 5:1–18] and 2 Chr 1:18–2:15 [Eng. 2:1–16]) which differ somewhat in detail. The Deuteronomistic narrative (1 Kgs 5:15 [Eng. 5:1]) credits Hiram with making the first overture upon Solomon's accession to the throne. A deal was made to exchange timber and manpower in return for large annual quantities of agricultural products. This is commensurate with the standard practice of the Phoenicians of supplying their foodstuffs from the hinterland so their population could engage in maritime activities.

The Chronicler (2 Chr 2:1 [Eng. 2:3]) has revised the entire transaction, giving the initiative to Solomon and making the foodstuffs logistic support for the workers on Solomon's building projects.

A joint sea venture involving ships and crews for a commercial fleet launched from Ezion-geber on the Red Sea (1 Kgs 9:26–28, 10:11, 10:22; 2 Chr 8:17–18, 9:10, 9:21) is also depicted in both Kings and Chronicles. The fleet operated on the Red Sea, possibly sailing to the land called Punt by the Egyptians. They specialized in luxury items, viz. silver, ivory, and exotic animals. The location of Ophir and Tarshish is uncertain. Many

*The traditional tomb of Hiram, king of Tyre.*

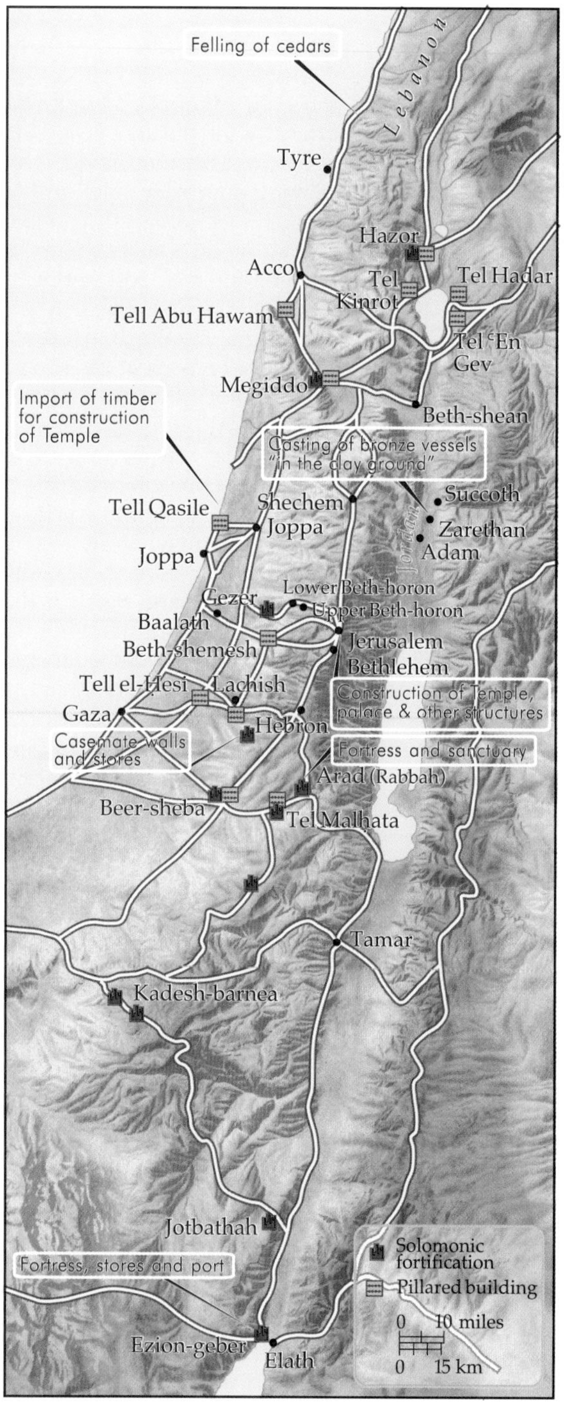


SOLOMONIC BUILDING PROJECTS

suggestions have been offered for Ophir but none can be substantiated. Tarshish is explained in various ways. In the Mediterranean there were several places by that name: Tarsus in Cilicia, a Tarshish in Sardinia and, of course, Tartessos in Spain. The Chronicler has the fleet visiting Tarshish (2 Chr 9:21), which could be an anachronism based on his own knowledge of Mediterranean sea trade in the Persian period. The term "ships of Tarshish" (1 Kgs 10:22) was perhaps misinterpreted by the Chronicler, who must have known about the Phoenician circumnavigation of Africa in the sixth century BCE.

Late in his reign Solomon was forced to transfer twenty cities "in the land of Galilee" to Hiram (*see* 1 Kgs 9:10–14). The phrase "the land of Cabul" indicates that these were towns on the Plain of Acco (Cabul=Kābûl; Josh 19:27).

The Chronicler could not accept the idea that Solomon might have relinquished a part of the kingdom (2 Chr 8:1–2). He presents a different picture in which Hiram gave the towns to Solomon, who then rebuilt them and resettled them with Israelites.

## Commercial and Economic Poli-cy.

The extraordinary wealth ascribed to Solomon's regime is surely exaggerated but still must have some basis in fact (*see* 2 Chr 1:15 || 1 Kgs 10:27; 2 Chr 9:27; *see also* 1 Kgs 10:14 || 2 Chr 9:14).

There is an acknowledgment that the southern land bridge had become the focus of commerce and trade (*see* 1 Kgs 10:15b || 2 Chr 9:14). The source of all this wealth, even if somewhat overstated by the historiographer, was control of the main arteries of commerce as achieved by the conquests of David. The Transjordanian highway from Arabia to Damascus passed through neighboring states that David had reduced to vassalage, including Damascus itself.

A recently discovered fort at Khirbet en-Naḥas near the mouth of Wâdī Feinân indicates organized copper production during the tenth century BCE.

The coastal trunk route (popularly and wrongly called *Via Maris*), linking Egypt with Syria and Mesopotamia, passed through Philistia, went by way of Gezer, Aphek, the eastern Sharon Plain and into the Jezreel Valley (near Megiddo). The main branch turned east to the fords of the Jordan near Beth-shean and Transjordanian Peḥel (Pella or Fiḥl) and up to Damascus, thence to Tadmor and Babylon. Solomon's control of these routes is expressed by his construction of strong cities at key junctures on these highways:

> Now this is the record of the forced labor which King Solomon levied to build the house of YHWH, his own house, the Millo, the wall of Jerusalem, **Hazor**, **Megiddo**, and **Gezer**. . . . So Solomon rebuilt **Gezer** and the ‹**upper Beth-horon**› and **lower Beth-horon** and **Baalath** and **Tadmor** in the steppe land; in the land and all the store cities, ‹fortified cities (with) walls, gates and bars› which Solomon had, even the chariot cities and the cavalry cities , and all that Solomon desired to build in Jerusalem, in **Lebanon**, and in all the territory under his rule.
>
> (1 Kgs 9:15–19; supplemented by 2 Chr 8:5)

Hazor, Megiddo and Gezer guard major junctions on the great north-south trunk route. At one time it was thought that the archaeological remains of three tenth-century BCE fortification systems confirmed this reference. Today there is much controversy on the subject but in reality, the evidence is being interpreted in a highly subjective manner and nothing firm can be concluded. The value of this written testimony in the sources is, in fact, beyond archaeological critique. It is inconceivable that the historiographer would invent details such as this no matter how much he wished to magnify his hero.

It is the parallel passage in Chronicles that preserves Upper Beth-horon. This would seem to be correct, both sites, upper and lower, being important vantage points on the best route from the plain to the hill-country saddle that joins Mount Judah with Mount Ephraim.

Baalath is evidently the town on the southwestern side of the so-called Danite inheritance (Josh 19:44). Baalath appears to have come under Israelite control only during the united monarchy. Baalath is most likely to be equated with Mount Baalah (Josh 15:11), on the alleged western boundary of Judah. It has been suggested to identify it with the Bronze and Iron Age site, el-Mughâr. From here one can trace a route to Jerusalem via Gezer and Beth-horon.

The problem of identifying chariots and cavalry cities has been mentioned above. The dispersal of cities with pillared buildings "in all the territory under his rule" gives a revealing picture of the geopolitical situation in the tenth century BCE. The control of these highways was a multifaceted source of income. The caravans doubtless paid for security and protection along the road. They also paid with their wares for water, fodder and food, all of which were supplied at the fortified cities. For a kingdom like Israel (and Judah), which had little in the way of mineral resources or valuable forests, the principal means of production were agriculture. The network of forts with their storehouses for supplying caravans was a convenient and lucrative market for agricultural produce. Grain, wine and oil along with other fruits and vegetables could be converted into "hard currency" (silver and gold) and other luxury goods. The arrival of a caravan at some strongpoint was an occasion for mutual exchange and benefit. Several caravans at once could comprise a "fair."

The reference to the import and export of horses and chariots has challenged commentators but there is no reason that it cannot be taken at face value. Horses from Kue had certainly been raised in eastern Anatolia and brought to the coastal plain of Adana (Cilicia). Egypt had had a long history of horse breeding ever since the New Kingdom pharaohs began to develop their chariot forces; Nubian horses were much in demand. Egypt was also known for its manufacturing industry with regard to chariots. The technology had been well

*Hazor, one of the cities fortified by Solomon. Shown here are remains of a pillared storehouse.*

developed and there is no reason that it could not have been revived during the XXI$^{st}$ Dynasty and especially during the XXII$^{nd}$ (*see* 1 Kgs 10:28–29). The mention of the North Syrian Hittite and Aramean kings is another link with the rise of those territorial states that had formed by the tenth century BCE.

**Internal Administration**. A number of passages describing the internal administration under David and Solomon have been singled out as having the character of true original sources: the list of David's wives and sons (2 Sam 3:2–5, 5:14–16); the list of David's cabinet officers (2 Sam 23:8–39); the list of Solomon's senior officials (1 Kgs 4:2–6); the list of Solomon's twelve administrative districts (1 Kgs 4:7–19); and Solomon's building activities (1 Kgs 9:15, 17–18). To these passages one may add the detailed description of the public works departments employed in the Solomonic construction projects, namely the "forced labor" (1 Kgs 5:13–14 [Heb. 5:27–28]) and the "burden bearers and hewers of stone" (1 Kgs 5:16–17 [Heb. 5:29–31]). The public works departments are described below. Solomon's "cabinet officers" appear in 1 Kings 4:2–6.

For conducting the kingdom's many building projects and for meeting the expenses of the central administration, the northern tribes were organized into twelve districts with a commissioner in charge of each (*see* 1 Kgs 4:7).

The districts as geographic entities are discussed in detail below and it is only necessary here to expound on one of the chief activities for which the commissioners were responsible, in fact their main function, which is usually overlooked, viz. the administration of the public labor conscription.

***The Departments of Public Works in Ancient Israel***. A crucial aspect of administration in ancient Israel has to do with a socioethnic factor that is generally ignored today, even though Old Testament studies have been so preoccupied with a "sociological" approach.

By the twelfth century BCE the principal rival peoples in the southern Levant were becoming well established in their respective areas: the Canaanites continued to dwell in the northern valleys and plains, the Philistines (with other "sea peoples"?) in the southern coastal plain, and the tribes of Israel in the hill country. The biblical tradition confirms that Israelites were unable to dislodge the Canaanites and Amorites in the lowland areas, for they had "chariots of iron" (Josh 17:18). A list of the areas where the non-Israelites continued to dwell is given in Judges 1 and similar allusions appear here and there in the Book of Joshua (15:63, 17:11–13). Judges 1:18–19 (LXX) confirms that Judah did not subdue the Philistines.

No tradition exists about the conquest of Shechem, whose situation may have been like Gezer (Judg 1:19), a Canaanite population living in symbiosis with the Israelites. Jebus-Jerusalem, Gezer and the Amorite towns that resisted the Danites were in the center of the country. Very early traditions reveal that the Ephraimites came into early contact with the indigenous population of the area where the Danites had been prevented from settling (1 Chr 7:20–24; Judg 1:35). Some clans from Benjamin also migrated to the same area (1 Chr 8:12–13; 2 Sam 4:3–4).

The dichotomy between Canaanites on the plains and Israelites in the hills characterizes the narratives throughout the books of Judges and Samuel. Judges 1:27–35 lists the unconquered areas by tribe. The main surviving Canaanite enclaves were in the Valley of Jezreel, and along the Phoenician coast. The Asherites gained acceptance among the Phoenicians (Sidonians), apparently as client farmers for a society whose manpower was heavily committed to maritime activities (Judg 1:31–32).

In the references to the tribal failures to dispossess the inhabitants of the plains, the institution of "forced labor" has been emphasized. It should be obvious that through the period of the Judges and till the end of Saul's reign, Israel had no control over the Canaanite population in those unconquered towns. Israel did not have a political infrastructure that could facilitate the establishment of such an administrative institution as forced labor or corvée.

On the other hand, the newly established kingdom of Israel is depicted in the census ordered by David. The territory covered represents all of the area directly under control of the monarchy in Jerusalem. Although the text of Joab's itinerary (2 Sam 24:5–7) is badly preserved in spots, the general course of the census can be discerned. The following entry is the most tantalizing: "All the cities of the Hivites and the Canaanites" (2 Sam 24:7), in other words, all those towns that had initially been unconquered (Judg 1:27–35). Here is the tacit admission that those elements of the pre-Israelite population who had maintained their social and political integrity up to now had finally succumbed to the new, united Israel. Specific details about how David subdued those Hivite and Canaanite cities is not found in any ancient source. The end result can be seen in the dispersal of Levitical settlements to places where they can represent the crown and temple in the enclaves of pre-Israelite population and in the Solomonic commissioners' districts. The united monarchy reached its apogee after Solomon had assured a steady flow of income from command of the world trade routes. This and a well-organized bureaucracy supported by the military establishment enabled him to harness the manpower now at his disposal. Besides the temple and the royal palace, Solomon built strong fortresses at key points throughout the realm (1 Kgs 9:15).

Today it is recognized that the districts in this roster divide into two groups: those defined in terms of tribal entities and those defined in terms of the towns included in them. The former were in hill-country areas while the latter were generally on the plains.

*Limestone relief depicting the head of a Phoenician nobleman, from Dor, Iron Age.*

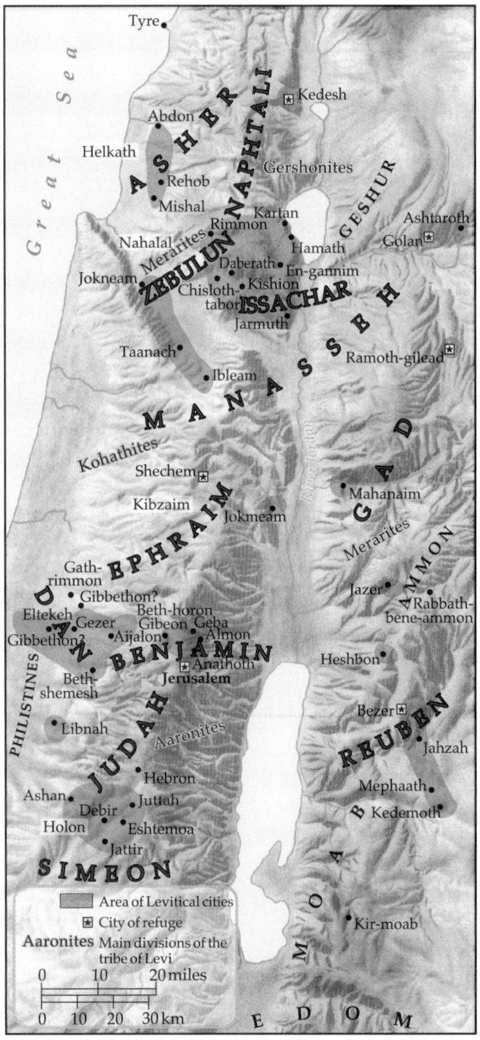


THE LEVITICAL CITIES (C. 975–940 BCE)

***The Press Gangs of the Levy.*** What is usually ignored in commentaries on 1 Kings is that the ensuing references to Solomon's manpower organization reflect *two* branches of public-labor conscription in accordance with the two types of districts in the list of district commissioners. Judges 1 stresses repeatedly that "when Israel became strong" the Canaanites were subjected to forced labor. These were mostly the inhabitants of the plains. This particular public institution and its activities are defined in 1 Kings 5: 27–28 (Eng. 5:13–14).

The clear intent of the context is that the newly subjected Canaanites and Hivites were those required to spend one out of every three months in Lebanon, cutting and transporting the lumber needed by Solomon. The commissioners in charge of the districts in the plains, those districts defined by their towns (which correspond largely to the unconquered towns in Judges 1!), were responsible for carrying out those tasks.

***The Corvée.*** The second government department is described in 1 Kings 5:29–31 (Eng. 5:15–17). The corvée was obviously recruited from the Israelite tribes; they worked in the hill country of Israel, quarrying stone and transporting it to the building sites; they also provided the labor force for the actual construction (1 Kgs 5: 15–17, 11:28). The quarries were naturally in the areas where the best building stone could be obtained, in the hill-country areas. The former tribesmen did not have to go as far away as Lebanon to do their work. Their burden was undoubtedly onerous but not as humiliating as that imposed on the former Canaanites and Hivites. The Chronicler could not countenance such a situation so he assigned even the corvée tasks of burden-bearing and quarrying to the foreigners (2 Chr 2:17–18). Each department had its own cadre of commissioners and overseers. The numbers of the participants cannot be used as valid indicators but the fact remains that there were two tables of organization operating side by side. The commissioners in charge of the formerly tribal, hill-country districts were the overseers of the quarriers, the teamsters and the construction workers comprised of the veteran Israelites. One of the most respected and brilliant of the overseers working with the corvée was Jeroboam the son of Nebat (*see* 1 Kgs 11:28).

When Solomon saw that Jeroboam was enjoying too much influence with his constituents, he sought to have him eliminated, so the young administrator fled to Egypt where he was granted political asylum (1 Kgs 11:40). At the confrontation between Rehoboam and the northern Israelites, the latter demanded an easing of the burdens imposed by the royal building projects. The new young king made the mistake of sending Adoniram, the commissioner in charge of the onerous forced labor, the levy imposed on the newly absorbed population, to try to browbeat the veteran Israelite tribesmen into submission. They were so incensed that they stoned him to death (1 Kgs 12:18). Then they turned to the popular administrator, Jeroboam, who had been their supervisor in the corvée department, and appointed him king.

The geographical analysis of the list of unconquered towns (Judg 1), the Davidic census (2 Sam 24) and the Solomonic districts (1 Kgs 4) reveals the dichotomy in the population of the Israelite united monarchy. Besides serving as a labor force, it stands to reason that many educated people of the pre-Israelite population, those who knew how to read and to write, would have gained positions in the newly founded Israelite administration. Their contribution to literacy in the ruling cadres and perhaps also to the development of a reservoir of literary traditions is impossible to ascertain but must be kept in mind when dealing with ancient Israelite culture.

**Building Projects.** The focus of the entire pericope about Solomon is the construction of the temple in Jerusalem. The logistic organization for this and the palace

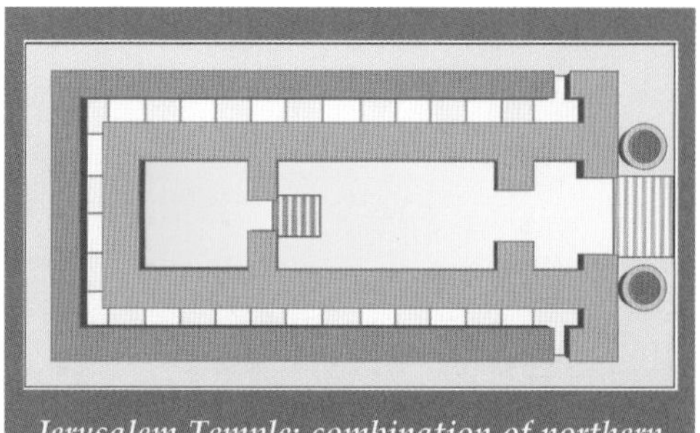

*Jerusalem Temple: combination of northern features (long room type) and southern orientation to the sunrise. Procession from courtyard along a straight axis towards the Holy and Most Holy, as common to Levantine temples.*

project were discussed in the previous section. The construction of fortified centers at the major highway junctions across the southern Levant, central Syria and as far as Tadmor on the road to Mesopotamia has been discussed above in conjunction with the economic program. It was explicitly stated that these were built as part of the forced labor activities described in the previous section.

The construction of the temple (1 Kgs 6: 1–38 || 2 Chr 3:1–5:1) and the royal palace (1 Kgs 7:1–12) are the centerpiece of the narrative, with an ideological chapter (1 Kgs 8:12-53 || 2 Chr 6:12-47) expressing the viewpoint that the temple would be a link between the people and YHWH and also a link for foreigners who may come from afar (1 Kgs 8:41–43 || 2 Chr 6:32–33).

The temple architecture appears to be a compromise or combination of northern and southern traditions. The building had a "long room" for the main internal hallway, with the cella at the western end. The few temples known from Judea (Iron Age: Arad; Hellenistic Age: Lachish, Beer-sheba) all have a broad room as the main hall with the

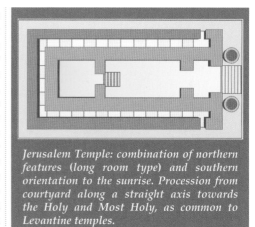

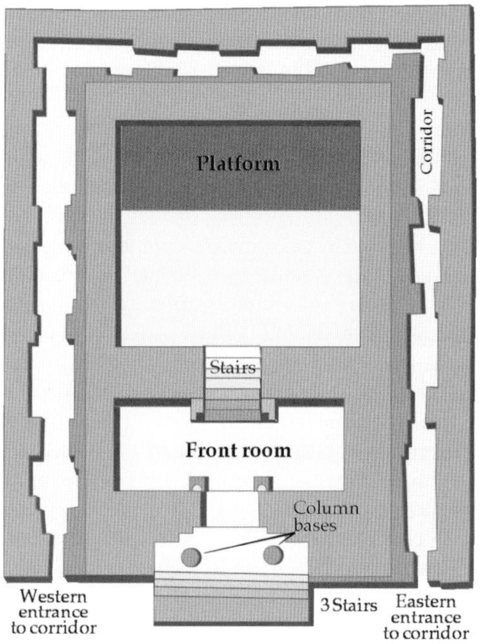


*Iron Age temple at ᶜAin Dārā (Syria), similar in plan to the Solomonic temple..*

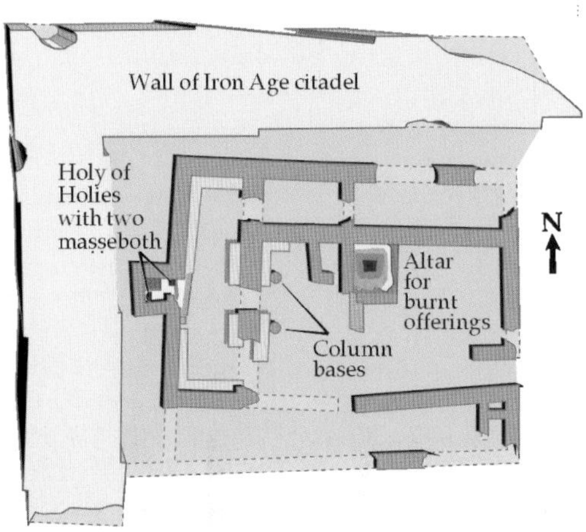


*The temple of Arad Stratum X, 9th century* BCE.

cella at the western side of that room, located midway along the western wall. On the other hand, it would seem that many Iron Age temples in the north (and some Bronze Age) have the cella at the northern end of the building. So the orientation (literally) of the Jerusalem temple toward the rising sun may reflect a Judean tradition.

The inauguration of a temple indicates a sophisticated ritual system with trained officiates who are specialists in the performance of the sacrifices. The Late Bronze ritual texts from Ugarit prove that elaborate rituals were well known in the Levant long before the tenth century BCE. Even if the relevant biblical texts (mainly in Ex, Lev, Num) are later (seventh or even fifth century BCE), there is no reason to doubt that they reflect more ancient practices. Furthermore, the "ritual" texts employ bookkeeping terminology well attested in epigraphic texts of the monarchial period.

**Opposition to Solomon**. The prophetic historian is highly critical of Solomon's policy regarding his foreign wives (*see* 1 Kgs 11:4–8; 2 Kgs 23:13).

Each foreign marriage was a diplomatic arrangement. The various princesses were undoubtedly accompanied by an entourage that included the ambassador and other advisers (economic and military attachés?) and a priest with his assistants. They were allotted places on the mountain opposite Jerusalem and that plot of land would enjoy extraterritorial status. The god of a nation ruled over his own turf. Whether each embassage brought along a load of soil on which to stand when worshipping (cf. 2 Kgs 5:17) is a moot point, but chapels were built to house the foreign cults.

The historiographer blames the adversaries who rose up against Solomon as part of the divine wrath because of the introduction and veneration of foreign cults.

***Tyre***. After twenty years of trading agricultural produce for technical assistance (1 Kgs 9:11; not in 2 Chr!), the relationship required adjustments. Solomon found it necessary to transfer twenty towns in the Galilee area to Tyrian control.

***Egypt***. The rise of Dynasty XXII (946–712 BCE) led by Shoshenq I (biblical Shishak, 945–924 BCE), saw a renewal of diplomatic relations with Phoenicia. The Shoshenq fragment discovered at Megiddo might be part of a victory stele from his campaign. Before the military invasion of Israel/Judah was conducted, Shoshenq had given political asylum to one of Solomon's most important enemies and may also have renewed a strong bond with the Philistines.

***Edom***. During the brutal conquest of Edom, a young prince of the royal line escaped and made his way across Sinai to Egypt (*see* 1 Kgs 11:14–18). Just incidentally, this narrative documents the route from Midian, the northern Hejaz, by way of the wilderness of Paran and across to Egypt. It would be a significant route in future centuries when the way from Babylon to Sinai would be developed.

The refugee was well received in Egypt. It is not said who the pharaoh was that granted asylum to Hadad and married him to his own sister-in-law. Whoever it was, he was ruling when David died and Joab was executed by Solomon. It is not clear just when and how the influence of Hadad was carried out in Edom or just how it began to affect Solomon's income (*see* 1 Kgs 11:21–22).

***Damascus***. Another, and more serious, challenger to the Solomonic hegemony arose in Damascus. This was Rezon, son of Eliada, who had fled from Hadadezer, the king of Zobah whom David eventually defeated. Rezon had gathered to himself a large band of discontents who had fled from David's brutal campaign in Damascus. The narrative is unclear as to just when Rezon had gained control of Damascus, but he is credited with opposing Solomon throughout his reign (1 Kgs 11:23–25). Using his hatred of Israel as a unifying ideology, he managed to raise himself to a place of seniority over Aram.

***Jeroboam son of Nebat***. Jeroboam has been mentioned above with reference to his position in the cadre that administered the corvée (*see* 1 Kgs 11:28).

From the account of his clash with Solomon, it would appear that there was already a conspiracy among prophetic circles of the northern tribes, centered around Shiloh, to break away from Jerusalem rule (1 Kgs 11:26–40). The story about Ahijah the Shilonite telling Jeroboam that he would have ten tribes reflects that plot. But when Solomon got wind of it, Jeroboam had to flee to Egypt where Shishak gave him political asylum (1 Kgs 11:40). Only after Solomon's death did he return to his native land.

*Stele fragment of Shishak, from Megiddo.*

## The Kingdom Split (931/930 BCE)

With the death of Solomon, Rehoboam his son was crowned king. He went to Shechem to be confirmed in his kingship over the northern coalition of tribes (1 Kgs 12:1). The drama of his confrontation with the northern leaders can only be fully grasped when the difference between Jeroboam as an officer of the corvée and Adoniram, the senior director of the forced labor, is understood. The northern spokesmen were not arguing for an easing of the burden on the newly absorbed Canaanites; they wanted an alleviation of the burdens of the corvée that was imposed upon them, i.e. quarrying and transporting stone. Rehoboam not only refused, he assigned the task of intimidating the refractory, insubordinate northerners to Adoniram, who was in charge of the onerous forced labor imposed on the unfortunate ex-Canaanites and Hivites. When they stoned Adoniram to death, Rehoboam got the message and withdrew. He was prevented from organizing a punitive expedition by prophetic intervention (1 Kgs 12:24).

**The Northern Kingdom**. So Jeroboam son of Nebat became king of a new dynasty among the northern tribes, henceforth called "Israel." He reigned for twenty-two years (non-accession system) from 931–930 to 910–909 BCE, Solomon's last year being counted as his first. In Judean synchronisms, the accession year system is used also for Jeroboam's years.

***Political Centers***. Two administrative centers were mentioned early on (*see* 1 Kgs 12:25). Shechem, in the navel of the Ephraimite hill country (note that it is a town of Manasseh), was a logical place for a capital. It had been the leading city of the Middle and Late Bronze ages. The mysterious move to Penuel (Tell edh-Dhahab esh-Sharqī) in the canyon of the Jabbok (Nahr

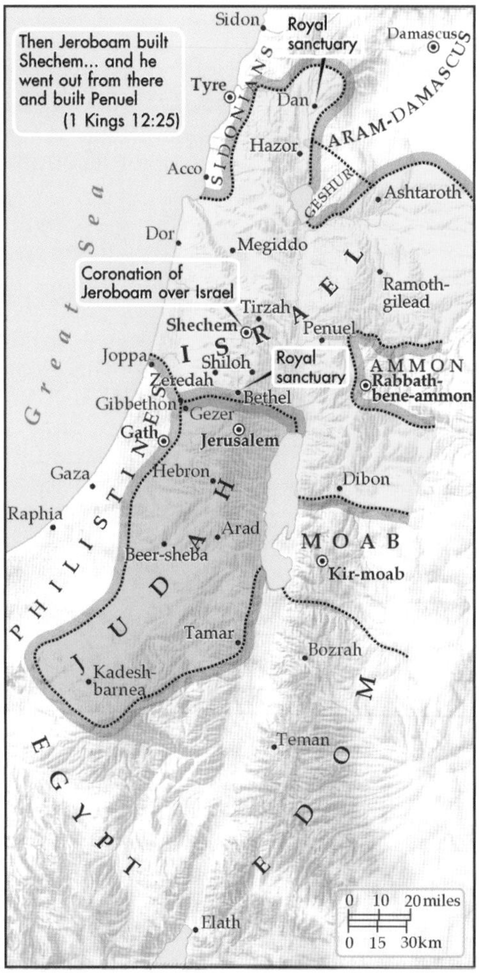


**THE DIVISION OF THE KINGDOM (931 BCE)**

ez-Zerqā) makes sense as a Transjordanian administrative center. Perhaps Jeroboam retired eastward in the face of the Egyptian invasion.

***Religious Centers.*** A much deeper impression is made on the tradition by Jeroboam's religious centers, which in fact were also administrative bases at the northern and southern extremities of his newly founded kingdom (*see* 1 Kgs 12:28–31).

Each site, viz. Bethel and Dan, had a long cultic history; the former with rich patriarchal associations and the latter as a cult place with a priestly tradition traced back to Moses. The calves became leading figures for the cult and new priestly cadres were established outside the Levitical tribe. The cultic complexes built there were called "houses of high places." It seems most likely that the high place was a platform on which were built altars and a shrine, and other installations. The platform and the associated structures uncovered at Dan (Tell el-Qâḍī=Tel Dan) are surely identical with the cult center initiated by Jeroboam I.

Having one shrine in the north and another in the south thus demarcated the extent of the new kingdom. This does not mean that the actual border must run along the foot of each tel. But the northern and southern districts had these two towns as their administrative centers.

Other important towns in the governance of the monarchy were Shiloh (*see* 1 Kgs 14:1–2), and Tirzah (apparently Tell el-Far$^{c}$ah North; *see* 1 Kgs 14:17):

It may be that during the Shishak campaign, Shechem was seriously damaged though the textual evidence is questionable. Afterwards, Jeroboam returned from Penuel in Transjordan and was forced to select an alternative site for his headquarters. In any case, Tirzah remained a seat of royal authority in subsequent generations (cf. 1 Kgs 15:21).

**The Southern Kingdom**. So Solomon's son, Rehoboam, returned to Jerusalem and continued to reign over Judah and Benjamin. Naturally, this included Simeon, which was settled in Judah, and also the other tribes such as the Kenites, the Kenizzites and the Jerahmeelites who had long since become absorbed into Judah. Rehoboam is credited with a reign of seventeen years (1 Kgs 14:21; 2 Chr 12:13) which would cover the period 931/930 to 913 BCE. The Chronicler gives data that are absent from the account in Kings. The authenticity of this additional material may be questioned but it does make a coherent picture and a neat chronology. But first there is the list of towns which Rehoboam is said to have fortified.

***Rehoboam's List of Forts*** (2 Chr 11:5–12). The list is problematic in many respects. The most glaring aspect is the lack of archaeological confirmation for this building activity. Some of the places mentioned, such as Azekah, have not produced signs of a tenth-century BCE fortification but it should be said that in fact the British excavators at the turn of the twentieth century did not really explore all the possibilities on that impressive mountaintop site. But an even more serious problem is Beth-zur (Kh. eṭ-Ṭubeiqeh) where modern, thorough excavations have not produced fortifications that can be related to Rehoboam's activity.

On the other hand, there is a clear possibility that Lachish was fortified at this time. Lachish, of course, is a key site. Level IV with its massive brick fortification wall and its triple-chambered gate, or perhaps just the "Palace A" in the center of the mound, could be assigned to the building activity of either Rehoboam, Asa or Jehoshaphat.

Because of the archaeological problems pertaining to towns in the list, other dates have been suggested for the original list, either the reign of Hezekiah or of Josiah. The list does not include all the possible fortified towns in Judah. For example Beth-shemesh and Libnah are ignored. Both are in the list of Levitical cities as well as some other towns in the southern Judean hill country. Perhaps those places were already fortified and may be used to supplement the Rehoboam list. It may be that the Chronicler found a town list and ascribed it to Rehoboam because he knew of some building activity. Or the building projects simply may not have been completed during Rehoboam's reign.

Another important point to note is that the Chronicler places the list of towns before the Shishak campaign. This is often denied but makes sense in the general framework depicted by the Chronicler and also conforms to the fact that Shishak's inscription does not record conquered cities in the Shephelah (except for Aijalon) or the hill country of Judah. On the other hand, the Negeb, where it may be assumed some towns were already fortified, was also not included in the Rehoboam list.

The list is recorded in 2 Chronicles 11:5–12. In some respects the collection of names seems almost random but some logical groupings do occur. The list starts with a line of towns along the eastern frontier of the northern Judean hill country, along the central watershed road from north to south:

**Bethlehem**, **Etam** (Kh. el-Khôkh), **Tekoa** (Kh. Teqû$^{c}$), **Beth-zur** (Kh. eṭ-Ṭubeiqeh).

After Beth-zur, there are two towns in the Vale of Elah on a lateral route leading into the Judean Hills on the road to Beth-zur:

**Socoh** (Kh. esh-Shuweikeh), **Adullam** (Kh. esh-Sheikh Madhkûr).

Then come two towns on the western border of the Shephelah:

(**Moresheth**?)-**Gath**, **Mareshah**.

These two towns seem to be marking another lateral road from west to east through the Shephelah; it happens to lead to the central hill country at Adoraim. The

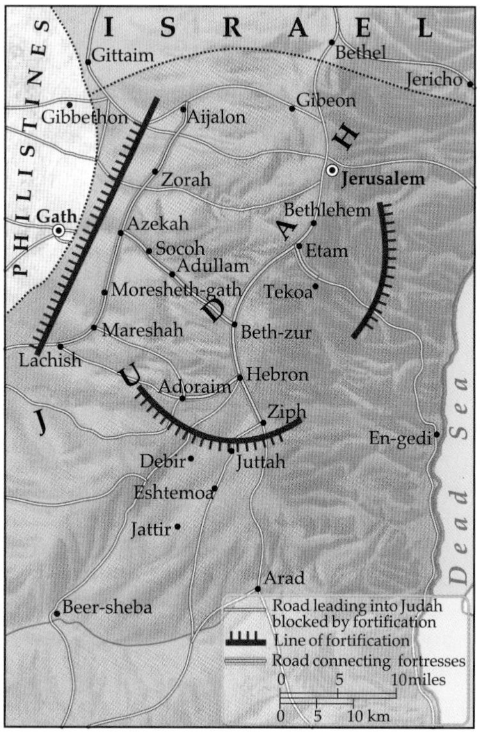


**THE FORTIFICATIONS OF REHOBOAM (C. 931–926 BCE)**

inclusion of a Gath is problematic. None of the proposed sites for Philistine Gath would suit this spot in the list. The suggestion that the intention is to Moresheth-gath, the home of the prophet Micah, is attractive from a geographical point of view. Only in Micah 1:14 is the full name, Moresheth-gath, actually given. The location can only be surmised on the basis of the *Onomasticon* (134:10–11 || 135:14–15) where "Morasthi" is said to be east of Eleutheropolis. That is supported by the place on the Medeba map. That is only somewhat conducive to the proposed identification with Tell Judeideh (Tel Goded) which is more to the north of Eleutheropolis, but not impossible. It would fit nicely, however, the pairing with Mareshah. The textual problem remains and a convincing explanation for the omission of Moresheth in the present text has not been found.

Next there follow two towns in the area south of Hebron, especially Adoraim (the only place where it is mentioned in the Bible):

**Ziph** (Tell Zîf), **Adoraim** (Dûrā).

Finally, the list culminates with a string of fortified cities on the western flank of the Shephelah, in order from south to north:

**Lachish** (Tell ed-Duweir=Tel Lakhish), **Azekah** (Kh. Tell Zakarîyeh=Tel ᶜAzeqa), **Zorah** (Kh. Ṣarᶜah), **Aijalon** (Yâlō).

At the end of the list comes Hebron, which may have been added for good measure, but also might have been included as the administrative hub of the Judean hill country.

In order to establish a firm administrative infrastructure, royal sons were appointed to positions of responsibility over the fortified cities (*see* 2 Chr 11:23).

***Priests and Levites***. The next significant event in Rehoboam's reign, according to the Chronicler, was the mass migration of the priests and Levites living in northern towns back to the territory of Judah (*see* 2 Chr 11:13–15). The Chronicler also records an influx of loyal supporters of the Jerusalem cult from among the northerners (*see* 2 Chr 11:16–17).

By noting that there were three years of loyal service to YHWH of Jerusalem (930–927 BCE), he wants to account for the period of time between the split of the kingdom until Shishak's campaign. The implication is that in the fourth year (926 BCE) a change occurred in the religious policies of the Rehoboam administration (*see* 2 Chr 12:1).

The Deuteronomist's account is even more severe; it goes into great detail about the apostasy (*see* 1 Kgs 14:22–24). Although the passage in 1 Kings does not construct a chronological framework for the cultic changes, it does follow the above remarks immediately with the reference to the campaign by Shishak in Rehoboam's fifth year.

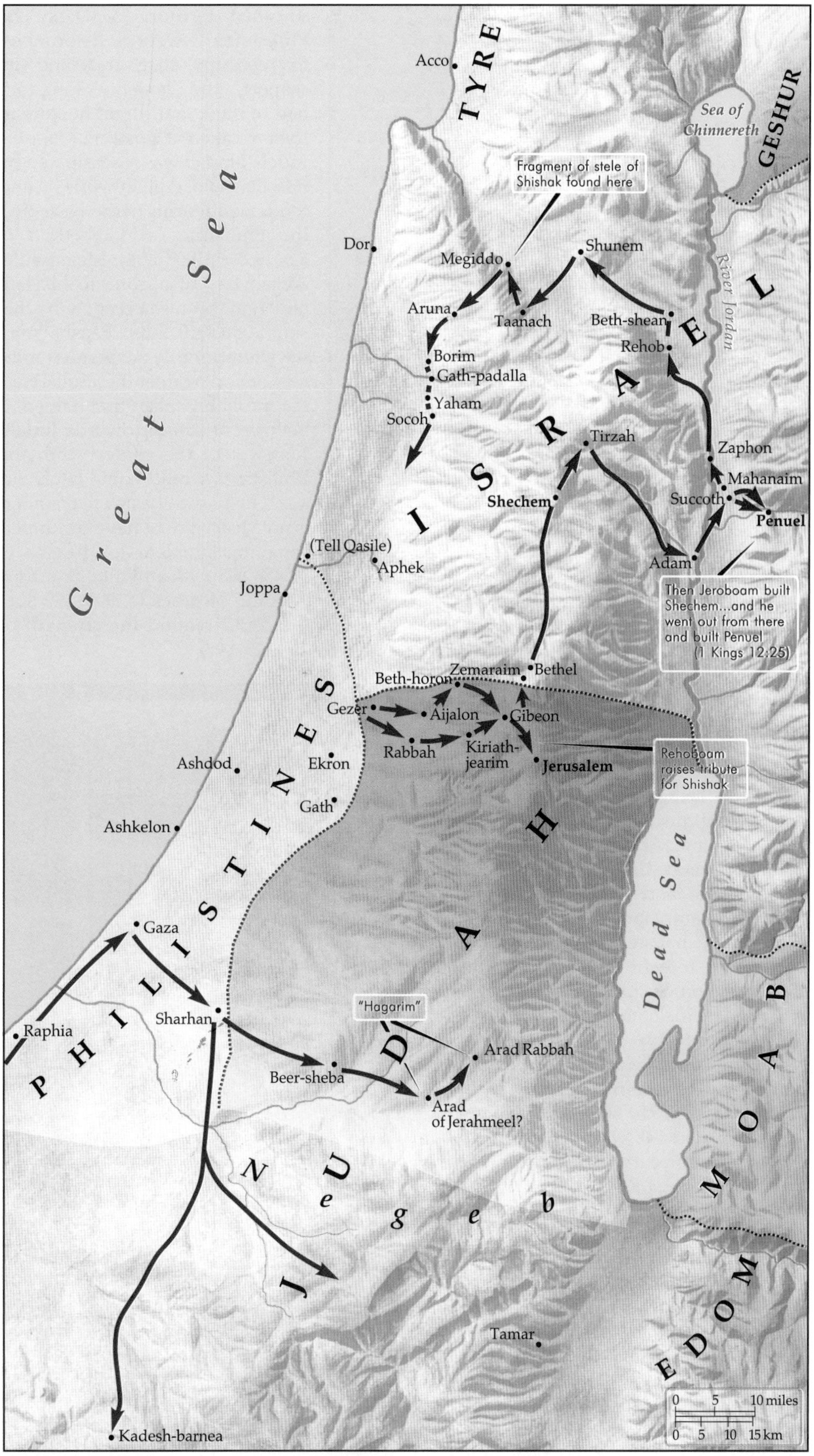


**A HIGHLY SPECULATIVE RECONSTRUCTION OF THE POSSIBLE COURSE OF SHISHAK'S CAMPAIGN (925 BCE)**

## Shishak's Campaign.

**Shishak's Campaign**. The statement about Shishak's campaign is short and laconic in the Deuteronomistic narrative (*see* 1 Kgs 14:25–26). By contrast, the Chronicler embellishes the event to a prophetic intervention that convinced the king and his leaders to change their religious attitudes and policies (*see* 2 Chr 12:2–12).

Neither passage gives significant details about the course of the campaign. Chronicles

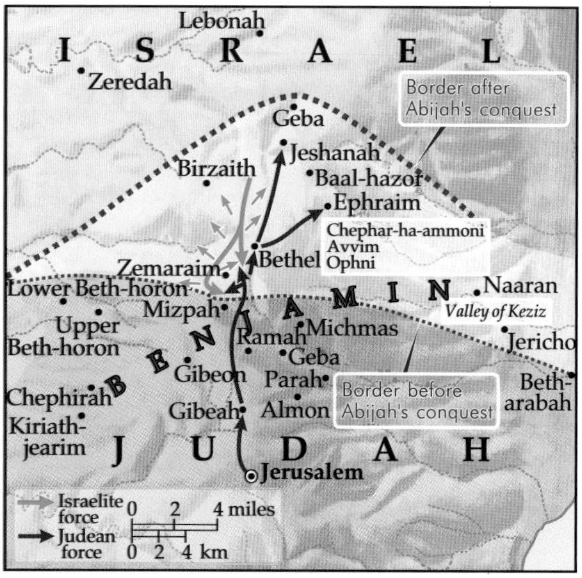


**Abijah's Conquest (c. 911 BCE)**

says at least that "He captured the **fortified cities** of Judah" (2 Chr 12:4) but he does not mention any of them. In addition, the Chronicler gives some details about the composition of the enemy army; besides Egyptians, there were "Lubim," Libyans; "Sukkiim," from the oases of Kharga and Dakhla; and "Cushites," Nubians.

**War Between North and South.** A state of belligerence between Judah and Israel continued throughout the reigns of Rehoboam, Abijah and Asa, the kings of Judah, and the short-lived dynasties of Jeroboam and Baasha in Israel. After Shishak's campaign, both kingdoms were doubtless exhausted. Their former means of earning foreign income by controlling the trade routes may have been seriously curtailed by the damage suffered during the Shishak campaign.

The first specific conflict described in the sources took place in the short, three-year reign (913–911/910 BCE) of Abijah (*see* 1 Kgs 15:7b; 2 Chr 13:2b–4), who began his reign in the eighteenth year of Jeroboam I (accession year reckoning; 1 Kgs 15:1–2; 2 Chr 13:1–2; 931 BCE minus 18 years = 913 BCE).

There is no firm identification for Zemaraim (2 Chr 13:4) but the suggestion is to place it at Râs eṭ-Ṭâḥûneh. After a bitter confrontation at Zemaraim the Israelites retreated, leaving the towns of Bethel, Jeshanah and Ephron (Ophrah) at the mercy of the Judeans (*see* 2 Chr 13:16–20).

Abijah thus pushed the border between the two nations north of Bethel, probably encompassing the district of Benjamin north of the "official" tribal border as reflected in the tribal town list (Josh 18:22–24).

Jeroboam I died not too long after this crushing defeat (909 BCE; 2 Chr 13:20; 1 Kgs 14:20) and was succeeded by his son, Nadab (909–908 BCE), who soon found himself at war with the Philistines. At stake was control of the corridor to Joppa and the so-called territory of Dan. The Philistines were determined to reoccupy that area and its seaport; the Israelite kingdom had to meet that threat in spite of their weakened position vis-à-vis Judah. Nadab was assassinated by Baasha son of Ahijah while he and the Israelite army were besieging the Philistines at Gibbethon (1 Kgs 15:27; in 908 BCE). Meanwhile, Abijah had also gone to his fate and had been succeeded by his son, Asa (910 BCE). Baasha may have temporarily suspended military action against the Philistines. He probably also maintained a belligerent stance towards Judah. Renewal of the contest with the Philistines would come later, but just when hostilities were resumed is not clear; it may have continued to be an ongoing problem for Baasha (1 Kgs 16:15; in 886 BCE). Meanwhile, Asa thus enjoyed a decade of peace (c. 909–899 BCE) in which he could rebuild the strength of Judah (2 Chr 13:23–14:7).

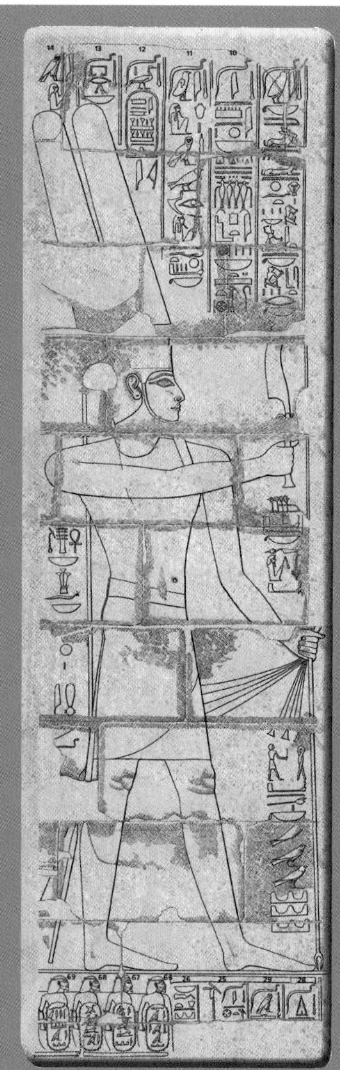

*Pharaoh Shoshenq I (Shishak) presenting the prisoners from his campaign in 925 BCE* (after Epigraphic Survey 1954).

## The Solomonic Administrative Districts

One of the most crucial passages for understanding the development of the kingdom of Israel in the tenth century BCE is the roster of Solomon's commissioners (1 Kgs 4:7–19). It has long been recognized as an accurate picture of the internal organization and socioethnic distribution of the population (*see* 1 Kgs 4:7–8a).

One of the authenticating features of the list is that two of the commissioners are said to have married daughters of Solomon. A folkloristic account would hardly have thought to invent just two such details as that. The two basic geographical principles in this list are: (1) it pertains only to the northern tribes—the reference to Judah at the end is tacked on but not integral to the list itself; (2) there are two types of districts, those defined as tribal areas and those defined by the towns within them with overlapping in a couple of instances. Six of the districts (Nos. 1, 8, 9, 10, 11, 12) are named after tribes and correspond to the areas settled by the Israelites during the Early Iron Age. The town lists and border descriptions for the tribe of Benjamin (Josh 18:21–27) and for the Galilean tribes, Asher, Naphtali and Issachar (Josh 19:10–39), most likely derived from the records of this Solomonic administration.

Six other districts (Nos. 2, 3, 4, 5, 6, 7) are defined only by the towns located in them. They are the areas of the former non-Israelite enclaves of Canaanites, Amorites and others. In two instances, the Solomonic lists are especially defective, namely for districts 2 and 12. It is highly likely that the original rosters for these two areas are preserved in the Book of Joshua as the tribal inheritances of Dan (Josh 19:40–46), Reuben (Josh 13:15–23) and Gad (Josh 13:25–27) respectively. The significance of the composition of the list with its two distinct types of districts will be expounded below. Meanwhile, the ensuing list stresses the geographical details of each district; the type of district, tribal or administrative, is denoted by the headings. Tribal districts are in italics while non-tribal districts are not. Still, it will be seen that this dichotomy is not thoroughly consistent and that is to be expected from any situation involving human social behavior. Nevertheless, the administrative mechanism of the royal organization for the accomplishment of the public building projects becomes clear when the list is properly analyzed.

### *First District: Mount Ephraim*

Ben-hur, in the hill country of **Ephraim**. (1 Kgs 4:8)

The first district included all the hill-country bloc called Mount Ephraim. It encompassed the tribal inheritance of Ephraim and the Cisjordanian hill regions of Manasseh. It may not have included the Dothan Valley (cf. discussion below concerning the third district). Furthermore, the tribal area of Benjamin is excluded, although at least its northern part was physically reckoned as part of Mount Ephraim.

This district also does not include the Ephraimite occupation of part of the coastal plain around Gezer.

Another name for this district is evidently "The House of Joseph" as seen in Solomon's appointment of young Jeroboam "over all the public work of the House of Joseph" (1 Kgs 11:28).

### Second District: "Danite Territory"

Ben-deker in **Makaz** and **Shaalbim** and **Beth-shemesh** and **Elon-beth-hanan**. (1 Kgs 4:9)

The second district is defined by the names of only three or four cities, only two of which can be identified with confidence: Beth-shemesh in the Sorek Valley and Shaalbim (Selbît) in the Aijalon Valley. Beth-shemesh appears as one of the Levitical cities of Judah but it is not surprising that there is some overlap between the two administrative concepts. As for Elon-beth-hanan, it might be an allusion to Aijalon in the neighborhood of Shaalbim, or to another town defined here by the family of Elon of the Hanan family. Makaz is completely unknown.

The short list of only four towns would leave a gap between this district and the third district in the northern Sharon Plain. Therefore, it is reasonable to assume that the list is incomplete at this point. But since the author of the Book of Joshua seems to have had at his disposal a copy of the Solomonic district list, it is fair to assume that his artificially created "Tribal Inheritance of Dan" is, in fact, the more complete list of the second Solomonic district.

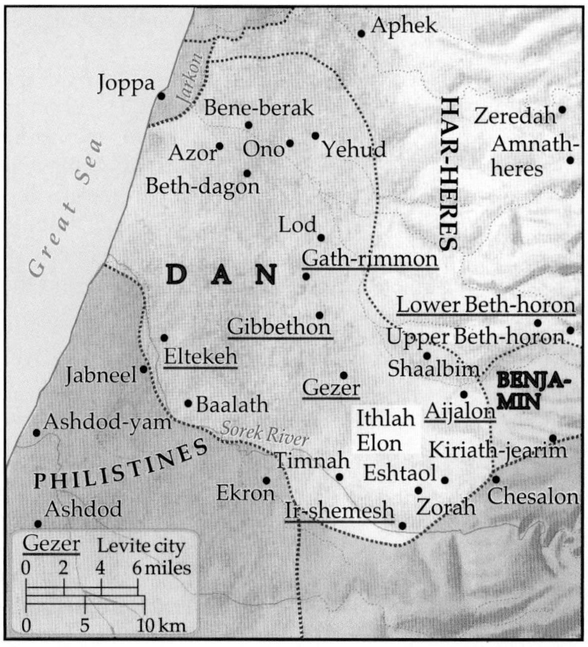


**The Reconstructed "Danite" Tribal District = Second Solomonic District**

### Third District: Northern Sharon Plain and Dothan Valley

Ben-hesed, in **Arubboth**, **Socoh** was his and all the land of **Hepher**. (1 Kgs 4:10)

Out of three entities of the third district, only Socoh (Kh. Shuweiket er-Râs) can be positively identified in the center of the Sharon. That district extended, therefore, from the Wâdī el-ᶜAujā (wrongly called Yarkon River) to the border of the fourth district which also cannot be defined explicitly. Reference to Socoh on the edge of the Sharon Plain brings to mind the neighboring towns of Yaḥma and Gath-(padalla) which played such a prominent role in the age of the XVIII$^{th}$ Dynasty, and which appear in the later tenth-century BCE inscription of Shoshenq I (biblical Shishak). That link in the great trunk route must have been one component in the third district. The town of Arubboth has been the subject of much controversy and various sites have been suggested. Most recent is the proposal to locate Arubboth at Khirbet el-Ḥammâm, in the pass between the Sharon and Dothan Valley. Excavations have suggested an identification with the Hellenistic-Roman Narbata; there was also a tenth-century BCE fortification wall around the citadel. The "Land of Hepher" is also controversial; the eponymous ancestor, Hepher, was the son of Manasseh and the father of Zelophehad (Num 26:32–33, 27:1; cf. 17:2–3). As such, Hepher was to have a share on the same level as the other eponymous sons of Manasseh (Josh 17:2). The daughters of Zelophehad, i.e. the granddaughters of Hepher, had inheritances in the northern hills beyond Shechem, as demonstrated by the Samaria Ostraca. Therefore, it was argued that the third district included the northern Samarian Hills. Tell Muḥaffar in the Dothan Valley has been proposed as the site of the city of Hepher (Josh 12:17). Therefore, it would seem that this third district included the northern Sharon Plain and the passage to the Dothan Valley as well as the adjacent hills.

The third district is, therefore, a possible exception to the sharp division in the nature of the districts. It is partly defined by towns and partly by the clan territory called "The Land of Hepher," a moderate hill-country area where Israelite clans must have taken part in the process of settlement.

### Fourth District: Naphoth Dor

Ben-abinadab, [in] all **the district of Dor**, Taphath the daughter of Solomon was his wife. (1 Kgs 4:11)

The fourth district is defined only by the important harbor town, Dor, situated on the Carmel coast. The definition Naphath and the

*Impression on a horn seal from Tel Dor, 10$^{th}$ century BCE.*

plural Naphoth only appear in association with that city (except for Josh 17:11). Its etymology is unclear. Logic and the terrain suggest that the Dor district was the district roughly from the Naḥal Tanninim to the slopes of the Carmel Ridge. However, the southern boundary could have been much closer to Joppa, perhaps even as far as the Wâdī el-ᶜAujā.

### Fifth District: Jezreel and Beth-shean Valleys

Baana the son of Ahilud: **Taanach** and **Megiddo**, and all **Beth-shean** which is beside **Zarethan** *below Jezreel*, from **Beth-shean** to **Abel-meholah** as far as the other side of **Jokmeam**. (1 Kgs 4:12)

This district includes the great northern valleys which formed a corridor from the Mediterranean to the Jordan Valley. It is defined by the previously Canaanite Taanach, Megiddo and Beth-shean. As a physical entity it is comprised of two basic units: (1) the Great Plain, perhaps called "the Valley of Megiddon" (cf. Zech 12:11), which extended to the site of Jezreel and (2) the Valley of Harod (not named in the Bible) and the Beth-shean Valley (also not a biblical term). The town of Jezreel sat on the edge of a shelf; east of it was a steep drop off to the level of the Harod spring (ᶜAin Jalûd). The stream from the latter, Wâdī Jalûd (Naḥal Ḥarod), flows past Beth-shean on its way to the Jordan. The fords across the river at this juncture were famous in antiquity as the most important passageway to Damascus, Tadmor and Mesopotamia. Beth-shean in the Bronze Age was part of a large pre-Israelite community with sites such as Tell eṣ-Ṣârem (Tel Reḥov) and Tell el-Ḥammeh farther south. The fact that the description here refers to "all of Beth-shean" shows that not just the city but its whole valley was intended. From the present text, the southernmost point in the Beth-shean Valley is Abel-meholah (Tell Abū Sûs) and also Jokmeam (Tell el-Mazâr?; not to be confused with Jokneam) which was opposite to Zarethan. (There is no need to emend the text.) After mentioning the larger unit, "all of Beth-shean contiguous to Zarethan," the scribe defined that zone further by using well-known reference points: below the shelf of Jezreel down to Abel-meholah and Jokmeam. The latter city was assigned to the Levites within Manasseh (1 Chr 6:53 [Eng. 6:68]). Zarethan (apparently Tell Umm Ḥammâd) is the well-known city near the

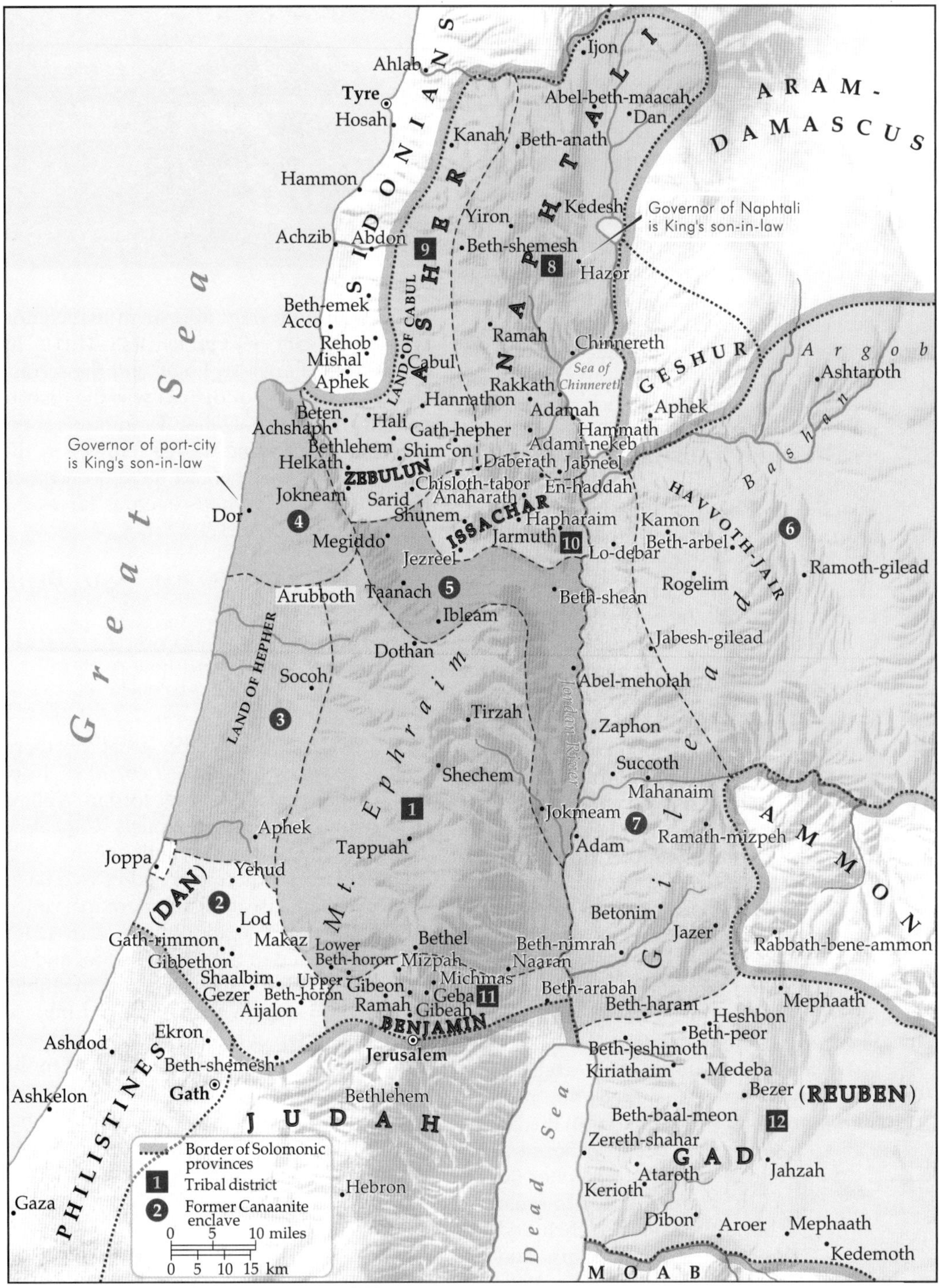


**The Solomonic Commissioners' Districts**

Adam ford across the Jordan (Josh 3:16), on the central plain of the eastern Jordan Valley near Succoth (1 Kgs 7:46).

The most notable feature of this district, then, is its function, not only as a great breadbasket for the kingdom (including Harosheth-ha-goiim) but also as the hub for the main thoroughfares across the southern Levant. The Bronze Age saw military campaigns by the pharaohs coming from Egypt to reassert their contested control over Canaan and also commercial and diplomatic caravans coming from Babylon on their way to Acco and thence to Egypt; the Iron Age saw caravans carrying rare and precious medicinal plants from Gilead to Egypt via the Dothan Valley (Gen 37:25). Furthermore, the same area is singled out as a major enclave of Canaanite cities that were not conquered by the Israelites (Manasseh) when they entered the land (*see* Judg 1:27–28).

This is a key focal point in the understanding of the function of the Solomonic commissioners who governed districts defined by their main cities. It was just such an area as this fifth district where the local population became subject to forced labor.

## Sixth District: Northern Gilead and Bashan

Ben-geber, in **Ramoth-gilead** (the towns of Jair, the son of Manasseh, which are in Gilead were his: the region of **Argob**, which is in **Bashan**, sixty great cities with walls and bronze bars [were] his). (1 Kgs 4:13)

The sixth district description was complemented by an explanatory gloss inserted by the editor, "sixty great cities with walls and bronze bars," taken from the traditional biblical description of the Bashan cities (Deut 3:4). The district was comprised, therefore, of the city of Ramoth-gilead (Tell er-Rumeith) in northern Gilead, the villages of Jair in northern Gilead and the region of Argob in Bashan, viz. the fertile agricultural region north of the Yarmûk River. The employment of the literary gloss is no indication that the entire list is nothing but a folkloristic creation. The format of the list has been compared with other ancient Near Eastern documents and shown to have a strong ring of authenticity.

## Seventh District: Eastern Jordan Valley

Ahinadab the son of Iddo: **Mahanaim**. (1 Kgs 4:14)

This district is allotted only one city, Mahanaim (Tell edh-Dhahab el-Gharbi). This is the logical place for a district capital since it was capital of Israel in the days of Ish-bosheth (Eshbaal) son of Saul (2 Sam 2:8), and was also used by David during the Absalom revolt (2 Sam 17:24). The district presumably extended to the north and to the south of the eastern Jordan Valley. Here the Deuteronomist's list was also defective but it is highly likely that the author of the Book of Joshua still had a better copy which he used to reconstruct his twelve-tribe system. Mahanaim appears in Joshua as a town of the tribe of Gad (Josh 13:26). It stands to reason, therefore, that the tribal list of Gad in Joshua may be the original list of the seventh Solomonic district in disguise.

The area of Gad extended from the border of the territory of Heshbon to the vicinity of Mahanaim, including Jazer. All the eastern Jordan Valley is attributed to Gad, from Beth-haram and Beth-nimrah to the Succoth Valley, "having the Jordan as boundary, to the lower end of the Sea of Chinnereth, eastward beyond the Jordan" (*see* Josh 13:25–27).

## *Eighth District: Naphtali*

Ahimaaz, in **Naphtali** (he also married Basemath the daughter of Solomon). (1 Kgs 4:15)

Naphtali was situated in eastern Lower and Upper Galilee, from Tabor and the Jezreel Valley on the south, through Upper Galilee to the river Litani on the north, including the mountainous block of Jebel Jarmaq (Mount Meiron), and also the northern Jordan Valley, viz. the Huleh, and including several places on the western shore of the Sea of Chinnereth, and the territory of

Hazor. There is no description of its western limits, from Tabor north. It is only clear that there was a border between Naphtali and Asher on that side (*see* Josh 19:33–38).

Note that the appearance of Judah as a southern reference point is absent from the Septuagint. It was probably added to the Masoretic Text by a Pharisaic hand in Hellenistic times (like several MT glosses) when "Beyond the Jordan" was reckoned as a Jewish enclave ("the district of the Jews across the Jordan" [Mt 19:1]). However, this gloss could have originated after the mid-eighth century BCE after Jotham had established a Judean presence there (2 Chr 27:5), but then why should it be absent from the Septuagint?

Although the eighth is a tribal district, with most of its villages and towns in the hill country of Lower and Upper Galilee, it still had a Canaanite enclave. According to Judges 1:33, there were two main Canaanite cities (in Upper Galilee) where the tribesmen of Naphtali did not dispossess the inhabitants, viz. Beth-shemesh and Beth-anath. Instead, the people of those cities were later made subject to forced labor. So like the Socoh/Hepher district, there were sites where the pre-Israelite population continued to live through the period of transition, as well as newly established hill-country sites occupied by the tribesmen when they first arrived.

### *Ninth District: Asher and Zebulun(?)*

Baana the son of Hushai, in **Asher** and in **Aloth** (=Zebulun?). (1 Kgs 4:16)

This entry is also corrupt. The use of the preposition "in" with Asher indicates that with the next geographical component it should also be a preposition and not part of the name as usually supposed (i.e. Bealoth). Still, the tribe of Zebulun would be expected here and palaeographic explanations have been suggested to amend the text to achieve a reading "Zebulun." Another question is whether the intention is Asher before or after the transfer of towns to Hiram of Tyre (1 Kgs 9:12–13). The Book of Joshua gives a town list for Asher (Josh 19:24–31) but it gives a complete border description for Zebulun (Josh 19:10–14) plus a list of some towns (Josh 19:15). That information would most likely have been taken from the list of the Solomonic districts. Meanwhile the copy of the list used in 1 Kings 4 is shown to be corrupt and incomplete at this point as well. The boundary of Zebulun will be discussed along with the other explicit boundary descriptions below.

### *Tenth District: Issachar*

Jehoshaphat the son of Paruah, in **Issachar**. (1 Kgs 4:17)

The district of Issachar (Josh 18:17–23) was located in the Great Valley and included the town of Jezreel. It extended eastward to the Jordan Valley between Beth-shean and the Chinnereth, northward to the Valley of Jabneel and westward to Mount Tabor (*see* Josh 19:18–22).

Their northern border is described in detail as the southern border of Naphtali (Josh 19:32–39) and will be discussed below. There is no southern border for this tribe; it would have had to run along the edge of the Harod Valley in the tenth century BCE. Earlier, the tribe of Issachar may have had settlements in the northern hills of Manasseh and also on the part of the Jezreel Plain known as Harosheth-ha-goiim. That they were an early arrival in the land is suggested by Genesis 49:15.

This has raised associations with the Amarna Letter 365 in which the ruler of Megiddo reports that he is using forced labor for cultivating the fields of Shunem. This is not to claim that those very same corvée workers were from the tribe of Issachar, but it opens the possibility that Issachar had arrived early and that they had accommodated themselves by serving as corvée workers in the agriculture of Harosheth-ha-goiim during the crisis years. Many of the Issachar towns listed above were concentrated in the plateau known today as Ramat Issachar. That plateau seems to only have been settled intensively in the tenth century BCE according to recent archaeological survey. When organizing the northern areas into administrative districts, the monarchy may have encouraged the Issacharites to move from their original places in the Jezreel Valley up to the tableland, thus freeing them from the onerous corvée now being imposed on the Canaanites down below. This also would be fostering the utilization of this hitherto underdeveloped plateau.

### *Eleventh District: Benjamin*

Shimei the son of Ela, in **Benjamin**; (1 Kgs 4:18)

This district is named after an important tribe, mainly for its situation on the north side of the topographical saddle joining the hill country of Judah with the hill country of Ephraim, "between the sons of Judah and the sons of Joseph" (Josh 18:11). The main approaches from the coastal plain to the central hill region came through their territory, viz. the plateau west of the watershed road. The borders on all sides of this tribe are explicitly described. Their towns are given in two segments with separate subtotals. This is obviously because the tribe was eventually split between Israel and Judah and the two districts reflect the settlements on each side of the border between the two kingdoms. The northern group has more unidentified names than the southern (*see* Josh 18:21–24).

The southern group includes the four Gibeonite towns but there are a few that do not appear elsewhere (*see* Josh 18:25–28). Although Jebus is included here, obviously it was a foreign enclave that was said to have been eliminated by the conquest of the city. There were no population elements in the Benjaminite area that had to be reduced to forced labor.

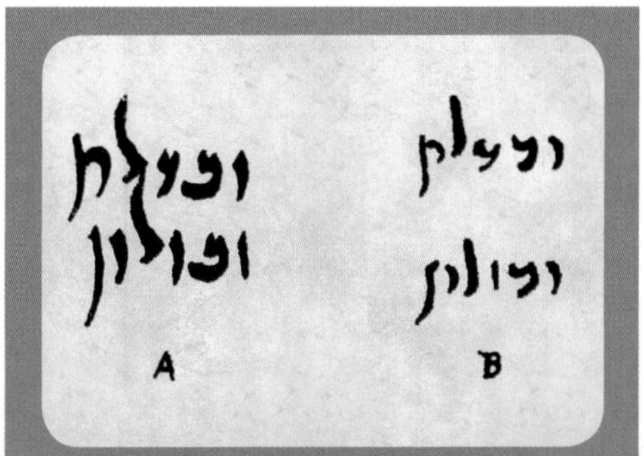

*Demonstration of possible corruption of Zebulun into Bealoth, in two scripts: (A) Samaria Papyri, 335 BCE, and (B) an archaic Exodus manuscript from Qumran, c. 250 BCE.*

### *Twelfth District: Gilead (LXX Gad)*

Geber the son of Uri, in the land of **Gilead**, the country of Sihon king of the Amorites and of Og king of Bashan; (1 Kgs 4:19a)

All that remains of the description of the twelfth district is a reference to a historical tradition: "the country of Sihon king of the Amorites and of Og king of Bashan." This is vague and not helpful because Bashan is already included in the sixth district. The defective list available to the editor of this roster may have had Heshbon, which had fallen out leaving only its literary gloss. In other words, for the southern district of Transjordan he probably had only the name of one central city, Heshbon, which was situated at the northern border of the Moabite tableland, the Mishor. The expression, "in the land of Gilead," is only a general term for Israelite Transjordan in that period. The interpretation of LXX, which reads "the land of Gad," is impossible. How can this serious lacuna be filled? Again the tribal inheritances in the Book of Joshua may be helpful. It has been noted above that the author of Joshua seems to have had a better list of the Solomonic districts from which he sought to construct a twelve-tribe system. He needed an inheritance for Reuben which he may have created by using a fairly complete roster of names that originally were the twelfth Solomonic district. It will be seen that the so-called Reubenite list would admirably complete the missing district (*see* Josh 13:16–23).

The theoretical inheritance of Reuben took in territory from the Arnon to Heshbon, including all of the plain around Medeba and farther north to Heshbon itself. The geographical division of the three Transjordanian districts can thus be reconstructed: the southern district extended over all the Mishor from the Arnon to Heshbon; the central district went from Jazer to Mahanaim, including all the eastern Jordan Valley; and the northern

*Solomonic stand.*

district ran from Ramoth-gilead to the Argob district in the Bashan.

### *Thirteenth District*

And one commissioner was in the land of **Judah**.
(1 Kgs 4:19b–20a [Eng. 4:19b])

The thirteenth-district commissioner for Judah was a literary embellishment to give the impression that Judah was also included. Judah can hardly have been in the original twelve-district system since the heading to the roster specifically refers to only twelve commissioners.

The dichotomy between the Israelites of tribal origin and the urban Canaanites was a social and geographical reality of the united monarchy. The non-Israelites who were subjected to the corvée lived mainly in the lowland areas such as the coastal plains and the Valley of Jezreel (a notable exception was Beth-shemesh and Beth-anath in Upper Galilee, Judg 1:32). Solomon's commissioners were assigned territories in accordance with this reality. The old-established tribal "inheritances" were recognized and respected; there was no intention to infringe on their integrity. On the other hand, the areas which had remained outside of Israelite tribal occupation until David's reign were now organized into new districts. The list of Solomon's twelve commissioners and their respective districts (1 Kgs 4:7–19) is one of the most ancient administrative documents in the Bible but it has been shown above that its text is corrupted in many places. In spite of some lacunae, it is possible, by using the data from the Book of Joshua, to reconstruct the geographical framework with reasonable certainty. It must also be noted that there are striking concentrations of Levitical towns in just those lowland and frontier areas of non-Israelite population. There was no attempt to create districts of equal economic potential. Besides sending the monthly provisions for Solomon's palace, the commissioners in the old tribal districts were responsible mainly for the "burden bearing/transport" (the best quarries were in those very hill-country zones) while the commissioners in the lowland districts were responsible for the corvée. Their subjects were mainly Canaanites and others of the pre-Israelite stock. The commissioner in Naphtali evidently had both Canaanites and Israelites to administer. Judah was not included in the twelve but it is assigned a commissioner. The district divisions of Judah (Josh 15:21–62) may represent a counterpart to the commissioners' districts but it seems obvious that Judah was considerably favored under the united monarchy.

The list of initially unconquered towns in Judges 1 is probably based on this list of the Solomonic districts. One should also note that the geographical allotments in the Book of Joshua are also based on the reality of the Solomonic roster even though the author of Joshua sought to present a different picture, viz. a twelve-tribe system without any gaps between the tribal allotments. The few tribal borders that he does describe actually demarcate some of the "tribal" districts in Solomon's list.

Attempts to deconstruct the roster of districts have been thoroughly refuted by demonstrating that the actual text of the various entries conforms to the standard formats of real cuneiform geographical and personnel lists from the ancient Near East.

## Tribal Border Descriptions

The Book of Joshua claims to present the territories of the twelve tribes as geographically defined. It is presumed to be the work of Joshua and the priesthood who made the assignments by lot. For a few tribes, there are some border descriptions giving landmarks and townships as stations along the demarcation lines. The date, origin and function of these border descriptions have been the subject of intense debate during the twentieth century. A few basic observations must precede any discussion of their authenticity:

1. Not all of the tribes are defined by boundary descriptions, in fact, only a few.
2. The author of the Book of Joshua evidently had at his disposal only a limited number of texts and those generally conform to the geographical picture reflected in the roster of Solomon's administrative districts. Sometimes the tribal districts can serve to supplement and round out the defective list of the commissioners' territories in 1 Kings 4:7–19.
3. There should be no hesitation in accepting the boundaries as authentic; but it cannot be demonstrated that they originated in the early process of tribal infiltration and settlement.
4. The villagers and landowners in each area knew very well the extent of their own fields and orchards and their own water sources, etc. Even if the texts reviewed here do not uniformly give local landmarks, the people living there knew what those landmarks were.

It has been suggested that the boundary descriptions represent a pre-monarchial league of northern tribes. It is true that the location of each tribe according to the borders in the Book of Joshua do seem to conform to the prevailing geographical situations in the various pre-monarchial narratives, e.g. hero stories of the Book of Judges, etc. However, the existence of such a league is impossible to prove; it is not an illogical surmise, but the social chaos that sometimes prevailed in pre-monarchial times according to those very same traditions does not square well with a central league authority that could establish boundaries on the ground and resolve disputes over territory. If such conflicts over land did exist, they have not been preserved in the sources.

When the commissioners' districts were being established under the newly united monarchy, it was seen that some of the districts were identical with tribal territories, mainly those in hill-country regions. So there must have been a system of tribal entities on which to base the new administration. It would logically follow that with regard to these districts the central government would recognize the prevailing situations on the ground and adopt them into the new administrative framework. Perusal of the Joshua passages reveals that on the whole, the author/editor had at his disposal the tribal boundaries only for those areas defined by tribal entities in the commissioners' list. A striking exception to this general rule is the tribal borders of Zebulun, which may, in fact, serve to repair the damage of an obviously corrupt passage in the district list (1 Kgs 4:16).

The boundary descriptions are distributed among the various "tribal allotments" (Josh 15:1–12, 16:1–8, 17:7–10, 18:12–20, 19:10–14, 19:25–29, 19:33–34). It has been argued, probably correctly, that the towns in the lists were extracted from the original source and linked together by verbs. The probability of this suggestion is strengthened by comparison of parallel passages in which most of the connecting verbs are different, although the place names are practically identical. This is especially striking with boundaries common to Judah and Benjamin, on the one hand, and between Benjamin and Ephraim, on the other. The order between the two descriptions of the shared border between Judah and Benjamin is also reversed. The Judean passage goes from east to west while that of Benjamin goes from west to east. The places are the fundamental data while the verbal forms are secondary. Nevertheless, it has been noted that these connecting verbs are the principal distinguishing feature that sets apart the tribal boundaries from the accompanying lists of towns. The verbs employed seem to have been technical terms used especially for such border descriptions. Business contracts with real-estate descriptions (like those from the cuneiform world) have not been found in ancient Israel. One cannot agree that the lists made up of towns joined together by the conjunction were also border descriptions of more distant tribes with which the editors were simply not sufficiently acquainted. The most decisive argument against that suggestion is that the order of towns in these lists, e.g. that of Issachar, does not produce a logical and continuous borderline like one finds in the real boundary descriptions.

The descriptions of the borders vary noticeably in the amount of detail included. Some contain many geographical points at short distances from one another, but others are quite brief and laconic. It is highly probable that all the original lists were much more detailed but that the author/editor of the Book of Joshua shortened them to suit his needs. This process is especially obvious with regard to the northern territories where the descriptions do not repeat a boundary common to more than one tribe. Sometimes, the cities included in the town lists were lifted from border descriptions or vice versa so as to prevent repetition. Therefore, we may assume that all of the boundary delineations were originally quite detailed, but in varying degrees they were simplified and shortened to produce the present lists. This assumption would explain the differences between those passages that describe a common border. It also eliminates three difficulties:

1. In parallel texts describing the same border one finds additional geographic features and the connecting verbs also differ. For example, in the boundary of Judah (Josh 15:7, 15:9), "to Debir from the Valley of Achor" and "Mount Ephron" are missing from the text describing the border of Benjamin

**The Borders of the Tribal Territories**

(Josh 18:15, 18:17); on the other hand "the shoulder north of Jericho," "at the steppe land of Beth-aven," and "the mountain south of Lower Beth-horon" occur only in the border description of Benjamin (Josh 18: 12–13) but they are missing from the border of the sons of Joseph (Josh 16:1–3). On the other hand, the latter text includes the Archites and the Japhletites though they are missing in the Benjaminite border. In another parallel passage describing the southern border of Ephraim one finds Upper Beth-horon (Josh 16:5), which does not appear in either of the other two lists. These variations can be readily explained by the assumption that the author/editor used one original detailed list, but shortened it in various ways for particular instances. Therefore, all of those geographical names could be considered as original.

2. The detailed description of the Benjamin-Judah boundary in the Jerusalem area requires special consideration. Jerusalem rose to prominence only in the reign of David, and many take this as evidence for dating the list under discussion to that period. But does it really seem likely that a king from the tribe of Judah would stress the capital as belonging to Benjamin? This difficulty can be removed by accepting the conclusion as stated above. The detailed account of Judah's border need not be considered something exceptional. It is simply a good example of an unabbreviated segment of a boundary description. All of the borders were similarly defined originally, but the author/editor did deem it necessary to preserve so much detail. The detailed description of the areas near Jerusalem is not, therefore, an argument for the date of the list, but only for that of its final edition and insertion in the Book of Joshua.

3. Most of the boundary delineations mention towns without specifying to which tribe they belong. It was not the city itself but its territory that is intended; however, it is often not stated around which side of the town's territory the border should pass. It must be assumed, therefore, that the original list recorded exact topographical features such as springs, hills, and streams but that the author/editor usually was content to use references to the towns only. The local inhabitants would recognize the specific landmarks, while the general reader would not need them. On the other hand, it is understandable that the border around Jerusalem, which is referred to in the list as Jebus (doubtless to give the text an archaic flavor), was deemed important because of its role as the capital and the general familiarity with the urban environs among the people.

It can hardly be denied that the original text of such detailed geographical lists did represent a real geographical-historical situation on the ground. Such texts could scarcely have served any other purpose than that ascribed to them in the Bible, viz. the exact delineation of the tribal territories. It is necessary to summarize the main factors for understanding the nature of these lists: (1) the boundary descriptions conform generally to the tribal inheritances as assumed in all the narratives in the books of Judges and Samuel. (2) They also conform to the land of Canaan as that term is defined in Numbers 34. The external tribal borders correspond to those of Canaan. The southern Judean and Canaanite borders are identical; the Mediterranean on the west and the Jordan on the east are both mentioned. Only in the north is there lack of conformity where the occupation limits of Naphtali and Asher fell far short of the northern Canaanite border. Apparently this is why Naphtali's northern boundary was not given and that of Asher on the north was only completed during the reign of David, as exemplified by the census list.

It is especially instructive to note that the descriptions of the Transjordanian tribes in Joshua 13 have no boundary delineations. It seems, in fact, that the author/editor of the Book of Joshua had at his disposal only two types of source material for this area, viz. town lists and territorial descriptions based on terminal reference points according to the formulation "from X to Y," completely different from the Cisjordanian lists under consideration. Note the case of Reuben (*see* Josh 13:16–17a) and also Gad (*see* Josh 13:25–26).

These are only descriptions of regions indicating the main population clusters. (3) The boundary descriptions divide up all of the land of Canaan without leaving any empty spaces between the various tribal inheritances. Even regions of foreign population were included within the respective tribal precincts; the same point of view is expressed in a negative way by the list of Canaanite cities in Judges 1. For the tribal situation that the author/editor of the Book of Joshua presents is a purely hypothetical viewpoint. He wanted it to look as though there were not really any gaps occupied by unconquered towns. But Judges 1 belies the validity of this picture. (4) The boundary list does not include all of the tribes in Cisjordan. Three tribes are notably missing: Issachar, Dan and Simeon. The descriptions of their respective tribal allotments consist only of town lists. The absence of boundary descriptions for these tribes does not create any empty spaces because their territories were included in the inheritances of neighboring tribes and this certainly must represent a historical reality. The original Danite territory is actually divided between Judah, Ephraim and Benjamin. The boundary of Judah extends from Kiriath-jearim past Chesalon and Beth-shemesh, whence it followed the Valley of Sorek to the sea. Ephraim's border ran from Beth-horon through Gezer to the coast (Josh 16:3). Evidently these two boundary lines were also Benjamin's southern and northern borders respectively, because as a matter of fact, the western border of this tribe is missing. Between Beth-horon and Kiriath-jearim no boundary points are mentioned (Josh 18:14). Issachar seems to have been included by the border lists in the territory of Manasseh. The northern boundary of Manasseh is missing, and in its place is the passage: "on the north they impinged on Asher, and on the east Issachar" (Josh 17:10); the text goes on to say that the various cities of the Jezreel Plain belong to Manasseh, although they were "in Issachar and in Asher" (v. 11).

However, the borders of Judah, too, are actually missing from the rosters under discussion. Not only are there no internal Judean boundaries even for the tribes that had become attached to Judah, e.g. Simeon, Caleb, Kenaz, etc., neither are there any external borders. The southern, eastern and western boundaries of Judah are identical with those of the land of Canaan, and that on the north corresponds to the southern boundary of Benjamin. The only section that appears nowhere else except in relation to the inheritance of Judah is the northwestern portion from Kiriath-jearim to the sea. It is most likely that this section is later than the original boundary lists in which segments passing through non-Israelite territory on the west were not described in detail. In any case, it is clear that this segment cannot be used as proof that Judah was included in the boundary descriptions. Meticulous analysis of the boundary list shows that, apart from the boundaries of Canaan which provide a general framework, it includes only six tribes: Ephraim, Manasseh, Benjamin, Zebulun, Asher and Naphtali. The list of unconquered Canaanite towns in Judges 1 pertains precisely to these same tribes, and this is hardly accidental. This has suggested that the list originated from a six-tribe coalition of northern tribes, that is, Israel in the limited sense of the term. The existence of such a league, whose boundaries and subdivisions could have been preserved in the Joshua border descriptions, is historically possible. During the monarchy Israel and Judah appear as two distinct units with separate organizational frameworks, and these seem to have preceded the unification; even a centralized government did not cancel these differences. In the pre-monarchial period the tribes of Mount Ephraim and Galilee worked together in concerted action, but there is no evidence that the Transjordanian and the southern tribes joined them. This was the situation during the battle of Deborah. Gideon sent for Manasseh, Asher, Zebulun and Naphtali (Judg 6:35), and sent messengers throughout Mount Ephraim (Judg 7:24). Can it be accidental that these are the same tribes for whom there are boundaries in Joshua?

Issachar is missing, even though the conflict took place in his territory. The same applies to the narrative of the dispute over the altar built by the Transjordanian tribes (Josh 22). They dwell outside of Canaan and build their memorial "over against the land of Canaan, in the districts of the Jordan, facing the side that belongs to the sons of Israel" (Josh 22:11). The resulting negotiations are carried on with the "people of Israel." Those "sons of Israel" have their cult center at Shiloh in Mount Ephraim and are led by the priest from there and the heads of the tribes. It is theoretically possible, therefore, that the boundary lists in the Book of Joshua derived originally from such a tribal alliance.

In the south the author/editor of Joshua recognized a separate existence for Judah, with two boundaries there, the southern of which was used elsewhere as the southern border of Canaan. The inclusion of Jebus (Jerusalem) in Benjamin was meant to add an archaic character to the description and to emphasize that this boundary is Israelite, not Judean. So the author/editor of the Book of Joshua supported the tradition that the border descriptions were written down and confirmed "before YHWH in Shiloh" (Josh 18:8). Whether such was the case cannot be proven; but if the initial committal to writing these lists took place during the early stages of the new monarchy, say, during the Davidic census, the realities on the ground could very well reflect the practical reality that prevailed between the villagers of the respective tribes vis-à-vis their neighbors. They surely knew which fields were theirs and which belonged to the adjacent villages and towns.

On the other hand, it seems obvious that the author/editor of Joshua had only the data that stood behind the roster of the Solomonic commissioners' districts. Wherever details were missing, he had to resort to literary devices to fill in the gaps (e.g. Josh 16:3, 16:8).

Only two boundary lines are notable for detailed description of areas not included in the original settlement process (as exemplified by Judg 1:26–36), viz. the northern extent of Asher (Josh 19:28–29) and the western extension of the border of Judah (Josh 15:10–12). Both of these are really exterior boundaries: the first, with Phoenicia on the north; and the second with Philistia on the south. From a comparison of Asher's border with the census by Joab (2 Sam 24:6–7) and the border of Judah with the theoretical list of Danite cities (Josh 19:43–44), it would seem likely that these boundaries were established during David's census. Those two borders certainly did not belong to any original tribal boundaries. This material was used by the author/editor to fill in the neat picture he wanted to create, viz. that of twelve tribes inhabiting all of Canaan and Transjordan.

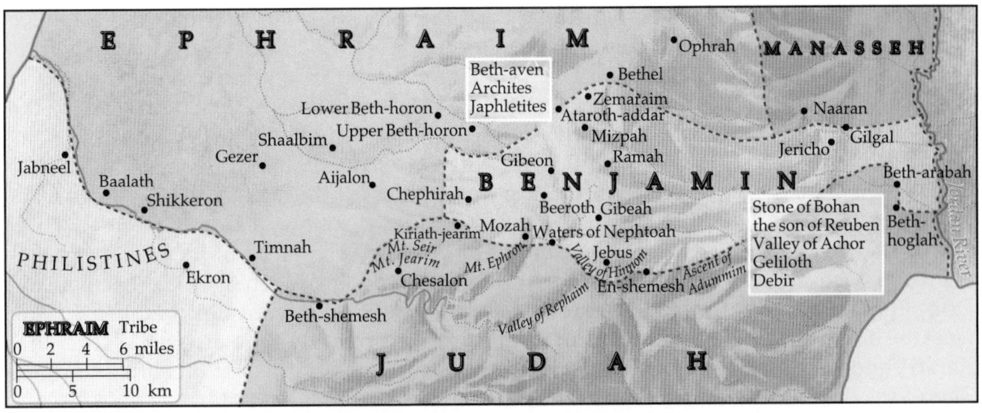


THE BORDERS OF THE TRIBE OF BENJAMIN AND ITS NEIGHBORS

**Benjamin** (Josh 15:5–11, 18:11–20). The tribal territory of Benjamin is listed as one of the Solomonic commissioners' districts (1 Kgs 4:18). It is the one adjacent to the capital city of Jerusalem. Therefore, it is most helpful for understanding the area in question during the united monarchy that the borders of this tribe are the best documented of all. The first passage appears as the northern border of Judah and runs from east to west so as to include the additional segment from Beth-shemesh to the sea, which was really the southern border of the so-called Danite inheritance (probably really the second of Solomon's districts; *see* Josh 15:5–11).

And the parallel passage describes the northern and southern borders of Benjamin giving the former from east to west, then swinging around to give the southern border from west to east (*see* Josh 18:11–19).

Some identifications can be suggested, e.g. Beth-hoglah, near ᶜAin Ḥajlā; Beth-arabah, near ᶜAin el-Gharabeh; Geliloth (instead of Gilgal, following Josh 18:17), "the ascent of Adummim" to be sought near the formation called Talᶜat ed-Damm south of the Wâdī Qelt (which is "the valley" referred to here); En-shemesh, probably ᶜAin el-Ḥod; En-rogel, apparently Bîr Ayyûb; "the valley of the son of Hinnom" is a deep ravine below the southern slope of today's "City of David" ridge; "the top of the mountain that lies over against the Valley of Hinnom, on the west, at the northern end of the Valley of Rephaim" is the ridge opposite the Old City of Jerusalem corresponding approximately to the plaza in front of the Montefiore milling station where one also gets a view down the Rephaim Valley to the southwest. The name of the Waters of Nephtoah is preserved in the village name of Liftā; Mount Ephron may be the block of hills including the modern Radar Hill; Baalah, equated with Kiriath-jearim, is the Iron Age tel on which is located Deir el-ᶜAzar in modern Abu Ghosh; looking southwest from Deir el-ᶜAzar, one can discern that Mount Seir must be the hilltop of modern-day Shoresh; Chesalon is preserved by Keslā on "the northern shoulder of Mount Jearim." The rest of this border does not pertain to Benjamin. Thus the border ran northwest from the shore of the Dead Sea, passed south of Jericho and followed the ridge south of Wâdī Qelt, and skirted the southern edge of the southern arm of Jerusalem, leaving the city in Benjamin while the associated fields to the south remained with Judah. Beyond Kiriath-jearim it was not concerned with Benjamin.

On the north Benjamin was contiguous to the House of Joseph, and this line is marked too by Ephraim's southern border (Josh 16:1–3, 16:5, 18:11–13). These parallel passages probably represent three shortened versions of the same list (*see* Josh 16:1–5).

The line of demarcation is quite clear: from the Jordan to a spring east of Jericho (apparently ᶜAin es-Sulṭân), thence to the mountain slope north of Jericho. It continued on northwestward towards Bethel (Beitîn) to the steppe land of Beth-aven (Tell Maryam?), followed the ridge south of Bethel (Luz) and descended westward to Upper Beth-horon (Beit ᶜÛr el-Fôqā) and to the hill south of Lower Beth-horon (Beit ᶜÛr et-Taḥtā). Between these last two towns mention is made of Ataroth-addar (Kh. Raddana) along with the territories of the Archites. In the passage concerning Benjamin the description stops at Beth-horon, but the parallel text about the House of Joseph preserved one more reference point between there and the sea, viz. Gezer.

**The House of Joseph = Ephraim and Manasseh** (Josh 16:1–8, 17:7–9). There is a dual approach to this area, as the "House of Joseph," reflecting an ancestral tradition (Gen 50:22–23) that Ephraim and Manasseh were descendants of the patriarch Joseph. This corresponds generally to the first commissioners' district, which bears the generic title, "Mount Ephraim" (1 Kgs 4:8), elsewhere "House of Joseph" (1 Kgs 11:28). The southern border of the House of Joseph (Josh 16:1–5) is defined first. The rest of that passage pertains to the northern boundary of Ephraim which separated it from Manasseh (*see* Josh 16:6–9).

The border description began with

an anchor point, Michmethath (Khirbet Makhneh el-Fôqā?) near Shechem. It looks as if the author/editor started to give the western segment and then changed his mind and turned eastward. As a result, the border is described in two segments, first the eastern and then the western. On the east are mentioned Taanath-shiloh (Khirbet Taᶜnā el-Fôqā), Janoah (Khirbet el-Yānûn), Ataroth, Naarah (Tell el-Jisr beside ᶜAin Dûq), Jericho and the Jordan. Towards the west the line followed Tappuah (Sheikh Abū Zarad), and the Brook Kanah (Wâdī Qanah). Therefore, the border between Ephraim and Manasseh began just south of Shechem and descended on a sharp diagonal line in each direction, southeast to Jericho and westward along the Wâdī Qanah which runs into the Nahr el-ᶜAujā (modern-day Yarkon). Just what did the author/editor of the Book of Joshua really think about the Nahr el-ᶜAujā? The key passage is in the section concerning Manasseh (*see* Josh 17:8–10).

As is well known, the Wâdī Qanah descends from the mountains of Samaria to the Sharon Plain where it joins the Nahr el-ᶜAujā. Although the el-ᶜAujā has its own beginning at the sources beside Tel Afeq (Râs el-ᶜAin=biblical Aphek/Antipatris), the author of Joshua 16:8 and 17:9–10 sees it as the continuation of its tributary, Naḥal Qanah, for he says: "and its extension is to the sea" (Josh 17:9b). Even if one must suspect that this clause is a schematic edition by the author/editor of Joshua to an older boundary description, which he made to round out the geographic picture, his statement would hardly be possible if he also looked on the Nahr el-ᶜAujā as a border of the tribe of Dan.

Between Jericho and the Jordan its line corresponded to the southern border of the House of Joseph, i.e. the northern border of Benjamin. Ephraim's tribal inheritance was thus restricted to the hill country; the respective portions of the Jordan Valley and the Sharon Plain on either side were reckoned to Manasseh. The remaining boundaries of the House of Joseph, viz. Manasseh, are mentioned only in a general manner: the sea on the west, and on the northwest the Asher district, and on the northeast that of Issachar. No precise borders are defined because apparently none were available to the author/editor. He was, after all, dependent on the data for the Solomonic commissioners' districts, albeit in a somewhat better version than that in 1 Kings 4.

**Zebulun** (Josh 19:10–14). The assumption that the tribal borders were once a part of the commissioners' districts in 1 Kings 4, gives special significance to the detailed border description of Zebulun. There is an obvious corruption in 1 Kings 4:16; "Bealoth," or more accurately "in Aloth," makes no sense in that context and the suggestion that the original should have been "Zebulun" has been made before. The proposal may receive further support from the fact that in 1 Kings 4:16–17, the enigmatic "in Aloth" is followed by the district named after Issachar. Likewise in Joshua 19:16–17, the tribal territory of Zebulun is followed immediately by that of Issachar. Therefore, it may be fortuitous that the Book of Joshua has preserved the Zebulun tribal description because it may very well represent the original district that was obscured by the textual corruption in 1 Kings 4:16 (*see* Josh 19:10–14).

The Hebrew boundary description begins with Sarid, but LXX testimony does not support this orthography. Some manuscripts of the Septuagint have Sedoud which all point to a Hebrew **Sᵊḏûḏ* (*Sadud) and that happens to be the proper cognate to the Arabic name of Tell Shadûd, a site located at a most logical place to fit the geographical indications in the text above. The tel in question is at the southeastern extremity of the tribal district and the border is said to continue westward from there to "the stream bed which is east of Jokneam (Tell Qeimûn)," evidently the Wâdī Muṣrârah which joins the Kishon opposite Jokneam. Thus part of the boundary extended along the Kishon, and the two places referred to on this line, viz. Maralah and Dabbesheth, may be identified with Tell Thôrah (Tel Shor) and Tell esh-Shammâm (Tel Shem) respectively. The description then returns northeastward and starts from *Sadud and follows the foot of the slopes of the Nazareth hills toward Mount Tabor; then it crosses those hills into the heart of Lower Galilee to the Sahl el-Baṭṭôf (Bet Netofa Valley). On this line are mentioned Chisloth-tabor (Iksâl), Daberath (Dabûrieh), Japhia (Yâfā), Gath-hepher (Kh. ez-Zurraᶜ=Tel Gat Ḥefer beside Meshḥed), Eth-kazin (unidentified), and Rimmon (Rummâneh). From here the boundary turns westward encompassing the western extension of the Sahl el-Baṭṭôf, passing north of Hannathon (Tell el-Bedeiwîyeh), "and it ends at the Valley of Iphtahel." It was originally suggested that the Valley of Iphtahel be identified with Wâdī Khalledîyeh/Wâdī el-Malik (=Naḥal Ẓippori) that drains the Sahl el-Baṭṭôf and opens out into the coastal plain in a deep and imposing gorge. Recent archaeological survey in that area revealed that the distribution pattern of Iron Age sites shows that an ancient route from Acco to the Sahl el-Baṭṭôf may have gone by way of Wâdī ᵓAbbelîn (Naḥal ᵓEvlayim). Therefore, it was suggested that Wâdī ᵓAbbelîn, connected at its northwest corner by a pass to the Sahl el-Baṭṭôf, should be identified with the Valley of Iphtahel. Nevertheless, the hills west of the Jezreel Valley and also those west of the Sahl el-Baṭṭôf are all within the territory of Asher, not Zebulun, so the older suggestion that it is the Wâdī el-Malik is more appropriate. In the forested hill country west of Bethlehem the boundary delineation is enclosed within the Valley of Iphtahel and the streambed opposite Jokneam. It should be noted that this is one of the most explicit border descriptions of all. There is also a list of other towns within the Asher district (Josh 9:15) but they are not of concern here.

**Asher** (Josh 19:24–29). For this tribe there is a concise boundary description, which has been combined with a town list (*see* Josh 19: 25–26). Thus the southern boundary started from Helkath (Tell el-Qassis), in the western Jezreel Valley, passed along the foot of the Mount Carmel ridge and ended at Shihor-libnath. Shihor is an Egyptian loanword for river and Libnath is most probably Tell Abū Huwâm. Into this boundary description is inserted the list of towns in the southern part of Asher's territory, taken from the assumed town list: Hali (Kh. Râs ᶜÂlī=Tel ᶜAlil), Beten (Tell el-Far=Tel Par near Ibtîn), Achshaph (Kh. el-Harbaj=Tel Regev), Allammelech (perhaps Tell en-Naḥl=Tel Naḥal), Amad (possibly Tell el-Idham) and Mishal (Tell Keisân=Tel Kison); they can all be placed at least tentatively, especially with the help of segments from the topographical list of Thutmose III (*see* Josh 19:27–30).

The description "returns," i.e. goes back to a previous starting point, and deals with the eastern boundary which touches Zebulun and the Valley of Iphtahel (Wâdī el-Malik) associated with it (Josh 19:14). Beth-dagon is mentioned first and should be sought somewhere between Helkath and the Valley of Iphtahel; among the proposed sites, Tell Tabûn (Beᵓer Tivᶜon) is the most likely.

Because the putative *Zephath (Josh 19:27c) and the following Beth-emek appear before Cabul, they have been sought to the south of the latter. But there are no verbs here and both places are probably part of the town list interwoven with the boundary description. A good case can be built for equating Zephath with a certain Sapheth of Crusader

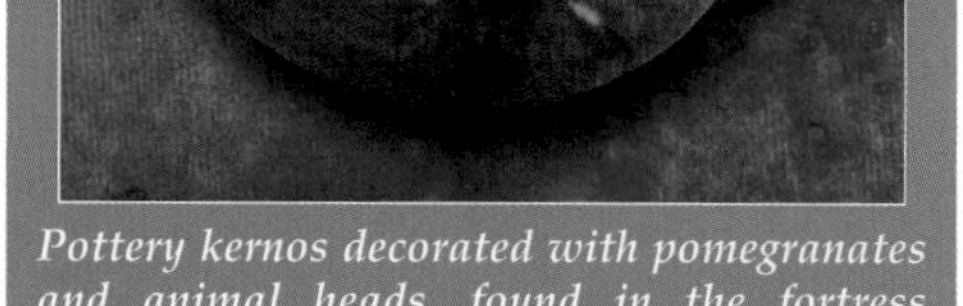

*Pottery kernos decorated with pomegranates and animal heads, found in the fortress remains at Ḥorbat Rosh Zayit, identified with biblical Cabul.*

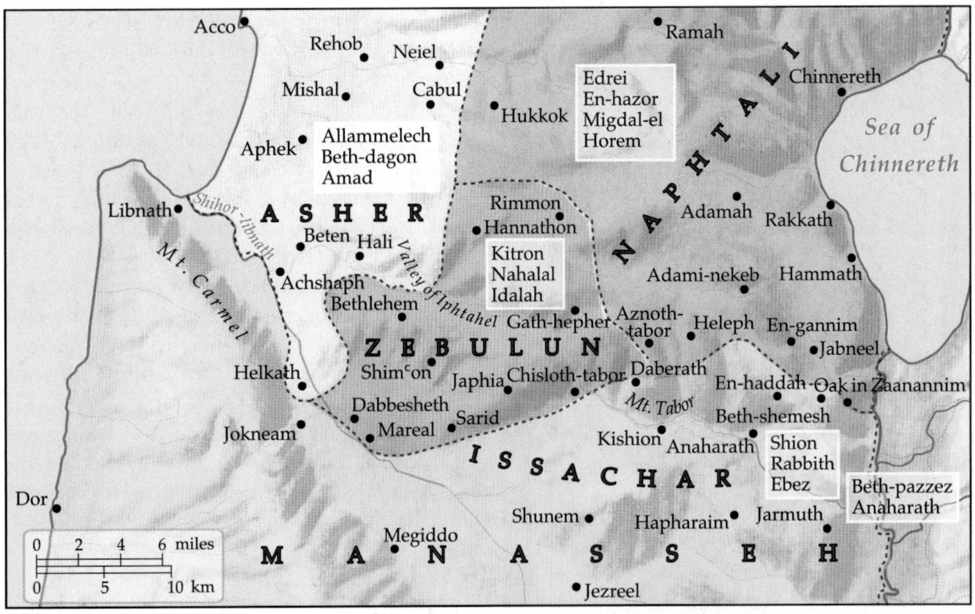


**The Borders of the Tribes in Galilee**

documents, which in turn may be located at Râs Kalbân on a peak between modern Yirkā and Yānûḥ. Beth-emek has been identified at Tell Mīmâs (Tel ᶜEmeq) located near ᶜAmqā. Neiel has been identified with Khirbet Yaᶜnîn (Ḥ. Yaᶜanin).

Next, Cabul (today the village of Kābûl, northwest of the Sahl el-Baṭṭôf) is mentioned; it is especially important since it is the only place clearly preserved by modern toponymy that pertains to the eastern border of Asher. The other places in Joshua 19:27–28, connected by the conjunctive "and," are generally considered not to belong to the border description but to have been part of a town list later added to it. Literally the phrase in Joshua 19:27 reads "and it (the border) went out to Cabul from the left." It is possible that "left" can be understood as "north" as in the Akkadian texts from Mari and in Arabic.

The name Cabul has survived in the name of the village Kābûl some 9 miles (14 km) southeast of Acco, situated on a low western spur of the Galilean hills. It is mentioned frequently in talmudic literature (*T. Šabb.* 7:17; *T. Moᶜed Qaṭ.* 2:5; *Y. Meg.* 4:78b; etc.). No evidence of Iron Age occupation has been found at Kābûl, however, so it has been suggested that biblical Cabul be identified with Khirbet Râs ez-Zeitûn (Ḥ. Rosh Zayit), 1 mile (1.5 km) northeast of Kābûl. Excavations at this latter site have revealed a town five acres in extent from the Early Iron Age replaced by a fort from the ninth century BCE. Cabul's position between the hills of Galilee and the coastal plain determined its function as the indicator of Asher's eastern border. The territory of Asher was apparently to the east of Cabul, thus including the foothills in the tribe's territory, while the border of Lower Galilee was probably to the west of Cabul at the foot of the hills.

For the Valley of Iphtahel, cf. the discussion *supra*, concerning its place in the description of the tribal territory of Zebulun.

The ensuing list of four towns are part of the northern cluster: Abdon(!) corrected from Ebron on the basis of Joshua 21:30 and 1 Chronicles 6:59 (Eng. 6:74), an emendation confirmed by the certain identification with Khirbet ᶜAbdā (Tel ᶜAvdon); Rehob (discussed below); Hammon identified with Khirbet Umm el-ᶜAmûd near ᶜAin Ḥamûl; Kanah, identified with the village of Qânā southeast of Tyre.

However, that cluster of towns in southern Lebanon today does not help to define the course of the northern segment of the eastern border with Naphtali (Josh 19:34). Only the final geographic point is preserved, viz. "as far as Great Sidon," i.e. at the Sidonian border somewhere near the river Litani. Finally, the northern segment is given. No modern site has been plausibly identified with Ramah but van de Velde's map shows a place spelled Ramah 3 miles (5 km) southeast of Tyre. Van de Velde is known for his scrupulous cartography but it is indeed strange that subsequent maps do not record this place. Perhaps it is to be equated with Râmieh, located 10.5 miles (17 km) east of Râs en-Naqûrā (Rosh ha-Niqra) and which appears on the Survey of Western Palestine map. The last two points are on the northern coast, viz. "the city of the fortress of Tyre" and Hosah. In the Septuagint the former is translated "the spring of the fortress of Tyre"; in Joab's census it is called simply "the fortress of Tyre" (2 Sam 24:7). The spring in question was undoubtedly the main source of fresh water for the island fortress of Tyre.

Verse 29 has twice the expression, "and the border (re)turned." Perhaps the second one was the result of a copyist's error; if it be omitted then the following text may be obtained:

> And the border turned towards Ramah and as far as the spring of the fortress of Tyre, Hosah.
>
> (Josh 19:29a)

Hosah has been identified with Usû, known from the second-millennium BCE Egyptian texts, the Amarna tablets and later Assyrian records (Sennacherib and Ashurbanipal). As a geographical name the Hebrew form is a *hapax* but as a personal name it appears among the Levitical gatekeepers (1 Chr 16:38, 26:10–11, 26:16). Perhaps some scribe substituted a name he knew for one with which he was unfamiliar. In any case, the coastal fortress town opposite Tyre, called Palaityros in Hellenistic texts, is most likely to be located at Tell Rashīdîyeh by the main coastal watercourse of Tyre.

The list of towns (Josh 19:29b–30) that begins with MT *mḥbl*, which can be rendered "*from the region of* Achzib," is certainly an addition to the text having a common origin with the list of towns not conquered by Asher (see Judg 1:31).

The geographical order in Joshua 19:29b–30a does not necessarily coincide with that of the preceding section: viz. *Maḥalleb(!), Achzib, Acco(!) (LXX C and Judg 1:31), Aphek and Rehob. It is, in fact, another cluster of northern towns. *Maḥalleb can be identified with Khirbet el-Maḥâlib on the banks of the Liṭâni River, 3.7 miles (6 km) northeast of Tyre. The implication is thus unavoidable that David indeed controlled this northern region and that the coastal territory of Tyre was quite restricted for a certain time during David's reign. Achzib is ez-Zîb (= Tel Akhzib); Acco, a correction based on LXX C, is Tell el-Fukhkhâr (= Tel ᶜAkko); Aphek cannot be Tell Kurdâneh, which is in the southern part of the Asher territory. A suggestion to place Aphek/Aphik at Tell Kabrī is most attractive since that site is located by the richest water source between the Carmel range and the modern Lebanese border. The town of Rehob in verses 28 and 30 is a problem. Are they two different places or, because Joshua 19:29b–30a is an obvious addition to the original, are they one and the same? In any case, their place among the towns in this part of the pericope suggests a site in northern Asher. Acco is the pivotal point in the division of Asher into two parts, a northern and a southern; could Rehob be located at Tell el-Bîr el-Gharbī as has been often proposed? It would be on an east-west line more or less with Acco and might, therefore, be reckoned with the northern group. Perhaps it is better to leave the question open.

The Asher territory was initially a significant district in the united monarchy administration. Later it was diminished by the transfer of twenty cities to Hiram, king of Tyre (cf. 1 Kgs 9:13).

**Naphtali** (Josh 19:32–34). For the tribe of Naphtali there is really only one detailed border description, viz. that along its

*Bronze figurine of a deity, Iron II, from Tel Kinrot (Kh. el-ᶜOreimeh), identified with biblical Chinnereth.*

southern boundary with Issachar. That boundary line is also the only one that helps to define the tribal territory of Issachar, although there is a commissioner's district named after it (1 Kgs 4:17). Naphtali's southern border description is followed by a general definition of the western and eastern boundaries but no northern boundary is given. There is also appended a town list.

The southern border description is as follows:

Their border was from **Heleph**, from the **Oak in Zaanannim** and **Adami-nekeb** and **Jabneel**, as far as **Lakkum**, and it ended at **the Jordan**. (Josh 19:33)

The description starts with Heleph (apparently Kh. ᶜIrbâdeh=Ḥ. ᶜArpad), 2.5 miles (4 km) northwest of Mount Tabor, then it mentions the Oak in Zaanannim, which is also known as the cultic center established by Heber the Kenite (Judg 4:11). Its location is unknown but one might suggest that it was not far from the Beth-shemesh of Issachar that is probably to be located at Khirbet Sheikh esh-Shamsâwī (= Ḥ. Shemesh). It has to be in a logical place to satisfy the account of Sisera's flight from the battle near Tabor. At this point two towns are inserted which are evidently somewhat north of the actual line of the border, i.e. they are a southern cluster of Naphtali sites. These are: Adami-nekeb (Khirbet et-Tell=Tel Adami) which is a prominent mound above Khirbet ed-Dâmieh, an impressive site which preserves a toponymic echo, and Jabneel which the Jerusalem Talmud (*Meg.* 1:1, 70a) identifies with Kfar Yamma, now Khirbet Yamma, on the grounds of Moshav Yavneᵓel. More appropriate archaeological remains were found at nearby Tell en-Naᶜam (=Tel Yinᶜam). Finally, Lakkum, which has been suggested for Khirbet el-Mansûrah, c. 11 miles (18 km) northwest of Tiberias. If such an identification be accepted, then the site can hardly have been a boundary marker. The actual boundary probably followed the line of the Wâdī Fajas, somewhat south of it to be more exact. Note that the actual boundary reference points are missing between the Oak in Zaanannim, the sacred site established by Heber the Kenite (Judg 4: 11).

The western border is only sketchily indicated. The descripton uses a common verbal construction for indicating that it is returning to a previous starting point. While Heleph was southeast of Mount Tabor, Aznoth-tabor is north of it so that the mountain is really the focus of the tribal borders where Zebulun, Issachar and Naphtali meet (*see* Josh 19:34a).

The western border has only two reference points, the first being Aznoth-tabor, which has been identified with Khirbet Umm Jebeil (=Tel Aznoth-tabor), 2.5 miles (4 km) north of Mount Tabor, situated on a small hill ideally suited as a starting point for a border description. The second site is Hukkok; if it can be placed at Khirbet el-Jemeijmeh (= Ḥ. Gamom), 3 miles (5 km) east of Cabul, then the text would be comprehensible. The line from Aznoth-tabor to Hukkok would indeed leave Zebulun on the south and Asher on the west.

The southern border is said to end at the Jordan but then the eastern border is defined in what appears to be an anachronistic manner:

and to Judah at the Jordan toward the east.
(Josh 19:34b)

The reference to Judah seems especially out of place. One might suggest, however, that the descriptions in Joshua date sometime after Jotham's power play in Transjordan, when a Judean presence was established (in particular the House of the Tobiads), a condition that continued into the Hellenistic and Herodian periods.

There is no northern border description for Naphtali. One finds, however, a town list which seems to follow a geographical order from south to north. It is discussed here because it may help to define the northern extent of the tribe's territory:

The fortified cities: **Ziddim**, **Zer** and **Hammath**, **Rakkath** and **Chinnereth**, and **Adamah**. . . .
(Josh 19:35–36a)

Joshua 19:35 seems to be corrupt (cf. the LXX, "And the fortified cities of the Tyrians"). And the first two names may not really be towns. Three places are on the shore of the Sea of Chinnereth: Hammath (Ḥammâm Ṭabarîyeh, the hot springs after which the place was named), Rakkath (presumably Kh. el-Quneitireh=Tel Raqqat, 15 miles [24 km] north of Tiberias), and Chinnereth (Kh. el-ᶜOreimeh=Tel Kinrot). Adamah is probably one of the larger sites close to Adami-nekeb and marks the transition from the area of the lake to the Darb el-Ḥawarneh, the ancient road that crosses Lower Galilee.

The remaining segment is concerned with Upper Galilee (*see* Josh 19:36b–38). Ramah is evidently Khirbet Zeitûn er-Râmeh, an Iron Age site beside the modern village of er-Râmeh at the foot of the massif Jebel Jarmaq (so-called Mount Meiron) above the talmudic Beth-haccerem Valley (esh-Shaghûr). Thus, Ramah marks the transition from Lower to Upper Galilee. Though Hazor (Tell el-Qedaḥ=Tel Ḥaẕor) is in the Ḥûleh Valley, it is in the northern half of the Naphtali territory. Kedesh (Tell Qádesh=Tel Qedesh) is in the hills of Upper Galilee ("Kedesh in Galilee," Josh 20:7; not to be confused with Kedesh of Naphtali, Judg 4:6). Edrei is not identified but En-hazor may be identified with the modern ᶜAinîthā near Bint Jbeil in southern Lebanon. Yiron is firmly located at Yārûn in southern Lebanon. Migdal-el has usually been ignored but there is a suggestion to identify it with Mejdel Islim, about 16 miles (26 km) east-southeast of Tyre. For Horem there are no suggestions.

Beth-anath appears in a topographical list of King Seti I. It also appears in an inscription of Ramesses II. Beth-anath was apparently in a mountainous region and the area took its name from the city. Eusebius (*Onom.* 52:24–26) identifies Bethanatha in the tribe of Naphtali with a village, Batanaia, 15 milestones from Caesarea [Philippi] where a health spa was located. This seems to point to Ṣafed el-Baṭṭîkh where a warm spring and pool were also found. Beth-anath was one of the Canaanite towns not disposed by Naphtali in the initial settlement (Judg 1:33).

The other town mentioned in Judges 1: 33, Beth-shemesh, may be identified with Khirbet Tell er-Ruweisī (=Tel Rosh) in the far north of Upper Galilee.

**Conclusion**. Although the theories of composition pertaining to the Book of Joshua are extensive and complex, the application of geographical analysis to its data may shed light on the social organization and distribution of the population during the monarchial age. It is highly likely that the pericopes discussed above derive from the same archival sources that preserved the list of Solomon's commissioners' districts.

# CHAPTER SEVEN
# Regional Conflicts
## NINTH CENTURY BCE

The ninth century BCE in the Levant was characterized by the ever-threatening shadow of Assyrian aggression. The Aramean and Neo-Hittite states were the first to feel the hot breath of the Assyrian monster. Greedy for tribute and for manpower to build new cities and temples, the Assyrian kings often pressed for exorbitant payments that led to armed resistance on the part of the local states. The northern kingdoms were eventually subdued, as were some entities in southeastern Anatolia. The central and southern Levant, on the other hand, saw collective resistance that succeeded in limiting the Assyrian aggression to campaigns of plunder and extortion. The enforced unity for defense against Assyria did not prevent the small states of the southern Levant from engaging in their own violent parochial quarrels.

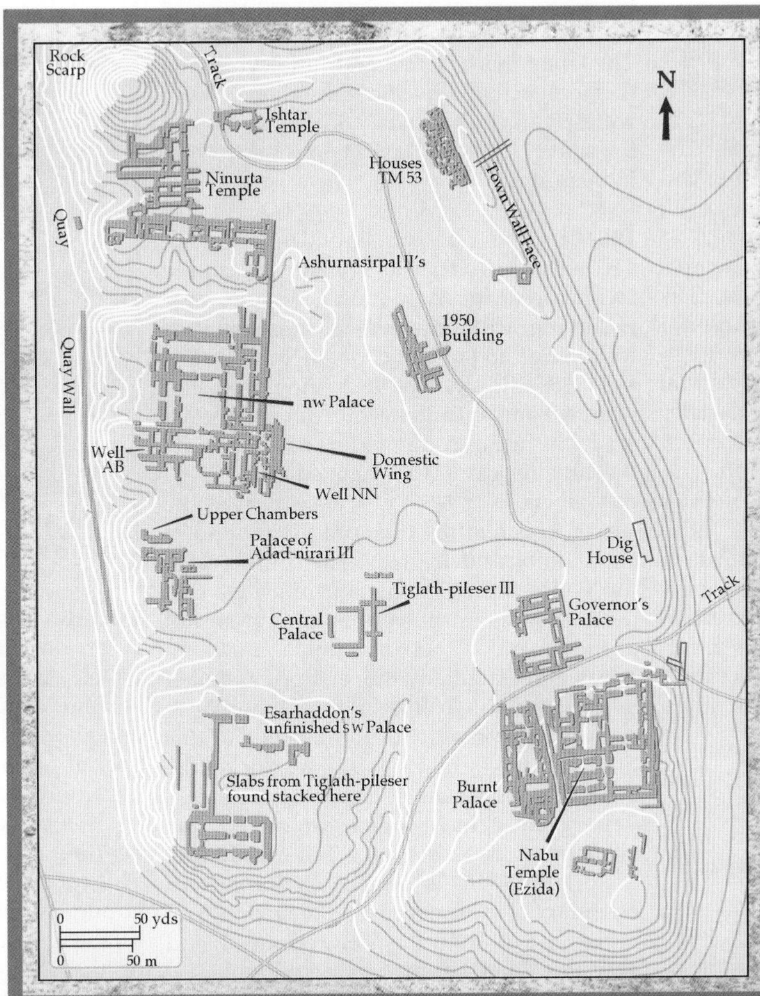

*Citadel of ancient Calah (Kalḫu; Nimrûd).*

## MESOPOTAMIA

**Ashurnasirpal II** (883–859 BCE). It has often been said that the founder of the early Assyrian Empire was Ashurnasirpal II, son of Tukulti-Ninurta II. Most of the evidence concerning his reign has been derived from the ruins of his chosen capital, Kalḫu, biblical Calah (Nimrûd). According to late biblical legend (Gen 10:11–12), the heroic figure, Nimrod, the "mighty hunter," began his rule at Babylon and then went into Assyria where he built cities, among them Nineveh and Calah. In fact, the ancient mound of Kalḫu bears the medieval and modern Arabic name, Nimrûd, showing that the biblical association had been alive there prior to the Arab conquest.

The massive wealth and the impressive public buildings of Kalḫu were financed by annual military campaigns of conquest, extortion and exploitation. Ashurnasirpal II inaugurated the principle of making at least one military campaign per year. To the east, in the area of the Upper Diyala in the Zagros Mountains, he conducted three campaigns against a coalition of tribes headed by a certain Nur-Adad. The Assyrians brought back extensive quantities of booty and large numbers of captives who were used in the work force for building the new capital. A garrison and supply depot were established deep in the Zagros Mountains.

On the northern front, there were several campaigns against the lands of Nairi (the Armenian highland). Eventually, he appointed a governor over the district and subsequently, these districts remained reasonably submissive and sent their tribute and corvée laborers to perform service in Assyria.

The other direction of the campaigns was toward the south along the Khabur and middle Euphrates. Ashurnasirpal embarked on an extensive foray to the west (between 875 and 867, c. 870 BCE), crossing the Euphrates. This first stage of the campaign was for intimidating the Aramean states in northern Syria, especially Bīt-Adini (Beth-eden, Amos 1:5).

The second stage was aimed primarily at the Neo-Hittite states with Carchemish as their senior. Their kings did homage and paid their tribute. Then Ashurnasirpal marched into the kingdom of Patina (also called Unqi; the Bronze Age Mugish, i.e. the ᶜAmuq Plain). The first stop was Ḫazazi (ᶜAzaz). The river Aprê (ᶜAfrîn) was crossed and the king progressed to Kunulua, the capital of Patina, most likely Tell Taᶜyinât. Lubarna, ruler of Patina, showed his dread of the Assyrian offensive capabilities and humbled himself before Ashurnasirpal.

The northern flank was now secure and it was possible to thrust southward via the Orontes Valley into central Syria. He evidently followed the route of the modern roads, crossing the mountains of Jebel Quseir southeast of Antakia. The Sanguru River is most likely the Nahr el-Abyaḍ near Jisr esh-Shughûr. Mount Saratini and Mount Qalpāni are probably also part of the Jebel Quseir. The southernmost outpost of the Patina kingdom was Aribua; in that capacity it most likely had a garrison and other symbols of a national border town. A location near Jisr esh-Shughûr is most logical. It is the only convenient ford on the Orontes and it has a direct eastward approach to Luǵutu and a westward approach to the Mediterranean via the Bdama pass through the Jebel Nosairah (Ansārîyeh).

Ashurnasirpal expropriated Aribua for himself and made it an Assyrian base. He then proceeded to launch a brutal campaign of conquest in the territory of Luǵuti. This is the land of Nughasse of the second millennium. The political status of the land of Luǵuti is not clear. By the reign of Shalmaneser III it seems to have formed the northern province of the kingdom of

Hamath, and it may have already been so at this earlier date.

After ravaging and savaging the land of Luǵuti, the king then turned his attention westward. The campaign culminated in a trek to the Amanus Mountains, where large quantities of lumber were gathered for use in the royal building projects back home in Assyria:

On a subsequent campaign to Khuzirina in 866 BCE, Ashurnasirpal received tribute from the king of Kummukh, Qatazilu. This expedition has been characterized as a peaceful progress rather than a massive feat of arms, and certainly its military and political effects cannot have been very extensive. On the other hand, the coastal cities of Phoenicia doubtless saw this occasion as an opportunity to open up markets to the east for their products being brought in by their westward-sailing commercial fleet.

**Shalmaneser III** (859–824 BCE). The policies of Ashurnasirpal II were continued by his son and successor, Shalmaneser III. The campaigns of this latter monarch to the west were marked by local attempts to resist the Assyrian aggressors. His inscriptions show that the Assyrians did their homework; they have a thorough knowledge of the political and social entities in the Levant. The political states in the northern and later in the central regions of Syria tried to band together to defeat the Assyrian invaders. The former were eventually subdued but the latter continued to resist Shalmaneser until late in his career. The Assyrian pressure forced the states of the central and southern Levant to work together against the common threat. Nevertheless, their own local conflicts and rivalries did not abate during the ninth century BCE.

**The Phoenician Coast.** The king list, mainly preserved by Menander of Ephesus, who had access to Phoenician sources, gives a number of Tyrian kings from the ninth century BCE (*Apion* 1.121–125).

| | |
|---|---|
| ʿAshtartrām | 890 BCE |
| Pilles | 880 BCE |
| ʾIttôbaʿal I (Ethobaal) | 880 BCE |
| Baʿal-azor II | 850 BCE |
| Mattan I | 840 BCE |
| Pygmalion | 830 BCE |

During the period when Tyre was the senior of the Phoenician cities, their kings could bear the title, "King of the Sidonians (=Phoenicians)" (1 Kgs 16:31).

The founding of Carthage ("New City") is credited in the ancient sources (Greek) to Tyre and the date given is in terms of the number of years before the first Olympiad, viz. 814/813 BCE. Presumably this was in the reign of Pygmalion.

The links between Tyre and Israel during the reign of Ethobaal (ʾIttôbaʿal) I will be discussed below.

Generally, the Phoenician cities chose to pay tribute to the Assyrian kings whenever it was demanded. At the battle of Qarqar, when the southern coalition made a stand against Shalmaneser III, there may have been a Byblian contingent fighting on the side of the coalition. But that is not certain. The Tyrians and Sidonians much preferred to protect their commercial interests between the Mediterranean and inland western Asia and in any case, their own military resources would have been limited.

## The Southern Levant

The kingdoms of Israel and Judah continue their respective dynastic successions. There were changes in dynasty in the north but the same House of David continues to rule in the south.

**Israel**. The son of Jeroboam, Nadab, succeeded his father in 910/909 BCE, in the second year of Asa (non-accession year reckoning; actual first official accession year reckoning) and reigned one actual year (1 Kgs 15:25; officially two years, non-accession year reckoning) until his murder in 909/908 BCE by his army commander, Baasha, while the Israelite army was engaged in the siege of Gibbethon (1 Kgs 15:27). Baasha was the son of Ahijah of the tribe of Issachar and of common birth (1 Kgs 16:2). The conflict with the Philistines at Gibbethon indicates that the two antagonists were vying for control of the "corridor" between Joppa and Beth-horon and essentially the territory assigned by the Book of Joshua as the "Inheritance of Dan." The issue was not resolved at this time and the conflict raged again during the latter days of Baasha's reign (1 Kgs 16:15).

Two sites have been suggested for Gibbethon. The first was Tell Melât (Tel Malot). Tell Melât is located near the eastern boundary of the inner coastal plain only 12.5 miles (20 km) from the Mediterranean, and 4.5 miles (7 km) south of modern Ramla. Tel Gezer sits boldly and alone on the horizon to its east. Surveys and trial probes at Tell Melât have yielded EB, MB, LB, Iron I, Iron II, Persian, Roman, Byzantine, and Arab materials. The ninth and eighth centuries BCE were well represented.

The second proposed site for Gibbethon is Râs Abū Ḥumeid (Ḥamîd), located 2 miles (3 km) southeast of Ramla and 4 miles (6 km) northwest of Gezer. The two contexts dealing with the conflict between Philistia and Israel indicate that Gibbethon must be located facing Ekron and although the original argument was made when it was thought that Ekron was at ʿAqir, the newly confirmed location of Ekron (Kh. el-Muqannaʿ=Tel Miqne) still leaves Tell Melât as the best site to fulfill that requirement.

Baasha exterminated all the members of the Jeroboam family so as to eliminate any rival claimants to the throne (1 Kgs 15:29). He reigned for twenty-four official years (non-accession year dating), actually twenty-three years (accession year dating). It was in Asa's actual twenty-fifth year (accession year dating), viz. 894 BCE, that Baasha's son Elah succeeded him (1 Kgs 16:8). The only further details of Baasha's reign have to do with his conflict with Asa and the subsequent loss of his northern territories (discussed below).

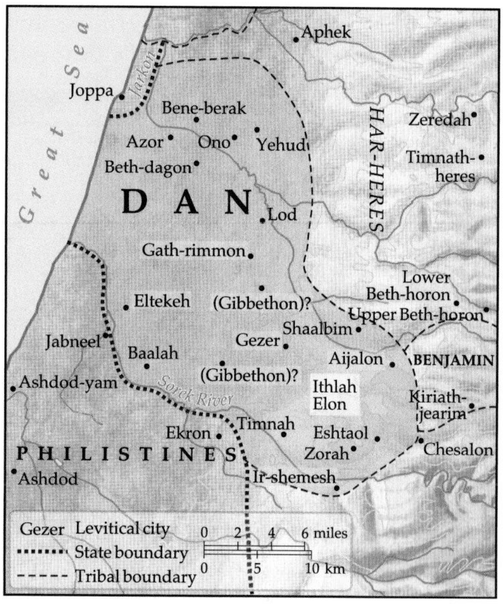

**Israel and the Philistines Clash at Gibbethon (909 BCE)**

**Judah**. In the twentieth year (Judean accession year reckoning) of Jeroboam I of Israel, Asa succeeded his father Abijah/Abijam (1 Kgs 15:9) and ruled forty-one actual years until 869 BCE. He is given special attention in the historical records, especially in Chronicles (2 Chr 14:1–4) because he is said to have discontinued worship at "the foreign altars and high places." This, of course, means that he was giving strong support to the Jerusalem temple establishment, which is a central concern of the Deuteronomistic history and also of the Chronicler. On the other hand, Asa did not just close down local cult places; he established royal centers in those same towns by means of a public program of fortifications, which incidentally must have provided employment for the local populations (in the off season of agricultural activity) under the supervision of newly appointed royal administrators, of course (*see* 1 Chr 14:5–6).

The most memorable event of Asa's reign was the repulsion of an attempted invasion of Judah by a foreign force. This is the account, preserved only in Chronicles, of Zerah the Cushite (2 Chr 14:9–15). A central question is the identity of the invader and his origin. Because of a prophetic allusion to

Libyans, it is assumed that the Cushites in 2 Chronicles 16:8 were Nubians.

In the actual battle account, no Libyans are mentioned, only "the Cushites" (2 Chr 14:11 [Eng. 14:12]). The invaders were overwhelmed and driven back (*see* 2 Chr 14: 11–14 [Eng 12–15]). The leader of the invaders, Zerah, has a perfectly good Semitic name. It is most likely that this Zerah was a member of the Cushite tribe from the northern Hejaz (2 Chr 21:16; Num 12:1), also called Cushan (Hab 3:7). These people would have had a special interest in supporting the Philistines against Judah in order to prevent the latter from interfering in the caravan trade from Arabia to the coast (a recurring theme that will appear repeatedly in subsequent events). Asa had built many fortified cities and those in the south would have provided supplies for passing caravans but the garrisons would have also exacted heavy payments for the right of passage. It would have been impractical for Asa to pursue the invaders across the Arabah to their homeland but he could punish severely the occupants of the western Negeb (the Hamites in origin; 1 Chr 4:39–40) who had undoubtedly provided logistic assistance for the invaders. The attempt to penetrate Judah by way of the Mareshah approach was aimed at crippling Judah's defenses and opening a way to the interior for murder and plunder.

The ensuing celebrations in honor of the great victory took place in the fifteenth year of Asa (2 Chr 15:10), i.e. 895 BCE. So, making allowance for the cultic and religious reforms inaugurated after the victory, it is obvious that the battle must have taken place late in 896 BCE. The references to the thirty-fifth and thirty-sixth years of Asa's reign (2 Chr 15:9–16:1) have to reflect a reckoning from the division of the monarchy. The proof of this contention is the fact that Baasha could not have attacked Asa in the latter's thirty-sixth year because Baasha had died in Asa's twenty-sixth year (2 Kgs 16:8; non-accession year reckoning in Israel; actually in the twenty-fifth year in accession year reckoning in Judah). The reckoning from the founding of the southern dynasty was soon abandoned but the Chronicler incorporated these two dates, perhaps because he linked them somehow with the genuine allusion to the thirty-ninth year of Asa as the beginning of his illness (2 Chr 16:11). During Asa's reign there had not been any hostilities until the thirty-fifth year of the kingdom of Judah which was actually the fifteenth year of Asa (2 Chr 15:10). During that time, Asa had been building up the defenses of his kingdom.

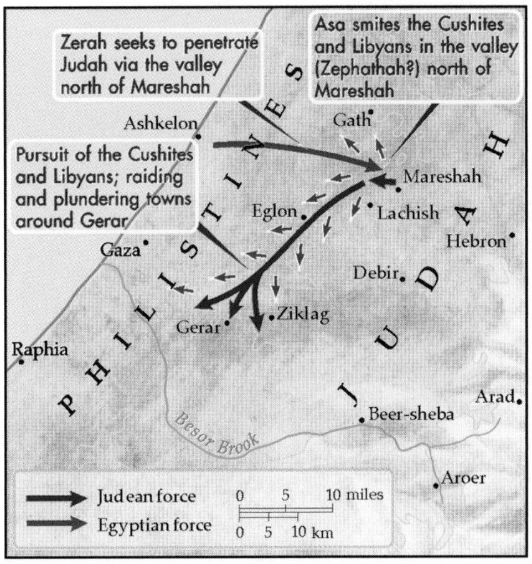


**THE CAMPAIGN OF ZERAH THE CUSHITE (C. 896/895 BCE)**

The military success against Zerah the Cushite apparently earned great notoriety for Asa so he attracted many people from the northern kingdom of Israel (*see* 2 Chr 15:8–10). The Simeon here is not the tribe settled in southern Judah. Rather, it is the town of Simeon (Josh 11:1, 12:20, 19:15) on the northwestern side of the Great Plain. After Megiddo had been destroyed by Shishak back in 925 BCE, it was not immediately reconstituted so that Shim$^{c}$ôn / Simeon (alias *Shôm$^{e}$rôn*) evidently became the main center for the indigenous population. In Josiah's day, Simeon appears again in a similar context (2 Chr 34:6) when Megiddo was an Assyrian administrative center.

Asa was thus enjoying great prestige in both Judah and Benjamin and the neighboring districts of Israel. The enhanced status found expression in new treaty arrangements between the people and the king with their God and with each other (2 Chr 15:1–15). On that basis, he had the political clout needed to carry out his cultic reforms throughout the kingdom, and even in the royal family, in favor of the Jerusalem religious establishment (2 Chr 15:16–18). This entailed the transfer of considerable material wealth from the monarchy to the temple.

Asa's enhanced reputation posed a threat to the northern kingdom. It is no surprise that the neighboring king, Baasha, whose rule was based on assassination of the scion of a popular royal family, felt compelled to take steps to prohibit the traffic from Israel to Jerusalem.

Shortly afterward comes the passage about Baasha's military action against Asa (*see* 2 Chr 15:19–16:1 || 1 Kgs 16:17). It (2 Chr 15:19) should be rendered, "There **had not been** war until the thirty-fifth year of the reign of Asa." As stressed above, this is in reality the fifteenth year of Asa when Zerah's invasion actually occurred. On the other hand, that gloss in Chronicles seems to be contradicted by the Deuteronomist who records that there was war between Baasha and Asa all their days (1 Kgs 15:16). There is seen an allusion to towns in Mt. Ephraim that had been captured by Asa (2 Chr 15:8). So to give any credence to 2 Chronicles 15:19, it must be assumed that the intention was to say that there had never before been an attempt to invade Judean territory from outside.

The 1 Kings description of Baasha's military move into central Benjaminite

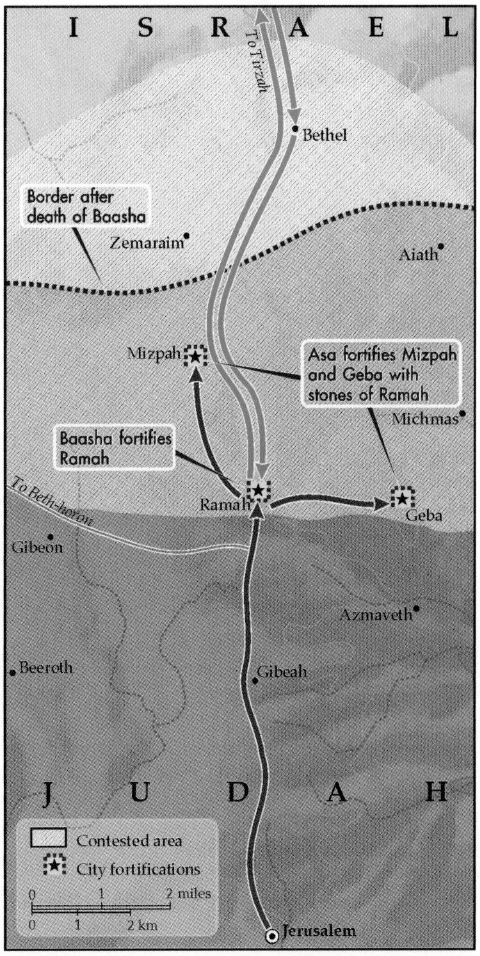


**BAASHA'S ATTACK ON ASA (C. 895 BCE)**

territory (1 Kgs 16:17) appears in the Deuteronomistic narrative like a bolt from the blue with no obvious rationale. But against the background of 2 Chronicles 15: 8–9 it makes perfect sense. The usurpation of the throne in Israel by Baasha (909/908 BCE) and the systematic extermination by him of the remaining members of the family of Jeroboam I (2 Kgs 15:29) must have created considerable unrest in the northern kingdom. Furthermore, the military conflict with the Philistines centered at Gibbethon when Baasha came to power (1 Kgs 15:27) was apparently still unresolved and a draining of assets may have remained so until the end of Baasha's reign in 885 BCE (1 Kgs 16: 15). Therefore, it is not surprising that many people of the north would be attracted to Asa because of his successes, both in the direct border conflicts with Israel and in his victory over Zerah. Asa looked like a winner; Baasha looked like a loser.

The passage in Chronicles is slightly condensed (a word here and there) from the Kings account but the parallel accounts are essentially identical. The Kings version is given here with the addition of the chronological note about the thirty-sixth year (actually it was the sixteenth year of Asa, i.e. 895 BCE), an obvious addition of the Chronicler (*see* 1 Kgs 15:16–17).

At this point, Asa turned to diplomacy in order to remove the Israelite threat (*see* 1 Kgs 15:18–19).

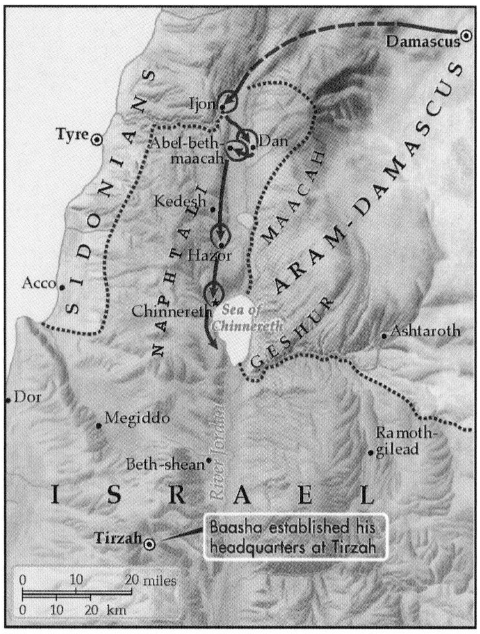


**The Campaign of Ben-hadad I (895/894 BCE)**

Emptying the treasure houses, not only of the palace but also of the temple, must have angered the priests and prophets of the Jerusalem religious establishment, which led to a prophetic rebuke and a resulting estrangement between the crown and the miter as recorded in Chronicles (2 Chr 16: 9–10).

The strategic result of the treaty with Ben-hadad was the invasion of northern Israel by the Arameans (*see* 1 Kgs 15:20 || 2 Chr 16:4). This diversion caused Baasha to withdraw his forces from Ramah. Henceforth he ruled what territory was still under his control from Tirzah (probably Tell el-Far$^{c}$ah North) at the head of the Wâdī Far$^{c}$ah (*see* 1 Kgs 15:22 || 2 Chr 16:5).

Asa was then able to assemble his manpower and dismantle the fortifications of Ramah (*see* 1 Kgs 15:22 || 2 Chr 16:1–6). He then built alternative strong points: Geba (modern Jeba$^{c}$), guarding the important pass over which the eastern road along the edge of the wilderness has to cross, and Mizpah (evidently Tell en-Naṣbeh), on the watershed road (Judg 21:19) facing northward toward Bethel. Henceforth, the recognized border between the two kingdoms was established between Bethel and Mizpah, i.e. on the ridge occupied by modern-day Ramallah and el-Bîrah.

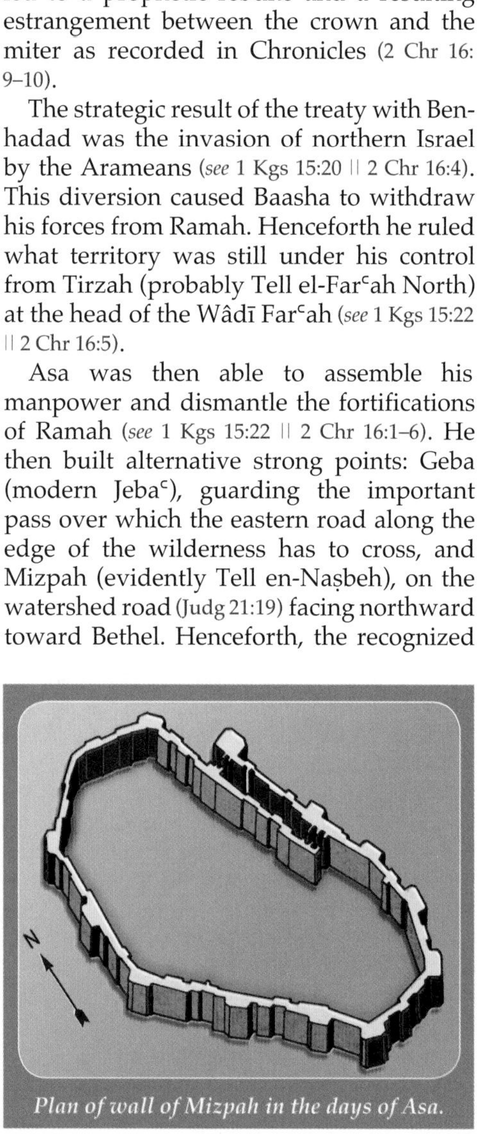


*Plan of wall of Mizpah in the days of Asa.*

## The Omride Dynasty

**The Internal Political Struggle.** The year 886/885 BCE found Israel still engaged with the Philistines at Gibbethon. The strain of that conflict and the alienation of Baasha and his family from the people sowed the seeds of discontent. Elah, son of Baasha, succeeded his father in the twenty-sixth year of Asa according to the non-accession system being used in Israel (1 Kgs 16:8–14). His official reign of two years was therefore only one real year. Elah seems to have preferred to stay at home while his generals conducted the war at Gibbethon. One gets the impression that Elah was a hero of the banquet table; while he was thoroughly inebriated, Zimri, the commander of half the chariot force, carried out an assassination plot and seized the throne. However, Zimri's coup lasted only eight days because when word of his conspiracy reached the army encamped against Gibbethon, the people crowned their senior army commander, Omri, who promptly rushed to the capital with a sufficient military force to establish a siege. Zimri saw that the jig was up and committed suicide by burning down the palace over his head.

In the twenty-seventh year of Asa king of Judah, Zimri reigned seven days at Tirzah. (1 Kgs 16:15a)

This twenty-seventh year was a non-accession year; the actual year (accession year system) was the twenty-sixth, 885 BCE.

There ensued a civil war between two factions. Half of the people supported a certain Tibni son of Ginath as a rival to Omri (whose patronymic is never given; *see* 1 Kgs 16:21–22).

The inauguration passage for Omri makes it clear that this internal conflict lasted for five actual (six official non-accession) years (*see* 1 Kgs 16:23).

The conflict had begun in 885 BCE, Asa's twenty-fifth actual year (accession reckoning) and ended in 880 BCE, Asa's actual thirtieth (accession system) year; these are called Asa's twenty-sixth and thirty-first years (non-accession system used in Israel), respectively. It had lasted about five actual years. It was in the thirty-first (actual thirtieth) year of Asa that Omri became sole ruler. His total years of reign were twelve (non-accession system), actually eleven (accession year system) from 885 to 874 BCE when Ahab became king in Asa's thirty-eighth (actual thirty-seventh) year (1 Kgs 16:29). As for Omri, his first six (actually five) years were spent ruling from Tirzah while contending with Tibni.

Throughout this time, the fate of the conquered territories in Galilee and Chinnereth is not known. Were these the towns mentioned later by Ben-hadad when he surrendered to Ahab (1 Kgs 20:34)? Or did Damascus take advantage of the internal strife in Israel to occupy further towns in Transjordan? Whatever the answer, the Damascus aggression against Omri must have taken place before he had achieved sole rule .

**Political/Military Program**. Once Omri found himself freed from the burden of civil strife, he was able to address the more pressing issues of external conflict. Besides liberating the Galilean territories, a potential source of economic and military power would be control of Transjordan. But Damascus had arisen as a major player on the local scene and it, too, shared the lust for wealth that could accrue from domination of the Transjordanian highways and their connections with Arabia, both via Wâdī Sirḥân and the Hejaz. Therefore, Omri launched a program of political, diplomatic and military action to prepare his nation for the showdown with Aram-Damascus. Although his reign is summarized in only five verses (1 Kgs 16:23–28), a great deal can be deduced from other sources to reveal the brilliant strategy of this ruler who became the eponymous founder of a new Israelite entity, still called in Assyrian sources "The Land of the House of Omri" a century later (under Tighlath-pileser III and Sargon II).

**Choice of a New Capital**. The first step was internal. He needed a new capital

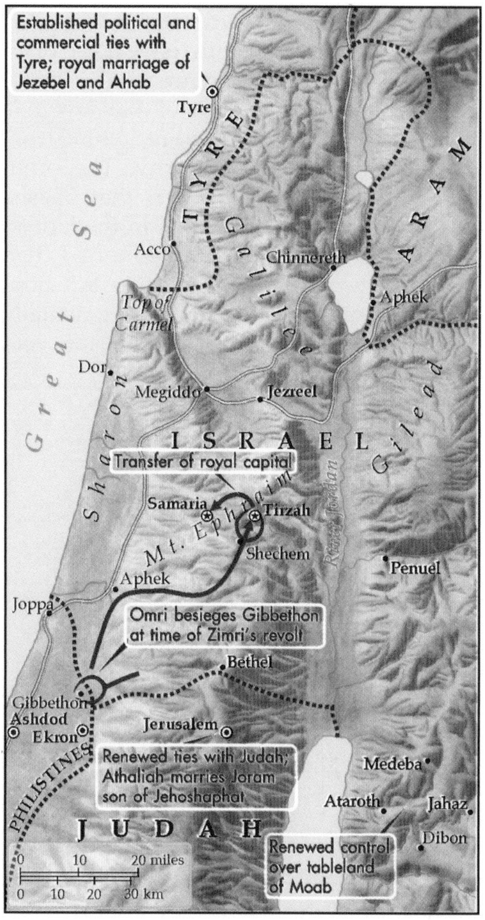


**The Rise of Omri (885/884 BCE)**

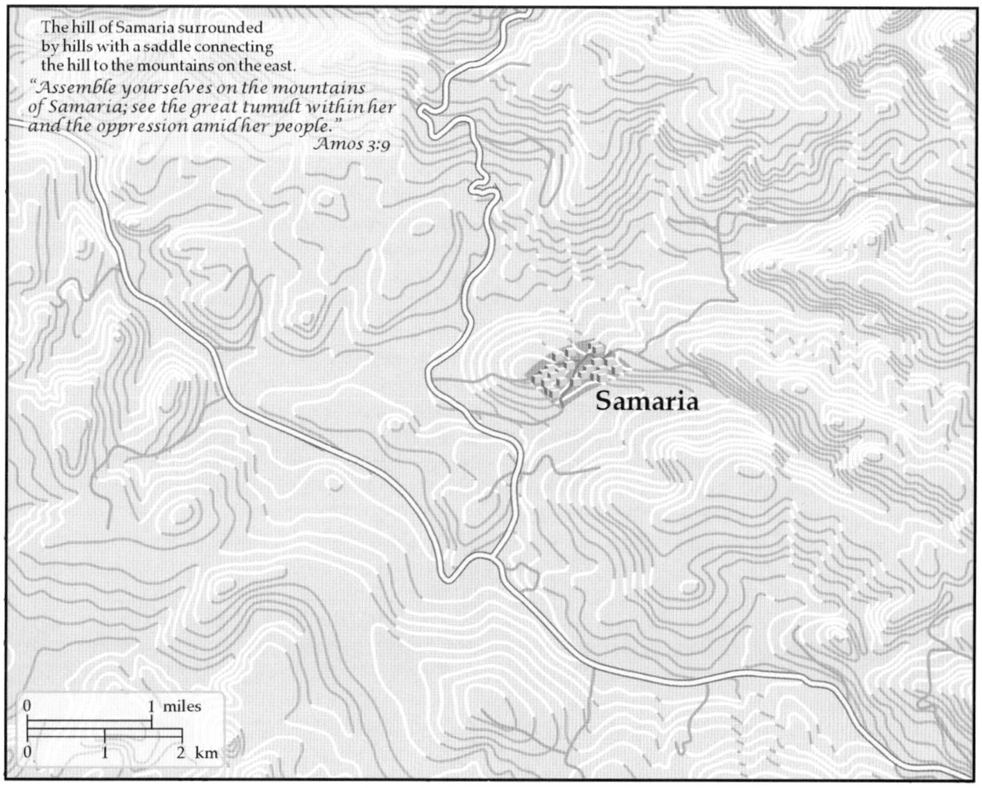


THE HILL OF SHEMER, WHERE OMRI BUILT HIS NEW CAPITAL NAMED SAMARIA

specifically linked to his new royal house (*see* 1 Kgs 16:24). Both Shemer and Omri may be linked to the tribe of Issachar and Omri might have been acting as the redeemer of clan property. In any case, the new city would be royal property by purchase. The very fact of its being named Samaria after the eponymous head of the occupying clan, is sufficient to prove that there must have been a settlement of some sort on the hill before Omri's purchase. Now it is clear that not just a village for oil production but also a walled enclosure and a significant public building existed on the site during the tenth century BCE, i.e. prior to Omri's purchase in the ninth century BCE.

In fact, a site named for an eponym such as Shemer, should be expected to have built-up remains. The excavators in the Joint Expedition of the 1930s made the fatal mistake of misinterpreting 1 Kings 16:24; they thought the earliest major construction phase had to be in the ninth century BCE. They should have assumed just the opposite. That hermeneutical error has caused needless misapprehensions in the archaeological interpretation of most northern Iron Age sites during the late twentieth century. Only now have the true pre-Omride remains at Samaria been properly discerned and defined.

**Political Alliances**. The next step was to forge a treaty alliance with the kingdom of Tyre, the leading maritime commercial power at that time on the eastern Mediterranean seaboard. Evidence for the treaty is the marriage of Jezebel, the daughter of Ethobaal, king of Tyre, with Ahab, the son of Omri. The influence of that princess, later queen, is a major focus in the historiography of the Omride dynasty, especially in the "Elijah Cycle" of prophetic legends, but attention to the religious tensions she created has obscured the important political and economic factors in the alliance. Omri, as ruler of an inland state, was planning to become the chief outlet for Arabian products to the Phoenician coast. He would also provide foodstuffs for the Phoenician maritime population, thus obtaining a market for his agricultural surpluses. To fulfill these goals, Omri was compelled to contest the Aramean control of the vital arteries in Transjordan. Transjordan was also a significant source for small cattle whose hair and wool would be in demand for the textile industry of Phoenicia, itself a major production center for colored dyes. Israel, in its turn, benefited from the architectural expertise of Phoenician artisans and craftsmen for the construction of cities and public buildings, as well as the production of specialty items such as decorative carved ivories. Tyre could also furnish many other imports from the Mediterranean world.

The second treaty was with the kingdom of Judah. It was obvious that if Omri planned to take on the Arameans, he could not afford to have a hostile neighbor on his southern border. This new political alliance was also sealed by a royal marriage, viz. between Athaliah and Joram, the firstborn of Jehoshaphat, son of Asa. Because of an obscure allusion to Athaliah as "daughter of Ahab" (2 Kgs 8:18=2 Chr 21:6), it has been thought that the title "daughter of Omri" (2 Kgs 8:26=2 Chr 22:2) was somehow a generalization. However, it would appear that the "daughter of Ahab" epithet is an editorial value judgment on the part of the Deuteronomistic editor. Athaliah was a member of the "house(hold) of Ahab" after her father's death.

Jehoram/Joram son of Jehoshaphat was only eleven years old when Omri died but Athaliah's age is unknown. Such royal marital unions were often arranged while the candidates were still in their minority, so there is no reason to doubt that the initiative could have been taken while Omri was still on the throne. If that were not the case, it would have made sense for Ahab to propose such a union in his own fourth year, when Jehoshaphat had become sole ruler of Judah and Jehoram was fifteen years old. The old king, Asa, had gone from the scene and his son could abandon his father's antagonism to Israel and practice a new *realpolitik*.

**Military Action**. The Bible says nothing about Omri making any military moves. Here is where an important extra-biblical source furnishes reliable details that illuminate Omri's strategy. It is the display inscription of Mesha king of Moab.

> Omr[5]i was king of Israel and he oppressed Moab many days because Chemosh was angry with his l[6]and. And his son replaced him and he also said, "I will oppress Moab. In my days he spoke ⌈thus⌉ [7]but I was victorious over him and his house and Israel suffered everlasting destruction.
> (Mesha Inscription ll. 4b–7a).

Omri's first move was to seize Medeba (modern Mâdabā) and its environs, the land of Medeba. This gave him control of a centrally located town on the north-south highway and also the extensive agricultural resources that surrounded it. This move had to take place sometime after 880 BCE when Omri was finally free of the civil war and could commit the resources needed for a Transjordanian campaign.

> But Omri conquered the lan[8]d of Mehadeba and he dwelt there during his reign and half the reign of his son, forty years, but Chemosh [9]returned it in my days. (Mesha Inscription ll. 7b–9a)

Israel also renewed contact with the ancient tribe of Gad that had inhabited a particular area on the western ridges of the central tableland of northern Moab. Their principal town was Ataroth. Actually there are two towns with this name, Ataroth and Atroth-shophan (Num 32:35) and there are two antiquity sites that preserve their names. They are barely 2.5 miles (4 km) apart, Khirbet ᶜAṭārûz (Ataroth) and Rujm ᶜAṭārûz (Atroth-shophan), both located on the ridge route leading from Libb westward towards the Dead Sea. The building of Ataroth for the Gadites took place during the almost thirty years (represented by "forty years," the round number for a generation in the Mesha text, as in the Bible) during which Moab was subject to Israel.

The man of Gad had dwelt in ᶜAṭarot (Ataroth) from of old and the king of Israel [11]built ᶜAṭarot (Ataroth) for him. (Mesha Inscription ll. 10–11a)

By this means, Omri had gained a firm footing in southern Transjordan and that enabled him to increase his support of the other Israelite tribes in Gilead, thus opening the way to divert Arabian caravans from Damascus to Israel, and on to Phoenicia, mainly via Beth-shean. Wool and goat hair from the large flocks of Moab and Gilead could be furnished to the Phoenicians who were manufacturing the colored dyes needed for a rich textile industry.

**Ahab Succeeds His Father**. Omri died and was succeeded by his son, Ahab, in the thirty-eighth year of Asa (1 Kgs 16:29). That was according to the non-accession year reckoning so for Asa it was actually in his thirty-seventh year in (874/873 BCE). Ahab's twenty-two official years were only twenty-one actual years.

**Internal Policies**. The ancient historiographers remembered the reign of Ahab as one of the worst periods of monarchial abuse in the history of ancient Israel (e.g. 2 Kgs 21:3). But this was the view of the Deuteronomist, a Judean writer. In Israel, Ahab aroused the ire of the prophetic circle led by Elijah and negative stories from the "Elijah cycle" form a major portion of the textual material included in the Deuteronomistic history (1 Kgs). In spite of all the negative hype, it is recorded that in the Chronicles of the Kings of Israel one would find an account of Ahab's building projects, viz. a "House of Ivory," evidently his royal palace in Samaria, and other cities which he built (1 Kgs 22:39). Some of his fortification projects were probably in northern Moab as described in the Mesha inscription.

**Introduction of Baal Worship**. Ahab introduced official Baal worship to his capital city establishing a sacrificial altar at the "house of Baal" which he built

*Selection of ivories from the royal palace in Samaria.*

in Samaria (1 Kgs 16:31–33). It should be remembered, nevertheless, that Ahab's sons, born to Jezebel, both had Yahwistic names and he continued the maintenance of the two national Yahwistic shrines at Dan and Bethel. The temple of Baal (and Asherah) in the capital city of Samaria, was a financial as well as a religious institution and represented the close commercial ties between the kingdoms of Tyre and Israel.

Early in his reign there is a report of a three-year drought (1 Kgs 17:1–19:21). The account of this drought is derived from the "Elijah cycle" of prophetic stories; still, there are some geographical details that can be taken at face value, viz. the presence of a holy place of sacrifice on Mount Carmel. According to the story, there had been a Yahwistic altar at that place (1 Kgs 18:30) before the altar to Baal was set up. Reference to the same cult place probably derives from a later report by Shalmaneser III (in 841 BCE).

**Social Injustice**. The internal administration of the kingdom was probably no better or no worse than neighboring states. However, the Elijah cycle preserves the account of a gross violation of human rights, the affair of Naboth and his vineyard (1 Kgs 21). The story, especially the disputed plot of ground, is linked to the assassination at Jezreel of Jezebel and her son Joram (2 Kgs 9:21, 9:25) so the vineyard must have been there. Emphasis in the narrative is on the citizen's right to maintain his family patrimony. Under the law, if the charges against Naboth had been true, the king would have had every right to confiscate the vineyard. However, the prophetic focus is on Jezebel's illegal scheme to violate ancestral law.

**Wars with Aram**. Mesha's inscription (line 6) says that Omri's son Ahab continued to maintain control of the northern tableland of Moab. On the other hand, Israel was still at a disadvantage with respect to Damascus. It would seem that the Aramean king had obtained the right to establish commercial enclaves in Samaria (1 Kgs 20:34).

About four years before the battle of Qarqar in 853 BCE, open conflict broke out between Damascus and Israel. The Aramean army invaded the hill country of Samaria and laid siege to Samaria itself (1 Kgs 20:1–22). Armies in that ancient period were always advised by prophets and this time the instructions were to organize a daring sortie from the city gate to take the besieging forces by surprise. While the king of Damascus and his vassals were enjoying an afternoon banquet and siesta, the very elite units of the Israelite troops led the attack on the unsuspecting besiegers. The latter were routed and forced to make a hasty retreat from the hill country of Ephraim, most likely via the Wâdī Farᶜah.

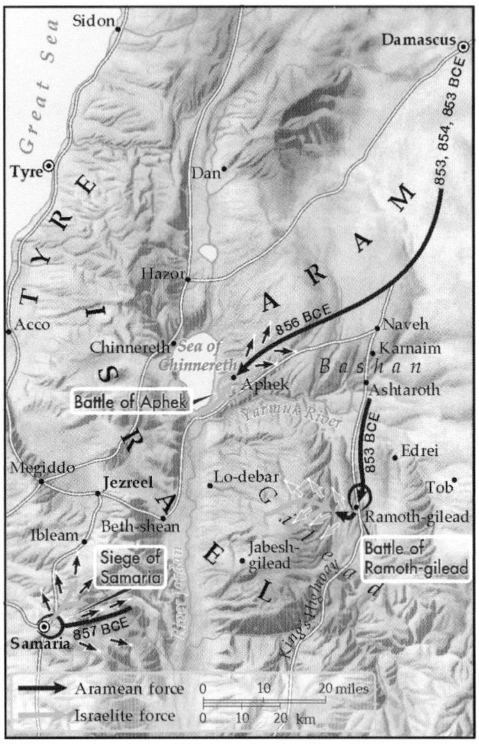


**AHAB'S WARS WITH ARAM (885–853 BCE)**

The Aramean king and his noblemen had been reclining in their pavilions nearby.

The tradition has it that this defeat led the king of Damascus to reorganize his federation of Aramean polities (1 Kgs 20:23–25), replacing the vassal kings by governors. A new army was raised and a more convenient venue was chosen. Instead of penetrating into the hill country, the Arameans chose to assemble at Aphek, on the east side of the Chinnereth (1 Kgs 20:23–43). Whether this Aphek is the site near the town of Fîq, on the plateau above the lake and east of Qalᶜat el-Ḥuṣn (Sussita/Hippus) at the head of Wâdī Fîq, it does not seem to have Iron Age remains. So it has been suggested that Aphek be located down at Khirbet ᶜÂsheq (ᶜEn Gev) near the mouth of the wadi on the edge of the lake. However, another Iron Age site northwest of Fîq, called Tel Soreq, does have Iron Age fortifications of the ninth and eighth centuries BCE and also Intermediate, Middle and Late Bronze materials, though it could not have been such a large city. Large-scale battles seem more likely to have taken place on the plateau above.

In any event, the result was a victory for Ahab. But he was rebuked by a prophet for having offered to accept generous terms from the defeated king of Damascus. This conflict evidently took place in c. 856 BCE because it is said:

So they sat for three years without war between Aram and Israel. (1 Kgs 22:1)

The reason for that three-year hiatus is found in the inscriptions of Shalmaneser III.

**Shalmaneser III vs. the Southern Coalition**. The king of Assyria turned his attention once again to the west. The Levant was calling him to further conquest.

From Aleppo, the Assyrian king moved south to attack the territory subject to Irḫulēni, king of Hamath, in central Syria.

I drew near to the cities of Irḫulēni the Hamathite; I conquered Adennu, Pargâ and Arganâ, his royal cities; I brought out his booty: his goods and the treasure of his palaces; I set fire to his palaces. I departed from Arganâ and drew near to Qarqar. I destroyed Qarqar, his royal city, and I set it on fire. (Kurkh II 87b–90a)

Tell Qarqur on the right (east) bank of the Orontes River, 4 miles (7 km) south of Jisr esh-Shughûr, has all the requisite archaeological remains for identification with Qarqar. Both ninth and eighth centuries BCE are represented.

The conquest of "Qarqar of Irḫulēni" is also portrayed on the Balawat gates. The other three cities destroyed before Qarqar must have been situated on a road between Aleppo and Jisr esh-Shughûr, but their exact location has not been determined. Parga and probably Adennu (in the form Adâ) are depicted on the Balawat gates. The two towns are alongside a body of water. Shalmaneser's route may have followed the Orontes on the west or more directly along the Quweiq River. It is not stated but there is the possibility that Ashurnaṣirpal II's colony of Aribua, probably located on the Orontes c. 6 miles (10 km) north of Qarqar, may have still been in Assyrian hands.

The composition of the western coalition should reflect the main political bodies of the central and southern Levant. At the head of the list is Hadad-ᶜid̲ri of Damascus, whom the Assyrians always considered their archenemy in the southern Levant. Hadad-ᶜid̲ri must have succeeded the Ben-hadad (Aramaic: Bar-hadad) who had given such good terms when he surrendered to Ahab. As the new king of Aram-Damascus, Hadad-ᶜid̲ri evidently became the driving force in the formation of the coalition and must be given credit for reading the political map correctly. He was surely aware of the Assyrian aggressions and extortions in northern Syria and southern Anatolia and realized that only by a concerted effort would it be possible to stop the Assyrian juggernaut.

Irḫulēni the Hamathite was the one who stood in the most immediate danger. His territories had already suffered Assyrian aggression, even under Ashurnasirpal II, and the kingdom of Hamath was clearly in

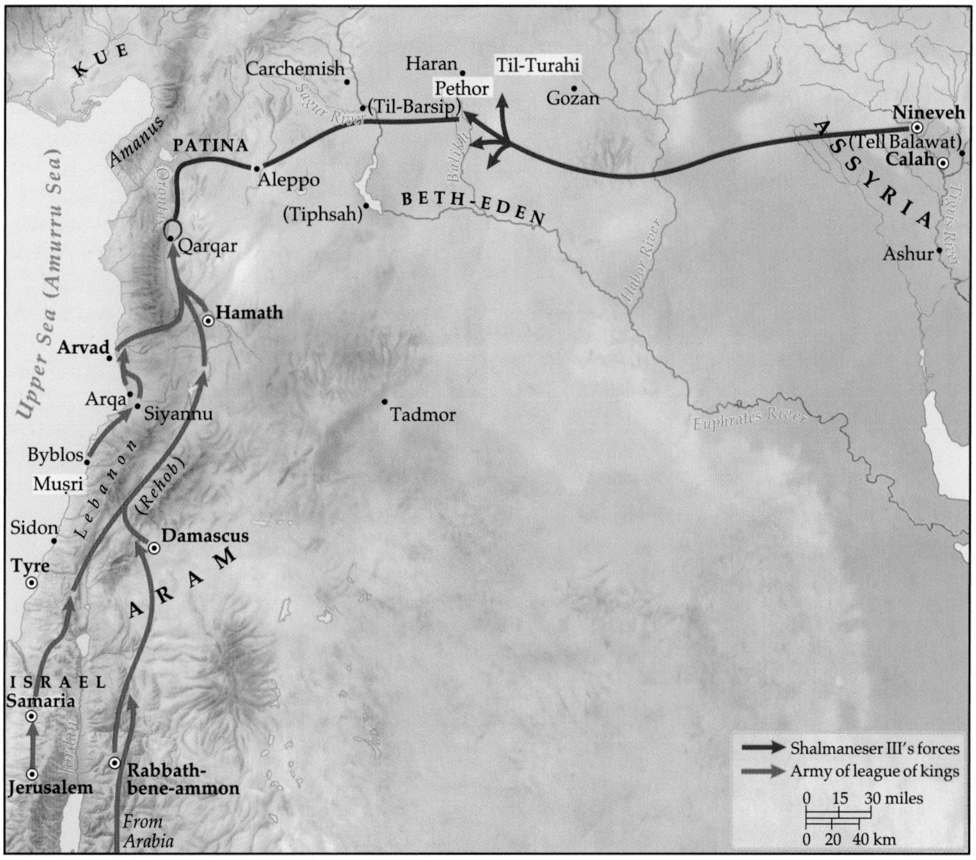


**THE BATTLE OF QARQAR (853 BCE)**

the crosshairs of Shalmaneser's avarice.

Ahab the Israelite might have come as the ally of Hadad-ᶜid̲ri even though it was Ahab who had gained an advantageous treaty with Damascus about two years earlier. On the other hand, it seems more likely that the traditional friendship between Hamath and Israel, going back to the tenth century BCE, may have motivated Ahab to come to the aid of his northern neighbor. There is nothing to be gained by speculating about the real number of chariots fielded by Israel.

The caption called for twelve enemies but only eleven seem to be listed. The solution may be in the final entry. Baasha son of Rehob was possibly ruler of a small princedom mainly in the Beqaᶜ, while some unknown force had come under the command of "X the Ammonite," both representing poetical entities tied closely to Aram-Damascus.

They attacked in order to [make] combat and onslaught against me. With the overwhelming forces that Ashur (my) lord had given to me, with the mighty weapons that the divine standard that goes before me had granted me, I engaged them. From the city of Qarqar to the city of Gilzaʾu I verily strew their corpses and I felled with the sword fourteen thousand troops, their fighting force. I rained down upon them a cascade alike the Storm God; I swamped (them). I made their corpses fill the open plain; their vast hordes I caused their blood to flow with the sword.... The open steppe was insufficient for laying out their bodies; the open space was used up with their burials. With their cadavers I dammed up the Orontes River like a bridge. In the midst of that battle I took away their chariots, their cavalry, their horses, i.e. their teams. (Kurkh II, 95b–102)

Such bombastic claims are meant to cover the fact that the Assyrians were stopped in their tracks. Subsequent events strongly suggest that the coalition had succeeded in its immediate goal. For the next three years (852–850 BCE), Shalmaneser did not cross the Euphrates. When he finally did turn his attention to Syria in his tenth regnal year (849 BCE), he had to first attack the towns of Carchemish and Bīt-Agusi, prior to his second clash with the central and southern coalition led by Damascus and Hamath. The resounding setback at Qarqar seems to have encouraged the more northerly states to behave independently. In regnal years 11 (848 BCE) , 14 (845 BCE) and 18 (841 BCE), he was opposed by the same coalition.

*King of Assyria at head of army; from bronze relief of Shalmaneser III at Tell Balawat.*

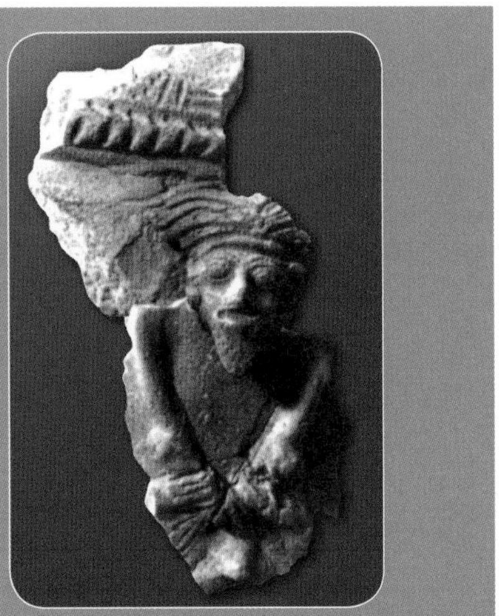

*Decorated fragment of a cultic stand, found in Area G, City of David, Jerusalem, Iron Age.*

**Judah (continued).** As mentioned above, Jehoshaphat became co-regent with his sick father, Asa, in 872 BCE. The introduction to his reign in 1 Kings uses the double dating system. His sole reign was reckoned from his father's death in the fourth year of Ahab in accordance with the accession year system (869 BCE). The total length of his reign was twenty-five official years in which his first year, overlapping his father, was not called an accession year. Thus the actual total number of regnal years was twenty-four (1 Kgs 2:41–42). When his father, who had had great animosity to the northern kingdom of Israel, died, it was a propitious time to make peace with Ahab and the marriage alliance between the two royal houses was probably initiated at this time.

The Chronicler provides a considerable amount of material about the reign of Jehoshaphat. Most of it is anchored in detailed information, e.g. names of officials, so that there is no reason to assume these verses are all the invention of the Chronicler. The naming of specific individuals, officials, and family members looks quite authentic.

Jehoshaphat recognized that he must overcome the estrangement that had occurred between his father and the Jerusalem religious establishment. Therefore, he focused his own energies on the centralized cult of YHWH (2 Chr 17:3–4) at the expense of local cult centers. His appointing officials, including clergy, to teach throughout the kingdom took place in his third year (*see* 2 Chr 17:7–9).

If, as is likely, this was the third year of his total reign, it was the last year of his co-regency with Asa, probably after Asa had died. But the previous two years, during his father's incapacitating illness, Jehoshaphat must have taken steps to strengthen his position as ruler. He placed military forces and loyal governors in the cities of Judah and in those along his northern border that had been taken from Israel by Asa (2 Chr 17:2). The appointment of six of his sons to positions over fortified cities of Judah (2 Chr 21:2–3) looks quite authentic also, but his eldest son, Jehoram, by the chief wife was only about sixteen in 869 BCE so the six brothers may have been mere youths or perhaps were born to lesser wives. It may be that those sons were placed in charge of six cities in 853 BCE when Jehoram became co-regent; their job would have been the support of their senior brother, especially if anything should happen to Jehoshaphat in the upcoming war with Aram. The extent of Jehoshaphat's kingdom was "from Beer-sheba to the hill country of Ephraim" (2 Chr 19:4). Beer-sheba was the administrative center of the southern district; on the north, all of the Benjaminite territory was encompassed, including those towns in southern Ephraim taken by Asa.

The sending out of the teachers to instruct the people in legal matters must be linked with his reform of the judiciary (2 Chr 19:4–11). He appointed judges in the cities of the kingdom. In Jerusalem he appointed Levites, priests and heads of leading clans to judge the residents of the capital and also to handle serious cases (such as blood feuds, etc.) brought to them on appeal from other cities throughout the kingdom (2 Chr 19:8). The chief priest, Amariah, had authority over all matters pertaining to the cult of YHWH (2 Chr 19:11). The affairs of the royal government were handled by Zebadiah the son of Ishmael, who was "commissar of the House of Judah." That title must correspond to the "(administrator) over the (king's) house" (Isa 36:3).

The reorganization of the military (2 Chr 17:14–19), again giving the names of authentic individuals, has the ring of truth even though the numbers of troops, etc., are undoubtedly artificial. Since Jehoshaphat had inherited a strong kingdom from his father, it is not surprising that he was able to capitalize on his father's previous military successes and further strengthen his kingdom (*see* 2 Chr 17:12–13).

The Chronicler was always sensitive to the geopolitical and military status of the kingdom of Judah. He makes specific reference to the Judean economic dominance of the region (*see* 2 Chr 17:11–12a).

The Philistines on the west and the Arabians on the east found it necessary and expedient to make these large payments to Jehoshaphat. That information, coupled with the references to extensive fortifications and military garrisons, makes the picture clear. The kingdom of Judah was controlling the caravan routes across the Arabah and the Negeb highlands to the Mediterranean coast. The Philistines and the Arabians were partners in commerce but Jehoshaphat had become a powerful middleman. For the trade caravans to pass, they had to pay duty and tribute to the kingdom of Judah. The Arabians in this context are undoubtedly the Meunites, a tribal confederacy that occupied southern Transjordan (probably from Maᶜin), across the northern Sinai expanses to el-ᶜArish. They will appear more explicitly in a subsequent military adventure against Jehoshaphat.

On the other hand, Edom was subject to Judean control. They did not have an independent king. Instead they had a ruler who was evidently commissioned by Judah and enjoyed his office by authority of Jehoshaphat (*see* 1 Kgs 22:48 [Eng. 22:47]).

This does not mean that he was not an Edomite. In fact, he could have been a well-respected leader among his own people and that may have prevented them from joining an anti-Judah expedition.

At this point the Chronicler deigns to incorporate a pericope that probably came from the Chronicles of the Kings of Israel (2 Chr 18:2–34 || 1 Kgs 22:3–35). It is the drama that played out when Jehoshaphat accepted Ahab's invitation to join him for the attempt to retake Ramoth-gilead.

**The Battle of Ramoth-gilead.** After the battle of Qarqar, where the coalition apparently stopped the Assyrian army in its tracks, the king of Aram-Damascus, Hadad-ᶜid̲ri, must have felt both relieved and buoyant. Since it was probably his predecessor, Ben-hadad, who had been forced to offer humiliating terms to Ahab, Hadad-ᶜid̲ri must have felt that now he could move against his neighbor, Ahab, and reassert Damascus' domination of the eastern trade routes. He had seized Ramoth-gilead, a key outpost along that route.

There had been three years of ceasefire between Israel and Aram-Damascus: "And they sat for three years without war between Aram and Israel" (1 Kgs 22:1). But "in the third year" Jehoshaphat, king of Judah, came to visit Ahab, king of Israel. This has to be 853 BCE after Ahab had returned from the great conflict at Qarqar. Ahab invited Jehoshaphat to join him in a combined effort to regain control of Ramoth-gilead and Jehoshaphat accepted (1 Kgs 22:2 || 2 Chr 18:2). This narrative is replete with prophetic anti-Omride elements, including the dire prediction of Micaiah (1 Kgs 22:5–28 || 2 Chr 18:4–27). The ensuing account of Ahab's death must be part of the same pericope (1

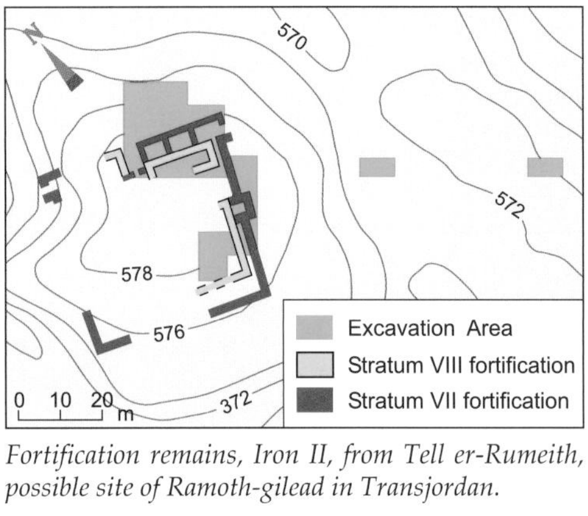


*Fortification remains, Iron II, from Tell er-Rumeith, possible site of Ramoth-gilead in Transjordan.*

Kgs 22:29–35 || 2 Chr 18:28–34). Still, it has the ring of authenticity. Before the battle, Ahab induced Jehoshaphat to wear his royal attire while he, himself, would dress as a common warrior. In the course of the fighting, the Arameans sought out Ahab and found Jehoshaphat by mistake but did not slay him. By accident an Aramean bowman took a shot and mortally wounded Ahab. The king of Israel had his charioteer station the chariot facing the field of battle so Ahab could oversee the conflict with his dying breath (1 Kgs 22:33–35 || 2 Chr 18:32–34).

> So Ahab lay down with his fathers, and Ahaziah his son reigned in his stead. (1 Kgs 22:40)

The expression "lay down with his fathers" means that Ahab was given the proper burial due to him, conducted by his heir. It by no means can be used to suggest that Ahab did not die a violent death in battle. There is not a scrap of evidence to negate the testimony that Ahab was engaged in military conflict with Aram-Damascus. The war stories of 1 Kings 20, 22 are legitimately assigned to Ahab's reign.

**Judah (continued)**. According to the Chronicler, Jehoshaphat returned safely to Jerusalem after the battle at Ramoth-gilead (2 Chr 19:1–4). He was rebuked by the prophet (v. 3) for supporting Ahab. The plan for reorganizing the court system (2 Chr 19) may have been a measure taken to counter this criticism. It would have been founded on the earlier project of teaching the people the proper statutes (2 Chr 17). The unifying power of this religious and judicial reform was essential in the face of new threats.

**Attempted Invasion**. The king of Damascus could take satisfaction in the death of Ahab, his archenemy in Israel. But it would have been impractical to launch a campaign of revenge against Jehoshaphat at this time. Therefore, he invoked his allies in southern Transjordan to do it for him. They launched an attempted invasion of Judah after Jehoshaphat's return from the battle at Ramoth-gilead (2 Chr 20:1–30).

The Chronicler's sequencing is of major importance here. His statement, "And it came to pass after this . . ." (2 Chr. 20:1) is more than a literary convention here. Furthermore, the details of the narrative fit just this particular time. The invasion took place in 853 BCE right after the death of Ahab. It is also significant that the Chronicler refers to the joint nautical venture with Ahaziah in the subsequent verses (2 Chr 20:35–37). Again the expression "after this" (2 Chr 20:35) is intentional; it is meant to confirm the sequence of events. The reign of Ahaziah was two official years (non-accession system) but only one calendar year, viz. 853/852 BCE. By placing the attempted Moabite-Ammonite invasion between the death of Ahab and the reign of Ahaziah, the Chronicler enables us to date that campaign to 853/852 BCE.

Opinions have varied concerning this narrative. It has even been suggested that the geographic details must derive from some local tradition of an otherwise unknown invasion by the Nabateans! There is at least a certain agreement that there was some ancient source behind the narrative. Even though the Chronicler may have embellished the material to suit his own theological goals, there is every reason to believe that he found the original embedded in the Chronicle of the Kings of Judah (*see* 2 Chr 20:1–2, 20:10–11).

Three points determine the correct interpretation of this passage:

1. The LXX reading "Meunites" is to be preferred and taken to represent an original Hebrew "from the Meunites" instead of the MT "from the Ammonites" who are already mentioned.

2. On the other hand "from Aram" is not to be amended to "from Edom." The Septuagint has "from Syria," and the implication is that the Arameans had incited the Ammonites and Moabites to launch this invasion. This can be seen as an offensive move designed to avenge Jehoshaphat's participation in the war against Aram alongside Ahab.

3. The Mount Seir in verses 10 and 22 is not to be sought to the east but rather to the west of the Arabah valley (cf. 1 Chr 4:42). The people of Mount Seir in this passage are those Meunites from LXX 2 Chronicles 20:1. They were the pastoral people living in southern Transjordan and who controlled the caravan routes across the Sinai desert. They paid tribute to Uzziah later on (2 Chr 26:7–8; cf. also 1 Chr 4:41) and afterwards paid tribute to Tiglath-pileser III.

The failure of the enterprise is credited to a falling out among the participants (*see* 2 Chr 20:22–23). The threatened invasion by way of En-gedi suggests that the southern, shallow part of the Dead Sea was dry at this time. From En-gedi, it was apparently expected that the invaders would attempt to penetrate Judah via the pass to "the steppe land of Tekoa." That is where Jehoshaphat and his forces had taken up positions against them (2 Chr 20:20).

The Deuteronomist skipped over this event as well as many other interesting details of the life of Jehoshaphat. Nevertheless, he does allude to the fact that Jehoshaphat engaged in military activity (2 Kgs 42:46 [Heb.]). The Chronicler included the narrative of chapter 20 because it served to balance the picture presented in 2 Kings 3 (a narrative from the Chronicles of the Kings of Israel). That latter campaign took place after the death of Ahaziah of Israel, when Joram of Israel took over his brother's throne (852 BCE). The Israelite motivation was revenge for Mesha's revolt and conquest of towns in the Moabite tableland north of the Arnon (as depicted in the Mesha inscription).

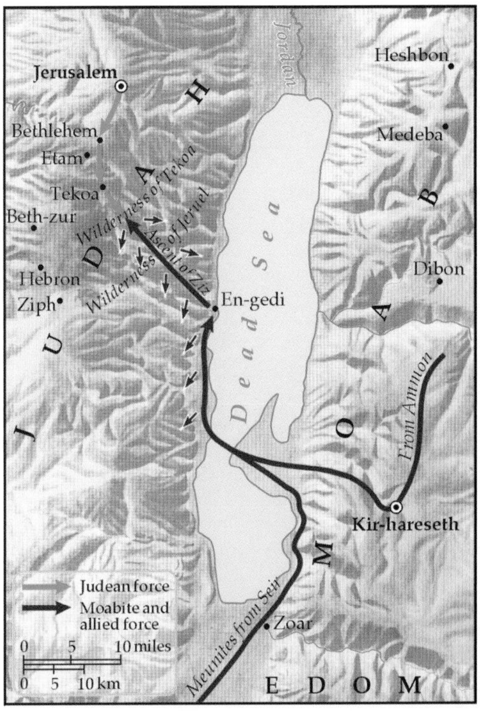


**Moabites and Their Allies Attempt to Invade Judah**

Jehoshaphat's motivation for joining Israel was to get revenge for the attempted invasion via En-gedi.

**The Ill-fated Fleet from Ezion-geber**. Both the Deuteronomist and the Chronicler make mention of Jehoshaphat's attempt to launch a fleet from Ezion-geber. However, the two versions differ in some essential features. Both confirm that the maritime effort was contemporary with Ahaziah, son of Ahab and king of Israel. That places the event squarely in 853/852 BCE. According to the Chronicler, the project was initiated after the failure of the Moabite/Ammonite/Meunite invasion. This left Jehoshaphat in control of the southern routes from Beer-sheba to Ezion-geber so he could plan such an enterprise knowing that there was no immediate threat to his security. The Chronicles version makes Ahaziah an actual partner (*see* 2 Chr 20:35–37).

Writing in the fourth century BCE, the Chronicler may have thought that the ships were intended to circumnavigate the Horn of Africa as was done by the Phoenicians during the reign of Pharaoh Necho II. But the account in 1 Kings makes it clear that it was "Tarshish ships" that were built. They were to go to Ophir, either a location in South Arabia or else in Somalia or some other point on the east African coast (*see* 1 Kgs 22:48–49).

The Deuteronomist avoids a prophetic rebuke for the partnership with Ahaziah and instead credits Jehoshaphat with refusing to accept Israelite crews. The original deal may have been Israelite participation only in the construction of the vessels. Ahaziah's offer implied that the Judean sailors had failed to

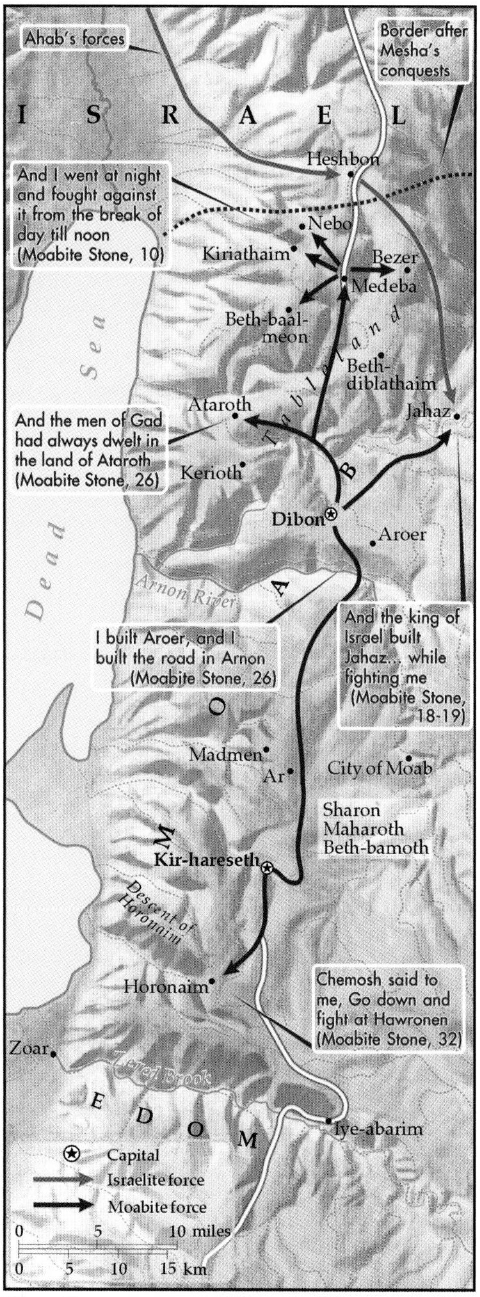


**The Campaign of Mesha, King of Moab**

manage the ships properly and thus led to their being wrecked.

**Mesha Revolts from Israel**. After the death of Ahab, the Moabite tableland from the Arnon once again became a bone of contention. Ever since the conquests of Omri in northern Moab, the king of Moab used to pay 100,000 lambs and the wool of 100,000 rams (2 Kgs 3:4). The numbers may be exaggerated but the economic ramifications are obvious. When Ahab died in the battle of Ramoth-gilead, Mesha, king of Moab, ceased to make his annual payments (2 Kgs 1:1, 3:5). He was an ally of the victorious king of Aram-Damascus. The attack on Judah described in 2 Chronicles 20 was at the behest of Hadad-$^{c}$iḏri; due to its disastrous conclusion, it is no wonder that the campaign is ignored in Moabite historiography. On the other hand, Mesha has provided the only example of a royal dedicatory inscription from the southern Levant. According to the opening lines (1–2):

> [1]I am Mesha$^{c}$ the son of Chemosh[-yat?] king of Moab, the Da[2]ibonite. My father reigned over Moab thirty years and I reign[3]ed after my father;

Mesha was the scion of a dynasty from Dibon, beside present-day Dhībân. The town was located on the northern side of the Arnon (Wâdī Mûjib). The ancient city stood on a prominent mound north of the modern village, cut off by the deep Wâdī Wâlā on the west and north, and by the Wâdī eth-Themed on the east, from the tableland surrounding it. From the inscription it can be deduced that Dibon and its environs were in Moabite hands in spite of Omri's conquest of the more northerly parts of the tableland. In the Transjordanian itinerary the town was called Dibon-gad (Num 33: 45) but it is not clear if the Gadites ever occupied it.

Just as Medeba was Omri's first foothold in Moab, so Mesha's rebellion was apparently launched by a thrust northward to liberate Medeba (Mesha Inscription, ll. 8b–9). That opened the way to rebuilding Baal-meon (Mā$^{c}$în, 5 miles [8 km] southwest of Medeba) and Kiriatēn (biblical Kiriathaim; el-Qureiyeh, c. 6 miles [10 km] west of Medeba on the bank of Wâdī $^{c}$Uyûn edh-Dhîb).

If this sequence is chronological, then it meant that the area still occupied by people of the ancient Israelite tribe of Gad were effectively cut off from the trunk route that led from Dibon past Libb to Medeba. There has been some misunderstanding about this passage. There is no reason to assume that the king of Israel built Ataroth "for himself." Obviously, he fortified the site for the men of Gad who had been exposed to the neighboring elements up until then.

> The man of Gad had dwelt in $^{c}$Aṭarot (Ataroth) from of old and the king of Israel [11]built $^{c}$Aṭarot (Ataroth) for him. (Mesha Inscription, ll. 10b–11)

Mesha conquered the town, killed all the inhabitants and annexed the city to the Moabite territory (which was considered the fief of Chemosh-Attar, god of Moab). An important object was confiscated via the "altar hearth of David." The Gadites had possessed an important cultic object that had evidently been given to them either by or in honor of King David, founder of the Jerusalem dynasty. The altar hearth was dragged over to Kerioth which must be represented by el-Qereiyât, today a village on the end of the same ridge occupied by Ataroth. Kerioth must have had a shrine to Chemosh marking the northwestern border of the Dibon district facing Ataroth with its shrine marking the southwestern border of the Israelite territory to the north. The principle of border shrines is reflected here: an original YHWH shrine facing a shrine to Chemosh. Mesha resettled Ataroth with people from two other unknown places of his own, Sharon and Maḥaroth.

Another isolated Israelite place was Nebo. The site must be near the peak of Jebel Nebā. Several candidates have been suggested: Khirbet el-Mukhaiyat, northwest of Medeba, where associated Iron Age tombs have been excavated; or other sites in the area such as Râs Ṣiyâgah, the high point just west of Jebel Nebā, Khirbet $^{c}$Ayûn Mûsā in the valley immediately north of Jebel Nebā or Ṣiyâgah, or Khirbet el-Muḥaṭṭah, c. 2 miles (3.5 km) north of Mukhaiyat on the next promontory north of Râs Ṣiyâgah, and within clear view of both $^{c}$Ayûn Mûsā and Râs Ṣiyâgah. Both Khirbet $^{c}$Ayûn Mûsā and Muḥaṭṭah have produced Iron Age pottery collected from surface surveys. It should not be surprising that Mesha was able to confiscate more cult objects of YHWH at Nebo and to bring them as trophies to the temple of his own deity (Mesha Inscription, ll. 14–18).

The final battle of the northern campaign was at Jahaz (Mesha Inscription, ll. 18b–21a), a town that must be to the northeast of Dibon, most likely at Khirbet el-Mudeiyineh on the Wâdī Themed, 1.5 miles (2.5 km) northeast of Khirbet Remeil. The site's size suggests that it is the largest predominately Iron Age settlement along the eastern periphery of the settled plateau.

During the ensuing years, and there is no way to know how many, Mesha embarked on an extensive building program to refortify cities and to refurbish temples. Much of his activity was focused on his capital, the citadel that had been mentioned before in line 3.

> I (myself) built for the citadel the "wall of the forests" and "the wall of [22]the rampart" and I built its gates and I built its towers and [23]I built a royal palace and I made the channels for the reservo[ir for] water in the mid[24]st of the city. But there was no cistern in the midst of the city, in the citadel, so I said to all the people, "Make [for] [25]yourselves each man a cistern in his house. And I hewed the shafts for the citadel with prisoner[26]s of Israel.
> (Mesha Inscription, ll. 21b–26a)

Other towns and temples throughout the kingdom were also beneficiaries.

> I built Aroer and I made the highway(s) in the Arnon. [27]I built Beth-bamoth because it was in ruins. I built Bezer because ⸢it was⸣ [28]a ruin. The men of Daibon were armed because all of Daibon was under orders and I rul[29]ed [over] one hundred towns which I had annexed to the land. And I buil[30]t [the temple of Made]ba and the temple of Diblatên and the temple of Baal-maon and I carried there [my] h[31][erdsmen to tend] the small cattle of the land.
> (Mesha Inscription, ll. 26–31)

Aroer ($^{c}$Arâ$^{c}$ir, 3 miles [5 km] southeast of Dhiban) is well known in the Bible as a border town (Deut 4:48; Josh 12:2; cf. Judg 11: 22) at the southern end of the tableland of Moab near the northern edge of the canyon formed by the Wâdī Môjib (Deut 2:36, 4:48; Josh 12:2, 13:16). Aroer was assigned to the tribe of Gad (Num 32:34), though elsewhere was

*Excavations at Aroer have revealed evidence of the Late Bronze and Iron ages among other periods. The most important excavated structure is a fortress that measures c. 60 yards (50 m) square, built of large stone blocks laid in header-stretcher, shown here. This might have been the fortress built by Mesha.*

supposedly in the Reubenite inheritance (Josh 13:16). During David's census, Aroer was the starting point for the Transjordanian population. Its strategic significance as a boundary marker is emphasized again in the description of Hazael's political control at the expense of Israel (2 Kgs 10:33).

The term "highway(s)" can be singular or plural. When mentioned in connection with Aroer, the association immediately presents itself with the main highway, the Roman *Via Nova Tirana*, which crossed the Môjib gorge nearby. On the other hand, an alternate road has recently been discovered to the east which might be included in this reference. It is even possible that only one highway is intended and that it was not along the line of the *Via Nova Tirana* at all, but to the east. The road may have originated at Balû$^{c}$ and crossed the wadis Unhealed and Suede on the way to either Aroer or nearby Laguna.

Beth-bamoth is probably to be equated with Bamoth-baal (Num 22:41; Josh 13:17) which must be a town with important cultic installations on the road between Dibon and Medeba. The important Iron I and II mound at the modern town at Libb is the most likely identification.

Bezer is known in the Bible as a Levitical city (Josh 21:36; 1 Chr 6:63, 78), the southernmost city of refuge in Transjordan (Josh 20:8), "in the steppe land on the tableland" (Deut 4:43). By far the most likely candidate for this identification is Tell el-Jalûl, c. 5 miles (8 km) east of Medeba. It is a massive tel and to the east of it is the steppe land cited in Deuteronomy 4:43. It is also on a line with other sites cited in the Mesha inscription: Nebo, Kiriathaim, Medeba. The fact that it had been in ruins suggests that Omri and Ahab had not reconstituted it when they occupied the land of Medeba.

Diblatên is the same as biblical Beth-diblathaim (Jer 48:22). Here it appears between Medeba and Beth-baal-meon, indicating that this town was somewhere in the vicinity of the other two sites. It also seems to be identical with Almon-diblathaim, between Dibon and the moun-tains of Abarim (Num 33:46–47) approximately halfway between Dibon and Nebo. It cannot be Libb (ancient Limbo) because in the church mosaic at Umm Raṣâṣ there is a "Beth Diblatain" and "Limbon." The most likely identification is Khirbet Deleilat esh-Sherqîyeh and/or Khirbet Deleilat el-Gharbîyeh c. 2.5 miles (4 km) northeast of Libb and c. 1 mile (1.5 km) apart. This proposal has the advantage of linking two related ruins with the dual ending present in both the Moabite and Hebrew names.

This list of sites reveals that there were sacred shrines at towns throughout the Moabite plateau.

The next pericope switches to a battle in the south. The text is given with some conjectural completions which match the remaining traces and letters and which also conform to the required space:

> And as for Ḥawronên, the [Ho]use of [Da]vid dwelt in it [wh]ile [32][it fought with me and] Chemosh [s]aid to me, "Go down, fight against Ḥawronen," so I went down [and I fo][33][ught with the city and I took it and] Chemosh [ret]urned it in my days.
>
> (Mesha Inscription, ll. 32–33)

Ḥawronên = Horonaim from prophetic oracles against Moab (Isa 15:5; Jer 48 [LXX 31]: 3, 5, 34; Jos *Ant.* 13.15.1, 14.1.4). Horonaim is associated with Luhith by parallelism (Isa 15:5) along an ascending roadway from Zoar at the southern edge of the Dead Sea to the Moabite plateau. A further geographical indication is the association with "the waters of Nimrim" (Isa 15:6; Jer 48:34) which is the modern Seil en-Numeirah, a stream cutting through the cliffs on the southwest edge of the Moabite plateau towards the Dead Sea. A Nabatean inscription from Medeba and a Hebrew contract from the time of Bar Kochba place Luhith in the southwest quadrant of the Moabite plateau, probably along a Roman road descending the plateau to continue around the southern end of the Dead Sea.

There was an ancient roadway from the Roman/Nabatean period leading to the Dead Sea from the modern town of Kathrabba, southwest of Kerak on the edge of the Moabite plateau. It probably follows the line of a more ancient road from the Iron Age, so both Horonaim and Luhith were most likely located along its course. Ai, just east of Kathrabba, has surface sherds from the Bronze, Iron, and Roman periods, so it and Kathrabba would make good candidates for the sites of Luhith and Horonaim. Furthermore, there are other Iron Age and Nabatean sites around these two towns, proving the importance of this area. Khirbet Meidân, a twin site with remains from both periods, is located on a strategic hill west of Kathrabba overlooking the Dead Sea and approaches to the plateau from it. Tell el-Miseh, an outpost or small fort on a high hill just southeast of Kathrabba, also has Iron Age and Nabatean pottery. This site has the most strategic view in this part of the Moabite plateau.

Other proposals for the location of Horonaim are the modern town of el-$^{c}$Irâq, 4 miles (7 km) south of Kathrabba at the head of the Seil en-Numeirah, or Medînet er-Râs or Khirbet Dhubâb in the southwest corner of the Moabite plateau near the Wadi Ḥasā. The latter is a tel on the north bank of the Wâdī Ḥasā with surface sherds suggesting almost continuous occupation from the Early Bronze Age.

In any case, this pericope deals with military action in southwestern Moab. The recent discovery that Ḥawrônên had been occupied by "the House of David" opens up the possibility that Mesha is referring to the conflict with invaders from the southwest. He boasts that he conquered Ḥawrônên but the context is too broken to deduce more than that. Since Mesha naturally gives only the details that glorify himself and his deity, it is not surprising that he does not describe the invasion by Judah, Israel and Edom (2 Kgs 3). However, it may very well be that Ḥawrônên had been occupied by the forces of Judah, the House of David, as a logistic base in support of the campaign on the Moabite plateau above.

**The Allied Invasion of Moab** (2 Kgs 3). After the untimely death of Ahaziah son of Ahab, his brother Joram became king (852 BCE). He approached Jehoshaphat with the proposal of a joint invasion of Moab. Each had his motive: Joram sought to regain control of the northern tableland and Jehoshaphat wished to get revenge for the attempted invasion of Judah by Moab and its allies (2 Chr 20). The narrative of the joint campaign is preserved in a narrative from the "Elisha Cycle" (2 Kgs 3) of northern origin. Therefore, the Chronicler does not present a parallel text. The ruler of Edom, a vassal of Judah, is called "king" in this narrative in contrast to the entry from the Chronicles of the Kings of Judah which calls him a "commissioner" (1 Kgs 22:48 [Eng 47]). In any case, the Edomites joined the van since they were subservient to Judah. The allies

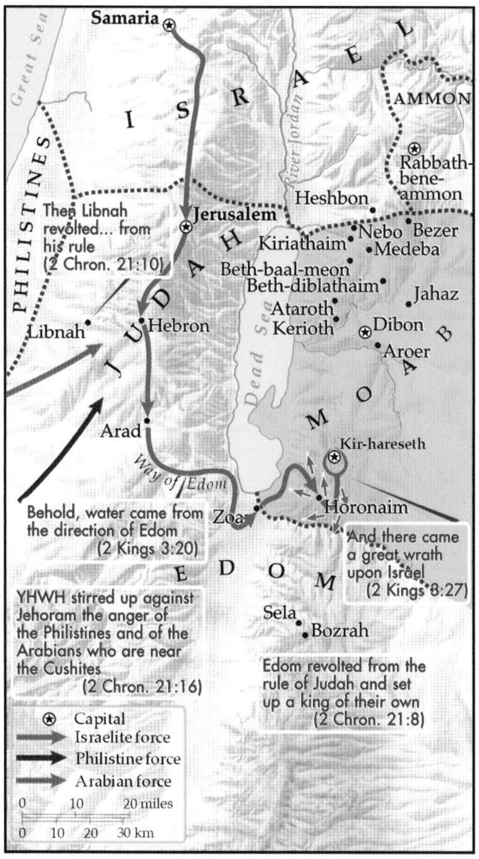


**Israel and Judah Invade Moab; Jehoram's Losses (852 and 848 BCE)**

chose to invade Moab from the south, to avoid the possible danger of a counterattack by the Arameans or the Ammonites. They marched by the "way of Edom," around the southern end of the Dead Sea (2 Kgs 3:8). On the desert road they suffered from extreme heat and thirst until they were saved by a flash flood, a phenomenon not uncommon in the canyons of the Arabah. Rain had fallen on the plateau above causing a sudden runoff down below.

It was most likely by "the ascent of Luhith . . . the road to Horonaim" (Isa 15:5; Jer 38:3, 5, 34) that they ascended from the Dead Sea to the plain above. It is this which Mesha probably refers to in his inscription. The invaders wreaked havoc on the southern Moabite countryside (*see* 2 Kgs 3:25).

Mesha was forced to withstand a siege in his southern capital, Kir-hareseth. The Targums render the name of this site as "fortified city" which points to the identification with Kerak. The town is also called Kir-heres (Jer 48:31, 48:36) but the Septuagint has "Kiradas" (Jer 31:31, 31:36) which strongly suggests that the original was "New Town." That certainly must have been the real name of this city; the MT variants "city of clay, potsherds," are simply pejoratives. But there is no reason to apply them to Dibon. The ensuing passage (*see* 2 Kgs 3:26–27) has caused much misunderstanding.

Commentators through the ages have assumed that Mesha sacrificed his own son. Even the Septuagint may have thought the same thing because instead of rendering "great wrath" on Israel, they rendered "repentence," as if the Israelites were so shocked that they regretted their actions and withdrew. However, the very idea that ancient Israel (at least in the Deuteronomist's view) would have felt remorse at the human sacrifice of an enemy is so outlandish that it must be rejected out of hand. The proper meaning of the very laconic passage was seen by Radak (Rav David Kimḥi).

The view of Rav Kimḥi's father, that the son in question was already a prisoner in Moab, is certainly not supported by the narrative. On the other hand, the interpretation by his brother, Rav Moshe, makes perfect sense and is beyond all doubt correct. When Mesha tried to make a breakthrough (to escape the siege and probably to go north to Dibon), he chose the part of the enemy ranks where the Edomites were stationed, probably thinking that they would be easier prey. But he misjudged his foe; the Edomites did not crack. However, Mesha did manage to take an important prisoner, viz. the son and heir of the Edomite king, who was already the co-regent. It was hardly intentional that the co-regent should have come in close contact with the attacking Moabites. But he was in the ranks and the Moabite onslaught had brought them as far as the reserve backup unit. The latter held their ground and did not let Mesha achieve his escape. The crown prince must have been at the head of this reserve unit and thus exposed to the Moabite charge. He was captured and dragged back into the city. Mesha then took him up on the wall and made him a human sacrifice.

The Edomites had come in support of Judah and Israel. It may be that they were also responsible for logistic support from their own flocks and food stores. The loss of the crown prince was a fatal blow to the Edomite morale. Their anger against the Israelite army was such that their own withdrawal from the campaign left the Judean and Israelite troops exposed and far from their home bases. They had no choice but to withdraw in ignominy. The sacrifice of the Edomite co-regent was denounced generations later by the prophet Amos (2:1).

## Decline of Judah.

After the ill-fated campaign against Moab, Jehoshaphat lived for about three years. At his death in 848 BCE, he was succeeded by his co-regent, Jehoram (*see* 2 Kgs 8:16).

Jehoram (Joram) was now sole ruler in Judah. It is of special significance that his wife was Athaliah from the house of Ahab (2 Kgs 8:18 || 2 Chr 21:6; 2 Kgs 8:26 || 2 Chr 22:2); that fact is emphasized in order to help explain the evil behavior of Jehoram. One of the subtle changes that took place in Judah was the shift to the non-accession year chronology in vogue in Israel. But the most drastic change was the murder of all the king's brothers who had been appointed by Jehoshaphat to govern cities throughout the kingdom (2 Chr 21:2–4). He was afraid that one of them might challenge his place as sole ruler. He also had other plans of a religious and administrative nature and needed to have his own appointees in place throughout the country.

The Edomites apparently continued to honor their commitment to Jehoshaphat as long as he was alive, this in spite of the tragedy that befell their co-regent. But when Jehoshaphat died and Jehoram became sole ruler, they renounced their obligations to Judah and openly rebelled (*see* 2 Kgs 8:20–22a || 2 Chr 21:8–10).

Zair may be a variant of Zoar, a town at the southernmost point of the Jordan Valley (Gen 13:10, 14:2, 8; Deut 34:3). Zoar is located on the border of the Moabite hill country (Gen 19:31–38; Isa 15:5; Jer 48:34). It must have been southeast of the Dead Sea (*War* 4.8: 4[482]). Jehoram evidently encountered the Edomites somewhere in the vicinity of Ghor eṣ-Ṣafîyeh.

The apostasy of Edom would leave Judah exposed in the south. To the west, Jehoram's kingdom was to suffer a more serious blow. Libnah, a leading priestly city in the Shephelah, renounced its allegiance to the crown; 2 Kings 8:22b just states that Libnah revolted at that time. The reason for the revolt is explained by the Chronicler (*see* 2 Chr 21:10b–11).

These evil deeds were attributed to his connection with the house of Ahab (2 Chr 21:13). The new cult centers were set up in the cities of the hill country (Libnah evidently had too much influence in the Shephelah) where Jehoram had appointed his own governors in place of his brothers and other officials loyal to the policies of Jehoshaphat. The local shrines diverted considerable income from the Jerusalem temple; religious offerings and tithes stayed in the local economy. In Jerusalem he had introduced foreign elements to the central cultural center at the expense of the Judean priesthood.

The weakening of Judah eventually led to a campaign of revenge by her neighbors who had long been compelled to make imbursements and gratuities to Jehoshaphat (2 Chr 17:10–11; *see* 2 Chr 21:16–17).

The Arabians (probably including the Meunites) in proximity to the Hejaz (the Arabian Cush) and the Philistines had a common commercial interest. The caravan trade across the highland routes from Transjordan through the Negeb to the Mediterranean coast was a source of appreciable revenue. Hitherto, Judah with the help of the Edomites (also west of the Arabah?) had guarded the trade routes and exacted payments from the caravans. The attack during the reign of Jehoram was aimed at removing the middleman.

The Deuteronomist gives nothing of this, nor does he mention that Jehoram died of a fatal disease of the bowels (possibly cancer?). The revolts by Edom and Libnah and the invasion by the Philistines and the Arabs are not dated to specific years of the reign. The revolts must have taken place after Jehoram's murder of his brothers and his institution of the new religious infrastructure which must have taken at least a year or maybe more. There was also the unsuccessful military campaign to the Arabah against the rebellious Edomites. So the Edomite and Libnah revolts and the enemy invasion happened a year or two after the beginning of the king's sole rule, i.e. about 846 BCE and the onset of his fatal disease. The disease is said to have lasted about two years meaning that its onset was in about 844 or 843 BCE, i.e. two years before Jehoram's demise and the murder of his heir, Ahaziah, at the hands of Jehu (841 BCE).

The Chronicles passage does not speak of conquered Judean cities or even of despoiled cities during the Philistine-Arabian campaign. The main goal was similar to the attempted invasion during the reign of Asa by Zerah the Cushite (2 Chr 14:8–14, 15:1–19, 16:8). The slaughter of the king's sons is seen as retribution for his murdering his brothers. Obviously not all of his wives could have been taken captive because Athaliah was alive and acting as queen mother during her son's short reign. Though the campaign itself seems logical, there is an impression that the Chronicler may have reworked his source to emphasize his belief in poetic justice as the fulfillment of prophecy (cf. the letter from Elisha).

Ahaziah (Jehoahaz) succeeded his father in 841 BCE and ruled less than a year (2 Kgs 8:25–29; 2 Chr 22:2–6) before he was murdered by Jehu. This and subsequent events will be discussed below.

## POLITICAL DEVELOPMENTS

**Damascus**. Hadad-$^{c}$id̲ri disappears after the battle in 845 BCE. By the time Shalmaneser III returns to the west, there is a new ruler in Damascus, Hazael "son of a nobody." The biblical "Elisha Cycle" preserves a tale about prophetic involvement in the coup d'état staged by the new ruler (*see* 2 Kgs 8:7–15).

Whatever the veracity of this narrative, there was a change in leadership in Aram-Damascus that is also confirmed by Shalmaneser's inscriptions. The pedigree of Hazael is not given, either in the Bible or in Assyrian sources. He was evidently someone close to the king, presumably his chief military commander. The king is called Ben-hadad (Aramaic Bar-hadad) and it is usually assumed that this is an error for Hadad-$^{c}$id̲ri or else that "Ben-hadad" was some kind of royal epithet like "son of Re$^{c}$" in Egypt. However, there is always the possibility that Hadad-$^{c}$id̲ri died shortly after 845 BCE and was succeeded by a son, Ben-hadad. This latter had become ill and that provided an occasion for Hazael to stage a military coup. It seems more likely that Hazael would dare to murder an inexperienced son rather than a venerable monarch such as Hadad-$^{c}$id̲ri, who had led his troops in so many fierce battles against the Assyrian monster. The allusion to Hadad-$^{c}$id̲ri's death in the Summary text on a statue of Shalmaneser III, viz. "Hadad-$^{c}$id̲ri went to his fate; Hazael, the son of a nobody, seized the throne," does not preclude the possibility that Hadad-$^{c}$id̲ri was succeeded by a Ben-hadad who was in turn assassinated by Hazael. The fact that this much telescoped text does not charge Hazael with Hadad-$^{c}$id̲ri's murder may suggest that Hazael came to the throne by some other means.

**Israel and Judah**. Whenever Hadad-$^{c}$id̲ri died, his erstwhile partner, Irḫulēni of Hamath, broke their alliance and submitted to Shalmaneser III. Henceforth, Hamath was a tribute-paying vassal of Assyria. Later, Hazael's son, Ben-hadad, would try to conquer the Hamath kingdom by force.

On the other hand, the simmering enmity between Aram-Damascus and Israel came to a head with Hazael's rise to power. Joram of Israel enlisted the aid of Ahaziah of Judah to reopen hostilities in Transjordan (2 Kgs 8:28). There is no need to doubt this statement or to excise the name of Ahaziah from the text. The battle was fought in the area of Ramoth-gilead (Tell er-Rumeith) and Joram was wounded. He left his troops at Ramoth-gilead and returned to Jezreel to recuperate. He was joined by Ahaziah (2 Kgs 8:28–29).

At this point, another narrative from the Elisha Cycle is inserted. It tells how

*"Woman-in-the-window" on ivory plaque, from Calah (Nimrud).*

Jezebel heard of it; and she painted her eyes, and adorned her head, and looked out of the window. And as Jehu entered the gate, she said, "Is it peace, you Zimri, murderer of your master?" (2 Kgs 9:30–31)

the prophet sent one of his prophets to Jehu, commander of the Israelite forces in Ramoth-gilead, to incite him to revolt and stage a coup against the scion of the House of Omri (2 Kgs 9:1–26). The story is well known: Jehu gained the support of his military officers and rode back to Jezreel with an entourage where he slew King Joram in the open field. The queen mother, Jezebel, was slain afterwards (2 Kgs 9:30–37). The king of Judah shared the same fate (*see* 2 Kgs 9:27–28; cf. 2 Chr 22:5–9).

And his cousins, the sons of his slain brothers, were also slain along with the leading government officials (2 Chr 22:8; cf. 2 Kgs 10:12–14). The "ascent of Gur" was the road leading up toward Beth-haggan (Jenîn) which is close to Ibleam (Khirbet Bel$^{c}$ameh). The young, mortally wounded king was evidently taken to Megiddo, an administrative center where some medical help might be available. The Judean queen mother, Athaliah, assumed the throne (2 Kgs 11:1; 2 Chr 22:10).

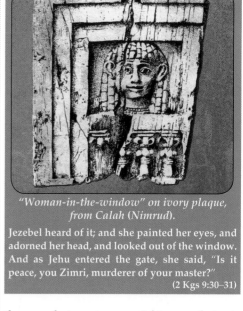

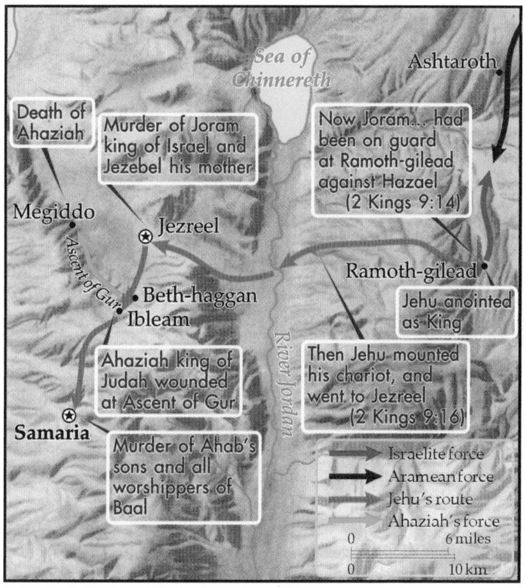


**THE REBELLION OF JEHU (841 BCE)**

## LATER DEVELOPMENTS

The assassination of both the king of Israel, Joram, and the king of Judah, Ahaziah, at the same time led to violent developments in the respective kingdoms. Jehu's revolt had doubtless been sparked by the strains of renewed conflict with Hazael of Damascus. The results were perhaps positive in the removal of an unworthy regime in Israel, but Judah saw an even worse government than before.

**The House of Jehu**. A coup d'état against the House of Omri/Ahab (2 Kgs 9–10), instigated by the leading prophets of the kingdom, opened the way to the establishment of a new dynasty, the House of Jehu. Jezebel's father, Ethobaal, king of Tyre and the

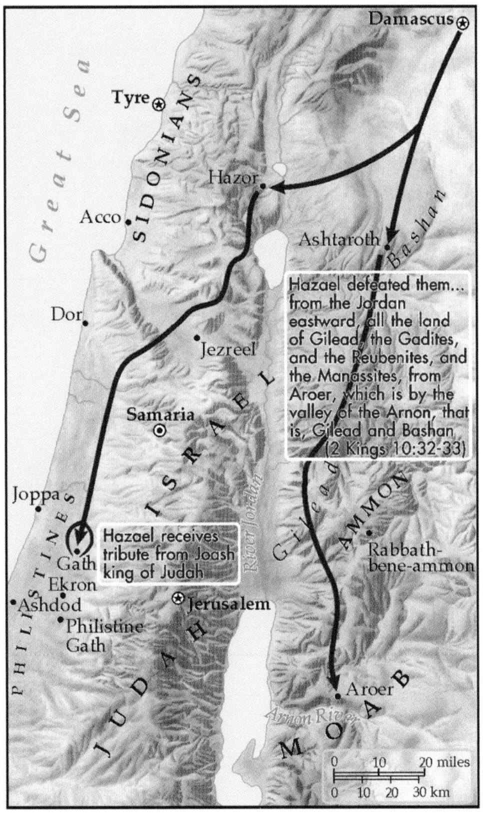


**ARAMEAN SUPREMACY (C. 841–798 BCE)**

Sidonians, must have died by then because Shalmaneser III received tribute from a new king in 841 BCE. The murder of Jezebel by Jehu naturally signaled the end of the close ties between Israel and Phoenicia but their mutual submission to the Assyrian invader at least kept them on the same side against Hazael.

Jehu reigned for twenty-eight years, non-accession reckoning, i.e. twenty-seven actual years (841–814 BCE). One of his first political steps was to eliminate the entire family of Ahab within his borders as well as forty-two relatives of Ahaziah from Judah (2 Kgs 10:1–14, 10:17). Then he also slaughtered the priests and prophets of Baal imported by the previous government (2 Kgs 10:18–28).

For a few years, Jehu's payment of tribute to Assyria may have provided him with some protection. But that was not to last. The final campaigns against Hazael's territory on the part of the Assyrians were in 838–837 BCE. For the next two decades, the Assyrians were preoccupied elsewhere and the revolt during the reign of Shamshi-Adad V meant that their influence west of the Euphrates was practically nil.

Now Hazael could flex his muscles. As the only power in the south-central Levant that did not bow the knee to Ashur, he was in a position to enforce his will on his neighbors and gain control of the previous highways from Arabia through Gilead (*see* 2 Kgs 10:32–33).

The conquest of Gilead was long remembered in Israel. Late in the eighth century BCE, the prophet Amos described it (*see* Amos 1:3–5). It seems most likely that the attack on Gilead was supported by the Ammonites as allies of Damascus. Note the oracle by Amos (*see* Amos 1:13–15). The mention of Aroer by the Arnon (2 Kgs 10:33) assures that Moab was also an active partner on the side of Damascus. Mesha had wrenched all of the tableland of Moab from the grasp of the house of Omri (cf. 2 Kgs 13:20).

But the depredations of Damascus on Israelite territory went far beyond just Transjordan. Jehoahaz, son of Jehu, succeeded his father in 814 BCE and reigned for seventeen non-accession years, sixteen actual years, until 798 BCE. During his reign the pressure from Damascus was intensified (2 Kg 13:22). Unfortunately, the Deuteronomist does not provide specific details. But the recently discovered Tel Dan inscription shows that during Hazael's reign, that northern Israelite town was in Aramean hands. The inscription makes reference to the assassination of the two kings of Israel and Judah in a broken but indisputable context:

> (7) [so that then they killed Jo]ram, son of [Ahab, (8) king of Israel, and [they] killed [Ahazi]yahu, son of [Joram, kin-] (9) g of the House of David;
>
> (Tel Dan Inscription, ll. 7–9)

The verb "to kill" (in 3rd masc. pl.) and the broken name of the king of Israel which ends in *-RM* alongside the name of a king of "the House of David" whose name ends in *-YHW* can only refer to Joram and Ahaziah. Furthermore, the parallel with "king of Israel" assures that the "House of David" can be none other than the kingdom of Judah. This coincides with the entry in the Mesha inscription where the "House of David" appears. The proper analysis of the verbs makes it clear that the Aramean author of the text does not claim to have been the slayer of the two kings. But their deaths were a result of his victorious actions in defeating many enemy kings. The Aramean author claims that his father engaged in warfare before him. Hazael is called "son of a nobody" by Shalmaneser III, a reference to his being a usurper. But Hazael may be claiming (falsely) that his predecessor was his father or else he may have been a son of Hadad-ʿid̠ri by some minor wife and thus the half-brother of the Ben-hadad whom he murdered. Perhaps these questions will never be definitively answered. In any case, the broken stele from Tel Dan shows that Israel had suffered the loss of its northern territories at that time.

*"Jehu son of Omri" (king of Israel) kneels before Shalmaneser III. A scene from the "Black Obelisk" of Shalmaneser III.*

## Further Developments in Judah.

As queen mother, Athaliah must have enjoyed an extraordinary position with regard to public ritual, and she probably also exerted influence on political matters. Her son Ahaziah's participation with Joram of Israel in the campaign against Hazael at Ramoth-gilead (2 Kgs 8:28), was most likely due to Athaliah's influence on her twenty-two-year-old monarch. When Ahaziah went to visit his wounded cousin, Joram, at Jezreel, he was assassinated at Jehu's command (2 Kgs 9:21–29). Another forty-two members of the Judean royal family were also murdered on Jehu's explicit instructions (2 Kgs 10:12–14).

The slaughter of the Omride royal family, viz. all of Athaliah's relatives, ended the erstwhile alliance between Judah and Israel. This permitted Athaliah to seize power in Jerusalem. She had the surviving males of the House of David put to death (2 Kgs 11:1=2 Chr 22:10). Ahaziah's son Joash was saved from the slaughter (*see* 2 Kgs 11:1–3 || 2 Chr 22:10–12).

Athaliah now ruled as absolute monarch for six actual years (non-accession reckoning). She followed a policy of internal rule modeled after that of Jezebel and Ahab in Israel; she had exercised powerful religious influence on her husband and their son (2 Kgs 8:18, 8:26–27; 2 Chr 22:3). Thus, she had inspired the building of a temple to Baal in Jerusalem or its environs (2 Kgs 11:18) and she had fostered the local cult places for Baal that her husband had permitted throughout the kingdom (2 Chr 21:11) and allowed her close followers ("her *sons*") to plunder the temple of YHWH and to make use of its implements (*see* 2 Chr 24:7).

The cults of Baal were evidently manned by officiates who had either come with her from Samaria or else had joined her circles during the reign of her husband, Jehoram. Opposition to her rule, which eventually led to her downfall, came from the cadre of priests in the Jerusalem temple, and also from leading military circles, including the elite Carite palace guards, with support of the body politic consisting of full-fledged Judean citizens. The Levitical military units charged with protection of the temple of YHWH were also recruited for the coup d'état (2 Chr 23:2).

In the seventh year of her reign (non-accession reckoning), Athaliah was deposed (2 Kgs 11:4–20 || 2 Chr 23:1–21). The rightful heir had been hidden in the sleeping quarters used by the temple personnel on their tours-of-duty in Jerusalem. The conspiracy was initiated by Jehoiada the priest whose wife was a daughter of Jehoram (probably not by Athaliah). Careful plans were laid beforehand. It was timed for the changing of the guards at the temple complex so that there would be a double complement of troops on hand. These were "Levites," according to the Chronicler (2 Chr 23:32). The seven-year-old Joash was proclaimed king within the temple precincts while surrounded by the armed supporters. Athaliah was taken completely by surprise and had no chance for any counter-measures on the part of her own supporters. She was seized and dragged out of the sacred complex to a palace gate where she was summarily put to death (2 Kgs 11:16, 11:20). The temple of Baal in Jerusalem was destroyed by the "people of the land" (2 Kgs 11:18).

Joash/Jehoash, son of Ahaziah by Zibiah from Beer-sheba, became king at the age of seven in the seventh year of Jehu, king of Israel (2 Kgs 11:21; 2 Chr 24:1). His reign was forty years according to the non-accession system, i.e. thirty-nine actual years (835–796 BCE). So long as his mentor, Jehoiada the chief priest, was alive, Joash maintained a stable rule but does not seem to have had the resources to expand his territory or to improve Judah's position in the regional matrix. Obviously, he had not recouped the losses of his grandfather, Jehoram, to the Philistines and the Edomites. It can probably be assumed that Libnah, a priestly city, had reaffirmed its loyalty to the crown.

The only affair given any attention in the biblical accounts is that of refurbishing the temple (2 Kgs 12:4–16; 2 Chr 24:4–14). It is not stated when the king initiated the program but in his twenty-third year (813 BCE) the work had not been done (2 Kgs 12:6).

## Prophetic Traditions

Interspersed in the Deuteronomistic narratives about the House of Omri and the House of Jehu, that is, the two principal dynasties of the northern kingdom of Israel in the ninth century BCE, there are folk legends about the activities of two prophets, Elijah and Elisha. It is not clear whether these prophetic stories were already incorporated into the Chronicles of the Kings of Israel or whether they were preserved in their independent source until the Deuteronomist wove them into his narrative. Some of the stories show the prophets taking an active part in the political and social conflicts of their time while others are mainly accounts of their miraculous lives as members of the "prophetic guild." There is no hint that they were involved in the writing of the chapters pertaining to the House of Omri or the House of Jehu in the ongoing Chronicles of the Kings of Israel. In other words, Elijah and Elisha are not credited anywhere with historiographic writing.

The main thrust of the Elijah stories is the conflict between Yahwism and the imported Baal cults brought in by Queen Jezebel and also a moral protest about the murder of Naboth. The Elisha narratives find the prophet taking an active role in political intrigues (inciting Jehu and Hazael to regicide) and counsel to the kings (concerning the siege of Samaria, the campaign against Moab and the advice to Jehoash about an offensive against Aram-Damascus).

This dichotomy between miracle stories and political actions characterizes all the narratives of the "Elijah/Elisha Cycle." Since the role of prophets in making political and military decisions is widespread in the ancient Mediterranean/Near Eastern world (from Assyria to Greece), there is no reason to doubt the reality of Israelite prophets being involved in such affairs as military sieges and campaigns and the overthrow of regimes.

In the eighth and subsequent centuries BCE, there are prophets in Israel (Hosea) and Judah (Amos, Isaiah, Micah, Jeremiah, Habbakkuk, *et al.*) and in the post-exilic Yehud (Haggai and Zechariah, Malachi) as well as the prophet of the Exile, Ezekiel. Miracle stories are not a part of their repertoire. Instead, there are compositions assigned to their authorship (certainly reliable for the most part) and some indications that among them were authors of sections of the Chronicles of the Kings of Judah (for example, Isaiah in the reigns of Uzziah and Hezekiah). In many of the prophetic books there is material of a geopolitical and geographic importance. Their involvement in the historical events of their own day will be woven into the mainstream of historical and geographical discussion in subsequent chapters.

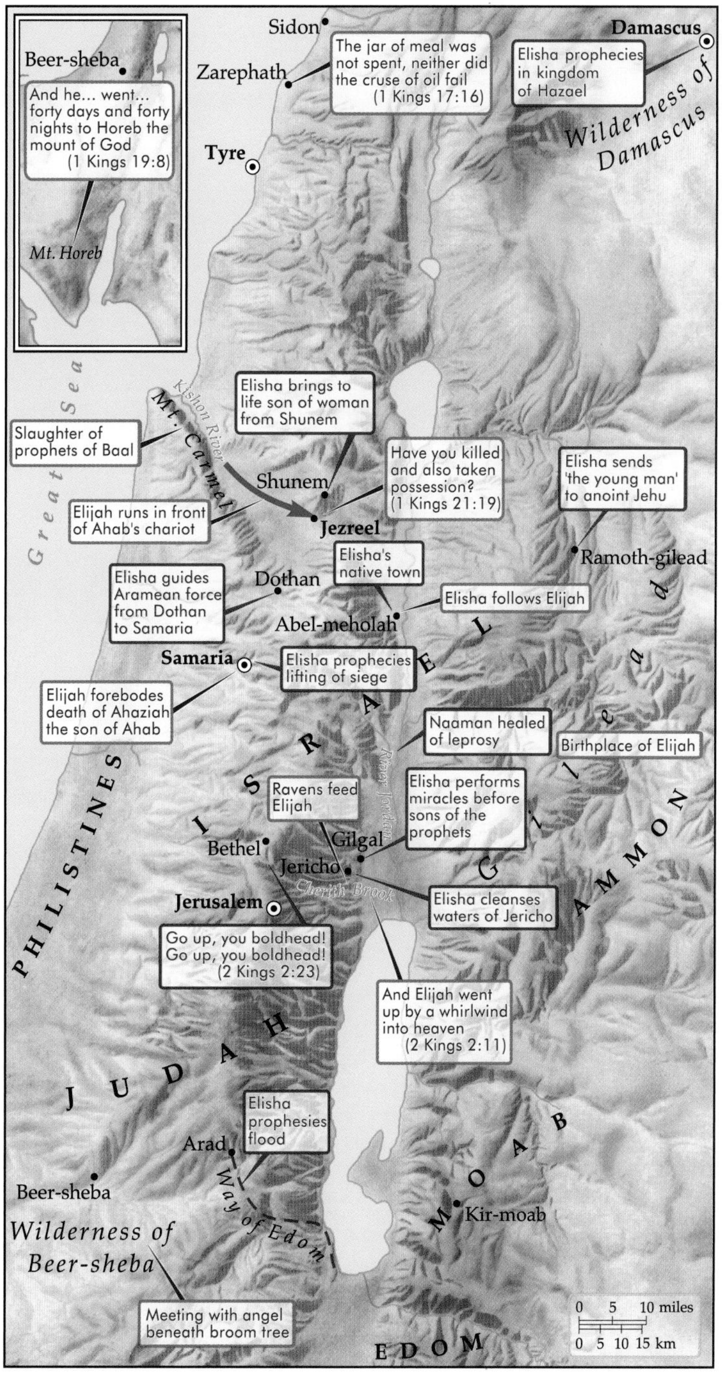


"Ninth-century Prophetic Legends"

*Carved ivory from Samaria (time of Ahab).*

# CHAPTER EIGHT

# WINDOW OF OPPORTUNITY

## EARLY EIGHTH CENTURY BCE

The later campaign of Adad-nirāri III, "against Manṣuate" in 796 BCE, was a turning point in the affairs of the central and southern Levant. However, it was preceded by some tumultuous events at the beginning of the eighth century BCE.

## ARAM-DAMASCUS' PERIOD OF SUPREMACY

**Against Israel**. Jehoahaz son of Jehu (814–798 BCE) was still ruling in Israel as the eighth century BCE began. His kingdom had been subjected to the depradations of Hazael of Damascus, who was still the dominant figure in central Syria. Although Shalmaneser III had sought to cut off Hazael's access to the Tadmor route to Mesopotamia, the final decades of the ninth century BCE had seen a weakening of Assyrian power in the west due to dynastic troubles at home. Thus far, the renewed campaigns of Adad-nirāri in the very final years of the century had been focused on North Syria. So Hazael had enjoyed a free hand in his drive to dominate the southern Levant and its lucrative trade routes. This is expressed by the biblical narrative in theological rather than geographical terms (*see* 2 Kgs 13:3–5).

The oppression of Israel by Hazael and Ben-hadad (Aramaic: Bar-hadad) undoubtedly included the occupation of Israelite towns in the north such as Dan (as evidenced by the stele found there). The occupation of Gilead and the linkup with Damascus' ally in Moab was mentioned earlier (2 Kgs 11:32). Unfortunately, the editor of Kings did not see fit to give additional geographical details. But the subsequent campaign against Gath (evidently of the Philistines) shows that Hazael enjoyed free rein to traverse Lower Galilee, the Jezreel Valley and the Sharon Plain. The "deliverer" granted to Israel may be a reference to the Assyrian king, Adad-nirāri III, who subdued Damascus in 796 BCE (cf. below).

**Against Philistia and Judah**. Joash (835–796 BCE; 2 Kgs 12:1–22; 2 Chr 24:1–27), who reigned for thirty-nine actual years (non-acession reckoning) in Judah, had begun to show an indifference to the Jerusalem priesthood, apparently after the death of his mentor, Jehoiada (probably in 800/799 BCE; *see* 2 Chr 24:17–18).

This new policy gave precedence to the local shrines at the various cities throughout the kingdom (to please the local governors). As a result, the Jerusalem religious leaders denounced the king (*see* 2 Chr 24:19–22).

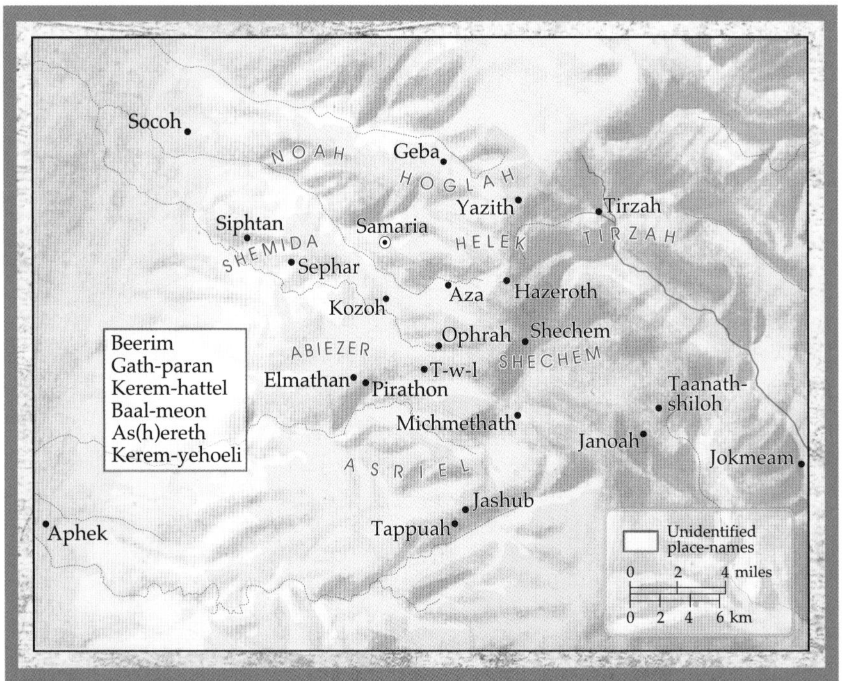

THE SAMARIA OSTRACA

The Chronicler sees the invasion by Hazael as punishment for the apostasy of the king and his ministers (*see* 2 Chr 24:23–25). The parallel version in Kings implies that Hazael personally led the campaign (*see* 2 Kgs 12:18–19 [Eng. 17–18]).

In this regard, however, it is likely that the Chronicler has given more faithful details from the original Chronicles of the Kings of Judah. The western campaign by the Arameans must have been Hazael's last and was probably led by his son Ben-hadad who may have been a co-regent (already for several years?). On the other hand, the Kings version stresses the high indemnity payments made by Joash in order to save the city from destruction and it is strange that the Chronicler ignores this.

The Jerusalem leadership was incensed, not only because of the incited murder of an innocent spokesman, Zechariah son of Jehoiada, but also because their treasures had been forfeited. Apparently the military leadership of those apostate officials (mayors of cities) was woefully inadequate; thus they had been beaten in a clash with a much smaller Aramean force. Therefore, the Jerusalem senior cadre conspired against Joash and murdered him on his sickbed (*see* 2 Kgs 12:21–22 [Eng. 19–21] || 2 Chr 24:23–26).

Hazael's campaign must have taken place in late 797 BCE because the attack by Adad-nirāri against Damascus took place in 796 BCE and in the interim, an Aramean plot against the ruler of the Hamath kingdom had evidently come to fruition.

**Against Hamath**. After the sweeping campaign against Philistia (Gath) and Judah, it would appear that the aged Hazael finally went to his fate (2 Kgs 13:24). This may be deduced by the evidence for an extensive campaign by his son, Bar-hadad, against the archrival of Damascus, namely the kingdom of Hamath on the Orontes. The event is recorded in the inscription of Zakkur, king of Hamath and Luǵath, which was discovered at Âfis (Aphish) in North Syria. It is suggested here that the deliverance was achieved by the appearance of Adad-nirāri on the scene. This would place the siege against Zakkur early in 796 BCE before the arrival of the Assyrian army. Thus one must assume that Hazael had passed away and that his son, Bar-hadad, had succeeded him. Buoyed up by the successes of the Aramean army on the southern coast (against Gath and Jerusalem), Bar-hadad had thought to turn the might of his victorious troops against his neighbor to the north. The prowess of Damascus on the battlefield had made its impression on the Neo-Hittite and Aramean states in North Syria so that they had agreed to join in a coalition against Zakkur. One can only speculate as to the change from a dynasty of rulers at Hamath with Neo-Hittite (Anatolian) names to a newcomer with an Aramaic name. Thinking that the Assyrian threat was far away, the Syrian allies all ganged up on Zakkur at Hadrach (location still unknown; perhaps to be identified with modern Ḥoms?), possibly because he was a usurper (from Aphish?) who thought to obtain Assyrian support for his seizure of power in central Syria. Notably, the siege operations described by Zakkur (rampart and moat) resemble those used against Gath of the Philistines in the Aramean campaign.

## Adad-nirāri's Last Campaign to the West

The Eponym Chronicle records a campaign by Adad-nirāri to Manṣuate in 796 BCE. That list seems to focus on one geographic entity that was central to the campaign without giving further details. It was this campaign that must have entailed the rescue of Zakkur from the coalition that was besieging him. The Antakya stele records that Adad-nirāri and his field marshal (*turtānu*), Shamshi-ilu, established the boundary between Zakkur of the land of Hamath and Atarshumki, the ruler of Arpad. The latter is to be identified with the Bar-gusi of the Zakkur text; Bīt-Agusi is the Assyrian name for the kingdom of which Arpad is the chief city. This stele seems to reflect a policy on the part of Adad-nirāri to woo Bīt-Agusi/Arpad from the alliance with Damascus. At the same time, the Assyrian monarch wanted to preserve the security of Zakkur. The fact that both Adad-nirāri and Shamshi-ilu appear together shows that the latter, who was now the powerful governor of Bīt-Adini with Til-Barsip as his main capital, was probably the actual commander during the campaign of 796 BCE although Adad-nirāri seems to have

*In 1907–08 there was published a fragmentary stele found at Âfis in northern Syria, known as the Zakkur Inscription. Its Aramaic text gives details about an act of aggression initiated by Bar-hadad son of Hazael king of Damascus. It describes the league of partners recruited by Bar-hadad, the initial siege of Hadrach, and the deliverance wrought by the deity worshiped by Zakkur, king of Hamath and Luġath (a territory in central Syria = Bronze Age Nughasse).*

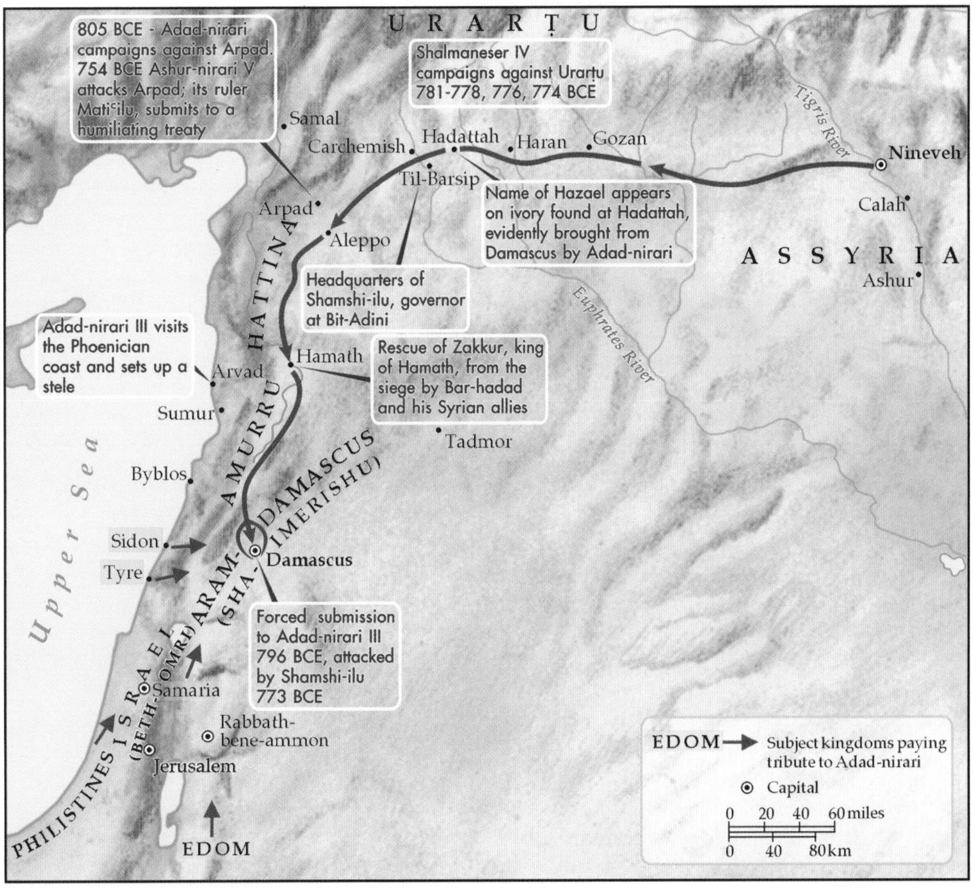


**The Campaign of Adad-nirāri III to Damascus**

accompanied the expedition.

Details of this campaign, found on a stele discovered in a shrine at Tell er-Rimâḥ west of Mosul, describe the subduing of Amurru, viz. Ḫatti land, which would refer to the scattering of the coalition that threatened Zakkur. As a follow-up, the Assyrians must have moved on Damascus (using Manṣuate as a base of operations) and extorted the large tribute. When the new king of Israel, Jehoash/Joash son of Jehoahaz, heard of the approach of the Assyrian force, he sent tribute. Undoubtedly, Jehoash intended to buy the support of Adad-nirāri against Bar-hadad. The latter was so weakened by the Assyrian attack that he soon became easy prey for his Israelite neighbor (cf. below).

Meanwhile, the Assyrian king states that he made the grand tour of Phoenicia. This would seem to confirm the king's personal participation in the campaign in spite of the prominence of his general, Shamshi-ilu.

**Period of Assyrian Weakness.** Already during the reign of Adad-nirāri III, the central government was weakening in favor of regional governors throughout the empire. This is even more evident during the subsequent reigns. A new enemy on the north, the east Anatolian kingdom of Urarṭu, was casting greedy eyes on the fertile territory with its lucrative trade routes in northern Mesopotamia and Syria. During the reign of Shalmaneser IV (782–773 BCE), the Eponym Chronicle records a series of campaigns to Urarṭu (781–778, 776, 774 BCE). The last campaign also included the land of Namri suggesting that Urarṭu's influence had reached that area. The campaigns were probably conducted under the command of Shamshi-ilu, the powerful general who ruled the western territories with Til-Barsip as at least one of his capitals. His personal inscriptions were found there on two stone lions guarding the city gate. His principal title was "field marshal," but he also claims to have been the "great herald" and the administrator of temples and commander of a vast army host, but especially the governor of the lands of Ḫatti, of Guti and all of Namur. He also claimed to have defeated Urarṭu as well as Mushku (on the Anatolian Plateau). He had already been in office during the reign of Adad-nirāri III during which time he exercised considerable authority alongside the king.

In 775 BCE, Shalmaneser IV made a foray to the Cedar Mountain and in 773 BCE Shamshi-ilu conducted an attack on Damascus. This latter event is dated by the Eponym Chronicle and in an inscription on a stele discovered near Pazarcik in Turkey.

It would make sense to assume that Jeroboam II's subjugation of Damascus took place in the wake of this Assyrian attack. Damascus probably exhausted its resources and was unable to resist the Israelite threat.

During the reign of Ashur-dan III, three campaigns were devoted to Hadrach (772, 765, 755 BCE) but in the interim a revolt was squelched in Gozan (763, 759–758

*Ivory cosmetic spoon found in the house of* M-k-b-r-m, *a merchant of Hazor under Jeroboam II.*

BCE) as well as elsewhere (e.g. Arrapkha). In the reign of Ashur-nirāri V there was a campaign to Arpad (754 BCE). The ruler, Mati$^{c}$-ilu son of Atarshumki, evidently was thoroughly cowed and forced to submit to a humiliating treaty of vassalage to Ashur-nirāri.

During the period following Adad-nirāri III, the many instances in the Eponym Chronicle in which the king and the army stayed "in the land," are indicative of the imperial weakness and explain why Babylon in the south and Urarṭu in the north dared to encroach on Assyria's borders. In the west, Shamshi-ilu seems to have maintained himself as virtual monarch while giving lip service to the king of Assyria. He was evidently the "holder of the scepter in Beth-eden" (Amos 1:5).

## The Resurgence of Israel and Judah

**Israel Tips the Scales Against Damascus.** Jehoash son of Jehoahaz (798–782 BCE; 2 Kgs 13:10–25; sixteen actual years by the accession year system) was now in a position to retaliate against his archenemy in Damascus. Prophetic tradition has it that Jehoash defeated Aram-Damascus three times (2 Kgs 13:18–19). One of these was a decisive victory at Aphek in the Golan (2 Kgs 13:17); the others (cf. Amos 6:13) were apparently at Karnaim (Sheikh Sa$^{c}$d) and Lo-debar (=Lidebir; Josh 13:26; possibly Kh. ed-Duweir=Tel Dover). The territorial gains achieved at Israel's expense by Hazael were all nullified and the towns restored to Israel (2 Kgs 13:25). Damascus had been too weakened by Adad-nirāri and the subsequent conflict with Hamath to prevent Jehoash and Jeroboam II from regaining almost full control over Transjordan (1 Chr 5:17). There are no dates for these three victories over Damascus but they probably fell in the decade between the battle with Judah at Beth-shemesh and the death of Jehoash in 782/781 BCE. This was a time of coregency with his son, Jeroboam II. When he became sole ruler Jeroboam continued the offensive and "restored the border of Israel from Lebo-hamath as far as the Sea of the Arabah" (2 Kgs 14:25). Such a hegemony was probably achieved only after the attack by Shamshi-ilu against Damascus in 773 BCE. It is possible that Hamath itself may have become subordinate to Israel alongside Damascus (2 Kgs 14:28). Gadites and Reubenites are now found in Bashan and across the eastern steppe land towards the Euphrates (1 Chr 5:9–11).

At this time a new alliance between Israel and Judah was evidently initiated. It was probably the result of Amaziah's coming to the throne of Judah after the death of his father in 796 BCE (2 Kgs 14:9). One of the interesting side effects of this new rapprochement was that both kingdoms switched their reckoning of regnal years from the non-accession to the accession year system.

**Judah Reconquers Edom But Is Defeated by Israel.** Amaziah (796–767 BCE, 29 actual accession years) also must have taken heart from the sharp decline in the power of Damascus. He decided on a campaign to reclaim Judah's own dominance over Edom. Such a program of aggression with its promise of booty may have served to unite the forces of Judah behind the monarchy and thus to heal the breach that had opened between them during the final months of the reign of Joash. He also decided to hire mercenaries from Israel who could share in the prospective loot. But a prophetic adviser on his military staff expressed strenuous objections to the use of mercenaries from the neighboring state and Amaziah elected to send his mercenaries home empty-handed (2 Chr 25:5–10).

Amaziah and his forces defeated the Edomites in the "Valley of Salt" (2 Kgs 14:7; cf. 1 Sam 8:13), that is, probably the southern end of the Dead Sea (Salt Sea). The exact location of the conflict is impossible to determine. The Sela from which the Edomite captives were cast down must be the site of Sila$^{c}$, 2.5 miles (4 km) northwest of Buṣeirah (ancient Petra was known as Reqem, Raqmu in Nabatean; it was never Sela).

The disappointed Israelite mercenaries vented their wrath on Judah by plundering towns located in the sensitive area along the border between the two states (*see* 2 Chr 25:13). Amaziah returned from his conquest of Edom full of confidence in his troops and his own prowess as a commander. He took pride in the booty that he had brought back from Edom and initiated worship of the Edomite cultic statues to the wrath of the prophetic circles in Jerusalem (2 Chr 25:14–16). The plundering of towns on his northern border so angered him that he issued a challenge to Jehoash, king of Israel, which was answered with sarcasm and scorn (2 Chr 25:17–20). The two kings faced off in the Sorek Valley by Beth-shemesh with disastrous consequences for Amaziah (*see* 2 Chr 25:23–25 || 2 Kgs 14:11b–14, 17).

An important detail, often missed by historians, is that Amaziah was not only captured on the field of battle, he was also taken hostage back to Samaria by Jehoash (Joash) king of Israel (in 792 BCE). This is the significance of the remark that Amaziah lived fifteen years longer than his captor. Further implications will be discussed below.

Meanwhile, the leaders of Judah took Azariah/Uzziah, the son of Amaziah, and made him king in his father's place (2 Kgs 14:21a || 2 Chr 26:1a). The editor of the Deuteronomistic history placed this statement after the record of Amaziah's demise in accordance with his practice of listing all the kings in chronological order. The Chronicler follows suit. But both texts make reference to the construction of a base at Elath/Eloth by Azariah/Uzziah, which took place fifteen years after the death of Jehoash/Joash of Israel. Here the Deuteronomist obscured the fact that Azariah/Uzziah actually began to rule at

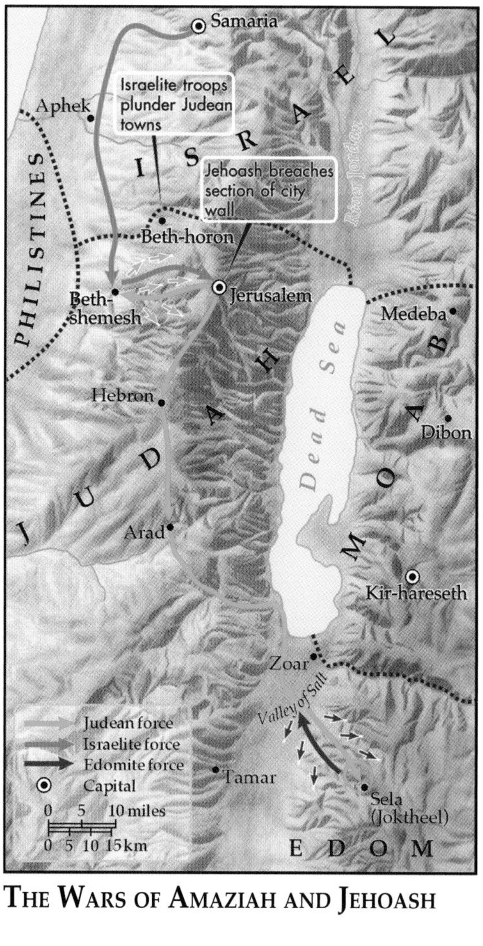


**The Wars of Amaziah and Jehoash**

age sixteen, from the time his father was taken prisoner to Samaria. This forced parallel rule is confirmed by the various dates for the kings involved.

**Israel Expands Its Territory.** Jeroboam II (793–753 BCE) was evidently appointed co-regent by his father on the eve of the coming battle with Amaziah at Beth-shemesh. For ten years he ruled in tandem with his father and probably gained military experience during his father's campaign against Damascus when three major victories were achieved (cf. above). Then as sole ruler, Jeroboam continued the offensive and restored Israel to the dominant position in the central Levant (*see* 2 Kgs 14:25–28).

He expanded Israel's territory from the watershed in the Lebanese Beqa$^c$ (at Lebo-hamath=Lebweh) to Transjordan as far as the Dead Sea (the Sea of the Arabah). In this southern direction it would appear that the Moabite tableland remained out of his control. That is confirmed by the later oracles of Isaiah (Isa 15–16) and Jeremiah (Jer 48).

Damascus was now in an inferior position to Israel and it would appear that Hamath was also somehow linked to Jeroboam's control. The enigmatic reference to Hamath belonging to Judah can perhaps be explained by a passage of Tiglath-pileser III that will be discussed below. It harks back to the time when Jeroboam had died and Azariah had taken over the leadership in the central Levant.

Jeroboam's control of Transjordan is exemplified by the census that was taken there in his days (1 Chr 5:17). It was probably in this period when the Reubenites successfully expanded eastward even unto the edge of the desert that extends to the Euphrates (*see* 1 Chr 5:9). (Compare below the critiques of the prophet Amos for discussion of some matters of internal administration and social policy during the reign of Jeroboam II.) It was a time of increased prosperity with an influx of luxury goods as a result of Israel's control of the trade routes in Transjordan and along the coastal plain and even up through the Lebanese Beqa$^c$ Valley.

**Judah's Unprecedented Expansion.** As mentioned above, when Amaziah was taken prisoner to Samaria by Jehoash king of Israel, the people appointed Azariah/Uzziah as king. The Deuteronomistic editor put this statement in his history after the death of Amaziah that actually occurred twenty-five years later. But when it is properly understood that Azariah's enthronement took place in 792 BCE (accession year), the later synchronisms of his reign fall nicely into place (*see* 2 Kgs 14:21 || 2 Chr 26:1).

This king is consistently called Azariah in Kings and Uzziah in Chronicles. He is mentioned as Azariah in an inscription of

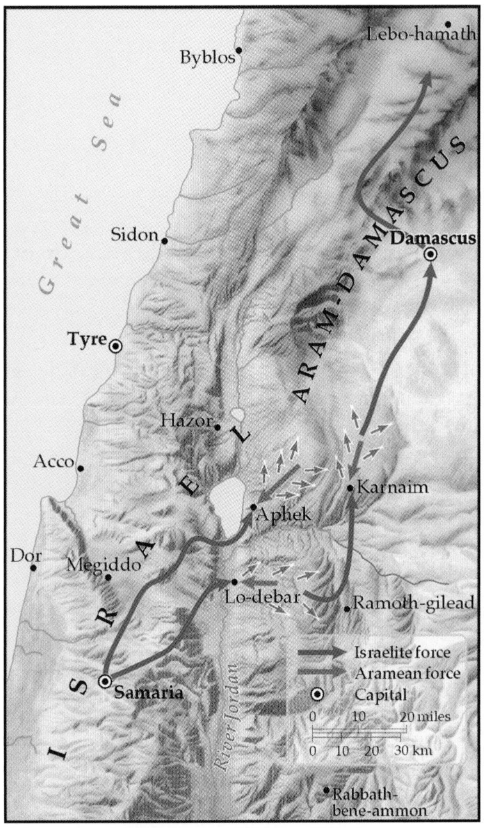


**THE CONQUESTS OF JEHOASH AND JEROBOAM II (C. 790–782 BCE)**

Tiglath-pileser III. Due to the imprisonment of his father, he became *de facto* co-regent in 792 BCE although he was assigned an accession year as a true successor. His entire reign lasted fifty-two years from his accession year in 792/791 to his death in 740/739 BCE. The overlap with Amaziah was from 792 to 767 BCE and during the last decade of his reign, he had his son, Jotham, as co-regent (due to his own illness).

Throughout the first decade of his reign the young king was probably learning his job. He had an adviser, Zechariah, who is otherwise unknown unless he might be the maternal grandfather of Hezekiah (2 Kgs 18:2) though that seems unlikely. This Zechariah who served as a mentor for Azariah/Uzziah must have been especially influential during the first decade of the king's reign, before Amaziah was sent home from captivity in Samaria.

It is not stated when during his reign Azariah/Uzziah launched his campaign against the northern inner coastal plain and the territory of Ashdod. He also succeeded in imposing his control over the Arabian elements, specifically the Meunites (according to LXX), which action gave him a monopoly over the trade routes across Sinai and as far as Egypt (*see* 2 Chr 26:5–8).

The military campaign across the northern inner coastal plain achieved control of Gath (Tell eṣ-Ṣâfī), which had apparently been rehabilitated after Hazael's devastating conquest though on a lesser scale, and Jabneh (Yebnā=Yavneh), and Ashdod (Esdûd). Forts and outposts were established in the Ashdod territory and the agricultural land was undoubtedly exploited.

In the south, gaining the upper hand against both the Philistines and the Arabians implies renewed Judean control of the caravan routes that connected those two socioethnic groups on the west and the east. The current middlemen, the Meunites (LXX), were evidently the Arabian tribe that plied the caravan routes and probably grazed their flocks across the Sinai expanses. It is not clear when this was achieved, but by 767 BCE (at the death of Amaziah) Azariah/Uzziah was able to refortify Elath/Eloth on the Gulf of Akkabah. This was undoubtedly the main Judean outpost for supervision of the caravan movements from Arabia.

The allusion to the fact that Amaziah lived fifteen years after the death of Joash must indicate that he had been released to his home after the death of the latter. This was probably a gesture on the part of Jeroboam II. Was it intended to facilitate a rapprochement with Judah or was it an attempt to complicate matters for Azariah/Uzziah? Perhaps it is better to assume that the release of Amaziah from captivity in Samaria was meant as an expression of goodwill. It could thus point to a new era of cooperation between the two kingdoms, each of which was achieving tangible results in the conquest and subjugation of the neighboring rival states. The combination of Jeroboam and Azariah/Uzziah created a dynamic power center in the southern Levant. From the border of Egypt to the central Orontes Valley their combined influence was predominant. This was a window of opportunity in the first half of the eighth century BCE. The two kingdoms achieved a high standard of economic and political development. Sadly, according to the critiques by the prophet Amos and slightly later by the northern prophet Hosea, the social life of both kingdoms fell far short of the ideals enshrined in their ancient traditions. A gap developed between the wealthy elite and the lower classes and religious observance often took on the flavor of empty routine rather than serious moral committal.

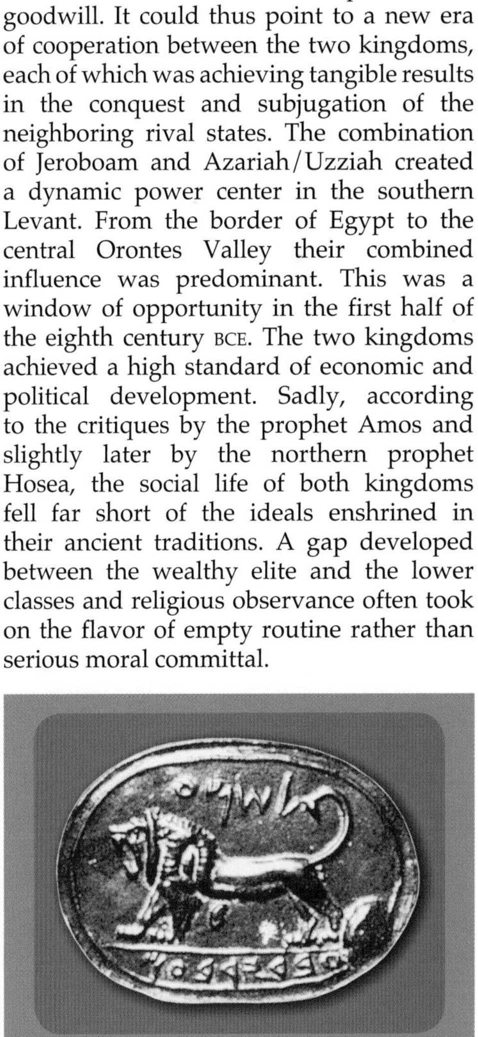

*Seal impression inscribed, "(Belonging) to Shema$^c$ servant of Jeroboam," from Megiddo.*

In Judah, the "emeritus" king Amaziah would appear to have fostered the cultic practices for which he was disliked by the temple establishment. Whatever his machinations, they led to a plot against him (*see* 2 Chr 25:25–28 || 2 Kgs 14:17–21).

It is noted that after the burial of Amaziah in 767 BCE, fifteen years after the death of Jehoash of Israel, Azariah/Uzziah built Elath/Eloth and established firm control over it (*see* 2 Kgs 14:22 || 2 Chr 26:2).

This is commensurate with the previous statement that Azariah/Uzziah achieved dominance over the routes across Sinai and as far as the border of Egypt. Especially significant is the tribute imposed on the Meunites who were plying the caravan routes from Arabia to the Mediterranean coast.

Of special interest is the Chronicler's description of the king's building programs and his agricultural projects. He expended some of his extensive income in the fortification of Jerusalem (*see* 2 Chr 26:9). His royal agricultural enterprises were located in the main topographical zones of the kingdom of Judah (*see* 2 Chr 26:10a).

To the east, in the Wilderness of Judah (Judg 1:16; Ps 63:1), more correctly the Steppe, Uzziah kept his extensive flocks and herds. It should be noted that the towers and cisterns ascribed to him here are in that eastern zone and not in the Negeb to the south, although the verse is often misquoted with reference to the latter area (*see* 2 Chr 26:10b).

To the west, two geographical entities are described—the Shephelah and the Plain (cf. the synonymous "sea coast"; Deut 1:7). As we would expect from those regions, the royal agricultural enterprises concentrated on cultivation of field crops. There Uzziah had his cultivators.

Though the Shephelah was generally recognized as an integral part of Judah, the coastal plain was Philistine territory. The expansion westward (2 Chr 26:6) discussed above had led to the acquisition of further land, probably most of it reckoned as crown property. It is hardly credible that the "tableland" north of the Arnon in Transjordan is meant here.

Of special interest is the royal wine production (*see* 2 Chr 26:10c). The "vinedressers, husbandmen," were

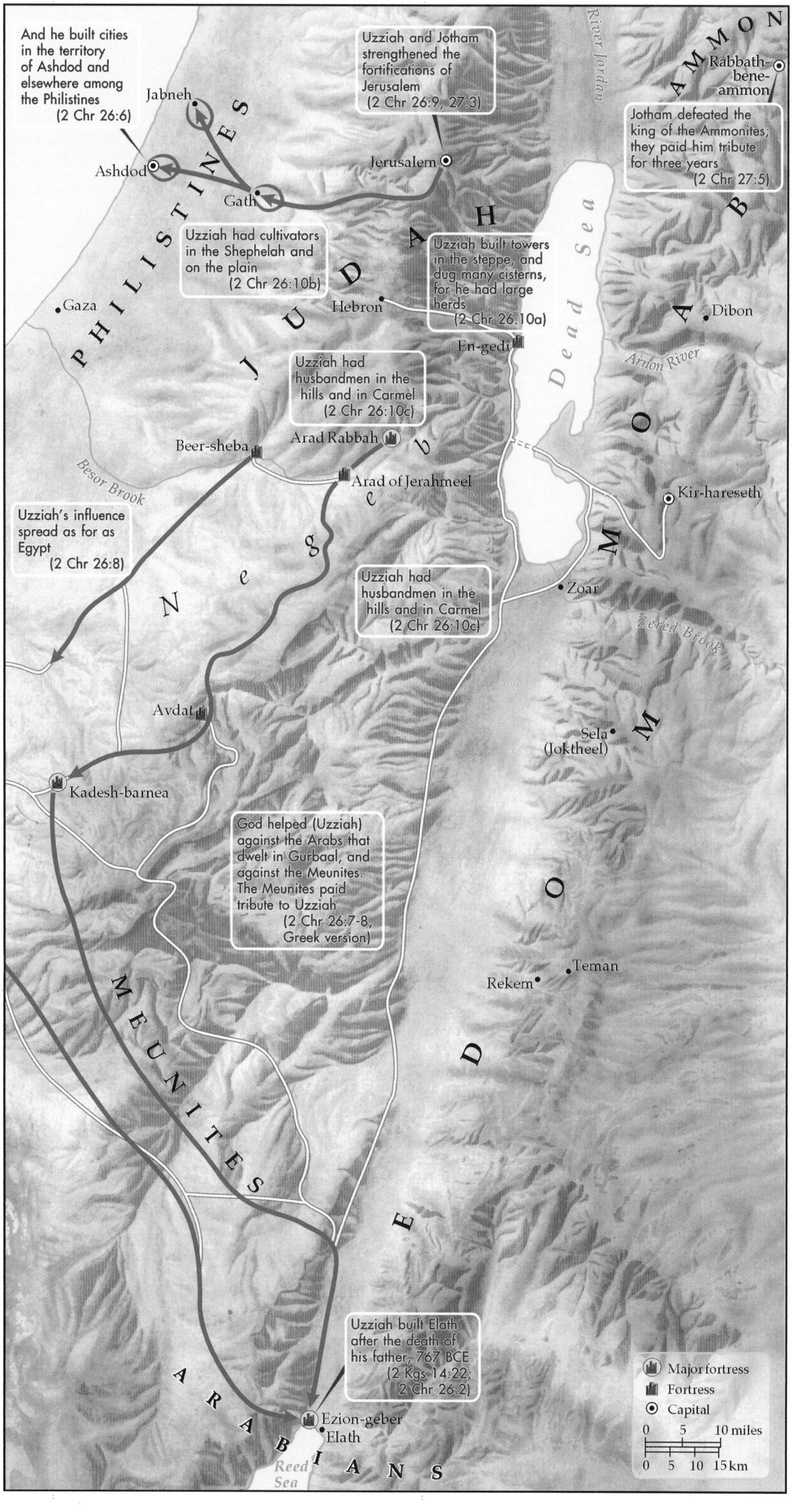


**UZZIAH'S SUCCESSES (782–750 BCE)**

located "in the Hills and in the Carmel." Such a unique delineation of the Hill Country deserves comment. Evidently, this author, whether the Chronicler himself or more likely his ancient source, viewed the area south of Hebron as a separate district. "The Carmel," with the definite article, must mean the area in which Carmel (Kh. el-Kirmil) was a principal town, certainly neither Mount Carmel, which was not under Uzziah's control at all, nor "garden land, fruitful lands." The area envisioned as "the Carmel" probably corresponds to the two districts in the southern hill country of Joshua 15 (vv. 48–52, 55–57). That zone has a character distinct from the main hill regions north of Hebron; its soil is less productive, and the altitude is lower. It could even be referred to as "Negeb land" (Josh 15:19; Judg 1:15) and may be identical to the "Negeb of Caleb" (1 Sam 30:14).

While Joshua 15 reckons the above-mentioned district "in the Hill (Country)" (Josh 15:48), the Chronicles passage under discussion distinguishes it from "the Hills." One might see this as recognition that Uzziah's realm included both the Hill Country of Judah (originally centered on Bethlehem) and a portion of the Hill Country of Ephraim (in which the tribe of Benjamin was located, 1 Sam 1:1). But the point should not be pressed. Perhaps the Chronicler or his source meant intentionally to avoid the officially sanctioned term, "the Hill," used so widely. At any rate, his description of the Judean hilly regions as being composed of two units, the Carmel and the Hills, is unique but not really obscure and it does match the physical characteristics of the two areas.

The significant detail in the passage pertains to the location of the vinedressers, which of course means that the royal vineyards must be in the same place. They are in the Hill Country. To be sure, there is some evidence for the presence of vineyards in the Shephelah, e.g., at Timnah (Judg 14:5) in the Valley of Sorek (Judg 16:5), the very name of which indicates viticulture (="red wine"). But the only specific royal holdings recorded for us in that area were olive and sycamore groves (1 Chr 27:28). It is not surprising that the vinedressers of the king should be in the Hill Country. That zone was and is famous for its viticulture. Some of the town names there also attest to it, e.g., Anab in the south (Josh 11:21, 15:50; Kh. ʿUnnâb eṣ-Ṣaghîr); Eshcol in the center, near Hebron (Num 13:23–24; Deut 1:24); and Beth-haccerem (Josh 15:59a LXX; Jer 6:1; Neh 3:14; Kh. Ṣâliḥ=Ramat Raḥel), as well as Qaryat el-ʾInab, the Arabic name of biblical Kiriath-jearim, in the north.

How the crown acquired these vineyards is not stated. It could hardly have been by conquest, since the Judean Hill Country and the "Negeb" hills south of Hebron came under David's control by invitation (2 Sam 2:

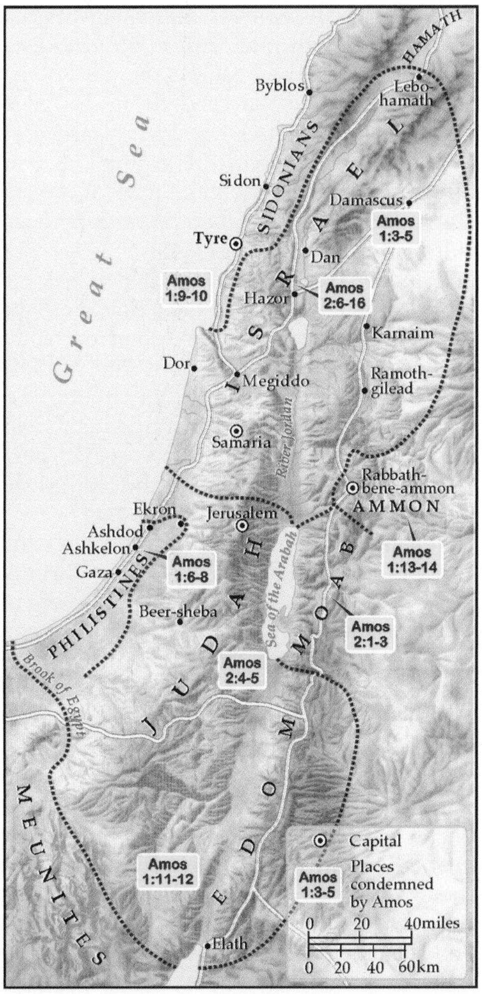


**ISRAEL AND JUDAH IN THE DAYS OF JEROBOAM II AND UZZIAH (MID-8TH CENTURY BCE)**

4). On the other hand, the royal family may have inherited vineyards through David's wives, e.g. Ahinoam the Jezreelite and Abigail, widow of Nabal from Carmel (2 Sam 3:2–5), and others. Further, such acquisitions may have been made in Benjamin through Michal, daughter of Saul (1 Sam 18:20–25; 2 Sam 3:13–16). And finally, Bethlehem was in any case David's hometown so he must have had private holdings in its vicinity. The wine of Deir Cremisan, about 2.5 miles (4 km) northwest of Bethlehem, is quite well known to this day.

Azariah/Uzziah was also known for his reorganization of the military (*see* 2 Chr 26:11–15). After all of his success in expanding the kingdom and in multiplying its riches and its agricultural production, Azariah/Uzziah was smitten with leprosy (2 Kgs 15:5). The explanation for this malady is only preserved by the Chronicler, who recounts the priestly version of the event. According to that account, it was because the king had become overly proud and is said to have attempted to usurp the ritual prerogatives of the high priest (*see* 2 Chr 26:16–21).

This event took place in 750 BCE. Jotham's first year was identical with that particular year of his father so the reckoning is not an accession year. The synchronization of Jotham beginning in the second year of Pekah is due to the latter's anti-Assyrian stance. Jotham was certainly carrying out the policy of his stricken father with regard to the Assyrian threat. Later, Tiglath-pileser III would make mention of Azariah's senior position in the central Levantine alliance.

Though scholars have often expressed skepticism, the personal name of the anti-Assyrian ruler can be none other than Azariah of Judah. As the senior partner in the Levantine alliance, he is blamed for the transfer of the territory decribed here from Assyrian control (harking back to the time of Adad-nirāri no doubt). During his lifetime, Jeroboam II was surely the senior partner but with his son's assassination and the removal of the usurper by another usurper in 752 BCE, it must have been Azariah/Uzziah who seized the helm of leadership. The relationship between Hamath and Jerusalem had a long history dating back to the founding of the Davidic dynasty so an association between Azariah and his counterpart in the central Levant would have been according to precedent. It is interesting to note that the Assyrians had accurate intelligence about the political alignments in North Syria even before the appearance of Tiglath-pileser III on the scene. The Assyrian monarch surely kept in mind the role of Judah in the Levantine alliances when he made his own foray into the southern Levant.

One is thus led to wonder if the enigmatic reference to Judah in the summary passage for Jeroboam II may not have had some

*Aerial view of the early 8th century BCE citadel at Arad, stratum IX, probably from the reign of Uzziah.*

*Aramaic inscription on stone tablet commemorating the reburial of King Uzziah's remains, Second Temple period.*

connection with Azariah's role in the Levantine alliance (*see* 2 Kgs 14:28).

With the death of Azariah/Uzziah in 740 BCE, the window of opportunity for Judah and Israel to dominate the southern Levant and to enjoy great prestige in the central Levant was closed. Israel was split apart by the events discussed below and Judah became embroiled in disputes with its neighbors that led to the loss of all its geopolitical advantages in the south and west.

**Turmoil in Israel**. Jeroboam was succeeded by his son, Zechariah (2 Kgs 15:8–12). This was in the thirty-eighth year of Azariah/Uzziah, i.e. 753 BCE. Zechariah's six months of reign extended into 752 BCE, the thirty-ninth year of Azariah/Uzziah, when a certain Shallum assassinated him (*see* 2 Kgs 15:8, 15:10).

Being a "son of Jabesh" might refer to Shallum's hometown instead of his patronymic. In that case, a Transjordanian interference in the affairs of Samaria would be indicated. Whether the murder was carried out at Ibleam or not, it was a short-lived reign. After one month, another rival made his move and slew the usurper (*see* 2 Kgs 15:13–14).

Menahem son of Gadi may have had Transjordanian connections, but he had been at Tirzah before seizing the throne. He apparently did not enjoy the support of his own hometown so he punished them severely. The LXX Old Greek serves to correct the MT.

> Then Menahem struck **Tirzah** (MT Tiphsah) and all who were in it and its borders from **Tirzah**, because they did not open [to him]; therefore he struck [it] and ripped up all its women who were with child.
> (2 Kgs 15:16)

His ten years of tenure (752–742 BCE) were a crucial period during which he ruled in Samaria (*see* 2 Kgs 15:17), while a rival, Pekah, was ruling in Transjordan (cf. below). The thirty-ninth year of Azariah/Uzziah was 752 BCE. In 743 BCE Menahem offered tribute to Tiglath-pileser III in order to gain Assyrian support (*see* 2 Kgs 15:19).

Menahem was succeeded by his son, Pekahiah (*see* 2 Kgs 15:23). His two years were 741 to 740 BCE. But then, this young king was also put to death by another rival, Pekah son of Remaliah, who had apparently been ruling in Gilead (*see* 2 Kgs 15:25).

It is not clear how Pekah had become such a trusted officer of Pekahiah. Perhaps a rapprochement was engineered after the death of Menahem. But the hapless Pekahiah fell victim to treachery on the part of his father's rival. The coup d'état was staged in the fifty-second year of Azariah/Uzziah, i.e. in the last year of the old Judean king's reign (740 BCE; *see* 2 Kgs 15:27).

Pekah met his death in 732 BCE after the invason of Israel by the Assyrians. Twenty years prior to that, 752 BCE, marks the year of the assassination of Shallum by Menahem. The double dating procedure used here makes a synchronism for the date on which Pekah became sole ruler, but gives the total of years from the time he began in tandem with Menahem. Further confirmation derives from the notation that Jotham began his reign (as co-regent) in the second year of Pekah (2 Kgs 15:32). It was during the twelve-year period when Pekah was ruling in Gilead (and possibly in Galilee) and Menahem and his son ruled in Samaria that the prophet Hosea made a tripartite distinction (*see* Hos 5:5b).

By 740 BCE Israel was once more united under one ruler, Pekah the son of Remaliah, and Judah was ruled by Jotham who had formerly been co-regent with his father. This, "the year of King Uzziah's death" (Isa 6:1), was to be a turning point in Levantine history.

## The Prophet Amos—Political Critique

An important religious denunciation and political critique of the actions by various states in the southern Levant has been preserved in the Prophecy of Amos, chapters 1 and 2. A review of this passage shows that the prophet and doubtless his contemporaries were aware of the late ninth-century BCE events that preceded the rise of Israel and Judah to a position of seniority in the region under the leadership of Jeroboam II and Uzziah respectively (*see* Amos 1:1).

Jeroboam II was still alive so the prophet's public career must have begun on or prior to 753 BCE. The "earthquake" is not mentioned anywhere else in biblical or non-biblical sources. It would have been a dramatic touch if an earthquake had been felt just at the time that Uzziah had unlawfully entered the temple hall to offer incense on the golden altar (2 Chr 26:16–21). The king was also smitten with leprosy at that time and forced to retire from public life. But assuming that there just might be a connection between the earthquake and the king's personal blasphemy, the latter took place in 750 BCE when Jotham had to take over the reins of administration. And if Uzziah's brazen sacrilege had taken place during the ritual celebrations at the beginning of the seventh month (Tishri), it would have been in 751 BCE, just two years after the death of Jeroboam II. These speculations are obviously no more than that but they challenge the imagination nonetheless.

The first target of the prophet's rage was the archenemy of Israel, Aram-Damascus to the northeast (*see* Amos 1:3–5). This harks back to the conquest of Gilead by Hazael during the latter part of the ninth century BCE. Note that the dynastic state is called "the house of Hazael" in accordance with common practice concerning Levantine states. The "Valley of (Beth-)Aven" may be a pejorative, "Valley of Iniquity," and may refer to the Lebanese Beqa$^c$. The one holding a scepter in Beth-eden would have to be the Assyrian general Shamshi-ilu, who had Til-Barsip as his main capital and who ruled almost independently in the west. Kir (Qîr) is more difficult. Various ingenious explanations of the term have been offered but none are convincing. It was the original home of the Arameans (Amos 9:7), and the place to which they were exiled by Tiglath-pileser III (2 Kgs 16:9). Kir is also mentioned (along with Elam) in Isaiah 22:6. The history of the Arameans and their origin in the steppe land west and south of the Euphrates Valley (including the Jebel Bishri), suggests that this is a name for this steppe land.

Next the prophet turns to the southwest (*see* Amos 1:6–8). The reference is to selling prisoners to the Edomites by the Philistines during the invasion of Judah in the reign of Jehoram son of Jehoshaphat (2 Chr 21:16–17). This allusion by Amos in fact gives additional credence to the Chronicles passage. It has long been noted that only four of the traditional five cities of Philistia are mentioned here. This is because the fifth city, Gath, had been devastated by Hazael (2 Kgs 12:18; 2 Chr 24:23) and later the much-degraded settlement that remained was captured by Uzziah king of Judah (2 Chr 26:6). Amos was well aware of the fate that had befallen Gath of the Philistines and held it up as a warning (*see* Amos 6:2). He was fully informed about the political and military events of the late ninth to early eighth centuries BCE.

From the southwest, attention is now directed to the northwest, to a neighbor with whom Israel had been linked by a treaty, that is until the murder of Jezebel by Jehu in 841 BCE (*see* Amos 1:9–10).

In retaliation for Jehu's seizure of the throne in Israel, Tyre must have taken captives from the Galilean districts

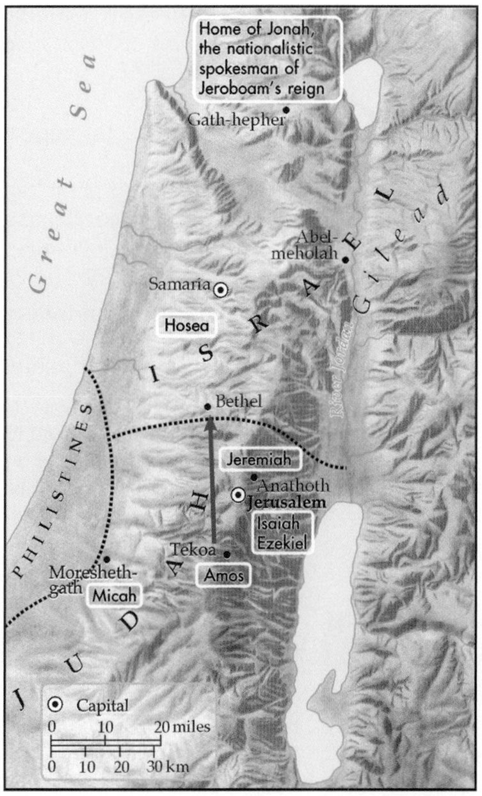


**The Great Writing Prophets**
**(8th and 7th Centuries BCE)**

bordering on its territory. Perhaps some of them were inhabitants of the Plain of Acco. In any case, the demand for slaves on the part of Edom tempted the Tyrians to make a profit at the expense of their former ally. The Edomites would hardly have had a need for such slave labor. They were evidently selling the hapless prisoners to foreign markets, probably in southern Arabia or maybe even in southern Mesopotamia.

The allusion to Edom leads the prophet to turn now to the southeast, to the land of Edom itself (*see* Amos 1:11–12). In view of Amaziah's aggression against Edom and his cruel slaughter of prisoners at Sela (2 Chr 25:12), it seems ironic that Amos should castigate the Edomites for violating a kinship of brotherhood. Of course, the prophet is denouncing mainly the previous actions during their revolt against Jehoram son of Jehoshaphat and the acceptance of prisoners for sale in the slave markets to which they had access. Teman is evidently a synonym for Edom though it probably specifically denoted a more southerly part of it. The present passage does not require that Teman be applied to the northern district around Bozrah. Bozrah itself, the ancient capital of Edom, is modern Buṣeirah, the place of a major Iron Age site in northern Edom c. 28 miles (45 km) north of Petra. It guards both the major north-south watershed route through Transjordan and a major route leading westward to the Wâdī ᶜArabah and thence to the Negeb of Judah and the Mediteranean coast.

Buṣeirah is situated just west of the main highway on a projecting spur, steep on three sides (north, west and east), with easy access only from the south. This natural defensive position was enhanced by strong walls enclosing a site of some 3,200 square meters. No natural water source has been found within the confines of the fortified site; the main supply was probably the spring at ᶜAin Jenîn, about half a mile (1 km) to the east, which until recently was also the source for the modern village. The context of Isaiah 63:1ff. suggests a derivation of the place name from **BṢR*, the verb of which signifies gathering grapes. The plateau below the site on the west would have been an ideal place for vineyards in antiquity. Of course that could just be a play on words while the real meaning of the name could have been "fortified place."

To the east, Amos directed his wrath against the Ammonites (*see* Amos 1:13–15). It would appear that the Ammonites had joined Hazael in the conquest of Gilead and had cruelly seized territory adjacent to their recognized kingdom.

Finally, the last of the foreign nations to come under the prophet's scrutiny is Moab (*see* Amos 2:1–3). The reference to the sacrilege of burning the bones of the king of Edom must surely refer to Mesha's sacrifice of the crown prince of Edom (2 Kgs 3:26–27), who is specifically defined as the heir (and probably co-regent). This brought the wrath of the Edomites on the forces of Israel and compelled them to withdraw.

Up to this point, the prophet has condemned acts of political and military aggression and sacrilege. When he turns his attention to his own people, to Judah and to Israel, he concentrates on internal policies and social behavior (*see* Amos 2:4–5).

The nature of the Torah (law) and the statutes in this passage is impossible to define. It would surely include what scholars call the J material and probably other priestly regulations that later became part of the P document. In any event, Judah is credited with having such regulations. The condemnation is that they have been vouchsafed such moral and religious material but they have neglected or outright rejected their own tradition in favor of various cults and forms of worship from foreign sources.

The culmination of the prophet's oracles is the moral condemnation of the kingdom of Israel for the gross violations of social justice. The wealthy upper classes are exploiting the poor and the disadvantaged. They are corrupting the legal process and defrauding the economically helpless (*see* Amos 2:6–16).

One is led to speculate about the situation reflected in the Samaria Ostraca whereby one person received shipments from more than one place and from more than one clan district. How did they acquire sources of production and income beyond their own inherited patrimony? Is it possible that the social corruption described by the prophet Amos is reflected in the payments recorded in the Samaria Ostraca?

Amos also makes reference to three cult centers that were active in his own day and that had earned his disapproval (*see* Amos 5:5). Concerning Beer-sheba, evidently the principal center in the Negeb of Judah, he uses an enigmatic expression (*see* Amos 8:14).

One other important point stressed by Amos has clear relevance for the subsequent invasion of Tiglath-pileser III (*see* Amos 3: 9–11). During the ninth century BCE there were many instances when the Assyrian army chose to forego the siege of well-fortified and well-stocked cities. But in the mid-eighth century BCE Tiglath-pileser III would implement a new strategy. His army would establish administrative and logistic bases in each new conquered district. The next campaign would not be overextended and could establish a well-organized and well-supplied siege operation until even the most heavily provisioned fortified city would have to surrender.

The Samaria Ostraca. *A collection of over a hundred inscribed potsherds (ostraca) were found in 1910 during the excavations at ancient Samaria. Of these, sixty-three have legible texts. They were administrative notations of shipments, wine or oil, that had been sent in to various officials from their estates out in the hills of Manasseh. All of the sherds had been discarded and were found in a fill beneath the floor level of the so-called "Ostraca House." The formulations on all the texts have the same general format, beginning with the (king's) regnal year and listing the recipient of the shipment. However, the remaining details divide the inscriptions into two groups. One type names the commodity being sent, a jar of either "old wine" or "purified oil." The other group lists only the sender of the shipment. Both groups give the name of the town from which the commodity was being sent, but the same group that omits the commodity adds the name of the clan district in which the town is located.*

# CHAPTER NINE

# IMPERIAL DOMINATION

## MID-EIGHTH TO MID-SEVENTH CENTURIES BCE

The ensuing century was dominated by the full-blown might of the Assyrian Empire. The political states of the Levant were faced with the choice of becoming tribute-paying vassals or of being destroyed politically, socially, and economically. The goal of Assyria's aspiration was the control of the entire Fertile Crescent and its adjacent areas and the economic exploitation of the sources of production and the domination of all trade routes crisscrossing the ancient Near East. The result was the largest empire ever seen in the area and the uprooting of vast populations and their transfer to foreign territories.

The second half of the eighth century BCE saw the rise and expansion of the Assyrian nation in the east and the appearance of Cushite rulers from Nubia who took over the political control of Egypt and established Manetho's XXV$^{th}$ Dynasty. The southern Levant eventually became the scene of the clash of these two powers and the small states found themselves tossed like flotsam on the waves of extortion, violence and terror.

*Tiglath-pileser III and a vassal king kneeling before him, on relief from the king's palace at Calah.*

## ASSYRIA UNDER TIGLATH-PILESER III

The period of weakness at the center of the Assyrian monarchy was brought to an end in 745 BCE when a new ruler of dubious lineage, Tiglath-pileser III (745–727 BCE), came to power in the wake of a revolt in Calah that had taken place in 746 BCE. It was evidently the result of power struggles between certain groups among the elite. The inscriptions of this monarch had been extracted from his palace by Esarhaddon and the expropriated slabs were mostly found in the building site (the Southwest Palace) being prepared for the latter king. Some slabs were copied from the ruins of another site (the Central Palace), presumably the site of Tiglath-pileser's original palace. Some of the inscriptions belong to an annalistic text (with probably three versions) while others are Summary Texts giving information in a geographical and political order rather than chronological. A stele of this king was found in Iran, evidently set up there at the end of the campaign against Madai/Media in 737 BCE; its inscriptions are excerpts from an older edition of the annals and often supply important data. The gaps in chronological information from Tiglath-pileser's inscriptions are enormous but the surviving texts (some originals in museums, some in scholarly copies and squeezes) can reasonably be ordered in accordance with the Assyrian Eponym Chronicle, where all of Tiglath-pileser's years of reign are preserved.

Tiglath-pileser III gained the throne in the month of Ayyaru (May) and by the month of Tashritu (September) he went forth on a campaign (745 BCE) in the area between the Euphrates and the Tigris, i.e. northern Babylonia. One of his first steps to strengthen the central monarchy was to strip the authority from the powerful governors who had been acting heretofore as virtually independent rulers. The following year (744 BCE) he marched eastward to the land of Namri. Once he had dealt with the areas adjacent to Assyria proper, he mounted a campaign to the west, aimed at smashing the coalition formed between the city-state of Arpad (Tell Rif$^{c}$at) and the kingdom of Urarṭu along with Melīd and Gurgum. In the Iran Stele text it is recorded:

> In my third regnal year, Mata$^{c}$-ilu [son of A]tarshumki fomented a seditious rebellion and he violated [his treaty. To] the kings that are [...] of the land of Ḫatti [...] the land of Urarṭu [he incited to] enmity to the land of Ashur. He made all the lands [hostile].
>
> Sarduri the Urarṭian, [Suluma]l the Me[lidian] and Tarḫularu the Gurgumite [came] to his aid. [Between] the mountain of Kistan and the mountain of Ḫalpi, the provinces of Kummuḫ, they trusted [in their own strength] and ordered the battle array. For seven double hours, day and night, I marched forth and did not allow the hosts of the land of Ashur to rest; water I did not give (to them); I did not make camp for my exhausted hosts. I engaged [th]em (the enemy) in battle. Their defeat I achieved. As for the camp of their forces I captured it. To save [their] lives they fled.
>
> (Stele IB, 21′–32′; cf. also Summ. 3: 15′–21)

The text of the annals is too fragmentary to preserve the connection with Mati$^{c}$-ilu of Arpad. However, the Eponym Chronicle for this regnal year (743 BCE) says (composite text):

> Tiglath-pileser, king of the land of Assyria: at the city of Arpad; the defeat of the land of Urarṭu was accomplished.

Obviously, Tiglath-pileser III was not inside the city of Arpad since the next three years were devoted to reducing it. The Iran Stele and Summary Texts all speak of a battle that took place to the north of the territory of Arpad, in the region of Kummukh. So what is this strange allusion to Arpad? After the battle in Kummukh Tiglath-pileser would not have missed the opportunity to show the flag in North Syria. In the rush to meet the allied armies he apparently had not brought siege equipment and his troops had been subjected to a grueling exertion. Nevertheless, the apostasy of Mati$^{c}$-ilu of Arpad could not be ignored until the following year. As often on Assyrian campaigns up to now, the king did not try to conquer the heavily fortified city of Arpad. But with his vast army he surely must have given notice to the neighboring states that

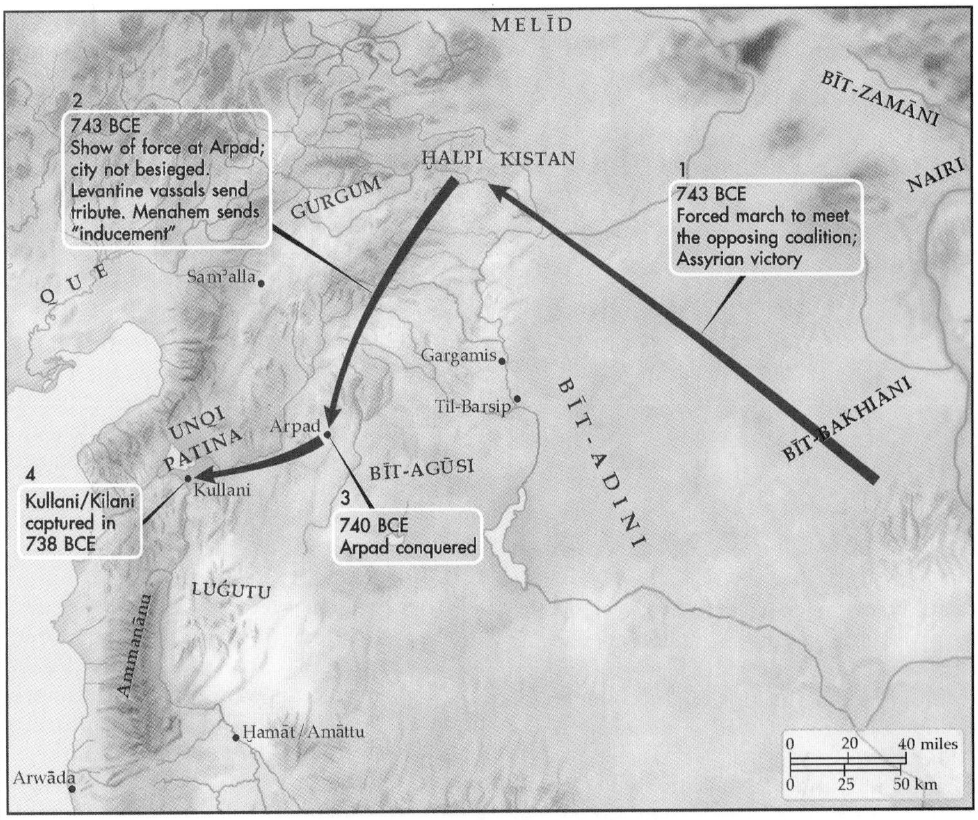


**TIGLATH-PILESER III CAMPAIGNS IN THE WEST (743–738 BCE)**

they had better demonstrate their continued loyalty to Assyria. Previously, they had paid their tribute to (the deposed?) Shamshi-ilu. But the change in monarchs was no license to withhold payments of tribute.

The payment of a thousand talents of silver by Menahem of Israel must have taken place during this period. It resembles the payments made by other rulers who were newly installed on their thrones, mainly usurpers: Hoshea of Israel, Ḫulli of Tabal, and Metenna of Tyre. The payment could have been sent to Tiglath-pileser III upon his appearance in North Syria in 743 BCE; or it could have been made in 742 BCE just before Menahem died. Nothing in the Assyrian inscriptions contradicts such a suggestion. Menahem was apparently aware of his failing health and wanted confirmation in his rule in order to assure the succession of his son, Pekahiah, which took place in 742 BCE (the fiftieth year of Azariah, 2 Kgs 15:23).

Except for the entries in the Eponym Chronicle, no records have survived for the fourth and fifth regnal years (742 and 741 BCE). The Chronicle entries (composite texts) are:

(Eponym) Nabû-daʾʾinanni, the field marshal: to the city of Arpad.

(Eponym) Bēl-Ḫarrān-uṣur, the palace herald: to the same city, in three years it was conquered.

For the following year (740 BCE) the entry is:

(Eponym) Nabû-Ēṭiranni, chief steward: to Arpad.

The receipt of the tribute in Arpad would strongly suggest that the tribute was received in 740 BCE. The ensuing lines deal with the treachery of Tutammu, ruler of Unqi, and Tiglath-pileser's severe action against him. This must be what happened in the eighth regnal year (738 BCE) when the king of Assyria captured Kullani, the capital of Unqi. Thus there are three discrete passages, the first concerning Ulluba (739 BCE), the second concerning tribute received at Arpad (740 BCE) and the third about severe military action against Unqi (738 BCE). Because of the confused chronological order, it seems more likely that the texts in Annals 20 and 21 (on the same stone) and Annals 25 (which overlaps the end of Annals 21 by one line) are part of a summary text and not part of what has been defined as Annals C. The tribute from western states received at Arpad is from local rulers who obviously do not want to feel the ire of Tiglath-pileser. Instead, they wish to recognize his political and especially economic control of the area. The list in Annals 21:4′–10′ and 25:1′–2′ must surely be a shorter version even though the length of the lines cannot be exactly determined. Therefore, it is significant that Menahem does not appear in this context. The name of the ruler of Tyre is not preserved but was most likely Hirom/Hiram.

By all reckoning, the year 738 BCE was crucial in the affairs of the western states. The year 739 was spent in a campaign to the north, "... against Ulluba whose capital city was captured." The focus of the 738 campaign was, according to the entry in the Eponym Chronicle (composite text):

(Eponym) Adad-bēlu-kaʾʾin, the governor: Kullāni was conquered.

The result of critical evaluation of the texts of Tiglath-pileser III for the years 743 BCE through 737 BCE is that there is no compelling reason to assume that either Azariah or Menahem was alive in 738 BCE. The chronology adopted herein for the kings of Israel and Judah during the mid-eighth century BCE is thoroughly vindicated.

## CONFLICTS IN THE SOUTHERN LEVANT

The land of Judah was governed by Jotham, son of Azariah/Uzziah, for the last ten years of the reign of the senior king (*see* 2 Kgs 15:5 || 2 Chr 26:21). Altogether, he reigned sixteen years, from 750 to 735 BCE inclusively (his first year was not an accession year since he was co-regent; *see* 2 Kgs 15:32–33). Even after Jotham was deposed in favor of his son, Ahaz (cf. *infra*), he continued to live to his twentieth year, 732 BCE (2 Kgs 15:30).

As co-regent with Azariah/Uzziah he continued the building projects initiated by his father (*see* 2 Chr 27:3–4 || 2 Kgs 15:35). By 743 BCE, Tiglath-pileser III had brought the Assyrian might back to the west and the local states either made their peace with him or looked for ways to foster an armed resistance. At first, Rezin of Damascus had paid tribute along with Menahem of Israel. Pekah, who was ruling in Gilead, bided his time. After Menahem's death, he seems to have made some accommodation with the successor, Pekahiah, son of Menahem. But after two years, at an opportune moment, he slew his rival and became sole ruler in Israel with his headquarters in Samaria (740 BCE). When Tiglath-pileser came back from his campaign in Ulluba and poured out his wrath on the kingdom of Patina/Unqi (738 BCE), and restored control over the nineteen districts of Hamath, Rezin again sent tribute. Pekah never appears in the Assyrian tribute lists.

But during this time Jotham, who must have shared his father's antipathy to Assyrian domination, made a move of his own. It appears that he took advantage of Pekah's move to Samaria in order to gain a foothold for Judah in Gilead, for the first time since the United Monarchy. He was able to conduct a census there (1 Chr 5:17). He was then able to subjugate the kingdom of Rabbath-bene-ammon (*see* 2 Chr 27:5).

Those three years must have been after Pekah had moved to Samaria so it has to be after 740 BCE. It would be logical to assume that Jotham made his military move in 739 BCE while Tiglath-pileser was busy in Ulluba. Then, whatever happened, he could present the Assyrian monarch with a *fait accompli*. The three years in which Ammonite tribute was paid to Jotham would thus be 739, 738 and 737 BCE. The grain products in this tribute (wheat for humans, barley as fodder) were doubtless designated for the newly established Judean garrisons in Transjordan,

*Signet ring inscribed, "(Belonging) to Jotham" thought to be that of Jotham, king of Judah, found at Tell el-Kheleifeh (bib. Ezion-geber).*

not only for their own consumption but also as provisions to be furnished to passing caravans on the Arabian and south Arabian routes. Jotham was thus encroaching on the profits formerly enjoyed by the king of the Ammonites.

Rezin of Damascus had made his tribute payment to Tiglath-pileser III in 740 BCE. The Assyrians were getting too close, and Arpad had knuckled under. It is not at all certain that Rezin paid tribute in 738 BCE since the list incorporated in the Assyrian annals for that year is most likely an old archive document from 742 BCE. The frightful expansion of Assyrian domination over central Syria as achieved in 738 BCE with the fall of Unqi and the annexation of the nineteen districts of Hamath probably stimulated Rezin to look for allies to form an anti-Assyrian coalition. By 737 BCE, with Tiglath-pileser on campaign in Madai, Rezin had probably managed to recruit Hiram, king of Tyre, and Pekah, now sole ruler over Samaria. Jotham, with his father's anti-Assyrian proclivities, might be expected to join them; but Jotham was seriously cutting into the political influence of Pekah and threatening the foreign income of Damascus. It was probably in 736 BCE that Rezin and Pekah joined forces and turned against Jotham. Both were angered that Judah had occupied Gilead (*see* 2 Kgs 15:37).

Perhaps Jotham would have been willing to throw in his lot with the anti-Assyrian conspirators, but the Jerusalem ruling class would have none of it. So they evidently forced Jotham to retire and installed his twenty-year-old son, Ahaz (735–716 BCE), as king. This is indicated by the chronological references to the respective years of their reigns. Jotham survived until his twentieth year (732 BCE), three years after Ahaz became king (*see* 2 Kgs 16:1–2).

Actually, the sixteen years of Ahaz's reign are counted from the year that Jotham died (2 Kgs 15:38 || 2 Chr 27:9), viz. 732 BCE. Incidentally, his first son, Hezekiah (twenty-five years old in 715 BCE when he began his reign), had been born in 740 BCE, when Ahaz was only fifteen. But this is not an unusual phenomenon for the kings of Judah. This youthful king was unwilling to join his northern neighbors in resistance to the Assyrians (*see* 2 Kgs 16:5; Isa 7:1–2).

Although the allies were unable to conquer Jerusalem, they evidently had taken many prisoners on the way (*see* 2 Chr 28:5–8). But Pekah, the usurper from Gilead, was opposed by native Ephraimites led by a prophet, and he was forced to return all the prisoners. Jericho was chosen as the venue for the repatriation of the captives (2 Chr 28: 9–15). These additions of the Chronicler to the story of Ahaz's reign make reference to specific personages, even the son of the king. So although the numbers of killed and captives are typically exaggerated, there is a ring of authenticity to the account.

Other actions were also taken against Judah, stripping it of all the territorial achievements of Azariah/Uzziah. Rezin of Aram-Damascus sent an expeditionary force to assist the Edomites in capturing Elath, thus robbing Judah of its southern maritime and caravan connection with southern Arabia:

> At that time **Rezin** king of **Aram** recovered Elath for **Edom(!)** (MT Aram), and cleared the Judeans out of Elath entirely; and the **Edomites** came to Elath and have lived there to this day. (2 Kgs 16:6)

He was obviously restoring Elath for **Edom** so the text must be emended at that point—a classic case of confusion between *resh* and *dalet*.

The Edomites themselves took courage and launched an invasion of southern Judah on their own (*see* 2 Chr 28:17).

On the western front, the Philistines attacked the Negeb and the Shephelah of Judah, probably in concert with the Edomites (*see* 2 Chr 28:18).

The Negeb towns are not named and only a set of towns in the Shephelah is given. They are all located on solid Judahite territory and each one guarded a major approach to the Judean hill country. The order seems to be a bit haphazard. Perhaps they had originally been listed in two columns and later just copied into the Chronicler's text. The northern routes via the Latrun or Beth-horon road were guarded by Gimzo (Jimzū; mentioned only here) and Aijalon (Yâlō); the Sorek Valley had Timnah (Tell el-Baṭâshī=Tel Baṭash) and Beth-shemesh (Tell er-Rumeileh=Tel Bet Shemesh); Socoh (Kh. ᶜAbbâd=Ḥ. Sokho beside Kh. esh-Shuweikeh) is in the Valley of Elah (Wâdī es-Sanṭ). The Timnah of the Judah and Tamar story (Gen 38:12; Kh. Tabbâneh=Ḥ. Tivna) might be the site just inland from Socho except that it is not in the Shephelah but on the slopes of the hill country. Gederoth is listed in the Lachish district of the southern Shephelah (Josh 15: 41). Like most towns in that district, it is not identified. The approach to Hebron via Makkedah (Kh. el-Qôm) or Eglon (Tell ᶜAiṭûn=Tel ᶜEton) runs through that district.

The two conspirators had their own plan for making Judah become a sympathetic ally. The prophet Isaiah records a message to the young King Ahaz (*see* Isa 7:3–6). This Tabeel (Isa 7:6) must have been someone who would be acceptable to the people of Judah but who would cooperate with Rezin and Pekah. It is interesting to note that a "land of Ṭāb-ʾel" is mentioned in a late eighth-century BCE letter from an Assyrian official responsible for reporting local problems in Transjordan to the Assyrian headquarters (after Tiglath-pileser III's conquest of Gilead). The eponym Ṭāb-ʾel is most likely the founder of the "House of Tobiah" of later history. Now the Tobiads had connections with the priesthood in post-exilic and Hellenistic times. But they may also have had a connection with the royal family of Judah. The original Ṭāb-ʾel, the Tabeel of Isaiah 7:6, may have been given the responsibility, or perhaps it was his

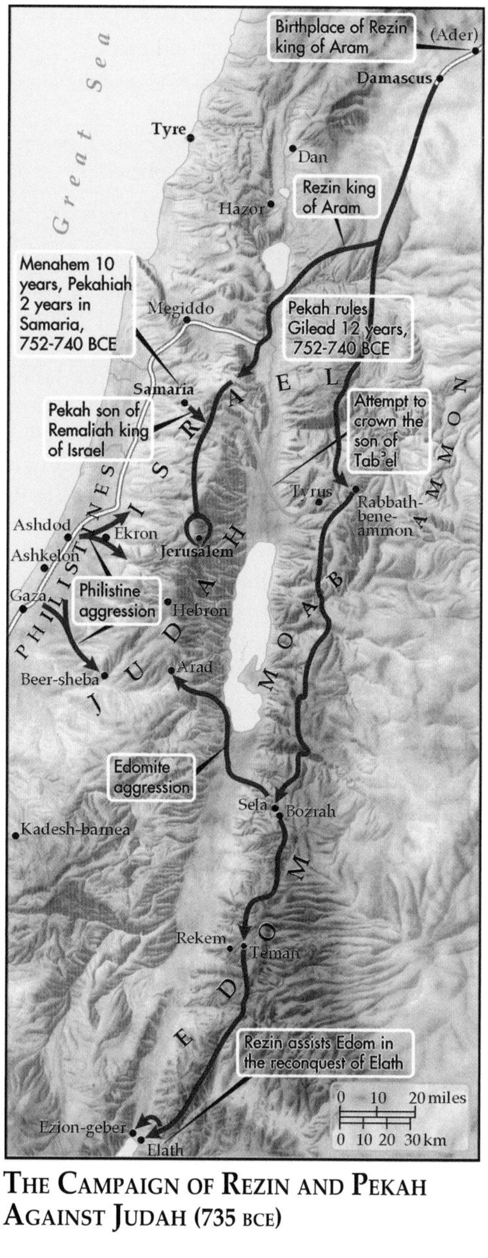


**THE CAMPAIGN OF REZIN AND PEKAH AGAINST JUDAH (735 BCE)**

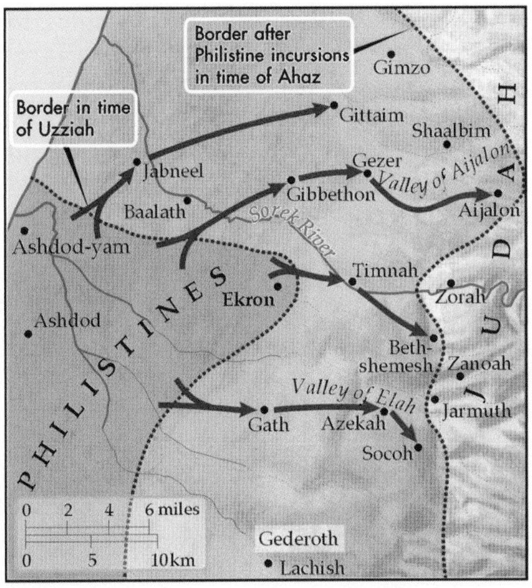


**Philistine Conquests in the Days of Ahaz (735 bce)**

son, for the oversight of the newly occupied territory in Transjordan following Jotham's thrust into that area. The son of Tabeel would surely share Jotham's anti-Assyrian attitude and thus would be amenable to taking the throne away from Ahaz.

Faced with attacks from all sides and an attempt to dethrone him, Ahaz decided to seek help through diplomacy (*see* 2 Kgs 16: 6–8; cf. 2 Chr 28:16, 20–21). It stands to reason that Tiglath-pileser III had plans to subdue the southern Levant even without the inducement from Ahaz. Damascus was a prime target, but the chance to control the entire corridor of trade from Egypt and Arabia was thoroughly commensurate with Assyrian ambitions.

In his tenth regnal year (736 bce), Tiglath-pileser went to the foot of Mount Nal and in his eleventh regnal year (735 bce), he launched a major campaign against Urarṭu. It must have been during that interlude in Assyrian campaigns to the west that Rezin and Pekah conducted their war against Ahaz supported by Edomites and Philistines.

## Assyrian Intervention in the Southern Levant

**Against Philistia.** Finally, in 734 bce, Tiglath-pileser III gave his attention to the eastern Mediterranean seaboard. Hirom (Hiram), ruler of Tyre, had entered the alliance with Rādiyān (Rezin) and this important coastal center could not be allowed to secede.

As for [Hi]rom the Tyrian, who had given his word to Rādiyān, [. . .]; Maḫalab, his fortress city, along with many towns, I conquered; [their] spoil [I took]. [Into] my presence he came and he kissed my feet. Twenty talents of [gold], multicolored [garments], linen garments, eunuchs, male and fem[ale] singers, *X* [horses] of Egyp[t, I received]. (Summ. 9:5–8)

Mitinti of Ashkelon had also broken his oath of allegiance to Ashur. It is not stated when he became smitten with fear but it is likely that it occurred in 734 bce.

Mitinti the Ashkelonite [violated] the loyalty oath [and] he re[belled] against me. He saw [the panic(!) of Rāḍiyān and in an attack of [madness(?)] [his heart] feared and his own panic [attacked him]. Rōkibtu, son of [...] sat on his throne [as king ...].
(combined text: Ann. 18:8′–10′ and Ann. 24:12′–16′)

The Eponym Chronicle for 734 bce refers to Philistia:

Bēl-dān of Kalḫa: to the land of Philistia.

The main narrative of the military action in Philistia is on a badly broken summary inscription. It is given here with some conjectural restorations:

Ḫanūnu of Gaza feared my powerful weapons and escaped t[o the land of] Egypt. The city of Gaza, [his royal city, I conquered/entered. *X* talents] of gold, 800 talents of silver, people together with their possessions, his wife, [his] sons, [his daughters ...,] his property (and) [his] gods [I despoiled/seized]. A statue of the great gods, my lords, and my (own) royal image out of gold I fashioned. Within the palace of Ga[za I set it up;] I counted (it) among the gods of their land. [The]ir [regular offerings] I established. As for him, [the fear of my lordship over]whelmed [him]; like a bird he flew back from Egypt. [. . . I returned him to his position. His . . .] I assigned [to the customs house of the land] of Assyria. I received [gold,] silver, multicolored garments, large [horses . . .]. My royal stele [I set up] in the city of the Brook of Egypt, a river[-bed ... *X* + 100 talents] of silver I carried off and I [brought] them to Assyria.

This fascinating affair reflects a special aspect of the Assyrian policy. As in the case of Hirom of Tyre, Hanun (Ḫanunu) was given a second chance. He had fled to Egypt but "flew back like a bird." Synchronization with the affairs of Egypt at this time strongly indicates that Hanun had fled to the court of Tefnakht at Sais sometime in the late spring of 734 bce. But during his stay there, the delta was invaded by Piye (Pi-ᶜankhy) of Cush who conquered Memphis between the end of July and September. When Hanun saw that his Egyptian protector and patron was in danger of being defeated, he decided to try his luck with Tiglath-pileser so he returned and was reinstalled as king of Gaza.

The establishment of a statue of the gods of Ashur and of the king, Tiglath-pileser III, in Gaza were intended as symbols of the extent of the empire. For good measure, another statue was set up in the "town of the Brook of Egypt" (el-ᶜArîsh). The king of Assyria thus sought to establish his hegemony on the entire eastern Mediterranean coast down to Naḥal Muṣri (the Brook of Egypt). It was his intention to profit from all the commercial activity between Egypt and the Levant. Controlling el-ᶜArîsh would also facilitate the domination of the caravan routes from Transjordan and Arabia. During the ninth and eighth centuries bce the dominant ethnic group in that area (Mt. Seir; 2 Chr 20: 10) was the Meunites. They were the pastoral people living in southern Transjordan, the Negeb highlands and in the Sinai expanses who operated the caravan routes across the Sinai desert. They paid tribute to Uzziah (2 Chr 26:7–8; cf. 1 Chr 4:41) and afterwards paid tribute to Tiglath-pileser III.

**Arabian Tribute.** As a result of the new Assyrian presence in northern Sinai and southern Philistia, distant tribes of Arabia sent tribute:

A leader from among these Arabian groups was appointed as warden, evidently in charge of the commercial traffic to and from Egypt. His post must have been at the city of Naḥal Muṣri (el-ᶜArîsh).

Most of the Arabian tribal groups in Tiglath-pileser's list can be recognized in the lists of the sons of Keturah and of Ishmael (Gen 25; 1 Chr 1).

**Tribute from Local States.** It was probably while Tiglath-pileser was making the arrangements at Gaza, reinstating Hanun and setting up his statues, that several states in the immediate area sent tribute, viz.:

[Ma]ttanbiᶜil the Arvadite, Sānipu the Ammonite, Salāmānu the Moabite, [Mi]tinti the Ashkelonite, Jehoahaz (Ahaz) the Judean, Qausmalaka the Edomite, Muṣ ... [... Ḫ]anunu the Gazaite.
(Summ. 7:10′–12′)

Ahaz had pinned his hopes on submission to Tiglath-pileser. His tribute payment may or may not be identical to the "inducement" that he had sent earlier. It is quite possible that the tribute in the Assyrian records is a new payment, this time as an acknowledged vassal (*see* 2 Chr 28:20–22).

Tiglath-pileser III did not "besiege" Ahaz; what he did was to "afflict" him. This means that he did not make the Philistines withdraw from the towns in the Negeb and the Shephelah that they had recently occupied (2 Chr 28:18). Two towns close to Gezer, viz. Aijalon and Gimzo, were still in Philistine hands. Perhaps the Assyrian monarch remembered that

*The capture of Gezer on a palace relief from Nimrud and only known from Layard's copy, shown here, might have occurred during Tiglath-pileser's Philistine conquests.*

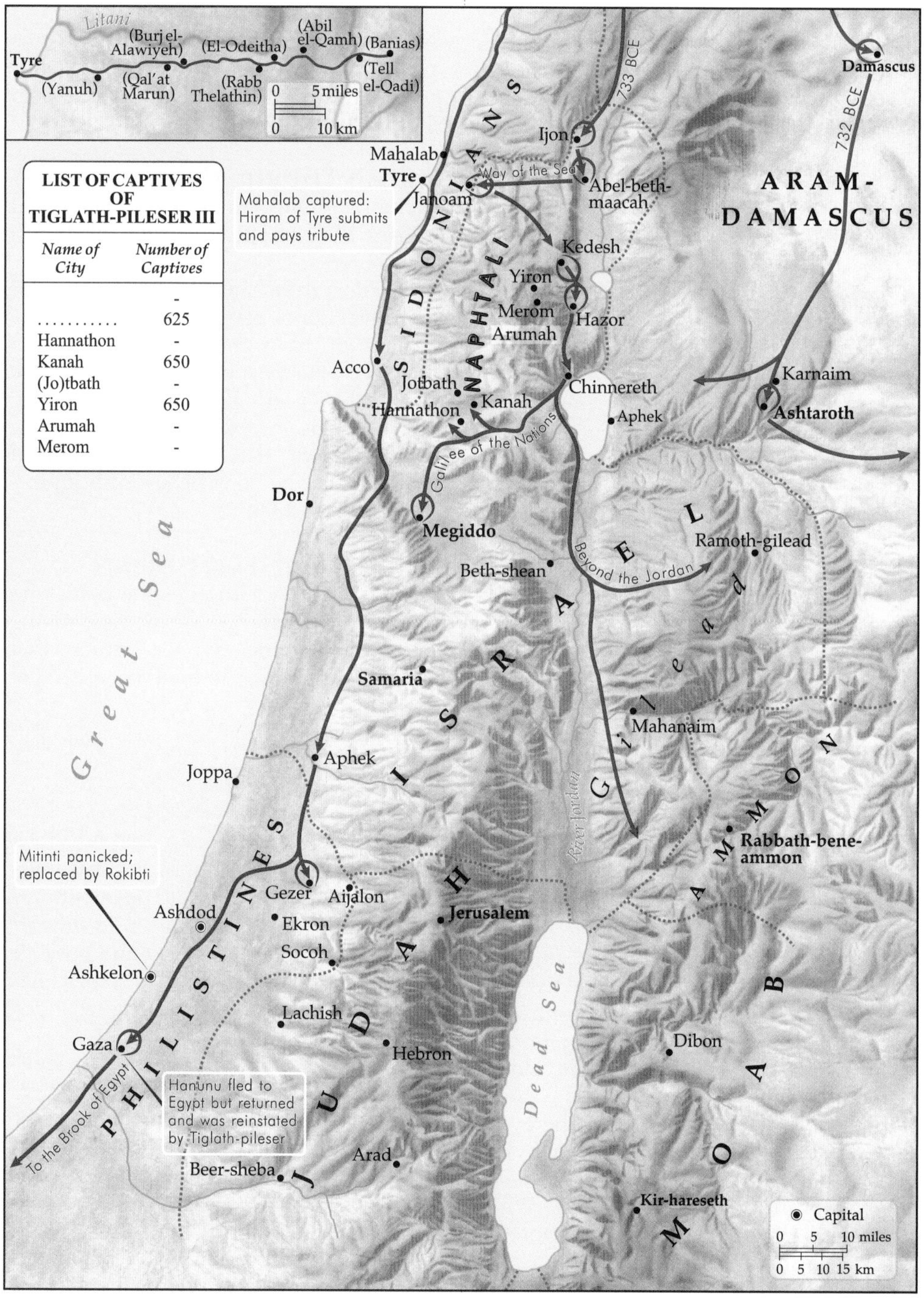


**THE CAMPAIGNS OF TIGLATH-PILESER III (734–732 BCE)**

Ahaz's grandfather, Azariah/Uzziah, had at one time assumed the leadership of a central Levantine coalition which sought to present a united front against the Assyrian program of eventual conquest of the entire southern Levant. So Tiglath-pileser found it expedient to leave Ahaz with a seriously curtailed territory. The representative of Assyrian interests in the south would be Ḫanunu of Gaza. As an inducement to insure Ḫanunu's loyalty, the king of Assyria allowed him to keep the Judean towns that he had taken just a year or so before.

**The Damascus Campaigns.** The Eponym Chronicle entries for 733 and 732 BCE indicate campaigns focused on Damascus:

$^{I}$Aššur-daʾʾinanni of the city of Māzamua: to the land of Damascus.

$^{Id}$Nabû-bēlu-uṣur of the city of Siʾmê: to the land of Damascus.

All things considered, it appears more likely that the attack on the "land of the House of Omri" occurred during 733 BCE as preparation for the final siege of Damascus. The Assyrian inscriptions mention the annexation of the country but there is a biblical itinerary that has all the earmarks of authenticity and needs to be addressed first (*see* 2 Kgs 15:29).

The initial course of the campaign can be deduced from this passage. Tiglath-pileser launched the attack from the Lebanese Beqa$^{c}$ Valley, first taking Ijon (Tell ed-Dibbîn on the plain called Marj $^{c}$Ayyûn) and Abel-beth-maachah (Abil el-Qamḥ=Tel Avel Bet Ma$^{c}$akha). Then he turned westward across Upper Galilee to Janoah (Yanûḥ), in the foothills above Tyre. Thus he assured his lines of communication with Tyre. Marching back across Upper Galilee, he conquered Kedesh. Merom appears in a very fragmentary Assyrian list of prisoners from this campaign. It is the only identifiable town in the list that could be in Upper Galilee. Presumably it is the same as Maron (LXX Josh 11:1, 12:19; MT Madon) which is probably Tell el-Khirbeh near the hill of Marûn er-Râs. The next station in the itinerary was Kedesh, obviously "Kedesh in the Galilee in the hill country of Naphtali" (Josh 20:7). He could now concentrate on the siege of Hazor (Tell el-Qedaḥ=Tel Hazor) without fear of harassment from Upper Galilee.

Forces were sent into Gilead and to "Galilee, all the land of Naphtali." The Gilead action is confirmed by two lines of evidence. First, there is the reference to exiles from the Transjordanian tribes in the genealogical lists of 1 Chronicles (*see* 1 Chr 5:6, 5:26).

The exiles were sent to well-known, legitimate Assyrian venues from the eighth century BCE so there is no reason to doubt these statements. Halah was a town and district northeast of Nineveh; Habor is the river el-Khâbûr, a tributary to the Euphrates. Each of these are glossed; Hara is Aramaic for "the mountain" referring to Halah while "the river of Gozan" (Tell Ḫalaf on the Khābûr) glosses Habor. Note that in the same passage, "Pul, king of Assyria," is glossed by "Tiglath-pil(n)eser, king of Assyria."

Three passages in the inscriptions of Tiglath-pileser III make reference to "the city of Gilead" as part of the kingdom of Hazael. The city in question is most certainly Ramoth-gilead (Tell er-Rumeith).

As for Galilee, there is a very poorly preserved roster of captives deported from some towns there. Maron in Upper Galilee has already been mentioned above. A conjectural composite text of the list is as follows:

Of sixteen districts of the land of the House of Om[ri] wi[th the spoil of the city of Ga?]barā six hundred and twenty five, the spoil of the city of [GN *x*, the spoil of the city of] Hannathon 650, the spoil of the city of Beth[lehem(?) *x*, the spoil of the city of Ya]ṭbite 656, the spoil of the city of Sam[$^{c}$ôna *x*, the spoil of] the city of Arûmā....

(Ann. 18:3′–7′ || Ann. 24:11′)

That badly preserved list bristles with problems but at least it can be said that it indicates the capture and plundering of several towns in Lower Galilee. That area is not included in the biblical itinerary of 2 Kings 15:29. Obviously, the full extent of this attack on the northern districts of the kingdom of Israel (the "House of Omri") remains mostly undocumented. It is noteworthy that the references to the plundering of the kingdom speak of "the House of Omri," and not of Samaria.

*This Assyrian relief from Calah shows the exile of inhabitants from Ashtaroth, chief city of Bashan, one of the cities taken by the army of Tiglath-pileser III in 732* BCE.

Menahem had been called a Samarian, not an Israelite (as was Ahab in the mid-ninth century BCE). The division between Samaria and "Israel" articulated by the prophet Hosea (5:5b) thus finds an oblique confirmation.

Isaiah also describes the territories mentioned in 2 Kings 15:29, the first to fall under a conqueror's heel (*see* Isa 8:23 [Eng. 9:1). Biblical semantics require that "Way of the Sea" be a route leading *to* the sea; this fits perfectly the road from Abel-beth-maacah to Janoah. The "land beyond the Jordan" is Gilead, of course, and "the district of the foreigners" is the equivalent of Harosheth-ha-goiim (Judg 4:2), mainly the Jezreel Valley. The term *gālîl*/*g$^{ə}$lîlā$^{h}$* simply means "district," e.g. *g$^{ə}$lîlôṯ happ$^{ə}$lištîm*, "the districts of the Philistines" (Josh 13:2; cf. Joel 4:4), and *g$^{ə}$lîlôṯ hayyardēn*, "the districts of the Jordan" (Josh 22:10–11). Therefore, *g$^{ə}$lîl haggôyîm* need not be part of *haggālîl*, the traditional Galilee although the Septuagint understood it as such: "Galilee of the nations" (also cited Mt 4:15). It is far more appropriate to its context to interpret it simply as "the district of the foreigners (non-Israelites)."

Damascus was now completely isolated. But it apparently managed to hold out during the attack of 733 BCE, possibly because of the intervention by an ally, Samsi, queen of the Arabians.

> [Of] Rāḍiyāni [I caused his defeat; his he]avy [spoil I took], his counsellor, [his courtier, I caught. With the blood of his] wa[rriors] the river [Abana(?)], the raging [torrent, I re]ddened like crimson. His [court]iers, his charioteers and [all] their weapons I smashed [X] of their horses, [$X_2$] of his [ass]ault troops, his archers, his shield and lance [be]arers I seized; their battle array [I di]spersed. He himself, in order to save his life, fled alone [like] a mongoose and entered the gate of his city. His foremost officials, I impaled alive on stakes and caused his country to behold it. For forty-five days I established my encampment [in the sur]roundings of his city and I trapped him like a caged bird. His [luxur]ious plantations, orchards without number, I chopped down. I did not leave a single one.
> (Ann. 23:1′–17′; with some conjectural restorations)

Tiglath-pileser went to great lengths to describe his actions around Damascus. This was obviously to avoid admitting that he had failed to conquer the city. The simile of the caged bird becomes a standard topos in such cases. It is not the first time that the Assyrians had failed to take a besieged city. However, the other cities in the Damascus area were overrun, evidently including *āl Astartu* (Ashtaroth=Tell $^{c}$Ashtarah) as inscribed on the relief of a besieged city. Within a year, they were to finally realize that ambition and to bring to an end the reign of Rezin. But in the meantime, it would seem that there was an intervention on the part of Samsi, queen of the Arabians.

For the following year (732 BCE) when the Eponym Chronicle again indicates a campaign against Damascus, there is no record of a prolonged siege and capitulation of the city. Damascus had finally seen its downfall before the victorious army of Tiglath-pileser III.

The annalistic text for regnal year 14 is missing. Only the biblical reference states explicitly that Damascus was actually conquered (*see* 2 Kgs 16:8–10a). Kir, the place of exile, is still debated. Many ingenious suggestions have been made for its location or interpretation, but none is convincing. Two Summary Texts make reference to the annexation of the entire kingdom of the House of Hazael. A composite of the two is as follows:

> The broad [land of the House of] Hazael in its entirety, from the mountain of [Leb]anon to the heart of the city of Gilea[d], Abel-shittim which is on the border of the land of the House of Omri, I annexed to the area of the land of Assyria. My eunuch I appointed over them as governor.
> (Summ. 9:3–4; Summ. 4:6′–8′)

In the wake of this crushing defeat, Pekah was assassinated by Hoshea, son of Elah (732 BCE; *see* 2 Kgs 15:30). Tiglath-pileser III confirms that he did not touch the city of Samaria:

> [As for the land of the House of Omri, of which i]n my former campaigns I razed all [its] cities [to the ground, its people and] its cattle I had despoiled, the city of Samaria alone did I leave, ‹they slew› Pekah their king. (Summ. 13:17′–18′)

In another somewhat broken passage he seems to confirm that "they" (the people of Samaria) slew Pekah and that he appointed Hoshea to the kingship there.

> As for the land of (the House) of Omri, [. . .] its [the aux]iliary [troops . . .] the totality of its people [. . . to] the land of Assyria I transported. As for Pekah, their king, [they] sl[ew him;] Hoshea I appointed [to the kingship o]ver them. As for 10 talents of gold, *X* talents of silver [with their possessi]ons, I accepted them. (Summ. 4:15′–18′)

Finally, Tiglath-pileser notes that Hoshea had come before him, apparently to receive

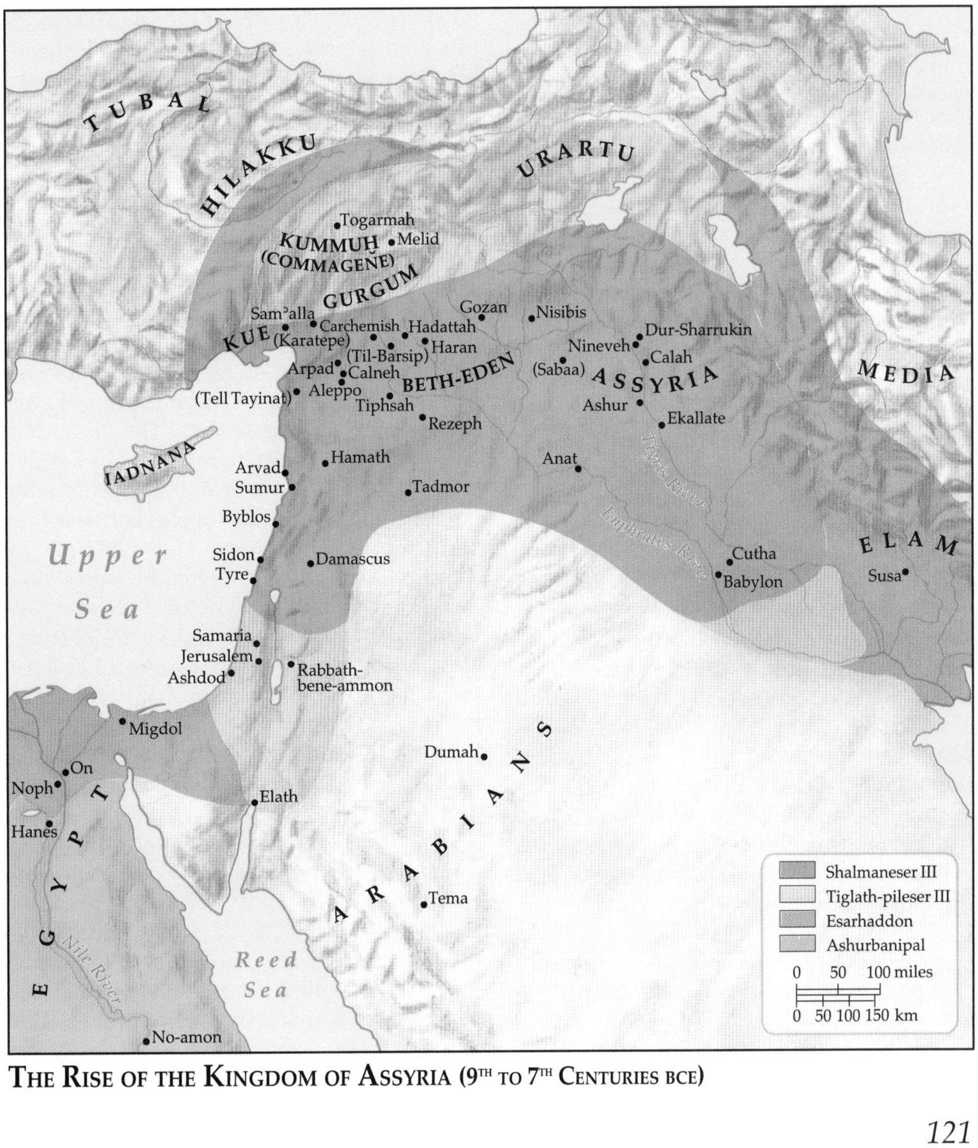


**The Rise of the Kingdom of Assyria (9th to 7th Centuries BCE)**

*Assyrian army attacks a city, on relief from the palace of Tiglath-pileser III at Calah.*

confirmation in his new post as king of Samaria.

> [The land of the House of Omri], in [its] entiret[y I conquered . . . with] their [pro]perty t[o the land of Assyria I transported. . . . Hoshea, to] the kingship over them [I appointed. He himself to the city of] Sarrabāni [came] into my presence. . . .
>
> (Summ. 9:9–11)

It has been duly noted that Sarrabāni was the correct reading here and that it evidently signified that Hoshea came before Tiglath-pileser III while the latter was campaigning in Babylonia. In accordance with the Eponym Chronicle the king of Assyria campaigned to Sapia/Shapia (in the territory of Bīt-Amuqāni) during the year 731 BCE and the Babylonian Chronicle reports:

> The third year of (Nabû)-mukin-zēri: When Tiglath-pileser went down to the land of Akkad, he ravaged Bīt-Amuqāni and captured (Nabû)-mukin-zēri.
>
> (Chronicle I, ll. 19–21)

Now Sarrabāni is also in the territory of Bīt-Shilāni which is associated with Bīt-Amuqāni. So it was observed that Hoshea must have gone to Babylonia to meet Tiglath-pileser III in 731 BCE. That was the year after he had slain his predecessor.

Hoshea came into possession of the throne in the twentieth year of Jotham (2 Kgs 15:30), i.e. in 732/731 BCE. So in that same year he evidently presented himself before Tiglath-pileser in southern Babylonia in order to get recognition as a loyal vassal of Assyria.

## The Last Days of Israel

The final years of the kingdom of Israel/Samaria are somewhat obscured by a paucity of unequivocal written sources. The successor to Tiglath-pileser III was Shalmaneser V, from whose five-year reign there remains practically no documentation. Therefore, the course of events in Samaria has been the subject of many efforts and explanations. The Babylonian Chronicle devotes only four lines to his reign.

> On the twenty-fifth day of the month of Tebet, Shalmaneser took his seat on the throne of the land of Assyria ‹and Akkad›. The city of Samaria he ravaged. Fifth (regnal) year, Shalmaneser died; five years Shalmaneser ruled. (col. I, 27–32)

Meanwhile, the Book of Kings includes a brief summary of the reign of Hoshea and his relations with Shalmaneser and the subsequent siege and capture of Samaria. The editor of the Deuteronomistic history, in his effort to arrange the kings of Israel and Judah in chronological order, did not realize that there was a twelve- year overlap between Menahem/Pekahiah and Pekah. So on his own initiative he sought to make four synchronisms (2 Kgs 17:1, 18:1, 18:9 and 18:10) which are twelve years in error. This has led to untold confusion among scholars and made it virtually impossible to properly reconstruct the course of events (*see* 2 Kgs 17:1–6).

How to coordinate this biblical passage with what little is known from Assyrian sources is a challenging issue. The reference to Shalmaneser's coming up against Hoshea does not require a personal visit by the Assyrian king. It will be seen with regard to Sargon II that even if the Eponym Chronicle says the king stayed in the land (712 BCE), an Assyrian army was sent to the west under the command of the *turtānu* (Isa 20:1). Therefore, the statement here in Kings does not require that the Assyrian monarch actually came to Samaria himself. Not long after his accession to the throne, he evidently sent an army to the west to assure that the change in rulers was having no affect on the loyalty of the sworn vassals of Levantine states. So in 726 BCE, Hoshea's tribute was now addressed to Shalmaneser V. The treachery of Hoshea probably took place in 725 BCE. Another disputed detail is the recipient of Hoshea's message sent by (two) ambassadors to Egypt. It has been suggested that "So" is a short form of the name Osorkon, in this case, Osorkon IV. The spelling, Shilkanni, in the cuneiform records of Sargon II, shows that Osorkon's pronunciation was quite different. The only truly credible suggestion is that "So" is a reference to the western capital of Sais established by Tefnakht. The required emendation is "to So ‹to the› king of Egypt" (2 Kgs 17:4). There is nothing intrinsically "gratuitous" about this logical and sensible correction to the text. The Pharaoh in question was surely Tefnakht, who had reasserted his authority in the delta after the withdrawal of Piye/Pi-ᶜankhy in 734 BCE. Tefnakht must have had a reign of at least eight years and that was probably from 733 to 726/725 BCE. He also had authority to deal with a land donation northeast of Bubastis so he surely had authority over the entire delta.

It has long been logically inferred that the three years when the objective of an Assyrian campaign is broken off from the Eponym entries must refer to Samaria. Obviously, this is only a conjecture and it takes for granted the biblical statement about a three-year siege of Samaria by Shalmaneser V. But why not? Until conflicting evidence of an unequivocal nature is forthcoming, it is just as reasonable to assume that the Eponym Chronicle really did refer to Samaria. The treasonous intrigue with the king of Egypt would thus fall near the end of Tefnakht's tenure, i.e. 725 BCE, just when Shalmaneser V was staying "in [the land]"; the following three years of siege would be 725, 724 and 723 BCE.

> Now in the ›~~fourth year of King Hezekiah, which was the~~‹ seventh year of Hoshea son of Elah king of Israel, Shalmaneser king of Assyria came up against Samaria and besieged it.
>
> At the end of three years they captured it; in the ›~~sixth year of Hezekiah, which was the~~‹ ninth year of Hoshea king of Israel, Samaria was captured.
>
> (2 Kgs 18:9–10)

This insert into the discussion of the reign of Hezekiah was made on the initiative of the Deuteronomist; its two synchronisms with the reign of Hezekiah are erroneous by twelve years. However, the actual notice about the three-year siege of Samaria is based on an accurate record, evidently from a northern source that most likely was brought to Jerusalem, or composed there by an Israelite prophet who had come seeking refuge. Since Hoshea began to rule in 732/731 BCE, his sixth year would be 726/725 and his ninth year would be 723/722 BCE. These years correspond to those entries in the Eponym Chronicle for which the name of the place being attacked is broken away. Can this be a pure coincidence? Surely not.

From 2 Kings 17:4 it would appear that Hoshea was arrested and taken prisoner to

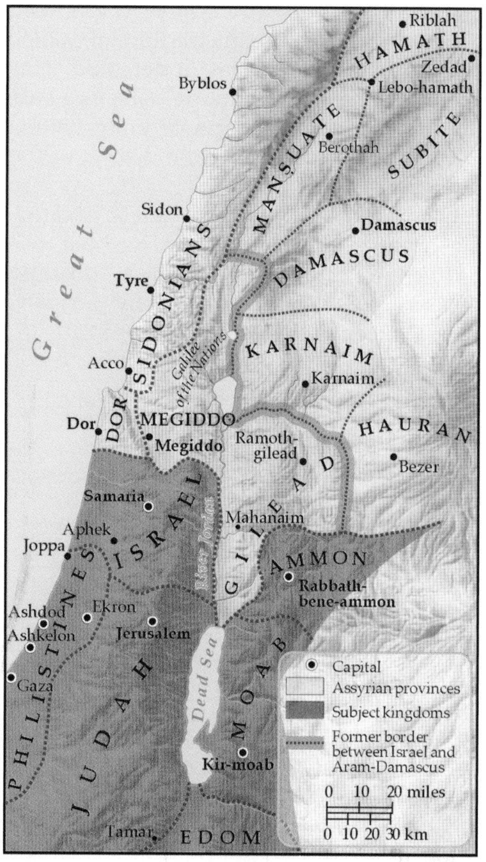


**The Assyrian Districts in the Days of Tiglath-pileser III (732 BCE)**

Assyria at the very beginning of the siege. The Israelite king may have come forth to plead for forgiveness from Shalmaneser hoping to get the same treatment afforded by Tiglath-pileser III to Hanun of Gaza. If so, he was sadly mistaken.

## The XXVth Egyptian (Cushite) Dynasty

The last quarter of the eighth century BCE saw a dramatic development in Egypt. Strong rulers of the land of Cush were able to exploit the internal fragmentation of authority in Egypt that marked Dynasty XXIV and to establish their control over upper and then also lower Egypt.

The first documented incursion of a Cushite ruler is that of Piye (Pi-ᶜankhy). According to the most recent data analysis, this campaign was launched in 734 BCE. That would have been just the year that Tiglath-pileser III carried out his attack on Philistia, Gaza in particular. It is no wonder that when Hanun of Gaza fled to Egypt, he decided to return to Gaza and try his fortunes as a suppliant to Tiglath-pileser III. He must have sought refuge with Tefnakht or perhaps one of the eastern delta rulers, but when he saw the approach of the Nubian king, he realized that his protector was himself in mortal danger.

Later contacts with the southern Levant will be dealt with in the ensuing discussion of Assyrian military actions in the last two decades of the eighth century BCE.

## The Reign of Sargon II

Though Shalmaneser V apparently died a natural death, his demise was the occasion for serious disturbances in Assyria. The winner was Sargon II (722–705 BCE) who mentioned that he "... pardoned 6,300 guilty Assyrians and showed mercy on them and settled them in Hamath." Those were evidently military personnel that had opposed Sargon's bid for power. But the transition was quick. Shalmaneser V is said to have died in the month of Tebet and Sargon is said to have taken his seat on the throne of Assyria on the twelfth day of that same month and three months later, Marduk-apla-iddina II (Merodach-baladan) became king of Babylon. Thus began the career of the true successor (in deed if not in fact) of Tiglath-pileser III. His reign was marked by the construction of a new capital, Dūr-Sharrukin (Khorsabad), at home and by dynamic campaigning on all the major fronts of the empire. His military exploits are legion but the focus herein will be those activities that directly impinged on the Levant.

What appears to be Sargon's first military engagement must not be overlooked. In 720 BCE the king of Elam, Khumbanigash I,

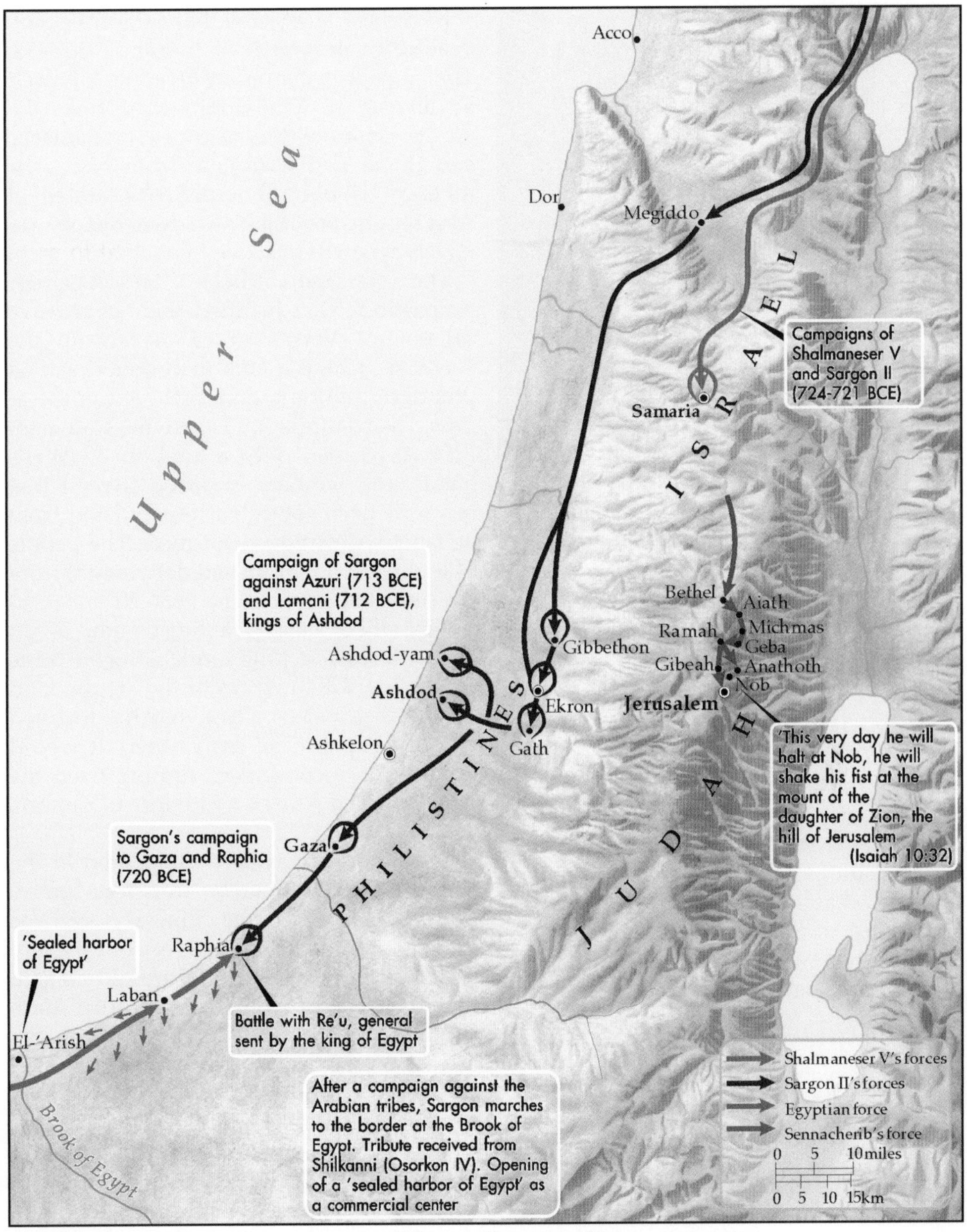


**The Campaigns of Shalmaneser V and Sargon II (724–712 BCE)**

inflicted a serious defeat on the Assyrian army in the district of Dēr (Tell ᶜAqar) on the plain east of the Tigris. According to the Babylonian report, it was a humiliating rout:

> Khumbanigash, king of Elam, in the district of Dēr, fought with Sargon, king of the land of Assyria; he brought about the retreat of the land of Assyria, their massive defeat he accomplished.
>
> (Chronicle I, 33–35)

In most of his own inscriptions, Sargon claims to have defeated Khumbanigash. It makes good sense to assume that the news of that defeat on the field of battle spread rapidly and encouraged people in the Levant to dare to rise in revolt. The preparations may have been underway earlier, upon the death of Shalmaneser V and the ensuing disturbances.

In his second regnal year, Sargon reports that Ilu-biʾdi (also called Iaʾu-biʾdi) of Hamath organized a coalition. This is further elaborated in other passages which show that Samaria was clearly implicated. Obviously, the reorganization of the Samarian province had only been started by the time Shalmaneser V had died.

> Il[u-biʾdi of Ha]math, not the rightful holder of the throne, not fit(?) for the palace, who in the shepherdship of his people, did [not attend to their] fate, [but] with regard to the god Ashur, his land (and) his people, he sought evil, not good, and he treated [them] with contempt. He assembled Arpad and Samaria, and he turned (them) to his side....
>
> (The Ashur "Charter" 17–28)

A more detailed list of the states that joined Ilu-biʾdi shows how widespread was the revolt:

> **Iaʾu-biʾdi from Hamath**, a peasant and not a candidate for the throne, a miserable Hittite, plotted to become king of **Hamath**, persuaded the cities of **Arpad**, **Ṣimirru**, **Damascus** and **Samaria** to desert me, caused them to work together and he organized an attack. I called up the masses of the troops of Ashur and laid siege to him and his warriors in Qarqar, his beloved city. I conquered it and I burned it. Himself I flayed. The rebels I slew in their cities and restored peace and quiet. I assembled two hundred chariots, six hundred cavalry from among

*Sargon II, on relief from his palace at Khorsabad.*

the people of Hamath, and I added (them) to my royal contingent.

(Great Display Inscription, ll. 33–36a)

The coastal provinces and also Damascus and Samaria were involved. Those were provinces of the Assyrian Empire but still their populations were anxious to escape from Assyrian domination. The link between Ilu-biʾdi of Hamath and Samaria confirms that all the other references to a conquest of Samaria by Sargon have to do with this military campaign of 720 BCE. It is not that Sargon II is usurping a deed of Shalmaneser V. Nor is it necessary to see a conflation of two Assyrian kings in 2 Kings 17:3–6. For examples of Sargon's own claim, the following passages are significant:

The city of Samaria I besieged and I conquered. 27,290 people who resided in it I took as booty. I conscripted fifty chariots from them and the rest I had instructed in their proper behavior. My eunuch I appointed over them, and I imposed on them the tribute like the previous king.

(Great Display Inscription, ll. 23–25)

[The Sa]marians who conspired with a [hostile] king to not render servitude [and to not re]nder tribute, opened hostilities. In the strength of the great gods, my [lor]ds, I engaged them. [2]7,280 people with their char[iots] and the deities, their helpers, I counted as spoil. Two hundred chariots for [my] roy[al] contingent I conscripted from among them. The rest of them I settled within the land of Assyria. The city of Samaria I resettled and made it greater than before. People of the lands conquered by my own hands I installed there. My eunuch I appointed over them as governor and I reckoned them as people of Assyria.

(Nimrud Prism, Fragment D, 25–41)

Sargon also claimed to be "the subduer of the land of Judah the location of which is far away" (Nimrud Prism). The inscription mentions other military achievements spanning the years 720 to 716 BCE while the Judah reference precedes the mention of the rebel king of Hamath. It therefore seems natural to assume that Sargon's contact with Judah has to do with the campaign to the west in 720 BCE.

It has been suggested that Sargon's action against Judah is reflected in Isaiah 10:27–32. The passage declaims an itinerary followed by an enemy who approached from the north, i.e. from the territory of Samaria, and threatened Jerusalem from Nob. The itinerary is part of a pericope aimed at Assyria and its role in current history (*see* Isa 10:5–11).

The passage echoes the Assyrian propaganda that justified their aggressive campaigns. Verses 13 to 14 recount the Assyrian achievements in conquering and plundering all the nations of the ancient Near East. The continuation is a divine statement that Assyria is only a tool in YHWH's hands; the remnant of Jacob (Israel) that has now been subjected to expulsion from its land, will still have a future. The people of Jerusalem are promised deliverance from the Assyrian threat (*see* Isa 10:24–27).

Next there ensues a description of an enemy force marching south along the route that follows the margin of the steppe land on the east, perhaps to avoid the fortified city of Mizpah (Tell en-Naṣbeh). It would be a military contingent coming from the newly formed Assyrian province of Samaria (*see* Isa 10:28–32).

The itinerary has been elucidated in the framework of the known Iron Age routes. The places along the itinerary can be identified with varying degrees of certainty but those that are confirmed are sufficient to define the general course of the route: Aiath (Kh. Ḥaiyân?), Migron (perhaps Kh. Tell el-ʿAskar), Michmash (Mukhmâs), Ramah (er-Râm), Geba (Jebaʿ), Gibeah of Saul (probably Tell el-Fûl), Gallim (probably Kh. Kaʿkûl), Laishah (the Iron Age fort on French Hill?), Anathoth (Râs el-Kharrûbeh), Madmenah and Gebim (unidentified; ʿIsāwîyeh could be one of them), Nob (Râs el-Meshârif or eṭ-Ṭûr).

The assignment of this itinerary to the campaign of Sargon II is conjectural but not impossible. The fact that Judah does not play an active role in other Sargonic royal texts suggests that its submission was immediate and that no extensive military force was necessary. Perhaps a force was sent south from Samaria to threaten Jerusalem into obedience to the Assyrian authority. Ahaz had been a loyal tribute bearer to Tiglath-pileser III. If he lapsed during the attempted rebellion of Hoshea, there is no record of it anywhere.

The final battle of this campaign of 720 BCE was fought at Raphia:

Rēʾê, his [commander] set forth to his a[i]d to conduct battle and war against me. In the name of Ashur, my lord, I accomplished their defeat. [Rēʾ]ê fled alone like a shepherd whose flock has been robbed, and he disappeared. [Ḫa]nunu I seized by (my own) hand, in captivity I conducted him to my city, Ashur. [The city of] Raphia I razed, I destroyed and I burned with fire. Nine thousand and thirty-three people with their extensive property I plundered.

(Annals 53–57)

It seems that Hanun was also deeply involved in an intrigue with Egypt. But this time, it was with Piye (Pi-ʿankhy) who had secured control of the delta. The Cushite king had pushed his authority from No-amon (Thebes; modern Luxor) to the northernmost extremity of Egypt and now he saw the chance to capitalize on his new position to establish ties with the southern Levant. The original entry of the Annals is best preserved in a display inscription:

Ḫanunu king of Gaza with Rēʾê the commander of the land of Egypt set forth to do war and battle against me at Raphia. Their defeat I accomplished. Rēʾê feared the sound of my weapons and he fled, his whereabouts unknown. Ḫanunu king of Gaza I seized with (my own) hand.

(Great Display Inscription, ll. 25–26)

For the tenth regnal year (712 BCE) the Eponym Chronicle states that Sargon "(remained) in the land." On the other hand, the Annals, the Display Inscriptions and the Nimrud Prism all speak of a campaign against Ashdod. However, the annalistic text assigns it to the eleventh regnal year (711 BCE) while the Nimrud Prism assigns it to the ninth regnal year, which in its system means 712 BCE. The arguments in favor of 712 BCE seem reasonable, especially in the light of the Eponym Chronicle which records that Sargon was "in the land." That entry is supported by the biblical reference to the campaign (*see* Isa 20:1).

On the other hand, Sargon's scribes/historians apparently were unwilling to give the *tartannu* his due. The best-preserved text is the Great Display Inscription:

As for ᴵAzūri, king of Ashdod, his heart schemed to not bring tribute; to the kings around him he wrote calumny against the land of Ashur in order that they commit wickedness. I abolished his lordship over his people. ᴵAḫimīti, his favorite brother, I appointed to the kingship over them. But the Hittites, congenital liars, hated his lordship;

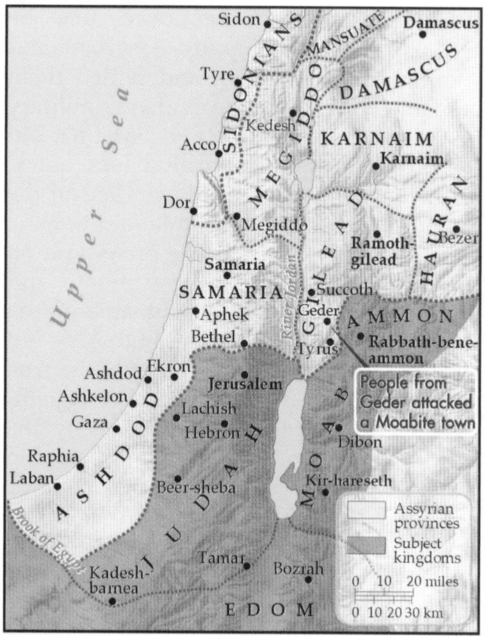


**THE DISTRICTS OF ASSYRIA IN THE DAYS OF SARGON II (733–716 BCE)**

ᴵYamāni, unqualified for the throne, who like them knew no respect for lordship, they elevated over them. In the anger of my heart, I did not assemble the mass of my troops; I did not organize my camp. With my warriors who never abandon my side even in a peacef[ul pla]ce, to the city of Ashdod I went and he, ᴵYamāni, heard from afar of the coming of my expeditionary force and up to the border of the land of Egypt which is on the border of the land of Meluḫḫa he fled; and his place was not found. The city of Ashdod, the city of Gath, the city of Ashdod-yam I surrounded, I captured; his gods, his wives, his sons, his daughters, the property, the possessions of the treasury of his palace, with the people of his land, I counted as spoil. I re[organized] those cities anew. People of lands of the conquest of my hand that are in the midst of the ex[tremity? of the] sunrise I [settled] within (them). [My eunuch as governor I placed over them.] I reckoned them as Assyrians; they pulled my harness.

The king of the land of Meluḫḫa that is in the midst of [. . .] - - - the land of Uriṣṣu, an inaccessible place, a [difficult] way which from distant days until now, his fathers never sent their mounted messengers to the kings, my fathers in order to inquire of their welfare, [heard] from f[ar] the might of the god Ashur, the [god Nabû, the god Marduk] and the fearful splendor of my royalty overwhelmed him; in a stock and manacles, [fe]tters of iron he cast him (Yamāni). To the heartland of Assyria, a distant road, to my presence [they] bro[ught] him.

(Great Display Inscription, ll. 90–111)

The parallel version in the Nimrud Prism has a few additional details of particular importance.

To the kings of the land of Philistia, the land of Judah, the land of Ed[om], the land of Moab, dwellers by the sea, bearers of tribute and audience gifts of ᵈAshur, my lord. ‹They wrote› treacherous words, treasonous speech, to cause enmity against me.

To Pharaoh, king of Egypt, a ruler who could not save them, they sent their greeting gift and they entreated him for reinforcements.

(Nimrud Prism VII.b, ll. 5b–33a)

It would seem obvious that the appeal to other states in the southern Levant did not bear fruit. None of them came to the aid of Ashdod. When Yamāni realized that he would have to stand alone against the Assyrian might, he fled.

The appeal to Pharaoh indicates that they had applied to one of the delta rulers, evidently Osorkon IV, though a ruler in Sais is also possible.

There is no date given for the removal of Azūri and his replacement by Aḫimīti, his brother. That could have been an administrative act during any of the years between 720 and 712 BCE. But one might surmise that it happened not long before 712 BCE. The correspondence between the Ashdodites and the neighboring kings must be behind the warning of Isaiah to Hezekiah about the Assyrian superiority over Cush and Egypt (Isa 20).

The description of Yamāni's flight to Egypt is also illuminating. He did not find refuge with Pharaoh. Instead he had to flee "up to the border of the land of Egypt which is on the border of the land of Meluḫḫa," i.e.

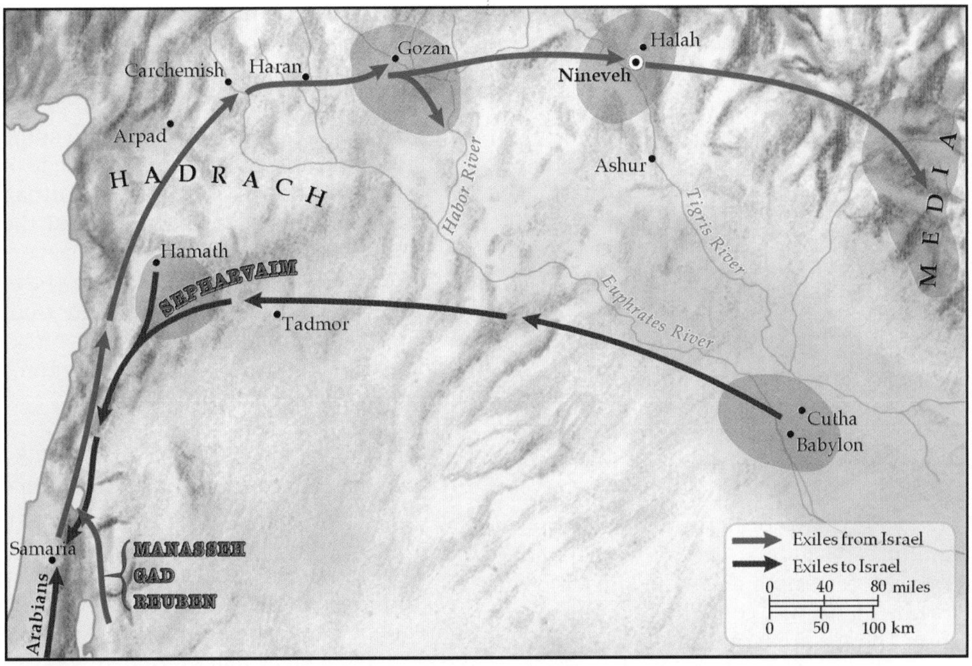


**The Exile of Peoples to and from Israel under the Assyrians (734–712 BCE)**

as far as Aswân, biblical Syene (Ezek 29:10, 30:6). For about five years he did receive political asylum with Shabako king of Cush.

The year 705 BCE was Sargon's seventeenth regnal year. The very broken entry in the Babylonian Chronicle shows that the king was in Tabal, but the Eponym Chronicle has:

(Eponym) Nasḫur-bēl governor of the city of Amedi: the king [went forth(?)] in confrontation with ᴵQurdî the Kulummāyu.

The venue of this fatal battle was the land of Tabal but the enemy is otherwise unknown. There is speculation that Qurdî was a Cimmerian. The evidence is scanty but Qurdî (formerly Eshpai) is otherwise unknown as is his ethnicon Kulummāyu. It is certainly possible that Sargon was called to Tabal by one of his local vassals or provincial governors, or perhaps by Midas himself. The death of this powerful ruler is thus shrouded in mystery. As the news spread across the empire, peoples everywhere saw an opportunity to throw off the oppressive Assyrian yoke.

## Hezekiah of Judah Stands Alone

During the reign of Sargon II, king of Assyria, the small kingdom of Judah had continued to pay tribute as a vassal state. It may have been necessary for Sargon to make a show of force (Isa 10:28–32) in 720 BCE but otherwise, there was no apparent need to coerce Ahaz to continue his payments. Ahaz died in 715 BCE and was succeeded by his son, Hezekiah, who reigned twenty-nine years (715–686 BCE, accession year system). The Deuteronomist records three late artificial synchronisms that are twelve years in error: his accession in the third year of Hoshea (2 Kgs 18:1), his fourth year with Hoshea's seventh year (2 Kgs 18:9), and his sixth year with the ninth year of Hoshea (2 Kgs 18:10). The late, final (exilic) editor of the history had data at his disposal from the Chronicles of the Kings of Israel, which must have been brought from Israel (Shechem?) to Jerusalem, but he did not know about the twelve-year overlap between Pekah and Menahem. The firm reference to Hezekiah's fourteenth year when Sennacherib came to attack Judah in 701 BCE (2 Kgs 18:13) is the chronological anchor for this period.

The Chronicler gives considerable detail about the beginning of Hezekiah's reign that is missing in the Deuteronomistic history. The authenticity of this material is often challenged and requires the scrutiny of external evidence for its general confirmation. There is an account of the restoration of the worship services in the Jerusalem temple (thus cancelling the arrangements made by Ahaz; 2 Chr 29:3–36). This is followed by the conduct of a great Passover as a national festival (2 Chr 30). Both of those events are decried by critics of the Chronicler who consider them inventions from the post-exilic period.

The Passover pericope includes geographical information that has an authentic ring (*see* 2 Chr 30:1). The messengers were said to have gone "from Beer-sheba to Dan" (2 Chr 30:5) and they received a varied response (*see* 2 Chr 30:10–11, 30:18).

Naphtali is not mentioned. It could well be that that area had been so long under foreign domination (Aramean and Assyrian) that there was no one interested in the ancient ties to Jerusalem. The text of the invitation letter itself, if it is fiction, does fit the circumstances of the times, making mention of the Assyrians as their

*Conquest of Ekron, on relief from palace of Sargon II at Khorsabad.*

captors and not confusing later enemies of the Jews.

Only if the northern areas, such as Samaria, Megiddo, etc., were under Assyrian governors and not under a rival Israelite monarchy, could this activity make sense. The Assyrian officials would not care about religious festivals unless they affected the tribute payments and law and order in their provinces.

The next act on the part of Hezekiah was to make a sweeping reform of the countryside by closing the local cult centers (*see* 2 Chr 31:1). In this, the Chronicler's report (2 Chr 31:1) is already recorded in the Deuteronomistic history, albeit with little detail (*see* 2 Kgs 18:4; cf. 2 Kgs 18:22).

It would also seem highly probable that Judah had recovered most, if not all, of the towns that had been overtaken by the Philistines during the crisis with Tiglath-pileser III (2 Chr 28:18). That can be deduced from the fact that other Philistine towns in the inner coastal plain had been punished by Sargon II, viz. Gibbethon, Ekron and Gath. This is obviously hinted in Isaiah's oracle (*see* Isa 14:28–29).

Ahaz is obviously depicted as the "rod that smote" Philistia. This in spite of the fact that no mention of any counter-military activity on the part of Ahaz is recorded in the Deuteronomistic history or in the Book of Chronicles.

Hezekiah's policy of obedience under Sargon II had allowed him to reap tremendous profits from the caravan trade (*see* 2 Chr 32:27–29). There is ample evidence for the extensive buildup of the kingdom of Judah during the late eighth century BCE. This was expecially evident in the Shephelah facing Philistia.

As discussed above, Isaiah had warned Hezekiah not to respond to the cry for assistance from Ashdod, in 712 BCE (*see* Isa 20:1–6).

Instead, Hezekiah paid his tribute as expected. So long as Sargon was alive and active, the nations of the Levant feared to violate their respective oaths to the god Ashur and to the king of Assyria. Even the new king of Cush, Shebitku, had made a conciliatory jesture by extraditing Yamāni. That action was hardly a secret among the Levantine states, especially in Philistia. So it appeared that the eastern Mediterranean seaboard was solidly in the Assyrian political and economic camp. However, when the news spread about the death of the tyrant, Sargon, and the apparent sacrilege of his body not receiving its honorable burial, this was taken by peoples throughout the empire as a signal for rebellion. Soothsayers and prophets everywhere must have heralded Sargon's demise as a sign from heaven, a call to freedom from the Assyrian yoke. But they did not reckon with Sargon's vigorous heir, Sennacherib.

**Rebellion Against Assyria (705–701 BCE).** The biblical allusion to Hezekiah's rebellion seems to be expressed as an act of bravery and honor (*see* 2 Kgs 18:7). A first glance might even give the impression that YHWH was with the king in his decision to rebel. Subsequent implications from the Assyrian record make it clear that Hezekiah was not only a party to but even the ring leader in all the plans made by the conspirators of the southern Levant, including the reliance on promises of support from the XXV[th] Dynasty. On the contrary, the prophetic writers glossed over much of Hezekiah's political connivance. It is absolutely certain that Hezekiah accepted Pādî, king of Ekron, as a political prisoner (cf. *infra*) but the biblical passages pertaining to Hezekiah's reign maintain absolute silence about that drastic and ultimately stupid maneuver. In fact, all the biblical pericopes describing the war with Assyria go overboard in glorifying Hezekiah and Jerusalem. They show little compassion for the savaged residents of other Judean towns, many of whom were pinned to the ground alive while the skin was peeled off their backs by the Assyrian conquerors. Nevertheless, there are some distinct protests (*see* Isa 30:1–5; also Isa 31:1–3).

Though it is not agreed by all that these passages refer to the preparations for the war with Sennacherib, there is really no reason to exclude them. As will become obvious from the inscriptions of Sennacherib, Shebitku, the Cushite ruler of Dynasty XXV, promised support to the rebels. The city-states of Phoenicia and Philistia as well as inland states like Ammon, Moab, and Edom joined in the revolt and ceased to pay their tribute. That, too, will become obvious from Sennacherib's account of how those nations hastened to Phoenicia to pay up their back taxes (cf. *infra*).

There may have been several factors that led the vassal states in the east and in the west to assume that Assyria had stretched its resources beyond its capabilities and that it was no longer able to suppress the uprisings that they were planning.

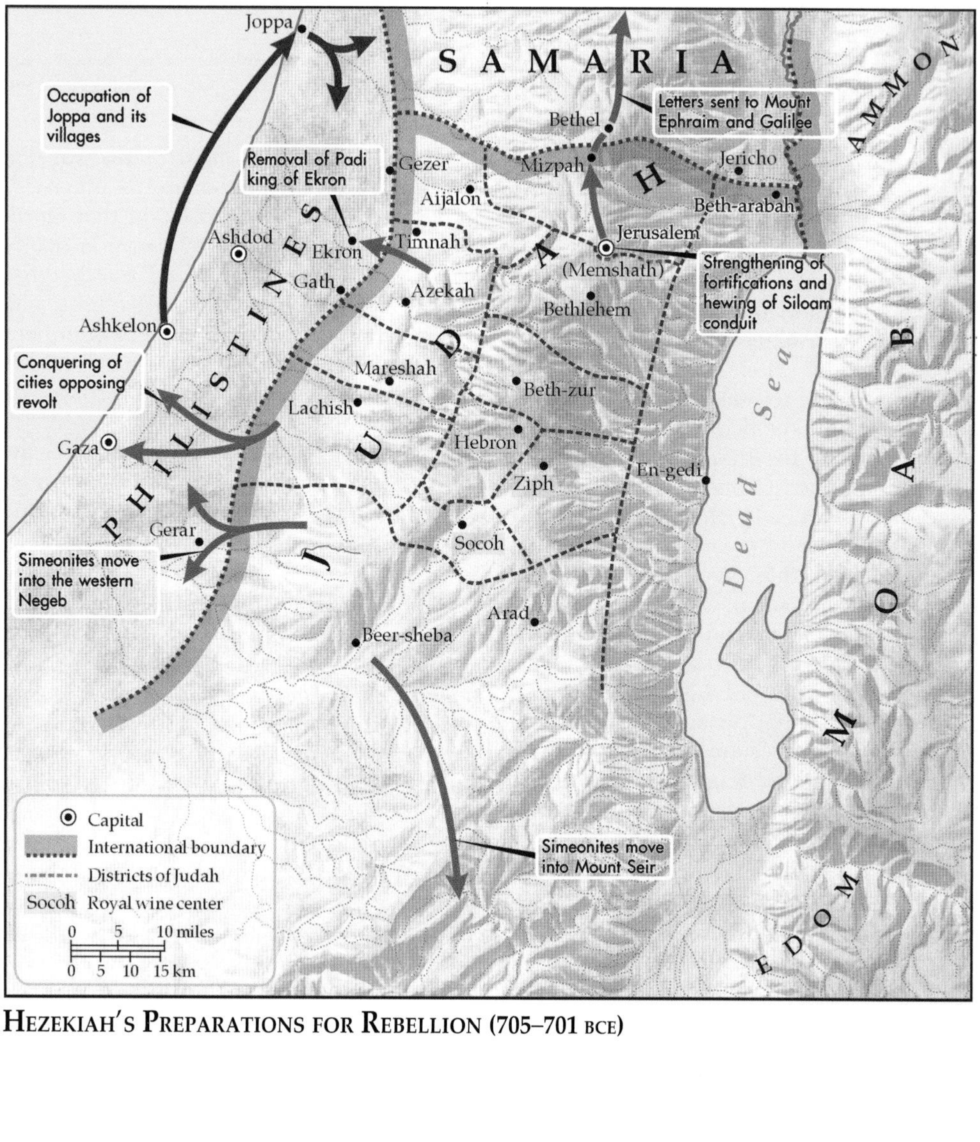


**HEZEKIAH'S PREPARATIONS FOR REBELLION (705–701 BCE)**

*Especially prominent among the provisions stored by Hezekiah throughout the kingdom were four-handled wine jars from the royal wineries, found in nearly every site of military importance in the north and west of Judah. The four place names (clockwise from top left: Ziph, MMŠT, Hebron and Socoh) stamped on these jars represent centers where wine was collected from the royal vineyards. All four places are in the Judean hill country, two in the south, one in the center, and one presumably in the north. The jars do not represent an exact measure but were of a more-or-less standard size. Their inscription,* **lmlk**, *simply means "royal property."*

During the final stages of the completion of Sargon's new capital, Dūr-Sharrukin, a plague broke out. Some allusions in broken contexts suggest that the epidemic had appeared in Damascus and in Riblah in the Lebanese Beqaᶜ. There was also a drain on economic resources and manpower during Sargon's extensive military campaigns and his public building projects.

Hezekiah used his resources to make Judah an armed camp, with newly fortified towns and fresh weapons (2 Chr 32:5). Provisions were stored in the fortresses throughout the kingdom (2 Chr 32:27–30).

Engineering projects for assuring the water supply in the fortified cities were also undertaken, in particular the Siloam tunnel from the Gihon spring (*see* 2 Chr 32:2–18, 30–31; cf. also 2 Kgs 20:20).

The king of Ashkelon gained control of Joppa and its agricultural hinterland. The people of Ekron supported the anti-Assyrian plot but their ruler, Pādî, did not. He was deposed and handed over to Hezekiah to be imprisoned in Jerusalem. Gath and Gezer apparently became Judean strongholds as attested by the finds of *lmlk* jar handles at each of these sites; Azekah was another. Lachish and Libnah were the chief centers in the southwestern Shephelah.

*The Siloam tunnel, Jerusalem.*

Ṣil-Baal, king of Gaza, refused to cooperate, so Hezekiah sent his troops to occupy Philistine strong points in the western Negeb (*see* 2 Kgs 18:8). The Simeonites were encouraged to settle there (1 Chr 4:39–41) and also to take (western) Mount Seir from the Amalekites (1 Chr 4:42–43).

In collusion with the leading officials of Ekron, Hezekiah agreed to imprison their ruler, Pādî, since he refused to support the rebellion against Sennacherib.

> The officials, the nobles and the people of ᶜ**Amqarōna** (= Ekron), who had thrown into iron fetters Pādî, their king, a sworn vassal of Ashur, and *handed him over to Hezekiah the Judean; he kept him in prison illegally as an enemy....*
>
> (Babylonian Chronicle II 73[69]–77[72])

During the frantic preparations for war, Hezekiah fell ill, but Isaiah assured him he would recover and live fifteen more years (2 Kgs 20:1–11; Isa 38:1–22), i.e. from 701 to 686 BCE (*see* 2 Kgs 20:1–6).

An embassage also arrived from Merodach-baladan who was still plotting against Sennacherib even though he was a political refugee in Elam (*see* Isa 39:1–2 || 2 Kgs 20:12–13).

## Sennacherib's Third Campaign

Sennacherib, Sargon's successor, was busy for the first few years with conflicts in the east and especially in Babylonia. His military campaigns are not dated according to eponyms or even regnal years; they are simply listed as "first campaign," "second campaign," etc.

When it became known that Sargon II was dead, Merodach-baladan, the Chaldean chieftain whom Sargon had driven out of Babylonia (710 BCE), had come back from exile, laid claim to the throne of Babylon, and mustered a large force, with chariotry and cavalry from Elam under the direction of their king, who was persuaded by prospects of plunder to support his protégé.

The first campaign of Sennacherib was, therefore, directed against Babylonia. Its record is preserved in a detailed annalistic account (the Bellino Cylinder) dated to the eponym of Nabû-lēʾi (702 BCE), as well as the later, more concise versions (Rassam, Taylor and Chicago prisms). The campaign began late in the year 703 BCE when Merodach-baladan had assembled a large force of Chaldeans, Arameans, and Elamites and had taken up positions at Kish. Sennacherib sent ahead to Kish a contingent which immediately engaged the enemy stationed there. The king in the interval proceeded to attack another enemy force at Cutha; he captured the city and then rushed to the aid of his embattled troops in the plain of Kish. Merodach-baladan fled the scene of battle and the allied army was defeated. Sennacherib continued on to Babylon, where he plundered the rich palace stores but left the city itself unharmed. He continued southward in pursuit of Merodach-baladan in the marshes, burning a string of towns along the way. Nonetheless, Merodach-baladan was not apprehended. Sennacherib then concentrated on eliminating rebellious factions in the larger cities: Uruk, Nippur, Kish, Khursagkalama, Cutha, and Sippar. He placed Bel-ibni on the Babylonian throne, a Babylonian by descent who had been raised at the Assyrian court. On the return march (already in 702 BCE), he captured and plundered numerous Aramean groups and he forcibly extorted tribute from Ḫirimmu. Finally he received voluntary tribute from Nabu-bel-shumati, ruler of Ḫararate.

It seemed necessary, shortly afterwards, to conduct a campaign eastward into the Zagros Mountains against the Kassites. He was also sent tribute from the Medes. Obviously, this campaign was concerned with restoring Assyria's military and commercial interests from that quarter.

Much sooner than the rebels had expected, Sennacherib appeared in the west. He was now on his third military campaign and arrived with his army in 701 BCE. The Rassam Cylinder was written in the eponymy of Mitunu (700 BCE) and gives the earliest official account of the third campaign. The campaigns of Sennacherib are usually studied in the more complete texts (with all eight known campaigns) of the Chicago and Taylor prisms. The Chicago Prism was inscribed in the eponymy of Gaḫilu/Giḫilu (689 BCE). The Taylor Prism was written two years earlier, in the eponymy of Bēl-ēmuranni (691 BCE). It is those combined texts that will be cited in the ensuing discussions. The principal citations are from the Chicago text with the line numbers of the Taylor Prism in brackets. The campaign is reported in logical, mainly chronological stages. On occasion some later incident or detail, not

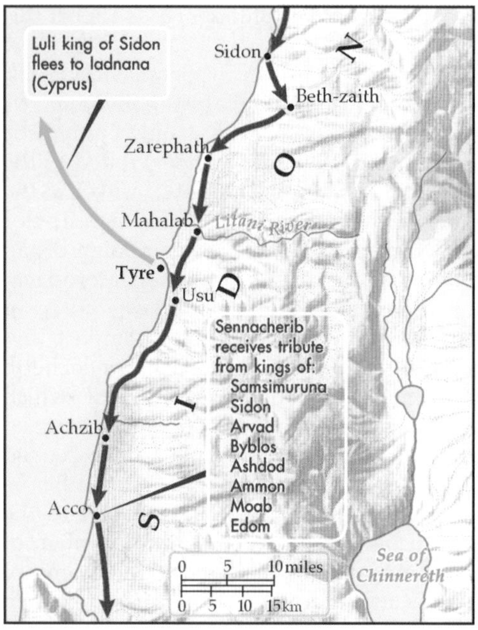


**Sennacherib's Reconquest of Phoenicia (701 bce)**

known to the recorder in the immediate wake of the campaign, is added in the later editions of Sennacherib's military career. When transcribing geographical and personal names, the evidence of other inscriptions and of comparative Semitics have been employed. In the translations and discussion, biblical spellings are used as much as possible though consistency is not always feasible or desirable.

The progress of the campaign is recorded in logical geographical and chronological order but some departures from the norm will be noted.

**The Conquest of Phoenicia**. The first objective was conquest of the Phoenician coast; the rebellious leader, (E)lulî/Elulaios of Sidon, fled to Iadnana (Cyprus) where he later met his death. Ethobaal was appointed in his place.

In my third campaign I marched to **the land of Ḫatti**. As for (E)lulî, king of **Sidon**, the terror inspiring splendor of my lordship overwhelmed him and he fled far away in the midst of the sea; there he met his fate. (II 37[34]–40[37])

The demise of (E)lulî/Elulaios in Cyprus is not recorded in the Rassam Cylinder from 700 bce. It first appears in the text of Cylinder C from the eponym of Nabû-dūru-uṣur (697 bce). That would lead to the assumption that the rebel Phoenician king died between 700 and 697 bce. A later text, Bull Inscription 4, evidently to be dated late in 694 or early in 693 bce, has an interesting variant about (E)lulî/Elulaios's flight and death:

As for (E)lulî king of Sidon, [my ter]ror inspiring spl[endor] overwhelmed him and he fled from within the city of Tyre to the land of Yadana (Cyprus) in the midst of the sea and he met his fate.

Although (E)lulî/Elulaios is called king of the city of Sidon, he is surely the Elulaios king of Tyre (*Ant.* 9:283–287). Much speculation has been spent on the reason for this later Assyrian entry. A plausible suggestion is that (E)lulî/Elulaios was king of Tyre but that Tyre was the senior Phoenician city at that time. Thus (E)lulî/Elulaios was at the same time king of the Sidonian nation, i.e. all the Phoenicians. Note that Sidonian(s) is the biblical generic name for Phoenicians.

When Sennacherib showed up with his vast army, (E)lulî/Elulaios evidently chose not to attempt to withstand a siege in his island fortress. Instead he fled to Kition which was his ally or, more likely, his vassal. However, Tyre did not surrender along with the other Phoenician cities. No one knows how the city finally must have reached an accommodation with the Assyrian overlord, but the appointment of (E)ttôbaᶜlu (Ethobaal) to the kingship suggests that a satisfactory arrangement was made.

Another overzealous composer of the Bull Inscriptions waxes eloquently on the fate of (E)lulî/Elulaios:

And (E)lulî, king of the city of Sidon, fled to the land of **Iadnana** which is in the midst of the sea; in that same year, by the flaming splendor of the weapon of Ashur, my lord, he went to his fate. (Layard 59–62 and Bull 2 and 3, ll. 17–19)

The reference to "that same year" seems to indicate that the scribes had more detailed notes from the campaign and that they exercised discretion in their use.

The other Phoenician cities were intimidated by the arrival of the mighty Assyrian army and they capitulated:

The terror of the weapon of Ashur, my lord, overwhelmed the city of **Great Sidon**, the city of **Little Sidon**, the city of **Beth-zaith**, the city of **Ṣariptu** (Zarephath), the city of **Maḫalliba**, the city of **Usû**, the city of **Achzib**, the city of **Acco**, his mighty fortified cities, where there was feed and water supply for his fortresses; they bowed in submission at my feet. I installed (E)tthō-baᶜl on the throne of their kingship over them; I imposed on him the tribute of my lordship, annually without cessation. (II 41[38]–49[46]; Rassam 33–35)

The fall of the Phoenician cities inspired fear in many of Hezekiah's erstwhile allies; they rushed to Usû to pay their tribute and renew their allegiance to Sennacherib.

*Seal impression: "(belonging to) Ebedeliab son of Shibᶜat, servant of Mitinti, son of Ṣidqâ."* (provenance unknown)

The sumptuous gifts and heavy tribute, fourfold, of Menaḥem the Šamši-Merōnite, (E)ttho-baᶜal the Sidonian, ᶜAbdi-līti the Arvadite, Urumilki the Gublite, Mittinti the Ashdodite, Bod-ᵓilu the Ammonite, Kemosh-nadbi the Moabite, Ayarâmu the Edomite, all the kings of the land of Amurru, they brought before me and they kissed my feet. (II 50[47]–59[58]; Rassam 36–38)

**The Conquest of Philistia**. Next comes an entry that seems to be out of chronological order. It is included in the Rassam Cylinder so its place in the composition was decided early on and it is not a later detail added in subsequent editions. But its inclusion here is associative. The list of those who hurried to pay up their back taxes and to profess allegiance brought to mind a glaring case of one Philistine king who did not submit. It seems highly unlikely that Sennacherib could have sent a delegation to Ashkelon from Usû (unless by sea?) to depose the recalcitrant ruler and replace him by another.

And as for *Ṣidqâ* the king of **Ashkelon** who had not submitted to my yoke, the gods of his house, himself, his wife, his sons, his daughters, his brothers, the seed of his house, I deported and I had him led off to Assyria. *Šarru-lū-dāri*, son of Rōkibti their former king, I placed over the people of Ashkelon, the payment of tribute, the gifts of my lordship, I imposed on him. He pulled my yoke. (II 60[58]–68[65];Rassam 39–40)

But the Ṣidqâ incident is included here, both for the contrast with the other local kings who had submitted and also because the next phase of the campaign brought Sennacherib to a strategic area where the stubborn ruler of Ashkelon had overstepped his bounds, viz. Joppa and its hinterland. There was no problem for Sennacherib's army to pass through the districts ruled by Assyrian governors, viz. at Megiddo and Samaria. They would have had supplies prepared in advance and would have seen to it that the roads were secure. The historian scribe does not bother to record the itinerary, whether along the coast or through the Jezreel and Sharon plains. The latter is more probable, of course, because the *kurkar* ridges and the swamps from Dor to Joppa did not make for easy passage.

In the course of my campaign, **Beth-dagan**, **Yāpô** (Joppa), **Bene-berak**, **Azor**, cities of Ṣidqâ who did not bow quickly at my feet, I surrounded, I conquered, their spoil I took away. (II 68 [65]–72 [68]; Rassam 4)

These cities, Joppa and its supporting towns, were essential for the securing of an efficient logistic supply line via the seaport. They represent the western extremity of the corridor from Joppa to Gibbethon. The latter, or eastern part, was most likely firmly in Assyrian hands already being controlled by the governor of Samaria.

One of the prime cities of the revolt was Ekron. Its leading citizens wanted to rebel but their king, Pādî, refused. So they put him in irons and handed him over to Hezekiah who kept him imprisoned until the threats of Sennacherib forced him to release the hapless vassal. The biblical accounts ignore this incident and that is hardly accidental. It would severely tarnish the image of King Hezekiah, the persecuted saint and hero of the deliverance of Jerusalem.

> As for the officials, the nobles and the people of ᶜ**Aqqarōna** (=Ekron), who had thrown into iron fetters **Pādî**, their king, a sworn vassal of Ashur, and *handed him over to Hezekiah the Judean; he kept him in prison illegally as an enemy*, their heart feared.
> (II 73 [69]–78[73]; Rassam 42–43)

Sennacherib's text assigns the call for Egyptian and Cushite help to the leaders of Ekron. But there can be no doubt that Hezekiah was party to the invitation.

> They called out for the **kings of the land of Egypt**, an army of bowmen, charioteers, and horses of the **king of the land of Cush**, a host without number; they came to their aid. In the vicinity of the city of **Altaqô** (Eltekeh) they were arraigned in battle order against me and they were sharpening their weapons. Trusting in Ashur, my lord, I engaged them in combat and I accomplished their defeat. The charioteers and the sons of the kings of Egypt with the charioteers of the king of Cush, my own hands captured alive. (II 78[73]–III 6[82]; Rassam 43–45)

The textual versions that speak of "**kings**" of Egypt has been chosen here because it may reflect the situation under Dynasty XXV. Some local rulers in the delta were still in place although they now owed service to the king of Cush. It does not appear that the Cushite king was in the field with his troops or else he managed to avoid capture. Princes, sons of the Egyptian kings, were captured along with charioteers from Cush. No Cushite ruler is said to have been captured.

The venue for this clash was "in the vicinity of the city of Eltekeh." This latter site is not identified securely; it appears in the "Danite" town list (Josh 19:44) and it was one of the Levitical cities assigned to the "tribal inheritance" of Dan (Josh 21:23). The proposal to locate it at Tell esh-Shallâf (Tel Shalaf) suits admirably the function of Levitical cities as frontier outposts. Tell esh-Shallâf is about 2 miles (4 km) north of Jabneh; it marks the fork of the major road from Jabneh with one branch continuing northward to Beth-dagon and the other turns northeast toward Lod. It is a relatively high mound compared to others in the vicinity and affords a view of the coastal plain, the Mediterranean, and the Shephelah in all directions except the northeast, where three or four small hills block the view. A wide range of Iron Age pottery has been found in surface surveys. Eltekeh, if located here, would have been marking the frontier of Solomon's second district (the so-called Danite territory) facing Philistia to the south (a typical Levitical function). It also looks down on a plain suitable for the battle depicted by Sennacherib.

It has been argued that the battle at Eltekeh actually took place late in the campaign (after the conquest of Lachish)

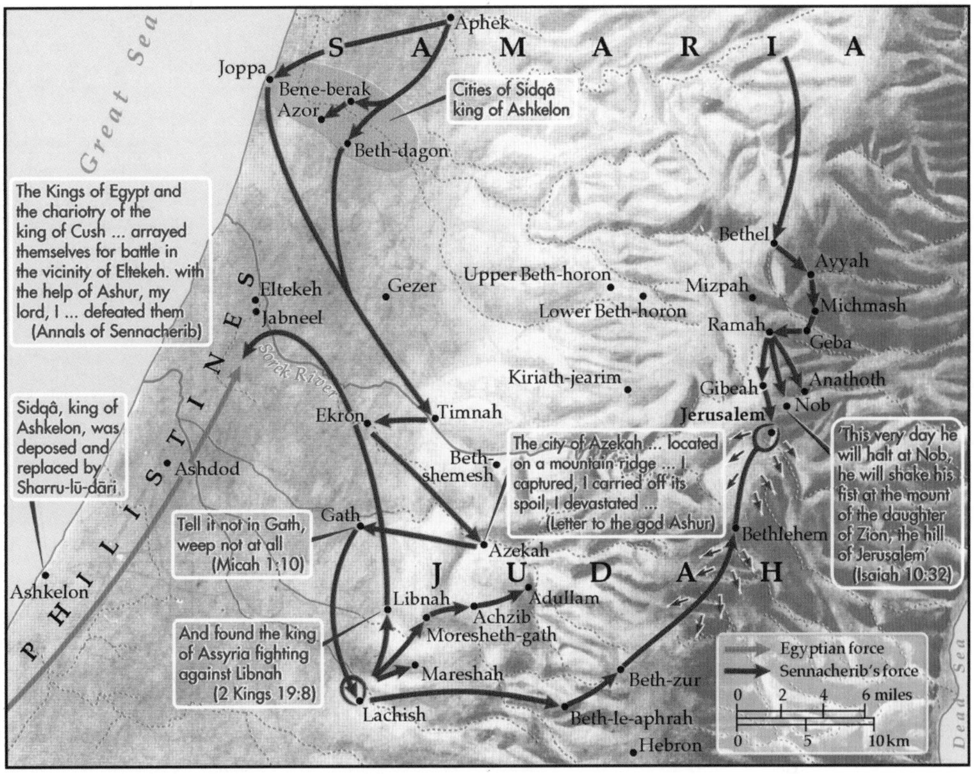


**SENNACHERIB IN PHILISTIA AND JUDAH (701 BCE)**

but that it is included here by association with the story of Ekron. However, the venue is quite far north and it seems unlikely that the enemy force could have reached such a northern position at so late a date in the Assyrian campaign.

The next stage of the campaign was the conquest of two towns, Eltekeh and Timnah.

> The town of **Altaqô** (Eltekeh), the town of **Tamnâ** (Timnah), I surrounded, I captured, their spoil I took away. (III 6 [II 82–83]; Rassam 46)

Eltekeh gave Sennacherib control over the main highway leading up from the south. Thus Joppa and its hinterland were isolated from Philistia. So he was protecting his western flank. Then Timnah (Tell el-Baṭâshī=Tel Baṭash) was captured. Its position in the Valley of Sorek between Beth-shemesh and Ekron (Josh 15:7) meant that it could provide a link between Ekron and the kingdom of Judah. By taking this town, Sennacherib was securing his eastern flank so that his forces could not be surprised from the direction of Judah while they were engaged in a serious attack on Ekron. It was essential for the Assyrians to conquer this leading center of the rebellion. The advocates and supporters of the anti-Assyrian policy had to be punished severely as an example to all the other states and peoples in the southern Levant.

> To the city of ᶜ**Amqarôna** (Ekron) I drew near; the officials and nobles who had committed a sin, I slew; on stakes around the city I impaled their bodies. The citizens of the city, who committed misdeeds and transgressions, I counted as spoil. As for the remainder, who did not bear any sin or misconduct, who had no guilt, I commanded their release. **Pādî**, their king, I brought out from the city of Jerusalem and I seated him on the throne over them. I imposed upon him the tribute of my lordship.
> (III 7 [III 1]–III 17 [III 11]; Rassam 46b–48)

The release of Pādî leads to the campaign against Judah. Before continuing with the official annals, it is necessary to consider another cuneiform inscription, on two fragmentary tablets from Nineveh. That the two pieces belonged together was discerned many years ago. In spite of later objections, the assumption that this is a "Letter to God," reporting on the results of Sennacherib's western campaign, still seems the most likely. The restoration of the name of Hezekiah in a broken space has serious drawbacks but it is still not impossible. Signs on the edge of a break are notoriously difficult to reconstruct. So with due reservations, the text in question in the British Museum is considered here as belonging to the Sennacherib campaign. Its reference to URU *A-za-qa-a* = *āl Azaqâ* seems to indicate the Shephelah town of Azekah (Josh 15:35). The presumed location of Azekah (Kh. Tell Zakarîyeh=Tel ᶜAzeqa) on a high perch overlooking the twisting course of the Vale of Elah (Wâdī es-Sunṭ) certainly matches the fragmentary description in the tablet under discussion:

> The city of **Azekah**, his stronghold, which was between my [bo]rder and the land of Judah [. . .] situated on top of a mountain peak like iron knives without number, high as the sky [. . .] . . . rivaling the highest mountains, to the sight of the eyes, as if from heaven. (K 6205 + BM 82-3-23,131; 5–7)

The capture of this city is followed by what appears to be a very broken reference to another city:

### The Conquest of Lachish

*According to the attention paid to it in Sennacherib's palace, the conquest of Lachish must have been reckoned as the most spectacular operation of the campaign. Since Jerusalem was not taken, it was necessary to pick another site for the glorification of the Assyrian army during the third campaign. Therefore, in the central palace, facing the entering visitors, in the reception hall of Sennacherib's palace, the craftsmen installed a series of reliefs depicting the most impressive city conquered during the Judean war (left). The details of these reliefs have been brilliantly elucidated by the excavations at the site. After two generations of futile debate, it is now universally recognized that Lachish Stratum III represents the destruction layer that resulted from Sennacherib's attack in 701 BCE. The identification of the scene is confirmed by the inscription over the representation of King Sennacherib himself:*

**Sennacherib, king of the world, king of the land of Assyria, sat on a throne; the booty of Lachish passed before him.**

*During the siege of Lachish it is stated in the biblical narrative that Hezekiah sent a message of submission and acquiescence in the payment of tribute (2 Kgs 18:14–16). It may have been at this time that Pādî was released and sent back to Ekron.*

[The city of GN, a] royal [city] of the land of Philistia which Hezekiah(?) had taken over and had fortified it [...] (K 6205 + BM 82-3-23,131:11)

The name Hezekiah is restored here with some hesitation in the light of serious criticisms. The identity of the town whose name is missing has also been the subject of controversy. There is no reason that it should be identified with Ekron. In view of the conquest of Azekah, the most logical city is Gath (Tell eṣ-Ṣâfī=Tel Ẓafit). As part of the kingdom of Ashdod (at least since Sargon II's campaign in 712 BCE), it would be considered by Sennacherib as his territory and Azekah could be described as being "between **my** [bo]rder and the land of Judah." The fact that six jar handles with the royal seal impression have been found at Tell eṣ-Ṣâfī indicates that the place had seen some kind of occupation during the late eighth century BCE. It would have been a logical outpost for Hezekiah in his preparations against the Assyrian invasion. That it was no longer a "royal city" made it fair game. It is also due south of Ekron and due west of Azekah. The seizure of Azekah would leave Gath unprotected from the east. Sennacherib had occupied Timnah and blocked the Sorek Valley before laying siege to Ekron. Then, if this tablet describes incidents in the campaign, it means that Sennacherib took Azekah and effectively blocked the Elah Valley before tackling the stronghold at Gath (Tell eṣ-Ṣâfī). Even if the Judean outpost there was of moderate size (not yet proven), the situation on top of a steep, isolated hill would require some effort for its subdual. The two main approaches to Judah from the west were now dominated by Assyrian-held strong points.

**The Ravaging of the Kingdom of Judah**. Taking up the story again from the annals, the attack on the kingdom of Judah is briefly described:

As for **Hezekiah the Judean**, who did not submit to my yoke, I surrounded **forty-six** of his strong walled cities and the numberless small towns in their surroundings, by laying down ramps and applying battering rams, onslaughts by foot troops, tunnels, breeches and siege ladders, I conquered them. Two hundred thousand one hundred and fifty people, small and great, male and female, horses, mules, donkeys, camels, oxen and small cattle without number I brought out of them and I counted them as spoil. (III 18 [III 12]–III 30 [III 23]; Rassam 49–51)

Unfortunately for the historical geographer, there is no cuneiform list of the forty-six cities claimed in this passage. There is, however, no reason to think that the number is inaccurate. The laconic biblical statement (*see* Isa 36:1 || 2 Kgs 18:13; 2 Chr 32:1) does describe the massive tragedy that befell the Judean kingdom, but the subsequent context focuses on the deliverance of Jerusalem and thus shows a shocking indifference to the fate of the host of victims from the rest of the country.

One passage from the prophet Micah (1:8–16) has been taken as a heartfelt lament over the Assyrian conquest of the Shephelah and its environs. The poem is built on word plays related to each of the place names (*see* Mic 1:8–15). Most of the towns in this lament are known, e.g. Gath (Tell eṣ-Ṣâfī), Lachish (Tell ed-Duweir=Tel Lakhish), Mareshah (Tell Ṣandaḥanna=Tel Maresha) and Adullam (Kh. esh-Sheikh Madhkûr).

However, the rest are still not firmly located. One of them, Achzib, appears in the same Shephelah district as Mareshah (Josh 15:44). Considering that the towns of that district may be recorded in an anticlockwise manner, it would lead to Khirbet Tell el-Beiḍā (Ḥ. Lavnin) and that would place the town close to Adullam and the Valley of Elah as suggested by its equation with the Chezib (Gen 38:5) of the Tamar and Judah story.

Moresheth-gath, the home of the prophet Micah, is shown on the Medeba Map to the north of Eleutheropolis (Beth-guvrin) with the superscript taken from Eusebius (*Onom.* 134:10):

Morasthi, whence was the prophet Micah.

Eusebius himself places Morasthi "to the east of Eleutheropolis" (*Onom.* 134:1–2). Actually, the Byzantine Morasthi was probably at Khirbet Umm el-Baṣal, 1 mile (1.5 km) north of Beth-guvrin while the Iron Age town was up above at Tell Judeideh (Tel Goded).

Five of the places have no solid basis for identification but they have often been the subject of speculation. Since none of them appear in Joshua 15 or in other contexts, the only guidelines must be the order in this chapter and the possibility of some toponymic survival. Beth-le-aphrah would most likely be one of the sites such as Khirbet eṭ-Ṭayyibeh on the western slopes of the southern hill country of Judah.

Shaphir is placed by Eusebius "in the mountains, a village between Eleutheropolis and Ashkelon" (*Onom.* 156:23–24). The contradiction between "in the mountains" and "between Eleutheropolis and Ashkelon" is hard to reconcile. An old suggestion is the cluster of villages called es-Sawāfîr. Eusebius' two conditions might be met by placing Shaphir at Tell esh-Sheikh Aḥmed el-ᶜAreinī (Tel ᶜErani; also Tell el-Menshîyeh). It is between the two cities but also just on the edge of the Shephelah hills to the east. All suggestions are conjectural.

Zaanan has been equated with Zenan (Josh 15:37) but neither has been identified. The latter place is in a district with Lachish and Makkedah.

Neither is there any help forthcoming for the identification of Beth-ezel. The meaning is obscure and the versions seem not to have understood it.

Finally, Maroth also remains a mystery. There is no justification for the suggested equation with Maarath (Josh 15:59) which is in the hill country, far from the area of Micah's interest.

The Micah passage is suggestive but no more than that. The prophet's selection of places marked for destruction is not transparent. It can be assumed that he is dealing with sites within his own personal acquaintance.

**The Fate of Jerusalem**. The biblical passages relating to the war with

Sennacherib are mainly concerned with the fate of Jerusalem and its apparently "miraculous" deliverance from physical conquest. Sennacherib's own inscriptions make the admission that the city was not stormed and overcome.

> As for him (i.e. Hezekiah), like a caged bird in Jerusalem, his royal city, I confined him; I linked together siege forts against him; whoever came forth from the gate I turned back in humiliation.
> (III 27 [III 20]–III 30 [III 23]; Rassam 52)

The expression, "like a caged bird," was used by Tiglath-pileser III on the occasion of his first, and unsuccessful, attempt to conquer Damascus (cf. *supra*). But in this present case, the king of Assyria never came back to finish the job. On the other hand, this passage makes it clear that a blockade had been set up around the city. Given Jerusalem's isolated position on ridges east of the watershed highway, that would not be so difficult to do. However, there is no reason to deduce from this text that a circumvallation wall or moat had as yet been constructed and certainly no siege ramp.

> He (the king of Assyria) will not come to this city and he will not shoot an arrow there and he will not advance a shield against it and he will not pile up a siege ramp against it. (cf. 2 Kgs 19:32 || Isa 37:33)

The prophet who contributed the Sennacherib pericopes to the Deuteronomistic history included dialogues with Assyrian leaders in order to demonstrate that the conflict was not just between Judah and Assyria but between YHWH and Ashur, god of the Assyrians. Much has been written about the Assyrian personnel in this delegation. They were the three highest-ranking military officers in the Assyrian hierarchy. Each commanded his own division and two of them were district governors of provinces in northwestern Mesopotamia. Their mission was entirely commensurate with known Assyrian practice (*see* 2 Kgs 18:17–20).

The Judean response was negative but one wonders if the release of Pādî from prison and the offer of tribute may not have come at this time. The biblical writers did not want to admit any sign of submission on the part of Hezekiah because they had a Yahwist agenda, thoroughly evident in these passages. After returning to Sennacherib, this time in the vicinity of Lachish, the officers went back to Jerusalem with renewed demands. This time, according to the biblical narrative, there was a divine response in the form of an oracle through the prophet Isaiah (the main historan for this period). The oracle predicted Sennacherib's withdrawal and subsequent assassination (2 Kgs 19:20–34).

The last Judean town mentioned in the biblical narratives is Libnah. The Assyrian army had moved its operations there after the fall of Lachish (*see* 2 Kgs 19:8–10).

The identification of Libnah with Tell Bornâṭ (Tel Burna) has previously been discussed. The entrée to the Judean hills from the central coastal plain via Tell Bornâṭ and Mareshah (Tell Ṣandaḥanna) is secondary to more important routes such as that passing by Lachish or by Azekah. Nevertheless, it must have been part of Sennacherib's plan to seize the major sites leading eastward into Judah. It is not stated but can probably be assumed that Libnah was taken.

At this point a report is mentioned that a new Cushite expeditionary force was about to arrive in the war zone. The Cushite ruler is Taharqa (bib. Tirhakah) who was sole ruler over Egypt and Cush from 690 to 664 BCE. He was the son of Piye (Pi-ᶜankhy). It would appear that his older brother, Shebitku, had ordered him to bring troops from Cush northward to Egypt presumably to send them on to the southern Levant. Taharqa has left a series of inscriptions at the Nubian town of Kawa. One of those texts describes his passing by the ruined temple of Kawa on his way northward. The syntax of the passage makes it absolutely certain that Taharqa was twenty years old at the time. His being called forth at that crucial time suggests that he was crown-prince designate and could have been called "king of Cush" in biblical terms like the crown prince of Edom murdered by Mesha and mentioned by the prophet Amos (Amos 2:1). He would not necessarily have been officially the co-regent.

It is also suggested that Taharqa did not actually engage the Assyrian army. On the other hand, there is the folk tale preserved by Herodotus about Sennacherib's attempt to invade Egypt (Herodotus II, 141). The Assyrian army is said to have reached Pelusium which was the city marking the entry to Egypt during the Persian period when Herodotus was there. There was an oracle in a dream assuring the Egyptian leader of victory and then an invasion of the Assyrian camp by thousands of field mice who ate all their accoutrements (bowstrings, chariot harness, etc.). Thus disarmed, the Assyrians are said to have withdrawn. That the mouse was a well-known symbol of plague in Semitic and Greek tradition is well known. Such a folk memory in mid-fifth-century Egypt makes an intriguing comparison with the biblical statement (*see* 2 Kgs 19:35–36).

There is nothing in the Assyrian records to echo these statements. The admission that Jerusalem was not forcibly entered shows that something extraordinary did in fact occur. But neither is there anything in the inscriptions of Dynasty XXV to shed light on the problem.

The biblical treatment of the whole affair is concluded by an allusion to the assassination of Sennacherib which took place in 681 BCE. The biblical version obviously is second- or third-hand because,

*Taharqa (biblical Tirhakah), "king of Cush."*

although the general facts are correct, the names of the assassins are garbled. The biblical Adrammelech was really Arad-mullissu. If the assassination report was an integral part of the Hezekiah/Sennacherib pericope (source B), then the composition of the latter cannot be before 681 BCE.

For practical purposes, nevertheless, Sennacherib achieved his main objectives for the campaign. The rebellions were crushed. Loyal vassals were confirmed and/or appointed in all the key city-states. Hezekiah was thoroughly subdued if not captured. The steady flow of tribute was assured.

The kingdom of Judah was in ruins. At least forty-six towns and their villages had been ravaged and vast numbers of the population were taken into exile as forced labor or for military service. The biblical emphasis on the deliverance of Jerusalem and King Hezekiah overshadows the suffering of the people as a whole. It also obscures the brutal fact that Hezekiah's policy decisions, viz. organizing an anti-Assyrian coalition, calling for Egyptian/Cushite help, were a fateful miscalculation. If YHWH loved His temple and His city, He showed little compassion for the rest of the Judean population.

Sennacherib's records make it quite clear that Judah's territory was severely diminished. Large sections were transferred to the control of the loyal Philistine rulers:

> As for his (Hezekiah's) towns which I plundered, I detached from his country and gave them to Mitinti, king of Ashdod, to Pādî, king of Ekron, and to Ṣil-Baal, king of Gaza. Thus I diminished his territory. On top of their annual tax, I added tribute and gifts of my royalty and I imposed it upon them.
> (Chicago Prism III, 30[23]–37[29]; Rassam 53–54)

The best textual variant here, "upon them," rather than "upon him" shows that the increased payments were imposed on all the vassals in the region. The other versions of this passage would indicate that it was Hezekiah's tribute that was vastly increased in spite of the curtailment of his territory. Such was hardly the case.

The later Assyrian records of Sennacherib make no mention of the death of Hezekiah. This is in contrast to the reference to the demise of (E)lulî, king of Sidon/Tyre. It has been correctly observed that Assyrian silence on the death of Hezekiah is a strong testimony that the king of Judah did not pass away shortly after the war of 701 BCE.

## The Aftermath

**The Judean Succession**. Probably due to the illness from which Hezekiah had only recently recovered (cf. *supra*), an heir was appointed as soon as he had reached the age of twelve (*see* 2 Kgs 21:1). Calculation of the regnal years for the Judean kings reveals that Manasseh died in 642 BCE so his fifty-five years of reign lead back to 697 BCE as the year that his father appointed him as co-regent.

King Manasseh of Judah is a much maligned figure in the Book of Kings. The Deuteronomistic editor(s) sought to blame Manasseh for the ultimate downfall of the Judean kingdom (2 Kgs 23:26–27). As will be noted below, the Chronicler preserves an account of Manasseh's arrest and deportation to Babylon (2 Chr 33:10–17) during which time he repented, was restored to his kingdom and launched a program of restoration and reconstruction. If the Chronicles passage be taken seriously, then it becomes necessary to explain just how a king so vilified in the Book of Kings could have been given such a reprieve by the Chronicler. It has long been admitted that the Chronicler's statements about building projects and military activities probably are derived from a genuine ancient source. There is no reason not to accept this evaluation in spite of many critical objections by twentieth-century scholars.

As a matter of fact, the course of world events during Manasseh's reign may provide the key to his pattern of behavior, both the "bad" and the "good" from the traditional point of view. The co-regency between Manasseh and Hezekiah is an important case in point. It will play a significant role in our discussion.

**Manasseh, King of an Economically Depressed State.** The circumstances prevailing in Judah during Manasseh's early career were not auspicious. His father, Hezekiah, had suffered terrible losses in a senseless rebellion against Sennacherib, king of Assyria. The biblical sources play up the fact that Jerusalem was not conquered by the Assyrian army (2 Kgs 18–19 || Isa 36–37; cf. also 2 Chr 32:1–22). However, they do not refer to the crushing burden imposed upon Judah as a result of the conflict. Not only were forty-six walled cities of Judah and their dependent villages ravaged by Sennacherib's troops, thus wrecking the entire infrastructure of the kingdom, but large portions of economically and militarily strategic territory were detached from Judah and given to those local rulers

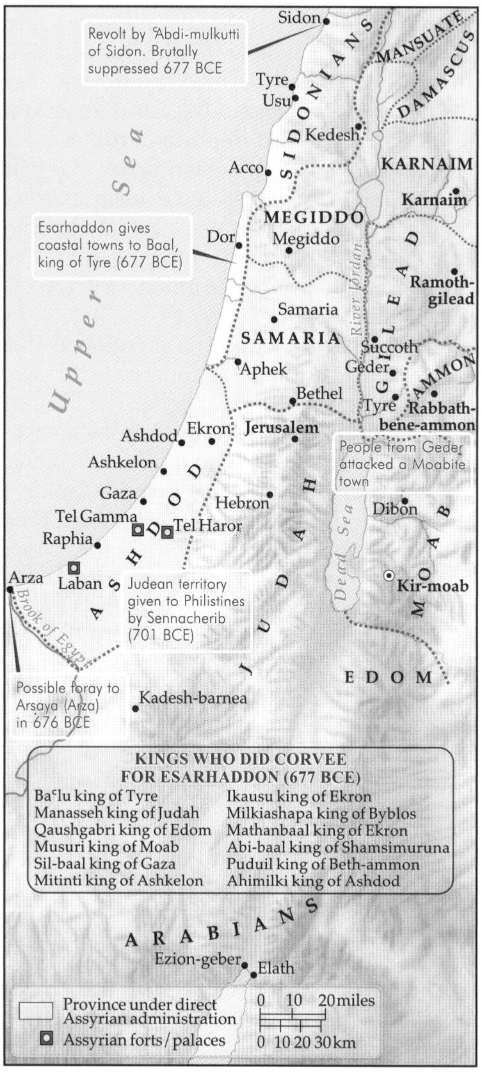


**Judah and Its Neighbors During the Reign of Manasseh (701–643 BCE)**

who had remained loyal to Assyria.

The same year that saw Judah's catastrophic defeat by the Assyrians (701 BCE) had also witnessed King Hezekiah falling victim to a serious illness. For the next ten years, Judah had to struggle under the burden of heavy war debt and diminished economic resources. There is no indication that Sennacherib did anything to alleviate Hezekiah's financial straits. It would have been contrary to Assyrian interests to allow the former leader of the western rebellion a chance to gain surplus income with which to rearm and refortify.

With Hezekiah's death in his twenty-ninth year (687 / 686 BCE), Manasseh assumed the responsibility for reviving the economy of Judah. The steps he took to achieve this goal were detrimental to the Jerusalem priesthood and the associated religious establishment and thus they are denounced in the prophetic history (*see* 2 Kgs 21:2–7).

Obviously, Manasseh could never have taken such drastic steps while his father was alive. Hezekiah's links with the temple and with the prophets (particularly Isaiah) were too strong. It is not simply fortuitous that the prophetic historian pointed out the parallel between Manasseh's new policy and that of Ahab, king of Israel, in the ninth century BCE. The obvious implication that Manasseh was entering into political and commercial relations with Tyre has not been lost on historians. These new political / economic ties were expressed in terms of the foreign cults established in Jerusalem. Many of the shrines to the various deities were doubtless associated with the embassies established by the diplomatic missions that came to Jerusalem (cf. during Solomon's reign, 1 Kgs 11:4–8; and for the location of the many shrines in Manasseh's day, cf. 2 Kgs 23:13–14). There is no reason to assume that Manasseh was adopting Assyrian cults imposed upon him as a vassal of the empire; it was not Assyrian policy to require such cultic practices on the part of their subject states.

The economic logic behind these moves is obvious. It is well known that Judah had no raw materials or manufactured goods worthy of export other than its agricultural produce (cf. Ezek 27:17). On the other hand, the Phoenicians, whose population was largely engaged in maritime-related activities (Ezek 27:8–9), were in constant need of foodstuffs to maintain their industrialized society (cf. e.g. 1 Kgs 5:25 [= Eng. 5:11]). Therefore, it seems clear that Manasseh was seeking markets for his agricultural products. He was also seeking links with other neighboring countries such as the Transjordanian kingdoms, which had not suffered from the war with Sennacherib and were thus potential markets for Judah. Their own economies were undoubtedly still based to a great extent on pastoral pursuits; with ready access to the highway from Arabia to Damascus, they could also tap in to the regional caravan trade.

## Assyrian Activity Renewed in the West

The Assyrians' primary goal in the west was complete, uncontested mastery of the rich commerce that flourished in the eastern Mediterranean Basin. To achieve their aims, they had to maintain their domination over the maritime states of the Phoenician and Philistine coast and also to control the caravan trade coming from north and south Arabia to the seacoast and to Egypt. The Cushite pharaohs of the XXV[th] Dynasty were doing everything in their power, mainly by diplomatic machinations and enticement, but also by promises of military support, to frustrate the Assyrian ambitions. Therefore, the expulsion of the Cushites from Egypt became a high-priority objective of Assyrian policy.

**Esarhaddon (681–669 BCE)**. During the last decade of Sennacherib's reign, he was deeply engaged in conflict with Elam and the unruly Chaldeans. This had given the Cushite Taharqa (690–664 BCE) an opportunity to stir up trouble among the countries of the Levant. Sennacherib's son, Esarhaddon, who came to the throne in a wave of violence, had to deal with the results of Taharqa's activities. On the Arabian scene, Esarhaddon was approached by Hazael, king of the Arabs, who reaffirmed his allegiance and requested the return of the Arab cult statues that Sennacherib had taken to Assyria to ensure Arabian fidelity.

**Hazael, the king of the Arabs**, came with heavy gifts to Nineveh, the city of my lordship, and kissed my feet; he implored me to return the images of his gods and I had mercy on him. . . . *When fate carried Hazael away, I set Yata^c, his son, upon his throne....*
(Nin. A, IV, 6–14)

The leniency toward Hazael may have been related to Esarhaddon's placatory policy toward the Babylonians. Hazael was an important figure in the commerce to Babylon from the west across the north Arabian desert. It would have also been a wise adjunct to Esarhaddon's policy in the west. He was about to begin the project of restoring Assyrian supremacy after the erosion of imperial authority due to Taharqa's subversive activity.

In view of the trouble attending the transition of power after the murder of Sennacherib, the king of Sidon, ^cAbdi-mulkutti, chose to rebel against the Assyrian authority (679 BCE). If the Esarhaddon Chronicle is to be trusted, the king made a preemptive strike down the Philistine coast to secure the southern approaches against Egyptian intervention. The Esarhaddon Chronicle records that in Esarhaddon's second year (679 BCE),

The second year: the major-domo co[nscripted conscript]s in the land of Akkad. That same [ye]ar the town of Arṣaya was captured; its [sp]oil was de[spoiled. The peopl]e were made prisoners, the king and [his] son were apprehended.
(Chronicle 14:6–8)

However, the campaign against Arṣaya consistently appears in the annals after the beheading of the rebellious king of Sidon. Therefore, the Chronicle record for this event has been challenged. Instead of being an early campaign to establish a firm Assyrian presence on the north Sinai coast facing Egypt before moving against the rebellious Sidon, it could have been an initial step towards launching the first campaign against Egypt, i.e. sometime prior to 674 BCE (perhaps in 676 BCE).

In Esarhaddon's fourth year (677 BCE), the city of Sidon was sacked.

The fourth year: Sidon was captured and plundered;
(Chronicle 14:12)

(As for) ^cAbdi-mulkutti king of the city of Sidon, who revered not my lordship, who heeded not the proclamations of my lips, who trusted in the raging sea, and threw off the yoke of Ashur, I swamped like a flood over the city of Sidon, the city of his trust situated in the midst of the sea. Its wall and its citadel I removed and cast into the sea and I destroyed his dwelling place.
(Prism B = Nin. A, II, 65–70)

The fact that ^cAbdi-mulkutti had been seduced to rebel against Assyrian domination by Taharqa of Egypt was clearly a matter of utmost importance to Esarhaddon. It was surely at this time that the king of Assyria began to make diplomatic and logistic preparations toward the final removal of the pharaohs of Dynasty XXV from the eastern Mediterranean sphere. That same year, Esarhaddon demonstrated his authority over the Levantine rulers by forcing them to furnish corvée workers to deliver logs and stones from Lebanon for his newly planned palace.

I called up the kings of the land of Ḫatti and of Beyond the River: Ba^clu king of the city of Tyre, Manasseh king of **the city** (sic) of Judah, Qausgabri king of **the city** (sic) of Edom, Muṣuri king of **the city** (sic) of *Moab*, Ṣil-Baal king of the city of Gaza, Mitinti king of the city of Ashkelon, Ikausu king of the city of Ekron (*et al.*) ... 22 kings of the land of Ḫatti, the seashore and the islands; all these I sent out and I made them transport under terrible difficulties, to Nineveh, the city of my lordship, as material for my palace: big logs, long beams (and) thin boards from cedar and pine trees, products of the Sirara (Anti-Lebanon) and Lebanon mountains, which had grown for a long time into tall and strong timber, (and) from their quarries in the mountains, statues of protective deities made of *ašnan* stone, statues of female *apsastu*, thresholds, slabs of limestone, of *ašnan* stone, of large and small grained breccia, of *alallu* stone (and) of *girinḫiliba* stone.
(Prism B = Nin. A, V, 54–76)

Manasseh was one of these. Note that the timber and stone were delivered to *Nineveh*, the capital of Assyria. The king of Sidon does not appear in this list; he was under arrest while his conquered city-state was being dealt with; in the following year (676 BCE), he was finally beheaded and his head brought to Assyria (Chronicle 1:6–7). Perhaps also, the occupation of Arṣa(ya) (at el-^cArîsh) took place at this time:

The town of **Arṣa** on the border of the **Brook of Egypt** I plundered; Asḫuli, its king, I cast in fetters, and brought to the land of Ashur. . . .
(Nin. A, III, 39–42)

The appointment of Yautha^c as successor to the deceased Hazael, king of the Arabs, must have occurred some time prior to the writing of the Heidel Prism, which was written in the month of Iyyar of Esarhaddon's fifth year (676/675 BCE), because it is recorded there: "When fate carried Hazael away, I set Yautha^c, his son, upon his throne...."

During the ensuing year (675 BCE), the Assyrian government was distracted by troubles with Elam and the Chaldeans. At this time the attempt to unseat Yautha^c may have taken place. Esarhaddon found it necessary to intervene directly in the affairs of the north Arabian tribal league. The pertinent record does not appear in the Heidel Prism but it is found in the Thompson Prism, which was written in the month of Adar, 673 BCE. Therefore, it has been rightly observed that the episode must have occurred between 676 and 673 BCE.

*Stele of Esarhaddon, king of Assyria; before him, Pharaoh Taharqa and Ba^clu of Tyre.*

Afterwards, Wahb induced all the Arabs to revolt against Yautha^c in order to establish (his own) kingship, but I, Esarhaddon, king of Assyria, ... sent my combat troops to the aid of Yautha^c and they subdued all the Arabs; Wahb with the troops of his entourage they cast in fetters and brought to me.
(Prism B = Nin. A, IV, 23–31)

There were many reasons besides the demand for tribute payments that would have induced Esarhaddon to support his loyal vassal. Not the least of these would be the fact that the highest priority in Assyrian policy at that time was to expel the troublesome Cushite pharaohs, not only from the Levant, but also from Egypt. This required that the Assyrians move a large body of troops across Sinai *en masse*; to do so they would need the logistic support of the Arabs.

Finally, in Esarhaddon's seventh year (674 BCE), an attempt was made to carry the war to Egypt. The results were disastrous:

Seventh year: on the fifth day of the month Adar, the army of the land of Assyria was defeated in the land of Egypt.
(Chronicle 1: iv, 16)

The annals do not discuss this Assyrian defeat.

Esarhaddon's failure on the first attempt to invade Egypt could have been due, at least in part, to improper logistic support. If fact, Wahb's att0empted coup against Yautha^c may have been a contributing factor. It was certainly crucial to the Assyrian war planners that the Arabs have a stable and loyal leadership capable of providing the needed assistance on the forthcoming campaign.

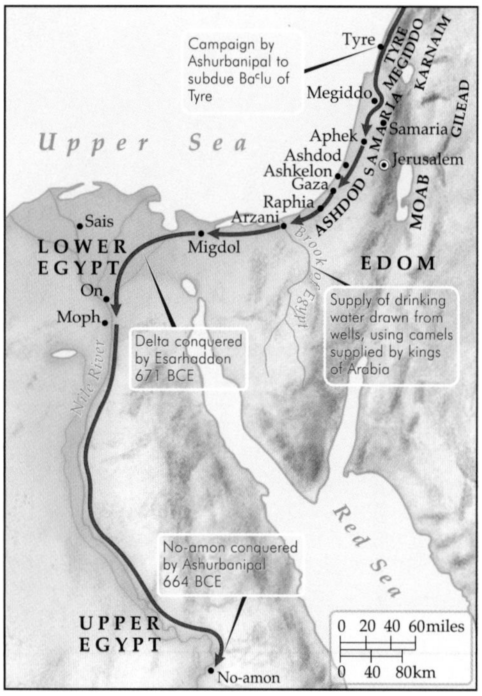


**The Conquest of Egypt by Assyria (669–663 BCE)**

In 671 BCE Esarhaddon achieved his initial goal by conquering the Egyptian delta. But on the way, he had to punish Baᶜlu, king of Tyre, who had been supporting the Cushite Taharqa:

In my tenth campaign, Ashur strengthened me and directed my face towards the lands of Magan [and Meluḫḫa] which are called the land of Cush and the land of Egypt in the common tongue. I called up the numerous troops of Ashur which are stationed in [. . .]. In the month of Nisan, the first month, I departed from my city Ashur. I crossed the Tigris and the Euphrates in the time of their flood; I strode across difficult mountains like a wild ox. In the course of my campaign I threw up an earthwork against Baᶜlu king of **the land** (sic) of Tyre who had trusted his friend Taharqa, king of the land of Cush, and threw off the yoke of Ashur and answered me with insolence; food and water, ‹the harvest of the field› the sustenance for their lives, I withheld. From (sic) the land of Egypt I called up the camp, to the land of Nubia I set my course. Thirty double hours distance from Aphek, which is in the region of the land of Sama‹ri›a(?) to the city of Raphia, towards the Brook of the land of Egypt, a place having no river, by ropes, by chains (and) buckets, I caused the troops to drink well water. When the command of Ashur, my lord, came to my ear, my heart rejoiced. I cal[led up] the camels of all the kings of Arabia; [water bottles I] placed on them; 20 (or 30?) double hours distance, a marching distance of 15 days, I went....

(Tablet K 3082 + S 2027 + K 3086 from the British Museum, Obv. 6–Rev. 18)

The victory in Egypt is also described in the Babylonian Chronicle:

In the tenth year, in the month of Nisan, the army of Ashur marched to Egypt; in the month of Tammuz, on the third, sixteenth and eighteenth days—three times—there was a massacre in Egypt. On the twenty-second day, Memphis, the royal city, was taken. (The Babylonian Chronicle, IV, 23–28)

The annals place special emphasis on the assistance of the Arabian kings with their camel corps. There can be no doubt that their support was a major contributing factor in transporting the Assyrian army across Sinai. They were essential to the success of the campaign. However, participation in such a bloody war so far from their native land may not have been as rewarding as the Arabs had hoped. Their dissatisfaction found expression in the rebellion of Yauthaᶜ, king of the Arabs (Kedar). That event is passed over by the annals and also by the chronicles. It is only attested retrospectively in the records of Ashurbanipal, in his annals and in more detail in a letter to the god Ashur:

When (Y)authaᶜ son of Hazael, king of Arabia, in the reign of Esarhaddon, king of Assyria, the servant, the creature of your hands, became hostile and cast off the yoke of his sovereignty, by trust in you, in the greatness of your exalted might, Esarhaddon, king of Assyria, my father, my begetter, called up his armies and sent them against him. In an open battle he accomplished his defeat and they carried away his gods. (Y)authaᶜ, to save his life, abandoned his camp, fled alone and escaped to distant parts.

(Letter of Ashurbanipal to the god Ashur, VAT 5600: 3–12)

Esarhaddon felt prepared to renew his war against Taharqa by 669 BCE. The Sinai route was now firmly in his control due to his previous successes in the delta. However, the king himself fell ill and died on the way:

In the twelfth year, the king of Assyria marched to Egypt; on the way he became ill and on the tenth day **he died**. (Babylonian Chronicle, IV, 30–31)

**Ashurbanipal (669–627 BCE).** The son of Esarhaddon continued his father's program. The year 667 BCE saw him marching to Egypt to punish Taharqa, who had tried to unseat the delta rulers appointed by Esarhaddon. The subject rulers of states in the Levant paid their tribute and joined in the van.

In my first campaign, I marched against the land of Magan and the land of Meluḫḫa. Taharqa, king of the land of Egypt and the land of Cush, whom Esarhaddon, king of Assyria, my own progenitor, had defeated and whose country he had taken over—Taharqa forgot the might of Ashur, Ishtar and the great gods, my lords, and put his trust in his own power. He attacked the kings (and) regents whom my own father had appointed in Egypt in order to kill, to rob and to take over the land of Egypt; he entered and took residence in the city of Memphis, the city which my own father had conquered and incorporated into Assyrian territory. A swift messenger came to Nineveh to report to me. Because of these deeds my heart raged and my soul was aflame. I lifted my hands and I prayed to Ashur and the Assyrian Ishtar. I called up my great forces which Ashur and Ishtar have entrusted to me and set a straight course for the land of Egypt and the land of Cush. During the course of my campaign [Baᶜlu king of Tyre, Manasseh king of Judah, Qausgabri king of Edom, Muṣuru king of Moab, Ṣil-Baᶜal king of Gaza, Mitinti king of Ashkelon, Ikausu king of Ekron...] 22 kings from the sea coast, from the midst of the sea and from the mainland, servants who are my subjects, brought their heavy tribute to me and kissed my feet. I made those kings with their forces (and) their ships accompany me by sea and by land.

(Rassam Cylinder, I, 52–89)

The climax of the war with Egypt came in 664/663 BCE when Ashurbanipal's army conquered No-amon (Thebes) and expelled Tanwetamani (664–656 BCE), the last of the Cushite rulers (cf. Nahum 3:8).

Psammetichus I succeeded his father as ruler of Sais and for some time he seems to have maintained his loyalty to Assyria.

Not long afterward, Ashurbanipal's third campaign was directed against Baᶜlu of Tyre.

On my third campaign I resolutely marched against Baᶜlu, king of Tyre, who dwells in the midst of the sea, who did not keep my royal decree, who did not heed the dictums of my lips. I blockaded him with redoubts, I seized his lines of communication. Their sustenance I restricted and I made it scarce. I forced them to submit to my yoke.

(Rassam Cylinder, II, 49–55)

Baᶜlu of Tyre surrendered quickly and managed to maintain his position as commercial leader of the eastern Mediterranean states. The ruler of Arvad, Yakinilû, also saw fit to submit to Ashurbanipal and he and his sons were well favored by the Assyrian king. Approaches were also made by the rulers of Tabal and Hilakku (Cilicia). It had become clear to the Phoenicians that the Cushite rulers of Egypt were no longer there to support them. The exact date of this campaign is impossible to determine. It must have been not long after the capture of No-amon.

Now, with Psammetichus installed in Sais as a loyal vassal of Assyria, it must have seemed that Ashurbanipal should be able to enjoy some stability along the Mediterranean seaboard. However, Psammetichus discovered the advantage of using bronze-clad mercenaries from Caria and from eastern Greece and employed them in gaining ascendancy over the other delta princes until he was the ruler of all of Lower Egypt (Herodotus II, 147–152). By 656 BCE Psammetichus had succeeded in imposing his rule over all of Egypt and had his daughter adopted as a priestess of No-amon.

The Assyrian garrisons were expelled from Egypt with the aid of mercenaries sent by Gyges, a professed friend of Ashurbanipal. These mercenaries were most likely Carians and eastern Greeks who had already been serving the ruler of Lydia.

Egypt of the XXVIᵗʰ Dynasty was now thoroughly independent of Assyria. One cannot know whether Psammetichus also used his new freedom to begin inciting the Levantine rulers to favor Egypt at the expense of Assyrian interests or not. What is known about the Levant is that Ashurbanipal had to deal with a new outbreak of hostility on the part of the Kedarites. Yauthaᶜ, to whom Ashurbanipal had originally returned the cult statues of

*King Ashurbanipal pouring libation over dead lions, on relief from the palace of Ashurbanipal at Nineveh.*

Kedar, took occasion to begin attacking the land of Amurru, i.e. the Levantine provinces of the Assyrian Empire:

> Aft[erwards] he violated my oaths, he did not keep my treaty, he threw off the yoke of my overlordship, he restrained his feet from seeking my health and he withheld my gifts. The people of Arabia he incited to revolt. They were repeatedly plundering Amurru. My forces [which were] stationed [on the bor]der of his territory, I dispatched against him. They accomplished their defeat; the Arabs, as many as had sallied [forth], they were smiting with weapons.... (Cyl. B, VII 93–VIII 2)

Another Kedarite leader, Ammuladdin, also took part in these razzias against Amurru, but he was defeated and apprehended by the king of Moab, a loyal vassal of Assyria:

> As for Ammuladdi‹n›, king of Kedar, who like him (Yautha$^{c}$) had become hos[tile] and was continually plundering the kings of the land of Amurru, invoking my name (and the names of) Ashur, Sin, Shamash, Bel, Nabu, Ishtar of Nineveh, Ishtar of Arbela, the queens of Kidmuri, Ninurta, Nergal, (and) Gerru, by the invocation of [my] name [which] Ashur made great, Kamash-khalta, king of [Moab], a servant loyal to me, accomplished his defeat in a pitched battle. (Prism B, VIII 39–45)

These actions may or may not be divorced from the revolt by Ashurbanipal's brother, Shamash-shum-ukin. They evidently took place no later than 652 BCE, but at least one can say that the unrest they represent on the part of the Kedarites reveals that the ground was ripe for a rebellion and the subsequent pro-Babylonian stance taken by Yautha$^{c}$'s successor, Abiyaṯe$^{c}$, makes sense in this context.

In 653 BCE there was a raid made by the Elamites but the Assyrian army repulsed them and pursued them to their home turf. There they were soundly defeated and their leader, Teuman, was captured and beheaded. If this was meant to be a coordinated attack to assist Shamash-shum-ukin, king of Babylon, it was abortive.

The rebellion against Ashurbanipal by his younger brother, Shamash-shum-ukin, king of Babylon, came in 652/651 BCE. It was obviously preceded by considerable political intrigue. Ashurbanipal stressed the disaffection of subject peoples throughout the empire, especially in the west:

> And he, Shamash-shum-ukin, the unfaithful brother who did not keep my treaty, caused to revolt the people of Akkad, Chaldea, Aram ... servants subject to me ... and he caused to revolt the kings of Guti, Amurru and Meluḫḫu ... all together; they made accord with him. (Rassam Cylinder, III, 96–106)

The Kedarite league moved to support Shamash-shum-ukin:

> At the command of Ashur, Ishtar and the great gods, my lords, *I overcame and defeated Abiyaṯeʾ and Aymu*, son(s) of Teʾri, who had come to the aid of Shamash-shum-ukin, my hostile brother; the survivors entered Babylon but because of the distress and hunger, they ate each other's flesh. To save their lives, they came forth from Babylon, and my forces that had been positioned against Shamash-shum-ukin, *defeated them a second time....*
> (Rassam Cylinder, VIII, 30–41)

**Manasseh Reinstated**. After conquering Babylon and exterminating his mutinous brother, Ashurbanipal began to reorganize his shaky empire (648 BCE). While still at Babylon, he took steps to deal with the seditious factions that had supported Shamash-shum-ukin. In this light, one must view a crucial notice about Manasseh, preserved only in Chronicles. The veracity of this passage has long been supported by several scholars (*see* 2 Chr 33:11–17).

Since it pertains finally to various aspects of realia, building projects in Jerusalem and elsewhere, the passage in question should be treated with respect. However, there is also a geographic detail which authenticates the context, viz. the reference to Babylon. Why should a later writer have Manasseh brought to Babylon instead of Nineveh, which was still remembered in the Persian period as the erstwhile capital of Assyria?

Manasseh was surely arrested along with other western rulers suspected of treason. He was brought to Babylon for interrogation before Ashurbanipal. This gives an exact date to the event, since Ashurbanipal was in Babylon precisely in 648 BCE after defeating his brother. In Manasseh's case, he evidently managed to convince Ashurbanipal of his innocence. The Chronicler gave a profound religious interpretation to these events but if a paraphrase may be permitted, a political interpretation may also be made:

> And when he was in distress he entreated the favor of Ashurbanipal and humbled himself greatly before the **king of Assyria**. He besought him and the **king** received his entreaty and heard his supplication and brought him again to Jerusalem into his kingdom.

The ensuing building projects and the reconstitution of Judah's fortresses must have taken place after 648 BCE. Manasseh was evidently a trusted vassal now and was expected to protect Assyrian interests. He must have been promised financial aid to enable him to restore the defenses of his kingdom. As a token of his political orientation, he also broke his diplomatic ties with the neighboring states, especially the Phoenicians who had been supporting the rebellious brother in Babylon. This is the political motivation behind Manasseh's removal of foreign cults. He was closing the embassies and consulates of his immediate neighbors. Manasseh's reinstatement is not without striking parallels in Assyrian policy, especially during the reign of Ashurbanipal, the best examples being the reinstatement of Necho I to his kingship in Sais and the reinstatement of Ba$^{c}$lu king of Tyre.

The Kedarites, twice defeated during the war, were still in line for further punishment. No longer could their current leadership be entrusted with control of the caravan trade across north Arabia to Babylon. Ever since the extermination of the Meunites (2 Chr 4:41) as part of Hezekiah's preparations for the war with Sennacherib, the Kedarite federation of north Arabia had had no real competitors. Even afterwards, in the Persian period, the Kedarites continued to dominate the trade routes to Gaza and to Egypt.

Ashurbanipal's famous war against the Arabs took place in 644–643 BCE. It is unnecessary to go into details here, but it is important to note that on his way back from the campaign, Ashurbanipal saw fit to cross over to the Phoenician coast in order to punish the kingdom of Tyre by attacking two of its mainland cities:

> On my return, I conquered **Usû** whose site is on the shore of the sea; the people of Usû who did not obey their governor (and) were not paying their tribute, the quota of their land, I attacked. I condemned the insubordinate people; their gods and their people I carried off to Ashur. The insubordinate people of **Acco**, I slew. Their corpses I impaled on stakes, around the city I placed them. The remainder I took to the land of Ashur. (Rassam Cylinder IX, 115–128)

It could very well be that at this time Dor (Duʾru) was constituted an independent governor's district. The king of Tyre had fallen out of favor and it makes sense to assume that Ashurbanipal would no longer allow him to have the benefits from control of the southern coastal seaports. This could explain why Dor then appears on seventh-century BCE rosters of towns that are all the seats of Assyrian governors.

Manasseh, king of Judah, was untouched! This may be taken as an indication that he was no longer on the suspect list. He had been returned to his kingdom in 648 BCE and was engaged in the reorganization of his administration, military, fiscal and religious. Obviously, he had not completed these projects by his death in 642 BCE. It remained to his grandson, Josiah, to carry through the far-reaching reforms for which Manasseh had evidently begun to prepare the infrastructure.

# CHAPTER TEN

# Crisis and Turmoil

## Late Seventh to Early Sixth Centuries BCE

The later years of Ashurbanipal in Assyria and Psammetichus (Psamtik) I in Egypt have furnished very little inscriptional evidence. It would almost seem that the ancient Near East was settling down to a time of flourishing commerce and general peace. The policy of Psammetichus towards the Levant during this period mainly was one of commercial interest. A striking cultural feature throughout the area is the process, already begun in some circles in the late eighth century BCE, of the search for origins. The Cushites of Dynasty XXV left inscriptions that show a decided attempt to imitate the very oldest Egyptian dialects. The Assyrians make special efforts to collect the literary heritage of Mesopotamia, especially to the library of Ashurbanipal. This interest in the "archaeological past" was further increased under the Babylonians. Aegean names begin to replace the Semitic names borne by Philistine rulers and subjects. The composition of at least two of the Pentateuchal sources (viz. D and P) probably originated in the seventh century BCE, though the latter was surely expanded in the post-exilic period. The development of the national epic to explain the ethnic and religious essence of the Israelite/Judean people was coming to fruition. These cultural activities were perhaps stimulated by the many crises that befell the countries of the eastern Mediterranean (such as the Assyrian conquest of Phoenicia, Philistia, Judah and Egypt). Mercenaries from the Aegean found their way to Egypt and eventually to Babylonia. East Greek merchants evidently visited the seaports and sometimes established small colonies along the eastern Mediterranean shoreline. The thriving commerce and international interaction among peoples in the seventh century BCE must have been a strong catalyst. The peoples of the area benefited from the stability of firm Assyrian control.

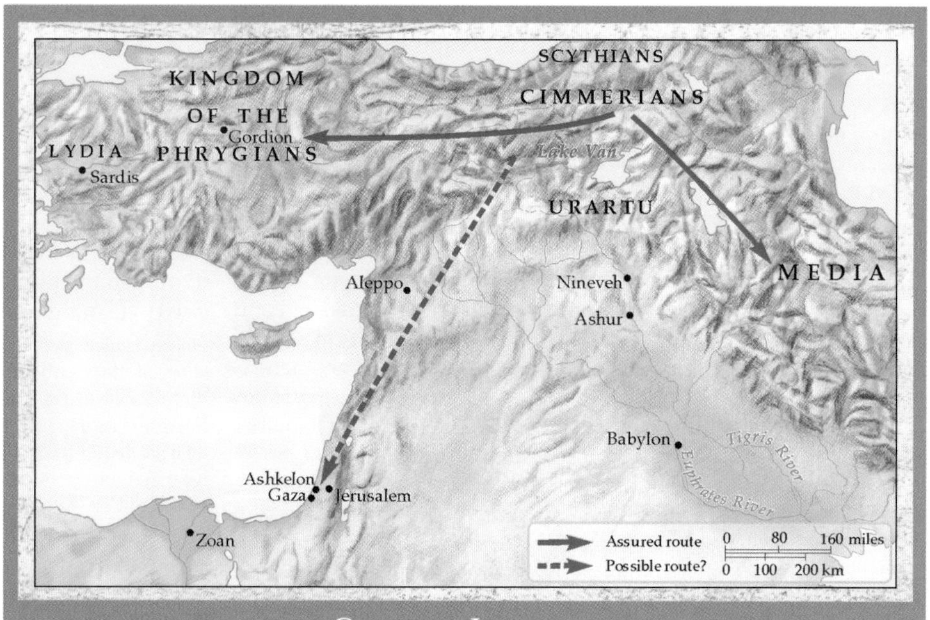


Cimmerian Invasions

Nevertheless, dangerous shadows were falling across the region. There were new enemies on the northern borders of the kingdoms of Anatolia. These tribal hordes imposed a threat to the Anatolian and Iranian kingdoms and their echoes reached the royal palace at Nineveh.

## Trouble from the North

**Cimmerians**. The Assyrian victories in Egypt and against Tyre had motivated the beleaguered states of Anatolia, viz. Ḫilakku, Tabal and Lydia, to seek Assyrian support. They were under constant threat from the Cimmerians. These latter were Indo-Europeans from the Ukraine who had been pushed south from the Ukraine region by the Scythians who, in turn, were being pressed westward by other peoples of the Eurasian steppe farther east (Herodotus 4.12.2).

The Cimmerians may originally have come from the steppes of southern Russia. Homer indicates that they were from a foggy land possibly located along the northern shore of the Black Sea on the Crimean Peninsula (*Od.* 11.13–19; cf. Strabo *Geog.* 7.4.3). They were viewed in the Bible as the descendants of Gomer in the "Table of Nations" (Gen 10:2–3; 1 Chr 1:6). Gomer is called a son of Japheth and grandson of Noah; he was made the father of Ashkenaz (the eponymous ancestor of the Scythians), Riphath (still unknown; Josephus places him in Paphlagonia; *Ant.* 1: 126), and Togarmah (Til-garimmu, modern Gürün). In the sixth century BCE Ezekiel pictures Gomer's descendants as being allied with those of Togarmah in support of Magog, Meshech, and Tubal, brothers of Gomer in the early genealogies. They are to suffer defeat in the eschatological punishment of Gog, king of Magog (Ezek 38:2–6). That legendary material shows the impact that the Cimmerians had made on the inhabitants of the Fertile Crescent. They descended upon the Urartians in the region of Lake Van during the late eighth century BCE. The Cimmerian threat so worried the Assyrians that an elderly Sargon II (722–705 BCE) led an attack against them during his campaign in Tabal and forfeited his life. In 679 BCE Esarhaddon had managed to defeat them near Tabal.

The clashes with the Assyrians evidently caused the Cimmerians to move farther west into central Anatolia. They attacked Sinope, a Greek colony located along the shore of the Black Sea. In c. 676 BCE they destroyed Gordion, the capital of the Phrygian kingdom and home of the legendary King Midas. Strabo records that Midas committed suicide by drinking bull's blood (Strabo *Geog.* 1.61).

The Assyrians took a dim view of the Cimmerians: "the seed of barbarians are they; they do not recognize the [o]ath of the god." In 657 BCE, an astrologer predicted, in a report to Ashurbanipal, that the Cimmerians would overrun the west but Assyria would successfully withstand them.

Mugallu, Esarhaddon's former enemy, was now ruler of Tabal and apparently also of Melid. He sent his daughter with a dowry to Nineveh, but afterwards he entered into an intrigue with Tugdamme (Gk. Lygdamis), leader of the Ummanmanda, an Akkadian term usually applied to "foreign hordes," including the Cimmerians and Scythians. The ruler of Ḫilakku also sent his daughter to Nineveh with a dowry.

Gyges, king of Lydia, was said to have received a dream from the gods telling him to resort to Ashurbanipal for aid against the Cimmerians. So long as he invoked the name of Ashurbanipal, he was successful. But when he shunned Assyria and even sent mercenaries to Psammetichus, Ashurbanipal cursed him and his kingdom was overrun by the Cimmerians. This incident is indicative of the way *realpolitik* in the seventh century BCE could be expressed in terms of dreams, oracles, magical curses and divine intervention.

The Cimmerians attacked Gyges, king of the Lydians, three times. The first onslaught was sometime between 668 and 665 BCE. After this first confrontation, Gyges pleaded for military aid from Ashurbanipal. The second Cimmerian attack against Lydia came in 657 BCE and Gyges apparently held his own (with some kind of Assyrian help?).

Then Gyges turned his diplomatic affections elsewhere and neglected the Assyrians. Ashurbanipal received a report that the Assyrian garrisons in Egypt had been expelled by Psammetichus I with the aid of mercenaries sent by Gyges. These mercenaries were most likely Carians and eastern Greeks who had already been serving the ruler of Lydia. Herodotus claims that the first "bronze-clad" warriors to come to Egypt were Ionian and Carian pirates (Herodotus 2.147–152; cf. Diod. Sic. 1.66.12).

Ashurbanipal responded by cursing the faithless Gyges. Several years later, Lydia was overrun by the Cimmerians and Gyges was killed (c. 645 BCE). After the death of Gyges and the fall of Sardis, the Lydian capital city, the Cimmerians pushed on into Ionia and attacked Smyrna, Magnesia, and Ephesus.

Gyges was succeeded by his son who, Ashurbanipal says, resumed good relations with Assyria. From these incidents it is clear that Assyria was still on the defensive on the Anatolian frontier, worried by the Cimmerian hordes and anxious to ally itself with any Anatolian state that would resist and hamper Cimmerian progress.

**Scythians**. On the heels of the Cimmerians came the Scythians. These are the Ashkenaz, the bringers of destruction in certain prophecies of Jeremiah (4:5–31, 5:15–17, 6:22–26). In later Jewish literature they are a symbol of savagery (2 Macc 4:47; 3 Macc 7:5; 4 Macc 10:7).

They are called Ashkuzāya/Ishkuzāya by the Assyrians and they appear first in the annals of Esarhaddon who encountered them in northwest Iran (676–674 BCE). According to Herodotus (4.1), the Scythians overpowered the Medes and ruled for twenty-eight years. Actually, that was accomplished with the aid of the Assyrians. A Scythian king, Bartatua (Protothyes) was offered the daughter of Esarhaddon and apparently supported Assyria against the Medes for the next two decades (i.e. to 653–652 BCE). Ashurbanipal defeated the Medes and left the Scythians in control. Herodotus' twenty-eight years probably began by about 645 BCE after the great civil war in the Assyrian Empire. The next ruler, Madyes, defeated the Cimmerians (Herodotus 1.103.3) and even is said to have turned south towards Egypt (Herodotus 1.104.2–1.105.4). Psammetichus is said to have met them in Syrian Palestine and by agreeing to pay a large indemnity was able to ward them off (Herodotus 1.105.1). During their withdrawal, the temple at Ashkelon was plundered (Herodotus 1.105.2). If the prophecy of Jeremiah about horsemen from the north (Jer 4:5–31, 5:15–17, 6:22–26) is truly a warning of the impending Scythian invasion, then it must have taken place no earlier than 627 BCE when the prophet claims to have begun his ministry.

## PHILISTIA

During these later years of Ashurbanipal's reign, there is no epigraphic evidence for the progress of life in Philistia.

The most important evidence for Philistine activity in the mid-seventh century BCE derives from the excavations at Ekron (Tell el-Muqannaᶜ=Tel Miqne). The city enjoyed its largest surface area ever, and was filled with important buildings. Of special note is the temple, evidently to Asherah, on the high center of the mound. The peripheral area all around the town was taken up by residencies with all the installations for the production of oil. The Ekronites had acquired the local monopoly over oil production since the good olive-growing areas had been wrenched from Judah by the edicts of Sennacherib. Their oil was undoubtedly being exported to meet the needs of Assyrian forces stationed in the southern Levant.

*Four-horned altar from Ekron, 7th century BCE.*

*Dedicatory inscription of Achish, king of Ekron.*

A dedicatory inscription in the main temple at Ekron gives the dynasty of Pādî, the ruler reinstated by Sennacherib.

The house which ˀIkayaus son of Pādî son of YSD son of ˀAdaˀ son of Yaᶜîr, ruler of ᶜAqqarôn built for Potgaya, his lady. May she bless him and may she gua[r]d him and may she lengthen his days and may she bless his [l]a⌜n⌝d.

The return to an Aegean name for the ruler of Ekron may be an expression of that archaizing tendency found among many peoples of the Fertile Crescent during the seventh century BCE. With the Philistines, that process may have been stimulated by the presence of East Greeks, as merchants and later as mercenaries.

At Ashkelon the excavations suggest that the city was known for its wine production, not only in the classical periods but also in the Iron Age.

The biblical records give some information about the southern Levant in the late seventh century BCE. If the Chronicler's narrative may be trusted, Manasseh had concluded his reign as a loyal vassal of Assyria and had been able to begin strengthening his kingdom by fortifications.

## THE KINGDOM OF JUDAH

**Amon, son of Manasseh**. This king was twenty-two years old in 642 BCE and ruled for two years (accession year system) to 640 BCE. The two brief parallel records of his reign differ in that the Kings account refuses to recognize the "repentance" of Manasseh and depicts Amon as simply continuing the policies of his father (*see* 2 Kgs 21:19–24).

On the other hand, the Chronicler charges Amon with turning back to the negative practices of Manasseh before his being carried captive to Babylon (*see* 2 Chr 33:21–25).

Meshullemeth, the mother of Amon, was the daughter of Haruz from Jotbah (2 Kgs 21:19). It is highly likely that Jotbah be identified with Jotapata, the fortress where Josephus was besieged by Vespasian (*War* 3:141–334), which has been identified with Khirbet Jifât on the ridge north of the Bet Netofa Valley. The ruins and finds here match Josephus' description but recent surveys have not found Iron Age remains at the site. Nevertheless, there are no convincing alternatives for its location. In any case, it is significant that a wife of the king of Judah in the mid-seventh century BCE may have come from a Lower Galilean town.

Amon's name is traditionally derived from the root *ᵓMN*, "faithful," but one should note that Amon was twenty-two years old in 642 BCE meaning that he was born in 664 BCE, the year when No-amon was conquered by Ashurbanipal. Levantine troops, including those of Judah, took part in that campaign. Could it be that the prince born that year was given his name in honor of the great military event of such far-reaching influence? A royal son bearing the name of Egypt's chief deity would match Manasseh's earlier policy of disloyalty to the traditional religion of the Jerusalem priesthood. Amon's return to the worship of foreign deities was clearly not an act of faithfulness to YHWH. Furthermore, it could be interpreted as a reversion to an anti-Assyrian stance on the part of the government.

It was the members of the government, those close to the king, who carried out the assassination. The larger body, apparently the landowners from throughout the kingdom, saw to it that the successor was from the royal family; they also probably made sure that the child king would be properly advised and guided.

**Josiah, son of Amon.** In this emergency, the heir to the throne was a minor child, eight years old. Josiah managed to reign for thirty-one years until he met his untimely death (2 Kgs 22:1–23:30; 2 Chr 34–35). He was eight years old in Tishri 641 BCE, so he must have been born in 649 BCE, during the great civil war that wracked the Assyrian Empire. His mother was from Bozkath, a town that appears between Lachish and Eglon in the southern district of the Shephelah of Judah (Josh 15:39). There is no firm suggestion for its identification. The political nuances of that marriage are obscure.

Little detail has been preserved in the Deuteronomistic account about the early life of King Josiah but a few details can be deduced. Josiah is credited with having four sons: Johanan, Jehoiakim, Zedekiah, and Shallum=Jehoahaz (1 Chr 3:15). Of his eldest son, Johanan, nothing else is known. He may have died at an early age since the three other sons succeeded their father in turn, starting with the youngest. The second oldest, Jehoiakim (originally Eliakim), was twenty-five years old when he began to reign (2 Kgs 23:36; 2 Chr 36:5) in 609 BCE so he must have been born in 634 BCE. His father, Josiah, would have been about fifteen years old. So the firstborn, Johanan, was probably born a year or so earlier when the king was thirteen or fourteen. Perhaps the child, born to a very young anonymous wife, was premature or had some defect that caused his demise. Infant mortality was probably high in any case. The mother of Jehoiakim was Zebidah from Rumah (2 Kgs 23:36 || 2 Chr 36:5). Two brave Galilean Jews are said to have come from there (*War* 3.7.21) so at least in the Herodian period the town was considered to be in Galilee. This points to Khirbet er-Rûmah (Ḥ. Ruma) in the Bet Netofa Valley north of Sepphoris. There is also a Rumah in Judah (Josh 15:52) but because of Eusebius' Douma (*Onom.* 78:21), which is a real town in the proper area (Kh. ed-Deir Dômeh), the Hebrew form of the name is usually corrected to Dûmah. There certainly was, and still is, a town of Dûmah (Dômeh) in the Judean hills. On the other hand, the textual support for Rumah in the Masoretic Text is solid. Therefore, one is hard pressed to decide whether Jehoiakim's mother came from Lower Galilee or the southern Judean hills; it remains an open question.

The favorite son, Jehoahaz, was the youngest. He was twenty-three years old in the summer of 609 BCE when he enjoyed a short three-month reign so he must have been born in 632. He was the son of Hamutal, the daughter of Jeremiah of Libnah. The child was conceived, therefore, in 633 BCE which happens to be Josiah's eighth year as king since he began his reign in Tishri of 641 BCE. The wedding was most likely in 633 BCE. It can hardly be a coincidence that the young King Josiah was influenced during that year by his father-in-law from the priestly city of Libnah (see 2 Chr 34:3a). In the terminology of the Chronicler this would imply a return to the religious practices of the Jerusalem temple.

A drastic difference is observable between the Kings and Chronicles versions of Josiah's political and religious reforms. The Deuteronomist's telescoping of the whole process into one great burst of energy in the eighteenth year of Josiah's reign is hardly credible. The Chronicler's description of a gradual process beginning in Josiah's eighth year of reign and progressing through his twelfth year to the eighteenth makes much more sense. If the Deuteronomist considered Josiah to be such a model ruler, how is it that he waited eighteen years before launching his reforms? (see 2 Chr 34:3b).

The twelfth year of Josiah would be 629/628 BCE. At this time, the purification of Jerusalem and Judah was followed by an extension of the reforms into the northern territory. The king of Judah was daring to rid himself of rival clerical institutions and organizations living in Assyrian provinces. It had been suggested that this coincided with the death of Ashurbanipal. Meanwhile, further research has shown that that Assyrian king died in 627 BCE, but it has

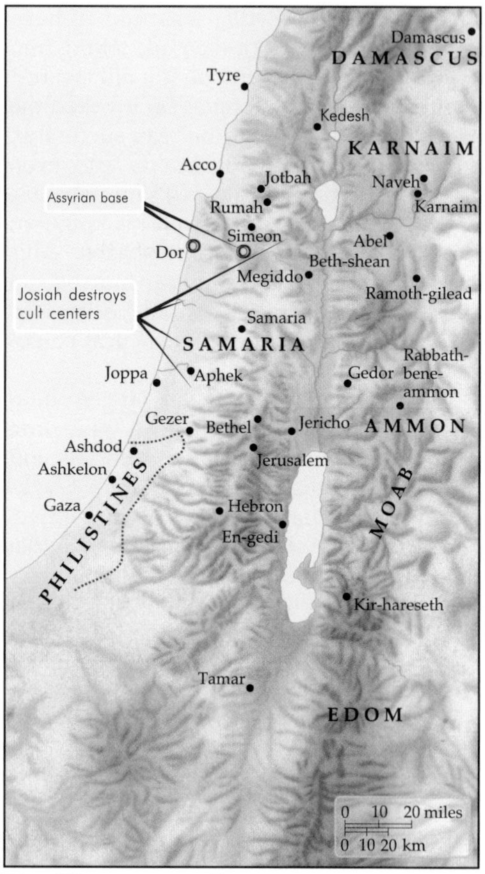


**THE KINGDOM OF JOSIAH**

been inferred that he might have turned the reins of power over to Ashur-etil-ilani in 630 BCE. In such case, it may have taken some months for the implications of that move, viz. the weakness of the central Assyrian authority (especially in the west), to be comprehended in states like Judah. But the chronology of the end of Ashurbanipal's reign is quite obscure. Nevertheless, the weakening of the central authority in these years seems evident although the parallel situation in Babylon is one of apparent tranquillity under the mysterious Kandalānu.

There were always problems with the Deuteronomist's version of this religious reform, e.g. how could Josiah be classified as such a good king when only after eighteen years did he remove the foreign cults from his kingdom? The expansion of the reform movement into the north during Josiah's twelfth year also makes more sense than the way the Deuteronomist has lumped all these events into one package in the reform of the eighteenth year. He evidently wanted to depict everything as the result of the discovery of the scroll in the temple compound while the Chronicler brings in the discovery of the book as a *result* of the reform in progress. Considering the three precise dates given by the Chronicler, the eighth, the twelfth and the eighteenth years, there is no reason to assume that he concocted the significance of the first two. Thus, it is reasonable to assume that the Chronicler has based his description on his primary source, the Chronicles of the Kings of Judah. Further support for that assumption is the geographical description. Such details can hardly be the result of invention. It is not true that there is an "absence of any indication of an additional source" for the Chronicler's narrative of the Josianic reform. Even though the Deuteronomist's depiction of the great purge has been misplaced to the eighteenth year, it has valuable geographical data and will be discussed here under the twelfth year.

The first stage was the cleansing of the Jerusalem temple of all foreign cult implements (*see* 2 Kgs 23:4). The next step was to rid the territory of the Judean kingdom of its rival cult centers (*see* 2 Kgs 23:5).

Then follows the cleansing of the temple courts. One would assume that this would have followed immediately after the cleansing of the temple building itself before going outside Jerusalem (*see* 2 Kgs 23:6–7).

The cadres of legitimate priests from the countryside were brought to the capital (or to the closest priestly city?) where they were given their rations like the temple functionaries but were not permitted to perform the rituals of Jerusalem (*see* 2 Kgs 23:8).

The geographic definition of the kingdom of Judah, "from Geba to Beer-sheba" designates the Geba in Benjamin (Jeba[c]) to the administrative center of the Negeb of Judah, Beer-sheba. The northern city in this expression is certainly within the well-known bounds of Benjamin and not a hypothetical Geba in Ephraim. There also had been cultic installations at the city gates of Jerusalem and apparently also at a citadel gate of the city administrator (*see* 2 Kgs 23:8b).

These latter cult places permitted travelers to offer thanks for a safe arrival or to ask a blessing for a safe departure. They also functioned on behalf of court trials held at the gates (especially that beside the gate of the city manager?; *see* 2 Kgs 23:9).

Special mention is made of the king's abolishing the Topheth sanctioned by previous monarchs as a place of infant sacrifice (*see* 2 Kgs 23:10). A special team of horses dedicated to sun worship was also removed from the temple precincts (*see* 2 Kgs 23:11).

There evidently had been some altars set up for royal use by former kings on the roof or in the temple courtyards. These had to be abolished as well (*see* 2 Kgs 23:12).

Special notice should be taken of the cultic installations on the hill opposite Jerusalem. These had been the sites of diplomatic legations and the homes of foreign princesses who had joined the retinue of royal wives (*see* 2 Kgs 23:13–14; cf. 1 Kgs 11:1–8).

The narrative concludes with Josiah's actions against the cultic centers to the north of his own kingdom, first the "royal chapel" (Amos 7:13) at Bethel, founded by the first king of the northern monarchy (*see* 2 Kgs 23:15). The prophetic anecdote about the tomb of the prophet is attached to the Bethel entry and this is followed by a general, nonspecific, reference to worship centers in Samaria (*see* 2 Kgs 23:19–20).

Josiah's campaign against rival cultic cadres was a bloody affair indeed. Functioning priests from the countryside in Judah were brought to Jerusalem and given rations but forbidden to officiate. On the other hand, the rival priesthoods of shrines in northern Israel (some of whom may have been brought from elsewhere in the Assyrian Empire) were considered too much of a threat to the new religious regime. They were mercilessly slaughtered and burnt on their own altars.

The Deuteronomist's account seems to lack a basic logical order, certainly only partially geographical. By contrast, the comparable narrative in Chronicles is more concise and has a certain cohesion (*see* 2 Chr 34:3–7). The Simeon here (2 Chr 34:6) refers not to the tribe but to the town located at Khirbet Sammûniyeh (today Tel Shimron) on the northwest side of the Jezreel Valley. Its appearance in a Josianic context is explicable inasmuch as Megiddo had long since become an Assyrian base and could not represent the residents in the Jezreel Valley.

It is not stated, though often assumed by historians of this period, that Josiah was imposing his political hegemony over the areas of those northern tribes. That is never stated in any of the narratives, Kings, Chronicles or among the contemporary prophets. Doubt is even cast of the story of the religious purge on the grounds that Assyrian governors would not have tolerated the use of armed force by a local vassal in the districts under their control. Was the Assyrian presence so weakened or diminished that a small-time monarch could move at will through the neighboring territories? If the Chronicler is correct, then the massacres took place before the death of Ashurbanipal after which political rivalries shattered the tranquility of Assyria and Babylonia. Some of the regional governors may have been spending more time at their family estates in the homeland in order to seek influence in coming conflicts. Maybe Assyrian troops had been called home to support the tottering monarchy. There is no answer to these vexing questions.

By 627 BCE Ashurbanipal had passed away. Coincidentally, Kandalānu of Babylon also died. From c. 640 to 627 BCE, the Assyrian and Babylonian homelands seem to have enjoyed a time of security, prosperity and tranquillity (a minor rebellion in southeastern Mesopotamia will be mentioned subsequently). The biblical narratives of Josiah's reign are the only significant testimony to activities among the small states of the Levant.

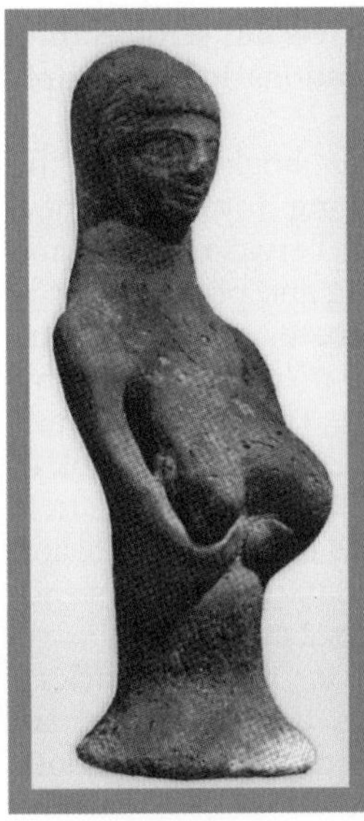

*Fertility figurine found in the Jewish Quarter excavations in Jerusalem, Iron II.*

Perhaps it is a coincidence that the prophet Jeremiah began his ministry in this same year (627 BCE; *see* Jer 1:1–2, 25:3).

From the time of Kandalānu's death in 627 BCE, Babylon entered a period of open revolt and Assyrian preoccupation with the ensuing struggles for the Assyrian and Babylonian thrones must have given the peoples of the west a chance to develop their own independence, at least in those vassal states that had not been converted to full status as Assyrian provinces. Nevertheless, the Assyrian presence in north and central Syria must have been such that even in the Persian period, the Levant could be called Athura/Assyria (hence Syria).

Little is known about Josiah's latter years. During this time he may have been fortifying major cities such as Lachish in the Shephelah and the known seventh-century BCE sites in the Negeb (unless the latter were begun under Manasseh).

By 623 BCE, when Nabopolassar had overcome the rivalries for the Assyrian and Babylonian hegemony and established himself as uncontested ruler of Babylon, western states like Judah must have been able to enjoy their freedom. Judah's subservience to Assyria must surely have ended. Against this background, one may understand the great "renewal" of the covenant with YHWH in the eighteenth year of King Josiah. If the Chronicler is to be believed, the major suppression of rival clerical institutions had been accomplished. The Jerusalem priesthood, allied with the monarchy, was in firm control. The time had come to formulate a new religious-political constitution for the state. In effect, this was tantamount to cancelling the vassal relationship to Assyria. Though no record of such a document is extant, well-known documents from Assyria illustrate the kind of treaty imposed on vassals, and since Manasseh's day, Judah was most assuredly committed to such vassalship. The rationale for Josiah's new covenant/treaty was expressed in the narrative about the discovery of the covenant scroll during the refurbishing operations in the temple (*see* 2 Kgs 22:3–10).

The finding of this book became the occasion for establishing formally a new contract relationship between king and deity and between king and people (*see* 2 Kgs 23:1–3). The age-old debate about the nature of the scroll that was promulgated at this time cannot be solved. The strongest odds are in favor of it being the present Book of Deuteronomy or something very close to it. The full Pentateuch has too many exilic and post-exilic features to have been in existence in its present form by 622 BCE.

As discussed above, the Chronicler's account, which places this new covenant after the regional program of religious suppression, is surely correct (*see* 2 Chr 34: 8, 34:29–30). The favorite wife, Hamutal, evidently gave birth to Zedekiah in 618 BCE (2 Kgs 24:28; Jer 52:1; 2 Chr 36:11) when Josiah was thirty-one years old.

The extent of the territory controlled by Josiah is impossible to establish with certainty. In the south, the fort at Kadesh-barnea was in Judean hands some time during the end of the seventh or the beginning of the sixth century BCE. This is attested by the Hebrew ostraca, including one (No. 6) that is almost entirely Egyptian symbols for commodities and amounts. The one Hebrew word there, "thousands" (l. 12, col. III), is enough to prove that the scribe was Judean. Such symbols had been adopted by Hebrew scribes at least as early as the eighth century BCE as attested by the Samaria ostraca. Such ostraca with hieratic writing at Kadesh-barnea and Arad are by no means evidence of an Egyptian presence there.

## The Fall of Assyria—The Rise of the Neo-Babylonian Kingdom

After the death of Ashurbanipal in 627 BCE, his son, Ashur-etil-ilani, was faced with considerable internal strife but his loyal eunuch, Sin-shumu-lishir, managed to place him on the throne. There ensued a period of conflict over the control of southern Mesopotamia, especially the routes to the Persian Gulf. The contender was Nabopolassar, the Chaldean leader who claimed the throne of Babylon as early as 626 BCE but who did not gain firm control there until 623. Meanwhile, Ashur-etil-ilani had been replaced by his eunuch, Sin-shumu-lishir, who in turn was succeeded by another royal prince, Sin-sharra-ishkun. The Babylonian Chronicle and year dates on local contracts and related documents are the framework for reconstructing these events. In spite of certain gaps due to missing tablets in the series, the Babylonian Chronicles provide a rich treasure of

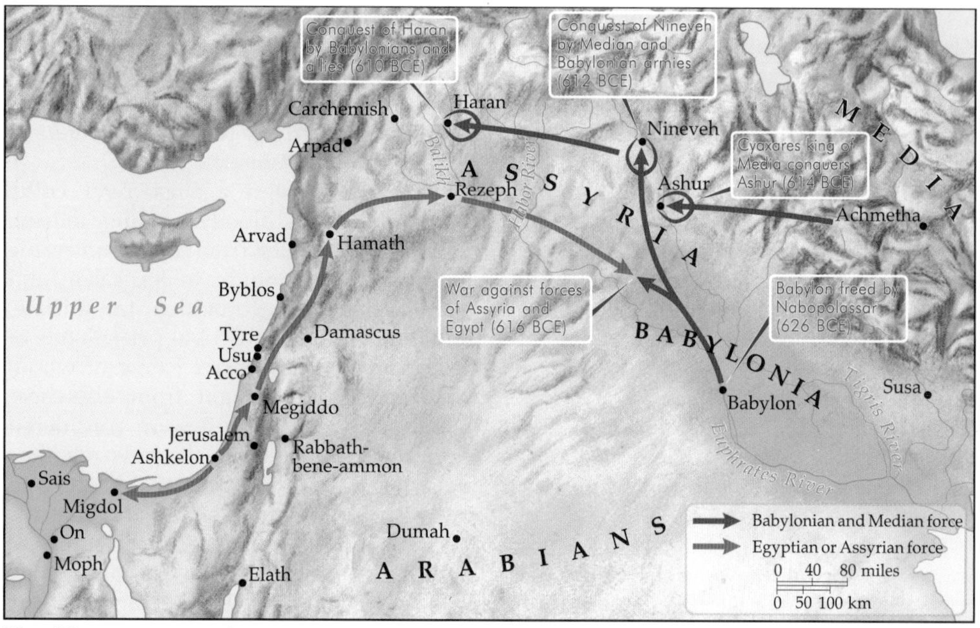


**The Downfall of Assyria (628–609 BCE)**

chronological information that can also be linked to the affairs of Egypt and of the kingdom of Judah. By 623 BCE Nabopolassar was firmly ensconced in Babylon. The Assyrians still had loyal governors as far west as Haran, Gozan and Kummukh. For the next several years, there is a dearth of texts; several tablets of the Chronicle series are missing. The story picks up again in 616 BCE with war along the Euphrates. This year saw a major development in the geopolitics of the Fertile Crescent which must have had great implications for the Levant: an Egyptian army showed up in Mesopotamia to support the Assyrians against the Babylonians.

Nabopolassar launched a campaign northward along the bank of the Euphrates:

> Year ten—Nabopolassar called up the army of the land of Akkad in the month of Iyyar; he marched along the bank of the Euphrates; the land of Suḫu (and) the land of Ḫindānu did not do battle against him; they placed their tribute before him.
>
> In the month of Ab the army of the land of Ashur assembled in the city of Gablini; Nabopolassar went up against them. Month of Ab, day twelve, he did battle against the army of the land of Ashur. The army of the land of Ashur retreated before him. He accomplished a severe defeat over the land of Ashur; he thoroughly plundered their spoil. The Manneans who had come to their aid and the senior officers of the land of Ashur were captured. On that same day he conquered the city of Gablini.
>
> In the month of Ab the king of Akkad (and) his hosts went up to the city of Manie, the city of Saḫiri and the city of Baliḫu; he plundered their booty and he despoiled their extensive booty and he abducted their gods.
>
> In the month of Elul the king of Akkad and his army in his train turned back; on his way he took away to Babylon the city of Ḫindānu and its gods.
>
> In the month of Tishri the army of the land of Egypt and the army of the land of Ashur came after the king of Akkad as far as the city of Gablini. They did not overtake the king of Akkad so they turned back from following them. (Chronicle 3:1–11)

The appearance of an Egyptian force in the upper Euphrates area means that Psammetichus I had been able to move troops across the Levant to come to the aid of the Assyrians. He must have been well informed of the war facing Sin-sharra-ishkun who probably had sued for his assistance. The question arises, what was the price demanded by Psammetichus for his help? The wily Pharaoh with his mercenary army of Aegean warriors must have been engaging in strong commercial activity among the states of the eastern Mediterranean seaboard throughout this time. Assuming that it was Sin-sharra-ishkun who had invited him, the local Assyrian governors must have been instructed to furnish logistical support for the Egyptian troops as they crossed Syria to the Euphrates. It is not necessary to assume that Psammetichus had established hegemony over the Levant—yet. But that was surely his goal.

Towards the end of that year, in the month of Adar, the Babylonians campaigned northward along the Tigris. They once again forced the Assyrian army to withdraw from the field in a fierce battle at Madānu in the vicinity of Arrapkha. The following year saw another Babylonian thrust northwards along the Tigris. They encamped near Ashur but were driven off by the Assyrian army. They fell back to Takritain (Tikrit) where they established a strong defensive perimeter. The ensuing Assyrian attack was repulsed with heavy losses to the northerners.

The year 614 BCE saw the destruction of Ashur by the Medes. They had first drawn close to Nineveh and destroyed a town in its vicinity. Then they turned to Ashur and took it. The Babylonian army had come forth to assist the Medes but arrived too late. Nabopolassar and the Median leader

Cyaxares had a meeting there and came to an alliance agreement. During the next year, a rebellion broke out on the part of the middle Euphrates kingdom of Suḫû. The king of Babylon was compelled to take action against them but finally withdrew after an Assyrian army appeared on the scene.

It was the following year (612 BCE) that marked the real turning point. The Median army came down and linked up with the Babylonian army. Together they marched to Nineveh where they conducted a three-month siege from the month of Sivan to the month of Ab. They achieved a great victory and Sin-sharra-ishkun met his death. After the Medes returned to their homeland, the Babylonian army pursued the Assyrians as far as Nisibin, a major city in the northern Jezîrah. The kingship of Assyria was assumed by Ashur-uballit II in Haran, the great crossroads city on the upper reaches of the Balikh River.

The following year was spent on a campaign of plunder in Assyria. Then in 610 BCE, the Babylonian and Median armies converged on Haran and drove away the combined Assyrian and Egyptian forces who apparently retreated westward to Carchemish. Haran was taken by the Babylonians and thoroughly plundered. Nabopolassar was now in virtual control of all of Mesopotamia. In this same year, Necho II became king of Egypt with the demise of his father, Psammetichus.

## Egyptian Intervention & Occupation of the Levant

There is no solid evidence for an Egyptian presence in the Levant up to this time except as supporters of the Assyrian rump government. Besides Herodotus' reference to the encounter between Psammetichus and the Scythians (above) there is also his description of a prolonged siege of Ashdod:

> Psammetichus reigned for fifty-four years, during thirty minus one of which he was occupied in addition laying siege to Ashdod, a large city of Syria, until he took it. (Herodotus 2.157.1)

There is certainly nothing in Egyptian or Assyrian or any other inscriptions to confirm this assertion. The fifty-four-year reign is supported by Manetho and the cuneiform records. Ashurbanipal confirmed him in his venue at Sais in 654 BCE and his death was in 610 BCE when Necho II succeeded him. Such a twenty-nine-year siege would have had to begin no later than 640 BCE but the presumed Scythian invasion found Psammetichus somewhere south of Ashkelon in about 627 BCE if the Jeremiah warning is relevant. So a prolonged siege of Ashdod may be possible but hardly twenty-nine years long. Assuming, as some have, that Herodotus or his source misunderstood and that it was in Psammetichus' twenty-ninth year of reign, the siege would fall in the mid-630s BCE. Considering that the later years of Ashurbanipal were probably marked by uncertainty and instability at home, it might be possible to assume that Psammetichus was making his move to gain control of the Levant. One would certainly expect some hint of this siege in the prophecy of Zephaniah, who spoke of four cities of Philistia (Zeph 2:4–7). A long-lasting Egyptian hegemony in the late seventh century BCE can hardly be predicated on Herodotus' reference. And there is no reason to think that Josiah was a vassal of Egypt at any time. But it is obvious that Psammetichus had every intention of reaping full benefit from the downfall of the Assyrian government on the Tigris. In 609 BCE his son and heir, Necho II, came forth with his army with the intention of helping Ashur-uballit regain his foothold in Haran. However, there is clear evidence that the minor kingdoms in the southern Levant did not want him to achieve his goal. Herodotus makes it clear:

> and Necho, encountering the Syrians with the land army, defeated them at Magdolo; after the battle he took the great Syrian city of Kadytis (Gaza). (Herodotus 2.159.2)

There is no excuse for correcting Magdolo to Megiddo to relate it to the battle with Josiah of Judah. The itinerary from Magdolo (biblical Migdol) to Gaza is confirmed by the prophet Jeremiah (*see* Jer 47:1).

From these two references it is certain that the "Syrians," i.e. the inhabitants of the southern Levant, made an effort to prevent the Egyptian army from crossing Sinai. They had mustered their forces and met Necho and his troops at Magdolo. But they did not succeed and the Pharaoh advanced across Sinai to conquer the city of Gaza. One would like to know the composition of the "Syrian" army. There must have been Philistines even though Herodotus does not say so explicitly. Elsewhere he speaks of "the Syrians called 'Palestinian'" (Herodotus 3.5.1).

In this context, the attempt by Josiah, king of Judah, to stop the Egyptian advance makes perfect sense. He and the neighboring states had seen clearly that if the Egyptians should succeed in their plans, the Levant would be changing masters, from the Assyrians to the Egyptians. They had no desire for that to happen.

The king of Judah had hoped to stop the Egyptian advance by opposing Necho's

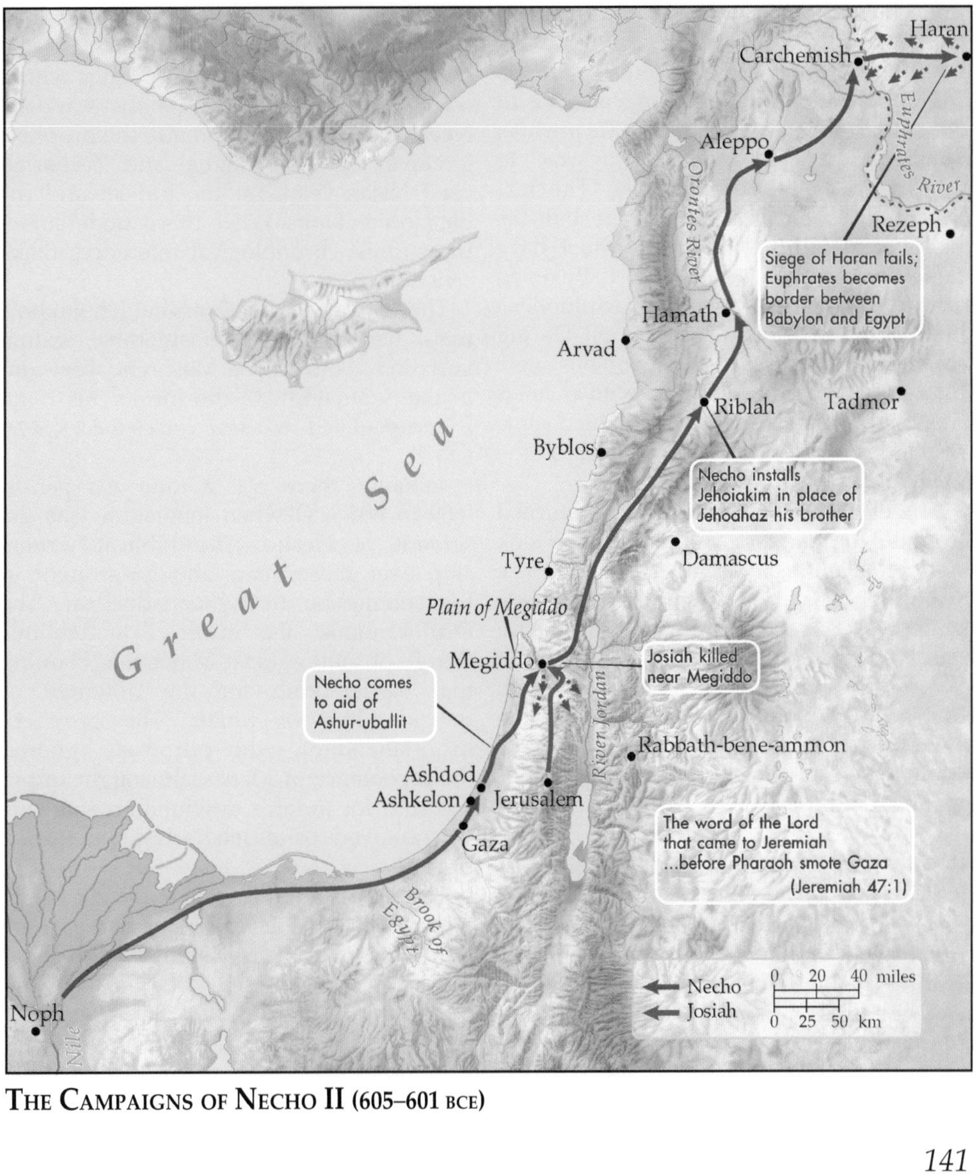


**The Campaigns of Necho II (605–601 BCE)**

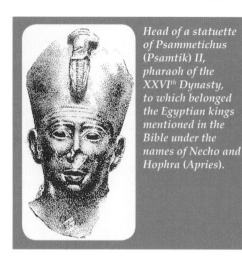

*Head of a statuette of Psammetichus (Psamtik) II, pharaoh of the XXVI[th] Dynasty, to which belonged the Egyptian kings mentioned in the Bible under the names of Necho and Hophra (Apries).*

army in the Valley of Jezreel at Megiddo. How large an army he may have been able to muster is an open question. The Egyptians surely had Aegean mercenaries in their front ranks. However, it was not a hoplite but an archer who struck the fatal blow. The conflict was settled abruptly by the death of Josiah (*see* 2 Kgs 23:29).

The Chronicler gives an expanded version of the tragedy and undoubtedly introduces his own interpretation. After the fact, it is always easy to discern the will of God (*see* 2 Chr 35:20–24).

Necho's campaign to recapture Haran was not successful in the end. His troops had overpowered the Babylonian garrison stationed there but a prolonged siege of the place failed to take it. Meanwhile, Nabopolassar marched northwards to relieve his beleaguered troops. The text is slightly broken at this point but the Egyptians and the Assyrians must have finally withdrawn because the Babylonian army could then turn northward to plunder a number of towns in the Izala region. During the next few years, the Babylonians were distracted by the need to deal with enemies on other fronts. So Necho had gained some respite to consolidate his control of the Levant.

Three months later, when Necho returned from his campaigning in the north, he took charge of political affairs in Judah. The young Jehoahaz, who had just been made king, was deposed and taken to Egypt. His brother Eliakim, whose regnal name became Jehoiakim, was placed on the throne by Necho and Judah was now an Egyptian vassal. The nation was put under heavy tribute and its "spring of independence" was over.

## Judah as a Vassal of Egypt

For the next four years, from 609 to 605 BCE, Judah was under Egyptian domination. During this time the Babylonian army was engaged in campaigns to the north and northeast. Necho took steps to establish an obedient vassal in Judah and this was probably just an example of his policies with regard to other recalcitrant states (in Philistia?). The fate of the Assyrian governors throughout the Levant at this time is unknown.

**Jehoahaz**. Upon the death of Josiah, the son apparently favored by him (born to Hamutal) was appointed in his place. Or was it the influence of Hamutal and her father who was associated with the priesthood? (*see* 2 Kgs 23:30b–33; cf. 2 Chr 36: 1–3a).

Perhaps it is significant that "the people of the land" chose Jehoahaz. He is given a negative evaluation by the historian. Could this be because he favored his patrons and began to support the city leaders of the countryside against the Jerusalem cliques? In any case, Necho had other ideas. His choice fell on the eldest son, Eliakim, whose regnal name became Jehoiakim. One is led to speculate as to whether an opposing party had informed Necho of the situation in Judah and argued the case for the senior brother.

**Jehoiakim**. The king appointed by Necho, Jehoiakim, was twenty-five years old when he began to reign. His accession year was 609/608 BCE. A problem in this period of Judean history is that Kings uses the traditional Tishri reckoning of regnal years even for the Babylonian kings whose own regime used Nisan as the standard New Year. On the other hand, the prophets Jeremiah, Ezekiel, Haggai and Zechariah used Nisan years for the Judean and the Babylonian kings. When this is understood, the various chronological references make sense.

The few passages concerning Jehoiakim's reign have suffered considerable textual variations both in the Masoretic Text and in the Septuagint. In the former his reign is encapsulated in a few verses (*see* 2 Kgs 24: 1–6).

Actually, there was a four-year period (609 to 605 BCE) when Jehoiakim was the servant of Necho. The biblical writers skip over those years and go straight to the submission to Nebuchadnezzar. The Deuteronomist also inserts a tendentious charge of guilt against Manasseh, blaming that earlier king for the downfall of the kingdom of Judah. The prophet/historian/editor, who purposely ignored the repentance of Manasseh, sought to pin the guilt for Judah's downfall on someone far removed from Jehoiachin, the exiled prince.

The Septuagintal version of the Jehoiakim pericope in Chronicles has preserved here the passage from 2 Kings 24:1b–4 about the military units sent to punish Judah on the eve of its ruin. But that insertion is hardly based on the original Hebrew text of Chronicles because the Chronicler would surely not lay the blame for the kingdom's collapse on Manasseh.

On the other hand, a serious textual corruption did take place in the Hebrew text of Chronicles during its transmission. The Deuteronomist account makes it clear that Jehoiakim died in Jerusalem and the Babylonian Chronicle says nothing about taking Jehoiakim prisoner to Babylon. In contrast, the biblical and the Babylonian records make it clear that Jehoiachin was taken prisoner to Babylon. So it is obvious that 2 Chronicles 36:6b–7 was originally part of the Jehoiachin pericope in the original Chronicles of the Kings of Judah but was misplaced during manuscript tradition. When copying the Jehoiachin pericope, a scribe's eye jumped from the words "king of Babylon," in what originally should have been 2 Chronicles 36:*9b to the same phrase in the present 2 Chronicles 36:10. So 2 Chronicles 36:*9b=36:6b–7 was skipped. The scribe who proofed that manuscript wrote the missing passage in the margin and when the text was recopied, the scribe inserted the marginal entry but in the wrong place, i.e. in the Jehoiakim pericope because it, too, had referred to the coming of the king of Babylon. The present text of Chronicles has caused endless controversy that was unnecessary. The corrected texts will be presented below. First the Chronicles pericope for Jehoiakim without the Septuagint addition and without the misplaced passage:

> Jehoiakim was twenty-five years old when he became king, and he reigned eleven years in Jerusalem; and he did evil in the sight of YHWH his God. Against him Nebuchadnezzar king of Babylon came up. ›**6b–7**‹ Now the rest of the acts of Jehoiakim and the abominations which he did, and what was found against him, behold, they are written in the Book of the Kings of Israel and Judah. And Jehoiachin his son became king in his place.
> (2 Chr 36:5–8)

The insertion of 6b–7 caused the scribe to leave out the three years of servitude to the king of Babylon. The Septuagint translators apparently sought to rectify the situation by carrying over the passage from 2 Kings 24:1b–4. They were on the right track but should have realized that the Deuteronomistic editorial note blaming Manasseh was certainly against the viewpoint of the Chronicler.

From these conflicting texts it can be confirmed that Jehoiakim was appointed by Necho. He must have behaved as a loyal vassal until the arrival of Nebuchadnezzar in 605 BCE (*see* 2 Kgs 23:33–35). His three years of vassalage to the Babylonians will be seen below to fit into the chronology of the Babylonian Chronicle very well.

Meanwhile, little is documented about the dominance of Pharaoh Necho in the Levant. The Aramaic letter from the ruler of Ekron, written in the face of the Babylonian invasion, is addressed to "the lord of kings, Pharaoh." So that local king had come to recognize Pharaoh as his overlord.

*Hebrew ostracon from Meẓad Ḥashavyahu: letter of a worker employed in the harvest who complains that his garment was confiscated; he entreats the governor to return his property. The text of this ostracon, the most important found at the site, is composed in brilliant Judean syntax.*

Another possible indication might be the archaeological discoveries at the small coastal fort of Meẓad Ḥashavyahu. The East Greek pottery, including household wares in that style but locally made, alongside native Judean pottery, testifies to the presence of Aegean foreigners. Perhaps they were mercenaries in Necho's service. But the Hebrew ostraca, in good Judean Hebrew (Yehudit), show that the commander of the fort and the officials supervising corvée labor in the region were all Judeans, mainly with Yahwistic names. The paleography of the ostraca there seems most appropriate to the very late seventh century BCE, not earlier as originally supposed. But the Judean ceramics also indicate that there were people, most likely soldiers, from Judah there as well. They could have been there during Jehoiakim's subservience to Necho or to Nebuchadnezzar, or even later during the reign of Zedekiah. Aegean mercenaries receiving supplies from Arad at the very end of the Judean monarchy (i.e. reign of Zedekiah) will be discussed below. The fate of Judah in these final years can be seen against the backdrop of the ensuing struggle for control of the Levant.

Necho is credited with developing an Egyptian navy and starting the excavation of a canal to connect the Nile with the Red Sea (Herodotus 2.158–159). He is also said to have initiated a Phoenician naval expedition from the Red Sea around the continent of Africa to the west. It supposedly took three years and seems confirmed by the report that when sailing west, the sun was on the right of the seafarers (Herodotus 4.42.4). The building of triremes for fleets on both the Mediterranean and the Red Sea was obviously inspired by the need to operate in the East Mediterranean in spite of Babylonian domination of the littoral.

## Nebuchadrezzar's Conquest of the Levant

Leaving the western front for a time, the king of Babylon turned his attention to the districts of Urarṭu, viz. Bīt Ḫanuniya (608 BCE). He plundered and burned cities in that mountainous area. The following year saw the son of Nabopolassar take the field for the first recorded time. Nebuchadrezzar accompanied his father as he led the army to a mountainous area, the name of which is not complete. The king returned to Babylon in the month of Tammuz while Nebuchadrezzar attacked fortresses and plundered them, returning in the month of Elul. The following month, Nabopolassar marched once again to the west.

> In the month of Tishri, the king of Akkad called up his host. To the city of Kimuḫu on the bank of the Euphrates, he came. He crossed [the river] and he laid siege to the city; in the month of Kislev he captured the city. He plundered its [loot]. His garrison he stationed within. In the month of Shebat he returned to his land. (Chronicle 4:12–15)

It is probable that this Kimuḫu was somewhere south of Carchemish along the Euphrates, as indicated by references in the annals of Ashurnasirpal and other texts of Ashurbanipal. An alternate view is that it is the same as Kummukh (Samsat), the Neo-Hittite city-state that became classical Commagene. In any case, Necho apparently had no intention of being outflanked from the north or from the south. In the following calendar year his army came forth and besieged the Babylonian garrison at Kimuḫu for four months until they capitulated and were slain. Then in the fall:

> In the month of Tishri the king of Akkad called up his hosts and he went along the bank of the Euphrates. At the city of Quramatu, which is on the bank of the Euphrates, he pitched his camp. He had his troops cross over the Euphrates and they captured the city of Shunadiru, the city of Elammu and the city of Daḫammu, cities in "Beyond the River." They plundered their loot. In the month of Shebat the king of Akkad returned to his land. (Chronicle 4:19–23)

> The host of the land of Egypt that was in the city of Carchemish crossed the Euphrates and they came against the army of Akkad that had been left in the city of Quramati and they repulsed the army of Akkad and they turned back. (Chronicle 4:24–26)

The army of Egypt, of which the main force was foreign mercenaries, was able to fend off once again a thrust by the Babylonians. But the tide was soon to turn. Incidentally, the use of the expression "beyond the river" as a designation of the territory west of the Euphrates is not so frequent in Babylonian records, which prefer the name "the land of Ḫattu."

Nabopolassar reigned until his twenty-first year. Apparently, his health was

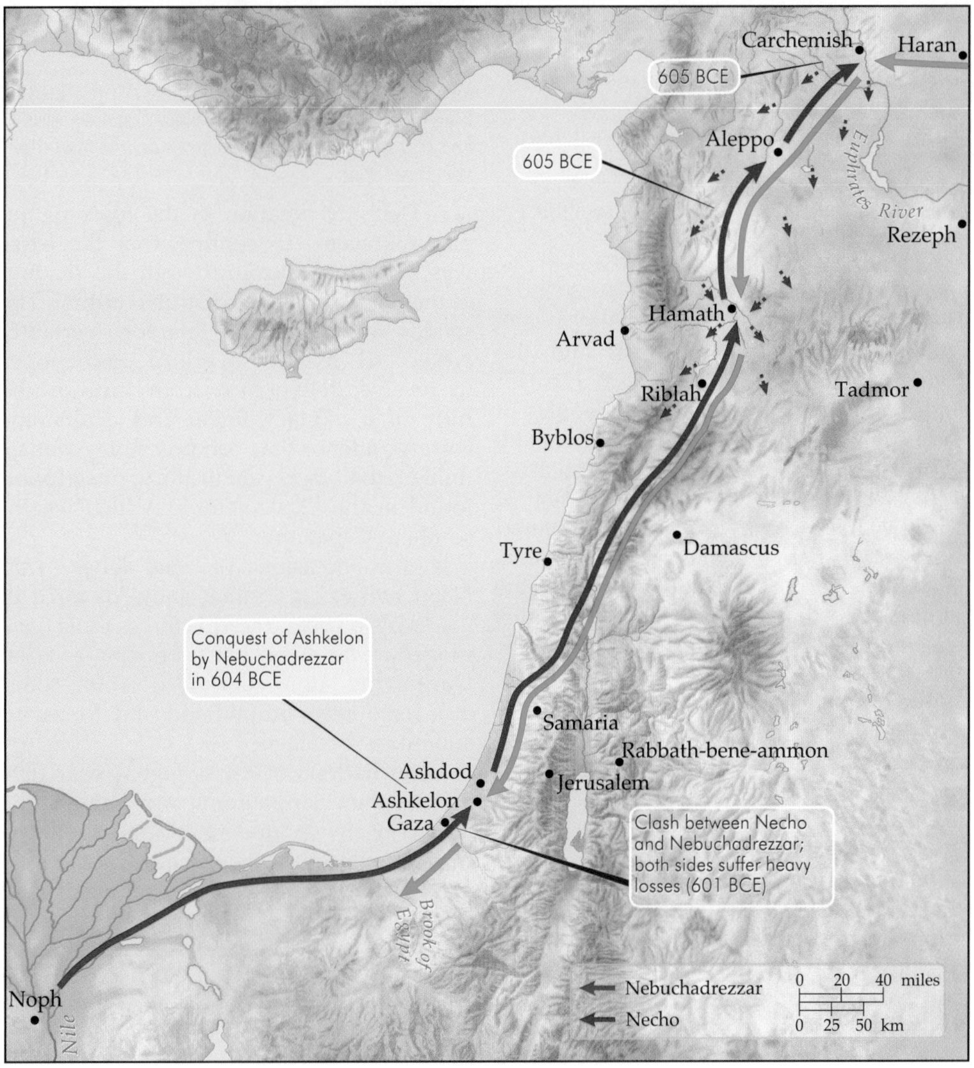


**The Campaigns of Nebuchadrezzar (605–601 BCE)**

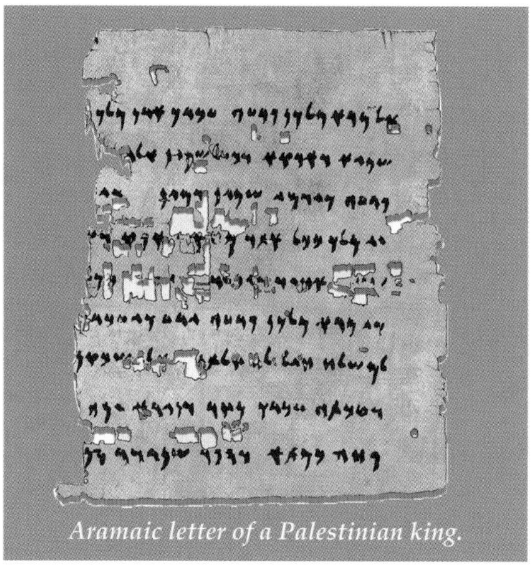
*Aramaic letter of a Palestinian king.*

not good so he sent the crown prince, Nebuchadrezzar, at the head of the army. The narrative begins in the last lines of Chronicle 4 and continues to Chronicle 5. The following passage uses Chronicle 4: 27–28 to fill in some lacunae in Chronicle 5.

> The twenty-first year: the king of Akkad was in his land. Nebuchadrezzar, his eldest son, the son of the king in the dynastic succession, called up the army of Akkad and he took the lead of the army and went to Carchemish on the bank of the Euphrates. He crossed the river [to attack the army of Egypt] which was stationed at Carchemish. [In open battle] they smote one another and the army of the land of Egypt was broken before him; he accomplished their [defeat]. He fi[nish]ed them off until none were left. As for the remainder of the army of the land of Egypt [which] had escaped the debacle and whom a weapon had not caught, the army of Akkad caught up with them in the district of Hamath and they accomplished their [de]feat. Even one man [did not return] to his land.
>
> On that day Nebuchadrezzar conquered the entire district of Hamath.
>
> (Chronicle 4:27–28 and Chronicle 5:1–8)

The capture of Carchemish and the routing of the Egyptian army at Hamath had a profound impact on the peoples of the Levant (Ḫatti land). It was duly noted, of course, in the small kingdom of Judah (*see* Jer 46:1–2). Jeremiah is using the system of Nisan years in accordance with the method in vogue in Babylon (the prophets of this period and of the post-exilic period do the same). According to the Tishri years, this was the third regnal year of Jehoiakim (e.g. Dan 1:1).

Josephus telescopes these events by crediting Nebuchadrezzar with conquering the entire Levant down to Pelusium after the victory at Carchemish (*Ant.* 10:86). He was surely basing his comment on 2 Kings 24:7 which was only realized after the death of Jehoiakim. On the other hand, there is no doubt that many of the local states, such as Judah, responded to Nebuchadrezzar's display of force in the fall of 605 BCE and paid their tribute.

The Babylonian Chronicle now records the demise of Nabopolassar and the assumption of the throne by Nebuchadrezzar. The old king died on the eighth of Ab (15 August 605 BCE) and by the first of Elul (7 September 605 BCE) Nebuchadrezzar had assumed the crown. The year 605 BCE was his accession year. There were still pressing matters to attend to in the land of Ḫatti so he returned to his army in central Syria.

> In the accession year, Nebuchadrezzar went back to the land of Ḫatti. Until the month of Shebat he marched about victoriously in the land of Ḫatti. In the month of Shebat he carried off the extensive tribute of the land of Ḫatti to Babylon.
>
> (Chronicle 5:12–13)

This military activity in Nebuchadrezzar's accession year (until the month of Shebat 604 BCE) probably included the threat to Jehoiakim and the latter's submission and payment of tribute (*see* 2 Kgs 24:1a). And note also that Nebuchadrezzar's actions in his accession year correspond to Jehoiakim's fourth regnal year (*see* Jer 25:1–2). The unusual expression, "the initial year" (Jer 25:1), is different from the standard "in the first year of his reign" (2 Chr 29:3), and so Jeremiah is indicating Nebuchadnezzar's accession year. That year (605 BCE) is also the fourth year of Jehoiakim according to the Nisan reckoning used by Jeremiah.

The Aramaic papyrus from Saqqara sent by a certain Adon from Ekron would fit nicely in this year. Key phrases from the text are as follows:

> To the lord of kings, Pharaoh, your servant Adon king of [Ekron . . .] . . . [. . . the forces] of the king of Babylon have come; [they] have reached Aphek and [. . .] . . . [. . .] to send a force to deliver me; don't abandon m[e]. . . .

A Demotic notation in the folds of the papyrus seems to confirm that the letter was sent from Ekron, though the reading of the place name was disputed at first. The sender recognizes the Pharaoh (certainly Necho II) as his overlord and hopes to receive deliverance from him in the form of a military force. This diplomatic correspondence was composed in Aramaic unlike the local dedicatory inscription found in the Ekron temple, which was in southern Canaanite.

If the occasion of the letter was Nebuchadrezzar's initial show of force in his accession year, then his forces must have ranged as far as northern Philistia at least. During the same foray, Jehoiakim could also have been intimidated and forced to submit to vassalage.

Nebuchadrezzar's first regnal year (604 BCE) saw him campaigning once again in the west. The city conquered on this expedition may be subject to dispute but the fact that such a place needed to be reduced is of importance.

> First year of Nebuchadrezzar: In the month of Sivan he called up his army and he went to the land of Ḫattu. Until the month of Kislev he marched around victoriously. The kings of the land of Ḫattu, all of them, came into his presence. Their extensive tribute he received.
>
> To the city of ⸢Ashke⸣lon he went; in the month of Kislev [he to]ok [it]. He captured its king; he plundered its loot; he [despoiled] its spoil. The city, he turned into a mound and a heap. In the month of Shebat he went away and he [returned] to Baby[lon].
>
> (Chronicle 5:15–20)

The brutal conquest of Ashkelon must have spread fear among all the people of the southern Levant. This event most likely led to a national fast proclaimed in Judah (*see* Jer 36:9). The ninth month is, of course, Kislev, the same month in which Nebuchadrezzar was besieging Ashkelon. The ninth month of the year 604 BCE would fall in the fifth year of Jehoiakim by either reckoning, Nisan or Tishri although Jeremiah uses the Nisan system.

The text for the second year is badly preserved since it comes near the bottom of the tablet of which the corners are broken. The following reconstruction is tentative and admittedly problematic but perhaps not impossible.

> [Sec]ond [year]: Month of Iyyar, the king of Akkad organized his large army and [to the land of Ḫatti he went; over against the city of Gaza] he encamped. He moved forward large siege towers [. . . from the month] of Iyyar until the month of [. . . he marched about victoriously . . .].
>
> (Chronicle 5:21–23)

Obviously, the name of the beleaguered city will probably never be known. The conjecture expressed here certainly makes sense. After Ekron in late 605 BCE, a major effort was required to conquer Ashkelon in 604 BCE. The following year, it would be logical to reduce Gaza, the closest Philistine city to the Egyptian border.

The entry for Nebuchadrezzar's third year (602 BCE) is very broken and the traces only support a reference to the bringing home of a large booty. The inscription of Nebuchadrezzar at Wâdī Brîsâ, high in the Lebanese mountains west of Riblah, tells about the king's efforts to bring cedar trees from Lebanon for the temple of Marduk in Babylon. That project must have been carried out during this period.

If Jehoiakim made his first tribute payment in 604 BCE, his second in 603 BCE, then his final payment must have been this same year (602 BCE). During the following year the Babylonian army was otherwise engaged and had no time to collect tribute.

> The fourth [ye]ar: The king of Akkad called up his army and went to the land of Ḫattu. [He went about] vic[toriously] in the land of Ḫattu. In the month of Kislev he took the lead of his army and went to the land of Egypt. The king of Egypt heard and he [called up] his army. In open battle they smote each other's breast. They inflicted a great defeat on each other. The king of Babylon turned away and returned to Babylon.
>
> (Chronicle 5:5–7)

So in 601 BCE, Nebuchadrezzar again faced an Egyptian army. This time the clash took place in open territory, somewhere on the Egyptian frontier, probably in northern Sinai. From the laconic Babylonian report, both sides suffered heavy losses. It may also be significant that it was the king of

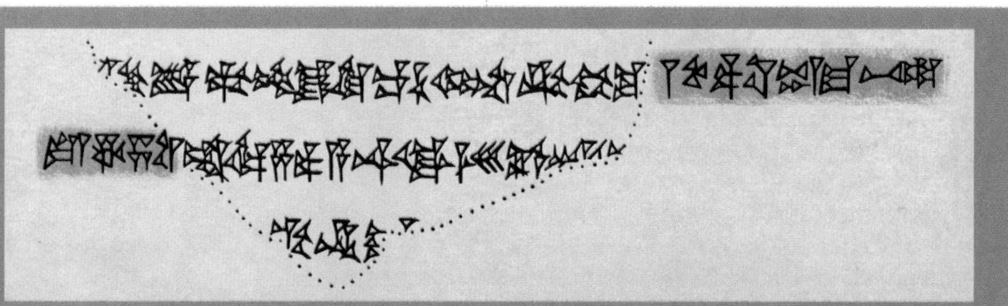

*Nebuchadrezzar Chronicle (5:21–23) showing possible reconstruction of the name Gaza.*

Babylon that abandoned the field and went home. Egypt certainly had inflicted an awful beating on the Babylonian force. The mercenary troops from the Aegean must have been a decisive factor. There is no record of this battle from the Egyptian side. Surprisingly, there is no direct allusion to the battle in the Hebrew texts, only an enigmatic statement in 2 Kings 24:7.

There can hardly be any doubt that this was when Jehoiakim dared to abandon his vassal treaty with Babylon (2 Kgs 24:1b). That proved to be a serious miscalculation but in the meantime, the pro-Egyptian faction in Jerusalem must have dominated policy for the moment. The year 600 BCE saw Nebuchadrezzar staying in his land; "the chariotry and his abundant horses he reorganized."

Babylon responded by sending bands of Arameans, Moabites, and Ammonites, along with some Chaldean units to harass Judah (2 Kgs 24:2). The biblical writer interpreted this as punishment from YHWH, of course (*see* 2 Kgs 24:2; also 2 Chr 36:5a–5d LXX). Was this action taken in 600 BCE while the king was in Babylon? It seems quite likely that local troops were employed to begin softening up the small kingdom of Jehoiakim.

In the following year (599/598 BCE), the king of Babylon was ready to take the field but perhaps not ready to launch a major offensive against Egypt. Since the previous battle had evidently taken place in northern Sinai, the Babylonian setback may also have been due to lack of cooperation on the part of Arabian tribes who plied the caravan routes from Babylon to the Mediterranean. Therefore, they became the object of the Babylonian fury:

> The sixth year: In the month of Kislev, the king of Akkad called up his army and he went to the land of Ḫattu. From the land of Ḫattu he sent his army. He directed them to the desert. They plundered extensively the many lands of the Arabs, their property, their cattle and their gods. In the month of Adar the king returned to his land.
>
> (Chronicle 5:9–10)

The action against the Arabs occasioned an oracle from the prophet Jeremiah (see Jer 49:28–33; LXX Jer 30:23–28). The Hazor in this passage is otherwise unknown. There is no hint that these Arabians were threatening the Transjordanian kingdoms of Ammon and Moab. Thus, it has been suggested that they were inhabitants of the Syrian desert adjacent to central Syria. However, it is hard to escape the impression that the punishment of the Kedarites (Qedarites) had something to do with the previous debacle in Sinai. The Kedarites were generally to be found in northern Arabia astride the caravan route from Babylon to the west.

The stage was set for the final blow against Jehoiakim. The Babylonian Chronicle records the expedition:

> The seventh year: In the month of Kislev the king of Akkad called up his army; he went to the land of Ḫattu. Against the city of Judah he encamped and in the month of Adar he took the city and captured the king. A king of his own choosing he appointed in it. Its heavy tribute he ca[rrie]d off. To Babylon he brought it in. (Chronicle 5:11–13)

The full Babylonian army marched forth in the month of Kislev (17 December 598 to 15 January 597 BCE). Naturally, the Babylonian record uses the Nisan reckoning to number the years of the king. This practice is followed by the prophet Jeremiah (*see* Jer 52:28).

**Jehoiachin**. By this time, Jehoiakim had already died. It is possible that he was assassinated. Jeremiah had predicted a violent death for him (Jer 22:18–19, 36:30). He was to be thrown out of the city gate where his body would suffer the heat of the day and the frost of the night. That would conform well to the month of December.

The young crown prince, Jehoiachin, succeeded his father at this crucial time (*see* 2 Kgs 24:8). The parallel passage in 2 Chronicles gave his age wrongly as eight years but it seems to have been more accurate regarding the exact length of his reign (*see* 2 Chr 36:9).

The city's surrender according to the Babylonian Chronicle was on 2 Adar (Saturday, 16 March 597 BCE). If Ezekiel 40:1 means that the exile of Jehoiachin began on the tenth of the first month, Nisan, then the young king's reign can be calculated as lasting from 21 Marheshvan to 10 Nisan (9 December 598 to 22 April 597 BCE). So Jehoiakim's death was at that time. There is no hint in the Deuteronomistic account or in Chronicles about a violent death for Jehoiakim. In any case, he was buried in the royal burial place.

This young king was forced into a virtually impossible position. His father had brought disaster on his country. It must have been obvious to many of the Judean leaders that the jig was up. Word of the Babylonian expedition must have preceded its advance. Now this lad, who, nevertheless, already had several children, was forced to make some hard decisions.

Jehoiachin's mother was Nehushta, the daughter of Elnathan from Jerusalem (2 Kgs 24:8). This Elnathan may be identical with Elnathan, son of Achbor, a senior government official (Jer 26:22, 36:12, 36:25). She had given birth to Jehoiachin in 615 BCE when her husband was nineteen years old. If Nehushta was the daughter of this Elnathan, her grandfather was probably Achbor son of Micaiah, who played a prominent role in Josiah's reform (2 Kgs 22:12, 22:14). Nevertheless, he is not credited with a high moral or religious stance. Nehushta was obviously acting as queen regent during her son's short reign.

During the interval when the Babylonian army was on the march, the neighboring forces sent against Judah (2 Kgs 24:2) had either overrun or were besieging the Negeb forts (*see* Jer 13:18–19).

Jehoiachin, his own family, the queen mother, high government officials, and most of Jerusalem's skilled workers were deported to Babylon (*see* 2 Kgs 24:8–13). The Book of Kings continues to reckon the years of the foreign ruler according to its own Tishri system. The parallel passage in Chronicles had suffered the loss of an important passage that was erroneously inserted in the pericope about his father, Jehoiakim. That passage has been inserted in the following text. It is obvious that this solves the problem of the contradiction concerning Jehoiakim who by all acounts was not taken to Babylon.

> At the turn of the year King Nebuchadnezzar ‹*king of Babylon came up against him and bound him with bronze chains to take him to Babylon. Nebuchadnezzar also brought some of the articles of the house of YHWH to Babylon and put them in his temple at Babylon.*› And he brought him to Babylon with the valuable articles

*One may assume that the military action on the part of the neighboring forces sent against Judah resulted in the destruction of Arad Stratum VII where an officer named Elyashib (Eliashib) son of ᵓOshiyahu had been in command, as demonstrated by his seals found on a floor of that stratum and the many letters addressed to him.*

of the house of YHWH, and he made his kinsman Zedekiah king over Judah and Jerusalem.

(2 Chr 36:10; note insertion of vv. 6b–7)

## Life on the Edge
## The Kingdom of Judah in the Vise of Levantine Geopolitics

**Zedekiah**. Another son of Josiah, i.e. the uncle of Jehoiachin, Mattaniah by name, was placed on the throne by Nebuchadnezzar (2 Kgs 24:17–25:26; 2 Chr 36:11–21), who gave him the throne name of Zedekiah. His reign of eleven years was a difficult time for the small kingdom of Judah. The Negeb forts were lost and yet heavy tribute was expected by the Babylonians. Zedekiah was said to have been twenty-one years old, i.e. he was born to Hamutal in 618 BCE and was nine years old when his father fell in battle. He grew to maturity during the troubled reign of his elder brother, Jehoiakim, and apparently learned from him the methods of government (2 Kgs 24:19) and his behavior in office reveals that he had not fully grasped the geopolitical situation in the southern Levant.

The final entries of the last tablet from the Nebuchadrezzar Chronicle show that the Babylonian activities did not abate after the punishment of Judah. During 598/597 BCE the king of Akkad went to the land of Ḫatti as far as Carchemish. The entry for 596/595 BCE, the king's ninth year, though quite broken, suffices to record a campaign along the Tigris but the precise objectives are not preserved. It appears that the campaign was to ward off an invasion by the king of Elam. Perhaps this was the occasion for Jeremiah's oracle against Elam (Jer 49:34–39). During 595/594 BCE the king stayed in the land and from the month of Kislev to the month of Tebet there was a rebellion in Akkad. The identity of the leading culprits is not preserved. It is only stated that the rebel army was soundly defeated and the enemies were overwhelmed by the hand of the king. After that, the king marched again to the land of Ḫatti and the local kings there had to report up and pay their extensive tribute. The impression is that Nebuchadrezzar purposely made an expedition to the west to demonstrate to the rulers there that the rebellion in Babylon had changed nothing. The king of Babylon was still in charge. His presence in Ḫatti land with his large army would still any rumors about his being weakened or deposed. This was the same year that Necho II died in Egypt and was succeeded by Psammetichus II.

However, Psammetichus II first had to deal with problems on his southern frontier and in his third regnal year (593 BCE) he launched a campaign, using an army with many Aegean and Semitic mercenaries. The king himself only went as far as Syene (Aswan); his generals led the campaign into Nubia. It was a great success and filled Egypt with a new confidence. This was a fateful year and the newly revived military prowess of Psammetichus II had its impact on the states of the southern Levant.

According to the Nisan reckoning used by Jeremiah, there was considerable diplomatic ferment in Zedekiah's fourth year (593/592 BCE). The initial passage has suffered textual corruption in most of the major Hebrew manuscripts but a few minor Hebrew texts and also the Syriac version give the correct reading. The passage begins with Jeremiah 27:1 where the Masoretic Text has "In the beginning of the reign of **Jehoiakim** son of Josiah." But in the rest of the pericope, only Zedekiah is mentioned (vv. 3, 12). The continuation, verse 28:1, has the correct date, in the fourth year of Zedekiah (cf. below). With this justifiable emendation, Jeremiah was commanded to denounce the flurry of diplomatic activity that was going on in the fourth year of Zedekiah. The corrected text is as follows:

In the beginning of the reign of «**Zedekiah**» (!) son of Josiah king of Judah, this word came to Jeremiah from YHWH, saying:

Thus YHWH said to me: "Make yourself thongs and yoke-bars, and put them on your neck and you shall send them to the king of **Edom**, the king of **Moab**, the king of the **sons of Ammon**, the king of **Tyre**, and the king of **Sidon** *by the hand of the envoys who have come to Jerusalem to Zedekiah king of Judah.* Give them this charge for their masters: Thus says YHWH of hosts, the God of Israel: This is what you shall say to your masters:

"It is I who by my great power and my outstretched arm have made the earth, with the men and animals that are on the earth, and I give it to whomever it seems right to me. Now I have given all these lands into the hand of Nebuchadnezzar, the king of Babylon, my servant, and I have given him also the beasts of the field to serve him." (Jer 27:1–6)

To Zedekiah king of Judah I spoke in like manner: "Bring your necks under the yoke of the king of Babylon, and serve him and his people, and live."

(Jer 27:12; cf. also Jer 28:1)

In that same year, ›*at the beginning of the reign of Zedekiah king of Judah,*‹ **in the fifth month of the fourth year**, Hananiah the son of Azzur, the prophet from **Gibeon**, spoke to me. (Jer 28:1)

If this latter passage is referring to the very beginning of the fifth month, the rebuke of Jeremiah by Hananiah was on 27 July 593 BCE. Evidently the anti-Babylon/pro-Egypt faction had been impressed by the news of Psammetichus' military successes in Nubia.

The very last entry preserved in the Nebuchadrezzar Chronicle reports that in his eleventh year (594/593 BCE), the king of Babylon called up his army and went to the land of Ḫatti. It is most unfortunate that the subsequent tablets of this series have not been discovered. There was certainly a need for him to make a show of force every year because the local states were teeming with sedition, most probably under the influence of the new Egyptian king.

The upstart of all this is that Zedekiah was ordered to go himself to Babylon!

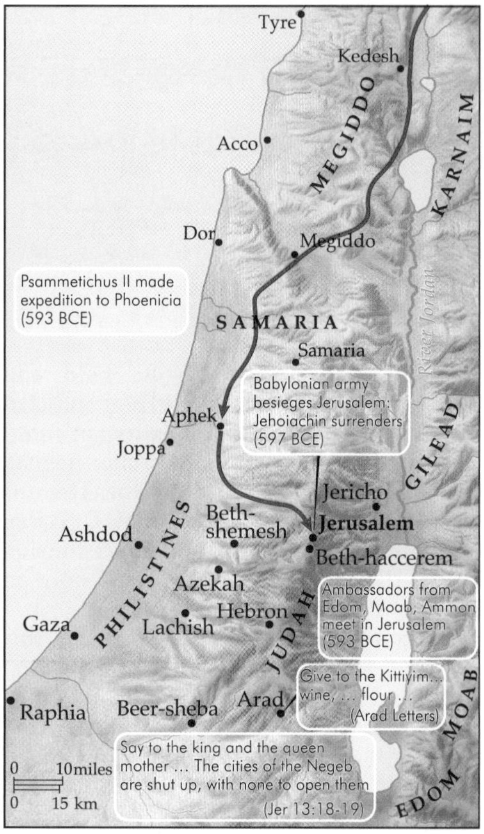


**The Closing Years of the Kingdom of Judah (599–586 BCE)**

Evidently he had to give account of his behavior (*see* Jer 51:59). So the year 593 BCE was pregnant with important events. The new king of Egypt had demonstrated that he had a powerful army. The local states in the southern Levant, from Tyre and Sidon on the coast to Ammon, Moab and Edom on the eastern frontier, were coming to Jerusalem to confer with Zedekiah. It would be a reasonable hypothesis that somehow there was brewing an attempt to enter into a new treaty relationship that might have had the backing of Egypt. The supporters of such a plan were evidently the opponents of Jeremiah who constantly warned them of the danger of angering the king of Babylon. In any case, Zedekiah's trip to Babylon did not result in his arrest. He evidently managed to convince Nebuchadrezzar that he could be trusted. Under the circumstances, it would seem that he received permission to rehabilitate some of the damaged forts in the Negeb. For example, that would explain the renewal of the fortress at Arad. The stratum that represents the suffering incurred when the country was being punished in 600/599 BCE was Stratum VII. Stratum VI is a renewal of the fortress of Stratum VII. The former commander, Elyashib son of ʾOshiyahu, occupied his same apartments where the floor levels had been raised. The collection of ostraca found in one of his rooms makes frequent reference to the issuance of food supplied to "Kittiyim," e.g.:

To Elyashib: And now, give to the Kittiyim three baths of wine, and write the name of the day. And from the remainder of the first flour, load one homer

(?) of flour to make bread for them. Give them the wine from the *aganot* jars. (Arad Letter No. 1)

The term "Kittiyim" must represent mercenaries from the Aegean area or perhaps from Cyprus. It is hardly likely that Zedekiah's economic situation would have supported the hiring of such troops at his own initiative. Most probable is the assumption that the king of Babylon was using the mercenaries to patrol the southern frontier. The local Judean forts were required to furnish them with supplies for the road when they passed by on their rounds of inspection. Such mercenary units would have been charged with intelligence gathering as well as inspecting the condition of the Judean military units posted along the border and on the lines of communication. This would help to explain how Nebuchadrezzar was so well informed about the behavior of the Judean king and about the Egyptian attempt to interfere with the subsequent siege of Jerusalem.

Incidentally, in the fourth year of Zedekiah (593 BCE) Ezekiel dates the beginning of divine revelation to him; it must have begun on 31 July 593 BCE (*see* Ezek 1:1–3). Ezekiel was dating his oracles by the years of Jehoiachin's exile and the fifth year corresponds to the fourth regnal year of Zedekiah. During the following year, on 17 September 592 BCE, the prophet shared his vision of the iniquities of Judah which will surely bring punishment upon them (*see* Ezek 8:1). But a year later, when approached by the leaders of the Judean community in exile, he refused to give them an oracle (*see* Ezek 20:1–3).

The occasion for their inquiry to the prophet (14 August 591 BCE) may have been the news that Psammetichus II had made a foray into the Levant. Such an excursion is only documented in a Demotic chronicle and the contents of the relevant pericope only speak of the priests designated to accompany the king:

In the fourth regnal year of Pharaoh Psamtik Neferibre, they sent to the great temples of upper and lower Egypt, saying: Pharaoh ... is going to the land of Ḫaru.... (Papyrus Rylands IX, xiv, 16 ff.)

The "campaign" of Psammetichus II would have taken place in 592/591 BCE, in the wake of his victory in Nubia. Details of the trip are not recorded in any other source and the entries from the Babylonian Chronicle for these years are not extant. Therefore, only the biblical references are available and as can be readily seen, they can only be used to supply inferences about what was happening in the southern Levant.

In mid-February 589 BCE Hophra, "Happy-hearted is Re" (589–570 BCE), succeeded Psammetichus II.

By 589 BCE the anti-Babylonian party in Jerusalem had prevailed upon the king to break his oaths of fealty to Nebuchadrezzar (*see* 2 Kgs 24:20b).

By this act, Zedekiah sealed the fate of his kingdom and of himself. Such a step was completely unacceptable to the Babylonian monarch (*see* 2 Kgs 25:1–3). It was on 5 January 588 BCE when the Babylonian army established a siege of Jerusalem (*see* Ezek 24:1–2).

Pharaoh Hophra came forth to the aid of Zedekiah, who must have been his nominal ally, but his troops were repulsed by superior Babylonian forces (*see* Jer 37:5–8). The precise date of the Egyptian interference is not recorded. During the interim when the Babylonians raised the siege to intercept the Egyptian force, the prophet Jeremiah tried to go out of the city to tend to some newly acquired property but he was arrested (Jer 37). The siege was already renewed in the year 587 BCE (Nisan reckoning for both Judah and Babylon; *see* Jer 32:1–2).

Neither are there any details about where the confrontation had taken place. The missing tablets of the Babylonian Chronicle would doubtless have supplied the information (*see* Ezek 17:11–16).

Throughout the territory of Judah, the fortified towns were under siege or threat. The Edomites cooperated with Nebuchadrezzar and moved against the Judean forts in the Negeb. An Arad letter dramatically illustrates the steps taken to defend a key fortress, Ramath-negeb (Kh. Gharrah=Tel ᶜIra) from Edomite attack.

... from Arad fifty and from Qinah and you will send them to Ramath-negeb [under the char]ge of Malkiyahu son of Qerab-ʾur, and he will hand them over to the charge of Elishaᶜ son of Jeremiah in Ramoth-negeb, lest anything happen to the city. And the word of the king to you is incumbent on your very lives! Behold I have written to warn you today: (Get those) men to Elishaᶜ! Lest Edom should come there. (Arad Inscription No. 24: rev. 12–20)

The obverse was almost completely obliterated but the address "To Elyashib (Eliashib)" was legible. As mentioned above Elyashib was commander of the fort at Arad in the last phase of its existence as an Iron Age fort (Stratum VI).

The other place from which men were to be drawn was Kinah (Qinah), a settlement in the Negeb district of Judah (Josh 15:22) and is most likely to be identified with Khirbet Ghazzah (Ḥ. ᶜUzza) south of Arad located above the canyon of the Wâdī el-Qeinī (Naḥal Qina). Ramath-negeb is also in the same district though it is only mentioned as a reference point for the extent of the Simeonite inheritance: "as far as Baalath-beer, Ramath-negeb" (Josh 19:8; cf. defective 1 Chr 4:33). Looking east from Beer-sheba (Simeon's central town) one sees Khirbet Gharrah on the horizon; it is directly north of Baalath-beer (Kh. el-Meshâsh=Tel Masos).

The Edomite perfidy was long remembered in Jewish tradition (*see* Ps 137:7; also Obad 1:8–10). During the time of the siege against Jerusalem, the Babylonian army committed other assets to the reducing of the remaining fortified centers in Judah. At a late stage in the action, only two forts remained in the Shephelah (*see* Jer 34:7).

Lachish was the key headquarters in the Shephelah. It had eye contact with Azekah and its communications were conducted via fire signals. At some point in the conflict, an officer subservient to the commander at Lachish, almost certainly located at Mareshah, informed his superior at Lachish that he was looking carefully for the signals from Lachish because he was concerned with the fate of Azekah. This finds expression in one of the ostraca (Lachish Letter No. 4) discovered in the gatehouse of Stratum II at Lachish (see *infra*).

Beth Harapid has not been located but its association with Mareshah is also suggested by the appearance of "Mareshah and Rapid" on one of the many Aramaic ostraca that have shown up in the antiquities market during the past decade, most likely from Makkedah (Kh. el-Qôm) in the trough valley marking the eastern edge of the Judean Shephelah district.

The sender of the letter could not see Azekah but Lachish did have eye contact with it. Mareshah seems to be the most suitable venue for the writing of the Lachish Letters. The devastation of the Shephelah towns, especially Lachish but also Mareshah

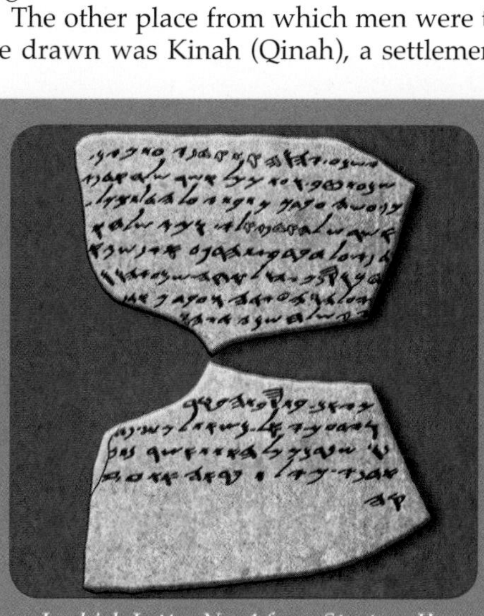

*Lachish Letter No. 4 from Stratum II.*

May YHW[H] cause my [lord] to hear, this very day, tidings of good. And now, according to everything which my lord has sent, this has your servant done. I wrote on the sheet/door according to everything which [you] sent [t]o me. And inasmuch as my lord sent to me concerning the matter of Beth Harapid, there is no one there.

And as for *Sᵉmakyāhû* (Semachiah), *Shᵉmaᶜyāhû* (Shemaiah) took him and brought him up to the city (i.e. Jerusalem). And your servant is not sending him there any[more], although when morning comes round [*I may send there* (?)].

And may ‹my lord› be apprised that we are watching out for the fire signals of Lachish according to all the signs which my lord has given, because we cannot see Azekah.

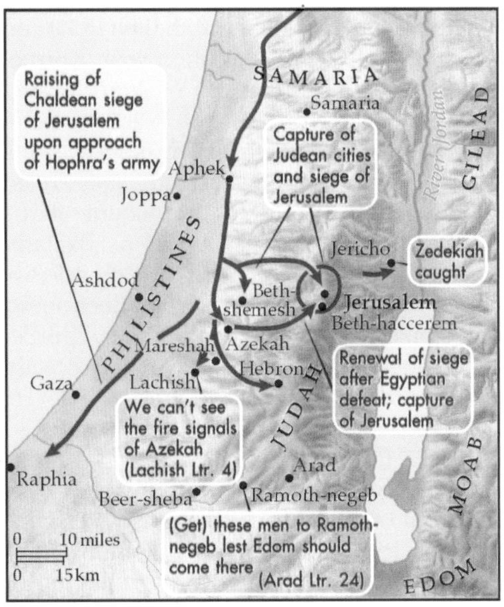


**THE FINAL CAMPAIGN OF NEBUCHADNEZZAR AGAINST JUDAH (15 JANUARY 588 BCE TO 19 JULY 586 BCE)**

and others, is seen in archaeological excavations. There is no further record of this conquest due to the lack of chronicle tablets for these years.

Finally the city wall of Jerusalem was breached and the king and his fighting men tried to escape (*see* Jer 39:2). Note that by both Jeremiah's Nisan-to-Nisan reckoning and the Deuteronomist's Tishri-to-Tishri calculations, the collapse of Jerusalem's defenses came about in 586 BCE (*see* 2 Kgs 25: 3–7; cf. Jer 52:5–7).

Nebuchadnezzar had taken over the regional headquarters, used formerly by Necho, at Riblah (Ribleh) near the watershed in the Beqa$^{c}$ Valley. The date of the city's being breached was 18 July 586 BCE (*see* 2 Kgs 25:8–9).

Again, by both systems, the nineteenth year of the king of Babylon was 586 BCE. Further support for the date of the city's destruction comes from Ezekiel's reference to his vision vouchsafed fourteen years later on the twenty-fifth anniversary of the beginning of Jehoiachin's exile (*see* Ezek 40:1). Some of the refugees who were transported to Babylon by the Chaldeans brought the tragic message to Ezekiel (8 January 585 BCE; *see* Ezek 33:21).

**Gedaliah/Gedalyahu**. Gedaliah, son of Ahikam and grandson of Shaphan, was appointed by Nebuchadnezzar to govern Judah (*see* 2 Kgs 25:22–26; Jer 40:5–41:18). Gedaliah first appears in connection with the prophet Jeremiah's release from captivity after the capture of Jerusalem by the Babylonians in 586 BCE (*see* Jer 39:11–14).

Gedaliah may have been serving under Zedekiah as the palace administrator, one of the highest executives in the government. A seal impression on an unstratified bulla found at Lachish reads, "(Belonging) to Gedalyahu / who is in charge of the palace," a title designating the chief minister of the king. Although Gedalyahu son of Ahikam is nowhere designated as such in the Bible, this would help to explain why he was appointed governor of Judah by Nebuchadrezzar. And the phrase, "to take him to the **house**" (Jer 39:14), may actually refer to the palace where Gedaliah was in charge. Thus Jeremiah found his place among the people who were designated for lenient treatment.

Gedaliah at first had some success in his efforts at reorganizing life in the devastated province (*see* 2 Kgs 25:23–24 || Jer 40:7–8). Nebuchadrezzar had ordered Nebuzaradan, the commander of his guard, to free Jeremiah and let him choose where he would go (Jer 40:1–5). Other citizens who had encouraged submission to Babylon were also allowed to stay. Excavations at Tell en-Naṣbeh have disclosed no signs of destruction for this period, in sharp contrast to Jerusalem and the cities of Judah (*see* Jer 40:6).

When the commanders of Judean troops who had escaped the Babylonians reassembled at Mizpah, Gedaliah encouraged them to settle down and proceed with harvesting the crops, which they did (*see* Jer 40:9–12). Among these were Ishmael son of Nethaniah and Johanan son of Kareah, Judahites who had fled to Moab, Ammon, Edom, and elsewhere and returned to participate in the abundant harvest (Jer 40:12).

However, not all the prominent Judahites were satisfied with Gedaliah. Johanan son of Kareah led a deputation to Mizpah warning Gedaliah of a plot against him. Baalis king of Ammon had persuaded Ishmael son of Nethaniah son of Elishama, a royal prince, to assassinate Gedaliah. Johanan proposed the countermeasure of assassinating Ishmael, thereby preserving the continuing process of reconstruction. Gedaliah, however, refused to believe that Ishmael wished to do him harm. Instead, he welcomed the delegation from Transjordan that came to him in the seventh month (October 586 BCE). After banqueting with Gedaliah, Ishmael and his men assassinated him and many of his supporters as well as the Babylonian soldiers stationed there (Jer 40:13–16, 41:1; 2 Kgs 25:25).

The following day eighty pilgrims came from Samaria to make offerings to YHWH. Ishmael murdered seventy of them and only spared the ten because they offered him rich stores of food. He then took with him a large number of hostages, including daughters of the royal house. But Johanan son of Kareah and his troops pursued them to "the great pool at Gibeon" and rescued the hostages. Ishmael and his close associates managed to escape (Jer 41:4–15).

The Ammonite king in this narrative, Baalis, is mentioned only in Jeremiah 40: 14. His motive for sending Ishmael to assassinate Gedaliah is obscure but hardly benign. Either he was anti-Babylonian in his foreign policy, or at least was seeking to encourage a candidate of his choice. Ishmael, of the royal family, may have been

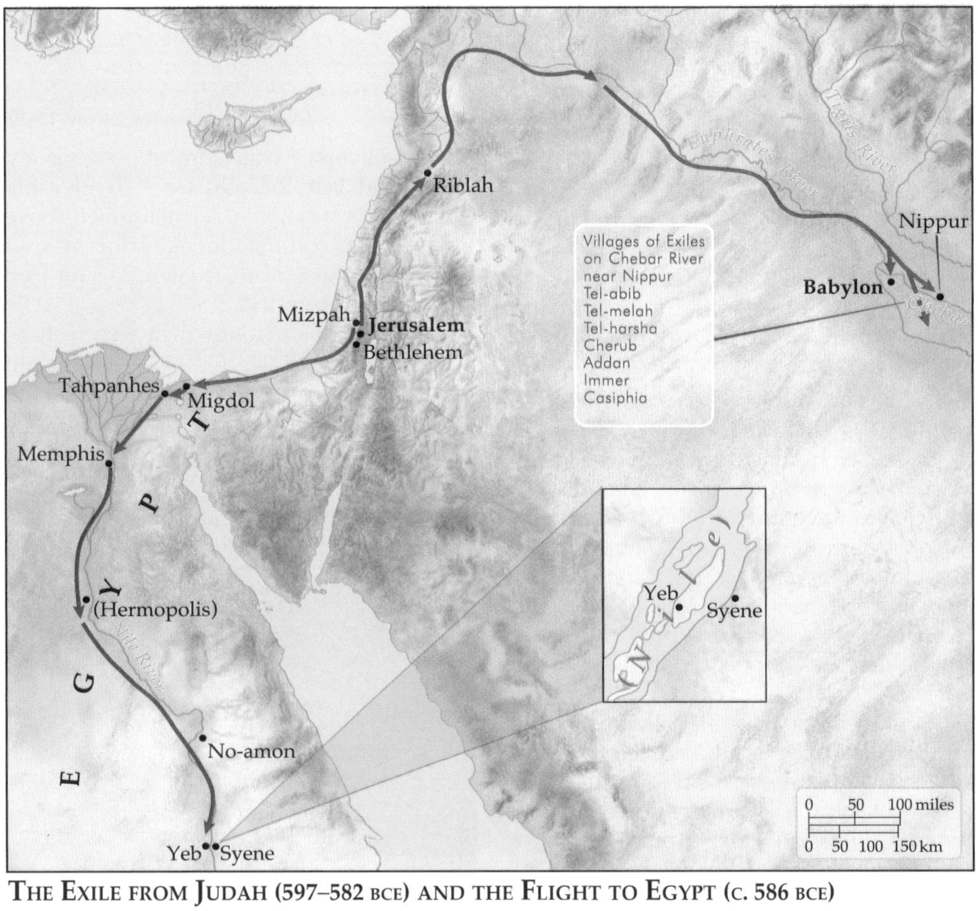


**THE EXILE FROM JUDAH (597–582 BCE) AND THE FLIGHT TO EGYPT (C. 586 BCE)**

from one of the families that established themselves in Transjordan during the eastward thrust of Jotham in the mid-eighth century BCE.

Fearing Babylonian reprisals in the wake of Gedaliah's assassination, Johanan, his commanders, and the people they had rescued fled to Egypt. Near Bethlehem they asked Jeremiah for an oracle as to what they should do. Ten days later the prophet spoke: they were to stay in the land and YHWH would protect them. The people, however, rejected this oracle and continued on to Egypt, taking Jeremiah with them (Jer 42:1–43:7; 2 Kgs 25:26). They came to Tahpanhes (="The temple of the Nubian"). As a result of the destruction of the Judean kingdom, Judean refugees found asylum in several Egyptian cities (Jer 44:1): Migdol, Tahpanhes, Noph (=Memphis), and the land of Pathros.

## Further Conflicts in the Levant

It was shortly after the fall of Judah that Nebuchadrezzar launched a campaign against Tyre. Josephus, citing Phoenician records preserved by Greek writers, is the main source for this siege.

> Moreover, statements matching those of what Berosus says are found in the archives of the Phoenicians, concerning this king Nabuchodonosor, that he subdued all Syria and Phoenicia; likewise Philostratus writes in that history which he composed, where he mentions the siege of Tyre; as does Megasthenes also in the fourth book of his History of India. (*Apion* 1:143–144)

> Nabuchodonosor besieged Tyre for **thirteen years** in the days of Ethobaal (Ittô-Baᶜl), their king. (*Apion* 1:156)

The Jewish historian made further reference to the siege of Tyre in his treatise *Against Apion*.

> Diocles also, in the second book of his Accounts of Persia, mentions this king; as does Philostratus, in his Accounts both of India and Phoenicia, say, that this king besieged Tyre thirteen years, while at the same time Ethobaal reigned at Tyre. (*Apion* 10:228)

The following entry must be emended in accordance with a Latin variant, *anno regni sui*, so that it is in the seventh year of Ethobaal that the siege was begun.

> for in the seventh year of his (Ethobaal's) reign, Nebuchadnezzar began to besiege Tyre. (*Apion* 1:159)

Since the siege is said to have lasted thirteen years, the allusion to the lack of material gain from the efforts of the king and his troops by Ezekiel can help to confirm the dates (*see* Ezek 29:17–19). This date, "the twenty-seventh year, in the first [month], on the first of the month" (Ezek 29:17), corresponds to 26 April 571 BCE. It was the Babylonian New Year's day and the prophecy was probably announced with reference to the recent conclusion of the siege of Tyre which must have been sometime in 572/571 BCE. It would appear that in fact the king of Tyre, by now Baal

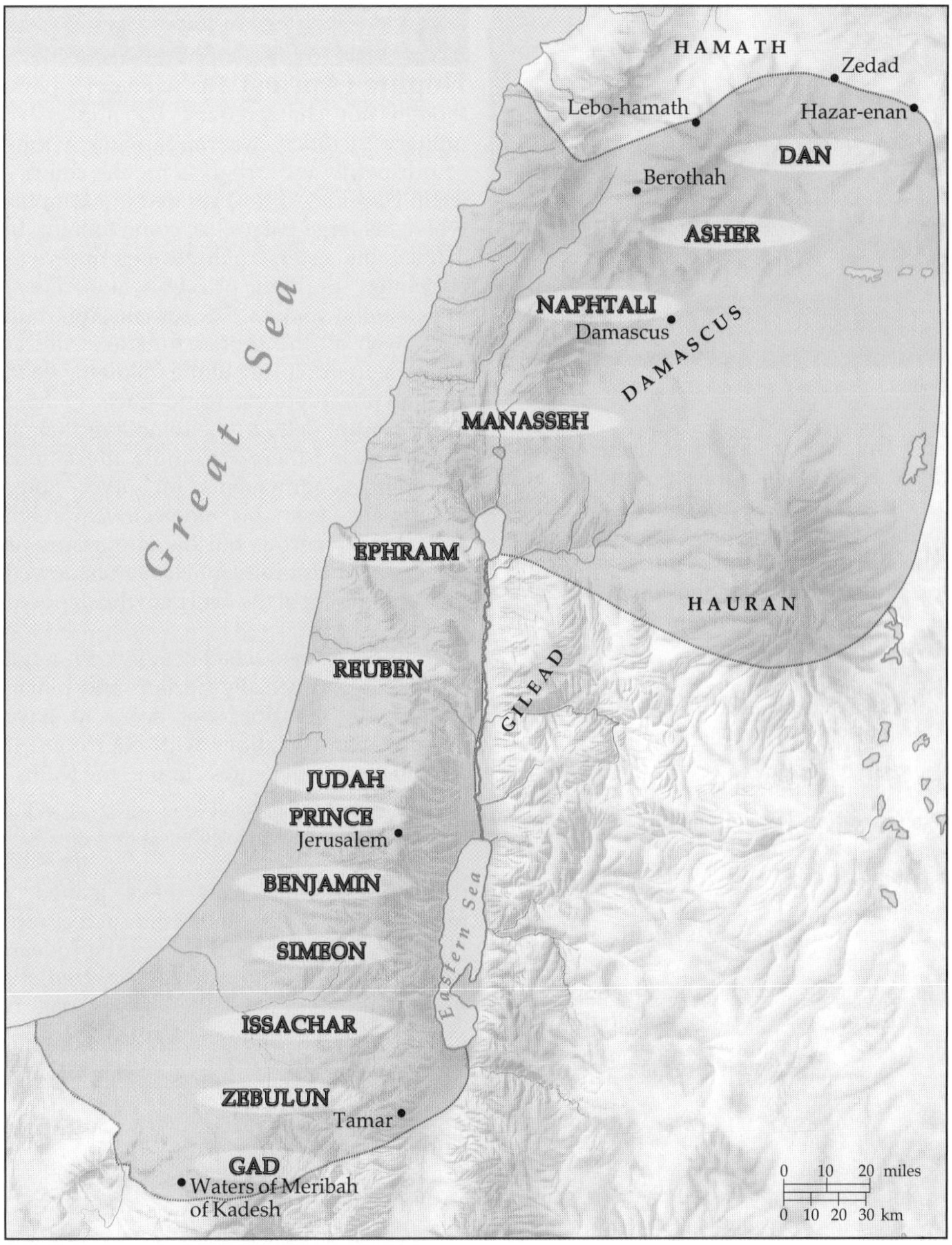


**Ezekiel's Vision of the Restored Tribes (573 BCE)**

II, had made a negotiated settlement. Nebuchadnezzar in any case would need the support of the Phoenician fleet if he intended to invade Egypt.

An Egyptian counteroffensive in the form of a naval operation against Phoenicia and Cyprus is said to have taken place in the reign of Hophra (=Apries; Diod. Sic. 1.68.1). It would have been designed to undermine the Babylonian flank. It was partly successful and Cyprus was reduced in the action. This action may have been the catalyst for the Babylonian invasion of Egypt.

But meanwhile, early on in the campaign against Tyre, Nebuchadnezzar had had to make a foray into the Lebanese Beqaᶜ and on down to Transjordan.

> ...on the fifth year after the destruction of Jerusalem, which was the **twenty-third** of the reign of Nebuchadnezzar, he made an expedition against Coele-Syria; and when he had possessed himself of it, he made war against the Moabites and the Ammonites; and when he had brought all those nations under subjection, he fell upon Egypt, in order to overthrow it; and he slew the king that then reigned, and set up another; and on the other hand, he took those Judeans that were captives in it, and led them away to Babylon. (*Ant.* 10:181–182)

This twenty-third year of the king was 582 BCE. The behavior of Baalis in the instigation of the murder of Gedaliah was indicative of Ammonite enmity to the rule of Babylon. Perhaps they and the Moabites thought that Transjordan would be able to remain aloof from Nebuchadnezzar's control. The campaign of 582 BCE evidently disabused them of such notions, at least for the time being.

It is certainly not coincidental that the additions to the Book of Jeremiah record a third deportation of Judean residents at this same time (*see* Jer 52:30).

Josephus, for his part, seems to have had access to translations of an original

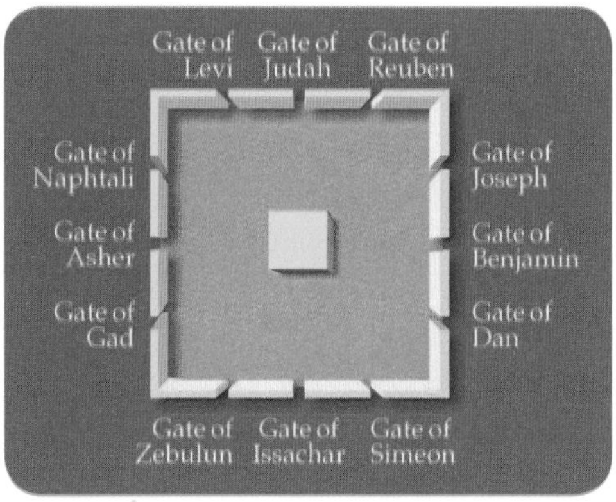


*Ezekiel's vision of Jerusalem* (Ezek 48:30–35).

Babylonian source. Ezekiel seems to allude to the conclusion of the siege of Tyre in his oracle (*see* Ezek 29:17–20). This oracle is dated to 26 April 571 BCE, the New Year's Day of Nebuchadrezzar's thirty-fourth regnal year. Josephus insists that the Babylonian king campaigned against Egypt but he does not give a date.

Late Coptic and Ethiopic romances describe an invasion of Egypt, ostensibly by Cambyses. But it is obvious that there is much in the context of these accounts that points to Nebuchadrezzar as the true invader. Two invasions separated by nearly fifty years have been telescoped. Nebuchadrezzar is mentioned in the narratives and the Egyptian Pharaoh who suffered this attack was Hophra (Apries), not Amasis. This contradicts the evidence of the cuneiform text discussed below.

The extremely broken Babylonian tablet BM 33041 and the fragment BM 33053 record a battle between Nebuchadrezzar and Amasis.

> ...In the thirty-seventh year Nebuchadrezzar king of Babylon [... to] Egypt to make war did [go. Ama]sis king of Egypt [called up his] ar[my ...]? from the city of Put, Greeks, from] distant districts in the midst of the sea [...]? numerous who were in the land of Egypt [. . .] bearers of arms, horses [. . . to] his aid he summoned. ?[. . .] and a line (row?) in front of him, for making [...] he trusted [...].

Obviously, the text is so fragmentary that no specific details of the battle can be discerned. From the scattered words and phrases, it would seem that the text describes Amasis' defense using foreign mercenaries: from Put (Libyans), Greeks and perhaps others. All those troops may have been aligned in a phalanx before him as the battle was joined. The one sure reading, "In the thirty-seventh year," places the event in 568 BCE. This would be two years after Amasis had overthrown Hophra (Apries). It is not likely, however, that the campaign caused any appreciable damage to the new king's position. Amasis himself is credited with campaigning in the East Mediterranean and conquering Cyprus (Herodotus 2.182.2; Diod. Sic. 1.68.6). Before tracing further the events that affected the Levant, it is necessary to review briefly the developments that transpired in Egypt.

## DEVELOPMENTS IN EGYPT

**Hophra (Apries)**. The reign of Hophra, though not characterized by impressive military victories, was apparently a time of prosperity and progress for the country itself. Hophra (Apries) resided at Memphis where his large palace has come to light. In 586 BCE his sister Ankh-nes-neferibre was appointed as high priestess and regent in No-amon and in 578 BCE an Apis bull was given all the proper funerary rites at Saqqara. In the spring of the following year, Hophra awarded extensive tracts of land in the central delta to the temple of Ptah at Memphis; and there are ample attestations of similar endowments for other gods. Monuments from his nineteen-year reign are fairly numerous but his importance as ruler of Egypt is pretty much overshadowed by the notoriety of the usurper who deposed him.

Hophra (Apries) relied heavily on foreign mercenaries, especially Carians and Ionian Greeks, but he does not seem to have enjoyed warm relations with his troops. If Jeremiah's assessment is close to the truth,

> They cried there, "Pharaoh king of Egypt, a big noise; he has let the appointed time pass by."
> (Jer 46:17)

then this pharaoh may have gained a reputation for arrogance and indecision. His downfall was predicted by the Judean prophet and was probably expected by most of the adjacent peoples (*see* Jer 44:30).

In 570 BCE Hophra (Apries) became embroiled in a dangerous adventure (Herodotus 2.161–163). Far out on the North African coast, the Greeks had developed a large and thriving colony, at Cyrene, taking over large tracts of land and creating great friction with the native Libyans. One of the Libyan leaders, Adicran, appealed to Apries for help (Herodotus 4.159.4). Hophra saw a threat in the growing power of the Greek colony at Cyrene, and prepared for a showdown with his western neighbors by establishing a firm presence at the Kharga and Bahriya oases. Then he sent an expeditionary force against the North African colony itself. This army was made up of native Egyptians, evidently because it was deemed unwise to employ Greek mercenaries against other Hellenes. The Egyptian force suffered a resounding defeat by the Cyreneans. News of this disaster led to open revolt back in Egypt, and a native general, Amasis (Ahmose), was sent to placate the troops but instead he was chosen king by the army. Hophra tried to use his Greek and Carian mercenaries to suppress the rebels but to no avail (Herodotus 2.169). There are conflicting evidences concerning the fate of the deposed king. Hophra is said to have been captured and kept prisoner in Sais, which became the capital of the newly enthroned Amasis (570 BCE). Apparently, when Nebuchadnezzar attempted to take advantage of the situation in Egypt and to invade, Hophra may have somehow gotten to the Babylonian side. But the invading army was repulsed, and Hophra (Apries) was captured and put to death (Herodotus

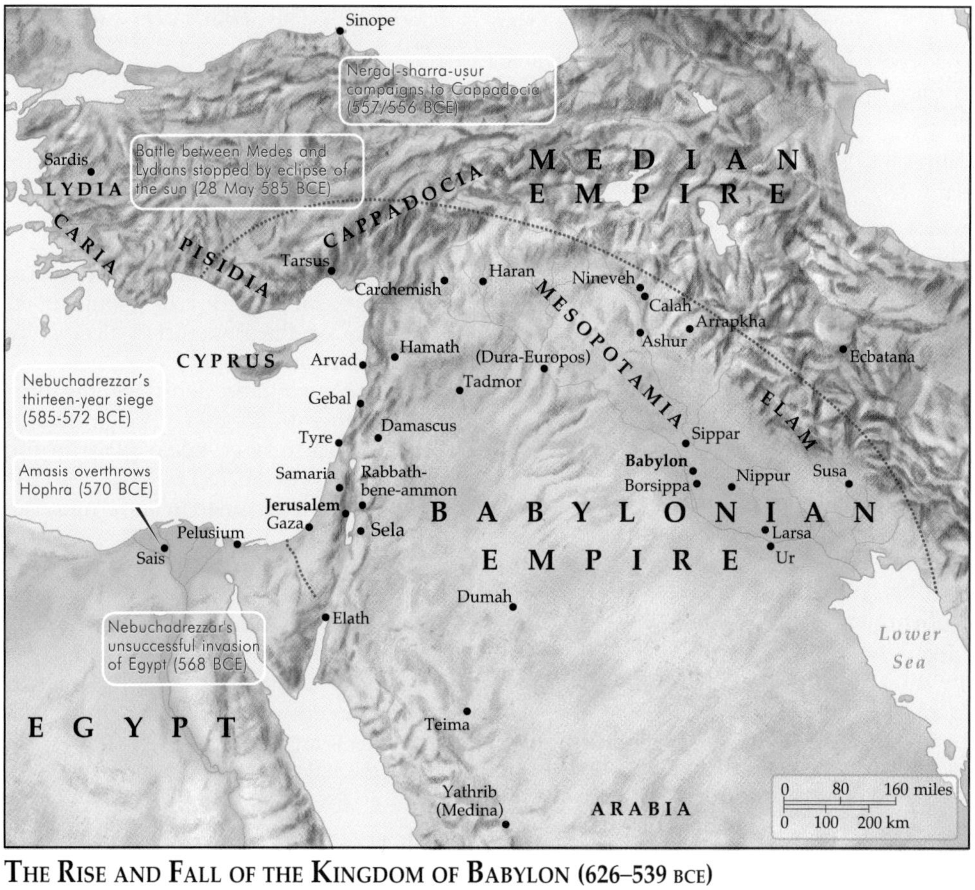


**THE RISE AND FALL OF THE KINGDOM OF BABYLON (626–539 BCE)**

2.161–167; Diod. Sic. 1.68.1). Reconciling the Greek and the Babylonian sources is a difficult task under present circumstances.

**Amasis (Ahmose).** The civil war between Hophra (Apries) and Amasis (Ahmose) cannot have lasted more than a few months and was limited to the northwestern delta; Herodotus (2.169), who seems to have telescoped two defeats of Hophra, says the final battle took place at Momemphis somewhere in the western delta. However, a great red granite stele dated to the third year of Amasis recounts the victory of Amasis and located the battle at Seḫet-mafk, "Malachite field," near Terenuthis (Terrâneh) on the Canopic branch of the Nile. Unfortunately that stele is very badly abraded because it was uncovered where it was being used as the threshold of a Cairo building. Although Herodotus' narrative about Amasis (570–526 BCE) is loaded with spice and gossip, it must contain a valid historical nucleus. He is depicted as a man of the people, albeit a lover of heavy drinking and the riotous life. But the tomb inscription of his mother indicated that she was a royal confidant of Hophra (Apries); and Amasis himself had noble titles. The native Egyptians supported him against the foreign mercenaries who tried to defend the cause of Hophra (Apries). According to the stele Apries was taken alive and brought to Sais, which had been his own capital. Now it was taken over by Amasis. The stele indicates that he gave him an honorable burial. The continuation suggests that Apries had escaped and joined an invasion of Egypt. The enemy troops are depicted as Greeks. Ultimately, the attack was repulsed and Hophra (Apries) was finally apprehended where he had taken refuge on a ship that was still operating in the delta. The cuneiform fragment in the British Museum discussed above ascribes to the thirty-seventh regnal year of Nebuchadrezzar's reign (568/567 BCE) a military campaign against Amasis. Can the two sources, the Egyptian and the Babylonian, be reconciled? The badly damaged state of both texts makes this virtually impossible. But if the Kittiyim of the Arad letters (discussed *supra*) were really Aegean mercenaries now in Babylonian service, then Nebuchadrezzar's invasion of Egypt in 568 BCE could very well have been led by crack troops of Greek origin.

On the whole, Amasis was a man of peace. He did seem to have subjugated certain towns on Cyprus but that was his only recorded conquest. In the west he entered into an alliance with Cyrenaica, and he arranged to marry a noble lady from Cyrene named Ladice. His increasing dependence on Hellenes as a driving force in his government and economy won him the epithet of "Philhellene" (Herodotus 2.178.1). He contributed generously to the rebuilding of the temple at Delphi, and made lavish donations to several other Greek temples. His friendship with Polycrates, the tyrant of Samos (Herodotus 3.41–43), is indicative of his efforts to expand Egyptian commerce to the most important centers of the eastern Mediterranean. On the other hand, he also had to placate his native Egyptian citizens who had put him on the throne. Greek merchants in the delta were becoming much too influential. To avoid the potential friction of a process like that at Cyrenaica, Amasis curtailed this development by confining the activities of the Greek merchants to the great city of Naucratis, southwest of Sais. There the population was exclusively Greek. Temples were built there by the different communities of colonists, and Naucratis became the great emporium of Aegean-Egyptian commerce. This policy on the part of Amasis was a political masterpiece. It satisfied the native Egyptians and funneled the trade with Greece through an efficient channel.

**Psammetichus III.** Amasis died in 526 BCE and was followed by his son, Psammetichus III. Within a year this monarch was to see the invasion of his country by Cambyses, king of the newly developing Persian Empire.

## The Final Stages of the Neo-Babylonian Dynasty

**Amēl-Marduk.** The successor to Nebuchadrezzar was his son, Amēl-Marduk. The name in Akkadian means "Man of (the deity) Marduk." The name is mentioned twice in the Hebrew Bible as Evil-merodach (viz. 2 Kgs 25:27 || Jer 52:31), which probably represents a close approximation to the contemporary pronunciation. His short two-year reign is not documented by any royal inscriptions. The only valuable Akkadian witnesses are dated business documents.

The exact date of the beginning of his reign is hard to determine. The death of Nebuchadrezzar is reckoned as early in October 562 BCE because of documents from Uruk dated to the sixth month of his forty-third year. The latest of these is day 12, sixth month of year 43 (8 October 562 BCE), and a tablet, probably from Sippar, has the same date but assigned to the accession year of Amēl-Marduk. On the other hand, there are two tablets, at least one of which is from Sippar, dated to the twentieth day of the month of Duʾʾuzi (Tammuz) and the *X* day of the month of Ab, both assigned to the accession year of Amēl-Marduk. So there may have been a period of co-regency. In any case, the first regnal year of Amēl-Marduk began on the first of Nisan = 6 April 561 BCE. This is a valuable datum for explaining the one reference to this king in the Hebrew Bible. It is the account of how Evil-merodach released Jehoiachin from his imprisonment (*see* 2 Kgs 25:27–30 || Jer 52:31–34).

*The god Marduk on a piece of* lapis lazuli, *from Babylon.*

As usual with the Deuteronomistic history, Tishri years are calculated. Thus, the thirty-seventh year of Jehoiachin's reign falls in 561 BCE. The very specific dating, viz. "in the twelfth month on the twenty-seventh day of the month," is 27 Adar 37 (2 April 561 BCE), just four days before the Babylonian New Year when Evil-merodach was inaugurated officially as king of Babylon, thus beginning his first regnal year. Obviously, the release of Jehoiachin was part of an amnesty proclaimed by the new king on the eve of his official coronation. This point has often been missed by commentators.

Unlike his father and his successors Nergal-sharra-usur and Nabonidus, Amēl-Marduk has left no epigraphic information whatsoever about military campaigns. His reign is only documented by a few vase fragments and about one hundred contract tablets datable to his reign.

**Nergal-sharra-usur (Neriglissar).** This wealthy and high-ranking in-law of the royal family (married to Kaššaya, daughter of Nebuchadrezzar) was assigned a four-year reign by Berossos but the Uruk King List gives him only three years and eight months; his last dated documents are in April 556 BCE and thus they tend to support the statement in the King List, i.e. an accession year of seven months, plus three calendar years and one month into his fourth year.

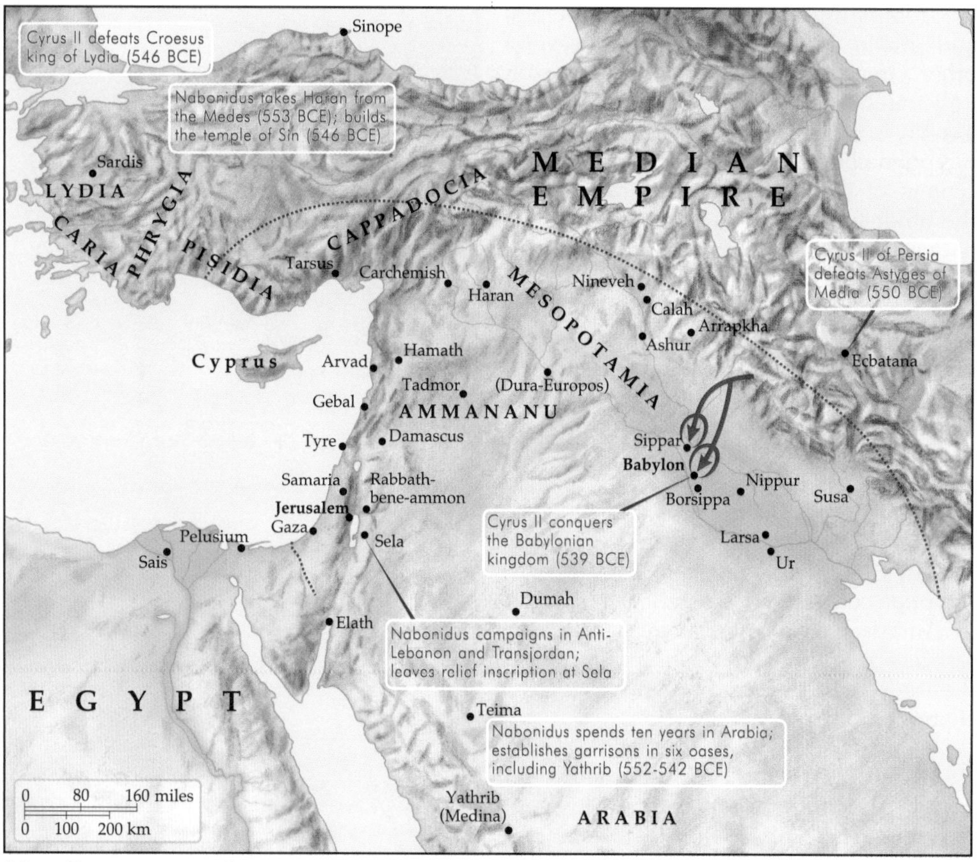


**NEO-BABYLONIAN CONFLICTS**

An entry in the court- and state-calendar of Nebuchadnezzar mentions an official named Nergal-sharra-usur with the title "man (ruler) of Sîn-māgir." The personal name Sîn-māgir is apparently an eponym for a geographical entity shortened from Bīt-Sîn-māgir, a place in southern Mesopotamia. This Nergal-sharra-usur has been recognized as Nebuchadnezzar's son-in-law and eventual successor. The province of (Bīt)-Sîn-māgir has been identified as being located north of Babylon. It seems quite likely that this Nergal-sharra-usur is the same person engaged in the disposition of the prisoners and the spoil after the conquest of Jerusalem in 586 BCE. A certain Nergal-sharezer was included in the list of Babylonian officials connected with the fall of Jerusalem and the subsequent release of the prophet Jeremiah (Jer 39:3, 39:13). The text of Jeremiah 39:3 appears to be somewhat corrupt. Nergal-sharezer is mentioned twice in this verse: the second matches Jeremiah 39:13, where he appears as an official with the strange title "Rab-mag." There is no Akkadian parallel to such a term. To resolve the dilemma, it has been proposed that the name in verse 39:3 be emended to read "Nergal-sharezer [prince] of Sin-magir, the Rab-mag."

King Nergal-sharra-usur has left a number of building inscriptions but the most important text from his reign for the history of the Levant is the so-called Neriglissar Chronicle.

That small tablet bearing an extract from the Babylonian Chronicle describes a military expedition in Nergal-sharra-usur's third year (557/556 BCE). The details, in the style of the Assyrian annals, give the decided impression that the text was composed close to the event.

> In the third year [in month *x*, day *y*] Appuashu, king of Pirindu, [call]ed up his [vast] host; for loot and plunder he set his face [to] "Beyond the River." (Chronicle 6:1–3)

In 557 BCE, in response to a raid planned by Appuashu of Pirindu into the northern Levant, Nergal-sharra-usur called his army to march to Ḫumê (eastern Cilicia, formerly Que in the Assyrian sources), which the Babylonians had inherited after the fall of Assyria.

After suffering a catastrophic defeat, Appuashu was pursued by Nergal-sharra-usur for over 15.5 miles (25 km) of difficult mountainous terrain along the coast to his royal residence and capital at Uraʾ, which was sacked. The town must be located near or at the site of the Hellenistic Seleucia (modern Silifke) on the right bank of the Calycadnos (modern Göksu) River.

> When he had gone from the city of Uraʾ to the city of Kirshi, the royal capital of his fathers, six leagues of difficult mountainous terrain and an excruciating pass, he seized the city of Kirshi, a mighty fortress, his royal capital. Its wall, its palace and its people he burned with fire. (Chronicle 6:15–19)

Nergal-sharra-usur then carried his pursuit a further 40 miles (65 km) up the valley to the north to burn Kirshu (Meydancikkale, near modern Gülnar). The identification of the latter has been confirmed by the discovery at Meydancikkale of two fragmentary Aramaic inscriptions, one of which refers to "Kirshu the fortress."

Afterwards, in a rare amphibious assault on an island two miles offshore, on Pitussu (modern Kargincik Adasi), Nergal-sharra-usur captured a large garrison of troops.

> The city of Pitussu, an island in the midst of the sea and six thousand fighting troops who had gone up into it, in boats he captured. They demolished its city and he captured its people. (Chronicle 6:20–23a)

Control of that island would be essential for domination of the route westward from Cilicia.

> That same year, from the pas[s] of the city of Sallunê towards the border of the city (sic!) of Lydia, he burned with fire. Appuashu escaped; he did not apprehend him. In the month of Adar the king of Akkad returned t[o] his [land]. (Chronicle 6:23b–27)

Finally, he laid waste by fire the passes leading to Sallunê and the Lydian border. Sallunê (modern Selinde) is the westernmost city of Cilicia. Lydia at this time, west of the Halys, probably also included the later Pamphylia. Nergal-sharra-usur was evidently protecting Babylonian interests in Cilicia.

Although Appuashu himself escaped, Nergal-sharra-usur's action reasserted Babylonian control over Pirindu and strengthened its position as a third party between Lydia and the ever-encroaching Medes.

In the month of Adar (February) of 556 BCE, Nergal-sharra-usur set off on the journey of some fifty days back to Babylon. As mentioned above, the latest documents dated by him were written on 12 April 556 BCE at Babylon and 16 April at Uruk. If he died later that month, that would accord with the Uruk King List ascription of a reign of three years and eight months. Xenophon's assertion (Xenophon *Cyr.* 4.1.8) that a predecessor of Nabonidus died in action against the Medes cannot be substantiated.

**Lābâshi-Marduk**. The young son of Nergal-sharra-usur succeeded him in May 556 BCE and his last attested document is in June of the same year. The four texts that refer to him speak of the accession year. There never was a first year. The Uruk King List assigns him three months. His successor, Nabû-naid, says of him:

> Lābâshi-Mar[duk] his young son, not well behaved, as against the will of the god, sat on the royal throne. (Babylon Stele: IV, 37′–42′)

The story of his assassination is missing, probably due to a break in the text.

**Nabû-naid (Nabonidus)**. The removal of Lābâshi-Marduk was the result of a military coup d'état. The conspirators elected one of their number, a high-ranking military officer, Nabû-naid, to be the king. This man was the son of a certain Nabû-balāssu-iqbi who had the titles of "magnet" and "military governor" in the king's inscriptions. He was evidently the chief of an Aramean ethnic group. Nabû-naid's mother, Adda-guppi', had served in some capacity in the courts of Nebuchadrezzar and Nabû-sharra-usur and she was the devotee of the moon god Sin in Haran.

It has been thought that Nabû-naid was identical with the Labynetos who negotiated the peace arrangement between the kingdoms of Lydia and Media after the eclipse of 28 May 585 BCE (Herodotus 1.74.3) because elsewhere Herodotus (1.77.2) says that the king of Babylon during the war between Cyrus and Croesus of Lydia (547 BCE) was Labynetos. If Nabû-naid was sufficiently mature and of high enough rank to fulfill such a prestigious diplomatic mission, then he must have been exceedingly old when he became king in 556 BCE. This is not impossible but casts doubt on the identification of Nabû-naid the king with the negotiator in 585 BCE or with another Nabû-naid that served as a witness on business documents in 597 BCE.

One thing is certain, when Nabû-naid came to the throne, there were three major powers in the Near Eastern/East Mediterranean world: Egypt, Babylonia, and Media. There were also two lesser kingdoms of considerable importance, Cilicia (Ḫumê) in southeastern Anatolia and Lydia in northwestern Anatolia. Haran, the great hub of caravan traffic in the northern Jezîrah (Aram-naharaim), had come under Median domination by 610 BCE when the temple of Sin, the Eḫulḫul, was destroyed (fifty-four years prior to Nabû-naid's accession year). Nabû-naid's external policy was initiated with an eye to the ever-growing strength of his northern neighbor, the Medes.

Against the background of the attention paid in his latter texts to the events of the Median Empire and its conflicts, and Nabû-naid's attention to Haran, it becomes obvious that the king was concerned with his northern borders. Haran was not only the site of his mother's beloved deity. It was also a major link between Mesopotamia (the Jezîrah) and the Levant.

During the king's second year (if the broken passage in Chronicle 7 is properly understood) there is the statement:

> [...] In the month of Tebet in the land of Hamath it was cold. (Chronicle 7: I, 9)

The passage is too broken to draw any conclusions but the logical inference would be that there was an expedition to central Syria, most likely in the winter of the second regnal year (winter 554/553 BCE).

In a propoganda text, a passage that had been dealing with "people of the land of Ḫattu" goes on to record:

> In the month of Adar, in the third regnal year [...in Bab]ylon he took the lead of his army [his hosts he] called up, in the thirteenth day [to...] Ammanānu they arrived. [The]ir [...] and their heads he cut off. (Pa IV, 226–231)

Thus a campaign to Ammanānu is dated to the third regnal year. Ammanānu is possibly the Lebanon but more likely the Anti-Lebanon. This association with the third year makes it possible to interpret the entry in the Nabonidus Chronicle:

> [Third regnal year ... the month of] Abu, the land of Ammanānu, a [difficult] mountain [...] orchards, every kind of fruit [...] from within them, to Babylon [he sent. The king beca]me ill and he got well. In the month of Kislev the king [called up] his army [...] to Nabû, Bēl-dān, brother [...] of the land of Amurru against [...the city/land of E]dom he encamped; the vast army [in the g]ate of the city of Ruqdini [...] he smote it. (Chronicle 7:11–17)

The reading "[...the city/land of E]dom" seems confirmed by the discovery of a Neo-Babylonian relief bearing the name of Nabû-naid high on the red sandstone cliff of Qal<sup>c</sup>at es-Sila<sup>c</sup>, a rocky outcrop near the modern village of Sila<sup>c</sup> in southern Transjordan. The scene depicts the Babylonian king doing homage to divine symbols typical of Nabû-naid's stele from Haran. Of the thirty-five-line text, only the opening words are decipherable thus far:

> I am Nabû-naid king of Babylon.

To all indications, Nabû-naid was securing the eastern frontier of the southern Levant with a view to continuing eastward towards Teima.

The most noteworthy event in the career of Nabû-naid was his ten-year stint in Arabia. The sources are clear with regard to the actuality of the decade in the desert but there is a plethora of unanswered questions and a bundle of speculations as to his motives. The date for the beginning of the campaign is fixed in the so-called "Verse Account," a poetic propaganda tract putting Nabû-naid in a negative light while exalting Cyrus the Great.

> With the arrival of the third year, he entrusted the camp to his firstborn; he placed under him the troops of all the lands; he withdrew his hand; he entrusted the kingship to him and he himself took distant roads; the forces of the land of Akkad departed with [him]; to the city of Tēmā by way of the Amurrites, he set his sight. (Pl. II, 17′–23′)

On stelae that were set up in Haran, the king himself tells his story (for consumption by the people of Haran). Because of chaos in Babylonia, he was led to abandon his country for a sojourn in the desert:

> And I took myself away from my city, Babylon. The road to the city of Tēmā, the city of Dadānu, the city of Padakku, the city of Ḫebrā, the city of Yadiḫ and as far as the city of Yatrib, I traversed for ten years. (composite text; 3.1:I, 22–26)

The cities mentioned in Arabia are: Tēmā =Teima, an important oasis that served as a way station on the caravan routes that came together there; Dadānu=biblical Dedan (Isa 21:13; Ezek 38:13), the ruins of Khuraybah just north of the modern village of el-<sup>c</sup>Ulā in the Hijâz; Padakku=Fadak, a town known in the time of early Islam, not firmly identified today but surely between Dedan and Tēmā

*Upper part of Nabû-naid stele, found at Haran.*

along with the next town, Ḫēbrā=Khaybar, both of which were subdued in the sixth and seventh years of Islam; Yadiḫ=Yadî<sup>c</sup>, a geographical entity mentioned by the Arab geographer Yaqut; and finally Yatrib which is Yathrîb, the ancient name of Medina. Throughout these years the king was accompanied by troops of Akkad (Babylonia) and also the land of Ḫattu, i.e. the Levant. It is stressed that during all those years on campaign in the desert, the logistical support was always forthcoming from the mountains and from the sea.

During the stay in Arabia, there were occasions for serious military action but there were also diplomatic activities with neighboring nations in the East Mediterranean and the Near East. The "great powers" were aware of his location in Tēmā and saw fit to send their ambassadors there. All this points to an active period of commercial and diplomatic endeavor.

> At the word of Sin and Ishtar, mistress of battle without whom hostility and peace cannot come into being in the land and a weapon cannot be employed, stretched out her hand over them and the king of the land of **Egypt**, the la[nd] of **Media**, the land of **Arabia**, all the enemy kings were sending to me for peace and good relations. The people of Arabia who *took up*(?) weapons against the [people] of the land of Akkad [...] in order to plunder and to take property rose up and at the word of Sin, Nergal smashed their weapons and all of them bowed at my feet. (composite text; 3.1:I, 38/45–II, 2/8)

Two legends concerning the stay in Arabia have survived in Jewish sources. The Book of Daniel builds a homily applying the theme of a desert exile to Nebuchadrezzar (Dan 4:28–37). The Book of Daniel does not know of Nabû-naid at all. On the other hand, there are fragments of an Aramaic text found at Qumran that records a prayer presumably by Nabû-naid concerning a seven-year affliction.

The appointed time for concluding the stay in Arabia is expressed as follows:

> Ten years arrived; the period was fulfilled, the day which the king of the gods, Nanna[r] had commanded, in the month of Tishri the seventeenth day, "The day on which Sin responds graciously" is its interpretation. (3.1: II, 11/18–13/20–21)

Unfortunately, the latter passage does not mention the regnal year of Nabû-naid but

*Relief and trilingual inscription of Darius I at Behistun.*

it is significant that the day commemorated is the holy day of the god Sin at Haran, i.e. the seventeenth of Tishri. On the other hand, the holy day of Marduk in Babylon was on the seventeenth day of Nisan. This is remarkable testimony that Haran was on a Tishri-to-Tishri calendar in contrast to the Babylonian calendar which was Nisan to Nisan.

Since the ten-year stay in Arabia began in the third year, ten years later brings the story to the thirteenth year even if that is not stated. There are sufficient evidences from other quarters to confirm that Nabû-naid had returned to Babylon by the early part of his thirteenth year. For one thing, Bēl-sharra-usur, the son of the king, had been left in charge of Babylon and the military units, apart from the elite "Akkadian" troops, had been placed under his command. The son of the king appears in some thirty-four archival documents where he is tending to affairs of the regime; all of them are dated according to the regnal years of his father, Nabû-naid. Their dates span the fourth to the thirteenth years of the king. Now, it is most unhelpful that further such documents, recording acts carried out by the king himself after the mid-thirteenth regnal year, are not attested. That may be due to accidental excavation but there are many texts of other categories from these later years. In any case, analysis of letters shows some important details. By the thirteenth year, for example, there was a sudden turnover in the cadre of government and temple officials at Uruk. It seems obvious that the king, upon his return, decided to retire those who had served while his son was in charge and replace them with new men. Furthermore, the correspondence from Uruk, even though usually undated, shows, on the basis of the prosopographical data, that Bēl-sharra-usur corresponded with the officials who served earlier while his father had dealings with those who were appointed by the thirteenth year.

This does not mean that the king was angry or suspicious of his son. Quite the contrary. It is possible that Bēl-sharra-usur was sent with an army to the military base at Dūr-karāshu north of Sippar in order to try and defend the northern border. During his last years, the aged king was certainly leery of his neighbor to the north, who was now Cyrus the Persian who had defeated Astyges, his father-in-law, in 550 BCE, Nabû-naid's sixth year. Three years later, in Nabû-naid's ninth year (547 BCE), Cyrus crossed the Tigris on his way westward. This was apparently his expedition aimed at the conquest of Lydia.

From mid-543 to mid-539 BCE, Nabû-naid devoted a great deal of his energy to the rebuilding of the Eḫulḫul, the temple of Sin at Haran. That project was not only a religious move. In addition to honoring the deity to whom his late mother had been devoted, the king was strengthening his presence in Haran, an essential crossroads linking the principal territories of the Neo-Babylonian kingdom, the Jezîrah between the Tigris and the Euphrates, and the land of Ḫatti, the Levant. The construction of the temple symbolized Babylonian assertion of control over the city and its environment.

All of these events had a profound effect on the people of the Levant. Many of their militarily qualified personnel had served in the Arabian campaign and some were posted as garrisons in the outposts mentioned above, i.e. controlling the route to Yathrib, the gateway to southern Arabia and its riches. Others had been living for a generation or more in Babylonia itself. They had developed a full economic and social life.

The measure of unrest engendered by Nabû-naid's policies toward the temples of the various urban centers is not an issue to be addressed here. There are reasons to believe that some segments of the population were turning their eyes to Cyrus and anticipating "liberation" at his hands. But some of the documentation to that effect is in fact Persian propaganda after the fact. Be that as it may, the Persian conqueror launched his campaign in the seventeenth year of Nabû-naid, in the month of Tishri, i.e. October 539 BCE.

> In the month of Tishri, when Cyrus did battle at Opis on the bank of the Tigris against the army of the land of Akkad, the people of the land of Akkad retreated. He looted the loot; the people he slew.
>
> On the fourteenth day, Sippar was captured without a battle. Nabû-naid escaped.
>
> On the sixteenth day, Ugbaru, the governor of Gutium, and the army of Cyrus entered Babylon without a battle. Afterwards, when Nabû-naid withdrew, he was captured in Babylon.
>
> Until the end of the month, the shield bearers of the land of Gutium surrounded the gates of Esaggil. The cancellation of anything pertaining to Esaggil or the (other) temples was not required and no appointed time was missed.
>
> In the month of Marheshvan, on the third day of the month, Cyrus entered Babylon.
>
> (Chronicle 7: III, 12b–18)

Josephus, citing Berossos (*Apion* 1:150–151), confirms the seventeenth year for the end of Nabû-naid's career with the capture of Babylon. Instead of being captured in Babylon, Berossos says he had fled to Borsippa (Barsip), some 12.5 miles (20 km) south of Babylon. He also says that Nabû-naid was transferred to Karmania (Kerman in south-central Iran) by Cyrus.

Bēl-sharru-usur is not mentioned in any of the Greek sources. It must be emphasized that in Babylonian documents, he is never called "king" and he never exercises functions that were restricted to the king's prerogative alone. The legend in the Book of Daniel, chapter 5, is a dramatic homily indeed but obviously filtered through a long period of transmission. Nabû-naid never appears in the Book of Daniel; the father of Bēl-sharra-usur (Belshazzar) is said to be Nebuchadrezzar (Dan 5:11, 5:18). Nowhere in the Babylonian documents is it stated that Bēl-sharra-usur was present in Babylon at the time of its conquest. In Daniel, it was a certain "Darius the Mede" who took over the city. That might be a distant echo of the actual governor, Ugbaru, who was ruler of Gutium, on the eastern side of the Tigris, and may have already been a vassal of Cyrus. But as is typical of the Book of Daniel, the author(s) cannot cite the real personages of the original events.

Xenophon makes the assertion that Cyrus had subjected the Arabians before attacking Babylon:

> En route to Babylon he subjugated Phrygians in Greater Phrygia, and he subjugated Cappadocia, and subdued the Arabians. (Xenophon *Cyr.* 7.4.16)

This is hardly credible. There is no hint at such a thing in any of the Akkadian sources and when Cambyses encountered the Arabs in Gaza (525 BCE) it was a new acquaintance and a special agreement was reached.

The various Greek versions about the capture of Babylon, especially the story about diverting the waters of the river which ran through the city (Herodotus 1.190–191; Xenophon *Cyr.* 7.5.1–36), may have a historical kernel. But those reports show that considerable "editorial" influence has been applied during transmission of the event through the Greek world.

## The Medes and the Persians

With the fall of Babylon, the entire Neo-Babylonian kingdom fell into the hands of Cyrus II, king of Persia. This inaugurated an empire greater than any that the Near East had ever seen before. The conquerors and sustainers of that new political giant were Indo-Aryans, the Medes and the Persians, occupants of the Iranian plateau around Hamadan and Fars (Parsa) and in the central western mountainous area around modern Kermanshah.

The Median language, known only in the survival of various personal names and some place names, supplemented by some Median loan words in Persian, is an old northwest Iranian dialect (suggested as the ancestor of modern Kurdish). The role of the Medes in history begins with their interaction with the invading forces of the Assyrian monarchs.

Medes first appear in a Neo-Assyrian account of a military campaign by Shalmaneser III in 835 BCE in central-western Iran. The further allusions to Assyrian campaigns in the Zagros region through the eighth and seventh centuries BCE indicate that the Medes were concentrated in the area of modern Kermanshah and along the main caravan route leading to modern Hamadan (ancient Ecbatana). North of the territory occupied by the Medes was a kingdom of people called the Manneans. South of the great highway lay the kingdom of Ellipi which also appears frequently in Assyrian records.

The ninth- and eighth-century BCE Assyrian royal inscriptions indicate that the Medes were as yet not organized into a unified kingdom but rather a society of smaller polities ruled by so-called "kings" who were more like tribal chiefs. During the seventh century BCE, Assyrian and Neo-Babylonian records point to a truly unified kingdom dominated by the Medes.

**Cyaxares**. Herodotus gives a detailed story of the formation and development of the Median state (Herodotus 1.96–103). However, his narrative is steeped in legend and folklore. The alleged founder of the kingdom was a certain Deioces. He was said to have been famous for his just decisions in cases brought to him, so he was invited by the Medes to be the chief arbitrator of their legal disputes. He is said to have accepted and to have demanded kingship and a capital city to be built at Ecbatana. He is supposed to have reigned for fifty-three years. The name may be reflected in the records of Sargon II where a Bīt-Dayukku appears as a Median polity. The person of Dayukku and his family were eventually captured and exiled to Hamath. The Sargonic evidence only confirms that such a name was in use among the Medes in the eighth century BCE. The personage cannot be identified with Herodotus' Deioces. This latter was succeeded by his son, Phraortes, who is supposed to have conquered the Persians, something doubtful in itself. He was reputedly killed in battle against the Assyrians. There is no Assyrian record of him. His son, Cyaxares, is credited with the reorganization of the Median army. It was he who opened hostilities against the internally weakened Assyrian kingdom, destroyed Ashur and, in alliance with Nabopolassar, destroyed Nineveh in 612 BCE. While the Neo-Babylonian dynasty carried the war westward to the Euphrates, Cyaxares was apparently not idle. The other major Assyrian cities along the Tigris such as Calah/Kalḫu were plundered and destroyed. This must have been the work of the Medes. The temple of Sin at Haran was allegedly destroyed by the Medes, who had come in 610 BCE to assist the Babylonians in the conquest of the city and the expulsion of the Assyrians and their allies, the Egyptians. Although the Babylonian Chronicle says of the king of Akkad (Nabopolassar), "he plundered vast booty of the city and the temple," the Medes are blamed by Nabû-naid for the actual destruction of the Eḫulḫul.

The Urartian kingdom had surely been decimated already by the Scythians. The way was apparently open for Cyaxares to advance into central Anatolia. In spite of the lack of other documentation for the Median westward expansion, the allusion by Herodotus to the Halys as the border between Lydia and Media (Herodotus 1.72.2) and the ensuing five-year war between Alyattes and Cyaxares (Herodotus 1.74) proves that Cappadocia was under Median control by 590 BCE. During the sixth year of the war, after a seesaw conflict with many vicious encounters, an eclipse of the sun caused a cessation of hostilities and an appeal to mediators for reconciliation. The eclipse has been identified as that of 28 May 585 BCE. Since the parties had been warring for over five years, the Median ruler had obviously extended his authority over central Anatolia by at least 591 BCE. This he accomplished while Nebuchadrezzar was consolidating his control over the Levant and confronting the Egyptian interference there.

The mediation between Lydia and Media was conducted by "Syenneisis the Cilician and Labynetos the Babylonian" (Herodotus 1.74.3). Although Herodotus calls the last king of Babylon Labynetos (Herodotus 1.188.1), it is not likely here that he is referring to Nabû-naid. What is more reasonable is the assumption that Herodotus knows only one late Babylonian king and he applies that name here. So in 585 BCE the ruler of Cilicia and the king of Babylon mediated between the Medes and the Lydians. They determined that a royal marriage between the rival parties would be the best way to assure that the new treaty would be honored by both sides. Thus the daughter of Alyattes of Lydia, Aryenis, was married to Astyges, the son of Cyaxares (Herodotus 1.74.3–5).

*Two Persian nobles, relief from Persepolis.*

**Astyges**. Herodotus gives Astyges a reign of thirty-five years. Since the date of his removal from office is fixed by the Babylonian Chronicle at 550 BCE, his reign would have begun in 585 BCE. This would also determine the death of Cyaxares at 585 BCE. Herodotus assigns Cyaxares forty years, meaning that he would have come to the throne in 625 BCE, during the troubled end of Assyrian control in Babylonia. Astyges is considered to have been a weak ruler but this is easy to say after he was defeated by Cyrus the Persian. However, the legendary tradition is that Astyges had a daughter, Mandane, presumably born to his Lydian wife. Mandane is reported to have been wed to Cambyses, a Persian, evidently Cambyses I of the Achaemenid line.

**Cyrus II (the Great)**. In the official genealogy propagated by Cyrus II, his royal ancestors are listed as rulers of Anshan (Malyān), located less than 60 miles (100 km) from Pasargade and Persepolis, the famous capitals of the Persian Empire. Anshan was the old name from early Mesopotamian times and Akkadian scribes continued to use it in Cyrus' earlier inscriptions. Later the district is called Parsa (modern Fars).

I am Cyrus, king of the world, great king, mighty king, king of Babylon, king of the land of Sumer and Akkad, king of the four quarters, son of Cambyses, great king, king of the city of Anshan, grandson of

*Median nobles, Persepolis.*

Cyrus, great king, king of the city of Anshan, great-grandson of Čišpiš, great king, king of the city of Anshan. (Cyrus Cylinder = K2.I: 20–21)

Darius I complicates matters with his own version, doubtless designed to support his legitimacy to rule:

Thus speaks Darius the king: My father was Hystaspes, the father of Hystaspes was Arshama, the father of Arshama was Ariyaramnaᵓ, the father of Ariyaramnaᵓ was Čišpiš, the father of Čišpiš was Achaemenes. (Bisitun Inscription §2, ll. 1–2)

There are various explanations for this anomaly but whatever the truth behind these lists, there is also the narrative by Herodotus (1.107–122) about Mandane, wife of Cambyses, who gave birth to a son named Cyrus. The legendary material in Herodotus' account may be safely ignored but if the skeleton of the narrative is true, it would make this Cyrus, son of Cambyses (I), the grandson of Astyges and great-grandson of the Lydian Alyattes.

In any event, Astyges lost his kingdom to Cyrus II. The chronological peg is the reference in the Babylonian Chronicle:

[Astyges mu]stered [his army]; he went against Cyrus for conquest. As for Astyges, his army revolted against him, he was made prisoner; they han[ded (him) over] to Cyrus. Cyrus ‹went› to the land of Ecbatana. The [vast] silver, gold, possessions and property of the land of Ecbatana he plundered; he took it to the country of Anshan. The property and possessions of the army of [Astyges he did not take(?)]. (Chronicle 7: II, 1–4)

Since this entry comes before that of the seventh year, it must belong in the sixth year of Nabû-naid, viz. 550 BCE. The Akkadian clearly states that Astyges was coming to attack Cyrus. Herodotus says that Cyrus, who had been a vassal of Astyges, was responding to an advance of the Median army (Herodotus 1.127–130). But the Babylonian Chronicle 7 is a pro-Cyrus document so the text may be formulated to look like Cyrus' action was one of self-defense. The unifying theme is the defection of most of the Median army to Cyrus and the subsequent capture of Astyges.

Cyrus must have spent the early years of his reign, from 559 to 554 BCE, unifying the different polities and tribes among his people the Persians, who may have been mainly tribal herdsmen at the beginning. Their presumed subjugation to Astyges, king of Media, as maintained by Herodotus (1.127), is not documented in any Persian document. However, the Median domination of Haran is attested in a "Dream Text" recorded on two cylinders and many fragments. One cylinder was found in the Ebabbar temple to Shamash in Sippar; the other was found in Babylon and was probably commemorating the Ishtar temple there. The contents of the inscription, viz. the references to the rebuilding of certain temples, require a date sometime in the thirteenth or more likely in the sixteenth year of Nabû-naid. Therefore, the allusion to Cyrus' revolt against the Medes is narrated in retrospect:

In the accession year of my eternal kingship, Marduk the great lord and Sin the luminary of heaven and earth revealed to me a dream. Both of them were standing. Marduk spoke to me, "Nabû-naid, king of Babylon, on the horse, your mount, carry bricks. Build the Eḫulḫul; install Sin, the great lord, in his dwelling place within it." Reverently I spoke to the Enlil of the gods, Marduk, "As for that temple of which you commanded to build, the barbarian surrounds it; his forces are massive." Marduk spoke to me, "As for that barbarian of whom you spoke, himself, his land and the kings who support him will not exist."

With the arrival of the third regnal year, they stirred up Cyrus, king of the land of Anshan, his young servant. With his small army he dispersed the vast barbarians; Astyges, king of the barbarians, he captured. He brought him in captivity to his land. (2.12: I, 15–29)

So Cyrus' uprising began in the third regnal year of Nabû-naid and came to its conclusion in the sixth regnal year. The "Dream Text" above has simply telescoped the events in retrospect.

The reference to Cyrus as the "young servant" of Marduk has long ago been noted as a parallel to the biblical passage where Cyrus is called the anointed one of YHWH:

Thus says YHWH to Cyrus His anointed one, whom I have taken by the right hand, to subdue nations before him and I will loosen the loins of kings; to open doors before him so that gates will not be shut;

I will go before you and level the hills (LXX); I will smash the doors of bronze and chop through the iron door bolts. I will give you the treasures of darkness and hidden caches, so you may know that it is I, YHWH, the God of Israel, who has called you by your name. (Isa 45:1–3)

An entry in the Nabonidus Chronicle for Nabû-naid's ninth regnal year (547 BCE) records the beginning of Cyrus' western campaign:

In the month of Nisan, Cyrus, king of the land of Persia, called up his army; below the city of Arbela he crossed the Tigris; in the month of Iyyar [he went] to the land of Ly[dia]; its king he slew; his property he took away; his own garrison he posted (there) [. . .]. (Chronicle 7:15–17)

The mustering of the army and the crossing of the Tigris took place in April 547 BCE and the arrival at the border of Lydia came about in May. According to Herodotus (1.76–91) there had been a fierce but indecisive battle between the Persian and Lydian forces after which Croesus, king of Lydia, retired to Sardis and sent his allied troops to winter quarters. Cyrus did not choose to make camp for the winter; instead he made a surprise dash to Sardis and forced Croesus to fight with depleted forces. Afterwards, the Persians even breached the citadel of Sardis where Croesus was holed up. The fate of Croesus is the subject of folkloristic legends. The dates in the Babylonian Chronicle place the Babylonian army in Cappadocia by the beginning of summer. Details about the number of battles that took place during the ensuing months are not available. There seems no reason to doubt the surprise tactic used by Cyrus. After the fact, note should be taken of the famous story of the oracle from the shrine of Apollo at Delphi who told Croesus that if he attacked the Persians, he would destroy a great empire (Herodotus 1.53). Croesus had sought help from his erstwhile allies, the Spartans, the Egyptians and the Babylonians. Amasis and Nabû-naid apparently had no desire to lock horns with the rising power of the Persians and the Medes. Neither did the Lacedemonians relish a war in Asia Minor.

During an unspecified number of years, the Persians, mainly under the generalship of Harpagus, who had brought the Median army over to Cyrus, fought to overcome the Greek cities of Ionia and Aeolia and also the Carians, Caunians and the Lycians (Herodotus 1.162–177). Asia Minor thus came under Persian rule. After this, Herodotus says that Cyrus attacked the Assyrians (Herodotus 1.178); he goes on to describe what he knows about the city of Babylon.

The conquest of Babylonia and the taking of the city of Babylon have been discussed above. Prior to that campaign, it is conjectured that Cyrus devoted a few years (between c. 546 and 540 BCE) to conquests in central and eastern Iran. This is assumed because those areas seem to have been part of the empire when Darius I came to the throne.

The year 539 BCE marked a major turning point in the history of the Near East and the East Mediterranean. Peoples and nations from all points of the compass were to feel its influence. Such would especially be true for the polities of the Levant.

# CHAPTER ELEVEN
# PERSIAN DOMINATION
## LATE SIXTH TO FOURTH CENTURIES BCE

The conquest of Babylon by Cyrus II (the Great) in 539 BCE gave the Persian monarch mastery over the entire Neo-Babylonian Empire from east of the Tigris to the Sinai desert. There are no records of any need to campaign in the Levant in order to establish control by the new masters (unlike the campaigns of Nebuchadrezzar after 605 BCE). Under the Neo-Babylonians there was no known governor responsible for the entire Ḫatti land. At least no such official is documented. With the acquisition of the Babylonian Empire, Cyrus appointed a commissioner for both Babylon and "Beyond the River." Probably at the same time there was a subordinate commissioner in charge of only "Beyond the River." Subsequently, the Levant became a satrapy of the Persian imperial administrative system, first linked to Babylonia and later as an independent unit (possibly 482 BCE). The two centuries of Persian history saw the Levant playing its ancient role as a land bridge and as the main focus of eastern Mediterranean maritime activity.

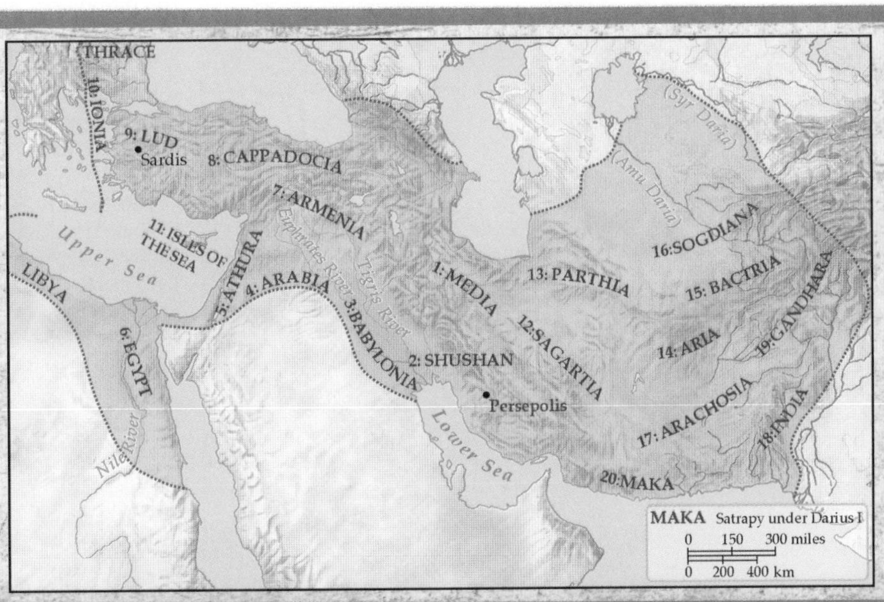


*The Persian Empire according to Herodotus and some Persian lists of tributary nations, 538–332 BCE.*

Unfortunately, the Persian monarchs did not adorn their palaces with stone slabs bearing texts equivalent to the Assyrian annals of a past era. The Persian royal inscriptions, although usually bi- or trilingual, do not provide much in the way of historical narrative. An exception is the Bisitun (Behistun) Inscription of Darius I that describes his efforts to reunite the empire. Some bits of information can be derived from the other texts and the lists of subject peoples help to understand the geography and ethnography of the empire.

Dating to the Persian period (539–333 BCE) are epigraphic witnesses in at least a dozen languages and several scripts (especially Akkadian, Elamite, Aramaic and Greek). However, the majority of real historical data are found in compositions from the Greek world, especially Herodotus in the fifth century BCE and Xenophon and the sources utilized by Diodorus for the fourth century BCE, plus numerous lesser works of varied substance. The chronology of the Persian kings is well established, based largely on the Ptolemaic Canon and the hundreds of legal and business documents in cuneiform discovered in southern Mesopotamia. The latter are mainly useful for the date formulae and for the social information they contain. Although most of the Greek writers are concerned more with happenings in the Aegean world and Asia Minor, the Greeks, especially of Athens, were active participants in the events of the eastern Mediterranean. Therefore, the Hellenic historians furnish considerable detail about Asia Minor, Egypt and the Levant. There is also today an abundance of Greek epigraphic material from which useful information is obtained, even though much of it is later in date (usually based on earlier sources). Nevertheless, the Greek writers must be handled critically; they often give precedence to a good story over dry historical fact. The few Semitic texts from the Phoenician and Cypriot cities contribute something but not much historical detail. Numismatics also has a significant role to play.

Herodotus (3.89–95) credits Darius I with organizing the empire into twenty satrapies, that is, provinces ruled by a governor with the title satrap ("protector of the kingdom"). The presumed duties of the satrap in the idealized reign of Cyrus II, as seen through Greek eyes, are given by Xenophon (*Cyr.* 8.6.11–13).

Jewish literature recognizes a hierarchy of administrative officers (*see* Esth 3:12, 8:9). Note the ethnarchs, "officers over each people" (=*millet*). Some of these terms seem flexible in the sources, especially "governor," which may be a generic term that can be used for various ranks in the hierarchy, even the satrap of a satrapy.

The Levant as a satrapy figures often in the East Mediterranean conflicts but direct data on the internal affairs and ethnographic composition of the smaller administrative units and ethnic polities within the province are scanty. The most detailed information in that respect comes from some biblical books and passages (Hebrew and Aramaic) but their chronological span is limited, mainly to the mid-fifth century BCE.

## POPULATION AND POLITICAL ORGANIZATION

Each satrapy was divided into provinces. It is evidently these to which the Book of Esther refers (Esth 1:1); there is no reason to assume that the author thought of Xerxes' empire as having 127 satrapies. The provinces were ruled by governors.

Some of the varied assortment of ethnic components is reflected in Ezra 4:9b–10. This list does not include all those exiled peoples settled in the Levant by the earlier Assyrian monarchs. By the time of the Persian annexation, those Semitic, mainly Aramaic-speaking, and non-Semitic peoples were becoming melded into a population known to outsiders, such as the Greeks, as "Syrians." That is especially clear in Herodotus' description of the satrapy.

Though Herodotus does not give a list of ethnic groups in his fifth satrapy, in contrast to other satrapies, he does mention several

**The Province "Beyond the River" with Some Documented Districts in the South**

geographical regions included within it, viz.

In this province was all of Phoenicia and that part of Syria which is called Palestine, and Cyprus.

(Herodotus 3.91, 1; cf. also 1.105; 2.104, 109; 3.5; 4.39)

**Phoenicians**. A major socioethnic component of the province that maintained its distinctiveness was the population of the city-states on the Lebanese coast. They are the original Canaanites, called by the Greeks Phoenicians. Their own inscriptions in the Phoenician language testify to their ethnic consciousness.

Two passages reveal that Herodotus reckoned the territory of Phoenicia as part of Syria:

Syria borders on Egypt, and the Phoenicians, to whom Sidon belongs, live in Syria.

(Herodotus 2.116.6)

To this statement can be compared his allusion to the Phoenician contingent in the Persian fleet (Herodotus 7.89; 8.67). Still, Herodotus never says that the Phoenicians are Syrians.

It is not possible to establish with precision the northern and southern limits of Phoenicia according to Herodotus. He stated that Poseideion was on the border between the Cilicians and the Syrians (not the Phoenicians), so he evidently considered the coast just south of Poseideion as Syrian, not Phoenician. Perhaps Phoenicia proper began somewhere just north of Byblos. Neither does Herodotus give an exact southern boundary for Phoenicia; he only wished to impress his readers with the fact that even the wealthy cities of Phoenicia were all within the Persian Empire. It would appear that the Sharon Plain was awarded to ʾEshmunʿazor, king of Sidon, by the Persian monarch during the fifth century BCE.

Along the Phoenician coast the famous city-states continued to exist and to grow in wealth and influence due to their role as the naval arm of the Achaemenid Empire in the Mediterranean. Arvad, Sidon and Tyre had developed a central meeting place, inhabited by citizens from each of the three cities known to the Greeks as Tripolis.

In Phoenicia is a noteworthy city, Tripolis by name, the appellation of which is suitable to its nature; because three cities are in it, having an interval of a stadia from one another; and these are denoted the Arvadians and the Sidonians and the Tyrians. And this city has the greatest reputation of the Phoenician cities, in which the Phoenicians assembled to convene a council and to deliberate concerning the most important matters.

(Diod. Sic. 16.411)

In Assyrian records, this town was called Ellišu. In the Bronze Age it was called Ullāsa.

The spread of Phoenician colonies along the coast of the fifth satrapy is illustrated by a passage from the *Peripolous* of Pseudo-Scylax. This is the ancient catalog for navigators listing seaports, river mouths and other geographical aids around the Mediterranean Sea. Though the work purports to be from the hand of the famous navigator of the fifth century BCE, it is assumed by most scholars to date from the mid-fourth century BCE. Nothing can be learned from it about the political boundaries of the province Beyond the River, but it does confirm the influence of Tyre and Sidon in the maritime communities along the whole of the Levantine coast. Chapter 104 begins: "After Cilicia there are the Syrian people. And in Syria the Phoenicians dwell along the shore." After some remarks about the narrowness of the Phoenician-occupied coastal zone, the text gives a list of coastal towns and other landmarks starting from the Thapsakos River (evidently the Orontes) and going south. Unfortunately, the text of this passage (par. 104) is very poorly preserved. There are some scribal omissions and numerous glosses have apparently been inserted by later copyists. The ends of the lines have been lost in many cases because of the mutilation of the page. The most impressive aspect of the whole picture is the number of towns belonging to

*Pottery figurine head in Greek Archaic style, Persian period, from Dor.*

either Tyre or Sidon. However, the coast as a whole is not reckoned as part of Phoenicia but rather as part of Syria. It was the Syrian people whom one encountered first after Cilicia. The same situation is reflected in other sources (Herodotus 3.91; Xenophon *Anab.* IV, 4:6; Strato *Geog.* XIV, 676; Pliny *Nat. Hist.* 5.79; Ptol. *Geog.* 5.14). Pseudo-Scylax does not deal in political borders, either in the north or the south. However, it is clear that in the south there was a strip of coast called Syria just as there was in the north. Confirmation for this is found in other classical writers (cf. Arr. *Anab.* 2.25.4; Diod. Sic. 19.93.7). Although Herodotus does not give the southern border of Phoenicia either, he certainly assigned the three Philistine cities of Ashdod, Ashkelon and Gaza to the latter, i.e. to "that part of Syria called Palestine" (Herodotus 3.5, 7.89). Pliny (*Nat. Hist.* 5.69) and Ptolemy (*Geog.* 5.14.3, 5.15.2) placed the southern border of Phoenicia between Dor and Caesarea, specified by Ptolemy as the Chorseas River. Joppa, Ashdod and Ashkelon are excluded by them from Phoenicia.

So the fact that various coastal settlements were assigned to the Tyrians or the Sidonians does not place them within the political boundaries of Phoenicia. The same composition refers to other towns around the Mediterranean that are called "city (or harbor) of the Phoenicians," e.g. Carthage and Myriandros, when it is obvious that they were independent. Phoenicia proper was a coastal zone midway along the eastern shore of the Mediterranean. In addition, there were numerous colonies founded by Tyre or Sidon. The absence of any reference to the Tower of Straton by Pseudo-Scylax suggests that the text was composed before that city (the later Caesarea) was founded by Straton (ᶜAbdashtart), king of Sidon (370–358 BCE). Sidonian suzerainty over Dor, Joppa and the Sharon Plain, as indicated by the ᵓEshmunᶜazor Inscription (l. 9), would evidently date to the fifth century BCE and provides the background for Pseudo-Scylax.

**Philistines**. The term Palestine as used by Herodotus with reference to the fifth satrapy is the country south of Phoenicia, extending down to Gaza. But he seems to have known this term in both a wider and a narrower sense. In one place (Herodotus 3.5 and 91) it has a restricted meaning excluding Phoenicia. On the other hand, when he says,

> This part of Syria, together with the country which extends southward to Egypt, is all known as Palestine. (Herodotus 7.89)

he is being more inclusive because he is referring to the territory occupied by the Arabians. But in the same paragraph he distinguished between the Phoenicians and the "Syrians of Palestine." Although there is an intermediate strip between Gaza and Ienysus, which was held by Arabians, this does not prove that it was not included in the concept of Palestine. One may compare Phoenicia as part of Syria though not occupied by people called Syrians. The peoples of the fifth satrapy furnished a major contingent to the Persian fleet during the invasion of Greece under Xerxes (481–479 BCE):

> . . . the Phoenicians, with the **Syrians of Palestine**, contributed 300 (ships). The crews wore helmets very like the Greek ones, and linen corsets; they were armed with light, rimless shields and javelins. These people have a tradition that in ancient times they lived on the Persian Gulf, but migrated to the Syrian coast, where they are found today. This part of Syria, together with the country, which extends southward to Egypt, is all known as Palestine. (Herodotus 7.89.1)

Herodotus knows nothing of the peoples and provinces located inland from the coast. For some of these in the southern Levant there is epigraphic and biblical material.

**Judeans**. Since there is relatively more information about the Judeans who lived in the ancient territory of Judah and some adjacent areas, they will be treated in the historical review below. Apart from the early chapters of Ezra, most of the other post-exilic information dates to the fifth century BCE with a cluster (mainly Ezra and Nehemiah) in the middle two decades of that century.

**Samaritans**. Several of the local provinces are mentioned in the Book of Nehemiah. Samaria is the oldest, having been created by Sargon II. Its boundaries probably were the Jezreel Valley in the north, the Jordan River in the east, and the province of Yehud in the south. The Samaria Papyri from Wâdī Dâliyeh have made it possible to reconstruct the dynasty of governors who ruled the province of Samaria. Three of these bore the name Sanballat, the first being a contemporary of Nehemiah. According to the Yeb (Elephantine) Papyri, control of the province was passed on to Sanballat's sons, Delaiah and Shelemiah. The next in line was another Sanballat, the son of one of the previous brothers and the father of Hananiah. This latter was ruling in Samaria in 354 BCE as indicated by Samaria Papyri. His son was the third Sanballat, who was appointed by Darius III in c. 334 BCE. It may be necessary to insert another person into the list, viz. Yeshua bar Sanballat, perhaps a brother of Hananiah.

**Ammonites**. Another district governor who played a prominent role in the Book of Nehemiah was Tobiah "the Ammonite slave" (Neh 2:19). His province was located in southern Gilead and was ruled by a dynasty of governors of the Tobiad family. Their headquarters were at Tyre in Transjordan. The epithet "Ammonite slave" has been interpreted as Tobiah's title as a Persian official governing the Ammonite region even though Nehemiah's reference to Tobiah seems to be pejorative in intent. Tobiah would thus be a counterpart to Sanballat in Samaria and Nehemiah in Judah. He was evidently a Judean whose family estate was established during the reign of Jotham. He was a member of a distinguished Judean family with connections to Jerusalem's aristocracy (Neh 6:18) and to the priesthood (Neh 13:7). His name is Yahwist ("YHWH is good"), as was his son's name (Johanan). So he may have achieved such prominence in the Persian bureaucracy that he was appointed as governor of what was formerly the kingdom of the sons of Ammon. In any case, the mention of this Tobiah is only an indirect inference to the survival of distinctive Ammonites in the Persian period.

**Edomites and Moabites**. There is some epigraphic evidence for people of Edomite origin in fourth-century BCE ostraca from southern Judea. The main groups of texts consist of small dockets recording quantities of grain being rendered as taxes (Beer-sheba) or being issued as fodder for horses or donkeys. A flood of similar documents has come to light in recent years

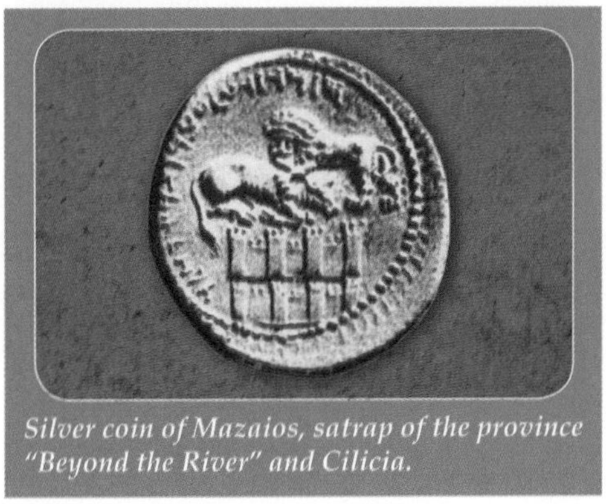

*Silver coin of Mazaios, satrap of the province "Beyond the River" and Cilicia.*

*Tomb of Cyrus the Great in Pasargadae.*

from somewhere in the Shephelah, probably Khirbet el-Qôm, ancient Makkedah.

In the early Hellenistic period there was an eparchy in southern Judea called Idumea (Diod. Sic. 19.95.2, 19.98.1). There is no evidence that such an official district existed in the Persian period; e.g. the Edomites are not mentioned in Nehemiah. But the possibility to establish such an entity certainly developed as a result of the Edomite population already present in that area, as witnessed by the ostraca.

**Arabians**. "Arabia" is the name of the third area whose ruler appears in the Book of Nehemiah. Its ruler was the enigmatic Geshem the Arab. His name has been found on a silver bowl from the temple at Tell el-Mashkhûta, 12.5 miles (20 km) east of Ismailiya in Lower Egypt. So the evidence points to the ruler of an influential Arabian kingdom, the biblical Kedar, which controlled the trade routes from Arabia to the Mediterranean and held sway over the coastal strip from Gaza to Ienysus. They had been permitted to establish colonies in the eastern Egyptian delta at least as early as the reign of Darius I.

Later allusions to joint Egyptian and Arabian hostilities against the Achaemenids in Phoenicia suggest that the "kingdom" of Geshem was not always loyal to Persia. During the latter part of the fifth century BCE a Persian satrap in Asia Minor sent a fleet of three hundred triremes to Phoenicia because he had received word that the king of the Arabians and the king of the Egyptians were plotting to seize Phoenicia (Diod. Sic. 3.46.6), though that may have been something of a pretense (Diod. Sic. 3.37.4–5).

**Cyprus**. There is no indication as to when Cyprus was joined to the satrapy "Beyond the River." A late tradition mentions that the Cypriots, along with Cilicia and Paphlagonia, voluntarily supported Cyrus in his campaign to conquer Babylon (Xenophon *Cyr.* 8.6.8). During the Ionian revolt (498 BCE) Cyprus was ostensibly part of the Persian Empire but most of the Greek cities sided with their compatriots in the Aegean (Herodotus 5.116) while the Phoenician cities supported the Persians. It certainly was reckoned with Beyond the River in Herodotus' day, in the mid-fifth century BCE (Herodotus 3.91). He lists the Cypriot naval unit in third place (because it was the third largest), while the Egyptian contingent came second. Thus the Cypriot group was separated from the Phoenician-Palestinian. Some political/administrative connection between Cyprus and Phoenicia might go back to Assyrian times but there is no evidence that it belonged to Beyond the River during the Neo-Babylonian period.

From an ethnic point of view, Cyprus was inhabited by Phoenicians, Greeks and Eteocypriots. While the Greek cities in the Aegean area had generally gone through an evolution from monarchy to tyranny and some on to democracy or oligarchy, the cities of Cyprus continued to maintain local monarchies throughout the archaic and classical periods. The Phoenician cities also supported local monarchies. The principal rivals during the Persian period were Greek Salamis on the eastern coast and Phoenician Kition on the southeastern shore.

## HISTORICAL OUTLINE

**Cyrus II and Cambyses** (539–521 BCE). ***Babylon and Beyond the River.*** Cyrus the Great conquered Babylon in 539 BCE, thus bringing to an end the great Neo-Babylonian, or Chaldean, kingdom. One of his first administrative arrangements was to place the entire Babylonian realm, including both Mesopotamia and the province Beyond the River, under the charge of a governor. It was evidently deemed advisable at that time to maintain the unity of the newly acquired territories. It is not known, however, if the small states in the province Beyond the River also submitted right away to Persian rule, though many subject peoples may have been happy about the fall of Babylon (Isa 13, 14:4–1, 21:1–10, 46:1–48:22; Jer 50, 51).

As lord of Babylon, Cyrus also claimed suzerainty over the peoples of the entire kingdom:

> [At his (Marduk's)] exalted [command] the entirety of the kings seated on thrones of all the whole world from the upper sea to the lower sea, dwellers in [distant] dis[tricts], all of the kings of the land of Amurru, the dwellers in tents, brought their heavy tribute; in the midst of Babylon they kissed my feet.
> (Cyrus Cylinder K2.1)

There is no detailed record of the submission of the various peoples in the province Beyond the River to their new Persian rulers. However, Cyrus' generosity in allowing various populations to return to their original home reflects a new policy:

> From [Babyl]on to the city of Ashur and Susa, Akkad, the land of Eshnunna, the city of Zabbān, the city of Meturnu, Dēr as far as the border of the land of Guti, the temple cities [bey]ond the Tigris of which their shrines had been in ruins from of old, the deities who dwelled in their sanctuaries, I returned to their places; I established them in permanent shrines. All of their peoples I assembled; I returned them to their abodes. (Cyrus Cylinder, K2.1)

This strengthens the case for the authenticity of the similar "Declaration" pertaining to the Judeans (*see* Ezra 1:2–4; cf. also 2 Chr 36:23).

His new policy, a reversal of the old Assyrian practices, supporting the ethnic identity and the religious institutions of the subject peoples, must have aided the process of winning their loyalty. Major cities, or city-states, such as Tyre and Sidon, must have continued to enjoy a good measure of autonomy, especially those upon whom the Achaemenids were to be dependent for their naval forces in the Mediterranean. Gubaru ruled over the combined provinces from the fourth year of Cyrus, 535/534 BCE, until the beginning of Darius I's reign, in 520 BCE.

One result of Cyrus' new policy toward the peoples of his empire was the restoration of the Judean temple community in Jerusalem. Sheshbazzar was "the prince of Judah" (Ezra 1:8) and "governor" (Ezra 5:14) of Judah. Cyrus entrusted him with the temple vessels stored in Babylon since Nebuchadnezzar's day

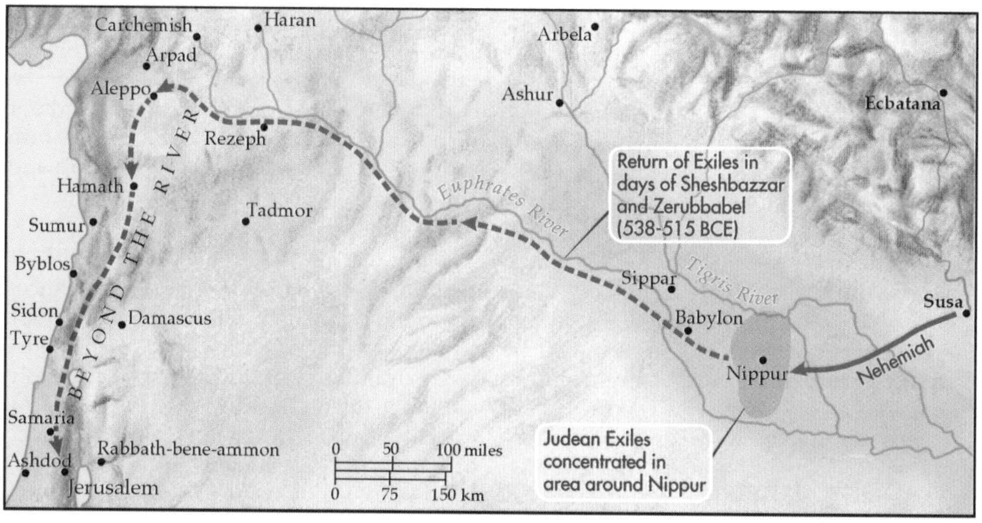


THE RETURN TO ZION

(Ezra 1:7–11). In a purported correspondence, he is credited with laying the foundation (Ezra 5:16; evidently the substructure for the sacrificial altar). Sheshbazzar is surely to be identified with Shenazzar (1 Chr 3:18), a son of Jehoiachin and uncle to Zerubbabel. He must have been about sixty years old when he immigrated to Jerusalem. His name was obviously of Babylonian origin, most probably from Sîn-ab(a)-usur.

Zerubbabel, son (or grandson) of Shealtiel (Ezra 3:2, 3:8, 5:2; Neh 12:1; Hag 1:1, 1:12, 1:14, 2: 2, 2:23; Zech 3:8; cf. 1 Chr 3:17–24), apparently replaced his uncle Sheshbazzar sometime prior to the reign of Darius I (Ezra 2:2). He had the title "governor of Judah" (Hag 1: 1, 1:14, 2:2, 2:21) and he was involved in the reconstruction of the altar on the temple mount (Ezra 3:2–3).

Regular sacrifices were reconstituted from the beginning of the seventh month in the first day of the month, i.e. Tishri (17 September 538 BCE). Basic plans were made for the building of the temple in the second year but when neighboring peoples asked to have a share in the enterprise, they were rebuffed. Henceforth, they continued to hamper the progress of the project until the reign of Darius I (Ezra 4:1–5).

**Egypt**. At the far southwest of the Persian domains, Egypt was also added to the empire by the conquest of Cambyses in 525 BCE (Herodotus 3.1–29). Amasis had died the year before and was succeeded by his son Psammetichus III. The tyrant of Samos, Polycrates, who had been a treaty partner with Amasis, shifted his allegiance and sent a fleet of forty ships to support Cambyses. On the route to Egypt along the Sinai coast, Cambyses requested and was granted the assistance of the Arabian king (evidently of Kedar) who controlled the zone from Kadytis (Gaza) to Ienysus (el-ᶜArîsh). The Arabs furnished water for the Persians and later were exempted from taxes (Herodotus 3.4–5). Besides the Arabian support, a leading mercenary general, Phanes of Halicarnassus, had defected to Cambyses and provided firsthand intelligence data of the utmost importance. The conquest itself and the many conflicting evidences about Cambyses' behavior do not concern the present narrative about the fortunes of Beyond the River. As is well known, Cambyses campaigned to Nubia and wanted to operate in North Africa but his mercenaries balked at fighting their countrymen. When news arrived that a usurper had seized the throne in Persia, Cambyses started home but died of an accidental wound on the way.

**Darius I** (521–486 BCE). Not only Herodotus but also Darius himself in the Behistun Inscription provide versions of the story of the latter's election to the succession and his subsequent struggle to put down rebellions and to consolidate the empire once more.

*King Darius seated on his throne with crown prince Xerxes behind him, from Persopolis.*

***Disturbances throughout the Empire***. Rebellions broke out in various parts of the empire when Darius came to power. A certain Nidintu-bel assumed the name Nebuchadnezzar III and led Babylon in revolt from October to December 522 BCE. While Darius was reestablishing his authority in Babylon after the defeat of this rebel, other subject peoples rose in revolt, possibly including Athura (Assyria) and Egypt. The Behistun inscriptions speak of serious fighting to subdue Armenia. The victory by one of the king's generals at "Izala in Assyria" (mountainous area in the northern Jezîrah) brought Armenia back into line and perhaps this also brought pacification to the Levant although it is questionable whether there were any real disturbances in the province Beyond the River. Egypt would be visited later by Darius (519 BCE). Another usurper, named Arkha, took the title of Nebuchadnezzar IV and stirred Babylon to another revolt from September to November 521 BCE. Although Gubaru no longer appears in cuneiform records, he still might have been the Gobryas who was sent to quell a fresh uprising in Elam during the third year of Darius.

***Reorganization***. After making firm his control, Darius I reorganized the empire. It may be at this time that the province Beyond the River was constituted as a sub-satrapy. By March 520 BCE, Ushtannu is documented as the governor of Babylon and Beyond the River. At this time there was some internal rivalry in the latter province, as evidenced by the tensions between Judah (Yehud) and its neighbors concerning the reconstruction of the temple in Jerusalem (Ezra 4:1–5). There is hardly a coincidence; the prophet Haggai (Hag 1) urged the Judeans to renew their efforts toward building the temple just when Darius had stabilized his rule by quelling the second Babylonian revolt (under Nebuchadnezzar IV). After so much trouble in the empire, Tattenai, who was evidently governor of Beyond the River under the higher authority of Ushtannu, and his colleagues, including his Iranian secretary Shethar-bozenai, can hardly be blamed for suspecting the Judean motives (Ezra 5:3–17). The strong building rising on the temple mount may have evoked the impression of a fortified citadel. Egypt had also been in revolt (*see* Ezra 5:3–4).

Incidentally, two other details about Achaemenid administration are revealed in this affair. Tattenai sent to Babylon for the pertinent records since this was the administrative headquarters for both provinces. His superior was located there. However, the actual record was found at Ecbatana. The scribes in Babylon have remembered that before his first official year, Cyrus had returned to Ecbatana. Though the actual decree was not found, a brief memorandum turned up in the files confirming the issuance of the original decree (Ezra 6:1–5). The Persian emperor, Darius, became convinced that the Jews were not guilty of rebellion so he ordered Tattenai to permit and even assist the building of the Jerusalem temple. A short time afterward there arrived a delegation of Jews from Babylonia bringing funds to support the work in Jerusalem (Zech 6:9–14).

One may note a parallel between Darius' concern for the temple in Jerusalem with his intervention on behalf of the priesthood of Apollo in Magnesia.

King of kings, Darius, son of Hystaspes, thus speaks to Gadatas, slave: I learn that you do not obey my commands in all things. That you cultivate my land by transplanting the fruits of Beyond the Euphrates to the lower district of Asia, I commend your purpose, and because of this there shall be laid up for you great favor in the king's house. But because you neglect my policy in behalf of the gods I will give you, if you do not change, proof of my wronged feelings, for you exacted tribute from the sacred cultivators of Apollo and commanded them to dig unhallowed ground, not knowing the mind of my ancestors toward the god, who spoke [the wh]ole tru[th] the Persians.

An official there named Gadatas had imported some fruit trees from the province "Beyond the Euphrates" but he had also "exacted tribute from the sacred cultivators of Apollo and commanded them to dig unhallowed ground." Darius warned Gadatas to desist from such behavior; the text, which is inscribed in Roman orthographic and paleographic style, was set up in the Apollo temple—proof of

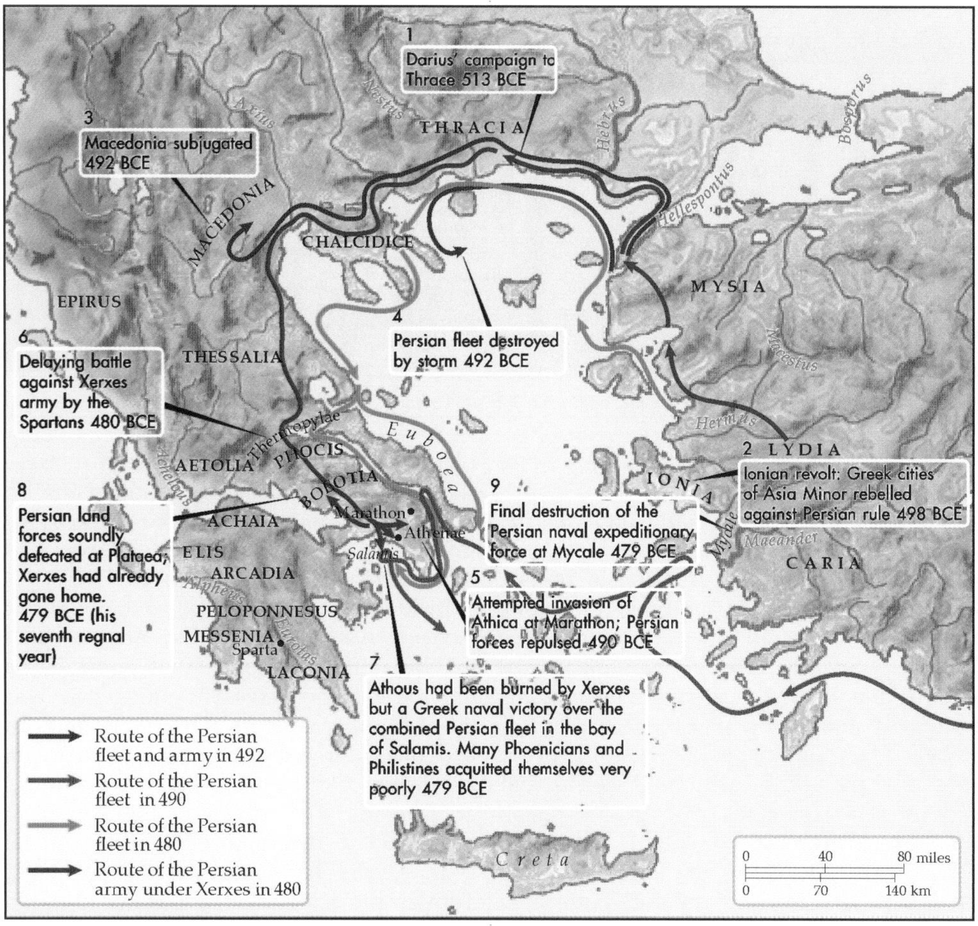


**WARS IN THE WEST—DARIUS I AND XERXES (AHASUERUS)**

temple prerogatives.

Darius must have passed through the province Beyond the River on his way to Egypt in 519/518 BCE. He may have taken this opportunity to clarify the problems that had arisen under Tattenai's supervision. But the assumption that Zerubbabel was executed as a rebel is belied by the passages showing Darius' support for the Judean governor (Ezra 6:7; cf. Hag 2:23; Zech 4:6–10). Nevertheless, it should be noted that in the case of the suspicions on the part of Tattenai and his colleagues with regard to the Judeans' intentions in rebuilding the temple, they seem to coincide with some possibly rebellious behavior on the part of Aryandes, the satrap of Egypt, Libya and Cyrene, appointed by Cambyses. He had begun to mint silver coinage (Herodotus 4.166). He had also initiated military action against Barca (Herodotus 4.200, 4.204). These may have been displays of independence on his part. One source claims that the Egyptians had risen in revolt against Aryandes (Polyaenus, *Strategica* 7.11.7; who calls him Oryandros) and Darius marched on Memphis to quell the insurrection. In any event, Darius I did go to Egypt as witnessed by many inscriptions and stelae. Any direct impact on the negotiations regarding building the temple in Jerusalem is unattested. The Jerusalem temple was finally completed by 12 March 515 BCE (*see* Ezra 6:15–19). The Passover was then celebrated on 20 April 515 BCE.

The last year for which a cuneiform document referring to Tattenai as governor of Beyond the River is 502 BCE. His four sons, Napsannu, Ṣīḫâ (or Ṣīḫai?), Šamšâ (or Šamšai) and Nabû-šarru-usur, are known to have had estates in various parts of Babylonia, especially in the vicinity of Borsippa. These are documented well into the fifth century BCE.

***Wars in the West.*** Documentation for the ensuing decades in the province Beyond the River is lacking. Events in the eastern Mediterranean from the late sixth century to the early fifth century BCE were to eventually have a profound effect on the peoples of the Levant. In 513 BCE Darius I made his first expedition to conquer Thrace. The subjection of the Thracian peoples was achieved, partly by submission and partly by conquest; but Darius' attempt to defeat the Scythians beyond the Danube was a disaster and he was forced to retreat.

In 498 BCE there was a revolt among the Hellenic cities of Ionia. With token assistance from Athens and Eretria, the Milesian rebels burned and looted most of the city of Sardis though the Persian garrison held out. Soon after, the western Greeks withdrew but the Ionians continued the war (Herodotus 5.99–103). They seized Byzantium in the Hellespont thus isolating the Thracian satrapy.

Many Carians and Lycians joined the rebels and the spirit of revolt spread to the Greek cities of Cyprus. The Phoenician cities remained loyal to Persia and the imperial fleet and army went to their aid. In the naval battle, the Ionians defeated the Phoenicians but on land the victory went to the Persians while the opposing generals were both slain. During 497–496 BCE the island was reconquered by the Persians (Herodotus 5.104–116). During the next two years the Persians gradually reduced the rebel cities and in 494 BCE their Phoenician fleet defeated and dispersed the Greek ships that were supporting Miletus. The latter city was subjected to a prolonged siege and afterwards was ravaged and burned. In 493 BCE the remaining islands such as Chios were subjected. With the crushing of the revolt, Ionia gradually lost its predominance in international trade and the center of political, military and economic gravity shifted to mainland Greece, principally to Athens and Sparta.

In order to achieve Darius' goal of domination of the Aegean, an expedition was launched in 492 BCE against the islands. Thrace and Macedonia were also reconquered. That campaign ended in the famous defeat at Marathon (490 BCE). The Persian objective had probably been to install a pro-Persian tyranny at Athens. The defeat did not really diminish the imperial strength and was followed by the extensive preparations for a full-scale invasion of mainland Greece.

***Egyptian Revolt.*** In 486 BCE, while the Persians were amassing their forces for the war against Hellas, news arrived at the Persian court that a new rebellion had broken out in Egypt (Herodotus 7.1, 3). Shortly after that Darius died and was succeeded by the eldest son of his royal wife (Atossa, the daughter of Cyrus II; Herodotus 7.3.4), viz. Xerxes (biblical Ahasuerus). Meanwhile, a business document from Babylon attests to a certain "Ḫutta--ᵓ son of Pagakanna governor of Babylon and Beyond the River." The date of the transaction, "Month of Ulūlu, day twenty-four, year thirty-six of Darius king of Babylon and of the lands," proves that the provinces of Babylon and Beyond the

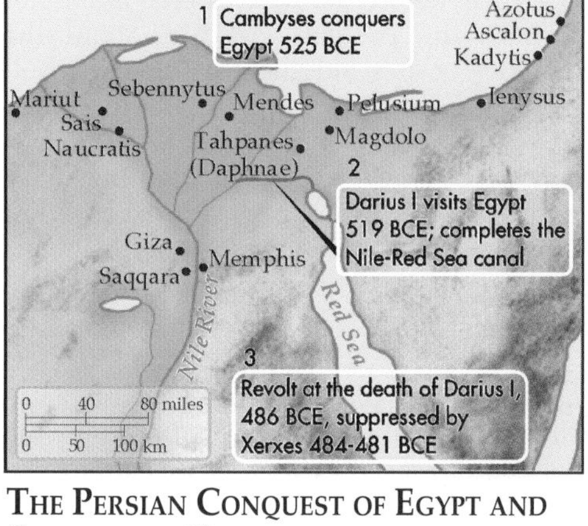


**THE PERSIAN CONQUEST OF EGYPT AND SUBSEQUENT REVOLTS (525–484 BCE)**

River had not been separated yet, and they were still under one satrap.

**Xerxes** (485–465 BCE). ***Reconquest of Egypt***. The suppression of the Egyptian rebellion occasioned the passage of a Persian army through the coastal territories of Beyond the River, most likely with the active support of the Phoenician navy. Darius had been assembling a large force for his renewed war in the Aegean and the forces eventually sent included a large contingent of ships from the Phoenicians and Philistines. But those military assets that Darius had spent three years in gathering must have been at least partially directed to the reconquest of Egypt. It took Xerxes another four years (484–481 BCE; Herodotus 7.20.1) to rebuild his armies and the navy for the planned invasion of Hellas. After smashing the Egyptian revolt, Xerxes appointed his brother, Achaemenes, as satrap of Egypt (Herodotus 7.7).

It is interesting to note that during the accession year of Xerxes (between November 486 and March 485 BCE) an accusation was made against the Jews:

> Now in the reign of Ahasuerus (Xerxes), in the **beginning of his reign**, they wrote slander against the residents of Judah and Jerusalem. (Ezra 4:6)

This particular entry is not evidence that the author/editor of the Book of Ezra is confused about the chronology. He simply wished to gather together in one place some notes on various times when the authorities of Beyond the River had caused trouble for the Jewish community. These were background for the earlier conflict over the building of the temple. Like the Egyptian rebellion, there is no detailed documentation about the incident. It just seems more than a curiosity that accusations against the Jews should coincide with a rebellion in Egypt. The previous troubles about the temple also coincided with suspicious activities on the part of the then satrap of Egypt.

***Babylonian Rebellions***. Subsequently, two revolts broke out in Babylon, the first in 484 and the second in 482 BCE. The second insurrection was violently suppressed. The king sent his brother-in-law, Megabyzus, to crush the latter revolt. The Babylonian estates of the local nobles were confiscated and awarded to Persians. Babylonia also lost its status as the senior province of the former Neo-Babylonian Empire. The separation of Beyond the River from Mesopotamia was evidently carried out at this time. If so, then Herodotus' fifth satrapy would have been constituted as an independent administrative unit in 482 BCE. This means that, although Herodotus claimed to know of an organization into twenty satrapies by Darius I (Herodotus 3.89–95), the actual situation depicted by him had come into effect sometime prior to his own visit to the Levant and Egypt but certainly not as early as the beginning of Darius' reign.

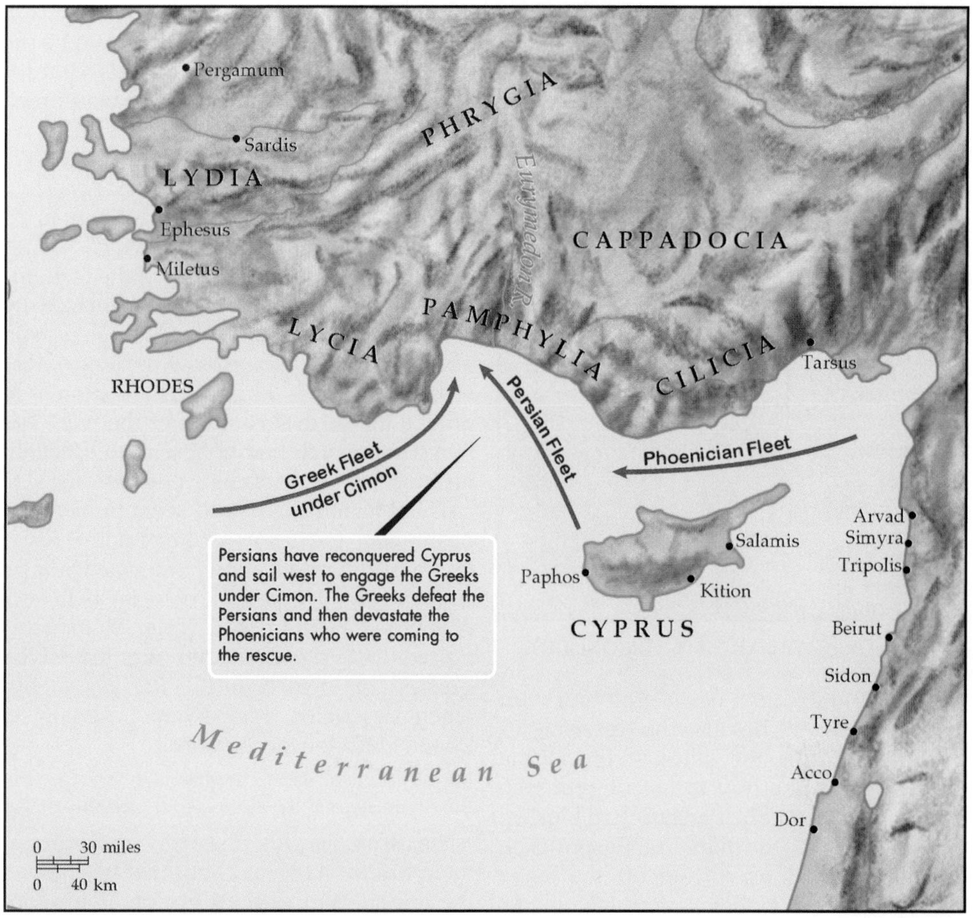


THE BATTLE OF EURYMEDON (466/465 BCE)

***The Great Persian War***. The campaign which culminated in the Greek naval victory in the bay of Salamis and the land victory at Plataea (followed by an additional victory at Mycale) took place far from the province Beyond the River, but Phoenician, Philistine and Cypriot ships were deeply involved in the fighting. Their performance was disgraceful and many commanders were severely punished by Xerxes (Herodotus 7.195; 8.11, 68, 100).

***Aftermath***. The peoples of the eastern Mediterranean preserved a number of humorous stories about Xerxes' bad temperament and about serious family problems in the aftermath of the First Persian War. That humiliation had taken place in the king's seventh year. Therefore, it is not fortuitous that a Hebrew novella about troubles in the royal family and the subsequent beauty contest to find a new virgin to distract the king from his troubles is placed in the seventh year (Esth 2:16). Herodotus (9.108–113) preserves the tale of the king's infatuation with his brother's wife and later with his brother's daughter. Queen Amestris discovered the latter affair and demanded the mutilation of the hapless girl.

This war resulted in the balance of power in the Aegean shifting to the Greek cities (there was never a "Greek Nation"), especially Athens. That city-state eventually became the head of the Delian league (478 BCE; Thuc. 1.4.96–97), which developed afterwards into an Athenian thalassocracy. Meanwhile, in the first year of the Delian alliance, a combined Greek fleet under Pausanias (the Spartan victor at Plataea) sailed to Cyprus and conquered most of the island (Thuc. 1.4.94; Diod. Sic. 11.44.1–2). In the decade of constant strife from 478 to 466 BCE one of the high points was the naval battle at the mouth of the Eurymedon in southern Asia Minor. Its exact date cannot be determined. The Persians had previously recouped their losses in Cyprus (perhaps by 470 BCE) and later (possibly in 466/465 BCE) sailed westward to engage the Hellenic allied fleet. The Greek commander by now was Cimon. Before the Phoenician ships could reach the Eurymedon to strengthen the Persian fleet, the Greeks inflicted a resounding defeat on them. Then they were ready when the Phoenicians finally did arrive and those, too, suffered disaster (Thuc. 1.4. 100, 1; Diod. Sic. 11.60.3–62).

**Artaxerxes I** (464–424 BCE). In August of 465 BCE, Xerxes was assassinated in his bed. His son must have been involved in the plot but leading courtiers had assumed most of the power. The new king, Artaxerxes I, managed to eliminate the assassins (who planned to usurp his throne) and then began to reorganize the imperial administration and to replenish his devastated naval assets (Diod. Sic. 11.62.2).

***Egyptian Revolt***. The middle decades of the fifth century BCE were saturated in

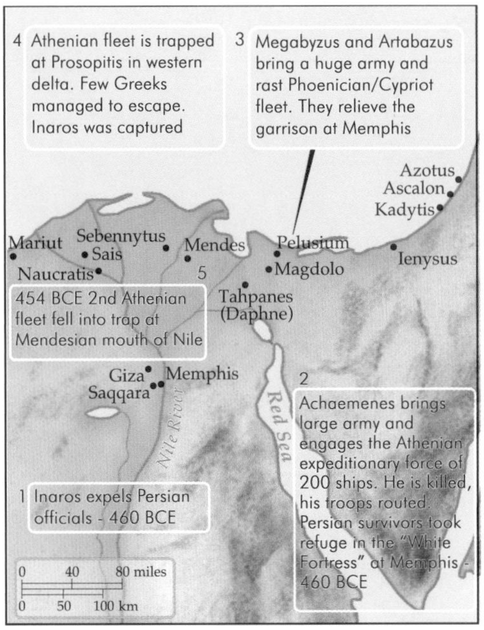


**Revolt of Egypt and Its Reconquest**

blood. Not only did a new revolt break out in Egypt (460 BCE), but also the Athenian sea power, including the allies of the Delian league, joined the fray to help Egypt gain its independence. The Persians had blocked the trade route through the Bosporus to the Black Sea, thus cutting off the major supply line for Hellenic grain. Now the Greeks hoped to establish a firm link with an independent Egypt to foster their trade and to acquire their grain supplies from the rich delta.

The leader of the revolt was Inaros, of Libyan background (Thuc. 1.104), called son of Psammetichus. He was supported by Amyrteus of Sais, probably a descendant of the family of pharaohs from Dynasty XXVI; he is probably the grandfather of the Amyrteus of Dynasty XXVIII (404–399 BCE). Inaros was supported first of all by native Egyptian and Libyan troops but mercenaries were also gathered from other peoples of the area. They expelled the Persian fiscal bureaucrats from the delta and established their own control. They also dispatched ambassadors to Athens requesting military aid and promising that the Greek efforts would be amply rewarded. However, Memphis had a strong Persian garrison and it stayed loyal to the empire along with most of Upper Egypt. The rebels besieged the Persians, who had holed up in the "White Fortress" at Memphis (Thuc. 1.104; Diod. Sic. 11.71).

The satrap of Egypt was Achaemenes, brother of Xerxes and uncle to Artaxerxes. He assembled a large army and entered Egypt, encamping close to the Nile. A contingent of two hundred ships arrived from Athens to strengthen the Egyptian side. The battle was joined at a place called Papremis (Herodotus 3.12), somewhere in the western delta. Achaemenes was slain and his forces thoroughly routed. The Persian survivors of the clash took refuge in the White Fortress at Memphis; the garrison there continued to hold out. It would be the key to Upper Egypt and was thus vital for Inaros to capture it. Therefore, he was forced into a prolonged siege (Diod. Sic. 11.74).

Artaxerxes countered his defeat with a political and a military response. A certain Megabyzus was sent to Sparta to try to bribe them into attacking Athens, which would presumably require the recall of the Hellenic forces in Egypt. When those efforts were not crowned with success, Megabyzus, son of Zophyrus and son-in-law of Xerxes, was ordered to amass a huge army and navy to pursue the further conduct of the war. The Persian monarch had no intention of losing his most rich and strategic possessions.

This Megabyzus would seem to have the position of governor of Beyond the River (Syria) if the implications in the account by Ctesias (*Persica* §§34–38) are to be believed. After the Egyptian war, when Megabyzus retired to Syria, the latter was called by Ctesias "his own country" (*Persica* §36). But when describing Megabyzus' mission to Egypt, Herodotus only says:

> Megabyzus, who served as general in Egypt against the Athenians and the allies. (Herodotus 3.160.2)

He assembled his vast army and brought them to Cilicia (456 BCE) but that he enjoyed the full support of the Cypriots is unclear. He ordered them and the Phoenicians on the mainland to produce a mighty fleet of triremes. The Greeks in the delta were still besieging the garrison in the White Fortress at Memphis. By 454 BCE, Megabyzus and his colleague, Artabazus, sent their army overland via Syria and Phoenicia with the fleet accompanying them offshore. They entered the delta and proceeded to Memphis, where they broke the siege. The Athenians and Egyptian/Libyan forces withdrew in terror. The Attic ships were moored at the island of Prosopitis in the western delta. The Persian fleet also entered by one of the branches of the Nile. They diverted the Nile waters from the anchorage of the Greek fleet and thus gained access to the island. The Athenians set fire to their ships and tried to make a stand. Thucydides (1.4.110) says most of them perished although a few escaped by way of Libya to Cyrene and on to home. Diodorus (Diod. Sic. 11.77.4) makes out that the Persian generals preferred to let the Greeks leave honorably rather than suffer heavy losses to their own troops conquering them. Thucydides' account is obviously more trustworthy. Meanwhile, another Athenian fleet had been dispatched to Egypt not knowing about the defeat of their compatriots. These latter ships put in to shore at the Mendesian mouth of the Nile. The Persian troops attacked them from the land and the Phoenician fleet attacked them from the sea. Only a few ships managed to escape (Thuc. 1.4.110). Thus, the Athenian adventure to Egypt came to an ignominious conclusion.

Inaros was captured along with his close associates and eventually executed in Persia. His cohort, Amyrteus, did manage to escape and continued to wage a guerrilla campaign from the delta marshes.

***Counterattack in Cyprus***. Three years later (449 BCE) a new fleet of Athenians and other members of the Delian league comprising two hundred vessels sailed to Cyprus under the leadership of Cimon. Sixty ships were detached and sent to aid Amyrteus in the marshes of Egypt. The rest laid siege to Marion and Kition. Cimon died during the siege and his death was concealed for thirty days while the Athenian forces organized their retreat. They were running out of supplies. Megabyzus prepared a large naval force in Cilicia made up of Phoenician, loyal Cypriot and Cilician ships. Perhaps in desperation, the Hellenes won a double victory on sea and land. It is claimed that they captured one hundred ships (Thuc. 1.4.112; Diod. Sic. 11.62, who wrongly associates this information with the earlier battle of Eurymedon).

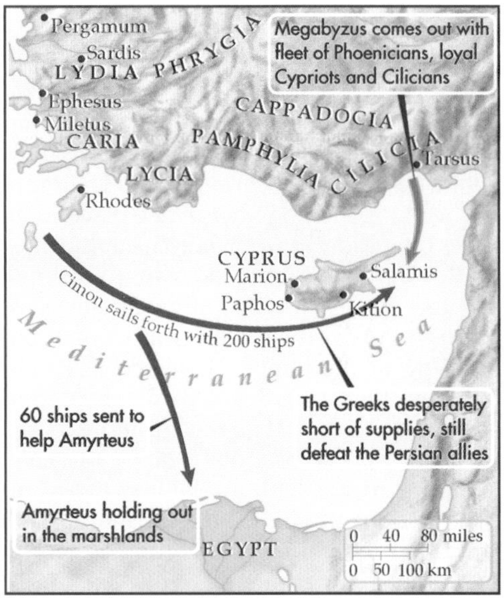


**The Sea Battle off Cyprus (449 BCE)**

***The "Peace of Callias."*** Both the Athenians and the Persians lost their will to continue the bloody and expensive hostilities. As a result, in 448 BCE the so-called Peace of Callias was negotiated. The fourth-century BCE alleged copy of the treaty seems to indicate that the Persians agreed to keep their ships out of the Aegean and the Athenians agreed to let the Persians dominate the Mediterranean. The status of the eastern Greek cities of Asia Minor is not clear; some compromises must have been reached.

***Sidonian Affairs***. At this point, some conclusions may be reached about the dating of the ʾEshmunʿazor Inscription. The approximate dates for the Sidonian kings of the mid-fifth century BCE, based on paleographic, numismatic and historical

*The ʾEshmunᶜazor Inscription. This Phoenician text, inscribed on the lid of a huge coffin of Egyptian manufacture, describes the premature demise of a young king of Sidon, ʾEshmunᶜazor II.*

considerations, can be established as follows:

| | |
|---|---|
| ʾEshmunᶜazor I | 479–470 BCE |
| Tabnit | 470–465 BCE |
| ʾEshmunᶜazor II | 465–451 BCE |
| Bodᶜashtart | 451–? BCE |

The first ʾEshmunᶜazor probably represents the attempt at rehabilitation after the stunning losses of men and materiel in the Aegean war in the Bay of Salamis. Tabnit would overlap the transition from Xerxes to Artaxerxes and probably was the ruler during the ignominious defeat at Eurymedon (466 BCE). The second ʾEshmunᶜazor would have been ruling during the suppression of the Egyptian revolt by Megabyzus. The inscription does not say explicitly but one wonders if the young king might have lost his life in the fighting off Salamis in 449 BCE.

Both Tabnit and ʾEshmunᶜazor II were buried in coffins brought from Egypt. They must have been booty, perhaps acquired during the suppression of the earlier Egyptian revolt in 484 BCE. In any case, when ʾEshmunᶜazor II speaks in his funerary text of the land grant which had been awarded to him by "the lord of kings" (l. 18), it was "for the measure of the mighty deeds which I did" (l. 19). Now this could hardly have been during the Persian war in the Bay of Salamis (479 BCE) or at the mouth of the Eurymedon in 466 BCE. Neither could it have been for taking part in the disastrous battle off Cypriot Salamis in 449 BCE. So the only alternative, when Phoenicians scored fantastic victories over the Greek fleet, was during Megabyzus' campaign to Egypt, in 454 BCE.

Two important conclusions can be drawn from this line of reasoning: up to the Egyptian revolt in 460 BCE and later, Dor and Joppa had been independent of Sidon. Were they subject to Tyre? Probably not. In other words, Dor in particular may have enjoyed a period of independence as a Phoenician seaport in the mid-fifth century BCE. The second point is that the Sharon Plain, which included the hinterland of Joppa, was under Sidonian jurisdiction during the ensuing decade(s), from which time there is a limited amount of information from the biblical books of Ezra and Nehemiah.

***The Jewish* Millet.** Some information about internal affairs in Beyond the River during the reign of Artaxerxes is provided by the books of Ezra and Nehemiah. The sending of Ezra, "a scribe skilled in the law of Moses" (Ezra 7:6), to Jerusalem in 458 BCE (Ezra 7:7) with proper credentials from the emperor himself (Ezra 7:11–26) may possibly represent an attempt on the part of the crown to secure the loyalty of various ethnic groups in the province Beyond the River. It can hardly be a coincidence that Ezra's commission to come to Judea was in the same year that Artaxerxes sent his ambassador, Megabyzus, to Sparta on a diplomatic mission aimed at undermining the power of Athens in the Egyptian rebellion. At the same time, the Persian monarch was taking steps to have the Phoenicians produce a new fleet of ships for use in the projected invasion of Egypt. It also behooved him to see to it that the various ethnic groups (*millets*) were loyal to the empire. Therefore, the commissioning of a highly qualified academic (scribe) of priestly lineage to deliver a constitutional document to the Jewish *millet*, thus strengthening its sense of identity and dependence on the crown, makes perfect sense (*see* Ezra 7:1–9).

They left Babylon on 8 April 458 BCE and arrived in Jerusalem on 4 August. This is a good example of the *millet* system as practiced by the Persians, whereby every district had its own script and every people its own language (Esth 1:22 *passim*). The religious and cultural traditions of each ethnic group in the empire were fostered and supported by the imperial authority. Naturally, the authenticity of the royal commission as presented in the Book of Ezra has been challenged but it certainly has all the earmarks of a valid administrative document. Thus, Ezra was authorized to establish the Torah as the statutory law of the Jewish *millet* (*see* Ezra 7:25–26).

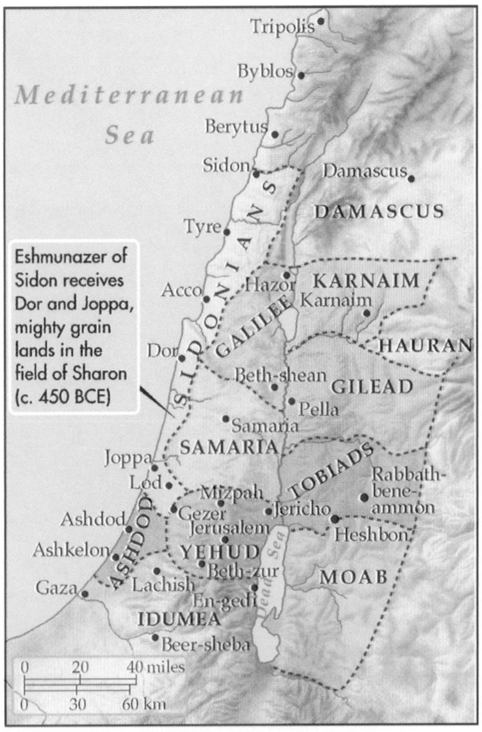


**PERSIAN GRANT TO SIDON (C. 451 BCE)**

Artaxerxes was giving official sanction to the Torah as the civil code of the Yehud province but Ezra was also charged with enforcing the law that he was bringing over, "all the people who are in Beyond the River" (Ezra 7:25). The entire Jewish *millet* in the province Beyond the River was to be subject to this legal text, not just those living in the small territory called Yehud. This was the beginning of the process whereby the Torah "instruction" acquired the status in the Jewish *millet* like the unchangeable laws of the Medes and Persians (*see* Esth 1:19; Dan 6:9 [Eng. 6:8]).

The promulgation of this Torah as depicted in the Masoretic Text of Nehemiah

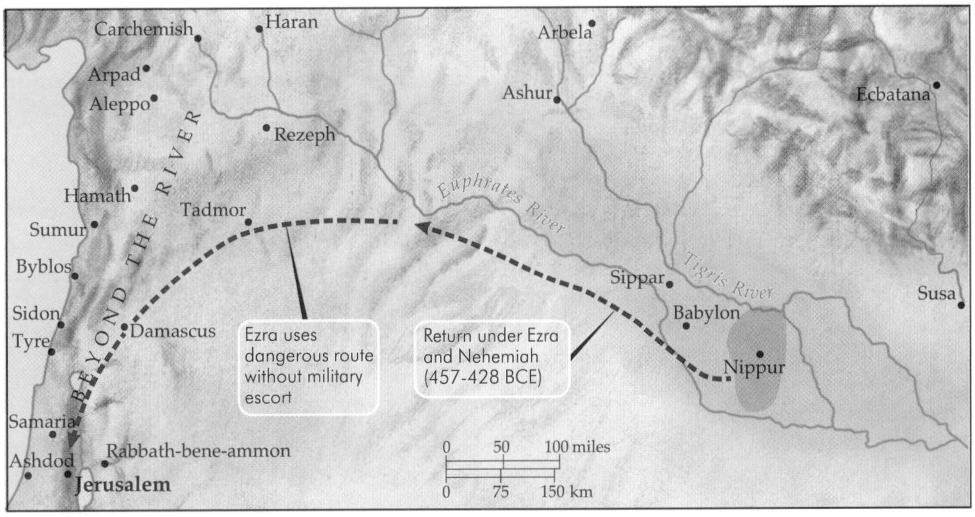


**THE RETURN TO ZION UNDER EZRA AND NEHEMIAH**

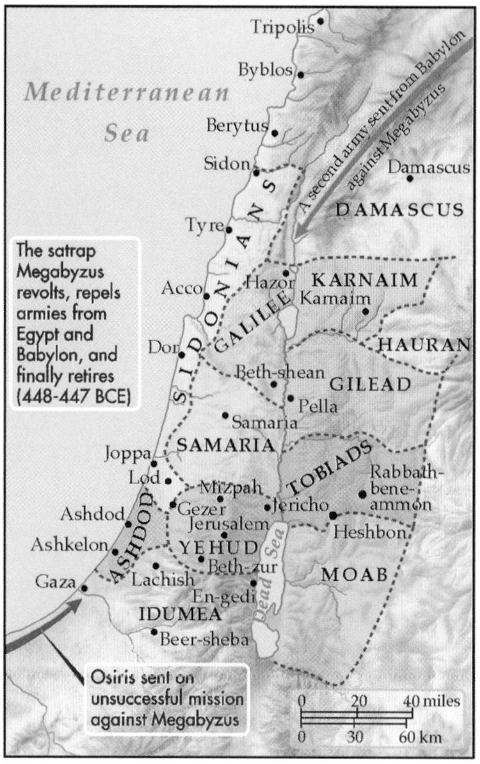


**Megabyzus' Revolt (448–447 BCE)**

(7:72b [Eng 7:73b]–8:12) appears in 1 Esdras (9:37b–55) immediately after the chapter comparable to Ezra 10 about the crisis of intermarriage. The name Nehemiah is entirely missing from 1 Esdras. As the texts stand in the Masoretic Text, the reading of the law took place thirteen years after Ezra's arrival, which does not make sense at all. Unfortunately, the Hebrew Vorlage used to make the translation of 1 Esdras was defective because it does not have the conclusion of the pericope. Although the composer of 1 Esdras is later and really does not know where to insert the passage about the reading of the Torah, he was surely correct to leave Nehemiah out of the passage about the public reading of the Torah. The public reading of Ezra's Torah took place years before Nehemiah even arrived in Jerusalem.

The "treasurers of the province Beyond the River" were enjoined to assist Ezra in carrying out his mission (Ezra 7:21–24). Most of the districts and ethnic groups in the province Beyond the River seemed to have remained loyal to Persia and were not sympathetic to the Egyptian cause.

A major issue addressed in the Ezra memoir was mixed marriages. Such liaisons were evidently quite widespread throughout the province and Ezra, in his capacity as executor of the Torah, took action. A public assembly was called to address the issue in month 9, day 20 (Ezra 10:9), and the commission appointed to resolve this problem completed its work in month 1, day 1 of the eighth year of Artaxerxes (Ezra 10:17), i.e. 27 March 457 BCE. Thus, the activities attributed to Ezra were completed in a single year.

***Megabyzus' Revolt.*** Not long after the restoration of Egypt and Cyprus to Persian control, Megabyzus, the king's relative, is said to have become angered over the harsh policies followed by the Persian monarch against the Egyptian political prisoners. The whole story is preserved only by Ctesias (*Persica*, Epit. 68–70). Although the writings of that Greek physician who spent time in the Persian court are highly suspect, the present narrative makes considerable sense in spite of the typical "soap opera" features. Furthermore, some of the personages who play a role in the story really existed, as demonstrated by cuneiform records.

Megabyzus is said to have returned to his own territory (which must be assumed to be the province Beyond the River) and declared a revolt against Persian authority. In this he was supported by his sons, Zopyrus and Artyphius. Ironically, a force from Egypt, led by a certain Usiris, is said to have been sent against him but was unsuccessful. A second force, this time commanded by a Persian, Menostanes, the brother of Artaxerxes and satrap of Babylon, came out but achieved even less. Eventually, Megabyzus was reconciled to the emperor but did not remain as satrap of Beyond the River. If the main lines of the narrative are to be believed, there was at least some military action in Beyond the River, first an invasion from Egypt followed by another from Babylon. Greek and Persian records say nothing about how all this affected the peoples of Beyond the River. The local officials were doubtless hard-pressed to maintain law and order.

***Jerusalem and Yehud.*** There certainly must be some connection between these events and the correspondence preserved in Ezra 4:7–23. The passage is inserted into the Book of Ezra as another "footnote" like the preceding mention of a complaint in the accession year of Xerxes (Ezra 4:6). The author wished to point out that obstructions to the building of the temple in the reign of Darius I had set a precedent for future conflicts with the authorities of Beyond the River. Each "footnote" had a date to the reign of the contemporary king. There should have been no reason to accuse the author of being confused in his chronology. He knew exactly what he was doing (*see* Ezra 4:7).

None of these officials have the title of governor of the province. The officials of the province in this pericope are clearly loyal to the emperor and not in revolt against his authority, so it seems more likely to associate that passage with events just after the Megabyzus rebellion. The initial complaint was sent to King Artaxerxes by Rehum the commander and Shimshi the scribe (Ezra 4:7–23). However, the concern with the walls of Jerusalem point to the events just prior to or just after the arrival of Nehemiah. The officials of the province Beyond the River made the following accusation:

> And now be it known to the king that the Jews who came up from you to us [i.e. Ezra and those who accompanied him] have gone up to Jerusalem. They are finishing the walls and repairing the foundations. (Ezra 4:12)

Their allusion to Jerusalem as "a rebellious city, hurtful to kings and provinces" (Ezra 4:15, 4:19) must certainly be understood against the background of the Megabyzus rebellion. The king's reply, that "mighty kings have been over Jerusalem, who ruled over the whole province Beyond the River" (Ezra 4:20), recalls to mind the kingdom of Judah's role in previous conflicts between Egypt and Mesopotamia. The Judean revolt against Sennacherib in 701 BCE and against Nebuchadnezzar in 587 BCE was instigated by offers of Egyptian support. Therefore, when the Jews began to fortify their citadel a few years after Egypt and even Beyond the River had been in revolt, it was bound to appear suspicious.

The freshness and vividness of the report brought to Nehemiah in the month of Kislev in the twentieth year (of Artaxerxes; Tishri reckoning), i.e. November/December 446 BCE (Neh 1:1), that "*the wall of Jerusalem is broken down and its gates are burned with fire*" (Neh 1:3), suggests that severe steps had been taken to neutralize the Jerusalem fortress (Ezra 4:23). It seems strange that Nehemiah waited three months, until Nisan (Neh 2:1), i.e. April 445 BCE (still in the twentieth year, according to Tishri reckoning), before

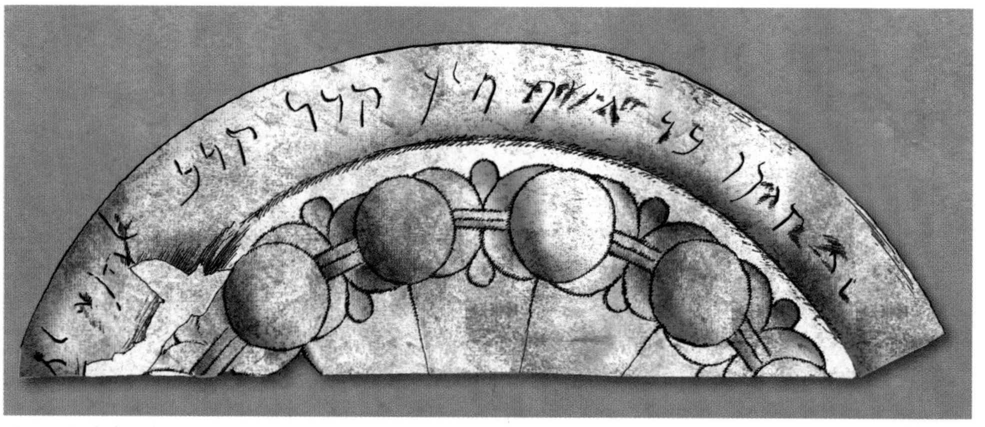

*Aramaic dedication inscription of Qaynu son of Gashmu (Geshem), king of Qedar, on a silver bowl from Tell el-Mashkhuta (Egypt).*

making his request to the king. Perhaps Artaxerxes had been away at another of his official residences and only came to Susa in the spring.

By 444 BCE Nehemiah had arrived in the satrapy Beyond the River, with credentials from Artaxerxes appointing him governor of the Yehud province. By virtue of this new authority he set about to repair the walls of Jerusalem in the face of opposition by the governors of the neighboring districts (Neh 2:10). Nehemiah served as governor of the territory of Judah (Neh 5:14) for twelve years, from the twentieth to the thirty-second year of Artaxerxes (444–432 BCE).

The theme of Nehemiah's conflict with his hostile neighbors (Neh 2:19, 4:1–8 *passim*) happens to provide some geographical information about the districts bordering on Yehud (*see* Neh 2:10, 4:1 [Eng. 4:7], 6:1). Sanballat "the Horonite" was governor of Samaria. The descendants of Sanballat, who inherited his office, are known now from the Wâdī ed-Dâliyeh Papyri.

Tobiah "the Ammonite slave" evidently was a descendant of the family that gained a foothold in Transjordan in the aftermath of Jotham's aggression in 739 BCE. This Tobiah was the son of an influential Jewish family with connections in Jerusalem. His capital was Tyre, which apparently was called "the Tyre of the House of Tobiah" in Gilead (*Ant.* 12:233; ᶜIrâq el-ᵓEmîr). He seems to have been the Persian-appointed governor of Ammon that had been joined to the province of Gilead. His family "dynasty" continued into the Hellenistic period.

Geshem the Arab was apparently also recognized as the governor of the Arabian district, which Herodotus included in the southern part of his fifth satrapy (cf. *supra*). From the discovery of Geshem's name on a silver bowl dedicated to a temple at Tell el-Mashkhûta, on the eastern border of Egypt, it became known that he was also king of the Kedar federation of Arabian tribes.

Nehemiah's fellow governors invited him to a conference (*see* Neh 6:2). However, Nehemiah declined the invitation. The entire hinterland of Joppa (part of the Sharon Plain) was controlled by the Phoenician king of Sidon, so, in spite of a considerable Jewish population in Ono and the neighboring towns (Neh 11:33–35), Nehemiah was justifiably suspicious that he was liable to fall into a trap. There is no reason to assume that the plain of Ono was ever a part of the Yehud province during the Persian period.

The hill region south of Beth-zur was not included in the province of Judah; in Hellenistic sources it is referred to as Idumea. Since Geshem the Arab was interfering in the affairs of Judah along with the governors of Samaria, Ammon and Ashdod, it is probable that Idumea, which borders on Judah, was within his sphere of authority.

Thus, the Book of Nehemiah testifies to four provinces bordering on Judah: Samaria in the north, Ammon-Gilead in the east, Arabia-Idumea in the south, and Ashdod in the west. The provinces of Ammon and Arabia may have been constituted in the wake of the campaign by Nabû-naid (cf. *supra*).

Nehemiah returned to Persia in the thirty-second year of Artaxerxes (433 BCE; Neh 13:6). An unspecified time later (perhaps a year?), he says he returned to Yehud (Neh 13:6). How long he stayed in the west is not stated.

**The Province of Yehud.** In Aramaic the district of Judah over which Nehemiah was appointed governor was called Yehud. The actual territory included in the official district or province was seriously diminished from the pre-exilic Judean state, e.g. the southern Judean hill country had become detached. The southern boundary of Yehud passed between Beth-zur and Hebron (which had become predominantly Edomite). On the other hand, the northern boundary seems to have corresponded to the pre-exilic line north of Mizpah and Bethel; Jericho was included on the east. To the west the province included at least part of the Shephelah, as far as Keilah. The finding of stamped jar handles corresponding to some found at Ramat Rahel moves the western

*Concerning the limits of the Jewish population in the Persian period, it is also possible to derive some information from the diffusion of storage jar handles bearing seal impressions inscribed "Yehud" (with some variations in orthography) and "Jerusalem." In the main these impressions have been discovered at Jerusalem, Ramat Rahel, Bethany, Jericho, En-gedi, Mizpah, Azekah and Gezer.*

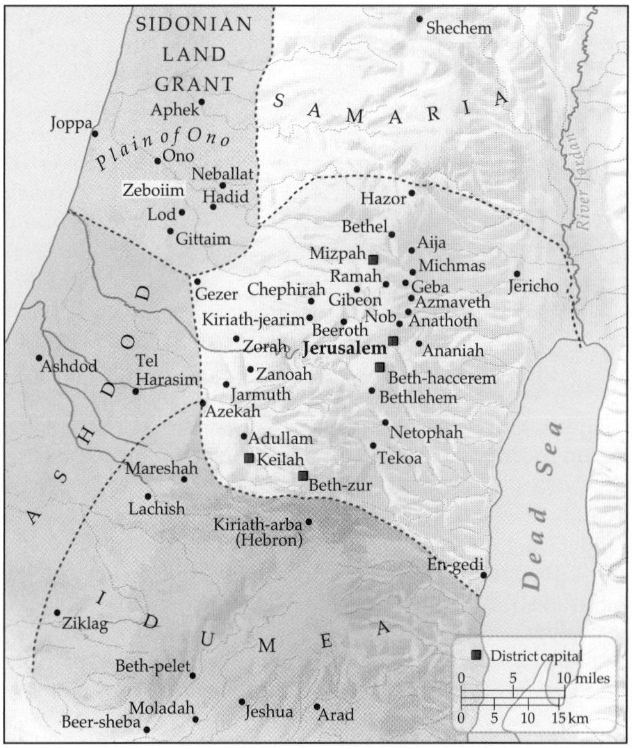


**THE PROVINCE OF YEHUD**

limits into the inner coastal plain.

Lod, Hadid and Ono in the northern Shephelah of Lod appear in the list of returnees (Ezra 2:33; Neh 7:37), but at least from the mid-fifth century BCE that area of the Joppa hinterland (the Plain of Ono) must have been under Sidonian control. People recognized by Nehemiah as Jews were living in various Negeb settlements as well, probably some of those who were not deported by the Babylonians. However, these Negeb settlements were obviously not reckoned as part of the Judean province. Neither were some of the towns in the southern Shephelah. From the cuneiform tablets discovered at Gezer, it would appear that in the seventh century BCE there was an immigrant population from Assyria. Recently, more such texts have been discovered at Hadid. In the Persian period Gezer may have reverted to Judea. At least many returnees settled in the Shephelah of Lod, i.e. the Plain of Ono.

A certain number of the Judean settlements in this period are known to us from the roster of "the people of the province who came up out of the captivity" (Ezra 2:1–35; Neh 7:6–38). A list of the returnees has been preserved (Ezra 2:1–64 || Neh 7:6–38); in addition to the many family and clan affiliations, it also includes a number of towns:

Bethlehem (Ezra 2:21; Neh 7:26), Netophah (Ezra 2:22; Neh 7:26), Anathoth (Ezra 2:23; Neh 7:27), [Beth-] Azmaveth (Ezra 2:24; Neh 7:28), Kiriath-jearim (Ezra 2:25; Neh 7:29), Chephirah (Ezra 2:25; Neh 7:29) and Beeroth (Ezra 2:25; Neh 7:29), Ramah (Ezra 2:26; Neh 7:30) and Geba (Ezra 2:26; Neh 7:30), Michmas (Ezra 2:27; Neh 7:31), Bethel (Ezra 2:28; Neh 7:32) and Ai (Ezra 2:28; Neh 7:32), Nob (read Nob instead of Nebo!; Ezra 2:29; Neh 7:33), Magbish (Ezra 2:30; not in Neh),

*Coin of the province "YHD."*

another Elam (Ezra 2:31; Neh 7:34), Harim (Ezra 2:32; Neh 7:35), Lod (Ezra 2:33; Neh 7:37), Hadid (Ezra 2:33; Neh 7:37) and Ono (Ezra 2:33; Neh 7:37), Jericho (Ezra 2:34; Neh 7:36), Senaah (Ezra 2:35; Neh 7:38).

The majority are in the former Benjaminite region north of Jerusalem: Nob (instead of Nebo), Anathoth, (Beth-)azmaveth, Ramah, Geba, Michmas, Ai (apparently Aiath / Aija; Khirbet Ḥaiyan), Bethel and the four Gibeonite towns—Gibeon, Chephirah, Kiriath-jearim and Beeroth. South of Jerusalem only two towns are mentioned, Bethlehem and Netophah, and on the east, Jericho. The Shephelah of Lod is represented by Lod, Hadid and Ono.

The settlements can be further filled in by the place names that appear on the roster of those who participated in building the walls of Jerusalem (Neh 3:1–32): Mizpah in the north; Beth-haccerem, Beth-zur and Tekoa in the south; Zanoah and Keilah on the west. Only two settlements also appear in the record of returnees, viz. Gibeon and Jericho. Besides Jerusalem itself four towns are referred to as furnishing full contingents of workers, viz. Mizpah, Beth-haccerem, Beth-zur and Keilah. This might suggest that the list of builders was made up according to the administrative centers. Some of these places seem to reflect towns that had survived the Babylonian destruction; Mizpah is the most significant since it had already been the headquarters of the local governor under the Neo-Babylonians, e.g. Gedaliah.

The list of those who rebuilt the city's defenses mentions specific communities (Neh 3:1–32). Certain men in this roster bore the title "officer of (half) the work battalion of. . . ." The distribution of these towns may be compared to that of the official "Yehud" seal impressions, found on jar handles from Mizpah in the north, Jericho in the east, En-gedi in the south, and Gezer in the west. Using the size of the work battalions as a key, it might be possible to reconstruct something of a local organization within Yehud.

| Districts | Sub-districts |
|---|---|
| Keilah | (1) Zanoah, (2) Keilah |
| Beth-zur | (3) Beth-zur, (4) Tekoa |
| Beth-haccerem | (5) Beth-haccerem |
| Jerusalem | (6) Jerusalem, (7) Gibeon |
| Mizpah | (8) Mizpah, (9) Jericho |

Therefore, the Jewish communities in the Persian period can be classified geographically into two categories, those within the province of Yehud, and those living outside it (Neh 4:12 [HMT 4:6]). Ezra was sent to enforce the Torah as the binding code for *all* the Jews in the province of Beyond the River (Ezra 7:25–26), not just in Yehud. The Jerusalem leaders were strict about who should participate in building the temple (Ezra 4:1–3) but Nehemiah recognized settlements in Kiriath-arba (Hebron), the Negeb, the Shephelah, and the Plain of Ono (Neh 11:25–36). In the list of returnees (Ezra 2: 1–34; Neh 7:6–38) many towns are recorded, some of which can hardly have been in Yehud. Society was comprised of three groups: Israel, Priests and Levites (Ezra 9:1; 1 Chr 9:1–16) and the Nethinim (Ezra 2:43, 2:58, 2: 70, 7:7, 8:17, 8:20 [2x]; Neh 3:26, 3:31, 7:46, 7:60, 7:73, 10:29 [Eng. 10:28], 11:3, 11:21 [2x]; 1 Chr 9:2).

After Nehemiah (Neh 5:14; c. 445-425 BCE), the names of several subsequent governors in charge of Yehud during the fifth and fourth centuries BCE are known. Even though they do not all have Hebrew names, there is no reason to doubt that they were Jewish, though the connection with the Davidic family was broken.

The Elephantine Papyri contain references to a Judean governor named Bagohi who, because of his typical Persian name (Bagoas in Greek sources), was usually thought to be a Persian. However, among the returnees from exile there was a family named Bigvai (containing the same Iranian element, *baga* meaning "god"; Ezra 2:2; Neh 7:7, *passim*), and the fact that the Bagohi of the Elephantine correspondence is involved in the problems of the Jewish garrison at Yeb (Elephantine) makes it clear that he was surely Jewish.

The names of two additional governors are known from seal impressions discovered at Ramat Rahel (biblical Beth-haccerem), viz. Jehoezer (*Yhwᶜzr*) and Aḥzai (*ʾḥzy*), who bear the title of governor. A Jehoezer seal has also been found at Tel Ḥarasim in the inner coastal plain, giving a new, westward limit for seal impressions from the Yehud province.

Another person, Hananiah, is called "the commander of the fortress" (Neh 7: 2) and it has been suggested that he also appears in the Elephantine Papyri. It is interesting to note that seal impressions from a person of this name have been found at Tel Ḥarasim and also in Babylon! In none of these instances is Hananiah called the "governor."

A coin, several examples of which were found at Beth-zur and Tell Jemmeh (Tel Gamma), bears the inscription, "Yehezkiah, the governor of Judah," who is apparently the Ezekias, a high priest in the early Hellenistic period, mentioned by Josephus (*Apion* 1:187–189). Another high priest, named Yohanan, put his name on other coins of the fourth century BCE. From this it can be deduced that the high priesthood had enhanced its political status to the point where its incumbents could serve as governors of Yehud.

This would indicate that throughout the Persian period Judah remained an autonomous province, usually (and perhaps always) under Jewish governors, the earliest originally from the House of David and later from the priestly families. Later Achaemenid policy apparently precluded the encouragement of potential local dynasts.

**Darius II** (423–405 BCE). Once again assassination and violence attended the transfer of power upon the death of Artaxerxes I. The winner was Ochus, satrap of Hyrcania, who took the throne name of Darius II. In the west two powerful satraps, Tissaphernes and Pharnabazos, vied for seniority and both maintained interference in the great Peloponnesian war between Sparta and Athens and their respective allies. The goal of Persian policy was restoration of political and financial control over the Greek cities and islands of Asia Minor. Local rebellions in the western Anatolian states often distracted them from their main objectives. Persian money was heavily invested in supporting the Spartan navy.

The papyri from the Jewish garrison at Elephantine (Yeb) reveal an incident (410–408 BCE) whereby the governors of Jerusalem, Bagohi, and the sons of Sanballat, governor of Samaria, were enlisted to use their influence with Arsames, governor of Egypt. Local priests of Khnum had bribed Persian authorities at Syene to permit and even abet the destruction of the Jewish temple to Yahu at Yeb. Eventually, a permit to restore the sanctuary was obtained. Arsames had absented himself from his satrapy for some time.

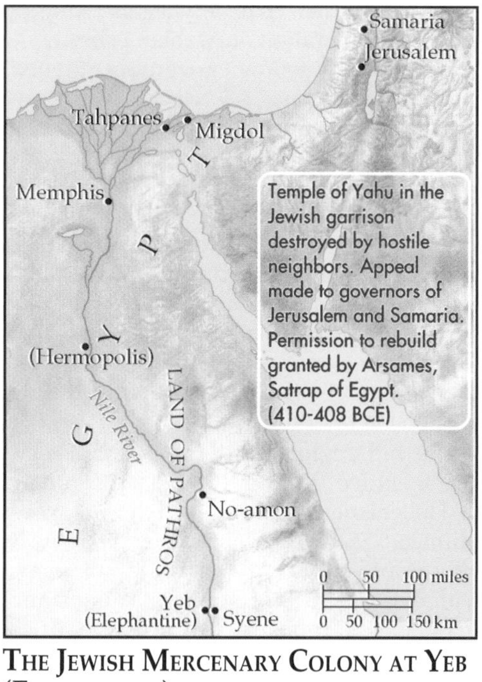


**THE JEWISH MERCENARY COLONY AT YEB (ELEPHANTINE)**

Darius died leaving the kingdom to his son, Artaxerxes II. Unfortunately, there was another son, the favorite of Darius' queen. This latter prince, named Cyrus, was given an appointment as satrap in the west with extensive authority over the principal districts and local states. That situation would lead to a war between the brothers that could have changed the course of Persian history.

**Artaxerxes II** (404–359 BCE). The year 404 BCE marks the beginning of a chain of events of far-reaching consequences for the province Beyond the River.

***Dynasty XXVIII in Egypt*.** In 404 BCE Darius II died and Amyrteus (404–399 BCE) led Egypt in a successful revolt. He was probably a descendant of the Amyrteus who had held out in the marshes during the older rebellion. His capital was Sais and he is reckoned as the only pharaoh of Dynasty XXVIII (404–399 BCE). Almost nothing is known about his reign except some statements in the Demotic Chronicle. There he is accused of violation of divine law for which he was deposed and his son not allowed to follow him. The Egyptians managed to maintain their independence for the next sixty years in spite of repeated Persian attempts to reconquer them. The history of Dynasties XXVIII to XXXI depends a great deal on the Demotic Chronicle, a source that must be used critically.

***The Revolt of Cyrus the Younger*.** The accession of Artaxerxes II Memnon and the subsequent conflict between him and his brother, "Cyrus the Younger," not only saw an insurrectionist army marching across the province of Beyond the River, it shook the great Persian monolith to its very foundations and taught the Greeks that a well-disciplined force could easily penetrate to the heart of the empire (Xenophon, *Anab.*).

By the end of the fifth century BCE, Syria, i.e. Beyond the River, was apparently being governed by a satrap called Abrokomas, who appears in Xenophon's account of the "ascent" by Cyrus the Younger (Xenophon, *Anab.* 1.3.20; 4.3.5, 18, 7.12). When Cyrus and his huge mercenary army arrived in Cilicia, he pretended that his aim was to attack this Abrokomas. The latter was thought to be waiting for him behind the Syrian Gates (Xenophon, *Anab.* 1.3.20). Diodorus (Diod. Sic. 14.20.5) only calls him "some Satrap of Syria." Although four hundred Greeks transferred their allegiance from Abrokomas to Cyrus, it was still reported that he had a strong force at his command (Xenophon, *Anab.* 1.4.3, 5). Abrokomas was a field commander on a par with the other three senior officers supporting King Artaxerxes at Cunaxa (Xenophon, *Anab.* 1.7.12). Of these latter, Tissaphernes was the well-known satrap of Asia Minor (who hated Cyrus the Younger), Arbakes was satrap of Media, and Gobryas (Gubaru) was "governor of Akkad" or

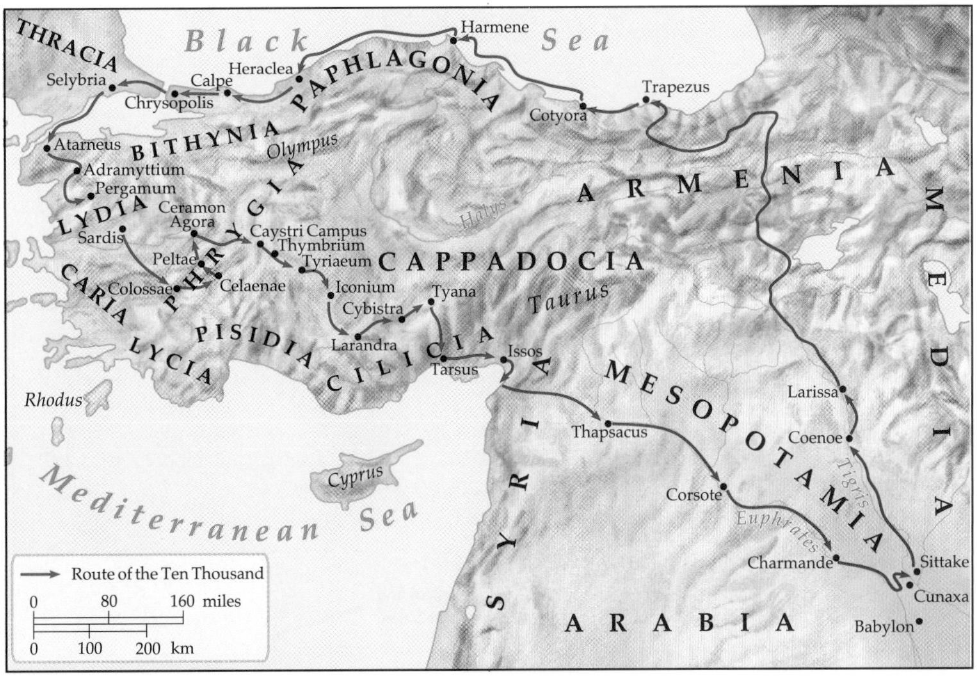


THE *ANABASIS* OF XENOPHON

"governor of Babylon" according to cuneiform texts from the reign of Darius II. The latest text of this Gubaru is 417 BCE; during the campaign of Cyrus the Younger, an addition to the *Anabasis* (7.8.25) has an otherwise unknown Rhoparas as governor of Babylon.

As Cyrus and his troops marched across northern Syria to cross the Euphrates at Thapsacus, mention is made of

> the palace of Belesys who had been ruler of Syria,
> (Xenophon, *Anab.* 1.4.11)

which was laid waste by Cyrus. Cuneiform records make it possible to reconstruct something of the career of Bēlshunu son of Bēluṣuršu. From his appearance on various dated business documents it can be seen that he was at one time a governor of the city of Babylon (but not the satrap of Babylonia / Akkad) from 421 to 414 BCE. He is documented as the "governor of Beyond the River" from 407 to 401 BCE. One need not think of this palatial estate and its well-tended park as the satrapal headquarters; it was more likely a private retreat maintained by the governor for his own use. By that time, he may have reached considerable seniority and thus retired. A person of his name is listed as furnishing sacrifices in 400 BCE in Babylonia. It seems reasonable to assume that Bēlshunu was relieved (not in disgrace) and replaced by Abrokomas, whose military skills were needed to organize the forces required for a new invasion of Egypt.

The land that Xenophon called "Syria" included Phoenicia and the northern coast as far as Myriandros. It extended eastward to the Euphrates. That Abrokomas was supposedly waiting behind the Cilician Gates does not mean that the border of his satrapy was there. The boundary between Cilicia and Syria is not given by Xenophon. In the east, when Cyrus and his troops were marching from Thapsacus (Tiphsah) to the mouth of the Khabur, he is said to have been in Syria; from there to Pylae he is in a region called Arabia. Whether this latter belonged to Syria or to Babylonia is not made clear. From Pylae onward, he is in Babylonia. After the failure of Cyrus' bid for power, Abrokomas returned to Syria.

The first decade of the fourth century BCE saw wars and intrigues between the Spartans and the various Persian satraps and generals. Most of the action was in Asia Minor. Artaxerxes was learning that the archers depicted on Persian gold coins were more effective than armies and navies.

***Dynasty XXIX*.** Nephrites became king of Egypt in 398 BCE. His capital was Mendes. The discovery of a scaraboid bearing his name at Gezer is hardly sufficient to suggest that he extended his control to include southern Palestine, but it does show a renewed interest in the Levant and a possible attempt to take advantage of the Persians' distraction in Asia Minor. He was followed by Achoris (393–380 BCE) who found a ready ally against the Achaemenids when Evagoras of Cyprus threw off the Persian yoke in 391 BCE (Diod. Sic. 15.2.3). Evagoras, in his turn, lost his support from the Athenians with the "Peace of Antacidas" ("the King's Peace"; Xenophon, *Hell.* 5.1.31) when the Persian monarch dictated humiliating terms to the Greek cities (386 BCE). Still, a Greek general was sent to Egypt to assist in preparing the Egyptian forces to face an impending Persian attack (Polyaenus, *Strategica* 3.11.7).

***Attack and Counterattack*.** Abrokomas joined Pharnabazos and Tithraustes in a concerted drive to reconquer Egypt (c. 385–383 BCE). While the Persian forces were engaged, Evagoras captured Tyre and won

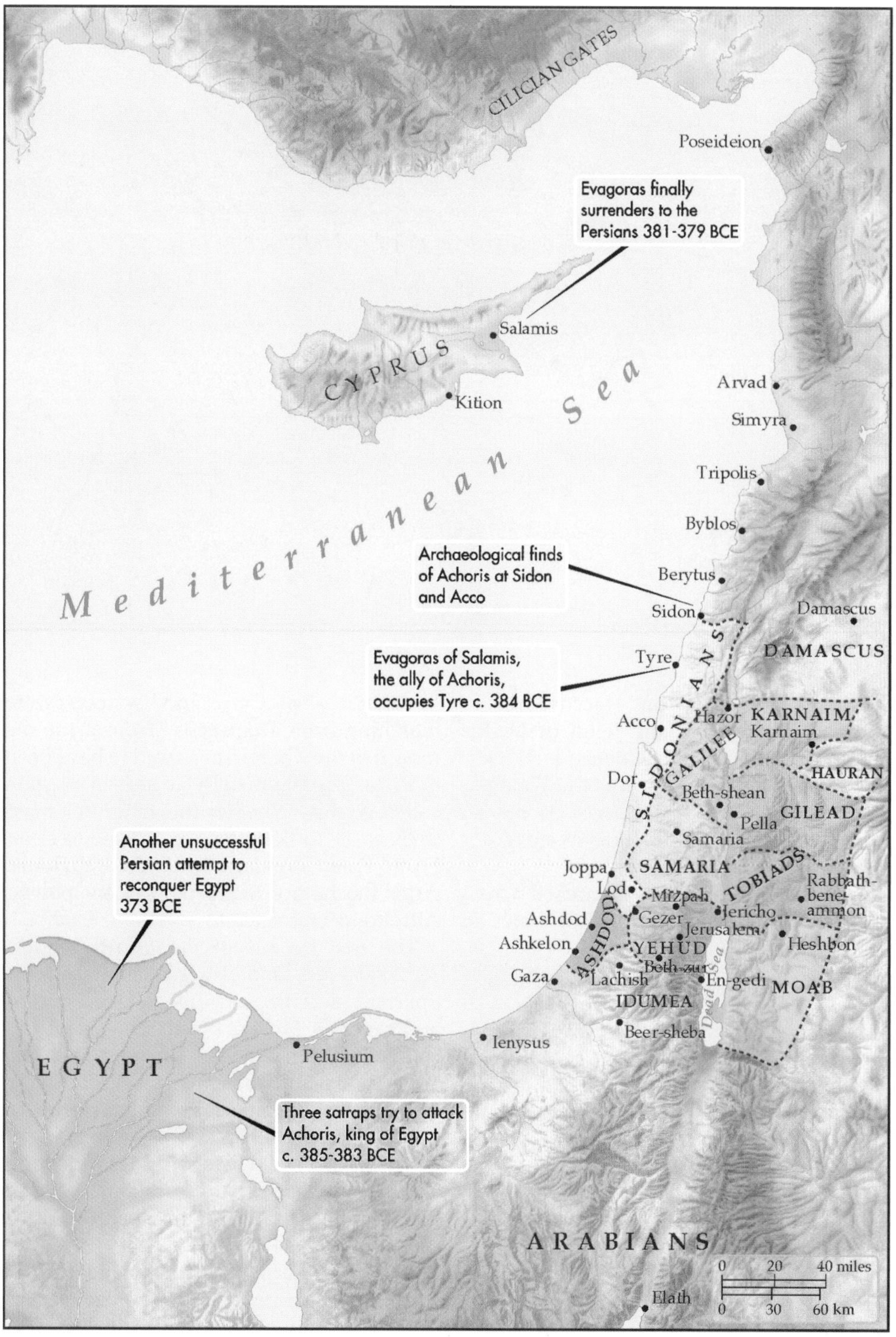


**ACHORIS AND EVAGORAS**

over a large part of Phoenicia and Cilicia (Diod. Sic. 15.2.4; Iso. *Evag.* 62; Iso. *Paneg.* 161). In addition to his alliance with Egypt, he had ample support from Hecatomnus, ruler of Caria. If the suggested emendation in Diodorus (Diod Sic. 15.2.3) be accepted, then Evagoras' forces included troops sent by "the king of the Arabians." The role of the province Beyond the River once again assumed a major geopolitical role in the struggle between Egypt and Mesopotamia. The Persian forces, their supply lines cut, were beaten severely and forced to retreat from Egypt (Iso. *Paneg.* 140). Pharaoh Achoris has left some monuments in the province Beyond the River, viz. an inscription at the ʾEshmunʿazor temple north of Sidon and an altar stand of polished gray granite (from Syene) at Acco.

A renewed Persian force invaded Cyprus and finally forced Evagoras to surrender (381–379 BCE) though the terms were much lighter than those demanded by him earlier (Diod. Sic. 15.8–9). In Egypt, Nectanebos became the founder of the XXX[th] Dynasty (380 BCE).

Pharnabazos, satrap of Cilicia, began mustering troops for a new assault on Egypt as early as 379 BCE but it was only in 373 BCE that he finally brought his forces together at Acco (Diod. Sic. 15.41.3; Polyaenus, *Strategica* 3.9.56; Isaeus, *Nicostratus* 7). Though he is credited with amassing a large navy, 300 ships, and extensive land forces, 12,000 Greek mercenaries and many Orientals, he was unable to do more than to establish a bridgehead near the Mendesian mouth of the Nile. He was unable to enter via Pelusium and a strong Egyptian counterattack forced him to withdraw.

Although the Phoenicians had done their part in this invasion by providing the naval support, they were not overly sympathetic. Within a few years, during the "satraps' revolt," they leagued up with the Egyptians against the Persians. From about 368 to 360 BCE the satraps' revolt nearly destroyed the Persian Empire altogether. It is impossible to determine to what degree Syria, i.e. Beyond the River, was actively engaged in the strife. Most of the rebel satraps governed districts in Asia Minor, but the Syrians and the Phoenicians also took part (Diod. Sic. 15.90.3).

***Dynasty XXX***. The XXIX[th] Dynasty was marked by considerable inner dissension among the ruling family, which led to its displacement by a new ruling family based at Sebennytus. Tachos (Teos) became king of Egypt (362 BCE) and mobilized a great army including ten thousand Greek mercenaries (361 BCE; cf. Diod. Sic. 15.90.2; 15.92.3). His ground troops were commanded by the Spartan general Agesilaüs and his naval forces were led by an Athenian admiral, Chabrias. In collaboration with the rebel satraps, he executed an invasion of the province Beyond the River and gained control of the major seaports of Palestine and Phoenicia. He was supposed to join another satrap, Aroandas, in Syria and march eastward in support of Datames who was crossing the

*Stele fragment bearing the name of Pharaoh Achoris, Dynasty XXIX (393–380 BCE), from Acco.*

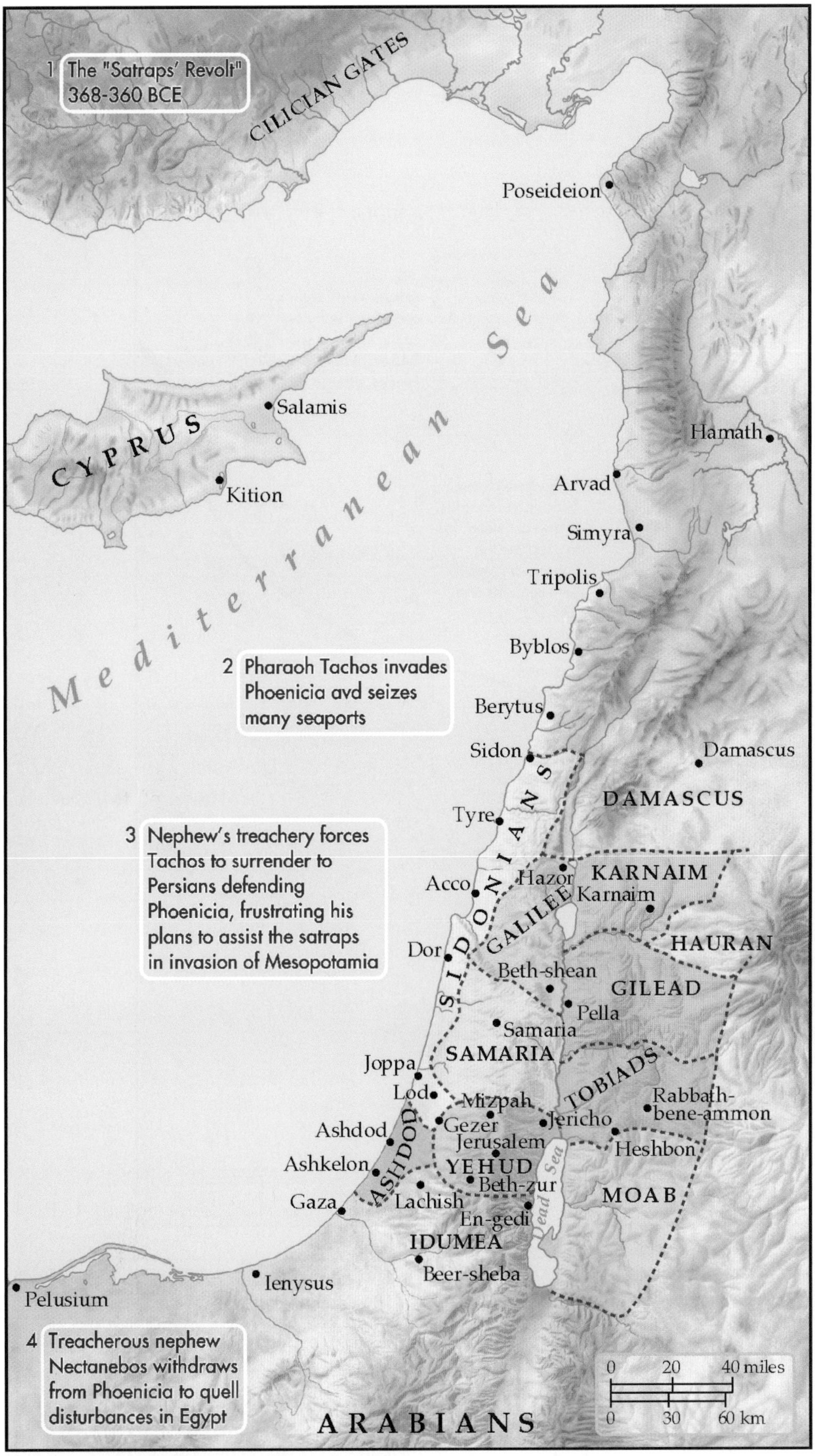


THE INVASION BY PHARAOH TACHOS (301 BCE)

Euphrates with an advanced guard. Ochus, a younger son of Artaxerxes, was struggling to maintain control of Phoenicia in the face of the Egyptian attack, but the Greek mercenaries were steadily gaining ground against him. However, Tachos' nephew, Nectanebos, rebelled against his uncle and this forced Tachos to surrender himself to Ochus at Sidon. In turn, disturbances in Egypt caused Nectanebos to withdraw from Phoenicia (Diod. Sic. 15.92). Persian authority was gradually restored in the west as the rebel satraps were betrayed or captured, one by one.

**Artaxerxes III** (358–338 BCE) **and Arses** (338–336 BCE). Ochus, who was not the firstborn prince, managed to eliminate all his rivals (his older brother was executed for plotting against Artaxerxes II) and succeeded his father as Artaxerxes III (358 BCE). During the next several years he was engaged in quelling various disturbances throughout the empire, especially in Asia Minor. By 351 BCE he had gained firm control over his western provinces, including Phoenicia, and was in position to launch a new invasion of Egypt.

The satrap of Syria at this time was another Belesys (Bēlshunu), possibly a grandson of the one who had governed the province in the late fifth century BCE (Diod. Sic. 16.42.1). The province Beyond the River reached as far as Cilicia in the north and included Phoenicia and North Syria as far as the Euphrates. The satrapy evidently had remained unchanged in geographical extent.

Artaxerxes III had no more luck in Egypt than did his predecessors. He too was forced to retire after a year of hard fighting (Diod. Sic. 16.40.3, 44.1, 48.1). This failure (c. 351–350 BCE) sparked an extensive revolt by the Phoenician cities, the so-called Tennes Rebellion, after the name of the king of Sidon. The Phoenician representatives assembled at Tripolis and voted to throw off the Persian yoke. A large fleet of warships and a mighty mercenary army was financed by the vast wealth of Sidon. The Phoenicians were followed by nine Cypriot kings and parts of Cilicia also joined in the revolt (Diod. Sic. 16.41). Belesys, the satrap of Beyond the River, had the job of quelling the rebellion. Accompanied by Mazaios, satrap of Cilicia, he made an unsuccessful assault on Phoenicia (Diod. Sic. 16.42.1). The exact date of this attempt cannot be determined.

Artaxerxes saw that his two satraps were ineffective so he decided to intervene personally. At the beginning of 345 BCE he assembled a huge force at Babylon and marched against Sidon. The populace had made preparations for an extended siege but they were betrayed to the Persians by Tennes their king (Diod. Sic. 16.43). They set fire to their ships and to their homes in order to escape capture. Artaxerxes sold the ruins to speculators, who paid a handsome price for the right to search for melted gold and silver (Diod. Sic. 16.43–45). It is a difficult question as to how widespread was the destruction wrought at archaeological sites of the Persian period in the inner southern Levant as a result of the Tennes Rebellion. There were too many different possibilities based on the various invasions and rebellions that took place in the fourth century BCE.

Belesys disappeared from the scene; nothing is known about what happened to him. Mazaios, though retaining his satrapy in Cilicia, was also given charge of Beyond the River. Many of his known coins are of Phoenician, particularly Sidonian, style and are numbered from 16 to 21, representing the last six years of Artaxerxes III's reign (345–339 BCE). Another series of Mazaios' coins confirms his rule over Cilicia and Syria; they are inscribed: "Mazdai who is over Beyond the River and Cilicia."

Artaxerxes III finally did conquer Egypt (343 BCE) and so strengthened his position in the West that even the Cypriot kings had to fall back into line (Diod. Sic. 16.46–51). The punishment of Egypt was severe and seems to have included extensive damage to temples and other religious institutions. But Artaxerxes himself was assassinated in 338 BCE and followed by Arses; this brought an end to all hopes of a great Persian revival. Egypt apparently took advantage of the situation and revolted (c. 337 BCE). This interim period may correspond to the short reign of a certain Khabbabash, a ruler attested by a few inscriptions, especially an Apis sarcophagus dated to his second year, in Egypt.

**Darius III** (336–330 BCE). Arses was murdered in 336 BCE and replaced by Darius III. This latter set about energetically to recoup the losses sustained since Ochus' demise and by 334 BCE he had even regained control over Egypt.

Mazaios seems to have maintained his position as satrap of Beyond the River throughout these final years. He has a series of Sidonian coins numbered 1 through 4. It is suggested that they date to the three years of Arses' reign (338–336 BCE) and the first four years of Darius III (336–333 BCE). But others have questioned whether he still held sway over Cilicia. Certain sources (Curt. 3.4.3; Arr. *Anab.* 2.4.5) refer to a certain Arsames who evidently led the Persian forces at Tarsus in 333 BCE. Arrian's account of the Persian commanders at Granicus (1.12.8; 334 BCE) and at Issos (11.11.8; 333 BCE) includes an Arsames who was a leading cavalry officer. He died at the battle of Issos. This is probably the same person who was in charge of Tarsus. Diodorus (Diod. Sic. 17.19.4) refers to an Arsamenes, a satrap, at the battle of Granicos; he had his own cavalry. If this is really a variant spelling of Arsames, then the allusion may be explained in one of two ways. Either the term satrap means something less here than ruler of a full province, or else there has been a transposition of names by which Arsamenes has displaced the next officer, Arsites, in this passage. It is probable that Mazaios was still governor of both Cilicia and Syria but that Arsames was his deputy in the northern province. Mazaios does not appear at any stage in the Macedonian conquest of Cilicia, Phoenicia or the rest of Syria. Nevertheless, he was a field commander at the battle of Gaugamela (331 BCE). After the Persian defeat he withdrew to Babylon with a remnant of his forces and finally surrendered the city to Alexander (330 BCE). He was rewarded with the governorship of Babylonia, which he ruled until his death in 328 BCE.

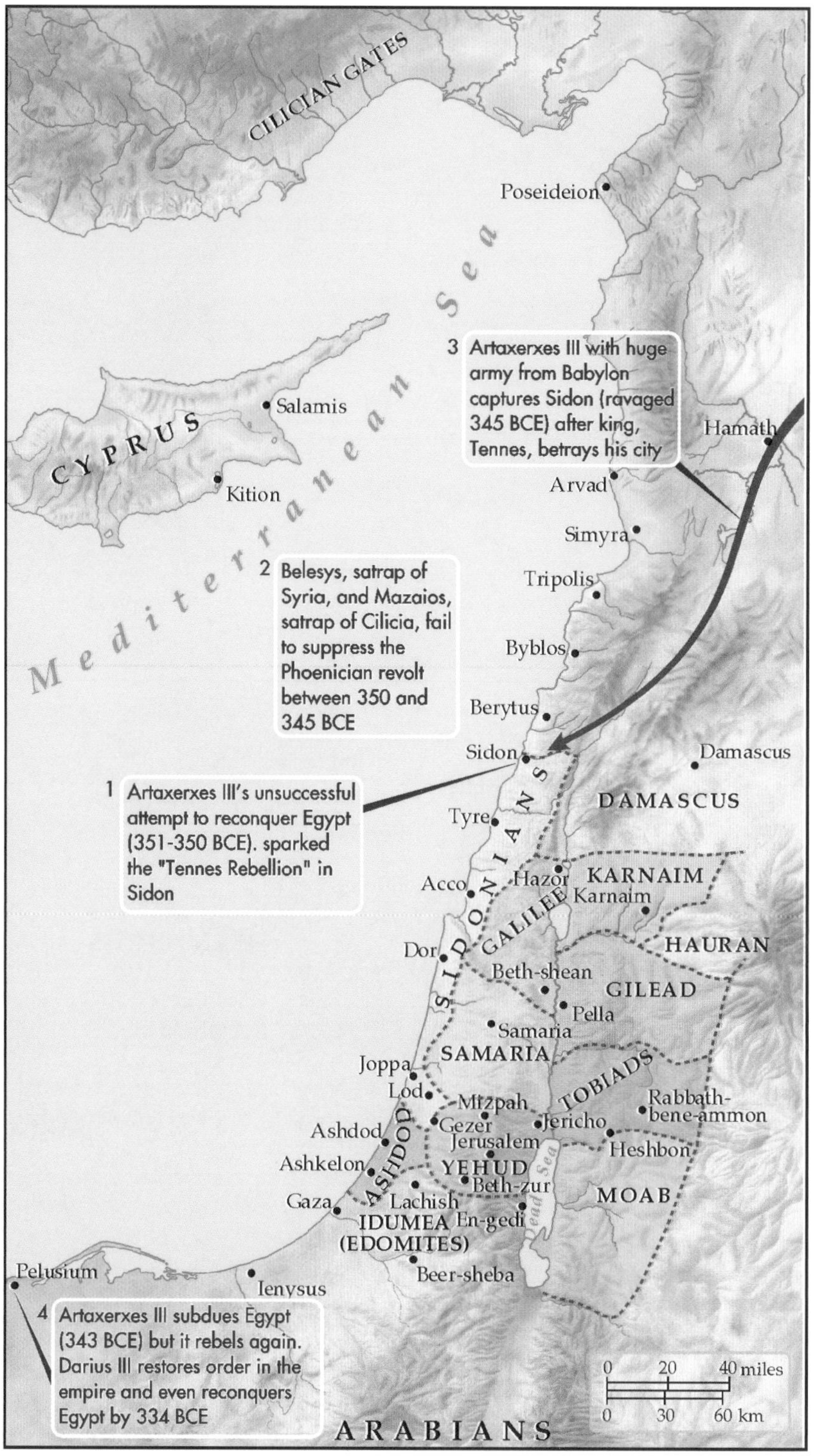


THE "TENNES REBELLION"

In the meantime, Alexander had marched southward from Issos and received the surrender of the Phoenician cities of Arvad (Arados), Byblos and Sidon. The province evidently maintained its identity until it was divided between the Seleucids and the Ptolemies. Henceforth, the history of the Levant in its role as a land bridge continues in the rivalry between the Hellenistic kingdoms and later in its function during the age of the Roman Empire.

| Governors of Babylonia and Beyond the River | |
|---|---|
| Gubaru/Gobryas | 535–525 BCE |
| Ushtannu/Hystanes | 521–516 BCE |
| *Ḫutta*[--] son of Pagakanna | 486 BCE |

| Governors of Beyond the River | |
|---|---|
| Tattenai/Tattennu | c. 518–502 BCE |
| Megabyzus | 456–c. 445 BCE |
| Bēlshunu/Belesys I | 407–401 BCE |
| Abrokomas | 401–c. 383 BCE |
| Bēlshunu/Belesys II | 369–c. 345 BCE |
| Mazaios | 343–332 BCE |

## CHAPTER TWELVE

# ALEXANDER AND THE EARLY HELLENISTIC PERIOD

The period of Persian domination of the Near East and of the Levant in particular came to an abrupt end with the remarkable campaign of Alexander, son of Philip, king of Macedonia. His conquest of Anatolia, the Levant, Egypt, Mesopotamia and the land of Persia up to the border of India earned him the title Alexander the Great. In 334 BCE Alexander marched his army of 35,000 men into Asia to challenge the Persians and fulfill his father Philip's pledge, "to avenge Greece by attacking Persia." He passed from Europe to Asia at the Hellespont.

> [Alexander] personally sailed with sixty fighting ships to the Troad, where he flung his spear from the ship and fixed it in the ground, and then leapt ashore himself the first of the Macedonians, signifying that he received Asia from the gods as a spear-won prize.
> (Diod. Sic. 17.17.1)

The Persians marched toward the Macedonians and camped at the river Granicus in western Anatolia. The river served as the Persians' first line of defense. Alexander hastened to meet them and stopped with the river separating the opposing forces. The Persians held the high ground and waited to attack the Macedonians, when they crossed the stream. However, Alexander surprised his Persian adversaries and crossed at daybreak, dashing up the hill to engage the enemy (Plut. *Alex.* 16.3–4). The fighting proved fierce, but the Macedonians prevailed.

After routing the Persian forces, Alexander continued south taking Sardis, currently in the hands of the Persians and the capital of Lydia (Diod. Sic. 17.21.7; Arr. *Anab.* 1.17.3–8; Plut. *Alex.* 17.1). He pursued the fleeing Persian general Memnon to Miletus on the Aegean coast, and following a brief siege captured the city. After the fall of Miletus, the Persians concentrated their forces at Halicarnassus, the most important city of Caria in southwestern Anatolia. There the fortifications also fell before the Macedonian onslaught, and Alexander moved along the southern Mediterranean coast taking the coastal cities of Lycia (Telmessus, Xanthus, Patara, Phaselis) and Pamphylia (Side, Aspendus, Perga).

Turning inland, Alexander subdued the Pisidians at Sagalassus and the cities of Phrygia, in which he visited its ancient capital of Gordion. An ancient oracle had foretold that the one who could loosen an impenetrable knot at Gordion would become the ruler of the world. According to the legend, Alexander unsheathed his sword and cut it (Plut. *Alex.* 18.1; Arr. *Anab.* 2.3). At Gordion Alexander was joined by his commander Parmenion, who arrived from Sardis. The combined forces marched south through Cappadocia and the narrow pass of the Cilician Gates in the Taurus Mountains. Descending onto the Cilician plains, they captured Tarsus, the capital of Cilicia.

*Alexander the Great (left) and Darius at the Battle of Issus, on mosaic from Pompeii, 2nd–1st centuries BCE.*

The Macedonians carried out punitive raids in the region of Cilicia and then marched eastward through the Syrian Gates in the Amanus Mountains. Alexander received word that Darius had arrived at Issus in his rear (Diod. Sic. 17.33.1–4), so he returned to meet the Persian king in battle. In 333 BCE Alexander and his army defeated the Persians, though heavily outnumbered, on the plain of Issus in a bold cavalry attack. Darius fled abandoning even his wife and family (Curt. 3.11.21–23; Arr. *Anab.* 2.11.9–10; Diod. Sic. 17.33.5–35.4).

Following the defeat, Alexander sent his general Parmenion to Damascus, where Darius' treasury had been moved (Curt. 3.13.1ff.; Arr. *Anab.* 2.11.10; Plut. *Alex.* 24). Plundering the Persians' war chest and replenishing his own (Grabbe 1992:1: 206), Alexander turned south through the Levant conquering the Phoenician cities on the Mediterranean coast. His military strategy was clear. Before continuing east in pursuit of Darius, Alexander had to assure that his rear flank along the western coast was secure. He first subdued Cyprus and the coastal cities of Phoenicia (Aradus, Byblos and Sidon) that offered no resistance. On the other hand, the island city of Tyre refused to surrender. Centuries earlier Tyre had likewise withstood the advance of the Babylonian Nebuchadnezzar and had survived his siege for thirteen years (*Apion* 1:156).

Tyre was allied with Darius and supplied the Persians with their main navy in the conflict with the Greeks. Secure in its isolated location and the hope of assistance from its colony at Carthage, Tyre refused to allow Alexander to enter the city to offer sacrifices in the Tyrian temple to Heracles-Melkart, the Macedonian's mythical ancestor (Diod. Sic. 17.40.2). Alexander was angered by the ignominy, and he laid siege to Tyre for seven months (Curt. 4.2.1–4.18; Just. *Epit.* 11.10.10–14; Plut. *Alex.* 24.2–25.2; Arr. *Anab.* 2.16–24). His troops managed to build a mole connecting the island to the mainland and succeeded in conquering the city in July 332 BCE (Diod. Sic. 17.46.5).

After the fall of Tyre, the Macedonian continued towards his primary objective to the south: Egypt. He met no resistance at the Persian administrative city of Acco or the remaining Phoenician cities on his march south. Only the independent city of Gaza is mentioned among the coastal cities of Palestine that challenged Alexander. Yet,

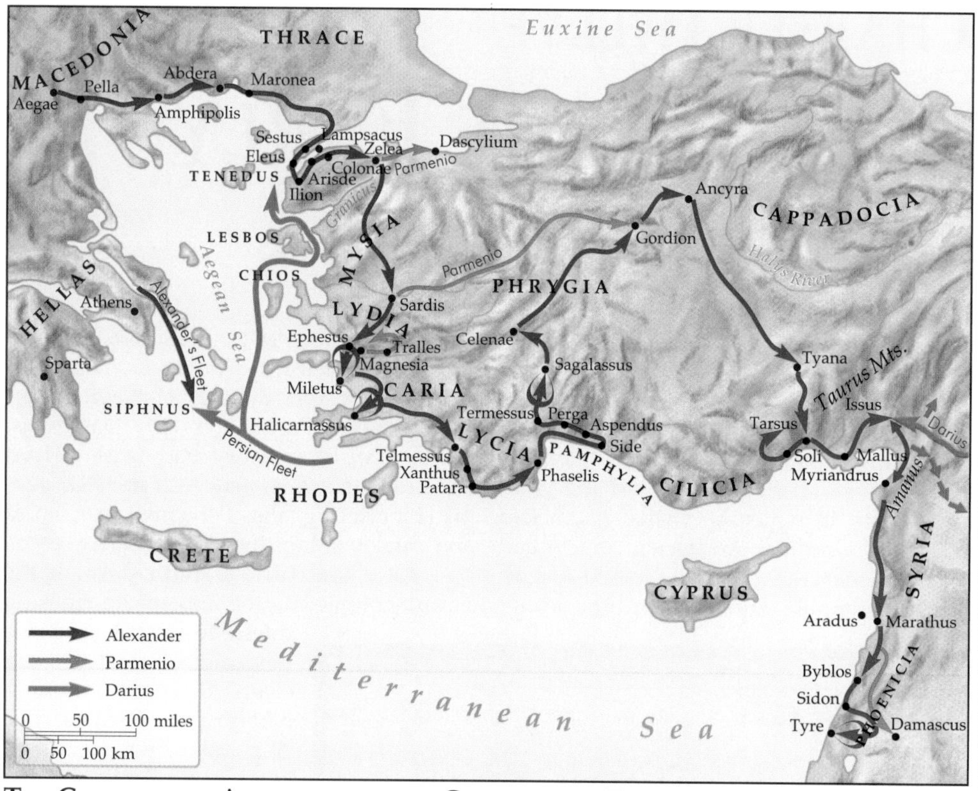


**The Campaign of Alexander to the Conquest ot Tyre (July 332 bce)**

it was only a temporary obstacle and was subdued after a two-month siege (Diod. Sic. 17.48.7; Arr. *Anab.* 11.25.4–27.7; Curt. 4.6.7–20; *Ant.* 11:325; Plut. *Alex.* 25.3).

Alexander continued to Egypt where he likewise met no resistance. According to Diodorus, the Egyptians had suffered impieties and harsh rule under the Persians. So, they welcomed Alexander, and Egypt fell to the Macedonians without a fight (Diod. Sic. 17.49.2; Curt. 4.7.1; Arr. *Anab.* 3.1.2). After his visit to the temple of Amon (Diod. Sic. 17.51.1–4; Curt. 4.7.25; Just. *Epit.* 11.11.2–12; Plut. *Alex.* 27.3–6), Alexander returned on the same coastal route by which he had marched to Egypt.

In spite of the tales that followed Alexander's conquests, the Macedonian likely had little interest in the hinterland of Judea. His concerns were to the east, where he would put an end to Darius and the Persian domination of the Near East. On the march through Phoenicia to Egypt his only pauses were the sieges of Tyre and Gaza. The Greek historian Arrian also reports that Alexander interrupted the siege of Tyre to deal with Arabs who had attacked his forces in the Anti-Lebanon (Arr. *Anab.* 2.25.4; Curt. 4.2.24; Plut. *Alex.* 24.6).

Alexander made an example of Tyre for those who resisted his advance. Of the survivors, thirty thousand were sent to slave markets, and the Macedonian conqueror crucified two thousand Tyrian men. The overwhelming superiority of Alexander's forces and the ferocity of their onslaught convinced local leaders that resistance was futile. Not surprisingly, Arrian records that with the fall of Tyre, "the remainder of Syria known as Palestine had already come over to him" (Arr. *Anab.* 2.25.4). The Macedonian expected local satrapies to transfer allegiances to their new sovereign. It is against this background that Josephus records the Samaritan Sanballat's offer of fealty to Alexander and material support in the siege of Tyre (*Ant.* 11:321–324).

We also have legends of meetings between Alexander and the leadership in Jerusalem. While such contact is not unimaginable, there are difficulties in all the accounts. The challenge is to identify if there are historical kernels embedded within the Alexander tales. Josephus' legend of Alexander's visit to Jerusalem appears very much like a Jewish version of similar Greek tales. Not only is the story found in Josephus (*Ant.* 11: 317–345), but also in a recension of the Greek Alexander Romance of Pseudo-Callisthenes (ii.24). These legends about Alexander were likely the creation of Alexandrian Jews who hoped to bolster their civic status in the Hellenistic city. Other Alexander legends appear in rabbinic literature (b. *Tamid* 31b–32b; *Gen. Rab.* 61:7), including accounts parallel to Josephus' story of Alexander's journey to Jerusalem.

The 21$^{st}$ of the month (Kislev) is the day of Mount Gerizim, when mourning is forbidden. On this day the Samaritans begged a temple from Alexander of Macedon and said to him: Sell us five *kurs* of earth on Mount Moriah. He gave it to them. When they came, the inhabitants of Jerusalem came out and drove them away with sticks and told Simon the Just. He put on priestly vestments and the leading men of Jerusalem with him and a thousand councilors clothed themselves in white and the priestly neophytes clashed the sacred vessels. And as they went among the hills [the Macedonians] saw torches of light. The King said: What is that? The informers said to him: Those are Jews who have revolted against you. When they came to Antipatris, the sun shone. They came to the first sentry-post. They said to them: Who are you? They said: We are people of Jerusalem and we have come to welcome the King. When Alexander of Macedon saw Simon the Just, he alighted from his chariot and knelt before him. They said to him: Do you know this man? He is a mere mortal. He said: I behold the image of this man when I go to war and conquer. [Alexander] said: What do you seek? [Simon] replied: Gentiles have misled you and you have given to them the house in which we pray for your kingdom. He asked: Who are they who have deceived me? He replied: The Samaritans who stand before you. He said: I hand them over to you. They pierced their heels and hung them on the tails of their horses and dragged them over thorns and thistles till they reached Mount Gerizim. They ploughed and sowed it with horse-beans as [the Samaritans] had thought to do to the Temple. And the day they did this they made a festival.

(Scholion on *Meg. Ta$^{c}$an.* 21 Kislev; cf. b. *Yoma* 69a)

Both Josephus and the rabbinical accounts place Alexander's encounter with the Jewish high priest in the literary-historical context of the Macedonian's encounter with Sanballat and the Samaritans. According to Josephus, Manasseh, the brother of the high priest Jaddus, married the daughter

*Papyrus fragment in Aramaic script that mentions "Sanballat governor of Samaria," 4th century* BCE*, found in the manuscript cave, Mughâret Abū Shinjeh, in Wâdī ed-Dalîyeh.*

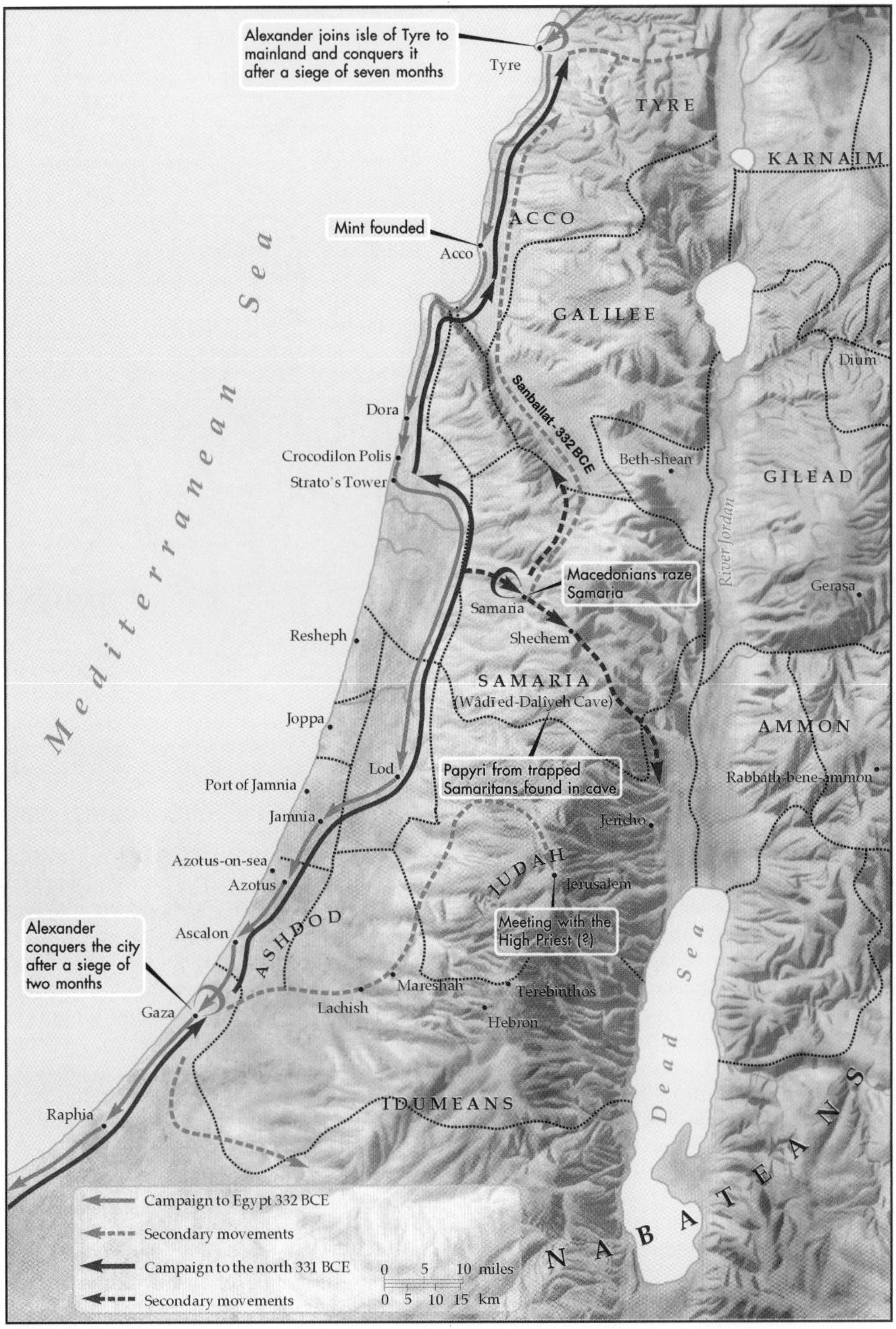


**Alexander Completes the Conquest of the Southern Levant (332–331 BCE)**

of Sanballat. Marriage to a Samaritan excluded Manasseh's fitness for service in the Jerusalem temple. Sanballat sought to compensate his son-in-law with the promise of a temple comparable to the Jerusalem temple (cf. *Ant.* 11:322–323). Alexander is described granting Sanballat's request, and the king sanctioned the building of a Samaritan temple on Mount Gerizim. Recent archaeology has identified the foundations of an early Hellenistic temple on Mount Gerizim.

Previously, scholarship assumed that the name Sanballat in Josephus' tale had been confused with another earlier Samaritan leader by the same name who opposed Nehemiah (Neh 2:10, 4:1, 6:1). However, Samaritan papyri found in a cave in Wâdī ed-Dalîyeh include documents from the latter part of the fourth century BCE. They indicate there was another Sanballat, who was governor of Samaria at the time of Alexander's conquest, lending some measure of historical credulity to Josephus' report.

Although there are other similarities, the rabbinical traditions concerning Alexander's journey to Jerusalem are distinguished from Josephus' report in several important details. According to Josephus, Alexander encountered the high priest Jaddus at Mount Scopus on the northern outskirts of Jerusalem (*Ant.* 11:329). Rabbinical tradition, on the other hand, identifies the priest who came to meet Alexander as Simon the Just—even though Jewish tradition records that he served as the high priest over one hundred years later, viz. c. 200 BCE (cf. *Ant.* 12: 43, 157; m. *ʾAbot* 1:2).

The location of the encounter also varies. According to the Scholion on *Megillat Taʿanit*, the high priest does not wait until Alexander is on the outskirts of the city at Mount Scopus; he descends instead from the hill country to Antipatris, where Alexander is encamped. Alexander's southern march toward Gaza (and return along the same route) would certainly have passed east of the headwaters of the Yarkon River at Aphek-Pegae-Antipatris. Notwithstanding the pure fiction of Alexander's falling prostrate, or kneeling before the Jewish high priest, the report of the initiative taken by the Jewish leaders to approach the king seems more plausible than Josephus' presentation that Alexander ascended to Jerusalem to offer sacrifices in the temple. However, the city name in rabbinical legend, Antipatris, is an anachronistic toponym reflecting the time of composition, rather than the time of the event. This is the name given to the city in the Roman period by Herod the Great in honor of his father (*Ant.* 16:143; *War* 1:417), almost three hundred years after Alexander the Great's march through the region.

Finally, the rabbinic legend concludes with the Jews from Jerusalem receiving permission from Alexander to punish the Samaritans on Mount Gerizim. Scholars have rightly recognized the influence of Alexander's punishment of the commander of the garrison in Gaza (cf. *Ant.* 11:320; Curt. 4.6; Arr. *Anab.* 2.25.4) upon the rabbinic description of the retribution meted out on the Samaritans. Furthermore, as Josephus testifies, the Samaritan temple on Mount Gerizim was not destroyed in the days of Alexander but remained standing until it was razed by the Hasmonean John Hyrcanus (c. 110 BCE; cf. *Ant.* 13:281; *War* 1:65).

Nevertheless, we would be remiss if we discarded entirely the historical essence of the rabbinical legend of Alexander's antipathy toward the Samaritans—a detail missing from Josephus' *Antiquities*, but perhaps hinted in his citation from Hecataeus.

> The honor in which [Alexander] held our nation may be illustrated by the statement of Hecataeus that, in recognition of the consideration and loyalty shown to him by the Jews, he added to their territory the district of Samaria free of tribute. (*Apion* 2:43; cf. 1 Macc 10:30, 38; 11:34)

The change of Alexander's disposition toward the Samaritans is attested also by Curtius Rufus. Upon the Macedonian's return to Gaza, he received

> . . . news of the death of Andromachus, to whom he had given the charge of Syria. The Samaritans had burned him alive. To avenge his murder he

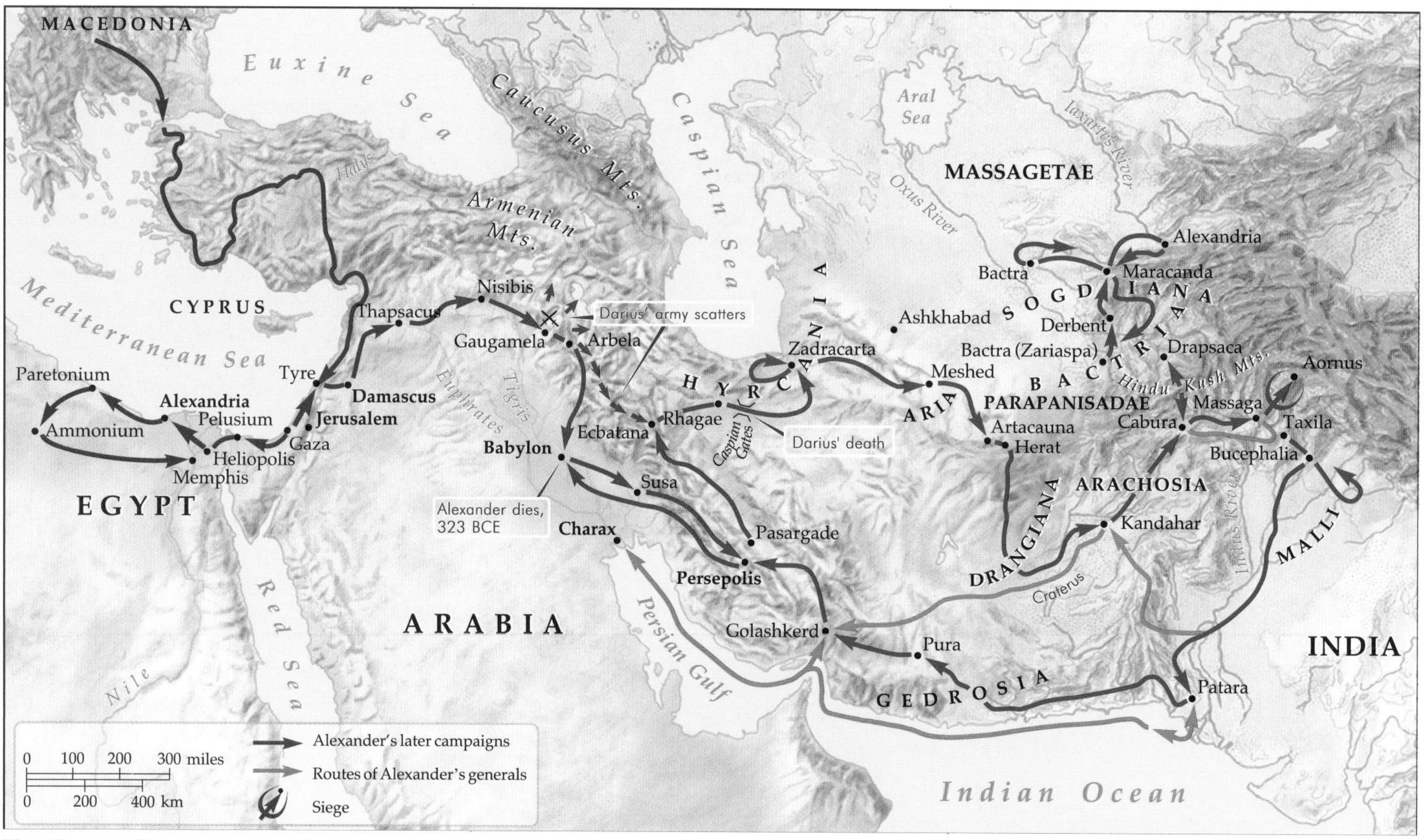


**THE LATER CAMPAIGNS OF ALEXANDER**

> hastened to the spot with all possible speed and on arrival those who had been guilty of so great a crime were delivered to him. (Curt. 4.8.9–10)

The church historian, Eusebius, likewise in the Armenian version of his *Chronicon* reports,

> [Alexander] appointed Andromachus, whom the inhabitants of the city of the Samaritans killed; and on his return from Egypt Alexander punished them, and having taken the city, settled Macedonians therein. (*Chron.* 2.23)

Together with Josephus' passing excerpt from Hecataeus, we may possess multiple witnesses to a historical event in the Samaritan uprising that led to retribution by Alexander.

Further, archaeological evidence for these events may be in hand, if we accept the proposal that it was Alexander's reprisal, which appears to have been the occasion of the patricians' flight into the wastelands of the Wâdī ed-Dalîyeh, where they were massacred by Macedonian troops, leaving to us a cache of papyri strewn among Samaritan bones." These same events centuries later became the genesis for the rabbinical legend intended as an anti-Samaritan apologetic.

Where and when Alexander encountered the Jewish hierarchy during his conquest of the region remains uncertain. Nevertheless, there is no reason to doubt that the Jewish leaders, like their regional counterparts, met with Alexander and submitted to his rule. Their participation in Alexander's campaign suggests that a formal relationship had already been established between the Macedonian and his new Jewish subjects. As he passed through the Near East, Alexander required the satrapies of Darius to swear allegiance to their new sovereign. Their change in allegiance was signaled by the redirection of tribute payments formerly given to the Persians into the Macedonian treasury (*Ant.* 11:317). Refusal to comply would have been met with severe retribution. So, some initiative by the local Jewish leaders in Jerusalem to submit to Alexander would have been expected to prevent the disaster that befell Tyre and Gaza.

## JUDEA UNDER THE DIODOCHI (323–301 BCE)

Alexander's sudden death in 323 BCE resulted in the necessary distribution of powers among his subordinates. The period from 323 to 281 BCE is designated by historians as the period of the Diadochi, named for Alexander's "successors," the generals who divided up his kingdom.

One general, Laomedon, was given the satrapy "Beyond the River," i.e. Syria. We have little information concerning the reason for the rise of this general to control such a strategic region as Syria, but his hold on the province was brief. In 320 BCE Ptolemy I Soter invaded Syria and wrested control away from Laomedon. The next twenty years proved to be a time of instability and political change in the region, with control of the Syrian lands changing five times—320, 315, 312, 302 and 301 BCE.

The initial seizure of Syria by Ptolemy likely brought little notice. Formal division of Alexander's kingdom had yet to materialize and the change in political leadership was viewed by the local population as little more than a change of satraps within the undivided kingdom. Laomedon's weak resistance to Ptolemy reinforced the perception of superficial change. He was unable to muster much of an army to resist Ptolemy's advance, and he eventually fled the country.

A more dramatic shift in political power occurred with the appearance in the region of Antigonus I Monophthalmus ("the One-eyed"), who succeeded Antipater to establish an independent kingdom in Asia, and who aspired to rule a unified empire at the expense of the Diadochi. His strategy for control of Alexander's empire included control of the Mediterranean Sea. He needed conquest of the important Phoenician coast to control shipping in the eastern Mediterranean.

Ptolemy tried to thwart Antigonus' design by strengthening his fortresses in Syria and withdrawing his navy to Egypt. Antigonus countered by establishing shipyards in Tripolis, Byblos and Sidon in Phoenicia, together with another in Cilicia to prepare for the looming conflict (Diod. Sic. 19.58.4). He then attacked the fortresses in Syria. Tyre fell in fifteen months with the agreement that Ptolemy's soldiers were allowed to leave (Diod. Sic. 19.61.5). Others fell with little resistance, but Joppa and Gaza had to be taken by force (Diod. Sic. 19.59.2).

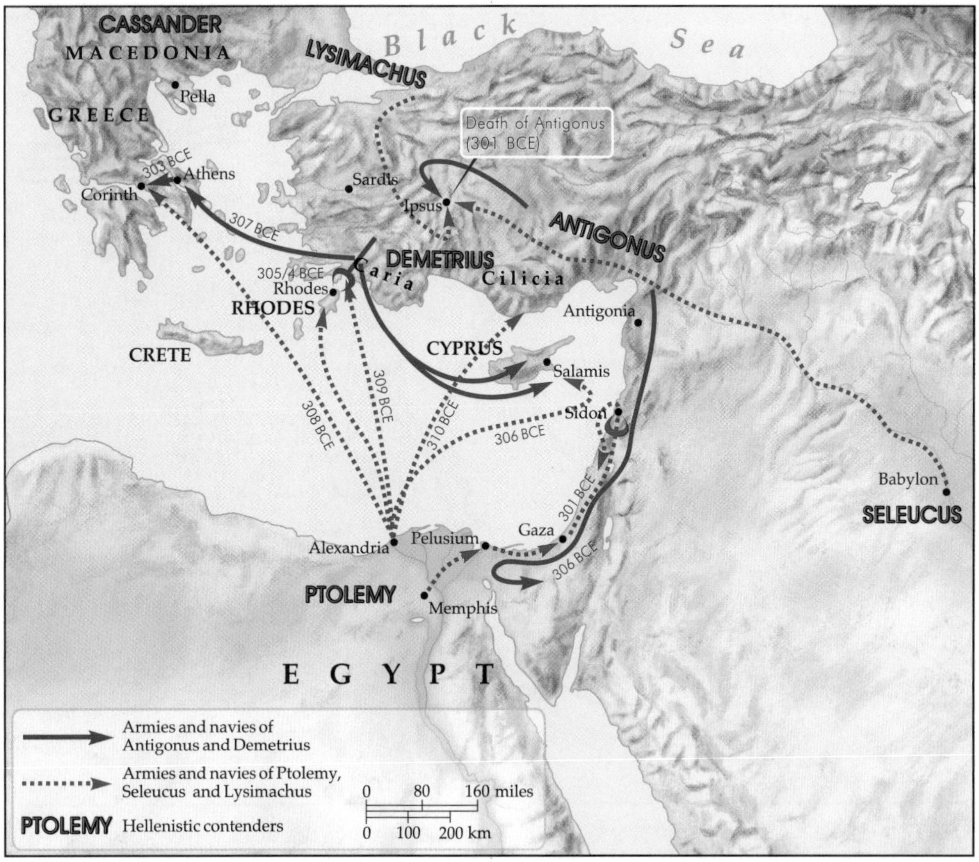


**The Wars Between Antigonus I and the Diadochi of Alexander (315–301 BCE)**

*A major turning point was the death of Antigonus at the Battle of Ipsus, 301 BCE.*

Antigonus drove out Seleucus, the satrap of Babylon, and by 315 BCE occupied most of Syria and Phoenicia. Seleucus fled to Egypt and formed an alliance with Ptolemy against Antigonus. These two divided up the eastern territories and presented Antigonus with an ultimatum, but he refused to concede his hold on the lands he occupied. Seizing an opportunity when Antigonus was occupied in Asia Minor, Ptolemy challenged and defeated Antigonus' son, Demetrius, on the field of battle at Gaza in the summer of 312 BCE. He also returned Seleucus to power in Babylon.

Demetrius was forced to withdraw from southern Syria, but Ptolemy did not retain possession of the lands for long. Antigonus returned from the region of Phrygia in Asia Minor at the head of a large army. Ptolemy's retreat from Palestine included the destruction of the fortified cities of Acco, Joppa, and Gaza (Diod. Sic. 19.93.7) to deny their use by Antigonus. Although Antigonus retook southern Syria, he was unable to dislodge Seleucus from Babylon. This marked the beginning of the Seleucid Empire, which would dominate the history of antiquity in the east. A treaty in 311 BCE effectively divided Alexander's territory.

In 302 BCE an alliance against Antigonus was forged among the Macedonians, who now bore the title of kings. Ptolemy reentered the territory of southern Syria, but while he laid siege to Sidon false rumors reached him that Antigonus had been victorious over Seleucus and Lysimachus. In an act of cowardice, Ptolemy withdrew to Egypt and did not participate with the other Macedonians in their decisive defeat of Antigonus at the Battle of Ipsus (301 BCE; Diod. Sic. 20.113.1–5). Thus, when the victors divided up Antigonus' lands, Ptolemy was excluded and the whole of Syria was given to Seleucus. Nonetheless, upon Seleucus' arrival to claim his new territory, he found Ptolemy occupying southern Syria. Rather than continue the armed conflict, Seleucus allowed his former ally and friend to remain in southern Syria (Diod. Sic. 21.1.5). Yet, the disputed territories would remain a bone of contention between the Ptolemaic and Seleucid kingdoms for the next one hundred years.

*Round tower built of "headers," from Samaria, Hellenistic period.*

## Judea Under the Ptolemies (301–200 BCE)

The occupation of Ptolemaic forces in southern Syria effectively divided the region, although the precise line of demarcation is uncertain. The northernmost city mentioned in the Zenon Papyri is Tripolis. This Hellenistic witness accords with Strabo's description in the Roman period of travel along the coast from Seleucia of Syria to Phoenicia (Strabo *Geog.* 16.2.2). The frontier was near ancient Orthosia and the Eleutherus River just north of Tripolis. Mention by Zenon of a visit by Egyptian officials to the Massyas Valley and a man of Damascus living in Palestine suggests that these areas also fell within Ptolemaic control (cf. Polyb. 45.8–46.1), since we have no Seleucid cities in the Zenon Papyri.

The needs of the Seleucid and Ptolemaic kingdoms differed. Seleucus needed possession of northern Syria to provide access to the Mediterranean. He founded Antioch with its seaport of Seleucia in 300 BCE. On the other hand, Egypt's need was shipping, which often necessitated ports-of-call at the coastal cities from Alexandria to Tripolis in Phoenicia. From Tripolis it was but a short journey to Cyprus, also a Ptolemaic possession. The island served as a springboard to the southern coast of Asia Minor, which was also under Ptolemy's control, or Rhodes and Greece to the west.

Ptolemaic control of "Syria and Phoenicia" (Let. Aris. 22) was executed through garrisons (e.g. Tyre, Acco, Joppa, Gaza, Samaria) and the establishment of *cleruchies*, frontier settlements comprised of soldiers who served both as the first line of defense for the Ptolemaic kingdom and for the cultivation of the land. It is in the context of a *cleruchy* in the Transjordan that we first hear of Tobias, a local leader of the Jewish community in the Transjordan.

In more distant lands Ptolemaic administration was in the hands of a local governor, a *strategos*. While Polybius likewise describes a Ptolemaic *strategos* in Syria and Phoenicia (Polyb. 5.87.6), no mention of *strategoi* is heard in the Zenon Papyri. It has been suggested that such administrative posts were unnecessary in lands that were viewed as mere extensions of Egyptian territory. Instead, affairs-of-state were carried out by "orders, regulations, laws and letters." The territory itself was divided into districts (*hyparchies*) that were administrated by a government appointee (*oikonomos*), whose primary task was overseeing economic affairs in the region. Local village leaders (*komarchs*) functioned primarily to assure the gathering of taxes and forwarding them to Alexandria.

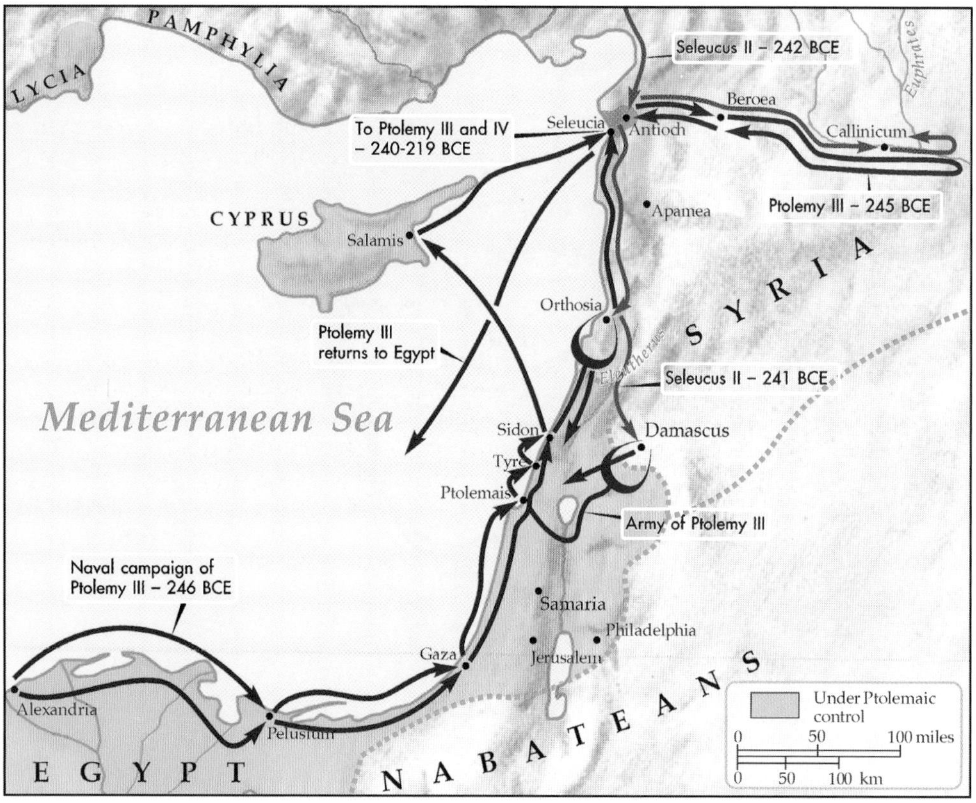


**THIRD SYRIAN WAR (246–240 BCE)**

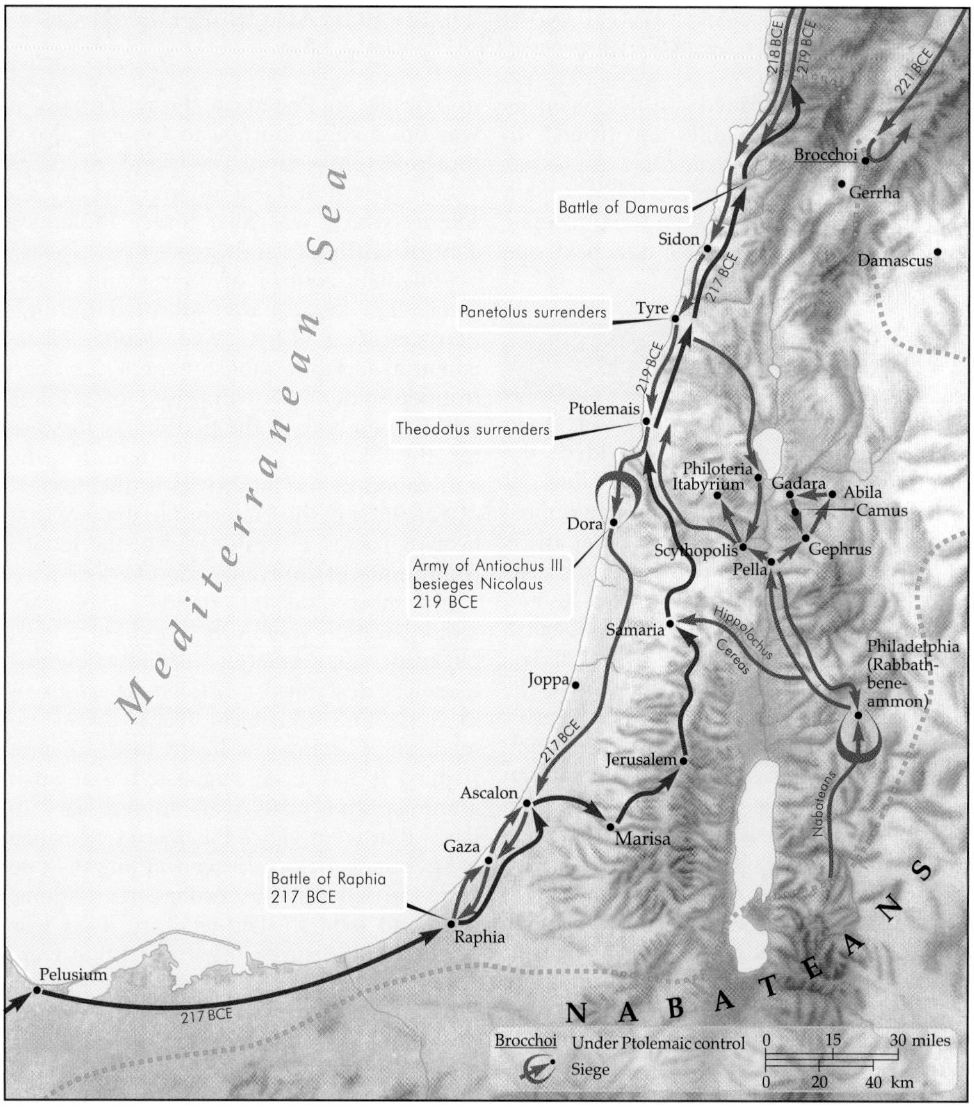


**FOURTH SYRIAN WAR: THE FIRST CAMPAIGN OF ANTIOCHUS III (219–217 BCE)**

**Syrian Wars.** Soon following Ptolemy I Soter's death (283 BCE), Seleucus I Nicator was assassinated near Lysimachia in Thrace (281 BCE). Ptolemy was succeeded by his son, Ptolemy II Philadelphus, who enjoyed a lengthy and prosperous reign from 282 to 246 BCE. Seleucus' successor, Antiochus I Soter (281–261 BCE), had greater difficulty securing his kingdom. He immediately faced an internal revolt in Syria, the continuing threat from Egypt, and an invasion by Gauls (278–277 BCE) in the early years of his reign. After establishing stability in his kingdom, Antiochus turned his attention to the contested lands of southern Syria.

The next seventy-five years witnessed five Syrian wars that brought the Ptolemaic and Seleucid kingdoms into open conflict. The First Syrian War (274–271 BCE) was instigated by Magas, governor of Cyrene, half-brother of Ptolemy II and son-in-law of Antiochus I, who rebelled against Ptolemaic rule with the help of Antiochus. While he gained a temporary measure of independence, his efforts were short-lived and left little lasting impact on the Ptolemaic kingdom. During this time, Ptolemy enlarged his territory into Asia Minor and also conquered the Nabateans. The valuable spice trade was now under his control and directed through the port city of Gaza, a Ptolemaic stronghold.

The Second Syrian War (c. 260–253 BCE) followed the death of Antiochus I (261 BCE) and took place largely on the Aegean coast of Asia Minor. A peace treaty between Antiochus II Theos and Ptolemy II resulted in territorial losses by Ptolemy to both Antiochus and the king of Macedonia and Rhodes. Ptolemy sealed the peace treaty by offering his daughter Bernice in marriage to Antiochus. The Seleucid king disowned his wife Laodice and her children to marry Bernice. Bernice had a son by Antiochus, who she hoped would succeed her husband. Yet, by the end of his life Antiochus had abandoned Bernice and their young son in Antioch, and he returned to live with Laodice and their son Seleucus II in Asia Minor. Laodice poisoned Antiochus, and upon his death she declared Seleucus to be the rightful heir to his father's throne. The death of Antiochus II resulted in a struggle for succession and the Third Syrian War or, as it is sometimes called, the Laodicean War (246–241 BCE).

The local population of Asia Minor favored Seleucus II Callinicus, son of Laodice, to be the rightful claimant to Antiochus' throne. Nonetheless, Ptolemy III Euergetes marched into Asia Minor to protect his sister Bernice and her young son, whom she had also put forward as Antiochus' rightful heir. Bernice and her son were murdered, and when Ptolemy received word of an uprising in Egypt, he was forced to retreat from Asia Minor. Seleucus attempted to take advantage of

*Silver tetradrachm of Ptolemy II Philadelphus (282–246 BCE).*

Ptolemy's distraction with local affairs. Yet, he was unable to expand Seleucid control over Coele-Syria. The resulting peace treaty maintained the Ptolemaic advantage in the lands of southern Syria.

Over the next twenty years there was little change in the territorial relationship between the two kingdoms. A new challenge to the Ptolemaic grip on Phoenicia and Syria occurred with the ascension of Antiochus III Megas, following the murder of his older brother, Seleucus III Ceraunus, in 223 BCE while on a military campaign against Attalus I of Pergamum (Polyb. 4.48, 5.40; App. *Syr.* 66). Young Antiochus was a talented and energetic leader. He attempted to exploit the political vulnerability in Egypt with the death of Ptolemy III and succession by the seventeen-year-old Ptolemy IV Philopator in 222 BCE. Antiochus' initial attack was repulsed by Ptolemy's general, Theodotus, in 221 BCE. Two years later, the Seleucid king would strike again and begin the Fourth Syrian War (219–217 BCE).

Antiochus initially seized large portions of southern Syria that extended down to the border of Egypt. Ptolemy IV had shown little interest or ability in military matters, but the Egyptian king was able to negotiate a peace settlement that bought him time to reinforce his military position in the hope of repulsing Antiochus' aggression. In the lead up to battle, his general Theodotus defected and took his best soldiers with him (cf. 3 Macc 1:2; Polyb. 5.61). On 22 June 217 BCE, Ptolemy met Antiochus on the battlefield in the pivotal Battle of Raphia, near the southern boundary between Palestine and Egypt. Against all odds, Ptolemy defeated Antiochus and the Seleucid army with the help of new recruits from among the local Egyptian population.

Antiochus retreated from southern Syria and the border between the two kingdoms remained virtually unchanged. The Third Book of Maccabees—a work that in spite of its title narrates events in the Ptolemaic period—mentions briefly the Battle of Raphia (3 Macc 1:1–7).

> When Philopator learned from those who returned that the regions that he had controlled had been seized by Antiochus, he gave orders to all his forces, both infantry and cavalry, took with him his sister Arsinoë, and marched out to the region near Raphia, where the army of Antiochus was encamped. (3 Macc 1:1)

Daniel also remembers the battle in his apocalyptic presentation.

> Then the king of the south, moved with anger, shall come out and fight with the king of the north; and he shall raise a great multitude, but it shall be given into his hand. (Dan 11:10; cf. Polyb. 5.79–80)

After his victory at Raphia, Third Maccabees reports that Ptolemy paid a visit to Jerusalem and the temple (3 Macc 1:8–15). There is little question that details in the story are imaginary and that it has been shaped by other Greek tales originating in the period. We may even witness elements from a similar story of pagan hubris in the precincts of the temple in the episode of Heliodorus (2 Macc 3:7–40). Nevertheless, there is inscriptional evidence of Ptolemy's visit to several cities within the province of Syria following his victory. Such a witness may suggest some historical essence to our account, even if it is difficult to distinguish fact from fable. In any event, there seems little reason to suspect that Ptolemy would have omitted Jerusalem in his itinerary through the province.

In the years that followed the Battle of Raphia, the Ptolemaic kingdom weakened while that of Antiochus grew ever stronger. The Seleucid king concentrated his energies on the eastern reaches of his kingdom. He subdued the lands from Asia to India and deigned the Persian title, "Great King." Thereafter, he would be ascribed Antiochus the Great. When Ptolemy IV died in 205 BCE and was followed by the five-year-old Ptolemy V Epiphanes, Antiochus determined that the time was advantageous to challenge the Ptolemaic hold on Phoenicia and Syria.

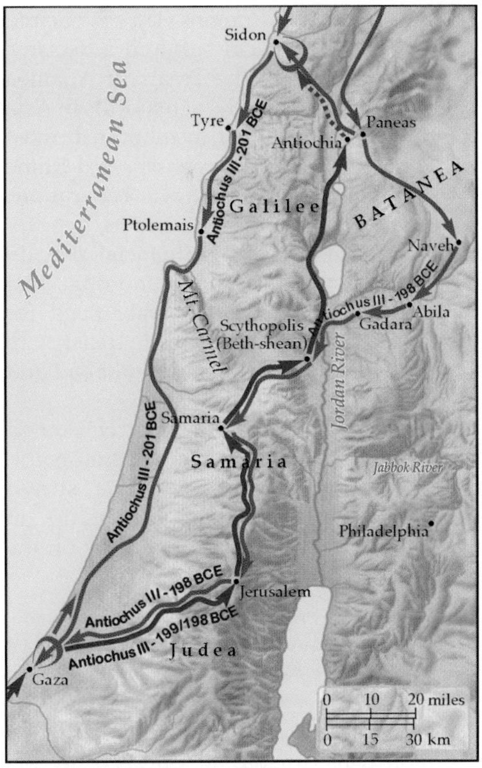


**FIFTH SYRIAN WAR: THE FINAL CONQUEST OF PALESTINE BY ANTIOCHUS III (201–198 BCE)**

He conspired with Philip V of Macedonia concerning the division of the Ptolemaic kingdom. In 201 BCE Antiochus initiated the Fifth Syrian War, and in a short matter of time he had secured control of the region. During the winter of 201/200 BCE, the Egyptian general Scopas led the Ptolemaic response to Antiochus' aggression. Scopas retook the south and Jerusalem, punishing the Seleucid stronghold in Jerusalem. He continued as far north as Paneas, near the headwaters of the Jordan River. There Antiochus the Great crushed the army of Scopas and recaptured the lands of Phoenicia and Syria, finally changing the border between the Seleucid and Ptolemaic kingdoms. Josephus describes the welcoming reception the Jewish population gave to Antiochus and his forces, opening the gates of Jerusalem and even joining the Syrians in their siege of the Ptolemaic garrison left in Jerusalem by Scopas (*Ant.* 13:133).

## JUDEA UNDER SELEUCID RULE

Simon (the Just) II's political intuition to support Antiochus III when he arrived in Jerusalem did not go unrewarded. In one of his first acts as the new sovereign, Antiochus sent a letter to his governor, recounting the material support by the Jewish rulers and the people.

> The Jews, from the very moment when we entered their country, showed their eagerness to serve us and, when we came to their city, gave us a splendid reception and met us with their council and furnished an abundance of provisions to our soldiers and elephants and also helped us to expel the Egyptian garrison in the citadel. (*Ant.* 12:138)

In recognition of this aid, Antiochus instructed that gifts be made to the temple in Jerusalem and that repairs be made to restore any damage it had suffered. The second-century BCE work, Ben Sira, also attests to the repairs of the temple in the days of the high priest Simon.

> The leader of his brothers and the pride of his people was the high priest, Simon son of Onias, who in his life repaired the house, and in his time fortified the temple. He laid the foundations for the high double walls, the high retaining walls for the temple enclosure. (Sir. 50:1–2)

Antiochus also affirmed the internal political structure of the country, exempting the leadership and those active in the temple cult from taxes.

> And all the members of the nation shall have a form of government in accordance with the laws of their country, and the senate, the priests, the scribes of the temple and the temple-singers shall be relieved from the poll-tax and the crown tax and the salt-tax which they pay. (*Ant.* 12:142)

*Aramaic inscription, "Tobiah," carved in a cliff near ʿIrâq el-ʾEmîr, likely marks the burial place of a prominent Jewish family living in Transjordan in the 3rd century BCE. Members of this aristocratic clan played an important role in the Ptolemaic period and events leading up to the Hasmonean revolt against the Seleucid, Antiochus IV.*

It is not the aristocracy alone that realized the benevolence of the new sovereign. In order to restore the population of the war-torn city, the king granted all of its inhabitants and those who would return before the beginning of the new year an exemption from taxes for three years. The ancestral customs pertaining to purity laws in the temple were reaffirmed: "It is unlawful for any foreigner to enter the enclosure of the temple which is forbidden to the Jews, except to those of themselves in accordance with the law of the country" (*Ant.* 12:145; cf. m. *Kelim* 1:8).

The Jewish people for their part reciprocated Antiochus' gestures with their loyalty. In response to an uprising among the people of Lydia and Phrygia in Asia Minor, Antiochus determined to relocate two thousand Jews and their possessions from "Mesopotamia and Babylonia to the fortresses and most important places" (*Ant.* 12:149). These colonists were intended to foster loyalty in a troubled region and were rewarded with land and exemption from taxes for ten years. Although Josephus' report of the friendship between Antiochus and the Jewish people in those early years may be overdrawn, even a less glowing portrayal would stand in stark contrast to the failures that marked the tenure of his sons.

The struggle between the Oniads and the Tobiads once again surfaced in the political and religious upheaval in the opening decades of the second century BCE. Simon (the Just) II was the son of Onias II, who had reneged on the tributes to Ptolemy and had aroused the anger of the Egyptian ruler. Into that historical context, Josephus had introduced Joseph the Tobiad. In contrast to Onias who was portrayed as greedy, Joseph was:

> an excellent and high-minded man and had brought the Jewish people from poverty and a state of weakness to more splendid opportunities of life during the twenty-two years when he controlled the taxes of Syria, Phoenicia [cf. *Ant.* 12: 175: and Judea] and Samaria. (*Ant.* 12:224)

Thus, Joseph was able to wrest the role of *prostates* from the Oniad priests. Under the Seleucids, the Oniads would seek to rejoin their lost political power with their priestly rule.

Josephus affords little attention at this point in his history of the rise of Rome as an international power. Soon after Antiochus had defeated Ptolemy at the Battle of Paneas, Rome defeated Philip V of Macedonia (197 BCE), and at the Isthmian Games in 196 BCE they declared the "freedom of the Hellenes." This would mark the beginning of the rise of Roman imperialism and the decline of the Hellenistic rulers in the east. Antiochus refused to acknowledge Rome's emancipation and to relinquish control of the Greek cities in his kingdom. In anticipation of the looming threat from the west, the Seleucid made peace with Ptolemy V Epiphanes by giving his daughter, Cleopatra, in marriage to the seventeen-year-old Egyptian ruler (194 BCE).

Now that he had achieved peace in his kingdom, Antiochus felt free to undertake westward expansion into Asia Minor and Greece. His activities were correctly perceived as a challenge to Rome. At Magnesia ad Sipylum, in 190 BCE, Antiochus clashed with the Romans led by Scipio Asiaticus. The Seleucid suffered a decisive defeat. The terms of the Treaty of Apamea (188 BCE) required the loss of his lands in Asia Minor. He likewise had to relinquish most of his fleet and battle elephants, and Rome forced upon him excessive war reparations (Polyb. 21.42; Diod. Sic. 29:10; Livy 38.38; App. *Syr.* 38–39). The weight of his financial penalty would lead to Antiochus' undoing. Not long after, the king's desperate need for money led him to sack a temple treasury in Elymais, during which he was mobbed and killed by outraged locals.

Antiochus the Great left a weakened empire to his son, Seleucus IV Philopator. The changing winds of fortune stirred internal conflicts in the leadership in Jerusalem. Jason the Cyrene reports on the actions of the warden of the temple:

> But a man named Simon, of the tribe of Benjamin, who had been made *warden of the temple* (cf. LXX Jer 20:1; 2 Chr 24:11), had a disagreement with the high priest [Onias III] about the administration of the city market. (2 Macc 3:4)

Simon was unable to succeed in his dispute with Onias, so he appealed to Apollonius of Tarsus, the current governor of Phoenicia and Syria, accusing Onias of hoarding funds in the treasury in Jerusalem. In the current political and financial crisis facing the Seleucid kingdom, the response was to be expected. Seleucus sent his chancellor, Heliodorus, to Jerusalem to confiscate the treasury. Onias attempted to thwart Heliodorus' efforts by explaining, "there were some deposits belonging to widows and orphans and also some money of Hyrcanus, son of Tobias, a man of very prominent position" (2 Macc 3:10–11). He continued that Simon had misrepresented the facts to Apollonius.

Nevertheless, Heliodorus insisted that the king's edict be carried out and set forth to inspect the treasury. The historical details of Heliodorus' failed attempt to confiscate the temple treasury have been lost in the legend of the frightening apparition to the Seleucid chancellor in the temple. The priests and people are portrayed in fervent prayer for divine intervention to prevent his efforts.

> When [Heliodorus] suddenly fell to the ground and deep darkness came over him, his men took him up and put him on a stretcher and carried him away, this man who had just entered the aforesaid treasury with a great retinue and all his bodyguard but was now unable to help himself; and they recognized clearly the sovereign power of God. (2 Macc 3:27–28)

Whatever the reason for his failure, Simon persisted in his accusations against Onias, "saying it was he who had incited Heliodorus and had been the real cause of the misfortune" (2 Macc 4:1). The high priest recognized that Simon's accusations of sedition would not disappear unless he addressed the king personally, and he intended to do so. However, before he could personally appeal to Seleucus, the king was murdered. Subsequently, it seems that Onias did appeal to Antioch, but was unsuccessful, because he does not return to Jerusalem. In the episode involving Menelaus and Andronicus, we hear that Onias was "in a place of sanctuary at Daphne near Antioch" (2 Macc 4:33).

Mention by Onias of the wealth of Hyrcanus kept in the temple treasury may hint at the political divide lying at the heart of Jerusalem's political intrigues. Onias spoke with great respect for Hyrcanus in the presence of the Seleucid chancellor,

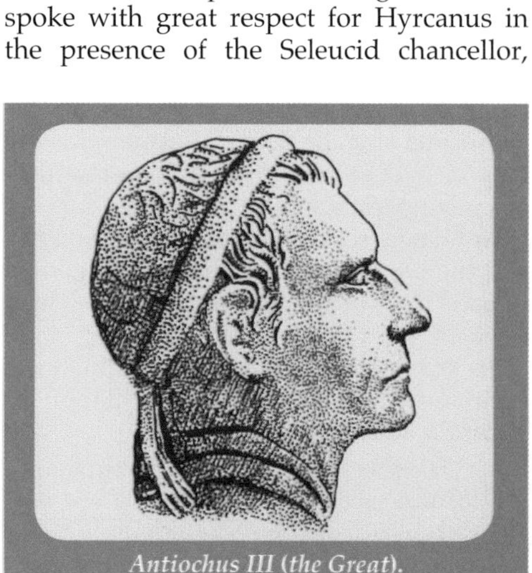

*Antiochus III (the Great).*

even though the Tobiad's pro-Ptolemaic sympathies were well known. The very fact that his wealth was placed in the Jerusalem temple indicates good relations between the Oniad priesthood and the alienated son of Joseph. Josephus likewise attests to a shift in popular opinion (*Ant.* 12:237–241).

Earlier the people had supported the pro-Seleucid Oniad priests and the older sons of Joseph against Hyrcanus and his pro-Ptolemaic faction. At some point after the ascension of Antiochus IV Epiphanes, popular opinion (and that of the Oniads) had realigned with Hyrcanus, and no longer supported the Tobiads or their pro-Seleucid supporters (e.g. Simon, Menelaus and Lysimachus). The Tobiads remained identified with those who offered to Antiochus "that they wished to abandon their country's laws and the way of life prescribed by these, and to follow the king's laws and adopt the Greek way of life" (*Ant.* 12:240; cf. *War* 1:31–32).

Seleucus was succeeded by his brother, Antiochus IV Epiphanes, in 175 BCE (Polyb. 26; Livy 41.20; Diod. Sic. 29.32; 31.16). He inherited a kingdom with dire financial problems, and this predicament would shape his policies toward Jerusalem. The change of political power in Antioch brought intrigues in Jerusalem.

> Jason the brother of Onias obtained the high priesthood by corruption, promising the king at an interview three hundred and sixty talents of silver and, from another source of revenue, eighty talents.
> (2 Macc 4:7b–8)

Although the sale of priestly offices was not uncommon in the Hellenistic world, this was the first time that the Jerusalem high priesthood had been the object of bargaining (cf. 2 Macc 11:3). Moreover, it represented a breach of Antiochus the Great's promise of internal autonomy: "And all the members of the nation shall have a form of government in accordance with the laws of their country" (*Ant.* 12:142). The faction led by Jason determined to introduce Hellenism into Jerusalem society over the objections of the more conservative elements that preferred traditional Jewish customs.

The new high priest's intention was not merely to acquire the high priesthood. He wanted to transform Jerusalem into a Hellenistic *polis*.

> In addition to this he promised to pay one hundred and fifty more [talents] if permission were given to establish by his authority a gymnasium and a body of youth for it, and to enroll the men of Jerusalem as citizens of Antioch. When the king assented and Jason came to office, he at once shifted his countrymen over to the Greek way of life.
> (2 Macc 4:9–10)

> [Antiochus] authorized them to observe the ordinances of the Gentiles. So they built a gymnasium in Jerusalem, according to Gentile custom, and removed the marks of circumcision, and abandoned the holy covenant. They joined with the Gentiles and sold themselves to do evil. (1 Macc 1:12b–15)

Jason's petition to the king was to change the status of Jerusalem into a Hellenistic *polis*. The city would be renamed after the king and its citizens known as Antiochenes (2 Macc 4:19). In order to achieve these aims, the high priest's request required the dissolution of the long-standing agreement with both the Ptolemaic and Seleucid rulers that Jewish ancestral customs were to be regarded as the law of the land (2 Macc 4:10).

The gymnasium and ephebeum were not built on the periphery of Jerusalem, but in the city's center. The institutions were intended to alter the very nature of life in the holy city.

> The priests were no longer intent upon their service at the altar. Despising the sanctuary and neglecting the sacrifices, they hurried to take part in the unlawful proceedings in the wrestling arena after the signal for the discus-throwing, disdaining the honors prized by their ancestors and putting the highest value upon Greek forms of prestige.
> (2 Macc 4:14–15)

Three years later Jason himself would be the victim of conspiracy, when he was jettisoned by the pro-Hellenistic faction. The Tobiad aristocracy supported Menelaus (*Ant.* 12:239–240), brother of Simon, in his bid to secure the high priesthood. Menelaus was supposed to convey Jason's tribute to Antiochus, but he betrayed the high priest. "When presented to the king, [Menelaus] extolled him with an air of authority, and secured the high priesthood for himself, outbidding Jason by three hundred talents of silver" (2 Macc 4:24). Although Jason had been brought to power by the pro-Seleucid Hellenizers, the continued close relationship of the Oniads with Hyrcanus perhaps made him suspect. Under the circumstances, the deposed priest had little choice but to flee to the Transjordan (2 Macc 4:26: the land of Ammon), presumably to seek refuge with the pro-Ptolemaic Hyrcanus.

Menelaus' new position came with the condition of substantially increased tribute payments to the king. According to Second Maccabees, the priest was called to Antioch because of failure to pay (2 Macc 4:27–28). He may have also wanted to pay into the treasury directly to prevent the same type of treason by which he had obtained the office. Lacking sufficient funds on hand, his brother and deputy, Lysimachus, stole vessels of gold from the temple to finance Menelaus' high tribute payments.

As we have noted, the former high priest Onias was in sanctuary at the temple of Apollo and Artemis in Daphne. When he heard of Menelaus' corruption, he confronted the priest before Andronicus, the deputy Antiochus left in charge while the king was away in Cilicia. Menelaus countered Onias' accusations with a bribe to Andronicus to murder Onias (2 Macc 4:24). When Antiochus returned he was presented the charges of treachery against Andronicus, and he executed his deputy

*Seleucid war elephant.*

on the site of Onias' murder (2 Macc 4:38; *contra War* 1:33; 7:423; *Ant.* 12:237; Diod. Sic. 30.7.2). However, the kingpin Menelaus escaped punishment for his complicity both in the murder of Onias and the plundering of the Jerusalem temple.

Lysimachus was not so fortunate. When his unlawful deeds became public knowledge, riots broke out in Jerusalem, and the high priest's brother was killed by a mob near the treasury (2 Macc 4:39–42). A delegation from Jerusalem presented their charges before Antiochus in Tyre against Menelaus, claiming his participation in Lysimachus' theft. The high priest countered the charges with bribes and was acquitted. Not only was Menelaus exonerated, Antiochus executed his accusers from Jerusalem (2 Macc 4:43–50).

At this time, Egypt was ruled by the weak boy-king Ptolemy VI Philometor, and Antiochus saw an opportunity to invade Egypt. He launched the Sixth Syrian War (170/169 BCE), defeating Ptolemy's forces at Pelusium. He continued to Memphis where he conquered the ancient capital of Egypt. However, he was repulsed at Alexandria and had to withdraw to Syria. On his retreat, Antiochus visited Jerusalem in need of funds. "Antiochus dared to enter the most holy temple in all the world, guided by Menelaus, who had become a traitor both to the laws and to his country" (2 Macc 5:15).

> That raid of Antiochus [Epiphanes] on the temple was iniquitous, that it was impecuniosity which drove him to invade it, when he was not an open enemy, that he attacked us, his allies and friends, and that he found there nothing to deserve ridicule.
> (*Apion* 2:83)

Antiochus attempted a second campaign the following year (168 BCE) and again captured Memphis. While laying siege to Alexandria, an emissary from the Roman Senate delivered an order to withdraw and return to his own lands (Polyb. 29.27; Diod. Sic. 31.2; Livy 45.12; App. *Syr.* 66; Justin. *Epit.* 34.3). The Seleucid king thus failed in his efforts to add Egypt to his kingdom.

The king's failure to conquer Egypt

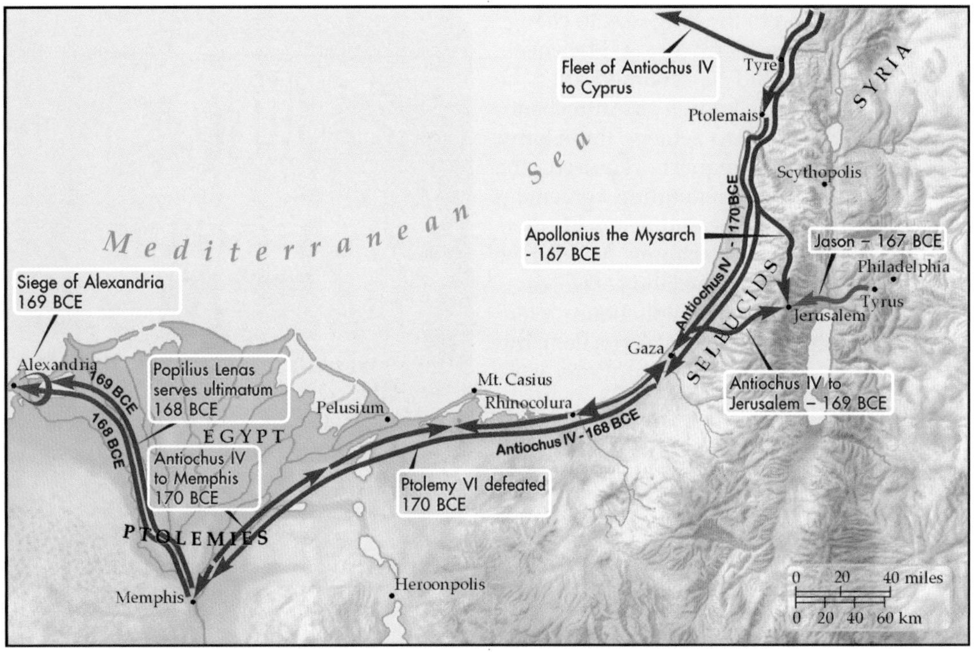


**Egyptian Campaigns of Antiochus IV (170–167 BCE)**

spawned false rumors that he had been killed in the Egyptian campaign. Mistakenly assuming a change in the balance of power in the region, the deposed high priest Jason retook Jerusalem. Menelaus had to take refuge in the citadel of Jerusalem (2 Macc 5:5). Jason eventually had to abandon Jerusalem once again into the region of Ammon (2 Macc 5:7). However, when faced with the prospect of Antiochus' retribution, Hyrcanus the Tobiad took his own life. This left Jason unprotected, and he fled to Egypt, where he eventually continued to Sparta and died in exile (cf. 1 Macc 12:7).

Antiochus received word of the disturbances in Judea and assumed the country was in open rebellion. He could hardly allow his reversals in Egypt to give the impression of weakness to his subjects.

> So, raging inwardly, he left Egypt and took [Jerusalem] by storm. And he commanded his soldiers to cut down relentlessly every one they met and to slay those who went into the houses. Then there was killing of young and old, destruction of boys, women, and children, and slaughter of virgins and infants. Within the total of three days eighty thousand were destroyed, forty thousand in hand-to-hand fighting; and as many were sold into slavery as were slain. (2 Macc 5:11–14)

The author of First Maccabees only remarks that "[Antiochus] went up against Israel and came to Jerusalem with a strong force" (1 Macc 1:20). Like other ancient historians, Jason the Cyrene, whose literary work is the source for Second Maccabees, has exaggerated the slaughter in Jerusalem, though there is little reason to question that Antiochus responded to the uprising in Jerusalem with force. Both reports recount with outrage, the king's desecration of the temple, when he entered the temple.

> He took the holy vessels with his polluted hands, and swept away with profane hands the votive offerings which other kings had made to enhance the glory and honor of the place.... So Antiochus carried off eighteen hundred talents from the temple and hurried away to Antioch, thinking in his arrogance that he could sail on the land and walk on the sea, because his mind was elated.
> (2 Macc 5:16, 21; cf. 1 Macc 1:21–23)

The king now took steps to assure that rebellion would not take hold in Judea. He sent Apollonius, captain of the Mysians, with a considerable force (1 Macc 1:29–30; 2 Macc 5:24). He took steps to assure the continued loyalty of the people to the Seleucid ruler. First Maccabees records that at this time, "they fortified the city of David with a strong wall and strong towers, and it became their citadel" (1 Macc 1:33). In addition, Antiochus stationed a garrison of foreign troops within the fortifications (1 Macc 1:38). These two initiatives by Apollonius on the orders of the Seleucid king would prove to be irritants to the people of Jerusalem for decades.

Reaction from the local citizenry was as expected. First Maccabees describes the flight of some of the residents of Jerusalem, who could not tolerate the introduction of foreign practices into the holy city.

> On every side of the sanctuary they shed innocent blood; they even defiled the sanctuary. Because of them the residents of Jerusalem fled; she became a dwelling of strangers; she became strange to her offspring, and her children forsook her.
> (1 Macc 1:37–38; cf. 2 Macc 5:27)

Yet, for Menelaus and those who sided with him, the introduction of foreigners and their practices into Jerusalem was merely a continuation of the Hellenizing initiative begun by Jason to transform the city into a true Greek city.

Scholarship has debated the origin and intent of Antiochus IV Epiphanes' harsh subsequent decrees. Certainly, his intolerance towards Jewish piety is exceptional, when compared with the king's dealings with other peoples in his kingdom. However, perhaps to the king's mind, the imperial assurance that ancestral Jewish customs would continue undisturbed had been abrogated to fulfill Jason's request to "shift his countrymen over to the Greek way of life" (2 Macc 4:10).

The author of First Maccabees observes that not everyone was disturbed by the new developments. "Many even from Israel gladly adopted his religion; they sacrificed to idols and profaned the Sabbath" (1 Macc 1:43). Yet, for most of the citizens, even the assured penalty of death could not persuade them to profane the holy covenant and heed the king's edict.

> And the king sent letters by messengers to Jerusalem and the cities of Judah; he directed them to follow customs strange to the land, to forbid burnt offerings and sacrifices and drink offerings in the sanctuary, to profane sabbaths and feasts, to defile the sanctuary and the priests, to build altars and sacred precincts and shrines for idols, to sacrifice swine and unclean animals, and to leave their sons uncircumcised. They were to make themselves abominable by everything unclean and profane, so that they should forget the law and change all the ordinances. And whoever does not obey the command of the king shall die. (1 Macc 1:44–50)

The aftermath of the royal decree is described in First and Second Maccabees and Josephus (*Ant.* 12:248–256). According to First Maccabees 1:54, on the fifteenth of Kislev in 167 BCE, a desecrating sacrilege (cf. Dan 12:11) was set upon the altar with the sacrifice of unclean animals in the sanctuary of Jerusalem. The temple in Jerusalem was now consecrated to Zeus Olympius. Other altars were built around the country, and books of the law were burned (1 Macc 1:54–55). If a person was found in possession of the law or discovered to still practice it, the penalty was death (1 Macc 1:57). Even women who circumcised their sons were executed (1 Macc 1:60).

Antiochus could not have known that his edicts would have an unintended affect. Rather than accelerating the Hellenization of the people of Judea, the forceful imposition of foreign customs and institutions solidified opposition to Seleucid rule and eventually led to the liberation of the Jewish nation.

# CHAPTER THIRTEEN

# The Hasmonean Struggle for Independence (167–142 BCE)

The response to Antiochus IV's Hellenizing campaign was quick and forceful. The writings of Josephus and 1 Maccabees recount that Mattathias son of John, a priest and leader in the village of Modiin (el-Midya; Eus. *Onom.* 132:16) near Lydda, was one of the first offered an opportunity to submit to the king's edict (*Ant.* 12:265–271). The location of Modiin may have contributed to its early place of imperial coercion. It lies in the transitional area of three distinct geographic regions. It marked the northeastern limits of the Shephelah. A mile north of the settlement was Wâdī en-Naṭuf, the northern border of the Judean Shephelah. North and east of the area are the western slopes of the Samarian hill country.

The Seleucids had hoped that Mattathias' leadership status in the community would influence others to follow (*Ant.* 12:268). However, he refused and when one of his own countrymen did step forward to offer a sacrifice on the newly constructed pagan altar at Modiin, Mattathias killed both the willing suppliant and the imperial emissary (1 Macc 2:23–26).

Anticipating reprisals from the Seleucids, Mattathias fled with his sons into the nearby hill country of Samaria (1 Macc 2:28; *War* 1:36; cf. 1 Macc 2:29; 2 Macc 5:27; *Ant.* 12:271). The author of 1 Maccabees does not specify the place of Mattathias' retreat, but most of the early skirmishes between the Seleucids and the Maccabean forces were located north and west of Jerusalem. Later, the Seleucid general Apollonius sent his troops south from the city of Samaria into nearby regions in which it seems Judas was active (1 Macc 3:10; cf. 2 Macc 15:1). On another occasion, Josephus also notes that Judas retreated into the region of Gophna within the border of Samaria (*War* 1:45).

Initial Seleucid reprisals were against pious Jewish families who had withdrawn into the wilderness areas of Samaria. Jason the Cyrene states that the reason for their sanctuary in remote caves was to avoid defilement (2 Macc 5:27). Their intentions may also be reflected in the words of another Hellenistic-period priestly figure. Taxo encouraged his sons,

> Let us fast for three days; and on the fourth day let us go out to a cave in the country, and let us die rather than transgress the commandments of the Lord of lords, the God of our fathers.
>
> (TMos 9:6; cf. Isa 32; Dan 11:33)

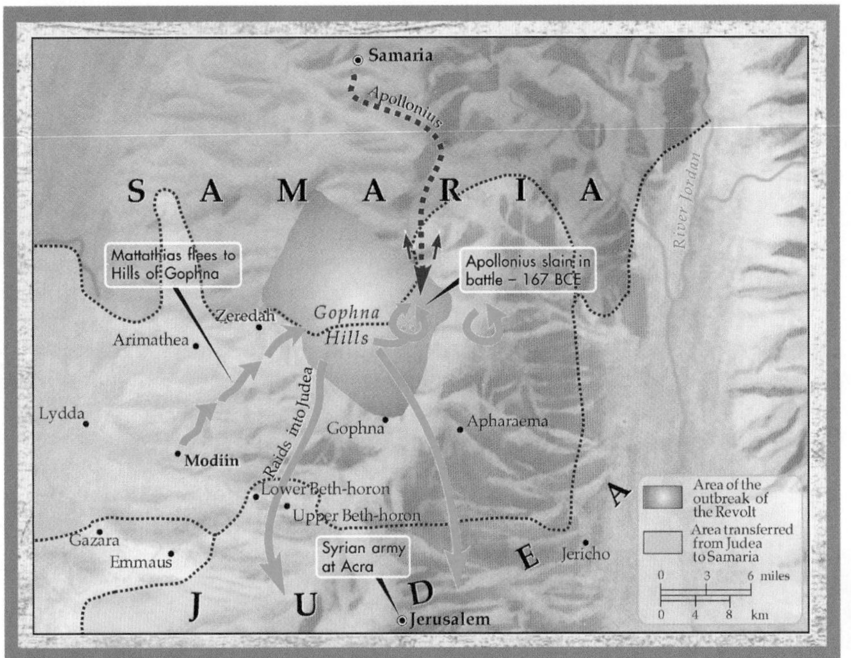


The Beginnings of the Hasmonean Revolt (167 BCE)

Their separation was not intended for martyrdom or asceticism but a desire to distance themselves from the spiritual pollution affecting the nation.

The author of 1 Maccabees calls these pietists Hasideans, a Greek designation of unknown origin, but likely a Greek rendering of the Hebrew *ḥasid*. These observant Jewish families were hiding in caves to conceal their observance of the Jewish Sabbath (cf. 2 Macc 6:11) and refusal to comply with Antiochus' proscriptions. The Seleucid forces encouraged the Hasideans to surrender and come out of their caves, but when they refused the Seleucids built fires at the openings of the caves in order to drive them out. The Hasideans' strict reading of the regulations for the Sabbath did not allow them to come out of the caves, "Each of you stay where you are (on the Sabbath); do not leave your place on the seventh day" (Ex 16:29; *Ant.* 12:274). So they remained in the caves and perished (1 Macc 2:38; *Ant.* 12:275).

Mattathias realized that the refusal to fight on the Sabbath made the Jewish forces vulnerable: "If we all do as our brethren have done and refuse to fight with the Gentiles for our lives and our ordinances, they will quickly destroy us from the earth" (1 Macc 2:40). The Jewish partisans concluded that defensive struggle on the Sabbath was permitted (1 Macc 2: 41), lest adherence to the ancestral tradition result in the loss of life. Mattathias then incorporated the remaining Hasideans and rallied others from the local population into a popular uprising to challenge the Seleucid military. From their position in the Samarian hill country, they attacked the Seleucid forces, pulled down pagan altars and forcibly circumcised the uncircumcised sons of Israel.

## The Early Battles

### The Battle of Gophna (1 Macc 3:10–12; *Ant.* 12: 287).

In the following year (166/165 BCE), Mattathias became ill and died. His third son, Judas Maccabeus (1 Macc 2:49–3:1), succeeded him in leadership. When Apollonius, *strategos* of the eparchy of Samaria (*Ant.* 12:287; 2 Macc 5:24), heard of Mattathias' death, he set out from the city with a contingent of conscripts to engage Judas in battle. On this and future occasions Judas proved to be a worthy adversary. The author of 1 Maccabees is scant on details concerning this first battle, while 2 Maccabees omits it altogether. The lack of details raises questions regarding the author's first-hand knowledge of the events and whether the descriptions are based upon eyewitness accounts.

Presumably Apollonius would have traveled south along the central ridge route from Samaria through Shechem towards Jerusalem. The Seleucid commander took with him mercenaries from among "the

*Tetradrachm of Antiochus IV Epiphanes.*

Gentiles and those from Samaria." The Greek phrase may represent a corruption of an original Hebrew, "[from Galilee of the] Gentiles and from Samaria." If so, then the phrase may point to the contiguous nature of the "region of the Gentiles" and the hill country of Samaria (see below on 1 Macc 5:15). Others read the difficult phrase as an apposition, "the Gentiles, who are in Samaria," and suggest that the phrase belongs to other pejorative references to the Samaritans found in Second Temple Jewish literature (e.g. Sir. 50:26; Mt 10:5).

Apollonius and his forces crossed the northern border of the district of Ephraim (near Apharaema—later a district of Gophna). This is the vicinity of the beginning of Jewish settlements (1 Macc 10: 30, 11:34), whose residents may have given warning to Judas of Apollonius' advances (1 Macc 3:11).

Lacking direct eyewitnesses, the author of 1 Maccabees shaped his account heavily with language from the biblical account of David's fight with Goliath. While the historical facts of an armed conflict and Apollonius' death are not in question, the descriptive details given in the account are less certain.

Apollonius' contingent was defeated and he himself killed (cf. LXX 1 Sam 17:50). The proximity of the skirmish to non-Jewish settlements along the southern border of Samaria is suggested by the ability of the Seleucid soldiers to escape to nearby villages and the lack of any pursuit by Judas and his men. Instead, they seized the spoils of Apollonius' fallen soldiers. According to the author, Judas reportedly took possession of Apollonius' sword and used it in all his future battles (*Ant.* 12:287; 1 Macc 3:12; cf. LXX 1 Sam 17:51, 54; 21:10–11).

**The Battle of Beth-horon** (1 Macc 3:13–24; 2 Macc 8:1–7; *Ant.* 12:288–292). Responsibility for putting down the rebellion now fell to the governor-general of Coele-Syria and Phoenicia, Ptolemy son of Dorymenes (2 Macc 8:8). He sent his army under the command of Seron (1 Macc 3:13), who was probably stationed in Ptolemais (cf. Strabo *Geog.* 16.2.25; Diod. Sic. 16.41.3) or Dora. The only record of the battle is that given in 1 Maccabees 3:13–24. It may also be hinted in the brief summary of Judas' exploits (2 Macc 8:1–7) prior to the report of the battle of Emmaus. Josephus likewise summarizes the battle, although he mistakenly read from 1 Maccabees 3:23 (cf. 3:17) to suggest that Judas attacked Seron's encampment below Lower Beth-horon (*Ant.* 12:288–292).

Seron avoided the mountainous regions that had proven treacherous for Apollonius. Instead, he approached along the more public coastal route that followed between the sand and swamps of the Sharon Plain and the hill country of Samaria. At Lydda, Seron turned east—passing by or through Judas' hometown of Modiin—to begin the ascent up the Beth-horon ridge that historically linked Jerusalem and the hill country to the coastal plain (*Ant.* 12:228).

It seems that the author of 1 Maccabees was not a participant in the conflict, because he does not provide details of the size of the armies, or military strategy as he does elsewhere. *Josippon* (17:24) notes only that the Hasideans did not participate. The fear among Judas' followers together with his speech to bolster their confidence may indicate that they were significantly outnumbered (1 Macc 3:17). Nevertheless, the element of surprise and their position of attack from higher ground gave Judas' forces a decided advantage.

The Maccabee positioned his unit near the village of Upper Beth-horon from which they could observe the Seleucid advance below (1 Macc 3:17). Withdrawing farther up the ridge, Judas surprised Seron's army at some point between Lower Beth-horon and the hills above Upper Beth-horon that reach to 2,180 feet [703 m] and lead to the central Benjamin Plateau [2,206 ft./712 m]. Seron clearly was motivated to keep this route open so that the Hellenistic contingent in the citadel would not be hemmed in.

Judas and his forces fell upon the Seleucids "suddenly" (1 Macc 3:23; cf. Josh 10:9). Josephus states that Seron fell in battle (*Ant.* 12:292), an interpretation of the report in his sources, "Seron and his camp were crushed before [Judas]" (1 Macc 3:23).

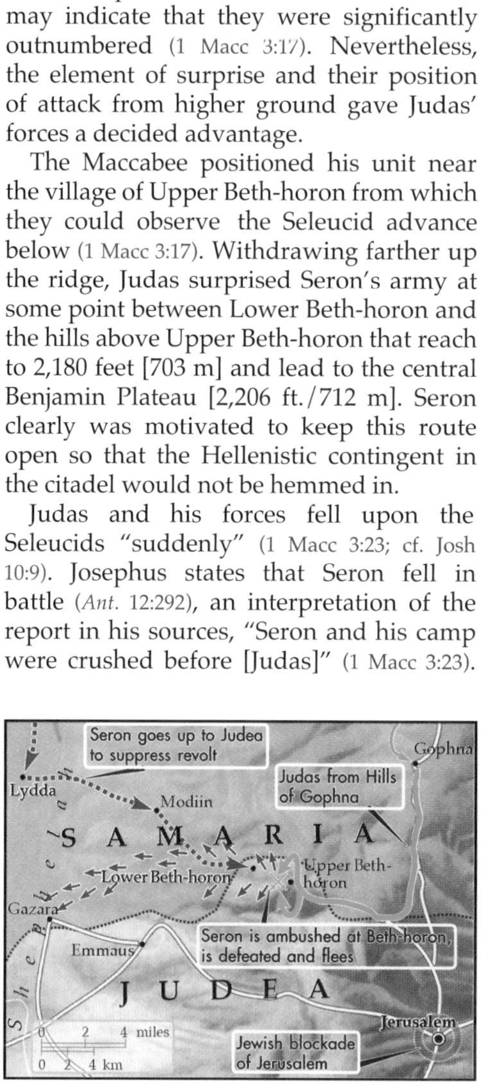


**THE BATTLE OF BETH-HORON (166 BCE)**

Although the detail of Seron's death is lacking in 1 Maccabees 3:23–26, the absence of any mention of the Seleucid in subsequent reports in 1/2 Maccabees or Josephus, strengthens Josephus' understanding. With the commander fallen, the Syrians quickly retreated down the Beth-horon ridge. The attacks from above by pursuing Jewish forces resulted in heavy Syrian casualties (1 Macc 3:24). The Syrians fled to the coastal plains chased by Judas and his men. The Seleucids turned south seeking refuge in the land of the Philistines (cf. 1 Macc 3:41; Sir. 50:26; Herodotus *Hist.* 3.5.1), that is the region of western Idumea with its coastal cities still allied to Antiochus and the Seleucid kingdom.

**The Battle of Emmaus** (1 Macc 3: 38–4:25; 2 Macc 8:8–29; *Ant.* 12:293–312). Word of Seron's defeat reached Antiochus, who was determined "to make an end of Jerusalem and destroy the Jewish race" (*Ant.* 12:296; 1 Macc 3:35). However, he lacked sufficient financial and military resources. Tributes from the rebellious eastern provinces had failed to be collected. His financial straits were also exacerbated by his well-known extravagance (Polyb. 26.1.8–11; 30.25.1–26.3). Antiochus was further limited from sending a full military response to Judea, because of the outbreak of rebellion in the eastern provinces. While the author of 1 Maccabees suggests Antiochus' campaign to Persia was intended merely to fill the imperial coffers, the king's personal oversight of the army against the rebellion in the east was also one of measured necessity. In any event, for the time being he left the region west of the Euphrates to the Egyptian border—and the well-being of his son Antiochus V—in the hands of his kinsman Lysias (1 Macc 3:32; *Ant.* 12:295).

Once again, Lysias delegated Ptolemy (2 Macc 8:9) the responsibility to suppress the Jewish rebellion. Ptolemy selected Nicanor son of Patroclus (cf. 2 Macc 8:9) to be his commanding general and Gorgias as his aide. Following the coastal route through the Sharon Plain taken by Seron, they arrived at Emmaus (Kh. ᶜImwas).

Jason of Cyrene numbered the Seleucid army at 20,000 men (2 Macc 8:9). The description by 1 Maccabees of 47,000 men (1 Macc 3:39) was likely inflated under the influence of the biblical description of David's defeat of the Arameans in 1 Chronicles 19:18. Nicanor learned from his predecessors' mistakes. Apollonius had been ambushed while approaching along the northern watershed route, and Seron likewise had been surprised while ascending the western approach on the Beth-horon ridge route. In both instances the hilly terrain and the element of surprise had mitigated their numerical advantage.

Nicanor pitched his camp "near Emmaus in the plain" (1 Macc 3:40). From this point

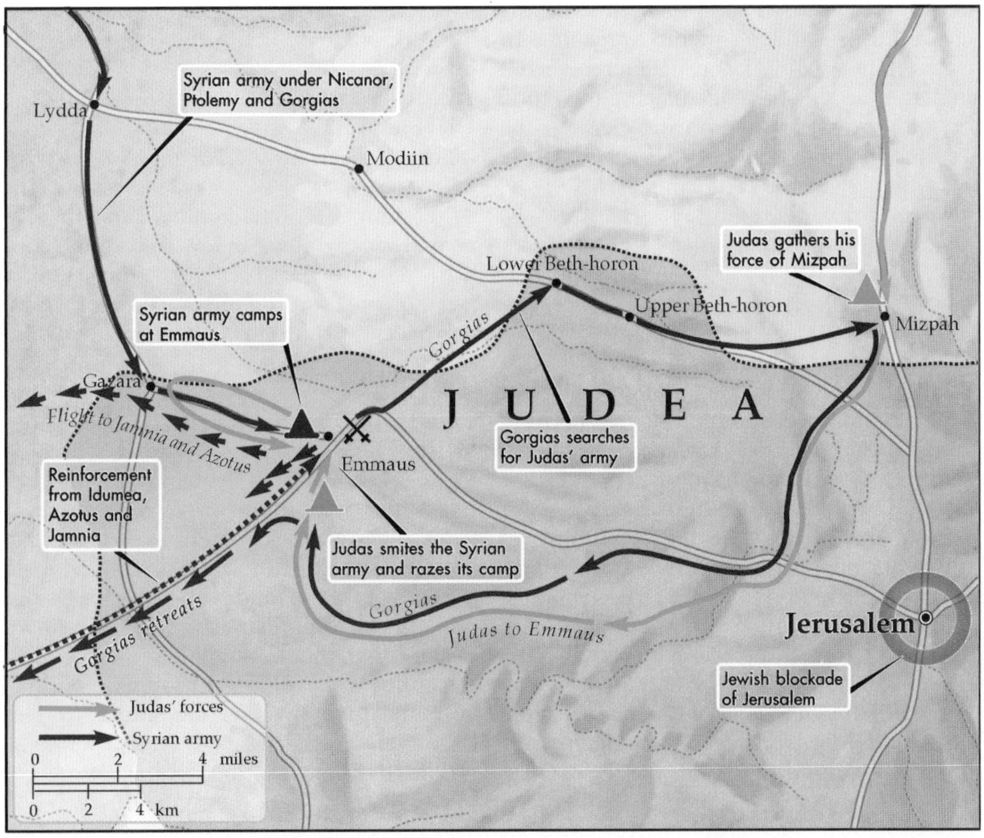


**The Battle of Emmaus (165 bce)**

he could choose the time and route of ascent which best suited his military strategy. His location also retained access to communication and supply lines north through the coastal plain. This would be the same staging area for Vespasian's forces, when they prepared for the assault on Jerusalem (*War* 4:444–445, 5:67). Nevertheless, the author of 1 Maccabees is clear that the location of the encampment was not at Emmaus itself, but nearby (cf. *Ant.* 12:298: "When they had gone as far as the city of Emmaus, they encamped on the plain"). Scholarly opinions differ precisely where Nicanor positioned his troops on the plain; according to one proposal, the Seleucid encampment was in the Aijalon Valley. The Seleucid forces were joined there by sympathizers from Idumea and the coast of Philistia, local traders who hoped to capitalize on the slave trade of the captured Jewish fighters.

Judas gathered his forces at Mizpah (1 Macc 3:46; i.e. Tell en-Naṣbeh) on the northern edge of the central Benjamin Plateau opposite Jerusalem. The author recalls Samuel's call to prayer at Mizpah after the return of the ark of the Lord (1 Sam 7:5–11), when he reminisces, "Israel had a place of prayer at Mizpah."

Word of the gathering of Jewish forces at Mizpah was relayed to the Seleucids by men from the citadel (1 Macc 4:1–2). The Syrians divided their army and Gorgias took a contingent of foot-soldiers and cavalry by night in the hope of a preemptive strike on Judas at Mizpah. When Judas got word of the approaching units of Gorgias, he took his men under the cover of darkness down the Kiriath-jearim ridge and encamped "south of Emmaus" before daybreak (1 Macc 3:57). Josephus corrects the confused chronology of 1 Maccabees that gives the impression that Judas had arrived at Emmaus prior to Gorgias' night march.

> But the enemy sent Gorgias with five thousand foot-soldiers and a thousand horsemen to fall upon Judas by night . . . and when the son of Mattathias became aware of this he decided to fall upon the enemy's camp himself, and to do this when their force was divided. Having, therefore, supped in good time and left many fires in his camp, he marched all night toward those of the enemy who were in Emmaus.
> (*Ant.* 12:305–306)

At Mizpah Judas left the campfires burning to give the false impression that the Jewish forces were still there. Upon entering the abandoned camp at Mizpah, Gorgias assumed that Judas had fled with his men into the security of the hill country. However, Judas had maneuvered around Gorgias' advancing troops and arrived south of Nicanor's troops at Emmaus. His attack would now take advantage of the division of Seleucid forces resulting from Gorgias' ill-fated preemptive strike.

The author of 1 Maccabees makes a point that the Jewish forces were victorious in spite of being insufficiently armed (1 Macc 4:6; *Ant.* 12:307). Josephus notes that Nicanor's men were caught unsuspecting by Judas' attack at daybreak (*Ant.* 12:308). So, even though better equipped, the Syrian forces were routed, but Nicanor was able to escape and would return later to challenge Judas (1 Macc 7:26). Once again the Syrians chose to flee into territories that were allied with the Seleucid kingdom. They escaped from the shoulder hills of the Shephelah through Gazara (Tell Jezer; 1 Macc 9:52) and turned south into the Philistine plain to the coastal cities of Jamnia and Azotus (1 Macc 4:15). Judas did not pursue them into these hostile areas, but instead turned his attention to the remaining forces of Gorgias. When the Syrian contingent arriving from the hills above Emmaus saw that the main camp had been destroyed, they likewise retreated without a battle to the coastal plain.

**The Battle of Beth-zur** (1 Macc 4:28–61; 2 Macc 11:1–14; *Ant.* 12:313–315). When word of the Seleucid defeat at Emmaus reached Lysias, he mustered an army under his own command and marched to Idumea (1 Macc 4:29). The steep terrain and deep ravines above the Aijalon Valley had thwarted previous Syrian attempts to engage successfully Judas' troops in the mountain strongholds. The Jewish partisans had taken advantage of the topography to equalize the military advantage of the Seleucids. On this occasion, Lysias chose a different course of attack.

Escape by the Syrians on the previous occasions had been into the southwestern region of Idumea, where they found allies among the Idumeans and the Hellenized Sidonians who colonized Marisa (Tell Ṣandaḥanna; cf. 1 Macc 5:66; 2 Macc 12:35). Lysias advanced his troops into this area and used it as a point of access onto the southern extension of the watershed route in the hill country of Idumea. The elevation of the hills near biblical Hebron is higher than Jerusalem, giving the Seleucid forces an additional advantage on their march to Jerusalem. Judas' watchmen doubtless kept a watchful eye on Lysias' movements south through the Shephelah and his ascent into the southern hills (1 Macc 4:30).

Once his army was positioned on the plateau of the watershed route, Lysias was now able to begin his approach towards Jerusalem and the citadel that remained besieged. His first step toward Jerusalem

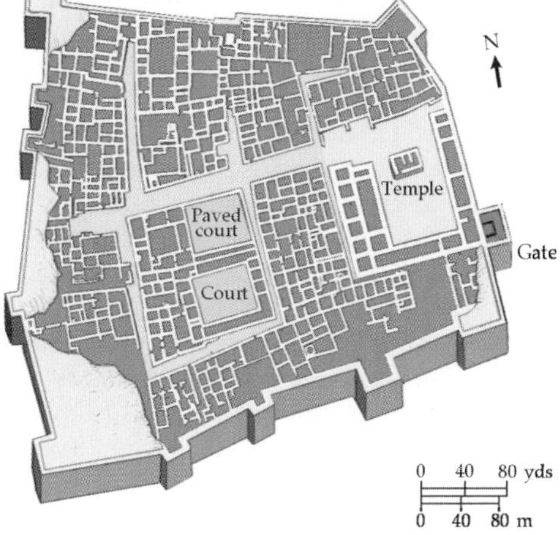


*Plan of Marisa, Hellenistic period.*

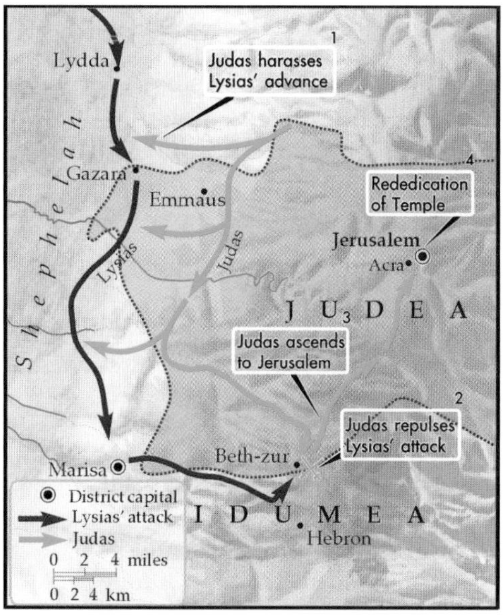


**The Battle of Beth-zur and the Rededication of the Temple (165 bce)**

was to take Beth-zur. Second Maccabees 11:5 leaves the impression that Beth-zur was already fortified and resisted Lysias' advance. The more reliable testimony in 1 Maccabees gives no suggestion of a significant struggle, "they came into Idumea and encamped at Beth-zur" (1 Macc 4:29). Moreover, it is only after Lysias' defeat that 1 Maccabees reports Judas fortified Beth-zur: "he stationed a garrison there to hold it. He also fortified Beth-zur, so that the people might have a stronghold that faced Idumea" (1 Macc 4:61).

Judas recognized the threat Lysias posed to Jerusalem and gathered his forces to counter the advancing Seleucid army. Unfortunately, the historical details are minimal in the sources. Much of the language of the conflict in 1 Maccabees is colored by biblical vocabulary from the account of Jonathan, son of Saul (cf. 1 Sam 14:1–15). However, Josephus does provide an independent and reliable detail that may indicate something of Judas' military strategy. At Beth-zur, the Maccabee saw a portion of Lysias' forces and engaged what were described as "the enemies' advance units" (*Ant.* 12:314). According to Josephus, their defeat convinced Lysias to withdraw and return to Antioch, "where he remained to enlist mercenaries and make preparations to invade Judea with a greater army" (*Ant.* 12:315).

It should not surprise us that the first-century Jewish historian has followed the author of 1 Maccabees' reason for Lysias' withdrawal to Antioch (cf. 1 Macc 4:35). Nevertheless, there are indications that Lysias' return to Antioch was precipitated primarily by the death of Antiochus IV and not reversals on the battlefield. Lysias had been appointed viceroy of the region west of the Euphrates and guardian of Antiochus V Eupator, son of Antiochus Epiphanes. The king's death now required Lysias' presence in Antioch to assure the protection of the crown prince and a smooth transition of power. Thus, while Jason the Cyrene erred in his sequence of events, placing the battle of Beth-zur after the purification of the Temple, his independent sources correctly placed the death of Antiochus (2 Macc 9:1–29) between the battle of Emmaus (2 Macc 8:8–29) and the battle of Beth-zur (2 Macc 11:1–14).

## Hasmonean Campaigns Outside of Judea

Political events inside and outside of Judea led to unrest among the neighboring lands and hostilities toward the Jewish communities living there. The author of 1 Maccabees attributes the cause for Gentile disturbances to the rebuilding of the altar and purification of the sanctuary in Jerusalem (1 Macc 5:1). The political uncertainty resulting from the sudden death of Antiochus Epiphanes may also have contributed to instability in the region. In any event, all of the reports agree regarding Maccabean military incursions into the surrounding regions.

Reference to Judas' military campaign into Akrabattene in Idumea (1 Macc 5:3) is difficult. Akrabattene is not in Idumea, but instead in Samaria (cf. *War* 2:235; 4:504; 4:511; 4:551). Some have suggested that the Greek toponym refers to the Ascent of Akrabbim (LXX Num 34:4; Josh 15:3; Judg 1:36). This suggestion fails on two points. First, there is no material evidence of Jewish communities in the region of Akrabbim whose persecution would have required Judas' rescue. Second, the Ascent of Akkrabim itself is outside the region of Idumea.

On the other hand, Akrabattene in the hill country of Samaria is known in literature of the Hellenistic-Roman period (cf. Jdt 7:18; Jub 29:14; m. *Maᶜas. Sh.* 5:2). Its mention in connection with Idumea may have resulted from the seizure of lands in the area of Akrabattene by Idumeans, or confusion in the sources of the toponym—Idumea—with a village by a similar name near Shechem in the toparchy of Akrabattene. In his pre-Byzantine *Onomasticon* Eusebius mentions both the toparchy of Akrabattene (cf. Eus. *Onom.* 14:10, 108:20, 156:30, 160:14) and a village within it called Aduma (Eus. *Onom.* 86:24).

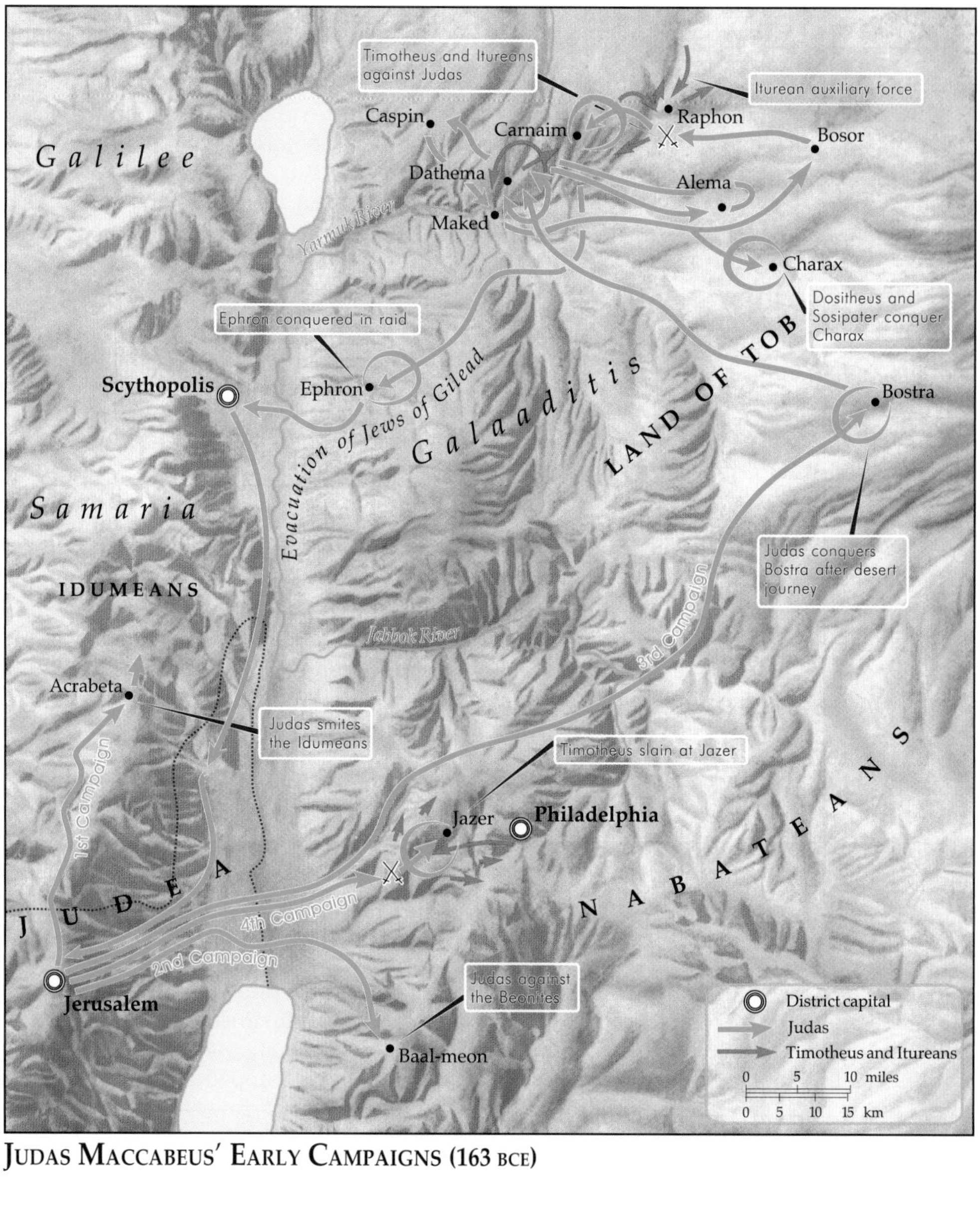


**Judas Maccabeus' Early Campaigns (163 bce)**

Whatever the cause for the confusion, it seems more likely that Judas' first military excursion outside of Judea was north into Akrabattene, where Jewish settlement is later understood (*War* 3:53–56).

Judas then ventured into the Transjordan in aid to the Jewish communities dwelling beyond the Jordan River. The first adversaries mentioned are the "sons of Baean" (1 Macc 5:4). Scholarship is divided over the identification of these people and their location. After destroying their fortified towers, Judas turned north into Ammon where he defeated the inhabitants and their leader Timotheus (1 Macc 5:6–8). The literary sources are in disagreement whether this Timotheus is the same mentioned later, or whether he died in battle during Judas' first campaign into the Transjordan (1 Macc 5:34, 37, 40; 2 Macc 8:30, 10:24; *Ant.* 12:329–330, 12: 341). Judas conquered Jazer (Kh. eṣ-Ṣar; cf. Eus. *Onom.* 12:3, 104:13) and the surrounding villages (cf. Num 21:32), and then returned to Judea (1 Macc 5:8).

## Simon's Expedition into Western Galilee

(1 Macc 5:14–15, 20–23). At this point hostilities broke out against the Jews living in Gilead (Galaaditis) and in the Galilee. Judas and Jonathan marched to rescue the Jews who had fled to Dathema in the Transjordan, while their brother Simon went to help the Jews in the Galilee.

The description of hostile neighbors of the Jews living in the Galilee suggests Hellenistic settlements bordering the Jewish villages of western Galilee, "Ptolemais and Tyre and Sidon, and all Galilee of the foreigners" (1 Macc 5:15). The three cities lie on the Phoenician coast bordering western Galilee. The final geographic designation is more problematic. The author's use of "foreigners" for non-Jewish residents in the north is atypical. He normally employs the term for inhabitants of the coast of Philistia (e.g. 1 Macc 3:41, 5:66 *et passim*) and even the biblical Philistines themselves (1 Macc 4:30).

Simon drove the hostile Gentile forces back to "the gate of Ptolemais" and then relocated the Jews of Galilee and Arbatta to Judea. The Greek reading in the narrative is awkward. One would have expected repetition of "from" with Arbatta. In addition, the toponym Arbatta is otherwise unknown. Arbatta is likely a corrupted reading of Narbata, which is also mentioned by Josephus (*War* 2:291) and appears as a toparchy near Caesarea (*War* 2:509).

If the author of 1 Maccabees did mean Narbata, then 1 Maccabees attests to the use of the Hebrew *galil* as a common noun, "region, district," and not "Galilee." Indeed, our author probably borrowed earlier from the nearly identical wording he found in the Septuagintal translation of Joel 4:4 [HMT 3:4]. Not only is this verse the singular occasion in the Septuagint where we find the phrase "Galilee of the foreigners," but it

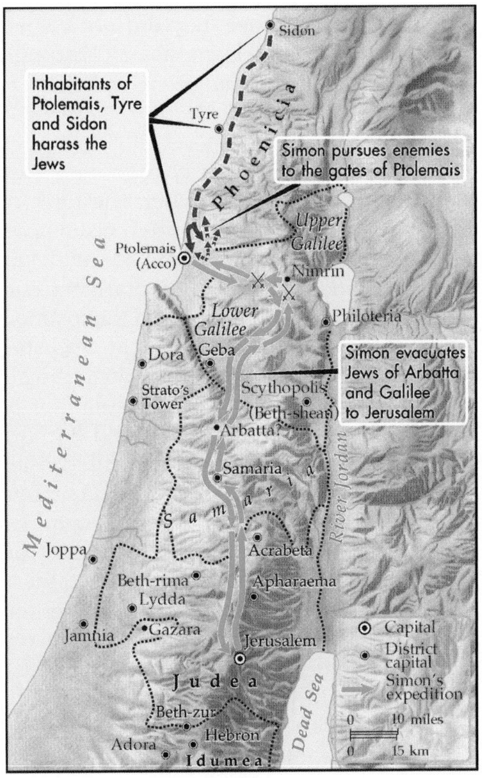


SIMON'S EXPEDITION TO WESTERN GALILEE

likewise appears in collocation with "Tyre and Sidon."

Thus, there is no compelling reason to read "Galilee of the Gentiles" in 1 Maccabees 5:15. Instead, it is a more generic description of an unspecified (but at the time familiar) "region, district of foreigners." Subsequent mention of Arbatta (i.e. Narbata) may point us to the coastal region south of the Jezreel Valley in the vicinity of the Sharon Plain. The threat from Hellenistic populations bordering the Galilee on the west and south (cf. 1 Macc 5:55) accords with the scholarly opinion that Simon relocated those Jews at most risk—those from western Galilee, while Jews living in the eastern Galilee remained.

## Judas' Campaign in Gilead

(1 Macc 5:3–13, 24–55; 2 Macc 10:24–37, 12:10–11; *Ant.* 12:335–349). During the same time, Judas Maccabeus and his brother Jonathan "crossed the Jordan and went three days' journey into the wilderness" (1 Macc 5:24). Here they encountered the Nabateans, with whom they were on peaceful terms and who reported on the imprisonment of Jews in the cities of Gilead, i.e. Galaaditis: "Bozrah and Bosor, in Alema and Chaspho, Maked and Carnaim" (1 Macc 5:26).

Judas attacked first the small Hellenistic city of Bozrah (Baṣûra esh-Sham; cf. Eus. *Onom.* 12:14, 13:14, 84:9, 85:8–9) that lay strategically on the crossroads of the wilderness route from Damascus through the Hauran and controlled east-west travel across the Jordan River from the Mediterranean to the cities of Mesopotamia. The author of 1 Maccabees reports that Judas conquered the city, destroyed every male (cf. Gen 34:25) and burned it with fire.

Next Judas and his men marched overnight to the fortress of Dathema (1 Macc 5:29; cf. 1 Macc 5:9) and surprised the forces there. He selected this city for his initial incursion among the cities of the Bashan and used it as his base for attacking the surrounding Gentile cities. The identification of Dathema is still debated.

The description that Judas' forces were able to complete a night march of 30 miles (50 km) from Bozrah to Dathema and surprise the local forces at dawn is an indication of the mobility and quality of the Jewish forces. Judas divided his men into three groups and, surprising the local forces from the rear, severely defeated the army of Timotheus (1 Macc 5:34; cf. 1 Macc 5:6).

From Dathema Judas attacked Alema (1 Macc 5:35). It is earlier listed in 1 Maccabees 5:26 to be one of the cities mentioned by the Nabateans. Site identification of Alema will depend upon the manuscript reading selected as a basis for the toponym, and so remains uncertain.

Judas next turned to the surrounding cities of Chaspho, Maked and Bosor (1 Macc 5:36). Josephus' *Antiquities* 12:340 combines the names of the first two cities, i.e. Chasphomake, in all of the extant manuscripts with only two Gentile cities specified. The site of Chaspho has been suggested at two locations, el-Mezerib on the Yarmuk River and Khisfîn. This latter site accords with the identification of Chaspho in 1 Maccabees 5:26, 36 and Caspin in 2 Maccabees 12:13. If the two accounts of Judas' conquest in the area describe the same event, then the significant differences in detail may be the result of abridgement or defective transmission. According to Jason the Cyrene, Caspin is adjacent to a lake that was a quarter-mile wide and ninety-five miles from Charax (2 Macc 12:16–17).

Maked is likely to be identified with Tell el-Jemid and located between Chaspho and Bosor. Bosor (Bozrah) marked the frontier of Trachonitis and "the eastern edge of the area settled by the Jews." Timotheus

*Seleucid coin with Apollo on reverse.*

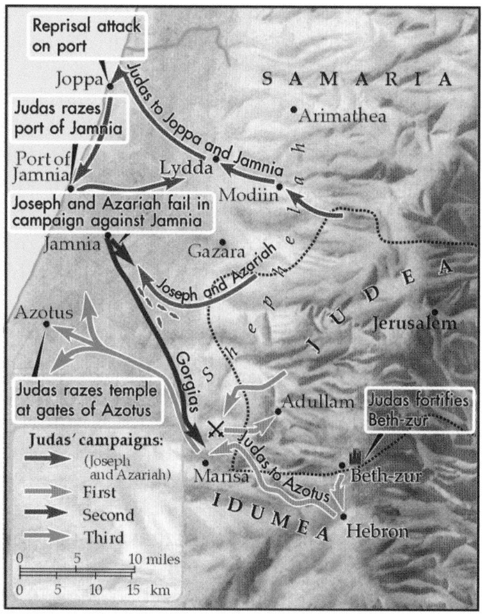


**Judas on the Coastal Plain and in Idumea (163 bce)**

recovered from his initial defeat and was reinforced by Syrian troops from Damascus and Arab mercenaries. They arrived at the fortified city of Carnaim (Sheikh Saᶜd; Eus. *Onom.* 112:3) and advanced east to the banks of the Raphon Brook (Nahr el-Ihreir), a tributary of the Yarmuk River. Timotheus camped there not expecting Judas to cross the stream. The Maccabee's unexpected advance led to the rout of the Seleucid forces, and he pursued them on their retreat to Carnaim. Judas captured the city and "burned the sacred precincts with fire, together with all who were in them" (1 Macc 5:44).

Judas gathered the Jews living in the province of Galaaditis to evacuate them to Judea. He met little resistance until they approached Ephron (eṭ-Ṭaiyiba; 2 Macc 12:27), a well-fortified city 12 miles (19 km) southeast of the Sea of Galilee that guarded the highway leading to the fords of the Jordan River. Judas destroyed the city and crossed over to Scythopolis. He continued his march to Judea, gathering conscripts as he went. Upon his return to Jerusalem, Judas ascended Mount Zion and offered burnt offerings in the rededicated Temple (1 Macc 5:54).

Judas had left Joseph, son of Zechariah, and Azariah to defend the population of Judea. He had given them clear instructions not to engage the local Gentile forces (1 Macc 5:18–19). The author of 1 Maccabees attributes their disobedience of this order to their pride, "Let us also make a name for ourselves; let us go and make war on the Gentiles around us" (1 Macc 5:57). However, their military initiative may have been in response to hostilities towards the Jews living in Jamnia (cf. 2 Macc 12:3–9). Whatever the justification for Joseph and Azariah's action, the author of 1 Maccabees interprets their defeat in religious terms, that they were defeated because they did not belong to the family of the Hasmoneans, "through whom deliverance was given to Israel" (1 Macc 5:62; *Ant.* 12:332–335, 353; *contra* 2 Macc 8:22, 12:36–40).

In military terms, the engagement was at an inopportune time when the bulk of Jewish forces had been diverted elsewhere. Moreover, even Judas Maccabeus with his military skills and personal charisma had yet to attempt a direct attack on the fortified cities along the coastal plain of Philistia. Jason the Cyrene does report on reprisals by Judas against Joppa and Jamnia, but in these Judas attacked the ships and harbors of these cities and not just the fortified cities themselves (2 Macc 12:6, 9). The language of these attacks more closely resembles guerrilla tactics than a military assault on the fortified cities. In any event, when these two marched on Jamnia, Gorgias routed the Jewish forces, which suffered heavy casualties on their retreat to Judea.

The report of Judas' accomplishments in the Transjordan brought new conscripts. The previous attack by Lysias by way of Idumea and the watershed route highlighted a strategic vulnerability in the defense of Jerusalem. Judas took the occasion to remedy this weakness. First, he "struck Hebron and its villages and tore down its strongholds and burned its towers round about" (1 Macc 5:65). These Idumean residents in the Hebron region had apparently assisted Lysias in his campaign. Judas then descended the ridge route that had been used by Lysias.

To access the Judean Shephelah and coastal areas he "passed through Marisa." The description that Judas "passed through" signals that the toponym means the province and not the city. So, it seems also regarding the report of Judas' attack on Azotus, where "land of the foreigners/Philistines" stands in apposition to the city name. The Maccabee attacked the province of Azotus and not the fortified city itself. Judas' primary concern seems to have been to shore up the defenses of the Judean Shephelah and the ridge routes leading through it to the hill country. He fortified Beth-zur (1 Macc 4:61, 6:26), and he camped in the lowland city of Adullam (2 Macc 12:38; Kh. ᶜId el-Minya; Eus. *Onom.* 24:21), where his reception by the local population indicates the growing popular support for the insurgency.

## Judas' Final Battles

### The Battle of Beth-zechariah (1 Macc 6:28–63; 2 Macc 13:1–23; *Ant.* 12:362–381; *War* 1:41–46).

Antiochus IV died during his campaign into the provinces east of the Euphrates, likely at Tabae (Isfahan) in 164 bce (App. *Syr.* 66; cf. *Ant.* 12:354–361; 1 Macc 6:1–4, 8–13; 2 Macc 9:1–29). A struggle for power followed, involving Philip, whom Josephus records "was appointed regent of his kingdom" and given the "diadem, robe and seal-ring" with instructions to pass them on to the heir, Antiochus V Eupator (*Ant.* 12:360). The actions of the dying king, whatever their motivation, essentially stripped Lysias of his power.

Earlier Lysias had been appointed guardian of the king's son and regent of the lands west of the Euphrates to Egypt. The unexpected death of Antiochus IV and his appointment of Philip as "ruler over *all* the empire" (1 Macc 6:14) threatened the legitimacy of Lysias. Lysias quickly designated Antiochus V Eupator king in order to secure his own position of influence as the guardian of the young king. Yet, the son of Antiochus IV would only survive for two years, murdered by his cousin, Demetrius, the son of Seleucus IV.

During this period of preoccupation within the Seleucid kingdom for the succession of power, Judas sought to address the vexing problem of the citadel in Jerusalem that had been built by Antiochus IV and "positioned above" (*Ant.* 12:362) the Temple. The Syrian garrison and their Jewish sympathizers (1 Macc 6:21; *Ant.* 12:362) in the citadel had continued to disrupt services in the sanctuary (1 Macc 6:18). So, Judas decided to take steps to remove the Hellenistic enclave in the citadel. Faced with this threat, the garrison sent for help from young Antiochus Eupator, who reacted by gathering troops and leading them with Lysias to Judea (*Ant.* 12:367). The size of the force is exaggerated in all of the sources, but it is clear that it included a substantial portion of the Seleucid army, including foot-soldiers, cavalry and elephants.

Together with Antiochus Eupator, Lysias retraced his previous strategy to approach Jerusalem from the southern end of the watershed route through Idumea and the

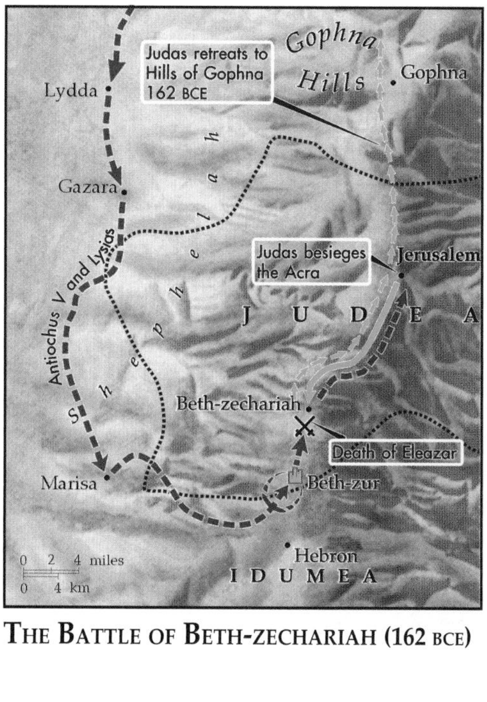


**The Battle of Beth-zechariah (162 bce)**

*Alexander on horseback fights an Indian king on an elephant. Scene on silver decadrachma.*

ascent beginning near Marisa. Jason the Cyrene records Judas' troops ambushed the Seleucid army on its approach to Judea (2 Macc 13:14–17).

Judas' ambush did little to prevent the assault of the Seleucid army. They attacked the newly fortified defenses at Beth-zur (1 Macc 4:61) that held out this time against the Seleucid king. Word of the enemy advances were forwarded to Judas who withdrew from his siege of the citadel and moved south along the watershed route to assist the Jewish forces at Beth-zur. The Maccabee encamped at Beth-zechariah (Kh. Beit Zakarîyeh; *Ant.* 12:369; *War* 1:41), 11 miles (18 km) south of Jerusalem and 6 miles (10 km) north of Beth-zur, "opposite the camp of the king" (1 Macc 6:32).

Early the next morning the forces met in battle. The vivid detail provided by the author of 1 Maccabees suggests that he was an eyewitness. In the ensuing fight Eleazar, the brother of Judas, perished when he impaled an elephant that he mistakenly thought was carrying the king. The elephant fell on him and killed him instantly. At the sight of the fallen Hasmonean, the Jewish forces panicked and fled north into the hill country of Gophna (*War* 1:45; *contra Ant.* 12:374).

The watershed route north to Jerusalem now lay undefended, and the Seleucid army advanced to lay siege to the Temple. The author of 1 Maccabees describes the battle for the sanctuary (1 Macc 6:51–54). Jason of Cyrene makes no mention of the siege of Jerusalem but writes solely about the attack on Beth-zur.

> [Antiochus Eupator] advanced against Beth-zur, a strong fortress of the Jews, was turned back, attacked again, and was defeated. . . . The king negotiated a second time with the people of Beth-zur, gave pledges, received theirs, withdrew, attacked Judas and his men, was defeated. (2 Macc 13:19, 22)

Jason's description of the king's "defeat" is doubtless an exaggeration of the Seleucid's inability to breach the defenses of Beth-zur.

The dissimilarity in the historical witnesses is manifest also in the histories of Josephus. His earlier account in *Jewish War* says almost nothing about the defense of Beth-zur, "after capturing the small town of Bethsuron. . ." (*War* 1:41). Likewise, the Jewish historian records a minimal stay by the king in Jerusalem in *War* 1:46 with no mention of fighting. His later account written in *Antiquities* 12:367–378 supplies details on the attack at Beth-zur (*Ant.* 12:367–368) and Jerusalem, "the siege of the temple in Jerusalem kept him there a long time, for those within stoutly resisted" (*Ant.* 12:377). Such differences by the same author show the influence of 1 Maccabees upon Josephus' subsequent rewriting of the conflict in *Antiquities*.

All of the witnesses agree that Antiochus and Lysias' retreat from Jerusalem coincided with word that Philip had arrived in Antioch (1 Macc 6:55–56; 2 Macc 13:23). The new regent posed a real threat to the young king and his guardian. So, they withdrew from Jerusalem immediately to return to Antioch.

The king could hardly abandon the region with the conflict still raging in Judea. Lysias sued for peace with the king's commitment to allow the Jewish population the freedom to "live by their laws as they did before; for it was on account of their laws which [the Seleucids] abolished that they became angry and did all these things" (1 Macc 6:59). According to the author of 1 Maccabees, the king also promised not to repeat his father's indignity in the desecration of the Jewish sanctuary. However, when he witnessed the strength of the fortifications, "he broke the oath he had sworn and gave orders to tear down the wall all around" (1 Macc 6:62). In other words, although the sanctuary and its service continued undisturbed, the walls that had been used for insurrection were breached.

## The Battle of Capharsalama (1 Macc 7:19–31; 2 Macc 14:15–18; *Ant.* 12:405).

Two years later Demetrius I claimed the Seleucid throne. He was the son of Seleucus IV Philopator and grandson of Antiochus III, but he had been imprisoned in Rome since childhood under terms of the Treaty of Apamea (188 BCE; Polyb. 18.39.5). When he heard of the political chaos surrounding the succession to Antiochus IV, he appealed to the Roman Senate to allow him to return to Syria. His request was denied. Nevertheless, he escaped with the help of the Greek historian Polybius and fled to Syria (Polyb. 31.19–21).

Landing in Tripolis (1 Macc 7:1; 2 Macc 14:1; *Ant.* 12:389), Demetrius challenged Antiochus Eupator's claim to the diadem (*Ant.* 12:389; 2 Macc 14:1–2). While Demetrius shared broad support from the military and local Syrian population, Rome remained suspicious of him, because he had ignored the will of the Senate. Nevertheless, Demetrius soon executed Antiochus V Eupator and Lysias and assumed the throne in 162 BCE, claiming the title Demetrius I Soter (1 Macc 7:1).

One of Demetrius' first initiatives upon taking power was to quell the continuing unrest in Judea. The author of 1 Maccabees describes an appeal made by the priest Alcimus, and a group of his pro-Greek supporters.

> Judas and his brothers have destroyed all your friends, and have driven us out of our land. Now then send a man whom you can trust; let him go and see all the ruin which Judas has brought upon us and upon the land of the king, and let him punish them and all who help them. (1 Macc 7:6–7)

The new king sent Bacchides, regent of the "lands west of the Euphrates" (1 Macc 7:8) back to Judea in the company of Alcimus. At first, the Hasideans welcomed the delegation, because they reasoned, "a priest of the line of Aaron has come with the army and will not harm us" (1 Macc 7:13–14). Judas remained wary, however, of Bacchides' show of force, and his fears were soon realized when sixty of his countrymen were killed in a single day.

Bacchides moved his troops north from Jerusalem and camped at Beerzaith (Kh. Bir Zeit; *Ant.* 12:397) on the edge of the Gophna region (cf. 1 Macc 7:19). He took punitive action against the local population, who he believed had been in collaboration with Judas and the insurrection. Shortly thereafter, Bacchides returned to Antioch. It may be that he felt his presence was no longer needed, or Demetrius may have recalled Bacchides and his forces to assist with the rebellion in the eastern provinces led by Timarchus.

Whatever the reason for his departure, Bacchides placed "Alcimus in charge of the country and left him with a force to help him" (1 Macc 7:20). Alcimus continued Bacchides' oppressive measures, cementing popular opposition to his rule as the high priest. Judas renewed the insurgency campaign from the hill country, and Alcimus soon realized that he could not overcome Judas alone. So, he journeyed to Antioch and appealed for Demetrius' help. The king sent Nicanor (1 Macc 3:38; 2 Macc 14:12), a member of the royal family, to eliminate Judas and his followers. Employing the guise of peace negotiations, Nicanor attempted to apprehend Judas. When his treachery proved unsuccessful,

*Coin of Demetrius I.*

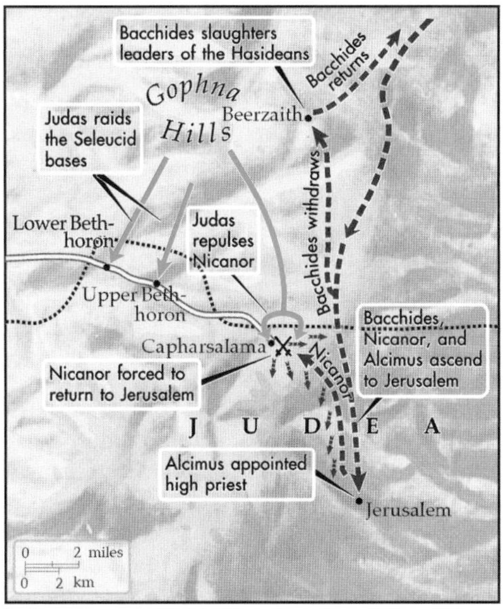


**The Battle of Capharsalama (162 bce)**

he moved his forces "to meet Judas in battle near Capharsalama" (1 Macc 7:31). The battle between Nicanor and Judas is not mentioned in 2 Maccabees which has led some to suggest that the battle is to be identified with the conflict at Dessau (2 Macc 14:16). However, confusion between these two toponyms is doubtful. Instead, it seems more likely that Dessau is a derivative of Adasa, site of a later battle between Nicanor and Judas (1 Macc 7:39–50). If so, Jason of Cyrene may have preserved an epitomized account of an additional skirmish between Nicanor and Judas in the area of Adasa.

The location of Capharsalama has likewise been the subject of debate. Early explorers to the Holy Land were drawn to ruins near the Byzantine monastery of Deir Salaam largely on the basis of toponymics (j. $^c$*Abod. Zar.* 5:4). However, the lack of Hellenistic and Roman period material remains, together with the topographical details of the narrative in 1 Maccabees, indicate Nicanor's intent was to clear the passage from Jerusalem to the coastal plain through Beth-horon (1 Macc 7: 39). Scholarship has thus identified a hill opposite biblical Gibeon, Khirbet $^c$Id, which is known locally as Khirbet Selma, as the likely site of Capharsalama. It may also be that this is the Salem "west of Jerusalem" mentioned by Eusebius in his *Onomasticon* (152:4).

The author of 1 Maccabees reports Nicanor's defeat (cf. j. *Ta$^c$an.* 2:13, 66a; j. *Meg.* 1:6, 70c.; b. *Ta$^c$an.* 18b; *Meg. Ta$^c$an.* 13 Adar), while Josephus' report has been corrupted and reads, "[Nicanor] defeated [Judas] and forced him to flee to the Citadel in Jerusalem" (*Ant.* 12:405). Rightly challenged was the reading of Josephus; 1 Maccabees is clear in its presentation that it is Nicanor who is defeated, even if his loss was not great. Moreover, the Citadel was currently in the hands of the Syrians (*Ant.* 12:406). So, Judas could hardly have sought refuge there.

**The Battle of Adasa** (1 Macc 7:39–50; 2 Macc 15:25–36; *Ant.* 12:406–412). Angered by his military reversals, Nicanor publicly expressed his contempt for the Jerusalem priests and threatened to burn the Temple if Judas were not apprehended (1 Macc 7: 33–35; *Ant.* 12:406). He probably detected the popular sentiment for the insurgency and hoped to force the public to realize that their misguided allegiance could lead to the destruction of the sanctuary. At the same time, reinforcements were sent from Antioch that required the Seleucid general to take a contingent to escort them and ensure their safety as they ascended into the Judean hill country from Beth-horon. Nicanor's choice of route via the Ascents of Beth-horon also signaled his intention to open this vital passageway from Jerusalem to the coastal plain.

He met no resistance on his journey to Beth-horon, where the troops from Syria met him. They then began the treacherous ascent to Jerusalem. Concern was likely for attacks from the north in the direction of the Gophna hill country, where Judas had operated with impunity. However, in a brazen demonstration of confidence, Judas positioned his troops on the open plain at Adasa near Gibeon, the point where the central plateau meets the Ascents of Beth-horon. Instead of the guerrilla tactics he had employed recently, Judas now felt he could confront the Seleucid forces in a traditional style of battle (1 Macc 7:43; cf. 1 Macc 10:78).

Three locations have been proposed for the site of Adasa: the Byzantine ruins of Khirbet $^c$Adasa southwest of er-Ram; Khirbet $^c$Adasa northeast of Tell el-Fûl on the road to Ḥisma; and Khirbet $^c$Adasa near Râs esh-Sharqi, where Hellenistic pottery was discovered.

Josephus says that Adasa was "thirty stadia" (*Ant.* 12:408 [3.5 mi./5.7 km]) from Beth-horon (Upper; i.e. el-Fôqā). Eusebius may also attest to the late Roman settlement of Adasa in this vicinity, in his confusion of the biblical Hadashah (Josh 15:37) with a village known to him north of Jerusalem, "It is now a village near Gophna" (Eus. *Onom.* 26:1). Although far from certain, Adasa

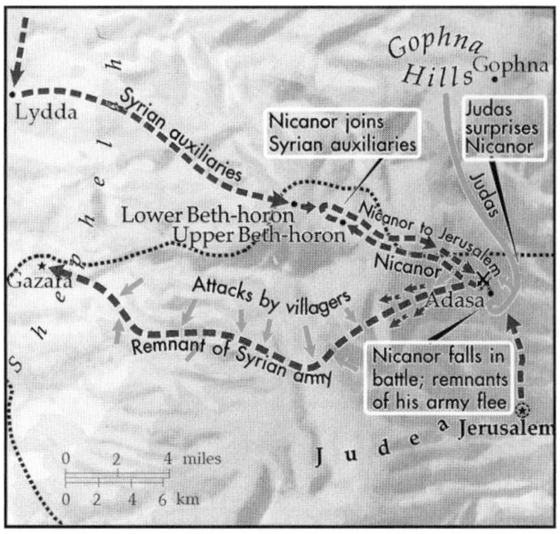


**The Battle of Adasa (161 bce)**

may also be identified with the mishnaic "Hadashah in Judea" (m. *Erub.* 5:6).

According to the author of 1 Maccabees, Nicanor was one of the first to fall in battle (1 Macc 7:43). Josephus provides an unusual testimony to Nicanor's valor and states that he fell towards the end of the battle: "finally Nicanor himself fell, fighting gloriously" (*Ant.* 12:409). Both reports agree that Nicanor's death brought panic among his forces that caused them to flee (1 Macc 7:44; *Ant.* 12:409). Judas' recent victories had regained the popular support of the local population. They came out of their houses and attacked the fleeing forces of Nicanor trying to escape to the Seleucid fortress at Gazara.

The victory was decisive, although the assessment by the author of 1 Maccabees, "not one survived" (1 Macc 7:46), is probably an exaggeration. The victory was a stinging blow to Seleucid prestige, and it also served to justify the national day of celebration, "Nicanor Day," which became a fixture in the Jewish calendar on the thirteenth of Adar (*Meg. Ta$^c$an.* 13 Adar). Nicanor's head and hand were impaled and displayed outside of the walls of Jerusalem. Albeit unusual, this was not a unique action in the pagan world. In this instance, however, it may also have been intended to signal the punishment for Nicanor's blasphemy in raising his hand against the Lord and his Temple (cf. *Seder Olam* 3 end; 2 Macc 7:34).

*Archaeological remains of the Citadel in Jerusalem showing the northwest corner of the First Wall and the Hasmonean middle tower.*

## The Battle of Eleasa and the Death of Judas (1 Macc 9:1–22; *Ant.* 12:420–434).

Judas regained control of Jerusalem, with the typical exception of the Citadel where the remnant of Nicanor's troops and their pro-Greek sympathizers remained fortified. He capitalized on his victory to strengthen his alliance with Rome (1 Macc 8:1–32). The Maccabee hoped a friendship treaty with the Roman Empire would counter the anticipated response from Demetrius I. However, the Syrian king had seized control of Babylonia, and open resistance to his rule in the eastern provinces had abated, at least to the extent that he was able to divert troops to deal with the unrest in Judea.

The treaty between Judas and Rome was a worrisome development for Demetrius. Rome had never officially recognized his claim to the throne. The empire's agreement with Judas signaled direct Roman engagement with the region and its support for the opposition. Rome had attempted a similar strategy with Timarchus, the rebellious satrap in Babylonia. Demetrius had to move quickly to remove the rebellion and reassert his political claim on Judea in support of Alcimus and his allies. Once again, the king called upon his trusted general, Bacchides, to lead troops into Judea (1 Macc 9:1). The king's delegation of the governor of the province with "twenty thousand foot soldiers and two thousand cavalry," is a measure of the concern with which the Jewish insurgency was viewed in Antioch.

The Seleucid army under the leadership of Bacchides proceeded south to find Judas and confront the Jewish forces in Judea. The geographical description of this march has been the subject of extensive debate, "they went by the road which leads to Gilgal and encamped against Mesaloth in Arbela" (1 Macc 9:2). Already by the first century CE, it seems that the toponyms in the report were in question. Josephus "corrected" his source to read, "[Bacchides] came to Judaea and encamped at Arbela, a city of Galilee" (*Ant.* 12:421).

Seleucid attention was not on the Galilee, but on the rebel forces in the hill country north of Jerusalem. The report of 1 Maccabees aptly begins the details for Bacchides' campaign from the point that he ascends into this region.

The army approached Judea through the Jordan Valley. Judas had defended against campaigns from the north, west and south. No adversary had yet to ascend into the hill country from the east. So, Bacchides' swift advance from the vicinity of Jericho may have been a surprise that prevented attacks during the difficult ascent. The route in question originates from the fords of the river Jordan near biblical Gilgal, unsettled in the Hellenistic-Roman period. Here the ascent continues north of Rammûn, near which are the ruins of Khirbet Jiljal whose

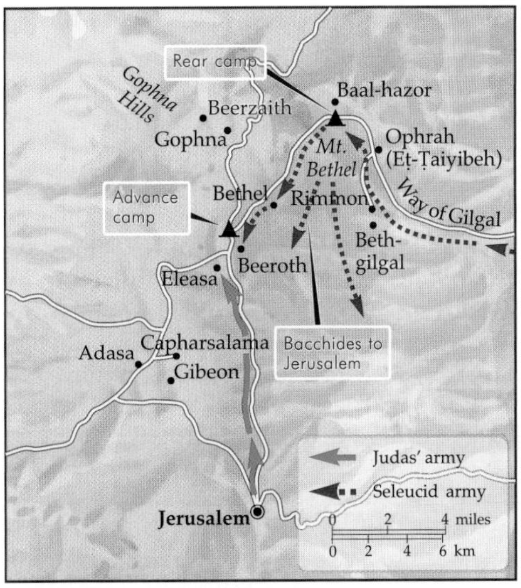


**The Campaign of Bacchides (161 BCE)**

name may preserve the memory of an ancient settlement nearby with the name of Gilgal. The Bible mentions a city near Bethel called by this name, "and [Samuel] went on a circuit year by year to Bethel, Gilgal and Mizpah" (1 Sam 7:16). Nehemiah likewise testifies to a Beth-gilgal in the vicinity, "from Beth-gilgal and from the fields of Geba and Azmaveth" (Neh 12:29). In the late Roman period Eusebius echoes a similar understanding regarding a Gilgal near Bethel. In his remarks about the site of Gilgal east of Jericho, he adds, "there seems to be another Gilgal around Bethel" (Eus *Onom.* 66:6–7). The language of his comment makes it unclear whether Eusebius actually knew a settlement by that name in his day or was merely parroting the biblical text.

From Bethel, the Syrians commanded a view of the area and control of the strategic north-south and east-west roads. Their first objective was to consolidate control of this strategic area by subduing or removing any resistance, "[Bacchides] killed many people" (1 Macc 9:2). Subsequent mention of Jerusalem was not intended to indicate that Bacchides journeyed to the city before his battle with Judas. Instead, the author depicts the establishment of a foothold in the hill country at Bethel, "they encamped opposite Jerusalem" (1 Macc 9:3b) from which the Syrians possessed a vantage of the Holy City. The general soon received reports on the location of Judas (*Ant.* 12:422), and so repositioned his forces, "then they marched off and went to Berea" (1 Macc 9:4a).

The Seleucid army moved east onto the watershed route at Berea. The author of 1 Maccabees 9:5 reports that Judas was at this time at Eleasa, identified by some scholars with Il$^{c}$asa, a kilometer from el-Bira.

On the other hand, Josephus' narrative is confused. He records that Judas encamped at Berzetho (*Ant.* 12:422). It may be reasoned that this is the result of Josephus' reliance upon a Lucianic (or pre-Lucianic) version of 1 Maccabees derived from a Hebrew original that confused *vav* for *zayin* in the earlier Hebrew text and read Beerzaith for Beeroth that some have proposed was the ancient spelling of the site. Josephus' identification of Beerzaith for Judas' position may also be a consequence of the mention of Bacchides' encampment on his first campaign to Judea (cf. *Ant.* 12:397). Since he wrongly assumed that Beerzaith was again the location of Judas' encampment, he felt no need to repeat the toponym or to provide any topographical description about the relocation of Bacchides' troops. He also makes no mention of Eleasa, perhaps under the impression that the place was located at Beerzaith, where both armies were encamped. However, the geographical testimony of 1 Maccabees 9:5 to Berea (el-Bira) and Eleasa (Il$^{c}$asa) is to be preferred. The sites are close, separated by a small plateau and valley that served as the site for the decisive battle.

From Eleasa Judas and his men could see the numerical disparity between the forces. In spite of the Maccabee's entreaty, some of his men slipped away leaving him "no more than eight hundred" (1 Macc 9:6). The Seleucid army advanced onto the battlefield with the cavalry forming "two wings on the flanks of the phalanx units" (cf. 1 Macc 9:12). A corresponding division of Judas' troops would have only aggravated the military disparity. In the previous battles with Apollonius and Nicanor, Judas had offset the numerical disadvantage by attacking the commanding unit. When Bacchides was identified in the right wing of the cavalry, the Jewish troops followed their previous battle strategy.

The Syrian unit feigned retreat in order to draw Judas and his men in and to encircle them with the two wings of the cavalry. Bacchides wanted to ensure the capture or death of Judas and his company. Judas and his men chased the right wing, "as far as Mount Azotus" (1 Macc 9:15). It is highly improbable that the battle ventured onto the coastal plain to Azotus. Equally problematic in reading Azotus in our account, the Hellenistic coastal city is never described in the ancient literary witnesses on a "mount."

Having retreated to the slopes of nearby hills, Bacchides' unit turned on Judas and his men, who were hemmed in by the encircling cavalry units. Many men from both sides fell, but in the end the Seleucids prevailed and Judas died in battle. Both 1 Maccabees and *Antiquities* report that Jonathan and Simon retrieved the body of Judas and buried him in Modiin. However, the circumstances by which they secured the body differ in the accounts. The author of 1 Maccabees provides no special details for the retrieval of the body which may have happened while the battle still raged or shortly thereafter. Josephus speaks of a truce with the Syrians to enable Judas'

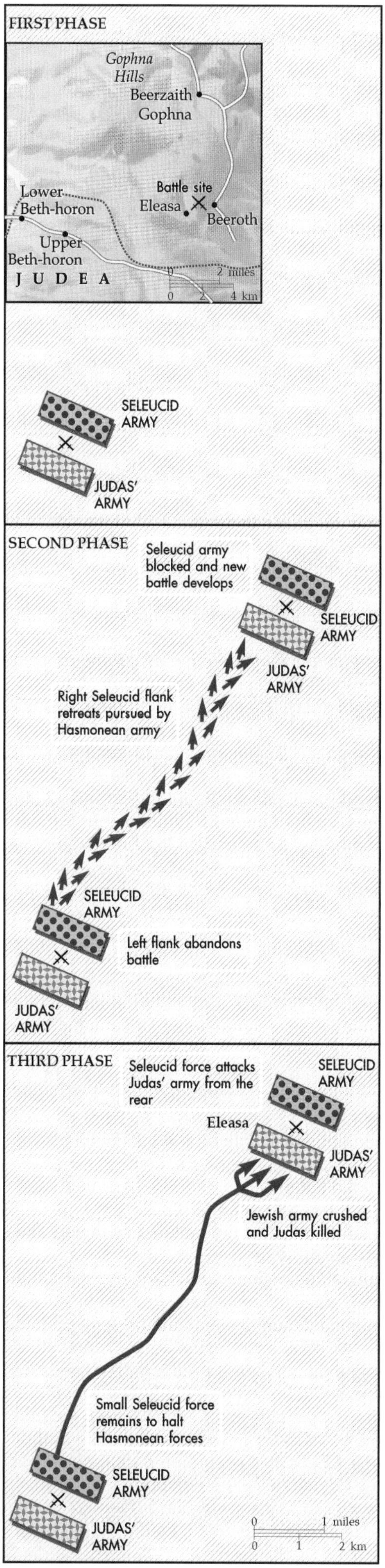


**THE BATTLE OF ELEASA AND THE DEATH OF JUDAS (161 BCE)**

brothers to secure his body. With the Jewish insurgency alive and after the desecration of Nicanor's body by Judas and his men, it is difficult to imagine Bacchides allowing a hero's burial for the Maccabee. Whatever the circumstances surrounding the return of Judas' body to his hometown, Josephus and 1 Maccabees identify his burial in Modiin, in a tomb whose location remains unknown.

## THE CAMPAIGNS OF JONATHAN AND SIMON

### Jonathan's Battles with Bacchides

(1 Macc 9:28–53; *Ant.* 13:1–22). After the death of Judas Maccabeus, his followers compelled Jonathan to assume the leadership of the resistance. When Bacchides heard that Jonathan and Simon were continuing their brother's struggle, he attempted to apprehend them as well. The area of their previous refuge in the hill country of Gophna was no longer safe, so Jonathan and Simon fled to the Judean Wilderness, a region that had proven to be a safe haven since the days of King David for political or religious refugees. The insurgency was now centered in the arid, barren steppeland near Tekoa. "They camped by the water of the pool of Asphar" (1 Macc 9:33), identified as the pool and cistern of Khirbet Bir ez-Za[c]farân. It lay on the southern border of Judea with Idumea.

Conflict with the Syrian forces was inevitable and Jonathan recognized their vulnerability to wage a guerrilla campaign with large amounts of baggage and stores. So, he sent their supplies with his brother, John, to their old allies, the Nabateans, perhaps to their stronghold in Petra. However, a local clan, the sons of Jambri from Medeba (*contra Ant.* 13:11; cf. Num 21: 30–31), waylaid the caravan. The supplies were lost and John killed. Later Jonathan and Simon ambushed the clan during a wedding party to avenge the blood of their brother. Then they returned and crossed to the marshy banks on the west side of the river Jordan, placing the waters between themselves and any pursuit by the Arab clansmen. The point of crossing was at the fords north of the Dead Sea.

Bacchides got word of the Jewish encampment and brought "a large force on the Sabbath day to the banks of the Jordan" (1 Macc 9:43). Familiar with the Jewish restrictions on the Sabbath, the Syrian likely hoped that Jonathan's forces would not fight. However, Jonathan encouraged his men to defend themselves against the approaching threat with words that depict their location:

> The battle is in front and the waters of the Jordan behind us; and marsh and thicket are everywhere with nowhere to turn. (1 Macc 9:45)

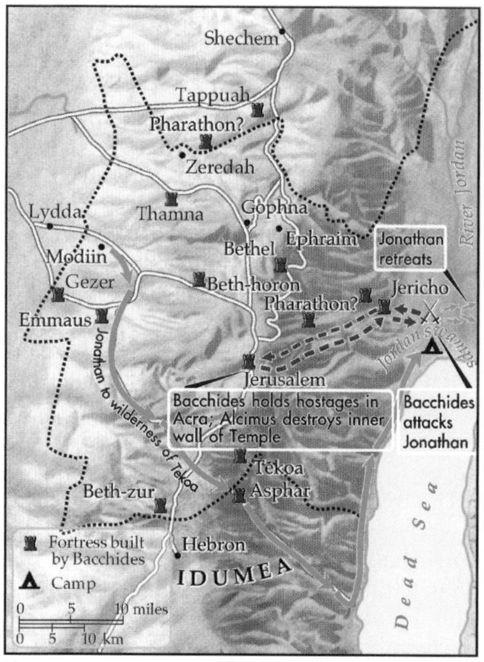


**JONATHAN IN THE WILDERNESS OF JUDEA AND THE FORTIFICATIONS OF BACCHIDES (160–155 BCE)**

Jonathan tried to employ the battle tactics of his late brother by striking out at the unit that included the commander. However, "Bacchides eluded him and went to the rear" (1 Macc 9:47). Realizing that they were outnumbered, Jonathan led his men in a retreat across the Jordan. Bacchides thought it wiser not to follow.

Anticipating the renewal of the insurgency, Bacchides turned his attention to fortifying the defenses of Jerusalem and Judea.

The role of Gazara (Tell Jezer) as a pre-existing fortified city of refuge allied with the Hellenistic kingdom is suggested by its mention as the destination for fleeing Seleucid troops (cf. 1 Macc 4:15, 7:45). The author of 1 Maccabees describes this city, together with the Citadel in Jerusalem and Beth-zur, receiving "troops and stores of food" (1 Macc 9:52). He does not repeat the mention of Bacchides' addition of "high walls and gates and bars" (1 Macc 9:50) in connection with these three cities, which were already royal fortresses (e.g. Citadel: 1 Macc 1:33; Beth-zur: 1 Macc 4:61, 6:26). They were not in need of extensive fortification, only the replenishing of their stores and the increase of the troops stationed within them.

### Jonathan at Beth-basi and Machmas

(1 Macc 9:54–73; *Ant.* 13:26–34). Alcimus held the office of high priest during the years 161 to 159 BCE, and he remained allied to Demetrius Soter and the Seleucid kingdom until his death (1 Macc 7:5, 9:1; 2 Macc 14:3–13; *Ant.* 12:385; *Gen. Rab.* 65:26). The author of 1 Maccabees reports that he attempted to remove the balustrade that separated the inner court of the sanctuary from the Court of the Gentiles (1 Macc 9:54–56; *Ant.* 12:413; cf. m.

*Mid.* 2:3; *Gen. Rab.* 55:22). The significance of this act was an attempt to remove the distinction between Jews and Gentiles in the area of the Temple. According to the author, as a result Alcimus became gravely ill and died before he could complete his intentions. His death seems to have brought some modicum of peace to the tensions between the pro-Greek aristocracy and the insurgents. Bacchides returned to Demetrius in Antioch and remained there for two years.

The Seleucid general returned to Judea at the behest of the pro-Greek aristocracy on one more occasion in an attempt to apprehend Jonathan and Simon. Their conspiracy of treachery failed, and Jonathan gathered fifty of those responsible and put them to death (1 Macc 9:61; *contra Ant.* 13: 25, 31). He then withdrew once again into the Judean Wilderness to Beth-basi (Kh. Beit Bassa; *contra Ant.* 13:26) and rebuilt the fortifications that had been torn down.

Bacchides learned of Jonathan's encampment and besieged the Hasmoneans "many days and made machines of war" (1 Macc 9:64). Jonathan was able to steal out of the city unnoticed, leaving Simon in command of the remaining forces. At this juncture the narrative in 1 Maccabees is corrupted. Most manuscripts of 1 Maccabees present Jonathan attacking what seems to be local beduoin, "Odomera and his brothers and the sons of Pasiron in their tents" (1 Macc 9:66). However, it seems unlikely that Jonathan would have initiated further hostilities while Simon and his troops were under siege. Josephus, instead, records that after escaping from the city, Jonathan "gathered together a large force from among those who sympathized with him" (*Ant.* 13:28).

Jonathan surprised the forces of Bacchides. At the same time, "Simon and his men sallied out from the city and set fire to the machines of war" (1 Macc 9:67). Upon hearing that the Syrian general had decided to withdraw from the country,

*Hellenistic cavalryman; painted tombstone from Sidon.*

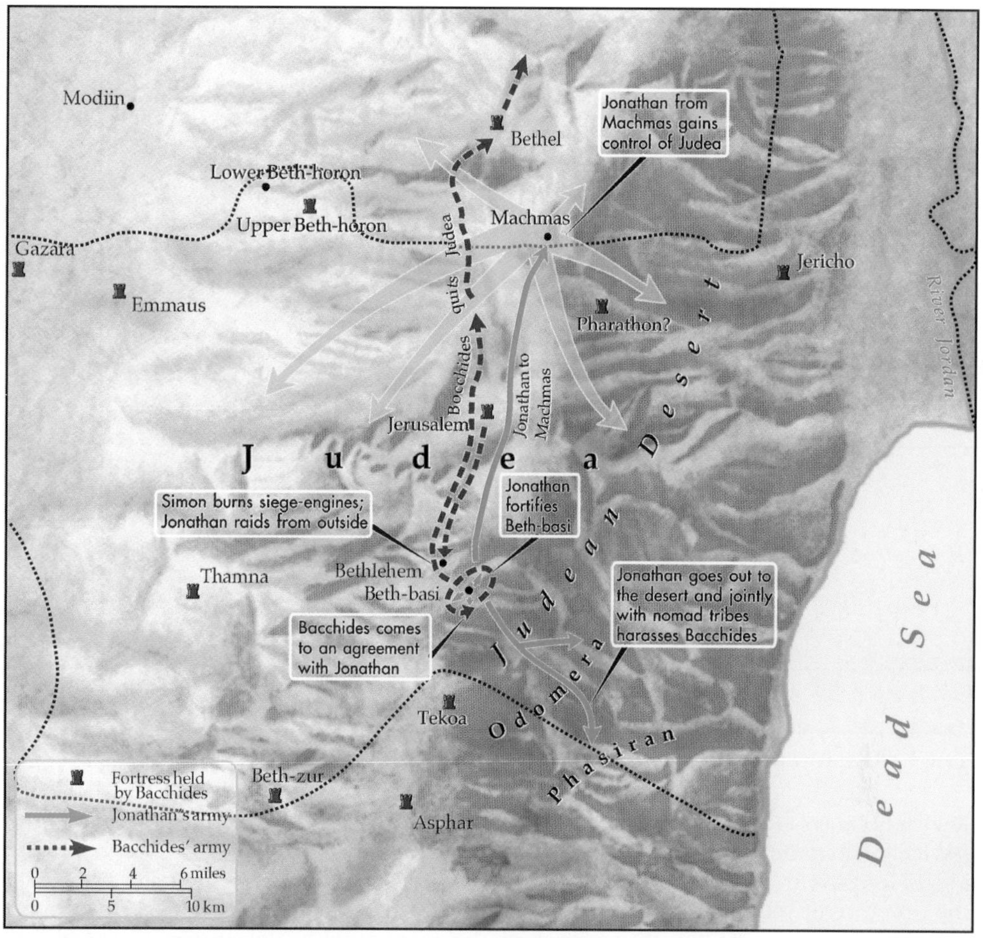


**The Siege of Beth-basi and Jonathan at Machmas (156–152 bce)**

Jonathan negotiated for peace. All captives were released and hostilities ceased. In the absence of Seleucid domination, Jonathan and Simon were now able to return to the areas north of Jerusalem where they had previously dwelt. Jonathan established his residence at Machmas (Mukhmas; Eus *Onom.* 132:3; cf. 1 Sam 13:2, 14:5–31), "and began to judge the people, and he destroyed the ungodly out of Israel" (1 Macc 9:73; *Ant.* 13:34).

**Judea Under Jonathan (152–142 bce) and the Battle of Jamnia** (1 Macc 10: 1–89; *Ant.* 13:35–61, 80–102). Judea experienced relative political stability until the arrival and conquest of Ptolemais by Alexander Balas in 152 bce. According to 1 Maccabees (10:1) and Josephus (*Ant.* 13:35), he was the son of Alexander IV Epiphanes (cf. Strabo *Geog.* 13.4.2). The Greek historians, however, present him as an impostor (Diod. Sic. 31.32a; Livy *Per.* 52; App. *Syr.* 67) presented to the Roman Senate by Ptolemy VI of Egypt and the kings of Asia Minor, none of whom supported Demetrius' claim to the diadem (Justin. *Epit.* 35.1.6; Polyb. 3.5.3). Alexander found ready allies among the Roman Senate as the pretender for the Seleucid throne. His first move was to occupy Ptolemais with the welcome of disaffected inhabitants (1 Macc 10:1).

Both Demetrius and Alexander understood the strategic importance of Jonathan's allegiance for control of Judea. They appealed to the Hasmonean with generous offers for his support. Demetrius first promised Jonathan the authority to conscript an equipped army and pledged to release Jewish hostages held in the Citadel in Jerusalem (1 Macc 10:6). With the king's permission, Jonathan also began to restore the walls of the Temple Mount (1 Macc 10: 10–11; *contra Ant.* 13:41) that had been breached by Antiochus Eupator (*Ant.* 12:383; 1 Macc 6: 62). The extent of the imperial offer caused alarm among the king's foreign allies who occupied the fortified cities of Judea, so that many of them, in fear for their lives, abandoned the country, with the exception of Beth-zur and the Citadel in Jerusalem (1 Macc 10:14; *Ant.* 13:42).

Alexander countered Demetrius' gesture with a personal offer to the Hasmonean. Jonathan's acceptance of personal promotion rather than Demetrius' public largesse may indicate that the historical source for this report originated among anti-Hasmonean circles. Alexander awarded Jonathan the position of high priest—for at this time there was no high priest (*Ant.* 13:46)—and the political designation of the king's friend.

Jonathan accepted Alexander's proposition and marked the beginning of his high priesthood at the Feast of Tabernacles in 152 bce. This turn of events alarmed Demetrius, so he responded with an even more generous offer to relinquish royal taxes on the populace, to recognize the

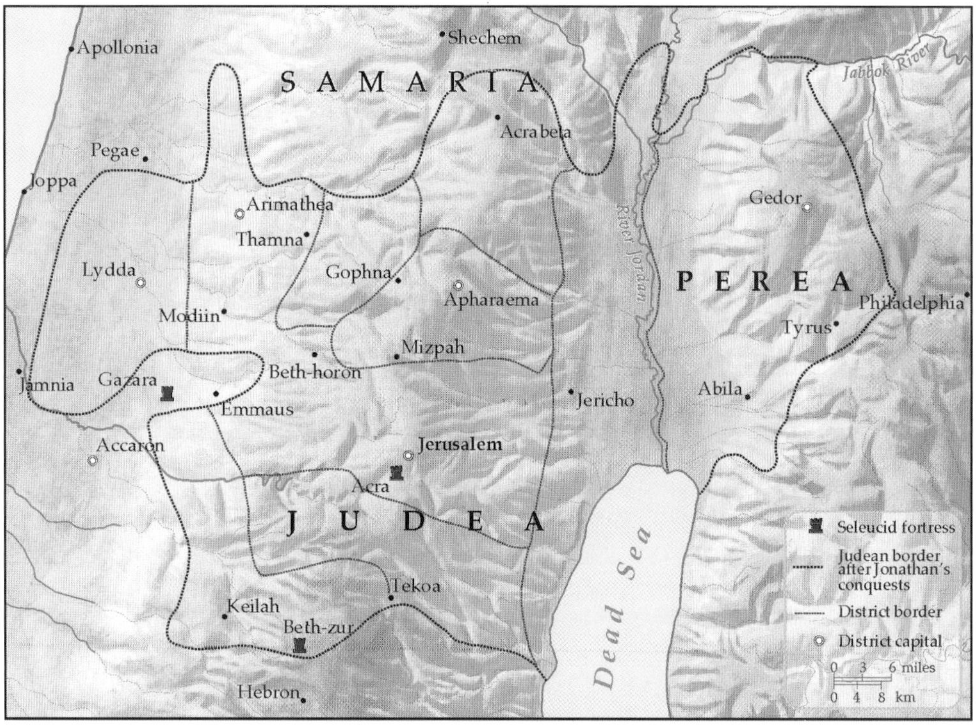


**The Expansion of Judea in the Days of Jonathan (152–142 BCE)**

Jewish holidays and Sabbath and to include Jewish inhabitants within the realm into the king's forces. He likewise offered to add to the province of Judea the city of Ptolemais and three districts under the control of Samaria (1 Macc 10:38–39: Apharaema, Lydda and Haramatha; *contra Ant.* 13:50; cf. 1 Macc 11: 34; *Ant.* 13:127).

It has been proposed that Demetrius' territorial offer (and that of his son's, cf. 1 Macc 11:34) was only a royal recognition of Jonathan's *de facto* administration of Jews living in these districts even before the days of Demetrius I. In any event, the king also volunteered to finance the rebuilding of Jerusalem from the royal coffers. However, Jonathan did not trust the sincerity of the king's pledge and remained allied to Alexander, the royal pretender.

Demetrius and Alexander met on the battlefield in the summer of 150 BCE. According to the ancient sources (*Ant.* 13:58–61; Justin. *Epit.* 35.1.10–11; App. *Syr.* 67), the king rode his horse deep into a swamp, where he fell. Soldiers of Alexander encircled the wounded king and killed him. The diadem passed to Alexander, who immediately forged a political alliance by his marriage to the daughter of Ptolemy VI Philometor, king of Egypt.

Jonathan was invited to meet with the two kings during the royal wedding in Ptolemais. The Hasmonean showered his hosts with gifts, and "[Alexander] honored him and enrolled him among his chief friends, and made him general and governor of the province" (1 Macc 10:65; *Ant.* 13:85). The son of Mattathias now possessed royal recognition of his priestly and political status as the leader of Judea.

Three years later (147 BCE) Demetrius II Nicator, son of Demetrius I, journeyed from Crete to Cilicia (*Ant.* 13:86; cf. *Ant.* 13:145), on the border of Syria, to challenge Alexander and reclaim his succession to the throne. The king withdrew from Phoenicia to Antioch "in order to make his position there secure before Demetrius should arrive" (*Ant.* 13:87; Justin. *Epit.* 35.2.3). The author of 1 Maccabees reports that Demetrius appointed Apollonius the governor of Coele-Syria (1 Macc 10:69). Josephus' presentation of Apollonius as the governor still loyal to Alexander is difficult. Yet, if the historian's single-sentence entry of Alexander's retreat (*Ant.* 13:87) is a confused intrusion into the description of Demetrius' initiatives, then the report may likewise indicate that it was Demetrius who retained (*Ant.* 13:88) Apollonius in a position that he already filled (1 Macc 10:69), presumably under Alexander Balas (i.e. treason), and perhaps even for Demetrius' father (cf. Polyb. 31.19.6, 31.21.2). Sense is then restored to the presentation of Apollonius' campaign against the king's ally—Jonathan, the high priest of Judea.

The governor moved quickly against Jonathan. He encamped at Jamnia (Yebnā) and sent a challenge to Jonathan to capitulate or fight on the open plain, "where there is no stone or pebble, or place to flee" (1 Macc 10:73). The language of the governor's challenge represents his familiarity with the Hasmonean's style of guerrilla campaign in the hill country of Judea.

Jonathan and Simon mustered their forces and marched first on Joppa. The residents of this harbor city initially resisted because of a garrison stationed in the city by Apollonius. They opened their gates, however, when it was clear Jonathan intended to storm the city. Jonathan now stood between Apollonius on the southern plain and any reinforcements or supplies in the north. Apollonius' predicament was not lessened by the presence of Ptolemy VI, who stood ready in Egypt to assist those allied with the king's son-in-law.

As Jonathan's troops edged southward, Apollonius feigned retreat in a withdrawal from Jamnia to Azotus (1 Macc 10:77; *contra Ant.* 13:92). He appeared to be continuing farther, but then turned to engage Jonathan's pursuing army on the coastal plain. During his retreat, Apollonius had strategically positioned one thousand of his cavalry (*Ant.* 13:94) to ambush Jonathan's troops. As fighting ensued Jonathan found Apollonius in front and the enemy's cavalry attacking from the rear (*Ant.* 13:94). Jonathan reformed his troops into a janus-faced phalanx formation (*Ant.* 13:94) to counter the Syrian attack on two fronts. The battle continued from the early morning into evening, and the Syrian cavalry weakened. This freed Simon to prevail against the Syrian foot-soldiers, while Jonathan routed the cavalry.

Apollonius' infantry fled amid the chaos and confusion and were met by their own cavalry who likewise scattered onto the plain. Together they sought refuge in Azotus (Isdûd) and entered the temple of Dagon (cf. 1 Sam 5:2–5), hoping to receive sanctuary. Instead, Jonathan destroyed Azotus and the surrounding villages and burned the pagan temple (*Ant.* 13:99–101; 1 Macc 10:82–85).

Fresh from a decisive victory, Jonathan proceeded on to the coastal city of Ascalon (Ashkelon). The residents of this coastal city

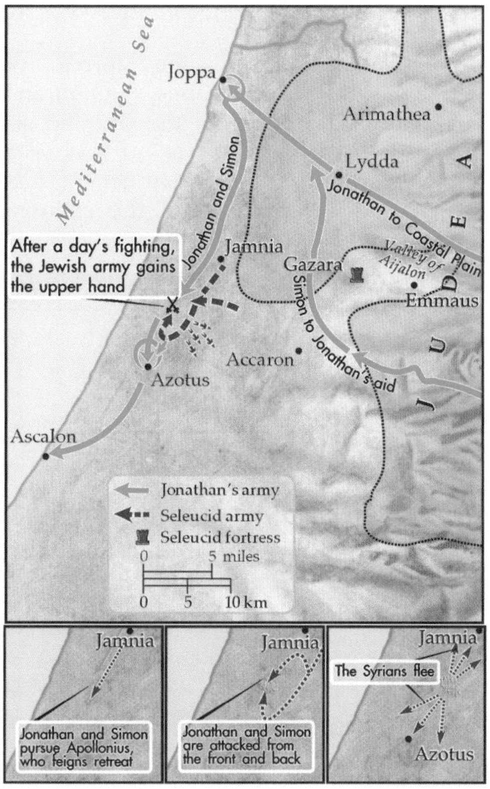


**The First Conquest of Joppa and the Battle of Jamnia (147 BCE)**

had maintained peaceful relations with the Hasmoneans, and the elders surrendered the city without a fight. When Alexander received word of Jonathan's feats, he rewarded him with honorary tributes and the coastal city of Accaron (Ekron [Tel Miqne]) "and its district as land for settlement" (*Ant.* 13:102; cf. 1 Macc 10:89). The language of Jonathan's reward indicates that Alexander's gift of property was a personal rather than political gesture.

## Jonathan's Intervention in Syria and the Battle of Hazor (1 Macc 10: 57–65; *Ant.* 13:103–105, 133–142, 146, 148–153, 158–162; 1 Macc 11:63–74).

The next three years (147–144 BCE) of Jonathan's high priesthood were a delicate balance between the changing fortunes of familial treachery and political intrigues within the Seleucid kingdom. Soon after Jonathan's destruction of Azotus (147 BCE), Ptolemy VI Philometor visited the ruins of the coastal city on his journey by ship to Seleucia (1 Macc 11:4–5). The reason given for his visit to Syria differs significantly in the literary witnesses.

According to the author of 1 Maccabees, who consistently demonstrates a pro-Alexander bias, Ptolemy was guilty of treachery. He stationed a garrison of his troops at each port-of-call, quietly wresting control of the coastal cities from his son-in-law without a fight. Jonathan met the Egyptian king in Joppa, where they spent the night, and the Hasmonean then accompanied him as far as the Eleutherus River (Nahr el-Kebir), north of Tripolis (Pliny *Nat. Hist.* 5:17), the border between Phoenicia and Seleucid Syria (Strabo *Geog.* 16.2.12). "So, King Ptolemy gained control of the coastal cities as far as Seleucia by the sea" (1 Macc 11:8). The author then presents Ptolemy continuing his treachery with an offer to Demetrius, his son-in-law's rival,

> Come, let us make a covenant with each other, and I will give you in marriage my daughter who is Alexander's wife, and you shall reign over your father's kingdom. (1 Macc 11:9)

Josephus paints a starkly different picture. According to the Jewish historian, Ptolemy's visit to Antioch was not intended to unseat Alexander, but to aid his son-in-law against the threats of Demetrius who was in Cilicia. For unstated reasons, Alexander had plotted the attempted assassination of Ptolemy at Ptolemais by the hand of his close friend, Ammonius (*Ant.* 13:106–108). Ptolemy demanded Ammonius' punishment, but Alexander refused. Thus, the Egyptian realized the origins of this treachery and broke off his relationship with Alexander.

According to Josephus, it was only after the failed plot that Ptolemy changed allegiances,

> having taken his daughter from [Alexander], he promptly sent to Demetrius, proposing a friendly alliance, and promising to give him his daughter as wife, and to restore to him his father's throne. (*Ant.* 13:110)

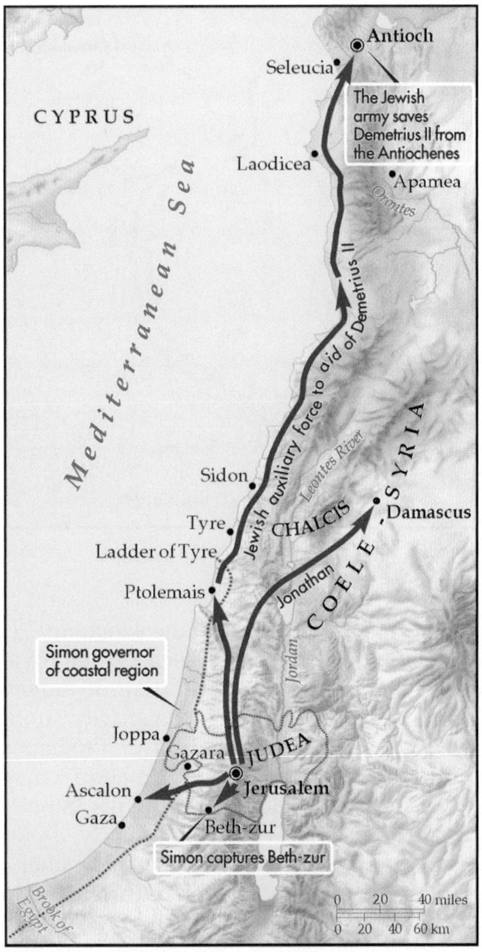


**THE INTERVENTION OF JONATHAN IN SYRIA (150 BCE)**

The Jewish historian's version of events accords with that of other Greco-Roman authors (e.g. Polyb. 28:21.4–5; Diod. Sic. 33.1.3, 12.1; Justin 35.2.2).

Whatever the genesis of the political crisis in the Seleucid Empire, the historical witnesses are in agreement that when Ptolemy arrived in Antioch, Alexander was absent (Diod. Sic. 32.9d,10.1; 1 Macc 11:16; *Ant.* 13: 113). Ptolemy entered Antioch undefended and vacant of its king. So, he claimed the diadem and declared himself king of both Egypt and Asia (cf. 1 Macc 11:13; Polyb. 39.7; *contra Ant.* 13:114–115). The Egyptian's actions represent an intriguing reversal of a similar episode, when Antiochus IV years before (169 BCE) at Memphis had declared himself also king of Egypt, and the young Ptolemy his subordinate (cf. 1 Macc 1:16).

Ptolemy soon met Alexander on the field of battle. The Egyptian was wounded, but his forces prevailed, and Alexander fled to Arabia. The Seleucid was quickly apprehended and assassinated by an Arab sheikh, Zabdiel (1 Macc 11:17; *Ant.* 13:118; cf. Diod. Sic. 32.9d, 10.1), who sent his head to Ptolemy. Unfortunately, the wounded Egyptian king only survived his former son-in-law by a few days. "So Demetrius became king in the one hundred and sixty-seventh year" (i.e. 145 BCE; 1 Macc 11:19).

Jonathan's political position was tenuous. His allies were dead, and the figure he had earlier opposed was now seated on the throne in Antioch. The high priest moved to take advantage of the political diversions in Syria and attacked the Citadel in Jerusalem. Perhaps, he assumed that Demetrius II would follow his father's pledge to empty the bastion of the Seleucid garrison and turn it over to the high priest (1 Macc 10: 32)—an offer his benefactor Alexander never matched. It seems that the son of Demetrius likewise thought it better to maintain a military presence in the Citadel and demanded the Hasmonean cease his hostilities.

The new king invited Jonathan to Ptolemais, where the Judean impressed Demetrius with extravagant gifts, "taking silver and gold and clothing and numerous gifts. And he won [the king's] favor" (1 Macc 11:24). Demetrius reaffirmed Jonathan's position as high priest and "chief friend" (1 Macc 11:27). The high priest's political position as general and governor of the province, while not explicitly mentioned, seems also to have been reaffirmed in the bestowing of "many other honors as he had formerly had." No mention is made of political appointees in Judea by Demetrius.

As for the province of Judea, Jonathan requested and received reaffirmation of the territorial additions and exemption from taxation first offered by Demetrius I Soter (cf. 1 Macc 10:25–45).

> We have confirmed as their possession both the territory of Judea and the three districts of Apharaema and Lydda and Haramatha; the latter, with all the region bordering them, were added to Judea from Samaria. To all those who offer sacrifice in Jerusalem, we have granted release from the royal taxes which the king formerly received from them each year, from the crops of the land and the fruit of the trees. And the other payments henceforth due to us of the tithes, and the taxes due to us, and the salt pits and the crown taxes due to us—from all these we shall grant them release. (1 Macc 11:34–35)

The author of 1 Maccabees omits any mention of Demetrius' abuses of power. Pagan historians record that the kingdom soon fell into disarray, when the king drowned himself in self-indulgences and delegated his powers to corrupt subordinates (Justin. *Epit.* 36.1.1; Diod. Sic. 33:9).

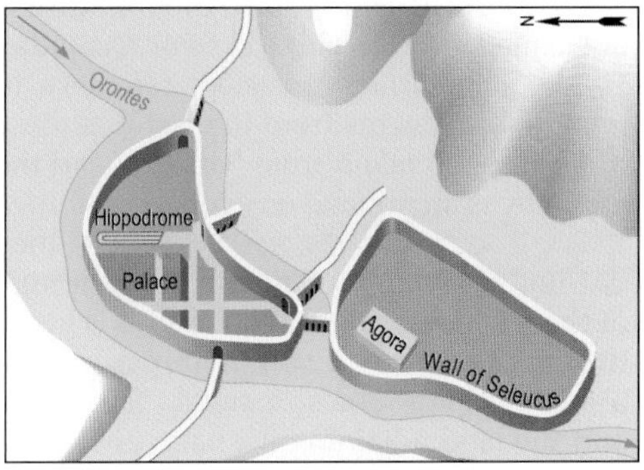


*Plan of Antioch in the Hellenistic period.*

Josephus only records that the population of Antioch grew to hate the king, "because of the ill-treatment they had received at his hands" (*Ant.* 13:135).

At the king's request Jonathan sent three thousand men to Antioch to assist him in controlling the rebellious local population. The Hasmonean hoped to leverage this assistance to gain the removal of the troops and their supporters from the Citadel (*Ant.* 13:133; 1 Macc 11:41). Riots broke out in Antioch, and the Jewish soldiers made their way to the housetops, while the crowds opposing Demetrius filled the streets. Greatly outnumbered, the soldiers set fire to some of the wooden houses in an effort to drive the rioting Antiochenes from their attacking positions. The fire spun out of control and there was a large loss of life. Out of the tragedy, peace was finally achieved between the Antiochenes and Demetrius. The Jewish army returned to Jerusalem with the king's appreciation for their assistance, but without mention of a pledge to dismantle the Citadel.

> [Demetrius] broke his word about all that he had promised; and he became estranged from Jonathan and did not repay the favors which Jonathan had done him, but oppressed him greatly. (1 Macc 11:53)

Meanwhile, unrest festered on another front. A provocateur named Diodotus of Apamea (Diod. Sic. 33.4a; Strabo *Geog.* 16.2.10; Livy *Per.* 52), who was surnamed Tryphon, sought to take advantage of the discontent among the local population, as well as current and former soldiers in Demetrius' army. Veterans had been discharged from duty and replaced with foreign mercenaries. Others had not been paid. Diodotus found the son of Alexander in the hands of Malchus in Arabia and returned him to Syria. Although the boy was only two years old, with Tryphon as his guardian he was proclaimed king: Antiochus VI Epiphanes Dionysus.

The disgruntled soldiers came to the young king's support. They declared war against Demetrius, "engaging him in battle, overcame him and took possession both of the elephants and of the city of Antioch" (*Ant.* 13:144). An envoy of the young king was sent to Jonathan and reconfirmed his position as high priest, appointed him over "the four districts" and made him "one of the friends of the king" (1 Macc 11:57).

The fourth district granted by Antiochus is not named in 1 Maccabees 11:57 or *Antiquities* 13:145. The earlier consistent reference to *three* districts stems from the fact that these three were all taken from Samaria, and the toparchy is mentioned on every occasion (cf. 1 Macc 10:30, 38; 11:28, 34; *Ant.* 13:127). Yet, they did not necessarily comprise the sum total of the territorial grant. Scant notice is given that in Demetrius I Soter's initial pledge, a fourth region is also named, "Ptolemais and the land adjoining it I have given as a gift to the sanctuary in Jerusalem to meet

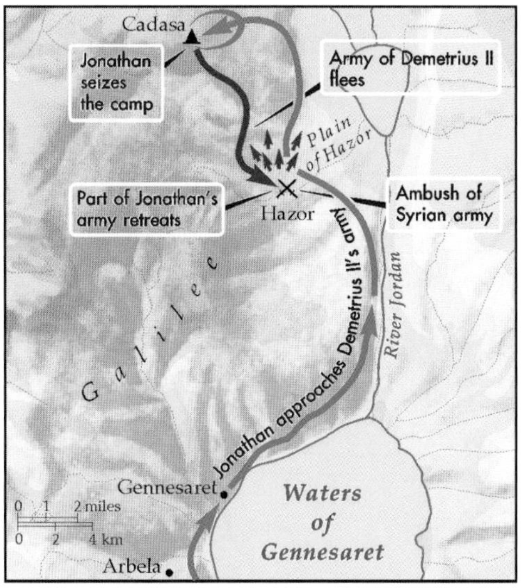


**The Battle of Hazor (144 BCE)**

the necessary expenses of the sanctuary" (1 Macc 10:39). Jonathan had declined the royal offer, and there is no indication of Judean administration of the coastal city until Antiochus VI. The omission of Ptolemais from Demetrius II's affirmation may indicate that he did not follow his father's generosity (cf. 1 Macc 11:34). Similarly, as we have noted, he did not repeat his father's promise to cede occupation of the citadel to Jonathan (cf. 1 Macc 10:32).

The language of the affirmation by Antiochus VI regarding the four districts echoes the initial pledge of Demetrius I Soter, but in the absence of any mention of Samaria, Ptolemais is now also numbered. Such an identification is also strengthened by Antiochus' offer to extend Hasmonean administration to the coastal plain. "Simon his brother [Antiochus] made governor from the Ladder of Tyre to the borders [i.e. the brook] of Egypt" (1 Macc 11:59).

Jonathan was commissioned to travel throughout Phoenicia and Coele-Syria into the Transjordan to conscript military support for the new king. Josephus describes Jonathan's efforts but states that the cities of Phoenicia and Syria, "while they received him splendidly, gave him no troops" (*Ant.* 13:148). Returning to the coastal regions where Jonathan already possessed alliances, at Ascalon "the people of the city met him and paid him honor" (1 Macc 11:60). However, Gaza determined to maintain its independence (*Ant.* 13:150). So, it shut its gates to Jonathan. He besieged the city, and burned and plundered its suburbs until the residents of Gaza relented and formed an alliance with him (1 Macc 11:61–63).

Word of Jonathan's efforts on Antiochus VI's behalf reached Demetrius, and he determined to put an end to the Hasmonean. His generals marched with a large army to Cadasa in Upper Galilee (Tel Qedesh; Eus. *Onom.* 116:8). According to Josephus, their strategy was to draw Jonathan out to the field of battle, because "he would not suffer the Galileans who were of his own people to be attacked by the enemy" (*Ant.* 13:154).

Jonathan left Simon to defend the hill country of Judea, because there remained forces loyal to Demetrius garrisoned at Beth-zur and the Citadel in Jerusalem (*Ant.* 13:155; cf. 13:42). Simon attacked the fortress at Beth-zur, and after a lengthy siege accepted its surrender. Once again, the Hasmoneans held the fortress that their brother Judas had fortified (1 Macc 4:61).

At the same time, "Jonathan and his army encamped by the waters of Gennesaret" (1 Macc 11:67; *Ant.* 13:158). The next morning they ascended from the Gennesaret plain arriving near the foothills of Upper Galilee.

In the later Roman period, travel through the Upper Jordan Valley passed along the northern shore of the Sea of Galilee, crossed the Jordan River near Bethsaida, and then continued north on the eastern edge of the Jordan Valley, along the foothills of the Golan Heights. Jonathan followed the older ascent beginning from the plain of Gennesaret at the northwest corner of the Sea of Galilee. He climbed over the Rosh Pinna Sill and continued onto the western edge of the plain near the site of biblical Hazor.

Demetrius' troops had anticipated Jonathan's route and stationed an ambush in the hills overlooking the Huleh Basin (cf. *Ant.* 5:199). The main body of the Syrian army moved onto the "Plain of Asor" to engage Jonathan's troops. This mention of the "Plain of Asor" led to the discovery of the site of biblical Hazor. When Jonathan advanced to meet Demetrius' army, the enemy hidden in the hills attacked. Jonathan's men found themselves fighting on two fronts. In fear many fled, but some stood their ground. When those who were fleeing witnessed the tide turning in the battle, they returned and together pursued Demetrius' troops to the main camp, Cadasa. With the fighting done and assured of his victory, Jonathan returned to Jerusalem.

## Jonathan's Final Campaigns

Following his army's initial defeat at Hazor, Demetrius had little choice but to send a larger force to challenge Jonathan, an important ally of Antiochus VI, his rival contender for the throne. When word reached the Hasmonean of Demetrius' plans, he decided to attack in the region of Hamath, "for he gave them no opportunity to invade his country" (1 Macc 12:25). The narrative makes it clear that the Syrians were at the southern edge of the region of Hamath, and not actually at the city itself on the Orontes. Nevertheless, why Jonathan ventured to the northern reaches of Phoenicia remains a matter of scholarly discussion.

We have no indication that Jonathan (or

the author of 1 Maccabees) had in mind Zechariah's prophecy:

> For to the Lord belong the cities of Aram, even as all the tribes of Israel; Hamath also, which borders thereon, Tyre and Sidon, though they are very wise. (Zech 9:1b–2)

Nor does our narrative indicate that Jonathan moved his defenses north, because "he began to regard the whole of the Promised Land as his rightful inheritance. Enemies coming from outside should not by right be allowed to tread on it." The author of 1 Maccabees gives no hint of recognition that Lebo-hamath was the border of Canaan (Num 13:21, 34:8; Ezek 47:15–17; 2 Chr 7:8).

Indeed, Jonathan's preemptive measures do not seem to involve territorial concerns at all. The Greek term in our passage indicates an *opportunity of time*. In other words, Jonathan did not want to allow the approaching forces the *time* to establish a formal military campaign but to strike them *en route*. This seems also to be Josephus' understanding, "For he determined not to allow them time enough to invade Judaea" (*Ant.* 13:174). The very manner of Jonathan's attack upon Demetrius' forces, an ambush on their camp at the break of day, suggests that Jonathan's northern strategy was not intended to demonstrate a territorial claim or religious statement on the open field of battle, but to exploit the element of surprise.

Nevertheless, Jonathan's advance to the region of Hamath on the border of Phoenicia and Syria certainly happened with Tryphon's advised consent. His earlier campaign on Antiochus' behalf "as far as Damascus," and the later march of his army "to Damascus . . . and through all that region" suggests at a minimum the freedom Jonathan possessed to move uninhibited throughout Coele-Syria and Phoenicia (1 Macc 10:69; Curt. 4.8.9; Diod. Sic. 19.93.1; 1 Esdr 2:13, 4:48, 8:64; 2 Macc 3:5, 10:11; *Ant.* 11:25, 13:65; Diod. Sic. 18.6.3). This no doubt came as a result of Jonathan's recent victories and Tryphon's realization that Jonathan's support of Antiochus VI was strategic in thwarting Demetrius' military forays into Judea.

Demetrius' generals discovered Jonathan's ambush and withdrew north across the Eleutherus River to "safe ground" (*Ant.* 13:179; cf. Thuc. 8.39.4). The coastal region of Seleucia had remained loyal to the house of Demetrius (1 Macc 11:44–51; *Ant.* 13:111, 135–141; Justin. *Epit.* 35.1.3, 2.3; Diod. Sic. 32.9c, 33.4; Livy *Per.* 52). If this was the direction for their retreat, then it is understandable why Jonathan would not have pursued beyond the Eleutherus River. Instead, both 1 Maccabees and Josephus report that the Hasmonean turned his forces on local inhabitants (1 Macc 12:31; *contra Ant.* 13:179). Neither account gives a reason for Jonathan's actions, but perhaps he discovered their collaboration with Demetrius.

Jonathan then marched his forces across Coele-Syria to "Damascus and through all that region" (1 Macc 12:32; cf. *Ant.* 13:179). The author inserts a brief account of Simon's campaign on the coastal plain. Mention of Simon's efforts within the account of his brother's victorious defense of the country is probably intended to anticipate his succession of Jonathan in a short while. Demetrius had his sympathizers among the coastal cities, but no opposition to Simon is mentioned at Ascalon, a city whose history of good relations with the Hasmoneans has already been noted (cf. 1 Macc 10:86). However, the fact that Simon felt any need to give the city attention, may signal real reasons for concern (cf. Philo *Leg.* 205).

Joppa, on the other hand, had been taken earlier by force (1 Macc 10: 75–76). Once again, Simon found the need to secure it without warning, "for he had heard that they were ready to hand over the stronghold to the men whom Demetrius had sent" (1 Macc 12:34; *Ant.* 13:180). To assure their continued loyalty, Simon stationed there a garrison of his soldiers.

Jonathan turned his attention to fortifying Jerusalem and Judea. Three initiatives are reported of Jonathan and "the elders of the people" (cf. m. *Sanh.* 1:5; m. *Sheb.* 2:2). First, they determined to repair (1 Macc 12:36; lit. raise; cf. *War* 3:284) the walls of Jerusalem (cf. 2 Chr 32:5). Specifically, the author of 1 Maccabees describes repair to a wall facing the Kidron Valley, "part of the wall on the valley to the east had fallen" (1 Macc 12:37). He notes that this section of the wall was called Chaphenatha, a designation that is not repeated in any other ancient source and whose etymology is not explained.

Next the residents of Jerusalem erected "a high barrier between the citadel and the city to separate it from the city, in order to isolate it so that its garrison could neither buy nor sell" (1 Macc 12:36). The continued presence of the Hellenistic enclave had proven to be an irritant. Particularly now at the outbreak of conflict with allies of those occupying the Citadel, its presence posed a grave security concern for the city. Jonathan and the leaders of the city determined to remove the stronghold from Jerusalem.

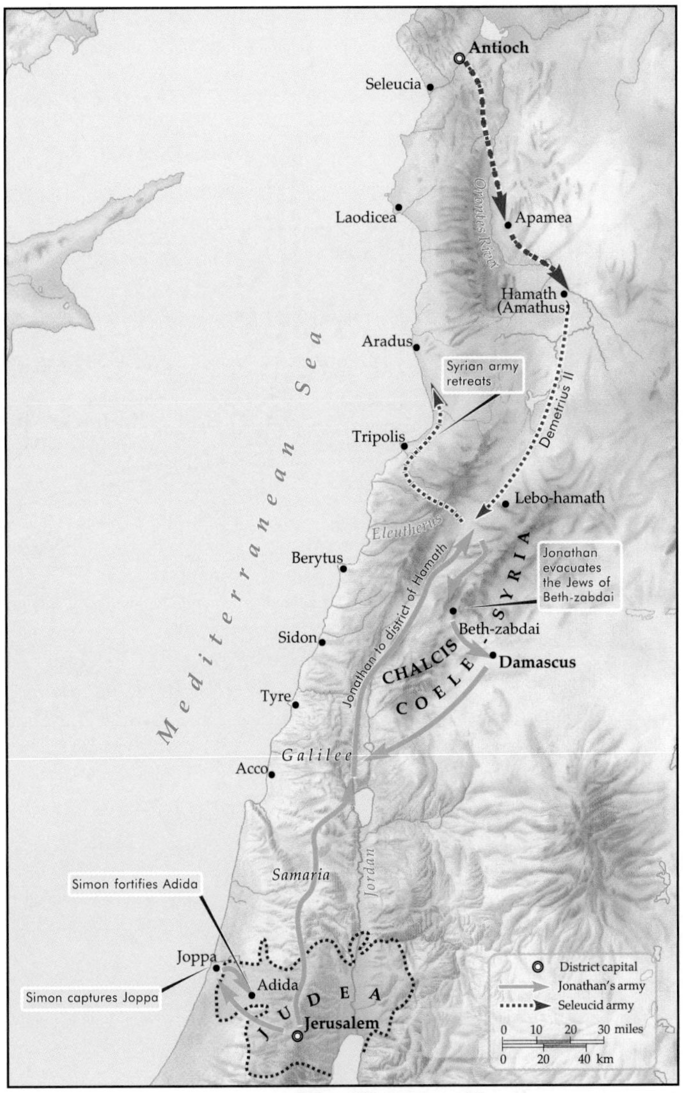


**The Hamath Campaign (143 bce)**

We do not know the nature of the *barrier* erected, nor how the blockade was intended to cut off supplies from those in the Citadel. These questions are largely dependent upon where the Citadel was located, itself a matter of considerable scholarly debate. What we do know is that this time Jonathan chose not to attack the Citadel, but to starve its occupiers into submission. He would succeed, but he would not live long enough to see the realization of his strategy. Instead, shortly after his brother's death, Simon accepted the garrison's surrender with much celebration and fanfare, and he rid the city once and for all of the hostile enclave first established by the hated Antiochus IV Epiphanes (1 Macc 13:49–51; cf. 1:33).

Finally, we are given another account of Simon's activity with the construction of Adida, in the Shephelah: "he fortified it and installed gates with bolts" (1 Macc 12:38). The toponym Adida represents the biblical name Hadid that appears in the lists of priestly courses, together with Lod and Ono, in post-exilic biblical references (cf. Ezra 2:33; Neh 7:37, 11:34).

Josephus makes no specific mention of Simon's efforts at Adida in his parallel narrative, reporting only "[Jonathan] sent

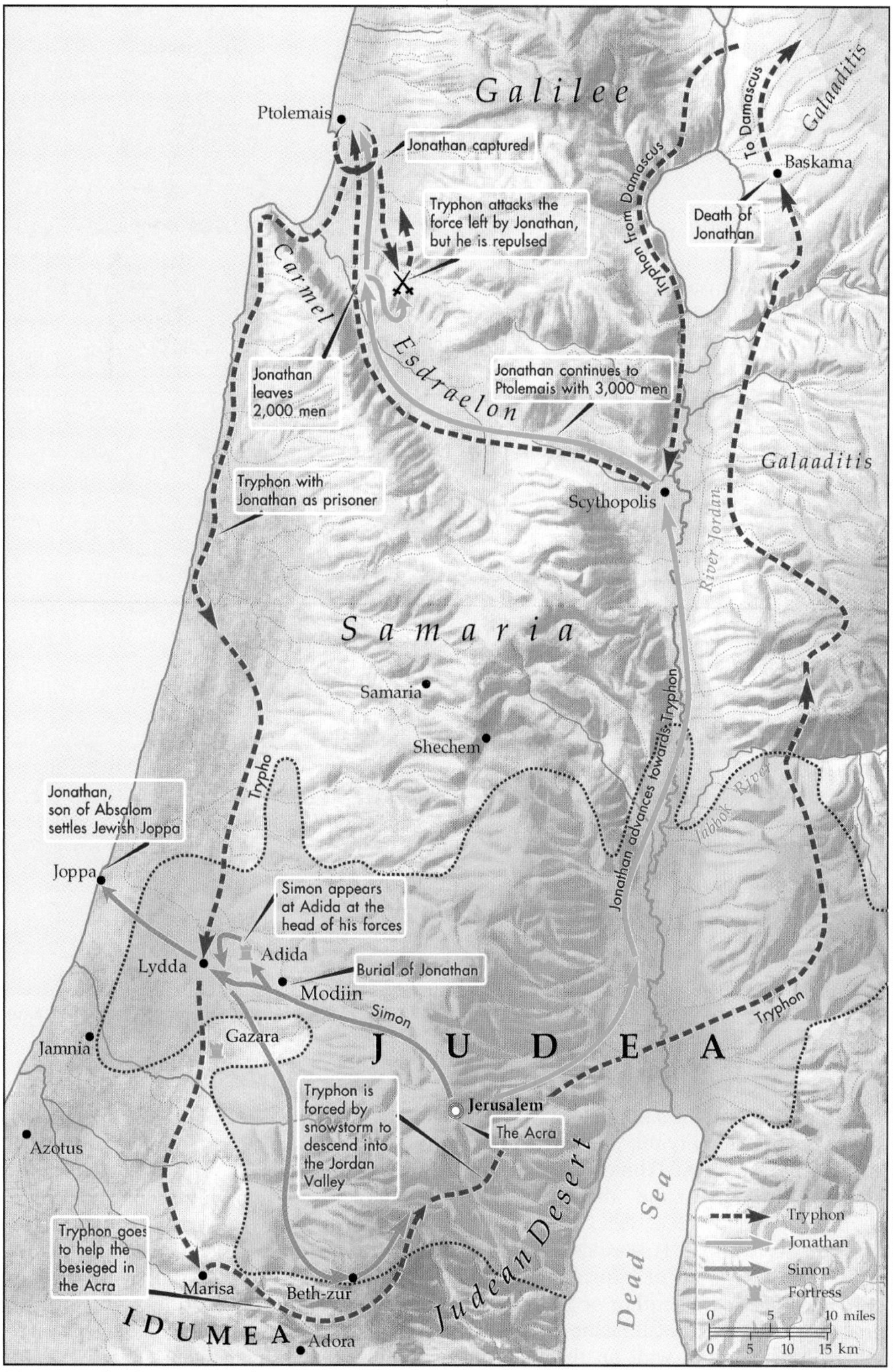


**Tryphon's Campaign Against Jonathan (143–142 BCE)**

Simon to make the fortresses in the country secure" (*Ant.* 13:183). A short time later, we hear of Simon at Adida in his battle with Tryphon, when the Syrian marched from Ptolemais with Jonathan in chains. According to the Jewish historian, they met at Adida, "a city which is situated on a hill, with the plains of Judea lying below it" (*Ant.* 13:203).

Josephus is mistaken that Adida adjoins "the plains of Judea." It lies outside of the Judean Shephelah, and belonged to a region designated in the Mishnah as "the Shephelah of Lod" (m. *Sheb.* 9:2).

Adida is situated at the northernmost edge of the paleocene limestone hills that define the geological nature of the Shephelah. The application of the topographical term by the author of 1 Maccabees to describe the setting for Adida is not drawn from biblical testimony, but instead is a remarkable indication of the local understanding of what constitutes the Shephelah.

Of particular note is the Hasmoneans' decision to fortify Adida. Simon's efforts are the first mention we have of the settlement in post-biblical literature. It was surely meager in size and its location not particularly compelling. The fortifications at Adida seem more to be a response to the looming military threat and a desire to provide some defense for nearby Modiin, the familial home of the Hasmoneans. Since Gazara was still likely in Seleucid hands (1 Macc 9:52, 13:43; *Ant.* 13:15, 215), Adida served Simon's defenses of the Ascents of Beth-horon and Jerusalem.

The site remained militarily important. Later Aretas, the Nabatean king, would defeat Alexander Jannaeus at Adida (*Ant.* 13:392), and Vespasian considered it sufficiently important to station troops there in preparation for his siege of Jerusalem. "Vespasian, with a view to investing Jerusalem on all sides, now established camps at Jericho and at Adida, placing in each a garrison composed jointly of Romans and auxiliaries" (*War* 4:486). These garrisons guarded the eastern and western access routes into the hill country north of Jerusalem.

Adida survived into the Byzantine period. Eusebius' entry on Adithaim in his *Onomasticon* mentions, "another village called Aditha east of Diospolis [Lod]" (Eus. *Onom.* 24:23). The bishop of Caesarea's etymological connection between the biblical city of Adithaim and Adida is likely the source for the confused epigraph of the village on the sixth-century CE Medeba Map, "Adiathim, now Aditha."

Tryphon's initiative had always been one of self-interest. It only remained a question of opportunity. The author of 1 Maccabees intimates that the regent took steps to seize the diadem before Demetrius' campaign and capture in Parthia (cf. 1 Macc 14: 1–3), while Josephus' *Antiquities* (13:184–186) follows the chronology of the Greek and Latin historians (e.g. App. *Syr.* 67–68; Oros. *Historiae* v 4.16–17) that Tryphon's takeover and Antiochus VI's death came only after Demetrius had marched east and was no longer a rival for the throne.

When Tryphon did move to usurp the throne, he was concerned that Jonathan would not lend his support. So, he sought to remove the Hasmonean leader. He marched his army to Scythopolis, where Jonathan met him with an imposing force. Whether it was wisdom or cowardice, the Syrian considered it better to remove Jonathan through treachery than on the field of battle. He invited Jonathan to dismiss the majority of his troops and to accompany him to Ptolemais.

> I will hand it over to you as well as the other strongholds and the remaining troops and all the officials, and will turn round and go home. For this is why I am here. (1 Macc 12:45)

At first blush, Tryphon's statement appears to undermine our earlier identification of the fourth district granted by Antiochus to be Ptolemais. If Ptolemais had already been granted to Jonathan, the regent's purpose seems superfluous. Yet, a closer examination of his words indicates that his stated purpose was to execute *the transfer* of Ptolemais to Jonathan. The verb is not used in any of the previous grants to cede territory, and it need not convey such an idea here. Indeed, it is the earlier promise of Ptolemais by Antiochus that gave lie to the ruse by Tryphon. Jonathan's willingness to accompany Tryphon, who is still viewed as the faithful regent for Antiochus VI, indicates the Hasmonean's prior expectation of the transfer of Ptolemais into Jewish hands.

Tryphon's stated purpose is to execute the promise of Antiochus VI. If so, we may witness a temporal lapse between the imperial edict and its implementation. One need look no further than the well-known account of Cyrus' edict to rebuild the Temple in Jerusalem, the lapse in those efforts because of local opposition, and the eventual completion under Darius I, to witness that a king's edict is not necessarily implemented without delay when it reached the provinces. Along the same lines, we hear nothing more of Antiochus' intention to appoint Simon to be the *strategos* "from the Ladder of Tyre to the borders of Egypt" (1 Macc 11:59). The absence of evidence is not proof, but Simon's later military campaigns in the coastal region appointed to him suggest that at least some of these areas did not recognize his authority.

As Jonathan entered Ptolemais, the citizens seized him and shut the gates. Those of his men who had entered the city were killed immediately, while others were shut out. Tryphon sent his troops to attack Jonathan's men who remained on the Great Plain (1 Macc 12:49; cf. 1 Macc 5:52) and the two thousand men that Jonathan had left in Galilee (*Ant.* 13:193). These troops already had word that Jonathan had been taken and believed he was dead. They withdrew "in close formation," dissuading Tryphon's men from attacking. "So they all reached the land of Judah safely, and they mourned for Jonathan and his companions and were in great fear" (1 Macc 12:52).

Under the mistaken assumption that Jonathan was already dead, Simon requested and received support from the people to assume Jonathan's place of leadership. They responded, "You are our leader in place of Judas and Jonathan your brother" (1 Macc 13:8). Simon hastened to finish the defenses of Jerusalem begun by Jonathan, "to complete the walls of Jerusalem, and he fortified it on every side" (1 Macc 13:10). He also sent a detachment to occupy Joppa.

Tryphon's subsequent actions give no indication he relished a confrontation with Simon. He marched south from Ptolemais onto the Sharon Plain with the intent to enter the hill country of Judea on his way to Jerusalem. However, near Lydda he encountered Simon's forces that were encamped at Adida. Access to the Ascents of Beth-horon was now impossible without a fight. Once again, Tryphon with Jonathan as his hostage attempted to manipulate Simon through deceit.

When it was clear that Simon would defend the route, Tryphon "circled around by the way to Adora" (1 Macc 13:20). Josephus records the same tactic in his inflated description, "[Tryphon] marched all through the country; and afterward deciding to go up to Jerusalem through Idumea, he finally came to Adora, a city in Idumea" (*Ant.* 13:207). The line of Tryphon's southern march remained on the eastern edge of the coastal plain by way of Lydda and Gazara to Marisa, the primary Idumean city in the Judean Shephelah. Advancing in parallel to Tryphon, Simon shadowed the Seleucid troops while moving southward in the limestone trough road of the Judean Shephelah, "and [Simon's] army kept marching along opposite [Tryphon] to every place he went" (1 Macc 13:20).

Arriving to the border of the hostile territory of the Idumeans, Simon stopped. At the Hellenistic city of Marisa, Tryphon began the climb unchallenged into the hill country. However, he did not follow the ascent from Marisa to the watershed route used earlier by Judas (1 Macc 5:66) or Lysias (1 Macc 6:31). Instead, a later Roman road from Eleutheropolis to Hebron through Tel ᶜEton likely followed the ascent chosen by Tryphon from the coastal plain to Adora (Dura). Adora was an important Idumean city that later would be appointed the capital of the toparchy of Idumea, when Gabinius established the five administrative councils in 58 BCE (*War* 1:170; *Ant.* 14:91).

Word was sent from the men in the Citadel, begging Tryphon "to come through the wilderness and to send them food." No indication is given where Simon was at the time. Earlier he personally fortified Beth-zur, and his presence there would assist to explain Tryphon's choice of an ascent more to the south (and more distant from Beth-zur) than others earlier recorded. Thus, the fortress of Beth-zur once again served to defend the southern approach to Jerusalem.

At every juncture, Tryphon is portrayed by the author of 1 Maccabees and Josephus as evading direct conflict with the Hasmoneans, whether it was Jonathan at Beth-shean, Simon at Adida or his continuation through the coastal plain until he was able to ascend into the hill country uncontested in Idumea. Perhaps, this is the background for the urging from the men in the Citadel. Tryphon's passage to Jerusalem was blocked. So, they urged him to use the route *through the wilderness*, language hardly suitable to describe the primary road from Adora to Jerusalem through Hebron, Beth-zur and Bethlehem. However, a secondary route from Hebron traversed through the Judean Wilderness to Tekoa and returned to the watershed route at Bethlehem. Travel

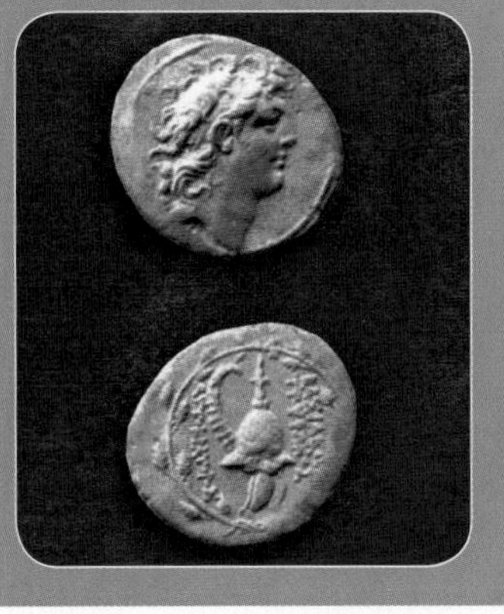

Coin of Diodotus Tryphon.

on this line would circumvent Beth-zur, if Simon's troops were indeed there.

In any event, Tryphon's arrival in Jerusalem was thwarted by a substantial snowstorm, an event not unheard of in the higher elevations of Judea. Although it receives less precipitation, at 2,883 feet (930 m) above sea level, Hebron is almost 620 feet (200 m) higher than Jerusalem, which has on average two snowfalls per year. Tryphon abandoned any attempt to reach the Citadel in Jerusalem, and instead returned to the Transjordan. No details are provided concerning his route. It is not unreasonable to surmise that he returned as he had come, through the coastal plain and the Jezreel Valley to Beth-shean. At the fords of Beth-shean he climbed into the heights of Gilead.

Josephus gives an unusual report that "reaching Coele-Syria, [Tryphon] hurriedly invaded Galaaditis" (*Ant.* 13:209). No indication is given by the Jewish historian why the need to "hurry" or who was "invaded." The author of 1 Maccabees is silent on these details, but does agree with Josephus that, "when he approached Baskama, he killed Jonathan, and he was buried there" (1 Macc 13:23). The place of Jonathan's burial in Gilead is not specifically mentioned and its location is uncertain.

Simon retrieved "the bones of Jonathan and buried him in Modiin, the city of his fathers" (1 Macc 13:25). After the period of mourning, Simon built an impressive memorial at the site of the family tomb.

> Simon also built for his father and brothers a very great monument of polished white marble, and raised it to a great and conspicuous height, made porticoes around it, and erected monolithic pillars.... In addition to these he built for his parents and his brothers seven pyramids, one for each, so made as to excite wonder by their size and beauty.
> (*Ant.* 13:211)

The author of 1 Maccabees adds that upon the pillars, "he put suits of armor for a permanent memorial, and beside the suits of armor carved ships, so that they could be seen by all who sail the sea" (1 Macc 13:29). Both authors testify that the memorial remained until their time. Eusebius likewise testifies that the ornamental tomb was still shown in his day (Eus. *Onom.* 132:16).

# CHAPTER FOURTEEN

# THE HASMONEAN KINGDOM

## 142 TO 76 BCE

The death of Jonathan meant the loss of an accomplished leader who had been able to exploit the internecine struggles within the Seleucid kingdom for the benefit of the people of Judea. Although true independence was not realized in Jonathan's lifetime, the expansion of territories under his administration and the increased autonomy he exercised within Judea laid the foundation for the emergence of an enlarged, independent Hasmonean state under the leadership of his brother, Simon, the last living son of Mattathias.

Soon after Tryphon's murder of Jonathan, the ancient histories also attribute his responsibility for the untimely death of the young Antiochus VI (1 Macc 13:31; *Ant.* 13: 218-219; Livy *Per.* 55; cf. Justin. *Epit.* 36.1.7; App. *Syr.* 67–68; Diod. Sic. 33.28). Yet, the sequence of events varies. According to the author of 1 Maccabees, the death of Antiochus VI (1 Macc 13:31) followed Tryphon's winter campaign into Judea and his return "to his own land" (1 Macc 12: 39–13:24). Only after the removal of Antiochus VI did Demetrius II Nicator march into Media, where he was defeated and captured by Mithridates I, the king of the Parthians (i.e. Arsaces VI: 1 Macc 14:1–3; *Ant.* 13:184–186; cf. Strabo *Geog.* 15.1.36; Justin. *Epit.* 36.1.1–6; 38.9.2).

On the other hand, Josephus followed the Greco-Roman authors by presenting Demetrius II's campaign across the Euphrates *before* the death of Antiochus VI. According to his version of events, after Tryphon heard of Demetrius' defeat and captivity, then he ceased "to support Antiochus, but, instead, plotted to kill him and seize the throne himself" (*Ant.* 13: 187). The numismatic evidence challenges Josephus' sequence of events and lends support to the story line presented by the author of 1 Maccabees. Coins minted in the name of Demetrius extend until 140 BCE, while those of Antiochus VI Dionysus only until 142 BCE. Coins would hardly have continued to be minted in the name of Demetrius after his defeat and captivity.

Reconciliation of these very different chronologies requires further study. It may be noted, however, that there are hints even within Josephus' own account of his awareness of reports that Tryphon had seized the throne *before* Demetrius II's campaign beyond the Euphrates. He describes Demetrius' motivation for his campaign, "if he should subdue the Parthians and acquire a force of his own, he would make *war on Tryphon* and drive him out of Syria" (*Ant.* 13:186). Josephus no longer presents Antiochus VI as Demetrius' contender for the throne, suggesting that in his source the young king has already perished.

*Bilingual (Hebrew and Greek) inscription: "Boundary of Gezer."*

Simon sensed the internal weakness in the Seleucid kingdom and sought to take advantage of it to liberate the Jewish people from "the servitude to the Macedonians." Incensed by Tryphon's senseless murder of his brother, Simon changed allegiances to Demetrius II and appealed for relief from the oppression being brought on the region by Tryphon (1 Macc 13:36–40; cf. *Ant.* 13:213). Demetrius replied to Simon as "the high priest and friend of kings."

Previous Hasmonean opposition to Demetrius II's rightful rule, likely the meaning of "errors and offenses committed to this day," was pardoned, and the strongholds—some of which were built to defend against Demetrius himself—remained the possession of Simon and the Jewish people. Equally important for the population of Judea, Demetrius extended, "whatever other tax has been collected in Jerusalem shall be collected no longer."

At the same time, Simon sent emissaries to Rome and Sparta (1 Macc 14:16–24) seeking international recognition of his high priesthood and leadership. Both of these kingdoms renewed the "friendship and alliance that they had established with Judas and Jonathan" (1 Macc 14:18). Josephus and 1 Maccabees agree that a new degree of independence is achieved under Simon.

> In the one hundred and seventieth year [142 BCE] the yoke of the Gentiles was removed from Israel, and the people began to write in their documents and contracts, "In the first year of Simon the great high priest and commander and leader of the Jews."
>
> (1 Macc 13:41–42)

The reckoning of legal contracts is usually dated from the beginning of a king's reign. Since the sons of Mattathias were not of Davidic lineage, they refrained from deigning the title king. Instead, we find Simon variously designated high priest (1 Macc 13:42; 14:27) and governor (1 Macc 11:59, 13: 42, 14:42, 14:47). The people also acclaim him their leader (1 Macc 13:8, 13:42).

The new era for Judea marked not only Simon's assumption of the high priesthood but the liberation demonstrated by the relinquishment of taxation upon the people of Judea. "This liberation and exemption from tribute came to the Jews in the hundred and seventieth year of the Syrian kingdom" (*Ant.* 13:213). Tyre and Sidon likewise established their eras from the beginning of their freedom from the Seleucid rule.

Bolstered by the affirmations to his leadership, Simon moved to complete his defenses in anticipation of military opposition from Tryphon.

> He fortified the cities of Judea, and Beth-zur on the border of Judea, where formerly the arms of the enemy had been stored, and he placed there a garrison of Jews. He also fortified Joppa, which is by the sea, and Gazara, which is on the borders of

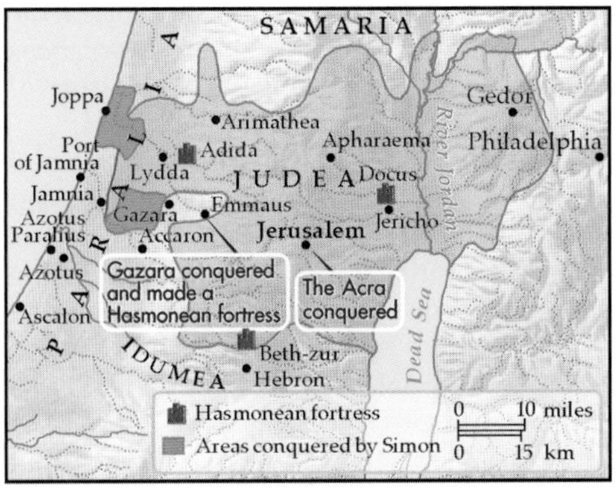


**The Conquests of Simon (142–135 bce)**

Azotus, where the enemy formerly dwelt. He settled Jews there, and provided in those cities whatever was necessary for their restoration. (1 Macc 14:33–34)

The Hasmonean had personally overseen the conquest of Beth-zur before his brother's death (1 Macc 11:65–66). Now he fortified this strategic point in Jerusalem's southern defense. Simon had also led troops against Joppa (1 Macc 10:74–75; 12:33). Yet, the loyalty of its residents remained a question. So, he sent troops to Joppa to strengthen the defensive posture of this important port city (1 Macc 13:11; *Ant.* 13:202). He also expelled the occupants and replaced them with his own sympathizers.

Gazara still lay in hostile hands (1 Macc 9: 52), situated in the territory of Azotus (1 Macc 14:34). It was located on the route between Jerusalem and Joppa, the capital's seaward outlet to the Mediterranean. Historically, the site of Old Testament Gezer also controlled the Aijalon Valley and consequent access to the Ascents of Beth-horon and Jerusalem. So, the security of Jerusalem and its economic livelihood were vulnerable, while Gazara remained a Seleucid stronghold.

Simon encamped against Gazara (cf. *Ant.* 13:215; *War* 1:50; *contra* 1 Macc 13:43; cf. 13:53) and surrounded it with troops. . . . Simon reached an agreement with them and stopped fighting against them. But he expelled them from the city and cleansed the houses in which the idols were, and then entered it with hymns of praise. He cast out of it all uncleanness, and settled in it men who observed the law. He also strengthened its fortifications and built in it a house for himself. (1 Macc 13:43–48)

Simon's actions regarding the idols of Gazara are no doubt connected to a heightened concern for ritual defilement with his personal residence now there. As the high priest, he had to maintain a higher degree of ritual purity (cf. m. *ʿAbod. Zar.* 3: 6–7; m. *Šabb.* 9:1). He also strengthened the fortifications of the city. Gazara now gained newfound strategic importance in the country second only to the capital, because it was the residence of the leader of the nation and stood in guard of the Holy City.

The last vestige of Antiochus IV Epiphanes' Hellenizing efforts was the Citadel in Jerusalem. No Hasmonean leader had successfully vacated the fortress. The strategy of blockading the occupants within the fortress, which had begun under Jonathan, now achieved triumph. According to 1 Maccabees, some of the occupants inside died of starvation. "Then they cried to Simon to make peace with them, and he did so. But he expelled them from there and cleansed the citadel from its pollutions" (1 Macc 13:50; cf. *Meg. Taʿan.* 23 Iyyar).

Both 1 Maccabees and Josephus depict the surrender of the Citadel. Josephus also supplies details of Simon's subsequent actions against the symbol of the pro-Greek faction in Jerusalem.

[Simon] also took the citadel at Jerusalem by siege, razing it to the ground that it might not serve his foes as a base to occupy and do mischief from it, as they were then doing. Having done this, he thought it would be an excellent thing and to his advantage to level also the hill on which the citadel stood, in order that the temple might be higher than this. . . . And so they all set to and began to level the hill, and without stopping work night or day, after three whole years brought it down to the ground and the surface of the plain. (*Ant.* 13:215–217; cf. *War* 5:139)

As we have noted, the location of the Citadel is still a matter of debate. Thus, no physical evidence of the dismantling of the Citadel or the leveling of the place on which it stood has been identified from modern excavations in the area of the Temple Mount. Josephus' claim that Simon utterly destroyed the Citadel disagrees with the subsequent report of 1 Maccabees that Simon, "settled Jews in [the Citadel], and fortified it for the safety of the country and of the city, and built the walls of Jerusalem higher" (1 Macc 14:37).

The absence of Demetrius II gave rise to a new pretender to the Seleucid throne. His brother Antiochus VII was on the isle of Rhodes (1 Macc 15:1), when he received word of Demetrius' capture (App. *Syr.* 68). According to Justin he was still a young boy (Justin. *Epit.* 36.1.8). Yet, according to Josephus, Cleopatra Thea, the wife of Demetrius I (and former wife of Alexander Balas), invited her brother-in-law to Seleucia, to marry her and to take the throne from Tryphon (*Ant.* 13:222). Her initiative was likely motivated out of fear for hers and her children's lives. Tryphon still controlled much of Syrian territory, but his treachery had shifted the support of the army to Cleopatra (*Ant.* 13:222; Diod. Sic. 33.28; Strabo *Geog.* 16.2.10).

While still in Rhodes, Antiochus VII received a letter from Simon seeking reaffirmation of the concessions awarded by Demetrius II. In reality Antiochus' concessions were merely an accommodation to the political realities of the moment. As yet, he possessed no political power. He could afford to be magnanimous. In time, however, he would attempt to rescind his generosity when the diadem was securely his.

I confirm to you all the tax remissions that the kings before me have granted you, and release from all the other payments from which they have released you. I permit you to mint your own coinage as money for your country, and I grant freedom to Jerusalem and the sanctuary. All the weapons which you have prepared and the strongholds which you have built and now hold shall remain yours. Every debt you owe to the royal treasury and any such future debts shall be canceled for you from henceforth and for all time. (1 Macc 15:5–8)

We are informed that Simon was granted the right to mint coins (1 Macc 15:6), a particular act denoting political independence. Yet, no coins from this period have been discovered, which has led to a debate regarding the reliability of the account.

In 139 bce Antiochus VII Sidetes defeated Tryphon on the field of battle near Antioch. Tryphon fled through Phoenicia to Dor (Burj eṭ-Ṭantura). The royal fortress of Dor was located in the Seleucid eparchy of Paralia (the coastal plain) that extended from the Ladder of Tyre to the Brook of Egypt. Here Tryphon was besieged in the royal fortress. "[Antiochus] surrounded the

*It has been proposed that remnants of the walls of the Seleucid Citadel in Jerusalem are identifiable in the eastern wall of the Temple Mount, north of "the seam," shown here, that demarks the southern extension added by Herod the Great. This suggestion challenges Josephus' report that the Citadel was totally dismantled and the elevation on which it stood leveled. However, by the first century* ce *Herod's expansion on the Temple Mount would have encompassed and fully integrated any previous Seleucid or Hasmonean construction. So, it is possible that the Jewish historian was unaware of remnants from the Citadel that were incorporated into Herod's building, and he unknowingly exaggerated Simon's attempt to remove entirely the Citadel of Antiochus IV Epiphanes.*

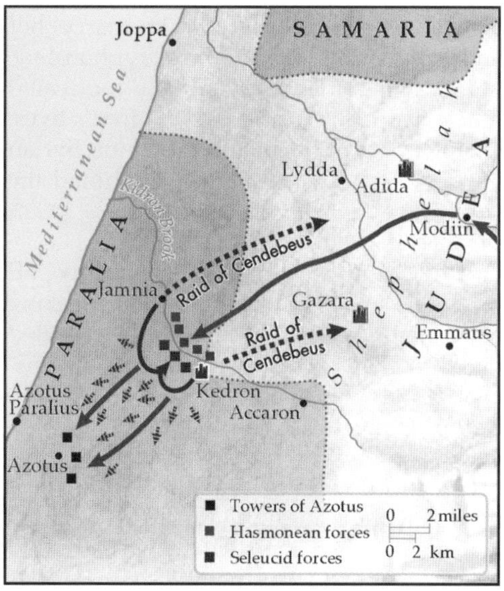


**The Battle of Kedron (137 bce)**

city, and the ships joined battle from the sea; he pressed the city hard from land and sea, and permitted no one to leave or enter it" (1 Macc 15:14; *Ant.* 13:223).

At this point in the narrative of 1 Maccabees the *senatus consultum* in response to Simon is reportedly received in Jerusalem. It guaranteed the Jewish people possession of the territory of Judea (1 Macc 15:15–24). It also established a friendship alliance and non-aggression pact between Rome and Judea. Its placement at this point in the narrative may have been the author's attempt to explain Antiochus VII's sudden change in attitude toward Simon. Whereas his previous generosity had been a mere political accommodation, Antiochus now realized that it would not be a simple matter to dispose of Simon and the Jewish territorial claim to Judea. Rome's support of the Hasmonean right to Judea stood as an impediment to the Seleucid's grand design.

Whatever his motivation, 1 Maccabees depicts Antiochus rejecting the offer of military and material assistance by Simon.

> Simon sent to Antiochus two thousand picked men, to fight for him, and silver and gold and much military equipment. But he refused to receive them and broke all the agreements he formerly had made with Simon, and became estranged from him.
> (1 Macc 15:26–27)

Josephus lacks any hint of this refusal of military assistance, and instead records the cordial correspondence between Antiochus VII and Simon during the siege of Dor, which serves as an epitome of the letter recorded in 1 Maccabees 15:1–9.

> [Antiochus] also sent envoys to Simon, the high priest of the Jews, to propose a friendly alliance. And Simon gladly accepted his offer, and lavishly supplied the soldiers who were besieging Dora with great sums of money and provisions, which he sent to Antiochus, so that for a short while he was considered one of his closest friends.
> (*Ant.* 13:223–224)

Eventually, in both accounts Antiochus VII reversed his attitude towards Simon and Judea. He sent an emissary, Athenobius, to demand that Simon relinquish his control of the coastal cities of Joppa and Gazara, which lay outside of the territory of Judea, as well as the Citadel in Jerusalem. His demand threatened the political and economic life of the Hasmonean state. The Seleucid acted to reduce the measure of Simon's political territory, in order to control Jerusalem's access to international trade and to curb the new freedoms recently realized. Judea would once again be subject to the pleasures of the Seleucid kings.

> Now then, hand over the cities which you have seized and the tribute money of the places which you have conquered outside the borders of Judea; or else give me for them five hundred talents of silver, and for the destruction that you have caused and the tribute money of the cities, five hundred talents more. Otherwise, we will come and conquer you.
> (1 Macc 15:30–31)

The single sum indemnity demanded by Antiochus, which signified Antioch's sovereignty over these cities, was countered by Simon's offer to pay a lower sum (1 Macc 15:35; cf. *Ant.* 17:320).

During this time, Tryphon escaped by ship to Orthosia (Pliny *Nat. Hist.* 5.17; Ptol. *Geog.* 5.14) north of Tripolis. He continued on to Apamea (*Ant.* 13:224), where he would eventually be captured and killed (cf. App. *Syr.* 68; Strabo *Geog.* 14.5.2). For the time being, the cessation of hostilities on the coast allowed Antiochus VII to turn brief attention to Simon, who had refused his demands. The new king appointed Cendebeus viceroy of Paralia (1 Macc 15:38), the coastal region that extended just north of the disputed city of Joppa and from Gaza to the Brook of Egypt. While Antiochus pursued Tryphon, it would fall to his new appointee to wrest the disputed cities from Hasmonean control.

The Seleucid commander marched with his infantry and cavalry into the territorial triangle of Joppa-Jamnia-Azotus that divided the province of Paralia in two. He had been instructed by Antiochus to establish a base of operations opposite the territory of Judea (1 Macc 15:39; cf. 4:61; 5:37). Based outside of Judea, Cendebeus executed raids against the surrounding local population. Josephus provides few geographical details in *Antiquities* or his earlier account in *War* about Cendebeus' campaign. The author of 1 Maccabees records that Cendebeus set up camp at Kedron (Qatra; cf. Eus. *Onom.* 68:22).

Kedron was strategically located southeast of Jamnia and well positioned for military forays (1 Macc 15:40; cf. LXX Dan 11:10, 25) against Jamnia and towns in the Shephelah of Judea. The well-fortified Hellenistic city of Azotus, which remained allied to the Seleucid kingdom, was also nearby in case retreat became necessary (cf. 1 Macc 16:10). It has been suggested that another base of operation may be indicated by 1 Maccabees (15:39)—i.e., Shaaraim, which was rendered literally "gates" in Josephus' Greek source.

The biblical city of Shaaraim is mentioned near the site of Gederah/Kedron in Joshua 15:36. Additionally, on another occasion in the Septuagint, the translators likewise misread the proper name Shaaraim for "gates" in their rendering in 1 Samuel 17:52. If correct, together Kedron and Shaaraim provided Cendebeus a staging area for incursions from the lower Sorek Valley.

The Seleucid raids on the Jewish villages provoked a military response from the Hasmoneans. John Hyrcanus traveled from Gazara to Jerusalem to report to his father what Cendebeus had done. The author of 1 Maccabees states that Simon, because of his advancing age, delegated his sons, Judas and John, to take his place to defend the nation (1 Macc 16:1–3; *contra Ant.* 13:226; *War* 1: 52). John and his brother quickly mustered troops to surprise the Seleucids at Kedron. The Jewish army comprised of infantry and cavalry bivouacked in Modiin to prepare for their advance on Cendebeus (1 Macc 16:4). This is the first mention of a Jewish cavalry.

The Jewish forces began their march 15 miles (25 km) from the low hills surrounding Modiin, past Gazara and into the lower portions of the Sorek Valley. Early in the morning they continued onto the plain opposite Kedron, while the Seleucid army stood to meet them on the other side of the Sorek stream that courses by Kedron. Hyrcanus' men were afraid to cross the streambed in their advance on the Seleucid army, so Hyrcanus led them across and into battle.

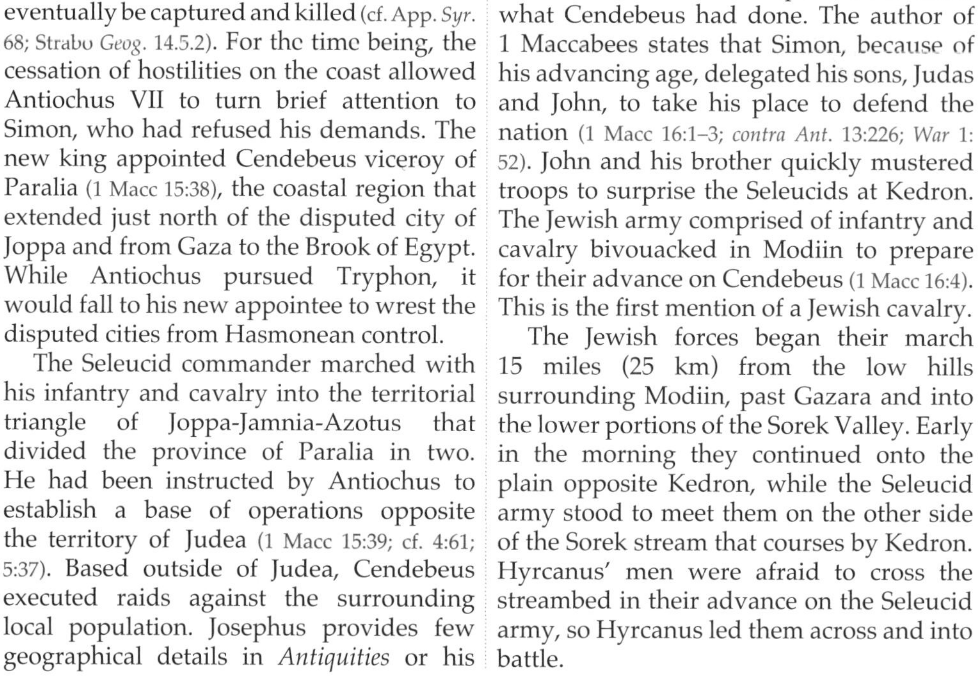

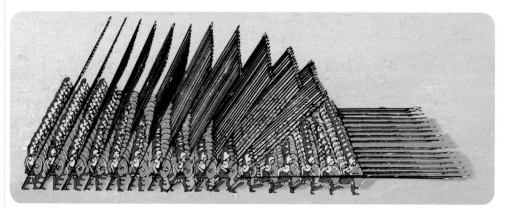

*Macedonian phalanx.*

The Seleucid formation was typical with a phalanx flanked by two units of cavalry. Significantly outnumbered, John divided his cavalry and infantry, interspersing them (1 Macc 16:7), perhaps imitating a Roman battlefield formation. In the fighting Judas was wounded in battle, but John led his troops in a rout of the Seleucids. Cendebeus retreated to Kedron, while others fled "into the towers that were in the fields of Azotus" (1 Macc 16:10). The text is unclear concerning the object of Hyrcanus' retribution, "he burned it with fire." The singular pronoun suggests Kedron, but Azotus may also have been intended (cf. 1 Macc 10:84). In any event, it is interesting that the description of "towers in the fields of Azotus" may be depicted on the Byzantine Medeba Map that has several towers pictured in the territory surrounding Azotus.

External danger now abated, but Simon and his family would ultimately fall at the hands of his own family. His son-in-law, Ptolemy the son of Abubus, was appointed governor of Jericho. He decided to remove Simon and his sons through treachery in order to seize control of the country for himself. In February 134 BCE Simon and two of his sons, Judas and Mattathias, were visiting Ptolemy at Dok (Jebel Qarantal), a small fortress built by Ptolemy (1 Macc 16:15) overlooking Jericho. The governor spread a banquet for the family, and when Simon and his sons became drunk, Ptolemy and his men killed them. Ptolemy then sought aid and support from Antiochus Sidetes. He also sent men to apprehend John Hyrcanus who was at Gazara and to secure the Temple in Jerusalem.

According to 1 Maccabees, Hyrcanus killed the men sent to apprehend him. Josephus, instead, describes Hyrcanus' flight to Jerusalem, where he gained support from the people and rebuffed Ptolemy's attempt to seize either the Temple or the remaining son of Simon. John was awarded the high priesthood of his father and marched on Ptolemy at Dok. In a dramatic portrayal, Josephus describes Ptolemy's murder of Simon's wife and daughters at Dok and his escape because of the sabbatical year to Zenon, tyrant of Philadelphia (*Ant.* 13:230–235).

## JOHN HYRCANUS (135–104 BCE)

The rule of John Hyrcanus extended over thirty years, longer than any other figure in the Hasmonean dynasty. The sons of Mattathias, who formed the first generation of Hasmonean leadership in Judea, were occupied primarily in the defense of the fledgling state. Now the volatile and quick-paced changes in the struggle for power in the Seleucid kingdom diverted much of Antioch's attention away from Judea, which resulted in a period of relative calm

*Coin of John Hyrcanus.*

during Hyrcanus' tenure. The narrative of 1 Maccabees concludes with the death of Simon and the unsuccessful attempt by the Hasmonean to avenge his father's murder. The final lines present a brief sketch of Hyrcanus' achievements (1 Macc 16:23–24). Other historical witnesses for his rule are the works of Josephus—which were for the most part reliant upon the annals of Nicholas of Damascus—and occasional references in rabbinical literature (e.g. m. *Maᶜaś. Š.* 5:15; m. *Soṭah* 9:10; m. *Parah* 3:5; m. *Yad.* 4:6).

Antiochus Sidetes returned to Judea to finish the uncompleted task of Cendebeus to return Joppa and Gazara to Seleucid domination (*War* 1:61). He invaded Judea in the first year of Hyrcanus' rule and ravaged the country (*Ant.* 13:236). He then besieged Jerusalem, but the strength of the walls prevented easy victory. Josephus' passing mention of the scarcity of water for the Seleucid troops during the siege may indicate that the waters of the Gihon that flow through Hezekiah's Tunnel into the Pool of Siloam were within the city walls in that day, and thus inaccessible to Jerusalem's attackers (*Ant.* 13:237).

The main thrust of the Seleucid attack came from the northern side of the city—historically its point of vulnerability—with towers upon which "were mounted companies of soldiers" (*Ant.* 13:238). The vigorous efforts of those defending their city led to a protracted siege. According to Josephus, the fighting ceased in an unusual manner. Upon the arrival of the Jewish Feast of Tabernacles, Hyrcanus appealed to Sidetes for a seven-day truce. "Antiochus, deferring to his piety toward the Deity, granted and moreover sent a magnificent sacrifice" (*Ant.* 13:243; cf. Plut. *Mor.* 184 E–F). The intent of this legend in *Antiquities* seems to be an explanation of Antiochus' moniker, the Pious, which Josephus repeats earlier (*Ant.* 7:393). Neither the legend nor the moniker appear in the epitomized version of the siege of Jerusalem in *Jewish War* 1:61. The generous description of Antiochus may also be an anticipation of Hyrcanus' participation in the king's campaign to Parthia (*Ant.* 13:249–253), an event also lacking in *Jewish War*.

Both of Josephus' histories, however, depict the end of the Seleucid blockade of Jerusalem upon the condition that the high priest agree to pay tribute for "Joppa and the other cities bordering on Judea" (*Ant.* 13:246). This concession is an acknowledgement that the cities belonged to the Seleucid kingdom. Josephus in his earlier account described Hyrcanus' payment as a bribe "to Antiochus to raise the blockade" (*War* 1:61). Yet, the high priest's strategy proved to be the better part of wisdom. Rather than challenging the militarily superior king, the Hasmonean would await the inevitable change in power to reassert his claim at a time (and under conditions) more advantageous to Judea.

Antiochus also demanded the return of a Seleucid garrison to Jerusalem, but Hyrcanus refused. Unlike Joppa and the cities on the borders of Judea, there had never been a question about Judea's claim to Jerusalem. It was recognized as an integral part of Judea and administrated by the high priest. The high priest countered the king with an offer of hostages to guarantee that no further insurrection would originate from Jerusalem or Judea. Before their departure the Seleucids pulled down the walls or battlements (*Ant.* 13:247; cf. Diod. Sic. 34.1; *Meg. Taᶜan.* 21 Kislev) of the city, which may explain why Hyrcanus found it necessary later to rebuild the walls of Jerusalem after Antiochus Sidetes' death (cf. 1 Macc 16:23).

Josephus recounts that Hyrcanus marched with Sidetes on his Parthian campaign, an indication of the improved relationship between Antioch and Jerusalem. According to the testimony of Nicholas of Damascus that Josephus preserves, Antiochus even remained encamped two days on the Lycus (Greater Zab) River at Hyrcanus' request, so that the Jewish conscripts not transgress the Sabbath and Pentecost that fell the next day (*Ant.* 13:251–252). The story may be fanciful, but the calendaric detail underpinning the legend could also give us a hint of the pro-Sadducean predilections of John Hyrcanus, which eventually led to open conflict with the Pharisees (cf. Lev 23:11; b. *Menaḥ.* 65a). After Hyrcanus' return to Judea, Antiochus VII Sidetes perished in battle. Demetrius II, who had been released from Parthian captivity and put forward as an imperial contender to Antiochus, succeeded his brother and resumed the throne in Antioch that he had previously held.

When word of Antiochus' death in 129 BCE reached Hyrcanus, he assumed that the attention of the Syrian kingdom would be focused on the war in Parthia and the succession of power in Antioch. Little concern would be given to local skirmishes among the Syrian cities in the Transjordan. We have few geographical details about Hyrcanus' military incursions into the

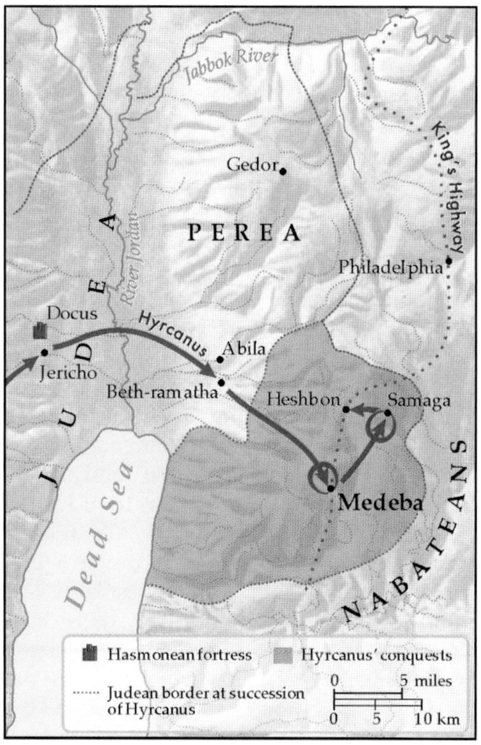


**The Conquests of Hyrcanus Beyond the Jordan (128 bce)**

Transjordan. He first captured Medeba (Josh 13:9; 1 Macc 9:36; Eus. *Onom.* 128:19) after a lengthy and difficult siege, and then he proceeded eight miles northeast to take Samaga (*Ant.* 13:255; Kh. Samik). Both of these cities lay beyond the Jewish settlements of Perea, a territory previously administrated by the Tobiads (*Ant.* 12:160; 12:239–240).

Josephus makes no mention in the present campaign of Heshbon, the metropolis of the region. Since it is later listed as one of the cities of Alexander Jannaeus (*Ant.* 13:397), but without any record of the son of Hyrcanus' conquest, it is reasonable to assume that John Hyrcanus himself took Heshbon at this time. Hyrcanus' immediate interest in these cities was access to the historic King's Highway that ran from Damascus to the Gulf of Elath. The Hasmonean's seizure of the Nabatean cities of Medeba and Heshbon were a challenge to the Nabatean kingdom's control of the Transjordan and the vital economic trade routes that ran through it.

Hyrcanus next turned his attention to Samaria, the region north of Judea that prevented contiguous Jewish settlement between Judea and Galilee. Jewish communities in southern Samaria in the Hellenistic period are attested in the transfer to Judea of the three Samarian nomes of Lydda, Haramatha and Apharaema by successive Seleucid kings. The Gophna hills in Samaria had also been a safe haven for Hasmonean fighters in the early days of the revolt. Yet, from the Persian period Samaritan-Judean relationships had been a source of unrest (cf. Ezra 4).

The language of Josephus' narrative employs the pejorative jargon of the Jewish people regarding the Samaritans. The Old Testament tradition presents the residents as a mixture of Jews who had intermarried with gentiles brought by Shalmaneser from "Babylon and Cuthah" (2 Kgs 17:24–41; *Ant.* 9:288). Thus, in rabbinical literature the Samaritans are regularly referred to derisively as "Cutheans" (e.g. m. *Ber.* 7:1; 8:8) and their region "the land of the Cutheans" (*Lam. Rab.* 3:7).

Hyrcanus attacked Shechem and Mount Gerizim, site of the Samaritan temple (2 Macc 6:2; cf. *Meg. Ta<sup>c</sup>an.* 21 Kislev). He also subdued Idumea taking Adora (cf. *Ant.* 13:396) and Marisa (cf. *Ant.* 12:353). In an unprecedented step, he allowed them to remain in their country, if they would agree to submit to circumcision "and were willing to observe the laws of the Jews" (*Ant.* 13:257). Proselytism on such a scale was unprecedented in the ancient world. Nevertheless, "from that time on they have continued to be Jews" (*Ant.* 13:258).

Once regional matters were in hand, Hyrcanus followed the example of his predecessors to renew his alliance with Rome. He rightly understood that this was necessary to offset the pressures from Antioch to reacquire the cities lost under Demetrius and Antiochus. Rome reaffirmed, "that Joppa and its harbours and Gazara and Pegae and whatever other cities and territories Antiochus (Sidetes) took from them in war (cf. *Ant.* 13:246), contrary to the decree of the Senate, be restored to them" (*Ant.* 13:262). Laws imposed upon Judea by

*Remains of Samaritan temple on the top of Mount Gerizim. In the Hellenistic period the Samaritans had built a temple to rival that in Jerusalem (cf. John 4:20). Josephus notes that it had been modeled after the Jewish temple, and "Alexander permitted their governor Sanaballetes to build [it] for the sake of his son-in-law Manasses, brother of the high priest Jaddua"* (Ant. *13:256; cf.* Ant. *11:322–324).*

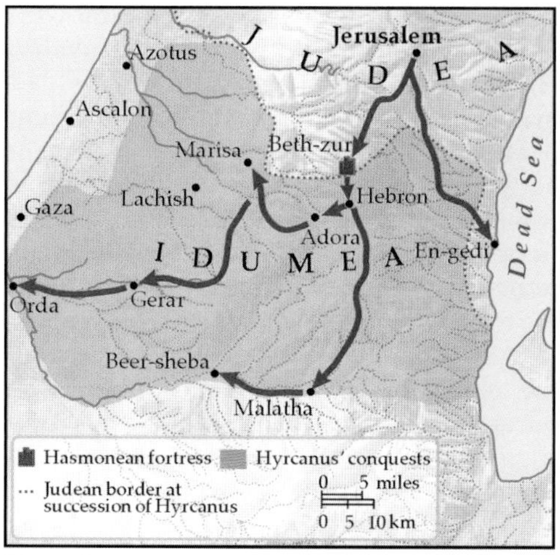


**The Conquests of Hyrcanus in Idumea (112 bce)**

Antiochus were also revoked. In effect, Hyrcanus' strategy of accommodating rather than confronting Antiochus Sidetes had succeeded. With Antiochus now gone, the status quo reverted to the situation prior to his campaign in Judea.

Rome even ceded control of Pegae (bib. Aphek) to Judea. Since biblical times the strategic importance of this site was recognized. Travel north and south on the coastal plain narrowed at this juncture. West of the Rosh ha-<sup>c</sup>Ayin springs, the Nahr el-Aujā flowed from its source and prevented travel through the coastal plain. The narrow passageway to the east, between the springs and the lower slopes of the Samarian Hills, controlled the most important international route in the region.

In an earlier age this area had been a point of struggle between the Philistines on the coast and the Israelites in the hill country (1 Sam 4–6). Later Herod the Great would found a nearby city and name it for his father—Antipatris—to secure this vital passageway. In the Hellenistic period it retained its Greek name Pegae (springs) that rendered the meaning of its semitic toponym, Aphek (Râs el-<sup>c</sup>Ain). Zenon in the journals of his travels notes that it was the site of a frontier guard.

In Antioch a dizzying series of changes kept the empire preoccupied with the succession of power. "The war between them gave Hyrcanus leisure to exploit Judea undisturbed, with the result that he amassed a limitless sum of money" (*Ant.* 13:273). With the diversion of attention in Syria, Hyrcanus extended his domination of Samaria by marching on the city that gave its name to the region.

> Advancing to Samaria, on the site of which now stands the city of Sebaste, founded by King Herod, [Hyrcanus] blockaded it by a surrounding wall and entrusted the siege to his sons Aristobulus and Antigonus, who pressed it so vigorously that the inhabitants were reduced by the extremities of famine to make use of the most unheard of food.
> (*War* 1:64)

The residents of Samaria appealed

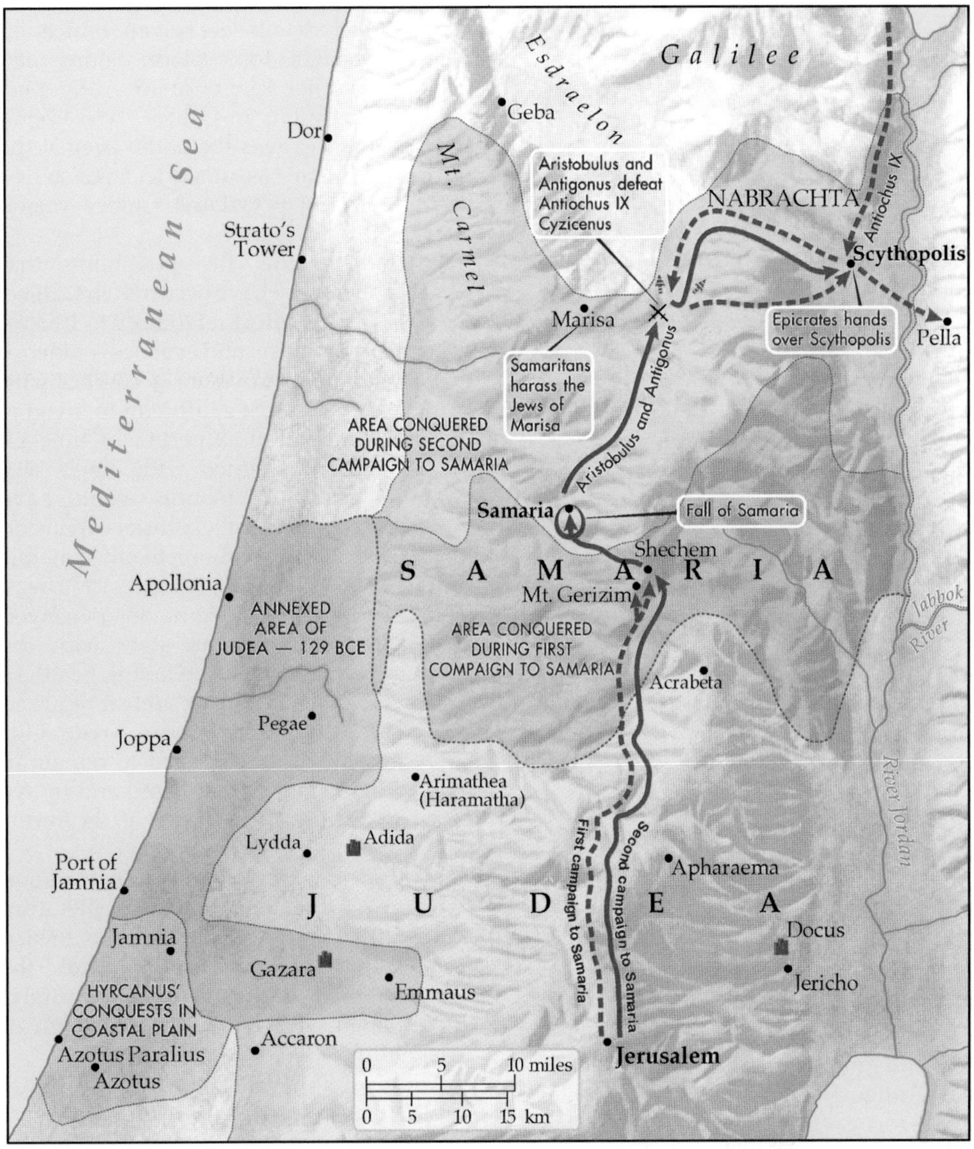


**The Conquests of Hyrcanus in Samaria and the Coastal Plain (126–104 bce)**

to Antiochus IX Cyzicenus (*contra War* 1:65: Aspendius) for help. He came to their aid but was turned back by the sons of Hyrcanus at Scythopolis (*Ant.* 13:277). They appealed a second time and the Syrian king sought the assistance of the Egyptian Ptolemy Lathyrus. Ignoring his mother's protests, he sent six thousand men to march with Cyzicenus, "who ravaged Hyrcanus' territory like a brigand" (*Ant.* 13:278). The Seleucid did not challenge Hyrcanus face-to-face but launched secondary strikes in an attempt to draw the Jewish army away from its siege of Samaria.

Antiochus Cyzicenus departed to Tripolis and left the command of his forces to Callimandrus and Epicrates. The former fell in battle, while Josephus reports that Epicrates relinquished control of Scythopolis for a bribe. In his earlier report in *Jewish War* 1:66 the historian relates that the Jewish forces took Scythopolis by force. In any event, the result was Judean domination of the region of Scythopolis, the Jezreel Valley and the coastal Plain of Sharon, or in the words of Josephus, "the whole country south of Mount Carmel" (*War* 1:66). The city of Samaria likewise fell to the Hasmonean siege (*Meg. Taᶜan.* 21 Kislev). Hyrcanus "effaced it entirely and left it to be swept away by the mountain-torrents" (*Ant.* 13:281).

No further report is given of territorial expansions under Hyrcanus. Josephus' concluding paragraphs concern the high priest's deterioriating relationship with the Pharisees and his gift of prophecy. According to a legend preserved by Josephus that is also recounted in rabbinical literature, Hyrcanus was alone in the Temple while his sons were battling Cyzicenus. "[He] heard a voice saying that his sons had just defeated Antiochus. And on coming out of the temple he revealed this to the entire multitude, and so it actually happened" (*Ant.* 13:282–283; cf. b. *Soṭah* 9:33a; j. *Soṭah* 9:13; *Cant. Rab.* 8:9; t. *Soṭah* 13:5). Josephus volunteers that to Hyrcanus alone was granted,

> to unite in his person three of the highest privileges: the supreme command of the nation, the high priesthood, and the gift of prophecy. For so closely was he in touch with the Deity, that he was never ignorant of the future. (*War* 1:68–69)

The accumulation of "the three crowns" (cf. Philo, *Moses* 2) that was incorporated as a central tenet of early Christian Christology is first attributed to John Hyrcanus. Nevertheless, Josephus concludes that it was his son, Aristobulus and not Hyrcanus, who "transformed the government into a monarchy, and was the first [of the Hasmoneans] to assume the diadem" (*War* 1:70; *contra* Strabo *Geog.* 16.2.40). In other words, unlike his sons, John Hyrcanus never assumed the title king.

## Aristobulus I (104–103 bce)

In contrast to his father, the reign of Aristobulus was the briefest of the Hasmonean Dynasty. In many respects, as told by Josephus, his life resembled a Greek tragedy. Hyrcanus left the high priesthood to his eldest son, but the realm to his wife. Ignoring his father's wishes, Aristobulus' first act was to put his brothers in chains and his mother in prison, where she soon died of starvation—and thus eliminated his rival for the diadem. Antigonus, the brother with whom he had fought side-by-side in battle (*Ant.* 13:276; *War* 1:64–65) maintained the king's affection and was not imprisoned.

Aristobulus appears first in Josephus' narrative in the campaign against Antiochus Cyzicenus when he proved himself to be an accomplished soldier (*Ant.* 13:276–277). Nothing is heard of his personal involvement in the military campaigns during his brief tenure as king. There are repeated references to his illness (*Ant.* 13:304, 307; *War* 1:73, 81–84) and it may be that he was not well enough to lead the army. Antigonus seems to have led them in his place. Once when Antigonus returned from a victorious campaign to Jerusalem, he even found it necessary to serve in place of his brother as high priest for the Feast of Tabernacles (*Ant.* 13:304).

Salome (*Ant.* 13:320), the wife of Aristobulus, suspected Antigonus' ambitions

*Entrance hall to tomb cave I at Marisa (biblical Mareshah), Hellenistic period.*

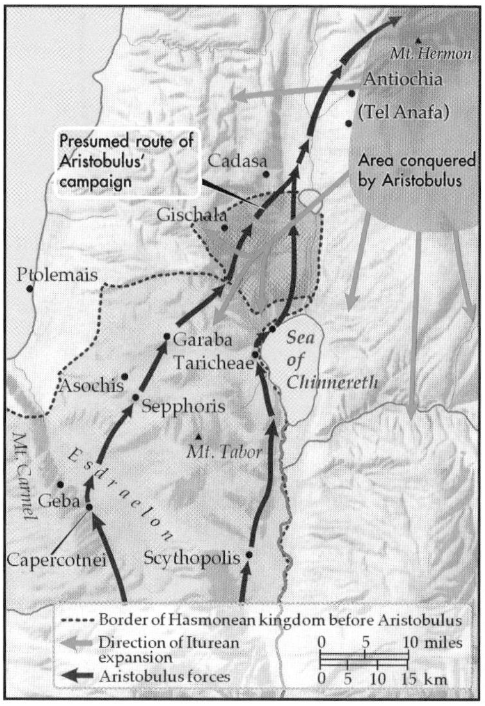


**Aristobulus Conquers the Itureans (104–103 bce)**

and plotted his demise. The king had instructed his brother not to enter the royal residence armed. Yet, when he sent for his brother, Salome persuaded the messenger to request that Antigonus come adorned with the "fine armour and military decorations" that he had procured on a recent campaign in Galilee (*War* 1:76). She did this knowing the bodyguards were under instructions to kill Antigonus, if he attempted to enter the royal fortress armed (cf. *War* 1:118).

Events proceeded as Salome had planned, and Antigonus was killed in a passageway from the Temple precincts into the Baris called "Strato's Tower." Confusion between the name of the passageway and a Hellenistic village by the same name, where later Herod built Caesarea, was the seed for a narrative sidebar concerning a local prophet named Judah (*Ant.* 13:311–313; *War* 1:78–80), the first historical figure identified by Josephus to be an Essene. The grief-stricken king mourned the tragic death of his brother and grew more ill until he finally died (*Ant.* 3: 316–318).

Immediately the queen released the imprisoned brothers of the dead king. There is no mention of any child born to Aristobulus, and some scholars suggest that Salome's act to appoint "as king Jannaeus, also known as Alexander" (*Ant.* 13:320) was likewise a proposal for levirate marriage. However, such a marriage is never indicated by Josephus, and recently it has been demonstrated that although the wives of Aristobulus and Jannaeus shared similar names, they should not be identified.

One of the important legacies from the short reign of Aristobulus was his defeat of the Itureans, Arab tribes who settled in the second century BCE in southern Lebanon. No geographical details are given indicating where the fight took place. Some read Josephus' earlier reference to Antigonus' military campaign "in Galilee" (*War* 1:76) to suggest that this was the battle against the Itureans, who are assumed to have settled in the sparsely populated Galilee region after the days of Simon.

Notwithstanding the possibility that some fighting may have occurred in Galilee, there are no historical references to Iturean settlement in Galilee, and even less evidence that Aristobulus provoked a conflict with them there. Indeed, it is difficult to imagine that after such a short period of time on the throne and plagued with illness and domestic crises, Aristobulus would have initiated a campaign of territorial expansion (*Ant.* 13:318). It seems more likely that this conflict was a defensive reaction to Iturean incursions into the Galilee, having perceived a weakened Hasmonean state with the death of Hyrcanus and the failing health of his successor. The Itureans' defeat required territorial concessions, but Aristobulus offered them, "if they wished to remain in their country, to be circumcised and to live in accordance with the laws of the Jews" (*Ant.* 13:318).

In the previous century, a common opinion repeated in scholarly literature argued that Simon evacuated the Jewish communities of the Galilee, and the region remained (virtually or entirely) unpopulated with Jews until the reign of Aristobulus.

Quite simply, the assumption that Aristobulus conquered Iturean settlements in the Galilee has no foundation in the archaeological data. To the contrary, a recent survey by the Israel Antiquities Authority in the Upper Galilee region, which adjoined Iturea, found an absence of evidence for Iturean settlement.

The statement that the Galilee was "more Gentile than Jewish" is a generalization that takes little account of the complex regional dynamics that distinguished Upper and Lower Galilee. In late antiquity Jewish settlement was more pronounced in Lower Galilee than Upper Galilee, and there certainly is no material evidence to suggest that the Lower Galilee was emptied of Jewish population or overwhelmingly outnumbered by pagan settlements. The historical witnesses point us to the same conclusions.

Jonathan earlier marched to Hazor to battle the generals of Demetrius II who were encamped at Kedesh (*Ant.* 13:158–162). Josephus reports that Jonathan responded to the external Seleucid threat in the north, because "he would not suffer the Galileans, who were of his own people, to be attacked by the enemy" (*Ant.* 13:154). The historian's statement assumes a Jewish presence in Galilee *after* Simon's removal of Jewish communities in western Galilee.

In addition, in the first year of Alexander Jannaeus' reign, Josephus reports that Ptolemy Lathyrus, king of Cyprus, took advantage of the Sabbath to attack Asochis (*Ant.* 13:337; *War* 1:86; Tel Ḥannaton), an observant Jewish village in the Bêt Neṭôfa Valley of lower western Galilee. It is difficult to explain the sudden appearance of such established, observant villages in such a short time, if until the previous year Galilee had lacked a Jewish presence.

Finally, Josephus reports that Alexander Jannaeus was "brought up in Galilee from his birth" (*Ant.* 13:322). The high priest would hardly have sent his son to be raised in a pagan environment. Thus, the historian provides yet another testimony to a Jewish presence in the Galilee *before* Aristobulus' campaign.

The results of an etymological study concerning the toponym, Gennosar, may be of some corollary importance. The political titles employed by the Hasmoneans were traced to conclude that the term *sar* ("Prince") began to be used in Judea in the time of Simon or his son John Hyrcanus for the office held by them. The name Gennosar was derived from agricultural lands owned by the Hasmonean high priestly family on the northwest shores of the Sea of Galilee. These lands became known as the "gardens of the Prince," the toponym later being attached to the adjoining body of water, Lake Gennosar (*War* 3:515; *Ant.* 13:158).

The use of the title *sar* in the toponym attests both to the multilingual environment in Galilee in the late Hellenistic period—the Aramaic equivalent for the Hebrew would have been *rav*—and to a Jewish presence in the lower eastern Galilee after the events recorded in 1 Maccabees 5:21–23. If correct, the place of Jannaeus' boyhood may very well have been Hasmonean properties in the vicinity of the Sea of Galilee.

Individually these unrelated passages might carry little weight. However, in the absence of material evidence to the contrary their attestations together suggest a continued Jewish presence in the Galilee *after* Simon's rescue of the communities living in western Galilee near hostile pagan cities and *before* Aristobulus' conflict with the Itureans. Moreover, they suggest that when the Jewish historian records that Aristobulus offered the Itureans "to remain in their land" he meant the region of Iturea and not Galilee.

## Alexander Jannaeus (103–76 BCE)

The fratricidal violence that dominated the reign of Aristobulus continued at the inauguration of his brother's rule. Jannaeus executed a brother whom he thought to be a contender for the throne and allowed another, less ambitious brother to live (*Ant.* 13:323; *War* 1:85). The king then decided to march on cities on the Mediterranean coast:

*Limestone head of Tyche, Hellenistic period, from Dor.*

Ptolemais, Dor, Strato's Tower and Gaza (*Ant.* 13:324). Seafaring motifs decorated the Hasmonean family tomb in Modiin (1 Macc 13:29–30), and an inverted anchor appears on the obverse of Jannaeus' coins. Perhaps, the king's military campaign against the coastal cities was an initiative to fulfill the Hasmonean dynasty's desire to be a maritime power. The king's name, Alexander, also prompted him to adopt the Macedonian star associated with his illustrious namesake, Alexander the Great.

At the same time in Syria, Antiochus VIII Grypus and Antiochus IX Cyzicenus were destroying each other's armies in a nine-year war (105–96 BCE) for the Seleucid throne. They received a plea for help from Ptolemais, but neither could spare forces for the defense of the city. Zoilus, the ruler of Dor and Strato's Tower, saw the diversion in Syria as an opportunity to expand his own influence. He marshaled troops to Ptolemais but made little difference. The besieged city then appealed to Ptolemy Lathyrus, ruler of Cyprus, who had been exiled from Egypt by his mother, Cleopatra III (*Ant.* 13:328). Upon reconsideration, however, the city leaders changed their mind when they realized that an allegiance with Ptolemy would embroil them in Ptolemy's struggle with his mother. Cleopatra would never allow her estranged son to gain a foothold in the region for fear that he would use it to launch attacks against Egypt.

Ptolemy landed at Sycamina (Tell es-Samak; Strabo 16.2.27; Pliny *Nat. Hist.* 5.75; Eus. *Onom.* 108:30), unaware of the change of heart by the citizens of Ptolemais. Instead, Zoilus and the people of Gaza met him to seek his assistance in the defense of their cities, likewise under attack from Alexander Jannaeus. The Hasmonean was able to delay their pact with Ptolemy by pretending to seek a friendly alliance with Ptolemy, all the while secretly negotiating with Cleopatra. When Ptolemy discovered Jannaeus' ruse, he attacked Asochis (i.e. Shiḥin) and Sepphoris in the Lower Galilee. He overran the former (*War* 1:86), but seems to have been unable to capture Sepphoris (*Ant.* 13:338).

Ptolemy advanced to challenge Jannaeus at Asophon, "not far from the river Jordan" (*Ant.* 13:338; Tell es-Saᶜidiyeh). Jannaeus had maneuvered north through the friendly territory of Jewish Perea. He encamped on the eastern side of the Jordan to await Ptolemy, "thinking that he would the more easily take the enemy if they had the river behind them" (*Ant.* 13:340). After some hesitation, Ptolemy's troops crossed to meet Jannaeus. The fighting was fierce and both sides suffered heavy losses, but eventually Ptolemy's army prevailed.

Ptolemy now invaded Judea, committing atrocities with impunity (*Ant.* 13:345–347). He would have marched on Jerusalem, but Cleopatra intervened. She sent her navy with another son to Phoenicia and her army, under the direction of two Jewish generals, Chelkias and Ananias, sons of Onias the high priest at Heliopolis (cf. *Ant.* 13:285-287), to attack Ptolemy in Judea (*Ant.* 13:349). Meanwhile, she herself landed at Ptolemais and besieged the city. Ptolemy sought to take advantage of his mother's absence from Egypt and moved south to retake his homeland. Although Josephus provides no details, Cleopatra's army must have confronted her son's advance, because the historian records that Chelkias died in the pursuit of Ptolemy (*Ant.* 13:351). Cleopatra also returned part of her navy to Egypt and turned her son back at Pelusium (*Ant.* 13:358). Expelled once again from Egypt, Ptolemy spent the winter at the coastal city of Gaza and then returned to Cyprus.

Cleopatra finally captured Ptolemais and stood unchallenged to occupy Judea and add it to her kingdom. Yet, Ananias encouraged her to retain Jannaeus' rule over Judea and establish a treaty with him, which she did "at Scythopolis in Coele-Syria" (*Ant.* 13:355). Bolstered by his new alliance with Egypt, Jannaeus turned his attention to the borderlands of his kingdom. First, he ventured into the Transjordan. After a lengthy siege he took Gadara (Umm Qeis) and Amathus (Tell ᶜAmta; cf. *Ant.* 14:91; Eus. *Onom.* 22:23), "the greatest stronghold of those occupied beyond the Jordan" (*Ant.* 13: 356; *War* 1:86).

The king then campaigned on the coast in an attempt to isolate Gaza. He struck Rhinocorura (el-ᶜArish; Eus. *Onom.* 148:3; cf. *Ant.* 13:395), Raphia (Eus. *Onom.* 50:18) and Anthedon, i.e. Agrippias (Teda; Pliny *Nat. Hist.* 5.14), the coastal city that would later be granted by Augustus to Herod and rebuilt in honor of Marcus Vipsanius Agrippa, Caesar's general and son-in-law (cf. *War* 1: 87, 118). Gaza could now no longer seek aid from Egypt or the sea.

Jannaeus inflicted revenge upon the Gazans, who had invited the intervention of Ptolemy, who in turn had ravaged Judea. The besieged Gazans looked for help from the Nabatean Aretas II, but this hope never materialized. Apollodotus, the *strategos* of Gaza, led a fierce defense of the city, but his brother Lysimachus betrayed him and opened the city gates to Jannaeus. At first Jannaeus seemed he would take the city without further violence, but when the rage from the painful siege took hold of the troops, they destroyed the city and killed many of its citizens.

After the year-long siege in Gaza, Jannaeus returned to Jerusalem to find unrest among the populace. Josephus does not provide the reason for their disaffection, but it may be related to the king's continued close relationship with the aristocratic Sadducees and alienation from the Pharisees, who gave expression to more popular sentiments. In this Jannaeus followed in the footsteps of his father (cf. *Ant.* 13:296).

Josephus narrates an event at the Feast of Tabernacles in which the people demonstrated their displeasure with his actions by pelting the priest-king with citrons and by shouting that he was not fit to be priest (cf. *Ant.* 13:292; m. *Sukk.* 4:9; b. *Qidd.* 66a; cf. t. *Sukk.* 3:16; b. *Sukk.* 22b). Jannaeus responded with rage, killing six thousand people and erecting a wooden partition-wall (cf. *Ant.* 8:95; *War* 5:226, 6:125) to distance the people from the priests officiating in the Temple.

The internal unrest did not dissuade Jannaeus' drive to enlarge his kingdom. His next move was to encircle the Dead Sea and secure the rich bitumen trade from the Nabateans, a feat attempted but failed by Antigonus Monophthalmus (Diod. Sic.

*Coin of Alexander Jannaeus.*

*The* Pesher Nahum *scroll from Qumran.*

19:95–97). Hyrcanus had already secured a foothold in this region for his son. He had conquered the Judean Wilderness and the portions of Moab east of the Dead Sea to the Arnon Valley (*Ant.* 13:255; *War* 1:63). Jannaeus now subdued the Nabateans living in Moab and Gilead and forced them to pay tribute.

The king then continued in Gilead to return a second time to Amathus, destroying the city that had been abandoned by its king, Theodorus (*War* 1: 89; *Ant.* 13:374). Jannaeus campaigned against the Nabateans north into Gaulanitis, where he fought Obedas (*Ant.* 13:375; *War* 1:90), the king of the Nabateans, near the village of Garada. The Hasmonean was ambushed and nearly lost his life, but he was able to escape to Jerusalem.

Sensing the king's vulnerability, the people now rose up in open rebellion (*War* 1:91–92; *Ant.* 13:376). A six-year civil war broke out with a large loss of life. Josephus' estimate of fifty thousand dead may be inflated, but it underscores the seriousness of the conflict. So desperate were the people that they even sought the intervention of the Seleucid king, Demetrius III Akairos. Regarding these events, the Qumran Congregation interpreted Nahum 2:11b:

> [Interpreted, this concerns Deme]trius king of Greece who sought, on the counsel of those who seek smooth things, to enter Jerusalem. [But God did not permit the city to be delivered] into the hands of the kings of Greece, from the time of Antiochus until the coming of the rulers of the Kittim.
> (4Q469 f3–4i:2–3)

Perhaps, the Pharisees and their supporters considered it preferable to return to the pre-Hasmonean arrangement with Jewish autonomy in religious matters, while leaving the political affairs to Syria. Similar sentiments would be voiced to Pompey (*Ant.* 14:58–60) and Caesar Augustus (*Ant.* 17:342–343; *War* 2:111–113; Strabo *Geog.* 16.2.46). In any event, the Seleucid king was eager to oblige their offer.

Demetrius encamped near Shechem in preparation to march on Jannaeus in Jerusalem (*Ant.* 13:377–378; *War* 1:92–95). The country stood divided, a dilemma exemplified by Josephus' picture of the facing armies. Disaffected Jews had joined Demetrius in his campaign against Jannaeus. Sympathizers of the Hasmonean called out to them and appealed to their fellow Jews to abandon Demetrius and throw their support to Jannaeus. At the same time, Pisidian and Cilician mercenaries among Jannaeus' soldiers appealed to their fellow Greeks in Demetrius' camp to likewise defect. Neither side succeeded to undermine the morale of the other, so the fighting ensued.

Demetrius was victorious in battle, but his success engendered sympathy for Jannaeus among the Hasmonean's Jewish opponents. When they witnessed the king retreating into the hills, they reversed allegiances causing alarm to Demetrius. Josephus implies that it is for this reason Demetrius withdrew to Syria. He may have also been forced to retreat because of threats from his brother Philip in Syria, a rival contender for the throne (cf. *Ant.* 13:384).

Jannaeus now besieged Bemeselis (*War* 1:96; *Ant.* 13:380), where the rebels, who had continued the struggle against the Hasmonean, had shut themselves up. The king stormed the city and brought the captives to Jerusalem, where Josephus recounts a horrifying episode. In the only record of a Jewish ruler executing by crucifixion, Jannaeus hung eight hundred men and slaughtered their wives and children before their dying eyes. All the while, the king feasted with his concubines and watched the carnage. Although earlier scholarship cast doubt on the reliability of Josephus' record, this event is likewise remembered in *Pesher Nahum* on Nahum 2:12.

> Interpreted, this concerns the furious young lion [who executes revenge] on those who seek smooth things [Pharisees] and hangs men alive . . . formerly in Israel. Because of a man hanged alive on [the] tree, He proclaims, "Behold I am against [you says the Lord of Hosts]."
> (4Q169 f3–4i:6–8)

The sectarian passage witnesses both to the historicity of Josephus' account and to the revulsion by those who had earlier praised the king (4Q448).

Josephus himself seems to have attempted to mitigate the outrage of Jannaeus' actions by criticizing the citizenry for "bringing foreigners" to assist them in the overthrow of the king (*Ant.* 13:381–382; cf. 11Q19 64:6–9). In addition, Josephus attributes Jannaeus' weakened hold on his territory to their sedition. The king was forced to surrender "to the king of the Arabs the territory which he had conquered in Moab and Galaaditis and the strongholds therein, in order that he might not aid the Jews in the war against him" (*Ant.* 13:382).

In the aftermath of the civil war eight thousand fled and lived in exile, while Jannaeus ruled in Jerusalem (cf. *Meg. Taʿan.* 17 Adar). His brutality gained him the nickname "the Thracian," after the rulers of Thrace who were known for their cruelty. If the allusions in *Pesher Nahum* are to Jannaeus, then we may hear a corresponding Hebrew moniker that underscores his brutal nature, "Lion of Wrath" (4Q169 f3 4i:5-6; cf. 4Q167 f2:2).

Some time later (c. 84 BCE), Antiochus XII Dionysus, who had succeeded both his brothers, Philip and Demetrius, as king in Damascus, marched through Judea in his war against the Nabateans. Alexander dug a trench from Caphar Saba near Antipatris (*contra Ant.* 13:390–391) to Joppa, "and he erected a wall and set up wooden towers and firing platforms for a distance of a hundred and fifty stades" (*Ant.* 13:391). These defenses did little to impede Antiochus' march to Arabia. Later, however, the Seleucid king fell in battle against Aretas III, and his men fled to Kana near the southern end of the Dead Sea.

King Aretas of the Nabateans now ruled Coele-Syria, including Damascus. He marched on Judea and defeated Alexander at Adida (cf. *Ant.* 13:203). The Nabatean king negotiated terms for peace, and then withdrew to Damascus. Josephus concludes his history of Jannaeus' numerous battles with the Hasmonean's campaigns in the

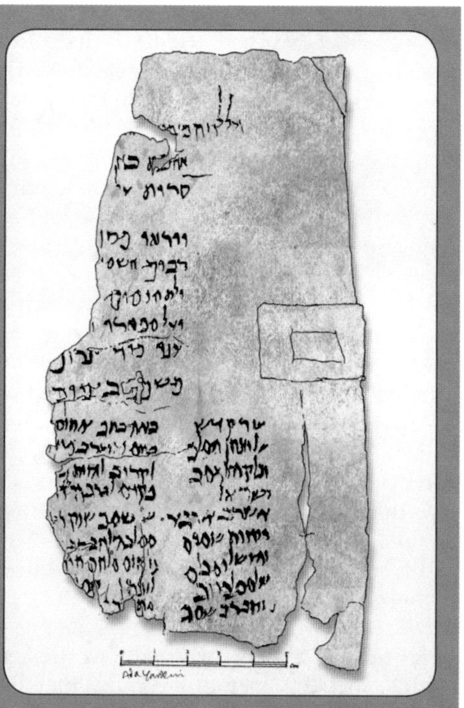

*A semi-cursive Hasmonean script in a liturgical poem from Qumran (4Q448) mentioning Jonathan the King (Alexander Jannaeus).*

Transjordan. He regained control of Moab, Gilead and portions of the Hauran, lands that he had been forced to cede to the Nabateans in his fight with Demetrius. Jannaeus' drive into Coele-Syria subsequent to the battle at Adida suggests that Aretas' victory was not decisive.

Jannaeus captured Dium, Pella (Ṭabaqaṭ Faḥil) and Gerasa (Jerash; *War* 1:104; *contra Ant.* 13:393), "where [*War* 1:104: Theodorus son of] Zenon's most valuable possessions were, and surrounded the place with three walls" (*Ant.* 13:393). Gerasa capitulated without a fight (cf. *War* 1:89), so Jannaeus moved on to Gaulana (cf. *Ant.* 4:173; *War* 1:90, 105) and Seleucia (Seluqiye; cf. *War* 4:1–2; *Life* 187). Finally, he took the fortified city of Gamala (cf. *War* 4:1–2) and the Valley of Antiochus. After three years (83–80 BCE), Jannaeus returned victorious to Jerusalem.

Jannaeus' rule now extended over the largest territory that the Hasmonean dynasty would realize. Josephus lists the regions and cities that comprised his kingdom at his death (76 BCE). On the coast he held Strato's Tower, Apollonia (Arsûf; Pliny *Nat. Hist.* 5.14), Joppa, Jamnia, Azotus, Gaza, Anthedon, Raphia and Rhinocorura. In other words, with the exception of Ascalon and Ptolemais, the Hasmonean controlled the coast of the Mediterranean from the Ladder of Tyre to the Brook of Egypt.

In the interior hill country, Jannaeus ruled Idumea, including Marisa and Adora, Judea, Samaria and Mount Carmel. No mention is made in this passage of the Great Plain, but the inclusion of Scythopolis and Mount Tabor together with Mount Carmel indicates that Jannaeus controlled all the access routes to the strategic Jezreel Valley.

A large area of the Transjordan is likewise listed in Jannaeus' kingdom. Gaulanitis included the cities of Seleucia and Gamala, while in Galaaditis, Gadara and Pella are specified. The region of Perea, where Jewish communities had existed for centuries, is not listed but surely assumed. Heshbon and Medeba, cities conquered by Hyrcanus, are specified in the list by Josephus with other cities in Moab that were included in the Hasmonean kingdom: e.g. Libba (Kh. Libb; cf. *Ant.* 14:18) and Zoar (Ghor eṣ-Ṣâfī; Eus. *Onom.* 42:1). Textual corruption in the manuscript readings of *Antiquities* 13:397, in which the cities in the Transjordan are listed, led to a debate in the last century concerning the southern limits of Jannaeus' kingdom.

Of particular note, Galilee and a few cities mentioned earlier in Jannaeus' conquests are omitted. Additional cities find no mention at this juncture but are later attributed to Jannaeus' campaigns. These cities are among those that Jannaeus' son, Hyrcanus II, relinquished to Aretas III (*Ant.* 14:18). It seems that Josephus' current list of regions and cities in Jannaeus' kingdom was not intended to be exhaustive. Instead, the historian's purpose was to emphasize the expansion of Jannaeus' kingdom.

At the time of his death Alexander Jannaeus ruled the whole of the coastal plain from the Kishon to the Brook of Egypt (excluding Ascalon), the whole of the mountains west of the Jordan from Dan to Beer-sheba, almost the whole area east of the Jordan from Paneas down to Zoar and the brook Zered. He had thus virtually restored the Kingdom of David and Solomon.

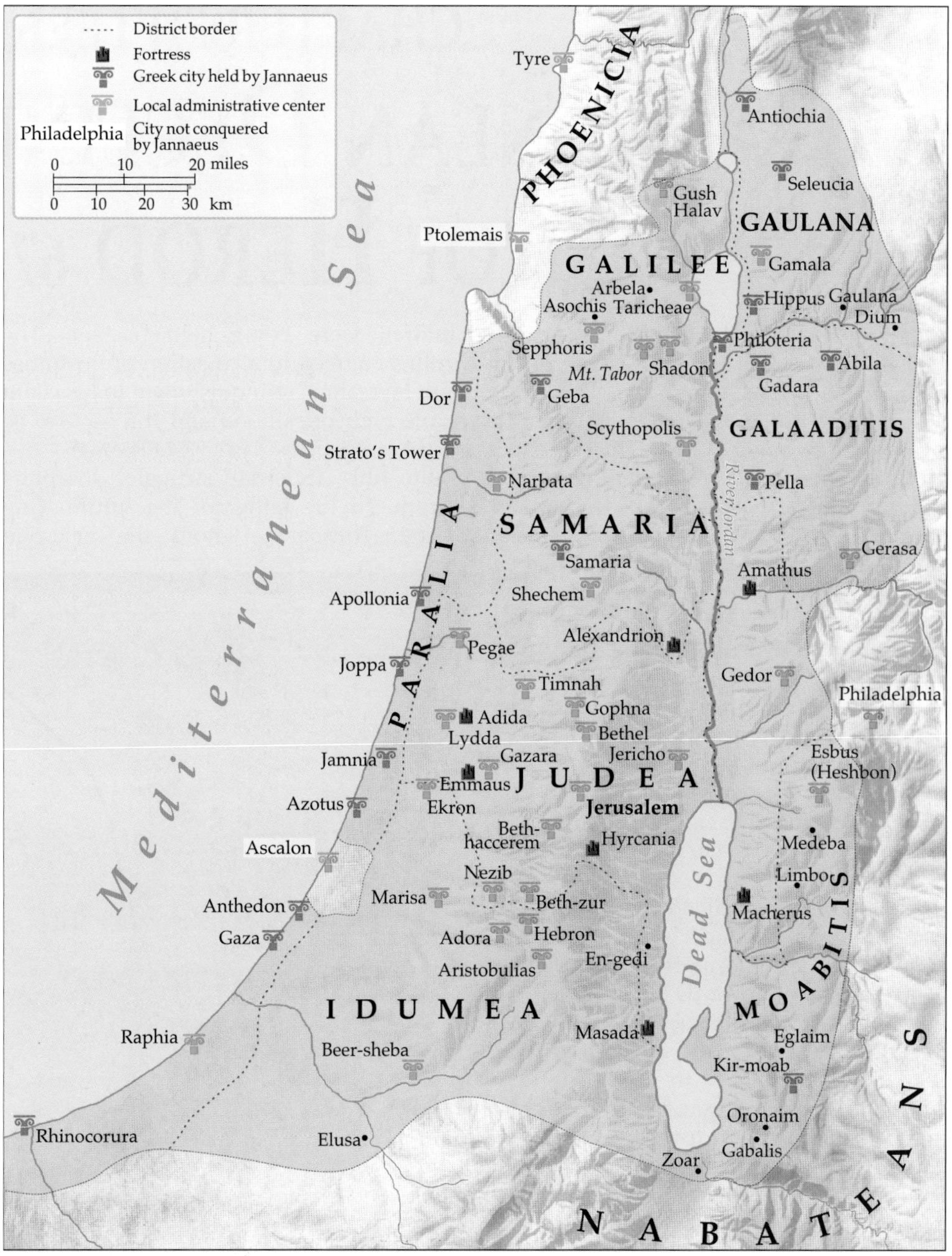

**The Kingdom of Alexander Jannaeus (103–76 BCE)**

*Marisa, general view of the tel.*

# CHAPTER FIFTEEN
# HASMONEAN DECLINE AND THE RISE OF HEROD 67 TO 37 BCE

Herod's rise to power occurred against the backdrop of the decline of the Hasmonean dynasty and the emergence of two intertwined rivalries: one domestic and one international. The final decades of Hasmonean rule in Judea witnessed a bitter contest between the descendants of Alexander Jannaeus (103–76 BCE) and Alexandra Salome (76–67 BCE). Alexandra had already designated her succession to their son John Hyrcanus II, but while she was still ailing Judah Aristobulus II rebelled and usurped the throne from his older brother. Hyrcanus may have been entitled to the throne by the rights of primogeniture, but as Josephus testifies, his younger sibling proved to be a more energetic leader (*War* 1:120).

Aristobulus was allied with the Sadducean aristocracy who had suffered under Alexandra's policy of appeasement towards their rival Pharisees, "for [the Pharisees] worked upon the feelings of the queen and tried to persuade her to kill those who had urged Alexander to put the eight hundred to death" (*Ant.* 13:410; cf. 13:380). Yet, at Aristobulus' request she allowed the Sadducean aristocracy to garrison themselves for protection in the royal fortresses, "with the exception of Hyrcania, Alexandrion and Macherus, where her most valuable possessions were" (*Ant.* 13:417).

As the queen's health failed, Aristobulus decided that the time had come to seize power. He slipped away by night to Gaba (*Ant.* 13:424, 5:157; Jeba<sup>c</sup>; Lat. Gabatha; cf. Tg. Judg 20:33; 1 Sam 13:33 *et passim*), leaving his wife and children in Jerusalem. Quickly the Hasmonean fortresses fell to Aristobulus, because they were already occupied by his Sadducean allies.

> For in barely fifteen days he had occupied twenty-two fortresses, and obtaining resources from these, he gathered an army from Lebanon, Trachonitis and the local princes. (*Ant.* 13:427)

Alexandra's death in 67 BCE brought open conflict between Hyrcanus and Aristobulus. Hyrcanus and his men suffered defeat when attacked near Jericho, and they fled to the Baris (Neh 3:1; *War* 1:118; cf. *Ant.* 15:403) in Jerusalem, where Aristobulus' wife and children were being held hostage. The brothers agreed to a cessation of hostilities with Hyrcanus' relinquishment to his claim to the high priesthood and throne (*Ant.* 14:4–6; *War* 1:121; cf. *Ant.* 14:41, 97; 20:243–244).

Into this fraternal struggle, Josephus introduced the father of the future King Herod, Antipater, whom the historian reports was of Idumean descent (*War* 1:123; *Ant.* 14:8-9; *contra* Just. *Dial.* 52; Eus. *Hist. eccl.* 1.7.11; Kokkinos 1998:100–112). Alexander Jannaeus had appointed the father of Antipater to be the *strategos* of all Idumea (*Ant.* 14:10), and his son succeeded him in the same position.

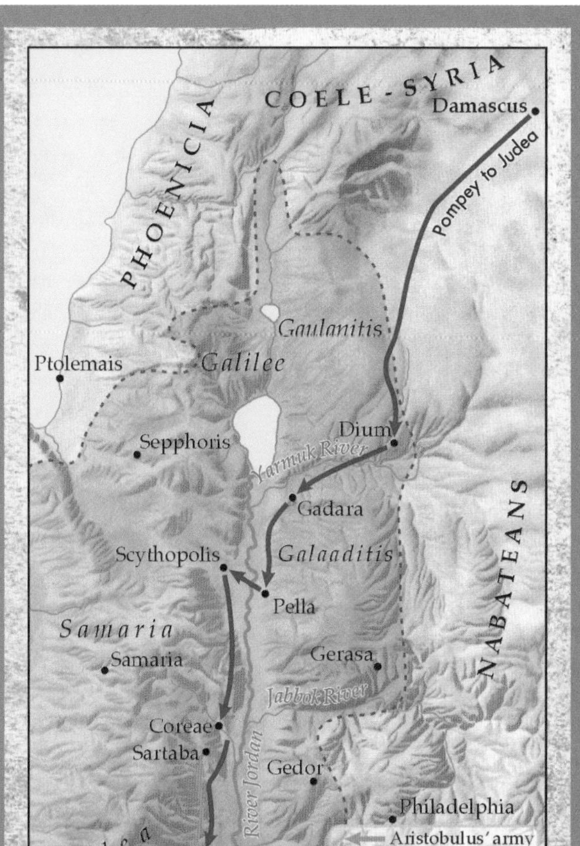


POMPEY'S CAMPAIGN IN PALESTINE (63 BCE)

The younger Antipater had allied himself with Hyrcanus in the hope of seeing his own influence increase. Consequently, the Idumean was unwilling to accept the recent turn of events without some challenge. He aroused suspicions in the mind of the deposed monarch towards his brother, and he persuaded the Nabatean king, Aretas, to lend his military support in an effort to help Hyrcanus regain the diadem. In exchange, Aretas was promised that he would receive the Nabatean cities seized by Hyrcanus' father, Alexander Jannaeus: Medeba (*Ant.* 13:255), Libba (Kh. Libb), Dabaloth (Beth-diblathaim; Kh. Deleilat), Arabatha (Rabbah), Agalla (Rujm el-Gilimé), Athone (et-Teniyé), Zoar (Ghor eṣ-Ṣâfî), Oronaim (el-<sup>c</sup>Irâq), Gobalis (el-Gebalin), Arydda, Alousa, and Oruba (*Ant.* 14:18; cf. *Ant.* 13:397).

During Passover 65 BCE, the Nabatean forces besieged Jerusalem where Aristobulus had withdrawn to the Temple Mount. The Sadducean priests who feared that Hyrcanus would revive the anti-Sadducean policies of his mother defended Aristobulus (*Ant.* 14:14–20; *War* 1:123–126). At the same time, Pompey was concluding his campaign against Tigranes in Armenia and had sent Marcus Aemilius Scaurus with Roman legions to Syria. Hearing of the civil war in Judea, Scaurus continued there (*War* 1:127), and both brothers made appeals with the promise of bribes for support from the Romans (*Ant.*14:30–31).

Scaurus considered Aristobulus more capable, decided in his favor and ordered Aretas to withdraw his siege from Jerusalem under the threat of Roman intervention. The Nabatean complied, but when his forces withdrew, Aristobulus attacked them at Papyron (*Ant.* 14:33; *War* 1:130; i.e. Calamon near <sup>c</sup>Ain Hajlā) near Jericho. While it appeared as if Rome had thrown its support to Aristobulus and his faction, Antipater awaited the arrival in the region of Pompey, whom the Idumean rightly discerned wielded the real power.

Pompey spent the winter of 64/63 BCE in Syria (Plut. *Pomp.* 39.2–3; Diod. Sic. 40.2) where he entertained delegations from Hyrcanus and Aristobulus (*Ant.* 14:34). The Roman general declined to make a hasty determination and invited both parties to return again in the spring to Damascus. The principals themselves returned to make claims and trade accusations. Other leaders of the people urged Pompey not to allow either brother to be king,

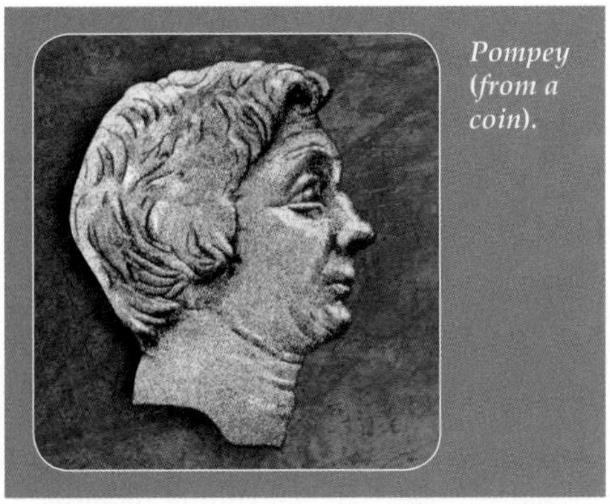

*Pompey (from a coin).*

saying that it was the custom of their country to obey the priests of the God who was venerated by them, but that these two, who were descended from the priests, were seeking to change their form of government in order that they might become a nation of slaves. (*Ant.* 14:41; cf. PssSol 17:21)

Once again, Pompey refused to take a position openly on the competing claims. In reality, he had decided in favor of Hyrcanus, but he was afraid that Aristobulus would sabotage his planned campaign into Arabia. He announced that he would wait until after dealing with the Nabateans, when he visited Judea to decide between the feuding brothers. Pompey feared Aristobulus' rash nature, and so ordered him to remain in the Roman camp near Dium.

The Hasmonean in an act of reckless impiety ignored Pompey's order and left without permission (*Ant.* 14:47; War 1:132). The Roman general pursued him passing through Pella and Scythopolis. He camped at Coreae (*Ant.* 14:49; Tell Zamadi; Tel Mazar) near the Judean fortress of Alexandrion to which Aristobulus had taken refuge. Aristobulus' men urged him not to provoke the Romans, and he attempted to negotiate a settlement with Pompey, who demanded that Aristobulus relinquish in writing his Judean fortresses. Aristobulus conceded but then withdrew to Jerusalem in preparation for what he saw as inevitable conflict, while Pompey dismantled Alexandrion (Strabo *Geog.* 16.2.40).

Once more Aristobulus attempted to mollify Pompey, who was now encamped near Jericho, with an offer of full submission to the will of the Romans, agreement to accept a Roman garrison in Jerusalem, and payment of an indemnity (*Ant.* 14:55). The Roman pardoned Aristobulus, but when Pompey's legate Gabinius went to Jerusalem to collect the payment and to station the garrison there, the Hasmonean's men shut the gates of the city and refused to receive him. Pompey promptly arrested Aristobulus and marched on Jerusalem from the north, "where it was weak. For it is surrounded by a broad and deep ravine which takes in the temple, and this is very strongly protected by an encircling wall of stone" (*Ant.* 14:57; cf. *War* 5:136–141; Dio Cass. 37.15.2–3).

The city was divided between the supporters of Hyrcanus and Aristobulus. The Pharisees and the greater populace of Jerusalem had supported Hyrcanus and were not in favor of opposing the Romans. In the end, they prevailed and opened the gates of Jerusalem to Pompey and his forces without a fight (PssSol 8:16). The Sadducean contingent and the remnants of Aristobulus' supporters destroyed the bridge leading from the sanctuary precincts to the western hill and Hasmonean palace, and they retreated to the Temple Mount (cf. *War* 2:344).

> Pompey pitched his camp on the north side of the temple where it was open to attack. But even here stood great towers [i.e. of the Baris], and a trench had been dug, and the temple was surrounded by a deep ravine; for there was a steep slope on the [western] side toward the city after the bridge was destroyed, and at this spot Pompey by great labor day by day had caused earthworks to be raised. (*Ant.* 14:60–61)

The Romans built the siege structures virtually unopposed, because they took advantage of the restrictions on defensive actions by the Jews on the Sabbath, "for the Law permits us to defend ourselves [on the Sabbath] against those who begin a battle and strike us, but it does not allow us to fight against an enemy [on the Sabbath] that does anything else" (*Ant.* 14:63; *War* 1: 145–147; Dio Cass. 37.16.2). Pompey conquered the Temple Mount in the third month of the siege (*Ant.* 14:66; cf. *War* 1:149) "on the Fast Day" (cf. Strabo *Geog.* 16.2.40; Dio Cass. 37.16.4) and entered the sanctuary.

Josephus reports that Pompey and his men entered the Holy of Holies but touched nothing (cf. Cic. *Flac.* 67; PssSol 2:1–2, 8:16–26; *contra* Dio Cass. 37.16.4). Later, Jewish opinion would interpret Pompey's violent death in Egypt as divine judgment for his hubris in entering the Holy of Holies where only

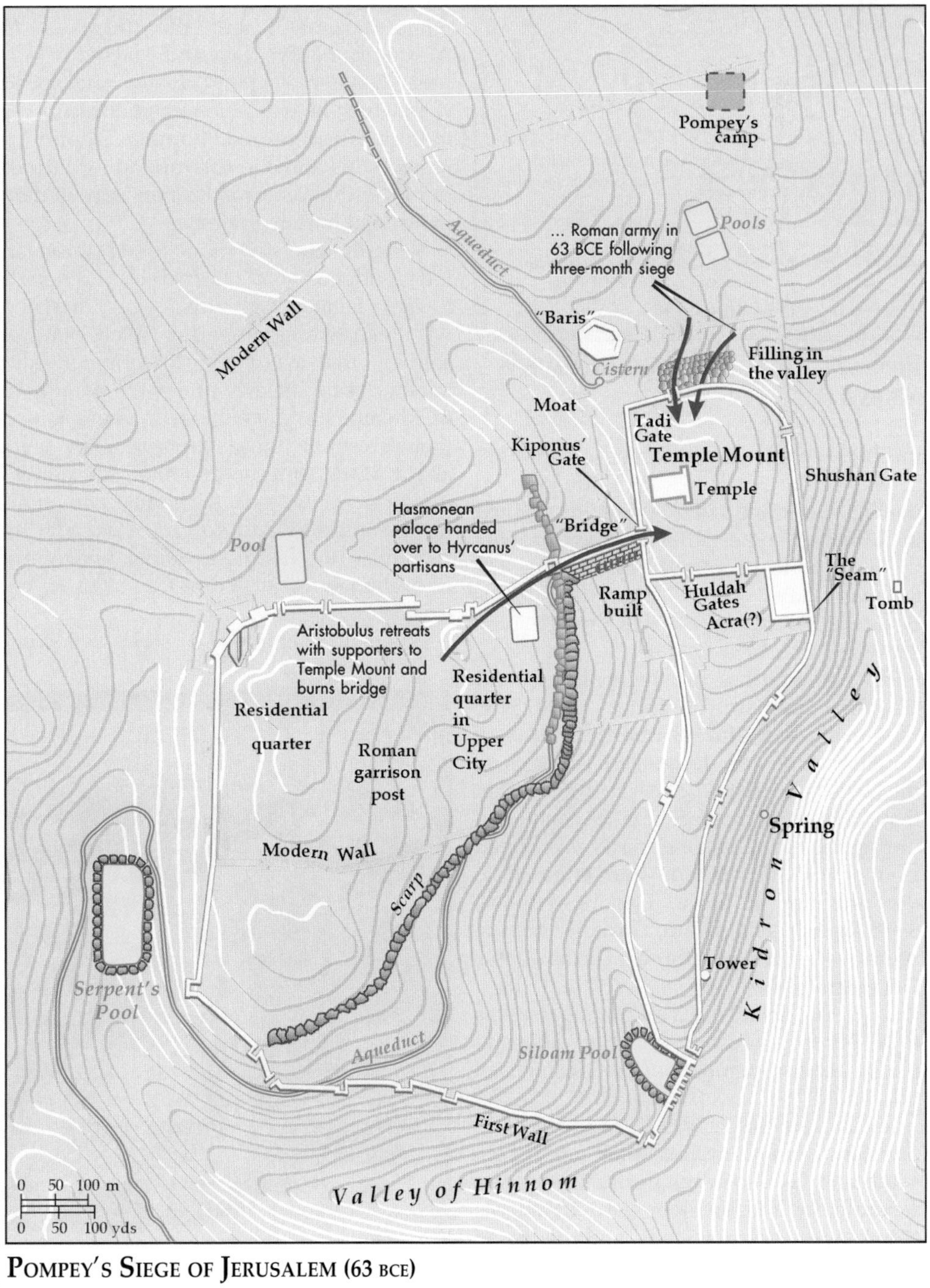


**Pompey's Siege of Jerusalem (63 BCE)**

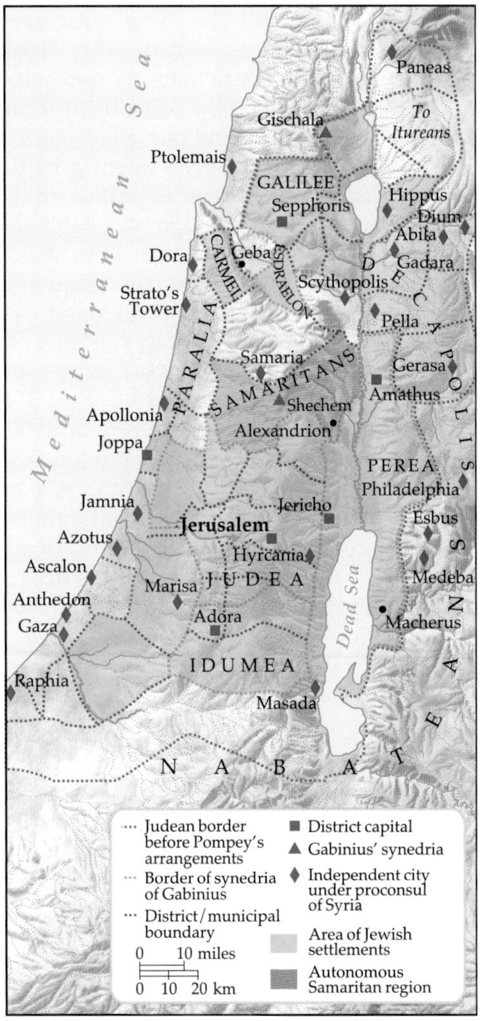


**POMPEY'S TERRITORIAL ARRANGEMENTS (63–55 BCE)**

the high priest was permitted on the Day of Atonement (PssSol 2:25–31). Little physical damage was done to the Temple, as testified by Josephus' report that Pompey ordered the Temple to be ritually purified on the following day (*Ant.* 14:73). Then the Romans reinstalled Hyrcanus as High Priest (*Ant.* 14:73; *War* 1:153; cf. Dio Cass. 37.16).

The boundaries of the political and territorial domain of Judea were now "confined within its own borders" (*Ant.* 14:74). Hyrcanus was designated ethnarch of the Jewish people (*Ant.* 14:148; cf. 20:244) rather than king, and a number of cities conquered during the Hasmonean dynasty were freed from Jewish domination and annexed to the province of Syria: Gadara, Hippus, Scythopolis, Pella, Dium, Samaria, Marisa, Azotus, Jamnia, Arethusa, Gaza, Joppa, Dora, Strato's Tower (*Ant.* 14:75–76; cf. *War* 1:156–157). The denial of access to the sea seems to be Pompey's response to accusations of piracy against members of the Hasmonean household (*Ant.* 14:43; Dio Cass. 40.18).

Jewish settlement was divided into two parts, Judea (with Idumea and Perea) in the south and Galilee in the north. These were separated by the hostile region of Samaria, Greek cities and townships, and the loss of the Esdraelon (Jezreel) Valley, which had included a hereditary Hasmonean estate (cf. *Ant.* 14:202–210). Jerusalem was also relegated to a Roman tributary city (*Ant.* 14:74) from which Hyrcanus was given oversight of internal affairs in Judea.

Hasmonean infighting is blamed by Josephus as the primary cause for the loss of lands and liberties realized by their fathers.

> For we lost our freedom and became subject to the Romans, and the territory which we had gained by our arms and taken from the Syrians we were compelled to give back to them, and in addition the Romans exacted from us in a short space of time more than ten thousand talents; and the royal power which had formerly been bestowed on those who were high priests by birth became the privilege of commoners (i.e. Herod). (*Ant.* 14:77–78)

Aristobulus and his family were led off to Rome in chains, but Josephus reports that his son Alexander escaped and began an extended insurgency campaign (*Ant.* 14:82). In 57 BCE Alexander led an armed force of 10,000 men and 1,500 horses to retake Jerusalem and the fortresses of Alexandrion, Hyrcania and Macherus (*Ant.* 14:82–90; *War* 1:160–168). The size and speed with which he was able to gather his forces indicates the continued popular support for Aristobulus and the corresponding lack of public enthusiasm for Roman intervention in internal Jewish affairs.

Nevertheless, any hope of Hasmonean independence was dashed by Pompey's former legate, Gabinius, who marched with his own legion and a "select body of soldiers that were about Antipater, and another body of Jews under the command of Malichus and Peitholaus. These joined themselves to those captains that were about Mark Antony, and met Alexander" (*War* 1:162; *Ant.* 14:84). Gabinius laid siege to Alexandrion and forced Alexander to relinquish the fortresses under his control in exchange for a pardon (*Ant.* 14:82–90; *War* 1:160-168).

Pompey appointed a series of commanders to govern the region from Syria to Egypt, but none took such an active engagement of the internal affairs of Judea as Gabinius (*Ant.* 14:82). Scholars have suggested that he followed the *divide et impera* example of Lucius Aemilius Paulus in Macedonia to weaken local resistance to Roman rule.

On the other hand, Gabinius' administrative organization was not simply intended to weaken Jerusalem's authority, but to strengthen localized governance in response to the rebel threat. Pompey's measures had left Hyrcanus unable to rule effectively from Jerusalem. Left with the existing political structure, the high priest would not have survived the threat of a popular insurrection. Gabinius chose to consolidate and strengthen authority in the districts under the leadership of local figures (e.g. Peitholaus in Jerusalem, Malichus in Galilee, Antipater in Idumea), all subordinate to the weakened high priest in Jerusalem.

Gabinius divided the region into five districts (*Ant.* 14:91; *War* 1:170) ruled from central cities: Jerusalem for Judea, Amathus for Perea, Jericho for the Jordan Valley, and Sepphoris for Galilee. Scholars debate the identity of the fifth city. Reading Gadara in our passage is difficult, because the well-known city in the Transjordan lay only 12 miles (20 km) from Amathus, the capital of Perea, too close to have served as the captial for another district.

A reading of Gazara likewise presents difficulties. Situated on the border of Judea, it would hardly have been chosen as the center of an administrative district. It has been argued, instead, that the city intended by Josephus was Adora. With the removal of western Idumea and Marisa from Jewish control, Adora was left as the most important city of eastern Idumea, a distinct region that remained attached to Judea during the Roman period.

*Wall of the Hasmonean fortress at Alexandrion.*

Gabinius' synedria ("districts") resemble Herod's "parts": Judea (incl. Samaria), Galilee, Perea and Idumea (cf. *Ant.* 15:216), and the emergency organization of Jewish defenses prior to the revolt in 66 CE (*War* 2: 566–568). The new administrative structure was intended to limit the centralized power of the high priest in Jerusalem, but also to provide enough authority in the districts under his administration to ward off the challenges of his enemies. However, Gabinius' plan did not survive the tumultuous power struggle in Judea. When Aristobulus arrived from Rome in 56 BCE in his short-lived attempt to overthrow Hyrcanus, he was joined by Peitholaus, ostensibly responsible to the high priest for the administration of Jerusalem (*Ant.* 14:93; *War* 1:172). After Alexander's return in the following year to lead a bloody rebellion against the Romans that required Antipater's intervention, "Gabinius then settled affairs at Jerusalem to suit the wishes of Antipater" (*Ant.* 14:103; *War* 1:178). It was only a matter of time until Antipater would be elevated to procurator of Judea (*Ant.* 14:143).

In the meantime, Gabinius expanded upon the policies of Pompey. Josephus provides two more lists of rebuilt Hellenistic cities under Gabinius' administration: "Samaria, Azotus, Scythopolis, Anthedon, Raphia, Adora, Marisa, Gaza and not a few others" (*Ant.* 14:88; *War* 1:166 adds, Apollonia, Jamnia, and Gamala [variants: Gabala, Gadara, Gaza]). Clearly, there was confusion in Josephus' sources between the cities rebuilt by Gabinius and those already refounded by Pompey (cf. *Ant.* 14:75–76; *War* 1: 156 and *Ant.* 14:88; *War* 1:166).

When Aristobulus escaped from captivity in Rome with his younger son Antigonus, he attempted to resist Roman rule in Judea. After suffering a defeat they retreated to Macherus (el-Mishneqeh; Strabo *Geog.* 16.2.40; Pliny *Nat. Hist.* 5.72; m. *Tam.* 3:8; j. *Šeb.* 9:2:38d), the Hasmonean fortress east of the Dead Sea. They held out only two days, after which Aristobulus was taken captive and returned to Rome.

Alexander reemerged to lead an uprising in the next year and overran Galilee and Samaria as well as Judea. At Gabinius' behest, Antipater appealed to the rebels in Alexander's ranks to abandon their imprudent challenge to Rome. His efforts seem to have garnered a measure of success, because when Gabinius later marched against Alexander at Mount Tabor, he easily defeated the Hasmonean (*Ant.* 14: 102). Thus, Gabinius and his Jewish allies—Hyrcanus and Antipater—maintained Roman hegemony over Judea. Only with the diversion of the civil war between Julius Caesar and Pompey, and with the incursion of Parthian armies from the east (*Ant.* 14:119–126), did the Roman grip on Judea loosen.

Hyrcanus and Antipater earlier lent

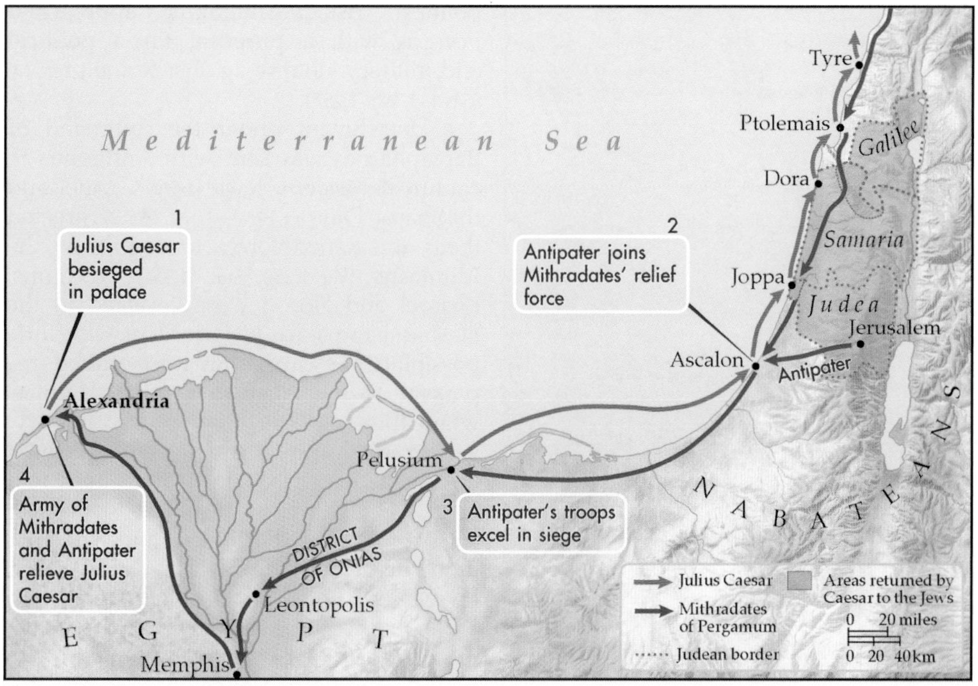


**JULIUS CAESAR AND JUDEA (47 BCE)**

their support to Pompey in his struggle with Caesar. Pompey's defeat and death in Egypt (48 BCE), however, brought a necessary realignment of allegiances by Hyrcanus and Antipater. The latter quickly distinguished himself by marshalling the Jewish forces in Judea to assist Mithradates of Pergamum to gain passage to Pelusium in Caesar's defense (*Ant.* 14:127). He likewise displayed uncommon valor on the battlefield alongside Mithradates against the anti-Caesarean elements in Egypt (*Ant.* 14:133–136). When Caesar visited Syria to establish his administration there, he denied the claim of Antigonus, the younger son of Aristobulus, that he was the rightful heir to his father's throne (*Ant.* 14:137). Instead, Caesar reaffirmed Hyrcanus as high priest and ethnarch of the Jewish people (*Ant.* 14: 191).

Moreover, Caesar granted Jews living in the Diaspora special privileges by which they were allowed to maintain their ancestral customs (*Ant.* 14:213–216; Suet. *Jul.* 42:3). Hyrcanus was granted permission to rebuild the walls of Jerusalem that had been destroyed by Pompey (*Ant.* 14:144, 14:200; *War* 1:199; cf. *Ant.* 14:156). Antipater was rewarded with Roman citizenship (*Ant.* 14:137–138) and elevated from administrator (*Ant.* 14:127) to procurator of Judea (*Ant.* 14:143).

Antipater took advantage of his position to place his two sons as governors, Phasael in Jerusalem and Herod in Galilee. The Jerusalem aristocracy resented the new influence wielded by the Idumean family. Herod's actions in Galilee in particular were a point of agitation. Galilee had often been an area of unrest and brigandry. Josephus reports that one of Herod's first actions was to capture and execute a group of Galileans led by Ezekias who had resisted Roman rule (*Ant.* 14:159–167; *War* 1:204–209).

Herod summarily executed these men without bringing them before the Sanhedrin, who under Jewish law retained the exclusive power to execute capital punishment (*Ant.* 14:167; m. *Sanh.* 7:1). Herod's disregard for the Sanhedrin's authority epitomized their concerns about the autocratic power wielded by the Idumeans. Herod was called to trial in Jerusalem, but a letter was sent to Hyrcanus from Sextus Caesar, governor of Syria, who cautioned the Hasmonean ethnarch that Herod, a Roman citizen, was not to be touched (*Ant.* 14:171–179; see b. *Sanh.* 19a/b). When Hyrcanus saw that the Sanhedrin was intent on punishing Herod, he advised him to flee. Herod avoided punishment by the Sanhedrin, but in the ensuing intrigues Antipater was poisoned by the Jerusalem aristocrat, Malichus (*Ant.* 14:277–281; *War* 1:226).

Into this internecine fighting returned Antigonus, son of Aristobulus II, who had stayed with his brother-in-law Ptolemy, son of Mennaeus, ruler of Chalcis, since his father's death (*Ant.* 14:297; cf. 14:126). He saw the political leadership in discord and sought to exploit it for his own gain. He marched into Galilee, which gladly threw its support behind the reestablishment of the Hasmonean line of Aristobulus. Tyrian

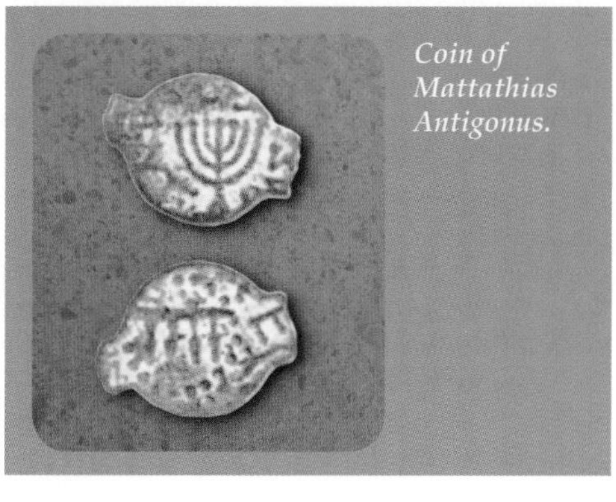

*Coin of Mattathias Antigonus.*

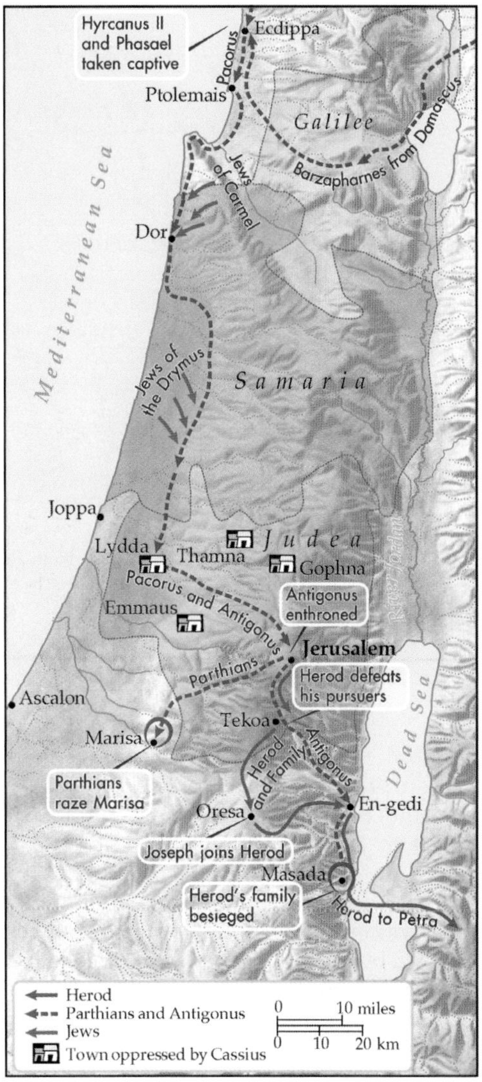


**The Parthian Invasion and the Escape of Herod (40 bce)**

troops allied with Antigonus captured three fortresses in Galilee (*Ant.* 14:297–299; *War* 1:238–240), while the Hasmonean pushed farther into Judea. Herod marched against Antigonus and drove him back out of the country, although for the time being the Galilean fortresses remained in Tyrian hands (cf. *Ant.* 14:306–322).

Herod was greeted in Jerusalem, and "Hyrcanus and the people wreathed his head with crowns" (*Ant.* 14:299; *War* 1: 240). Previous fissures in the relationship between Hyrcanus and Antipater's sons were quickly forgotten. All shared a common threat from Antigonus. Hyrcanus took steps to strengthen the personal ties by betrothing his granddaughter, Mariamme, to Herod (*Ant.* 14:300, 351–353).

In 40 bce Parthian forces invaded Syria to challenge Rome's eastern frontier. Led by Pacorus son of Orodes II of Parthia, and assisted by Labienus, a former legate of Julius Caesar, the Parthians exploited the hatred for the Romans among the local populations in the east. Sweeping through the Levant, Pacorus ventured south in an effort to secure the coastal areas of the eastern Mediterranean. At considerable political risk, Antigonus approached Pacorus with a proposal for a political and military alliance against Rome (*Ant.* 14: 331–333; *War* 1:257).

A detachment under the command of Barzapharnes was sent with Antigonus to capture Jerusalem. Jews from Carmel and the Sharon Plain (cf. Strabo *Geog.* 16.2.27) greeted them and joined forces to overthrow the Idumeans (*War* 1:250; *Ant.* 14:334). Hyrcanus, Phasael and Herod were besieged in the Hasmonean palace of Jerusalem with little possibility of escape. They were offered free passage to the Parthian camp in Galilee, where they could negotiate peace.

Hyrcanus and Phasael were inclined to accept this offer, since there appeared no possibility of escape. Herod was less trusting of the Parthians and tried to dissuade his brother. He was unsuccessful. Hyrcanus and Phasael traveled to Barzapharnes in Galilee. The two were received cordially by the Parthian and then brought to Ecdippa (Achzib; Pliny *Nat. Hist.* 5.75; Ptol. *Geog.* 5.15.5; Eus. *Onom.* 30:12: "Ecdippa that is nine miles from Ptolemais on the way to Tyre"), "overlooking the sea" (*Ant.* 14:343). The Parthians waited to strike Hyrcanus and Phasael, until after they were assured that Herod was captive. In the meantime, Phasael got word of their treachery. He had the opportunity to escape, but he did not want to abandon Hyrcanus nor jeopardize his brother. Instead, he unsuccessfully appealed to Barzapharnes, who imprisoned Hyrcanus and Phasael.

When Herod got word of Phasael's arrest by the Parthians, he fled south with the women, children and servants to bring them to safety at the Hasmonean fortress of Masada (*Ant.* 14:358). During their escape Herod fought off the pursuing Parthian forces.

> But he found in this flight the Jews even more troublesome than the Parthians, for they perpetually harassed him, and at a distance of sixty furlongs (7 miles) from the city brought on a regular action that was prolonged for a considerable time. Here Herod eventually defeated them with a great slaughter and here subsequently, to commemorate his victory, he founded a city, adorned it with the most costly palaces, erected a citadel of commanding strength, and called it after his own name Herodion.
> (*War* 1:265; *Ant.* 14:359–360)

Herod continued to Oresa (Kh. Khureisa) where he met his brother Joseph (*War* 1:266; *Ant.* 14:361). There were simply too many in the party to place them all at Masada. Most were released to flee for safety into Idumea, whose residents remained allied with the sons of Antipater. His closest relatives, however, including his mother Cypros, his betrothed Mariamme and the others he took to Masada.

Antigonus returned to Judea in a rampage of bloodshed. Jewish properties in Jerusalem were plundered, and the Parthians destroyed the Idumean city of Marisa (*Ant.* 14:364–365). In Galilee, Phasael and Hyrcanus had miscalculated Parthian treachery. Instead of negotiating peace, the Parthians handed the men over to Antigonus. The sources vary regarding the circumstances of Phasael's death (*Ant.* 14: 365–369; *War* 1:269–272), but Antigonus assured that Hyrcanus would no longer be his rival for the high priesthood. Hyrcanus' ear was mutilated, which permanently disqualified him (*Ant.* 14:366; cf. 3:278–279; Lev 21:17–23; t. *Parah* 3:8).

Antigonus now stood as the sole claimant to be high priest. His Parthian benefactors also granted him the title of king. Coinage from his brief rule provides both his Hebrew name, Mattathias, and a bilingual inscription on the coins resembling that of Alexander Jannaeus.

Herod left Masada for the Arabian capital of Petra, where he sought the support of the Nabatean king, Malchus. He left Petra empty-handed but determined to make his way to Rome and appeal to the Senate. He traveled to Rhinocorura (Polyb. 5.80.3; Diod. Sic. 1.60.5; Strabo *Geog.* 16.1.12, 31; 16.4.24; Pliny *Nat. Hist.* 5.68) at the Brook of Egypt, where he received word of Phasael's death (*Ant.* 14:374; *War* 1:277). He continued to Pelusium and Alexandria in search of a ship to Rome. Finally, Herod secured passage on a ship to Pamphylia and Rhodes. At Rhodes, Herod found the city in ruins from the war against Cassius, and he "did not hesitate to help it even though he was in need of funds, but actually exceeded his means in restoring it" (*Ant.* 14:377–378; *War* 1:280). He then embarked to Brundisium (Brindisi), the port on the southeastern coast of Italy.

In Rome, Herod found ready allies in Octavian and Mark Antony, who both had been assisted by Herod's father, Antipater (*Ant.* 14:127–136; 14:326). The Senate was convened to consider events in Judea. Antigonus was,

> . . . declared an enemy, not only because of the first offense he had committed against them (i.e. assisting in his father's insurrection), but because he had received his kingly title from the Parthians, thus showing no regard for the Romans. (*Ant.* 14:384)

The alliance between Antigonus and the Parthians had made him an enemy of Rome. Mark Antony urged the Roman Senate that in light of the Parthian threat from the east it would be advantageous to have Herod on the throne. Herod's loyalty to Rome was

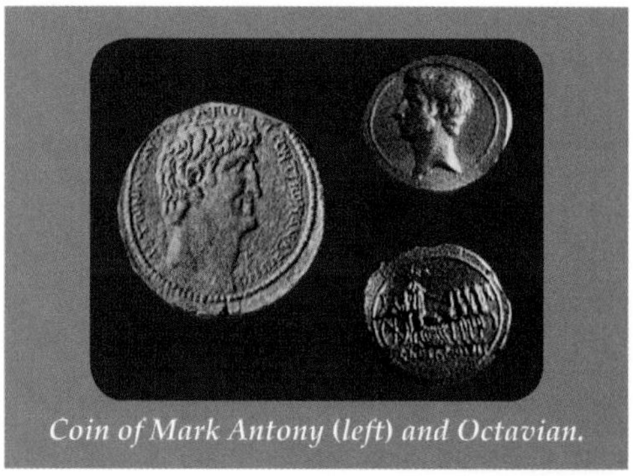

*Coin of Mark Antony (left) and Octavian.*

well known. The Senate, thus, proclaimed in the summer of 40 BCE that Herod should be king of Judea, and it granted to Herod the possessions of Hyrcanus II: Judea, Joppa, eastern Idumea, Perea, Galilee and the Jezreel Valley (*Ant.* 14:91; *War* 1:170).

Landing at the port of Ptolemais, Herod marched through Galilee. He chose to move quickly through the countryside and to avoid the strongholds where support for Antigonus was entrenched. He would deal with them later when the southern parts of the country, and more importantly his family, were secure. His army, comprised of Jews and foreign mercenaries (*Ant.* 14:394), proceeded south through the coastal plain into western Idumea. They met little resistance except at Joppa, port city for Jerusalem. Herod besieged Joppa, taking it by force. His attention now turned to the interior hill country. He rescued those at Masada and enlisted the local inhabitants of Idumea, who joined his ranks, "because of their friendship with his father" (*Ant.* 14:398; cf. 14:8–10).

The coastal regions and Idumea were now in Herod's hands. His campaign strategy followed that of earlier conquerors (e.g. 1 Macc 4:28–61; *Ant.* 12:313–315) who had chosen to ascend into the hill country through Idumea because of hostile forces positioned in the Judean hill country.

> Antigonus occupied the most suitable places for passage with snares and ambushes, but did not the least, or at best only slight, damage thereby to the enemy. (*Ant.* 14:399)

Garrisoned at the Idumean fortress of Oresa, southeast of Hebron, Herod began his approach to Jerusalem. No resistance is recorded on Herod's march north along the watershed route to the outskirts of Jerusalem. He encamped to the west of the city, where Silo, an officer of the general Ventidius, and his Roman troops joined Herod. The new king appealed to the defenders of the city to surrender, promising not to punish those who had opposed him. Antigonus tried to dissuade the Romans in their support for Herod,

> that it would be contrary to their own notion of right if they gave the kingship to Herod who was a commoner and an Idumean, that is, a half-Jew, when they ought to offer it to those who were of the (ruling) family, as was their custom. (*Ant.* 14:403)

Neither appeal succeeded in averting conflict.

During the winter months, the Roman army was dismissed and quartered "in the districts which had been added to [Herod's] territory (App. *Bell. Civ.* 5.75), namely Idumea, Galilee and Samaria" (*Ant.* 14:411). Josephus indicates that during this time Herod returned to remove Antigonus' sympathizers in the surrounding districts. He sent Joseph to Idumea with two thousand infantry and four hundred cavalry, while he proceeded to Galilee to deal with the resistance there. Herod captured Sepphoris

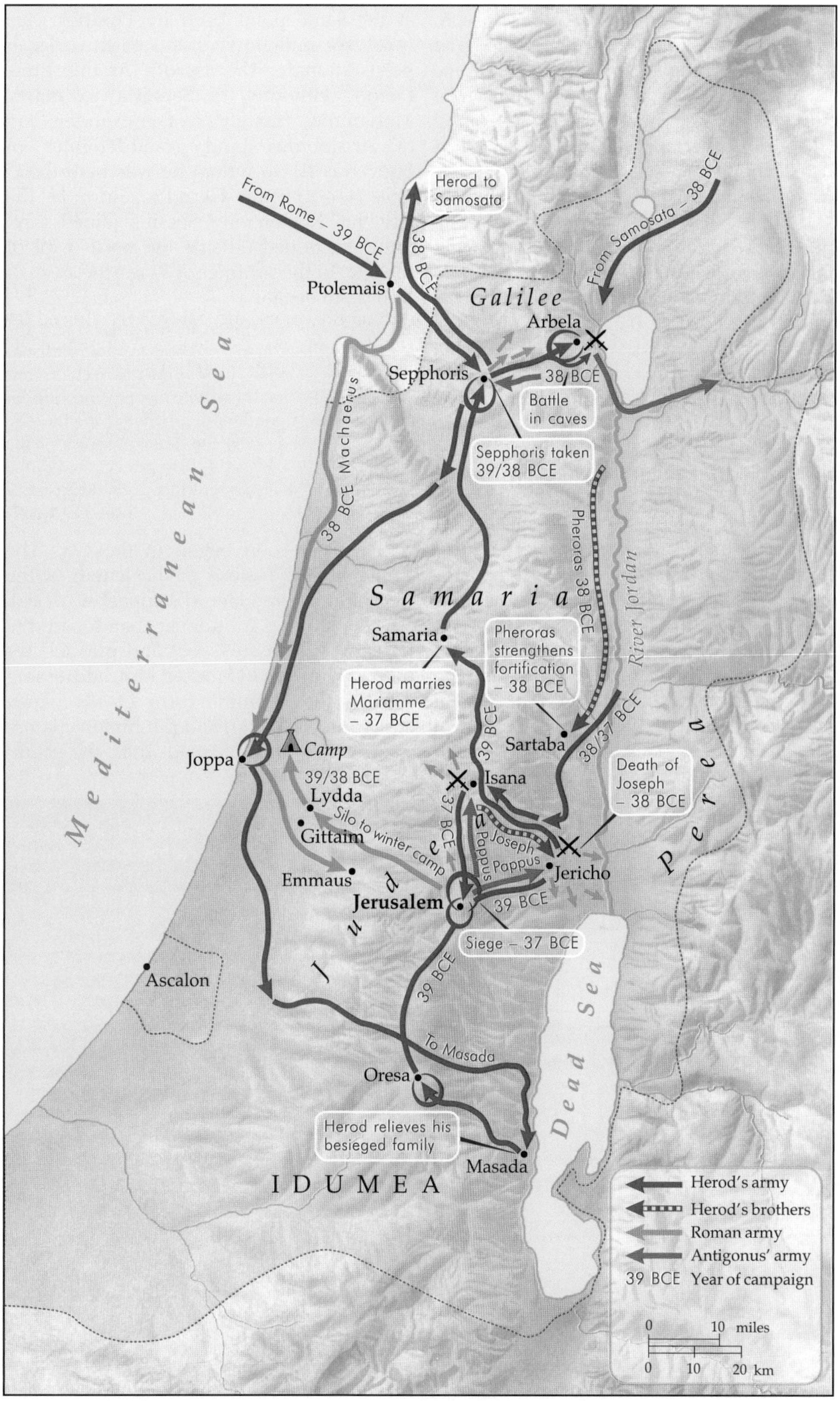


**THE RISE OF HEROD (40–37 BCE)**

in a snowstorm, when Antigonus' garrison there withdrew without a fight (*Ant.* 14:414; *War* 1:304). In the caves near the Jewish village of Arbela, however, Herod faced those who were steadfastly opposed to his reign (*Ant.* 14:415–417). He strengthened his hold on Galilee and now was prepared to move on Jerusalem (*Ant.* 14:421–430). Yet, he could not do it alone. He would need help from Rome to take the well-fortified city.

Silo had been withdrawn to Syria to assist Ventidius against the Parthians. When Pacorus was killed and the Parthians routed, Machaeras was sent in the summer of 38 BCE with two legions to assist Herod. However, the Roman became entangled in bribes and intrigues, and Herod found it necessary to appeal to Mark Antony directly in Samosata near the Euphrates. Herod returned with additional help from Antony under the direction of Sossius, the new governor of Syria.

In his absence, Herod's brother, Joseph, was killed in fighting near Jericho. The death of the king's brother sparked hope in Antigonus' partisans. Rebellion broke out in Galilee and Herod's supporters were drowned in the Lake of Gennesaret. Open insurrection spread throughout Judea. When Herod arrived at Mount Lebanon, he received word of his brother's death. He charged through Galilee destroying any resistance. At Jericho he took revenge upon Antigonus' forces that had fought his brother.

Antigonus sent his forces under the command of Pappus, who had beheaded Herod's brother, to Samaria. Pappus encamped near Isana (*Ant.* 14:458; *War* 1:334; Kh. el-Burj el-Isaneh), 20 miles (32 km) north of Jerusalem on the watershed route. Herod overran Pappus' troops and they fled to the nearby village, where Herod's army slaughtered them. The following day Herod cut off the head of Pappus in revenge for what he had done to Joseph (*Ant.* 14:464; cf. 14:450).

It had now been almost three years since the Roman Senate had declared Herod king (37 BCE; cf. *Ant.* 14:388). He was once again encamped on the western hill of Jerusalem and decided to attack the Temple Mount at the same point used by Pompey (*Ant.* 14:60). He built towers and earthworks in preparation for the assault. At this time, Herod withdrew to Samaria to marry Mariamme, "daughter of Alexander, son of Aristobulus [and granddaughter of Hyrcanus II], to whom he was betrothed" (*Ant.* 14:467). Upon Herod's return to the city, his Roman ally Sossius joined him. They encamped outside the north wall of the city. In the summer of 37 BCE the siege of Jerusalem began.

> The first wall was taken in forty days, and the second in fifteen more; and some of the porticoes around the temple were burnt, which Herod accused Antigonus of setting on fire, making an effort to draw upon him the hatred of the Jews by this charge. And when the outer precincts of the temple and the Lower City had been captured, the Jews fled into the inner precinct of the temple and the Upper City. (*Ant.* 14:476–477)

Slaughter soon began in the city. The Romans were furious at the length of the siege and ignored Herod's appeals to desist. At this point, Antigonus abandoned the Baris, fell at Sossius' feet and pleaded for mercy. The Roman mocked him, addressing him in the feminine form of his name, Antigone (*Ant.* 14:481) and put him in chains.

Herod was concerned that the plundering by the Romans and desecration of the temple would alienate the new king from the people he would now have to rule. He appealed for calm and even took from his own wealth to reward the soldiers, rather than have them plunder the captives. Josephus remarks that the date of Herod's victory in Jerusalem fell on the same day as that of Pompey, "in the third month, on the day of the Fast, as if it were a recurrence of the misfortune which came upon the Jews in the time of Pompey" (*Ant.* 4:487–488). While the year of the fall of Jerusalem can be ascertained in 37 BCE, the month and day are less certain.

Antigonus was led away in chains to Antioch. In the first case on record, Rome beheaded a conquered king; Sossius executed Antigonus at Herod's request (*Ant.* 14:490; *War* 1:357; Dio Cass. 49.22) bringing an end to the Hasmonean dynasty.

> The Hasmonean line came to an end after a hundred and twenty-six years (i.e. 163–37 BCE). Theirs was a splendid and renowned house because of both their lineage and their priestly office, as well as the things which its founders achieved on behalf of the nation. But they lost their royal power through internal strife, and it passed to Herod, the son of Antipater, who came from a house of common people and from a private family that was subject to the kings. (*Ant.* 14:490–491; cf. *Ant.* 14:78)

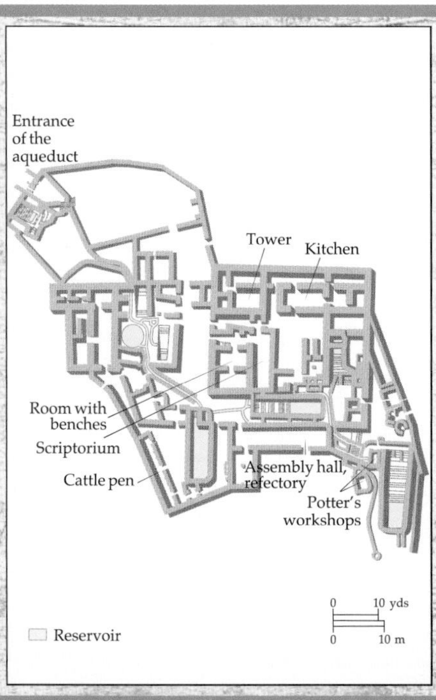


*The Qumran caves and plan of Kh. Qumran.*

**QUMRAN.** In 1947 Bedouin shepherds discovered a cache of seven parchment scrolls hidden in a cave (Cave 1Q) in the barren steppe land of the Judean Wilderness. In the winter of 1949, an expedition led by G. L. Harding and Father R. de Vaux, sponsored by the Jordanian Department of Antiquities, the Palestine (Rockefeller) Archaeological Museum, and the École Biblique et Archéologique Française of Jerusalem, excavated the first cave, which yielded parchment fragments. This remarkable find set off a frantic search for additional scrolls among the hundreds of caves that pock the limestone and marl cliffs along the western shore of the Dead Sea by both the Bedouin and scholars. Caves two through eleven (2Q–11Q) were discovered between 1952 and 1956, with the majority of the caves being initially discovered by the Bedouin. Beginning in 1951 and from 1953 to 1956 an expedition led by de Vaux on behalf of the École Biblique excavated the site of Khirbet Qumran (the 1951 excavations were co-directed with Harding, who represented the Jordanian Department of Antiquities), which was situated adjacent to the caves. Subsequent excavations and surveys of Khirbet Qumran and the caves surrounding the site have yielded no further scrolls, but have brought to light information on the life of the community that inhabited Qumran in the late Hellenistic and Early Roman eras.

The library of scrolls discovered among the eleven caves around Qumran preserved invaluable works for the study of the Hebrew Bible and Judaism of the late Second Temple period. The library of scrolls contains biblical works (all books of the Hebrew Bible apart from Esther and Nehemiah have been discovered), Jewish works previously known apart from Qumran (e.g., *Jubilees*, Tobit, and portions of *1 Enoch*), and Jewish works previously unknown, some of which came from the Qumran Community and others which do not appear to have been composed by the group at Qumran.

While scholarship continues to debate the meaning and significance of the Dead Sea Scrolls, one of the most contentious issues is the identity of the Congregation referred to in some of the writings discovered within the caves: "That every Israelite may know his place in the Congregation of God, an eternal society" (1QS 2:22). Although every imaginable affiliation has been suggested, the identification of this group as the Essenes continues to represent the opinion of most scholars.

The Qumran library remains one of the most important archaeological discoveries of the twentieth century. It provides a treasure trove for biblical scholars and others interested in the developments of Jewish thought in late antiquity. Of inestimable value are the writings that reflect the sectarian thought of the Congregation at Qumran. These documents of biblical interpretation and apocalyptic speculation shed light on the spiritual life and thought of the Congregation. Moreover, their similarities and differences with other contemporary groups and individuals assist us to better understand the varieties of religious expressions and streams of Jewish thought in the late Hellenistic and early Roman eras, including nascent Christianity. Furthermore, the ideology and vocabulary of the Qumran sectarian scrolls provides an important, yet often overlooked, theological repository for the developing ideas and expressions of the Hellenistic Christian communities.

# CHAPTER SIXTEEN

# HEROD AND HIS SONS

## 37 BCE TO 6 CE

It took Herod almost three years to realize the kingdom granted to him by the Roman Senate. After the capture of Jerusalem (37 BCE), his rule would extend another thirty-four years (*Ant.* 17:191; *War* 1: 665; cf. *As. Mos.* 6:6), longer than any other sovereign during the days of the Jewish Second Commonwealth. Historians commonly identify three periods of his reign. During the first twelve years (37–25 BCE), Herod consolidated power. There still existed those both inside and outside of Herod's kingdom who resisted his rule. The second period (25–13 BCE) was a time of great prosperity. His relationship with Rome deepened, founded on the strength of his relationship with Caesar Augustus. It was also during this time that Herod accomplished most of his extensive building. The size of his kingdom reached its greatest extent, including lands not even ruled by Alexander Jannaeus. The final years of Herod's reign (13–4 BCE) were marked by domestic strife and the king's declining health.

## HEROD'S EARLY YEARS (37–25 BCE)

The first years of Herod's rule were a deft balancing act within the changing political fortunes of the Roman Empire. This era marked the final phase of the Roman civil wars and Octavian's defeat of Mark Antony at the Battle of Actium (31 BCE). Against this backdrop, Herod also faced challenges closer to home. Cleopatra VII, Queen of Egypt, used her considerable influence over Antony to obtain parts of Herod's kingdom. Her aim was to reestablish Egyptian control over lands that had previously been in the possession of the Ptolemies: Judea and the lands of the Nabateans.

When the Roman Senate in 40 BCE awarded Herod the diadem, it also granted him the lands of the ethnarch Hyrcanus: Judea (including eastern Idumea), Perea, Galilee and the Jezreel Valley. Appian's record that in 39 BCE Antony expected Herod to collect imperial taxes in (western) Idumea and Samaria (App. *Bell. Civ.* 5.8.75) indicates that the new king also possessed responsibility for these areas. Since there is no record of a separate occasion when these regions were given to Herod, it seems likely that they were included in the lands awarded by the Roman Senate in 40 BCE.

Control over western Idumea and Samaria gave Herod access to important coastal settlements. Although the Parthians had razed Marisa (*Ant.* 14: 364; *War* 1: 269), Jamnia and Azotus remained important possessions on the plains of Idumea (1 Macc 4: 15; cf. *Ant.* 12: 308). Control of Samaria brought with it the important ports of Joppa and Apollonia. Likewise, the strategic site of Arethusa-Pegae (*War* 1:156; *Ant.* 13: 261; m. *Parah* 8:10; t. *Ter.* 1:15) controlled trade routes through the coastal plain. It is here that later Herod would establish Antipatris in honor of his father (*War* 1: 417).

*Scale model of Herod's Temple at Jerusalem's Holyland Hotel (now at the Israel Museum).*

Even with the increase of Judean territorial dominion under Herod, the Hasmonean aristocracy had not given up hope that one day a member of the priestly family would reascend the throne. Indeed, Herod's divorce from Doris and marriage to Mariamme, granddaughter of Hyrcanus, was intended to secure his offspring the claim to the priestly dynasty (*War* 1: 241). In the meantime, a Hasmonean was absent both from the throne and the position of high priest.

When Herod came to power, the elderly Hyrcanus was still in Parthian captivity, having been taken hostage when Antigonus ruled Judea (*Ant.* 15:11–20; cf. *Ant.* 14:366; *War* 1:273). Now Herod took steps to negotiate his release in order to gain favor with the Hasmoneans. The Parthians had mutilated Hyrcanus' ear to prevent him from being a contender for the throne of Antigonus. His disfigurement still prevented him from returning to his duties as high priest, leaving him as little threat to Herod.

The king could have appointed other members of the Hasmonean family to follow Antigonus, but his suspicious nature led him to appoint "an unknown priest named Ananel" from Babylon (*Ant.* 15:22; cf. m. *Para* 3:5). Alexandra, Herod's mother-in-law and daughter of Hyrcanus, objected to this ignominy suffered by the Hasmoneans and used her friendship with Cleopatra to coerce the appointment of her young son, Jonathan Aristobulus III (*Ant.* 15:23–24; *War* 1:437). Under pressure from Alexandra and Mariamme, Herod relented and replaced Ananel with Aristobulus, when the young Hasmonean was barely seventeen years old (*Ant.* 15: 39–41).

During the Feast of Tabernacles that year (c. 35 BCE), Aristobulus began his service in the Temple. The crowds in Jerusalem received the young priest with great affection, which only confirmed Herod's suspicions (*Ant.* 15: 51–52). The king realized that he could not personally remove Aristobulus, lest he arouse the hostility of his wife's family and the people who loved the new high priest. Instead, Herod arranged the young man's murder, while he was being entertained at Alexandra's palace in Jericho. On an occasion when the young men were playing sport in the swimming pools that had been built by Alexander Jannaeus, they held Aristobulus underwater until he drowned (*Ant.* 15:55; *War* 1:437).

Alexandra recognized who was behind her son's murder and brought charges through Cleopatra to Antony. Antony eventually exonerated Herod of the charges, but the events did little to improve Herod's relationship with Mariamme or her

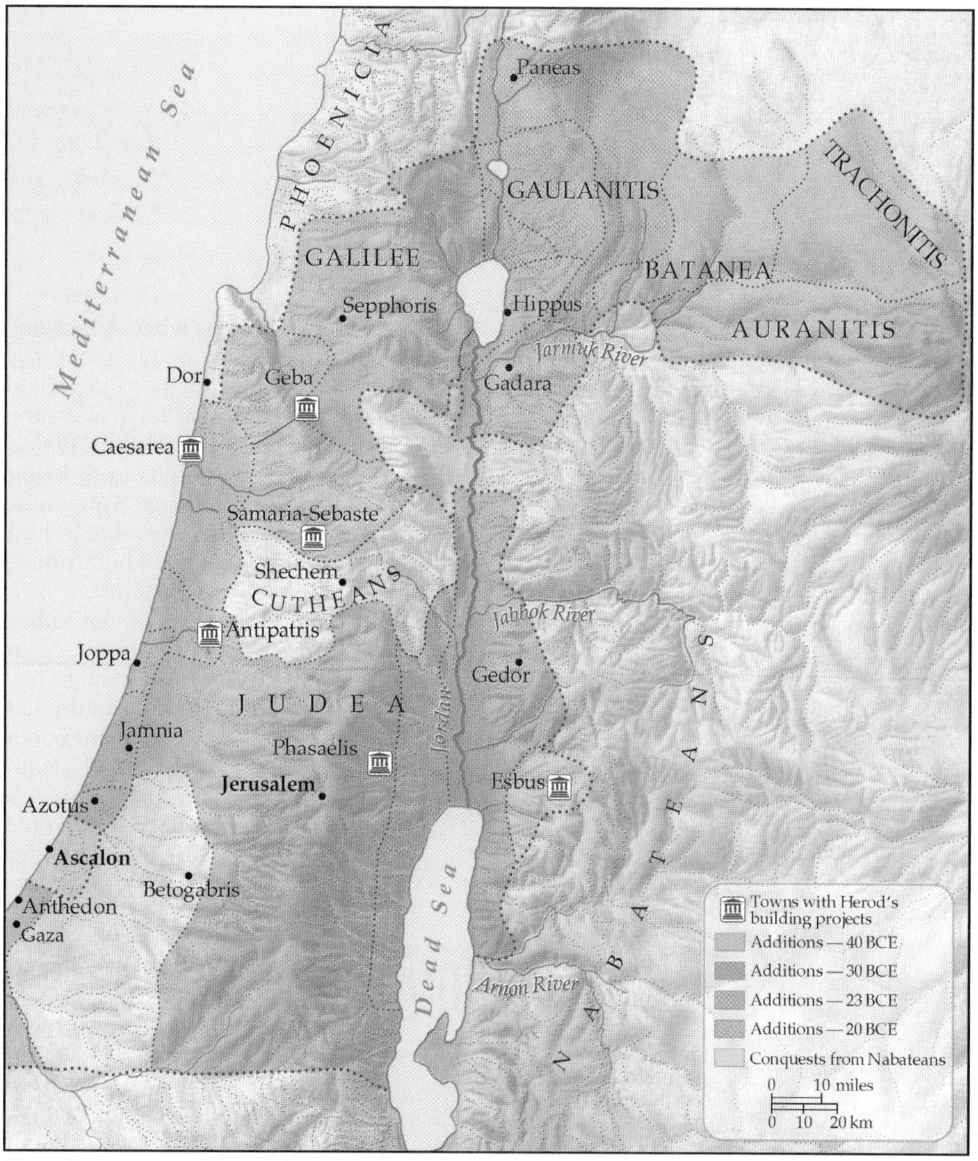


**The Growth of Herod's Kingdom (40–4 bce)**

family. Resentment and suspicion would grow until Herod's tragic removal of all he suspected of sedition.

As we mentioned, Cleopatra sought to expand her kingdom at the expense of the neighboring rulers. "She asked Antony for Judea and Arabia, requesting him to take them away from their royal rulers" (i.e. Herod and Malchus II, king of Arabia; *Ant.* 15: 92; *War* 1:360). Although Antony resisted the full scope of Cleopatra's designs, he granted Cleopatra the coastal regions that included Herod's up to the Eleutherus River north of Beirut, with the exception of Tyre and Sidon (*Ant.* 15:95; *War* 1:361; Plut. *Ant.* 36.2–3).

The queen's territorial ambitions left Herod in danger of having no access to the sea with the loss of his ports and coastal settlements. Antony also awarded her lands around Jericho and in the Transjordan (*Ant.* 15:96; *War* 1:361; Dio Cassius 49.32). Herod was able to mitigate this loss of territory by arranging to lease from Cleopatra, " those parts of Arabia that had been given to her and also the revenues of the region about Jericho" (*Ant.* 15: 96). According to Josephus, Herod paid two hundred talents to lease his own lands and also served as a surety for the tributes from Arabia (*War* 1: 362; *Ant.* 15: 132). Herod struggled to collect the payments due from Malchus, and he was preparing to march against him when he received word of the impending battle between Octavian and Antony.

Herod offered to fight alongside Antony, but his benefactor instructed him to deal with Malchus instead. Herod's first battle with the Nabateans was at Diospolis (*Ant.* 15:111; *War* 1:366). It has been suggested that the site should be identified with Dium in the Transjordan. If so, the amended reading likely resembled a similar toponymic reference in another campaign, "Alexander (son of Aristobulus II) marched again to the city Dium" (*Ant.* 13:393; cf. *Ant.* 14:75; Tell Ashᶜari).

Although Herod's forces routed the Nabateans at Dium, the next battle at Canatha in Coele-Syria proved disastrous (*War* 1:367–368; cf. *Ant.* 15:112). So devastating was Herod's defeat that he was incapable of mustering a sufficient army to wage open war. He had to resort to guerrilla warfare.

> Camping in the mountains and always avoiding open battle, he still did considerable damage by his incessant and energetic movements, and he was also very careful of his own men, using every means to make good his losses. (*Ant.* 15:120; cf. *War* 1:369)

Herod's preoccupation with the Arabs proved fortuitous. At the Battle of Actium Herod's benefactor was defeated. Antony returned to Egypt where he died by his own hand. Ironically, his demise also removed one of the greatest external threats to Herod's kingdom—Cleopatra. Although Herod had not fought alongside Antony at Actium, he had remained a trusted ally sending money and grains (*Ant.* 15:190). Now, the changing political fortunes in the Roman Empire required that Herod move quickly and decisively (Plut. *Ant.* 72).

Herod rallied his forces and crossed the Jordan to attack the Nabatean forces near Philadelphia (Rabbath-ammon; *War* 1: 380–385; *Ant.* 15:147–155). Many fell on both sides, but Herod prevailed. The Nabateans attempted to sue for peace, but Herod pressed forward until they surrendered and declared Herod their ruler (*Ant.* 15:160). Next he dealt with intrigues closer to home. He discovered that Hyrcanus had conspired with Alexandra to escape to Malchus (*Ant.* 15:167). Hyrcanus was brought before the Sanhedrin (cf. m. *Sanh.* 2:1), accused of treason and executed (*Ant.* 15: 173).

Herod had effectively removed the Hasmonean threat to his throne. He now had to face Octavian. He traveled to Rhodes, leaving his mother, sister and all his children protected at Masada (*Ant.* 15:184), while Mariamme and Alexandra remained under guard at Alexandrion (*Ant.* 15:185–186). When Caesar received the king, Herod removed his crown but otherwise remained adorned in royal regalia (*Ant.* 15: 187; *War* 1:387). He made no apology for his friendship and loyalty to Antony. Indeed, he stated that if he had not been otherwise engaged with the Arabs in the Transjordan, he would have fought alongside Antony. In that event, the outcome might have been different. Nevertheless, he now offered Caesar the same loyalty he had given to Antony.

Herod's loyalty to Rome had been demonstrated time and again. There was no reason to suggest that he would not likewise serve the new emperor. "[Caesar] then restored his diadem to him, at the same time urging him to show himself no less a friend to him than he had formerly been to Antony" (*Ant.* 15:195). Herod pledged his loyalty to the new emperor and then accompanied him to Egypt, showering Caesar and his friends with extravagant gifts. The Judean king returned home with greater power than he had left, much to the consternation of his opponents.

Augustus not only retained Herod as king of Judea, he rewarded him with the return of the lands taken by Cleopatra. Herod was also given additional Greek cities: "Gadara,

Hippus (cf. *Ant.* 14:75), and Samaria, and on the coast also Gaza, Anthedon, Joppa (cf. *Ant.* 15:294) and Strato's Tower" (*Ant.* 15: 217; *War* 1:396). The addition of these Greek cities increased the non-Jewish population responsible to Herod's rule.

Herod proved to be an able and loyal client king to Rome. In 23 BCE Caesar once again enlarged Herod's kingdom and entrusted to him the northeastern region of Trachonitis, Batanea and Auranitis (*Ant.* 15:343–344; *War* 1:398). Zenodorus had leased these lands (*Ant.* 15:344; *War* 1:398) after Antony executed Lysanias, son of Ptolemaeus, the last king of the Itureans, in 35 BCE (*Ant.* 15:92; *War* 1: 440; Dio Cass. 49.32.5; cf. Plut. *Ant.* 36.3). The area was known for its brigandage. According to Josephus, not only did Zenodorus do nothing to prevent it, he even shared in the spoils (*Ant.* 15:345).

Augustus transferred to Herod the administration of these territories to restore order, and the Judean king "put a stop to their criminal acts and brought security and peace to the surrounding peoples" (*Ant.* 15:348). Three years later when Zenodorus died, the emperor rewarded Herod by appointing him the procurator of all of Syria and granting to him the remaining lands from Zenodorus' tetrarchy. This included Gaulanitis, Paneas and the Ulatha region (*Ant.* 15:359–360; *War* 1:400).

To establish an increased measure of control, Herod settled the region with Idumeans and Jews from Babylonia. These new lands included in Herod's kingdom brought new settlements with little previous history. Here Herod did not have to face a deposed aristocracy or religious qualms as he did in Judea. The population was indebted to Herod's efforts on their behalf. The gratitude that they felt was exhibited in the continued loyalty they gave to Herod and his successors. For later members of the Herodian dynasty, Agrippa I (*Ant.* 18:237; *War* 2:181) and his son, Agrippa II (*Ant.* 20:138; *War* 2:247), this region was the testing ground for their administrative abilities. Once proven here, Rome granted them control of larger segments of Herod's previous kingdom.

## Herod's Building Projects

Herod possesses few rivals for the monumental achievements of his building projects. Most of these were carried out during the golden years of his rule, 25 to 13 BCE. These years were ones of relative political stability in which Herod was able to focus his resources to demonstrate that he was worthy of the trust Rome had placed in him. Indeed, the scale of his efforts seems intended to impress his Roman benefactors. It should thus be no surprise that Herod ascribed the names of Mark Antony, Caesar Augustus and Marcus Agrippas to buildings and cities he constructed throughout his kingdom.

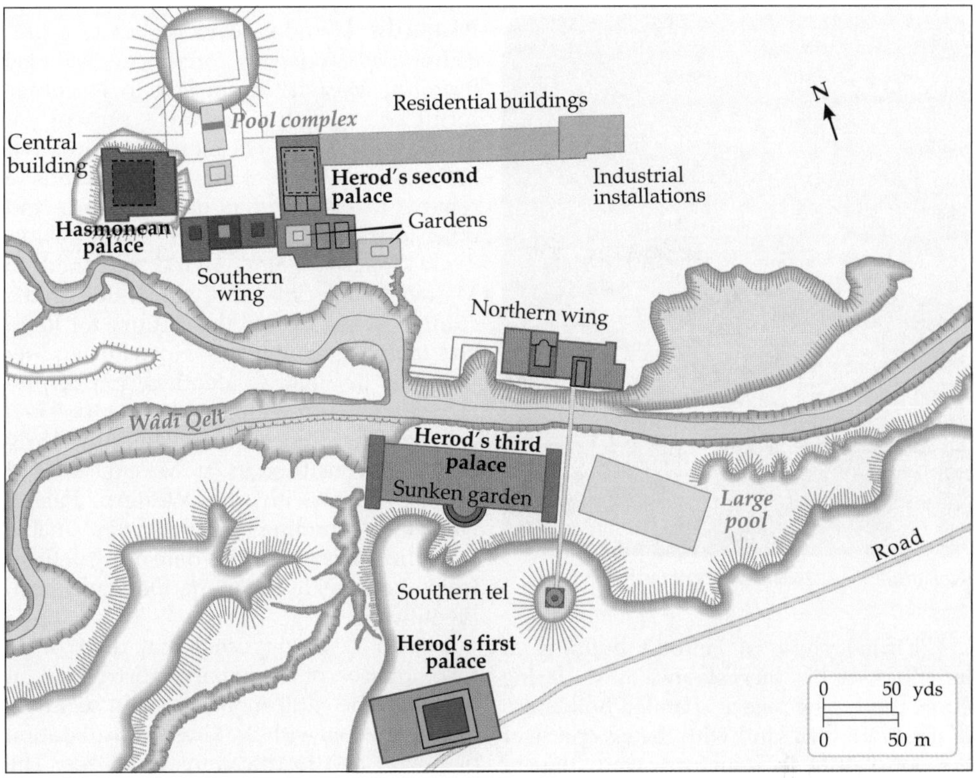


**Roman Jericho (Tulul Abū el-$^{c}$Alayiq)**

Herod's architectural endeavors extended from Idumea to Epirus in western Greece. Nevertheless, he lavished most of his efforts on Jerusalem, Judea, Samaria and cities on the Mediterranean coast. The writings of Josephus are the primary historical witness to Herod's efforts. Epigraphical evidence and archaeological investigations during the twentieth century have likewise provided details about Herod's building projects.

Herod's contributions included new settlements (e.g. Phasaelis, Antipatris) and the transformation of previous Hellenistic villages into full-fledged cities (e.g. Caesarea, Sebaste). He also strengthened fortifications in the Judean wilderness that lined the eastern frontiers of his kingdom (Alexandrion, Cypros, Dok, Hyrcania, Masada, Macherus). One of the puzzling omissions in Herod's efforts is the relative absence of his building efforts in Galilee. He began his political career as the governor of Galilee. Yet, the king left few monuments to commemorate his beginnings. Equally remarkable is the lack of Herodian fortifications in Galilee, which would seem to challenge the repeated perception that Galilee was a hotbed of political dissent during the reign of Herod.

**Jericho**. Herod spared no expense in the construction of elaborate palaces throughout his kingdom. In Jericho he followed the lead of the Hasmoneans, building elaborate winter palaces along Wâdī Qelt. Three stages of Herodian construction have been identified. In 35 BCE Herod built a palace south of Wâdī Qelt and west of Tulul Abū el-$^{c}$Alayiq, while the Hasmonean palaces remained in use. His palace contained bathing installations and a peristyle courtyard. In recent excavations of Herod's palace at Jericho, the archaeologists uncovered a stepped pool with an adjoining pool lacking steps. The installation's style matched that of the ritual immersion baths (*miqva'ot*) discovered in the Hasmonean palace at Jericho. This comes as little surprise, since Herod's wife belonged to the Hasmonean clan. However, what is exceptional about the mikveh in Herod's palace at Jericho is that it is the only one found in a Herodian palace that was accompanied with an *otzar* ("reservoir").

The king's initial, modest palace at Jericho survived the devastating earthquake in 31 BCE, but the nearby palaces of his predecessors did not. The second phase of Herod's winter palaces was built on the ruins of these Hasmonean buildings. Yet, not everything was destroyed. In a measure of irony that only Herod could fully appreciate, the large Hasmonean swimming pools, in which he had conspired to have the young Aristobulus drowned, survived the earthquake and were integrated into Herod's renovations. This palace included a peristyle courtyard and Roman-style bathhouse typical of Herod's residences. It also included a winepress and columbarium (dovecote) to provide for the dining in Herod's triclinium hall.

The final phase of Herod's palace in Jericho was the largest and most ornate. Concrete walls were faced with Roman-style plastering, *opus reticulatum* and *opus quadratum*, perhaps indicating the direct involvement of Roman builders and architects in the construction.

*Remains of the Herodian palace at Jericho.*

The final phase of Herod's building at Jericho was his largest and most daring effort there. The palace spanned both sides of the Wâdī Qelt, and with the exception of the pool, all of its structures were aligned with the winter streambed. A bridge led from the southern side of the ravine where Herod had constructed a sunken garden and pool below the high tel. The northern wing of the palace had a large reception hall, rooms and, typically for a Herodian palace, a Roman-style bathing complex.

As indicated, to the south of Wâdī Qelt were three wings to Herod's new palace. A large sunken garden was framed by a rectangular structure and oriented to parallel the wadi. To the east of the gardens was a large pool measuring 295 by 138 feet (90 by 42 m). The scale of the pool has led excavators to suggest its use for swimming and boating, and competition associated with these sports.

Excavations carried out on the southern tel, Tulul Abū el-ᶜAlayiq, confirmed that the structures on the summit belonged to Herod's third palace at Jericho. Crossing the bridge that spanned Wâdī Qelt, one ascended the staircase to the top of an artificial mound. On it was constructed an impressive structure with a cistern and bathhouse in its basement. The structure itself consisted of a round hall built in a *tholos* shape with semicircular exedrae on four corners. A porticoed porch faced north looking over the gardens, wadi and lower palace. What struck the excavators was the considerable effort afforded in the construction of the artificial mound and staircase to access a single structure. They surmised that the round structure perched upon the artificial mound was intended to serve as a second reception hall. Its height gave it a commanding view over the nearby palm trees towards the surrounding plain of Jericho. Here Herod entertained his guests in similar fashion to his residence at Masada with wonderful vistas and baths.

**Masada**. Herod's development of a preceding Hasmonean presence is also found at Masada. According to Josephus, fortifications were already present at Masada during the Hasmonean period (*War* 7:285). Herod was sent there by Hyrcanus to remove rebels who had taken Masada and other fortresses in the country (*War* 1:237–238; *Ant.* 14:296–298). Later, Herod returned to Masada to leave his family protected on the summit, when he fled the country for Petra and then Rome in 40 BCE. Notwithstanding Josephus' testimony, identification of pre-Herodian construction on Masada has been elusive. It was once thought that the early phase of construction at Masada should be identified with the Western Palace. However, soundings in 1989 were unable to confirm this notion. To date no structures from the pre-Herodian period have been identified.

Instead, it is suggested that there were three phases of Herodian construction at Masada. The earliest construction seems to have coincided with the king's consolidation of power and fortifications in 35 BCE. The second phase consisted of the extensive palace complex on the northern end of the mountain. The final phase of building at Masada primarily entailed casemate walls and some storage facilities.

The three-tiered northern palace provided a magnificent view north towards En-gedi. Access between the terraces was through a staircase on the western side of the mountain. About 65 feet (20 m) below the upper terrace, the only remnants to

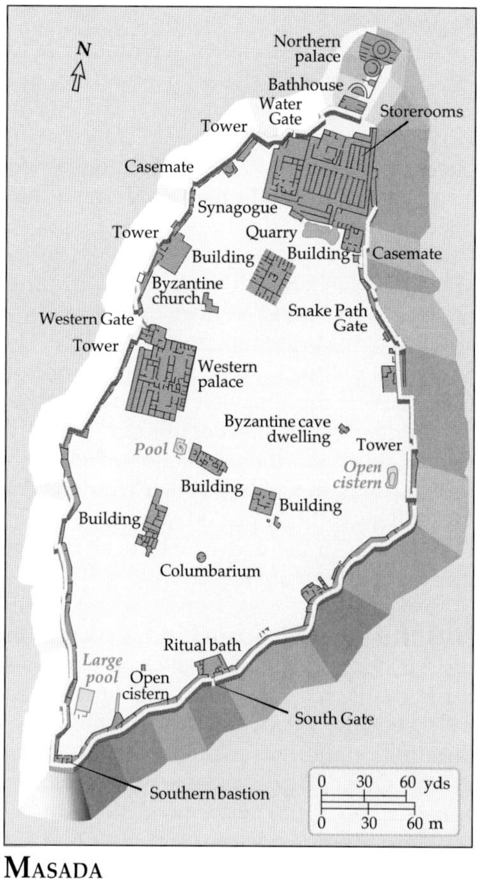


MASADA

*View of Masada, looking southeast.*

be seen from the middle terrace are the foundations laid in concentric circles. Here was a reception hall, resembling a *tholos*, which was surrounded by a portico of columns. Adjacent to the hall were two rooms where there was a stepped pool, apparently the remains of a mikveh. The staircase continued down to the lowest terrace, the best preserved of the three. It consisted of a square courtyard surrounded by porticoes.

On the eastern edge of the lower terrace, a staircase led to a small bathhouse. It possessed the expected components: a *calidarium* (hot room) built above a heating chamber (*hypocaust*), a *tepidarium* (warm room), and a cold plunge bath (*frigidarium*). The presence of this and other bathing installations at Masada stand in contrast to the arid setting on the summit. An obvious challenge for any residence on Masada was the lack of water. A sophisticated water-collection system (*War* 7:291) diverted winter rains from nearby wadis and channeled them into lower cisterns. These waters were then transported to reservoirs on the summit. The water storage capacity is remarkable with the lower cisterns alone estimated to have a capacity of 40,000 cubic meters.

**Caesarea**. While Herod's construction at Jericho and Masada followed the Hasmoneans, such was not the case in Caesarea and Sebaste. These were cities indebted to Herod for their founding. Augustus awarded Strato's Tower to Herod in 31 BCE. Almost ten years later the king transformed the Hellenistic village into a major port. He built extensively in the city (22–10 BCE) and the adjoining harbor that he named Sebastos.

Caesarea was a well-planned city with a Hippodamian grid street plan and installations typical of a Greco-Roman *polis*, including a theater, amphitheater and agora. Josephus preserves a detailed description of Herod's efforts at Caesarea (*Ant.* 15:331–341; 16:136–141; *War* 1:408–414). The historian lavished particular praise on Herod's construction of the harbor, the size of which exceeded the legendary port of Piraeus in Athens.

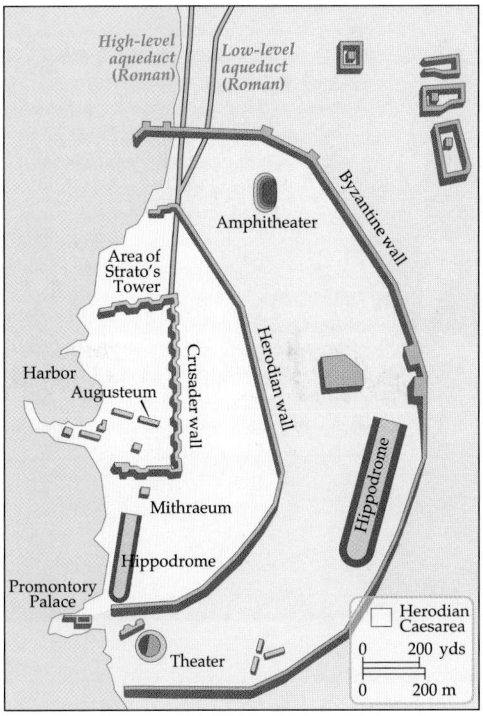


CAESAREA

Overlooking the harbor and perched upon a vaulted platform, Herod erected a temple in honor of the goddess Roma and Caesar Augustus.

To the west of the theater and at the southern end of a hippodrome, Herod built his Promontory Palace. As with the other Herodian palaces, it included Roman-style baths. What is uncommon in this palace is that the *frigidarium* (cold plunge bath) served as the architectural focal point for the palace. A large peristyle colonnaded courtyard surrounded a freshwater pool cut into the *kurkar* sandstone on the edge of the Mediterranean Sea. The palace was beautifully decorated with extensive mosaic floors some of which were uncovered intact. Although it is not the only *villa maritima* on the Mediterranean, its spectacular location on a promontory projection and surrounded on three sides by the sea makes it one of the most impressive. Similar to Herod's royal residence in Jerusalem, the Promontory Palace in Caesarea would later become the residence for the Roman governors of the province of Judea (cf. Acts 23:35; Mk 15:16).

**Sebaste (Samaria).** Caesarea served as the seaward outlet for the Herodian city of Sebaste, built upon the ancient ruins of biblical Samaria (1 Kgs 16: 23–24). Josephus describes Herod's contributions to Sebaste in his record of how the king honored his Roman benefactors.

> He was not content, however, to commemorate his patrons' names by palaces only; his munificence extended to the creation of whole cities. In the district of Samaria he built a town enclosed within magnificent walls twenty furlongs in length, introduced into it six thousand colonists, and gave them allotments of highly productive land. In the center of this settlement he erected a massive temple, enclosed in ground, a furlong and a half in length consecrated to Caesar; while he named the town itself Sebaste [i.e. the Greek equivalent to Augustus]. (*War* 1:403)

Archaeological excavations have uncovered the remains of Herod's building. Two towers dating from the time of Herod protected the city gate to the west. Built upon Hellenistic foundations, these towers are likely part of the walled fortifications mentioned by Josephus. Moreover, columns can still be seen from the colonnaded street that stretch over 875 yards (800 m) across the Herodian city.

On the western edge of the acropolis stood the Augusteum, the second of three (Caesarea, Sebaste, Paneas) temples built in honor of the Roman emperor. The vantage from the summit provides an unimpeded view of the Mediterranean Sea. Remains from a stadium and forum may likewise point us to the early Roman development of Sebaste.

**Herodium.** The largest and most impressive of Herod's palaces was that of Herodium (Jebel Fureidis). Josephus reports that Herod built the site to memorialize his victory over those pursuing him in his flight from Antigonus and the Parthians in 40 BCE (*Ant.* 14:359–360, 15:323–325; *War* 1:265). Herodium also served as the capital of the toparchy (*War* 3:55; Pliny *Nat. Hist.* 5.70) and the location for Herod's mausoleum.

Herod's construction at Herodium added to the height of an existing hill with concentric supporting walls and four towers. The increased height of the hill apparently was intended so that it could be seen from the environs of Jerusalem. On its summit Herod built his Upper Palace.

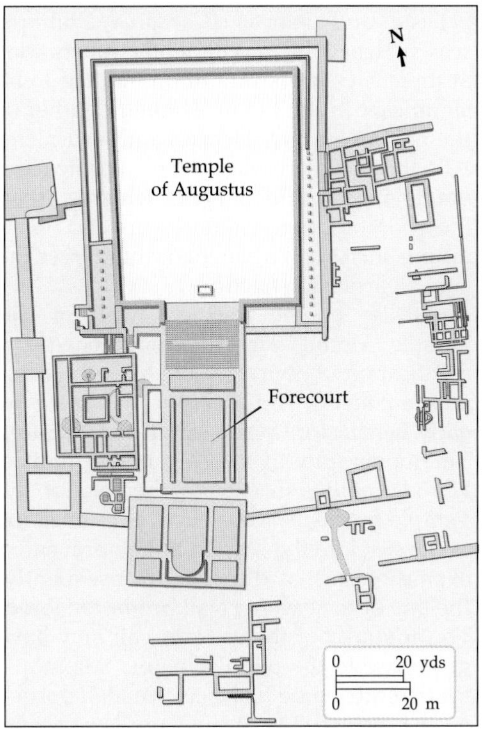


SEBASTE—TEMPLE OF AUGUSTUS

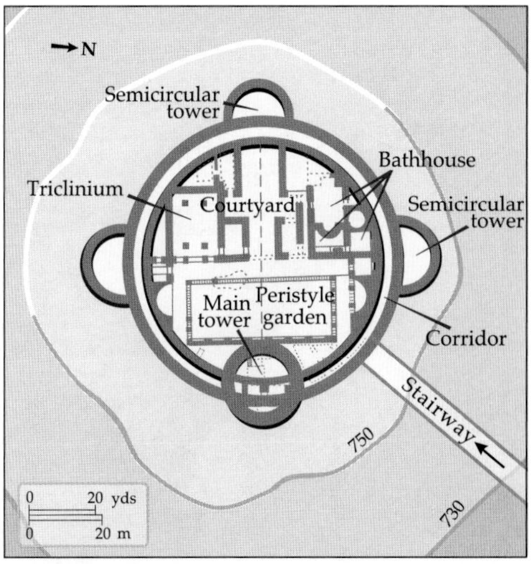


HERODIUM—THE PALACE-FORTRESS

At the base of the hill Herod built a complex of buildings constructed around a colonnaded pool and formal gardens. Herod's palatial residence at Herodium is one of the largest in the Roman world, and here the king entertained Marcus Agrippas on his visit to Judea in 15 BCE (*Ant.* 16:12–13). Although located in an arid setting, like his other desert palaces, Herodium did not lack an ample supply of water. Aqueducts brought water from springs adjacent to Solomon's Pools (cf. *War* 1:420).

Josephus records that Herod was buried at Herodium, but his tomb has yet to be discovered (*Ant.* 17:199; *War* 1:673). Certain location for the burial place of Herod must await further investigation.

*Herodium: view of the mountain palace-fortress from Lower Herodium.*

**Jerusalem.** Herod's architectural contribution to the city of Jerusalem left a lasting imprint on the shape of the city. The Hasmoneans had earlier restored the walls of Jerusalem and once again incorporated the western hill into the walled city. The line of their wall approximated the earlier defensive efforts of Hezekiah (2 Chr 32:5). Inadvertently, restoration by the Hasmoneans of walls on a line close to their previous course likely contributed to the confusion witnessed in the first century regarding the size of Jerusalem during the time of David. Josephus seems to have

*It is difficult to distinguish Herod's efforts at Mamre (Ramet el-Khalîl). Yet, the archaeologists have remarked on the similarity between the Herodian-style stone masonry found in situ at Mamre and that seen in the Herodian Machpelah in Hebron, a structure that stands mostly intact. The pilasters decorating the upper section of the walls of the Machpelah in Hebron and Mamre are also important for our understanding of the architectural style of the upper walls surrounding the Temple Mount that were destroyed in the Roman destruction of Jerusalem in 70 CE.*

*(above) Ḥaram el-Khalîl (Cave of Machpelah) in Hebron.*

*(left) Northern pilaster wall of the Herodian enclosure at Mamre (Ramet el-Khalîl).*

mistakenly thought that David's conquest of the Jebusite city included the western hill (cf. *Ant.* 7:64–65; *War* 5:137). This confusion over the size and development of Jerusalem would lead in the late Roman and Byzantine periods to the mistaken application of the biblical toponym "Mount Zion" to the western hill (e.g. Eus. *Onom.* 74:19).

Archaeologists are divided regarding responsibility for the construction of what Josephus calls the Second Wall. Herod or his Hasmonean predecessors (cf. *Ant.* 14:476) added a wall that enclosed the northern market area. Although the precise line of the Second Wall has yet to be determined, its beginning and end points are described by Josephus:

> The Second Wall took its beginning from that gate which they called " Gennath, " which belonged to the first wall; it only encompassed the northern quarter of the city, and reached as far as the tower Antonia. (*War* 5:146)

Herod's Jerusalem was a bicameral city. On both the eastern and western hills Herod was responsible for the construction of monumental enclosures fortified on their northern exposures. Very little remains of Herod's royal palace on the western hill in the vicinity of today's Citadel and the Armenian Seminary in the Old City of Jerusalem. Only the foundations have been identified from what Josephus describes as a remarkable structure.

> [Herod's] own palace, which he erected in the Upper City, comprised two most spacious and beautiful buildings, with which the Temple itself bore no comparison; these he named after his friends, the one Caesareum and the other Agrippeum. (*War* 1:402; cf. *Ant.* 15:318)

The two buildings named for Herod's benefactors housed his *triclinia* and rooms for sleeping. They looked out on open-air courts with gardens and pools.

> All around were many circular cloisters, leading one into another, the columns in each being different, and their open courts all of greensward; there were groves of various trees intersected by long walks, which were bordered by deep canals, and ponds everywhere studded with bronze figures through which the water was discharged and around the streams were numerous cots for tame pigeons. (*War* 5: 180–181)

Three monumental towers named for Hippicus, Phasael and Mariamme (*War* 5: 164–171) guarded the northern entrance into Herod's royal palace. The lower portions of one of Herod's towers can still be seen today at the Citadel near Jaffa Gate.

Herod's greatest architectural achievement was the renovation and expansion of the Jerusalem Temple. It may perhaps signify something of Herod's delicate balance between Rome and the Jewish nation that his construction of three temples in honor of Caesar Augustus at Caesarea, Sebaste and Paneas [Caesarea Philippi] was matched by monumental sanctuaries at three sites Jewish tradition marked to be significant in the life of Abraham, father of the nation: Mamre, Hebron and Jerusalem. All three sanctuaries were constructed employing a Roman-style temenos plan incorporating a walled enclosure and open-air precincts with a sanctuary built over the site of particular sanctity.

Outside of the northern wall of the Temple Mount, Herod strengthened the fortification known previously as the Baris and renamed it Antonia (*War* 1:118) after his early benefactor, Mark Antony (*Ant.* 15:409). The topography of the eastern hill limited Herod's ability to expand the area of the Temple precincts. The severity of the slope to the east into the Kidron Valley prevented expansion in that direction. Consequently, the line of the eastern wall predates Herod. The antiquity of the eastern wall may have given rise to the popular name, Solomon's Portico, attributed to the colonnaded portico on the eastern side of the Temple precincts (Acts 5:12). Evidence of Herod's extension of the eastern wall southward can be seen in "the Seam" c. 100 feet (32 m) north of the southeastern corner of the Temple Mount.

Herod had to construct an artificially elevated platform to support the expanded precincts. With these modifications, Herod was able to increase significantly the surface area of the enclosed Temple Mount (cf. *War* 1: 401). Nevertheless, it seems that for ritual purposes Herod's expanded area was never reckoned according to Jewish law (cf. m. *Mid.* 2:1).

According to Josephus, Herod built a Royal Stoa the width of the platform along the southern end. Recent excavations have discovered that this stoa was accessed from a staircase supported by one of the largest arches in the classical world, "Robinson's Arch, named after the nineteenth-century explorer who discovered it. Three other gates provided access to the platform from the direction of the upper city. However, the primary means of access for pilgrims was to ascend the monumental staircase and to enter the Huldah Gates on the southern face of the Temple Mount. The needs of ritual purity for pilgrims ascending to the Temple led to the construction of numerous ritual bathing installations near the Huldah Gates.

Of course, the jewel in the crown of Herod's building in Jerusalem was the Temple itself. Josephus praises Herod's efforts (*Ant.* 15:391–420). Even the Talmud, the repository of those who were hardly Herod's supporters, remarked, "He who has not seen the Temple of Herod has never seen a beautiful building" (b. *Bab. Bat.* 4a). Today scholars disagree concerning the specifics of Herod's Temple. This is understandable, because the ancient literary witnesses differ. Since a scientific archaeological investigation of the Temple Mount has never been conducted, those differences remain unresolved.

## The Declining Years of Herod

Herod's domestic troubles overshadowed his reign. In his waning years they culminated in a series of tragic events. The king executed his beloved wife Mariamme in 29 BCE on charges of infidelity (*Ant.* 15: 232–236; *War* 1:438–443). A few years later he also put to death his mother-in-law, Alexandra (*Ant.* 15:247–252). Herod's guilt over Mariamme's death continued to haunt him. It also poisoned his relationship with his two sons by Mariamme, Alexander and Aristobulus. They had spent six years being educated in Rome, and the popular expectation was that these sons born into the Hasmonean line would succeed Herod on the throne. In 17 BCE Herod traveled to Rome to bring his sons back to Judea.

Their return was not welcomed by everyone. Herod's sister, Salome, had been at the center of the allegations against Mariamme (*Ant.* 15:213, 231). She probably had a right to be concerned for her own welfare should the sons of the deceased queen take the throne. Herod's brother, Pheroras, and the king's eldest son, Antipater, likewise were suspicious of the boys' return. Years of intrigues, accusations, and machinations ensued between the parties. The domestic strife in Herod's court became so bad that even Augustus had to intervene in an attempt to bring reconciliation.

Three years before Herod's death, Alexander and Aristobulus were brought before a tribunal in Syria where they were condemned to death. They were brought to Sebaste where they were executed by strangulation and their bodies buried at the fortress of Alexandrion (*Ant.* 16:356–394; *War* 2:101–110). Hope for a return to the Hasmonean dynasty died with the two sons, and now the focus of succession fell to Herod's oldest son, Antipater. Yet, Herod had other sons, and Antipater's position was not secure. His alliance with his uncle Pheroras was later perceived as sedition, and upon Pheroras' death, accusations were laid against Antipater.

*Coin of Herod the Great.*

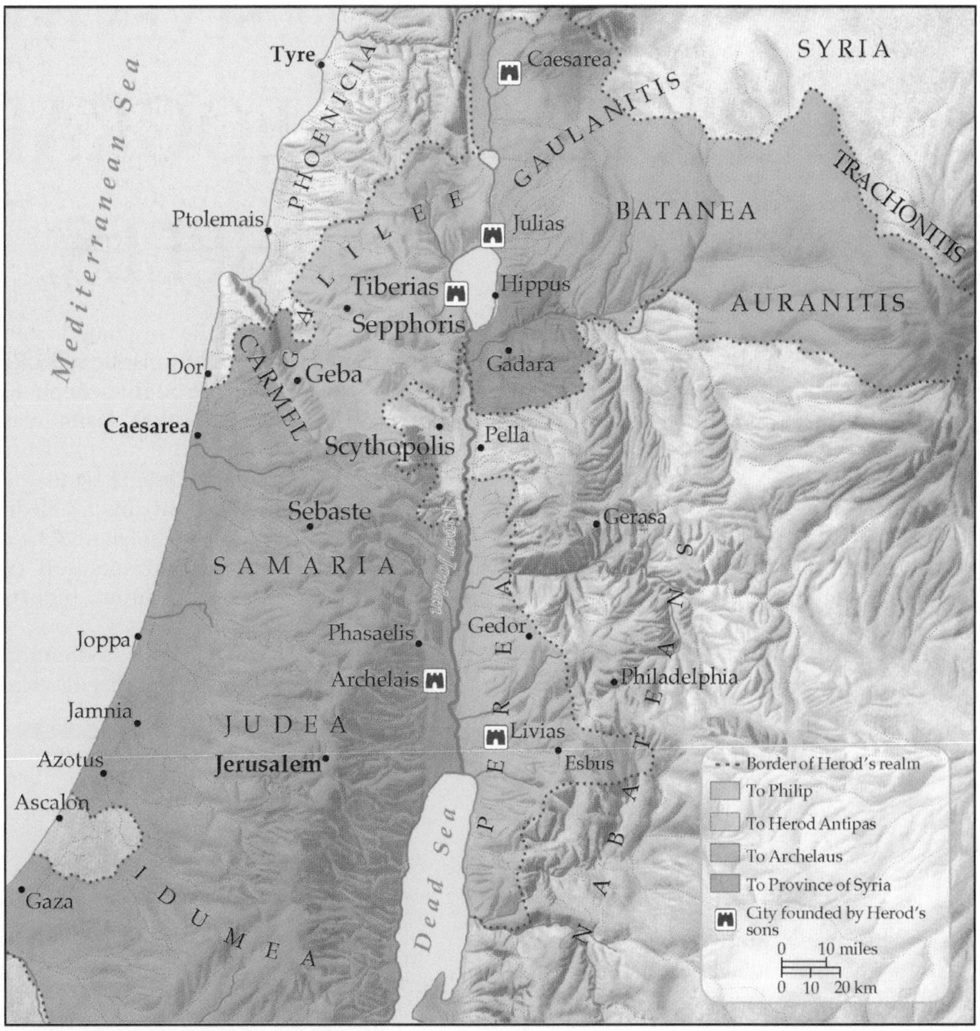


**The Division of Herod's Kingdom (4 BCE–6 CE)**

## Herod's Death and the Division of His Kingdom

In the meantime, Herod's health declined. He attempted to get relief from the hot springs of Callirrhoe (*War* 1:657; *Ant.* 17: 171; Pliny *Nat. Hist.* 5.16). Yet, the mineral springs brought little relief. Premature rumors of Herod's death were constant through the kingdom. Josephus records one event when two sages, upon hearing of Herod's passing, led the pulling down of an eagle Herod had erected over a gate of the Temple—an offense to the Jewish prohibition against graven images (*Ant.* 17: 151; *War* 1:651). Although frail, the king had enough strength to oversee their execution.

In his last days, Herod received permission from the emperor to execute Antipater. He executed his eldest son a mere five days before his own death (*Ant.* 17: 191). Josephus likewise reports that Herod realized there would be little mourning at his death. So, he arrested the leading men of the country and instructed Salome that they should be executed upon his death in order to assure the mourning of the nation (*Ant.* 17: 174–175). She would later rescind that order (*Ant.* 17:193).

Herod died in 4 BCE. Josephus records a regal funeral procession from Jericho to Herodium where the king's body was laid to rest (*Ant.* 17:196–199). In his last days Herod changed his will a final time (*Ant.* 17:188–189). He requested from Caesar that his kingdom be divided among his three surviving sons. The king nominated Archelaus to be ethnarch and given the territories of Judea, Idumea and Samaria. The eldest son also received the two great cities founded by Herod, Caesarea and Sebaste. Herod Antipas was designated tetrarch and given Galilee and Perea. Herod Philip was also designated tetrarch. He received the lands on the northeastern edge of his father's kingdom: Batanea, Trachonitis, Auranitis, Gaulanitis, Paneas and the Ulatha region. Salome was left in the care of Archelaus. For her years of steadfast faithfulness, she was granted the cities of Jamnia, Azotus, on the coastal plain, and Phasaelis, in the Jordan Valley.

# CHAPTER SEVENTEEN
# HISTORICAL GEOGRAPHY OF THE GOSPELS

The narrative of the New Testament from its beginning to end assumes the reader is familiar with the physical setting that served as a stage for the unfolding drama. In many instances the location and nature of the recorded sites have been lost in time. Modern archaeology together with a careful reading of the ancient witnesses can assist in illuminating our understanding of the persons, places and events reported in the New Testament. On the following pages we will carefully consider significant events that may benefit from a historical and geographical reading of the text.

## THE BIRTH OF JESUS AND THE FLIGHT INTO EGYPT

Mark and John open their Gospels with the ministry of John the Baptist, while Matthew and Luke provide details of Jesus' birth. Even though the two birth narratives give different historical perspectives, they both identify the place of Jesus' birth at Bethlehem (Mt 2:1; Lk 2:15)—the ancestral home of King David (1 Sam 17:12). The relationship between Jesus and David is a particular emphasis of Matthew: "An account of the genealogy of Jesus the Messiah, *the son of David*, the son of Abraham" (Mt 1:1; 12:23 *et passim*).

By contrast, John's Gospel lacks both the title "son of David" and any mention of a Bethlehem birth. When the subject of Jesus' birthplace is raised, the Evangelist leaves unanswered the objection of some:

> Still others asked, "How can the Christ come from Galilee? Does not the Scripture say that the Christ will come from David's family and from Bethlehem, the town where David lived?" (Jn 7:41–42)

Luke records that Joseph and Mary were residents of Nazareth in Galilee (Lk 1:26, 2:4), and that they traveled to Bethlehem in compliance with a census ordered by Caesar Augustus when Quirinius was governor of Syria (Lk 2:2). Joseph's enrollment at Bethlehem suggests that he originated from the Judean region south of Jerusalem. Luke does not explain what brought Joseph to Nazareth in the years before Jesus was born.

We also possess scant information outside of the New Testament about this Galilean village (see Eus. *Onom.* 138:14; Epiph. *Adv. haer.* 30.11.10). Josephus makes no mention of Nazareth, and rabbinic tradition reports only that it was a village of priests (*Mishmarot* 18; *Qoh. Rab.* 2:8). The scarcity of its mention is not surprising. Modern archaeological work in Nazareth paints a picture of a remote, insignificant village that would have attracted little attention.

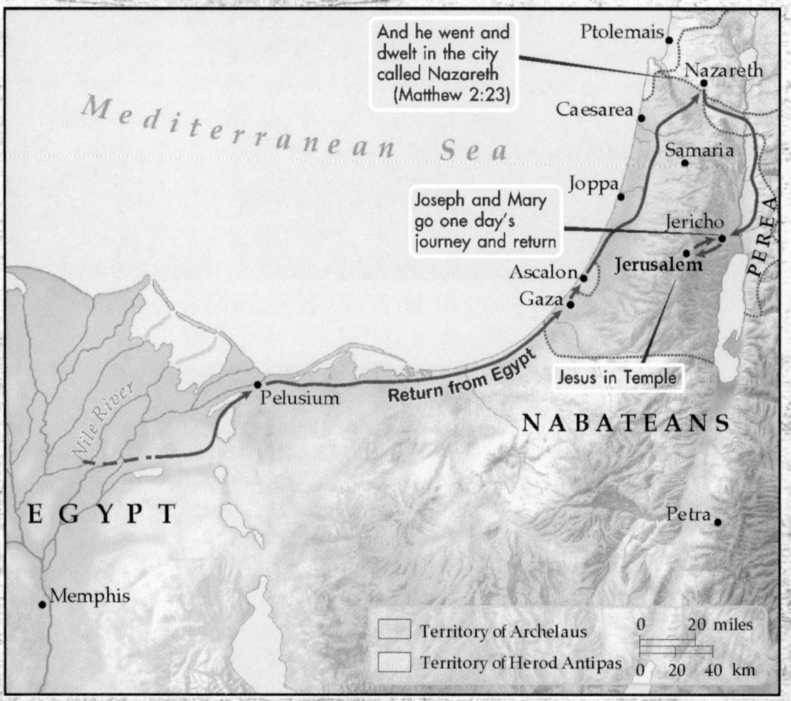

THE RETURN FROM EGYPT; THE BOY JESUS IN THE TEMPLE

Both Matthew and Luke present Jesus' birth during the last years of Herod the Great, who died in 4 BCE (Mt 2:1; Lk 1:5). New Testament scholarship has tried to reconcile Herod's presence in the birth narratives with Luke's report that Jesus was born at the same time as the Roman census when Quirinius was governor (Lk 2:2). Luke and Josephus are familiar with another census that took place in 6 CE (Acts 5:37; *War* 7:253), but there is no mention in Jewish or Roman sources of an earlier census under Quirinius during the reign of Herod the Great.

External corroboration is also lacking for Matthew's account of Herod's execution of the young male children in Bethlehem. Matthew is our only record of the event. Nevertheless, Herod's actions described by Matthew fit the king's paranoid personality sketched by Josephus. Herod executed members of his own family out of fear that they might attempt to usurp the throne. On one occasion, certain Pharisees prophesied to the wife of Pheroras—the brother of Herod—that, "by God's decree Herod's throne would be taken from him, both from himself and his descendants, and the royal power would fall to her and Pheroras and to any children that they might have. . ." (*Ant.* 17:41–45). Herod responded by killing the Pharisees involved and the members of his family who had expressed sympathy with this prophecy.

Matthew 2:13–15 reports that Joseph was warned by an angel to take his family to Egypt to escape Herod's murderous intentions. Only when the king had died was it safe to return to the Land of Israel. In the meantime, Rome had awarded authority in the region of Judea and Samaria to Archelaus, son of Herod (*War* 2:93; *Ant.* 17:317). He followed in his father's cruel footsteps. So, according to Matthew, Joseph was warned in a dream not to return to the environs of Jerusalem.

> And he [Joseph] went and dwelt in a city called Nazareth, that what was spoken by the prophets might be fulfilled, "He [Jesus] will be called a Nazarene." (RSV Mt 2:23)

This final verse of Matthew's report concerning Jesus' birth and childhood has challenged Christian readers for centuries. The crux of its interpretation revolves around the meaning of *nazoraios* that is routinely translated Nazarene, and the identification of the prophecy that Matthew claims is fulfilled with the family's settlement in Nazareth.

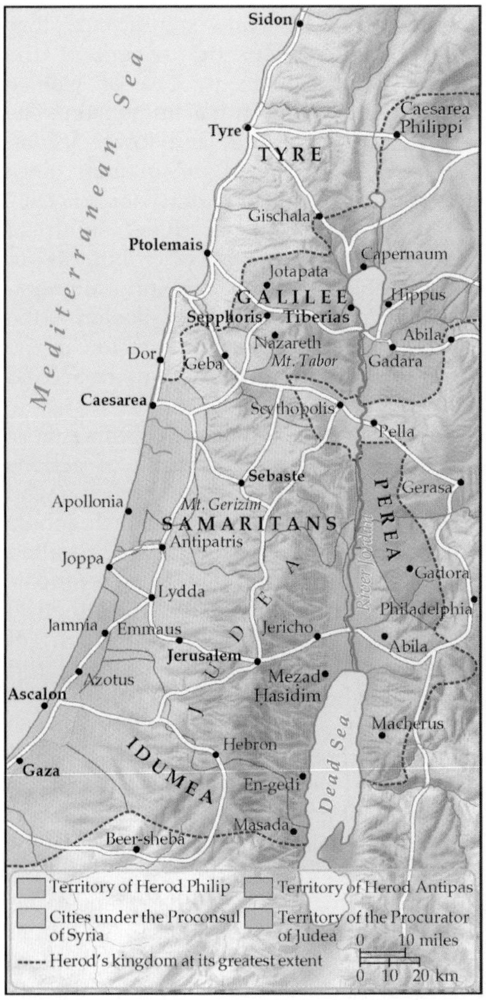


**The Southern Levant in the Time of Jesus**

We will not review the many and varied solutions that have been proposed. We venture here only two observations about the language of the verse that may assist towards narrowing Matthew's possible intent. First, the "o" in the second syllable of *naẓoraios* indicates that the Hebrew word behind our Greek term was *natzor*, i.e. one kept, protected, and not *netzer* (branch) or *nazir* (Nazirite). Second, translators of our verse rarely take note that the passive Greek verb can be intended to communicate a divine passive in which God is assumed to be acting. The verse may thus be rendered, "The one whom I have kept (i.e. *natzori*) shall be called (i.e. by God)." Accordingly, Matthew's elliptical allusion is to a prophetic passage that describes one who has been kept, protected and whom the Lord has called.

Scholarship on this verse has focused most of its attention on trying to explain the significance of the collocation of *naẓoraios* and *naẓaret*. Yet, nowhere else in the New Testament do these terms appear alongside each other. Could it be that Matthew has brought the elliptical Old Testament prophecy, not because of the name of the Galilean village, but because the angelic warning and protective actions of Joseph were reminiscent of an ancient prophecy?

A cruel son of Herod remained in power in Jerusalem, and it was not yet safe to return there. At the angelic warning, Joseph took Mary and Jesus to Nazareth out of concern for their continued safety. Their relocation to the security of this remote Galilean village, where Jesus could grow to adulthood, reminded Matthew of a verse concerning the Isaianic Servant of the Lord:

> *I, the Lord, have called you* in righteousness; I will take hold of your hand. *I will keep you* and will make you to be a covenant for the people and a light for the nations. (Isa 42:6)

So, Matthew concludes his abbreviated description of Jesus' infancy with a report that Jesus was taken to a remote village in the Galilee and preserved there by the Lord, until the appointed time for the beginning of his prophetic ministry. We witness a similar literary device by Luke to summarize and conclude his report concerning the childhood of John the Baptist: "And the child grew and became strong in spirit; and he lived in the desert until he appeared publicly to Israel" (Lk 1:80).

Of additional value for Matthew, however, the Evangelist uses Isaiah 42:6 to anticipate the next episode in his record of Jesus' life—the heavenly call at his baptism (Mt 3:16–17). Scholars have already demonstrated that according to the Evangelists the heavenly voice drew from the same block of scripture in Isaiah 42 to proclaim the prophetic significance of Jesus' baptism: "Here is my servant, whom I uphold, my chosen one in whom I delight; I will put my Spirit on him" (Isa 42:1).

## The Ministry of John and the Baptism of Jesus

**Geographical Setting.** In all of the Gospels the ministry of Jesus begins with his participation in the baptism of John. The geographical setting for John's ministry varies in the four Gospel accounts. In both Christian tradition and modern scholarship this has resulted in uncertainty regarding the location of John. All of the accounts cite Isaiah 40:3 to introduce the reason for the Baptist's presence in the wilderness. "A voice cries: In the wilderness prepare the way of the Lord." Like the Qumran Congregation (1QS 8:13–14), John believed that preparation for the Lord should take place in the wilderness.

Mark reports that John was "in the wilderness" (Mk 1:4) without any specification where that wilderness lay. The Greek term, similar to its Hebrew counterpart, need not indicate an arid, uninhabitable place, i.e. desert. It may also describe unpopulated, pasturing areas belonging to residents of a nearby city (cf. Lk 8:29). So, we hear of a "wilderness" near Bethsaida (Lk 9:10–12), where Mark describes green grass (Mk 6:39). We find a similar breadth of usage for the Hebrew term in the Old Testament (Gen 21:14; Joel 2:22; Isa 42:11).

Mark does record that crowds came to John from "all Judea and Jerusalem" (Mk 1:5; cf. Mt 3:5; Jn 1:19), which may or may not imply proximity to the arid regions in the lower Jordan Valley. It is difficult to know how much weight Mark intends for us to give to these geographical details about the crowds. Are they instead the Evangelist's periphrastic style of emphasizing John's role as the Voice of Isaiah 40:3? In the Isaiah passage the Voice is to speak to Jerusalem and the cities of Judea (Isa 40:9).

If Mark is employing here a technique of verbal allusion, it would not be uncommon. For example, elsewhere he omits explicit testimony to the popular notion that the Baptist was Elijah *redivivus* (cf. Mal 4:5 [HMT 3:23]; Mt 11:14; Lk 1:17). Yet, Mark was certainly aware of this opinion, because he describes John's clothing with clear intent to present John in Elijah's attire (Mk 1:6; Mt 3:4; 2 Kgs 1:8). On that occasion, Markan detail is not intended to merely describe John's clothing but to signal to his readers the eschatological importance of John's prophetic role. The challenge for the modern reader remains how to read these Markan details. Matthew on both of these occasions shares Mark's features, but he alone of the Synoptic Gospels—perhaps anticipating the mention of the Jerusalem and Judean crowds or reflecting the earlier Judean wilderness setting of Isaiah 40:3—specifies that John was in "the wilderness of Judea" (Mt 3:1).

While Luke agrees with Mark's portrayal that John is in the wilderness, he lacks Mark and Matthew's geographical reference to Judean and Jerusalem crowds. Instead, Luke notes only, "[John] went into all the region about the Jordan" (Lk 3:3). The Fourth Gospel contributes unique geographical

*John the Baptist, from the Hagia Sophia, Istanbul.*

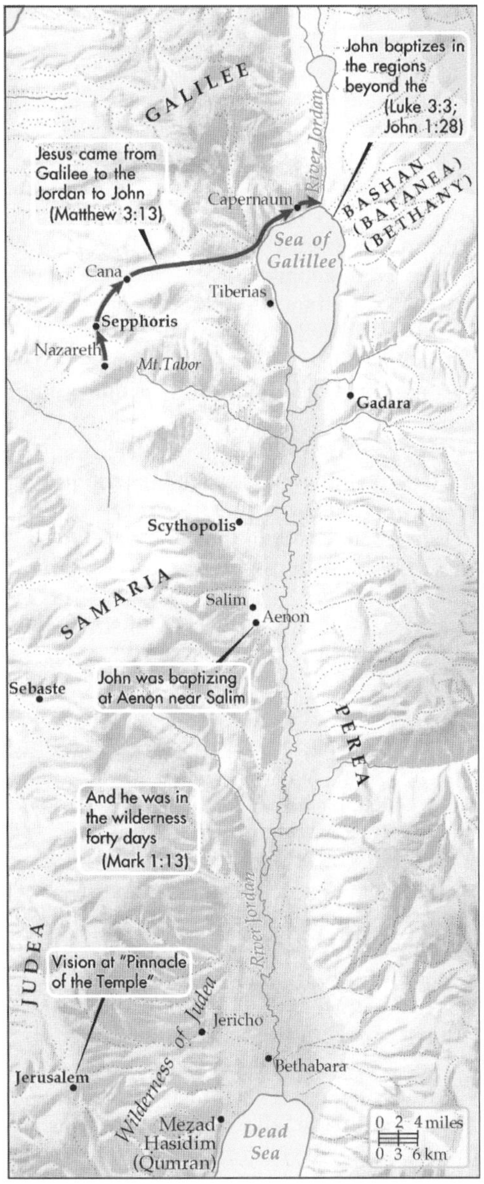


**The Baptism of Jesus and the Sojourn in the Wilderness**

details about the location of John's ministry, before and after its description of John's baptism of Jesus. At points the Evangelist parallels the Synoptic Gospels, and at other points he presents independent traditions. Of the setting prior to Jesus' baptism, John's Gospel records that the Baptist was at "Bethany beyond the Jordan" (Jn 1:28). Sometime later he is reported at "Aenon near Salim" (Jn 3:23). So, in apparent agreement, John and Luke present the Baptist moving between different venues and not limited to any single location.

The site of Bethany in the Transjordan finds no mention in early literature outside of John's singular reference. Origen reports in c. 200 CE that no such place exists (Orig. *Comm. John* VI.24). In spite of his admission that "[Bethany] is found in almost all of the copies [of John's Gospel]," he proposed a textual emendation for the verse to read Bethabara. Eusebius' *Onomasticon* (58:18) a century later describes Bethabara: "Where John was baptizing, beyond the Jordan. The place is shown where even today many of the brothers still endeavor to receive a bath." Eusebius embraced this textual solution first heard from Origen, because he makes no mention of Bethany in connection with John's baptism. While these early Christian conjectures exchanged the known for the unknown, manuscript support for Bethabara prior to Origen is nonexistent. Bethany appears in our earliest and best manuscripts of John's Gospel. Confusion in the later Byzantine period is compounded by the Medeba Map, which preserves "Bethabara, the sanctuary of Saint John the Baptist" on the *western* bank of the Jordan River, not as the New Testament describes Bethany, "beyond (i.e. *east of*) the Jordan."

John's reference to Aenon shares Bethany's absence in the early sources. The Medeba Map describes an Aenon in the Transjordan and identifies it with the site of Sapsaphas. A second "Aenon near Salim" is depicted on the west side of the Jordan River not too distant from Scythopolis (i.e. Beth-shean). This latter site is attested also in Eusebius' *Onomasticon* 40:1–4 and Egeria's *Travels* 15:1–4. A third suggestion for Aenon, perhaps owing to the fact that mention of Aenon occurs within the Fourth Gospel's narrative about Jesus in Samaria, identifies the Baptist in the interior of the hill country of Samaria. Its location is remembered near the modern-day Arab village of Salim (Jdt 4:4). While the toponymic challenge of springs (=Aenon) near Salim may be resolved, it is difficult to understand how the interior of Samaria served as the venue for John's ministry to call Jews to repentance and ritual immersion. Identification of an early Roman location for the springs of Aenon remains uncertain.

Returning to Bethany, it is suggested that the reference in John 1:28 is not to a village, but to the region of Bashan in the Transjordan. Designation of the region of biblical Bashan—extending from Mount Hermon in the north to the southern boundaries of the Lower Golan—with the term Batanea is also heard by Greek writers from Josephus (*Life* 54; *Ant.* 9:159) to Eusebius (*Onom.* 44:9–11). Additionally, according to the Septuagint the region of Bashan is demarked like Bethany, "beyond the Jordan" (Deut 4:47; Josh 9:10).

If "Bethany beyond the Jordan" does signal the region of ancient Bashan (Batanea), then it indicates that John's ministry reached regions northeast of the Sea of Galilee. A northern setting for John better suits the description that two of his disciples, Andrew and Peter, together with Philip came out from Bethsaida to follow Jesus the day following his baptism (Jn 1:44). The location of John's disciples at Bethsaida on the northern shores of the Sea of Galilee is not easily reconciled with the traditional location of Jesus' baptism in the lower Jordan Valley near Jericho.

It may be of some significance that in rabbinic opinion, the waters of the Jordan River above the Sea of Galilee were preferable for ritual immersion. The waters of the Yarmuk and lower Jordan rivers were reckoned unsuitable, since they included "mixed waters" (m. *Para* 8:10). In other words, these rivers south of the Sea of Galilee received tributaries of questionable purity. The rabbinic estimation accords with the lack of any allusion to the practice of Jewish ritual immersion in the lower Jordan River in the days of the Second Temple.

John's ministry in the north seems a more fitting setting for his critique of actions involving the Herodian families, who resided in the Galilee and the north. John's popularity and outspoken critique resulted in his imprisonment by Herod Antipas, tetrarch of Galilee. Josephus' parenthetical remarks concerning the fortress of Macherus indicated that the historian did not know where John was executed. Mark's description that "leading officials of Galilee" (Mk 6:21) were present during the banquet when John was condemned strengthens the contention that John was imprisoned and executed in Antipas' Galilean palace in Tiberias.

John's calling to the crowds to repent and ritually immerse in the regions of the Jordan above the Sea of Galilee may also explain the large crowds (*Ant.* 18:118) that Jesus encountered on the plains near Bethsaida, where he withdrew upon hearing of the Baptist's death (Mt 14:13). According to Mark, when Jesus saw the crowds he had compassion for them, "because they were like sheep without a shepherd" (Mk 6:34). With these words the Evangelist hints both to the relationship of the crowds with the recently deceased John, and the popular

*The River Jordan—traditional site of Jesus' baptism.*

notion among some that John was the anticipated prophet-like Moses (Deut 18:18; Jn 1:25; cf. 4Q175 1:5–8). Mark's creative use of the phrase—"sheep without a shepherd"—is intended to echo the same words spoken by the Lord to Moses in Numbers 27:17 to emphasize the need for new leadership after his death.

What we witness, then, with the topographical setting for the Feeding of the Multitudes in the Synoptic Gospels (Lk 9: 10–17 *parr.*) is not unlike the Fourth Gospel's fragmented description of Jesus' return beyond the Jordan.

> Then Jesus returned beyond the Jordan to the place where John had been baptizing in the early days (i.e. Batanea / Bashan; Jn 1:28). Here he stayed and many people came to him. They said, "Though John never performed a miraculous sign, all that John said about this man was true." And in that place many believed in Jesus. (Jn 10:40–42)

## The Travels of Jesus

**From Nazareth to Capernaum.** Prominent east-west valleys (Beth-haccerem, Hannathon, Bêt Neṭôfa, Turân) that traverse the lower region are one of the topographical features that distinguishes Lower Galilee from Upper Galilee (*War* 3: 35). The valleys of the Lower Galilee are the result of prehistoric tectonic activity. These geological striations extend from the Mediterranean coast north of Mount Carmel and reach inland to the Sea of Galilee and the upper Jordan Valley.

By contrast the Upper Galilee region lacks the open valley systems that mark the Lower Galilee, and so was not easily traversed. In addition, its mountainous terrain reaches heights that double those of the mountains of the Lower Galilee. The contrasting degree of accessibility left its mark on human settlement and movement in both regions. Archaeological surveys in the Lower Galilee indicate a greater degree of outside contact that is evidenced in the material culture of the populations residing there. In addition, while Josephus attests to the establishment of new urban centers (Sepphoris, Tiberias, Gabara: *Life* 188) in the Lower Galilee during the Hellenistic and early Roman periods, there is no similar evidence for urban centers in the Upper Galilee.

The topographical delineation between Upper and Lower Galilee is the esh-Shaghûr fault that is marked by the Beth-haccerem Valley, the northernmost of the transversal valleys in the Lower Galilee. The accessibility of the Lower Galilee region caused by these valleys had its impact on social development. There was sparse settlement in the interior of the Upper Galilee, while the early capital of the Galilee was Sepphoris, positioned in the Bêt Neṭôfa Valley (Sahl el-Baṭṭôf). Its importance was accentuated by its location at the crossroads

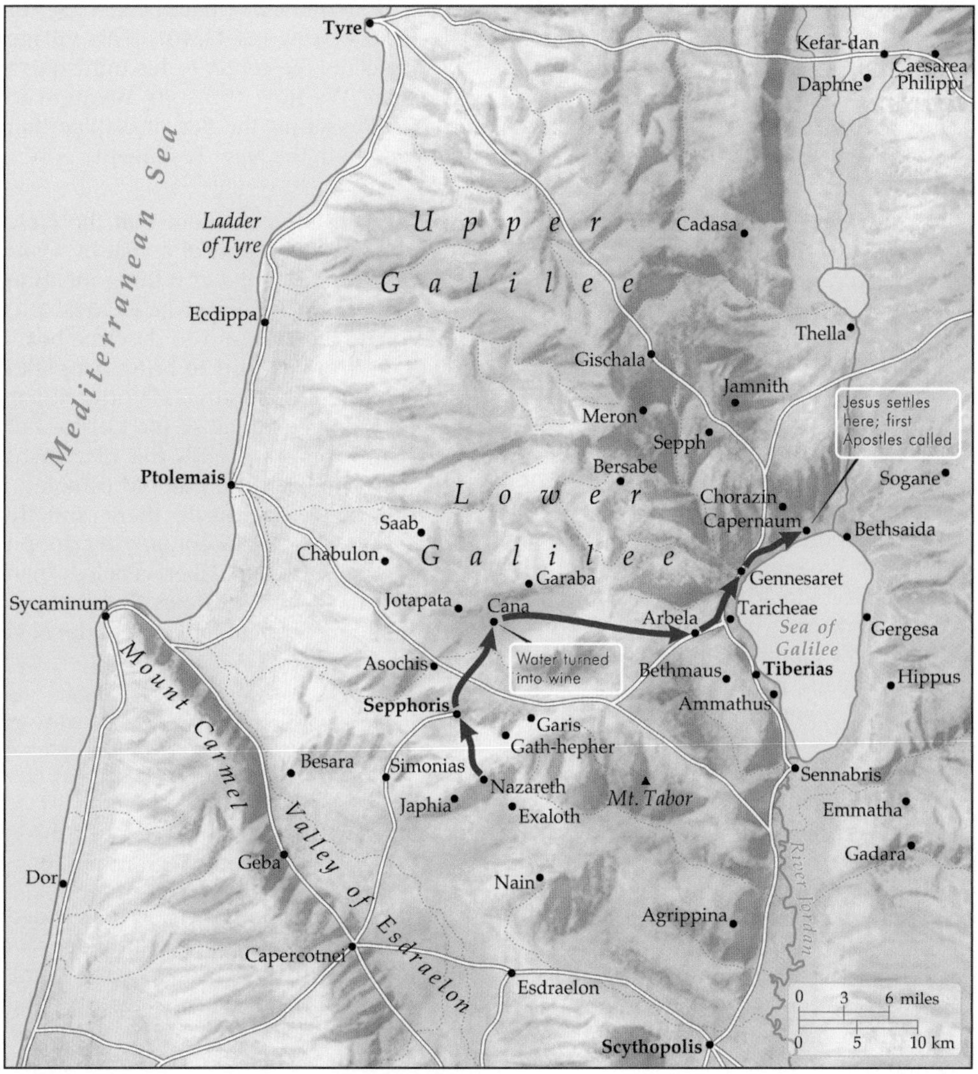


From Nazareth to Cana and Capernaum

of the Ptolemais–Taricheae (Magdala) trunk road and the secondary north-south route by way of Simonias to the Jezreel Valley and the international coastal highway.

In Matthew 4:13 the Evangelist reports that Jesus traveled from Nazareth to Capernaum. The journey north from Nazareth and east may pass through either the Bêt Neṭôfa Valley or the Turân Basin to descend from Nazareth's chalk ridge overlooking the Jezreel Valley to villages along the Sea of Galilee. However, indications of Jesus' presence in the Bêt Neṭôfa Valley suggest that he used the Ptolemais–Taricheae trunk road in his movement between his boyhood home and the Sea of Galilee.

In the beginnings of the Fourth Gospel Jesus' first miracle is recorded at Cana (Jn 2:1–11). Immediately following the miracle Jesus is reported to descend to Capernaum (Jn 2:12). According to John, on another occasion Cana and Capernaum are likewise juxtaposed in mention of Jesus' activity (Jn 4:46). It should also be remembered that Cana was the home of one of Jesus' twelve disciples, Nathana-el (Jn 1:45–49, 21: 2). Together these verses suggest Jesus' presence in Cana on more than one occasion and that the village may have been a regular waystation on his route from Nazareth to the Sea of Galilee.

The New Testament site for Cana of the Galilee is likely Khirbet Qanah in the Bêt Neṭôfa Valley. It guarded the ascent to Jotapata, the city of Josephus, who reports staying in Cana (*Life* 86). The fortified village lay on the road from Ptolemais to Taricheae (Magdala). The Hellenistic-Roman site is currently under excavation and should be distinguished from the medieval Christian pilgrimage site of Kafr Kana that from the time of Quaresmius (1620 CE) has been identified as New Testament Cana.

Eusebius (Eus. *Onom.* 116:4) identifies the New Testament village with the Old Testament Kanah of Joshua 19:28. However, this is merely a result of the similarity of the Septuagint's Greek rendering of the Hebrew name for the Old Testament village rather than a clear identification. The lack of any topographical information by Eusebius other than his biblical citation is patent for sites unknown to him. His knowledge of the Galilee was limited in any event. However, it seems that by the late Roman period the identity of either Old Testament Kanah or New Testament Cana was unknown.

*Capernaum—reconstruction of the synagogue.*

The journey from Nazareth to Capernaum is almost 30 miles (48 km), too lengthy for a single day's travel. Instead, Cana provided a convenient break in the journey, lying as it did on the Ptolemais–Taricheae (Magdala) road. Accessibility to the Sea of Galilee from Cana is indicated by Josephus' report of an overnight march from Cana to Tiberias in the company of two hundred men (*Life* 86–90). His report demonstrates that the route from Cana to the Sea of Galilee was known and in use. The Johannine account of the nobleman's appeal for Jesus to heal his son (Jn 4:46–54) assumes his travel from Capernaum to Cana, where Jesus was staying. While questions may exist concerning certain geographical details in the event, especially in terms of its relationship to its Synoptic counterpart, clearly the author of the Fourth Gospel saw no problem in describing a journey from Cana to Capernaum.

Khirbet Qanah lies a little more than 7 miles (11 km) north of Nazareth. Several ridge routes lead down the northern slopes of the Nazareth ridge into the Bêt Neṭôfa Valley. Travel to Cana likely led near to Sepphoris that lies in the middle of the valley. The route from Cana to Capernaum then courses north and east along the northern edges of the Bêt Neṭôfa Valley until it descends into Wâdī Arbel. This serpentine descent winds north of Qarné Ḥittim through the Arbel Pass. Passing at the foot of the Arbel cliffs the route turns north across the fertile Plain of Gennesaret and follows the shoreline past Magdala and Gennesar to Capernaum.

## The 1st Century Environs of the Sea of Galilee

Events recorded in the ministry of Jesus outside of Jerusalem are primarily located in the region around the Sea of Galilee, specifically in the north and northwest area of the lake. The Gospels are an important historical witness for Jewish settlement in this region. Scholarship seldom notes that for many of these settlements, their first mention in the literary witnesses is in the New Testament. After a confrontation in the synagogue in Nazareth, his boyhood home, Jesus relocated to Capernaum on the Sea of Galilee (Mt 4:13; Mk 1:21; Lk 4:31). This village would become the center of his ministry in the region. We now turn our attention to settlements around the Sea of Galilee that find mention in the New Testament.

**Tiberias**. It is no accident that the New Testament lacks a report of a visit by Jesus to Tiberias. Indeed, the city finds mention only in the Fourth Gospel (Jn 6:1, 6:23, 21:1) to designate the lake and to describe boats embarking from its port to bring people to Jesus. As Josephus reports, Herod Antipas founded the new capital of the Galilee but took insufficient care with the placement of the city. He built it on an old cemetery, rendering all who dwelt there ritually defiled (*Ant.* 18:36–38). Josephus' description of those who settled in Tiberias is less than complimentary, and he states that Antipas even had to force some to reside in the new regional capital.

> The new settlers were a promiscuous rabble, no small contingent being Galilaean, with such as were drafted from territory subject to [Antipas] and brought forcibly to the new foundation. Some of these were magistrates. Herod accepted as participants even poor men who were brought in to join the others from any and all places of origin.
> (*Ant.* 18:37)

It is suggested that the city was founded in 18 CE, although the coins of Antipas from Tiberias begin only from 20 CE. In any event, it was not until the second century that Tiberias was purified under the direction of Simeon bar Yohai to render it fit for a religiously observant population (*Gen. Rab.* 79h; j. *Shabb.* 9, 1–38d). In the late Roman and Byzantine periods it became a center of Jewish learning and the location for the compilation of the Jerusalem Talmud.

Antipas selected the site because of its location on the shores of the Sea of Galilee. It benefited from the economy of the lake and its accessibility to nearby trade routes. It also is near the warm springs of Hammath (*Ant.* 18:36; *Life* 85; *War* 2:614; cf. Pliny *Nat. Hist.* 5, 71; *Mo*ʾ*ed Qat.* 18a; j. *Meg.* 2:1–2), a site already settled before Tiberias. For the most part, the ancient remains of Tiberias lie beneath the modern city, and only meager finds from first-century Tiberias have been uncovered. The only sizeable structure identified by the archaeologists to the time of Antipas is the gate complex located at the southern entrance to Tiberias.

Josephus describes both a stadium (*War* 2:618) and a place of prayer, *proseuche* (*Life* 277, 280, 293), in Tiberias. Neither has been discovered. The precise sense of the latter term for Josephus is unclear. Although the historian mentions a large building (*Life* 277) for the location of the *proseuche* where the public gathered in Tiberias, he does not otherwise use the term in such a way that it necessitates the meaning of a fixed structure (*War* 5:388; *Ant.* 14:258). His citation from *Apion* describes prayers at Heliopolis offered in open-air (*Apion* 2:10). The Greek term shares the same breadth of meaning in the New Testament (cf. Acts 16:13, 16:16).

Josephus mentions also a palace built by Antipas that was gilded with gold and decorated with "figures of living creatures" (*Life* 65–66). The tetrarch's transgression of Jewish law later contributed to the building's destruction. It may have been at the palace in Tiberias that Antipas gave a banquet on his birthday, "for his courtiers and officers and the leading men of Galilee" (Mk 6:21). Events at that banquet led to the Baptist's tragic end.

**Magdala-Taricheae**. At the foot of the Mount Arbel cliffs, on the road from Tiberias along the lakeshore, lay the settlement of Magdala. Its Hebrew and Greek names, Migdal-Nunia ("fish tower"; cf. b. *Pesaḥ.* 46b) and Taricheae ("salted fish";

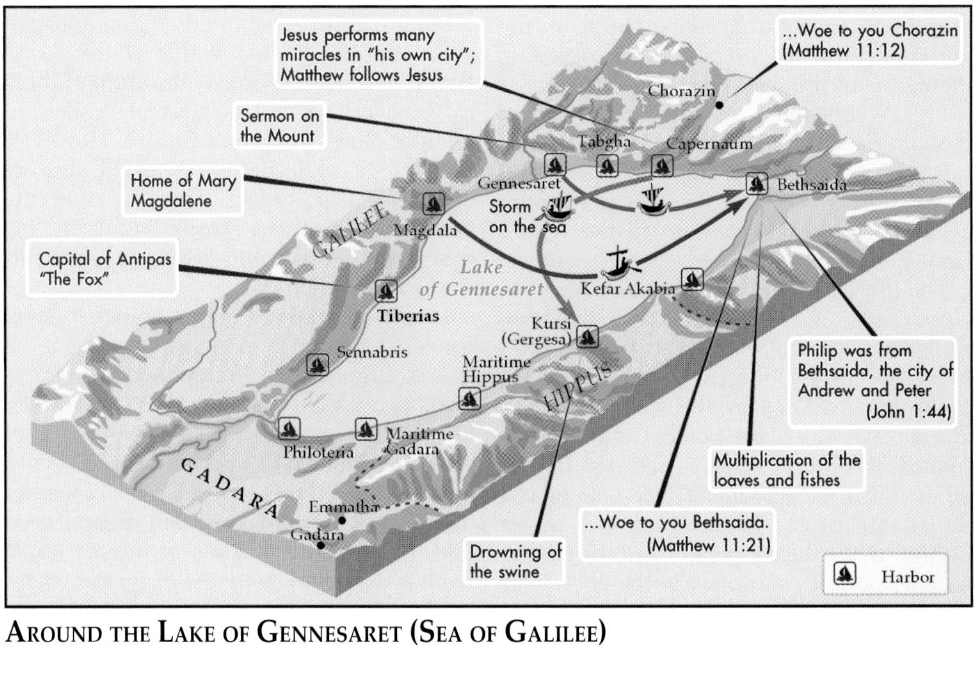


**Around the Lake of Gennesaret (Sea of Galilee)**

*Life* 188) reflect the dominant local industry of the first century. According to Strabo, "At the place called Taricheae the lake supplies excellent fish for pickling, and on its banks grow fruit-bearing trees resembling apple trees (Strabo *Geog.* 16.2.45).

Apart from a poorly attested reading of Matthew 11:39, no mention is made of Jesus' presence at Magdala (cf. Mk 8:10). We likewise do not hear that any of the disciples come from here. Yet, Jesus' embarkation on a fishing boat from nearby Gennesaret (Lk 5:1) would have brought him near to the tower of Magdala, which gave the town its name and where local fish were dried and salted. The only undisputed reference in the New Testament to Magdala is as the home of Mary Magdalene. She was among the women who followed Jesus from Galilee (Mt 27:56; Jn 19:25) and also with those who discovered Jesus' empty tomb (Lk 24:10).

Travel between Tiberias and Magdala is described both in rabbinic literature and Josephus, who speaks of "a road to Taricheae, which is thirty furlongs [c. 3.5 mi./5 km] distant from Tiberias" (*Life* 157). His description is to be preferred over Pliny's placement of Taricheae, south of the Sea of Galilee, "Taricheae on the south (a name which is by many persons given to the lake itself), and of Tiberias on the west" (Pliny *Nat. Hist.* 5:15).

Josephus presents Taricheae as the center of its own toparchy in 54 CE, when it was awarded by Nero to Agrippa II. Together with the toparchy of Tiberias, Taricheae comprised eastern Galilee (*War* 2:252). The historian, who was given the responsibility for the defense of the Galilee, includes Taricheae in a list of cities of Lower Galilee that he fortified in preparation for the war with Rome (*Life* 188; 156). To the present no walls have been discovered. Nor has there been certain identification of the *proseuche* (*Life* 280) or hippodrome (*War* 2: 599). He describes a sea-battle at Taricheae that resulted in a devastating Jewish loss. Residents fled to Tiberias thinking they would not be able to return. It may be that Taricheae was absorbed into Tiberias after the Jewish Revolt.

**Capernaum**. Our most plentiful literary witness to the village of Capernaum is the New Testament. Jesus moved to Capernaum after his rejection in Nazareth (Mt 4:13), and it was subsequently known as "his own city" (Mt 9:1). A number of Jesus' disciples were chosen there (Mt 4:13–22, 8:5–22, 9:1–34; Mk 1: 21–34, 2:1–17; Lk 7:1–10), and he is reported to preach in the synagogue on more than one occasion (Lk 4:31; Jn 6:59). Jesus is also found in the house of Peter, which is described in Capernaum (Lk 4:38).

The only other first-century witness to Capernaum comes from Josephus. He reports that he was carried to the village of Capernaum when he was wounded in battle near Bethsaida (*Life* 403). Otherwise, his only reference to the town is in his description of the western region of the Lake of Gennesaret. It is the first-century eyewitness description that challenged nineteenth-century explorers, who desired to rediscover this important city from the Gospels. After describing the fruitfulness of the plain of Gennesar, Josephus continues,

*The Sea of Galilee at sunset.*

> …besides being favored by its genial air, the country is watered by a highly fertilizing spring, called by the inhabitants Capharnaum; some have imagined this is to be a branch of the Nile, from its producing a fish resembling the *coracin* found in the lake of Alexandria. The region [i.e. Gennesar] extends along the border of the lake that bears its name for a length of thirty furlongs and inland to a depth of twenty. Such is the nature of this district.
> (*War* 3:519–521)

According to his description, the region that coursed along the northwest edge of the lake was known as Gennesar, and within its limits was an area of springs known by the name Capernaum. The historian makes no mention of a village in his description, perhaps an unconscious omission because his attention was focused on the natural surroundings.

Nevertheless, what early explorers found most puzzling was the mention of the springs of Capernaum. Those familiar with today's setting of Capernaum, recognize that within the vicinity of the site there are no springs. Instead, 3 miles (5 km) to the west are springs known locally as Tabgha, a corruption of its Greek name Heptapegon (i.e. seven springs).

Prior to modern exploration, the first Christian pilgrim to record their visit was Egeria (c. fifth century CE). Her itinerary is preserved in the writings of Peter the Deacon.

Egeria was followed three centuries later by Bishop Arculf (c. 700 CE). He directed his visit to Capernaum, not a great distance beyond "where the loaves were blessed" (i.e. Tabgha).

Only a few years later (c. 724 CE), he was followed by Willibald, who traveled in the same direction as Egeria and Arculf, leaving north from Tiberias along the shore of the lake. Two details from Willibald's journal are important for our consideration. First, he describes Capernaum with a great wall, while Arculf is explicit that the village had no walls. Further, Willibald relates that in Capernaum he was shown the house of "Zebedaeus with his sons John and James," while in Bethsaida he saw a church on the place of Peter and Andrew's house. While Willibald may have confused Capernaum for Bethsaida, he is in agreement with Arculf in his omission of a church at Capernaum in his day.

Modern archaeological excavations at Capernaum have uncovered a city laid out with a Hippodamian (orthogonal) street plan. Several insulae-style houses have been uncovered and partially restored. Excavators have determined that resettlement of the city began in the Persian period and grew throughout the Hellenistic and Roman periods. It fell into disrepair and was abandoned during the Islamic invasion in the seventh century CE. This state of affairs fits the description of the eighth-century visitors to Capernaum.

Two structures have drawn considerable attention. As we have noted, Byzantine Christian pilgrims were shown a church built upon the house of Peter. Excavations have uncovered a series of sanctuaries that likely correspond to these testimonies. Archaeologists suggest that the beginnings of veneration for this location began in a *domus ecclesia*. Epiphanius records that Joseph of Tiberias was authorized by the emperor Constantine to build the church in Capernaum (Epiph. *Adv. haer.* 30.4.1). The archaeological evidence suggests that the earlier house was transformed into a church,

*Aerial view of Capernaum.*

and it is likely this structure is that which Egeria visited in the early fifth century CE. In the second half of the fifth century an octagonal church was erected. As we have noted, the testimony of the eighth-century pilgrimage to Capernaum may indicate that the church no longer existed at this time.

The synagogue of Capernaum that dates to the fourth or fifth century is built in an early Galilean style and is the largest synagogue discovered in the Land of Israel. It was first partially excavated by Kohl and Watzinger. Their efforts were later followed by the Franciscan custody of the Holy Land. Two synagogues have been identified on the same location. The later limestone synagogue is the one visited by Egeria, who describes its many steps and cut stones. Forming the foundation of the Byzantine synagogue are the remains of walls from what is proposed to be an earlier synagogue, perhaps dating to the first century CE. This structure would then be the synagogue mentioned in the Gospels in which Jesus taught.

Finally, a malediction by Rabbi Issi in the third century CE against the heretics of Capernaum indicates that Judeo-Christians lived among the Jewish community of Capernaum in the late Roman period. Indeed, Epiphanius testifies that still in the fourth century CE among the Jewish communities of "Tiberias, Diocaesarea, also called Sepphoris, Nazareth, and Capernaum they take care to have no foreigners living among them" (Epiph. *Adv. haer.* 30.11.10). The continuance of an observant Jewish community in the Byzantine period in Capernaum may also be indicated by the discovery of a sixth-century CE Aramaic inscription in the floor of the synagogue at Hammath Gader, which mentions a donor named Yosse bar Dosti of Capernaum.

The historical and material witness of the community at Capernaum serves as a caution against the premature imposition by scholars of "the parting of the ways" upon Judaism and Christianity uniformly at an early period. At Capernaum and elsewhere in Roman-Byzantine Palestine, the archaeological evidence points to coexistence. At a minimum, the evidence adds further challenge to the erroneous assumption that the *Birkhat ha-Minnim* in its earliest form expressed Jewish antipathy towards nascent Christianity.

*In 1927 a stone seat was discovered south of the synagogue at Chorazin. This stone chair and others like it found at Hammath Tiberias and in a synagogue on the Greek isle of Delos have been suggested to represent what is sometimes referred to as "the seat of Moses." Presumably, from such a seat sermons were delivered in the synagogue. If so, Jesus may have had this in mind in his remark concerning his contemporaries, "The scribes and the Pharisees sit on Moses' seat" (Mt 23:2). Likewise, Luke's description of Jesus' actions in the synagogue of Nazareth accords with this presentation (cf. Lk 4:16–30). Jesus stood to read from the Torah and the Haftara. He then sat [i.e. on the seat of Moses] to expound upon the reading.*

**Chorazin**. Of the three Galilean cities (Capernaum, Chorazin and Bethsaida) Jesus mentions as places in which he performed miracles (Mt 11:21; Lk 10:13), only Chorazin is not located on the Sea of Galilee. It is about 2 miles (3 km) north of Capernaum on the basalt slopes of the Rosh Pinna sill and near the Ptolemais–Bethsaida road that crosses the Jordan River. According to Jewish sources, the wheat from this town (t. *Mak.* 3:8) was of exceptional quality (b. *Menaḥ.* 85a). Chorazin flourished in the second century CE, likely as a result of the increase of the Jewish population in the Galilee in the aftermath of the Bar Kochba rebellion (132–135 CE).

The archaeological evidence indicates that the town suffered a devastating earthquake in the early fourth century CE, but was rebuilt and continued to exist into the Byzantine period. This stands at odds with Eusebius' description at the beginning of the fourth century CE that Chorazin was already an abandoned village. "Chorazin. A village in the Galilee. Christ cursed it according to the Gospel. Now it is a deserted place two miles from Capernaum" (Eus. *Onom.* 174:23).

A Dutch officer, C. W. M. Van de Velde, who traveled in the Near East in the mid-nineteenth century, first identified the site of Khirbet Karazzeh with Chorazin. Kohl and Watzinger later included the synagogue of Chorazin in their survey of synagogues in Galilee. More recent excavations have uncovered houses and a ritual bathing installation. Nevertheless, only a small portion of the site has been excavated, and first-century Chorazin has yet to be identified.

Chorazin's late Roman period synagogue is in early Galilean style, similar to those at Capernaum and Barᶜam. Excavators have also found ornamental fragments belonging to the synagogue's Torah ark, where the congregation's scrolls were kept, and the platform (*bema*) on which the Torah would have been read on the Sabbath and other appointed days.

**Gergesa**. The reader of the Gospels is faced with a complex textual and topographical challenge in identifying the location of Jesus' encounter with the demoniac "on the other side opposite Galilee" (Mt 8:28–34; Mk 5: 1–17; Lk 8:26–37).

In spite of the strong textual witnesses for either Gadara or Gerasa, geographers struggle with these settings because of the topographical problems they present. According to all of the accounts, Jesus' encounter followed a boat ride from Capernaum, during which there was a sudden and violent storm (Mt 8:23–27; Mk 7: 35–41; Lk 8:22–25). Afterwards, Jesus and his disciples arrived to their destination, which is additionally described by Mark and Matthew as "the other side [of the sea]" (Mt 8:28; Mk 5:1). Typically in the New Testament "the other side" describes the northeast side of the lake opposite Capernaum and Gennesaret. In fact, on one occasion, Mark uses this same language and further specifies, "the other side, to Bethsaida" (Mk 6:45). Matthew and Mark's identification of the region corresponds to Luke's regional description, "opposite Galilee" (Lk 8:26).

Quite simply, neither Gadara nor Gerasa fit the description presented by the Gospels for the destination of Jesus' journey. Gadara (=Umm Qeis), the capital of a toparchy, was about six miles southeast of the Sea of Galilee, Gerasa (=Jerash, a city of Perea) about thirty-three miles. At such remote distances from the lake, these cities are not suitable candidates for the point of destination of a crossing of the Sea of Galilee from Capernaum.

It should be quickly added that the region of Gadara may likely have reached the southern shores of the lake. Coins of Gadara in the Roman period depict naval battles, suggesting that the district of Gadara extended to the lakeshore, where theatrical sea battles called "Naumachia" were held (e.g. Dio Cass. 43.23; Suet. *Jul.* 39; Suet. *Aug.* 43; Tac. *Ann.* 12.56, 14.15). During a drought in the 1980s, the low water level of the Sea of Galilee allowed investigation along the shoreline, which had been inundated in modern times because of a modern dam. Sixteen first-century harbors were identified around the lake, including that of Gadara near Tell Samara on the southeastern shore of the Sea of Galilee.

The discovery of Gadara's harbor supports the statement of Josephus that the region of Gadara extended along the southern shores of the Sea of Galilee to the point where the Jordan River exited the lake on its southwestern end. The Jordan River north of the Sea of Galilee and its southern exit from the lake were points of demarcation for the eastern frontier of the region of Galilee: "[Justus] went out, and set the villages that belonged to Gadara and Hippus on fire; *which villages were situated on the borders of Tiberias*, and of the region of Scythopolis" (*Life* 42).

Mention of Tiberias should not be read "lake of Tiberias" (i.e. *War* 3:57) but the capital of Galilee, as it appears in the following lines of Josephus' narrative (*Life* 43). The appearance of the city, similar to the mention of Scythopolis, is intended to signal the region about the city, in this instance Galilee. The historian's use of the region of Gadara to mark the limits of Galilee parallels a similar use of Gadara in his description of the borders of Galilee:

On the south the country is bounded by Samaria and the territory of Scythopolis up to the waters of Jordan; on the east by the territory of Hippus, Gadara and Gaulanitis, the frontier-line of Agrippa's kingdom. (*War* 3:37)

Nevertheless, while the toparchy of Gadara extended to the shores of the Sea of Galilee, its position was too far south for the event described in the Gospels.

In the investigation of the harbor of Gadara a large tower on the shoreline was discovered, which may have marked the northern frontiers of the city's territory. The limits of Gadara's shoreline are important, because there are no nearby slopes reaching the lake included in the region of Gadara that would fit the topographical description portrayed in the Gospel accounts: "The herd (of swine) rushed *down the steep bank* into the lake and were drowned" (Lk 8:33; cf. Mt 8:32; Mk 5:13).

Already at the beginning of the third century CE, Origen recognized the topographical problems of Gerasa and Gadara

*Roman remains at Gadara (Umm Qeis).*

*View of the ancient church remains at el-Kursi (Gergesa), looking northwest toward the Sea of Galilee.*

for our account. He offered a suggestion based on the topographical setting and local traditions: Gergesa, "an ancient city . . . by the lake now called Tiberias, by which is a cliff overhanging the lake, from which they show that the swine were cast down by the devils" (Origen *Comm. on John* 6:41). The site of this ancient village lies in the Wâdī Samekh delta just north of the only point at which the overlooking heights of Gaulanitis descend to the lake. "Gergesa" does appear in some Greek manuscripts for our account. However, the manuscripts in question antedate Origen and may reflect the influence of the church father's ingenuity, rather than witness to an early textual tradition.

While the textual witnesses to Gergesa antedate Origen, the tradition is undoubtedly pre-Origenian. Those who transcribed our manuscripts of the Gospels may have been familiar with Origen's writings, but that does not preclude the existence of Gergesa in the New Testament period, nor does it exclude the environs of the village from being a candidate for the destination of Jesus and his disciples.

Origen's description of Gergesa as an "ancient city" likely suggests that by his day, the village was in ruins. It also points to local traditions that are heard in Jewish and Christian sources. A century after Origen, Eusebius identified the location of "the border of Geshur" (Josh 13:11; Deut 3:14) north and east of the Sea of Galilee with Girgash beyond the Jordan, reflecting the Septuagintal reading (LXX Deut 3:14). He also mentions Gadara and Gerasa.

Girgash. A city beyond the Jordan located near Gilead (Josh 13:11), which the tribe of Manasseh took (Deut 3:14). This is said to be Gerasa, the famous *polis* in Arabia. Some say it is Gadara. The Gospel also mentions the (land of) Gerasenes. (Eus. *Onom.* 64:1)

Yet, in a subsequent entry Eusebius once again demonstrates his familiarity with the village of Gergesa and local traditions connected to it.

Gergesa. There the Lord healed the demoniacs. A village is now shown on the hill next to the Lake of Tiberias into which also the swine were cast down. (Eus. *Onom.* 74:13)

The church father's pre-Byzantine testimony to a village on the eastern shores of the Sea of Galilee is not a Christian invention. An early Jewish midrash makes a similar identification of Girgash [or Gergeshta] on the eastern shores of the lake.

R. Nehemiah said: "When the Holy One, blessed is he, shows Israel the graves of Gog and Magog, the feet of the Shechinah will be on the Mount of Olives and the graves of Gog and Magog will be open from south of the Kidron Valley to *Gergeshta on the eastern side of Lake Tiberias*. (*Shir ha-Shirim Zuta* 1.4 [p. 11])

For the purposes of our study, what is important is the familiarity of both Eusebius and the Jewish midrash with the location of Girgash / Gergeshta / Gergesa on the eastern side of the Sea of Galilee. These local traditons were important, because Origen's description of Gergesa as an "ancient city" may indicate that by his own day the village already lay in ruins. Nevertheless, later Christian tradition strengthened the identification of Gergesa (el-Kursi), and a church was built to commemorate the Gospel event.

There is little question that on the basis of topography, the region surrounding the ancient village of Gergesa (el-Kursi) better suits the details presented by the Evangelists. Its location fits Matthew and Mark's description of Jesus' destination "on the other side" and Luke's "opposite Galilee." The village does not possess the problems of distance from the northern portions of the Sea of Galilee inherent in the location of Gadara, or even more acutely with Gerasa. Moreover, only in the vicinity of Gergesa do the slopes of the heights descend steeply to the shores of the Sea of Galilee. Evidence for the village's existence in antiquity is heard in rabbinical literature and the pre-Byzantine Christian writings of Origen and Eusebius. Both of the Christian writers also attest to local pre-Byzantine Christian traditions that identified Gergesa with the Gospel event.

Gergesa's only obstacle is its non-appearance in pre-Origenian manuscripts of the Gospel account. Yet the dilemma of Gergesa belongs to a well-known pattern: in the copying of ancient texts, an unknown name will almost always be "corrected" to a known name. So, it seems that in spite of its location as the place of Jesus' encounter with the demoniac, at a very early stage

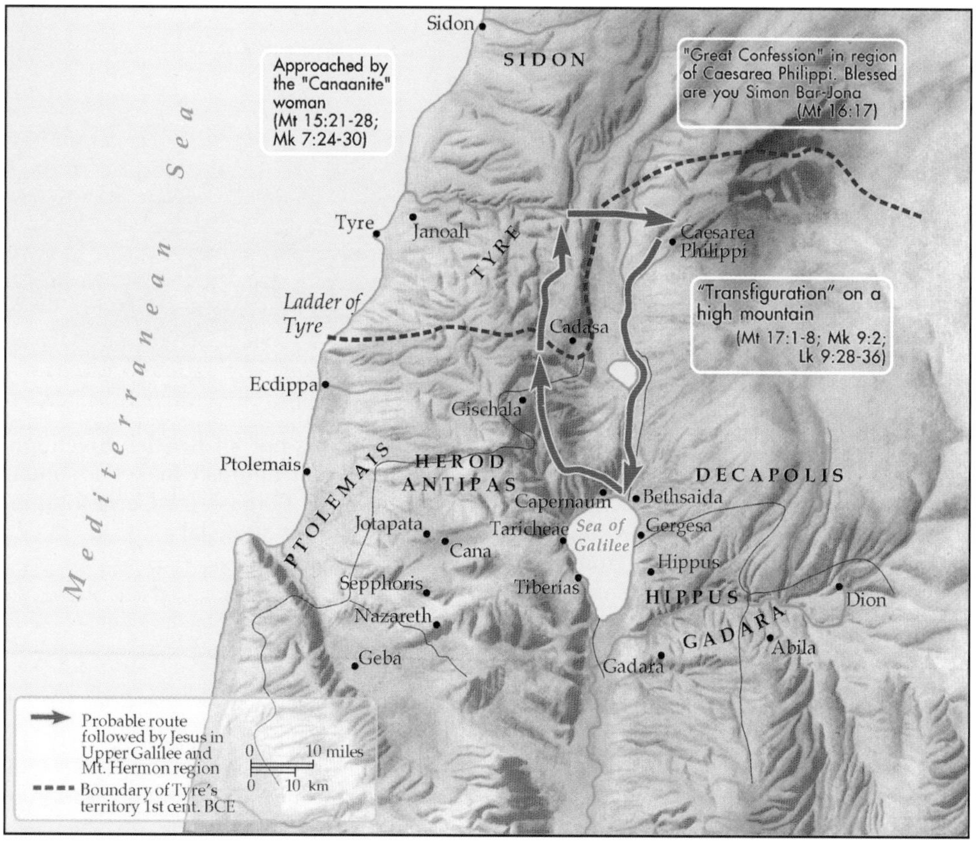


**Putative Travels in the Districts of Tyre and Caesarea Philippi**

the name of the lesser-known village of Gergesa was exchanged for one of the two renowned cities of the Decapolis: Gadara and Gergesa.

**The Decapolis.** The toponym, Sea of Galilee, is the product of a creative Christian interpretation of Isaiah, "but in the latter time he will make glorious the way of the sea, the land beyond the Jordan, Galilee of the nations" (Isa 9:1b [HMT 8:23b]). Mark's use of the Christian name for the lake (Mk 1:16, 7: 31) signals his embrace of this contemporary homily. It seems that the same Isaianic passage provided the narrative structure for Mark's presentation of Jesus' northern journey: "Then [Jesus] returned from the region of Tyre, and went through Sidon to the Sea of Galilee, through the region of the Decapolis" (Mk 7:31).

According to Mark, Jesus returned from Phoenicia on Isaiah's way of the sea—the trunk road from Tyre to the region of Caesarea Philippi—and then continued to the Transjordanian heights of the Hauran, which Mark identified with the region of the Decapolis. Jesus' circuitous journey concluded on the shores of the Sea of Galilee. There is little geographical logic in a route from Phoenicia to the Sea of Galilee through the Hauran. However, Mark's presentation uncannily follows the order of the topographical points in Isaiah's passage: the way of the sea, the land beyond the Jordan, Galilee of the nations. So, it seems that once again we witness Mark writing in his distinctive paraphrastic style to present Jesus' fulfillment of Isaiah's ancient prophecy.

The first historical witness to the place name Decapolis is Mark and Matthew's Gospels (Mk 5:20, 7:31; Mt 4:25). The history of this toponym has been the subject of renewed discussion. Josephus mentions "the Decapolis of Syria" in connection with a complaint brought to Vespasian by these cities against Jewish insurgents (*Life* 341, 410). He also describes Scythopolis as the largest city in the Decapolis (*War* 3:446). However, the historian does not provide any additional information about the nature of the designation (geographical or political), its origins or which cities were included.

Pliny (79 CE) provides the most detailed first-century description of the Decapolis.

Adjoining Judaea on the side of Syria is the region of the Decapolis, so called from the number of its towns, though not all writers keep to the same list; most, however, include Damascus, with its fertile water-meadows that drain the river Chrysorrhoe, Philadelphia, Raphana (all these three withdrawn towards Arabia), Scythopolis (formerly Nysa, after Father Liber's nurse, whom he buried there), Gadara, past which flows the river Yarmuk; Hippus mentioned already, Dion, Pella rich with its waters, Galasa [i.e. Gerasa], Canatha. (Pliny *Nat. Hist.* 5.16)

Pliny is the only writer to list *ten cities* included in the Decapolis. However, as he indicates, this list is not certain, and he acknowledges that there is disagreement among writers. His statement suggests that he is not writing from personal knowledge of the Decapolis. Instead, he is relying upon the conflicting reports of others.

The disagreement among historical witnesses is heard again in Ptolemy's *Geography*. Writing in the second century (c. 150 CE), Ptolemy includes eighteen cities in the Decapolis. His list contains nine of Pliny's cities (omitting Raphana) and adds nine more: Heliopolis, Abila, Saana, Hina, Abila Lysanias, Capitolias, Edrei, Gadora, and Samulis (cf. Strabo *Geog.* 5.14–22). Yet what is most remarkable is that we have no mention of the Decapolis by the first-century geographer, Strabo.

Strabo describes both Syria and Palestine at some length, and even names several of the Decapolis cities: Damascus, Gadara, Philadelphia, and Scythopolis. His silence is even more curious when we recall Strabo's interest in the Lycian League, a federation of twenty-three cities in western Asia Minor organized and supervised by the Romans.

The next significant literary witness to the Decapolis is Eusebius, who reports at the beginning of the fourth century CE, "Decapolis. In the Gospels. This is (the region) in Perea that surrounds Hippus, Pella and Gadara" (Eus. *Onom.* 80:16). Eusebius does not define the nature of the Decapolis. However, his description that it "surrounds" three cities suggests that Eusebius understood it to designate a geographical region, rather than a mere political league. Jerome's Latin translation of the *Onomasticon* specifies what may be implied in Eusebius' Greek, *regio decem urbium* (a region of ten cities). Jerome's use of *regio* to define the Decapolis echoes the earlier terminology by which Pliny described the Decapolis.

Nothing in the historical descriptions speaks of a political confederation. The only joint political effort in the Jewish Revolt is the complaint to Vespasian. These cities are not even mentioned to have sent soldiers to assist the Romans in the Jewish Revolt. Yet, modern scholarship has generally suggested that Pompey founded the league of cities when he liberated the region from Hasmonean domination in 63 BCE. While a number of the cities adopted Pompeiian eras, others did not. For example, Damascus retained its Alexandrian era.

Of greater significance, no mention is made of the Decapolis on coins for these cities, or in any first-century inscriptions yet discovered. One would have thought that with the political upheaval in the region during the first century, these cities would have proudly publicized their allegiance to the Roman Empire with mention of their membership in a political league founded by the great Roman general, Pompey. Further questions are raised about the early existence of a Roman league of cities by Augustus' assignment of Hippus and Gadara to Herod in 30 BCE (*Ant.* 15:217; *War* 1: 396). It is unlikely that the emperor would have transferred these cities to a Jewish king, if they belonged to a Roman league.

It may be of some significance that apart

from the references in Mark and Matthew, all of our historical references to the Decapolis occur in writings after the Jewish Revolt of 66–70 CE. In the complete absence of any historical or epigraphical evidence to the contrary, it seems that Mark and Matthew's Decapolis—similar to the Fourth Gospel's "Bethsaida in Galilee" (Jn 12:21)—is an anachronistic toponym. The tumultuous events surrounding the Jewish Revolt brought significant geopolitical changes to the region. These are reflected in changing, evolving regional toponyms.

We simply do not know what the genesis was for the origins of the Decapolis. It may have stemmed from the desire of these cities to define themselves in contradistinction to the neighboring regions heavily populated with Jews, who had recently rebelled against Rome. Use of the term in the Gospels may reflect the period in which the individual writings were composed (i.e. post–70 CE), because there is no corroborating evidence to suggest that the Decapolis was known in the days of Jesus. Those familiar with the history of the Land of Israel in an earlier age will recognize the same phenomenon in the Hebrew Scriptures' use of an anachronistic toponym to designate the coastal plain as "the land of the Philistines" (Gen 21:32) in the time of Abraham—centuries before the actual arrival of the Philistines. In both instances, they tell us more about the toponymic usage at the time of the composition than place names in the period described.

## The Last Days of Jesus

All of the Gospels agree that the Romans crucified Jesus outside of Jerusalem. Roman responsibility for the death of Jesus is also recounted in one of the earliest Christian baptismal creeds: "[he] suffered under [the Roman prefect] Pontius Pilate." Yet, the topographical and historical details surrounding Jesus' execution vary in the reports of the New Testament. It is not possible to engage here the complex issues of the literary relationship of the four Gospels as historical sources for the Passion narratives. Much is written about the subject elsewhere. Our interest is more narrowly focused to determine what can be known of the physical setting of Jerusalem, and what that setting can inform us about the historical events that unfolded on it.

One hundred years of archaeological activity in Jerusalem, begun at the end of the nineteenth century, have helped to illuminate the physical setting of Jerusalem during the New Testament period. Questions still remain, but new data have provided fresh insights. The results have sometimes challenged long-held traditions attached to sacred sites. Nevertheless, a clearer picture has emerged about those

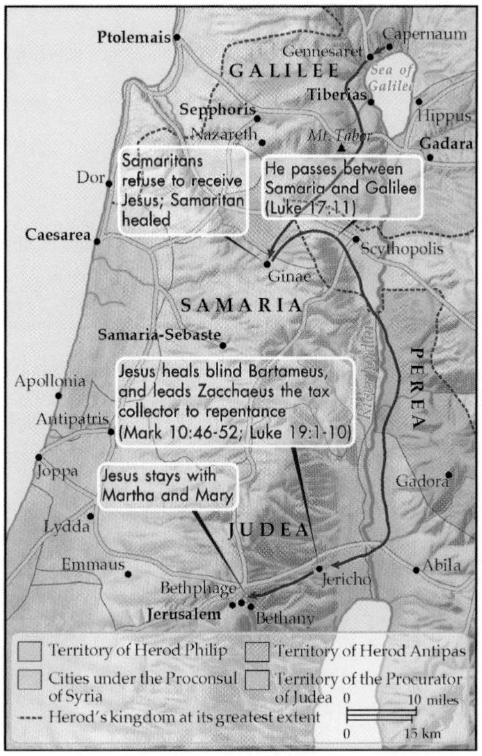


**Jesus' Last Journey to Jerusalem**

fateful days. We shall attempt to sketch the historical framework for the events of that week, with particular attention given to their topographical setting.

Jesus approached Jerusalem in the days leading up to Passover (Jn 11:55). His pilgrimage continued a family practice. During the days of the Second Temple, it was not a necessary requirement to travel to Jerusalem three times a year as obligated at Sinai: "Three times in the year shall all your males appear before the Lord God" (Ex 23:17; cf. 30:23). The impracticality of traveling long distances thrice yearly—particularly difficult from the remoteness of the Jewish dispersion—necessitated a figurative interpretation of the injunction, "to appear before the Lord" (Tob 1:6–10; *Midr. Tanh.* [Buber ed.] *Teẓawe* (51b); *Ant.* 4:203–204).

Nevertheless, Luke records the piety of Jesus' family—"Now his parents went to Jerusalem every year at the feast of the Passover" (Lk 2:41). Jesus' familiarity with the setting of Jerusalem indicates he was accustomed to—and perhaps a familiar figure in—the city at the time of Passover, "The Teacher says, 'Where is my guest room, where I am to eat the Passover with my disciples?'" (Mk 14:14; Lk 22:7–13).

The northern ford across the Jordan River, which would have been used by a pilgrim who desired to travel to Jerusalem through the Transjordan, lay within the territory of Scythopolis (cf. *Ant.* 12:348). This independent Greek city was situated between the geopolitical regions of Galilee and Samaria. The city and its territory belonged to the province of Syria and were not part of the lands granted to Herod's sons upon his death. As a statement of the geographical and political realities that existed in the days of Jesus, Luke's description that Jesus "passed between Samaria and Galilee" in Luke 17:11 is correct and can hardly be deemed evidence of Luke's "geographical ineptitude."

According to the Gospels, Jesus did not always use the same route in his pilgrimage to Jerusalem. Testimony on an earlier occasion (Jn 4:4–6) of Jesus' presence in the interior of Samaria suggests that at times he followed the watershed route through the central hill country. This route was the most direct, taking only three days from Galilee to Jerusalem (*Life* 268–270). Yet, because of violence between the Jews and Samaritans, it was often considered too dangerous (*War* 2:232–233; *Ant.* 20:118; Lk 10:30–37). A third route from Galilee mentioned in the ancient sources led along the foothills of Mount Ephraim to Antipatris and ascended the Beth-horon ridge to Jerusalem (*War* 2:228). However, we have no mention of this route in connection with Jesus' pilgrimages to the Holy City.

Mention of his travel through Jericho (Mt 20:29; Mk 10:46; Lk 19:1) indicates that Jesus' pilgrimage from the Galilee led him through the region of Perea in the Transjordan and along the Roman road from Jericho (cf. Lk 10:30) that followed near the biblical Ascent of Adummim (Josh 15:7). That route would have taken him within sight of the former Hasmonean and Herodian palaces at Jericho. Indeed, it seems that the physical presence of the former residence of Archelaus, son of Herod, may have been the cue for Jesus to adopt the well-known story of "the Herodian son who would be king" (*Ant.* 17:342–343; *War* 2:111–113; Dio Cass. 55.27.6; Strabo *Geog.* 2.46) as the inspiration for his parable: "A man of noble birth went into a far country to receive a kingdom and then return" (Lk 19:12).

Only Luke relates that Jesus told the parable as they passed out of Jericho, and likewise only in the Third Gospel does

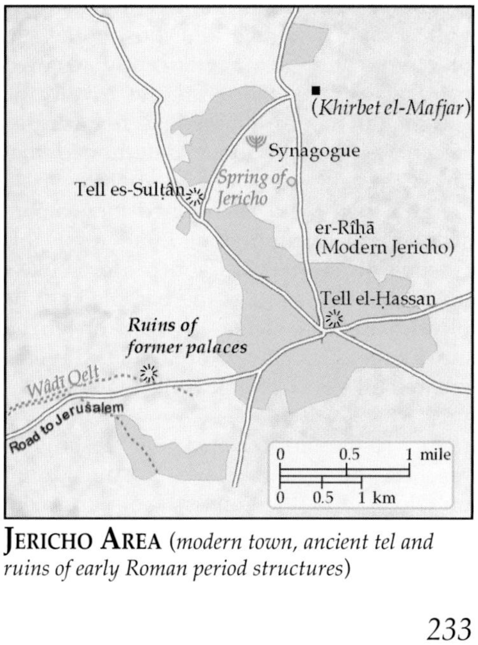


**Jericho Area** (*modern town, ancient tel and ruins of early Roman period structures*)

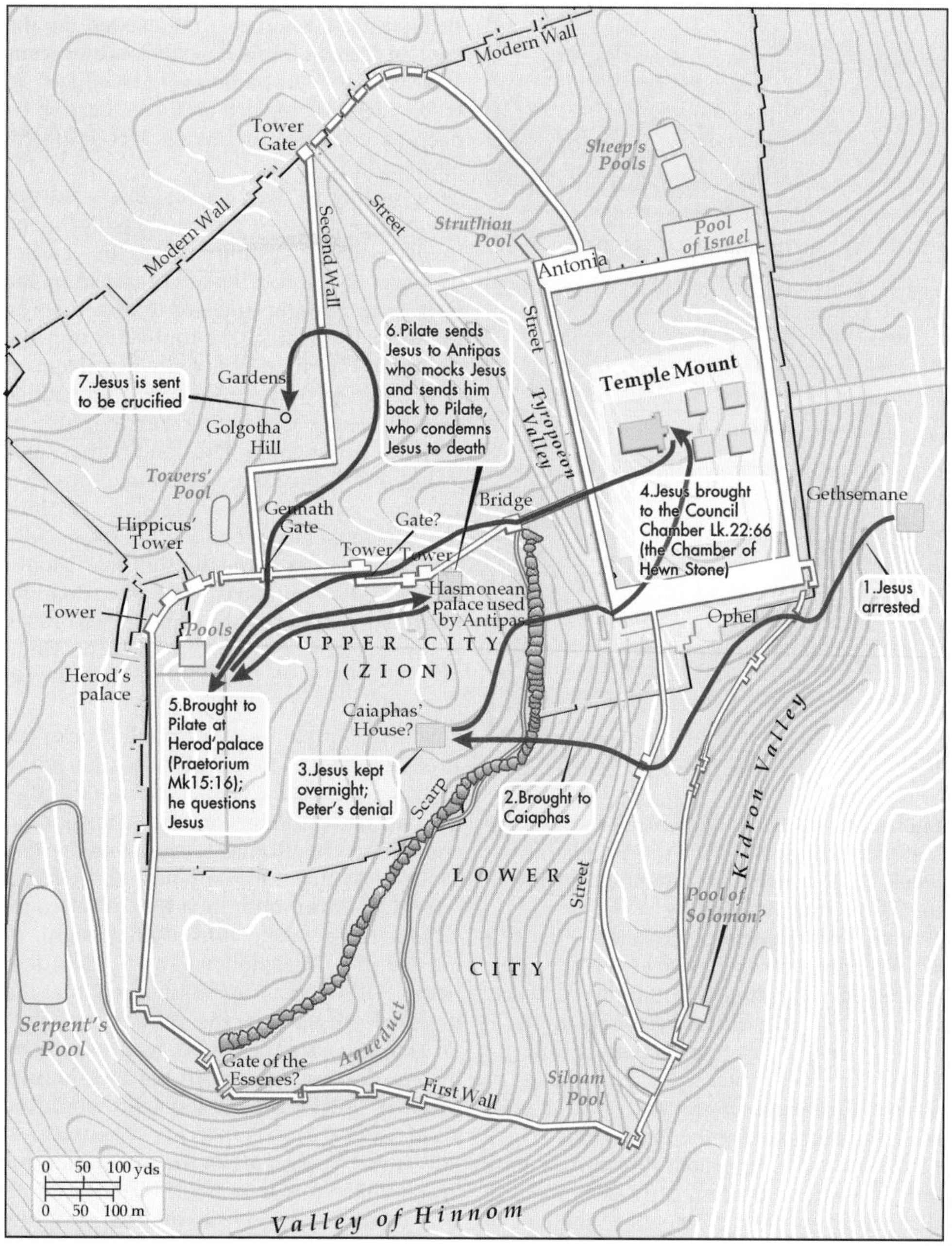


**The Arrest, Interrogation and Execution of Jesus**

Jesus use the story of the Herodian scion as the narrative structure for his parabolic creativity. The collocation of the parable with strong historical allusions to the son of Herod and the magnificently restored residence that symbolized the royalty he sought but never attained, is remarkable. Recent excavations have determined that an earthquake destroyed the palaces in 48 CE, and they were abandoned long before scholarship assumes that Luke wrote his Gospel. It seems the source for Luke's unique combination of the parable and the physical setting of the environs of Jericho must have originated from a time when the palace still stood, or at least its memory was fresh.

As Jesus approached Jerusalem he reached the eastern slopes of the Mount of Olives. On the outskirts of Jerusalem lay the villages of Bethany (Neh 11:32; Eus. *Onom.* 58:15) and Bethphage (Lk 19:29). The latter was positioned between Bethany and Jerusalem and marked the outer limits of the Holy City (m. *Men.* 11:2; b. *Pesaḥ.* 63b). Its name was derived from the Semitic word for unripened figs (see Eus. *Onom.* 58:13) and may indicate agricultural activity in the vicinity (Mk 11:20). In the same vein, the toponym "Mount of Olives" (Zech 14:4) was also determined from local produce.

The New Testament records that Jesus stayed in Bethany (Mt 21:17; Mk 11:11), perhaps in the home of Lazarus, Mary and Martha (Lk 10:38; Jn 11:1). The large influx of visitors (cf. *Ant.* 18:313) during the pilgrimage feasts meant that many pilgrims had to stay outside of the Holy City (*Ant.* 17:213–214). Bethany is situated less than 2 miles (3 km) from Jerusalem (Jn 11:18), making it a convenient place for daily access to Jerusalem and the Temple. The Gospels portray Jesus' trips back and forth between Bethany and Jerusalem (Mk 11:11–12). However, even pilgrims who stayed outside of the city were required to eat within the city walls the offering sacrificed on the Passover eve—14/15 Nisan (m. *Pesaḥ.* 7:9, 7:12, 10:3). The disciples' efforts to arrange the meal within the city walls of Jerusalem (Lk 22:7–13) are one of the clearest indications that for the Last Supper Jesus followed the rabbinic stipulations regarding the Passover meal.

During the week leading up to Passover, Jesus was teaching daily in the Temple (Lk 19:47). Study of the Scripture within the temple precincts is recorded in Jewish tradition (m. *Tamid* 5:1; m. *Yoma* 1:7). It was also a place of study familiar to Jesus from his youth (Lk 2:48–49). The colonnaded porticoes surrounding the Temple likely included these places of study (cf. Acts 5:12). In addition, the platform atop the steps of ascent leading from the south into the Huldah Gates of the Temple Mount was a place where teaching was reported (t. *Sanh.* 2:2; m. *Sanh.* 11:2). The Mishnah describes three courts of law, "One used to sit at the gate of the Temple Mount, one used to sit at the gate of the Temple Court, and one used to sit in the Chamber of Hewn Stone" (*Sanh.* 11:2). The first of these locations may be identified near the broad platform atop the steps to the Huldah Gates.

It is in the vicinity of the Temple that Jesus challenged financial transactions that came under the responsibility of the Sadducean priesthood (Lk 19:45–46). Scholarship has tried to identify Jesus' actions within the temple courts. The expanded narrative of Mark does imply Jesus' actions were within the temple precincts and even directed against the Temple itself, "and he would not allow any one to carry anything through the temple" (Mk 11:16; cf. Jn 2:15). On the other hand, Matthew and Luke omit Mark's portrayal that Jesus' actions were aimed at the institution of the Temple, but instead at the priests entrusted with its care. Moreover, Luke's verbal description does not necessarily indicate Jesus' presence already within the temple precincts.

Luke's account is supported by the Jewish sources. The mishnaic tractate *Berakhot* 9:5 states that one was not even permitted to ascend to the Temple Mount with a purse, let alone that it was the site of a marketplace: "He may not enter into the Temple Mount with his staff or his sandal or his purse." It seems likely that Jesus' actions took place either in the area of shops, recently excavated adjacent to the southern and southwestern walls of the Temple Mount, or the enclosed Royal Portico built by Herod the Great (*Ant.* 15:411–416) in the southern portion of the Temple Mount. In an apocryphal story of the life of Jesus, we find him mentioned among the ritual baths near the shops south of the Temple Mount: "And [Jesus] took them and brought them into *the place of purification* itself and walked about in the temple" (P. Oxy 840; cf. Jn 11:55; Acts 21:24, 26).

The cause for Jesus' protest is not explicitly stated. A recent study of this episode in light of contemporary Jewish sources suggests that Jesus—like others of his contemporaries—objected to the House of Annas' evasion of personal tithes to the Lord and oppressive measures. Jesus was certainly not alone in his assessment that this priestly clan (Lk 3:2; Jn 18:13; Acts 4:6) had misused its position as stewards of the temple finances.

> The Sages said: The (produce) stores for the children of Hanin [=Annas] were destroyed three years before the rest of the Land of Israel, because they failed to set aside tithes from their produce, for they interpreted *Thou shalt surely tithe . . . and thou shalt surely eat* as excluding the seller, and *The increase of thy seed* as excluding the buyer. (*Sifre*; cf. j. *Pe'a* 1:6)

The description of the House of Annas being both "sellers" and "buyers" in *Sifre* may help to explain Matthew and Mark's expanded description of the targets of Jesus' rebuke. The Evangelists' combination of sellers and buyers is a derivation from an earlier hendiadys. While Luke states that Jesus expelled only "the sellers" (cf. Jn 2:14), the other two Evangelists speak of "those who sold and those who bought." The rabbinic witness suggests that in all of the Gospels Jesus is only concerned with the abuses of the temple hierocracy (see also *Tg. Isa.* 5:7–10; b. *B. Bat.* 3b–4a; *Ant.* 15:260–262, 20:181, 20:205–207).

Jesus' words and actions in the days leading up to Passover were interpreted as a challenge to the Sadducean temple establishment. Yet, his message shared a broad public appeal, and they could not arrest him openly (Lk 19:48). He gave voice to popular discontent (Lk 20:19), and a response by the temple establishment had to wait until a more opportune moment.

On the eve of Passover, preparations were made for the festive meal. While the priests offered other sacrificial offerings, Scripture stipulated that the people themselves were to sacrifice this offering in the Temple (Deut 16:2; m. *Pesaḥ.* 5:6; Philo *Spec.* 2.145). The sacrifice could only be performed on the 14th of Nisan, and it was to be eaten that evening (Deut 16:6). The Gospels are silent on the details of preparation leading up to the meal, likely because they were so commonplace as to need no report.

Pilgrims to Jerusalem ascended to the Temple and offered the sacrificial lambs—the *Pesach* (Mk 14:12; Lk 22:15; 1 Cor 5:7)—that were then served as the main course for those celebrating Passover in the Holy City (Deut 16:5–6). We have no clear indication where Jesus shared this meal. Mark (14:15) and Luke (22:12) merely describe that it was in a "room upstairs." Early Christian tradition located this room on the southern slopes of the western hill of Jerusalem, yet corroborating literary or archaeological evidence is lacking.

What is more clear is that after the hymns of praise were sung (Mt 26:30; Mk 14:26; i.e. the *Hallel* of Ps 113–118) that conclude the Passover meal, Jesus and his disciples then retreated to the slopes of the Mount of Olives (Lk 22:39; Mt 26:30; Mk 14:26). Matthew and Mark further specify that the place was called Gethsemane (Mt 26:36; Mk 14:32)—a topographical name unknown in any other first-century source (cf. Eus. *Onom.* 74:16).

Restrictions on the distance of travel on a holy day would not have allowed Jesus to return to Bethany that evening. The celebrants were required to remain within the boundaries of the city overnight. The Mount of Olives laid within "a sabbath's day journey" (Acts 1:12)—the limits of travel to which an observant Jew was restricted on the holy day. Jesus may have been drawn to a specific site on the Mount of Olives by custom (Lk 22:39) to a focal point of prayer where tradition remembered the place of King David's prayer (j. *Ber.* 4:8b [based on 2 Sam 15:32]).

After a time of prayer, the Gospels report that one of Jesus' followers—Judas Iscariot—led a contingent of the high priests and their soldiers to arrest him. Judas' role was not to identify Jesus, who was well known to the temple establishment, but to locate Jesus' entourage and to distinguish them from others who were likely encamped on the hillside. Under the cloak of darkness, Jesus was arrested and led away to the house of the high priest, Joseph bar Caiapha (Caiaphas).

Christian tradition has located the high priest's house on the southern portions of the western hill. Nevertheless, recent excavations carried out in today's Jewish Quarter of Jerusalem uncovered an inscribed weight measure from the home of Bar Kathros, another family of high priests. This family is remembered in the Babylonian Talmud in the context of criticisms toward high priestly dynasties from the Roman period. These priests were criticized for their oppression, secrecy and financial misconduct. In a saying remembered by the second-generation *tanna*, Abba Saul b. Batnit:

> Woe is me because of the house of Boethus;
> Woe is me because of their staves!
> Woe is me because of the house of Hanin (=Annas);
> Woe is me because of their whisperings!
> Woe is me because of the house of Kathros;
> Woe is me because of their pens!
> Woe is me because of the house of Ishmael the son of Phabi;
> Woe is me because of their fists!
> For they are High Priests and their sons are [temple] treasurers and their sons-in-law are trustees and their servants beat the people with staves.
> (b. *Pesaḥ.* 57a=t. *Menaḥ.* 13:21)

Three features from this talmudic witness are important for our concerns. First, the complaint against these families of treachery is coupled with mention of their control over the finances of the Temple. This corresponds to Jesus and the Sages' complaint against the House of Annas (Mk 11:17). Second, we hear a specific charge against the family of Hanin (Annas), which the Gospels describe secretly handed Jesus to the Romans. Their "whisperings" indicate "secret conclaves to devise oppressive measures" (b. *Pesaḥ.* 57a n. b2; cf. *Ant.* 20:199, 13:294). Finally, mention of the Bar Kathros family in the inscription and the Talmud assists to identify the vicinity of a family of priests (see *Ant.* 20:16) whose home in Jerusalem was destroyed during the Roman siege in the summer of 70 CE.

*Stone weight from the "Burnt House" in the Jewish Quarter inscribed, "(belonging) to Bar Kathros."*

Discovery of monumental homes near the Bar Kathros house has raised the possibility that this area may have been a neighborhood of other high priestly families. One designated by the archaeologists, "the Palatial Mansion," is remarkable for its size and elegance. It was a multi-storied home, over 5,500 square feet [c. 600 sq. m] in size. It contained imported vessels, and its plastered walls were covered with frescoes, newly refashioned to imitate contemporary Roman styles just prior to its destruction. A signature glass pitcher discovered within the ruins was the work of the renowned glass-maker, Ennion of Sidon. The residents of this house must have been a particularly notable and wealthy family, and the exceptional number of *miqva'ot* may indicate that they were a family of high priests.

We have no way of determining whether this home belonged to the family of Annas or Caiaphas. However, the opulence and accumulation of wealth exhibited in "the Palatial Mansion" characterize the economic position of the longest hierocratic dynasty in the first century CE (*Ant.* 20:198). They were the targets of harsh criticism in their day, as we have heard both from Jesus and Abba Saul b. Batnit.

At daybreak Jesus was brought to "the Sanhedrin" (Lk 22:66; cf. Mt 26:59; Mk 14:55). This is Luke's only use of the term in his Gospel. In Acts (4:15; 5:27, 34; 6:12, 15) he employs the term not to designate the council but the council-chamber, the Chamber of Hewn Stone mentioned in the Jewish sources (m. *Pe'a* 2:6; m. *Sanh.* 11:2; m. *Mid.* 5:4; j. *Sanh.* 19c).

*The Pontius Pilate inscription from Caesarea.*

Luke's reading of council-chamber rather than an indication of the participation of the full Sanhedrin in Jesus' condemnation and transfer to the Romans, concurs with testimony about the Sanhedrin's concern to preserve human life and strong reluctance to execute capital punishment.

> A Sanhedrin that puts someone to death in a week [i.e. in seven years] is called "destructive." Rabbi Eleazar ben Azariah says: "Even one person in seventy years." Rabbi Tarfon and Rabbi Akiva say: "If we had been members of the Sanhedrin, no one would ever have been put to death." (m. *Maksh.* 1:10)

In addition, the understanding that only the clan of Annas (i.e. Annas, Caiaphas, John and Alexander; cf. Acts 4:6) and those close to them were present in the Chamber of Hewn Stone and questioned Jesus, is more fitting with the subsequent steps taken by Jesus' accusers. Their actions would hardly have gained the required approval of the full Sanhedrin (Lk 23:50–51).

To deliver a fellow Jew into the hands of the Romans with the possibility of his execution was considered in Jewish opinion a transgression of such magnitude that it was eternally unforgivable (*S. ʿOlam Rab.* ch. 3 end). With the same overriding concern for a single human life (cf. m. *Sanh.* 4:5), we hear in the Jerusalem Talmud that even if the Romans have surrounded the city:

> And they say, "Give us one from among you and we will kill him. And if you do not, we will kill all of you." Even if all of you may be killed, you shall not hand over a single soul from Israel. (j. *Ter.* 8:10)

So, we hear later of the concern by these same Sadducean priests that their clandestine actions might become public knowledge (Acts 5:28).

Finally, still another piece of evidence demonstrates that Jesus could not have been condemned to death by the Sanhedrin. According to the mishnaic tractate *Sanhedrin* there were two graves reserved for those executed by order of the supreme council.

> They used not to bury [the condemned man] in the burying-place of his fathers, but two burying-places were kept in readiness by the court, one for them that were beheaded or strangled, and one for them that were stoned or burnt. (m. *Sanh.* 9:6)

The Gospel accounts are unanimous that Jesus was not laid in one of these two tombs (Mt 27:60; Mk 15:46; Lk 23:53; Jn 19:41).

After a period of initial inquiry, Jesus was taken to the Roman prefect, Pontius Pilate, and accused of political sedition (Lk 23:2). Normally, Pilate resided in Caesarea, the capital of the Roman province of Judea. However, to maintain a show of imperial power before the crowds gathered for Passover, the Gospels record that Pilate came to Jerusalem and resided at the Praetorium (Mt 27:27; Mk 15:16; Jn 18:28).

Christian tradition has identified the site of the Praetorium with the Antonia Fortress, built by Herod the Great and named after his early benefactor, Mark Antony (*War* 5: 238–245). Recent excavations, however, have determined that the *Lithostrotos* (Jn 19:13)—the pavement where tradition remembers Pilate condemned Jesus—under the present-day Church of Ecce Homo, dates from the time of Hadrian (c. 135 CE) and not from the New Testament period.

Instead, Pilate was probably staying in the palace of Herod the Great on the western hill. Both Philo (*Legat.* 38:299) and Josephus (*War* 2:31) report that Herod's palace in Jerusalem was the residence of the Roman governor. According to Mark, Herod's palace was also called the Praetorium: "The soldiers led Jesus away into the palace, that is the Praetorium" (Mk 15:16a). Later, we read that the Roman governor resided in Herod's seaside palace in Caesarea that is similarly called the Praetorium of Herod (Acts 23:35).

Luke reports that Jesus was charged with stirring up the population from Galilee to Jerusalem, encouraging the people not to pay taxes and claiming to be the king Messiah (Lk 23:2). When his accusers informed Pilate that he came from Galilee, the prefect sought to pass Jesus off to Herod Antipas, tetrarch of Galilee and Perea. Antipas was staying in the former Hasmonean palace (*Ant.* 20:190). Its location has not been confirmed, but it may have been north of the neighborhood of the priestly homes previously mentioned. In any event, all of these sites were closely situated.

Josephus and the Gospels record that Antipas executed John the Baptist, the cousin of Jesus (*Ant.* 18:119; Mt 14:3–12; Mk 6:17–29). John had openly criticized the marriage of Antipas and his second wife, Herodias. According to Josephus, the Herodian couple had divorced their spouses to legitimize a pre-existing adulterous affair, an action prohibited according to Jewish law (m. *Soṭah* 5:1; *Ant.* 18:109–110; Mt 14:4; Mk 6:18). The popularity of John's movement together with his open rebuke had resulted in his tragic murder. Jesus may have subsequently taken up his cousin's reprimand (Lk 16:18). Antipas had been seeking to meet Jesus face to face (Lk 13:31–33, 23:8), but at their encounter Jesus remained silent. It seems the tetrarch did not interpret Jesus as great a threat as his cousin, so he returned the Galilean to Pilate in mocking attire (Lk 23: 11–12).

Returned to Herod's palace, Pilate attempted to punish Jesus and release him, but the priestly family who had been the subject of Jesus' public rebuke pressed for his execution. The Roman prefect had a reputation as remembered by Josephus and Philo for his brutality, "a man of inflexible, stubborn and cruel disposition," guilty of "venality, violence, robbery, assault, abusive behavior, frequent executions without trial, and endless savage ferocity" (Philo *Legat.* 301–302; cf. 303–305; *Ant.* 18:55–59, 60–62; *War* 2:175–177).

There is an additional facet of Pilate's character. His small temple built in Caesarea in honor of Tiberius is the only known temple built by a Roman official for a living emperor. Pilate's efforts to ingratiate himself with the emperor—who according to Suetonius (Suet. *Tib.* 26) forbade temples dedicated to himself—reveals another aspect of the prefect's complex personality, a personal weakness at the point of persuasion put forward by Jesus' accusers. "If you release [Jesus], you are no friend of Caesar" (Jn 19:12). Pilate condemned Jesus to death by crucifixion, and he was summarily led a short distance outside of the city to be executed.

Since the medieval period the *Via Dolorosa* ("the way of suffering") has been traced through the streets of Jerusalem, beginning at the site of the Antonia, east of today's Church of the Holy Sepulcher. Yet, there are early Byzantine traditions that remember the place where Jesus was flogged on Mount Zion (Bordeaux Pilgrim 592). These Christian traditions have confusedly combined the event of Jesus' flogging with his brief confinement at the House of Caiaphas. Yet, the Gospels record that it was Pilate's soldiers who flogged Jesus while he

*Tiberius, emperor at the time of Jesus' death.*

was still in the Praetorium (Mt 27:26; Mk 15:15). With the recent recognition that the Roman prefect was at Herod's former palace on the western hill, the Byzantine tradition may be a vestige of a pre-Byzantine memory concerning the location of Jesus' Roman incarceration, flogging and condemnation to death.

If modern scholarship is correct, then the starting point for Jesus' way of suffering began on the western hill, today's Mount Zion. He was led from Herod's palace and out the city gates to be crucified. Excavations directed south of the Muristan in the Old City of Jerusalem discovered portions of the First Wall of Jerusalem described by Josephus. More important for our present interests is the discovery of the remains of a first-century gate, thought to be the one described by Josephus. He describes only one gate along the northern line of the First Wall, the Gennath Gate: "The second wall started from the gate in the first wall which they called Gennath (i.e. Garden Gate), and [the second wall] enclosing only the northern district of the town, went up as far as Antonia" (*War* 5:146).

If Jesus was taken from Herod's palace to the area north of the walled city as Christian tradition remembers, then it seems likely that he would have been taken out of the city through the Gennath Gate. Josephus does not discuss the etymology of the name of the gate, but the Fourth Gospel may assist. It supplies a unique topographical detail on the vicinity where Jesus was executed, "in the place where [Jesus] was crucified there was a garden" (Jn 19:41). John's description of an agricultural area north of the city corresponds to the etymology of the Gennath Gate. The gate opened northward beyond the First Wall of Jerusalem to an area of gardens. It is in this area that Christian tradition marks the place of Jesus' death, burial and resurrection.

Twenty years of excavations as part of restoration work within the Church of the Holy Sepulcher have helped to determine the early history of the site. It was the location of a limestone quarry during the Old Testament period.

Unfortunately, the traditional tomb of Jesus has been severely damaged over the centuries, and visitors can see little of the original hewn stone. Nevertheless, the so-called Tomb of Nicodemus and Joseph of Arimathea nearby is typical of a first-century *kokh* tomb. The topographical question at the center of the claims of the Church of the Holy Sepulcher is whether the site was inside or outside the walls of first-century Jerusalem. Since no conclusive evidence has been discovered from Josephus' Second Wall (which would determine the position of the present-day church vis-à-vis the city walls in 30 CE), the presence of Jewish tombs—which were required to be outside the boundary of a city—within the Church of the Holy Sepulcher may be the best evidence that the traditional site of Golgotha was indeed outside the walls of first-century Jerusalem. The site remains the best candidate for the place of Jesus' death, burial and resurrection.

## From the Empty Tomb to the Road to Emmaus

The Gospels are in agreement that Jesus died on a Friday afternoon as the Sabbath approached (Mt 27:45; Mk 15:33; Lk 23:44; Jn 19:31, 42). According to Luke 23:46, his dying words were uttered from Psalm 31:5 [HMT 31:6], the traditional deathbed prayer of an observant Jew: "Into your hand, I commit my spirit." Those who had accompanied Jesus were concerned that his corpse not remain exposed overnight. Josephus attests to a similar Jewish concern in the wake of Titus' crucifixion of countless innocent victims during the siege of Jerusalem.

> [The Romans] actually went so far in their impiety as to cast out the corpses without burial, although the Jews are so careful about funeral rites that even malefactors who have been sentenced to crucifixion are taken down and buried before sunset.
>
> (*War* 4:317)

The initiative to provide Jesus with a proper burial (cf. m. *Naz.* 6:5; 7:1 [Lev 21:1]) was taken by Nicodemus and Joseph from Arimathea (Mt 27:57; Mk 15:43; Lk 23:20; Jn 19:38–42), leading figures in the city. Nicodemus is well known from rabbinic literature and was a wealthy patrician of Jerusalem (Jn 7:50–52; b. *Giṭ.* 56a; t. *ᶜErub.* 3(4):17). The provision of a burial place for one who could not afford his own would have been part of these aristocrats' expected role to dispense charity.

Although there was urgency to assure that Jesus was properly interred before sunset, there was insufficient time to prepare his body. "It was the day of Preparation [for the Sabbath, i.e. Friday], and the Sabbath was beginning" (Lk 23:54). The women who had accompanied Jesus from Galilee took the responsibility for the preparation. So, they followed and noted the location of the tomb, determined to return after the Sabbath to complete their task.

Of all the variants in the resurrection accounts, two geographical notes in those reports cannot be overlooked: Jesus' reported resurrection appearance in Galilee and the site identification of Emmaus.

Paul of Tarsus penned the oldest literary witness to the Christian belief in Jesus' resurrection from the dead.

> For I delivered to you as of first importance what I also received that Christ died for our sins in accordance with the scriptures, that he was buried, that he was raised on the third day in accordance with the scriptures, and that he appeared to Cephas, then to the twelve. Then he appeared to more than five hundred brethren at one time, most of whom are still alive, though some have fallen asleep.
>
> (1 Cor 15:3–6)

*The rolling stone in Herod's family tomb, Jerusalem.*

The Apostle mentions several resurrection appearances by Jesus, some of which are not repeated elsewhere in the New Testament. However, he also refers to an individual appearance to Cephas (i.e. Simon Peter; Jn 1:42; 1 Cor 1:12, 3:22, 9:5; Gal 1:18, 2:9) that is included in Luke's story of Jesus' encounter with the two departing Jerusalem on the road to Emmaus. When the two returned that evening to Jerusalem to tell those gathered what had happened, they were told, "The Lord has risen indeed, and has appeared to Simon!" (Lk 24:34).

The report of an individual appearance to Simon Peter, as distinguished from the other followers of Jesus, is not preserved in Mark and Matthew, but it may be the genesis for Mark's specific mention of Peter in the instruction to the women at the empty tomb, "But go, tell his disciples *and Peter* that he is going before you to Galilee; there you will see him, as he told you" (Mk 16:7; cf. Mt 28:7). The fragmented endings in the manuscripts of Mark's Gospel present a challenge for text critics. However, the various endings of Mark include neither an individual appearance to Peter nor any appearance of Jesus in the Galilee.

The singling out of Peter in the Markan logion is likely to address the unreconciled breach between Jesus and Peter, which resulted from the disciple's denial of his master (Mt 26:69–75 *parr.*). Although the Fourth Gospel does not preserve Mark's logion and the anticipated encounter, reconciliation between Peter and Jesus is certainly central to the episode recorded in John 21:15–19. In other words, the Johannine account of Peter and Jesus on the shores of the Sea of Galilee is the literary complement to the unfulfilled

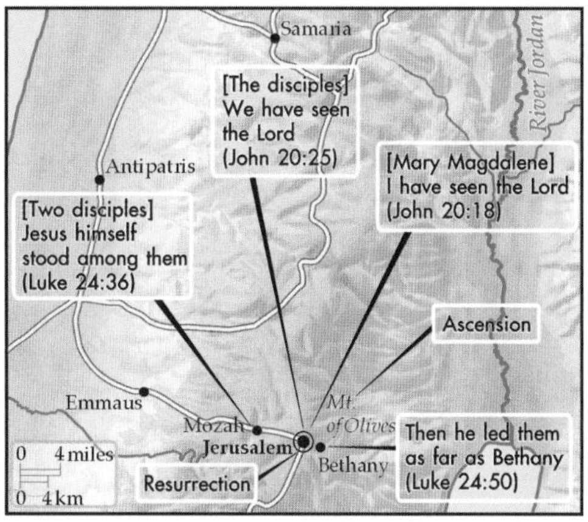


**The Resurrection and Ascension**

expectations raised in Mark's logion at the empty tomb.

Notwithstanding the Evangelists' motives in their concern for Peter, it should be noted that there is no reason to read Paul's statement as a testimony of Jesus' appearance to Peter *in Galilee*. Indeed, what is striking about the Pauline version of Christianity's most primitive resurrection tradition is the absence of any knowledge of a Galilee appearance by Jesus. Paul seems unaware of the traditions preserved in Matthew 28:16 or John 21:15–19 that Jesus appeared to the eleven in Galilee. Moreover, if recent scholarship is correct, that John 20:30–31 served at an earlier stage of composition to conclude the Fourth Gospel, then John's earliest testimony without the epilogue of chapter 21 agrees with Paul, Luke and the extant endings of Mark, all of which lack a report of Jesus' appearance to his followers in Galilee after the resurrection.

These witnesses concur with Luke's presentation—which is too often easily discarded by New Testament scholarship as the Evangelist's attempt to anticipate the literary structure of his sequel (cf. Acts 1:8)—that the followers of Jesus remained in Jerusalem until the outpouring of the Holy Spirit at Pentecost. According to the Third Gospel, Jesus instructed them, "And behold, I send the promise of my Father upon you; *but stay in the city*, until you are clothed with power from on high" (Lk 24:49).

As a brief aside, this type of expanded narrative witnessed in the post–Easter Galilee appearances of Matthew, John (and assumed in the logion of Mark), is seen elsewhere in the Synoptic tradition. The incidental mention of a term or toponym in one Gospel serves as the seed for a developed narrative tradition in a parallel account. This expansive style of storytelling shares affinities with contemporary Jewish Midrash, Targums and intertestamental literature that presents the Bible creatively re-written (e.g. Jubilees, Genesis Apocryphon, etc.).

In the arrest of Jesus, Luke's singular mention of the Sanhedrin (Lk 22:66) to designate the council-chamber, in Mark and Matthew became the historical kernel for the illegal night-meeting of the full Sanhedrin (Mt 26:59; Mk 14:55) and their condemnation of Jesus. This is not to suggest literary dependence, but only access to common sources. Although not of great significance, it should come as no surprise that John's Gospel agrees with Luke in his omission of any participation of the Sanhedrin or a night-trial by the ruling council in Jerusalem.

In the current narrative, Luke preserves a statement by the two angelic men at the empty tomb.

> Why do you seek the living among the dead? Remember how he told you, *while he was still in the Galilee*, that the Son of man must be delivered into the hands of sinful men, and be crucified, and on the third day rise. (Lk 24:5b–7)

Consider Mark's version of the same statement, "But go, tell his disciples and Peter that he is going before you to Galilee; there you will see him, as he told you" (Mk 16:7). While Matthew 28:7 agrees with Mark that the disciples are instructed to go to the Galilee, he does not preserve the notion that Jesus himself informed them of this earlier, concluding instead, "Behold, I have told you." It seems that first-century reports circulated concerning the encounter at the empty tomb with mention of Galilee, and these provided the narrative seeds from which "the Galilee appearance" traditions emerged. Yet, the earliest testimony in the New Testament reported by Paul is silent on the Galilee appearances of the resurrected Jesus.

As we began, mention by Paul of an appearance to Simon Peter is echoed in the report given to the two who returned from Emmaus, already on the eve of the first day of the week. The identification of the destination for those two has been the subject of speculation. Christian tradition since the Byzantine period has uniformly identified New Testament Emmaus with Nicopolis-ᶜImwas. This identification, however, is not without its difficulties. Luke describes the location of Emmaus, "sixty stadia (seven miles) from Jerusalem." The traditional site of Nicopolis-ᶜImwas exceeds that distance, situated approximately 22 miles (35 km) from Jerusalem.

The discrepancy in distance between Luke's description and the Byzantine city is likely the cause for the textual changes in some manuscripts to read "one hundred and sixty stadia" in Luke 24:13. The revised distance brought the location of New Testament Emmaus in line with the Byzantine identification of the site with Nicopolis-ᶜImwas. So, according to Eusebius' *Onomasticon*, "Emmaus: From whence came Cleopas, who is recorded in the Gospel according to Luke. This is now Nicopolis, the famous *polis* of Palaestina" (Eus. *Onom.* 90:15). However, the editorial committee of the United Bible Society's Greek New Testament determined that in spite of the difficulties in site identification, the best reading is the shorter distance of "sixty stadia" attested in better manuscripts. Our identification of New Testament Emmaus must fall within the spatial limits imposed by the best manuscript readings, thus excluding Nicopolis-ᶜImwas.

It seems that early Christian tradition exchanged the identity of a lesser-known village by the same name for the Byzantine metropolis. Josephus knew both locations. The site of Emmaus at Nicopolis-ᶜImwas is given as the location for the encampment of attacking foreign forces during the Hasmonean revolt (*Ant.* 12:98, 306; 13:15) and the First Jewish Revolt (*War* 5:42). However, Josephus knew another Emmaus closer to Jerusalem. After the Jewish revolt Vespasian assigned "eight hundred veterans discharged from the army a place for habitation called Emmaus, distant thirty stadia (3.5 miles) from Jerusalem" (*War* 7:217; m. *Sukkah* 4:5; j. *Sukkah* 54b; b. *Sukkah* 45a). The distance is precisely half of the distance (sixty stadia) described in Luke's Gospel, perhaps suggesting that Luke's measurement includes the return distance to Jerusalem. In any event, the description that the two returned that very evening to Jerusalem indicates that the village of Emmaus was nearby to Jerusalem and more likely the place mentioned by Josephus.

*Remains of the Roman road leading from Jerusalem to Emmaus.*

# CHAPTER EIGHTEEN
# THE EARLY DAYS OF THE CHURCH
## FIRST CENTURY CE

## JERUSALEM, JUDEA AND SAMARIA

The geographical expansion in the first decades of the Early Church is anticipated in a dominical saying recorded in Acts 1: 8: "You shall be my witnesses in Jerusalem and in all Judea and Samaria and to the end of the earth." Scholarship has rightly recognized that this verse serves as a literary framework for Luke's composition. Yet, it also describes the historical movement of the Christian faith beyond the confines of its Jewish context within the borders of the Land of Israel to Gentile audiences in the Greco-Roman world. As the Jerusalem Temple played a central role in the life of the Jewish Diaspora, so the Jerusalem Church continued to play a central role in the developing life of the Church.

*Greek inscription forbidding Gentiles to enter the Temple Mount.*

**In the Shadow of the Temple**. The opening chapters of the Book of Acts describe the followers of Jesus still gathered in Jerusalem. On the "day of Pentecost" (cf. the biblical "Feast of Weeks" [Ex 34:22; Num 28:26]), Luke reports that these followers were gathered together (Acts 2:1), without specification where in the city they were located. Christian tradition has typically identified the place of gathering with the same setting as the Last Supper in the upper city. These traditions do not predate the Byzantine period. Likely, they were derived from the similarities between the description of the setting of the Last Supper (Mk 14:15; Lk 22:12) and place of gathering in Acts 1:13. Yet, even if one were to assume the same setting for the Last Supper and the meeting in the first chapter of Acts, there is no indication that the Christians remained in the room for the events that followed. The language of the second chapter opens with a Hebraic-styled narrative break (i.e. "and when the day of Pentecost came") separating the events that follow from what has previously occurred.

Details in the narrative itself may hint to its location. The time of the event is important. According to Deuteronomy:

> Three times a year all your males shall appear before the Lord your God at the place which he will choose: at the feast of unleavened bread, at the feast of weeks, and at the feast of booths.... (Deut 16:16)

Josephus reports that at Pentecost the population of Jerusalem would increase significantly:

> Now, when that festival which we call Pentecost was at hand, all the places about the temple, and the whole city was full of a multitude of people that were come out of the country.... (*War* 1:253)

The historian's description of the influx of visitors to Jerusalem corresponds to Luke's testimony concerning Jewish pilgrims who were present in Jerusalem that day and witnessed the outpouring of the Holy Spirit:

> ...Parthians and Medes and Elamites and residents of Mesopotamia, Judea and Cappadocia, Pontus and Asia, Phrygia and Pamphylia, Egypt and the parts of Libya belonging to Cyrene, and visitors from Rome, both Jews and proselytes, Cretans and Arabians.... (Acts 2:9–11)

Luke reports that these pilgrims were amazed by what they saw and heard, and they sought an explanation. Peter stood and recounted recent events concerning Jesus' death and resurrection. In a measure of creative exegesis, he interpreted the manifestation of the Holy Spirit in light of the Hebrew Scriptures and invited those present "to repent and be baptized in the name of Jesus" (Acts 2:38).

For the current study, what is significant is the concluding report that three thousand people responded that day to Peter. Every aspect of the episode suggests a public setting. It is unlikely that such an event could occur in the confines of a private home on the upper slopes of the western hill of Jerusalem, where pilgrims from across the Roman world would have witnessed it.

Moreover, little attention has been given by scholarship to the practical challenge of immersing three thousand people in Jerusalem. Recent excavations near the southern entrance to the Temple Mount unearthed numerous *miqva'ot*, viz. ritual immersion baths. Many more of these installations were likely destroyed as a result of construction during the Byzantine and subsequent periods. Purity requirements for visitors to the Temple necessitated sufficient bathing facilities to serve the thousands of people who were obligated to ritually immerse before ascending (Lk 2:22; Acts 21:24). All of these elements point to the event of Pentecost somewhere within the vicinity of the Temple. This should not surprise us. Luke concludes his gospel with the observation: "They stayed continually at the temple, praising God" (Lk 24:53).

**Into Judea and Samaria**. In the wake of the death of Stephen (Acts 7–9), the Christian community in Jerusalem was scattered. Several episodes are recounted to describe the new faith of individuals and groups in Samaria and Judea. Philip (Acts 6: 5) proclaimed the gospel in Samaria where "multitudes paid close attention to what he said" (Acts 8:6). The toponym in this passage has been read to identify either the region of Samaria or its main city called by the same name. By the New Testament period the ancient city of Samaria (1 Kgs 16:24) had been rebuilt and renamed Sebaste by Herod the Great in honor of Caesar Augustus (*Ant.* 15:296; *War* 1:403; Strabo *Geog.* 16.2.34). Yet, even Josephus continues to use the biblical name, while already reporting that Herod had renamed the city (e.g. *War* 1:156 *et passim*).

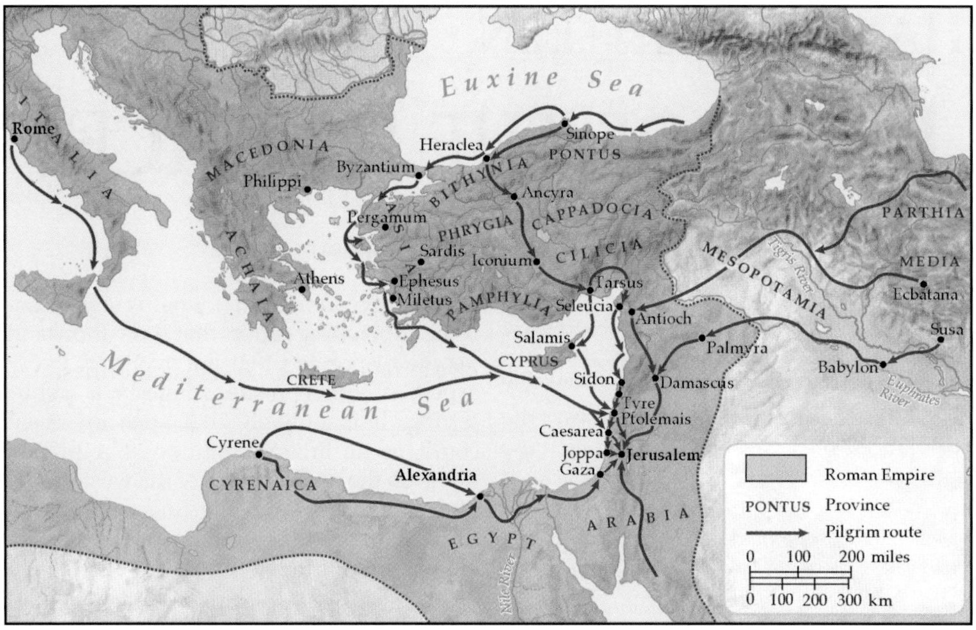


**The Pentecost Experience—Diaspora Communities Represented**

Our reading of whether Samaria in Acts 8:5 designates the city or the region largely is dependent upon variant manuscript readings that include or omit the article (i.e. *the* [main] city of Samaria [=Sebaste], or *a* city of Samaria). The stronger manuscript readings support the inclusion of the article. Other than the inclination to read this verse in light of Luke's topographical rubric in Acts 1:8, there seems little reason to read the location of events other than the Hellenistic city (cf. Just. *Apol.* 26).

No other points of geographical reference appear in the evangelistic journeys of Philip, Peter and John from Jerusalem into Samaria. The most direct northern route was the watershed route followed by the patriarchs. From Samaria, Peter and John ventured into "many villages of the Samaritans" which dotted the interior of the hill country of Samaria (Acts 8:25).

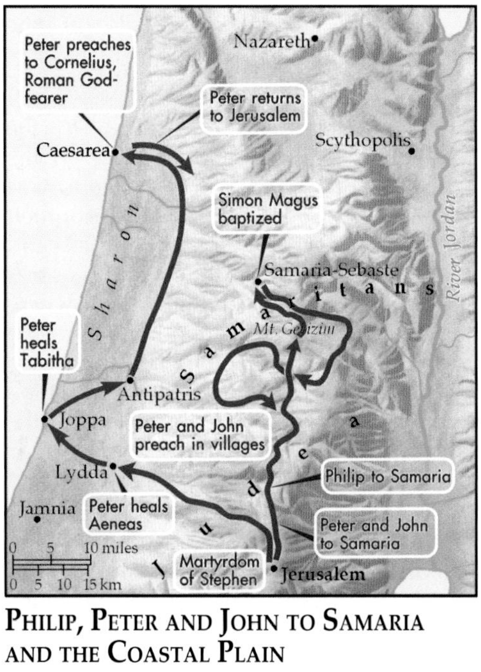


**Philip, Peter and John to Samaria and the Coastal Plain**

## Philip and the Ethiopian Eunuch.

Philip next ventured south on the road from "Jerusalem to Gaza" (Acts 8:26). The route from Jerusalem to Gaza would likely have descended south from Jerusalem near Bethlehem on the watershed route towards Hebron. Eusebius preserves the Christian tradition that it is on this ancient southern route that Philip encountered the Ethiopian eunuch. His mileage measurements attest to the existence of the road system in the late Roman period, which he used to measure distances from administrative centers—in this instance from Jerusalem and Eleutheropolis.

> Bethsoro is today a village at the twentieth mile on the way from which it is said the eunuch (belonging to) Candace (queen of the Ethiopians) was baptized by Philip. Another (village called) Bethsur, also in the tribe of Judah, one mile from Eleutheropolis.
>
> (Eus. *Onom.* 52:1)

The historian also indicates that Christian tradition in his day assumed that the caravan continued on the watershed route to springs near Beth-zur, and that it was here that the eunuch was immersed. This is likewise the opinion of the fourth-century Bordeaux Pilgrim (599) and Jerome (Eus. *Onom.* 53:1). It may also be reflected in the depiction of a church and springs at Beth-zur in the sixth-century Medeba Map.

It is unlikely that Philip and the caravan would have continued south in the Judean hills as far as Beth-zur (Kh. eṭ-Ṭubeiqa). Southwest of Bethlehem the ancient route divides. The watershed route continues to Beth-zur and Hebron, while a western spur follows the Ḥushah ridge and descends into the Elah Valley (Wâdī es-Sanṭ). The Romans paved this descent and evidence of these efforts can still be seen in steps cut into the Judean hills.

At the western end of the Elah Valley the sharp Cenomanian limestone hills are separated from the rounded Senonian chalk hills of the Shephelah by a fault line marked with a shallow trough that transverses the eastern edge of the lowlands. Roman milestones in this chalky trough are witness to the importance of the route. It remained in use during the late Roman and Byzantine periods providing access from Eleutheropolis to Lydda (Diospolis; 1 Macc 11:34; Acts 9:32) and points north.

Nearby and east of the intersection of the trough and the Elah Valley was the settlement of Socoh (Kh. esh-Shuweikeh). The site is mentioned in the Old Testament (Josh 15:35; 1 Sam 17:1), and in the Hellenistic period it was the home of the well-known sage, Antigonus (m. *ʾAbot* 1:3). It may have been in the vicinity of Socoh that Philip and the eunuch parted ways. The caravan would have continued south by way of Beth Govrin (Eleutheropolis) across the coastal plain to Gaza and the southern route through the wilderness to Egypt.

Luke provides an added description about the caravan route: "This is a wilderness [road]" (NRSV Acts 8:26b). The Evangelist's comment is commonly viewed as an indication of Luke's ignorance of the topographical realities of Judea.

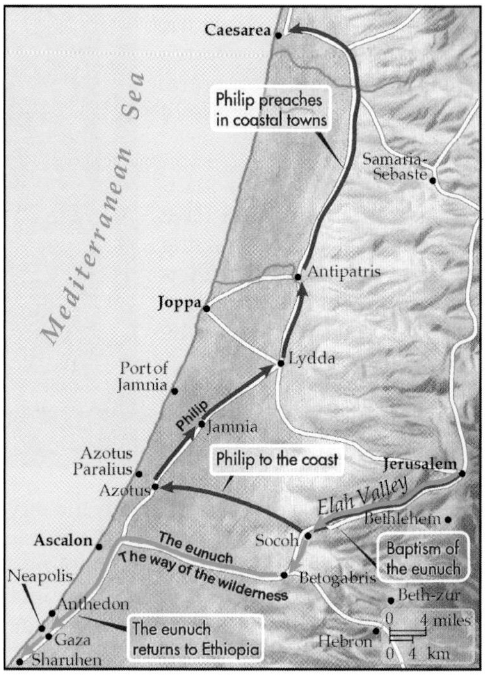


**Philip and the Ethiopian Eunuch**

It is worthwhile noting that there is another possible reading of Luke's presentation of the road in association with the term "wilderness." It may be a vestige of an expression similar to what we find commonly in Hebrew (e.g. Deut 2:8; Josh 8:15; 2 Sam 2:24). In these instances, use of the term is not intended to describe the local terrain but to indicate the destination, i.e. "to the wilderness." This description also aptly describes the route on which the caravan was traveling. It led south to the biblical wilderness (e.g. Gen 14:6, 21:14; Ex 3:1 *et passim*).

There are insufficient details in the

narrative to indicate where the eunuch was baptized. Luke only describes that the place as being alongside the road. Scholars have proposed that it took place at the springs of Wâdī el-Ḥesi. While there are springs at Wâdī el-Ḥesi between Beth Govrin and Gaza, they lie too far south for Philip's route to Azotus. It seems more likely that the waters indicated were one of the numerous springs in the Elah Valley, near the descent from the Judean hills. It is here the eunuch was baptized before he and Philip parted ways.

Philip continued his journey westward across the coastal plain to Azotus (1 Macc 4:15, 10:70–84; *Ant.* 13:92), the Hellenistic-Roman period settlement on the site of the ancient Philistine city of Ashdod (Josh 13:3). While we have no evidence of Roman roads linking the Elah Valley and Azotus, a local route is documented by way of Gath (*Ant.* 5:87; Eus. *Onom.* 68:4–7) and Saphir (Eus. *Onom.* 156:23), where one would join the international coastal route to Azotus.

**Peter on the Coastal Plain.** As part of Luke's account of the spread of the Gospel, he records Peter's ministry in the coastal regions (Acts 9:32–10:48). Peter is first mentioned at Lydda, where he healed Aeneas, "a paralytic who had been bedridden for eight years" (Acts 9:32). Next he was urged to come to Joppa, because Tabitha, a woman "full of good works and acts of charity" (Acts 9:36), had died. The Apostle prayed for her, and she came back to life. "And it became known throughout all Joppa, and many believed in the Lord. And he stayed in Joppa for many days with one Simon, a tanner" (Acts 9:41–42). It is at Simon's house in Joppa that Peter saw his vision of the sheet descending from heaven with clean and unclean animals on it. His experience was intended to prepare him for his meeting with the Gentile Cornelius in Caesarea, and the realization that "what God has cleansed, you must not call common" (Acts 10:15).

During this time, Cornelius, a Roman centurion, had a vision in which he was instructed to send for Peter. The Gentile is described as "a devout man who feared God with all his household, gave alms liberally to the people, prayed constantly to God" (Acts 10:2). Luke's description of the Roman suggests that he was a semi-proselyte, a God-fearer, who had elected to refrain from certain aspects of pagan life (e.g. idolatry, sexual immorality) and identified himself with the faith of the Jewish people. When Peter arrived and heard of Cornelius' experience, he remarked, "Truly, I perceive that God shows no partiality, but in every nation any one who fears Him and does what is right is acceptable to Him" (Acts 10:34–35). Peter's experience in Joppa and Caesarea is paradigmatic for the early church's dawning recognition that Gentiles would now be drawn to faith.

## The Apostle Paul

**Paul's Encounter on the Road to Damascus.** The Apostle Paul is introduced for the first time in the New Testament in Jerusalem during the stoning of Stephen (Acts 7:58). Paul's role in the execution of the first Christian martyr is unclear (cf. Acts 22:20). All we are told is that those who acted against Stephen, "laid down their garments at the feet of a young man named Saul." Concerning the Apostle's name, Paul never calls himself in his epistles by his Hebrew name (Saul). Instead, he always uses his Greco-Roman cognomen, Paul (Rom 1:1; 1 Cor 1:1, etc.).

In the chronicle of Paul's embrace of the Christian faith and subsequent missionary efforts, Luke refers to the Apostle as Saul until the beginning of his missionary activities to the Gentiles (Acts 13:9). Thereafter, the only occasions when Paul is referred to as Saul are in the repeated accounts of his experience on the road to Damascus, "Saul, Saul, why do you persecute me?" (Acts 22:7, 22:13, 26:14).

Insufficient geographical details are provided to know which route Paul chose to travel from Jerusalem to Damascus. Presumably he would have traveled by way of the Galilee and ascended to the Transjordanian highlands somewhere east of the Sea of Galilee. We also do not know precisely where he had his vision of Jesus. Two of the three accounts (Acts 9:1–19, 22:4–11, 26:12–18) of Paul's encounter in Acts relate that he was *nearing Damascus* (Acts 9:3, 22:6).

Blinded from his vision, Paul stayed a few days at a private home "on the street called Straight" (Acts 9:11) in Damascus, until

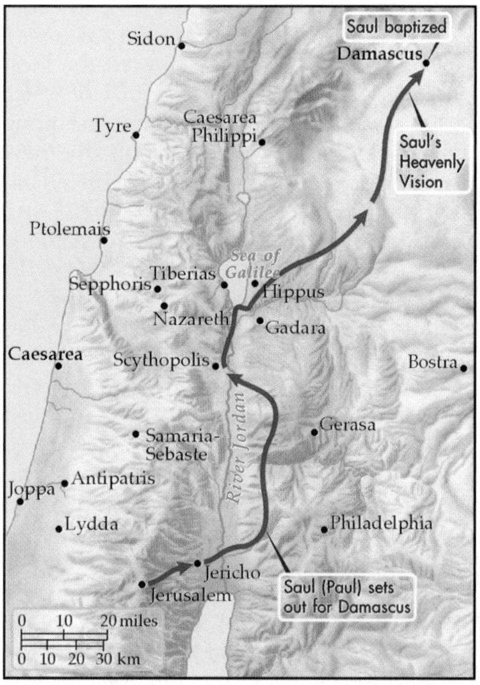


**Saul of Tarsus (Paul) on the Road to Damascus**

a disciple named Ananias arrived and laid hands on him "so that he might regain his sight" (Acts 9:12). It is to Ananias that the Lord first reveals the purpose of Paul's calling: "Go, for he is a chosen instrument of mine to carry my name before the Gentiles and kings and the sons of Israel . . ." (Acts 9:15). Paul's sight is restored, and he then is baptized and takes a meal. Soon, Paul publicly declares his new faith in Jesus to the skepticism of some of his fellow believers who have heard of his reputation and the consternation of the Jewish authorities.

Discovering a plot to kill him, Paul escaped by night and returned to Jerusalem where he once again engages in disputations, this time with Greek-speaking Jews. After renewed threats, he was taken to Caesarea, where he traveled by ship to Tarsus, the place of his birth (Acts 9:30, 21:39, 22:3).

We next hear about Paul when he is sought by Barnabbas in Tarsus and brought to the church in Antioch. Here the two ministered for a year (Acts 11:25–26). At the time of a great famine during the reign of Claudius, Paul and Barnabbas were appointed by the church in Antioch to take relief offerings to the believers in Jerusalem (Acts 11:27–30). When they returned to Antioch they brought with them John Mark. These three would once again join company in Paul's first missionary journey.

## Paul's First Missionary Journey

Luke reports in Acts 13:1–3 that Barnabbas and Paul were set apart for a special work by the congregation at Antioch. They began their mission from Seleucia, the Mediterranean port c. 17 miles (27 km) southwest of Antioch, and sailed c. 120 miles (200 km) to Salamis (*War* 2:358; ActsBarn 22–23), the eastern port city of Cyprus. The city had diminished in the Roman period when the capital of the island was moved to Paphos. Nevertheless, there remained a significant Jewish community in Cyprus (1 Macc 15:16–23; Philo *Leg.* 282; *Ant.* 13:284–287, 18:131, 20:142). In the synagogues of Salamis, Paul and Barnabbas "proclaimed the word of God" (Acts 13:5).

Traveling overland across Cyprus, the company arrived at Paphos on the southwestern coast of the island (Pliny *Nat. Hist.* 5.130). The fame of the ancient city was attached to its temple of Aphrodite mentioned by Homer (*Od.* 8.363), and the city grew in importance during the Ptolemaic and Roman periods. Sergio Paulus, the Roman proconsul stationed there, requested to hear from Paul and Barnabbas. He accepted the new faith in spite of the interference of Elymas, a magician, and after witnessing a miracle at the hands of Paul (Acts 13:6–12).

The company sailed from Paphos to

*City gates of Perga.*

Perga in the province of Pamphylia. No mention is made at this point of Attalia, the Mediterranean harbor c. 10 miles (16 km) southwest of Perga and the natural seaward destination from Paphos. It may be that Luke assumed in his narrative that Attalia was the point of disembarkation. It was the natural transit point on the way to Perga, the metropolis of Pamphylia (Strabo *Geog.* 14.42). Archaeological remains point to a road between Attalia and Perga built during the reign of Tiberius.

Scant record is given about Paul's initial visit to Perga. All we are told is that for an unexplained reason, John Mark abandoned the company to return to Jerusalem. His desertion would later be a point of friction between Paul and Barnabbas (Acts 15:37, 15: 39; Col 4:10; Phil 24; 2 Tim 4:11). We also have no evidence of a Jewish settlement in Perga, though there is mention of Jews in the province of Pamphylia (1 Macc 15:23; Philo *Leg.* 281).

*The ancient remains of Pisidian Antioch have been identified with the ruins just east of the modern city of Yalvaç. The city thrived after Augustus annexed the region and reestablished it as a Roman colony, populating it with veterans of the Roman legions V and VII. Shown here are the remains of the Augusteum.*

Travel from Perga followed inland along the Cestrus River to the *Via Sebaste*, built in 6 BCE by Caesar Augustus through Colonia Comama to Colonia Antiochia. The toponym Pisidian Antioch (Acts 13:14) is imprecise. The Roman colony was situated in the province of Phrygia near the frontier of Pisidia (cf. Strabo *Geog.* 12.6.4, 12.8.14; Pliny *Nat. Hist.* 5.24.94).

The Jewish community there may have resulted from the colonization of Phrygia and Lydia by Antiochus III (*Ant.* 12:147–153). On the Sabbath Paul and Barnabbas entered the synagogue, where Luke reports the congregation listened to the reading of "the law and the prophets" (Acts 13:15). Luke's account is the earliest written record of the Jewish practice to read the Hebrew Prophets (the *Haftara*) following the weekly reading of the Torah in the synagogue on the Sabbath (cf. Lk 4:16–30; m. *Meg.* 4:2).

Paul and the other visitors were invited to speak, and in his remarks the Apostle addressed those present, "sons of the family of Abraham, and those among you that fear God" (cf. Acts 16:14, 17:17, 18:7). The dual terms of address to signify Paul's hearers are repeated throughout his journeys and they suggest the diverse composition of the synagogue audiences. A number of Gentile God-fearers, semi-proselytes or sympathizers who had abandoned pagan practices, associated with the Jewish communities in the Diaspora and became the focal point of Paul's mission to the Gentiles (cf. *Ant.* 20:34–38).

The message of Paul and Barnabbas received a mixed reception in Pisidian Antioch, leading them to abandon the city and continue on the *Via Sebaste* c. 90 miles (150 km) to Iconium (Xenophon *Anab.* 1.2.19; Pliny *Nat. Hist.* 5:41; modern Konya). Once again, the Apostles entered the local synagogue to proclaim the word of grace (Acts 14:3; cf. Lk 4:22). Divided opinions among the people of the city regarding this new message grew to the point of violence, and the company had to flee [c. 20 mi./33 km] "to Lystra and Derbe, cities of Lycaonia, and to the surrounding country" (Acts 14: 6). Ancient Lystra has been identified at Zoldera near Hatun Saray about 24 miles south of Konya. The *Via Sebaste* reached Colonia Lystra, but the way to Derbe and the surrounding region was likely unpaved at the time.

Opposition to the message of the Apostles strengthened and followed them on their way. Indeed, the pursuit by Paul's Jewish opponents from Pisidian Antioch and Iconium to Lystra may indicate the ease of access between these cities on the *Via Sebaste*. At Lystra they stoned Paul and left him for dead, but he survived and set off with Barnabbas to Derbe (Acts 14:19–20; cf. 2 Tim 3:11).

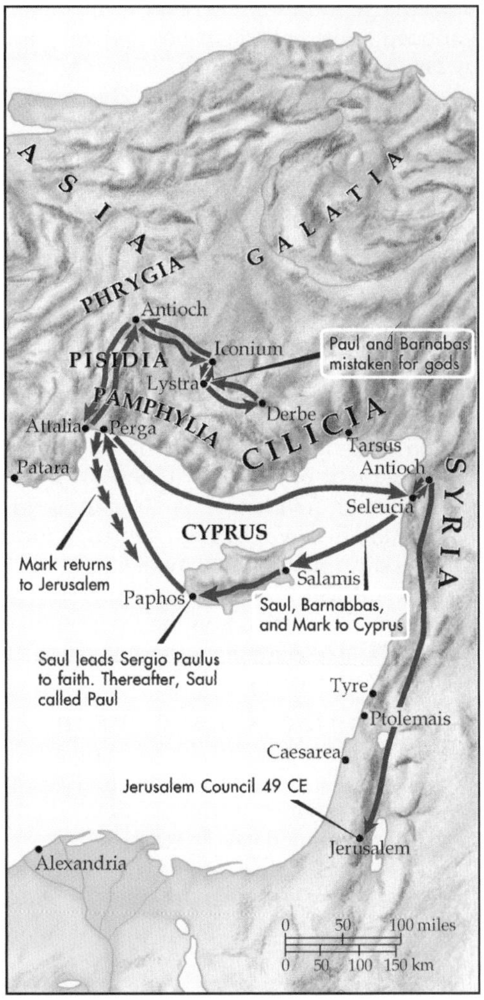


**The First Missionary Journey of Paul**

Luke records that the party returned on the same route by which they had arrived to Derbe. "They returned to Lystra and to Iconium and to Antioch" (Acts 14:21). Not only did they continue to preach in these cities, they appointed leaders for the fledgling congregations. Turning south they crossed the southwestern portions of the province of Galatia into Pisidia and finally to the province of Pamphylia, in which were the cities of Perga and Attalia (Antalya). From this port city they set sail and returned to Antioch in Syria, where "they declared all that God had done with them, and how he had opened a door of faith to the Gentiles" (Acts 14:27).

**Jerusalem Council**. As the number of Gentiles increased in the church, it brought to the fore the question of the Gentiles' relationship to the Law and the people of Israel. Some argued, "Unless you are circumcised and walk according to the custom of Moses you cannot be saved" (Acts 15:1 in Western texts; cf. *Ant.* 20:34–48). Paul, Barnabbas and others from Antioch were appointed to go to Jerusalem to meet with the Apostles and address these issues. The leadership in Jerusalem met and reached a decision. Rather than requiring conversion with circumcision and full adherence to the Law (cf. Gal 5:3), they applied minimal requirements to the Gentile Christians that approximated the basic statutes of the Noachide Laws (Acts 15:28–29; cf. Gen 9:4–6; Jub 7:20–21; Did. 3:1–6; t. ᶜ*Abod. Zar.* 8:4; *Sipra* on Lev 18:4).

## Paul's Second Missionary Journey

After returning from Jerusalem to Antioch, Paul told Barnabbas of his desire to return "to visit the brethren in every city where we proclaimed the word of the Lord" (Acts 15:36). However, the two disagreed about whether they should again take John Mark. Paul refused, because Mark had deserted them in Pamphylia (Acts 13:13). So, Paul and Barnabbas parted ways. Barnabbas sailed with Mark to Cyprus, while Paul invited Silas to accompany him.

Paul and Silas did not return on the same route that Paul had previously taken. This time they traveled overland from Antioch through the Amanus Mountains to the province of Cilicia. Luke merely reports that they arrived to Derbe and Lystra. No details are given about their journey, and few paved roads in Cilicia are known. The earliest Roman milestones discovered at the foot of the Taurus Mountains date from 75/76 CE. While Luke gives no account of Paul's route, it seems likely that the Apostle would have traveled north from Antioch in Syria (17 mi./28 km) to the pass of the Syrian Gates through the Amanus Mountains and entered the province of Cilicia to his birthplace at Tarsus (Acts 22:3).

The road from east to west follows the base of the foothills above the marshy and fertile plains but below the rocky terrain of the Taurus Mountains. At the junction of river and road lay the major settlements of the region: Adana (the modern capital), Misis (Mopsuestia), and Tarsus. Tarsus sits at the juncture of the east-west road and the route north through the Cilician Gates and on to the Anatolian Plateau.

*Roman milestone.*

*Anatolian Plateau: Paul traveled through here during his journey from Tarsus to Iconium, and between Iconium, Lystra and Derbe.*

Turning north they traveled 26 miles (42 km) to the narrow pass of the Cilician Gates in the Taurus Mountains, and then continued northwest onto the wide plains of the province of Lycaonia and the cities of Derbe and Lystra (Acts 16:1). In Lystra they met Timothy, a young man whose Greek father was well known in the area. However, his mother was Jewish (2 Tim 1:5), so Paul had Timothy circumcised (Acts 16:1–4; cf. Titus in Gal 2:3). Paul's actions may be one of the earliest historical witnesses to the rabbinical opinion that one's Jewish identity is determined by the mother. The company returned to the inland cities of Paul's previous missionary journey to report about the decision of "the apostles and elders who were at Jerusalem" (Acts 16:4–5).

At this point, they were "forbidden by the Holy Spirit" from continuing west to Asia. Instead, they ventured north and ministered in the provinces of Phrygia and Galatia (Acts 16:6). We are uncertain which Roman road might have been used by Paul on his northern journey through Phrygia to the edge of Bithynia. Further, with no explanation, we are told that the entourage was "compelled not to enter the region of Bithynia" (Acts 16:7).

Instead, they turned west "coming opposite" the northern regions of the district of Mysia and "came down to Troas," a Greco-Roman city on the coast of the Aegean Sea. It seems that Paul's circuitous route followed unpaved tracks on this stretch of his journey that led him through Adramyttium.

In the city of Alexandria Troas, 10 miles (16 km) south of ancient Troy, Paul received a vision of a man from Macedonia who appealed, "Come over to Macedonia and help us." The Apostle interpreted the vision as an indication that "God had called us to preach the gospel to them" (Acts 16:10). From Troas Paul set sail to Samothrace.

Paul and Silas took the most direct route of travel to Macedonia. They stopped overnight at the island of Samothrace, docking in the mole of the old northern harbor of the city by the same name. The following day they continued about 64 miles (107 km) to Neapolis, the port city for Philippi. The ancient witnesses are divided as to whether the location of Neapolis made it a part of Thrace (Strabo *Geog.* 7:330; Ptolemy 3:13) or Macedonia (Pliny *Nat. Hist.* 4:18). Positioned on a promontory on the Aegean coast and strategically on the *Via Egnatia*, Neapolis became an important crossroads between Europe and Asia in the Roman period. Philip of Macedonia had conquered it in 350 BCE to serve as the port for Krenides, which he conquered and renamed Philippi after himself. The assassins of Julius Caesar—Brutus and Cassius—also used the western bay of Neapolis in the battle of Philippi with Octavian and Mark Antony (App. *Bell. Civ.* 4:106; cf. *Ant.* 14:301).

Following the *Via Egnatia*, Paul journeyed 6 miles (9.5 km) to Philippi, where the Roman road actually served as the *decumanus maximus* for the city. On the Sabbath, they went outside of the city near the river that courses by Philippi, because supposedly there was a place of prayer. Paul encountered a God-fearer, "a woman named Lydia, from the city of Thyatira, a seller of purple" (Acts 16:14). She embraced the new message, but others among the local population were not so receptive.

*Alexandria Troas, the Gymnasium. Paul had a vision in Alexandria Troas to bring the Gospel to Macedonia.*

Paul and Silas were dragged into the agora of Philippi, beaten and jailed for teaching "customs which it is not lawful for us Romans to accept or practice" (Acts 16:21). A great earthquake at midnight freed Paul and Silas from their fetters, but they stayed in their cells. As a result, the jailer and all of his household "believed in God" (Acts 16:34). Subsequently, when it was discovered that Paul and Silas were Roman citizens, the magistrates expressed concern and regret at their mistreatment. They apologized, released the prisoners, but requested them to leave the city.

The company continued west on the *Via Egnatia* (c. 40 mi./67 km) through Amphipolis and (c. 24 mi./40 km) Apollonia to (c. 36 mi./60 km) Thessalonica (Acts 17:1). Thessalonica is located at the northern edge of the Thermaic Gulf. It was founded in 315 BCE by Cassander, king of Macedonia, in honor of his wife, Thessaloniki, stepsister of Alexander the Great. The ancient poet

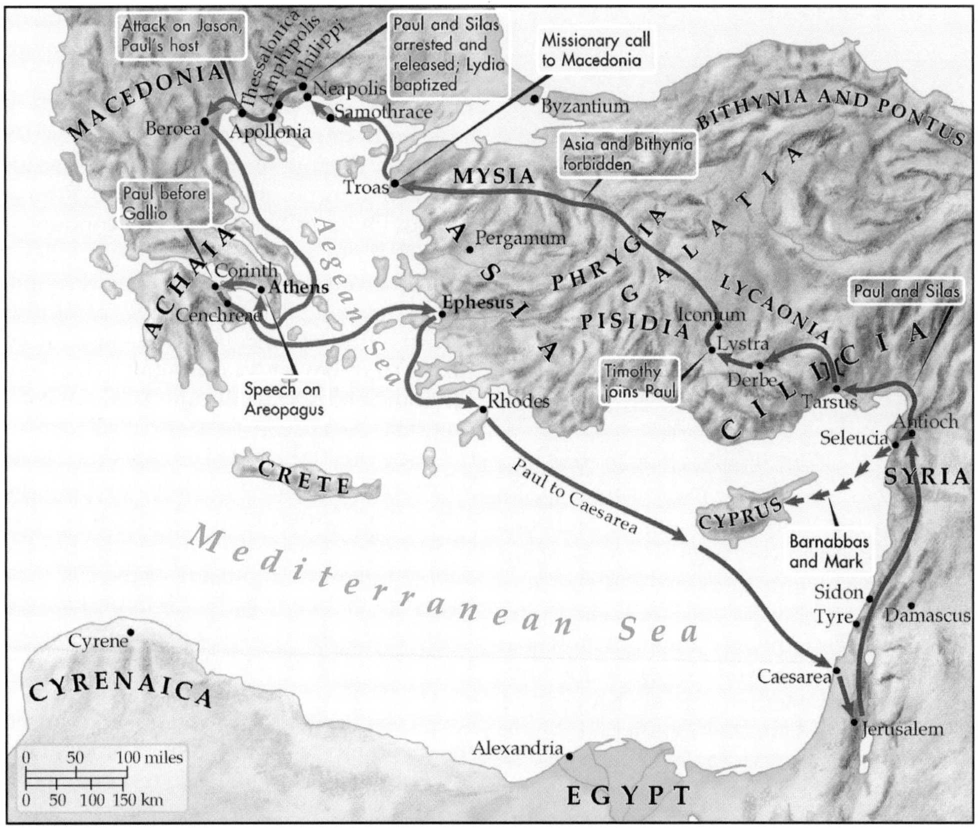


**The Second Missionary Journey of Paul**

Antipater celebrated it as "the Mother of Macedonia," and it served as a crossroads for international travel.

Although historical references to a Jewish presence in Thessalonica are scarce, there is inscriptional evidence for Jews and Samaritans in the city, and elsewhere in Macedonia. Luke reports that in Thessalonica there was a congregation of Jews, and Paul worshipped with them on the Sabbath "as was his custom." He argued with those present that it was necessary "for the Christ to suffer and to rise from the dead" (Acts 17:2). We witness once again the diverse composition of the audience

*Roman road and Hadrianic gate: Paul would have traveled on this road during his journey inland.*

with the mention of both Jews and God-fearing Greeks among those who embraced Paul's message. Nevertheless, accusations were brought by their opponents to the Roman authorities charging Paul, Silas and sympathetic local inhabitants with political sedition: "they are all acting against the decrees of Caesar, saying that there is another king, Jesus" (Acts 17:7).

In light of the growing danger, the two were whisked away at night c. 48 miles (80 km) to the neighboring city of Beroea (modern Verria). It lay several miles south of the *Via Egnatia* and was somewhat remote, reflecting Cicero's comment that the city was "off the beaten track" (Cic. *Pis.* 36.89). Once again, Paul and Silas proclaimed their message in the local synagogue. In spite of the fact that some believed, those from nearby Thessalonica arrived to incite the population. Paul was placed on a ship to Athens, while Silas and Timothy remained behind in Beroea (Acts 17:14–15). Investigations in recent years have discovered local routes of access from Beroea to the nearby ports of Methone and Pydna. Either of these may have served as Paul's point of embarkation for his voyage to Athens.

Passenger ships arriving to Athens would have docked at Kantheros, the western harbor for the port of Piraeus c. 3.5 miles (6 km) south of Athens (Philostratus *Vit. Apoll.* 4:17; Paus. *Descr.* 1.2.2). The degree of idolatry in the ancient city disturbed Paul and prompted his arguments with "Jews and devout persons" in the synagogue of Athens. No archaeological evidence for the first-century synagogue has been uncovered, though a later synagogue has been suggested.

Uncharacteristic of Paul's strategy in other cities, he brought his argument to the agora of Athens where he encountered Epicurean and Stoic philosophers. The Painted Stoa from which the Stoics derived their name was found in 1981 in the northwest corner of the agora. Paul was soon led to the Areopagus for a fuller hearing "of this new teaching." Scholarship is divided where Paul delivered his speech in Acts 17:22–31 in which he quotes the third-century Stoic, Aratus, "For we are indeed his offspring" (Aratus *Phaen.* 5) and refers to an Athenian altar "to an unknown God" (Acts 17:23). The name strictly signifies the "hill of Ares [Mars]" in Athens, but the term was also used to identify the judicial council without topographical constraints. By the fourth century BCE the council regularly met in the Royal Stoa, leaving unclear its place of meeting in the first century CE.

In any event, Paul addressed the men of Athens in the midst of the Areopagus, but his message was largely unsuccessful. Luke records that the difficulty for the Athenians was Paul's declared belief in the resurrection from the dead. Nevertheless, a member of the Areopagus, Dionysius, did become a Christian through Paul's efforts. Eusebius records that Dionysius became the bishop of Athens (Eus. *Hist. eccl.* 4.23).

From Athens Paul likely traveled west by ship c. 50 miles (83 km) along the coast to Corinth, where Silas and Timothy rejoined him. Julius Caesar rebuilt this important commercial city in 44 BCE. A century earlier it had led the Achaean League of cities in its attempt to resist Roman rule, but the league had been defeated, and Lucius Mummius laid waste to Corinth in 146 BCE. The revitalized colony of Julius Caesar grew and became the seat of the governor for the province of Achaia.

Corinth's international importance was enhanced by its strategic location on the isthmus between the Peloponnesus and central Greece. Strabo attests to the commercial benefits of its position.

> Corinth is called "wealthy" because of its commerce, since it is situated on the Isthmus and is master of two harbors, of which the one leads straight to Asia, and the other to Italy; and it makes easy the exchange of merchandise from both countries that are so far distant from each other....
>
> (Strabo *Geog.* 8.6.20)

Strabo describes the city's two harbors, Cenchreae, 6.5 miles (11 km) east of the city on the Saronic Gulf, and Lechaion, on the Corinthian Gulf. The *diolkos*, a narrow stone roadway, was built during the reign of Periander in the sixth century BCE to transport goods from one seaport to the other.

The most prominent topographical feature of Corinth is its towering acropolis, the Acrocorinth, rising to an elevation

*Seleucia Harbor: Paul would have traveled in and out of this harbor on his journeys.*

of 1,886 feet (575 m) above sea level. On its pinnacle was the renowned temple of Aphrodite that Strabo suggests also contributed to the wealth of Corinth.

> And the temple of Aphrodite was so rich that it owned more than a thousand temple slaves, courtesans, whom both men and women had dedicated to the goddess. And therefore it was also on account of these women that the city was crowded with people and grew rich; for instance, the ship captains freely squandered their money, and hence the proverb, "Not for every man is the voyage to Corinth." (Strabo *Geog.* 8.6.20)

As in the previous Greco-Roman cities on Paul's journey, the Apostle was drawn to the Jewish community in Corinth. We have no evidence for the beginnings of a Jewish presence in Corinth. Philo mentions a Jewish community there already in the time of Gaius Caligula (37–41 CE; Philo *Leg.* 281). In the Book of Acts, Luke refers to the synagogue of Corinth and identifies Priscilla and Aquila, a Jewish couple who had recently arrived, "because Claudius had commanded all the Jews to leave Rome" (Acts 18:2).

Suetonius likewise reports that Claudius expelled Jews from Rome: "Since the Jews constantly made disturbances at the instigation of Chrestus, [Claudius] expelled them from Rome" (Suet. *Claud.* 25:4). The Roman historian's testimony is interesting because it attests not only to Claudius' order of expulsion but to early activity by the fledgling Christian movement in Rome. The Claudian edict curtailing a Jewish presence in Rome stands in contrast to Josephus' presentation of the Emperor's restoration of the rights of the Jewish people (*Ant.* 19: 280–296) and his friendship with Agrippa I (*Ant.* 19:274; *War* 2:215).

Paul's activities in Corinth again stirred controversy. His proclamation that "the Christ is Jesus" provoked bitter Jewish opposition, so that he abandoned the synagogue and went to the home of a God-fearer named Titius Justus, who lived "next door to the synagogue" (Acts 18:7). No archaeological structures from the first-century synagogue have been identified, but in 1898 Benjamin Powell discovered a fragmented Greek inscription that reads, "Synagogue of the Hebrews." Initially, it was proposed that the inscription belonged to a first-century synagogue. Subsequent paleographic examination, however, determined that the inscription belonged to a later period.

Paul's efforts appear to have had some measure of success, because he stayed in Corinth for eighteen months. The church at Corinth later was the recipient of his epistolary activity. Jewish opponents to Paul brought him before Gallio, the proconsul of Achaia, but he refused to intervene (Acts 18: 12–17).

A short while after this dispute, Paul decided to depart for Syria, taking with him Priscilla and Aquila (Acts 18:18). Before embarking on his journey from Corinth's eastern port of Cenchreae (cf. Rom 16:1), Paul cut his hair apparently for reasons related to a personal vow. Luke does not specify the reason for the vow (Acts 18:18, 21:23), but mention that the Apostle cut his hair suggests that it was related to the vow of a Nazirite (Num 6:1–21).

New Testament scholarship has struggled to understand the significance of Paul's actions in Cenchreae. Typically, the Nazirite cut his hair at the end of the period of his vow. So, Paul's actions have been understood. The difficulty in the present episode is that the Nazirite was restricted to conclude the vow with the shaving of his hair only in Jerusalem (m. *Naz.* 6:7), and accompanied with the necessary offerings in the Temple.

During the first century CE, we hear that Queen Helena of Adiabene initiated a Nazirite vow abroad and completed it only after coming to the Land of Israel (m. *Naz.* 3:6). The Mishnah also records that Nazirites came to Jerusalem shortly after its destruction to complete their vows but found the Temple in ruins (m. *Naz.* 5: 4). The obligation to be in Jerusalem at the conclusion of the Nazirite vow has led some to speculate that Paul cut his hair in Cenchreae to mark the beginning of his vow. However, we have no evidence for such a practice, and there are questions whether or not this may even be a Nazirite vow.

What is often overlooked is that the requirement to shave one's hair in Jerusalem pertains to the conclusion of the Nazirite vow. If the Nazirites became ritually unclean during the period of their vow, they were required to shave their head to mark the renewal of their vow (Num 6:9). This act of renewal does not seem to have been limited to Jerusalem. While Luke does not tell us the reason for Paul's actions, the most probable explanation is that he cut his hair in Cenchreae to renew his Nazirite vow.

Paul launched from Cenchreae, on the Saronic Gulf, across the Aegean Sea to Ephesus, the most important Roman port on the Aegean coast of Asia Minor. Paul stayed in the Asian city only a brief time and refused the offer to stay longer. His haste may have been related to as yet unfulfilled duties pertaining to his Nazirite vow. The obligations of the vow could only be fulfilled with offerings in the Temple in Jerusalem (Num 6:13–20; *Ant.* 4:72). For our present study, what is important is the recognition that Paul's need to fulfill his Nazirite vow in Jerusalem helps us to explain his unusual itinerary.

Paul's stated destination is Antioch in Syria. Yet, rather than sailing directly from Ephesus to Seleucia, the port of Antioch, Paul is next in Caesarea—about 300 miles (483 km) to the south. His out-of-the-way port-of-call is neither an accident nor the result of unfavorable winds. Although Luke does not specify a visit to Jerusalem, there seems little question that such a visit is the reason for Paul's arrival to Caesarea (Acts 18:22). Otherwise, a journey from Ephesus to Antioch in Syria by way of Caesarea is inexplicable. After landing at Caesarea, *he went up* (i.e. to Jerusalem) and greeted the church (Acts 14:27; 15:3, 5). Later, *he went down* (i.e. from Jerusalem; Acts 11:27, 15:30) to Antioch.

## Paul's Third Missionary Journey

The Apostle's final missionary journey begins with little fanfare, no special appointment and no laying on of hands. "After spending some time [in Antioch] he departed and went from place to place through the region of Galatia and Phrygia, strengthening the disciples" (Acts 18:23). Luke's lack of geographical detail may correspond to the fact that this portion of Paul's journey is not part of the "we section" that presumably records the journeys to which the author of Acts was a firsthand witness (Acts 16:6–17, 20:5–15; 21:1–18, 27:1–28: 16 [and 11:28 in Codex Bezae]). Accordingly, we

*Priene: remains of this very early synagogue emphasize a Jewish presence in Asia Minor.*

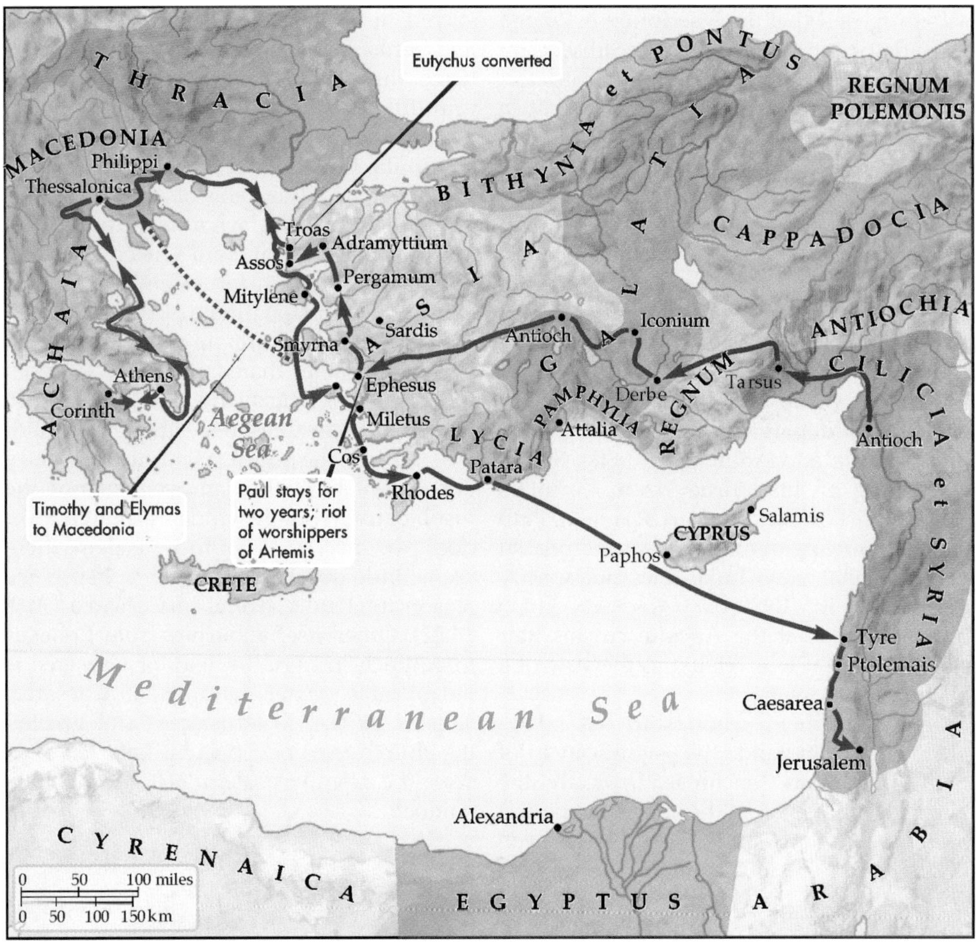


**The Third Missionary Journey of Paul**

are not told whether Paul traveled from Antioch by land or by sea. Neither are we told in which cities of Galatia and Phrygia Paul strengthened the disciples (Gal 4:13).

Next Paul passed "through the upper regions" and came down to Ephesus (Acts 19:1). The precise location of these "upper regions" or "inland regions" is unknown. Paul may have returned north retracing a portion of his previous journey. On the other hand, he may have taken a more direct route from Ephesus on the Royal Route first mentioned by Herodotus (*Hist.* 15.54.1) that connected Asia Minor through the Cilician Gates to Susa, the ancient capital of Persia.

A Jewish presence may be attested in Asia Minor already in the fourth century BCE. Clearchus of Soli, a student of Aristotle, records that his teacher encountered a Jew "who not only spoke Greek, but had the soul of a Greek," during his travels between 348 and 345 BCE (cf. *Apion* 1:176–182). According to Philo, by the first century CE Jews resided throughout Asia Minor (Philo *Leg.* 245): ". . . those countries which have large numbers of Jews in all their cities, namely Asia and Syria." Material evidence of Jews in Ephesus is lacking. Yet, Josephus relates that Jewish residents of Ephesus were granted citizenship in the early Hellenistic period of the Diadochi (*Ant.* 12:125; *Apion* 2:4). Under Roman rule Jews in Ephesus gained special privileges to practice their ancestral customs and received exemption from military service (Philo *Leg.* 40; *Ant.* 16:167–168, 172–173). Although a century of archaeological investigations at Ephesus has not unearthed the location of the synagogues there, historical attestations suggest that they did indeed exist.

Paul had promised the congregation in Ephesus on his previous visit that if he were able, he would return and spend more time with them. On this occasion Paul taught and ministered in Ephesus for two years. While there Paul met followers of John the Baptist, who "had not yet heard that the Holy Spirit had been received" (Acts 19:2 [in Codex Bezae]). These had only heard John's call to repentance and baptism in anticipation of the coming of the Redeemer, whose advent would coincide with the outpouring of the Holy Spirit (cf. 1QS 4:19-26). Paul informed the disciples that John's proclamation had been fulfilled in the person of Jesus. They accepted Paul's message, were baptized, and "the Holy Spirit came upon them" (Acts 19:6).

Luke records that Paul continued to speak daily in the synagogue and in the hall of Tyrannus, "so that all the residents of Asia heard of the word of the Lord, both Jews and Greeks" (Acts 19:10). After a while Paul determined "to pass through Macedonia and Achaia and to go to Jerusalem, saying, 'After I have been there, I must also see Rome'" (Acts 19:21). Following a riotous protest in the theater of Ephesus against Paul and the local church which was instigated by Demetrius, a silversmith who made shrines for the local cult to Artemis, the Apostle set out for Macedonia. The author does not indicate whether his journey from Ephesus began by land or by sea, but Paul continued through the region of Macedonia until he came to Greece (Acts 20:1).

Plots once again surfaced against Paul, so he determined to return to Syria through Macedonia. A number of his party went on before Paul and waited for him in Alexandria Troas (Acts 20:4–5). Presumably, Paul retraced his steps through Macedonia along the *Via Egnatia* to the port of Philippi (Neapolis) and from there sailed to Troas (Acts 20:3–6).

The ports-of-call on the journey to Syria indicate that Paul traveled primarily by ship from Troas to Antioch. The recorded stops are either island settlements or port cities on the Aegean coast of Asia Minor. The only exception is Paul's trek on the Republican road from Troas to Assos (Strabo *Geog.* 13.1.51, 57–58; Pliny *Nat. Hist.* 2.211, 5.32, 36.131–133), a city situated on the southern coast of the Troad, looking across the Gulf of Adramyttium toward the isle of Lesbos.

> We set sail for Assos, intending to take Paul aboard there; for he had arranged, intending himself to go by land (from Troas). And when he met us at Assos, we took him on board and came to Mitylene.
> (Acts 20:13)

The harbor city of Mitylene is the chief city on the eastern side of the isle of Lesbos. The ship moored there overnight and the next day continued c. 28 miles (47 km) to the island of Chios (Strabo *Geog.* 14.1.35; Herodotus *Hist.* 6:8; Thuc. 8:15; *Ant.* 16:18–19). The following day they "touched at Samos" (*Ant.* 16:23–24) just one mile off the coast of Asia Minor. A Jewish community is mentioned in Samos already in the period of the Hasmoneans (1 Macc 15:23).

Western and Byzantine Greek text traditions read that Paul did not stay at Samos but continued a short distance to the mainland, "and they remained in Trogyllium." Trogyllium was a small settlement situated on a promontory of the mainland that faced across the narrow channel c. 1 mile (2 km) from Samos. Whether Paul's ship stayed overnight at Samos or Trogyllium, it undoubtedly coursed through this strait on its way to Miletus.

The following day the ship traveled c. 28 miles (47 km) to Miletus (Strabo *Geog.* 14.1.6; Herodotus *Hist.* 1.17–20, 141; 6:6; Arr. *Anab.* 1.18), an Ionian city near the mouth of the Meander River. The famous port lies due south (c. 30 mi./50 km) of Ephesus. Its street design follows the rectangular grid plan associated with the local architect, Hippodamus. A Roman period synagogue has been suggested near the center of the city.

*A Jewish presence in Miletus is attested by an inscription found in situ on the fifth row of seats in the theater. The phrase is grammatically awkward and has been translated by some, "a place of the Jews who are (also called) God-fearers." In other words, the designation "God-fearers" describes members of the Jewish community. Others have noted that a pagan reference to the religious piety of the Jewish community within the setting of a Roman theater is at the least strange. Accordingly, the awkward grammatical structure of the inscription is corrected to read, "a place of the Jews and God-fearers." Such a reading would then designate seating for both Jews and Gentile God-fearers who had become closely identified with the Jewish community.*

Paul stayed in Miletus rather than nearby Ephesus, because he was in haste to be in Jerusalem for the day of Pentecost. Nevertheless, he invited elders from the congregation in Ephesus to visit him in Miletus. After their time together, Paul set sail for Jerusalem continuing ports-of-call at the Greek islands of Cos and Rhodes. Paul seems to have done little more than stay overnight in Cos (cf. 1 Macc 15:23; *Ant.* 14:112, 14:233; Strabo *Geog.* 14.2.19; *War* 1:424). A small island in the Aegean Sea, it was famous for being the birthplace of Hippocrates, the father of medicine, and a temple to Asclepius.

Likewise no mention is made of Paul's activities in Rhodes. Historical sources attest to a Jewish presence in Rhodes (Suet. *Tib.* 32:2; 1 Macc 15:23), and it is here that Herod the Great came to swear his loyalty to Caesar Augustus after the Battle of Actium and the death of Mark Antony (*Ant.* 15:187; *War* 1:387). Herod also contributed to the rebuilding of the temple of Apollo at Rhodes (*Ant.* 16:147; *War* 1:424).

From Rhodes Paul journeyed east to Patara, a harbor town on the southern coast of Lycia and 7 miles (12 km) east of the Xanthus River. Some manuscripts add "to Myra" in Acts 21:1 to the ports visited on Paul's journey (cf. Acts 27:5). Geographically, a stop in the well-known port of Myra is natural on the journey eastward to Phoenicia (cf. Acts 27:5–6).

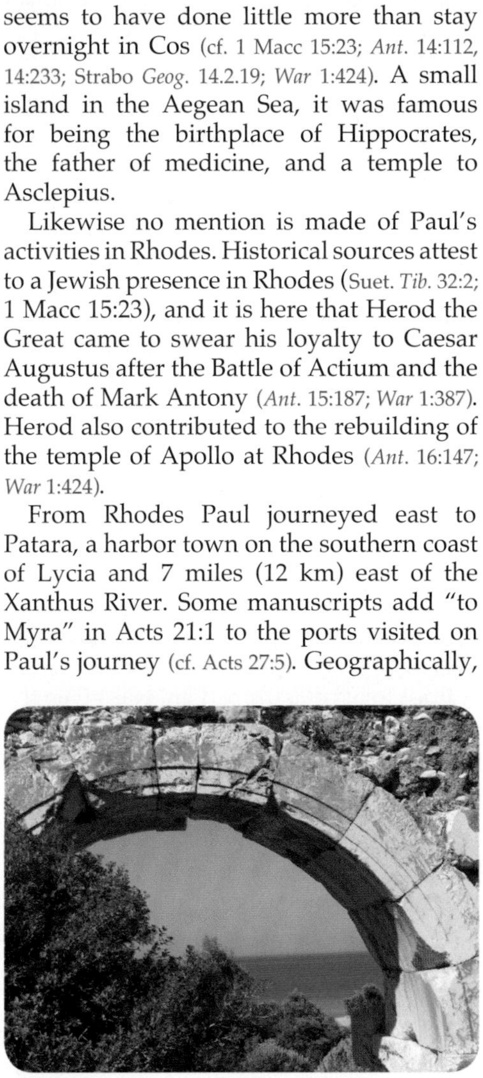

*Lighthouse at Patara, site visited by Paul.*

Leaving Asia Minor Paul found a ship going to Phoenicia. They sailed "within sight of Cyprus," but continued along the island's southern coast (Acts 21:3) and landed at the legendary Phoenician port city of Tyre. There is minimal inscriptional evidence of Jewish settlement on the Phoenician coast. Nevertheless, coins minted in Tyre were used in the Roman period for the Temple tithe in Jerusalem (m. *Bek.* 8:7; t. *Ketub.* [12] 13:4). Paul stayed in Tyre seven days after discovering a community of Christians (Acts 21:4). The believers in Tyre attempted to discourage Paul from going to Jerusalem, but he boarded a ship and continued southward along the coast towards the Holy City.

The ship stopped at the biblical port of Acco, which had been transformed into a Hellenistic *polis* and renamed Ptolemais during the rule of the Diadochi Ptolemy II (1 Macc 5:15; Eus. *Onom.* 30:10). Paul stayed with fellow believers in Ptolemais one day, and then he continued his journey to the final port-of-call at Caesarea. Paul stayed in Caesarea with Philip and his family, where he was again cautioned not to go up to Jerusalem. Nevertheless, Paul was determined to go to Jerusalem, and upon arriving in the Holy City he stayed with Mnason of Cyprus, "an early disciple" (Acts 21:16).

## The Arrest and Imprisonment of Paul

After some time Paul went up to Jerusalem to meet with James (cf. Eus. *Hist. eccl.* 2.1.2) and the elders of the church. He reported to them the events of his journeys and what the Lord had done among the Gentiles. James responded that,

> many among the Jews have also believed; they are zealous for the law (cf. Acts 22:3; Gal 1:14; Tit 2:14), and they have been told about you that you teach all the Jews who are among the Gentiles to forsake Moses, telling them not to circumcise their children or observe the customs. (Acts 21:20–21)

In order to dispel the false rumors surrounding Paul's message, they recommended that he offer to pay the expenses for four men concluding a Nazirite vow (m. *Naz.* 1:3).

They also proposed that Paul accompany the men and purify himself (cf. Jn 11:55), in other words, that he join the men in the rite of ritual immersion before ascending to the temple precincts (cf. Acts 21:26, 24:18; cf. P. Oxy 840). "Thus, all will know that there is nothing in what they have been told about you, but that you yourself live in observance of the law" (Acts 21:24b). As we noted in connection to Paul's own vow described in Acts 18:18, fulfillment of the Nazirite vow was purely voluntary, and sometimes intended to demonstrate one's commitment to Torah observance.

Paying the costs for devotees, who could not afford the expenses involved in the concluding rites of their Nazirite vows, was also considered an expression of religious piety. Josephus reports that King Agrippa I performed just such a charitable act upon his return to Jerusalem (cf. *Ant.* 19:293–294). His actions were indicative of his reported religious character.

> He enjoyed residing in Jerusalem and did so constantly; and he scrupulously observed the traditions of his people. He neglected no rite of purification, and no day passed for him without the prescribed sacrifice. (*Ant.* 19:331)

At the end of the prescribed seven days, the *period of purification* (Acts 21:27; cf. Codex Bezae: "When the seven days had ended"; Num 6:9, 18–19), Paul and the men went to the Temple, but Jews from Asia recognized him and stirred up the crowds against him with serious charges: "This is the man who is teaching men everywhere against the people and the law and this place; moreover he also brought Greeks into the temple, and he has defiled the holy place" (Acts 21:28). They accused Paul of bringing a non-Jew beyond the partition into the inner courts of the Temple, an act forbidden in Jewish law.

> Proceeding across this (outer court) towards the second court of the temple, one found it surrounded by a stone balustrade, three cubits (4.5 ft./1.4 m) high and of exquisite workmanship; in this at regular intervals stood slabs giving warning, some in Greek, others in Latin characters, of *the law of purification*, to wit that no foreigner was permitted to enter the holy place.
> (*War* 5:193-194; *Ant.* 15:417; Philo *Leg.* 212; cf. Eph 2:14)

Two remnants from this warning, sometimes called "the Thanatos [i.e. death] Inscription" have been discovered.

As violence broke out, a Roman tribune of the cohort that was responsible for maintaining order in Jerusalem arrived to arrest and take Paul to the barracks (cf. Acts 21:34, 23:10; i.e. Antonia Fortress). He was

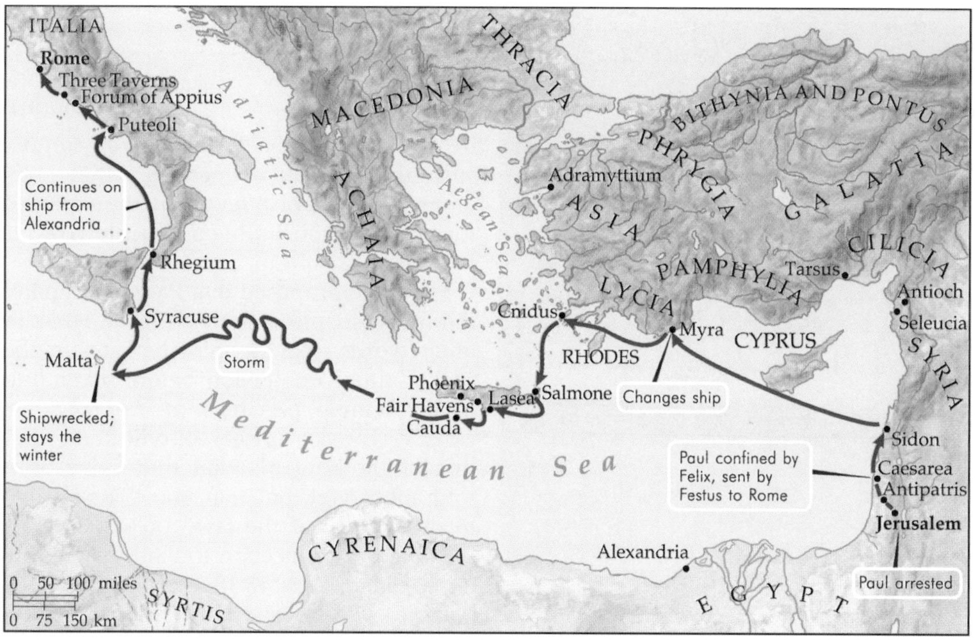


**Paul's Arrest and Imprisonment (59–62 ce)**

about to question Paul under the lash, when the Apostle informed him of his Roman citizenship. No details are given how Paul merited citizenship, only that he was born a Roman citizen. This presumes that his family had been settled in Tarsus for quite a long time.

On the next day, the commander wanted to determine further the basis of the accusations against Paul, so he brought him before the Sanhedrin. In a heated exchange Ananias, the high priest, had Paul struck on the mouth. Paul reviled the Sadducean leader, and those who stood by rebuked the Apostle that he would speak with such disrespect to the high priest. In a creative reply, full of irony, Paul responded, "I did not know, brethren, that he was the high priest; for it is written, 'You shall not speak evil of a ruler of your people'" (Acts 23:5). His use of Exodus 22:27 in this context conveys a stinging reproach of the high priest and reflects a turn of the passage heard from Israel's Sages.

> Why does Scripture specify "among your people"? [Isn't this phrase superfluous? We should understand this addition to imply, only] when they [the rulers] behave in a manner that befits "your people."
> (*Mek.* on Ex 22:28 *Mishpatim* 19)

*Cleopatra's Gate at Tarsus, the home of Paul.*

Paul's excuse was not that he did not know the high priest, but that Ananias had not behaved in a manner that "befits your people." The Apostle's rabbinic-styled use of Scripture anticipates his self-identification with the Pharisees, who were included in the Sanhedrin. Knowing that there were both Pharisees and Sadducees present, Paul defended himself: "Brothers, I am a Pharisee, a son of Pharisees; with respect to the hope and the resurrection of the dead I am on trial" (Acts 23:6; *Ant.* 18:14, 16; *War* 2:163, 165; cf. Dan 12:2–3; 2 Macc 7:14, 12:43).

As Paul undoubtedly anticipated, dissension broke out among the religious council. In the *mêlée*, the Roman tribune thought it best to remove Paul and return him to the barracks. A plot against Paul's life was uncovered, and the Romans transferred Paul at night to Caesarea (Acts 23:23–30). They arrived at Antipatris (Acts 23:31; *Ant.* 16:142–143; *War* 1:417) and the following morning continued their journey to Caesarea, where they turned Paul over to Felix, the governor of Judea. Tacitus mentions the appointment of Felix to the province of Judea.

> The [Herodian] princes now being dead or reduced to insignificance, Claudius made Judea a province and entrusted it to Roman knights or to freedmen; one of the latter, Antonius Felix, practiced every kind of cruelty and lust, wielding the power of a king with all the instincts of a slave; he married Drusilla, the granddaughter of Cleopatra and Antony, and so was Antony's grandson-in-law, while Claudius was Antony's grandson.
> (Tac. *Hist.* 5:9; cf. Tac. *Ann.* 12:45; *Ant.* 20:137)

Drusilla, the wife of Felix mentioned by Tacitus, was the daughter of Herod Agrippa I, and one of three wives that he married, who came from royal families (Suet. *Claud.* 28). Josephus recounts how Felix lured Drusilla away from her first husband, Azizus, king of Emesa (*Ant.* 19:354–355, 20:138–144; *War* 2:220). His marriage to the Jewish princess may explain why Felix was "well informed about the Way" (Acts 24:22), the name by which the fledgling Christian movement is sometimes called in Acts (Acts 9:12, 19:9, 19:23, 24:14, 24:22; cf. Did. 1:1–2).

The Romans held Paul in Herod's praetorium, the residence of the Roman procurators at Caesarea (Acts 23:35; cf. Mk 15:16). Charges were brought against Paul, and Luke reports his defense, first before Felix (Acts 24:1–26) and two years later before his replacement. Porcius Festus (Acts 24:27), "who succeeded Felix as procurator, proceeded to attack the principal plague of the country; he captured large numbers of the brigands and put not a few to death" (*War* 2:271). In *Antiquities*, Josephus provides a fuller description of steps taken by Festus during his two-year tenure (60–62 ce) to bring the brigandry in the countryside under control.

> When Festus arrived in Judea, it happened that Judea was being devastated by the brigands, for the villages one and all were being set on fire and plundered. The so-called *sicarii*—these are brigands—were particularly numerous at that time. ...They would also frequently appear with arms in the villages of their foes and would plunder and set them on fire. Festus also sent a force of cavalry and infantry against the dupes of a certain impostor who had promised them salvation and rest from troubles, if they chose to follow him into the wilderness. The force which Festus dispatched destroyed both the deceiver himself and those who had followed him.
> (*Ant.* 20:185–188)

Luke records that the new procurator went directly to Jerusalem to meet with the high priest and other Jewish leaders (Acts 25:1). There he heard the accusations against Paul and invited his accusers to return with him to Caesarea. In a hearing before Festus, Paul renewed his defense against those who had come from Jerusalem. "Neither against the law of the Jews, nor against the temple, nor against Caesar have I offended at all" (Acts 25:8). Festus desired to gain favor with his new Jewish subjects, so he encouraged Paul to accommodate their request that he go to Jerusalem and be heard again by the Sanhedrin. Instead, Paul exercised his right to appeal to Caesar, and Festus agreed (Acts 25:11–12).

Prior to his departure, Paul was given the opportunity to speak before King Agrippa II and his sister Bernice. Agrippa was the brother of Drusilla, the wife of Felix. Paul once again recounted the story of his encounter on the road to Damascus and his subsequent work among the Gentiles. He reiterated his innocence.

> My manner of life from my youth, spent from the beginning among my own nation and at Jerusalem, is known by all the Jews. They have known for a long time, if they are willing to testify, that according to the strictest party of our religion, I have lived as a Pharisee.
> (Acts 26:4–6)

This is now a second time that Paul

emphasized his identity as a Pharisee (cf. Acts 23:6; Phil 3:5). When he concluded, Agrippa shared Festus' opinion. "This man could have been set free, if he had not appealed to Caesar" (Acts 26:32).

At the first opportunity, Paul and the other prisoners being held in Caesarea were placed on a ship from Adramyttium, "which was about to sail to the ports along the coast of Asia" (Acts 27:2). It was likely bringing grain or cargo from Egypt back to Adramyttium, in the region of Mysia in northwest Asia Minor, between Pergamum and Alexandria Troas. The ship's return destination made it clear that it would not take them to Italy. Its stated intention "to sail to the ports along the coast of Asia" befits travel close to the coast of Asia likely because of the approaching winter season.

The first port-of-call was Sidon, on the Phoenician coast from which the ship "sailed under the lee of Cyprus" (Acts 27:4). The strong headwinds from the northwest prevented the ship from continuing northward along the coast of Syria and Asia. Instead, the crew used the isle of Cyprus to protect the ship from northern winds, and they passed the seacoast of Cilicia and Pamphylia (Acts 27:5). West of Cyprus the ship turned north, crossed the open seas and arrived at the important Lycian port of Myra.

The port of Myra was well known by the Roman grain fleet for its role in the storage and distribution to Asia. A large granary built by Hadrian still stands visible today. The centurion responsible for Paul's transport arranged for another passage on a ship that had arrived from Alexandria and was bound for Italy. However, strong headwinds also impeded this ship's progress. At Cnidus, a town on the southwestern tip of Asia Minor, the

*Harbor and Hadrianic granary at Myra: Paul is brought here from Caesarea on a "grain ship" and they change ships to Italy.*

ship turned south-southwest, to Salmone (Pliny *Nat. Hist.* 4.12.58, 4.12.71; Strabo *Geog.* 10.3.20, 10.4.3) on the eastern edge of Crete. The crew once more used the landmass of the island to protect the ship from the heavy northern winds. "Coasting along with difficulty, we came to a place called Fair Havens, near which was the city of Lasea" (Acts 27:8).

As Luke remarks, weather had delayed their passage, and it was already after "the Fast" (i.e. Day of Atonement). This is the author's way of noting the time of travel at the beginning of the winter season, making travel on the Mediterranean Sea difficult. The southern Cretan port of Fair Havens was not considered suitable for a winter dock, so the captain continued with the hope of reaching Phoenix on the southwestern tip of Crete. However, strong winds blew the ship off course, "under the lee of a small island called Cauda" (Acts 27:16).

The crew began throwing their cargo overboard to try and lighten their load in the stormy seas. Nevertheless, after a number of days they ran ashore on an island that they later learned was Malta (Acts 28:1; Strabo *Geog.* 6.2.11, 17.3.16; Diod. Sic. 5.12.2–3). It was here that Paul survived a snake bite to the amazement of his fellow travelers (Acts 28:2–6). Finally, after three months the party continued on to Italy on a ship that had originated from Alexandria. First they arrived at Syracuse. "And from there we made a circuit and arrived at Rhegium; and after one day a south wind sprang up, and on the second day we came to Puteoli" (Acts 28:13). As they traveled overland from Puteoli to Rome (cf. Strabo *Geog.* 17.17; *Life* 16), Paul was met by fellow believers who came to meet him at the Forum of Appius and the Three Taverns. Both of these towns are situated on the *Via Appia* leading to Rome.

When Paul arrived in Rome, he was placed under house arrest. However, he could receive visitors. First, local leaders of the Jewish community came to meet Paul.

> When they had appointed a day for him, they came to him at his lodging in great numbers. And he expounded the matter to them from morning till evening, testifying to the kingdom of God and trying to convince them about Jesus both from the law of Moses and from the prophets. And some were convinced by what he said, while others disbelieved. (Acts 28:23–24)

Luke concludes his story about Paul with the Apostle still under house arrest. According to Christian tradition, Paul was martyred during the persecution of Christians by Nero after the fire of Rome in 64 CE (cf. Tac. *Ann.* 15:44; Suet. *Nero* 16:2; Eus. *Hist. eccl.* 2.25). Yet, Luke gives no hint in his work of knowledge of Paul's death. Instead, at the time Luke concludes his work, Paul is still presented in the final lines of the Book of Acts engaged in active ministry.

> And he lived there two whole years at his own expense, and welcomed all who came to him, preaching the kingdom of God and teaching about the Lord Jesus Christ quite openly and unhindered. (Acts 28:30–31)

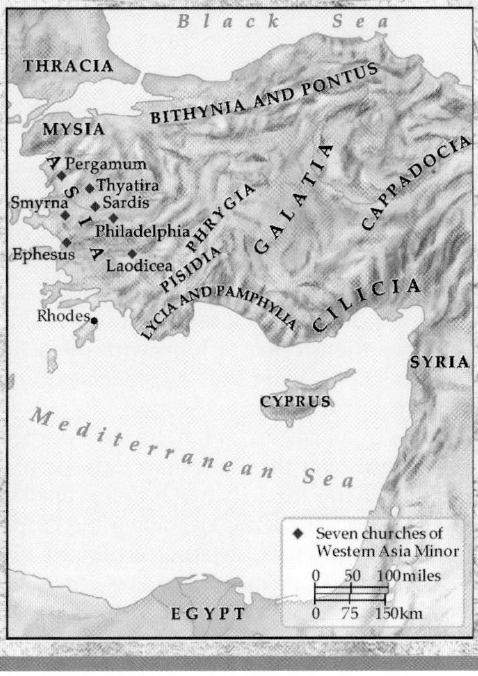


## THE SEVEN CHURCHES OF THE APOCALYPSE (Rev 1:4–3:21)

Incorporated into the larger work of the Apocalypse, the author includes seven letters to churches in Asia Minor. No explanation is provided why these churches are deemed worthy of the author's attention, or why others are excluded. It is suggested that they follow in a circular order, perhaps reflecting a mail route. In that regard, then, the letters were not to be read individually but as an encyclical. As a corpus they addressed the spiritual concerns of the church of Asia Minor. Physical evidence for this suggestion is lacking. However, the overlapping and repetitive nature of the letters does indicate that these letters reflect the spiritual challenges facing the church of Asia Minor in the reign of the Roman emperor Domitian during the last decade of the first century CE.

*The great library at Ephesus, one of the churches of Revelation.*

# CHAPTER NINETEEN

# THE FIRST JEWISH REVOLT AGAINST ROME 66 TO 74 CE

In a succession of inept and corrupt Roman procurators, Josephus narrates the deterioration of relationships between the Jewish people and the Roman Empire in the years leading up to open rebellion. Each appointee added to the excesses of his predecessor. The final and worst of the Roman procurators in the Province of Judea was Gessius Florus (64–66 CE; *Ant.* 20:252–253; Tac. *Hist.* 5:10) who followed Lucceius Albinus (62–64 CE; Tac. *Hist.* 2.58–59). The Jews complained to the Roman governor in Antioch, Cestius Gallus, but with no real success (*War* 2:280). The later Herodians did their best to avoid disaster but to no avail.

*Triumphal parade of Roman soldiers carrying the Temple vessels, relief on Arch of Titus, Rome.*

## THE END OF THE HERODIAN DYNASTY

**Agrippa I**. Shortly before the death of his grandfather, Herod the Great, six-year-old Agrippa I was sent to Rome with his mother. His father, Aristobulus, had been executed three years prior (7 BCE), one of the victims of Herod's violent paranoia (*Ant.* 16:392–394). Agrippa grew up among the royal court of Rome and experienced unlimited opulence. However, by the time Agrippa reached adulthood he found that his extravagant lifestyle had left him badly in debt. He eventually was forced to return to Judea (*Ant.* 18:143–147). His troubles led him to consider suicide, but his wife Cyprus appealed to his sister Herodias and Antipas for help, and they gave him the position of overseer of the markets (*Ant.* 18:149; cf. 14:261) in Tiberias. Yet, the opportunity afforded Antipas and the others that followed failed to satisfy the adventurous Herodian, and he eventually returned to Rome. There he befriended Gaius Caligula, son of the emperor Tiberius (*Ant.* 18:168).

Agrippa's financial woes continued to dog him until the death of Tiberius and the succession of Caligula to his father's throne in March 37 CE. Events leading up to his change in fortune had not looked promising. Tiberius threw Agrippa into prison, when it was reported to the emperor an overheard statement by Agrippa expressing hope "that Tiberius would relinquish his office with all speed in favor of Gaius, who was more competent in every respect" (*Ant.* 18:168). Upon assuming his father's throne, Caligula released Agrippa and gave him a gold chain of equal weight to the iron chain he had been forced to wear in prison (*Ant.* 18:224–237; *War* 2:181; Philo *Flac.* 25; Dio Cass. 69.8).

He also bestowed upon the Herodian scion the diadem (*Ant.* 18:237), and awarded him lands belonging to the former tetrarchy of Philip (cf. *Ant.* 18:27–28) and Lysanias (cf. *Ant.* 15:344; 19:275; 20:138; Dio Cass. 59.8.2). The new king stayed on in Rome for a short while, but then traveled to his new kingdom by way of Alexandria in the autumn of 38 CE (*Ant.* 18:238–239).

The reversal in fortunes for Agrippa stirred envy in Herodias (*Ant.* 18:240). She had witnessed the sudden and unexpected successes of her brother, who previously squandered all of his wealth and every opportunity that came his way, including Herodias and Antipas' own generosity. It was a bitter pill for a woman who wanted nothing more than to be queen. She pressured Antipas to likewise seek a royal title from the new emperor. Finally, he reluctantly agreed but his audience before Caligula brought a different outcome.

Agrippa's freedman, Fortunatus, had traveled to the emperor at the same time and laid charges against Antipas, including sedition. Although the charges were probably unfounded, circumstantial evidence left suspicions. Caligula deposed Antipas and sent the son of Herod and his wife to Gaul in 39 CE (*Ant.* 18:252; *War* 2:183). The misfortune of Antipas led to the increased good fortune of Agrippa. The emperor expanded Agrippa's kingdom by granting him Galilee and Perea, the territory of Antipas' former tetrarchy.

Agrippa's new charge brought a change in behavior, at least while resident in his kingdom. One of the king's first acts upon his arrival to the region was to visit Jerusalem.

> On entering Jerusalem, he offered sacrifices of thanksgiving, omitting none of the ritual enjoined by our law. Accordingly he also arranged for a very considerable number of Nazirites to be shaven (m. *Naz.* 2:5–6). Moreover, he hung up, within the sacred precincts, over the treasure-chamber, the golden chain which had been presented to him by Gaius, equal in weight to the one of iron with which his royal hands had been bound, as a reminder of his bitter fortune and as a witness to his reversal for the better, in order that it might serve as a proof both that greatness may sometimes crash and that God uplifts fallen fortunes. (*Ant.* 19:293–294)

This new-found piety marked the three years of his rule. Both Josephus and rabbinic literature attest to his concern for ritual matters (cf. *Ant.* 19:331; m. *Bik.* 3:4). Their picture stands in stark contrast to that of the New Testament. "About that time Herod [Agrippa I] the king laid violent hands upon some who belonged to the church. He killed James the brother of John with the sword" (Acts 12:1–2). Peter was also arrested at this time, but was able to escape.

As a Jewish sovereign, he took particular concern over the Temple in Jerusalem. It is likely in this capacity that he intervened with Caligula (*Ant.* 18:298–301), when the emperor decided to erect a statue of himself in the Temple (*Ant.* 18:261–262; *War* 2:185–187; Philo *Leg.* 188, 207–208; Tac. *Hist.* 5.9). Agrippa succeeded in persuading Caligula to rescind his edict,

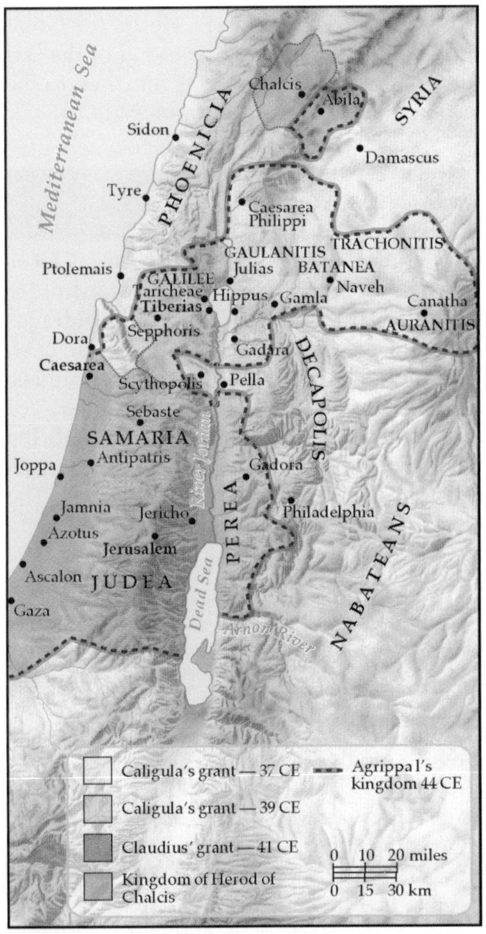


**The Kingdom of Agrippa I**

shortly before the emperor's death. The king was still in Rome, when Caligula was murdered by Chaerea, tribune of a cohort of the praetorian guard on 24 January 41 CE (*Ant.* 19: 105; cf. Suet. *Calig.* 56–58).

The new emperor, Claudius, not only confirmed Agrippa's kingdom, but he also added to it the territory of Judea and Samaria (*Ant.* 19:274–275; *War* 215-216). The Herodian monarch now ruled over a kingdom whose expanse equaled that of his grandfather's. He was also awarded consular rank (Dio Cass. 60.8.2–3). In Jerusalem, Agrippa's contribution to the city was to initiate the building of a new city wall, which Josephus describes as "the third wall" (*War* 5:147, 158, 260), encircling the northern suburbs of Jerusalem .

> Agrippa fortified the walls of Jerusalem on the side of the New City (i.e. Bezetha; cf. *War* 5:151) at the public expense, increasing both their breadth and height, and he would have made them too strong for any human force had not Marsus, the governor of Syria, reported by letter to Claudius Caesar what was being done. Claudius, suspecting that a revolution was at foot, earnestly charged Agrippa in a letter to desist from the building of the walls; and Agrippa thought it best not to disobey. (*Ant.* 19:326–327)

It is unlikely that Agrippa would have begun such a project without Claudius' previous knowledge. Tacitus implies that the project may have initially been granted through bribes. "Profiting by the greed displayed during the reign of Claudius, they had bought the privilege of fortifying the city, and in time of peace had built walls as if for war" (Tac. *Hist.* 5.12). The communication by the governor of Syria probably only brought to Caesar's attention the scale of Agrippa's project and led to the cessation of construction out of concern regarding its purpose.

The monumental scale of the new wall led Josephus to suggest that if Agrippa had been permitted to complete the wall, the outcome of Titus' later siege of Jerusalem might have faired differently.

> For [Agrippa] began to surround Jerusalem with a wall on such a scale as, had it been completed, would have rendered ineffectual all the efforts of the Romans in the subsequent siege. But before the work had reached the projected height, he died at Caesarea (44 CE), after a reign of three years, to which must be added his previous three years' tenure of his tetrarchies. (*War* 2:218–219)

The historian's mention of Agrippa's unexpected death in Caesarea, is paralleled in the New Testament.

> Then [Herod Agrippa] went down from Judea to Caesarea, and remained there.... On an appointed day Herod put on his royal robes, took his seat upon the throne, and made an oration to them. And the people shouted, "The voice of a god, and not of man!" Immediately an angel of the Lord smote him, because he did not give God the glory; and he was eaten by worms and died. (Acts 12:19–23)

Josephus' account also relates that Agrippa held a public audience in Caesarea. He was clothed in a garment woven with silver. Meeting early in the morning, "there the silver, illumined by the touch of the first rays of the sun, was wondrously radiant and by its glitter inspired fear and awe in those who gazed intently upon it" (*Ant.* 19: 344).

Those present addressed Agrippa as a god (*Ant.* 19:345). At this point, the New Testament writer relates that the king was immediately struck and died. Josephus reports, instead, that at this moment he looked up and saw an owl perched on a rope over his head.

> At once, recognizing this as a harbinger of woes, just as it had once been of good tidings (cf. *Ant.* 18: 195, 200), he felt a stab of pain in his heart. He was also gripped in his stomach by an ache that he felt everywhere at once and that was intense from the start. (*Ant.* 19:346)

The king withdrew to his bedchambers and died five days later. Although the two witnesses vary in details, the essence of their testimony presents the same event.

*Coin of Agrippa I.*

Josephus concludes his history of the reign of Agrippa I in *Antiquities* 19:351 with a slightly different reckoning than *War* 2: 218–219, and probably a more accurate accounting of the tenure of his rule.

> He reigned for four years (37–41 CE) under Gaius Caesar, ruling during three of them over the tetrarchy of Philip, and adding that of Herod [Antipas] during the fourth year. He reigned further for three years (41–44 CE) under the emperor Claudius Caesar, during which time he ruled over the territory mentioned above and received in addition Judea, Samaria, and Caesarea. (*Ant.* 19:351)

**Agrippa II**. Agrippa was survived by four children, a son named Agrippa and three daughters, Bernice, Mariamme and Drusilla (*Ant.* 18:132; *War* 2:220). Claudius wanted to place Agrippa II on his father's throne, but he was only seventeen years old, and his advisers counseled against it. So, the entire kingdom was returned to the supervision of the governor of Syria, and it was administrated by a Roman procurator from Caesarea (*Ant.* 19:363–365; *War* 2:220).

The only son of Agrippa I followed the custom of other Herodian children and was educated in Rome. He was there when he received word of his father's death (*Ant.* 19:360–363). As we noted, his young age prevented his immediate succession to his father's throne. However, in about five years he was awarded the kingdom of his uncle, Herod of Chalcis (*Ant.* 20:104). It seems that he also inherited his uncle's charge over the objects in the Temple and the selection of priests.

> Herod, the brother of the deceased Agrippa, who was at this time charged with the administration of Chalcis, also asked Claudius Caesar to give him authority over the temple and the holy vessels and the selection of the high priests . . . all of which requests he obtained. This authority, derived from him, passed to his descendants alone until the end of the war. Herod accordingly removed the high priest surnamed Cantheras (cf. b. *Pesaḥ* 57a=t. *Menaḥ* 13:21) his position and conferred the succession to his office upon Joseph the son of Carmei. (*Ant.* 20:15–16)

King Agrippa II appears to have delayed for two years his departure from Rome for his new kingdom. Not long after he was resident there, he received an imperial request from Claudius in 53 CE to relinquish his territory (*Ant.* 20:138) in exchange for new lands that included the former tetrarchy of Herod Philip (cf. *Ant.* 18:27–28, 106), i.e. Batanea, Trachonitis and Gaulanitis. In addition, he was granted the territory of Lysanias' former tetrarchy of Abila (*Ant.* 19:275) and the tetrarchy of Varus son of Soaemus (*War* 2:247; cf. Dio Cass. 69.12.2; Tac. *Ann.* 12:23). Agrippa's territory increased soon again upon the death of Claudius. In 54 CE Nero awarded him Tiberias and Taricheae in Galilee and Julias-Livias and Abila in Perea (*Ant.* 20:159; *War* 2:252; cf. *Ant.* 18:27).

Agrippa II closely adhered to Roman policy, and his loyalty to the succession

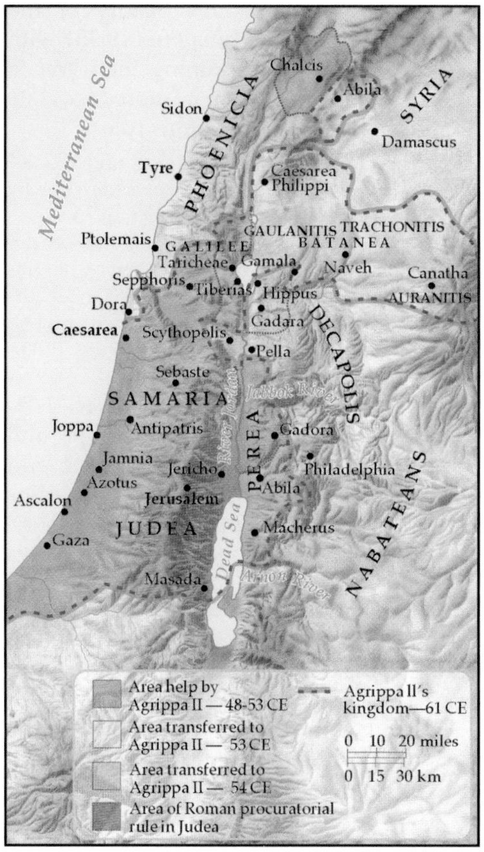


**The Kingdom of Agrippa II**

of Roman emperors is exemplified in his coins that regularly depict their images and names. He also renamed Caesarea Philippi to Neronias in honor of the Roman emperor (*Ant.* 20:211). Tacitus reports that he contributed auxiliary troops for the Roman campaign against Parthia (Tac. *Ann.* 13.7). The New Testament bears evidence to Agrippa's attentiveness to developments in Rome's administration of the region. Agrippa and Bernice visited Caesarea to greet the new Roman procurator, Porcius Festus (Acts 25: 13, 23; cf. *Ant.* 20:182; *War* 2:271). It is this visit that also allowed Agrippa and Bernice to hear the Apostle Paul (Acts 26:1–32).

The king's sister, Bernice, resided with her brother for years after the death of her husband, Herod of Chalcis. In Rome there persisted rumors of an unseemly relationship between the siblings (cf. *Ant.* 20: 145; Juvenal *Sat.* 6.156–160). Nevertheless, she had a rather public affair with Titus that took her to Italy in 75 CE (cf. Tac. *Hist.* 2.2), where she lived with him for some time at Palatine. When the son of Vespasian ascended the throne in 79 CE, he considered the relationship inappropriate for his new status, and he abandoned her (Dio Cass. 66.15.3–4; Suet. *Tit.* 7).

When the Jewish Revolt broke out in Jerusalem in 66 CE, Bernice was there but Agrippa was in Alexandria. He returned and tried to dissuade those who were inciting insurrection. In Josephus' reports concerning Agrippa II during the revolt, there is never a hint that the Jewish king weakened in his support of Rome. He committed auxiliary troops to Rome during the war against the Jewish insurgents. After the fall of Jerusalem, Titus removed his troops to Agrippa's capital at Caesarea Philippi.

> Here many of the prisoners perished, some being thrown to wild beasts, others compelled in opposing masses to engage one another in combat.... During his stay at Caesarea [Philippi], Titus celebrated his brother's birthday with great splendor, reserving in his honor for this festival much of the punishment of his Jewish captives. For the number of those destroyed in contests with wild beasts or with one another or in the flames exceeded two thousand five hundred. (*War* 7:23–24, 37–38)

Thus, Agrippa hosted Titus in the celebration of the defeat of his own people. Undoubtedly, he was rewarded for his loyalty with increased territories, but we have scant information on this period of his rule. Josephus once remarks that Agrippa's territory extended to Arcea (*War* 7:96–99), a town at the northern end of the Lebanon range and northeast of Tripolis. Yet, these northern territories are not mentioned in Josephus' earlier description of the kingdom of Agrippa II.

> . . . lastly the territories of Gamala, Gaulanitis, Batanaea, and Trachonitis, which form, moreover, part of Agrippa's kingdom. That kingdom, beginning at Mount Libanus and the sources of the Jordan, extends in breadth to the lake of Tiberias, and in length from a village called Arpha to Julias; it contains a mixed population of Jews and Syrians. (*War* 3:56–57)

The omission of Arcea or the regions farther north in the earlier written *War* could be because the northern territory had not been awarded to Agrippa at the time of its composition (c. 77 CE). This would explain Josephus' mention of Arcea in *Antiquities*, which was written several years later (c. 90 CE), and after the northern kingdom was included in Agrippa's kingdom. On the other hand, the silence concerning Arcea and the north in *War* could be simply a matter that its inclusion did not suit the more narrow purpose of Josephus' description in *War* 3:56–57.

Photias reports that Agrippa died in the third year of Trajan (100 CE), but other evidence seems to suggest that he died earlier, perhaps in 92/93 CE. More important than the precise year, the death of King Agrippa II signified the end to Herodian rule in Judea, which had spanned almost 140 years. Rome responded to Agrippa's death as it had to the death of the preceding Herodian kings, Herod the Great and Agrippa I. Upon the passing of the last Herodian, his kingdom was returned to the supervision of the province of Syria.

*Coin of Agrippa II.*

## The Outbreak of Violence

The abuses under the procurator Florus reached an intolerable level. According to Josephus, Florus "paraded his outrages upon the nation, and, as though he had been sent as hangman of condemned criminals, abstained from no form of robbery or violence" (*War* 2:278). Rather than quell the unrest, Florus allegedly sought to aggravate tensions, so that he could exploit them. The Jewish historian accuses Florus of desiring to inflame the rebellion so that in the ensuing chaos he could achieve his real aim: to pillage the funds of the temple treasure in Jerusalem.

In 65 CE an altercation between Jews and Greeks in Caesarea gave Florus his opportunity (*War* 2:284–292). A synagogue there adjoined land owned by Greeks. The Jewish adherents in the synagogue had attempted to purchase the land but failed. Friction increased between the Jewish community and the owner when he began to build on the property, impeding access to the synagogue. Events escalated until one Sabbath a troublemaker, at the instigation of contentious Greek elements, performed a satirical sacrifice of a bird on an overturned earthen vessel outside the synagogue. The reenactment reflected the sacrifice of purification for lepers dictated in Leviticus 14:4–9. It was intended as a jibe to revisit a pagan anti-Semitic explanation for the Exodus. As Josephus explains in *Against Apion*, it was fictitiously charged that the Israelites had not left freely from Egypt but had been expelled because they were lepers (*Apion* 1:229, 279, 304; cf. Justin. *Epit.* 36.2.12–15; Tac. *Hist.* 4.2, 5.3.1). Members of the synagogue reacted with outrage and the Roman troops were not able to control the riot that ensued.

Synagogue members expected Florus' retribution, so they took the Torah scroll and fled to Narbata (*War* 2:291, 509), while their leaders went to Florus at Sebaste. Rather than addressing the substance of their complaint against the Greeks' provocation, the governor imprisoned the Jewish representatives on charges of removing the Torah scroll from its rightful place in Caesarea. News spread quickly to Jerusalem. The Jewish response was restrained, but only until Florus followed his actions in Sebaste with orders to confiscate seventeen talents from the temple treasury under the guise of payment for imperial services (*War* 2:293, 2:403; cf. 2:331). Crowds rushed to the Temple shouting for Florus' dismissal. Instead of sending troops to Caesarea to confront the root cause for the disturbances, the governor thought he might benefit more from additional unrest. So, he sent troops to Jerusalem to provoke further hostilities.

The next day Florus gave orders to sack the upper city, because the priests and aristocratic leaders who met with the governor in Herod's palace refused to hand over those who had called out for his removal. The troops went from house to house plundering the city and killing its residents. Included were even those who had taken no part in the disturbances; nevertheless, they were brought before Florus, sentenced, scourged and crucified (*War* 2:305–308).

King Agrippa was in Alexandria, but his sister Bernice was in Jerusalem and witnessed the carnage. She implored Florus to desist. At one point in the violent chaos, her own life came into danger, and she had to flee to the royal palace. The procurator, in a ruse to draw the people beyond the protection of the city gates, offered pardon for previous offenses, if the crowds would welcome the new troops arriving from Caesarea. His real intent was to instigate another riot, so that he could move against the Antonia and the Temple with its treasures.

> The troops pushed in with the fugitives, mercilessly striking anyone who fell into their hands, and so thrust the crowd back through the quarter called Bezetha, trying to force their way through and occupy the temple and the Antonia. Florus, with the same object in view, led his men out from the court of the palace and struggled to reach the fortress (Antonia). (*War* 2:328)

Eventually, the Roman troops were forced to withdraw, and the Jewish partisans blocked access from the Antonia to the temple precincts (*War* 2:329). Florus returned to Caesarea and sent word to Cestius that the Jews had instigated rebellion. The Jewish leaders together with Bernice also sent messages to Cestius, but they laid the blame for the atrocities squarely with Florus (*War* 2:333).

King Agrippa soon returned from Alexandria and saw for himself the destruction that had been visited on his subjects. The people pressed him to appeal directly to Nero and not to allow Florus' charge of insurrection to go unchallenged. The king gathered the people to attempt to return some calm to the troubled city. He seated Bernice in view of the crowds at the Hasmonean palace, "which stood above the Xystus on the opposite side of the upper city; the Xystus was connected with the temple by a bridge" (*War* 2:344). Josephus records Agrippa's impassioned speech pleading for a cessation of the uprising by his subjects (*War* 2:345–401).

The people answered that their actions had not been against Rome or the emperor, but against Florus because of his atrocities. Agrippa replied,

*Judaea Capta coin.*

> But your actions are already acts of war against Rome; you have not paid your tribute to Caesar, and you have cut down the porticoes communicating with Antonia. If you wish to clear yourselves of the charge of insurrection, re-establish the porticoes and pay the tax; for assuredly the fortress does not belong to Florus, and it is not Florus to whom your money will go. (*War* 2:404–405)

The people responded favorably to the king's call for loyalty to Rome and the emperor. However, their reception changed abruptly when the Jewish sovereign called upon them to submit also to Florus—still the lawful representative of Rome—until the corrupt procurator could be replaced. "This exasperated the Jews who heaped abuse upon the king and formally proclaimed his banishment from the city; some of the insurgents even ventured to throw stones at him" (*War* 2:406).

Elsewhere during the summer of 66 CE, insurgents had assaulted the Roman garrison on Masada and captured the fortress (*War* 2:408). However, the clarion call for shirking Roman rule came at the instigation of Eleazar, son of Ananias, who persuaded the temple authorities,

> . . . to accept no gift or sacrifice from a foreigner. This action laid the foundation of the war with the Romans; for the sacrifices offered on behalf of that nation and the emperor were in consequence rejected. (*War* 2:409: cf. 2:197; *Apion* 2:77)

These same sacrifices are mentioned earlier by Philo in his *Embassy to Gaius* (c. 40 CE) in testimony to Caesar Augustus' affirmation of the Jewish faith.

> He gave orders for regular sacrifices of holocausts to be offered every day at his expense to the Most High God. These sacrifices continue to this day. Two lambs and a bull form the offerings with which Caesar glorified the altar, because he knew quite well that there was no image, visible or concealed, there. (Philo *Leg.* 317; cf. 157)

The cessation of these sacrifices marked the ascendancy of those who called for open rebellion and who rejected Roman authority over the nation.

Attempts were made by the priests to demonstrate "that all their ancestors had accepted the sacrifices of foreigners" (*War* 2:417). However, the leaders failed to dissuade the growing insurgency. When they realized that the rebellion would undoubtedly intensify, they sent deputations to Florus and Agrippa in order to distance themselves from the rebels. Agrippa intervened with two thousand cavalry from "Auranitis, Batanea and Trachonitis" to assist them. Now Jerusalem was divided between those occupying the upper city who favored peace, and "the lower city and the temple in the hands of the insurgents" (*War* 2:422).

> The objective of the royal troops [of Agrippa] was to capture the temple and to expel those who were polluting the sanctuary; Eleazar and the rebels strove to gain the upper city in addition to the ground that they held already. (*War* 2:424)

Outnumbered by the rebels, those who held the upper city were soon overrun. The house of the high priest Ananias and the additions built onto the Hasmonean palace by Agrippa and Bernice (cf. *Ant.* 20:189–190) were set ablaze. Likewise, the rebels burned the public archives "to destroy the money-lenders' bonds and to prevent the recovery of debts" (*War* 2:427; cf. 6:354). Their action underscores the social and economic rift between the insurgents and the aristocracy who desired to put an end to the rebellion.

Fighting ensued over the days that followed with the insurgents capturing the Antonia fortress, setting it on fire and putting the Roman troops to the sword (*War* 2:430). Allies to Agrippa fled for refuge to Herod's royal palace, where the remaining Roman army was garrisoned. A ferocious siege continued until the arrival of Menahem, son of Judah the Galilean (*Ant.* 17:271), who had broken into Herod's armory at Masada and returned with arms for the brigands (*War* 2:433–440). Negotiations allowed the Jewish allies to the king to leave, but the Roman forces had to withdraw farther inside the palace to the "royal towers, known as Hippicus, Phasael and Mariamme" (*War* 2:439; cf. 5:161–175, 7:1).

Events seemed to unfold in favor of

*The so-called "David's Tower" in Jerusalem, built in the Herodian period and identified by some scholars with the tower of Hippicus.*

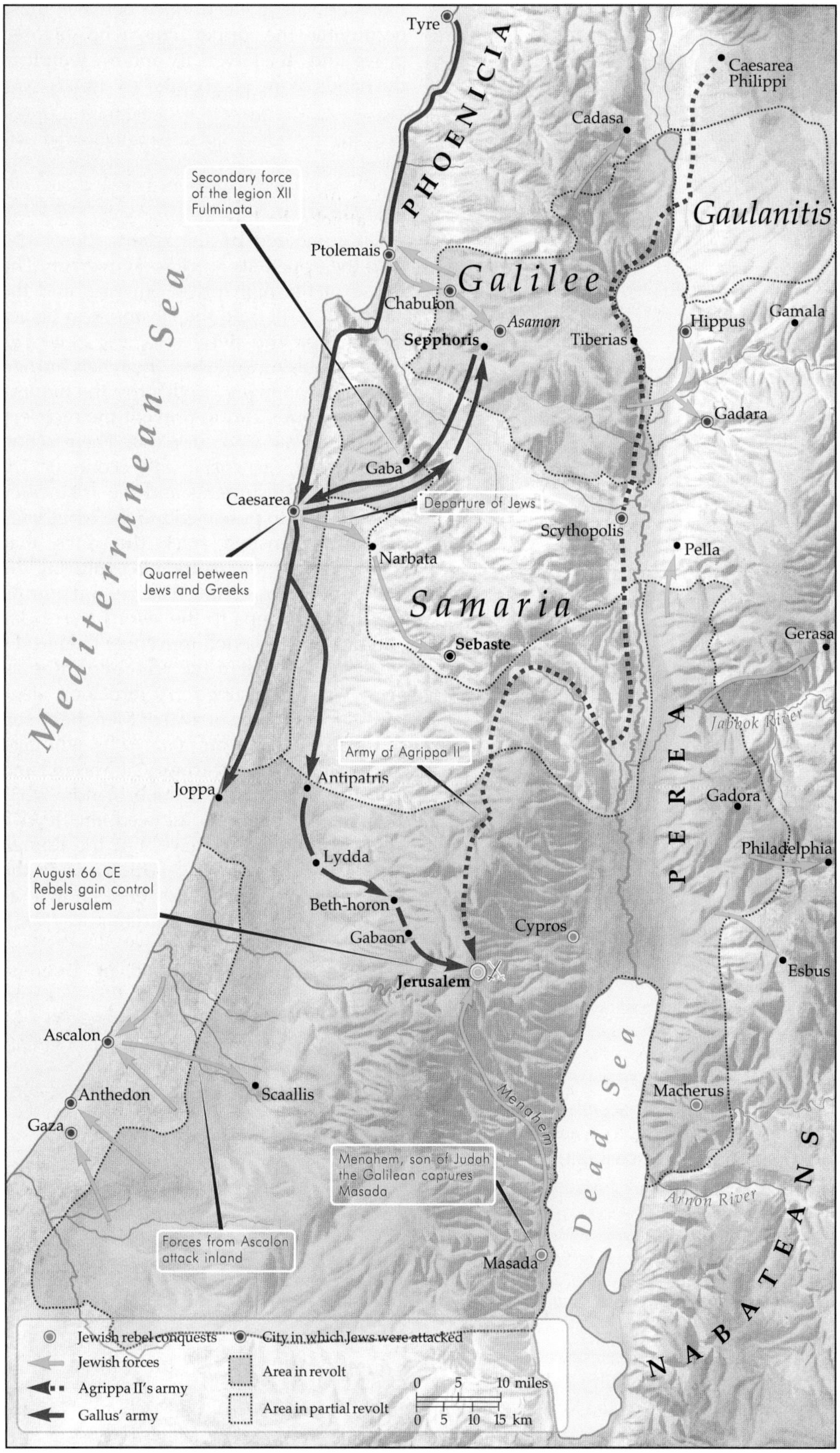


**THE OUTBREAK OF THE FIRST REVOLT AGAINST ROME (66 CE)**

the insurgency. Ananias was captured and killed (*War* 2:441). The heady successes steeled the hubris of Menahem and his iron-fisted tyranny. A rift soon resulted among the zealots. Some reasoned, why trade one tyrant for another? So, they plotted against him, and when he ascended to the Temple arrayed in royal regalia, Eleazar and his followers ambushed the tyrant. Menahem was captured, tortured and murdered, with many of his followers sharing his fate (*War* 2:442–448). Others fled to Masada, including Eleazar son of Jairus, who would later lead the defense of Masada (*War* 2:447; cf. 7:275).

Attention returned to the Roman garrison in the royal towers. In a negotiated truce, they were assured safe passage, if they would abandon the towers unarmed. They agreed, but no sooner had they left the protection of the towers than they were slaughtered. The only member of the garrison to survive was the commander Metilius, who offered to convert to Judaism with circumcision (*War* 2:454). Although the loss in life for the Romans was minimal in number, Jerusalem awoke the next morning to the realization that the full force of a Roman response would soon be felt. "To add to its heinousness, the massacre took place on the Sabbath, a day on which from religious scruples Jews abstain even from the most innocent of acts" (*War* 2:456; cf. *Meg. Taᶜan.* 17 Elul).

At the same time, fighting between Jews and Gentiles broke out throughout the region. In Caesarea thousands were killed, and Florus ordered the arrest of all who remained in order to remove any Jews from that Greek city (*War* 2:457). When word spread about the events at Caesarea, Jewish communities vented their anger by attacking their neighbors. Josephus describes the communal violence, listing disturbances in cities of the Transjordan in a line from south to north, then cities of the Galilee, and finally names of coastal cities from north to south.

> ...parties of Jews sacked the Syrian villages and the neighboring cities, Philadelphia, Heshbon and its district, Gerasa, Pella and Scythopolis. Next they fell upon Gadara, Hippus, and Gaulanitis, destroying or setting fire to all in their path, and advanced to Cadasa, a Tyrian village, Ptolemais, Gaba and Caesarea. Neither Sebaste nor Ascalon withstood their fury; these they burnt to the ground and they razed Anthedon and Gaza. (*War* 2:458–460)

His report that Jews living in these cities felt the confidence to strike out against their neighbors, suggests that there were large and well-established Jewish communities throughout the region.

The Gentile populations of Syria and Alexandria reacted with similar fury and murdered Jews living in those communities. Yet, Josephus notes they faced a quandary with converts to Judaism, who for all practical purposes identified themselves with the Jews, but whose legal status within the Roman Empire was in question.

> For, though, believing that they had rid themselves of the Jews, still each city had its *converts to Judaism*, who aroused suspicion; and while they shrunk from killing offhand this equivocal element in their midst, they feared these neutrals as much as pronounced aliens. (*War* 2:463)

Nevertheless, not every Greek city rose up against its Jewish citizenry. Antioch, Sidon, Apamea and Gerasa are mentioned by name among those who neither killed, nor imprisoned their Jewish residents (*War* 2:479–480).

With violence breaking out against Jewish communities throughout the region, the Roman legate, Cestius Gallus, now

*The Jewish partisans moved to secure the eastern frontier by capturing additional fortresses in the Judean wilderness. First, the fortress of Cypros (Tell el-ᶜAqabeh;* War 1:407, 417; Ant. 16:143) *that guarded Jericho was taken and the Roman garrison massacred* (War 2:484). *At Macherus, shown here, the neighboring Jewish residents negotiated with the Roman garrison for their safe passage, if they agreed to abandon this strategic fortress rebuilt by Herod overlooking the Dead Sea* (War 2:485–486).

moved against the center of the insurrection at Jerusalem (*War* 2:499). He marched from Antioch with a considerable force, including the legion XII Fulminata and two thousand men from the other Syrian legions (III Gallica, VI Ferrata, X Fretensis: Tac. *Ann.* 4:5). His forces were augmented by contributions from Antiochus IV of Commagene (*War* 2: 500, 7:219), Soaemus king of Emesa and King Agrippa II, who supplied foot soldiers and cavalry.

Agrippa accompanied Cestius, guiding him and his army south along the coast to Ptolemais. The first Jewish city to fall before Cestius' advance was the fortified city of Chabulon (Kabul; *War* 3:38; *Ant.* 8:142; *Life* 213, 227, 234) in Galilee that lay on the frontier between Ptolemais and the Jewish settlements in the region (*War* 2:503–506). While Cestius marched to Caesarea with the main contingent, advance units continued by land and sea and succeeded to capture Joppa. At the same time Cestius was securing the northern coastal regions, he also sent "a strong force of cavalry into the toparchy of Narbatene (cf. *War* 2:291: Narbata; 1 Macc 5:23; Kh. el-Ḥammam), which borders on Caesarea; these ravaged the country, killed a large number of the inhabitants, pillaged their property and burnt their villages" (*War* 2:509).

Segments of the legion XII Fulminata returned to the Galilee, where Sepphoris, in a portent to its capitulation before Vespasian (*War* 3:30–31), threw open its gates to Cestius' commander, Caesennius Gallus (*War* 2:510–511). The remaining Galilean settlements followed the lead of Sepphoris and did not resist. Josephus does describe an insurgency in Galilee that took refuge in the mountainous area called Asamon (possibly Jebel Jarmaq), opposite Sepphoris. From here the rebels used their position of advantage in sorties against the foreign troops (*War* 2:511).

After his forces had subdued the Galilee, Cestius marched from Caesarea to Antipatris, the Roman city built by Herod on the site of Hellenistic Pegae. Here Cestius learned that Jewish forces were gathered at "a certain Tower of Aphek" (*War* 2:513; Migdal ᵓAfeq). However, they fled rather than challenge the Roman legion. Likewise, when the Roman legate continued south on the eastern edge of the coastal plain, he found Lydda vacated; although, Josephus says that the residents had left to attend the Feast of Tabernacles in Jerusalem. Mention of the Jewish feast dates Cestius' march to October 66 CE.

Cestius began his climb into the hill country of Judea following the Ascent of Beth-horon (*War* 2:516; cf. Josh 10:10; 1 Macc 3:16, 7:39, 9:50). He encamped at Gabaon, biblical Gibeon (el-Jib; cf. *War* 2:544; *Ant.* 5:49–62, 7:283; Eus. *Onom.* 66:13–14). Jerusalem was full of pilgrims who quickly armed themselves to engage the Roman armies, even though the fighting fell on the Sabbath. The frontal assault by the Jewish forces was checked, and they withdrew to Jerusalem. Simon son of Giora struck at the rear against Roman reinforcements as they ascended from Beth-horon (*War* 2:517–522).

Agrippa realized that the insurgents could surround the main camp at Gabaon and mount an endless guerrilla campaign from their advantageous position in the hills. He tried to parley a truce with the Jewish rebels with the promise of amnesty, but his offer was rebuffed and his emissaries murdered. Cestius brought the remainder of his troops to join the fight and proceeded to the outskirts of Jerusalem. He pitched his camp at a place called Scopus (*War* 2:528, 542), the high hill overlooking Jerusalem where Titus would also pitch his camp a few years later in the Roman siege of Jerusalem (*War* 5: 67, 106–108).

It was now early November and Cestius received word of internal dissension among the Jewish rebels. He breached the Third Wall begun by Agrippa I (*War* 2:218–219; *Ant.* 19:326–327) and moved into the northern neighborhoods between the Third Wall and the Second Wall known as *Bezetha* (*War* 2:328, 530; 5:149, 151, 246), or *the new city* (*Ant.* 19:326). The rebels had withdrawn into "the inner city (i.e. within the First Wall) and the temple" (*War* 2:529). Cestius shifted to the western hill and camped opposite the royal palace.

The Romans began their siege of the Temple Mount and fighting continued for days (*War* 2:532–539). According to Josephus, Cestius was not fully aware of the desperation of the rebel forces. Inexplicably, he withdrew his forces without suffering a defeat. Emboldened by their enemy's retreat, the Jewish forces pursued the Romans first to the camp on Scopus, and then on to Gabaon (*War* 2:542–545). The specter of the Roman flight attracted new recruits. At Gabaon Cestius delayed the descent for two days, which gave the Jewish forces time to organize. On open ground the attacks had been minimal, but once the descent began toward Beth-horon they were unrelenting.

> Here, while even the infantry were hard put to it to defend themselves, the cavalry were in still greater jeopardy; to advance in order down the road under the hail of darts was impossible, to charge up the slopes was impracticable for horses; on either side were precipices and ravines, down which they slipped and were hurled to destruction; there was no room for flight, no conceivable means of defense.
> (*War* 2:548–549)

Only the onset of nightfall at Beth-horon saved Cestius and his generals from capture. Under the cloak of darkness they were able to slip away. At daybreak, the Jewish forces realized that the real prize had escaped. So, they pursued Cestius and his men as far as Antipatris (*War* 2:554). Here they broke off the chase and returned to the hill country. The aristocracy of Jerusalem, which had refused to support the rebellion, realized that the Roman response would not be long in coming. Some fled (*War* 2:556). Others now joined the rebels. Cestius sent a report of events to Nero at Achaia and sought to minimize his own responsibility by laying blame for the insurrection on Florus (*War* 2: 558).

When word reached Nero of the reverses in Judea, he was anxious not only about the stability of this small province, but also "forestalling a revolt of the neighboring nations, which were already catching the contagion" (*War* 3:3). Insurrection could quickly spread. He needed someone who would dispel any notions of Rome's weakness. In Vespasian, Nero found a seasoned veteran who would deal decisively with the rebellion.

> He had already earlier in his career pacified and restored to Roman rule the West when convulsed by the Germans; he had by his military genius added to the Empire Britain, till then almost unknown, and thus afforded Claudius, Nero's father (i.e. stepfather, cf. *War* 2:249), the honors of a triumph which cost him no personal exertion.
> (*War* 3:4–5; cf. Tac *Agr.* 13; Suet. *Vesp.* 4)

Vespasian dispatched his son Titus to Alexandria to call up the legion XV Apollinaris, while he traveled over land from Achaia, crossing the Hellespont to proceed to Syria (*War* 3:8). There he gathered Roman forces and auxiliaries supplied by the kings of neighboring nations.

Jewish preparations for war had also begun in earnest. Leadership of the supreme council in Jerusalem had been entrusted to two men: Joseph son of Gorion and Ananus son of Ananias, the former high priest (*War* 2:563), although leadership would soon

*Roman bust, thought to be that of Josephus Flavius.*

gravitate from Joseph to a wealthy brigand, Eleazar son of Simon. Ananus seems to be the same high priest who was deposed by Agrippa for his complicity in the death of James (*Ant.* 20:197–203).

The first order of business was to strengthen the walls of the capital (*War* 2: 648). The council also divided the country into six districts and appointed generals who were responsible to prepare defenses for these districts.

> Other generals were selected for Idumea, namely, Jesus son of Sapphas, one of the chief priests, and Eleazar, *son of the high priest Neus* (cf. *War* 2:409). . . . Joseph, son of Simon, was sent to take command at Jericho, Manasseh to Peraea, John the Essene to the province of Thamna, with Lydda, Joppa and Emmaus also under his charge. John, son of Ananias, was appointed commanding officer of the provinces of Gophna and Acrabeta; Josephus, son of Matthias, was given the two Galilees, with the addition of Gamala, the strongest city in that region. (*War* 2:566–568)

Not surprisingly, Josephus provides the most detailed report of Jewish preparations for war in the northern districts of Galilee and Gaulanitis, where the historian himself was responsible for fortification of the cities.

> Foreseeing that Galilee would bear the brunt of the Romans' opening assault, [Josephus] fortified the most suitable places, namely, Jotapata, Bersabe, Selame, Caphareccho, Japhia, Sigoph, the mount called Itabyrion, Taricheae, and Tiberias; he further provided with walls the caves in Lower Galilee in the neighbourhood of the lake of Gennesaret, and in Upper Galilee the rock known as Acchabaron, Sepph, Jamnith, and Meron. In Gaulanitis, he fortified Seleucia, Sogane and Gamala. (*War* 2:573–574)

Two cities are not included in Josephus' oversight. Sepphoris possessed the economic means to erect its own walls (*War* 2:574). Likewise, the village of Gischala in Upper Galilee had a local benefactor, John son of Levi, who offered to build its fortifications at his own expense (*War* 2:575).

John of Gischala is introduced as one of Josephus' primary detractors in the attempt to organize and lead the Galilee. John mustered a band of men and with them harried villages in the region (*War* 2: 588–589). More troubling to Josephus, John spread rumors "that Josephus intended to betray the country to the Romans, and in numerous similar ways he was scheming to ruin his chief" (*War* 2:594). Indeed, Josephus' later behavior at Jotapata and his service to Vespasian suggest that John's suspicions about Josephus' commitment to the war effort may not have been completely unfounded.

On the southwestern front of Judea, a preemptive campaign by the Jewish forces was launched against the Greek city of Ascalon with whom there had existed a long history of acrimony (*War* 3:10; cf. 2:460; Philo *Leg.* 205: "its inhabitants cherish an implacable and irreconcilable hatred for the Jews who live in the Holy Land and with whom they have a common frontier"). The miserable outcome of the Jewish attack was not the fault of the commanders, who Josephus lauds as "men of first-rate prowess and ability," but the inexperience of the fighters. "It was a case of novices against veterans, infantry against cavalry, ragged order against serried ranks, men casually armed against fully equipped regulars" (*War* 3:15). That same inexperience would be evident on the field of battle before Vespasian and the Roman legions.

Titus proceeded without delay to Alexandria to bring the legion XV Apollinaris on a forced march to the coastal city of Ptolemais, where he met Vespasian waiting with the legions V Macedonica and X Fretensis. Even before Titus joined his father, messengers arrived from Sepphoris (*War* 3: 30–34). A garrison had been stationed there at the time of the city's surrender to Cestius (*War* 3:30–31; cf. 2:510; *Life* 394). In response to the offer of support from the leaders of Sepphoris, Vespasian sent 1,000 cavalry and 6,000 infantry under the command of the tribune Placidus to strengthen the Roman presence in this strategic Galilean city (*War* 3:59). He now had a foothold in Lower Galilee, "it was the largest city of Galilee, a fortress in an exceptionally strong position in the enemy's territory, and adapted to keep guard over the entire province" (*War* 3:34). Josephus tried to thwart Sepphoris' concessions by attacking it, but all attempts were repulsed (*War* 3:61; *Life* 395). The Romans began to make sallies into the surrounding region. "Galilee from end to end became a scene of fire and blood; from no misery, no clamity was it exempt; the one refuge for the hunted inhabitants was in the cities fortified by Josephus" (*War* 3:63).

After Vespasian had consolidated his forces with those of Titus and the auxiliaries that joined them at Ptolemais, he began his campaign against Judea. He marched from Ptolemais to the frontiers of Galilee, while

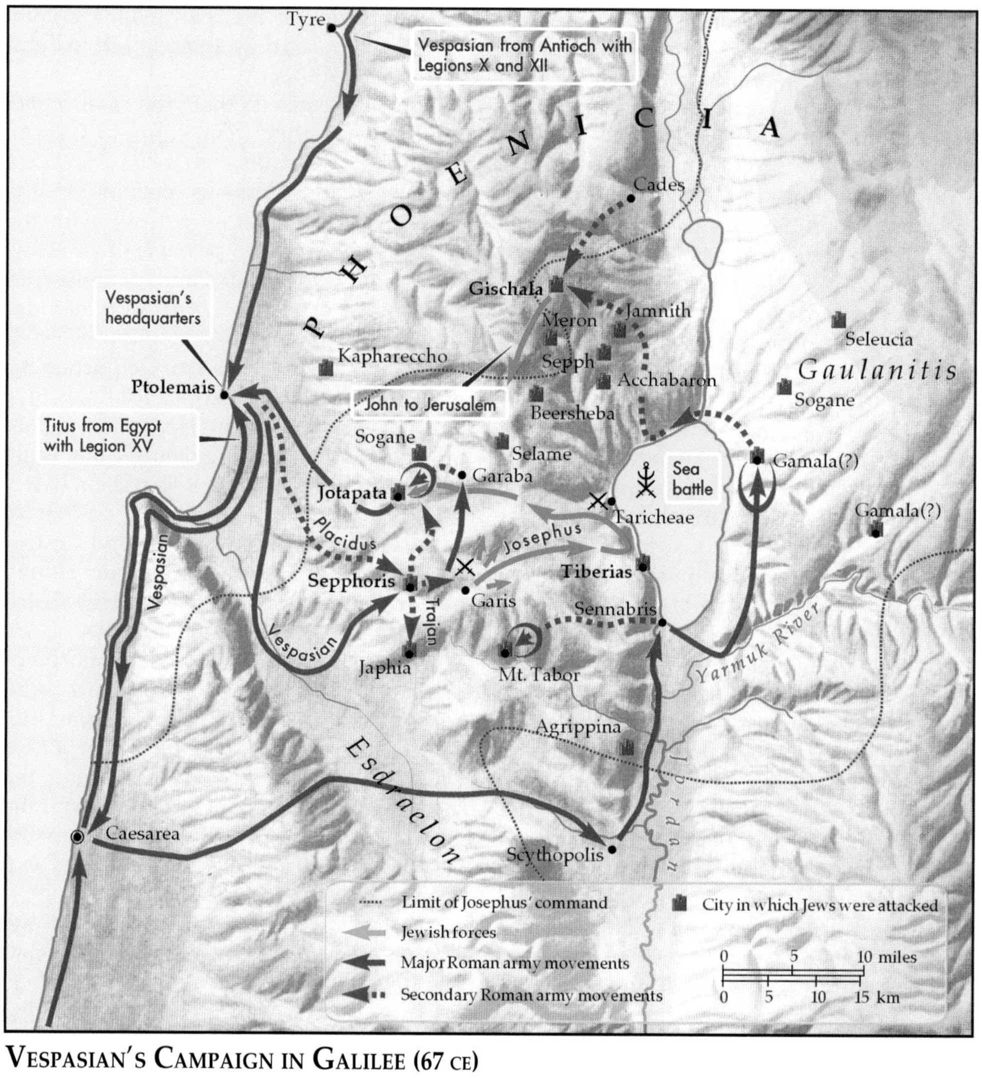


**VESPASIAN'S CAMPAIGN IN GALILEE (67 CE)**

Josephus was encamped at Garis (*War* 3:129, 5:474; *Life* 395, 412). The Jewish forces fled in fear, according to Josephus, even before they gained sight of the approaching Roman armies. So, the commander had little choice but to withdraw and take refuge in Tiberias.

Vespasian's first assault came against the western Galilean city of Garaba (ᶜArraba; *War* 3:132–134), a settlement due east of Ptolemais (*Life* 123). Here the Romans killed all males of arms-bearing age and razed the surrounding villages. Josephus quickly recognized the disparity in military might between his forces and the approaching Roman legions. He appealed to Jerusalem for reinforcements (*War* 3:139–140), while he himself moved to Jotapata to lead the city's defense against the Romans. The historian provides a lengthy description of the siege of Jotapata (*War* 3:145–339), perhaps because it was one of the few cities of the Galilee to muster a spirited defense against the Roman advance.

Eventually, the city succumbed to the Roman siege. Hiding in one of the cisterns that honeycomb the hilltop city, Josephus surrendered to the Romans rather than fight to the death or take his own life (*War* 3:392). Vespasian ordered Josephus to be kept alive, so that he could be sent to Nero. However, the Jewish general asked for a private audience with Vespasian in which he prophesied the Roman would soon become emperor.

You will be Caesar, Vespasian, you will be emperor, you and your son here. Bind me then yet more securely in chains and keep me for yourself; for you, Caesar, are master not of me only, but of land and sea and the whole human race. For myself, I ask to be punished by stricter custody, if I have dared to trifle with the words of God.

(*War* 3:401-402; cf. Suet. *Vesp.* 5; Dio 66.1)

In lending his prophecy concerning the Roman general, Josephus portrayed himself as "an interpreter of dreams and skilled in divining the meaning of ambiguous utterances of the Deity" (*War* 3:352; cf. 2:112–116; *Life* 208–212). Vespasian did not release Josephus from custody, but he "treated him with kindness and solicitude, being warmly supported by Titus in these courtesies" (*War* 3:408).

The Romans now had subdued those areas of western Galilee that lay outside of Agrippa's kingdom. Vespasian would soon march into Agrippa's territory against settlements around the lake, but only after his visit to the Jewish king. For the time being, he removed two legions, V Macedonica and X Fretensis, to Caesarea and the third legion XV Apollinaris to Scythopolis (*War* 3:409-412). While his troops were resting, Vespasian joined Agrippa at Caesarea Philippi.

He was being fêted himself and rendering thanksgivings to God for the successes that he had obtained. But when he learned that Tiberias was disaffected and Taricheae already in revolt—both cities formed part of Agrippa's realm—he thought that now was the time to march against these rebels in pursuance of his fixed intention of crushing the Jews wherever they rose, and also to oblige Agrippa and to repay his hospitality by recalling these cities of his to their allegiance. (*War* 3:444–445)

*Coin of the legion X Fretensis.*

Vespasian dispatched his son to retrieve the forces billeted at Caesarea and to meet him at Scythopolis. With the combined three legions and auxiliary forces the Romans advanced to Sennabris (Senn en-Nabra; *War* 3:447; cf. 4:455), a town at the exit of the Jordan River on the southwestern shore of the Sea of Galilee. Stationed within view of Tiberias, Vespasian offered peace to the people. As the company sent by Vespasian with the offer approached Tiberias, it was attacked by "Jesus, son of Saphat, the ringleader of this band of brigands" (*War* 3:450; cf. 2:566, 599). This brigand together with John of Gischala are named by Josephus as being at the center of his problems in Tiberias. Now arguments broke out among the people of Tiberias, whether to fight or to withdraw. In the face of overwhelming force, Tiberias threw open its gates to the Romans without a fight (*War* 3:443–461), while the brigands of Tiberias and the surrounding region fled to Taricheae (*War* 3:457).

Vespasian ordered part of the south wall to be thrown down and so opened a broad passage for his soldiers. However, as a compliment to the king, he strictly forbade any pillage or violence, and for the same reason spared the walls, after receiving from Agrippa guarantee for the future fidelity of the inhabitants. He thus brought new life to a city that had sorely suffered from the effects of sedition.

(*War* 3:461)

When Vespasian heard that the rebels had fled from Tiberias to Taricheae, he sent Titus to pursue them. Here was yet another city Josephus claimed he fortified. However, he remarks that in comparison to the defenses of Tiberias, those of Taricheae were meager. "For the fortifications [in Tiberias] had been built by him at the outbreak of the revolt in the plentitude of his resources and his power, whereas Taricheae only obtained the leavings of his bounty" (*War* 3:465). His excuse, however, was later contradicted by his own testimony given in his autobiography (*Life* 156), when he recounted that the fortifications at Taricheae were built before those of Tiberias. He also reasoned that the walls surrounding Taricheae were not imperative, because the city faced the lakefront, where the citizens maintained a considerable fleet. In any event, the fortifications did little to impede Titus' lightning strike and conquest of the city.

As he spoke [Titus] leapt on his horse, led his troops to the lake, rode through the water and was the first to enter the town, followed by his men. Terror-struck at his audacity, none of the defenders on the ramparts ventured to fight or to resist him; all abandoned their posts and fled, the partisans of Jesus [son of Sapphas] across country, the others down to the lake. (*War* 3:497–499)

The refugees that fled by boat were pursued by Vespasian and his troops on a flotilla of rafts (*War* 3:522). Josephus describes in graphic detail the carnage that resulted from the sea battle (*War* 3:530–531). The fall of Taricheae (*War* 3:462–502; cf. Suet. *Div. Tit.* 4) left only Gischala and Mount Tabor in Galilee participating in the Jewish resistance. Before dealing with them, Vespasian turned his attention to Gamala, the well-fortified city of lower Gaulanitis.

Josephus first mentions Gamala in connection with the campaign of Alexander Jannaeus (*Ant.* 13:394; *War* 1:105), and identifies it as the home of Judas son of Ezekias (*Ant.* 18:4), whom the historian subsequently describes as the founder of the Zealots, the Fourth Philosophy (*Ant.* 18:23; *War* 2:118; Acts 5:37). He begins his account of the siege of Gamala with a description of this settlement and its relationship with two other cities in the Transjordan.

Gamala was also in league with these rebels [i.e. Gischala and Mount Tabor], *a city situated on the other side of the lake, opposite Taricheae.* Gamala formed part of the territory allotted to Agrippa, like Sogane (el-Yehudiye) and Seleucia (Seluqiye); Gamala and Sogane were both in Gaulanitis, the latter belonging to what is known as Upper, the former to Lower, Gaulan; Seleucia was near the lake Semechonitis.

(*War* 4:2)

Josephus' description of Gamala is at the center of scholarly debate concerning its identification. Earlier scholarly opinion identified Gamala with Tell el-Aḥdab, near Jamleh on the Nahr el-Ruqqad, 11 miles (18 km) east of the Sea of Galilee.

Khirbet es-Salam near the village of Deir Qeruḥ then became a possible candidate for Gamala. A subsequent survey and excavations confirmed the remains of a fortified Hellenistic-Roman period city, situated on a rocky spur between Naḥal Daliyyot and Naḥal Gamla. The city included a synagogue and a ritual bath installation, and there is ample evidence of a siege and destruction dating from the Jewish Revolt. These conclusions led to a shift in scholarly opinion to embrace Khirbet es-Salam as first-century Gamala.

Nevertheless, there are some difficulties in reconciling Josephus' description of

*Khirbet es-Salam (Gamala?) in the southern Golan.*

Gamala with its identification at Khirbet es-Salam. Reconciliation of Josephus' picture of the summit of Gamala with the shape of Khirbet es-Salam is possible, though not without a creative reading of the Greek text. However, the reader is challenged with insurmountable obstacles in the historian's description of the location of Gamala and its district Gamalitike (*War* 3:56).

Presenting even greater difficulty, Josephus describes the city of Gamala in the geographical region of Lower Gaulanitis (*War* 4:2). While the historian does not give the line of demarcation between Upper and Lower Gaulanitis, the delineation between these two regions would likely derive from a visual impression (e.g. *War* 3:35: Upper and Lower Galilee).

Josephus' presentation of Gamala in Lower Gaulanitis and juxtaposed to Sogane, which lay in Upper Gaulanitis, brings the topographical challenge for Khirbet es-Salam into clear relief. Since the nineteenth century Sogane has been identified at el-Yehudiye. It lies only 3 miles (5 km) northwest of Khirbet es-Salam, and there is no geographical feature between these two villages to distinguish between Upper and Lower Gaulanitis. The site of Khirbet es-Salam would thus be located in the region of Upper Gaulanitis, and consequently excluded from consideration for first-century Gamala in Lower Gaulanitis, according to Josephus' description.

The ruins of Khirbet es-Salam may thus be identified with Solyma, another Jewish village with a similar name that participated in the revolt: "The region of Gaulanitis, as far as the village of Solyma, likewise revolted from the king" (*Life* 187). In his singular reference to this village in Gaulanitis, Josephus also describes his fortification of Seleucia and Sogane, two cities in the kingdom of Agrippa. On the three other occasions these two cities appear in collocation, they are mentioned with Gamala (*War* 2:574, 4:2, 4:4). This would suggest that the four settlements were not too distant, but Josephus' description is equally clear that between them, Gamala alone resided in Lower Gaulanitis.

Early in the conflict Agrippa convinced Seleucia and Sogane to abandon the revolt. Although Josephus remarks that he fortified these cities (*War* 2:574), they did not possess the natural defenses that lulled Gamala into overconfidence.

> Gamala refused to surrender, relying even more confidently than Jotapata upon the natural difficulties of its position. From a lofty mountain there descends a rugged spur rising in the middle to a hump, the declivity from the summit of which is of the same length before as behind, so that in form the ridge resembles a camel; whence it derives its name. ...Its sides and face are cleft all round by inaccessible ravines, but at the tail end, where it hangs on to the mountain, it is somewhat easier of approach.... It faced south, and its southern eminence rising to an immense height, formed the citadel; below this an unwalled precipice descended to the deepest of the ravines. There was a spring within the walls at the confines of the town. (*War* 4:5–8)

Their defenses allowed Gamala to resist Agrippa's siege for seven months. However, now the Herodian was joined by Vespasian and his Roman legions, presenting an irresistible threat. The severe topography surrounding the city prevented Vespasian's normal circumvallation of the besieged city. Instead, he posted sentries to prevent escape and began the task of filling in the trench in the saddleback that connected Gamala to the adjacent mountain (*War* 4:13).

Agrippa continued to appeal to his citizens to abandon their hopeless resistance, but when he was struck by a stone from a sling of a defender, it prompted vigilance on the part of the Romans to hasten the siege. Soon the Romans applied battering rams to three different quarters of the surrounding walls and broke into the city. Panic ensued as the soldiers chased the defenders to the upper sections of the city. "They fled to the upper parts of the town, where, rounding upon the pursuing enemy, they thrust them down the slopes and slew them while impeded by the narrowness and difficulties of the ground" (*War* 4:22–23).

The Romans were unable to repel the enemy because of the steepness of the slope before them. At the same time, they were unable to retreat because of the press of their comrades who followed. Some of the soldiers sought refuge on the roofs of the houses. The construction held a few, but the roofs soon gave way under the weight of the mass of escaping Romans. Those who survived the collapse were in no state to defend themselves. The Jewish defenders saw this turn of events as God's intervention. Vespasian was cut off from the main body of his troops and found himself in danger on the higher reaches of the slopes. Valiantly, but slowly, he and his men extracted themselves from the city.

*Roman battering ram.*

Vespasian's troops were discouraged by their losses. The general sought to bolster their resolve by observing that they had not suffered defeat because of a lack of military superiority, but a momentary lack of discipline.

> ...fault might be found with your inordinate ardor; for when the enemy fled to the higher ground, you should have restrained yourselves and not by pursuit exposed yourselves to the perils impending over your heads ... incautiousness in war and mad impetuosity are alien to us Romans, who owe all our success to skill and discipline. (*War* 4:44–46)

At this point in the siege of Gamala, Josephus reports that Vespasian undertook a diversion and sent a detachment under the command of the tribune Placidus (cf. *Life* 213, 411; *War* 3:59, 3:110, 4:419) to secure Mount Tabor. Josephus himself had fortified the summit (*War* 4:56). The Roman tribune found the ascent impractical and offered the defenders terms of peace. They ostensibly agreed to the Roman's proposal, but their real intent was to surprise the Romans under the guise of acquiescence.

> The craft of Placidus, however, won the day; for when the Jews opened hostilities he feigned flight and, having drawn his pursuers far into the plain, suddenly wheeled his cavalry round and routed them. Masses of them were slain; the remainder he intercepted and prevented from reascending the mountain. These fugitives abandoning Mount Tabor made off to Jerusalem. (*War* 4:60–61)

At Gamala those who were able, escaped through unguarded ravines. Others died from a lack of food and water. As the siege moved into November (67 CE), three soldiers crawled in the early morning and removed supporting stones for the eastern tower to the city. The crash of the collapsing wall caused panic among the locals, who awakened to the noise. They assumed that the Romans had broken into the city. On this occasion, however, the Romans proceeded slowly. Titus led the incursion and chased the locals to the citadel. Soon the entire Roman force followed. Seeking to avenge the loss of their comrades from the earlier disastrous assault, the Romans dispensed with every defender in reach.

> Despairing of their lives and hemmed in on every side, multitudes plunged headlong with their wives and children into the ravine that had been excavated to a vast depth beneath the citadel. Indeed, the rage of the Romans was thus made to appear milder than the frantic self-immolation of the vanquished, four thousand only being slain by the former, while those who flung themselves over the cliff were found to exceed five thousand. (*War* 4:79–80)

The fall of Gamala left Gischala (Jish) as the lone rebel holdout in the north to face the Romans. John of Gischala had incited the residents of this small town to revolt. When Titus arrived at Gischala, he appealed to the residents to surrender. John feigned surrender, but requested from Titus "in deference to the Jewish law, to allow them that day, being the seventh, on which they were forbidden alike to have resort to arms and to conclude a treaty of peace" (*War* 4:100). Titus not only agreed to the delay, but he withdrew his forces at a distance to nearby Cadasa (Tel Qedesh). John's delay tactic proved only to be a ploy to escape that night with his men to Jerusalem, where he would become a leader of the insurgents in their defense of the capital. At daybreak the residents of Gischala threw open their gates to Titus, and so by the end of 67 CE the last Jewish settlement in the north had fallen to the Romans (*War* 4:113).

The first season of fighting against the Romans had not gone well for the Jewish resistance. During the winter, recriminations and a struggle for power erupted in Jerusalem among the insurgents (cf. *War* 4:128–134). The population of Jerusalem swelled because of the influx of refugees and bands of brigands, who attacked those suspected of pro-Roman sympathies (*War* 4: 135–136). One of the first changes sought was the manner in which the high priest was selected. Previously, he had been chosen from established families and typically from circles opposed to armed conflict. Now the high priest was to be selected by lots. However, the candidate so awarded, Phannias son of Samuel, Josephus portrays to have been entirely ignorant of the office (*War* 4:147–157), "a man who not only was not descended from high priests, but was such a clown that he scarcely knew what the high priesthood meant" (*War* 4:156).

Outrage at these changes spurred the existing leadership led by Joseph son of Gorion, Simon son of Gamaliel (*Life* 190, 309), and two former high priests, Ananus and Jesus son of Gamaliel, to appeal to the people of Jerusalem to resist the zealots (*War* 4:158–192). Fighting broke out and the zealots cordoned themselves within the inner precincts of the Temple (*War* 4:196–207).

John of Gischala, who was ostensibly allied with the aristocratic leadership, was sent to negotiate on their behalf with the besieged brigands. In an act of betrayal to the high priest Ananus, he informed the zealots of the leadership's plans and encouraged them to seek support from the Idumeans. They sent a message alleging that the leadership of Jerusalem intended to hand the city over to the Romans. The Idumeans responded to the false report and rushed to the gates of Jerusalem, where they were denied access on suspicion of being in league with the rebel elements (*War* 4:224–282).

A violent storm allowed the zealots to slip out of the temple precincts undetected and to open the gates to the Idumeans (*War* 4:300). As they entered the city, they began to murder and pillage the residents of Jerusalem (*War* 4:305–313). Together with the

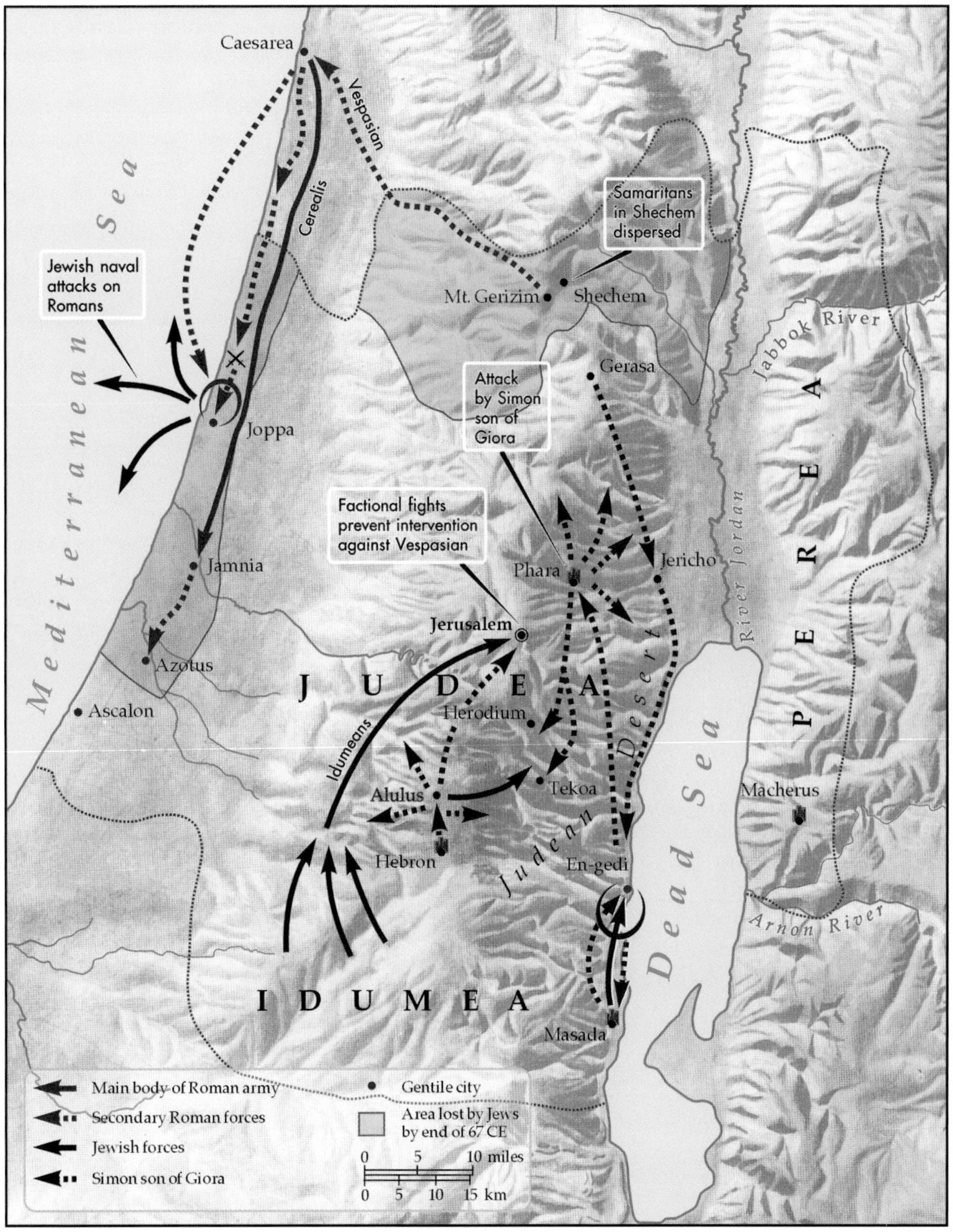


**VESPASIAN'S CAMPAIGN IN JUDEA; INTERNAL CONFLICT AMONG THE JEWS (67 CE)**

zealots they secured the city. The zealots took revenge against the high priests, executing Ananus and Jesus (*War* 4:314–333). As a vivid example of the injustice meted out by the zealots, Josephus details the execution of Zacharias son of Baris (*War* 4: 335–344), who even though acquitted at his trial was murdered by the zealots.

> Two of the most daring of them then set upon Zacharias and slew him in the midst of the temple, and exclaiming in jest over his prostrate body, "Now you have our verdict also and a more certain *release* [lit. *acquittal* or *death*]," forthwith cast him out of the temple into the ravine below.
> (*War* 4:343; cf. Mt 23:35; Mk 12:8)

It is during this time that Josephus recounts that many from the peace party abandoned the city in the realization that the zealots were leading the nation headlong into disaster (*War* 4:377–378; cf. b. *Giṭ.* 56a–b; *Midr. Lam. Rab.* 1, 5 §31; *ᵓAbot R. Nat.* 4). It may also be at this time, as Eusebius records, that Christians left the city for Pella (Eus. *Eccl. hist.* 3.5.2–3; Epiph. *Adv. haer.* 29.7).

Some of Vespasian's advisers encouraged him to take advantage of the infighting among the rebels (*War* 4:366–376). However, he considered dissension a godsend and elected to allow the insurgents to continue to weaken their own cause, as they reduced their numbers through murder and sedition. In the meantime, he marched on Gadora, capital of Perea (*War* 4:413). The leadership of the city offered to capitulate, while the rebels in their midst fled (*War* 4:415–417). When Vespasian returned to Caesarea, he dispatched Placidus (cf. *Life* 411; *War* 3:59, 110) with 3,000 infantry and 500 cavalry to subdue the remaining insurgents in Perea. The Romans overtook fleeing rebels at Beth-nimrah (Tell Nimrin). Others made their way towards Jericho, but Placidus caught them, as they tried to cross the Jordan.

> Placidus, following up his good fortune, hastened to attack the small towns and villages in the neighborhood, and taking Abila, Julias, Besimoth,

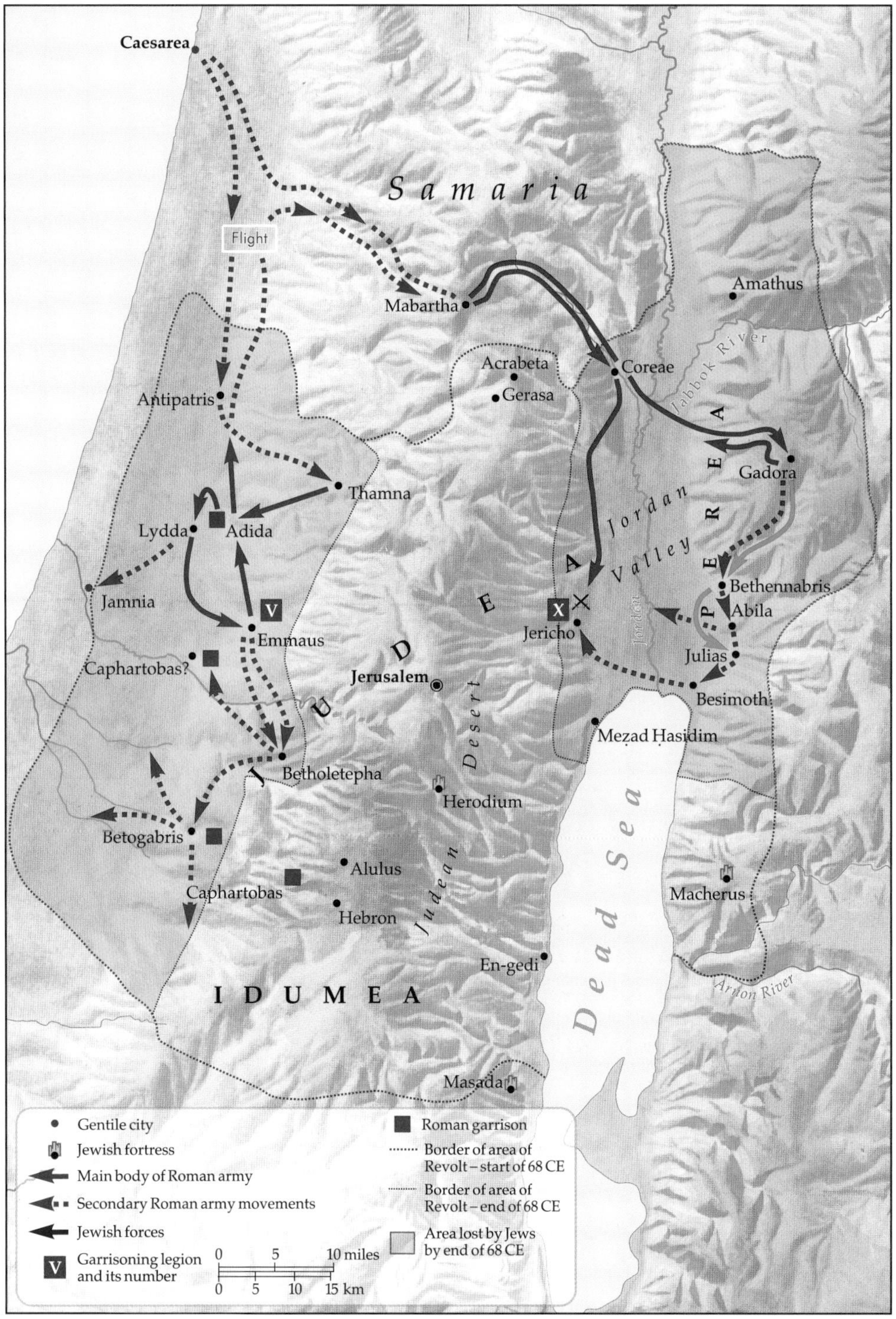


**THE ROMAN CAMPAIGN OF 68 CE**

> and all as far as the lake Asphaltitis, posted in each a garrison of such deserters as he thought fit; then embarking his soldiers on shipboard he captured those who had taken refuge on the lake. Thus, the whole of Perea as far as Macherus either surrendered or was subdued. (*War* 4:438–439)

Vespasian received word of continued dissension in the Roman Empire and the revolt against Nero by Julius Vindex, the prefect of Gallia Celtica (*War* 4:440; Dio Cass. 63.22ff.; Plut. *Galb.* 4 ff.). He decided to pursue his campaign in Judea more vigorously, lest his efforts be curtailed by instability elsewhere in the empire. At the first sign of spring in 68 CE, he moved the main body of the army from Caesarea to Antipatris. He attacked the toparchy of Thamna, and continued to Lydda and Jamnia, two districts that he had already subdued (*War* 4:130). Next he advanced into the territory of Emmaus, where he left the legion V Macedonica garrisoned, while the rest of his forces he moved to the province of Betholetepha (*War* 4:445; cf. Pliny *Nat. Hist.* 5.70 [cf. *War* 3:55]; Beit Nattif). He razed this settlement and the surrounding area on "the outskirts of Idumea," he built fortresses, and he captured two villages in the heart of Idumea: Betogabris and Caphartobas (Kh. ᶜAtraba; *War* 4:447).

Having subdued the region of southern Judea, western and central Idumea, Vespasian returned with his remaining forces to Emmaus. From here he entered Samaria,

> ...passing Neapolis or, as the natives call it, Mabartha (Nablus; Pliny *Nat. Hist.* 5.69 [Mamortha]), he descended to Coreae ... he reached Jericho, where he was joined by Trajan [father of the future emperor], one of his generals, with the force which he had led from Perea, all the country beyond the Jordan being now subjugated. (*War* 4:449–450)

Vespasian established camps at Jericho and Adida, "placing in each a garrison composed jointly of Romans and [foreign] auxiliaries" (*War* 4:486). His strategy now had Jerusalem hemmed in on every side. The Roman returned to Caesarea to make final preparations for the assault on Jerusalem, when he received word of the death of Nero (9 June 68 CE). With the death of the emperor, Vespasian lost the authority to wage war. He would have to wait until Nero's successor renewed his instructions to subdue the insurrection in Judea (*War* 4: 491).

In Rome a succession of emperors led to continued instability and caused the campaign of Vespasian in Judea to remain inactive for almost a year (*War* 4:491–502). On the Jewish side, developments were hardly at a standstill. The lull in the Roman advance allowed another rebel movement to emerge, led by Simon son of Giora, a native of Gerasa (*War* 4:503; cf. 2:521). Earlier he had been relieved of his command and expelled from Acrabatene by Ananus the high priest. He had joined ranks with the *sicarii* at Masada (*War* 2:652–654); but when he got word of the death of Ananus, he returned to the hill country to continue his campaign of insurgency and terror. Offering freedom to slaves and rewards for those already free, he soon drew a considerable force comprised of unsavory elements.

> He now overran not only the province of Acrabatene but the whole district extending to greater Idumea.... His objective was evident; he was training his force and making all these preparations for an attack on Jerusalem. (*War* 4:511–513)

The leadership in Jerusalem recognized the looming threat and faced him in battle. "Simon met them and in the ensuing fight killed many of them and drove the remainder into the city" (*War* 4:514). Unsure of his forces, however, he did not continue immediately to Jerusalem, but turned his attention to Idumea.

> The chieftains of Idumea hastily mustered from the country their most efficient troops, numbering about twenty-five thousand, and, leaving the mass of the population to protect their property against incursions of the *sicarii* of Masada, met Simon at the frontier. There he fought them and, after a battle lasting all day, left the field neither victor nor vanquished; he then withdrew to Nain and the Idumeans disbanded to their homes. (*War* 4:516–517)

Through force and trickery Simon was eventually able to gain control of Idumea. "Just as a forest in the wake of locusts may be seen stripped quite bare, so in the rear of Simon's army nothing remained but a desert" (*War* 4:536). The zealots in Jerusalem were afraid to fight Simon again, choosing instead to kidnap his wife and use her as a hostage to forestall his aggression. Although the zealots in Jerusalem in due course released his wife in answer to his threats, he remained encamped outside of the city walls determined to gain entrance.

Inside of the city, tyranny and treachery led to further division in the insurgency. Followers of Eleazar son of Simon (*War* 2:564; 4:225) together with Idumeans among them, mutinied and drove John and his contingent from the inner courts of the Temple (*War* 4: 567). John was preparing to counterattack, when the people led by the high priest Matthias (cf. *War* 5:527) invited Simon into the city to put an end to John's tyrannical rule. Josephus paints a picture of chaos and carnage that plunged Jerusalem into despair (*War* 4:577–584). Rather than preparing for the inevitable Roman attack, the factions fought and killed each other, all the time weakening the defense of Jerusalem (*War* 5:5–26).

After the succession of Vitellius, Vespasian determined that he himself was more qualified to be emperor. In a quick-paced series of events, Roman armies in the east pledged their support to the Roman general. By December 69 CE, "on reaching Alexandria Vespasian was greeted by the good news from Rome and by embassies of congratulations from every quarter of the world, now his own" (*War* 4:656). He was anxious to return to Rome, but before he left he attended to the unfinished business of Judea. He delegated his son Titus to command the legions in the assault on Jerusalem (*War* 4:658). The new commander set out with select forces by way of Pelusium, Rhinocorura and Raphia, "at which city Syria begins" (*War* 4: 662). He continued along the Philistine coast through Gaza, Ascalon, Jamnia, and then Joppa. From here he returned to Caesarea where he began to organize his forces for the assault on Jerusalem.

Titus now commanded his father's three legions still garrisoned in Judea, together with the legion XII Fulminata, which was returned to Judea after having been shamed under Cestius at the outset of the conflict (*War* 5:41). Titus approached Jerusalem from the north ascending into the hill country of southern Samaria to the toparchy of Gophna (*War* 5:50). Vespasian had previously subdued this region and troops were already garrisoned there. Turning south along the watershed route, they set out at dawn and after a full day's march camped at "the Valley of Thorns" near Gibeah, birthplace of Saul (Tell el-Fûl; *War* 5:51; Eus. *Onom*. 70:11–12).

Near disaster struck the Roman assault when Titus, who was on reconnaissance with a small company, got into trouble (*War* 5:50–66). He and his men found themselves cut off from the main body of the army near Psephinus' Tower (*War* 5:55, 133, 147, 159) and under attack by a Jewish contingent. The Romans were barely able to fight their way through to their comrades. In the evening, Titus was joined by the legion V Macedonica recently arrived from Emmaus. Titus edged closer to the outer walls of Jerusalem, moving his base camp to Mount Scopus, "from which was obtained the first view of the city and the grand pile of the temple gleaming afar" (*War* 5:67). The commander placed the legions XII Fulminata and XV Apollinaris with him on Mount Scopus, the legion V Macedonica to guard his rear, and the legion X Fretensis, which just arrived from Jericho to set up camp on the Mount of Olives, overlooking Jerusalem from the east.

As the legion X Fretensis was fortifying its position on the Mount of Olives, it was surprised by the Jewish partisans who struck suddenly in a sortie with fanatical fervor (*War* 5:75–76). Fighting was fierce, and it was only Titus' personal bravery that prevented the Roman legion from being routed. This and other skirmishes were only the precursor to the real battle, when the Romans would mount an assault against Jerusalem.

Infighting continued among the three-sided insurgency with Simon in the upper and lower city, John in the outer courts of the Temple and on the Ophel, and Eleazar in the inner precincts (*War* 5: 5–12). At Passover, John's men disguised themselves as pilgrims to bring offerings into the inner precincts of the Temple. Their real intent was to smuggle weapons into the inner precincts. They surprised Eleazar's men and took control of the entire temple area. "The sedition, hitherto of a tripartite character, was thus again reduced to two factions" (*War* 5:105).

*Seal with emblem of the legion X Fretensis.*

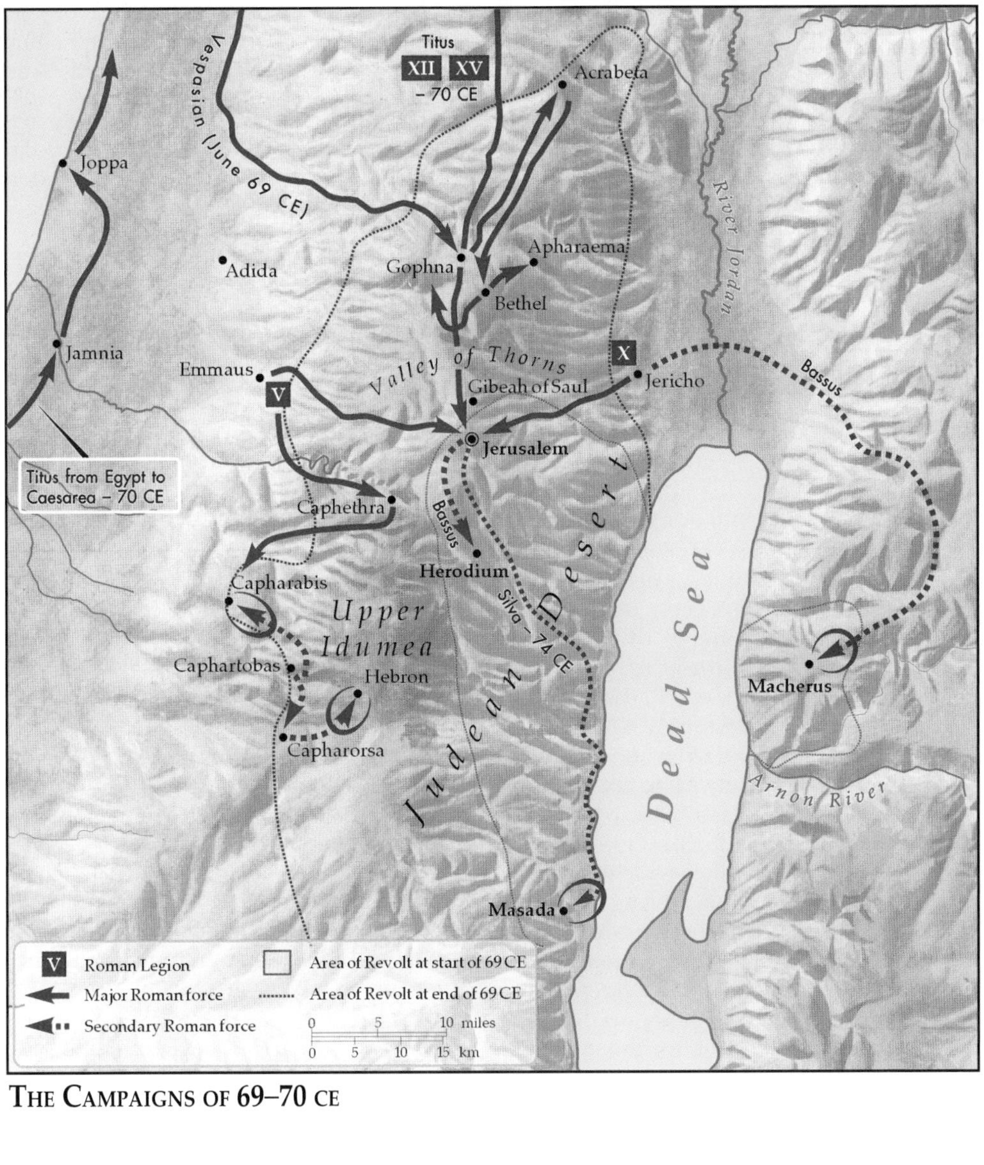


**The Campaigns of 69–70 CE**

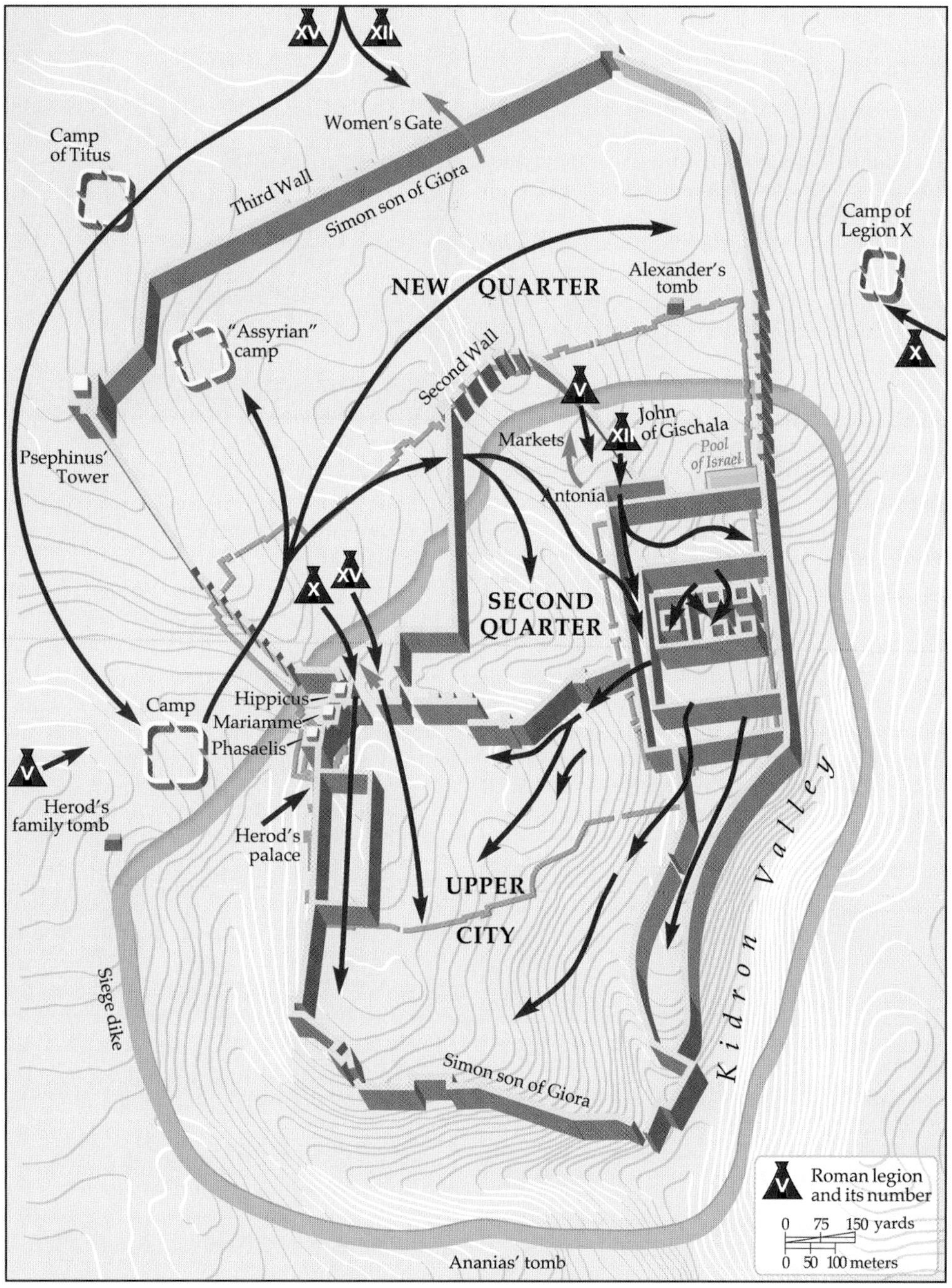


**The Siege of Jerusalem in 70 CE**

Titus threw himself into final preparations for the Roman offensive. Surrounded on three sides by deep valleys, Jerusalem has historically been most vulnerable from its northern approach. After examining the situation with the walls, Titus determined "to make the assault opposite the tomb of John the high priest" (i.e. Hyrcanus; *War* 5: 259, 304, 356; 6:169),

> . . . for here the first line of ramparts was lower ground, and the second was disconnected with it, the builders having neglected to fortify the sparsely populated portions of the new town, while there was an easy approach to the third wall, through which his intention was to capture the upper town, and so by way of Antonia, the temple. (*War* 5:260)

The Jews tried to thwart the workmen building the earthen ramparts, while the Romans protected them with catapults. Watchmen on the walls of Jerusalem cried out warnings to the people, who happened in harm's way. In a little-noticed testimony to the vernacular use of Hebrew on the streets of first-century Jerusalem, Josephus preserves a confused Greek rendering of their cry, "the son is coming" (*War* 5:272). His report unquestionably attests to the Hebrew warning "Stone's coming!" The play in Hebrew between *eben* (stone) and *haben* (the son) is well known, and even attested in the Gospels (e.g. Lk 3:8, 20:9–18). More importantly, the use of Hebrew in a time of peril to warn the general population indicates that Hebrew spoken by the watchmen was understood by everyone. It is of no little significance that this Hebrew word play is not possible in Aramaic. Consequently, our story is yet another piece of evidence that refutes the persistent scholarly opinion that *only* Aramaic was spoken on the streets of first-century Judea.

The Romans used battering rams to penetrate the outer wall, which from the attackers' perspective was reckoned the "first wall," but chronologically and from the perspective of the Jewish defenders within Jerusalem, the "third wall," begun by Agrippa I. After fifteen days, the wall was breached and the Romans occupied the area outside of the second wall (*War* 5:302). Five days later, this wall was also breached (*War* 5:331). The initial entry by the Romans into the city was repulsed, but four days later they secured the second wall (*War* 5:334–342). Josephus now appealed to his countrymen to abandon the rebellion (*War* 5:362–419).

Next the Roman commander assigned each of the four legions to build a rampart (*War* 5:356). Two were constructed against the upper city and two against the Antonia. However, these were undermined by the men of Simon son of Giora and John of Gischala, who guarded the upper city and Antonia, respectively (*War* 5:467–472). They dug tunnels under the earthen ramparts that were supported by wooden posts. The tunnels were then set ablaze and the ramparts collapsed. Titus' response was to ring Jerusalem with a stone wall and to cut off all supplies. Starvation set in. Those who tried to escape in desperation were either crucified or mutilated and returned to the city (*War* 5:512–518). "The soldiers out of rage and hatred amused themselves by nailing their prisoners in different postures; and so great was their number, that space could not be found for the crosses nor crosses for the bodies" (*War* 5:451).

Four new ramparts were built against the Antonia in twenty-one days. In early July, the Romans occupied the Antonia and drove John and the zealot forces back into the temple precincts. To this point, daily sacrifices in the Temple had continued, in spite of the surrounding travail of war and famine. According to Josephus (*War* 6:94) and rabbinical tradition (m. *Taʿan.* 4:6), sacrifices now ceased on the $17^{th}$ of the Hebrew month of Tammuz.

Titus now tightened his stranglehold on the Temple Mount, once again building ramparts in order to breach the massive walls surrounding the sanctuary. This time, however, the battering rams proved ineffective, so the Romans elected to breach the gates (*War* 6:220–235). According to Josephus, orders were given to preserve the Temple, but this may have been the historian's attempt to exonerate Titus from the blame of destroying the legendary structure (*War* 6:237–243). In the heat of battle, the Temple was set ablaze and soon was engulfed in flames. The Romans killed all who fell into their hands, while John of Gischala and his men fled to the upper city to join Simon son of Giora. Josephus records that the Temple was destroyed on the $10^{th}$ of Ab (*War* 6:250), at variance with rabbinical tradition that it fell on the $9^{th}$ of Ab (m. *Taʿan.* 4:6; cf. b. *Taʿan.* 29a; Dio Cass. 66.7.2).

Titus called for Simon and John to surrender, but they refused (*War* 6:323–353). So, the Roman began the methodical task of constructing ramparts, one against Herod's palace in the upper city and one against the Xystus. In comparison to the spirited defense of the Temple, the upper city fell with little resistance. After the lengthy five-month siege, the soldiers pillaged the city, murdering and looting as they went. John and Simon were captured. The former begged for his life and was imprisoned for the remainder of his life. Simon son of Giora was put in chains and taken to Rome for the triumph (*War* 6:433). Most of the city now lay in ruins. Only a portion of the first wall and the three towers were left as a testimony to the former strength of the city and the Roman power that brought the Jewish resistance to its knees.

## The Aftermath of the Revolt

Although Jerusalem had fallen, Jewish resistance to Rome continued in the outlying areas. Titus left the legion X Fretensis in Jerusalem, while he stationed the legion XII Fulminata, "beside the Euphrates near the confines of Armenia and Cappadocia," and retained the legions V Macedonica and XV Apollinaris with himself in Alexandria, Egypt (*War* 7.17–19). Josephus remarks that only the three fortresses of Herodium, Macherus and Masada remained in rebel hands. Responsibility for dealing with these would now fall to the new governor of Judea, Lucilius Bassus.

**The Siege of Macherus**. Herodium does not appear to have put up much resistance. Few details of the Roman siege are given, only that its garrison surrendered (*War* 7.163). Lucilius now turned his attention to the more serious fortifications at Macherus and Masada. Of the former, Pliny observed that Macherus ranked with Jerusalem in its natural defenses (Pliny *Nat. Hist.* 5.17). The site of Macherus (Qal$^{c}$at el-Mishneqeh) is located between Wâdī Zerqa Ma$^{c}$in and Wâdī Mûjib (Arnon). Josephus paints a vivid picture of its formidable setting.

> For the site that is fortified is itself a rocky eminence, rising to so great a height that on that account alone its reduction would be difficult, while nature had further contributed to render it inaccessible. For it is entrenched on all sides within ravines of a depth baffling to the eye, not easy to traverse and utterly impossible to bank up. The valley which hems it in on the west extends to sixty furlongs [3.5 mi./5 km], ending at the Lake Asphaltitis; and somewhere in this direction Macherus itself reaches its highest commanding peak. The ravines on the north and south, though less extensive than this, are equally impracticable for purposes of attack. That on the east is found to be no less than a hundred cubits in depth and is terminated by a mountain facing Macherus. (*War* 7:165–170)

Its natural defenses had earlier attracted the attention of Alexander Jannaeus, who Josephus reports was the first to fortify the mountain (*War* 7:171). It was used by Aristobulus II and his son, Alexander, in their rebellion against the Romans (*Ant.* 14: 83). So, after their insurrection was subdued, Gabinius demolished the fortress to prevent its use again in rebelling against Rome (*War* 7:171).

Herod the Great saw the strategic value of the fortress and rebuilt Macherus as part of his line of fortresses on the eastern front (*War* 7:172). After Herod's death, Macherus was awarded to his son Antipas. The fortress marked the frontier of his tetrarchy in Perea (*War* 3:46), and as we have noted Josephus erroneously reports that Antipas executed John the Baptist at Macherus (*Ant.* 18:119). The execution of John, who spoke out against the shame brought by Herod Antipas upon his estranged wife—the daughter of Aretas IV the Nabatean king, who went to war with Antipas over the matter—on the very frontier of the Nabatean kingdom, makes little sense.

Excavations in recent years have confirmed Josephus' historical presentation of the occupation of Macherus. Archaeological evidence indicates that the site was not settled before the Hasmonean period, nor after its conquest in 72 CE. Josephus reports that while the Romans built an embankment around the desert fortress,

> . . . the Jewish party shut up within now separated themselves from their alien colleagues and, regarding the latter as mere rabble, compelled them to remain in the lower town and to bear the first brunt, while they themselves seized and held the fortress above. (*War* 7:191–192)

The Romans broke through and burned the lower portion of the fortress, but only conquered the upper fortress through a ruse. They captured a young Jewish defender named Eleazar and threatened to crucify him, if the rebels did not surrender.

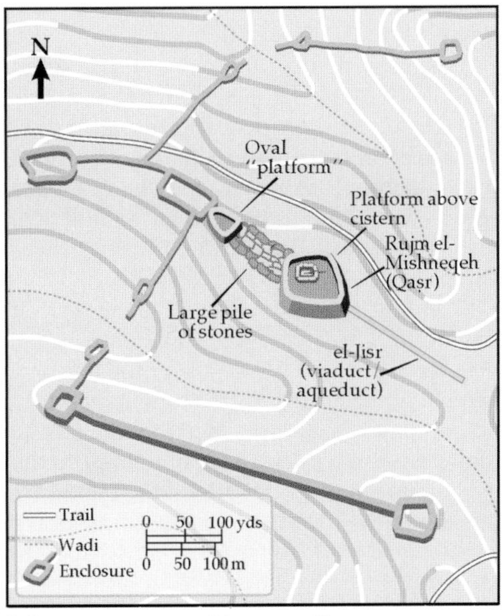


**Macherus with Roman Siege Installations**

The defenders agreed to abandon the fortress, if Eleazar and the other defenders were permitted to abandon the fortress unpunished. After their departure, the Romans systematically dismantled the Herodian fortifications.

**The Fall of Masada**. The final stronghold for the revolt stood on the mountain-fortress of Masada. The foundations for this daunting fortification were laid in the days of the Hasmoneans, and Herod himself used it for the safekeeping of his family (*Ant.* 14:361–362; *War* 1:264, 266). Herod enhanced its position, perhaps as part of the paranoia that marked his personality.

> For it is said that Herod furnished this fortress as a refuge for himself, suspecting a twofold danger: peril on the one hand from the Jewish people, lest they should depose him and restore their former dynasty to power [i.e. the Hasmoneans]; the greater and more serious from Cleopatra, the queen of Egypt. For she never concealed her intention, but was constantly importuning Antony, urging him to slay Herod, and praying him to confer on her the throne of Judea. (*War* 7:300–301)

Of particular note was Herod's three-tiered palace that cascaded down the northern precipice of the mountain and the sophisticated water-collection system (*War* 7: 291) that later served the rebel community, which occupied the fortress during the revolt.

At the outbreak of hostilities the *sicarii* overran the Roman garrison that had been stationed on Masada (*War* 2:408). They now represented the last holdout of the Jewish revolt against Rome. In the intervening years following the capture of Macherus, Lucilius Bassus had died and been succeeded as governor by Flavius Silva,

> . . . [who] seeing the whole country now subjugated by the Roman arms, with the exception of one fortress still in revolt, concentrated all forces in the district and marched against it. This fortress is called Masada; and the Sicarii who had occupied it had at their head a man of influence named Eleazar. He was a descendant of Judas who, as we have previously stated, induced multitudes of Jews to refuse to enroll themselves, when Quirinius was sent as censor of Judea. (*War* 7:252–253; cf. Lk 2:1–3; Acts 5:37)

The Romans' first order of business was to surround entirely the mountain with a circumvallation wall that still stands today. "[Silva] established garrisons at the most suitable points, threw up a wall all round the fortress, to make it difficult for any of the besieged to escape, and posted sentinels to guard it" (*War* 7:275).

The challenge now for Flavius Silva was how to ascend the summit without the certain danger his soldiers would meet on the severe incline. The sides of the mountain are nearly sheer vertical on the north, west and south, rising almost 1,000 feet (c. 300 m) above the plains alongside the Dead Sea. As Josephus describes, access was possible only by two trails on the eastern

## The Fall of Masada (73 ce)

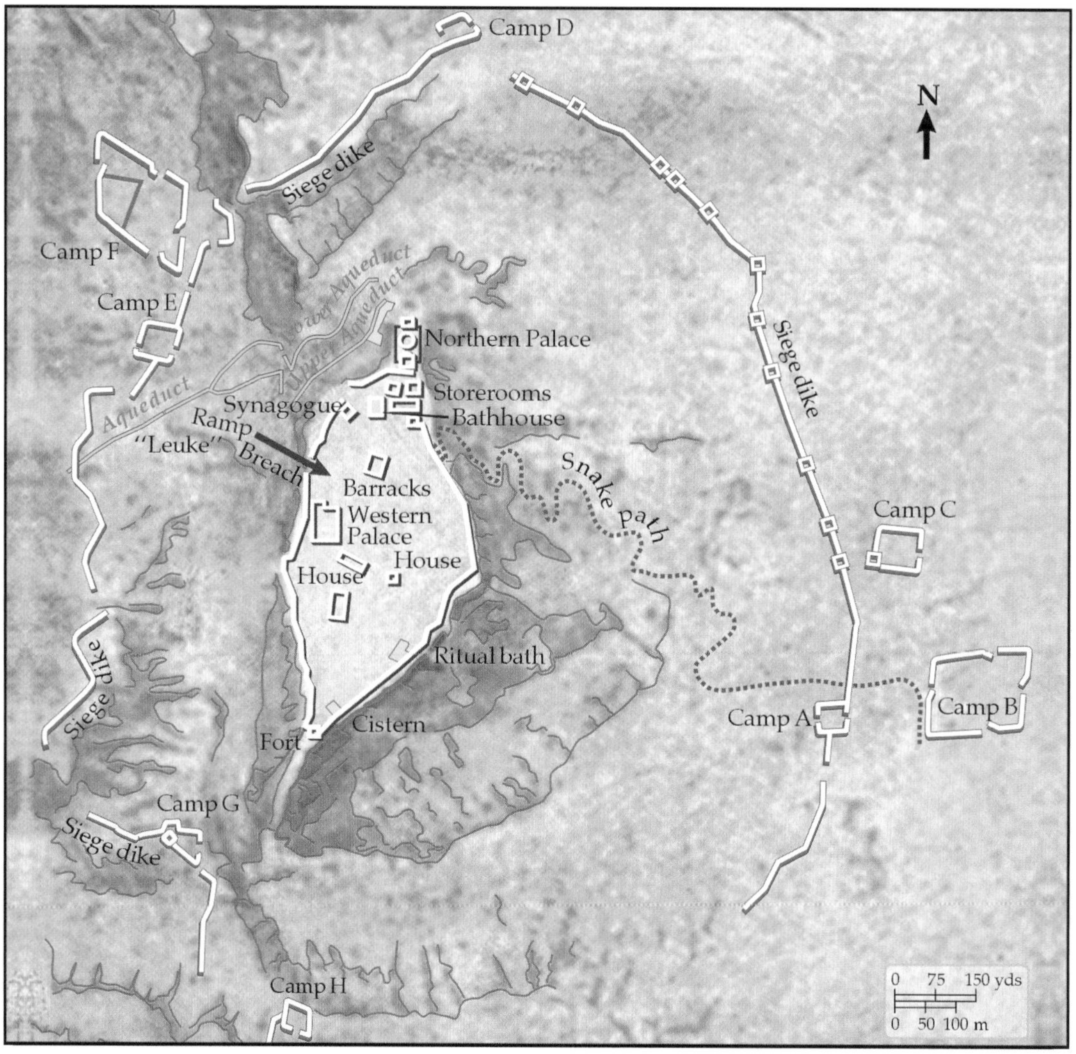

*Ostracon inscribed "ben Ya'ir," one of the "lots" used by the last defenders of Masada. This particular lot may have belonged to Eleazar son of Jair, commander of the Sicarii.*

and western faces of the mountain.

> Of these tracks one leads from the Lake Asphaltitis on the east, the other, by which the approach is easier, from the west. The former they call the snake, seeing a resemblance to the reptile in its narrowness and continual windings. ... One traversing this route must firmly plant each foot alternately. Destruction faces him; for on either side yawn chasms so terrific as to daunt the hardiest. (*War* 7:282–283)

The Roman general determined that there was one point of vulnerability for the fortress. The mountain's less severe western slope (*War* 7:305: White Promontory) allowed the construction of a siege ramp on which the Romans could employ a battering ram to breach the walls of Masada.

> Working with a will and a multitude of hands, they raised a solid bank to the height of two hundred cubits ... on top of it was constructed a platform of great stones fitted closely together. ... Silva, having further provided himself with a great battering-ram, ordered it to be directed without intermission against the wall, and having, though with difficulty, succeeded in effecting a breach, brought it down in ruins. (*War* 7:306–310)

Eleazar had anticipated that the battering ram would break through the stone walls, so he prepared a counter-defense, an inner wall constructed from wooden beams and earth.

> For it was pliable and calculated to break the force of the impact, having been constructed as follows. Great beams were laid lengthwise and contiguous and joined at the extremities; of these there were two parallel rows a wall's breadth apart, and the intermediate space was filled with earth. (*War* 7:311–312)

When Silva realized the counter-measures taken by the *sicarii*, he saw that it would be easier to assail the wood and earthen wall by burning its support beams. So, he ordered his soldiers to throw burning torches against the wooden wall.

A change in the direction of the wind caught the adjacent siege engines on fire. The zealots interpreted this as an act of divine deliverance, but their renewed hope was shattered when the winds shifted again, "and flung the flames against the wall, which now through and through was all ablaze" (*War* 7:318).

Realizing that the Roman conquest of the summit was merely a matter of time, Eleazar is reported by Josephus to have given a lengthy and impassioned speech to his compatriots. He appealed to them to take their own lives, rather than to submit to the ignominies sure to be afflicted on them by the Romans. While the historical accuracy of the words of Eleazar is certainly open to question, Josephus' purpose in the speech was to present the mind-set of those who occupied Masada. In that light, he presents the impetus for the revolt, "We determined neither to serve the Romans nor any other save God, for He alone is man's true and righteous Lord" (*War* 7:323). The religious fervor attributed by Josephus to the rebels is exemplified in their transformation of a pre-existing structure into a synagogue on Masada.

According to Josephus' account, which is the sole testimony we possess apart from the archaeological evidence, the head of each family took the lives of his loved ones. Ten men were then chosen by lots to take the lives of these men. Finally, one man was selected to take the lives of the other nine, and lastly his own. The defenders of Masada set the palaces ablaze, denying the Romans the material reward of their victory, and leaving only the food in storage as a sign that they had willingly died, and not for want. When the Romans ascended the summit, they found the victims and the destruction that marked the end of the insurrection.

> The fortress being thus taken, [Flavius Silva] left a garrison on the spot and himself departed with his army to Caesarea. For not an enemy remained throughout the country, the whole having now been subdued by this protracted war, which had been felt by many even in the remotest parts, exposing them to risk of disorder. (*War* 7:407–408)

## CHAPTER TWENTY

# THE BAR KOCHBA REVOLT

## 132 TO 135 CE

Sixty years after the fall of Jerusalem and the destruction of the Temple, hope stirred again among the Jewish people that they might shake off Roman domination. In contrast to the detailed eyewitness account of Josephus to the First Jewish Revolt, the literary witnesses to the Bar Kochba Revolt are meager and none are firsthand accounts to the revolt. Our literary sources for reconstructing the events of the Bar Kochba Revolt rest primarily on the witness of the third-century CE *Roman History* of Dio Cassius, the church father Eusebius, and scattered rabbinic testimony to the years in question. In 1952, documents and artifacts from the period of the Bar Kochba Revolt were discovered in Wâdī Murabbaʿat in the vicinity of the Dead Sea.

In 1961–1962, additional finds within the Judean Desert provided further information from the time of the revolt, particularly a cache of letters discovered in a cave in the cliffs of Naḥal Ḥever, which came from Bar Kochba himself. While the sources, both literary and material, are fragmentary for providing a detailed account of the revolt and those impacted by it, the Bar Kochba Revolt apparently involved and affected a greater number of participants than the First Jewish Revolt chronicled by Josephus (cf. Dio Cass. 69, 14:1–3; Eus. *Hist. eccl.* 4, 6:1; Jer. *Commentary on Daniel* 11: 24; j. *Taʿan.* 4:69a–b). Moreover, the fact that the revolt shares the name of its leader suggests the unique character of the revolt in which "a confederation of revolutionaries" amassed under the leadership of Shimʿon bar Kosiba (Bar Kochba).

One of the elusive questions at the center of the Bar Kochba Revolt is the cause for the rebellion. Here the historical sources differ. The *Historia Augusta* attributes it to Hadrian's ban on circumcision. Hadrian did ban castration, but the date of that prohibition is uncertain. The later relaxation of the prohibition regarding the case of Jewish circumcision by Antoninus Pius, while maintaining the ban on castration, lends credence to the notion that his predecessor had included Jewish circumcision in his prohibition.

Hadrian's prohibition expressed a general Roman revulsion regarding castration and was not directly aimed at Jewish practice. Nevertheless, it is understandable that it would be remembered in that way, in light of the suffering that soon followed. Statements in the rabbinical sources by those who lived at the time of the revolt, suggesting the need for secrecy in matters of circumcision "in a time of danger," indicate that the prohibition preceded the revolt, and was not generated as a means for punishing the Jewish people for their rebellion (cf. m. *Šabb.* 19:1; b. *Šabb.* 130a; b. *Yebam.* 46a–b; *Gerim* 1.6; m. *ʾAbot* 3:12).

*Bar Kochba letter found in Wâdī Murabbaʿat.*

Hadrian visited Palestine in 130 CE on his way from Arabia to Egypt. In acts of typical imperial benevolence he made several contributions to the province. A road was built connecting Jerusalem through Jericho to Trajan's trunk road from Damascus to Petra, and another from Jerusalem to Gaza. At Caesarea, the emperor ordered the establishment of a Hadrianeum. According to Epiphanius, he also constructed a Hadrianeum in Tiberias (cf. Epiph. *Adv. haer.* 30.12.2).

Yet, according to Dio Cassius, Hadrian's most ambitious contributions were to Jerusalem, and it is these efforts that the Roman author cites as the cause for the insurrection.

> At Jerusalem he founded a city in place of the one that had been razed to the ground, naming it Aelia Capitolina, and on the site of the temple of the god he raised a new temple to Jupiter. This brought on a war of no slight importance nor brief duration, for the Jews deemed it intolerable that foreign races should be settled in their city and foreign religious rites planted there. (Dio Cass. 69.12.1–2)

While there is no reason to question the historical event of Hadrian's foundation of Aelia Capitolina and a new temple to Jupiter, Dio's presentation of the reason for the Jewish revolt, that "the Jews deemed it intolerable that foreign races should be settled in their city and foreign religious rites planted there," seems untenable. Since Titus' conquest of Jerusalem in 70 CE, the legion X Fretensis had been garrisoned within the confines of Jerusalem. A Roman presence in the Holy City after sixty years can hardly have been the cause for sudden insurrection. Moreover, almost certainly foreign rites would have accompanied a Roman presence in Jerusalem. After such a long period of foreign residence within Jerusalem together with pagan rites, it does not seem the most likely cause for rebellion.

It seems, rather, that the provocation in Hadrian's new initiative was its consequence for the Jewish hopes that the Temple would one day be restored. The establishment of a Roman city with its pagan temple on the most sacred site in Jewish faith would have brought a strong response as one hears in the echoes of the Jewish hopes in the Epistle of Barnabas (usually dated 132–135 CE) and its interpretation of the Septuagintal rendering of Isaiah 49:17: "Lo, they who destroyed this temple shall themselves build it" (cf. 1QIsa$^{a}$). The epistle continues, "That is happening now. For owing to the war it was destroyed by the enemy; at present even the servants of the enemy will build it up again" (Ep. Barn. 16:3–4).

These lines probably reflect Jewish hopes aroused by Hadrian's intentions to rebuild the city of Jerusalem, and the corollary Jewish hope for the restoration of the Temple. Both the dreams for Jerusalem and

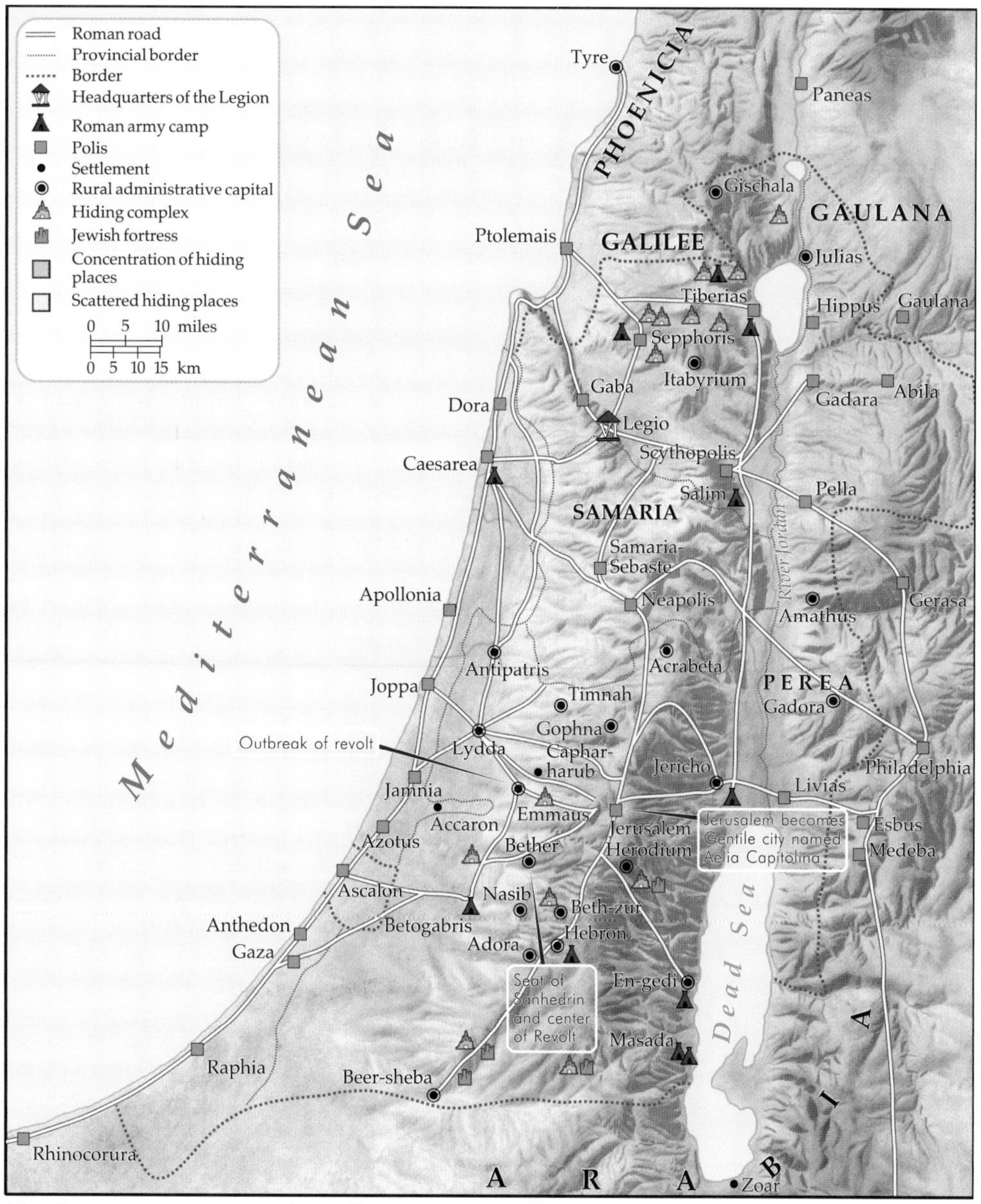


**The Beginnings of the Bar Kochba Revolt**

the rebuilt Jewish Temple were jeopardized by Hadrian's plans for Jerusalem. The strong connection between the Jewish Temple and the Bar Kochba Revolt is demonstrated in the coinage minted by the rebels. The large tetradrachmas bear an imprint of the façade of the Temple, at a time when the Temple Mount stood in ruins, indicating the rebels' desire to see the sacred mountain once again display a Jewish temple. Additionally, the inscription on these particular coins bore the legend "Jerusalem," suggesting the strong connection between the Jewish rebels' cause and their desire for the Holy City. Jerusalem, in fact, seems to have fallen into the hands of the Jewish insurgents for a brief period of time during the revolt (cf. App. *Syr.* 50); however, the Romans wrested the city back from the Jewish leaders and subsequently banned Jews from even entering into the region around the city (Eus. *Hist. eccl.* 4, 6:4 citing Ariston of Pella).

Eusebius posits Hadrian's efforts to create a pagan city and temple in Jerusalem, as well as the renaming of the city Aelia Capitolina, after the revolt in order to punish the Jewish people for their rebellion (Eus. *Hist. eccl.* 4.6.4). The mishnaic tractate *Taᶜanit* (4:6) apparently supports Eusebius' order of events. The passage lists five disasters that befell the people of Israel on the ninth of the month of Ab, including the destruction of the First and Second Temples; the final two disasters listed are "the capture of Bether and the plowing of the city" (i.e., Jerusalem).

Nevertheless, Hadrian's intentions for Jerusalem fit well with his benefaction for the entire region prior to the insurrection. The two perspectives of Dio and Eusebius need not conflict. Dio presents Hadrian's intentions prior to the outbreak of hostilities, and Eusebius to their eventual completion after the revolt had been subdued. Moreover, the presentation of Dio and the *Historia Augusta* likewise complement, for Hadrian's efforts to advance Hellenization in the region were not targeted at the Jewish people. His laws on the prohibition of castration (and thus circumcision) and his benefaction were not limited to the Jews; however, as the historical sources attest, Hadrian's actions may have had unintended consequences.

Dio comments that while Hadrian was on his visit in the province, the impulse for insurrection was restrained. This also seems to be the impression gained from rabbinic stories of positive encounters with the Roman emperor (e.g. *Midr. Gen. Rab.* 10,3; 28,3; 78, 1; *Midr. Lev. Rab.* 18,1; b. *Ḥul.* 59b-60a; b. *Šabb.* 119a, 152a). His departure, however, brought open rebellion.

> So long, indeed, as Hadrian was close by in Egypt and again in Syria, they remained quiet, save in so far as they purposely made of poor quality such weapons as they were called upon to furnish, in order that the Romans might reject them and they themselves might thus have the use of them; but when he went farther away, they openly revolted.
>
> (Dio Cass. 69.12.2)

The name of the leader of the revolt varies in the ancient witnesses. In fact, Dio never mentions the name of the Jewish leader; however, Eusebius provides his nickname:

> The Jews were at that time led by a certain Bar Chochebas, which means "star," a man who was murderous and a bandit, but relied on his name, as if dealing with slaves, and claimed to be a luminary who had come down to them from heaven to give light to the oppressed by miracles.
>
> (Eus. *Hist. eccl.* 4, 6:2)

Eusebius reflects familiarity with the popular title of this Jewish leader, Bar Kochba (i.e., "son of the star"), an epithet according to rabbinical literature conferred upon this individual by the second-century CE *tanna* Rabbi Akiva. According to a tradition passed on by Rabbi Shimon bar Yoḥai, Rabbi Akiva sought to interpret "a star will go forth from Jacob" (Num 24:17) as "Kosiba goes forth from Jacob" and when he saw bar Kosiba he said, "This is the King Messiah." Yohanan ben Torta responded to Akiva's proclamation by stating "Akiva, grass will grow from your cheeks and still the Son of David will not have come" (j. *Taᶜan.* 68:4).

Akiva's ascription of the moniker Bar Kochba to this figure stems according to the rabbinical tradition from the ancient prophecy in Numbers 24:17: "I see him, but not now; I behold him, but not near. A star will come out of Jacob; a scepter will rise out of Israel. He will crush the foreheads of Moab, the skulls of all the sons of Sheth." Akiva apparently verbalized popular sentiment concerning this figure, because one finds a star situated above the façade of the Temple on some of the tetradrachmas minted by Bar Kochba. Discovery of his correspondence from Naḥal Ḥever informs us that his actual name was Shimᶜon bar Kosiba. Incidentally, after the tragic events connected with the Bar Kochba Revolt and the devastation of the land of Israel, rabbinical literature offers a different play upon the name, identifying him as "son of the lie."

The appellation of the title "star" for

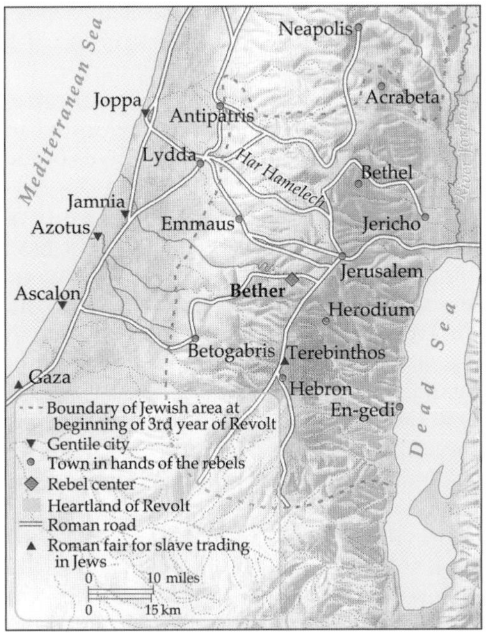


**The Third and Fourth Years of the Bar Kochba Revolt (133–134 CE)**

a messianic pretender revisits the use of Numbers 24:17 in the Dead Sea Scrolls to express their hope for a Redeemer figure. In a creative interpretation of Amos 9:11, the author of the Damascus Covenant employs Numbers 24:17 to introduce his redemptive figures.

> *The star* is the Interpreter of the Law who shall come to Damascus; as it is written, a Star shall come forth out of Jacob and a scepter shall rise out of Israel (Num 24:17). The scepter is the *Prince of the whole congregation,* and when he comes he shall smite all the children of Seth. (CD 7:19–21)

These titles express the redemptive hopes both for the Qumran Congregation and the people living in the days of Bar Kochba. Epithets such as "Star" and "Prince" were applied to messianic pretenders, who had yet to fulfill the expectations of the hoped-for messiah. Someone such as Rabbi Akiva could openly express his belief that Shimᶜon was the messiah. Such was usually not the course for the exalted individual himself.

Nevertheless, there is little question about Shimᶜon's acute self-awareness. As we witness in the passage from the Damascus Covenant, the title *nasi* was also applied to the redeemer. Routinely upon his coinage Bar Kosiba identified himself as Shimᶜon, Prince of Israel. The origins of the epithet *nasi* lie in the presentation of the redemptive figure in Ezekiel 12:10–13.

*Bar Kochba coin: on obverse, "Shimᶜon," and reverse, "of the Freedom of Jerusalem."*

In addition, documents from the time of Bar Kochba make it clear the rebellion's objective and Shimᶜon's role in that objective by proclaiming a new era: "For the redemption of Israel by Shimᶜon bar Kosiba, Prince of Israel." The incorporation of the façade of the Temple upon coins minted during the revolt, at a time when there existed no Temple in Jerusalem, further signals the expectation that Shimᶜon would lay the foundations for the new Temple in fulfillment of Zechariah's description of the future role for the Branch of David (see Zech 6:12–13).

Apart from shedding light upon Bar Kochba and the organization of his army and daily life in the land of Israel at the time of the revolt, the documents discovered in Wâdī Murabbaᶜat and Naḥal Ḥever provide important linguistic evidence as to the spoken and written languages prevalent within the land of Israel during the early second century CE. The documents discovered in Wâdī Murabbaᶜat and Naḥal Ḥever reflect a multilingual populace that communicated principally in Hebrew, Aramaic, and Greek. Of particular importance is the preservation of documents composed in Hebrew reflecting a colloquial, vernacular language akin to mishnaic Hebrew.

The Bar Kochba Revolt not only marked a shift in the population demographic of the land of Israel from the second century CE onward, but it also marked a significant linguistic transition within the land of Israel. The finds from around the Judean Desert connected with the Bar Kochba Revolt indicate the persistence of a mishnaic Hebrew dialect among the spoken languages of the land. In the aftermath of the Bar Kochba Revolt, the Jewish population of the land of Israel was decimated. Many Jews who previously resided in the land emigrated to the Diaspora (cf. Just. *Dial.* 1). At the same time Jews, principally from Babylon, began immigrating to the land of Israel together with a greater influx of non-Jewish peoples. This population shift significantly marked the linguistic register in the land of Israel.

Mishnaists view 200 CE as a watershed in the linguistic topography of the land of Israel. Prior to 200 CE, tannaitic Hebrew held the position of a colloquial language used by the Jewish people living within the land of Israel for both religious instruction and daily activities and interactions. After 200 Hebrew became principally used in the synagogue and rabbinical academies with Aramaic becoming the principal language used for religious instruction and daily interactions. This linguistic transition is further reflected in the appearance of Aramaic Targums within the synagogues of the land of Israel only after the Bar Kochba Revolt beginning in the Usha period (c. 140 CE) onward. Apparently prior to the revolt the inhabitants of the land of Israel understood the Scriptures in Hebrew without their translation into Aramaic (cf. Lk 4:16–21; t. *Sukkah* 2:11). The appearance of the Aramaic Targums within the synagogues coincides with the immigration of Jews from Babylon, who most likely brought their Aramaic Bibles (i.e. Targums) with them and the decline of spoken Hebrew in the aftermath of the Bar Kochba Revolt due to the population shifts.

The Bar Kochba Revolt also affected the character and nature of the Christian movement residing in Jerusalem. Eusebius reports that prior to the Bar Kochba Revolt all of the bishops of the Christian community in Jerusalem had been Jews, as well as those who comprised that community:

> . . . up to the siege of the Jews by Hadrian the successions of bishops were fifteen in number. It is said that they were all Hebrews by origin.... For their whole church at that time consisted of Hebrews who had continued Christian from the Apostles down to the siege at the time when the Jews again rebelled from the Romans and were beaten in a great war [i.e., the Bar Kochba Revolt]. (Eus. *Hist. eccl.* 4, 5:2)

As a result of the revolt, Hadrian forbade Jews from coming within the vicinity of Jerusalem. His edict affected all Jews, including the followers of Jesus:

> Thus when the city came to be bereft of the nation of the Jews, and its ancient inhabitants had completely perished, it was colonized by foreigners, and the Roman city which afterwards arose changed its

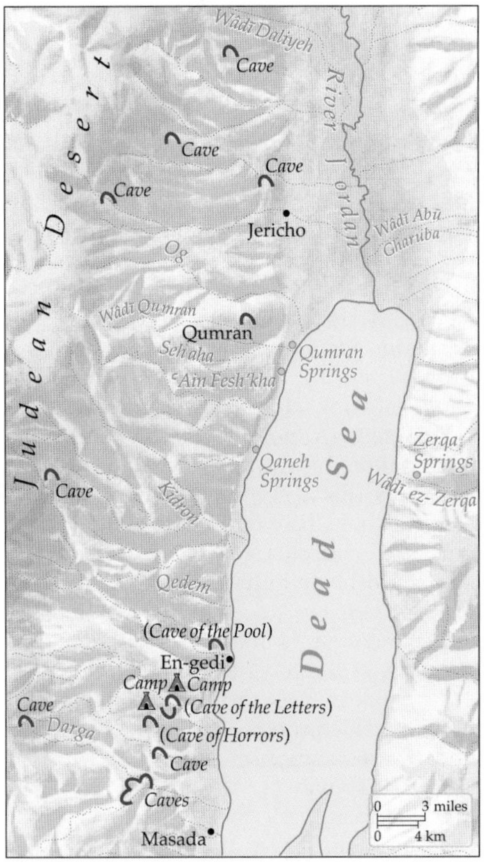


**The Bar Kochba Fighters in the Judean Desert Caves (135 CE)**

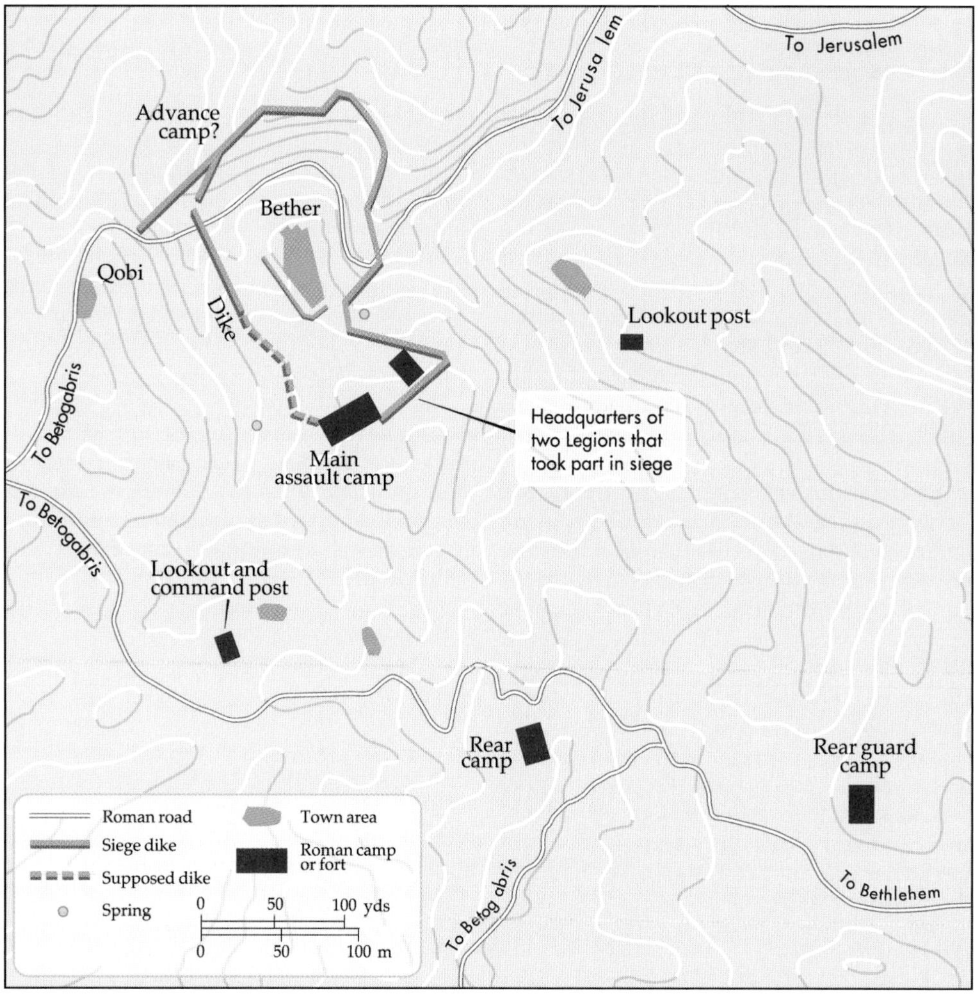


**The Siege of Bether**

name. . . . The church, too, in it was composed of Gentiles, and after the Jewish bishops the first who was appointed to minister to those there was Marcus. (Eus. *Hist. eccl.* 4, 6:4)

From this point on the Christian community in Jerusalem had a non-Jewish makeup; however, it is important to note the Jewish quality of the nascent Christian movement in Jerusalem prior to the revolt.

Bar Kochba's forces exploited the element of surprise and soon overran the Roman forces. "At first the Romans took no account of them. Soon, however, all Judea had been stirred up, and the Jews everywhere were showing signs of disturbance" (Dio Cass. 69.13.1). Although Dio does not give information of the full extent of Jewish advances, his testimony later that Julius Severus took "fifty of their most important outposts" indicates something of the extent of Bar Kochba's initial success (cf. Dio Cass. 69.14.3–4; *Midr. Lam. Rab.* ii,2,§4 [end]).

No mention is made in the historical accounts of the rebel capture of Jerusalem, but it is clear from the outset that the aim of the rebellion was the redemption of Israel and the restoration of Jerusalem with the Temple. Appian of Alexandria, who was a contemporary of these events, remarks of Jerusalem: "It was afterward rebuilt and Vespasian destroyed it again, and Hadrian did the same in our time" (App. *Syr.* 50). Other ancient witnesses make similar allusions (e.g. Just. *Dial.* 108.3). Hadrian's destruction of Jerusalem would not have been necessary if it had remained in Roman hands.

The documentary evidence suggests that the land functioned for two years under rebel administration. The measure of the initial rebel success was marked by the size of the Roman response and number of legions called into action against the revolt, the dispatch from Britain of Julius Severus, one of the leading Roman generals of his day, to lead the counter-offensive, and Hadrian's personal visit to the front in the midst of the war. Regarding the leadership of the campaign, Dio comments,

Then, indeed, Hadrian sent against them his best generals. The best of these was Julius Severus, who was dispatched from Britain, where he was governor, against the Jews. Severus did not venture to attack his opponents in the open at any one point, in view of their numbers and their desperation, but by intercepting small groups, thanks to the number of his soldiers and his under-officers, and by depriving them of food and shutting them up, he was able, rather slowly to be sure, but with comparatively little danger to crush, exhaust and exterminate them. Very few of them in fact survived. (Dio Cass. 69.13.2–3)

As Dio testifies, the Roman response was slow, but determined. His description of a campaign of deprivation eerily mirrors the setting discovered in "the Cave of Horrors." Soon the rebel campaign was relegated to guerrilla efforts in the hills and caves of the Judean wilderness.

In the writings from the caves we read the correspondence between Shimᶜon and his deputies. We also read of the religious fervor that was at the heart of the rebellion. Caravans of provisions were not allowed to travel on the Sabbath, and in the midst of the fighting there were still concerns for the celebration of Sukkoth. These sentiments contrast with the fury of the Roman soldiers. In a cave in Wâdī Murabbaᶜat the Hebrew Scriptures were found shredded by the Romans. Many of the fugitives died from starvation.

Eusebius describes the conclusion to the revolt at a previously little-known fortification, "the war reached its climax in the eighteenth year of Hadrian's reign (134–135 CE) at Bether, a very strong citadel not far from Jerusalem. It was a long siege, and the rebels were finally destroyed by starvation and thirst" (Eus. *Hist. eccl.* 4.6.3).

As for Bar Kochba, Eusebius concludes that "this instigator of Jews' madness paid the penalty he deserved." His meaning is clear that the leader of the revolt was captured and executed, although legendary depictions present Bar Kochba dying in battle.

The end of the insurrection found Judea thoroughly devastated. Dio reports that thousands died in the conflict, "and the number of those that perished by famine, disease and fire was past finding out. Thus, nearly the whole of Judea was a desert" (Dio Cass. 69.14.1). Innumerable Jews were sold as slaves at the annual market of the Terebinth at Hebron. Those who were not sold there were taken to Gaza and sold, or shipped to Egypt.

The large loss of life by the Romans made their victory bittersweet. Unlike Vespasian and Titus's victory sixty years before, on this occasion there would be no triumph, no *Judaea capta* coins, boasting of victory. The sober mood of the Romans at the conclusion of the revolt may be reflected in Dio's earlier testimony on the difficult state of affairs during the conflict. He records that Hadrian wrote a letter to the Senate on his visit to Palestine. In his opening the emperor voiced a particularly somber tone, which undoubtedly persisted to the end of the conflict.

Many Romans, moreover, perished in this war. Therefore Hadrian in writing to the senate did not employ the opening phrase commonly affected by the emperors, "If you and your children are in health, it is well; I and the legions are in health." (Dio Cass. 69.14.3)

# ABBREVIATIONS

## General

| | |
|---|---|
| BCE | before the common (or Christian) era |
| c. | circa |
| CE | common (or Christian) era |
| cent. | century |
| cf. | compare |
| chap(s). | chapter(s) |
| cm | centimeter(s) |
| col(s). | column(s) |
| EB | Early Bronze |
| e.g. | *exempli gratia*, for example |
| Eng. | English |
| *et al.* | *et alii*, and others |
| etc. | *et cetera*, and so forth |
| *et passim* | and throughout |
| ff. | and following |
| fig(s). | figure(s) |
| frg(s). | fragment(s) |
| ft. | foot, feet |
| Gk | Greek |
| GN | geographical name |
| HB | Hebrew Bible |
| Heb. | Hebrew |
| ibid. | *ibidem*, in the same place |
| *idem* | *idem*, the same |
| i.e. | *id est*, that is (to say) |
| in. | inch(es) |
| *infra* | below |
| Iron | Iron Age |
| km | kilometer(s) |
| LB | Late Bronze |
| l(l). | line(s) |
| lit. | literally |
| LXX | Septuagint |
| m | meter(s) |
| mm | millimeter(s) |
| MB | Middle Bronze |
| mi. | mile(s) |
| MS(S) | manuscript(s) |
| MT | Masoretic Text |
| No(s). | Number(s) |
| NT | New Testament |
| OT | Old Testament |
| p(p). | page(s) |
| pl(s). | plate(s) |
| PN | personal name |
| r. | reigned; ruled |
| rev. | revised |
| sq. | square |
| *supra* | above |
| Tg. | Targum |
| v(v). | verse(s) |
| yd (s). | yard(s) |

## Books of the Bible

### *Old Testament*

| | |
|---|---|
| Gen | Genesis |
| Ex | Exodus |
| Lev | Leviticus |
| Num | Numbers |
| Deut | Deuteronomy |
| Josh | Joshua |
| Judg | Judges |
| Ruth | Ruth |
| 1 Sam | 1 Samuel |
| 2 Sam | 2 Samuel |
| 1 Kgs | 1 Kings |
| 2 Kgs | 2 Kings |
| 1 Chr | 1 Chronicles |
| 2 Chr | 2 Chronicles |
| Ezra | Ezra |
| Neh | Nehemiah |
| Esth | Esther |
| Job | Job |
| Ps | Psalms |
| Prov | Proverbs |
| Eccl | Ecclesiastes |
| Song | Song of Solomon |
| Isa | Isaiah |
| Jer | Jeremiah |
| Lam | Lamentations |
| Ezek | Ezekiel |
| Dan | Daniel |
| Hos | Hosea |
| Joel | Joel |
| Amos | Amos |
| Obad | Obadiah |
| Jonah | Jonah |
| Mic | Micah |
| Nah | Nahum |
| Hab | Habakkuk |
| Zeph | Zephaniah |
| Hag | Haggai |
| Zech | Zechariah |
| Mal | Malachi |

### *New Testament*

| | |
|---|---|
| Mt | Matthew |
| Mk | Mark |
| Lk | Luke |
| Jn | John |
| Acts | Acts (or Acts of the Apostles) |
| Rom | Romans |
| 1 Cor | 1 Corinthians |
| 2 Cor | 2 Corinthians |
| Gal | Galatians |
| Eph | Ephesians |
| Phil | Philippians |
| Col | Colossians |
| 1 Thes | 1 Thessalonians |
| 2 Thes | 2 Thessalonians |
| 1 Tim | 1 Timothy |
| 2 Tim | 2 Timothy |
| Tit | Titus |
| Phlm | Philemon |
| Heb | Hebrews |
| Jas | James |
| 1 Pet | 1 Peter |
| 2 Pet | 2 Peter |
| 1 Jn | 1 John |
| 2 Jn | 2 John |
| 3 Jn | 3 John |
| Jude | Jude |
| Rev | Revelations |

## Intertestamental Works

| | |
|---|---|
| As. Mos. | Assumption of Moses |
| 1 Esdr | 1 Esdras |
| 2 Esdr | 2 Esdras |
| Jdt | Judith |
| Let. Aris. | Letter of Aristeas |
| 1 Macc | 1 Maccabees |
| 2 Macc | 2 Maccabees |
| 3 Macc | 3 Maccabees |
| 4 Macc | 4 Maccabees |
| Pss. Sol. | Psalms of Solomon |
| TMos | Testament of Moses |
| Tob | Tobit |

## Rabbinic Works

| | |
|---|---|
| *ʿAbad.* | *ʿAbadim, Avadim* |
| *ʿAbod. Zar.* | *ʿAbodah Zarah, Avodah Zarah* |
| *ʾAbot* | *ʾAbot, Avot* |
| *ʾAbot R. Nat.* | *Abot de Rabbi Nathan, Avot of Rabbi Nathan* |
| *ʿArak.* | *ʿArakin, Arakhin* |
| b. | Babylonian Talmud |
| *B. Bat.* | *Baba Batra, Bava Batra* |
| *Bek.* | *Bekorot, Bekhorot* |
| *Ber.* | *Berakot, Berakhot* |
| *Bik.* | *Bikkurim* |
| *Dem.* | *Demai* |
| *ʿErub.* | *ʿErubin, Eruvin* |
| *ʿEd.* | *ʿEduyyot* |
| *Gen. Rab.* | *Genesis Rabbah* |
| *Gerim* | *Gerim* |
| *Giṭ.* | *Giṭṭin, Gittin* |
| *Ḥag.* | *Ḥagiga, Hagigah* |
| *Ḥul.* | *Ḥullin, Hullin* |
| j. | Jerusalem Talmud |
| *Kelim* | *Kelim* |
| *Ker.* | *Kerithot, Keritot* |
| *Ketub.* | *Ketubbot* |
| *Kil.* | *Kilʾayim* |
| *Lam. Rab.* | *Lamentations Rabbah* |
| m. | Mishnah |
| *Maʿaś.* | *Maʿaśerot* |
| *Maʿaś. Š.* | *Maʿaśer Šeni, Maʿaser Sheni* |
| *Makš.* | *Makširin, Makhshirin* |
| *Meg.* | *Megillah* |
| *Meʿil.* | *Meʿilah* |
| *Mek. on Ex.* | *Mekhilta on Exodus* |
| *Menaḥ.* | *Menaḥot* |
| *Mid.* | *Middot* |
| *Midr.* | *Midrash* |
| *Miqw.* | *Miqwaʾot* |
| *Moʿed* | *Moʿed* |
| *Moʿed Qat.* | *Moʿed Qatan* |
| *Naš.* | *Našim, Nashim* |
| *Naz.* | *Nazir* |
| *Ned.* | *Nedarim* |
| *Neg.* | *Negaʿim* |
| *Nez.* | *Neziqin* |
| *Nid.* | *Niddah* |
| *Ohal.* | *Oholot* |
| *ʿOr.* | *ʿOrlah* |
| *Parah* | *Parah* |
| *Peʾah* | *Peʾah* |
| *Pesaḥ.* | *Pesaḥim* |
| *Pesiq. Rab* | *Pesiqta de Rab* |
| *Kah.* | *Kahana* |
| *Qidd.* | *Qiddušin, Qiddushin* |
| *Qod.* | *Qodašin, Qodashin* |
| *Roš. Haš.* | *Roš Haššanah, Rosh HaShanah* |
| *Sanh.* | *Sanhedrin* |
| *Šabb.* | *Šabbat, Shabbat* |
| *Šeb.* | *Šebiʿit, Sheviʿit* |
| *Šebu.* | *Šebuʿot, Shevuʿot* |
| *Šeqal.* | *Šeqalim, Sheqalim* |
| *Soṭah* | *Soṭah* |
| *Sukk.* | *Sukkah* |
| t. | Talmud |
| *Taʿan.* | *Taʿanit* |
| *Tamid* | *Tamid* |
| *Tem.* | *Temurah* |
| *Ter.* | *Terumot* |
| *Yad.* | *Yadayim* |
| *Yebam.* | *Yebamot* |
| Yoma | Yoma |
| *Zabim* | *Zabim, Zavim* |
| *Zebaḥ.* | *Zebaḥim, Zevahim* |
| *Zer.* | *Zeraʿim* |

## Church Fathers

| | |
|---|---|
| *Did.* | *Didache* |
| Epiph. *Adv. haer.* | Epiphanius, *Adversus haereses* |
| Eus. *Hist. eccl.* | Eusebius, *Historia ecclesiastica* |
| Eus. *Onom.* | Eusebius, *Onomasticon* |
| Ign. *Eph.* | Ignatius, *Letter to the Ephesians* |
| Ign. *Magn.* | Ignatius, *Letter to the Magnesians* |
| Ign. *Phld.* | Ignatius, *Letter to the Philadelphians* |
| Ign. *Trall.* | Ignatius, *Letter to the Trallians* |
| Just. *Apol.* | Justin, *Apology* |
| Just. *Dial.* | Justin, *Dialogue with Trypho* |
| Pap. | Papias |

## Classical Sources

| | |
|---|---|
| App. *Bell. Civ.* | Appian, *Civil Wars* |
| App. *Syr.* | Appian, *Syrian Wars* |
| Aratus *Phaen.* | Aratus, *Phaenomena* |
| Arist. *Mete* | Aristotle, *Meteorology* |
| Arr. *Anab.* | Arrian, *Anabasis* |
| Cic. *Pis.* | Cicero, *In Pisonem* |
| Cic. *Flac.* | Cicero, *Pro Flacco* |
| Curt. | Q. Curtius Rufus |
| Dio Cass. | Dio Cassius |
| Diod. Sic. | Diodorus Siculus |
| Herodotus | |
| *Hist.* | *Histories* |
| Homer *Od.* | Homer, *Odyssey* |
| Iso. *Evag.* | Isocrates, *Evagorus* |
| Iso. *Paneg.* | Isocrates, *Panegyric* |
| Josephus | |
| *Ant.* | *Jewish Antiquities* (= *Antiquitates judaicae*) |
| *Apion* | *Against Apion* (= *Contra Apionem*) |
| *Life* | *The Life* (= *Vita*) |
| *War* | *The Jewish War* (= *Bellum judaicum*) |
| Justin. *Epit.* | Justinus, *Epitome* |
| Juvenal *Sat.* | Juvenal, *Satirae* |
| Livy, *Epit.* | Livy, *Epitomae* |
| Livy, *Per.* | Livy, *Periochae* |
| *Or.* | Aelius Aristides, *Orationes* |
| Orig. *Comm.* | Origen, *Commentary on John on John* |
| Oros. *Historiae* | Orosius, *Historiae* |
| Polyaenus | Polyaenus, *Strategica* |
| Paus. *Descr.* | Pausinius, *Description of Greece* |
| Philo, *Flac.* | Philo, *In Flaccum* |
| Philo *Legat.* | Philo, *Legatio ad Gaium* |
| Philo *Spec.* | Philo, *De specialibus legibus* |
| Pliny *Nat. Hist.* | Pliny, *Naturalis historia* |
| Plut. *Alex.* | Plutarch, *Alexander* |
| Plut. *Ant.* | Plutarch, *Antony* |
| Plut. *Galb.* | Plutarch, *Galba* |
| Plut. *Mor.* | Plutarch, *Moralia* |
| Plut. *Pomp.* | Plutarch, *Pompey* |
| Polyb. | Polybius |
| Ptol. *Geog.* | Ptolemy, *Geography* |
| Thuc. | Thucydides |
| Suet. *Aug.* | Suetonius, *Augustus* |
| Suet. *Calig.* | Suetonius, *Gaius Caligula* |
| Suet. *Claud.* | Suetonius, *Claudius* |
| Suet. *Jul.* | Suetonius, *Divus Julius* |
| Suet. *Tib.* | Suetonius, *Tiberius* |
| Suet. *Tit.* | Suetonius, *Divus Titus* |
| Suet. *Vesp.* | Suetonius, *Vespasianus* |
| Strabo *Geog.* | Strabo, *Geography* |
| Tac. *Agr.* | Tacitus, *Agricola* |
| Tac. *Ann.* | Tacitus, *Annales* |
| Tac. *Hist.* | Tacitus, *Historiae* |
| *Vit. Apoll.* | Philostratus, *Life of Apollonius of Tyana* |
| Vitr. *De Arch.* | Vitruvius, *Scriptor de Architectura Latinus* |
| Xenophon | |
| *Anab.* | *Anabasis* |
| *Cyr.* | *Cyropaedia* |
| *Hell.* | *Hellenica* |

# INDEX

*Diacritics have been omitted from names in the index but can be found in the body of the book.*

## A


Aaron; Aaronites 41, 59, 78
Abarim Mountains 42, 103
Abba Saul b. Batnit 235
Abdashtart. *See* Straton
Abdera 174
Abdi-mulkutti 132, 133
Abdon 17, 48, 52, 57, 78, 84, 87, 91
Abel 27
Abel (in Gilead) 138. *See also* Abila
Abel-beth-maacah 10, 17, 21, 63, 67, 72, 73, 84, 87, 96, 120, 121. *Also* Abel-beth-maachah
Abel-keramim 56, 57. *See also* Abila
Abel-meholah 55, 83, 84, 107, 115
Abel-shittim 43, 44, 45, 53, 56, 121. *See also* Abila; Shittim
Abiathar 64
Abi-baal of Shamsimuruna 132
Abibalos (Abi-Baal) 75
Abiezer 55, 68, 108
Abigail 65, 113
Abijah (Abijam) 82, 94
Abila (in Gilead) 178, 179, 209, 212, 225, 232, 266
Abila (nr. Damascus) 251, 252
Abila (nr. Dead Sea) 194, 204, 225, 233, 251, 259, 260
Abila 44. *See also* Abel-shittim
Abila 57. *See also* Abel-keramim
Abila Lysanias 232
Abil el-Qamh 10, 120. *See also* Abel-beth-maacah; Tel Avel Bet Maakha
Abimelech 34, 35, 55, 56
Abishai 72
Abiyate 135
Abner 71
Abram; Abraham 13, 14, 33, 34, 35, 42, 45, 222
Abrokomas 169, 172
Abronah 39, 40
Absalom 84
Abu Ghosh 89
Abu Seyal 27
Abydos 27
Accad 12, 33. *See also* Akkad
Accaron 194, 195, 201, 202, 205, 266. *See also* Ekron
Acchabaron 256
Acco 15, 16, 17, 18, 19, 27, 28, 29, 30, 32, 50, 52, 54, 63, 67, 70, 72, 73, 74, 76, 81, 84, 87, 90, 91, 96, 98, 106, 111, 120, 122, 123, 124, 128, 132, 135, 138, 140, 146, 158, 163, 165, 166, 170, 171, 172, 173, 175, 177, 187, 197, 247. *See also* Ptolemais
Acco, Plain of 48, 74, 76, 115
Achaemenes; Achaemenids 160, 163, 164, 169
Achaia 162, 240, 244, 245, 246, 248, 255
Achan (son of Carmi) 44, 68
Achbor 145
Achish 64, 65, 66
Achmetha 140. *See also* Ecbatana
Achor Valley 44, 68, 87, 89
Achoris 169, 170
Achsah 48, 53, 66
Achshaph 18, 27, 29, 48, 54, 63, 84, 90, 91
Achzib (in Asher) 17, 28, 30, 50, 63, 84, 87, 91, 128. *See also* Ecdippa
Achzib (in Judah) 36, 129, 130. *See also* Chezib
Acra (in Jerusalem) 183, 186, 188, 192, 194, 198, 201, 211
Acrabatene 260. *See also* Akrabattene
Acrabeta 186, 187, 194, 205, 256, 260, 261, 266, 267
Actium 217, 218
Adad-nirari III 108, 109, 110
Adah 66
Adam; Adamah 20, 22, 44, 45, 50, 52, 55, 56, 61, 63, 68, 71, 76, 81, 84, 91, 92
Adami-nekeb 54, 55, 84, 91, 92
Adana 76, 243
Adasa 190, 191
Adda-guppi 153
Addan 148
Addar 15
Adennu 99
Ader 118
Adicran 150
Adida 197, 198, 199, 201, 202, 205, 208, 209, 260, 261. *See also* Hadid
Adithaim 198
Admah 11, 35
Adoni-bezek 50
Adoniram 78, 79
Adoraim; Adora 20, 69, 80, 81, 187, 198, 199, 204, 209, 212, 213, 266
Adrammelech 131
Adramyttium 169, 243, 246, 248, 249
Adriatic Sea 248
Adullam 36, 47, 48, 64, 69, 72, 80, 129, 130, 167, 188
Aduma 186
Adummim, Ascent of 89, 233
Aegae 174
Aegean Sea 160, 162, 174, 243, 244, 245, 246, 247, 248
Aelia Capitolina 265, 266. *See also* Jerusalem
Aeneas 240, 241
Aenon (in Transjordan) 226
Aenon (nr. Salim) 226
Aeolia 156
Aetolia 162
Afis 108
Africa 143
Afula 26, 28, 32
Agalla 210
Agrippa I 219, 245, 247, 248, 250, 251
Agrippa II 219, 229, 248, 249, 251, 252, 253, 255, 256, 257, 258
Agrippias 207. *See also* Anthedon
Agrippina 227, 256
Ahab 96, 97, 98, 99, 100, 101, 102, 103, 104, 105, 106, 107, 121, 132
Ahasuerus 162, 163. *See also* Xerxes
Ahaz 117, 118, 119, 120, 124, 125, 126
Ahaziah 101, 103, 105, 106, 107. *Also* Jehoahaz
Ahijah (father of Baasha) 94
Ahijah the Shilonite 79
Ahimaaz 84
Ahimelech 64
Ahimilki 132
Ahimiti 124, 125
Ahinadab 84
Ahinoam 65, 113
Ahlab 17, 50, 84, 87
Ahmose. *See* Amasis
Ahzai 168
Ai 26, 32, 34, 45, 46, 48, 95, 103, 123, 124, 167, 168. *Also* Aiath; Aija; Aioth. *See also* Et-Tell
Aijalon 29, 46, 50, 52, 57, 60, 61, 62, 63, 67, 69, 72, 78, 80, 81, 83, 84, 87, 89, 94, 118, 119, 120, 126
Aijalon Valley 17, 19, 20, 46, 52, 62, 83, 119, 185, 194, 201
Ailia 63. *See also* Jerusalem
Ailim 57
Ain 16, 71
Ain Dara 78
Ain el-Gharabeh 89
Ain el-Hod 89. *See also* En-shemesh
Ain el-Khudra 40. *See also* Hazeroth
Ain el-Qudeirat 15, 40. *See also* Kadesh-barnea
Ain es-Sultan 89
Ain Feshkha 267
Ain Ghadyan 22, 40
Ain Hajla 89, 210
Ain Husb 15, 22
Ainitha 92. *See also* En-hazor
Ain Jalud 55, 83. *See also* En-harod; Harod, Spring of
Ain Jenin 115
Ain Jidi 65. *See also* En-gedi
Ain Muweilih 15. *See also* Azmon
Ain Qedeis 15, 40. *See also* Hazar-addar
Ain Qeseimeh 15. *See also* Karka
Ajlun 23
Akhenaten. *See* Amenhotep IV
Akhetaten 30. *See also* Tell el-Amarna
Akiva, Rabbi 266, 267
Akkad (city) 160, 169. *See also* Accad
Akkad (region) 26, 122, 133, 140, 143, 144, 145, 146, 152, 153, 155
Akrabattene 186, 187. *See also* Acrabatene
Akrabbim, Ascent of 15, 186
Alalakh 31, 33
Alashia 12. *See also* Elishah
Alcimus 189, 190, 191, 192, 193
Aleiyan 42
Alema 72, 186, 187. *See also* Helam
Alemeth 69
Aleppo 15, 24, 33, 70, 74, 99, 109, 121, 136, 141, 143, 158, 160, 165
Alexander (son of Aristobulus II) 212, 213, 218, 263
Alexander (son of Herod the Great) 223
Alexander (the Great) 172, 173, 174, 175, 176, 177
Alexander Balas 193, 194, 195, 196, 201
Alexander IV Ephiphanes 193
Alexander Jannaeus 198, 204, 206, 207, 208, 209, 210, 214, 217, 257, 263
Alexandra (daughter of Hyrcanus II; Herod's mother-in-law) 217, 218, 223
Alexandra Salome 210
Alexandria (in Egypt) 24, 176, 177, 178, 181, 182, 213, 214, 224, 240, 242, 244, 246, 248, 249, 250, 252, 253, 254, 255, 256, 261, 263
Alexandria (on Iaxartes R.) 176
Alexandria Troas 243, 246, 249. *See also* Troas
Alexandrion 209, 210, 211, 212, 218, 219, 223. *See also* Sartaba
Allammelech 90, 91
Allan Valley. *See* Nahr Allan
Alma. *See* Alema
Almon 61, 69, 78, 82
Almon-diblathaim 42, 43, 103. *See also* Diblaten
Aloth 85, 90
Alousa 210
Alpheus 162
Alulus 259, 260
Alush 39
Alyattes 155, 156
Amad 90, 91
Amalek; Amalekites 11, 35, 42, 55, 57, 62, 63, 65, 66, 127
Amana River 18
Amanus Mountains 24, 94, 99, 173, 174, 243
Amariah 100
Amarna Tablets 29, 30
Amasis 150, 151, 156, 161. *Also* Ahmose
Amathus (in Jordan Valley) 207, 208, 209, 212, 260, 266
Amathus (on the Orontes) 197. *See also* Hamath
Amattu. *See* Hamath
Amaziah 110, 111, 112, 115
Amel-Marduk 151. *See also* Evil-merodach
Amenhotep IV 30
Amestris 163
Amki 29
Amman 24. *See also* Philadelphia; Rabbah; Rabbath-bene-ammon
Ammananu 117, 152, 153
Ammathus 227. *See also* Hammath
Ammia 29
Ammon; Ammonites 17, 23, 35, 43, 44, 45, 50, 56, 57, 61, 63, 65, 70, 71, 72, 73, 74, 75, 78, 84, 87, 101, 104, 106, 107, 112, 113, 115, 118, 120, 122, 124, 126, 128, 132, 138, 145, 146, 148, 149, 159, 167, 175, 182, 187
Ammonium 176
Ammuladdin 135
Ammurapi 34
Amnath-heres 83
Amon (son of Manasseh) 137, 138
Amorites 11, 13, 17, 23, 35, 37, 39, 42, 43, 49, 51, 52, 61, 67, 77, 82, 85
Amos 107, 111, 113, 114, 115
Amphipolis 174, 243, 244
Ampi 29
Amraphel 34
Amu Daria 157
Amuq Plain 93. *See also* Mugish; Patina; Unqi
Amurru 16, 29, 31, 33, 109, 128, 135, 153, 160
Amurru Sea 99. *See also* Mediterranean Sea
Amyrteus (of Dynasty XXVIII) 169
Amyrteus of Sais 164
Anab 69, 113
Anaharath 55, 66, 84, 91
Anakim 34
Ananel 217
Ananiah 167. *See also* Bethany
Ananias (disciple) 241
Ananias (Hasmonean general) 207
Ananias (high priest) 248, 253, 254, 262
Ananus 255, 256, 259, 260
Anat 121
Anathoth 65, 69, 78, 115, 123, 124, 129, 167, 168
Anatolia 12, 29, 76, 136, 153, 155, 173
Anatolian Plateau 24, 243
Ancyra 174, 240
Andrew 226, 228, 229
Andromachus 175, 176
Andronicus 180, 181
Anim 69
Ankara 24
Ankh-nes-neferibre 150
Annas, House of 235, 236
Anshan 155, 156
Antacidas 169
Antakya 109
Antalya. *See* Attalia
Anthedon 207, 209, 212, 213, 218, 219, 240, 254, 266
Antigonia 177
Antigonus (sage) 240
Antigonus (son of John Hyrcanus) 204, 205, 206
Antigonus, Mattathias 213, 214, 215, 216, 217, 221
Antigonus I Monophthalmus 176, 177, 207
Anti-Lebanon 14, 133, 152, 153, 174. *See also* Sirion
Antioch (in Pisidia) 242, 246
Antioch (in Syria) 177, 178, 180, 181, 182, 186, 189, 190, 191, 193, 194, 195, 196, 197, 201, 203, 204, 216, 240, 241, 242, 243, 244, 245, 246, 248, 250, 254, 255, 256
Antiochia 179, 206, 209. *See also* Daphne (in Palestine)
Antiochia (region) 246
Antiochus, Valley of 209
Antiochus I Soter 178
Antiochus II Theos 178
Antiochus III Megas (the Great) 178, 179, 180, 181, 189, 242
Antiochus IV Epiphanes 181, 182, 183, 184, 186, 188, 189, 195, 197, 201
Antiochus IV of Commagene 255
Antiochus V Eupator 184, 186, 188, 189, 193
Antiochus VI Epiphanes Dionysus 196, 197, 198, 199, 200
Antiochus VII Sidetes 201, 202, 203, 204
Antiochus VIII Grypus 207
Antiochus IX Cyzicenus 205, 207
Antiochus XII Dionysus 208
Antipas. *See* Herod Antipas
Antipater (son of Herod the Great) 223
Antipater I 176, 210
Antipater II 210, 212, 213, 214, 216
Antipatris 90, 175, 204, 208, 217, 218, 219, 225, 233, 240, 241, 248, 251, 252, 254, 255, 260, 266, 267. *See also* Aphek (in Sharon); Pegae
Antonia Fortress (in Jerusalem) 234, 236, 237
Antoninus Pius 265
Antonius Felix. *See* Felix
Antony, Mark 212, 214, 215, 217, 218, 219, 222, 247, 253, 262
Aornus 176
Apamea 178, 180, 189, 195, 197, 202, 254
Apharaema 183, 184, 187, 194, 195, 201, 204, 205, 261
Aphek (in Asher) 17, 50, 63, 84, 87, 91
Aphek (in Golan) 63, 73, 84, 96, 98, 110, 111
Aphek (in Sharon) 11, 19, 27, 28, 29, 30, 31, 32, 34, 36, 48, 50, 60, 61, 63, 65, 66, 71, 72, 76, 81, 83, 84, 94, 108, 110, 120, 122, 124, 129, 132, 134, 138, 146, 148, 167. *See also* Antipatris; Arethusa; Pegae; Ras el-Ain; Tel Afeq
Aphek(ah) (in Lebanon) 16
Aphik. *See* Aphek (in Asher)
Aphish 108, 109. *Also* Afis
Apiru 30, 49
Apollodotus 207
Apollonia (in Macedonia) 243, 244
Apollonia (in Palestine) 194, 205, 209, 212, 213, 217, 225, 233, 266
Apollonius (commander under Demetrius) 194
Apollonius (Seleucid commander) 183, 184, 191
Apollonius of Tarsus 180
Apollonius the Mysarch 182
Appian of Alexandria 268
Appuashu 152
Apries. *See* Hophra
Apum 27. *See also* Damascus (city)
Aqabah, Gulf of 41. *See also* Elath, Gulf of
Aqir 94
Aquila. *See* Priscilla and Aquila
Ar 102
Arab 65
Arabah 15, 17, 18, 21, 22, 23, 39, 40, 41, 43, 54, 63, 68, 71, 105
Arabah, Sea of the 113. *See also* Dead Sea
Arabatha 210. *See also* Rabbah; Rabbath-bene-ammon
Arabia; Arabians; Arabs 14, 15, 19, 21, 24, 95, 96, 99, 100, 104, 105, 111, 112, 118, 119, 121, 123, 125, 132, 133, 134, 135, 140, 145, 150, 152, 153, 154, 157, 158, 159, 160, 167, 169, 170, 171, 172, 176, 195, 196, 208, 211, 218, 239, 240, 246, 266
Arabian Desert 24
Arachosia 157, 176
Arad 10, 16, 25, 26, 36, 39, 41, 42, 43, 48, 52, 63, 65, 66, 69, 78, 79, 95, 104, 107, 110, 113, 118, 120, 126, 140, 143, 146, 147, 148, 167. *See also* Malatha
Arad of Jerahmeel 81, 112
Arad Rabbah 76, 81, 112
Arados; Aradus 172, 173, 174, 197. *See also* Arvad
Arair. *See* Aroer (in Reuben)
Aral Sea 176

Aram; Arameans 12, 33, 37, 61, 63, 70, 72, 79, 96, 98, 99, 100, 101, 104, 108, 114, 118
Aram-beth-rehob 72
Aram-Damascus 23, 73, 74, 84, 96, 99, 100, 101, 102, 105, 107, 108, 109, 110, 111, 114, 118, 120
Aram-naharaim 53. *See also* Mesopotamia
Aram-zobah 72, 73. *See also* Zobah
Ararat Mountains 24
Araunah the Jebusite 73
Arbakes 169
Arbatta 187
Arbela (in Galilee) 156, 160, 165, 191, 196, 209, 215, 227
Arbela (in Mesopotamia) 176
Arcadia 162
Arcea 252
Archelaus 223, 224, 233
Archites 89
Arculf 229
Ardata 29
Areopagus (in Athens) 244
Aretas I 198
Aretas II 207
Aretas III 208, 209, 210
Aretas IV 263
Arethusa 212, 217. *See also* Aphek (in Sharon); Pegae
Argob 23, 56, 84, 86
Aria 157, 176
Aribua 93, 99
Arimathea 183, 188, 194, 201, 205, 237
Arisde 174
Aristobulias 209
Aristobulus (son of Herod the Great) 223
Aristobulus I 204, 205, 206
Aristobulus II 210, 211, 212, 213, 263
Aristobulus III 217, 219
Arkha 161. *See also* Nebuchadnezzar IV
Arkite 13
Armant 27
Armenia 24, 26, 157, 161, 169, 210
Armenian Mountains 176
Arnon River/Valley 17, 23, 42, 43, 44, 45, 74, 85, 87, 102, 106, 112, 218, 251, 252, 259, 260, 261
Aroandas 170
Aroer (in Gad) 57
Aroer (in Negeb) 50, 52, 63, 65, 69, 95
Aroer (in Reuben) 17, 44, 50, 57, 63, 70, 72, 73, 74, 84, 87
Arpad 70, 109, 110, 116, 117, 118, 121, 123, 125, 140, 160, 165
Arpha 252
Arqa 27, 29, 99
Arqat 13
Arraba. *See* Garaba
Arrapkha 33, 110, 140, 150, 152
Arsaces VI. *See* Mithradates I
Arsamenes 172
Arsames 168, 172
Arsaya 132, 133. *See also* El-Arish
Arses 171, 172
Arsuf. *See* Apollonia (in Palestine)
Artabazus 164
Artacauna 176
Artaxerxes I 163, 164, 165, 166, 167, 168
Artaxerxes II 169
Artaxerxes III 171, 172
Artyphius 166
Arubboth 83, 84
Arumah 55, 56, 120
Aruna 81
Arvad 12, 13, 15, 18, 29, 74, 99, 109, 121, 128, 134, 140, 141, 143, 150, 152, 158, 163, 170, 171, 172. *Also* Arwada 117
Aryandes 162
Arydda 210
Aryenis 155
Arza 132
Arzani 134
Asa 80, 82, 94, 95, 96, 97, 98, 100, 105
Asahel 71
Asamon 254, 255
Ascalon 162, 164, 175, 178, 194, 195, 196, 197, 201, 204, 209, 212, 213, 214, 215, 218, 223, 224, 225, 240, 251, 252, 254, 256, 259, 261, 266, 267. *See also* Ashkelon
Ashan 71, 78
Ashdod 11, 15, 17, 19, 28, 30, 31, 32, 47, 50, 52, 57, 60, 63, 65, 69, 70, 73, 81, 83, 84, 87, 94, 96, 106, 111, 112, 113, 118, 119, 120, 121, 122, 123, 124, 125, 126, 128, 129, 131, 132, 134, 138, 141, 143, 146, 148, 158, 159, 160, 165, 166, 167, 170, 171, 172, 175, 241. *See also* Azotus
Ashdod (province) 124, 130, 132, 134, 167
Ashdod-yam 83, 94, 119, 123, 125
Asher; Asherites 17, 19, 44, 48, 50, 51, 52, 54, 55, 68, 77, 78, 82, 84, 85, 87, 88, 89, 90, 91, 92, 149
Ashereth 108
Ashkelon 15, 19, 27, 28, 29, 30, 31, 32, 36, 47, 50, 52, 57, 58, 63, 65, 69, 70, 73, 74, 81, 84, 95, 113, 118, 119, 120, 122, 123, 124, 126, 127, 128, 129, 132, 134, 136, 137, 138, 140, 141, 143, 144, 158, 159, 165, 166, 167, 170, 171, 172. *See also* Ascalon
Ashkenaz 12, 136, 137
Ashkhabad 176
Ashtaroth 11, 16, 17, 27, 29, 34, 35, 43, 50, 52, 63, 70, 72, 73, 74, 78, 84, 87, 96, 98, 105, 106, 120, 121
Ashtaroth-karnaim 35
Ashtartram 94
Ashur (city) 33, 99, 109, 121, 124, 125, 136, 140, 150, 152, 155, 160, 165
Ashur (region) 12, 119, 134. *See also* Assyria
Ashurbanipal 121, 134, 135, 136, 137, 138, 139, 140, 141
Ashur-dan II 75
Ashur-dan III 109
Ashur-etil-ilani 138, 140
Ashurnasirpal II 93, 94, 99
Ashur-nirari V 109, 110
Ashur-rabi II 70
Ashur-uballit II 141
Asia (province) 239, 240, 242, 243, 244, 246, 248, 249
Asia Minor 162, 169, 171, 178, 180, 246, 247, 249
Asochis 19, 206, 207, 209, 227. *See also* Hannathon; Shihin
Asophon 207. *See also* Zaphon
Asor, Plain of 196. *See also* Hazor, Plain of
Aspendus 173, 174
Asphaltitis, Lake 23, 260, 263, 264. *See also* Dead Sea
Asphar 192, 193
Asriel 68, 108
Assos 246
Assyria 30, 70, 72, 93, 94, 98, 99, 105, 106, 109, 110, 113, 114, 116, 117, 118, 119, 120, 121, 122, 123, 124, 125, 126, 127, 128, 129, 130, 131, 132, 133, 134, 135, 136, 137, 139, 140, 141, 142, 152, 155, 156, 167
Astyges 152, 154, 155, 156
Aswan 125, 146. *See also* Syene
Asyut 24, 27
Atarneus 169
Ataroth 44, 69, 84, 90, 96, 97, 98, 102, 104
Ataroth-addar 89
Atarshumki 109, 110
Athach 65
Athaliah 96, 97, 104, 105, 106, 107
Athenae 162. *See also* Athens
Athenobius 202
Athens 24, 157, 162, 163, 164, 165, 168, 174, 177, 220, 240, 244, 246
Athica 162
Athone 210
Athura 157, 161. *See also* Assyria
Atossa 162
Atroth-shophan 97
Attalia 242, 246
Attalus I 179
Augustus Caesar 208, 217, 218, 219, 220, 221, 222, 223, 224, 232, 253
Auranitis 23, 218, 219, 223, 251, 252, 253
Avaris 27, 38, 40
Avdat 112
Avvim 82
Axius 162
Ayyah 129
Ayyun Valley 21. *See also* Ijon Valley
Aza 108
Azariah (Hasmonean commander) 188
Azariah (king of Judah) 110, 111, 112, 113, 114, 117, 118, 120. *See also* Uzziah
Azekah 46, 47, 60, 63, 69, 72, 80, 81, 119, 126, 127, 129, 130, 131, 146, 147, 148, 167. *See also* Tell Zakariyeh
Azerbaijan 24
Azmaveth 65, 69, 95, 167, 191
Azmon 15, 16, 40, 42
Aznoth-tabor 55, 91, 92
Azor 32, 83, 94, 128, 129
Azotus 162, 164, 175, 185, 188, 191, 194, 195, 198, 201, 202, 203, 204, 205, 209, 212, 213, 217, 218, 223, 225, 240, 241, 251, 252, 259, 266, 267. *See also* Ashdod
Azotus Paralius; Azotus-on-Sea 175, 201, 202, 205. *See also* Ashdod-yam
Azuri 123, 124, 125


# B


Baal (king of Tyre) 132. *See also* Balu
Baal II 149
Baalah (in Dan) 94
Baalah (in Judah) 76, 89. *See also* Kiriath-jearim
Baalath 76, 83, 89, 119
Baalath-beer 63, 65, 71, 147
Baal-azor II 94
Baal-beth-meon 43
Baal-hazor 61, 82, 191
Baalis 148, 149
Baal-meon (in Mt. Ephraim) 108
Baal-meon (in Transjordan) 69, 102, 186. *See also* Beth-baal-meon
Baal-peor 43, 44
Baal-perazim 71, 72
Baal-zephon 37, 38, 39. *See also* Daphne
Baana the son of Hushai 85
Baasha (son of Ahijah) 82, 94, 95, 96
Baasha (son of Rehob) 99
Babel 12
Babylon (city) 33, 76, 79, 84, 110, 121, 125, 127, 132, 135, 136, 137, 140, 141, 142, 144, 145, 146, 148, 149, 150, 151, 152, 154, 155, 156, 160, 161, 165, 166, 168, 169, 171, 172, 176, 177, 217, 240
Babylon; Babylonia 30, 70, 116, 122, 123, 127, 133, 135, 136, 138, 139, 140, 141, 142, 143, 145, 146, 147, 148, 150, 152, 153, 154, 155, 156, 157, 161, 162, 163, 166, 167, 169, 172, 177, 180, 191, 219, 267. *Also* Babylonians
Babylonian world view 13
Bacchides 189, 190, 191, 192, 193
Bactra 176
Bactria 157, 176
Baean; Baenites 187
Baghdad 24
Bagohi 168
Bahriya Oasis 150
Bahurim 65
Baku 24
Balaam 43, 44
Balikh River 24, 33, 99, 140, 141
Balu 103, 132, 133, 134, 135. *See also* Baal (king of Tyre)
Bamoth-baal 43, 103. *See also* Beth-bamoth
Banias 10, 21, 54, 120. *See also* Paneas
Bar-gusi. *See* Atarshumki
Bar Hadad. *See* Ben-hadad
Bar-hadad 108, 109. *See also* Ben-hadad III
Barak 52, 53, 54, 55, 59
Baram 230
Barca 162
Baris (in Jerusalem) 211
Bar Kathros 235
Bar Kochba 265, 266, 267, 268
Barnabbas 241, 242, 243, 244
Barsip. *See* Borsippa
Bartatua 137
Bartameus 233
Barzapharnes 214
Bashan 18, 23, 34, 43, 45, 50, 56, 73, 74, 84, 85, 86, 98, 106, 110, 121, 187. *See also* Batanea
Baskama 198, 199
Basra 24
Bassus 261
Basura esh-Sham. *See* Bozrah (in Gilead)
Batanea 23, 179, 218, 219, 223, 226, 227, 251, 252, 253
Bath-sheba 71
Batrona 29
Bealoth 85, 90. *See also* Aloth
Beerim; Beer 55, 108
Beer-lahai-roi 21
Beer-lahai-roi 34
Beerot. *See* Beirut
Beeroth 46, 53, 61, 62, 69, 72, 89, 95, 167, 168, 169, 191, 192
Beersheba (in Galilee) 256
Beer-sheba (in Negeb) 14, 17, 20, 21, 33, 34, 35, 41, 42, 50, 52, 59, 61, 63, 65, 66, 69, 70, 71, 73, 74, 75, 76, 81, 95, 100, 101, 107, 112, 113, 115, 118, 120, 124, 125, 126, 139, 146, 147, 148, 158, 159, 165, 166, 167, 170, 171, 172, 204, 209, 225, 266
Beer Tivon. *See* Tell Tabun
Beerzaith 189, 190, 191, 192. *See also* Birzaith
Behistun 154, 157, 161. *See also* Bisitun
Beirut 17, 18, 24, 29, 73, 163. *See also* Berytus
Beitin 34, 45, 89. *See also* Bethel
Beit Jibril/Jibrin. *See* Beth Govrin
Beit Lahm 57. *See also* Bethlehem (in Galilee)
Beit Nattif. *See* Betholetepha
Beit Ur el-Foqa and Beit Ur et-Tahta. *See* Beth-horon, Upper and Lower
Bela 10, 11, 34, 35, 44, 68. *See also* Zoar
Belesys I 169, 172
Belesys II 171, 172
Bel-ibni 127
Bel-sharra-usur 154. *Also* Belshazzar
Belshunu 169. *See also* Belesys
Bemeselis 208
Ben-hadad I 96, 99, 100
Ben-hadad II 105, 106
Ben-hadad III 105, 108
Bene-berak 83, 94, 128, 129
Beni Hasan 27
Benjamin 17, 20, 36, 44, 49, 50, 52, 53, 54, 58, 59, 60, 61, 63, 65, 67, 68, 69, 70, 71, 77, 78, 80, 82, 83, 84, 85, 86, 87, 88, 89, 94, 95, 113, 139, 149
Beonites 186
Beqa Valley 21, 27, 99, 111, 114, 120, 149
Berea 191
Bered 21
Beriah (clan) 46, 61, 68, 69
Bernice (daughter of Agrippa II) 248, 251, 252, 253
Bernice (daughter of Ptolemy II) 178
Beroea (in Macedonia) 244
Beroea (in Syria) 178
Berothah 122, 149
Berothai 72, 73
Bersabe 227, 256. *See also* Beersheba (in Galilee)
Berytus 15, 158, 165, 166, 170, 171, 172, 197. *See also* Beirut
Berzetho 191
Besara 227
Besimoth 259, 260
Besor Brook 18, 21, 65, 95, 112
Beten 84, 90, 91
Bethabara 226
Beth-anath 17, 48, 50, 51, 63, 84, 86, 87, 92
Bethany 167, 226, 233, 234, 235. *See also* Ananiah
Bethany beyond the Jordan 226
Beth-arabah 53, 61, 65, 82, 84, 89, 126
Beth-arbel 36, 56, 84
Beth-ashbea 69
Beth-aven 62, 69, 88, 89
Beth-aven, Valley of 114
Beth-azmaveth 168. *See also* Azmaveth
Beth-baal-meon 17, 43, 44, 56, 84, 87, 102, 103, 104. *See also* Baal-meon (in Transjordan); Main
Beth-bamoth 102, 103. *See also* Bamoth-baal
Beth-basi 192, 193
Beth-car 60
Beth-dagon 83, 90, 91, 94, 128, 129
Beth-diblathaim 102, 103, 104. *See also* Dabaloth; Diblaten
Beth-eden 93, 99, 110, 114, 121. *See also* Bit-Adini
Beth-eglaim 36
Bethel 17, 28, 30, 32, 34, 36, 43, 45, 46, 48, 50, 51, 52, 53, 55, 58, 59, 60, 61, 62, 63, 65, 67, 69, 71, 72, 73, 80, 81, 82, 84, 87, 89, 95, 96, 98, 107, 115, 123, 124, 126, 129, 132, 138, 139, 167, 168, 191, 192, 193, 209, 261, 267
Beth-emek 17, 84, 87, 90, 91
Bethennabris 260
Bether 266, 267, 268
Beth-ezel 130
Beth-gader 69
Beth-gilgal 191
Beth Govrin 47, 63, 240, 241. *See also* Betogabris; Eleutheropolis
Beth-haccerem 59, 113, 146, 148, 167, 168, 209. *See also* Ramat Rahel
Beth-haccerem Valley 19, 51, 92, 227
Beth-haggan 55, 66, 105. *See also* Gina; Ginae
Beth-haram; Beth-haran 17, 27, 44, 53, 56, 71, 84, 87. *See also* Livias
Beth Harapid 147
Beth-hoglah 17, 53, 61, 87, 89
Beth-horon, Upper and Lower (Beit Ur, el-Foqa and et-Tahta) 17, 20, 29, 37, 45, 46, 58, 60, 61, 62, 69, 72, 76, 78, 81, 82, 83, 84, 87, 88, 89, 94, 110, 118, 129, 183, 184, 185, 190, 192, 193, 194, 198, 199, 201, 233, 254, 255
Beth-jeshimoth 17, 43, 44, 45, 50, 53, 56, 84, 87
Beth-le-aphrah 129, 130
Beth-lebaoth 71
Bethlehem (in Galilee) 55, 57, 84, 91
Bethlehem (in Judah) 20, 36, 47, 50, 52, 57, 58, 59, 60, 61, 63, 64, 65, 67, 69, 71, 72, 76, 80, 84, 101, 113, 126, 129, 148, 149, 167, 168, 193, 199, 224, 240. *See also* Ephrath
Beth-marcaboth 71
Bethmaus 227
Beth-nimrah 17, 44, 53, 56, 84, 87, 259
Betholetepha 260
Beth-omri 109. *See also* Omri, House of
Beth-pazzez 91
Beth-pelet 65, 167
Beth-peor 16, 17, 44, 84, 87
Bethphage 233, 234
Beth-ramatha 204
Beth-rapha 69
Beth-rechab 69. *See also* Rechab, House of
Beth-rehob 61, 72, 73, 74. *See also* Aram-beth-rehob
Beth-rima 187
Bethsaida 225, 226, 227, 228, 229, 230, 232, 233
Beth-shan. *See* Beth-shean
Beth-shean 17, 20, 26, 28, 29, 30, 32, 41, 50, 52, 54, 55, 61, 63, 66, 67, 68, 70, 72, 73, 74, 76, 81, 83, 84, 85, 87, 96, 98, 120, 138, 158, 165, 166, 170, 171, 172, 175, 187, 199. *See also* Scythopolis
Beth-shean Valley 20, 22, 31, 51, 83
Beth-shemesh (in Issachar) 55, 91, 92
Beth-shemesh (in Judah) 17, 28, 30, 32, 36, 50, 57, 58, 60, 61, 63, 69, 72, 76, 78, 80, 83, 84, 87, 88, 89, 110, 111, 118, 119, 129, 146, 148
Beth-shemesh (in Naphtali) 27, 50, 51, 63, 84, 85, 86, 87, 92
Beth-shittah 55
Beth-yerah 21, 26. *See also* Philoteria; Sennabris
Beth-zabdai 197
Beth-zaith 128
Beth-zechariah 188, 189
Beth-zur 28, 30, 32, 36, 69, 80, 101, 126, 129, 158, 165, 166, 167, 168, 170, 171, 172, 185, 186, 187, 188, 189, 192, 193, 194, 195, 196, 198, 199, 200, 201, 204, 209, 240, 266

Bet Netofa Valley 19, 90, 227, 228. *See also* Sahl el-Battof
Betogabris 218, 240, 260, 266, 267. *See also* Beth Govrin; Eleutheropolis
Betonim 17, 56, 84, 87
Beyond the Jordan 10, 85. *See also* Gilead
Beyond the River 14, 15, 16, 17, 74, 143, 157, 158, 159, 160, 161, 162, 163, 164, 165, 166, 167, 168, 169, 170, 171, 172, 176
Bezek 50, 55, 61, 63, 66
Bezer (in Bashan) 27, 29, 72, 122, 124
Bezer (in Reuben) 44, 56, 78, 84, 102, 103, 104
Bilad er-Ruhah. *See* Ramat Menashe
Bilhah 33, 44, 68
Bir Ayyub 89. *See also* En-rogel
Birzaith 68, 82. *See also* Beerzaith
Bisitun 157. *See also* Behistun
Bit-Adini 70, 93, 109, 117. *See also* Beth-eden
Bit-Agusi 70, 99, 109, 117
Bit-Amuqani 122
Bit-Bakhiani 70, 117
Bit-Dayukku 155
Bit-Gabbari 70
Bit-Hanuniya. *See* Urartu
Bithron 71
Bithynia 169, 240, 243, 244, 246, 248
Bit-Khalupe 70
Bit-Shilani 122
Bit-Sin-magir 152
Bitter Lake 37, 39
Bit-Zamani 70, 117
Black Sea 24, 164, 169, 177. *See also* Euxine Sea
Bodashtart 165
Boeotia 162
Boghazkoy. *See* Hattusas
Borashan 65
Borim 81
Borsippa 150, 152, 154, 162
Bosor 72, 186, 187
Bosporus 162, 164
Bostra 186, 241
Bozez 62
Bozkath 138
Bozrah (in Edom) 43, 73, 104, 115, 118, 124
Bozrah (in Gilead). *See* Bosor
Brocchoi 178
Brundisium; Brindisi 214
Brook of Egypt 14, 15, 16, 18, 39, 40, 73, 74, 113, 119, 120, 123, 124, 132, 133, 134, 141, 143, 195, 196, 201, 209. *See also* Wadi el-Arish
Bubastis 37, 38
Bucephalia 176
Bulgaria 24
Bull Site 32
Burj el-Alawiyeh 10, 120
Burj et-Tantura. *See* Dor, Fortress of
Buseirah 115. *See also* Bozrah (in Edom)
Busr el-Hariri. *See* Bosor
Busra Eski Sham. *See* Bezer (in Bashan)
Byblos 15, 16, 18, 26, 27, 29, 33, 51, 99, 109, 111, 113, 121, 122, 128, 140, 141, 143, 158, 160, 165, 166, 170, 171, 172, 173, 174, 176. *See also* Gebal
Byzantium 162, 240, 244

# C

Cabul 17, 84, 87, 90, 91. *See also* Chabulon
Cabul, Land of 76, 84
Cabura 176
Cadasa; Cades 196, 206, 227, 232, 254, 256, 259. *See also* Kedesh (in Galilee)
Caesarea 159, 218, 219, 220, 221, 222, 223, 224, 225, 227, 232, 233, 236, 240, 241, 242, 244, 245, 246, 247, 248, 249, 251, 252, 253, 254, 255, 256, 257, 259, 260, 261, 264, 265, 266
Caesarea Philippi 223, 232, 251, 252, 254, 257. *See also* Paneas
Caesennius Gallus 255
Caiaphas 234, 235. *See also* Joseph bar Caiapha
Caiaphas, House of 234, 236
Cairo 24
Calah 12, 33, 93, 99, 109, 116, 121, 150, 152, 155. *See also* Nimrud
Calamon 41, 210. *See also* Papyron
Caleb 20, 41, 47, 48, 50, 53, 65, 66, 68, 69, 70, 88
Caligula 245, 250, 251. *Also* Gaius Caligula
Callias, Peace of 164
Callimandrus 205
Callinicum 178
Callirrhoe 223. *See also* Zereth-shahar
Calneh 12, 121
Calpe 169
Cambyses 150, 151, 154, 155, 156, 160, 161, 162
Camus 178
Cana (in Galilee) 226, 227, 228, 232. *See also* Garis; Kafr Kana
Canaan; Canaanites 12, 13, 14, 15, 16, 17, 18, 19, 22, 23, 26, 29, 31, 32, 33, 34, 36, 37, 38, 40, 41, 42, 44, 45, 48, 49, 51, 52, 54, 71, 73, 77, 78, 79, 82, 84, 86, 88, 89, 158
Canatha 218, 232, 251, 252. *See also* Kenath
Capercotnei 206, 227
Capernaum 21, 225, 226, 227, 228, 229, 230, 232, 233
Capharabis 261
Caphareccho 256
Caphar-harub 266
Capharorsa 261
Caphar Saba 208
Capharsalama 189, 190, 191
Caphartobas 260, 261
Caphethra 261
Caphtor 66. *See also* Crete
Caphtorim 12, 13
Capitolias 232
Cappadocia 12, 150, 152, 154, 155, 156, 157, 163, 164, 169, 173, 174, 239, 240, 246
Carchemish 15, 33, 74, 93, 99, 109, 121, 125, 140, 141, 143, 144, 146, 150, 152, 158, 160, 165
Caria; Carians 134, 137, 150, 152, 156, 162, 164, 169, 170, 173, 174, 177
Carmel 50, 64, 65, 69, 112, 113. *See also* Khirbet el-Kirmil
Carmel; Carmel Range 20, 198, 212, 214, 223. *See also* Mount Carmel
Carmi 44, 68
Carnaim 186, 188. *See also* Karnaim
Carthage 94, 159, 173
Casiphia 148
Casius 15
Cassius 214
Casluhim 13
Caspian Gates 176
Caspian Sea 24, 176
Caspin 186, 187
Cassander 177, 243
Caucasus Mountains 24, 26, 176
Cauda 248, 249
Caunians 156
Cave of Horrors 267, 268
Cave of the Letters 267
Cave of the Pool 267
Cave of the Valley 11
Caystri Campus 169
Cedar Mountain 109
Celenae; Celaenae 169, 174
Cenchreae 244, 245
Cendebeus 202, 203
Cephas 237. *See also* Simon Peter
Ceramon Agora 169
Cerealis 259
Cereas 178
Cestius Gallus 250, 253, 254, 255, 256, 261
Cestrus River 242
Chabulon 227, 255. *See also* Cabul
Chalcidice 162
Chalcis 195, 197, 251, 252
Chaldean Kingdom. *See* Neo-Babylonian Kingdom
Chaldeans 33, 132, 133
Charax (in Gilead) 186
Charax (on Persian Gulf) 176
Charmande 169
Chaspho 187
Chasphomake 187
Chebar River 148
Chedorlaomer 34
Chelkias 207
Chephar-ha-ammoni 82
Chephirah 46, 69, 82, 89, 167, 168
Chephren. *See* Khafre
Cherith Brook 107
Cherethites 21, 66, 70
Cherub 148
Chesalon 58, 83, 88, 89, 94
Chesalon Valley 57
Chezib 36, 130. *See also* Achzib (in Judah)
Chicago Prism 127
Chinnereth 17, 50, 54, 63, 73, 84, 87, 91, 92, 96, 98, 120
Chinnereth, Sea of. *See* Sea of Chinnereth
Chinneroth 21
Chios 162, 174, 246
Chisloth-tabor 54, 55, 78, 84, 90, 91
Chorazin 227, 228, 230
Chorseas River 159
Christ, Jesus. *See* Jesus
Chrysopolis 169
Cilicia 12, 15, 76, 134, 152, 153, 155, 159, 160, 163, 164, 169, 170, 171, 172, 173, 174, 176, 177, 194, 195, 240, 242, 243, 244, 246, 248, 249. *See also* Hilakku
Cilician Gates 158, 170, 171, 172, 173, 243
Cimmerians 12, 136, 137
Cimon 163, 164
Cisjordan 20, 31, 32, 33, 45, 53, 68
City of Palms 53
Claudius Caesar 241, 245, 248, 251
Cleopatra (wife of Ptolemy V) 180
Cleopatra III 207
Cleopatra VII 217, 218
Cleopatra Thea 201
Cnidus 248, 249
Coastal Plain 14, 18, 112, 188, 194, 205
Coele-Syria 179, 195, 196, 197, 208, 209, 210
Coenoe 169
Colonae 174
Colossae 169
Commagene 121, 143. *See also* Kummukh
Constantine 229
Coreae 210, 211, 260
Corinth 177, 244, 245, 246
Cornelius 240, 241
Corsote 169
Cos 246, 247
Cotyora 169
Cozeba (Cezib) 69
Craterus 176
Cretans 239
Crete 13, 27, 66, 174, 177, 194, 240, 244, 246, 249. *See also* Caphtor
Crocodilon Polis 175
Crocodile River 19
Croesus 152, 153, 156
Ctesias 164, 166
Cun 27, 73
Cunaxa 169
Cush; Cushites (in Africa) 12, 82, 119, 123, 125, 126, 129, 131, 132, 134, 136. *See also* Nubia; Nubians
Cush; Cushan (in Arabia) 53, 95, 104. *See also* Hejaz; Midian
Cush (in Palestine) 27
Cutha 121, 125, 127
Cutheans 204, 218
Cyaxares 140, 141, 155
Cybistra 169
Cypros (fortress) 219, 254, 255
Cypros (mother of Herod the Great) 214
Cyprus 12, 15, 24, 128, 147, 149, 150, 151, 152, 158, 160, 162, 163, 164, 166, 169, 170, 171, 172, 173, 174, 176, 177, 178, 182, 195, 206, 207, 240, 241, 242, 244, 246, 247, 248, 249
Cyprus (wife of Agrippa I) 250
Cyrenaica 151, 240, 244, 246, 248
Cyrene 150, 151, 162, 164, 178, 239, 240, 244
Cyrus II (the Great) 152, 153, 154, 155, 156, 157, 160, 199
Cyrus the Younger 169
Cyzicenus 205

# D

Dabaloth 210. *See also* Beth-diblathaim
Dabbesheth 90, 91
Daberath 54, 55, 78, 84, 90, 91
Daburieh. *See* Daberath
Dadanu 153. *See also* Dedan
Dahammu 143
Dahshur 27
Dakhla 82
Damascus (city) 11, 15, 16, 19, 23, 24, 29, 33, 35, 72, 73, 74, 76, 79, 83, 96, 98, 99, 106, 107, 109, 110, 111, 113, 117, 118, 119, 120, 121, 122, 123, 124, 127, 131, 138, 140, 141, 143, 149, 150, 152, 158, 160, 165, 166, 170, 171, 172, 173, 174, 176, 177, 178, 195, 197, 198, 208, 210, 214, 232, 240, 241, 244, 251, 252, 265
Damascus (region) 15, 72, 73, 96, 98, 99, 101, 105, 106, 108, 109, 111, 120, 122, 124, 132, 138, 149, 158, 166, 170, 171, 172. *See also* Aram; Aram-Damascus
Damieh. *See* Adam
Dammam 24
Damuras River 178
Dan (city) 10, 16, 17, 21, 26, 27, 28, 30, 32, 35, 50, 52, 55, 58, 59, 63, 67, 72, 73, 74, 75, 80, 84, 87, 96, 98, 108, 113, 118, 125, 209. *See also* Laish
Dan; Danites (tribe) 17, 37, 49, 50, 51, 52, 54, 55, 57, 58, 67, 77, 78, 82, 83, 84, 88, 90, 94, 129, 149
Danunians 54
Daphne (in Egypt) 38, 39. *See also* Baal-zephon; Tahpanes; Tell Defeneh
Daphne (in Palestine) 227. *See also* Antiochia
Daphne (nr. Antioch in Syria) 180, 181
Darius I 154, 156, 157, 160, 161, 162, 163, 166, 199
Darius II 168, 169
Darius III 159, 172, 173, 174, 176
Darius the Mede 154
Dascylium 174
Datames 170
Dathema 186, 187
David 17, 42, 51, 58, 60, 61, 63, 64, 65, 66, 67, 68, 70, 71, 72, 73, 74, 75, 76, 77, 79, 84, 87, 88, 89, 91, 102, 103, 113, 209, 221, 222, 224
David, House (dynasty) of 59, 74, 94, 103, 106
Dayukku 155
Dead Sea 17, 18, 22, 23, 28, 32, 34, 36, 39, 42, 43, 44, 45, 46, 50, 52, 53, 55, , 61, 63, 64, 65, 69, 71, 72, 81, 84, 87, 101, 102, 103, 104, 110, 111, 112, 120, 122, 126, 129, 132, 158, 165, 166, 167, 170, 171, 172, 175, 183, 187, 192, 193, 194, 198, 201, 204, 207, 209, 212, 214, 215, 218, 223, 225, 226, 251, 252, 254, 259, 260, 261, 263, 265, 266, 267
Debir (in Judah) 20, 42, 46, 47, 48, 50, 52, 53, 57, 63, 65, 66, 69, 78, 87, 95
Debir (nr. Jordan R.) 89
Deborah 45, 53, 54, 67, 88
Decapolis 212, 232, 233, 251
Dedan 12, 153
Deioces 155
Deir 33
Deir Allah 55. *See also* Succoth
Deir el-Azar 89. *See also* Baalah (in Judah); Kiriath-jearim
Deir el-Balah 28, 30, 32
Deir el-Ballas 27
Deir el-Bersha 27
Delilah 57
Delos 230
Delphi 151, 156
Demetrius I Soter 177, 188, 189, 191, 192, 193, 194, 195, 196, 201
Demetrius II Nicator 194, 195, 196, 197, 198, 200, 201, 203, 206
Demetrius III Akairos 208, 209
Dendara 27
Der 123
Dera. *See* Edrei
Derbe 242, 243, 244, 246
Derbent 176
Dessau 190
Dhiban 42, 102. *See also* Dibon
Diblaten 102, 103. *See also* Beth-diblathaim
Dibon; Dibon-gad 17, 23, 42, 43, 44, 50, 52, 63, 65, 71, 84, 87, 96, 101, 102, 103, 104, 110, 112, 120, 124, 132. *See also* Dhiban
Dibseh. *See* Thapsacus; Tiphsah
Diocaesarea 230. *See also* Sepphoris
Dio Cassius 265, 266
Diodachi 176, 177
Diodorus 157
Diodotus of Apamea. *See* Tryphon
Dionysius 244
Diospolis 240. *See also* Lydda
Dium; Dion 175, 209, 210, 211, 212, 218, 232. *Also* Diospolis? 218
Dius 75
Di-zahab 39
Djahi 15, 31
Dodanim 12
Dok; Docus 201, 203, 204, 205, 219
Domeh. *See* Dumah
Domitian 249
Dophkah 39
Dor; Dora 15, 17, 19, 28, 30, 31, 32, 48, 50, 52, 54, 61, 63, 67, 68, 70, 72, 73, 74, 81, 83, 84, 87, 91, 96, 106, 111, 113, 120, 122, 123, 124, 128, 132, 135, 138, 146, 158, 159, 163, 165, 166, 170, 171, 172, 175, 178, 184, 187, 202, 205, 207, 209, 212, 213, 214, 218, 223, 225, 227, 233, 251, 252, 266
Dor (district) 51, 74, 122, 135. *See also* Naphoth Dor
Dor, Fortress of 201
Dorians 32
Dositheus 186
Dothan 28, 30, 36, 55, 84, 107
Dothan Valley 20, 36, 82, 83, 84
Drangiana 176
Drapsaca 176
Drusilla 248, 251
Drymus 214
Dumah 121, 138, 140, 150, 152
Dura 81. *See also* Adora; Adoraim
Dura-Europos 150, 152
Dur-karashu 154
Dur-Sharrukin 121, 123, 127. *See also* Khorsabad
Duru. *See* Dor (district)

# E

Eastern Sea 17, 149. *See also* Dead Sea
Ebenezer 60, 66
Eber 13, 34
Ebez 91
Ebla 25, 26. *See also* Tell Mardikh
Ebron 91
Ecbatana 150, 152, 155, 156, 160, 161, 165, 176, 240
Ecdippa 214, 227, 232. *See also* Achzib (in Asher)
Edfu 27
Edh-Dhaheriyeh 47
Edom; Edomites 14, 16, 19, 21, 22, 23, 37, 40, 41, 42, 43, 44, 50, 54, 61, 62, 63, 65, 69, 72, 73, 75, 78, 79, 81, 100, 101, 102, 103, 104, 105, 107, 109, 110, 112, 113, 114, 115, 118, 119, 122, 124, 125, 126, 128, 132, 134, 138, 146, 147, 148, 153, 159, 160, 172
Edrei 17, 45, 50, 56, 87, 91, 92, 98, 232
Egeria 229, 230
Eglaim 209
Eglon 46, 47, 48, 53, 57, 63, 65, 69, 95, 118, 138
Egypt 12, 14, 15, 19, 24, 25, 26, 27, 29, 30, 31, 33, 34, 36, 37, 38, 73, 74, 75, 76, 78, 79, 84, 111, 112, 116, 119, 120, 121, 122, 123, 124, 125, 129, 131, 132, 133, 134, 135, 136, 137, 138, 140, 141, 142, 143, 144, 145, 146, 148, 149, 150, 151, 152, 153, 157, 161, 162, 163, 164, 165, 166, 167, 168, 169, 170, 171, 172, 173, 174, 176, 177, 178, 179, 181, 182, 207, 211, 213, 217, 218, 224, 239, 240, 244, 248, 256, 261, 268
Egypt, River of 14, 16, 75
Egyptian world view 13

Egyptus 246. *See also* Egypt
Ehud 52, 53
Ekallate 121
Ekron 17, 19, 28, 31, 32, 47, 50, 57, 58, 60, 61, 63, 64, 65, 69, 70, 73, 81, 83, 84, 87, 89, 94, 96, 106, 113, 118, 119, 120, 122, 123, 124, 126, 127, 128, 129, 130, 131, 132, 137, 142, 144, 209. *See also* Accaron; Tel Miqne
Elah (son of Baasha) 94, 96
Elah Valley 20, 36, 46, 63, 69, 72, 80, 118, 119, 129, 130, 240, 241
Elam (town) 168
Elam; Elamites 12, 34, 114, 121, 123, 127, 132, 133, 135, 146, 150, 161, 239
Elammu 143
El-Arish 119, 123, 161. *See also* Ienysus; Rhinocorura
El-Ashmunein 27
Elath 21, 22, 23, 39, 43, 73, 74, 76, 110, 111, 112, 113, 118, 121, 132, 140, 150, 152, 158, 170. *See also* Eloth; Ezion-geber
Elath, Gulf of 22, 38, 41. *See also* Aqabah, Gulf of
El-Bira. *See* Berea
Elealeh 56
Eleasa 191, 192
Eleazar (son of Ananias) 253, 254
Eleazar (son of Jair[us]) 254, 263, 264
Eleazar (son of Simon) 256, 261
Eleazar Maccabeus 188, 189
Elephantine 27, 168. *See also* Yeb
Eleus 174
Eleutheropolis 63, 199, 240. *See also* Beth Govrin; Betogabris
Eleutherus River 177, 178, 195, 197, 218
El-Gebalin. *See* Gobalis
Elhanan, son of Jaare-oregim 63
Eliakim 138, 142. *See also* Jehoiakim
Elijah 107, 225
Elijah Cycle 98, 107
Elim 39
Eliphaz 62, 66
El-Iraq 103. *See also* Horonaim; Oronaim
Elis 162
Elisha 107
Elisha Cycle 103, 105, 107
Elishah 12
El-Jaia Cave 59. *See also* Rimmon, Rock of
El-Jib 59, 71. *See also* Gabaon; Gibeon
El-Kab 27
Elkanah 59, 60
El-Kursi. *See* Gergesa
Ellasar 34
Ellipi 155
Ellisu 158. *See also* Tripolis; Ullasa
El-Lubban 59. *See also* Lebonah; Lubban esh-Sherqiyeh
Elmathan 108
El-Mezerib 187
El-Midya. *See* Modiin
El-Mishneqeh. *See* Macherus
El-Mughar 76. *See also* Baalath
Elnathan 145
El-Odeitha 10, 120
Elon 52, 57, 83, 94
Elon-beth-hanan 83
Eloth 110, 111, 112. *See also* Elath
El-Paran 11, 35
El-Qereiyat 102. *See also* Kerioth
El-Qureiyeh. *See* Kiriaten; Kiriathaim
Eltekeh 69, 78, 83, 94, 129
Eltolad 71
Eluli; Elulaios 128
Elusa 209
Elyashib son of Oshiyahu 146, 147
El-Yehudiye 258. *See also* Sogane (in Gaulanitis)
Elymais 180. *See also* Elam
Elymas 246
Emar. *See* Tell Meskeneh
Emim 11, 34, 35
Emmatha 227, 228. *See also* Hammath Gader
Emmaus 183, 184, 185, 186, 192, 193, 194, 201, 202, 205, 209, 214, 215, 225, 233, 237, 238, 256, 260, 261, 266, 267
Enaim; Enam 36
En-dor 54, 55, 63, 66
En-gannim 78, 91
En-gedi 23, 63, 64, 65, 69, 101, 112, 126, 138, 158, 165, 166, 167, 168, 170, 171, 172, 204, 209, 214, 225, 259, 260, 266, 267
En-gedi, Stronghold of 64
En Gev 98. *See also* Khirbet Asheq
En-haddah 55, 84, 91
En-harod 55
En-hazor 91, 92
En-mishpat 10, 11, 35, 40. *See also* Kadesh; Kadesh-barnea
En-rogel 89
En-shemesh 89
Ephes-dammim 63
Ephesus 137, 163, 164, 174, 240, 244, 245, 246, 247, 249
Ephraim 14, 16, 17, 20, 37, 45, 50, 51, 52, 53, 54, 56, 57, 58, 60, 61, 63, 65, 68, 69, 70, 78, 82, 86, 87, 88, 89, 90, 137, 149
Ephraim (district) 184
Ephraim (village) 82, 192. *See also* Ephron; Ophrah (in Benjamin)
Ephraim, Hill country of 31, 32, 36, 45, 53, 58, 60, 68, 85, 98, 100, 113. *See also* Mount Ephraim
Ephraimites 49, 50, 52, 55, 57, 77. *See also* Joseph, House of
Ephrath; Ephrathah 36, 69. *See also* Bethlehem (in Judah)
Ephron (in Benjamin) 82. *See also* Ephraim; Ophrah (in Benjamin)
Ephron (in Gilead) 186, 188. *See also* Gephrus
Epicrates 205
Epirus 162, 219
Erech 12, 33
Eretria 162
Er-Ram. *See* Ramah (in Benjamin)
Er-Riha 233
Esarhaddon 14, 116, 121, 132, 133, 134, 136, 137
Esau 35, 36, 63, 66
Esbus 43, 44, 209, 212, 218, 223, 254, 266. *See also* Heshbon
Esdraelon 20, 198, 205, 206, 212, 227, 256. *See also* Jezreel Valley
Esdud. *See* Ashdod
Eshbaal 70, 71, 72. *See also* Ish-bosheth
Eshcol 113
Eshmunazer. *See* Eshmunazor
Eshmunazor I 165
Eshmunazor II 158, 165
\ Eshmunazor Inscription 19, 164, 165, 170
Eshnunna 33
Esh-Shaghur 92, 227. *See also* Beth-haccerem Valley
Eshtaol 57, 58, 67, 69, 83, 94
Eshtemoa 63, 65, 69, 78
Esna 27
Es-Saliyeh 42
Es-Sawafir 130
Essebon 43. *See also* Heshbon
Essenes, Gate of the 234
Etam (in Judah) 58, 69, 80, 101
Etam (in Simeon) 58
Eteocypriots 160
Eth-kazin 90
Etham 39
Ether 47, 71
Ethiopian eunuch 240
Ethobaal 94, 97, 105, 128, 149. *See also* Ittobaal I
Etruscans. *See* Tiras
Et-Taiybeh (in Transjordan). *See* Tob
Et-Taiyiba. *See* Ephron (in Gilead)
Et-Taiyibeh 62. *See also* Ephron; Ophrah (in Benjamin)
Et-Tell 32, 45, 46. *See also* Ai
Et-Teniye. *See* Athone
Et-Tur 124
Euboea 162
Euphrates River 14, 15, 17, 24, 33, 69, 70, 72, 74, 75, 93, 99, 109, 111, 116, 121, 125, 136, 140, 141, 143, 144, 148, 155, 157, 160, 165, 169, 171, 176, 178, 200, 240
Eurotas River 162
Eurymedon River 163, 165
Eusebius 19, 57, 231, 232, 240, 265, 266
Eutychus 246
Euxine Sea 174, 176, 240. *See also* Black Sea
Evagoras 169, 170
Evil-merodach 74, 151. *See also* Amel-Marduk
Exaloth 227
Execration Texts 27
Ezekias (Hasmonean leader) 213
Ezekias (high priest) 168
Ezekiel 16, 33, 107, 115, 142, 147, 148, 149, 150
Ezem 71
Ezion-geber 22, 23, 39, 40, 75, 76, 101, 112, 118, 132. *See also* Tell el-Kheleifeh
Ezra 165, 166, 168
Ez-Zib. *See* Achzib (in Asher); Tel Akhzib

# F

Fadak 153. *See also* Padakku
Fair Havens 248, 249
Faran. *See* Feiran
Farata 57. *See also* Pirathon
Fars 155. *See also* Parsa
Feinan 23, 41. *See also* Punon
Feiran 40
Felix 248
Fertile Crescent 14, 116, 140
Festus 248, 249, 252
Fiq 98
Flavius Silva. *See* Silva
Florus 252, 253, 254, 255
Fortunatus 250
Forum of Appius 248, 249

# G

Gaba 254, 266. *See also* Geba (nr. Mount Carmel)
Gaba; Gabatha 210. *See also* Geba (in Benjamin)
Gabala 213
Gabalis 209
Gabara 227
Gabinius 199, 211, 212, 213, 263
Gablini 140
Gabaon 254, 255. *See also* Gibeon
Gad; Gadites 17, 23, 42, 44, 50, 52, 54, 56, 65, 73, 74, 78, 82, 84, 85, 88, 97, 98, 102, 103, 106, 110, 125, 149
Gadara 178, 179, 207, 209, 210, 212, 213, 218, 223, 225, 226, 227, 228, 230, 231, 232, 233, 241, 251, 252, 254, 266
Gadara (district) 230, 231, 232
Gadatas 161
Gadi 114
Gadora 225, 232, 252, 254, 259, 260, 266. *See also* Gedor
Galaaditis 186, 187, 188, 198, 199, 208, 209, 210. *See also* Gilead
Gaius Caesar 251
Gaius Caligula. *See* Caligula
Galasa. *See* Gerasa
Galatia 242, 243, 244, 245, 246, 248
Galil-ha-Goiim 48. *See also* Galilee of the Gentiles/Nations
Galilee 15, 18, 19, 31, 48, 49, 51, 53, 55, 71, 76, 85, 88, 91, 92, 96, 108, 114, 120, 126, 158, 165, 166, 170, 171, 172, 175, 179, 186, 187, 191, 196, 197, 198, 205, 206, 209, 210, 212, 213, 214, 215, 216, 217, 218, 219, 223, 224, 225, 226, 227, 228, 229, 230, 231, 233, 236, 237, 238, 241, 250, 251, 252, 254, 255, 256, 257, 266
Galilee, Sea of. *See* Sea of Galilee
Galilee of the Gentiles/Nations 10, 120, 121, 122. *Also* Galilee of the Foreigners 187
Gallim 124
Gallio 244, 245
Gallus, Cestius. *See* Cestius Gallus
Gamala 209, 213, 251, 252, 254, 256, 257, 258
Gamalitike 258
Gandhara 157
Garaba 206, 227, 256, 257
Garada 208
Gargamis 117
Garis 227, 256, 257. *See also* Cana; Kafr Kana
Gath (in Sharon) 36, 37, 61, 71. *See also Gath-rimmon; Gittaim*
Gath (of Philistines) 17, 19, 29, 31, 32, 37, 50, 51, 57, 60, 61, 63, 64, 65, 69, 70, 71, 73, 74, 81, 84, 87, 95, 106, 108, 111, 112, 114, 119, 123, 125, 126, 127, 129, 130, 241. *See also* Tell es-Safi
Gath-carmel 29
Gath-hepher 55, 84, 90, 91, 115, 227
Gath-padalla 19, 29, 81, 83
Gath-paran 108
Gath-rimmon 37, 51, 60, 61, 71, 72, 78, 83, 84, 94. *See also* Gath (in Sharon); Gittaim
Gaugamela 172, 176
Gaul; Gauls 178, 250
Gaulana 23, 209, 266
Gaulanitis 23, 208, 209, 210, 218, 219, 223, 231, 251, 252, 254, 256, 257, 258
Gaza 14, 15, 16, 19, 21, 29, 31, 32, 35, 39, 42, 43, 50, 52, 55, 57, 58, 63, 65, 66, 69, 70, 73, 74, 76, 81, 84, 95, 112, 113, 118, 119, 120, 122, 123, 124, 126, 127, 131, 132, 134, 135, 136, 138, 141, 143, 144, 145, 146, 148, 150, 152, 154, 158, 159, 160, 165, 166, 167, 170, 171, 172, 173, 174, 175, 176, 177, 178, 179, 182, 195, 196, 204, 207, 209, 212, 213, 218, 219, 223, 224, 225, 240, 241, 251, 252, 254, 261, 265, 266, 267, 268. *See also* Kadytis
Gazara 183, 184, 185, 186, 187, 188, 190, 192, 193, 194, 195, 198, 199, 200, 201, 202, 203, 204, 205, 209, 212. *See also* Gezer
Geba (in Benjamin) 53, 55, 58, 59, 61, 62, 69, 71, 78, 82, 84, 95, 96, 123, 124, 129, 139, 167, 168, 191. *Also* Gibeath-elohim
Geba (in Samaria) 108
Geba (nr. Mount Carmel) 187, 205, 206, 209, 212, 218, 223, 225, 227, 232
Gebal 73, 74, 150, 152. *See also* Byblos
Geber, the son of Uri 85
Gebim 124
Gedaliah; Gedalyahu 148, 149, 168
Geder 48, 124, 132. *See also* Gerar
Gederah 69
Gederoth 118, 119
Gedor 69, 138, 167, 194, 201, 204, 209, 210, 218, 223
Gedrosia 176
Ge-harashim 69
Geliloth 89
Gennath Gate (in Jerusalem) 234, 237
Gennesar 21. *See also* Gennosar
Gennesaret 196, 227, 228, 229, 230, 233
Gennesaret/Gennesar, Plain of 21, 228, 229
Gennesaret, Lake/Waters of 196, 216, 228, 256. *See also* Sea of Galilee
Gennosar 206
Georgia 24
Gephrus 178. *See also* Ephron (in Gilead)
Gerar 16, 34, 35, 36, 37, 42, 43, 48, 50, 63, 65, 69, 95, 126, 204. *See also* Geder
Gerar Brook 18
Gerasa (in Samaria) 259, 260
Gerasa (in Transjordan) 175, 209, 210, 212, 223, 225, 230, 231, 232, 241, 254, 266
Gergesa 227, 228, 230, 231, 232. *Also* Gergeshta; Girgash
Gerrha 178
Gershonites 78
Geshem the Arab 21, 160, 166, 167
Geshur 23, 29, 50, 63, 70, 72, 73, 74, 78, 80, 81, 84, 96, 231
Gessius Florus 250
Gethsemane 234, 235
Gezer 17, 20, 24, 28, 29, 30, 32, 36, 43, 46, 47, 48, 49, 50, 51, 52, 57, 60, 61, 63, 67, 69, 71, 72, 73, 74, 75, 76, 77, 78, 80, 81, 83, 84, 87, 88, 89, 94, 119, 120, 126, 127, 129, 138, 158, 165, 166, 167, 168, 169, 170, 171, 172, 192, 201. *See also* Gazara
Ghor es-Safi. *See* Zoar
Ghor es-Safiyeh 104
Gibbethon 32, 60, 69, 78, 80, 82, 83, 84, 94, 95, 96, 119, 123, 126, 128
Gibea 69
Gibeah 53, 58, 59, 60, 61, 62, 63, 64, 65, 66, 69, 72, 82, 84, 89, 95, 123, 124, 129, 261. *Also* Gibeah of Benjamin; Gibeah of Saul
Gibeath-elohim. *See* Geba (in Benjamin)
Gibeath-kiriath-jearim 60
Gibeon 20, 28, 30, 45, 46, 47, 50, 53, 57, 58, , 59, 61, 62, 63, 64, 65, 69, 71, 72, 78, 80, 81, 82, 84, 89, 95, 148, 167, 168, 190, 191, 255. *See also* Gabaon
Gideon 52, 55, 56, 59, 88. *See also* Jerubbaal
Gihon Spring 203
Gilat 11
Gilead 10, 14, 15, 16, 17, 18, 23, 43, 44, 45, 54, 56, 57, 61, 63, 67, 68, 70, 73, 84, 85, 87, 96, 98, 106, 107, 108, 114, 115, 117, 118, 120, 121, 122, 124, 132, 134, 146, 148, 149, 158, 159, 165, 166, 167, 170, 171, 172, 175. *See also* Galaaditis
Gilgal 45, 46, 50, 52, 53, 55, 58, , 53, 61, 62, 63, 89, 107, 191
Giloh 32
Gimzo 69, 118, 119
Gina; Ginae 29, 233. *See also* Beth-haggan
Ginnosar. *See* Gennesar
Girgash 231. *See also* Gergesa
Girgashite 13
Gischala 206, 212, 225, 227, 232, 256, 257, 258, 259, 262, 266. *See also* Gush Halav
Gittaim 37, 51, 57, 60, 61, 69, 71, 80, 119, 167, 215. *See also* Gath (in Sharon); Gath-rimmon
Giza 162, 164
Gobalis 210
Gobryas 161, 169. *See also* Gubaru
Gog 136
Goiim in Galilee 48. *See also* Galil-ha-goiim
Golan (region) 14, 23. *See also* Bashan
Golan (town) 78. *See also* Gaulana
Golashkerd 176
Golgotha Hill 234
Goliath 63, 64
Gomer 12, 136
Gomorrah 11, 34, 35, 59
Gophna (town) 183, 184, 190, 191, 192, 194, 209, 214, 266
Gophna (province) 256, 261
Gophna, Hills of 183, 184, 188, 189, 190, 191, 192, 204
Gordion 136, 173, 174
Gorgias 184, 185, 188
Goshen (in Egypt) 37, 38, 39
Goshen (in Judah) 69
Gozan 70, 99, 109, 120, 121, 125, 140
Granicus River 172, 173, 174
Great Plain 51, 83. *See also* Jezreel Valley
Great Rift 14, 22. *See also* Rift Valley
Great Sea 16, 17, 18, 24, 29, 32, 33, 34, 36, 37, 39, 42, 43, 47, 50, 52, 54, 57, 60, 63, 64, 65, 66, 67, 69, 70, 73, 74, 78, 80, 81, 83, 84, 87, 94, 96, 98, 104, 106, 107, 111, 113, 115, 118, 120, 122, 129, 141, 149. *Also* Mediterranean Sea
Greece 24, 31, 32, 134, 151, 159, 162, 177, 246
Gubaru 160, 161, 169, 172. *See also* Gobryas
Gur, Ascent of 105
Gurbaal 112
Gurgum 116, 117, 121
Gurun. *See* Togarmah
Gush Halav 209. *See also* Gischala
Guti 109
Gutium 154
Guzanu. *See* Gozan
Gyges 137

# H

Habbakkuk 107
Habor River 24, 99, 120, 125, 140

Hadad 73, 79
Hadadezer 72, 73, 79
Hadad-idri 99, 100, 102, 105, 106
Hadashah 190
Hadattah 109, 121
Hadid 167, 168. *See also* Adida
Hadoram 72. *See also* Joram
Hadrach 74, 109, 125
Hadrian 236, 265, 266, 267, 268
Hagarim 81
Haggai 107, 142, 161
Halab. *See* Aleppo
Halah 120, 125
Halhul 20, 69
Hali 84, 90, 91
Halicarnassus 173, 174
Halpi 117
Halys River 24, 155, 169, 174, 176
Ham (city) 11, 34, 35, 50, 56, 68
Ham (son of Noah) 12
Hamadan. *See* Ecbatana
Hamath (in Naphtali) 63, 78. *See also* Hammath
Hamath (on the Orontes) 12, 15, 16, 74, 99, 109, 110, 117, 121, 123, 125, 140, 141, 143, 144, 150, 152, 155, 158, 160, 165, 171, 172, 197. *See also* Amathus
—(city-state; district) 13, 72, 73, 74, 75, 94, 99, 105, 108, 109, 110, 111, 113, 117, 118, 122, 123, 124, 144, 149, 153, 196, 197
Hamath-zobah 74
Hamites 95
Hammath; Hammath Tiberias 84, 91, 92, 228, 230. *Also* Hammam Tabariyeh
Hammath Gader 230
Hammon 17, 84, 87, 91
Hamutal 138, 140, 142, 146
Hananiah 168
Hanes 121
Hanin, House of. *See* Annas, House of
Hannathon 29, 63, 84, 91, 120. *See also* Asochis
Hannathon Valley 227
Hanun; Hanunu 71, 119, 120, 123, 124
Hapharaim 55, 66, 84, 91
Hara 120
Haramatha 194, 195, 204, 205. *See also* Arimathea
Haran 33, 74, 99, 109, 121, 125, 140, 141, 142, 143, 150, 152, 153, 154, 155, 156, 160, 165
Hararate 127
Har Hamelech 267
Har-heres 52, 60, 61, 67, 83, 94
Harim 168
Harmene 169
Harod, Spring of 55, 66, 83. *See also* Ain Jalud; En-harod
Harod Valley 20, 83
Harosheth-ha-goiim 10, 54, 84, 85, 121
Harpagus 156
Hasideans 183, 184, 189, 190
Hatti/Hattu, land of 14, 30, 109, 133, 143, 144, 145, 146, 153, 154, 157. *See also* Amurru
Hattina 109
Hattusas 29
Hattusili I 28
Hauran 15, 23, 122, 124, 149, 158, 165, 166, 170, 171, 172, 209, 232
Havilah 12, 62
Havvoth-jair 17, 23, 45, 50, 56, 68, 84, 87
Hawronen. *See* Horonaim
Hawwarin. *See* Ziphron
Hazael (king of Arabia) 133, 134
Hazael (king of Damascus) 103, 105, 106, 107, 108, 109, 110, 111, 114, 115, 120, 121
Hazar-addar 15, 16, 40, 42
Hazar-enan 16, 149
Hazarmaveth 12
Hazar-shual 71
Hazar-susah 71
Hazeroth 39, 40, 108
Hazi 29
Hazor (in Judah) 167. *See also* Baal-hazor
Hazor (in Naphtali) 16, 21, 26, 27, 28, 29, 30, 31, 32, 33, 48, 52, 53, 54, 67, 76, 77, 80, 84, 92, 96, 98, 106, 111, 113, 118, 120, 158, 165, 166, 167, 170, 171, 172, 195, 196, 206
Hazor, Plain of 196. *See also* Asor, Plain of
Heber the Kenite 54, 92
Hebra 153
Hebrews 30, 62
Hebron 11, 16, 17, 20, 28, 30, 32, 34, 35, 36, 38, 40, 42, 43, 46, 47, 48, 50, 52, 57, 58, 63, 64, 65, 68, 69, 70, 71, 72, 73, 74, 76, 78, 80, 81, 84, 87, 95, 101, 104, 110, 112, 113, 118, 120, 124, 126, 127, 129, 132, 138, 146, 148, 167, 175, 186, 187, 188, 192, 194, 199, 201, 204, 209, 222, 225, 240, 259, 260, 261, 266, 267, 268
Hebrus 162
Hecataeus, world view of 13
Hecatomnus 170
Hejaz 14, 40, 79, 95, 96, 104. *See also* Midian
Helam 72, 73
Helek 68, 108
Helena of Adiabene 245
Heleph 17, 55, 87, 91, 92
Heliodorus 180
Heliopolis 27, 38, 176, 228, 232. *See also* On
Helkath 17, 78, 84, 87, 90, 91
Helkath-hazzurim 71
Hellas 162, 163, 174
Hellenes 151
Hellespont 173, 255
Hepher (city) 48, 61, 63, 83
Hepher (clan; district) 68, 69, 83, 84, 85
Heptapegon. *See* Tabgha
Heraclea 169, 240
Herat 176
Hereth, Forest of 64
Hermopolis 148, 168
Hermus 162
Herod (of Chalcis) 251, 252
Herod (the Great) 201, 204, 210, 213–223, 224, 232, 233, 234, 236, 237, 239, 247, 262, 263
Herod Agrippa I. *See* Agrippa I
Herod Antipas 223, 226, 228, 232, 234, 236, 250, 251, 263
Herod Philip 250, 251
Herodias 236, 250
Herodium; Herodion 214, 221, 223, 259, 260, 261, 263, 266, 267
Herodotus 13, 15, 131, 157, 158, 159, 160, 161, 163, 164
Herod Philip 223
Heroonpolis 182
Heshbon 17, 42, 43, 44, 50, 52, , 61, 63, 68, 78, 84, 85, 87, 101, 102, 104, 158, 165, 166, 170, 171, 172, 204, 209, 254. *See also* Esbus; Tell Hisban
Heth 13, 42
Hezekiah 41, 80, 107, 118, 122, 125, 126, 127, 128, 129, 130, 131, 132, 221
Hezron 15, 44, 68
Hilakku 121, 134, 136. *See also* Cilicia
Hina 232
Hindu Kush Mountains 176
Hinnom Valley 20, 59, 89, 211, 234
Hippolochus 178
Hippus (city) 21, 98, 209, 212, 218, 219, 223, 225, 227, 231, 232, 233, 241, 251, 252, 254, 266. *See also* Qalat el-Husn; Sussita
Hippus (district) 228, 232
Hirah 36
Hiram; Hirom 75, 76, 85, 91, 117, 118, 119, 120
Hirimmu 127
Hittites 17, 33, 75, 124
Hivites 13, 32, 45, 46, 73, 77, 78, 79
Hoglah 68, 108
Holon 78
Holy Sepulcher, Church of the 237
Homs 109
Hophra 147, 148, 149, 150, 151
Horbat Adullam. *See* Adullam; Khirbet esh-Sheikh Madhkhur
Horbat Arpad. *See* Heleph; Khirbet Irbadeh
Horbat Gamom. *See* Hukkok; Khirbet el-Jemeijmeh
Horbat Lavnin. *See* Khirbet Tell el-Beida
Horbat Qedesh. *See* Khirbet Qedish
Horbat Rosh Zayit. *See* Khirbet Ras ez-Zeitun
Horbat Ruma. *See* Khirbet er-Rumah; Rumah (in Galilee)
Horbat Shemesh. *See* Khirbet Sheikh esh-Shamsawi
Horbat Sokho. *See* Khirbet Abbad; Socoh (in Shephelah)
Horbat Tivna. *See* Khirbet et-Tabbaneh
Horbat Tivna. *See* Khirbet Tabbaneh
Horbat Uzza. *See* Khirbet Ghazzah
Horbat Yaanin. *See* Khirbet Yanin
Horbat Yoqrat. *See* Iqrit
Horeb 39, 40, 107. *See also* Mount Sinai
Horem 91, 92
Horites 11, 34, 35, 69
Hormah 36, 42, 48, 50, 63, 65, 69, 70, 71. *See also* Zephath
Horns of Hattin 48. *See also* Qarne Hittim
Horonaim 23, 102, 103, 104. *See also* Oronaim
Hosah 17, 84, 87, 91
Hosea 107, 111, 114, 115
Hoshea 117, 121, 122, 124, 125
Hukkok 91, 92
Huleh Valley 19, 21, 84, 92
Hulli 117
Hume 152, 153. *See also* Kue; Que
Hur 20, 69
Hurrians 13, 35
Hushah 65, 69
Hushim 67. *See also* Shuham
Hutta[--] (son of Pagakanna) 162, 172
Hyrcania 168, 176, 209, 210, 212, 219
Hyrcanus I. *See* John Hyrcanus
Hyrcanus II 209, 210, 211, 212, 213, 214, 215, 217, 218, 220
Hyrcanus the Tobiad 180, 181, 182
Hystanes 172. *See also* Ushtannu

# I

Iadnana 121, 128. *See also* Cyprus
Iaxartes River 176
Ibleam 17, 50, 55, 63, 68, 78, 84, 87, 98, 105, 114
Ibzan 52, 57
Iconium 169, 240, 242, 244, 246
Idalah 91
Idumea 15, 158, 160, 165, 166, 167, 170, 171, 172, 184, 185, 186, 187, 188, 192, 198, 199, 201, 204, 209, 210, 212, 213, 214, 215, 217, 219, 223, 225, 256, 259, 260, 261
Ienysus 15, 158, 159, 160, 161, 162, 164, 170, 171, 172. *See also* El-Arish; Rhinocorura
Ijon 17, 27, 50, 63, 67, 73, 74, 84, 87, 96, 120
Ijon Valley 21. *See also* Ayyun Valley
Ikausu 132, 133, 134
Iksal. *See* Chisloth-tabor
Ilasa. *See* Eleasa
Ilion 174
Ilu-bidi 123, 124
Imaret el-Khureiseh 41
Immer 148
Inaros 164
India 157, 176
Indian Ocean 176
Indo-Aryans 155
Indus River 176
Ionia 12, 137, 156, 157, 162
Iphtahel Valley 17, 87, 90, 91
Ipsus 177
Iqrit 48
Ir-nahash 69
Ir-shemesh 83, 94
Iraklion 24
Iran 12, 24, 155, 156. *See also* Persia
Iraq 24
Iraq el-Emir 167
Irhuleni 99, 105
Isaac 34, 35
Isaiah 107, 115, 131
Isana 215, 216
Isawiyeh 124
Isdud. *See* Ashdod; Azotus
Isfahan 24. *See also* Tabae
Ish-bosheth 71, 84. *See also* Eshbaal
Ishmael; Ishmaelites 37, 119
Ishmael (son of Nethaniah) 148
Ishmael (son of Phabi) 235
Isles of the Sea 157
Israel; Israelites 13, 17, 21, 24, 32, 33, 34, 35, 36, 38, 40, 41, 42, 43, 44, 45, 46, 47, 48, 49, 51, 52, 55, 56, 59, 60, 61, 62, 63, 64, 66, 70, 71, 72, 73, 74, 75, 77, 78, 79, 80, 81, 82, 84, 85, 86, 87, 88, 89, 94, 95, 96, 97, 98, 99, 100, 101, 102, 103, 104, 105, 106, 107, 108, 109, 110, 111, 112, 113, 114, 115, 117, 118, 120, 121, 122, 123, 125, 204, 267, 268
Issachar 17, 20, 50, 51, 52, 54, 56, 68, 78, 82, 84, 85, 87, 88, 89, 90, 91, 92, 94, 97, 149
Issi, Rabbi 230
Issos; Issus 169, 172, 173, 174
Istanbul 24
Itabyrium; Itabyrion 178, 256, 266. *See also* Mount Tabor
Italia; Italy 240, 248, 249
Ithlah 83, 94
Ittobaal I 94. *See also* Ethobaal
Itureans 186, 206, 212, 219
Iye-abarim 41, 43, 102
Iyim 41
Izala 142, 161
Izbet Sartah 32, 60

# J

Jaan 73
Jaazer. *See* Jazer
Jabbok River 18, 22, 23, 35, 36, 44, 45, 56, 79, 179, 186, 194, 198, 204, 205, 210, 218, 252, 259, 260
Jabesh-gilead 50, 55, 56, 59, 61, 62, 63, 66, 67, 68, 84, 98
Jabez 69
Jabin 53, 54
Jabneel; Jabneh 17, 19, 69, 83, 89, 94, 111, 112, 129. *See also* Jamnia
Jabneel (in Naphtali) 54, 55, 84, 85, 87, 91, 92
Jacob 13, 33, 35, 36, 37
Jaddua; Jaddus 174, 175, 204
Jael 53, 54, 55
Jaffa 28, 30, 32. *See also* Joppa
Jahaz 42, 43, 44, 96, 102, 104
Jahzah 17, 43, 78, 84, 87
Jair (son of Manasseh) 45, 84
Jair the Gileadite 45, 52, 56
Jambri (clan) 192
James (apostle) 247
James (son of Zebedee) 250, 256
Jamnia 19, 175, 185, 187, 188, 193, 194, 198, 201, 202, 205, 209, 212, 213, 217, 218, 223, 225, 240, 251, 252, 259, 260, 261, 266, 267. *See also* Jabneel; Jabneh
Jamnia, Port of 175, 188, 201, 205, 240. *See also* Yavneh-yam
Jamnith 227, 256
Jannaeus. *See* Alexander Jannaeus
Janoah (in Ephraim) 17, 55, 87, 90, 108
Janoah (nr. Tyre) 120, 121, 232. *Also* Janoam; Yanuh
Japheth 12
Japhia 17, 54, 55, 87, 90, 91, 227, 256
Japhlet; Japhletites 68, 89
Jarkon River 18, 19, 83
Jarmuk River 218. *See also* Yarmuk River
Jarmuth (in Issachar) 17, 26, 50, 55, 66, 78, 84, 87, 91
Jarmuth (in Judah) 36, 46, 47, 48, 63, 69, 72, 119, 167
Jashub 68, 108. *Also* Jashib
Jason (high priest) 181, 182
Jason (Paul's host) 244
Jason the Cyrene 182
Jattir 50, 65, 69, 78, 80
Javan 12
Jazer 17, 43, 44, 50, 52, 56, 63, 73, 74, 78, 84, 85, 87, 186, 187
Jeba. *See* Geba (in Benjamin)
Jebel Akkar 16
Jebel Ansariyeh. *See* Jebel Nosairah
Jebel Bishri 14
Jebel Druze 16, 23
Jebel ed-Dahi 66. *See also* Moreh, Hill of; Nebi Dahi
Jebel Fuquah 66. *See also* Mount Gilboa
Jebel Fureidis. *See* Herodium
Jebel Hauran 23
Jebel Jarmaq 19, 48, 51, 52, 53, 84, 92, 255. *See also* Mount Meiron
Jebel Jelad 56
Jebel Madrah 41
Jebel Makmel 16
Jebel Marun er-Ras 19
Jebel Musa 39, 40
Jebel Neba 102
Jebel Nebi Harun 41
Jebel Nosairah 14, 93
Jebel Qarantal. *See* Dok; Docus
Jebel Quseir 93
Jebel Usdum 23. *See also* Mount Sodom
Jebus; Jebusites 13, 17, 42, 49, 50, 52, 53, 55, 57, 58, 59, 60, 61, 63, 64, 65, 66, 69, 70, 72, 77, 85, 87, 88, 89. *See also* Jerusalem
Jehoahaz (king of Israel) 106, 108
Jehoahaz I (king of Judah). *See* Ahaziah
Jehoahaz II 138, 141, 142. *Also* Shallum
Jehoash (king of Judah) 107. *See also* Joash
Jehoash (king of Israel) 109, 110, 111, 112. *See also* Joash
Jehoezer 168
Jehoiachin 142, 145, 146, 147, 148, 151
Jehoiada 106, 107, 108
Jehoiakim 138, 141, 142, 143, 144, 145, 146
Jehoram 47, 96, 97, 98, 100, 101, 103, 104, 105, 106, 107, 114, 115. *Also* Joram
Jehoshaphat (king of Judah) 80, 96, 97, 100, 101, 103, 104
Jehoshaphat (son of Paruah) 85
Jehu 105, 106, 107, 114
Jekabzeel 11, 35, 65
Jenin. *See* Beth-haggan
Jephthah 44, 52, , 56, 57
Jerahmeel; Jerahmeelites 21, 65, 66, 68, 69, 70, 74, 80
Jerash. *See* Gerasa (in Transjordan)
Jeremiah (prophet) 60, 107, 115, 137, 139, 141, 142, 146, 147, 148, 149, 152
Jericho 16, 17, 20, 22, 26, 28, 30, 42, 43, 45, 48, 53, 58, 72, 80, 82, 87, 88, 89, 90, 107, 118, 126, 138, 146, 148, 158, 165, 166, 167, 168, 170, 171, 172, 175, 183, 191, 192, 193, 194, 198, 201, 203, 204, 205, 209, 210, 211, 212, 215, 216, 217, 218, 219, 220, 223, 224, 225, 226, 233, 234, 241, 251, 252, 255, 256, 259, 260, 261, 265, 266, 267
Jeroboam I 78, 79, 80, 81, 82, 83, 94, 95
Jeroboam II 109, 110, 111, 113, 114, 115
Jerome 232
Jerubbaal 55. *See also* Gideon
Jerusalem 15, 16, 20, 24, 27, 28, 29, 30, 32, 35, 36, 37, 41, 42, 43, 45, 46, 48, 50, 60, 64, 67, 70, 71, 72, 73, 74, 75, 76, 77, 78, 79, 80, 81, 82, 84, 88, 89, 94, 95, 96, 99, 100, 101, 104, 106, 107, 108, 109, 110, 112, 113, 115, 118, 120, 121, 122, 123, 124, 125, 126, 127, 129, 130, 131, 132, 134, 136, 138, 139, 140, 141, 142, 143, 145, 146, 147, 148, 149, 150, 152, 158, 159, 160, 161, 162, 165, 166, 167, 168, 170, 171, 172, 174, 175, 176, 178, 179, 180, 181, 182, 183, 184, 185, 186, 187, 188, 189, 190, 191, 192, 193, 194, 195, 196, 197, 198, 199, 200, 201, 202, 203, 204, 205, 207, 208, 209, 210, 211, 212, 213, 214, 215, 216, 217, 218, 219, 221, 222, 223, 224, 225, 226, 233, 234, 235, 236, 237, 238, 239, 240, 241, 242, 243, 244, 245, 246, 247, 248, 250, 251, 252, 253, 254, 255, 256, 257, 259, 260, 261, 262, 263, 265, 266, 267, 268
Jerusalem Council 242
Jeshanah 82
Jeshua 167
Jesse 70

Jesus 224–238, 239, 241, 246, 249, 267
Jesus (son of Gamaliel) 259
Jesus (son of Sapphas/Saphat) 256, 257
Jether 69
Jethro 44
Jezebel 96, 97, 98, 105, 106, 107, 114
Jezirah 70, 153, 154
Jezirat Farun 40. *See also* Jotbathah (in Sinai); Tabeh
Jezreel (in Issachar) 20, 50, 55, 61, 63, 66, 68, 70, 83, 84, 85, 91, 96, 98, 105, 106, 107
Jezreel (in Judah) 65
Jezreel Valley 10, 20, 21, 23, 31, 36, 51, 52, 55, 66, 67, 70, 74, 76, 77, 83, 84, 85, 86, 90, 108, 139, 159, 205, 209, 215, 227. *See also* Esdraelon; Great Plain
Jimzu. *See* Gimzo
Jish. *See* Gischala
Jisr esh-Shughur 93, 99
Joab 71, 72, 73, 74, 77, 79, 89, 91
Joash (king of Israel) 109, 110, 111. *See also* Jehoash
Joash (king of Judah) 106, 108. *See also* Jehoash
Jogbehah 50, 55, , 55, 61, 63, 68
Johanan (son of Josiah) 138
Johanan (son of Kareah) 148, 149
Johanan (son of Tobiah) 159
John (apostle) 240
John Hyrcanus 175, 202, 203, 204, 205, 206, 208, 209, 262
John Hyrcanus II. *See* Hyrcanus II
John Mark. *See* Mark, John
John of Gischala 256, 257, 258, 259, 261, 262, 263
John the Baptist 224–228, 236, 246, 263
Jokmeam 78, 83, 84, 108
Jokneam 17, 20, 26, 28, 30, 48, 54, 78, 84, 87, 90, 91
Joktan 12
Joktheel 110, 112. *See also* Sela
Jonah 115
Jonathan (son of Absalom) 198
Jonathan (son of Saul) 62, 64, 186
Jonathan Aristobulus. *See* Aristobulus III
Jonathan Maccabeus 187, 191, 192, 193, 194, 195, 196, 197, 198, 199, 200, 201, 206
Joppa 15, 16, 19, 29, 43, 50, 52, , 50, 54, 63, 65, 66, 67, 70, 71, 73, 74, 76, 80, 81, 82, 83, 84, 94, 96, 106, 120, 122, 126, 127, 128, 129, 138, 146, 148, 158, 159, 165, 166, 167, 170, 171, 172, 175, 176, 177, 178, 187, 188, 194, 195, 197, 198, 199, 200, 201, 202, 203, 204, 205, 208, 209, 212, 213, 214, 215, 217, 218, 219, 223, 224, 225, 233, 240, 241, 251, 252, 254, 255, 256, 259, 261, 266, 267. *See also* Jaffa
Joram (king of Judah). *See* Jehoram
Joram (son of Toi) 72. *See also* Hadoram
Jordan 14, 24
Jordan River 16, 17, 21, 22, 27, 29, 34, 36, 43, 44, 45, 50, 52, 53, 54, 55, 56, 60, 61, 63, 65, 66, 67, 68, 71, 73, 76, 81, 83, 84, 87, 88, 89, 90, 92, 96, 98, 99, 101, 104, 105, 106, 107, 110, 111, 112, 113, 115, 120, 122, 124, 132, 141, 146, 148, 159, 167, 175, 179, 183, 187, 191, 192, 193, 194, 195, 196, 197, 198, 201, 204, 205, 207, 209, 210, 214, 215, 218, 223, 225, 226, 227, 230, 233, 240, 241, 251, 252, 256, 257, 259, 260, 261, 266, 267
Jordan Valley 20, 31, 33, 34, 44, 55, 67, 84, 85, 198, 212
Jorkeam 69
Joseph (brother of Herod the Great) 214, 215, 216
Joseph (husband of Mary) 224, 225
Joseph (son of Carmei) 251
Joseph (son of Gorion) 255, 256, 259
Joseph (son of Jacob) 33, 36, 37
\ , House of 37, 50, 51, 52, 68, 83, 88, 89, 90. *See also* Ephraim
Joseph (son of Zechariah) 188
Joseph bar Caiaphas 235. *See also* Caiaphas
Joseph of Arimathea 237
Joseph of Tiberias 229
Joseph the Tobiad 180, 181
Josephus 75, 137, 227, 229, 256, 257, 258, 262, 264, 265
Joshua 41, 45, 46, 47, 48, 67, 68
Josiah 74, 80, 95, 135, 138, 139, 140, 141, 142, 146
Jotbah; Jotbath 120, 137, 138. *Also* Jotapata 225, 227, 232, 256, 257, 258
Jotbathah (in Arabah) 76
Jotbathah (in Sinai) 39, 40
Jotham 55, 56, 85, 92, 111, 112, 113, 114, 117, 118, 119, 122, 149, 159, 167
Jubeihat 55. *See also* Jogbehah
Judah 13, 14, 16, 17, 20, 23, 37, 40, 42, 44, 47, 50, 52, 53, 57, 58, 60, 61, 62, 63, 64, 65, 66, 68, 69, 70, 71, 73, 75, 77, 78, 80, 81, 82, 84, 85, 86, 87, 88, 89, 92, 94, 95, 96, 97, 100, 101, 102, 103, 104, 105, 106, 107, 108, 110, 111, 112, 113, 114, 115, 117, 118, 119, 120, 122, 123, 124, 125, 126, 127, 129, 130, 131, 132, 135, 137, 138, 139, 140, 141, 142, 143, 144, 145, 146, 147, 148, 149, 159, 167, 168, 175. *See also* Judea
Judah, Hill country of 20, 31, 36, 80, 85, 113, 130. *See also* Mount Judah
Judah, Kingdom of 21
Judah (son of Jacob) 50
Judah and Tamar narrative 36, 37, 47, 69, 118
Judah Aristobulus. *See* Aristobulus II
Judas (son of Ezekias) 257
Judas Iscariot 235
Judas Maccabeus 183, 184, 185, 186, 187, 188, 189, 190, 191, 192, 202, 203
Judea 160, 165, 167, 174, 176, 177, 179, 183, 184, 185, 186, 187, 188, 189, 190, 191, 192, 193, 194, 195, 197, 198, 200, 201, 202, 203, 204, 205, 206, 208, 209, 210, 212, 213, 214, 215, 216, 217, 218, 219, 223, 225, 226, 233, 239, 240, 248, 250, 251, 252, 255, 256, 259, 260, 261, 263, 268
Judean Desert 193, 198, 259, 260, 261, 267
Judeo-Christians 230
Judges, Book of 49
Jungle of the Jordan 18
Julias (in Gaulanitis) 223, 251, 266. *See also* Bethsaida
Julias (in Perea) 251, 252, 259, 260. *See also* Livias
Julius Caesar 213, 214, 244
Julius Severus 268
Julius Vindex 260
Justinian 41
Juttah 69, 78, 80

## K

Kabri 28
Kabul 91. *See also* Cabul; Chabulon
Kadesh; Kadesh-barnea 10, 11, 15, 16, 17, 20, 23, 34, 35, 38, 39, 40, 41, 42, 43, 73, 76, 80, 81, 112, 118, 124, 132, 140. *See also* En-mishpat
Kadytis 15, 161, 162, 164. *See also* Gaza
Kafr Kana 227. *See also* Cana; Garis; Kanah (in Galilee)
Kalhu. *See* Calah
Kamon 50, 52, 56, 68, 84. *See also* Camus
Kana (nr. Dead Sea) 208
Kanah (in Asher) 17, 48, 84, 91
Kanah (in Galilee) 120, 227. *See also* Cana (in Galilee)
Kanah Brook 17, 18, 87, 90
Kanah Valley 20
Kandahar 176
Kandalanu 138, 139
Kantheros 244
Karatepe 121
Kargincik Adasi. *See* Pitussu
Karka 15, 16, 40, 42
Karkor 55, 74
Karmania 154
Karnaim (city) 11, 34, 35, 98, 110, 111, 113, 120, 122, 124, 132, 138, 158, 165, 166, 170, 171, 172. *See also* Carnaim
Karnaim (province) 15, 122, 124, 132, 134, 138, 146, 158, 165, 166, 170, 171, 172, 175
Karnak 38, 39. *See also* No-amon
Kartan 78
Kassites 127
Kathrabba 103
Kathros. *See* Bar Kathros
Kattath 51. *See also* Kitron
Kawa 131
Kazakhstan 24
Kedar; Kedarites 21, 23, 134, 135, 145, 160, 161, 167
Kedem, Land of 34
Kedemoth 17, 42, 43, 44, 78, 84, 87
Kedesh (in Beqa Valley) 16, 29
Kedesh (in Galilee) 17, 27, 48, 50, 52, 54, 63, 72, 73, 74, 78, 84, 87, 92, 96, 120, 124, 132, 138, 146, 206. *See also* Cadasa
Kedesh-naphtali 52, 54, 55, 92
Kedron 202, 203
Kefar Akabia 228
Kefar-dan 227
Keilah 20, 29, 63, 64, 69, 72, 167, 168, 194
Kenath 16, 27, 29, 45, 73. *See also* Canatha
Kenaz 47, 66, 68, 69, 70, 88
Kenites 21, 50, 62, 63, 66, 69, 70, 74, 80
Kenizzites 20, 47, 50, 53, 80
Kerak 64, 104. *See also* Kir-hareseth
Kerem-hattel 108
Kerem-yehoeli 108
Kerioth 84, 102, 104
Kerman. *See* Karmania
Kermanshah 155
Kesalon; Kesla. *See* Chesalon
Keturah 119
Keziz Valley 82
Kfar Yamma 92. *See also* Khirbet Yamma
Khabbabash 172
Khabur River 93, 169. *See also* Habor River
Khafre (Chephren) 25
Kharga Oasis 82, 150
Khashabu 29
Khaybar 153. *See also* Hebra
Khirbet Abbad 63. *See also* Horbat Sokho; Socoh (in Shephelah)
Khirbet Abda. *See* Abdon; Tel Avdon
Khirbet Adasa 190. *See also* Adasa
Khirbet Asheq 98. *See also* En Gev
Khirbet Atar 47. *See also* Ether
Khirbet Ataruz 97. *See also* Ataroth
Khirbet Atraba. *See* Caphartobas
Khirbet Awfar 56. *See also* Ophrah
Khirbet Ayun Musa 102
Khirbet Ayyun. *See* Ain
Khirbet Beit Bassa. *See* Beth-basi
Khirbet Beit Maqdum 46
Khirbet Beit Zakariyeh. *See* Beth-zechariah
Khirbet Belameh. *See* Ibleam
Khirbet Bir ez-Zafaran 192. *See also* Asphar
Khirbet Bir Zeit 68. *See also* Beerzaith; Birzaith
Khirbet Deir Shubeib 57. *See also* Eshtaol
Khirbet Deleilat. *See* Beth-diblathaim; Dabaloth
Khirbet Deleilat el-Gharbiyeh 103
Khirbet Deleilat esh-Sherqiyeh 103
Khirbet Dhubab 103
Khirbet ed-Damieh 92
Khirbet ed-Dawwara 32
Khirbet ed-Deir Domeh 138. *See also* Dumah
Khirbet ed-Duweir 110. *See also* Lo-debar
Khirbet el-Burj el-Isaneh. *See* Isana
Khirbet el-Hammam 83 . *See also* Narbata
Khirbet el-Harbaj 48. *See also* Achshaph; Tel Regev
Khirbet el-Jemeijmeh 92. *See also* Horbat Gamom; Hukkok
Khirbet el-Khokh. *See* Etam (in Judah)
Khirbet el-Kirmil 65. *See also* Carmel
Khirbet el-Mafjar 233
Khirbet el-Mahalib 91. *See also* Mahalleb
Khirbet el-Main 65. *See also* Maon
Khirbet el-Mansurah 92
Khirbet el-Meshash 42, 63. *See also* Baalath-beer; Tel Masos
Khirbet el-Mudeiyineh 102. *See also* Jahaz
Khirbet el-Muhattah 102
Khirbet el-Mukhaiyat 102
Khirbet el-Muqanna 63. *See also* Ekron; Tel Miqne
Khirbet el-Oreimeh 92. *See also* Chinnereth; Tel Kinrot
Khirbet el-Qom 46, 160. *See also* Makkedah
Khirbet el-Quneitireh 92. *See also* Rakkath; Tel Raqqat
Khirbet el-Quweiqiyeh 44
Khirbet el-Urmah. *See* Arumah
Khirbet el-Yanun. *See* Janoah
Khirbet en-Nahas 41, 76
Khirbet er-Rumah 138. *See also* Horbat Ruma; Rumah (in Galilee)
Khirbet esh-Sheikh Madhkur. *See* Adullam; Horbat Adullam
Khirbet esh-Shuweikeh 63, 118. *See also* Socoh (in Shephelah)
Khirbet es-Sar 73. *See also* Jazer
Khirbet es-Salam 257, 258. *See also* Solyma
Khirbet es-Suq 57
Khirbet es-Suweimeh 44
Khirbet et-Tabbaneh 36. *See also* Timnah (in Judah)
Khirbet et-Tayyibeh 130
Khirbet et-Tell (ed-Damiyeh). *See* Adami-nekeb; Tel Adami
Khirbet et-Tubeiqeh/Tubeiqa. *See* Beth-zur
Khirbet ez-Zurra. *See* Gath-hepher; Tel Gat Hefer
Khirbet Gharrah 42, 147. *See also* Ramath-negeb; Tel Ira
Khirbet Ghazzah 147. *See also* Horbat Uzza; Kinah
Khirbet Haiyan 124. *See also* Aiath; Aija
Khirbet Ibziq 50. *See also* Bezek
Khirbet Id 190. *See also* Capharsalama
Khirbet Id el-Minya. *See* Adullam
Khirbet Imwas 184. *See also* Emmaus; Nicopolis
Khirbet Irbadeh. *See* Heleph; Horbat Arpad
Khirbet Jazzir 43. *See also* Jazer
Khirbet Jelad 56
Khirbet Jifat 137. *See also* Jotbah
Khirbet Jiljal 191
Khirbet Kakul 124. *See also* Gallim
Khirbet Karazzeh 230. *See also* Chorazin
Khirbet Kerak Ware 26
Khirbet Khureisa. *See* Oresa
Khirbet Libb. *See* Libb; Limbo
Khirbet Makhneh el-Foqa 90. *See also* Michmethath
Khirbet Marjameh 32
Khirbet Medeiyineh 32
Khirbet Meidan 103
Khirbet Musheirefeh 48
Khirbet Qanah 228. *See also* Cana (in Galilee)
Khirbet Qedish 54. *See also* Horbat Qedesh; Kedesh-naphtali
Khirbet Qila 64. *See also* Keilah
Khirbet Qumran 216. *See also* Qumran
Khirbet Rabud 28, 30, 47, 48. *See also* Debir (in Judah)
Khirbet Raddana 32. *See also* Ataroth-addar
Khirbet Ras Ali. *See* Hali; Tel Alil
Khirbet Ras ez-Zeitun 91. *See also* Cabul; Horbat Rosh Zayit
Khirbet Safsafeh 66. *See also* En-dor
Khirbet Salih 113. *See also* Beth-haccerem; Ramat Rahel
Khirbet Samik. *See* Samaga
Khirbet Sammuniyeh 48, 139. *See also* Shimon (Simeon); Tel Shimron
Khirbet Sarah. *See* Zorah
Khirbet Seilun 59, 60. *See also* Shiloh
Khirbet Selma. *See* Khirbet Id
Khirbet Sheikh esh-Shamsawi 92. *See also* Beth-shemesh (in Issachar)
Khirbet Shuweiket er-Ras 83. *See also* Socoh (in Sharon)
Khirbet Tabbaneh 36, 118. *See also* Horbat Tivna; Timnah (in Judah)
Khirbet Tana el-Foqa. *See* Taanath-shiloh
Khirbet Tell el-Askar 124. *See also* Migron
Khirbet Tell el-Beida 36, 130. *See also* Achzib (in Judah); Horbat Lavnin
Khirbet Tell er-Ruweisi 51, 92. *See also* Beth-shemesh (in Naphtali)
Khirbet Tell Zakariyeh 129. *See also* Azekah; Tel Azeqa
Khirbet Tequ 80. *See also* Tekoa
Khirbet Tibnah 45. *See also* Thamna; Timnath-heres
Khirbet Umm el-Amud 91. *See also* Hammon
Khirbet Umm el-Basal 130
Khirbet Umm Jebeil 92. *See also* Aznoth-tabor; Tel Aznoth-tabor
Khirbet Unnab es-Saghir. *See* Anab
Khirbet Yamma 92
Khirbet Yanin 91. *See also* Neiel
Khirbet Zeitun er-Rameh 92. *See also* Ramah (in Naphtali)
Khisfin 187. *See also* Caspin; Chaspho
Khizam 27
Khorsabad 123. *See also* Dur-Sharrukin
Khumbanigash I 123
Khuraybah 153. *See also* Dadanu; Dedan
Khurru 15
Khursagkalama 127
Khuzirina 94
Kibroth-hattaavah 40
Kibzaim 78
Kidron Brook 202
Kidron Valley 59, 197, 211, 222, 234, 262
Kilani. *See* Kullani
Kimhi, Rav David (Radak) 104
Kimuhu 143
Kinah 147
King's Highway 23, 42, 73, 98, 204
Kir 114, 121
Kiradas. *See* Kir-hareseth
Kir-hareseth 63, 101, 102, 104, 110, 112, 120, 124, 138
Kir-heres. *See* Kir-hareseth
Kiriaten 102. *See also* Kiriathaim
Kiriathaim 17, 35, 44, 84, 87
Kiriath-arba 34, 36, 167, 168. *See also* Hebron
Kiriath-jearim 17, 46, 47, 57, 58, 60, 61, 63, 67, 69, 71, 72, 81, 82, 83, 87, 88, 89, 94, 102, 103, 104, 113, 129, 167, 168, 185
Kir-moab 17, 43, 50, 52, 65, 70, 72, 73, 74, 78, 80, 87, 107, 122, 132, 209
Kirshi; Kirshu 152
Kish 127
Kishion 54, 55, 78, 91
Kishon River 18, 54, 90, 107
Kistan 117
Kition 12, 15, 128, 158, 160, 163, 164, 170, 171, 172
Kitron 51, 91. *See also* Kattath
Kitron Nahalal 50
Kittim; Kittiyim 12, 146, 147, 151
Kohathites 78
Kom el-Ahmar 27
Kom Yajuz 57
Konya. *See* Iconium
Korah 68
Kozoh 55, 108
Kue 74, 76, 99, 121. *See also* Que
Kullani 117
Kumidi 29
Kummukh 94, 116, 121, 140, 143
Kunulua 93
Kurdistan 24
Kursi 228. *See also Gergesa*
Kuwait 24

# L


Laban 33, 37, 53, 123, 124, 132
Labashi-Marduk 152
Labienus 214
Labynetos 153, 155
Lachish 20, 26, 28, 29, 30, 32, 36, 43, 46, 47, 48, 50, 57, 63, 69, 76, 78, 80, 81, 95, 118, 119, 120, 124, 126, 127, 129, 130, 131, 138, 139, 146, 147, 148, 158, 165, 166, 167, 170, 171, 172, 175, 204. *See also* Tell ed-Duweir
Laconia 162
Ladder of Tyre 18, 195, 196, 201, 209, 227, 232. *See also* Ras en-Naqura
Lagash 33
Laguna 103
Laish 11, 16, 27, 35, 54, 58, 67. *See also* Dan
Laishah 124
Lake Gennosar 206. *See also* Sea of Galilee
Lake Van 136
Lakkum 92
Lamani 123
Lampsacus 174
Laodice 178
Laodicea (in Asia Minor) 249
Laodicea (in Canaan/Phoenicia) 17
Laodicea (in Syria) 17, 195, 197
Laomedon 176
Larandra 169
Larissa 169
Larsa 33, 150, 152
Lasea 248, 249
Last Supper 239
Latikia (Ladiqiyeh) 17. *See also* Laodicea (in Syria)
Latrun 118
Leah 18, 19,
Lebanon 24, 26, 33, 44, 76, 78, 99, 118, 133, 144, 153
Lebanon, Valley of 18. *See also* Beqa Valley
Lebanon Mountains 14, 19, 21, 133. *See also* Mount Lebanon
Lebo; Lebo-hamath; Lebweh 16, 17, 21, 27, 29, 73, 74, 110, 111, 113, 122, 149, 197
Lebonah 20, 55, 59, 82
Lecah 69
Lechaion 244
Legio 266
Lehi 58
Leontes River 195
Leontopolis 213
Lesbos 174, 246
Leshem 67
Levant 14
Levi; Levites 36; 58, 60, 71, 78, 81, 83, 100, 107
Libb; Libba 102, 103, 209, 210
Libnah 20, 47, 48, 69, 78, 80, 104, 105, 107, 127, 129, 131, 138
Libnath 90, 91
Libya 157, 162, 164, 239
Libyans 82, 95, 150. *See also* Lubim
Lidebir. *See* Lo-debar
Lifta 89. *See also* Nephtoah, Waters of
Limbo 103, 209. *See also* Libb
Litani River 10, 18, 19, 21, 84, 91, 120, 128
Livias 44, 223, 251, 266. *See also* Beth-haram; Julias (in Perea)
Lod 27, 60, 61, 69, 83, 84, 94, 129, 158, 165, 166, 167, 168, 170, 171, 172, 175. *See also* Lydda
Lo-debar 17, 56, 66, 68, 84, 87, 98, 110, 111
Lot 34, 35
Lower Sea 24, 150, 157. *See also* Persian Gulf
Lubarna 93
Lubban esh-Sherqiyeh 59. *See also* El-Lubban; Lebonah
Lubim 82. *See also* Libyans
Lucceius Albinus 250
Lucilius Bassus 263
Lud; Ludim 12, 13, 157
Lugath; Luguti; Lugutu 74, 93, 94, 108, 117
Luhith 23, 103, 104
Luli 128
Luxor. *See* No-amon; Thebes
Luz 89. *See also* Bethel
Lycaonia 242, 243, 244
Lycia; Lycians 156, 162, 163, 164, 169, 173, 174, 178, 246, 247, 248
Lycus (Greater Zab) River 203
Lydda 183, 184, 185, 186, 187, 188, 190, 192, 194, 195, 198, 199, 201, 202, 204, 205, 209, 214, 215, 225, 233, 240, 241, 254, 255, 256, 260, 266, 267. *See also* Diospolis; Lod
Lydia; Lydians 12, 136, 137, 150, 152, 153, 154, 155, 156, 162, 163, 164, 169, 173, 174, 180, 242, 244
Lygdamis. *See* Tugdamme
Lysanias (son of Ptolemaeus) 219
Lysanias (tetrarch of Abila) 250, 251
Lysias 184, 185, 186, 188, 189
Lysimachia 178
Lysimachus 177, 181, 207
Lystra 242, 243, 244


# M


Maacah 27, 50, 68, 72, 73, 74, 96
Maanith 57. *See also* Minnith
Maarath 130
Mabartha 260. *See also* Neapolis (nr. Shechem)
Macedonia; Macedonians 162, 173, 174, 176, 177, 178, 240, 243, 244, 246, 248
Macestus 162
Machbenah 69
Machaeras (Roman officer) 215
Macherus 209, 210, 212, 213, 215, 219, 225, 226, 252, 254, 255, 259, 260, 261, 263
Machir 45, 54, 67, 68
Machmas 192, 193. *See also* Michmas
Machpelah 34
Madaba 97. *See also* Medeba
Madai 12, 116, 118. *See also* Media
Madanu 140
Madmannah 65, 69
Madmen 102
Madmenah 124
Madon 48. *See also* Merom
Madyes 137
Maeander 162
Magas 178
Magbish 167
Magdala 228, 229. *See also* Taricheae
Magdolo 141, 162, 164. *See also* Migdol
Magnesia 137, 161, 174
Magnesia ad Sipylum 180
Magog 12, 136
Mahalab 119, 120, 128
Mahalleb 91
Mahalliba. *See* Mahalab
Mahalul 51. *See also* Nahalal
Mahanaim 17, 23, 35, 36, 44, 56, 61, 63, 65, 70, 71, 72, 73, 74, 78, 81, 84, 85, 87, 120, 122
Mahaneh-dan 57
Maharoth 102
Mahoz 19
Main 43. *See also* Baal-meon (in Transjordan); Beth-baal-meon
Maka 157
Makaz 83, 84
Maked 186, 187
Makkedah 46, 47, 48, 118, 130, 147, 160
Malachi 107
Malatha 204. *See also* Arad
Malchiel 68
Malchus 196
Malchus II 218
Malichus 212
Malli 176
Mallus 174
Malta 248, 249
Malul 51. *See also* Mahalul; Nahalal
Malyan. *See* Anshan
Mamilla 59
Mamortha. *See* Mabartha
Mamre 36, 222
Manahath 69, 72
Manasseh (brother of Jaddus) 174, 175
Manasseh (king of Judah) 132, 133, 134, 135, 137, 138, 139, 142, 149
Manasseh (son of Joseph; tribe) 16, 17, 20, 23, 31, 37, 44, 45, 50, 52, 54, 55, 56, 58, 59, 60, 65, 67, 68, 69, 78, 79, 82, 83, 84, 85, 87, 88, 89, 90, 91, 115, 125
Mandane 155, 156
Manetho 116
Manneans 155
Manoah 58
Mansuate 108, 109, 122, 124, 132
Maon 21, 64, 65, 69
Maracanda 176
Maralah 90
Marathon 162
Marathus 174
Marcus Agrippas 219, 221
Marduk-apla-iddina II 123. *See also* Merodach-baladan
Mareal 91
Mareshah 20, 47, 69, 80, 81, 95, 126, 129, 130, 131, 147, 148, 167, 175. *See also* Marisa
Mari 26, 28, 33
Mariamme (daughter of Agrippa I) 251
Mariamme (wife of Herod the Great) 214, 215, 216, 217, 218, 223
Marion 164
Marisa 178, 185, 186, 188, 189, 198, 199, 204, 205, 209, 212, 213, 214, 217. *See also* Mareshah
Mariut 162, 164
Maritime Gadara 228
Maritime Hippus 228
Mark, John 241, 242, 243
Mark Antony. *See* Antony, Mark
Maron 48, 53, 120. *See also* Madon; Merom; Meron
Maronea 174
Maroth 130
Martha (sister of Lazarus) 233
Marun er-Ras 21, 48
Mary (mother of Jesus) 224, 225
Mary (sister of Lazarus) 233
Mary Magdalene 228, 229
Masada 64, 69, 209, 212, 214, 215, 218, 219, 220, 225, 252, 253, 254, 259, 260, 261, 263, 264, 266, 267
Massaga 176
Massagetae 176
Massyas Valley 177
Mathanbaal 132
Mati-ilu 109, 110, 116
Mattan I 94
Mattaniah 146. *See also* Zedekiah
Mattathias (Hasmonean priest) 183, 200
Mattathias (son of Simon Maccabeus) 203
Mattathias Antigonus. *See* Antigonus
Matthew 228
Matthias 261
Mazaios 159, 171, 172
Medeba 17, 43, 44, 50, 56, 61, 63, 65, 70, 71, 72, 73, 84, 85, 87, 96, 97, 101, 102, 103, 104, 110, 192, 204, 209, 210, 212, 266
Medeiyineh 41
Medes; Media; Medians 116, 121, 125, 127, 136, 137, 140, 141, 150, 152, 153, 155, 156, 157, 169, 200, 239, 240. *See also* Madai
Median Empire 150, 152, 153
Medina 153. *See also* Yatrib; Yathrib
Medinet er-Ras 103
Mediterranean Sea 15, 16, 24, 28, 32, 76, 88, 158, 159, 162, 163, 164, 165, 166, 169, 170, 171, 172, 174, 175, 176, 177, 178, 182, 187, 194, 195, 197, 202, 205, 209, 212, 213, 214, 215, 221, 223, 224, 225, 227, 240, 244, 246, 248, 249, 251, 252, 254, 259, 267
Megabyzus 163, 164, 165, 166, 172
Megiddo (city) 16, 17, 20, 26, 27, 28, 29, 30, 32, 33, 34, 36, 48, 50, 52, 54, 55, 61, 63, 67, 68, 70, 72, 73, 74, 76, 80, 81, 83, 84, 85, 87, 91, 95, 96, 98, 105, 111, 113, 118, 120, 122, 123, 124, 132, 134, 138, 139, 140, 141, 142, 146
Megiddo (province) 122, 126, 128, 134, 146
Megiddo, Plain of 51, 141
Megiddon, Valley of 83. *See also* Great Plain
Meir 27
Meiron 48
Mejdel Islim 92. *See also* Migdal-el
Melchizedek 35
Melid 116, 117, 121, 136
Memnon 173
Memphis 27, 30, 119, 134, 148, 149, 150, 162, 164, 168, 176, 177, 178, 181, 182, 213, 224. *See also* Noph
Memshath 126. *See also* MMST
Menahem (king of Israel) 114, 117, 118, 121, 122, 125
Menahem (son of Judah the Galilean) 253, 254
Menander of Ephesus 75, 94
Mendes 162, 164, 169
Menelaus 180, 181, 182
Menostanes 166
Mephaath 17, 44, 78, 84, 87
Merarites 78
Meribah, Waters of 40. *See also* Kadesh-barnea
Merneptah 37
Merodach-baladan 123, 127
Merom; Meron 19, 21, 48, 54, 120, 227, 256. *See also* Madon; Maron
Merom, Waters of 21, 48, 54
Meroz 55
Mersa Gawasis 27
Mesaloth 191
Mesha 44, 97, 98, 101, 102, 103, 104, 106, 115
Meshech 12, 136
Meshed 176
Meshullemeth 137
Mesopotamia 12, 14, 19, 24, 25, 27, 29, 31, 33, 72, 83, 93, 108, 109, 136, 140, 141, 150, 152, 153, 157, 160, 163, 169, 171, 180, 239, 240
Messenia 162
Metenna 117
Methone 244
Metilius 254
Meunites 100, 101, 104, 111, 112, 113, 119, 135
Meydancikkale 152. *See also* Kirshi; Kirshu
Mezad Hashavyahu 143
Mezad Hasidim 225, 226. *See also* Qumran
Micah 58, 81, 107, 115, 130
Micaiah 100
Michal 113
Michmas; Michmash 53, 58, 61, 62, 69, 82, 84, 95, 123, 124, 129, 167, 168. *See also* Mukhmas
Michmethath 17, 20, 55, 87, 90, 108
Midas 136
Midian; Midianites 14, 23, 37, 39, 43, 44, 53, 55, 79
Migdal 27, 29
Migdal-eder 44, 68
Migdal-el 91, 92
Migdal-Nunia 228. *See also* Magdala; Taricheae
Migdol 39, 121, 134, 140, 141, 148, 149, 168. *See also* Magdolo
Migron 62, 124
Miletus 162, 163, 164, 173, 174, 240, 246, 247
Milkiashapa 132
Minnith 57
Miriam 40
Mishal 18, 27, 78, 84, 90, 91
Misis 243
Misrephoth 48
Mithradates I 200
Mithradates of Pergamum 213
Mitinti 119, 120, 131, 132, 133, 134
Mit Rahina. *See* Memphis; Noph
Mittani 28
Mitylene 246
Mizpah (in Benjamin) 53, 57, 58, 59, 60, 61, 62, 63, 69, 82, 84, 89, 95, 96, 124, 126, 129, 148, 158, 165, 166, 167, 168, 170, 171, 172, 185, 191, 194
Mizpah (in Gilead) 56. *Also* Mizpeh-gilead
Mizpeh (of Moab) 64
Mizpeh, Valley (or Land) of 21
Mizraim 12, 13. *See also* Egypt
MMST 127
Mnason of Cyprus 247
Moab; Moabites 14, 15, 16, 17, 34, 35, 41, 42, 43, 44, 50, 61, 63, 64, 65, 70, 71, 72, 73, 74, 75, 78, 80, 81, 84, 87, 96, 97, 98, 101, 102, 103, 104, 106, 107, 108, 110, 112, 113, 115, 118, 120, 122, 124, 125, 126, 128, 132, 134, 135, 138, 145, 146, 148, 149, 158, 159, 165, 166, 167, 170, 171, 172, 208, 209. *Also* Moabitis 209
Moab, City of 102
Moab, Plains of 43, 44, 45, 53
Modiin 183, 184, 185, 188, 191, 192, 193, 194, 198, 199, 202, 207
Moladah 71, 167
Momemphis 151
Moph 134, 140. *See also* Noph
Mopsuestia. *See* Misis
Morasthi 130. *See also* Moresheth-gath
Moreh, Hill of 18, 20, 54, 55, 66
Moresheth-gath 69, 80, 81, 115, 129, 130. *See also* Morasthi
Moses 16, 17, 41, 44, 58, 67, 227
Mount Arbel 228
Mount Atzmon 19
Mount Azotus 191
Mount Baalah 76. *See also* Baalath
Mount Bashan 17, 18, 87. *See also* Bashan
Mount Bethel 191
Mount Carmel 11, 17, 18, 19, 48, 50, 83, 87, 90, 91, 98, 107, 113, 179, 205, 206, 209, 227
Mount Casius 15, 182
Mount Ebal 20, 32
Mount Ephraim 18, 20, 32, 33, 55, 56, 59, 60, 61, 62, 67, 68, 76, 82, 83, 84, 88, 89, 95, 96, 126, 233. *See also* Ephraim, Hill country of
Mount Ephron 87, 89
Mount Gerizim 20, 55, 174, 175, 204, 205, 225, 240, 259
Mount Gilboa 20, 55, 66
Mount Halak 18, 42
Mount Hermon 14, 17, 18, 21, 50, 63, 206
Mount Hor (in Lebanon) 16
Mount Hor (in Negeb) 41, 42, 43
Mount Horeb 107. *See also* Mount Sinai
Mount Jearim 89
Mount Judah 18, 20, 34, 60, 61, 76. *See also* Judah, Hill country of; Judean Hills
Mount Lebanon 18, 24, 63, 216, 252
Mount Meiron 19, 48, 51, 84, 92. *See also* Jebel Jarmaq
Mount Nal 119
Mount Nebo 16, 17, 18, 23, 42. *See also* Pisgah
Mount of Olives 234, 235, 261
Mount Paran 39, 40. *See also* Mount Sinai
Mount Phogor 44
Mount Qalpani 93
Mount Saratini 93
Mount Scopus 64, 175, 255, 261
Mount Seir (in Edom) 11, 18, 21, 22, 23, 35, 36, 40, 42, 63, 68, 69, 101, 119, 119, 126, 127
Mount Seir (in Judah) 89
Mount Shechem 20
Mount Sinai 39, 40, 54. *See also* Horeb; Mount Paran
Mount Sodom 23
Mount Tabor 17, 18, 20, 53, 54, 55, 84, 85, 87, 90, 91, 92, 206, 209, 213, 225, 226, 227, 233, 256, 257, 258
Mount Zion 222, 236, 237
Mozah 69, 89
Mugallu 136
Mugish 93. *See also* Amuq Plain; Patina; Unqi
Muhai 41
Mukhmas. *See* Machmas; Michmas; Michmash
Mushki; Mushku 12, 109. *See also* Meshech
Musri 99
Musuri; Musuru 132, 133, 134
Mycale 162, 163
Myra 247, 248, 249
Myriandros/Myriandrus 159, 169, 174
Mysia 162, 174, 243, 244, 249


# N


Naaman 107
Naaran (Naarah) 46, 53, 61, 82, 84, 89, 90

Nabal 64, 65, 113
Nabatean Kingdom 204
Nabateans 101, 175, 178, 186, 187, 192, 204, 207, 208, 209, 210, 211, 212, 213, 217, 218, 223, 224, 251, 252, 254
Nablus. *See* Neapolis (nr. Shechem)
Nabonidus 33, 151, 152. *See also* Nabu-naid
Nabopolassar 139, 140, 141, 142, 143, 144, 155
Naboth 98, 107
Nabrachta 205
Nabu-balassu-iqbi 152
Nabu-bel-shumati 127
Nabuchodonosor. *See* Nebuchadnezzar; Nebuchadrezzar
Nabu-duru-usur 128
Nabu-naid 33, 152, 153, 154, 155, 156, 167. *See also* Nabonidus
Nabu-sharru-usur 162
Nadab 82, 94
Nafud Desert 24
Nag el-Madamud 27
Nahal Adorayim. *See* Wadi el-Jizair
Nahalal (Nahalol) 51, 78, 91
Nahal Ayyalon 19. *See also* Wadi Musrarah
Nahal Darga 267
Nahal Evlayim. *See* Wadi Abbelin
Nahal Harod. *See* Wadi Jalud
Nahal Hever 265, 266, 267
Nahal Kidron 267. *See also* Kidron Valley
Nahal Musri 119. *See also* Brook of Egypt
Nahal Og 267
Nahal Sehaha 267
Nahal Soreq. *See* Sorek Valley; Wadi Sarar
Nahal Tanninim 83. *See also* Crocodile River
Nahal Yoqneam. *See* Wadi Milh
Nahal Zin 41. *See also* Wadi Fuqrah
Nahariya 28
Nahash 61
Nahor 33
Nahr Allan 23
Nahr el-Abyad 93. *See also* Sanguru River
Nahr el-Auja 19, 60, 90, 204
Nahr el-Ihreir. *See* Raphon Brook
Nahr el-Kebir 29. *See also* Eleutherus River
Nahr ez-Zerqa. *See* Jabbok River
Nain 227, 260
Naioth 64
Nairi 93, 117
Naman (Belus) River 18
Namri 109, 116
Namur 109
Naphoth-dor 19, 83
Naphtali 16, 17, 19, 21, 48, 50, 51, 52, 53, 54, 55, 78, 82, 84, 85, 86, 87, 88, 91, 92, 96, 120, 125, 149
Napsannu 162
Naqb es-Safa 15
Naram-Sin 26
Narbata; Narbatene 83, 187, 209, 252, 254, 255
Nasib 266
Nasibina 70
Nathana-el 227
Naucratis 151, 162, 164
Naur 57
Naveh 63, 98, 138, 179, 251, 252
Nazareth 224, 225, 226, 227, 228, 229, 230, 232, 233, 240, 241
Nazareth Hills 19
Nazirite vow 245, 247
Neapolis (in Macedonia) 243, 244, 246
Neapolis (nr. Gaza) 240
Neapolis (nr. Shechem) 260, 266, 267. *See also* Mabartha
Neballat 167
Nebi Dahi. *See* Jebel ed-Dahi
Nebi Samwil 20
Nebo 43, 44, 56, 69, 102, 103, 104
Nebuchadnezzar II; Nebuchadrezzar 142, 143, 144, 145, 146, 147, 148, 149, 150, 151, 152, 153, 154, 155, 157, 166, 173
Nebuchadnezzar III 161
Nebuchadnezzar IV 161
Nebuzaradan 148
Necho I 135
Necho II 141, 142, 143, 144, 146, 148
Nectanebos 170, 171
Nefertiti 30
Negeb 16, 18, 20, 21, 23, 25, 34, 35, 41, 42, 43, 55, 61, 62, 63, 65, 66, 71, 80, 81, 95, 112, 119, 126, 127, 139, 145, 146, 147, 167, 168
Negeb of Caleb 20, 65, 66, 113
Negeb of Judah 21, 65, 74, 115, 118
Negeb of the Cherethites 65, 66
Negeb of the Jerahmeelites 65
Negeb of the Kenites 65, 66
Negev (modern) 21
Nehemiah 159, 160, 165, 166, 167, 168
Nehushta 145
Neiel 17, 87, 91
Neo-Babylonian Empire/Kingdom 155, 157, 160
Nephrites 169
Nephtoah, Waters of 89
Nergal-sharezer/Nergal-sharra-usur/Neriglissar 150, 151, 152, 153
Nero 229, 249, 251, 253, 255, 257, 260
Neronias 252. *See also* Caesarea Philippi
Nestus 162
Netaim 69
Netophah 65, 69, 167, 168
Nezib 20, 69, 209
Nicanor (commander under Demetrius I) 189, 190, 191, 192
Nicanor (commander under Ptolemy) 184, 185
Nicodemus 237
Nicolaus 178
Nicopolis 238. *See also* Emmaus; Khirbet Imwas
Nicosia 24
Nidintu-bel 161. *See also* Nebuchadnezzar III
Nile River 12, 14, 15, 16, 24, 37, 38, 39, 121, 134, 141, 143, 148, 151, 157, 162, 164, 168, 170, 176, 224, 240
Nimrin 187
Nimrim, Waters of 103
Nimrod 93
Nimrud 12, 93, 119. *See also* Calah; Kalhu
Nineveh 12, 33, 93, 99, 109, 120, 121, 125, 129, 133, 134, 135, 136, 140, 141, 150, 152, 155
Nippur 33, 127, 148, 150, 152, 160, 165
Nisibin 141. *See also* Nasibina
Nisibis 121, 176
No-amon 27, 30, 121, 124, 134, 138, 148, 150, 168
Noah 12, 13, 68, 108
Nob 60, 64, 69, 123, 124, 129, 167, 168
Nobah 45, 55
Noph 30, 33, 39, 121, 141, 143, 149. *See also* Memphis; Moph
Nubia; Nubians 12, 27, 82, 95, 116, 134, 146, 147, 161, 167. *See also* Cush; Cushites (in Africa)
Nughasse 93, 109. *See also* Lugath
Nuzi 33
Nysa. *See* Scythopolis

# O

Oak in Zaanannim 54, 55, 91, 92
Oak of Moreh 34
Oak of Tabor 61
Oak of the Pillar 55
Oaks of Mamre 34
Obedas 208
Oboth 41, 43
Ochus 168. *See also* Darius II
Ochus (son of Artaxerxes II) 171. *See also* Artaxerxes III
Octavian 214, 217, 218
Odomera 193
Og 43, 45, 48, 85
Olympus 169
Omri 96, 97, 98, 102, 103, 105, 106, 107
Omri, House of 120, 121, 122
On 33, 37, 38, 39, 121, 134, 140. *See also* Heliopolis
Onam 69
Onan 69
Oniads 180, 181
Onias II 180
Onias III 180, 181
Ono 60, 69, 83, 94, 167, 168
Ono, Plain of 37, 167, 168
Ophel (in Jerusalem) 234
Ophir 12, 75, 76, 101
Ophni 82
Ophrah (in Benjamin) 60, 61, 62, 63, 89, 191
Ophrah (in Manasseh) 52, 55, 56, 108
Orda 204
Oreb 55
Oresa 214, 215
Origen 231
Orodes II 214
Oronaim 209, 210. *See also* Horonaim
Orontes River 16, 21, 24, 29, 72, 93, 99, 108, 111, 141, 195, 197
Orthosia 177, 178, 202
Oruba 210
Osiris 166
Osorkon IV 122, 123. *See also* Shilkanni
Othniel 50, 52, 53
Othnielites 66
Oxus River 176

# P

Pacorus 214, 215
Padakku 153
Paddan-aram 33, 35, 36
Padi 126, 127, 128, 129, 130, 131, 137
Palaityros 91
Palatine 252
Palestine 15, 158, 159, 170, 174, 178, 232, 265
Palmyra 240
Pamphylia 152, 163, 164, 173, 214, 239, 240, 242, 246, 248, 249
Paneas 10, 179, 180, 212, 218, 219, 221, 222, 223, 266. *See also* Banias; Caesarea Philippi
Panetolus 178
Paphlagonia 160, 169
Paphos 163, 164, 241, 242, 246
Pappus 215, 216
Papremis 164
Papyron 210. *See also* Calamon
Papyrus Anastasi I 15
Parah 82
Paralia 201, 202, 209, 212
Paran 39
Parapanisadae 176
Paretonium 176
Parga 99
Parmenion; Parmenio 173, 174
Parsa 155. *See also* Fars
Parthia; Parthians 157, 198, 200, 203, 214, 215, 217, 221, 239, 240, 252
Pasargade 155, 176
Patara 173, 174, 176, 242, 246, 247
Pathros, Land of 149, 168
Patina 93, 99, 117. *See also* Amuq Plain; Mugish; Unqi
Paul (apostle) 237, 238, 241, 242, 243, 244, 245, 246, 247, 248, 249, 252
Pausanias 163
Pazarcik 109
Pegae 175, 194, 204, 205, 209, 217, 255. *See also* Antipatris; Aphek (in Sharon); Arethusa
Pehel 22, 27, 29, 76. *See also* Pella
Peitholaus 212, 213
Pekah 113, 114, 117, 118, 119, 121, 122, 125
Pekahiah 114, 117, 118, 122
Pella (in Macedonia) 174, 177
Pella (in Transjordan) 22, 28, 30, 158, 165, 166, 170, 171, 172, 178, 205, 209, 210, 211, 212, 223, 225, 232, 251, 252, 254, 259, 266. *See also* Pehel; Tabaqat el-Fahil
Peloponnesus 162
Peltae 169
Pelusium 14, 15, 37, 38, 131, 144, 150, 152, 158, 162, 164, 170, 171, 172, 176, 177, 178, 181, 182, 207, 213, 214, 224, 261. *Also* Pelusion
Penuel 35, 36, 44, 55, 68, 79, 80, 81, 96
Peor 44
Pepi I 25
Perea 10, 194, 204, 207, 209, 212, 213, 215, 217, 223, 224, 225, 226, 232, 233, 250, 251, 252, 256, 259, 260, 263, 266
Perga 173, 174, 242
Pergamum 163, 164, 169, 179, 240, 244, 246, 249
Persepolis 12, 155, 156, 157, 176
Persia; Persians 12, 24, 152, 155, 156, 160, 162, 163, 164, 165, 166, 167, 171, 173, 174
Persian Empire 157, 158, 160, 170
Persian Gulf 24, 140, 176
Peter (apostle) 226, 228, 229, 234, 237, 238, 239, 240, 241, 250
Pethor 33, 99
Petra 23, 41, 68, 110, 192, 214, 220, 224, 265. *See also* Rekem
Phanes of Halicarnassus 161
Phannias (son of Samuel) 259
Pharathon 192, 193. *Also* Phara 259
Pharisees 13, 203, 205, 207, 208, 210, 211, 224, 248, 249
Pharnabazos 168, 169, 170
Pharpar River 18
Phasael 213, 214
Phasaelis (in Jordan Valley) 218, 219, 223
Phaselis (in Lycia) 173, 174
Phasiran 193
Pheroras 215, 223, 224
Philadelphia (in Asia Minor) 249
Philadelphia (in Transjordan) 57, 178, 179, 182, 186, 194, 201, 204, 209, 210, 212, 218, 223, 225, 232, 241, 251, 252, 254, 266. *See also* Rabbah; Rabbath-bene-ammon
Philip (apostle) 226, 228, 239, 240, 241, 247
Philip (regent of Seleucid kingdom) 188, 189
Philip I Philadelphus 208
Philip V of Macedonia 179, 180
Philippi 240, 241, 243, 244, 246
Philistia; Philistines 12, 13, 15, 17, 19, 21, 31, 32, 35, 37, 39, 47, 49, 50, 53, 56, 57, 58, 60, 61, 62, 63, 64, 65, 66, 67, 69, 70, 71, 73, 74, 76, 77, 78, 79, 80, 81, 82, 83, 84, 87, 89, 94, 95, 96, 100, 104, 105, 106, 107, 108, 109, 110, 111, 112, 113, 114, 115, 118, 119, 120, 122, 123, 125, 126, 128, 129, 130, 137, 138, 141, 144, 146, 148, 159, 163, 185, 188, 204, 233
Philoteria 178, 187, 209, 228. *See also* Beth-yerah; Sennabris
Phinehas the son of Eleazar 59
Phocis 162
Phoenicia; Phoenicians 15, 17, 18, 49, 52, 55, 57, 75, 77, 79, 89, 94, 97, 98, 106, 109, 126, 128, 132, 134, 135, 146, 149, 158, 159, 160, 162, 163, 164, 165, 169, 170, 171, 172, 173, 174, 176, 177, 179, 180, 187, 194, 195, 196, 197, 207, 209, 210, 218, 223, 232, 247, 251, 252, 254, 256, 266. *See also* Sidonians
Phoenix 248, 249
Phraortes 155
Phrygia; Phrygians 136, 152, 154, 163, 164, 169, 173, 174, 177, 180, 239, 240, 242, 243, 244, 245, 246, 248
Pi-ankhy. *See* Piye
Pi-hahiroth 39
Pi-Ramesses 40
Pilate, Pontius 233, 234, 236
Pilles 94
Piraeus 244
Pirathon 52, 55, 57, 65, 108
Pirindu 152
Pisgah 16, 23, 42, 44. *See also* Mount Nebo
Pisidia; Pisidians 150, 152, 169, 173, 242, 244
Pithom 37, 38, 39
Pitussu 152
Piye 119, 122, 123, 124, 131. *Also* Pi-ankhy
Placidus 256, 258, 259
Plataea 162, 163
Pliny 232
Poleg 28
Polycrates 151, 161
Pontus Mountains 24
Polybius 189
Pompey 208, 210, 211, 212, 213, 216, 232, 262
Pontius Pilate. *See* Pilate, Pontius
Pontus 239, 240, 244
Popilius Lenas 182
Porcius Festus. *See* Festus
Poseideion 15, 158, 170, 171, 172
Praetorium 236, 237
Priene 245
Priscilla and Aquila 245
Pr-Ramesses 37
Prince (tribe) 149
Promised Land 14
Prosopitis 164
Protothyes. *See* Bartatua
Psammetichus I 134, 136, 137, 140, 141
Psammetichus II 142, 146, 147
Psammetichus III 151, 161
Psamtik. *See* Psammetichus
Pseudo-Scylax 158, 159
Psusennes I 40, 41
Ptolemais 178, 179, 182, 184, 187, 193, 194, 195, 196, 198, 199, 206, 207, 208, 209, 210, 212, 213, 214, 215, 223, 224, 225, 227, 228, 232, 233, 240, 241, 242, 246, 247, 251, 252, 254, 255, 256, 266. *See also* Acco
Ptolemais (district) 232
Ptolemies 172, 177, 182, 217
Ptolemy (son of Abubus) 203
Ptolemy (son of Dorymenes) 184, 185
Ptolemy (son of Mennaeus) 213
Ptolemy I Soter 176, 177, 178
Ptolemy II Philadelphus 178, 179
Ptolemy III Euergetes 178, 179
Ptolemy IV Philopator 178, 179, 180
Ptolemy V Epiphanes 179, 180
Ptolemy VI Philometor 181, 182, 193, 194, 195
Ptolemy IX Lathyrus 205, 206, 207
Puah 68
Puduil 132
Pul 120. *See also* Tiglath-pileser III
Punon 23, 41, 42, 43. *See also* Feinan
Punt 27, 75
Pura 176
Put 12, 150
Puteoli 248, 249
Pydna 244
Pygmalion 94
Pylae 169

# Q

Qalat el-Husn 98. *See also* Hippus
Qalat el-Mishneqeh. *See* Macherus
Qalat es-Sila 153
Qalat Marun 10, 120
Qana. *See* Kanah (in Asher)
Qanawat 45. *See also* Kenath
Qarne Hittim 228. *See also* Horns of Hattin
Qarqar 94, 98, 99, 100, 123
Qaryat el-Inab 113. *See also* Kiriath-jearim
Qaryatein. *See* Hazar-enan
Qatazilu 94
Qatna 29, 33
Qatra. *See* Kedron
Qaushgabri 132, 133, 134
Qedar; Qedarites 13, 15, 166. *See also* Kedar; Kedarites
Qinah 147. *See also* Kinah
Qir. *See* Kir
Que 117. *See also* Kue
Quirinius 224
Qumran 13, 59, 153, 208, 216, 226, 267. *See also* Mezad Hasidim
Quramatu 143
Qurdi 125
Quweiq River 99

# R

Raamah 12
Rabb Thelathin 10, 120
Rabbah; Rabbath-ammon; Rabbath-bene-ammon 17, 23, 28, 30, 43, 44, 50, 52, 55, 56, 57, 61, 63, 65, 68, 70, 71, 72, 73, 74, 78, 80, 81, 84, 87, 99, 104, 106, 109, 111, 112, 113, 117, 118, 120, 121, 122, 124, 132, 138, 140, 141, 143, 150, 152, 158, 160,

165, 166, 170, 171, 172, 175. *See also* Arabatha
Rabbith 91
Racal 65
Rachel 33, 36, 37, 61
Radak. *See* Kimhi, Rav David (Radak)
Radiyan 119. *See also* Rezin
Rakkath 84, 91, 92
Ram (son of Hezron) 68
Ramah (in Asher) 91
Ramah (in Benjamin) 20, 57, 58, 59, 61, 62, 63, 64, 69, 72, 82, 84, 89, 95, 96, 123, 124, 129, 167, 168. *See also* Er-Ram; Ramathaim
Ramah (in Naphtali) 17, 50, 63, 84, 87, 91, 92
Ramat Issachar 85
Ramat Menashe 20
Ramat Rahel 59, 113, 167, 168. *See also* Beth-haccerem; Khirbet Salih
Ramath-mizpeh 17, 44, 56, 61, 84, 87. *See also* Mizpah (in Gilead)
Ramath-negeb 71, 147. *See also* Ramoth-negeb
Ramathaim 59. *See also* Ramah (in Benjamin)
Ramesses II 30, 37, 38
Ramesses III 30, 31
Ramesses IV 30
Ramesses XI 40
Ramesses, City of 37, 38, 39. *See also* Pr-Ramesses
Ramesses, Land of 38. *See also* Goshen
Ramet el-Khalil. *See* Mamre
Ramieh 91. *See also* Ramah (in Asher)
Ramla (Ramleh) 37, 61, 94
Rammun 59, 191
Ramoth-gilead 36, 50, 52, , 63, 68, 72, 73, 74, 78, 80, 84, 86, 96, 98, 100, 101, 102, 105, 106, 107, 111, 113, 120, 122, 124, 132, 138
Ramoth-negeb 10, 147, 148. *See also* Ramath-negeb
Raphana 232
Raphia 42, 73, 80, 81, 95, 123, 124, 132, 134, 146, 148, 175, 178, 179, 207, 209, 212, 213, 261, 266
Raphon 186
Raphon Brook 188
Ras Abu Humeid (Hamid) 61, 94. *See also* Gibbethon
Ras el-Ain 60, 90, 204. *See also* Aphek (in Sharon); Pegae; Tel Afeq
Ras el-Kharrubeh. *See* Anathoth
Ras el-Mesharif 64, 124
Ras en-Naqura 18
Ras et-Tahuneh 82. *See also* Zemaraim
Ras Kalban 91
Rassam Cylinder 127
Ras Shaqqah 16. *See also* Mount Hor (in Lebanon)
Ras Siyagah 102
Rebekah 33, 34, 35
Rechab, House of 69
Red Sea; Reed Sea 18, 22, 24, 27, 37, 38, 39, 41, 43, 75, 112, 121, 134, 143, 162, 164, 176
Regnum Polemonis 246
Rehob (in Acco Plain) 17, 50, 78, 84, 87, 91
Rehob (in Beth-shean Valley) 27, 28, 29, 30, 32, 36, 55, 66, 81
Rehoboam 78, 79, 80, 81, 82
Rehoboth-ir 12
Rehum 166
Rekem 23, 43, 68, 112, 118. *See also* Petra
Remaliah 114, 118
Rephaim 11, 23, 34, 35
Rephaim Valley 20, 57, 71, 72, 89
Rephidim 39
Resen 12
Resheph 175
Retenu 15
Reu 123
Reuben; Reubenites 17, 42, 44, 45, 50, 52, 54, 61, 65, 68, 69, 73, 78, 82, 84, 85, 88, 106, 110, 111, 125, 149
Rezeph 121, 140, 141, 143, 160, 165
Rezin 117, 118, 119, 121
Rezon (son of Eliada) 79
Rhagae 176
Rhegium 248, 249
Rhinocorura; Rhinocolura 182, 207, 209, 214, 261, 266. *See also* El-Arish; Ienysus
Rhodes (city) 164, 177, 201, 214, 218, 244, 246, 247
Rhodes (island) 12, 163, 174, 177, 178, 248. *Also* Rhodus 169
Rhoparas 169
Riblah; Ribleh 122, 127, 141, 143, 148
Rift Valley 21, 22
Rimmon (in Benjamin) 61, 62, 191
—Rimmon, Rock of 58, 59
Rimmon (in Negeb) 71
Rimmon (in Zebulun) 78, 90, 91
Riphath 12, 136
Rodanim 12. *See also* Dodanim
Rogelim 84
Rokibti 120
Roman Empire 217, 218, 232, 240, 250, 260
Rome 180, 189, 191, 200, 202, 204, 212, 213, 214, 215, 216, 217, 218, 219, 220, 223, 224, 229, 239, 240, 245, 246, 248, 249, 250, 251, 252, 253, 254, 261, 263
Romans 266, 268
Rosh ha-Niqra 18. *See also* Ras en-Naqura
Rosh Pinna Sill 196
Rubbutu 29
Rud el-Air 27
Rujm Ataruz 97. *See also* Atroth-shophan
Rujm el-Gilime. *See* Agalla
Rujm el-Meshrefeh 64
Rumah (in Galilee) 138
Rumah (in Judah) 138
Rummaneh. *See* Rimmon (in Zebulun)

# S

Saab 227
Saana 232
Sabaa 121
Sabtah 12
Sabteca 12
Sadad. *See* Zedad
Sadducees 207, 210, 248
Safed el-Battikh 92. *See also* Beth-anath
Sagalassus 173, 174
Sagartia 157
Sagur River 99
Sahab 32, 57
Sahl el-Battof 90. *See also* Bet Netofa Valley
Sahveh Kiriathaim 11
Sais 119, 122, 134, 135, 140, 141, 150, 151, 152, 162, 164, 169
Sakha 27
Salamis 15, 158, 160, 162, 163, 164, 165, 170, 171, 172, 177, 178, 240, 241, 242, 246
Salecah 16, 73
Salem 11, 34, 35, 190. *See also* Jerusalem
Salim 226, 266
Sallune 152
Salmone 248, 249
Salome (sister of Herod the Great) 223
Salome (wife of Aristobulus I) 205, 206
Salt Sea 29, 35. *See also* Dead Sea
Salt, Valley of 110
Samaga 204
Samal 70, 109
Samalla 117, 121
Samaria (city) 68, 96, 97, 98, 99, 104, 105, 106, 107, 108, 109, 110, 111, 113, 114, 115, 117, 118, 120, 121, 122, 123, 124, 125, 128, 132, 134, 138, 143, 146, 148, 150, 152, 158, 160, 165, 166, 168, 170, 171, 172, 175, 177, 178, 179, 183, 187, 198, 204, 205, 209, 210, 212, 213, 215, 216, 218, 219, 221, 224, 233, 239, 240, 241, 266. *See also* Sebaste
Samaria (region/province) 15, 20, 98, 121, 122, 124, 126, 128, 129, 132, 134, 138, 139, 146, 148, 158, 159, 165, 166, 167, 168, 170, 171, 172, 175, 179, 183, 184, 186, 187, 188, 194, 196, 197, 198, 201, 202, 204, 205, 209, 210, 212, 213, 214, 215, 217, 219, 223, 226, 233, 239, 251, 252, 254, 260, 261, 266
Samaria Ostraca/Papyri 68, 108, 115, 159
Samaritans 159, 174, 175, 176, 184, 204, 212, 225, 233, 240, 244, 259
Samos 151, 161, 246
Samosata 215
Samothrace 243, 244
Samsat. *See* Kummukh
Samsi 121
Samsimuruna 128
Samson 52, 53, 56, 57, 58, 60, 67
Samuel 51, 59, 60, 61, 62, 63, 64
Samulis 232
Sanballat 159, 167, 168, 174, 175
Sanguru River 93
Sanhedrin 213, 235, 238, 248, 266
Sansannah 69
Sapheth 90. *See also* Zephath
Saphir 241
Sapia 122
Sapsaphas 226. *See also* Aenon (in Transjordan)
Saqqara 27, 39, 144, 150, 162, 164
Sarah; Sarai 34, 35
Sardis 136, 137, 150, 152, 156, 157, 162, 163, 164, 169, 173, 174, 177, 240, 246, 249
Sargon I 26
Sargon II 122, 123, 124, 125, 126, 127, 130, 136, 155, 159
Sarid 17, 54, 55, 84, 87, 90, 91
Sariptu 128. *See also* Zarephath
Sarrabani 122
Sartaba 210, 215. *See also* Alexandrion
Saudi Arabia 24
Saul (king of Israel) 51, 52, 61, 62, 63, 64, 65, 66, 67, 70, 71, 113
Saul of Tarsus 241, 242. *See also* Paul (apostle)
Scaallis 254
Scaurus, Marcus Aemilius 210
Scipio Asiaticus 180
Scopus 179
Scythians 12, 136, 137, 141, 155, 162
Scythopolis 178, 179, 182, 186, 187, 188, 198, 205, 206, 207, 209, 210, 211, 212, 213, 223, 225, 226, 227, 231, 232, 233, 240, 241, 251, 252, 254, 256, 257, 266. *See also* Beth-shean
Sea of Chinnereth 16, 17, 18, 19, 50, 54, 55, 63, 81, 84, 87, 91, 92, 96, 98, 105, 128, 206. *See also* Sea of Galilee
Sea of Galilee 21, 44, 226–232, 233, 237, 241, 257
Sea of Salt 23. *See also* Dead Sea
Sea of the Arabah 23, 110, 111. *See also* Dead Sea
Sea Peoples 31, 53, 54. *See also* Philistines
Seba 12
Sebaste 204, 218, 219, 220, 221, 222, 223, 225, 226, 233, 239, 240, 241, 251, 252, 254, 266. *See also* Samaria (city)
Sebennytus 162, 164, 170
Sehet-mafk 151
Seil en-Numeirah 103. *See also* Nimrim, Waters of
Seir 69, 104
Sela 16, 23, 42, 43, 110, 112, 115, 118, 150, 152. *See also* Joktheel
Selame 256
Selbit 83. *See also* Shaalbim
Seleucia (in Cilicia) 152
Seleucia (in Gaulanitis) 209, 256, 257, 258
Seleucia (in Syria) 177, 178, 195, 197, 201, 240, 241, 242, 244, 245, 248
Seleucid Empire/Kingdom 177, 200
Seleucids 172, 180, 182, 183, 184, 191, 202, 203
Seleucus I Nicator 177, 178
Seleucus II Callinicus 178
Seleucus III Ceraunus 179
Seleucus IV Philopator 180, 181, 189
Selinde. *See* Sallune
Selle 39. *See also* Sillu/Sillo
Seluqiye. *See* Seleucia (in Gaulanitis)
Selybria 169
Semechonitis (lake) 257. *See also* Sea of Galilee
Senaah 168
Seneh 62
Sennabris 21, 227, 228, 256, 257. *See also* Beth-yerah; Philoteria
Sennacherib 47, 123, 125, 126, 127, 128, 129, 130, 131, 132, 133, 137, 166
Senn en-Nabra. *See* Sennabris
Senwoseret I 27
Sepham 16
Sephar 108
Sepharvaim 125
Sepph 227, 256
Sepphoris 206, 207, 209, 210, 212, 215, 218, 223, 225, 226, 227, 228, 230, 232, 233, 241, 251, 252, 254, 255, 256, 266
Serabit el-Khadem 27, 39
Serah 68
Serbonis, Lake 15
Sergio Paulus 241, 242
Seron 184
Serug 33
Sestus 174
Seth 27
Seti I 15, 38, 39
Severus. *See* Julius Severus
Sextus Caesar 213
Sha-Imerishu 109
Shaalbim 17, 50, 52, 60, 61, 65, 67, 69, 83, 84, 87, 89, 94, 119
Shaalim 61, 68
Shaaraim 63, 202
Shabako 125
Shadon 209
Shalishah 61, 68
Shallum (king of Israel) 114
Shallum (king of Judah). *See* Jehoahaz II
Shalmaneser II 70
Shalmaneser III 93, 94, 98, 99, 105, 106, 108, 121, 155
Shalmaneser IV 109
Shalmaneser V 122, 123, 124
Shamash-shum-ukin 135
Shamgar the son of Anath 52, 53, 54, 57
Shamir 52, 68. *See also* Shemer; Shimron
Shamsha; Shamshai 162
Shamshi-Adad V 106
Shamshi-ilu 109, 110, 114, 117
Shanghar 34. *See also* Shinar
Shaphir 130
Shapia. *See* Sapia
Sharhan 81
Sharon (city) 102
Sharon Plain 17, 18, 19, 20, 31, 36, 48, 74, 76, 83, 96, 108, 128, 158, 159, 165, 187, 199, 205, 214, 240
Sharru-lu-dari 129
Sharuhen 65
Shasu 30, 32, 34, 37, 38, 41, 49
Shaveh-kiriathaim 35
Shealtiel 161
Sheba 12
Shebitku 126, 131
Shechem (city) 16, 17, 20, 27, 28, 29, 30, 32, 33, 34, 36, 43, 49, 50, 52, 55, 56, 59, 61, 63, 65, 66, 67, 68, 71, 72, 73, 74, 76, 77, 78, 79, 80, 81, 83, 84, 87, 90, 96, 108, 125, 167, 175, 183, 186, 192, 194, 198, 204, 205, 208, 209, 212, 218, 259
Shechem (clan) 68, 69
Shechem Valley 20
Sheikh Sad. *See* Carnaim; Karnaim
Shelah 69
Shelesh 68
Shem 12, 13, 34
Shema 68, 71
Shemer 56, 68, 97. *See also* Shimron
Shemida 68, 108
Shenazzar 161. *See also* Sheshbazzar
Shephelah (of Israel) 17, 18, 48. *Also* Shephelah of Galilee
Shephelah (of Judah) 17, 18, 19, 20, 31, 36, 37, 46, 47, 57, 58, 61, 63, 64, 67, 69, 80, 104, 112, 113, 118, 119, 126, 130, 138, 139, 147, 160, 167, 168, 183, 184, 186, 188, 190, 198, 202, 240
Shephelah (of Lod) 167, 168, 198. *See also* Ono, Plain of
Sheshbazzar 160, 161
Shigata 29
Shihin. *See* Asochis
Shihor, Lake 37, 38, 39
Shihor-libnath 90, 91
Shikkeron 89
Shilkanni 122, 123. *See also* Osorkon IV
Shiloh 17, 28, 32, 37, 50, 52, 55, 59, 60, 64, 79, 80, 87, 89
Shilshah 68
Shimeathites 68
Shimei (clan) 68
Shimei (son of Ela) 85
Shimon 27, 29, 48, 54, 55, 84, 91, 95. *See also* Simeon (city); Simonias
Shimron 68. *See also* Shamir; Shemer
Shimon bar Kosiba 265, 266. *See also* Bar Kochba
Shimon bar Yohai 266
Shimshi 166
Shinar 12, 34
Shion 91
Shiqmona 28, 30
Shishak 75, 79, 80, 81, 82. *See also* Shoshenq I
Shishak 95
Shittim 43, 44. *See also* Abel-shittim
Shobal 69
Shoresh 89
Shoshenq I 79, 83. *See also* Shishak
Shual 62, 68
Shuhah 69
Shuham 67. *See also* Hushim
Shunadiru 143
Shunem 17, 29, 54, 55, 66, 81, 84, 85, 87, 91, 107
Shur 33, 34, 35, 39, 62
Shushan 157. *See also* Susa
Shutu. *See* Seth
Siamon 40, 75
Sibmah 44
Sicels 31
Siddim, Valley of 11, 35
Side 173, 174
Sidon 12, 13, 15, 16, 18, 29, 33, 48, 55, 72, 73, 74, 80, 91, 98, 99, 107, 109, 111, 113, 121, 122, 124, 128, 132, 133, 146, 158, 159, 160, 163, 165, 166, 167, 170, 171, 172, 173, 174, 176, 177, 178, 179, 187, 195, 197, 200, 218, 225, 232, 240, 241, 244, 248, 249, 251, 252, 254
Sidon (district) 232
Sidonians 13, 50, 52, 54, 63, 67, 70, 73, 74, 75, 77, 80, 84, 94, 96, 106, 113, 120, 122, 124, 132, 158, 165, 166, 167, 170, 171, 172
Sidqa 128, 129
Sigoph 256. *See also* Sogane (in Galilee)
Siha; Sihai 162
Sihon 42, 43, 48, 85
Sila 110, 153. *See also* Sela
Silas 243, 244
Sil-Baal 127, 131, 132, 133, 134
Silifke. *See* Seleucia (in Cilicia)
Sillu/Sillo 39
Silo (Roman officer) 215
Siloam Tunnel 126, 127
Silva, Flavius 263, 261, 264
Simeon (city) 138, 139. *See also* Shimon; Tel Shimron
Simeon (tribe); Simeonites 17, 21, 36, 41, 42, 50, 52, 65, 66, 68, 69, 70, 71, 74, 78, 80, 88, 126, 127, 147, 149
Simeon bar Yohai 228
Simirru; Simyra 13, 15, 123, 158, 163, 170, 171, 172. *See also* Sumur
Simon Bar-Jona 232
Simonias 227. *See also* Shimron
Simon (of Benjamin) 180, 181
Simon (the tanner) 241
Simon (son of Gamaliel) 259
Simon (son of Giora) 255, 259, 260, 261, 262, 263
Simon Maccabeus 187, 191, 192, 193, 194, 195, 196, 197, 198, 199, 200, 201, 202, 203, 206
Simon Magus 240
Simon Peter 237, 238. *See also* Cephas; Peter
Simon the Just 174, 175
Simon (the Just) II 179, 180
Sinai 15, 19, 24, 35, 38, 39, 40, 41, 44, 74, 79, 111, 112, 119, 133, 134, 144, 145

Sinite 13
Sinjirli. *See* Samal
Sin-magir 152
Sinope 136, 150, 152, 240
Sin-sharra-ishkun 140, 141
Sin-shumu-lishir 140
Sinuhe, Tale of 27
Siphmoth 65
Siphnus 174
Siphtan 108
Sippar 127, 150, 151, 152, 156, 160, 165
Sirion 14, 18, 21, 24, 27. *See also* Anti-Lebanon
Sisera 54, 55, 92
Sittake 169
Siyannu 13
Smendes 40
Smyrna 137, 246, 249
So 122. *See also* Sais
Soaemus (king of Emesa) 255
Socho. *See* Socoh
Socoh (in Sharon) 50, 61, 63, 66, 74, 81, 83, 84, 85, 108
Socoh (in Shephelah) 57, 63, 69, 71, 80, 118, 119, 120, 240
Socoh (nr. Hebron) 126, 127
Sodom 11, 34, 35, 59
Sogane (in Galilee) 256
Sogane (in Gaulanitis) 227, 256, 257, 258
Sogdiana 157, 176
Solem 66. *See also* Shunem
Soli 174
Solyma 258
Solomon 14, 17, 51, 74, 75, 76, 77, 78, 79, 82, 86, 92, 129, 209
Solomon's Pools 221
Sorek River/Valley 18, 19, 20, 57, 58, 60, 72, 83, 83, 88, 110, 113, 118, 119, 129, 130, 202
Sosipater 186
Sossius 215, 216
South Arabia 22, 23
Sparta 162, 164, 165, 168, 174, 182, 200
Spartans 156
Stephen (the Martyr) 239, 240, 241
Steppe land of . . . *See* Wilderness of . . .
Stone of Bahan the son of Reuben 44, 68, 89
Strabo 232
Straton 159
Straton/Strato, Tower of 159, 175, 205, 207, 209, 212, 219, 220. *See also* Caesarea
Strato's Tower (in Jerusalem) 206
Stronghold, The 64, 65. *See also* Masada
Subartu 33
Subite 122
Succoth (in Egypt) 37, 38, 39
Succoth (in Jordan Valley) 17, 22, 23, 36, 44, 50, 52, 55, 61, 63, 68, 76, 81, 84, 87, 124, 132
Suhu 141
Sukkiim 82
Sumer 12, 25, 26, 33, 34, 155. *See also* Shinar
Sumur 13, 29, 74, 109, 121, 160, 165. *See also* Simirru, Simyra
Susa 33, 121, 140, 150, 152, 160, 165, 167, 176, 240. *See also* Shushan
Sussita. *See* Hippus; Qalat el-Husn
Sycamina; Sycaminum 207, 227
Syene 125, 146, 148, 168, 170
Syenneisis 155
Syracuse 248, 249
Syr Daria 157
Syria 14, 15, 26, 72, 75, 94, 108, 109, 116, 117, 118, 139, 140, 153, 158, 159, 164, 169, 170, 172, 174, 176, 177, 178, 179, 180, 182, 195, 196, 207, 208, 210, 212, 213, 214, 215, 219, 223, 224, 232, 233, 242, 244, 245, 246, 248, 251, 252, 254, 255
Syria (modern state) 24
Syrian Desert 24
Syrian Gates 173
Syrians of Palestine 159
Syrtis 248

# T

Taanach 17, 28, 29, 30, 32, 36, 48, 50, 54, 55, 63, 68, 74, 78, 81, 83, 84, 87
Taanath-shiloh 17, 55, 87, 90, 108
Tabae 188. *See also* Isfahan
Tabal 12, 117, 125, 134, 136. *See also* Tubal
Tabaqat el-Fahil 28. *See also* Pehel; Pella (in Transjordan)
Tabbath 55
Tabeel; Tab-el 118, 119
Tabeh 40. *See also* Jotbathah (in Sinai)
Taberah 40
Tabgha 228, 229. *See also* Heptapegon
Tabitha 240, 241
Tableland 17, 18, 87
Tabnit 165
Tachos 170, 171
Tadmor 33, 74, 75, 76, 83, 99, 108, 109, 121, 125, 141, 143, 150, 152, 160, 165
Taharqa 131, 132, 133, 134. *See also* Tirhakah
Tahpanes; Tahpanhes 39, 148, 149, 162, 164, 168. *See also* Daphne (in Egypt); Tell Defeneh
Tahtim-hodshi 73
Takhshi 29
Takritain 140
Talat ed-Damm 89. *See also* Adummim, Ascent of
Tamar 11, 15, 16, 35, 42, 43, 73, 80, 81, 110, 122, 124, 138, 149
Tamar (daughter-in-law of Judah). *See* Judah and Tamar narrative
Tanis 37, 38. *See also* Zoan
Tanwetamani 134
Taphnith 48
Tappuah 17, 48, 50, 55, 60, 68, 71, 84, 87, 90, 108, 192
Taricheae 206, 209, 227, 228, 229, 232, 251, 252, 256, 257. *See also* Magdala
Tarshish 75, 76
Tarshish (in Sardinia) 12, 76
Tarsus (in Cilicia) 76, 150, 152, 163, 164, 169, 172, 173, 174, 240, 241, 242, 243, 244, 246, 248
Tartessos (in Spain) 76
Tattenai; Tattennu 161, 162, 172
Taurus Mountains 24, 169, 173, 174, 243
Taxila 176
Taylor Prism 127
Tbilisi 24
Tebah 72
Teda. *See* Agrippias; Anthedon
Tefnakht 119, 122, 123
Tehran 24
Teima 150, 152, 153
Tekoa 20, 21, 65, 69, 71, 72, 80, 101, 115, 167, 168, 192, 193, 194, 199, 214, 259
Tel-abib 148
Tel Adami. *See* Adami-nekeb; Khirbet et-Tell
Tel Afeq 90. *See also* Aphek (in Sharon); Ras el-Ain
Telaim; Telem 62
Tel Akhzib. *See* Achzib; Ez-Zib
Tel Akko. *See* Acco; Tell el-Fukhkhar
Tel Alil. *See* Hali; Khirbet Ras Ali
Tel Avdon. *See* Abdon; Khirbet Abda
Tel Avel Bet Maakha. *See* Abel-beth-maacah; Abil el-Qamh
Tel Aviv-Jaffa 24
Tel Azeqa. *See* Azekah; Khirbet Tell Zakariyeh
Tel Aznoth-tabor. *See* Aznoth-tabor; Khirbet Umm Jebeil
Tel Batash 28, 30, 32, 58, 60. *See also* Tell el-Batashi; Timnah (in Shephelah)
Tel Bet Shemesh 58, 118. *See also* Beth-shemesh (in Judah); Tell er-Rumeileh
Tel Bira 28
Tel Burna. *See* Tell Bornat
Tel Chinnereth 28, 30
Tel Dan 28, 67, 106. *See also* Dan (city); Tell el-Qadi
Tel Dover. *See* Khirbet ed-Duweir
Tel Emeq. *See* Tell Mimas
Tel En Gev 76
Tel Erani 25, 32. *See also* Tell esh-Sheikh Ahmed el-Areini
Tel Esur 28
Tel Eton 32, 47, 118, 199. *See also* Eglon; Tell Aitun
Tel Gamma 35, 132. *See also* Tell Jemmeh
Tel Gat Hefer. *See* Gath-hepher; Khirbet ez-Zurra
Tel Gerisa 28, 30, 32
Tel Gezer 94. *See also* Gezer
Tel Goded. *See* Tell el-Judeideh
Tel Hadar 32, 76
Tel Halif 28, 30, 42. *See also* Tell el-Khuweilifeh
Tel Hannaton. *See* Asochis; Hannathon
Tel Harashim 32
Tel Harasim 167, 168
Tel Haror 28, 30, 32, 35, 132
Tel-harsha 148
Tel Hasi. *See* Tell el-Hesi
Tel Hazor. *See* Hazor; Tell el-Qedah
Tel Hefer 28, 30
Tel Ira. *See* Khirbet Gharrah; Ramath-negeb
Tel Kedesh (in Jezreel Valley) 28, 30
Tel Kinrot 76
Tel Kision 28, 32
Tel Kison. *See* Tell Keisan
Tel Kitan 28
Tell Abu Hawam 28, 30, 76, 90. *See also* Libnath
Tell Abu Hureirah 35. *See also* Tel Haror
Tell Abu Qudeis 54. *See also* Tel Qedesh
Tell Abu Sus 83. *See also* Abel-meholah
Tell Ahmar. *See* Til-Barsip
Tell Aitun 47, 118. *See also* Eglon; Tel Eton
Tel Lakhish. *See* Lachish; Tell ed-Duweir
Tell Amta. *See* Amathus (in Jordan Valley)
Tell Aqar 123. *See also* Der
Tell Ashari. *See* Dium
Tell Ashtarah 121. *See also* Ashtaroth
Tell Azeimeh 44
Tell Balawat 99
Tell Basta 27
Tell Beit Mirsim 28, 30, 32, 36
Tell Bornat 47. *See also* Libnah; Tel Burna
Tell Defeneh 39. *See also* Baal-zephon; Daphne (in Egypt)
Tell Deir Allah 28, 30, 32, 33, 36, 37. *See also* Succoth (in Jordan Valley)
Tell ed-Daba. *See* Avaris
Tell ed-Damiyeh 45
Tell ed-Dibbin 73, 120. *See also* Ijon
Tell ed-Duweir 47, 130. *See also* Lachish; Tel Lakhish
Tell edh-Dhahab el-Gharbi. *See* Mahanaim
Tell edh-Dhahab esh-Sharqi 55, 79. *See also* Penuel
Tell el-Ahdab 257
Tell el-Ajjul 28, 30, 32, 66
Tell el-Amarna 30
Tell el-Aqabeh. *See* Cypros
Tell el-Batashi 118, 129. *See also* Tel Batash; Timnah (in Shephelah)
Tell el-Beida 51. *See also* Nahalal
Tell el-Bir el-Gharbi 91. *See also* Rehob (in Asher)
Tell el-Far. *See* Beten; Tel Par
Tell el-Farah (North) 28, 30, 32, 80, 96. *See also* Tirzah
Tell el-Farah (South) 26, 28, 30, 35
Tell el-Fukhkhar 91. *See also* Acco; Tel Akko
Tell el-Ful 59, 62, 124. *See also* Gibeah (in Benjamin)
Tell el-Hammam 44. *See also* Abel-shittim
Tell el-Hammeh 83
Tell el-Hassan 233
Tell el-Hayyat 28
Tell el-Hesi 28, 30, 32, 47, 76
Tell el-Idham 90. *See also* Amad
Tell el-Jalul 103. *See also* Bezer
Tell el-Jemid 187. *See also* Maked
Tell el-Jisr. *See* Naaran (Naarah)
Tell el-Kefrein 44
Tell el-Kheir 39
Tell el-Kheleifeh 118. *See also* Ezion-geber
Tell el-Khirbeh 120
Tell el-Khureibeh 48
Tell el-Khuweilifeh 42. *See also* Tel Halif
Tell el-Mashkhuta 39, 160, 166, 167
Tell el-Mazar 83. *See also* Jokmeam
Tell el-Menshiyeh. *See* Tell esh-Sheikh Ahmed el-Areini
Tell el-Milh 42. *See also* Tel Malhata
Tell el-Miseh 103
Tell el-Qadi 10, 21, 67, 80, 120. *See also* Dan (city); Tel Dan
Tell el-Qassis. *See* Helkath
Tell el-Qedah 120. *See also* Hazor; Tel Hazor
Tell el-Umeiri 28, 30, 32
Tell el-Yehudiyeh 37
Tell en-Naam 92. *See also* Jabneel (in Naphtali); Tel Yinam
Tell en-Nahl 90. *See also* Allammelech; Tel Nahal
Tell en-Nasbeh 59, 96, 124, 148. *See also* Mizpah (in Benjamin)
Tell en-Nejileh 36
Tell er-Ratabah 38. *See also* Pithom
Tell er-Rimah 109
Tell er-Rumeileh 58, 118. *See also* Beth-shemesh (in Judah); Tel Bet Shemesh
Tell er-Rumeith 84, 100. *See also* Ramoth-gilead
Tell esh-Shallaf 129. *See also* Eltekeh; Tel Shalaf
Tell esh-Shammam 90. *See also* Dabbesheth
Tell esh-Shariah 30, 35, 42, 65. *See also* Tel Sera; Ziklag?
Tell esh-Sheikh Ahmed el-Areini 130. *See also* Tel Erani; Tell el-Menshiyeh
Tell esh-Sheikh Madhkur 64. *See also* Adullam
Tell esh-Shuna 26
Tell es-Safi 47, 51, 63. *See also* Gath (of Philistines); Tel Zafit
Tell es-Saidiyeh 28, 30, 32, 57. *See also* Asophon; Zaphon
Tell es-Samak 19. *See also* Sycamina; Sycaminum
Tell es-Sarem 83
Tell es-Sultan 233. *See also* Jericho
Tell Halaf. *See* Gozan
Tell Hamoukar 25
Tell Hisban 43. *See also* Esbus; Heshbon
Tell Iktanu 44
Tell Jemmeh 28, 30, 32, 35, 168. *Also* Tel Gamma
Tell Jezer. *See* Gazara; Gezer
Tell Judeideh 28, 30, 81, 130. *Also* Tel Goded
Tell Kabri 91
Tell Keisan 18, 28, 30, 32, 48. *See also* Achshaph?; Mishal; Tel Kison
Tell Kurdaneh 91
Tell Mardikh 25. *See also* Ebla
Tell Maryam 89. *See also* Beth-aven
Tell Melat 94. *See also* Gibbethon; Tel Malot
Tell Meskeneh 14
Tell Mezar 57
Tell Mimas 91. *See also* Beth-emek
Tell Muhaffar 83. *See also* Hepher (city)
Tell Nimrin. *See* Beth-nimrah
Tell Qadesh. *See* Kedesh (in Galilee); el Qedesh
Tell Qarqur 99. *See also* Qarqar
Tell Qasile 32, 60, 76, 81
Tell Qasileh 19
Tell Qeimun. *See* Jokneam
Tell Qudadi 19
Tell Ramada 28
Tell Rashidiyeh 91
Tell Rifat. *See* Arpad
Tell Samara 230
Tell Sandahanna. *See* Mareshah; Marisa; Tel Maresha
Tell Shadud 90. *See also* Sarid
Tell Sheikh el-Areini. *See* Tel Erani
Tell Tabun 90. *See also* Beer Tivon; Beth-dagon
Tell Tayinat 93, 121. *See also* Kunulua
Tell Terah 33
Tell Thorah 90. *See also* Maralah
Tell Umm Hammad 83. *See also* Zarethan
Tell Zakariyeh 46, 63. *See also* Azekah
Tell Zamadi. *See* Careae; Tel Mazar
Tell Zif 64. *See also* Ziph
Tel Malhata 28, 42, 76. *See also* Tell el-Milh
Tel Malot. *See* Tell Melat
Tel Maresha. *See* Mareshah; Tell Sandahanna
Tel Masos 28, 30. *See also* Khirbet el-Meshash
Tel Mazar. *See* Coreae; Tell Zamadi
Tel Megadim 28
Tel-melah 148
Telmessus 173, 174
Tel Mevorakh 28, 30
Tel Michal 28, 30
Tel Miqne 28, 30, 32. *See also* Accaron; Ekron; Khirbet el-Muqanna
Tel Mor 28, 30, 32
Tel Nagila 28
Tel Nahal. *See* Tell en-Nahl
Tel Nami 28, 30
Tel Par. *See* Beten; Tell el-Far
Tel Qashish 28, 30
Tel Qedesh. *See* Cadasa; Kedesh (in Galilee); Tell Abu Qudeis
Tel Qiri 28, 32
Tel Raqqat. *See* Khirbet el-Quneitireh; Rakkath
Tel Regev. *See* Achshaph; Khirbet el-Harbaj
Tel Rehov. *See* Tell es-Sarem
Tel Rosh Haniqra 26
Tel Rosh. *See* Beth-shemesh (in Naphtali); Khirbet Tell er-Ruweisi
Tel Sera 28, 32, 35, 42, 65. *See also* Tell esh-Shariah
Tel Shalaf. *See* Tell esh-Shallaf
Tel Shem. *See* Dabbesheth; Tell esh-Shammam
Tel Shimron. *See* Khirbet Sammuniyeh
Tel Shiqmona. *See* Tell es-Samak
Tel Shor. *See* Maralah; Tell Thorah
Tel Soreq 98
Tel Yinam. *See* Jabneel (in Naphtali); Tell en-Naam
Tel Zafit 28, 30, 32. *See also* Gath (of Philistines); Tell es-Safi
Tel Zeror 28, 30, 32
Tel Zippor 32
Tel Zora. *See* Khirbet Sarah
Tema 121. *See also* Teima
Teman 43, 73, 80, 112, 115, 118
Tenedus 174
Tennes Rebellion 171, 172
Teos. *See* Tachos
Terah 33
Terebinthos 175, 267
Terenuthis; Terraneh 151
Termessus 174
Thamna (in Judea) 192, 194, 214, 256, 260. *See also* Timnath-heres
Thamna (nr. Bethlehem) 193
Thapsacus; Thapsakos 14, 74, 169, 176. *See also* Tiphsah
Thapsakos River 158. *See also* Orontes River
Thebes. *See* No-amon
Thebez 56
Thella 227
Theodotus 178, 179
Theodorus 208
Theouprosopon 16
Thermopylae 162
Thessalia 162
Thessalonica 243, 244, 246
Thrace; Thracia 157, 162, 169, 174, 178, 208, 246, 248
Three Taverns 248, 249
Thutmose III 13, 15, 29, 36
Thyatira 249
Thymbrium 169
Tiberias 21, 223, 225, 226, 227, 228, 229, 230, 231, 232, 233, 241, 250, 251, 252, 254, 256, 257, 265, 266
Tiberias, Sea/Lake of 21, 231, 252. *See also* Sea of Galilee
Tiberius Caesar 236, 250
Tibhath 73
Tibni the son of Ginath 96

Tidal 34
Tiglath-pileser I 33
Tiglath-pileser III 67, 101, 111, 113, 114, 115, 116, 117, 118, 119, 120, 121, 122, 123, 124, 126, 131
Tigranes 210
Tigris River 24, 33, 70, 99, 109, 116, 121, 125, 136, 140, 146, 148, 154, 155, 156, 157, 160, 165, 169, 176, 240
Tikrit. *See* Takritain
Ti-Ku 37
Til-Barsip 70, 99, 109, 114, 117, 121
Til-garimmu 12. *See also* Gurun; Togarmah
Til-Turahi 99
Timarchus 189, 191
Timnah (in Arabah) 39, 43
Timnah (in Judah) 118, 209, 266
Timnah (in Shephelah) 36, 57, 58, 60, 63, 69, 72, 83, 89, 94, 113, 118, 119, 126, 129, 130
Timnath-heres 45, 46, 60, 68, 94. *Also* Timnath-serah
Timotheus 186, 187, 188
Timothy 243, 244, 246
Timsah Lake 37, 39
Tiphsah 14, 15, 74, 99, 114, 121, 158, 169. *See also* Thapsacus
Tiras 12
Tirhakah 131. *See also* Taharqa
Tirzah 17, 36, 48, 55, 56, 61, 63, 68, 69, 80, 81, 84, 87, 96, 108, 114
Tissaphernes 168, 169
Tithraustes 169
Titius Justus 245
Titus 237, 250, 251, 252, 255, 256, 257, 258, 259, 261, 262, 263, 265
Tob (city) 56, 72, 73, 98
Tob, Land of 56, 72, 73, 186
Tobiah/Tobias; Tobiads 15, 92, 118, 158, 159, 165, 166, 167, 170, 171, 172, 177, 180, 181, 204
Togarmah 12, 121, 136
Toi 72
Tola the son of Puah 52, 56, 68
Top of Carmel 96. *See also* Mount Carmel
Tophel 42, 43
Topheth 139
Trachonitis 23, 187, 218, 219, 223, 251, 252, 253
Trajan 252, 256, 260
Tralles 174
Transjordan 17, 22, 23, 28, 31, 32, 36, 42, 43, 45, 53, 56, 57, 62, 67, 68, 72, 85, 89, 96, 97, 101, 110, 111, 114, 115, 117, 119, 148, 149, 152, 167, 181, 187, 188, 196, 199, 203, 204, 207, 209, 218
Trapezus 169
Tripolis 15, 16, 158, 163, 165, 166, 170, 171, 172, 176, 177, 189, 195, 197, 205. *See also* Ellisu; Ullasa
Troas 243, 244, 246. *See also* Alexandria Troas
Trogyllium 246
Tryphon 15, 196, 197, 198, 199, 200, 201, 202
Tubal 12, 121, 136
Tubas 56
Tudkhaliya 34
Tugdamme 136
Tukulti-Ninurta II 93
Tulul Abu el-Alayiq 219, 220. *See also* Jericho
Turan Basin 227
Turkey 24
Tutammu 117
T-w-l 108
Tyana 169, 174
Tyre (in Lebanon) 10, 16, 17, 18, 19, 27, 29, 50, 52, 54, 63, 67, 72, 73, 74, 75, 76, 78, 79, 80, 84, 87, 91, 94, 96, 97, 98, 99, 105, 107, 109, 111, 113, 114, 117, 118, 119, 120, 121, 122, 124, 128, 132, 134, 135, 138, 140, 141, 143, 146, 149, 150, 152, 158, 159, 160, 163, 165, 166, 169, 170, 171, 172, 173, 174, 175, 176, 177, 178, 179, 181, 182, 187, 195, 197, 200, 209, 213, 214, 223, 225, 227, 232, 240, 241, 242, 244, 246, 247, 251, 252, 254, 256, 266
Tyre (in Transjordan) 159, 167. *See also* Tyrus
Tyre (district) 81, 96, 98, 134, 135, 225, 232
Tyriaeum 169
Tyropoeon Valley 59, 234
Tyrsenoi. *See* Tiras
Tyrus 118, 124, 167, 182, 194. *See also* Tyre (in Transjordan)

## U

Ugarit 29, 31, 33, 79
Ugbaru 154
Ulatha 21, 219, 223. *See also* Huleh Valley
Ullasa 27, 29, 158. *See also* Ellisu; Tripolis
Ulluba 117
Umm el-Basatin 57. *See also* Maanith; Minnith
Umm Qeis. *See* Gadara
Umm Rasas 103
Ummanmanda 136
Unqi 117, 118. *See also* Patina
Upe 29
Upper Sea 24, 99, 109, 121, 123, 124, 132, 134, 140, 157. *See also* Mediterranean Sea
Ur; Ur of the Chaldees 33, 150, 152
Ura 152
Urartu; Urartians 13, 109, 110, 116, 119, 121, 136, 143
Uriah the Hittite 71, 72
Uruk 127, 154
Uruk King List 151, 152
Ushtannu 161, 172
Usiris 166
Usu 29, 73, 74, 91, 128, 132, 135, 140. *See also* Hosah
Uzziah 17, 101, 107, 110, 111, 112, 113, 114, 117, 118, 119, 120. *See also* Azariah

## V

Valley, The 18. *See also* Jordan Valley; Jezreel Valley
Valley of Thorns 261
Varus (son of Soaemus) 251
Ventidius 215
Verria. *See* Beroea
Vespasian 137, 185, 198, 232, 238, 255, 256, 257, 258, 259, 260, 261, 268
Via Appia 249
Via Dolorosa 236
Via Egnatia 243, 246
Via Maris 73, 76
Via Nova Tirana 103
Via Sebaste 242
Vitellius 261

## W

Wadi Abbelin 90
Wadi Abu Agag 27
Wadi Abu Diba 62
Wadi Abu Gharuba 267
Wadi Allaqi 27
Wadi Arbel 228
Wadi Beit Haninah 20, 57
Wadi Beit Jibrin. *See* Zephathah Valley
Wadi Beiza 27
Wadi Brisa 144
Wadi ed-Daliyeh 159, 167, 174, 175, 176, 267
Wadi el-Ain 40
Wadi el-Arab 27
Wadi el-Arish 14, 15. *See also* Brook of Egypt
Wadi el-Auja 83
Wadi el-Farah 20, 22
Wadi el-Hasa. *See* Zered Brook
Wadi el-Hesi 241
Wadi el-Jizair 47
Wadi el-Malik 90. *See also* Iphtahel Valley
Wadi el-Mojib. *See* Arnon Valley
Wadi el-Shatt el-Rigal 27
Wadi en-Natuf 183
Wadi es-Sarar 57. *See also* Sorek Valley
Wadi es-Sunt/Sant 63. *See also* Elah Valley
Wadi es-Suweinit 59, 62
Wadi ez-Zerqa 267
Wadi Fajas 92
Wadi Farah 98
Wadi Feinan 41
Wadi Fiq 98
Wadi Fuqrah 41. *See also* Nahal Zin
Wadi Hasa 103. *See also* Zered Brook
Wadi Jalud 83
Wadi Kharit 27
Wadi Maghata 27
Wadi Milh 18
Wadi Mujib 102. *See also* Arnon River
Wadi Murabbaat 265, 267, 268
Wadi Musrarah 19, 90. *See also* Nahal Ayyalon
Wadi Nasb 27
Wadi Qanah 90. *See also* Kanah Brook
Wadi Qelt 89, 219, 220, 233
Wadi Qumran 267
Wadi Samekh 231
Wadi Sarar. *See also* Nahal Soreq; Sorek Valley
Wadi Sirhan 96
Wadi Tumeilat 38
Wahb 133
Washshukanni 28
Waters of Meribah of Kadesh 149
Waters of Nephtoah 89
Way of Edom 104, 107
Way of Gilgal 191
Way of Horus 38, 39. *See also* Way of the Land of the Philistines
Way of the Land of the Philistines 38, 39
Way of the Sea 10, 54, 120, 121, 232
Way of the Spies 39, 42
Way of the Wilderness 45, 58, 240
Way to Mount Seir 39
Way to Shur 21, 39
Way to the Arabah 39
Way to the Hill-country of the Amorites 39
Way to the Reed Sea 39, 43
Western Desert 24
Western Sea 16. *See also* Mediterranean Sea
Wilderness of Beer-sheba 107
Wilderness of Damascus 107
Wilderness of Jeruel 101
Wilderness of Judah/Judea 21, 64, 112, 192, 225, 226. *See also* Judean Desert
Wilderness of Kedemoth 43, 50
Wilderness of Maon 64, 65
Wilderness of Paran 11, 21, 24, 34, 35, 39, 40, 65, 79
Wilderness of Shur 39
Wilderness of Sin 39
Wilderness of Sinai 39
Wilderness of Tekoa 101, 192
Wilderness of Zin 16, 21, 39
Wilderness of Ziph 64, 65
Willibald 229

## X

Xanthus 173, 174
Xenophon 157, 169
Xerxes 157, 159, 161, 162, 163, 166. *See also* Ahasuerus

## Y

Yadi; Yadih 153
Yafa. *See* Japhia
Yaham 81
Yahma 83
Yahwism 55
Yakinilu 134
Yalo. *See* Aijalon
Yamani 125, 126
Yanoam 29
Yanuh 10, 120. *See also* Janoah (nr. Tyre)
Yarkon River 19, 60, 83, 90
Yarmuk River/Valley 18, 23, 98, 186, 210, 226, 256
Yarmuth. *See* Jarmuth
Yarun 92. *See also* Yiron
Yashub. *See* Jashub
Yathrib 150, 152, 153, 154
Yattir 48
Yautha 133, 134, 135
Yavneh-yam 19, 28, 30
Yavneh; Yebna. *See* Jabneh; Jamnia
Yazith 108
Yeb 148, 168. *See also* Elephantine
Yehud (city) 83, 84, 94
Yehud (province) 15, 107, 158, 159, 161, 165, 166, 167, 168, 170, 171, 172. *Also* Judah
Yeshua bar Sanballat 159
YHWH 13
Yiron 17, 84, 87, 92, 120
Yohanan (high priest) 168
Yohanan ben Torta 266
Yurza 29

## Z

Zaanan 130. *See also* Zenan
Zabdiel 195
Zacchaeus 233
Zacharias (son of Baris) 259
Zadracarta 176
Zagros Mountains 24, 94, 127
Zair. *See* Zoar
Zakkur 108, 109
Zalmonah 41, 43
Zanoah 36, 69, 72, 119, 167, 168
Zaphon 17, 44, 50, 52, , 57, 61, 63, 68, 71, 81, 84, 87. *See also* Asophon
Zarephath 107, 128
Zarethan 27, 45, 55, , 61, 63, 68, 76, 83
Zariaspa. *See* Bactra
Zealots 257
Zebadiah (son of Ishmael) 100
Zebedaeus 229
Zebidah 138
Zeboim/Zeboiim 35, 167
Zeboim ( gHyenas h) Valley 62
Zebulun 17, 50, 51, 52, 54, 55, 57, 78, 84, 85, 86, 87, 88, 90, 91, 92, 149
Zechariah (prophet) 107, 142
Zechariah (advisor to Azariah/Uzziah) 111
Zechariah (son of Jehoiada) 108
Zechariah (son of Jeroboam II) 114
Zedad 16, 122, 149
Zedekiah 138, 140, 143, 146, 147, 148
Zeeb 55
Zela 61
Zelea 174
Zelophehad 68, 83
Zelzah 61
Zemar 12. *See also* Sumur
Zemaraim 81, 82, 89, 95
Zenan 130. *See also* Zaanan
Zenodorus 219
Zephaniah (prophet) 141
Zephath (in Asher) 90
Zephath (in Negeb) 42, 50. *See also* Hormah
Zephathah Valley 20, 95
Zer 92
Zerah of Judah 69
Zerah the Cushite 94, 95, 105
Zered Brook 18, 23, 41, 43, 102, 112, 209. *See also* Wadi el-Hasa
Zeredah 80, 82, 83, 94, 183, 192
Zereth-shahar 17, 44, 84, 87. *See also* Callirrhoe
Zerubbabel 160, 161, 162
Ziddim 92
Ziklag 32, 63, 64, 65, 66, 69, 70, 71, 95, 167
Zilpah 33, 44, 51
Zimri 96, 105
Zin 15
Ziph 64, 65, 69, 80, 81, 101, 126, 127
Ziphron 16
Ziz, Ascent of 101
Zoan 33, 37, 38, 40, 41, 136. *See also* Tanis
Zoar 10, 11, 16, 34, 35, 42, 43, 50, 52, 53, 63, 65, 73, 101, 102, 103, 104, 110, 112, 209, 210, 266. *See also* Bela
Zobah (city) 65
Zobah (region) 61, 72, 73, 74, 79. *See also* Aram-zobah
Zoilus 207
Zoldera 242. *See also* Lystra
Zophim 44
Zopyrus 166
Zorah 52, 57, , 57, 58, 67, 69, 72, 80, 81, 83, 94, 119, 167
Zuph; Zuphim 59, 61
Zuzim 11, 34, 35